The link between theory and classroom practice has never been so strong!

EDUCATIONAL PSYCHOLOGY AND CLASSROOM PRACTICE: A Partnership

R. ____ C____, Duquesne University
Peter ____, Appleton Area School District, Appleton, Wisconsin

Written by an educational psychologist and an award-winning classroom teacher, the text offers a uniquely practical perspective.

True-to-life anecdotes provide realistic context for important principles.

Built-in casebook offers ample opportunity for reflection and critical analysis.

Exceptionally strong treatment of cognitive development highlights excellent topical coverage.

Comprehensive Annotated Instructor's Edition features detailed teaching suggestions, classroom scenarios, field observations, and more.

Full supplement package includes Cable News Network videotapes that tie actual CNN news segments to the material in the text.

McCown and Roop... the perfect partnership.

McCown and Roop...the perfect partnership.

THEORETICALLY SOUND, EXCEPTIONALLY RELEVANT ■ ■ ■ ■ ■ ■ ■ ■ ■ ■ ■

Designed to help aspiring teachers develop professionally, *Educational Psychology and Classroom Practice* describes how successful teachers deal with real classroom situations.

These stories of teaching expertise form a relevant framework for the principles of educational psychology. Plus they help guarantee the most applied, most effective presentation anywhere.

THE ANSWER TO A PRESSING NEED

As the field of educational psychology has grown, so has the need to involve experienced educators in training new teachers. The use of practicing professionals as role models gives deeper meaning to important principles and better prepares students for classroom success.

A UNIQUE WRITING PARTNERSHIP

The only text co-authored by a master classroom practitioner, the text represents a partnership between respected educational psychologist R. R. McCown and veteran teacher Peter Roop.

Peter Roop has been a practicing teacher since 1973. The winner of numerous teaching awards, including Wisconsin Teacher of the Year, he is also a well-known educational consultant and children's author. Mr. Roop has tapped a large network of accomplished teachers from the elementary and secondary levels to gather the classroom-based accounts for this text.

R. R. McCown is an educational psychologist and a professor at Duquesne University where he chairs the Department of Educational Foundations and Leadership. He is an educational consultant to numerous organizations and is also an authority on educational computing.

Chapter Overview

This chapter focuses on the instructional approaches a teacher might use to bring about desired outcomes. The relationship between instruction and learning is considered in the context of Gagné's instructional events, discovery learning, and reception learning. Transfer of learning is also examined to provide an understanding of the way in which students can apply material learned to one situation to new situations. Models that address issues of planning and presenting direct instruction lessons, the instructional form typically used in the classroom, are considered. The current emphasis in education is on the teaching of thinking skills. The chapter addresses this issue through an examination of models of instruction. ■

McCown and Roop…the perfect partnership.

AN OUTSTANDING COMBINATION OF THEORY AND EXPERTISE

Educational Psychology and Classroom Practice definitely lives up to its name. By integrating theory with realistic classroom situations, the text helps students use critical thinking to apply key principles to everyday classroom events.

DIARY OF A DAY ▪▪▪

The book begins with a detailed account of one teacher's routine day. Setting the stage for the *Teacher Chronicles* which appear in later chapters, the diary gives students a real sense of the kinds of problems teachers face, and how they develop solutions. Written by an experienced teacher brimming with enthusiasm, the diary helps establish the text's positive outlook and practical approach.

TEACHER CHRONICLES ▪▪▪▪▪▪▪▪▪▪▪▪▪▪▪▪▪▪▪▪▪▪▪▪▪▪▪▪▪▪▪▪▪▪▪▪▪▪

These unique teaching scenarios form the heart of the text. Every chapter contains three different chronicles (one to introduce each major section) that show the principles of educational psychology in action. Relating the experiences of practicing teachers, the chronicles describe classroom situations from the elementary level through high school. So no matter what age group your students plan to teach, they'll find relevant classrooms described throughout the text.

The chronicles make first-rate case studies in which students can interpret the events in light of theory. A valuable source of ideas and hypotheses, they give aspiring teachers practice in applying principles before they enter their first classroom.

To begin, we present Peter Roop's autobiographical account of a teacher's day, March 17, 1989. His classroom is not identical to any other classroom. His students do not represent a random sample of all students at all grades. No teacher's classroom does.

Peter performs the teaching functions that every teacher must perform in order to be effective. The way in which he does so reflects his knowledge of himself, his students, his curricula—his theory of teaching. As you read Peter's account, pay close attention to Peter's thoughts and actions. Read his diary to discover the problems he identifies and the decisions he makes. Read his attitude toward children and toward the profession of teaching, and the routines he uses to motivate and manage.

You may not agree with Peter's ideas of how instruction works. You may reject some of his decisions. You may not execute the functions of teaching in the same way Peter does, but your job will be similar in many ways.

The Diary of a Day

Chap. Obj. 2
Test Ques. 1.11–1.13; 1.24–1.26; 1.29–1.30

Focus Question: What does a day of teaching look and feel like?

The mix of ideas, experiences, and innovative approaches that teachers and students share make every classroom unique.

"thanks." He acknowledged the offer to do the artwork, but added a little twist consistent with his reputation. He used his street-smarts in school to the point that he hid other kinds of intelligences he might have possessed. The teacher's initial assignment happened to uncover one of Louis's other intelligences, the teacher lost no time in trying to capitalize on this discovery.

1. Do some students adapt to their environments better or just differently than others do? How has Louis adapted?
2. In what ways is Louis intelligent?
3. Would suggesting to Louis that he "draw a picture" depicting the content of a history lesson be a good test of his learning style?

GRANDMA TALES

Kevin was a storyteller. He loved to tell about his older brother the basketball star, his Native-American tribe, his aunt (with whom he lived), children around school, and recent trips. Kevin's reading was weak and his written work was a constant struggle, compared with that of other students in his English class. He was unable to organize his thoughts on paper. Storytelling was his only outstanding skill. He got no help at home. There seemed to be no way to head off an F at report card time.

Kevin's Native-American background was based on a strong oral tradition, that is obvious now, in retrospect. I could kick myself for not seeing it sooner. He could tell stories that captivated his listeners, stories with solid beginnings, intriguing middles, and powerful endings. Kevin could tell stories, but he had not yet equated storytelling with story writing.

We were discussing tall tales in preparation for a writing assignment. We went around the room sharing the tales in preparation for a story writing assignment: Paul Bunyan, Captain Stormalong, Pecos Bill, and Joe Magarac.

About halfway through the sharing, Amy noted, "You know, there aren't any tall tales about women."

Kevin piped up, "Have you ever heard about the time Grandma made the Great Lakes?" There was a glint in his eye that I read as a stalling tactic. I knew he hadn't read the assignment and was trying to throw me off the track by spinning some story.

And spin he did.

"Many years ago, where the Great Lakes are now, there was an open prairie. Grandma came along, saw this prairie, and decided to make her garden there. She reached inside her leather pouch and took out the five seeds: the long green bean seed, the fat pumpkin seed, the flat squash seed, the hard maize seed, and the round eye of a potato. Then she took her hoe and began to dig the right hole for each seed: A long skinny hole for the green bean, a fat hole for the pumpkin, a flat hole for the squash, a hole in granite for the hard corn seed, and a potato-shaped hole for the potato. It only took her one day to dig the five holes. She took all the dirt she dug and threw it to the east where she made mountains. Then, just as she got ready

Teacher Chronicle 4.2

McCown and Roop...the perfect partnership.

PRINCIPLES IN PRACTICE ■■

Each section introduced by a *Teacher Chronicle* is followed by a *Principles in Practice* feature, which reviews key concepts and then applies them to the preceding classroom events. This feature gives students a model for interpreting teaching situations in terms of principles. A good source for journal work or discussion, they include questions that require reflection and the development of hypotheses.

CASEBOOK ■■

An exciting in-text casebook is bound right into the book. Chapter 15, *Casebook of Successful Teaching* is the most extensive casebook of its kind, containing a generous number of lengthy teaching accounts from every grade level. Master teachers across the country pinpoint teaching challenges, test hypotheses, and discuss the results.

The cases help students understand theoretical principles by applying them to actual teaching situations. An excellent basis for classroom discussion or journal entries, they help students practice the critical thinking skills they'll need for teaching success.

and inconsistent. The children of permissive-indulgent parents tend to exhibit little self-reliance and to exhibit low levels of achievement in school, especially among the male children.

The behaviors of students, of teachers, and of parents reflect cultural values. A conflict of values, like the mismatch between learning and teaching styles, is another place where teachers may find an explanation of poor student performance.

Principles in Practice 4.2

Principles . . .

1. Cultural differences are reflected in differences in values.
2. A student's values provide guidelines for behavior.
3. Differences between the values held by a teacher and those of a student can create instructional problems.

. . . in Practice

Kevin, in Teacher Chronicle 4.2, had difficulties with writing assignments. His difficulties were puzzling to the teacher because Kevin was a very creative storyteller. The problem stemmed from a conflict of values so subtle that it took the teacher quite some time to understand Kevin's hesitancy to work on writing assignments. Once the teacher understood how much value Kevin's family placed on storytelling, and how little value was placed on writing, the teacher was able to adapt writing exercises to better fit Kevin's cultural background.

1. In what other instructional situations might the teacher need to account for Kevin's cultural background?
2. What should be the thrust of the teacher's message to Kevin's parents at the next parent–teacher conference?
3. How might a teacher find out about the communication values in order to enhance students' participation in classroom interaction?

LOST AND FOUND

We were working on reading color-coded maps. I had just finished explain
how to identify areas on a cross-section map of a mining area when I saw
look on Nick's face. Reading Nick's face was like reading one of the maps
had taken a wrong turn and was lost. I knew I had to steer him back on
right track. But first we had to find where he made the wrong turn. It
backtracking with him.

While the other students worked on a map assignment using the c
codes, I pulled up a chair and sat beside Nick.

I Am Leo

Every school has a number of specialist teachers who serve unique student needs. Remedial teachers in elementary schools provide students with individual help outside the regular classroom environment, most commonly in math and language arts. These educators develop effective teaching techniques while working one-on-one with students. As the following case, "I Am Leo," illustrates, realizing individual student's needs and seeking the critical moment for making an academic connection is vital for any teacher.
Sue Misheff, now a college professor, was a K–6 reading specialist.

David could not read or write. He could recognize only the letters in his first name; he could not say the alphabet. He could not concentrate on one thing long enough to count a number of items past ten. He often confused his left hand and his right hand. For all appearances, David had a potentially serious learning problem as a six-year-old kindergartner.

In addition to his apparent lack of ability to achieve in school, David's home life had been unhappy until his recent adoption into a loving family. And, as if to ensure that David would be noticed somehow, nature had not endowed David with tear ducts, so that a continual tear always lingered in his eye.

When he was first referred to my remedial reading program, I learned that David could make up a wonderful story and that he enjoyed listening to books while I read to him. David exuded curiosity and a willingness to interact with the printed word that belied his underlying problems; and so I began our sessions together with a great deal of hope and a belief that one among all of the techniques that I planned to use would help him to grow.

By Christmas, however, David had made little progress and I was starting to feel as if I'd failed. None of the language experience activities that I'd used had seemed to enlighten him at all about the various forms and functions of print. The kinesthetic tactics that were supposed to increase David's awareness of individual letter patterns had obviously failed to do their job, for he still could only recognize and write the letters of his first name. Although we had read and enjoyed a number of books together, I could see no evidence that David connected what we were doing when we looked at pictures and listened to stories with the words on the page. I did not feel that I'd given David a gift of literacy for the holidays.

In late January, however, something happened that confirmed every belief in the power of stories to change the lives of people that I'd ever held. David had decided to take home a book/cassette kit of Leo the Late Bloomer by Robert Kraus. He chose the book himself because, as he said, he liked the cover; and I planned to have him tell me the story by using the pictures and what he remembered from listening to the tape at our next session.

When David returned the following week, he sat down, opened his book, pointed to the little lion and said, "That's me. I'm Leo." I had not seen David react so positively to a story, and I marveled as he continued pointing to the characters in the pictures.

"My dad is like Leo's dad."

"And is your mom like Leo's mom?"

"Yeah, she is."

Connections: Chapter 2, Egocentrism; Chapter 3, Stage 4: Identify versus Inferiority; Chapter 7, Self-reflective Capability; Chapter 8, Self-efficacy, Attribution Training; Chapter 14, Diagnostic Tests

McCown and Roop...the perfect partnership.

SUPERIOR TREATMENT OF MAJOR CONCEPTS ■ ■ ■ ■ ■ ■ ■ ■ ■ ■ ■ ■ ■ ■ ■ ■ ■ ■

The text's topical coverage is outstanding. No other educational psychology book offers such comprehensive, understandable treatment of subjects such as cognition, exceptionality, and moral development.

COGNITIVE DEVELOPMENT

You'll find the most up-to-date treatment of cognition anywhere, with more applications and descriptions of age-level characteristics throughout. The only text with such extensive coverage of Piaget, it also offers a thorough look at behaviorism and social learning theory — a real plus when you consider the importance of observational learning.

EXCEPTIONALITY

The text looks at exceptionality from a number of perspectives. It describes various exceptionalities and explains how they can influence values and function. Also included are excerpts from a book in which learning-disabled children share their classroom experiences. These passages provide many insights, not only for special education teachers, but for all teachers with mainstreaming in their schools.

MORAL DEVELOPMENT

The text uses a unique classroom model to study moral development. This model is an effective tool for dealing with differences among students, particularly in today's multicultural classrooms.

Difficulties That L.D. People Might Have

Even though our vision is usually normal, sometimes our mind "sees" something different from what our eyes see. Some examples: We might see "but" instead of "put," "mose" instead of "nose," "6" becomes "9." We may read and write words backwards or upside down: "was" becomes "saw," "107" becomes "701," "spot" becomes "pots," "sung" becomes "snug."

SOMETIMESALLTHELETTERSAREJUMBLEDTOGETHER.

or

THEW ORD SARE NOTSP ACED COR RECT LY.
Sometimes it's hard to Write on the Lines.

Journal Entry: Have students reflect on the examples provided by L.D. students, riting the re sponsis fonetiklee.

Copying words and designs and cutting with scissors are hard when your fingers don't do what you want them to. Coloring within the lines is hard too!

We spell wrds xatle az tha snd to us! "Girl" becomes "gril," "house" becomes "howc." We like to add extra letters when we spell or leave out the letters we don't hear.

Our hearing is usually normal but sometimes we don't hear the endings or beginnings of words, or we hear a different word altogether! Instead of "Go to bed" we hear "the goat is read," "but" - "bat" - "bet" - "bit" all sound the same to us.

or

We hear too much!! Even soft sounds can seem loud to us and make it hard to concentrate. Hearing a clock ticking or water dripping can keep us from being able to finish our math. Or we hear everybody but the person who is talking to us.

We often have a hard time paying attention because noises and movements distract us. People think we are not paying attention when we don't follow directions. Actually we are paying attention too much!!

We get directions confused easily and become lost even in places we know. We forget what's "left" and "right," "up" and "down," "under" and "over."

Changes in our routine can also confuse us. This confusion can blow our whole day!

Sometimes we say and do things without thinking first. We often move too quickly and end up running into furniture or people!!

A lot of times we have difficulty sitting on our chairs. We feel like we need to jump and move around even when it's time to sit still. Our mind just keeps jumping and our body wants to too!

One day we know something, the next day we forget it. Remembering things like the days of the week, spelling words, or math facts are hard for us. But, some days we remember very well.

At times we know what we want to say but just can't get it out. It's that way when we write. Our mind and our hands just don't cooperate! Our mind thinks "animal" but our mouth says "maminal."

Sometimes we can do a math problem in our head, but, when we have to write it, we can't! We can add and multiply, but not subtract or divide.

McCown and Roop...the perfect partnership.

CAREFULLY DESIGNED PEDAGOGY ▪▪▪▪▪▪▪▪▪▪▪▪▪▪▪▪▪▪▪▪▪▪▪▪▪▪▪

The excellent learning devices in *Educational Psychology and Classroom Practice* do more than help students memorize principles. They reinforce comprehension, while requiring students to practice the thinking skills teachers use each day.

Diary of a Day, appearing in Chapter One, anticipates the *Teacher Chronicles* by detailing a real teacher's thoughts and actions during an actual classroom day. Notes in the margin of the student edition key the events to appropriate upcoming chapter sections.

Every chapter in the text features:

Chapter Outlines feature a brief sketch of upcoming topics.

Chapter Overviews help students develop realistic expectations of what they're about to learn.

Focus Questions at the start of every chapter help students anticipate the principles and practices to be presented. Designed to connect visually with the material that follows, the questions help motivate students and increase comprehension.

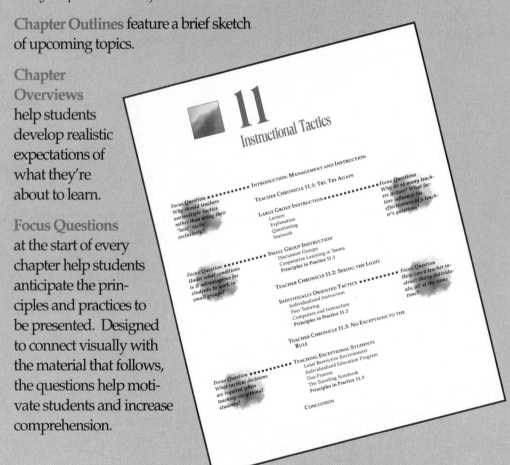

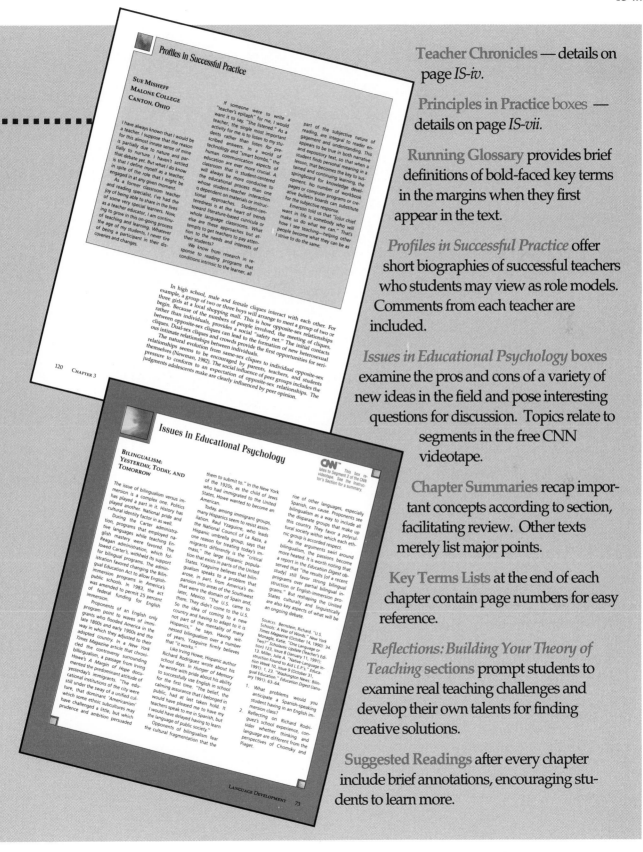

Teacher Chronicles — details on page *IS-iv*.

Principles in Practice boxes — details on page *IS-vii*.

Running Glossary provides brief definitions of bold-faced key terms in the margins when they first appear in the text.

Profiles in Successful Practice offer short biographies of successful teachers who students may view as role models. Comments from each teacher are included.

Issues in Educational Psychology boxes examine the pros and cons of a variety of new ideas in the field and pose interesting questions for discussion. Topics relate to segments in the free CNN videotape.

Chapter Summaries recap important concepts according to section, facilitating review. Other texts merely list major points.

Key Terms Lists at the end of each chapter contain page numbers for easy reference.

Reflections: Building Your Theory of Teaching sections prompt students to examine real teaching challenges and develop their own talents for finding creative solutions.

Suggested Readings after every chapter include brief annotations, encouraging students to learn more.

McCown and Roop...the perfect partnership.

A SUPERB ANNOTATED INSTRUCTOR'S EDITION ∎∎∎∎∎∎∎∎∎∎∎∎∎∎∎∎∎

The Annotated Instructor's Edition (AIE) gives you exactly what you need for a thorough, coordinated presentation. An extensive Instructor's Section, bound into the front of the book, is keyed by section to the student portion of the text.

Each chapter in the Instructor's Section features:

Chapter Objectives that specifically state what concepts students must master in order to understand the material fully.

Focus Questions to present reflective questions on key points as students read each chapter.

Chapter Outlines provide a framework for the presentation.

Chapter Summaries that highlight main points of each chapter.

Key Terms listed for planning convenience.

***Teacher Chronicle* Summaries** that provide a synopsis of each chapter's journal feature.

Possible Answers for *Principles in Practice* suggest answer guidelines for student responses to *Principles in Practice* boxes.

CNN Connections to *Issues in Educational Psychology* concisely summarize the appropriate segment from the specially assembled CNN videotape to accompany the text.

Activities and Exercises that describe in-class activities, discussion topics, teacher interviews, field observations, and journal entries.

Chapter 15 Casebook Previews that highlight connections between textual material and appropriate case material contained in Chapter 15.

Teaching Anecdotes that provide lively and engaging stories to spark class discussions and enhance lectures.

Transparency references to indicate appropriate acetate transparencies to use in conjunction with each chapter.

Teaching Resources that provide helpful lists of useful outside readings, films, videotapes, and audiotapes that may be used to enrich the presentation of each chapter.

Study Guide references to highlight the availability of this useful student resource.

Test Question listings to provide a list of appropriate test items at a glance.

---

tells you that she is busy trying to think about where to put her fingers and where the next letter ought to be. Can you develop a program of low-road transfer to help students like Dava develop automatic skills?

Chapter 15 Casebook Previews

See Responsibility Education.
See Science Is Only Real When You Do It.
See Beginning Each Day as a Learning Experience.
See Improvisation and Aesthetic Appreciation.
See Gifted Achievers and Underachievers.
See Writing Success in Science.

Teaching Anecdotes

Tell your students about the kindergarten teacher who had each of her children pick an object from a box each day and describe it. In the box, she had a collection of "junk" that she had gathered—everything from old records to nuts and bolts. After each child had described the object, the teacher asked him or her how the object might be used. At first, the children's guesses ranged far afield from the actual use of the objects. But as they became more skilled in describing, they also began to realize the functional attributes of the objects. Ask your students why the teacher took the time to do this exercise and what value it might have had for the children. (See p. 363.)

Tell your students about two high school students in English class. Reading was difficult for the first student, but he worked every night on his assignments and did well. The second student, for whom English had always been a "breeze," soon found herself struggling in the same class. Although her IQ was much higher than her fellow student's, she received lower grades for the first quarter of the year.

Ask your students what might account for the difference in performance. Which student might retain new material for longer periods of time—the first or the second? (See p. 370.)

Tell your students about the high school that began using a computer system to access various data bases. By using a computer students' research time was cut from weeks to days, and the computer searched for and located far more sources than the students previously had access to. Instead of being inundated with the amount of material, most students found the extra data helpful. Many students began using the computers during lunch and free periods with no specific assignment due, but rather to discover more on topics that interested them individually.

Ask your students why this might have happened. (See p. 371.)

clip, a bottle cap, and a pan of water. The students were to predict which objects would sink and which would float. After experimenting with the objects, the students were to use the material they had been studying about water displacement to get all of the objects to float.

Ask your students how this project might combine inductive and deductive thinking skills. (The final solution was to mold a boat from the clay and place the other objects inside.) (See p. 377.)

Tell your students about the teacher who describes her approach to teaching this way, "If I can make the students feel comfortable and enjoy being here, I can teach them anything."

Ask your students if this is an appropriate way to approach teaching. Why or why not? How would they respond to such a teacher? Ask them if this might be the way they feel as teachers themselves. (See p. 385.)

Transparencies

For transparencies to use with this chapter, see the Transparency Guides on page 362, page 376, and page 377.

Teaching Resources

Suggested Readings

Eggen, D. P., & Kauchak, P. D. (1988). *Strategies for teachers*. Englewood Cliffs, NJ: Prentice-Hall.

Gagné, R. M. (1985). *The conditions of learning* (4th ed.). New York: Holt, Rinehart & Winston.

Gagné, R. M., & Driscoll, M. P. (1988). *Essentials of learning for instruction* (2nd ed.). Englewood Cliffs, NJ: Prentice-Hall.

Gunter, M. A., Estes, T. H., & Schwab, J. H. (1990). *Instruction: A models approach*. Needham Heights, MA: Allyn & Bacon.

Films, Videocassettes, Audiocassettes

• *Student-Centered Classroom, Secondary*, 16mm, 20 min., color. This film gives an overall view of what a student-centered classroom may look like when interaction, materials, and activities generate self-directed individualization and small group process. Interaction is a language arts and reading program. Houghton Mifflin Co., Multimedia Division, 1 Beacon Street, Boston, MA 02107. HMC 1973.

• *Who Did What to Whom?: II. Recognizing Four Behavioral Principles in Action*, 16mm or videocassette, 20 min., color. Robert Mager is well known in the fields of education and business training for his excellent books on planning, thinking, and striving for objective-directed results. The program illus-

---

5. General Objective

Uses the psychomotor taxonomy to classify learning activities (pp. 349–351).

Specific Behaviors

5.01 Gives examples of reflex movements and level objectives and activities.

5.02 Gives examples of basic/fundamental movements and level objectives and activities.

5.03 Gives examples of perceptual abilities and level objectives and activities.

5.04 Gives examples of physical abilities and level objectives and activities.

5.05 Gives examples of skilled movements and level objectives and activities.

5.06 Gives examples of nondiscursive communication and level objectives and activities.

Focus Questions

• What is the difference between a strategic decision and a tactical decision?
• How can the outcomes of instruction be specified for students?
• What do instructional objectives do for teachers and students?
• What capabilities might students gain from instruction?
• How can the different areas and levels of outcomes be classified?
• What student behaviors allow teachers to infer that particular outcomes have been attained?

Chapter Outline

INTRODUCTION: STRATEGIC AND TACTICAL DECISIONS

TEACHER CHRONICLE 9.1: STUDENTS: THE MISSING INGREDIENT

INSTRUCTIONAL OBJECTIVES
The Behavioral Approach
The Goals Approach
    Goals
    Evaluative Statements
The General Objectives–Specific Behaviors Approach

USING OBJECTIVES
Cautions for Using Objectives
Alternative Views
Principles in Practice 9.1

TEACHER CHRONICLE 9.2: CONTENT OR PROCESS?

GAGNÉ'S OUTCOMES OF INSTRUCTION
Verbal Information

Intellectual Skills
    Discriminations
    Concrete Concepts
    Defined Concepts
    Rules
    Higher-Order Rules
Cognitive Strategies
Attitudes
Motor Skills
Principles in Practice 9.2

TEACHER CHRONICLE 9.3: A HARD NUT TO CRACK

TAXONOMIES OF OUTCOMES
The Cognitive Domain
    Level 1: Knowledge
    Level 2: Comprehension
    Level 3: Application
    Level 4: Analysis
    Level 5: Synthesis
    Level 6: Evaluation
The Affective Domain
    Level 1: Receiving or Attending
    Level 2: Responding
    Level 3: Valuing
    Level 4: Organization
    Level 5: Characterization
The Psychomotor Domain
    Level 1: Reflexive Movements
    Level 2: Basic/Fundamental Movements
    Level 3: Perceptual Movements
    Level 4: Physical Abilities
    Level 5: Skilled Movements
    Level 6: Nondiscursive Communication
Deciding on Objectives
Principles in Practice 9.3

CONCLUSION

Chapter Summary

Introduction: Strategic and Tactical Decisions
• Strategic decisions result in plans. Tactical decisions are made as the plan is executed. Strategic decisions begin with the teacher determining the outcomes desired for his or her students.

Instructional Objectives
• Instructional objectives can be specified in a number of ways. Instructional objectives prepared as specified by Robert Mager are called behavioral objectives. Behavioral objectives include a statement of terminal behavior, the conditions of performance, and the criteria used to judge attainment of an objective.

McCown and Roop...the perfect partnership.

Following the Instructor's Section is the annotated text section that features blue annotations in the margins. These blue notes for the instructor do NOT appear in the students' texts.

The wide range of margin annotations includes: ■

Lecture Notes — that can be used for additional ideas or for planning your presentation.

Teaching Anecdotes — that supplement the *Teacher Chronicles* and casebook, and include reflective questions.

Chapter 15 Casebook Previews — to suggest effective ways to use the classroom scenarios in the Chapter 15 casebook.

Journal Entries — that present ideas for journal work that complement the text and foster critical thinking.

Transparencies — to offer ways to enhance your presentation using the supplemental transparency package.

Test Questions — cross-referenced to the Test Bank and Computerized Test Bank Supplements.

Focus Questions — that connect each question to the text.

Field Observation — to provide ideas and guidelines for field work assignments.

Connection — cross references to related portions of the text provide continuity and unique opportunities for class discussion.

Study Guide — to highlight the availability of this useful student resource.

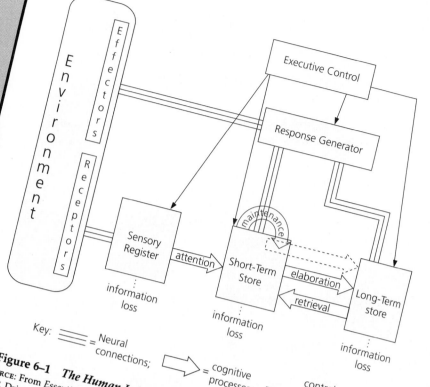

■ Figure 6–1   *The Human Information-processing Model*
SOURCE: From *Essentials of Learning for Instruction* (2nd ed., p. 13) by R. M. Gagné and M. P. Driscoll, 1988, Englewood Cliffs, NJ: Prentice-Hall. Copyright 1988 by Prentice-Hall. Adapted by permission.

Transparency: This figure is duplicated in the acetate transparency package. See T-8 The Human Information-processing Model.

Following the trail of information takes us from the environment (stimulus input), through the cognitive mechanism of the learner, and finally back to the environment (response output). Behaviorists focus exclusively on the stimulus, response, and associated environmental changes. Information-processing theorists focus primarily on what goes on inside the learner—the cognitive mechanism—to investigate learning processes.

Memory Structures

In this section we focus on the three memory structures in the human information-processing system: sensory register, short-term store (STS), and long-term store (LTS). Waugh and Norman (1965) were among the first theorists to suggest that there are different types of memory functions, which they called primary memory and secondary memory. The structures in Figure 6–1 were identified by Atkinson and Shiffrin (1968). The **Atkinson and Shiffrin model** of information processing, an extension of Waugh and Norman's notion, has undergone many modifications since it was first introduced, but its

Lecture Note: Have students in small groups identify information they would present in their classes and track the flow of that information through the various structures of the human cognitive mechanism.

Teacher Interview: Have each student ask a teacher to describe observable behaviors that allow him or her to infer various kinds of cognitive activities.

Chapter 15 Casebook Preview: Beginning Each Day as a Learning Experience.

McCown and Roop...the perfect partnership.

A COMPLETE SUPPLEMENT PROGRAM ■■■■■■■■■■■■■■■■■■■■■■■■■■■■

Every element in the supplement package is designed to maximize learning and foster reflective skills. In addition, transparencies and videotapes add color and drama to the course.

Test Bank
Over 1800 test items. Also available in computerized form for the IBM-PC and, with graphic capability, for the Macintosh computer.

Transparencies
A total of 25 acetate transparencies helps keep your presentation lively by supplementing the artwork in the text.

Student Study Guide
This carefully organized manual helps students use the text to full advantage by providing an additional set of learning aids. Each Study Guide chapter contains:

Summary — provides an overview of chapter content and its significance.

The Teacher's Corner — sets forth realistic teaching scenarios that require students to consider the solutions suggested.

Key Terms — lists all the highlighted terms from the text to encourage review.

Practice Makes Perfect — features short-answer questions dealing with key terms, as well as numerous multiple-choice problems that test major concepts.

Applying Your Knowledge — challenges students to develop their own solutions to specific teaching problems based on chapter material.

Our Turn — summarizes important theories and suggests related topics for student journal entries.

STUDENT STUDY GUIDE for

Educational Psychology AND Classroom Practice — A PARTNERSHIP

Rick R. McCown
Peter G. Roop

Gary Shank, Northern Illinois University

CNN Video Connections in Educational Psychology
A specially produced videotape highlights relevant issues from recent Cable News Network broadcasts. This one-hour tape contains actual news segments on topics from education and psychology. *Issues in Educational Psychology* boxes found in the text relate topically to the video segments and provide opportunities for reflection and critical thinking.

FREE WITH EVERY STUDENT TEXT!

Teacher Magazine Reader: Focus on Teacher Education
Allyn and Bacon is pleased to offer a special 16-page reader designed to supplement your course. Included free with every student edition, this full-color publication includes articles on cooperative learning and multicultural issues, as well as information on what teaching is really like — all from the favorite magazine of U.S. teachers.

Annotated Instructor's Edition

Educational Psychology and Classroom Practice: A Partnership

R. R. McCown
Duquesne University

Peter Roop
Appleton Area School District, Appleton, Wisconsin

SCHOOL OF EDUCATION
CURRICULUM LABORATORY
UM-DEARBORN

Allyn and Bacon
Boston   London   Toronto   Sydney   Tokyo   Singapore

Series Editor; Sean Wakely
Executive Editor: Mylan Jaixen
Developmental Editors: Alicia Reilly and Carol L. Chernaik
Cover Administrator: Linda Dickinson
Composition Buyer: Linda Cox
Manufacturing Buyer: Megan Cochran
Editorial-Production Service: Proof Positive/Farrowlyne Associates, Inc.
Cover Designer: Susan Slovinsky

Copyright ©1992 by Allyn and Bacon
A division of Simon & Schuster, Inc.
160 Gould Street
Needham Heights, Massachusetts 02194

Printed in the United States of America

10 9 8 7 6 5 4 3 2 1   96 95 94 93 92 91

ISBN: 0-205-13741-5

Brief Contents

Instructor's Preface

The authors of this text, an educational psychologist and a classroom teacher, have formed a partnership to meld the principles of educational psychology with the maxims of classroom practice. The result is the student text and this Annotated Instructor's Edition (AIE). We designed the AIE to mirror the text's emphasis on active learning and reflection. Recognizing that every effective instructor puts his or her imprimatur on a course, we have suggested a variety of ways that you might foster student understanding of the principles of educational psychology in the context of classroom practice.

ORGANIZATION OF THE TEXT

The text is organized into four parts.

Part I, the *Teacher as Learner*, contains Chapter 1. Our introductory chapter differs from introductions in other educational psychology texts. Chapter 1 features the "Diary of a Day," a complete account of decisions, actions, and reflections made by one of the coauthors as he taught his students on a recent St. Patrick's Day. It is a story of real teaching and, as such, provides a practical context for the remainder of the book. Topics and concepts from every subsequent chapter in the text are cross-referenced for your students in the margins of the Diary of a Day. These marginal cross-references are provided to demonstrate that the elements of teaching can be understood through the principles of educational psychology. Chapter 1 also includes an analysis of the Diary. Written from the perspective of educational psychology, the analysis identifies the hallmarks of effective teaching and provides a model for students to use when conducting their own analyses throughout the course.

Part II, Chapters 2–8, describes *Students as Learners.* Chapters 2, 3, and 4 discuss the developmental characteristics of students. Chapters 5, 6, 7, and 8 describe how students learn and the ways in which they are motivated to learn.

Part III, Chapters 9–14, describes the *Teacher as Decision-Maker.* Chapters 9 and 10 focus on planning decisions. Chapters 11 and 12 address the tactical decisions required for instruction and for classroom management. Chapters 13 and 14 examine evaluative decisions.

Part IV, Chapter 15, the *Teacher as Researcher,* is the "Casebook of Successful Teaching"—real cases of teaching in which master teachers identify problems, test possible solutions, and reflect on the results of their "experiments." The Casebook includes accounts written by teachers from across the country and across grade levels.

INSTRUCTIONAL FEATURES OF THE TEXT

Part I (Chapter 1) and Part IV (Chapter 15) differ in structure from Parts II and III. In Chapters 2–14 the following features are provided:

- A chapter opening that consists of **Focus Questions,** a **Chapter Outline,** and a **Chapter Overview.** The Focus Questions help orient students to the theory and practice described in that chapter. These questions, and the Chapter Outline and Chapter Overview build expectations for what is to come.
- **Teacher Chronicles,** which occur within the chapters, are true stories from the lives of teachers. The Teacher Chronicles provide a practical context for the discussion of the principles of educational psychology that follows. After the principles are examined, another feature called **Principles in Practice** appears. This feature identifies key principles of educational psychology and applies them to the events described in the preceding Teacher Chronicle.
- Each chapter in Parts II and III also contains a **Running Glossary of Key Terms** in the chapter's margins; a news feature related to the subject matter of the chapter, **Issues in Educational Psychology;** and a short commentary by a successful teacher called **Profiles in Successful Practice.**
- At the end of each chapter, a **Chapter Summary** briefly recounts important concepts, a page-referenced list of **Key Terms** helps students locate the concepts that appear in the chapter, and a **Suggested Readings** list offers them access to supplemental materials. Additionally, a feature called **Reflections: Building Your Theory of Teaching** presents opportunities for students to reflect on teaching situations taken from real classrooms and to formulate ideas about the ways in which they might deal with similar situations.

FEATURES OF THE AIE

The annotations in the AIE present ideas for you to consider as you plan your course. You will find twelve different kinds of annotations in the margins of the AIE. What follows is a brief description of each.

The **Chapter Objectives, Focus Questions,** and **Test Questions** that pertain to a particular section of the text are referenced at the beginning of each major section within a chapter. The other types of annotations occur throughout the margins of Chapters 2–14.

Lecture Notes include additional examples not found in the student text, alternative explanations, interactive questions, and discussion questions. Lecture Notes are ideas that can be used during lecture or recitation sessions.

Teaching Anecdotes are brief stories about real classroom events. They can be incorporated into lectures or used as the basis for discussion.

Chapter 15 Casebook Previews identify those cases from the Casebook of Successful Teaching that pertain to specific points in a chapter. Although these annotations refer to specific points, the cases themselves can be used more generally. For example, the cases could be analyzed for hallmarks of effective teaching (as is modeled by the analysis of the "Diary of a Day" in Chapter 1). Cases could be analyzed in order to identify principles within a chapter or across chapters. Cases could be analyzed as "classroom experiments." Students could be asked to identify the teacher's problem and the hypothesis tested by the teacher in an attempt to solve the problem, and to provide an explanation of the results of the test. Regardless of the kinds of analysis you choose, cases can be used as formative exercises, as supplemental readings, as cooperative learning assignments, or as term paper assignments.

Field Observations are ideas for the types of activities students might undertake as they observe in classrooms. A few of the Field Observations could take place in locations other than the classrooms.

Teacher Interviews suggest questions or issues that students might ask practicing teachers to address. Teacher Interviews could take place in the field, or teachers could be invited to class sessions.

Connections are cross-references. They identify pertinent material from other parts of the text.

Journal Entries are ideas for reflections that students can collect in a journal.

Transparency references indicate the appropriate acetate transparencies to use with the text.

Study Guide references list the chapters to assign for student review of the text.

The categories of annotations are not mutually exclusive. The ideas annotated as Journal Entries can easily be used as Lecture Notes. Teacher Interviews can be used instead of or in combination with Field Observations. Teaching Anecdotes can be used as minicases.

The AIE is simply a source of ideas, not a prescription. Use the ideas that spark your enthusiasm, modify those that need it, and discard those that do not fit your style.

ORGANIZATION OF THE INSTRUCTOR'S SECTION

Finally, the AIE includes an Instructor's Section that collects information on features and text supplements in one place. The Instructor's Section also includes features not available to students in the text or in supplements. The fifteen elements of each chapter in the Instructor's Section are briefly described in the text that follows.

- **Chapter Objectives.** Gronlund-type objectives (general objectives followed by specific behaviors) are supplied for each chapter. Neither the text nor the *Study Guide* presents objectives.
- **Focus Questions.** The Focus Questions that appear at the beginning of each chapter in the text are presented.
- **Chapter Outline.** A full, detailed outline of the chapter is presented.
- **Chapter Summary.** An abbreviated summary of the chapter is presented.
- **Key Terms.** The Key Terms defined in the running glossary of the text are presented.
- **Teacher Chronicle Summaries.** The Teacher Chronicles for the chapter are summarized for quick reference.
- **Possible Answers to Principles in Practice.** Possible answers to the questions that conclude each Principle in Practice feature in the chapter are provided to simplify evaluation.
- **CNN Connection to Issues in Educational Psychology.** A brief summary of the video segments associated with the chapter is presented.
- **Activities and Exercises.** Six types of activities or exercises are provided for each chapter:

  1. In-Class Activities. Simulations, demonstrations, role-playing, and cooperative exercises are provided for your consideration.
  2. Teacher Interviews. The Teacher Interview annotations for the entire chapter are collected for ease of reference.
  3. Field Observations. The Field Observation annotations for the entire chapter are collected to simplify field assignments.
  4. Journal Entries. The Journal Entry annotations for the entire chapter are collected to facilitate journal writing assignments.
  5. Discussion Topics. The Lecture Note annotations that identify discussion questions are collected to simplify the planning of group discussions.
  6. Application Scenarios. The Applying Your Knowledge exercises from the *Study Guide* are collected for use in planning reflective discussion exercises.

- **Chapter 15 Casebook Previews.** The cases referenced in the Casebook Preview annotations are collected to suggest pertinent cases from the Casebook of Successful Teaching.
- **Teaching Anecdotes.** The teaching anecdote annotations are collected, supplying you with additional "teaching stories" for use in constructing lectures or student activities.
- **Teaching Resources.** Suggestions for supplemental readings, films, videocassettes, and audiocassettes are provided.
- **Study Guide Assignment.** The *Study Guide* assignment for this chapter is listed.
- **Test Questions.** The items from the test bank written for the chapter are listed in order to simplify test construction.
- **Transparency Guide.** The appropriate figures from the transparency package are listed.

We hope this AIE provides or triggers ideas that will make your teaching fun and your students' learning meaningful. Please let us hear your ideas for improving the AIE, the text, or any of the supplements by writing to

McCown & Roop: A Partnership
Allyn and Bacon, Publishers
160 Gould Street
Needham Heights, MA 02194

1

Reflection and Teaching

Chapter Objectives

1. General Objective

Understands how intuitive and specific theories contribute to classroom practice (pp. 4–6).

SPECIFIC BEHAVIORS
1.01 Characterizes the nature of intuitive theory.
1.02 Characterizes the nature of scientific theory.
1.03 Describes the behaviors and characteristics of novice and expert teachers.
1.04 Illustrates how novice and expert teachers approach teaching situations.
1.05 Argues the position that effective teachers test ideas in their classrooms.

2. General Objective

Experiences vicariously the complexities of a teaching day (pp. 7–30).

SPECIFIC BEHAVIORS
2.01 Identifies the types and frequency of decisions implied in the Diary of a Day.
2.02 Identifies the established routines implied in the Diary of a Day.
2.03 Identifies the hypotheses tested in the Diary of a Day.

3. General Objective

Analyzes expert practice for the purpose of developing a personal theory of teaching (pp. 30–34).

SPECIFIC BEHAVIORS
3.01 Characterizes teaching themes as a product of classroom experiences.
3.02 Illustrates how flexibility and planning are related.
3.03 Argues the importance of teachers' knowing their students as individuals.
3.04 Understands the need for novice teachers to observe and analyze expert performance.

4. General Objective

Understands how the organization of the book can help in the development of a personal theory of teaching (pp. 35–37).

SPECIFIC BEHAVIORS
4.01 Uses focus questions to anticipate chapter content.
4.02 Uses the Teacher Chronicles as practical contexts for learning the principles of educational psychology.
4.03 Uses the Principles in Practice to reflect on teaching practice.
4.04 Uses end of chapter Reflections to build a theory of teaching.

Focus Questions

- What is a theory?
- How does an *intuitive* theory differ from a *scientific* theory?
- What are the differences between novice and expert teachers?
- What does a day of teaching look and feel like?
- How does teaching experience contribute to teaching expertise?
- What should aspiring teachers do about their lack of classroom experience?
- How will this book help an aspiring teacher develop professionally?

Chapter Outline

INTRODUCTION: EXPERT THEORIES
Learning to Read Classrooms

THE DIARY OF A DAY
Friday, March 17, 1989

EXPERIENCE AND EXPERTISE
A St. Patrick's Day Analysis
Using Expert Performance

SCIENTIFIC PRINCIPLES AND THE ART OF TEACHING

ORGANIZATION OF THE BOOK

QUESTIONS, CHRONICLES, PRINCIPLES, AND REFLECTIONS

Chapter Summary

Introduction: Expert Theories

- The chapter begins by distinguishing intuitive theories from scientific theories. Intuitive theories are the understandings that people have of everyday events, including the clinical practice of teaching.
- Berliner identifies characteristics that distinguish experts from novices. Expert teachers have intuitive theories that allow them to "read" classrooms better than novices. Educational psychology, a source of scientific theories, can help the novice learn how to read behavior in classrooms.

The Diary of a Day

- This account demonstrates the way Peter Roop carried out the functions of teaching in his classroom on March 17, 1989. The diary does not define the way that all teachers should teach, but it does demonstrate the functions all teachers must fulfill. The marginal comments accompanying the diary indicate that the principles of educational psychology address the events that occur in real classrooms.

Experience and Expertise

- Teaching experience is necessary for the development of teaching expertise, but experience does not guarantee expertise.
- The analysis of Peter Roop's teaching day yielded the presence of several themes. Peter allows his special interests to be part of, and therefore, enthuse his teaching. Other characteristics of his approach include flexibility, which is afforded by careful planning, and the belief that he must know his students as individuals in order to teach them effectively. Finally, Peter's testing of hypotheses has led to the development of effective classroom routines.
- New teachers lack the experience necessary to develop solutions to the problems they will most certainly face in their first classroom. A strategy for overcoming the lack of experience is to use the performances of experienced (and, better yet, expert) teachers as a guide to one's own performance. The solution of an expert teacher may not work as a model for every new teacher, but it will provide a hypothesis that can be tested. Testing hypotheses is a way to build the experience that leads to expertise.

Scientific Principles and the Art of Teaching

- Science provides us with knowledge of the principles that govern phenomena. Art is the exploitation of those principles for some purpose. Educational psychology informs us about the principles that govern behavior in classrooms. Teachers who test these principles in their own classrooms can learn to exploit them for positive outcomes.

Organization of the Book

- The book is organized into four parts: I. Teacher as Learner (the content of the present chapter); II. Students as Learners; III. Teacher as Decision-Maker; and IV. Teacher as Researcher. Chapters in the second and third parts contain features designed to relate theory to practice and to build a theory of teaching through reflection.

Key Terms

teaching	educational psychology
theory	reflection

CNN Connection to Issues in Educational Psychology

Will the United States remain competitive in the global economy? Can today's youth be tomorrow's standard bearers? These concerns are part of the reason why educational reform has become a key political issue for the 1990s . . . and why the teaching profession especially is under such close scrutiny. This segment focuses on the new requirements for teachers advocated by the National Board for Professional Teaching Standards and the controversy surrounding the Board's program.

Activities and Exercises

In-Class Activities

1. Assign several students to the selection committee of the Teaching Hall of Fame. One requirement for induction is that teachers must have had a lasting effect on a large number of students. As a measure of a teacher's influence, the selection committee considers how many former students chose to become teachers. Have other students each assume the identity of some of the students described in the Diary of a Day who have become teachers themselves. The selection committee is assumed to have read part of the memoir Peter wrote years ago and they should prepare interview questions for Peter Roop's "former students" that will enable them to decide on his nomination to the Hall of Fame.

2. Assign students to small groups. Each group is to assume the role of the editorial board for a new journal called the *Journal of Teaching Mistakes*. The task of the board is to work on the journal's prospectus. Specifically, the group should prepare two sections of the prospectus including: (a) a statement of philosophy that explains why it is useful to publish accounts of mistakes made by

teachers in the classroom, addressing specifically the question, ''What can an aspiring teacher learn from the mistakes made by practicing teachers?''; and (b) a set of guidelines on the nature and format of publishable articles.

You may wish to consider developing the *Journal of Teaching Mistakes* as a one semester project. Students could submit ''articles'' based on their own field observations and experiences.

Application Scenarios

Present the following scenarios to students:

- Diego is a new student entering your third-grade classroom. He is from California, which is quite far from your state. He seems very friendly and eager to meet his fellow students and wants to do well in school. What can you do to help him, without appearing to be meddling or favoring him? What are some problems, if any, that you might anticipate Diego to have getting to know his classmates? How can you help?

- It is the first day of seventh grade. Melissa stumbles self-consciously into your homeroom. It is apparent that she has matured over the summer. Her classmates notice, and they start buzzing. She is obviously very uncomfortable with the attention. Can you help? Should you do anything, or would it be better to ignore the matter, and hope that the furor dies down quickly? Why do you choose to do what you do?

- Charlie is a student in your first-grade class. You write ''Good Morning Students'' on the board. Charlie promptly bounces out of his seat and erases your message. When you ask why he acted as he did, he tells you that he erased the message because he could not read it. What would you do? What do you think will happen to Charlie?

Transparencies

For transparencies to use with this chapter, see the Transparency Guide on page 6.

Teaching Resources

Suggested Readings

Freedman, S. G. (1990). *Small victories.* New York: Harper & Row.

Kidder, J. T. (1989). *Among schoolchildren.* Boston: Houghton-Mifflin.

Marquis, D. M., & Sachs, R. (1990). *I am a teacher.* New York: Simon & Schuster.

Palonsky, S. (1985). *900 shows a year.* New York: McGraw.

Raphael, R. (1985). *The teacher's voice: A sense of who we are.* Portsmouth, NH: Heinemann.

Rubin, L. J. (1985). *Artistry in teaching.* New York: Random House.

Shulman, L. S. (1986). Those who understand: Knowledge growth in teaching. *Educational Researcher, 15*, 2, 4–14.

Films, Videocassettes, Audiocassettes

- *Methodology—The Psychologist and the Experiment,* 1975. An award-winning film (also available in videocassette). Although somewhat dated, this film explores the basic rules common to all research by documenting two different experiments. Independent and dependent variables, control groups, random assignments, and other basic statistical concepts are discussed. Available through Media Five Film Distributors, 1011 North Cole Avenue, Hollywood, CA 90038.

- *In Pursuit of the Expert Pedagogue,* 50 min. David C. Berliner and his colleagues, in a University of Arizona research project, try to understand the nature of expertise in pedagogy. Their strategy is to find and study expert or experienced teachers and to compare them with ordinary or novice teachers in order to discover how they differ in their behavior and their approaches to tasks. Early findings indicate that among the most important differences is problem-solving ability, which expert teachers share with experts in such other fields as chess or physics. Available through AERA Videotape Sales, P.O. Box 19700, Washington, DC 20036.

- *Free to Teach: Unchaining Teachers,* 26 min., color. A round table discussion in which eight teachers (members of the Advisory Council for the Teacher's Institute of Continuing Education) suggest ways to make changes in the education process. Suggestions include such areas as risk taking, working with students, and presenting education in the community. Available through Successful Teaching Practices Series, EBEC, 1982. Encyclopaedia Britannica Educational Corporation, 310 South Michigan Ave., Chicago, IL 60604.

Test Questions

Test Questions 1.1–1.71

Study Guide

Assign Chapter 1 of the *Study Guide.*

2
Cognitive and Linguistic Development

Chapter Objectives

1. General Objective

Understands the factors that influence intellectual development (pp. 42–45).

SPECIFIC BEHAVIORS
1.01 Defines maturation.
1.02 Defines active experience.
1.03 Defines social interaction.
1.04 Defines equilibration.
1.05 Explains the interaction between factors.
1.06 Identifies examples of how factors operate in and out of school.

2. General Objective

Understands the mental structures and processes of organization and adaptation (pp. 45–52).

SPECIFIC BEHAVIORS
2.01 Defines schemata.
2.02 Defines assimilation.
2.03 Defines accommodation.
2.04 Provides an example of the complementary nature of assimilation and accommodation.
2.05 Explains how equilibration regulates intellectual growth.
2.06 Distinguishes between physical experience and logico-mathematical experience.

3. General Objective

Demonstrates knowledge of Piaget's stages of cognitive development (pp. 52–60).

SPECIFIC BEHAVIORS
3.01 Reconciles the notion of stages with the idea of continuous development.
3.02 Recognizes ordinality as invariant, but rate of development as highly variable.
3.03 Describes the relationship between stages and schemata.
3.04 Characterizes the sensorimotor stage.
3.05 Characterizes the preoperations stage.

3.06 Characterizes the concrete operations stage.
3.07 Characterizes the formal operations stage.

4. General Objective

Judges the utility of variations of the Piagetian theme (pp. 60–67).

SPECIFIC BEHAVIORS
4.01 Recognizes the implications of Vygotsky's concept of the zone of proximal development.
4.02 Characterizes cognitive development from an information-processing perspective.
4.03 Identifies the developmental changes in attention.
4.04 Explains developmental changes in memory capacity.
4.05 Recognizes the relationship between operational efficiency, automaticity, and metacognition.

5. General Objective

Understands language development (pp. 67–72).

SPECIFIC BEHAVIORS
5.01 Distinguishes between the innatist, cognitivist, and social contextual theories of language development.
5.02 Recognizes the implications of interconnectedness and independence assumptions concerning language and thought.
5.03 Characterizes each stage of language development.
5.04 Identifies the hallmarks of language development.

6. General Objective

Understands the influences of bilingualism and dialect (pp. 72–78).

SPECIFIC BEHAVIORS
6.01 Identifies the importance of a "critical period" in second language acquisition.
6.02 Identifies the cognitive advantages and disadvantages of bilingualism.

6.03 Defines dialect differences.

6.04 Distinguishes between restrictive and elaborated linguistic codes.

6.05 Applies guidelines for promoting language development.

Focus Questions

- What factors influence intellectual development?
- How do students mentally organize their experiences in an adaptive way?
- How does a student's mental representation of his or her environment change as he or she develops?
- Can cognitive development be accelerated?
- In what ways are language and cognition related and unrelated?
- How do students, with varying capabilities, come to communicate competently?

Chapter Outline

INTRODUCTION: THE NATURE OF HUMAN DEVELOPMENT
Jean Piaget: A Curious Biologist

TEACHER CHRONICLE 2.1: MAGNETS

BASIC PIAGETIAN CONCEPTS
Influences on Cognitive Development
Maturation
Active Experience
Social Interaction
Equilibration
Intellectual Organization and Adaptation
Organization
Schemata
Adaptation
Assimilation and Accommodation
Equilibration
Experience and Knowledge
Physical Experience
Logico-mathematical Experience
Principles in Practice 2.1

TEACHER CHRONICLE 2.2: READY OR NOT?

PIAGET'S STAGES OF COGNITIVE DEVELOPMENT
Describing and Interpreting Cognitive Change
The Stages: Hallmarks of Change
Sensorimotor Stage
Object Permanence
Imitation
Preoperations Stage
Symbolic Representation
Perceptual Concentration
Irreversibility
Egocentrism
Concrete Operations
Reversibility and Decentration
Conservation
Multiple Classification
Formal Operations
Abstract Reasoning

THE PIAGETIAN THEME AND SOME VARIATIONS
Zone of Proximal Development
Information-processing Capabilities
Attention
Memory and Metacognition
Principles in Practice 2.2

TEACHER CHRONICLE 2.3: CRACKING THE CODE

LANGUAGE DEVELOPMENT
Theories of Language Development
The Innatist Theory
The Cognitivist Theory
The Social Contextual Theory
Hallmarks of Language Development
Syntax
Semantics
Pragmatics
Language Differences
Bilingualism
Dialect
Principles in Practice 2.3

CONCLUSION

Chapter Summary

Introduction: The Nature of Human Development

- The study of human development involves assessing the capabilities we possess as we grow into and develop our potential. There are several areas of human development that have been identified for the purpose of study: cognitive development, personal development, and social development. This chapter has focused on cognitive capabilities and the related area of language development.
- The most influential cognitive theorist is Jean Piaget, who began his studies of early cognitive development in the 1920s.

Basic Piagetian Concepts

- Piaget's theory of cognitive development is based on basic assumptions about the factors that influence cognitive development: maturation, that is, genetically determined growth; active experience with objects in the environment; social interaction with people in the environment; and equilibration, that is, the regulation of other factors.

- Piaget viewed cognitive development as being governed by the same principles that determined biological development. The human tendency to organize the environment yields schemata or knowledge structures. The tendency to adapt to the environment is played out through the processes of assimilation and accommodation. These processes allow one to modify schemata. Equilibration provides a balance between assimilation and accommodation in order to maintain schemata that yield to adaptive interaction with the environment.

- Two types of experience allow us to construct knowledge. Using the first, physical experience, we observe and manipulate objects in the environment to construct knowledge of the physical properties of objects. Using the second, the logico-mathematical experience—thinking about one's thoughts—we can build new knowledge. Both types of experience are important for cognitive development.

Piaget's Stages of Cognitive Development

- Piaget viewed cognitive development as being gradual. He established stages as hallmarks along the continuum of cognitive development. The order of these stages is universal; each person passes through them in the same way. The rate at which development proceeds varies considerably from person to person.

- The stages of cognitive development define critical characteristics of the schemata possessed at each stage. Later stages include the characteristics of earlier ones. The first stage of development, the sensorimotor stage, is characterized by sensations and motor actions. The second stage, preoperations, is characterized by symbolic representation. The third stage, concrete operations, is characterized by schemata that allow logical operations. The fourth stage, formal operations, introduces the capability of abstract reasoning.

The Piagetian Theme and Some Variations

- Piaget's view of cognitive development provides us with a definition of the ways in which children think. Teachers who wish to carefully identify children's capabilities must carefully observe each child. One variation on the Piagetian theme is Vygotsky's zone of proximal development, a notion that suggests that teachers look for and support areas of imminent "breakthroughs."

- Another variation on Piaget's theme comes from information-processing theory. Information processing helps teachers to focus on how a student attends to his or her environment, uses his or her limited memory capacity, and monitors his or her own cognitive activity (metacognition).

Language Development

- Innatist, cognitivist, and social contextualist views of language development define the relationship between language and cognition. The innatist view suggests that a person's utterances do not reflect his or her cognitive capability. Cognitivist theory suggests that cognitive development must precede language. Social contextualist theory suggests that after two years of age, language and cognition are interrelated. In all cases, the relationship between language and cognition is not a simple one. Students who speak well are not necessarily more advanced.

- A language is a set of grammatical rules covering phonology (sounds), syntax (putting words together to communicate ideas), and semantics (the meanings of words and sentences). In addition, language development involves pragmatics (the use of language in various contexts). Grammatical development occurs rapidly. Children can use relatively complex structures by the time they reach school. Pragmatic development continues indefinitely.

- Language differences contribute to the variation in classroom communications. Demographic trends suggest that bilingual education is likely to increase. Students who are immersed in a second language will respond differently to instruction based on whether the second language is the school's majority or minority language. Dialects should be recognized as legitimate forms of language. The use of a nonstandard dialect does not indicate substandard cognitive capabilities.

Key Terms

developmental psychology
cognitive development
  theory
social development theory
personal development
  theory
maturation
active experience
social interaction
equilibration
schemata
assimilation
accommodation
disequilibrium
physical experience
empirical abstraction
logico-mathematical experience
reflexive abstraction
constructivist theory
ordinality

sensorimotor stage
object permanence
imitation
operations
preoperational
symbolical representation
perceptual centration
conservation tasks
irreversibility
egocentrism
collective monologue
concrete operations
reversibility
decentration
conservation
multiple classification
formal operations
abstract reasoning
décalage
zone of proximal development

information processing
attention
short-term store
operating space
storage space
automaticity
metacognition
innatist theory
language acquisition device (LAD)
transformational grammar
deep structure
surface structure
cognitivist theory

social contextual theory
grammar
phonology
syntax
semantics
pragmatics
bilingualism
metalinguistic awareness
bilingual education
language immersion
dialect
restricted language codes
elaborated language codes

Teacher Chronicle Summaries

Teacher Chronicle 2.1: Magnets (p. 43)

Two teachers are discussing a third-grade student who is struggling with the abstractness of math concepts. One teacher suggests that the student manipulate objects to help him understand that numbers represent specific amounts.

Teacher Chronicle 2.2: Ready or Not? (pp. 51–52)

A teacher meets with a concerned parent to discuss why the parent's first-grade son is not reading, although his twin sister is. The teacher explains that the boy has not yet mastered letter-sound correspondence, but that he has an expansive vocabulary. The teacher feels that the boy does not have a reading problem; that he will read when he is ready.

Teacher Chronicle 2.3: Cracking the Code (pp. 65–67)

A teacher introduces a numerically coded message to a class of first graders who can make no sense of it. Through trial and error and teacher questioning, one student, who is bilingual, breaks the code.

Possible Answers to Principles in Practice

Principles in Practice 2.1

1. *What types of experiences, other than the manipulation of magnets, might have helped the first graders build appropriate schemata?*

Students might have been encouraged to work problems with objects, such as magnets or blocks, instead of numerals. For example, students might be instructed to line up three blocks in a row, make a second row underneath the first containing two blocks, place a line under the second row, and, under the line, place the number of blocks that indicates the answer—five blocks if the problem is addition, one block if subtraction.

Students might work simulation problems on a computer, typing in problems rather than writing them. This assumes some proficiency with the keyboard.

2. *How did the magnets allow assimilation and subsequent accommodation to occur?*

Using the magnets allowed students to manipulate numerals as they have manipulated other objects (assimilation). Manipulating the numbers in order to work problems led to a new idea of how numerals can be used to solve math problems (accommodation).

3. *What about Pat, now a third grader? What sort of experiences could the teacher set up to help him understand the concept of numbers?*

Pat could be given some practice in counting objects or be given objects to represent different numbers. For example, a tennis ball might represent ten units, a marble might represent one unit. Pat could be asked to represent the number *22* by selecting two tennis balls and two marbles. Pat might also be given the assignment to create his own number codes using objects he selects and then using these objects to work problems.

Principles in Practice 2.2

1. *How will Paul's experiences at car shows and on his grandfather's farm contribute to logical thinking?*

Any experiences will build Paul's schemata through assimilation and accommodation. As Paul continues to organize his experiences, he is constructing cognitive structures that will, at some point, allow him to perform logical operations. (Answering the question along these lines might include a discussion of décalage and Piaget's concept of operations.)

2. *In terms of Piaget's stages, is Paul at a different stage of development than his sister?*

Paul's sister possesses skills he doesn't possess. The question, however, is whether Paul thinks differently than his sister. The teacher's comments to Paul's mother can be used as an argument that Paul is capable of thought that is similar to his sister's. Therefore, it can be argued that even though one child can read and one can't, they are at the same stage of cognitive development.

Given the age of the twins, a student might argue that Paul is preoperational, while his sister is concrete operational. This line of argument would require the student to demonstrate that Paul's sister reasons logically and that Paul does not.

3. *Assuming that Paul's mother is capable of abstract reasoning, why did she misunderstand her son's reading problem?*

First, she assumed that her children would develop at the same rate—possibly placing too much emphasis on the role of heredity. Children, even twins, are different. Second, she discounted the influence that Paul's experiences in kindergarten had on him.

Principles in Practice 2.3

1. If Ernesto's metalinguistic awareness helped him think effectively about the code, why didn't that awareness prove as effective when he attempted to read or communicate?

Comprehending and producing a particular language requires knowledge of that language. In order to read English, a student must know the vocabulary and syntax of English. Understanding that language is coded information is different than knowing the code of a specific language.

2. Re-reading the utterances of the students, what do you understand the "speaking-in-class" rules to be in this classroom?

Students are called upon, but they also contribute answers freely, at least when the class is in a "problem-solving" mode.

Follow-up Question: How does this kind of classroom atmosphere affect a bilingual student such as Ernesto?

3. How much do you imagine other students in this class talk to Ernesto? What is his "social" position in this class?

Indications are that Ernesto is somewhat isolated from the rest of the class. His contributions to solving the code were met with some surprise from his classmates. He is probably not among the most popular children in the class.

Follow-up Question: How important are communication skills to social status in elementary classes? In junior high classes? In high school classes?

CNN Connection to Issues in Educational Psychology

The old notion of the United States as a "melting pot" is too simplistic. Large numbers of non-English speaking children in today's classrooms will not become "Americans" automatically. The challenges for educators are formidable. The video segments illustrate some of the controversies surrounding bilingual education and examine the ways in which our nation will address the needs of a rapidly growing multicultural population.

Activities and Exercises

In-Class Activities

1. Assign students to groups according to their anticipated teaching level: elementary, junior high, or high school. Inform students that each group is a "task force" established by the superintendent of their school district to create a better match between the characteristics of students and the district's curriculum. Their specific task is twofold. First, as prospective teachers, they must develop an efficient method of classifying their students

according to Piaget's stages. Second, they should provide a rationale for using Piaget's theory to help guide curricular decisions. The latter task will help the superintendent prepare a presentation for the school board.

2. Identify any bilingual students in the class or recruit other bilinguals from campus. In addition, select a panel of students. Have the panel hear testimony from the bilingual students concerning "what teachers need to know about bilingual students." The panel can take statements and ask questions. The students who do not testify or sit on the panel can play the role of reporters. At the conclusion of the testimony have each reporter write a headline about the panel discussion. These headlines could be used in follow-up discussions of issues that are important to bilingual students.

Teacher Interviews

Have students interview elementary teachers to collect hypotheses for hands-on activities, analyzing them for developmental appropriateness.

Have students interview teachers regarding their experiences and observations of developmental gaps.

Field Observations

Have students observe children in a playground, noting the age levels at which they play different games.

Have students observe young toddlers, perhaps in a day-care center, trying to distinguish *imitation* from *deferred imitation*.

Have students administer conservation tasks to preschool students.

Have students observe children of various ages in school, church, at a concert, etc.

Have students collect ten examples of nonverbal communication while observing both teachers and students.

Have students listen and document preschool "conversations."

Have students document the sentence constructions of children of various ages. Have them give children a complex sentence and ask the children to repeat it in order to observe changes in syntax that the children make.

Have students interview elementary, middle, and high school students from schools in different socioeconomic neighborhoods to discover different "codes," i.e., phrases, connotations, etc.

Journal Entries

Have students describe something that they've learned easily and something that was difficult to learn. Was the difficulty due to development or learning?

Have students discuss the extent to which they have talked with children at various age levels, noting the "level" at which they talk when addressing children of various ages.

Have students think about an accident they nearly had, commenting on what they learned from their experiences.

Have students reflect on how they will account for differences between their perceptions and those of their students when they have their own classrooms.

As a way of reflecting on their own thinking processes, have students reflect on the shortcuts they "discovered" and the shortcuts they were given by their teachers, commenting on whether it is better to discover or be given shortcuts.

Ask students to reflect on a teacher (or other adult) who influenced their use of language as a child or adolescent. Have them reflect also on the time when they wrote their first poems (or used poetic language). What was the social context? Had they fallen "in love" for the first time?

Discussion Topics (based on Lecture Notes)

Ask students who have baby-sat or have infant children to identify reflexes they have observed in those children.

Have students discuss how language and thought are different.

Ask students to speculate about the inferential abilities of good versus poor readers.

Ask students to discuss if there is a "grammar" of communication between people and their pets.

Ask students if they or any of their friends use different dialects at home and at school. Ask them to compare their speech in the dorm, fraternity or sorority house, or even in small group discussions with the speech they use to recite in larger groups with a professor or instructor present.

Application Scenarios

Present the following scenarios to students:

- Imagine that you are a fifth-grade teacher. Two of the boys in your class, Tony and Ben, are good friends. Tony is very tall and muscular for his age, and Ben is skinny and a bit uncoordinated. Tony is shy and tries to stay in the background, and Ben is chatty and is always looking for the limelight. Tony is good at working on a task until it is finished, and Ben tends to jump around. Can you devise a project for these two friends to work on together? Assume that you want each boy to help the other boy improve behavioral skills.

- Suppose that you are a ninth-grade algebra teacher. You have a very unusual class. Half of the class is clearly operating in the concrete operational stage, while the other half of the class is operating in the formal operational stage. What can you do to help each student learn algebra the way that is most productive for that student?

- Your sixth-grade class just added three transfer students at the break. Ming Chee is from Taiwan, and she speaks very little English. Jeffrey is from the Deep South, and his accent is so thick that you and the other students sometimes have trouble understanding what he says. Martha is from a neighboring town, but she is also hard to understand. She speaks very little, and when she does speak, she talks in very short, concrete phrases. How can you help each of these students develop their linguistic and communication skills?

Chapter 15 Casebook Previews

See Responsibility Education.

See Coup D'Etat in the Classroom.

See I Am Leo.

See Science Is Only Real When You Do It.

See Writers' Tea.

Teaching Anecdotes

Tell a story of the teacher who, during summer vacation, took classes in mime and karate. While he found them both challenging, he began dreading karate class. He just couldn't seem to coordinate his body movements and became increasingly frustrated. The mime class, although equally demanding physically, intrigued him and he became proficient enough to teach mime to his students in the fall. After reflecting on the difference between the two classes, the teacher felt he better understood his students' frustration in learning new concepts and skills.

Ask students how this experience made the teacher more effective. (See p. 42.)

Tell a story of the junior high math teacher who switched to teaching at the first-grade level. She learned that junior high and primary grade students have very different understandings of the concept of time. The first graders, while knowing the words *hour* and *half hour*, had no concrete understanding of what those lengths of time meant. They were constantly asking when recess would begin. The frequent interruptions decreased when the teacher compared one "half hour" with the amount of time it took the students to watch a popular TV program.

Ask students to explain/verify the teacher's experience. (See pp. 52–53.)

Tell the story of the kindergarten teacher who built a tepee in her classroom as a place for silent reading. After reading a story about Native Americans and buffalo, children began an elaborate game, which they played intensely for weeks. They became Native American parents and children, hunters and horses, buffalo and bears. Ask students whether they see this as imitation or deferred imitation. (See p. 55.)

Tell the story of the first-grade teacher who could not understand why Myra, a bright student, was having difficulty learning to read. She was also very demanding of attention. Myra had appropriate language skills, but couldn't sit still or concentrate for longer than five minutes. In her teacher's words, "She's driving me crazy." Myra was falling behind her classmates. When the teacher checked Myra's birth date, she understood the problem. Myra had turned six only three days before school started; she was nearly a year younger than the majority of her classmates. Why would Myra's age make such a difference in her ability to learn how to read? (See p. 52.)

Tell the story of the high school English teacher who, when asked for the four-thousandth time, "How long does the paper have to be?" responded sarcastically, "The paper must be 4.23 pages long." He felt bad the next day when an anxious student asked, "How do you figure out how long .23 of a page is?" (See p. 71.)

Transparencies

For transparencies to use with this chapter, see the Transparency Guide on page 53.

Teaching Resources

Suggested Readings

Anderson, P. S., & Lapp, D. (1988). *Language skills in elementary education* (4th ed.). New York: Macmillan.

Case, R. (1984). The process of stage transition: A neo-Piagetian view. In R. J. Sternberg (ed.). *Mechanisms of cognitive development.* New York: W. H. Freeman.

Cazden, C. B. (1988). *Classroom discourse: The language of teaching and learning.* Portsmouth, NH: Heinemann.

Flavell, J. H. (1985). *Cognitive development* (2nd ed.). Englewood Cliffs, NJ: Prentice-Hall.

Piaget, J., & Inhelder, B. (1969). *The psychology of the child.* New York: Basic Books.

Vygotsky, L. S. (1986). *Thought and language.* Cambridge, MA: MIT Press.

Wadsworth, B. J. (1978). *Piaget for the classroom teacher.* New York: Longman.

Wadsworth, B. J. (1989). *Piaget's theory of cognitive and affective development* (4th ed.). New York: Longman.

Films, Videocassettes, Audiocassettes

- *The First Years: What to Expect,* video, 19 min., color. The video examines the critical parent/child relationship in the first five years; the effects in adolescence of traits learned in early childhood, and the relationship between emotions and cognitive development.
- *Nature & Nurture,* video, 52 min., color. This program, one of the widely acclaimed Human Animal series, looks at identical twins separated at birth and reports some fascinating findings—that some 10 to 15 percent of these children are born with a slight tendency to be very outgoing or very apprehensive and there may be a chemical predisposition to anger or seeking high risk. The video concludes that biology is not everything; a supportive environment helps.

These two videos are available through Films for the Humanities and Sciences, Inc., P.O. Box 2052, Princeton, NJ 08543. ED-1412

Test Questions

Test Questions 2.1–2.142

Study Guide

Assign Chapter 2 of the *Study Guide.*

3
Personal and Interpersonal Growth

Chapter Objectives

1. General Objective

Understands the relationship between social and personal development (pp. 86–88).

SPECIFIC BEHAVIORS
1.01 Identifies how the epigenetic principle operates in personal and interpersonal development.
1.02 Recognizes Erikson's stages as social tasks.
1.03 Characterizes the nature of developmental crises.

2. General Objective

Understands the developmental crises associated with each of Erikson's stages (pp. 88–93).

SPECIFIC BEHAVIORS
2.01 Explains the issues of the stage labeled Trust Versus Mistrust.
2.02 Explains the issues of the stage labeled Autonomy Versus Shame and Doubt.
2.03 Explains the issues of the stage labeled Initiative Versus Guilt.
2.04 Explains the issues of the stage labeled Industry Versus Inferiority.
2.05 Explains the issues of the stage labeled Identity Versus Role Diffusion.
2.06 Explains the issues of the stage labeled Intimacy Versus Isolation.
2.07 Explains the issues of the stage labeled Generativity Versus Stagnation.
2.08 Explains the issues of the stage labeled Integrity Versus Despair.

3. General Objective

Recognizes how the resolutions of earlier developmental crises influence identity (pp. 93–97).

SPECIFIC BEHAVIORS
3.01 Differentiates Erikson's concept of psychosocial moratorium and negative identity.
3.02 Characterizes identity diffusion types.

3.03 Characterizes moratorium types.
3.04 Characterizes identity achievement types.
3.05 Characterizes foreclosure types.

4. General Objective

Understands the principles governing the development of moral judgments (pp. 98–104).

SPECIFIC BEHAVIORS
4.01 Distinguishes between what Piaget called morality of constraint and morality of cooperation.
4.02 Relates Piaget's conception of moral judgments to Kohlberg's stages of moral reasoning.
4.03 Infers behaviors reflected in Kohlberg's punishment-obedience stage.
4.04 Infers behaviors reflected in Kohlberg's instrumental exchange stage.
4.05 Infers behaviors reflected in Kohlberg's interpersonal conformity stage.
4.06 Infers behaviors reflected in Kohlberg's law-and-order stage.
4.07 Infers behaviors reflected in Kohlberg's prior rights and social contract stage.
4.08 Infers behaviors reflected in Kohlberg's universal ethical principles stage.
4.09 Distinguishes Kohlberg's morality of justice from Gilligan's morality of care and responsibility.
4.10 Infers behaviors reflected in Gilligan's individual survival level.
4.11 Infers behaviors reflected in the transition to and attainment of Gilligan's self-sacrifice and social conformity level.
4.12 Infers behaviors reflected in the transition to and attainment of Gilligan's morality of nonviolence level.

5. General Objective

Applies an integrative view of moral development to classroom interaction (pp. 104–112).

SPECIFIC BEHAVIORS
5.01 Explains the vertical and horizontal dimensions of moral growth.

5.02 Interprets Lickona's process of building self-esteem and social community.

5.03 Interprets Lickona's process of cooperative learning and helping relations.

5.04 Interprets Lickona's process of moral reflection.

5.05 Interprets Lickona's process of participatory decision making.

5.06 Illustrates the interrelatedness of the processes in Lickona's model of moral education.

6. General Objective

Understands the normative value of grade-level characteristics (pp. 112–122).

SPECIFIC BEHAVIORS

6.01 Integrates the physical, social, and cognitive characteristics typical of a primary grade student.

6.02 Integrates the physical, social, and cognitive characteristics typical of an intermediate grade student.

6.03 Integrates the physical, social, and cognitive characteristics typical of a junior high school student.

6.04 Integrates the physical, social, and cognitive characteristics typical of a high school student.

Focus Questions

- How does a student's sense of self contribute to his or her relationships with others?
- What are the possible outcomes of a student's search for identity?
- How does moral decision making change as a student develops?
- What classroom processes influence moral judgments, feelings, and behavior?
- How are the various areas of development—social, cognitive, physical—related to each other?
- How does knowledge of the development of the "typical student" help us understand individuals?

Chapter Outline

INTRODUCTION: SELF AND OTHERS

TEACHER CHRONICLE 3.1: A CHANCE TO CHAT

A THEORY OF PSYCHOSOCIAL DEVELOPMENT
The Stages of Psychosocial Development
Stage 1: Trust Versus Mistrust (birth–18 months)
Stage 2: Autonomy Versus Shame and Doubt (18 months–3 years)
Stage 3: Initiative Versus Guilt (3–6 years)
Stage 4: Industry Versus Inferiority (6–12 years)

Stage 5: Identity Versus Role Diffusion (adolescence)
Stage 6: Intimacy Versus Isolation (young adulthood)
Stage 7: Generativity Versus Stagnation (young adulthood–middle age)
Stage 8: Integrity Versus Despair (later adulthood–old age)
Identity: A Closer Look
Identity Types or Statuses
Interpreting Erikson's Theory
Principles in Practice 3.1

TEACHER CHRONICLE 3.2: THE FIRE DRILL

MORAL DEVELOPMENT
Piaget's Framework of Moral Reasoning
Morality of Constraint
Morality of Cooperation
Kohlberg's Stages of Moral Reasoning
Preconventional Morality (birth–9 years)
Stage 1: The Punishment-Obedience Level
Stage 2: The Instrumental Exchange Orientation
Conventional Morality (9 years–young adulthood)
Stage 3: The Interpersonal Conformity Orientation
Stage 4: The Law-and-Order Orientation
Postconventional Morality (adulthood)
Stage 5: The Prior Rights and Social Contract Orientation
Stage 6: The Universal Ethical Principles Orientation
Criticisms of Kohlberg's Theory
The Question of Stages
The Question of Generalizability—Gilligan's Theory
The Question of Applicability

AN INTEGRATIVE VIEW OF MORAL DEVELOPMENT
Lickona's Model of Moral Education
Building Self-esteem and Social Community
Cooperative Learning and Helping Relations
Moral Reflection
Participatory Decision Making
Principles in Practice 3.2

TEACHER CHRONICLE 3.3: LOOKS CAN DECEIVE

GRADE-LEVEL CHARACTERISTICS
Groups and Individuals
Key Capabilities in the Primary Grades (K–3)
Physical
Social/Emotional
Cognitive
Developmental Issue: Sex Roles
Key Capabilities in the Intermediate Grades (4–6)
Physical
Social/Emotional
Cognitive

Developmental Issue: Growth Spurt Begins
Key Capabilities in Junior High School Grades (7–9)
    Physical
    Social/Emotional
    Cognitive
Developmental Issue: Early and Late Maturation
Key Capabilities in the High School Grades (10–12)
    Physical
    Social/Emotional
Developmental Issue: Social Pressure and Anxiety
Principles in Practice 3.3

CONCLUSION

Chapter Summary

A Theory of Psychosocial Development

- Erikson proposes eight stages of psychosocial development. Each stage's developmental crisis is identified as a dichotomy of qualities, positive and negative. If the social experiences during that period are generally positive, positive qualities result. If experiences are generally negative, the crisis is resolved negatively.
- Erikson's Stage 5—identity versus role diffusion—can be resolved in ways other than the positive and negative qualities of the dichotomy. One additional resolution is to enter a state called psychosocial moratorium, which is really no resolution at all, but rather a postponement of life-style decisions. Another resolution is to adopt a negative identity, rebellion against authority.
- James Marcia extended Erikson's work as it applied to adolescents' search for identity. He identified four identity statuses. Identity diffusion types are confused, disorganized, and avoid commitment. Moratorium types (not to be confused with Erikson's psychosocial moratorium) have given a great deal of thought to identity issues, but have not yet arrived at any conclusions. Identity achievement types are those adolescents who have made life-style decisions on their own. Foreclosure types do not experience a crisis of identity; they simply adopt decisions made for them by others.
- If a teacher uses Erikson's theory to make decisions about a student's psychosocial needs, he or she should keep in mind the evidence that suggests that Erikson's framework is a better description of males than of females. There is also a good bit of overlap in the stages—crises that begin in toddlerhood and continue through the middle school years are quite similar.

Moral Development

- Piaget distinguishes between the moral reasoning of younger and older children. Younger children

follow the morality of constraint; they follow rules without question. Older children, who follow the morality of cooperation, take into account the context of behaviors in order to judge whether an action is right or wrong.
- Kohlberg based his framework on Piaget's views. Kohlberg identified stages of moral reasoning that exist at three levels. At the first level, preconventional morality, reasoning about right and wrong is based on the idea that correct behavior is that which avoids punishment and yields some kind of reward. The second level, conventional morality, is based on respect for authority and a desire to impress others. The third level is postconventional morality. The reasoning at this level recognizes the need for societal agreement and the consistent application of moral principles.

An Integrative View of Moral Development

- Lickona identified four overlapping processes that should occur in classrooms where moral education is addressed. The first process focuses on building healthy self-esteem through social support and a sense of belonging to the community of the classroom. The second process operates to establish cooperative learning; the emphasis is on students learning to help each other. The third process, moral reflection, is similar to Kohlberg's—and more similar to Gilligan's—moral reasoning. The final process encourages participatory decision making on questions of behavior in the community of the classroom.

Grade-Level Characteristics

- These composites of the developmental capabilities of students at various grade levels provide reference points for identifying the uniqueness of individuals. The physical, social/emotional, and cognitive characteristics of primary, intermediate, junior high, and high school students contribute to critical developmental issues at each level. The issues include sex role stereotypes, the growth spurt, early and late maturation, and social pressure and anxiety.
- Primary students differ from one another considerably in size; as a group they seek outlets for their abundance of physical energy. Peer relationships are being formed, but friendships change often and quickly. Cognitively, students are generally preoperational; some students may begin to display concrete operations late in the primary grades. Although their language skills are fairly well developed, their comprehension is very literal.
- Primary-grade children have learned sex role stereotypes. Typically, boys have been encouraged to achieve, be independent, compete, and control their emotions. Girls have been encouraged to be

warm, dependent, and nurturing. Sex role stereotypes can be combated by encouraging nonstereotypic behaviors in both female and male students.

- Students' diversity in physical size and appearance can have pronounced social effects in the intermediate grades, including name calling. Athletic activity can be a useful way of encouraging motivation. Status within a group is an important aspect of social interaction. Cognitively, students are becoming more logical in their thinking, moving from preoperations to concrete operations.

- Toward the end of the intermediate grades, rapid physical changes—typical of the growth spurt—are evident. This time of change can make many students feel uncomfortable with their bodies and, in turn, uncomfortable in their interactions with peers.

- Junior high students have recently or will soon begin experiencing the physical and emotional changes that are part of puberty. Close friendships with other individuals and within a small group become important. Close-knit peer relations are especially important when students experience family stress. Although Piaget's age estimates suggest that junior high students are becoming formally operational, a large percentage of these students are still concrete operational.

- The onset of puberty and the growth spurt during the junior high years produces differences between students who mature early and those who mature later. Females as a group mature earlier than males; females who mature early are very different from most peers. The same is true of late-maturing males. Owing to the importance of "fitting in" during junior high, these two groups suffer more social and emotional stress than other students.

- Although physical growth may continue past graduation, especially for males, virtually all high school students have become sexually mature. Cliques and crowds, which include members of both sexes, provide the social context for the development of close, opposite-sex relationships. It is important to remember that many high school students will still be concrete operational.

- The development of intimate relationships, questions about one's future, and other pressures increase the emotional stress experienced by high school students. It is not uncommon for teenagers to experience symptoms of depression. If serious depression results, the possibility of suicide cannot be ignored. A suicidal student must never be left alone.

Key Terms

self-concept
psychosocial development
epigenetic principle

critical periods
dichotomy
developmental crisis

autonomy
initiative
industry
identity
identity diffusion
intimacy
isolation
generativity
stagnation
integrity
psychosocial moratorium
negative identity
identity statuses
identity diffusion types
moratorium types
identity achievement types
foreclosure types
moral judgments
morality of constraint
morality of cooperation
preconventional morality

conventional morality
postconventional morality
individual survival
self-sacrifice and social conformity
morality of nonviolence
integrative model
vertical dimension
horizontal dimension
self-esteem
moral reflection
participatory decision making
stereotype
sex role stereotypes
growth spurt
puberty
clique
crowd
learned helplessness
suicidal students

Teacher Chronicle Summaries

Teacher Chronicle 3.1: A Chance to Chat (pp. 86–87)

A high school teacher talks with a female student who is concerned about her physical development. The teacher gives the student advice and boosts her self-confidence. The student has other unasked questions, but accepts her teacher's suggestion and leaves school feeling better.

Teacher Chronicle 3.2: The Fire Drill (p. 97)

A primary school teacher tells about a fire drill in which three of her students remained at their desks due to a conceptual misunderstanding about classroom rules. The children had been told not to get out of their seats during reading without raising their hands, so they sat through the fire drill.

Teacher Chronicle 3.3: Looks Can Deceive (pp. 110–112)

A teacher has a student in class whom, by all counts, she should like, but it turns out that she doesn't. He is a model student, but something about him makes her dislike him. When he unexpectedly falls behind in class assignments, the teacher is puzzled until she finds out the reason and comes to understand him much better.

Possible Answers to Principles in Practice

Principles in Practice 3.1

1. *What other suggestions would you make to Mary that might contribute to a positive resolution of her identity crisis?*

Mary might be encouraged to use some of her extra time to pursue interests or hobbies with others. One way would be to join an extra-curricular club (e.g., the French club, chess club, ecology club).

2. Based on what you've learned about Mary in Teacher Chronicle 3.1, what areas do you see as being strengths and weaknesses in her personality?

The teacher's description implies that Mary has a sense of industry, evidenced by her capability to do well in school and by her enjoyment of school. Mary also is able to trust people; she has at least one close friend her age and is able to confide in the teacher. Mary is not, however, confident in her social abilities, evidenced by the content of her chat with the teacher.

3. What would be the advantage of inviting Mary for another after-school chat, but this time to talk about her career goals?

If the teacher can help Mary establish some career goals, even very general ones, these decisions should help give her a clearer image of herself and, perhaps, more confidence.

Principles in Practice 3.2

1. Would participatory decision making have helped the children put the "stay-seated" rule in context?

It seems likely that participating in decision making might have helped students learn something about the conventions of social interaction, at least in the classroom. Also, group discussions of social problems in the class might have helped students come to a more relativist conception of correct behavior.

2. How could the fire-drill episode be used to address values with the students in Teacher Chronicle 3.2?

The class can talk about the fire-drill episode, and the reasons that the students remained in the classroom can be explored. Perhaps even more importantly, the feelings experienced by the students who remained behind should be shared. The teacher can explain that the students who remained should be commended for doing what they thought was the right thing, but the teacher should explain why the "stay-seated" rule does not apply during a fire drill.

3. If you were to take over Mrs. Stein's class, how would you implement Lickona's processes without losing the discipline she instilled in her students?

Implementation of Lickona's model implies a different classroom atmosphere than the one in Mrs. Stein's class. But it does not imply that students must be undisciplined. Someone taking over Mrs. Stein's class might retain her rules, but might discuss those rules in the context of building students' self-esteem and sense of community. The class could then be asked to decide whether the existing rules should be retained or new rules established.

Principles in Practice 3.3

1. Will this teacher limit him- or herself to a first impression the next time a student like William comes to class?

The teacher was deeply troubled by his or her reaction to William. Much soul-searching went on. Sharing William's concern over Mr. Walker gave the teacher a new view of the student. The teacher also helped William deal with his feelings of guilt. The teacher learned not to trust first impressions.

2. How do physical differences come into play in William's social circle?

Given the description in Teacher Chronicle 3.3, one could assume that William belonged to a high-status crowd and clique in the school. One could also speculate on the role physical appearance might play in determining whether a student is or is not welcome in William's social circle. The point of the story, however, is that speculation based on stereotypes can lead to inaccurate conclusions.

3. Why do social and moral problems seem so much more traumatic for high school students than for elementary school students?

If one reflects on the developmental crises identified by Erickson, high school students are more likely to be dealing with issues of identity in an environment highly charged with peer pressure. Add to that environment the stress of establishing opposite-sex relationships and of choosing a career, and it is not surprising that high school students experience more social and moral "trauma."

CNN Connection to Issues in Educational Psychology

Should schools/teachers take responsibility for the moral development of students? In recent years, the debate about the educational system's role in providing moral education has often fallen into two camps, each perceived derogatorily by the other as either amoral atheists or religious fanatics. The segments reflect the most current thinking on this issue. Educators are beginning to focus on ethics and morals, rather than religion.

Activities and Exercises

In-Class Activities

1. Have students assume the roles of teachers attending a state education conference. The Association for Advancement of Moral Education is conducting sessions at the conference. Tell students that they have been invited to attend a workshop sponsored by the association. The goal of the workshop is to develop in-service training to help teachers implement Lickona's model. Working in groups assigned to primary, intermediate, junior

high, or high school grades, have students generate recommendations for in-service training. Recommendations should be based not only on Lickona's model, but also on what they have learned about psychosocial development, moral development, and key developmental issues.

2. Assign students to teams for the purposes of a debate. A third group of students will adjudicate the debate. The issue of the debate can be defined along the following lines: Resolved: Public school curriculum should reflect Gilligan's morality of care and responsibility rather than Kohlberg's morality of justice.

Teacher Interviews

Have each student interview a practicing teacher regarding his or her efforts to establish a classroom atmosphere that enhances interpersonal relationships.

Have each student interview a preschool teacher regarding the kinds of physical activity and linguistic experimentation he or she observes students taking part in.

Have each student interview a teacher regarding the practices described in text.

Have each student interview a practicing teacher regarding his or her efforts to incorporate participatory decision making.

Have students interview an intermediate-grade teacher regarding the social implications of student appearance.

Have each student interview a junior high school teacher regarding his or her understanding of social characteristics and how they influence his or her teaching.

Have each student interview a junior high school teacher to find out how physical differences influence peer relations.

Have each student interview a high school teacher regarding the behaviors he or she has observed in depressed students.

Field Observations

Have students observe parents interacting with infants, noting the ways in which the parents hold, feed, change, play with, and talk to their children.

Have students interview working adults, making comparisons between those who are active in community activities and those who are not.

Have students interview grandparents or other senior citizens regarding their sense of integrity.

Have students interview children of varying ages using Piaget's stories.

Have students observe children in a school or neighborhood playground, documenting how children decide to take turns in the games they play.

Have each student observe a cooperative classroom and try to identify student behaviors designed to subvert cooperative efforts.

Have students observe primary-grade classes, noting the differences in physical size among students and whether those differences are associated with patterns of social interaction.

Have students observe children of varying ages at play in the neighborhood or on a school playground.

Have students interview intermediate-grade children regarding the reactions of other children to their physical appearance.

Journal Entries

Have each student reflect on those periods of growing up when he or she felt intensely focused on some aspect of his or her personality and how it was perceived by others, especially peers.

Have students reflect on teachers they have had who either listened to them and made them feel important and those who seemed disinterested in them or their problems.

Have students reflect on groups in their high schools whose members saw themselves as wanting to be members of some kind of profession—even if they were unsure of the specific profession they would pursue. Have them consider if there were other groups made up of people who aspired to practice a trade, and whether some of those groups were even labeled with reference to a future occupation.

Have students reflect on the extent to which they see themselves as dealing with Stage 5 issues of identity and Stage 6 issues of intimacy and isolation.

Have each student reflect on his or her own life-style decisions, and whether the decisions have met the demands of others in his or her social environment.

Have students respond to Kohlberg's dilemma.

Have students reflect on the ways that Kohlberg's and Gilligan's theories differ with regard to their values, noting the set of values that best reflects their own views.

Have students reflect on any students in their high schools who felt they were under tremendous pressure from home and who took "shortcuts" in order to maintain grades.

Have students reflect on the "worst" classes they were in during elementary, junior high, and high school, and the ways in which they differed.

Have students reflect on their own acquisition of sex role stereotypes.

Have students reflect on their thoughts and feelings as they entered puberty.

Discussion Topics (based on Lecture Notes)

Ask students to speculate on what children who are not allowed to make mistakes might learn.

Ask students to consider how important the attainment of concrete operational thought might be to children at this level.

Ask students to consider whether the attainment of formal operations is necessary to postconventional moral judgments.

Ask students to speculate about why a person's moral reasoning might change depending on the particular dilemma he or she is considering.

Ask students how the transitions in Gilligan's theory integrate affect and cognition.

Ask students to share their impressions of former teachers who would meet these criteria.

Ask students to comment on the ways in which they have used stereotypic knowledge in dealing with people.

Ask students to describe their own memories of social groups in elementary school. How were those social groups defined?

Ask students to describe cliques and crowds to which they belonged.

Application Scenarios

Present the following scenarios to students:

- Imagine that you are a ninth-grade teacher. You are concerned about three students in your class. Martha is very quiet and shy, and she doesn't seem willing to share her ideas with the class. She appears to be a loner, and she never eats with other people in the cafeteria. Mark works very hard on his schoolwork, and makes good grades, but he never seems to be satisfied with what he has achieved. He is constantly asking for extra credit assignments to help bolster his grades. Larry is very athletic looking, and seems coordinated, but he never seems to take an interest in trying out for any school or intramural sports. You have heard that he has told others that he doesn't think he is good enough. What would Erikson say about these students? How could you use his ideas to help these students if they asked you for advice?
- The money that your home economics class raised to sponsor a class picnic is missing. While it is not a great deal of money, you are concerned that someone in the class has probably stolen it. How can you use Piaget's ideas of moral development and Kohlberg's ideas of moral reasoning to resolve this problem?
- You have been asked by the Board of Education to set up a Peer Tutoring program in your school district. The School Board wants fourth graders to tutor first graders, and eleventh graders to tutor seventh graders. Knowing what you know about the developmental norms of each of these grade levels, how would you prepare the older students to work with the younger ones? How would you prepare the younger students for the tutoring experience? How would you evaluate the ongoing activities? What problems would you expect?

Chapter 15 Casebook Previews

See I Am Leo.
See Gifted Achievers and Underachievers.
See Science Is Only Real When You Do It.

See Improvisation and Aesthetic Appreciation.
See Responsibility Education.

Teaching Anecdotes

Tell the story of the high-ability student who shows off her intelligence every chance she gets, always getting a perfect score in math and A's on essays in English. The student's labs always work. Instead of accepting success, she finds opportunities to call attention to how well she performs.

Ask your students why she persists even in the face of resentment from her classmates. (See p. 87.)

Tell the story of the student who did so well in high school math that she was accepted at the local community college to continue math in her senior year. The student had done well in other courses, and had a job and a car. Yet after graduation, she decided to remain at the community college rather than attend one of the universities to which she had won acceptance. "I don't think I'll be able to make the grade," she said. "I'm really not that good."

Ask your students why she might have felt this way and what a teacher or counselor could have done to encourage her to realize her potential. (See p. 94.)

Tell the story of the Honor Council president who cheated to get a passing grade in English. Without a good grade he would have failed the semester and lost his position on the council. After he was caught, he told his fellow council members why he cheated. "I knew that one way or the other—either failing or getting caught cheating—I would be off the council."

Ask your students if they think the other Honor Council members "accepted" the president's explanation. (See p. 104.)

Starratt (1987) reports a small group exercise in which each student writes his or her name at the top of a sheet of paper. The paper is passed to the next student who writes something likable about the student named on the page. The page continues around the circle until each student has named something likable about every other student in the group. Students can be encouraged to place their own sheet in their locker or on a wall at home. Some teachers display the sheets on the walls of their classrooms. Others have their class return to the sheets to elaborate on earlier comments. Another variation is to have students write affirming notes to parents, while the teacher asks parents to write affirming letters back to their children.

Ask students to explain why this technique has proved effective. (See p. 106.)

Tell the story about the fifth-grade girl who towered above her classmates. Although she was well-liked, her physical development set her off from the rest of the fifth and sixth graders. She felt awkward and uncomfortable. Her teacher began to see a slip in her work and attitude. Then a long-term substitute teacher—a very tall woman—came into the building. One day the girl stopped by to see her and they chatted. Soon the student came by every afternoon for a talk. Her grades picked up and the smile returned to her face.

Ask your students why the contact with the teacher seemed to help. (See p. 119.)

Transparencies

For transparencies to use with this chapter, see the Transparency Guides on page 100 and page 106.

Teaching Resources

Suggested Readings

Erikson, E. H. (1963). *Childhood and society* (2nd ed.). New York: Norton.

Erikson, E. H. (1968). *Identity: Youth and crisis*. New York: Norton.

Gilligan, C. (1982). Why should a woman be more like a man? *Psychology Today*, June, 68–77.

Knowles, R. T. (1986). The acting person as a moral agent. In R. T. Knowles, & G. F. McLean (Eds.), *Psychological foundations of moral education and character development*. Lanham, MD: University Press of America.

Lickona, T. (1985). *Raising good children*. New York: Bantam Books.

Lickona, T. (1987). Character development in the elementary school classroom. In K. Ryan, & G. F. McLean (Eds.), *Character development in schools and beyond*. New York: Praeger.

Films, Videocassettes, Audiocassettes

- *Preventing Teen Pregnancy*, 28 min., color. This program recommends sex education beginning in the preteens, sexual abstinence by teenagers, and education about contraceptives. CC-1438.
- *The Discovery Year*, 52 min., color. Christopher Reeve hosts this look into the first year of a human life when personality develops. The program watches how three sets of parents respond to the different personalities of their infant daughters, and how they learn to adapt to and communicate with the individuals who are their children. EC-1626.
- *Bulimia*, 28 min., color. Bulimics alternate between gross overeating and vomiting. Low self-esteem, anger, and depression are both the cause and the result of their illness. In this Phil Donahue program, these issues are discussed. EC-1165.
- *Anorexia*. Females are ten times as likely as males to become anorexic—usually bright, verbal, aggressive teenagers and young women in their early twenties. The video explores how anorexia starts and how it can be detected and cured. CC-1164.
- *Telling Teens About Sex*, 28 min., color. Do today's teenagers know all about sex? Phil Donahue's audience of teenagers tells a panel of sex educators what they really know and what they would like to know. CC-1234.
- *Telling Teens About AIDS*, 52 min., color. Helping teachers and parents to confront the issue of AIDS with respect to their own children and speaking directly to teenagers, this program shows, without moralizing, how one seemingly innocent liaison can lead to death. Former NBA star Julius Erving is the host. CC-1688.
- *Child Abuse*, 19 min., color. A therapist who deals with sex offenders describes the common characteristics of offenders; and a clinical social worker explains how she gets children to re-create what has happened to them. The program offers tips on selecting a day-care center. A neurologist provides examples of disciplinary problems and offers clues to help identify abused children. EC-1449.

These seven videos are available through Films for the Humanities & Sciences, Inc., P.O. Box 2052, Princeton, NJ 08543. Or call 1-800-257-5126 (in NJ, 609-452-1128).

- *The Bizarre Trail of the Pressured Peer*, 28 min., color. This is a fast-paced, entertaining film designed for high school students that illustrates the potentially negative consequences of peer pressure. Classroom teachers will find that this film contains excellent discussion topics for health education, social development, and drug prevention programs.
- *The Skillstreaming Video: How to Teach Students Prosocial Skills*, video, 26 min., color. Illustrates an innovative approach for teaching students the skills they need for coping with typical social and personal problems.

These two productions are available through Research Press, P.O. Box 3177, Department K, Champaign, IL 61821. Or call (217) 352-3273.

- *Erikson on Erikson: Developmental Stages*, 18 min., color, 1977. Erik Erikson discusses with students of the Institute sexual modes, family interactions, and the individual's identity crises, citing examples and responses of Freud. The adult stage is discussed in chemical and psychoanalytic terms. Erikson Institute for Early Education, Chicago, IL.
- *Introduction to Moral Development*, 16 mm, 29 min., color, 1977. The genesis of moral development from the ideas of Piaget and Dewey is described by Lawrence Kohlberg. Various theories and their practicality as well as the six stages of moral development are described. Includes visits to both elementary and secondary classrooms (Values and Morality in School series). Films, Inc./Public Media, Inc., 5547 Ravenswood Avenue, Chicago, IL 60640. Or call (312) 878-2600, 1-800-323-4222.

Test Questions

Test Questions 3.1–3.109

Study Guide

Assign Chapter 3 of the *Study Guide*.

4
Developmental Diversity

Chapter Objectives

1. General Objective

Understands traditional views of intelligence (pp. 128–136).

SPECIFIC BEHAVIORS
1.01 Explains Piaget's dynamic view of intelligence.
1.02 Explains Wechsler's global view of intelligence.
1.03 Explains Guilford's multifactor view of intelligence.
1.04 Characterizes operation, content, and product as dimensions of multifactor intelligence.

2. General Objective

Understands that the construct of intelligence can be viewed from the perspective of subtheories (pp. 136–138).

SPECIFIC BEHAVIORS
2.01 Distinguishes Sternberg's triarchic theory of intelligence.
2.02 Summarizes the experiential subtheory of intelligence.
2.03 Summarizes the contextual subtheory of intelligence.
2.04 Summarizes the componential subtheory of intelligence.
2.05 Explains adaptive ability.
2.06 Explains environmental selection.
2.07 Explains environmental shaping.

3. General Objective

Recognizes the relationship between environments and personal styles of learning (pp. 138–142).

SPECIFIC BEHAVIORS
3.01 Discriminates between personality types.
3.02 Infers style differences along the continuum extrovert–introvert.
3.03 Infers style differences along the continuum sensory–intuitive.
3.04 Infers style differences along the continuum thinker–feeler.

3.05 Infers style differences along the continuum judger–perceiver.
3.06 Infers style differences between convergent and divergent thinkers.
3.07 Infers differences between impulsive, reflective, thematic, and analytic styles.
3.08 Identifies the implications of research on matching learning styles to instruction.

4. General Objective

Understands that the values in school may differ from the values of a student's family (pp. 142–150).

SPECIFIC BEHAVIORS
4.01 Explains how values contribute to macroculture and microculture.
4.02 Explains how achievement-related value conflicts and communication-related value conflicts influence classroom interaction.
4.03 Distinguishes between the home environments of high achievers and low achievers.
4.04 Relates the parenting style to a child's competence.
4.05 Characterizes the authoritative parenting style.
4.06 Characterizes the authoritarian parenting style.
4.07 Characterizes the permissive-indulgent parenting style.
4.08 Generalizes from parenting style to typical behavior in children.

5. General Objective

Analyzes the exceptionalities in order to prevent disabilities from becoming handicaps (pp. 150–164).

SPECIFIC BEHAVIORS
5.01 Identifies the characteristics of mental retardation.
5.02 Identifies the characteristics of learning disabilities.
5.03 Identifies the characteristics of emotional/behavioral disorders (E/BD).

5.04 Identifies the characteristics of communication disorders.

5.05 Identifies the characteristics of hearing impairment.

5.06 Identifies the characteristics of visual impairment.

5.07 Identifies the characteristics of physical disabilities.

5.08 Identifies the characteristics of gifted and talented.

Focus Questions

- What is intelligence and how does it contribute to differences among students?
- Can students be intelligent in different ways?
- Why do students approach learning tasks differently?
- How do cultural differences contribute to diversity among students?
- How is a disability distinguished from a handicap?
- What is exceptionality in general and what forms does it take in students?

Chapter Outline

INTRODUCTION: SEEING THE INDIVIDUALS IN A GROUP

TEACHER CHRONICLE 4.1: AREN'T I SMART?

VARIETIES OF INTELLIGENCE
  Piaget's Dynamic View
  Wechsler's Global View
  Guilford's Multifactor View
    Operation
    Content
    Product
  An Interim Report on Intelligence Theories
  Sternberg's Triarchic Theory of Intelligence
    The Experiential Subtheory
    The Contextual Subtheory
    The Componential Subtheory

LEARNING STYLES
  Principles in Practice 4.1

TEACHER CHRONICLE 4.2: GRANDMA TALES

CULTURES AND VALUES
  Achievement-related Value Conflicts
  Communication-related Value Conflicts
  Parenting Styles
  Principles in Practice 4.2

TEACHER CHRONICLE 4.3: LOST AND FOUND

EXCEPTIONAL STUDENTS
  Mental Retardation
  Learning Disabilities
  Emotional/Behavioral Disorders
  Communication Disorders
  Hearing Impairment
  Visual Impairment
  Physical Disabilities
  Gifted and Talented
  Principles in Practice 4.3

CONCLUSION

Chapter Summary

Introduction: Seeing the Individuals in a Group

- Knowledge about the developmental groups that students belong to is important for teachers. It is also important, however, for teachers to know each student as an individual. Knowledge of individuals helps teachers make sound decisions.

Varieties of Intelligence

- According to Piaget, intelligence changes as a person adapts to his or her environment. The modes of adaptation change as a student develops intellectually. Because ways of adapting change (see Piaget's stages in Chapter 2), so does intelligence. In Piaget's view, intelligence is dynamic, not static.
- Wechsler views intelligence as a general or global capacity that allows the individual to deal effectively with his or her environment. This global capacity is not simply the sum of several subscales on an intelligence test.
- Guilford viewed intelligence as comprising a whole range of factors. His three faces of intellect model combines five kinds of operations, four kinds of content, and six kinds of products to yield 120 separate factors.
- Piaget's, Wechsler's, and Guilford's views of intelligence focus on different aspects of intelligent behavior. Piaget warns against using just one "yardstick" to judge intelligence. Wechsler warns that intelligence is more than the sum of its parts. Guilford warns against ignoring divergent operations.
- Sternberg's theory of intelligence is made up of three subtheories. The experiential subtheory describes a person's capacity to handle new ideas and situations. The contextual subtheory describes one's ability to adapt to his or her environment. The componential subtheory describes the mental components of intelligent behavior.

Learning Styles

- Learning styles are the ways students prefer to learn. Personality types have been used to determine learning styles. The personality type approach suggests that teaching styles also exist. This discovery raises questions about the ways learning and teaching styles match up. Learning styles have been identified along the dimensions of convergent-divergent thinking, impulsive-reflective thinking, and thematic-analytic thinking.

Cultures and Values

- Different macro- and microcultures have different values. If students have values about achievement-related behavior that differ from the values reflected in a classroom, problems can occur. One source for an achievement-related value conflict is the value placed on individualism in most schools and the value of groupism held by students from some microcultures.
- The value systems of certain microcultures include the ''rules'' of social interaction. When the cultural background of a teacher and a student are different, misunderstandings can result.
- The family acts as a significant source of values for students. Parents communicate what is and is not valued by the way they raise their children. Certain parenting behaviors are associated with high and low achievement in their children. As is the case with other cultural influences, it is the values that the parents communicate, not their ethnic background, that is significant.

Exceptional Students

- Mental retardation is a condition within which intellectual functioning and adaptive behavior are significantly subaverage.
- A learning disability is a disorder of one or more of the psychological processes involved in general language use, reasoning, or computation. Learning disabilities are distinct from mental retardation, physical disabilities, and emotional disorders.
- E/BD students can display externalizing behavior or acting out in ways that disturb or injure others. Another category of disordered behavior is internalizing behavior, which refers to the emotional problems that may result in anxiety or depression. In the extreme, internalizing can manifest itself as autism or schizophrenia.
- Communication disorders are of two major types: speech disorders, which refers to some type of voice problem (e.g., stuttering); and language disorders, which make it difficult to understand or generate messages.
- Students who are hearing-impaired may be able to hear with the use of special amplification devices (the hard of hearing), or may have to learn special communication techniques (deaf students). Because of the special nature of communication among deaf

people, they tend to socialize more with other deaf people.
- Visual impairment can be defined legally or educationally. Educators define the degree of visual impairment in terms of the type of reading instruction required.
- Physical disabilities include skeletal, joint, muscle, or health problems that interfere with students' performances. Depending on the disability and its severity, seizures may result. Teachers should know first aid for seizures.
- Gifted and talented students are able to meet educational challenges better than most students. A distinction has been drawn between those who are gifted academically and those whose gifts allow them to be creative and productive in nonacademic ways. Just because gifted students are able to outperform most students does not mean they always do.

Key Terms

intelligence	permissive-indulgent style
construct	exceptional students
dynamic	Public Law 94-142
global view	least restrictive environment
three faces of intellect	ronment
experiential subtheory	mainstreaming
contextual subtheory	individualized education
componential subtheory	program (IEP)
learning styles	disability
convergent thinkers	handicap
divergent thinkers	mental retardation
impulsive	learning disabilities
reflective	emotional/behavioral disorder (E/BD)
thematic	order (E/BD)
analytic	externalizing
values	internalizing
macroculture	communication disorders
microcultures	hearing impairment
multicultural education	visual impairment
individualism	physical disabilities
groupism	gifted and talented students
authoritative style	dents
authoritarian style	

Teacher Chronicle Summaries

Teacher Chronicle 4.1: Aren't I Smart? (pp. 130–132)

A science teacher looks at her class list and sees that Louis, the most difficult student in school, is assigned to her class. The teacher is determined to help Louis, but he lives up to his reputation. Then, one day, the teacher discovers Louis's talent for drawing and uses this to establish a positive link with him.

Teacher Chronicle 4.2: Grandma Tales (pp. 141–142)

A Native-American boy struggles with written assignments in English and is facing a grade of F. His teacher, recognizing a skill in storytelling that stems from his background, helps him use this strength to pass the class.

Teacher Chronicle 4.3: Lost and Found (pp. 149–150)

On an assignment reading color-coded maps, a teacher tries to give individual help to a student having difficulties. The student, even with the extra help, cannot read the map. After working on the map at home, the boy solves his problem by letter-coding the colors. Unbeknownst to the teacher, the student is color blind and therefore could not do the work.

Possible Answers to Principles in Practice

Principles in Practice 4.1

1. Do some students adapt to their environments better or just differently than others do? How has Louis adapted?

On the basis of Sternberg's triarchic theory, we can say that people are intelligent in different ways. A person with high componential intelligence is likely to adapt well to the academic environment of the classroom. A person with high contextual intelligence, such as Louis, may not do well on academic tasks, but can find ways to adapt to situations. Louis adapts to the classroom environment by being disruptive. We could argue that Louis disrupts class to delay academic tasks on which he performs poorly.

2. In what ways is Louis intelligent?

Louis has the ability to express himself well through his artistic talents. Chronicle 4.1 also implies a degree of contextual intelligence.

3. Would suggesting to Louis that he "draw a picture" depicting the content of a history lesson be a good test of his learning style?

Because of his artistic talent and behavior, it is reasonable to assume that Louis can operate effectively on figural content and tends to think divergently. "Drawing a picture" of historical material is a reasonable hypothesis for his teacher to test.

Principles in Practice 4.2

1. In what other instructional situations might the teacher need to account for Kevin's cultural background?

Kevin's background seems likely to affect other situations that call for creative writing. His family values the group; therefore, tasks that reward individuals who compete successfully against others might cause Kevin some frustration.

2. What should be the thrust of the teacher's message to Kevin's parents at the next parent–teacher conference?

One tactic to take with Kevin's family is to remark on how much respect Kevin has for his family as evidenced by the writing problem he encountered. The teacher might also point out that Kevin is likely to encounter similar problems unless he can somehow reconcile the difference between the values that are important to his family and the values that he will continue to encounter in school. The teacher might recruit the family to help Kevin become more flexible. The teacher might also discuss steps that might be taken at school to accommodate Kevin's background.

3. How might a teacher find out about the communication values in order to enhance students' participation in classroom interactions?

One way to discover students' communication values is to conduct a "multicultural communication festival." The point of the festival would be to research various cultural conventions regarding social interaction. Students could also be asked to research other conventions used by their families and friends.

Principles in Practice 4.3

1. What other undetected disabilities might exist in this or other classes?

Any number of disabilities can go undetected for lengthy periods of time. Nick's color blindness is just one kind of visual impairment. Unless diagnosed through proper tests, poor eyesight or hearing may be taken for inattentiveness or laziness; learning disabilities or communication disorders may be mistaken for a general lack of ability; and an unrecognized gifted student may become bored to the point of becoming a troublemaker.

2. Why are learning disabilities especially likely to become handicaps?

The very nature of academic work in schools tends to put students with learning disabilities at a disadvantage. Unless the learning disability is diagnosed, it is unlikely that the students will make appropriate adaptations.

3. Why should teachers be aware of disabilities that cause problems with communication?

Communication skills are central to classroom interaction and learning. An inability to use symbol systems puts a student at a considerable disadvantage, especially when dealing with conceptual material.

CNN Connection to Issues in Educational Psychology

What is normal? Who fits in and who doesn't? Students at Gallaudet University, a school for the hearing impaired, turned those questions inside out in March 1988 when they strongly objected to a "hearing" university president. Communities of individuals with disabilities no longer accept their role as "abnormal"; nor do they accept the social and educational separation that has been imposed on them in the past. In the video, students will see some of the issues that surround students with a variety of disabilities.

Activities and Exercises

In-Class Activities

1. Assign students to one of three groups: teachers, parents, or school board members. Hold a meeting of the school board to hear testimony to decide on the implementation of a proposal submitted by Robert Sternberg. Sternberg proposes to write a new curriculum especially for students who are "street wise," but who have a history of failure in school. Parent and teacher groups can now be further divided into groups who will testify for or against the proposal. The school board hears testimony and renders a decision. If you choose to participate, you can play the role of Robert Sternberg or the superintendent of the district.

2. Assign students to work in pairs for a period of at least two hours; longer periods, if feasible, would be better. Have one student in each pair role-play a disabled person. For example, some students can be blindfolded or given glasses which distort or reduce vision. Some can be required to read material upside down. Some can wear earplugs. Some can be confined to a wheelchair or wear braces which restrict arm or leg movement. Some can be required to write with their nondominant hand, etc. The nondisabled student in the pair accompanies the disabled student when he or she leaves the classroom as a safety measure, but also to document those situations that turn the disability into a handicap. Some time after the role-playing session have students prepare a brief report on "disabilities and handicaps" that can be shared with classmates. (Help in setting up the role-playing might be available from campus Health Services or from the local chapter of organizations for disabled persons.)

Teacher Interviews

Have each student interview a teacher or curriculum supervisor to find out the criteria for entrance into instructional programs for exceptional students including those who are gifted and talented.

Have students ask teachers to identify their creative students by using the questions in text (p. 138) and then interview the creative students.

Have each student interview a teacher regarding the teacher's knowledge of his or her students' values and skills, observing the teacher's effectiveness in the classroom.

Have each student interview a teacher regarding the behaviors and attitudes of E/BD students. The students should ask how the teacher approaches his or her interactions with the students and write a definition of E/BD based on the interview.

Field Observations

Have each student observe a lesson or interview a practicing teacher regarding the types of operations stressed in classrooms.

Have students observe other students in a classroom, trying to identify impulsive, reflective, thematic, and analytic thinkers.

Have students observe other students in a classroom or interview a teacher regarding his or her use of student-selected activities.

Have students observe nonverbal communication in or out of classrooms to see if microcultural differences exist.

Have students observe teachers in living skills programs for mentally retarded adults or visit community living arrangements.

Have each student interview a blind person about his or her learning experiences while growing up.

Have each student visit a gifted and talented class or interview a teacher about the way he or she interacts with gifted and talented students.

Journal Entries

Have students generate some teaching hypotheses consistent with the three theories examined to this point (p. 135), comparing and contrasting the hypotheses.

Have students recall former classmates and try to categorize them.

Have students reflect on their own teaching styles. What are their current preferences? Who influenced those preferences? Their favorite teachers? Their least favorite teachers?

Have each student design a survey of learning styles for use in your classroom.

Have students reflect on their experiences of how cultural differences influence, positively or negatively, educational equity.

Have each student reflect on whether his or her upbringing engendered the values of individualism or groupism.

Have students reflect on the parenting styles they experienced growing up and the amount and nature of the care-giver contact they had with their teachers.

Have students reflect on the examples provided by L.D. students, riting the re sponsis fonetikalee.

Discussion Topics (based on Lecture Notes)

Have students discuss the differences between constructs and measurements, generally, and intelligence and IQ in particular. See also *Mismeasure of Man,* by Stephen J. Gould, p. 24.

Have students discuss their school experiences that encouraged divergent thinking.

In discussion, have students identify values they hold and then compare differences and similarities among members of the class.

Have students compare the L.D. students' view of intelligence with the theories of intelligence examined early in this chapter.

Have students carry out a simple conversation using fingerspelling. Have them start with ''Where are you going after class?'' Allow them five minutes to carry on the conversations and then have them share their feelings about the experience.

Application Scenarios

Present the following scenarios to students:

- You call them the Three Musketeers because they go everywhere together, but they are as different as morning, afternoon, and night. Robert works very hard on his studies. He places a great deal of emphasis on getting the homework assignments right, and even asks for extra work to take home if he has no homework on that night. Barry never seems to take a book home, and doesn't seem to care what grades he gets, as long as he passes. Michael is always inviting his friends to his house, where they play video games until suppertime. Analyze each of these students in terms of what sort of parenting styles are used on them. How have parenting styles affected their performances? What can you do to help?

- You are substitute teaching in a special education class in a small, rural school district. You have been warned that all sorts of students have been lumped together in this classroom. Some of the students are mentally retarded. Some are physically impaired. Several are emotionally disturbed, while others are struggling with learning disabilities. Given that you are there for just one day, what can you do to foster their education? What would you recommend for a more equitable long-range way of dealing with the needs of these students?

Chapter 15 Casebook Previews

See Writers' Tea.

See Science Is Only Real When You Do It.

See Student of the Week.

See Bringing the Real World into the Classroom.

See Gifted Achievers and Underachievers.

Teaching Anecdotes

Tell the story of Marshall who was an excellent reader, but struggled with math. He enjoyed problem solving when writing a story or working on the structure of a research paper. He couldn't seem to grasp mathematical problem solving. He grew increasingly frustrated with what he called ''the absoluteness of math.'' Everything seemed so black and white, right or wrong, there didn't seem to be a place for his kind of creativity in math class. (See p. 133.)

Tell the story of Roy, an attentive, alert student. He contributed to every discussion, often adding a divergent perspective. When the class performed lab assignments, Roy always managed to add a new ''twist'' to the assignment. At first, this tendency to go beyond the assigned task annoyed the teacher until she realized that Roy was expressing his creativity. What might have happened had the teacher insisted that Roy's labs strictly follow the lab sheet? (See p. 135.)

Tell the story of the student whose parents would not allow him to exchange valentine cards at school. His teacher, not wanting him to feel left out, devised a unit that included Valentine's Day letters, but revolved around the workings of a post office. Activities such as making stamps and mailing and delivering letters kept him involved, but did not require that he exchange valentines. Note how the teacher respected the parents' wishes without disrupting a traditional activity. (See p. 143.)

Tell the story of two teachers discussing a child who had become a discipline problem. The first teacher complained, ''She just doesn't seem to want to cooperate. She's always talking and refuses to do assignments in class.''

''I know,'' the second teacher said. ''When she is near her friends, you might as well forget teaching her.''

Just then, the student walked by. The teachers stopped talking as she passed. When she rounded the corner, the second teacher asked, ''Do you think we're too harsh because she doesn't speak English very well?''

Ask your students if they have ever had to ''overcome'' negative first impressions they've formed of people who were somehow different from themselves. (See p. 147.)

Tell the story of John, a high school student with multiple sclerosis who is confined to a wheelchair. His science teacher planned a snowshoeing field trip at a local nature center. A special van transported John to the nature center. John was placed on a sled and pulled by several friends who took turns.

Does this approach to the activity meet the least restrictive environment clause of PL 94-142? (See p. 151.)

Transparencies

For transparencies to use with this chapter, see the Transparency Guides on page 143 and page 144.

Teaching Resources

Suggested Readings

Banks, J. A., & McGee Banks, C. A. (Eds.). (1989). *Multicultural education: Issues and perspectives.* Needham Heights, MA: Allyn & Bacon.

Baron, J. B., & Sternberg, R. J. (Eds.). (1987). *Teaching thinking skills.* New York: Freeman.

Hallahan, D. P., & Kauffman, J. M. (1991). *Exceptional children: Introduction to special education.* Englewood Cliffs, NJ: Prentice Hall.

Sternberg, R. J. (1985). *Beyond IQ: A triarchic theory of human intelligence.* New York: Cambridge University Press.

Films, Videocassettes, Audiocassettes

- *Learning: A Matter of Style,* video, 30 min., color. Learning styles expert Rita Dunn explains her research and observations. Classroom examples show teachers how to accommodate different student learning styles. A videotaped case study helps apply what is presented in video. 614-106v2.
- *Training Intellectual Skills—A Triarchic Model,* audio, 45 min. Psychologist Robert Sternberg discusses his theory of intelligence and how it can be applied to the teaching of thinking skills. 612-20372c2.
- *Recent Research on Learning Styles and Practical Implications for Supervisors and Teachers,* audio. Learn how schools have boosted test scores and created more positive classroom environments by adapting teaching strategies to individual learning styles. 512-20232c2.
- *Social Expectations of the Learner and Students' Ability/Inability to Respond,* audio. How strongly do physical, sociological, and emotional elements influence the learning that takes place in your class? 612-87574c2.
- *What Do We Really Know About Learning Styles and Reading and Math Achievement,* audio. Hear the research on learning styles and learn how the findings can be applied easily and economically in your classroom. 612-20447c2.

These five productions are available through Association for Supervision and Curriculum Development, 125 North West Street, Alexandria, VA 22314-2798. Telephone orders: (703) 549-9110.

Test Questions

Test Questions 4.1–4.99

Study Guide

Assign Chapter 4 of the *Study Guide*.

5

Environment and Behavior

Chapter Objectives

1. General Objective

Judges the utility of behaviorist assumptions (pp. 170–175).

SPECIFIC BEHAVIORS
1.01 Explains the behavioristic view of learning.
1.02 Explains how the components of respondent conditioning operate to change behavior.
1.03 Justifies that learning is a change in behavior related to changes in the environment.
1.04 Supports the use of experimental procedures to determine causes of behavior.
1.05 Justifies the individual as the appropriate data source for explanations of behavior.

2. General Objective

Understands the components of learning from an operant perspective (pp. 175–180).

SPECIFIC BEHAVIORS
2.01 Distinguishes discriminative stimuli from reinforcing stimuli.
2.02 Explains the relationship between discriminative stimuli, reinforcing stimuli, and responses.
2.03 Distinguishes primary and conditioned reinforcers.

3. General Objective

Understands how the various types of environmental consequences influence behavior (pp. 180–186).

SPECIFIC BEHAVIORS
3.01 Distinguishes the effect of reinforcement from the effect of punishment.
3.02 Gives examples of positive reinforcement.
3.03 Gives examples of punishment.
3.04 Gives examples of time-out.
3.05 Gives examples of negative reinforcement.

4. General Objective

Judges the utility of various classroom contingencies (pp. 186–193).

SPECIFIC BEHAVIORS
4.01 Compares the effects of continuous versus intermittent reinforcement.
4.02 Interprets the effects of fixed interval schedules.
4.03 Describes variable interval and fixed ratio schedules of reinforcement.
4.04 Interprets the effects of variable ratio schedules.
4.05 Explains shaping.
4.06 Explains fading.
4.07 Explains techniques for eliminating behaviors.
4.08 Explains token economies.
4.09 Explains rule-governed behavior.

5. General Behavior

Understands the Premack principle to classroom situations (pp. 198–201).

SPECIFIC BEHAVIORS
5.01 Shows the circular nature of the concept of reinforcement.
5.02 Characterizes the relative nature of high-probability and low-probability behaviors.
5.03 Gives examples of high- and low-probability behaviors.
5.04 Explains how a reinforcement menu exemplifies the Premack principle.

Focus Questions

- What is a science of behavior?
- How does the environment control what is learned?
- How does behavior operate on the environment?
- Why do some behaviors persist while others cease?
- How can reinforcement be used to change behavior?
- Will your students perceive reinforcement the same way that you do?

Chapter Outline

Chapter Summary

Introduction: Behaviorism

- Operant conditioning is a behavioristic view of human learning. This explanation of learning relies on the observable environment and observable behaviors. Skinner's operant model of learning came from his study of Pavlov's work with behaviors that were reflexes to environmental stimuli. Skinner's theories address behaviors that lead to environmental consequences, and thus operate on the environment.

- The assumptions underlying operant conditioning are consistent with the principles of behaviorism. They address the necessity for careful control and observation of behaviors and the environments in which behaviors occur. Most important, from a teaching standpoint, is the assumption that the individual is the appropriate data source about behavior.

Components of Learning

- Discriminative stimuli are aspects of the environment that are dependent on the presence of reinforcement. Such stimuli can control behavior. The behaviors that teachers use to accompany reinforcement are potential signals of appropriate behaviors for students. Discriminative stimuli can also control superstitious behavior.

- Reinforcing stimuli are consequences that follow a behavior and that serve to increase the likelihood of that behavior. Reinforcement, either positive or negative, is not the only kind of consequence. Forms of punishment may also follow behaviors. Punishment decreases the likelihood of reoccurrence of a behavior.

- Primary reinforcers meet some basic need, such as food, water, or shelter. Conditioned reinforcers are, of themselves, neutral. They can become associated with primary reinforcers to such an extent that they influence behavior. Examples include money, grades, and other forms of recognition.

Consequences of Behavior

- Positive reinforcement is the addition of something desirable to the stimulus situation as a consequence of some response. The effect of positive reinforcement is to increase the likelihood that the behavior will reoccur. A consequence cannot be judged to be a positive reinforcement unless the probability of reoccurrence increases.

- Punishment is the addition of something undesirable to the stimulus situation as a consequence of a response. The effect of punishment is to decrease the likelihood that the behavior will reoccur. A consequence cannot be judged to be punishment unless the probability of reoccurrence decreases.

- Time-out is the removal of something the learner finds desirable as a consequence of a response. The effect of time-out is to decrease the likelihood that the behavior will reoccur. A consequence cannot be judged to be time-out unless the probability of reoccurrence decreases.

- Negative reinforcement is the removal from the stimulus situation of something the learner finds undesirable as a consequence of some response.

The effect of negative reinforcement is to increase the likelihood that the behavior will reoccur in the future. A consequence cannot be judged to be negative reinforcement unless the probability of reoccurrence increases.

Contingencies

- Reinforcement can be delivered intermittently on schedules that are variable or fixed. Schedules of reinforcement can also define contingencies in terms of number of responses or the period of time between responses. There are four types of intermittent reinforcement: variable interval, fixed interval, variable ratio, and fixed ratio.

Changing Behaviors

- Shaping is the use of reinforcement, preferably positive reinforcement, to encourage successively closer approximations of some target behavior. Because many of the behaviors teachers desire for their students are complex, behaviors must be shaped.
- Fading is the gradual withdrawal of discriminative stimuli while continuing to reinforce the response. Fading is a procedure teachers use when they wish to make student behavior less dependent on themselves or other aspects of the student's environment.
- Punishment is one way to decrease undesirable behaviors, but it can also lead to new, maladaptive behaviors. Response cost is a procedure by which a specified amount of reinforcers is removed to reduce or eliminate behaviors. Extinction, another procedure for eliminating behavior, is the removal of all reinforcement. The effectiveness of extinction depends on the schedule of reinforcement in place when extinction is begun.
- In a token economy, students earn objects (or tokens) as a result of appropriate behavior. The tokens can then be used to "buy" reinforcers. The reinforcers may include free time in the library, computer use, or something as simple as a pencil. In a token economy, the token acquires the status of a generalized reinforcer.
- Behavior prescribed by rules as appropriate or inappropriate is called rule-governed behavior. In a classroom, rules can be established, but the rules will only govern behavior if the consequences of following or violating the rules are delivered consistently.

Premack Principle

- The Premack principle states that a high-probability behavior can be used to reinforce a low-probability behavior. In practical application, if a teacher can find out what behaviors students prefer, those be-

haviors can be used to increase behaviors that the students find less preferable. One way to use the Premack principle is to establish a contract for student behavior.

Key Terms

behaviorism	punishment
unconditioned stimulus (US)	time-out
	negative reinforcement
unconditioned response (UR)	aversive control
	contingencies
conditioned stimulus (CS)	continuous reinforcement
conditioned response (CR)	intermittent reinforcement
respondent behavior	fixed interval schedule
respondent conditioning	variable interval schedule
operant behavior	fixed ratio schedule
operant conditioning	variable ratio schedule
operant analysis	shaping
discriminative stimulus	successive approximations
behavioral control	fading
reinforcing stimulus	response cost
primary reinforcer	extinction
conditioned reinforcer	token economy
generalized reinforcer	rule-governed behavior
law of effect	Premack principle
positive reinforcement	

Teacher Chronicle Summaries

Teacher Chronicle 5.1: Call in the Reinforcements (p. 175)

An elementary teacher has a student who is a "handful." Nothing the teacher does seems to help him manage the student. Then, one day, he discovers that the boy is fanatical about taking a football out for recess. Using the football as a reinforcement, the teacher manages the boy's behavior.

Teacher Chronicle 5.2: Just in Case (p. 180)

An elementary school student hates school and complains continually about stomachaches and headaches. The teacher is at a loss to explain why, so she begins keeping a log of when the complaints occur. A pattern emerges and the teacher uses this insight to help the student overcome her "illness."

Teacher Chronicle 5.3: Getting to Know You (pp. 192–193)

An elementary teacher has a student who is way ahead of her class in reading. The student is clearly uncomfortable being put on a pedestal for her peers to emulate. In order to keep the student involved with her classmates, the teacher lets the student have her own reading bookshelf, while she still participates in a reading group. This combination of individual attention and group participation helps solve the difficulty.

Possible Answers to Principles in Practice

Principles in Practice 5.1

1.   What other aspects of this situation might serve as discriminative stimuli?

The time of year might serve as a discriminative stimulus. It is only during football season that Rodney can take out the football. Any classroom routine that accompanies good weather, for example, nature hikes during science could serve as a discriminative stimulus.

2.   Are there other potential reinforcers the teacher might have tried to improve Rodney's behavior?

Rodney's responses might indicate a tendency to want to be "in charge" of things other than a football. The teacher might have tried to let Rodney be responsible for instructional materials, bulletin board supplies, and the like.

3.   Why should a teacher attend to discriminative stimuli when testing possible reinforcers?

Any stimulus perceived by a student when reinforcement is delivered can come to control the student's behavior. The teacher may perceive one stimulus as controlling the student's behavior; the student may perceive a different discriminative stimulus. A mismatch can cause a teacher to inaccurately identify the controlling stimulus.

Principles in Practice 5.2

1.   What are some possible explanations for the failure of the teacher's praise as a permanent solution to Leticia's discomfort?

The teacher's praise did work, but only temporarily. One explanation is that praise did not remove the aversive aspect of the situation for Leticia (her stomachache).

2.   What other actions might the teacher take to provide positive reinforcement for Leticia?

One idea would be to find a classmate whom Leticia likes and to allow Leticia to work cooperatively with that classmate. The teacher might also encourage Leticia's parents to feed her a more substantial breakfast.

3.   Assuming that it would be medically safe, what would be the advantage of "weaning" Leticia from her snacks?

If the snacks are the only reinforcement controlling Leticia's positive behavior in a classroom, there is a risk that her avoidance and escape behavior might redevelop in other classrooms. The basic idea is to avoid having Leticia become dependent on the reinforcement of a daily snack.

Principles in Practice 5.3

1.   Would a token economy have induced Marlene to participate in reading groups more quickly? Would a token economy have been preferable to the solution devised?

It depends on what the token economy "bought" for Marlene. Given the results of the teacher's experiment in Chronicle 5.3, it seems that if Marlene could have earned time for independent reading, a token economy might have been effective. It seems even more likely that a token economy would have encouraged greater interaction between Marlene and her classmates.

2.   Do you think Marlene felt empowered by the solution? Do you think that empowerment made a difference?

The solution implemented by the teacher gave Marlene choices. Therefore, it is reasonable to assume that she felt empowered to control her activities in class. The power to control the environment is, in most cases, reinforcing. One way to test the idea that empowerment is reinforcing is to give Marlene additional choices in the class.

3.   What other items would you put on a reinforcement menu for Marlene to choose from?

The opportunity to choose activities would be an attractive item on a reinforcement menu for Marlene. It is important to keep in mind that the items on the menu would be used to reinforce low-probability behaviors. In Marlene's case, a low-probability behavior is active participation in group activities.

CNN Connection to Issues in Educational Psychology

Punishment and negative reinforcement definitely work in the laboratory. But how do they—or should they—be used in a classroom? What approaches should teachers take, and how far should they go when confronted with disruptive behavior? In this videotape, students will see two different approaches to the use of punishment: time-out rooms and corporal punishment.

Activities and Exercises

In-Class Activities

1.   Assign students to work in small groups. Assign each group several key terms at the end of the chapter. The group's task is to write at least two questions for each key term that will then be used to stage a quiz show, which might be called "What's Your Response?" One of the questions should be definitional; the other question should require an application answer. Students could compete as teams as a way of reviewing the techni-

cal language of operant conditioning theory. At the conclusion of the game, students could be asked to reflect on how they might use a similar procedure in their classrooms in the future.

2. For purposes of a demonstration, select between three and six students to be "shapers" and equip each with a squirt gun. Seat the shapers at the front of the room in a semicircle with their backs to the class. Find one good sport to serve as the subject for the demonstration. The subject will stand in the middle of the semicircle of shapers. Before the demonstration begins, the shapers will decide on a behavior that they will attempt to shape in the subject (e.g., raising his or her right hand, touching his or her nose, facing the left or right wall). The catch is that the only tools the shapers can use to bring about the desired behavior are their squirt guns. As the demonstration begins, have the remainder of the students document the subject's behavior and how it changes as a function of being squirted. Allow the demonstration to continue for four to six minutes. After the demonstration discuss the difficulty of shaping behavior using only aversive stimuli.

Teacher Interviews

Have each student interview a teacher who uses time-out as a consequence to find out if the procedure works with all students, and if there is a pattern related to each student's desire for attention.

Have students interview a teacher to find out how complex behaviors are broken down so that they can be successively approximated.

Have each student observe or interview a teacher regarding the types of behaviors that can and cannot safely be ignored.

Field Observations

Have students record, in strictly behavioral terms, inappropriate student behaviors and antecedent and consequent events.

Have students observe behavior in classrooms, in a workplace, or among children on a playground to determine the contingencies of reinforcement.

Have students take note of the differences in atmosphere of classroom whose teacher relies heavily on threat and one in which the teacher relies more on positive reinforcement.

Have students observe a token economy, paying attention to the effects of intermittent reinforcement.

Have students observe a token economy or interview teachers who use this approach. Have them ask if the teachers have plans for stretching the ratio or fading.

Have students observe a classroom in which the teacher enjoys a good rapport with his or her students. Find out how he or she reinforces desirable behavior.

Journal Entries

Have students reflect on the types of reinforcing stimuli they can deliver in a classroom. Have them analyze their own interpersonal strengths and weaknesses. Not every teacher can communicate praise by laying a hand on a student's shoulder.

Have students reflect on a classroom they enjoyed and one that they didn't enjoy. Have them identify the differences in terms of the contingencies that operated in each room.

Have students reflect on their experiences in classes in which they were given pop quizzes and those in which tests were given according to a predictable schedule.

Have students reflect on classes in which their behavior was not very "adaptive." What contingencies operated in those situations?

Have students reflect on teachers they had whose actions did not match their words. How effective were such teachers?

Have students reflect on situations in which they had a choice of reinforcers and how that choice influenced their behavior.

Discussion Topics (based on Lecture Notes)

Discuss what it means when the probability of a response is decreased in terms of motivation.

Ask students to think back to theories of development, especially that of psychological development presented in Chapter 3. Discuss the question, What can developmental theory tell us about effective reinforcement?

Application Scenarios

Present the following scenarios to students:

- Your fourth-grade class wants to begin a recycling program for your school. They argue that recycling will help eliminate waste, help solve the trash and litter problem in the halls, and allow the school to raise some extra money for special projects. Isaac, one of your class leaders, is pessimistic. He feels that the students, particularly those in the lower grades, are just not mature and responsible enough to make such a program work. Use your knowledge of operant conditioning to design a series of reinforcements that would help the younger students cooperate with the program. How can your fourth graders help implement your ideas? What are some potential problems?

- Deena has a very short attention span. Her parents are concerned, so they have had her tested for hyperactivity. Deena is not hyperactive, but she gets bored easily. She likes to do schoolwork, but she expects to be rewarded for every right answer she gives. Set up a schedule of reinforcements to help Deena learn to do more work between explicit rewards. Use the principles of shaping, fading, and rule-governed behavior to set up this schedule.

- The boys in your class are furious. It seems that State University has finally been chosen for the NCAA basketball tourney, and the committee scheduled State's first game during school hours! Since State was one of the last teams chosen, they probably will lose that game, and the kids will not get to see them at all in the tournament. They plead with you to borrow the school TV so that they can watch the game. Can you use the Premack principle to help your students get ready for their final exams?

Chapter 15 Casebook Previews

See Around the World.

See Taking Control.

See Gifted Achievers and Underachievers.

See Science Is Only Real When You Do It.

See Student of the Week.

See Taking Control.

See Writers' Tea.

See Bringing the Real World into the Classroom.

Teaching Anecdotes

Tell the story of Tyler, a serious student who did his work on time, used free time wisely, and was a good role model. Yet, whenever Tyler received recognition or an award he acted very silly.

Ask your students why this might be so. (See p. 172.)

Tell the story of the teacher who used a secret code to manage Jeff who loved to tickle, poke, grab, and shove other students. Only the teacher and Jeff knew the code. The code worked this way: Whenever Jeff bothered someone, the teacher pulled on her left ear, a signal for him to stop. Whenever she "caught him being good," she pulled on her right ear. Why would such signals work with Jeff? (See p. 178.)

Tell the story of the teacher who kept putting a disruptive boy out in the hall. She figured that he would miss participating in class and control his behavior. She didn't realize that he provoked her when he was bored and wanted stimulation. He loved going to the hall, seeing the activity near the office, and talking with everyone who passed by. When the teacher discovered this attraction, she turned the tables. She began using the hallway as a reward when he cooperated in class. (See p. 181.)

Tell the story of Lawrence who tried to do everything he could to provoke a strong negative reaction from his teacher. Whenever he broke a rule, the teacher would yell at him, move his desk, or send him to the office. Whenever she tried persuading, rather than coercing, Lawrence would find a way to anger her. At conference time, the teacher gained an insight when

his mother said, "If you ever have any problems with him, feel free to wallop him. That's what we do at home all the time."

Was Lawrence consciously trying to make his teacher angry or was he simply displaying behaviors he learned at home? (See p. 183.)

Tell the story of the teacher who used bear-shaped note paper to send her first graders' weekly reports home. Good notes were written on the front and notes about negative behavior on the back. The teacher decided to stop writing the notes at midyear, but did not tell the students. Much to her surprise, only two students asked why they weren't getting their bears anymore. Why didn't more students ask about the notes? (See p. 194.)

Transparencies

For transparencies to use with this chapter, see the Transparency Guide on page 181.

Teaching Resources

Suggested Readings

Nye, R. D. (1979). *What is B. F. Skinner really saying?* Englewood Cliffs, NJ: Prentice-Hall.

Rachlin, H. (1991). *Introduction to modern behaviorism* (3rd ed.). New York: W. H. Freeman.

Skinner, B. F. (1948). *Walden two.* New York: Macmillan.

Skinner, B. F. (1974). *About behaviorism.* New York: Knopf.

Skinner, B. F. (1987). Whatever happened to psychology as the science of behavior? *American Psychologist, 42,* 780–786.

Films, Videocassettes, Audiocassettes

- *Pavlov: The Conditioned Reflex,* 25 min., b&w. This documentary shows Pavlov's pioneering work in behavioral psychology, including the famous dog experiment. It provides rare documentary footage of Pavlov at work, focusing on his revolutionary studies of the conditioned reflex. Available through Films for the Humanities & Sciences, Inc., P.O. Box 2052, Princeton, NJ 08543. Or call 1-800-257-5126 (in NJ, 609-452-1128). EC-112. VHS or Beta.
- *B. F. Skinner and Behavior Change,* video, 45 min., color. This video provides an introduction to the work of B.F. Skinner including behavior modification. The viewing of on-site interventions helps to bridge the gap between theoretical and human applications. Available through Research Press, Box 3177, Department K, Champaign, IL 61821. Or call (217) 352-3273.

- *Effective Behavioral Programming.* Eight videotapes demonstrating the use of behavioral procedures for training mentally handicapped persons. Nearly five hours of instruction. Available through Research Press, Box 3177, Department K, Champaign, IL 61821. Or call (217) 352-3273.
- *Learning About Learning*, 16 mm, 30 min., b&w. Outlines the work of Dr. Howard Kendler of New York University, Dr. Tracy Kendler of Barnard College, Dr. Kenneth Spence of the University of Iowa, Dr. Harry Harlow of the University of Wisconsin, and Dr. B. F. Skinner of Harvard University in exploring the different strategies employed in developing new theoretical concepts about human beings' ability to learn. Shows how the work of these men has influenced methods of instruction in schools and colleges. Focus on Behavior Series. NET: INUAVC 1962. Indiana University, Audio-Visual Center, Bloomington, IN 47405. Or call (812) 335-8087.

Test Questions

Test Questions 5.1–5.130

Study Guide

Assign Chapter 5 of the *Study Guide*.

6

Cognition: Codes of Understanding

Chapter Objectives

1. General Objective

Interprets the term *understanding* as it is used by cognitive psychologists (pp. 206–211).

SPECIFIC BEHAVIORS
1.01 Gives examples of the term used in an everyday sense.
1.02 Explains the term as it is used to describe human cognition.
1.03 Uses the analogy of the computer's information-processing capabilities to expand the use of the terms.

2. General Objective

Understands the functions of the structures of the cognitive mechanism (pp. 211–221).

SPECIFIC BEHAVIORS
2.01 Identifies the flow of information through the cognitive mechanism.
2.02 Distinguishes the functions of the three memory structures.
2.03 Explains the nature of information in sensory register.
2.04 Explains the nature of information in short-term store.
2.05 Explains the nature of information in long-term store.
2.06 Identifies the capacity of each memory structure.
2.07 Identifies the code of each memory structure.
2.08 Identifies the permanence of each memory structure.
2.09 Identifies the source of information in each memory structure.
2.10 Identifies how information is lost from each memory structure.

3. General Objective

Interprets the processes which transform information to the operation of the memory structures (pp. 221–231).

SPECIFIC BEHAVIORS
3.01 Infers that cognitive processes are necessary for active learning.
3.02 Infers that cognitive processes yield a mental representation in memory.
3.03 Explains how the process of attention is associated with memory structures.
3.04 Distinguishes the selective and automatic attention modes.
3.05 Explains encoding as a generic term.
3.06 Explains how the encoding processes are associated with memory structures.
3.07 Distinguishes between maintenance and elaborative rehearsal.
3.08 Explains the relationship between encoding processes and short-term store capacity.
3.09 Gives examples of the process of retrieval.
3.10 Explains the relationship between encoding and retrieval.
3.11 Relates encoding and retrieval to the generation of inferences—construction and reconstruction.
3.12 Explains the instructional importance of cognitive automaticity.

4. General Objective

Recognizes the instructional implications of prior knowledge (pp. 231–236).

SPECIFIC BEHAVIORS
4.01 Illustrates how prior knowledge is used to construct a meaningful cognitive representation.
4.02 Distinguishes between episodic and semantic prior knowledge.
4.03 Gives examples of episodic and semantic memories.
4.04 Explains how prior knowledge operates through schemata.
4.05 Characterizes procedural and conditional prior knowledge.

5. General Objective

Recognizes the use of imagery and mnemonics as applications of prior knowledge (pp. 236–246).

SPECIFIC BEHAVIORS

5.01 Identifies imagery as a form of elaborative encoding.
5.02 Distinguishes interactive and noninteractive imagery.
5.03 Infers the memorial advantages of bizarre images.
5.04 Generates rhyme mnemonics.
5.05 Generates letter (acronym) and sentence (acrostic) mnemonics.
5.06 Generates peg mnemonics (methods of loci and peg-word).
5.07 Generates story mnemonics.
5.08 Generates keyword mnemonics.
5.09 Identifies the mnemonic value of metaphors and analogies.

6. General Objective

Translates "ease of learning" from an information-processing perspective (pp. 245–246).

SPECIFIC BEHAVIORS

6.01 Explains metacognition.
6.02 Distinguishes learning content from learning to learn.
6.03 Summarizes, from an information-processing perspective, the task of instruction.

Focus Questions

- How do I know if my students understand what I am teaching?
- Why do students learn and remember some concepts more easily than others?
- How can I help my students comprehend, retain, and apply what they learn?
- Why are students more actively engaged in learning some times than at others?
- Why do students enjoy sharing their own experiences?
- How should I use what my students already know to enhance their learning?
- How can I make my students better learners?

Chapter Outline

INTRODUCTION: UNDERSTANDING
   Understanding—from a Cognitive Perspective
   Information Processing

TEACHER CHRONICLE 6.1: KNOT UNDERSTANDING

THE MODEL OF HUMAN INFORMATION PROCESSING: STRUCTURES
   Overview of the Model
   Memory Structures
      Sensory Register
      Short-Term Store (STS)
      Long-Term Store (LTS)
   Summary of Structures
   Principles in Practice 6.1

TEACHER CHRONICLE 6.2: NOW I SEE!

THE MODEL OF HUMAN INFORMATION PROCESSING: PROCESSES
   Attention
   Encoding
      Maintenance Rehearsal
      Elaborative Rehearsal
   Retrieval
      Reconstructive Retrieval
   Automaticity
   Principles in Practice 6.2

TEACHER CHRONICLE 6.3: WARMING UP WITH POLLIWOGS

PRIOR KNOWLEDGE
   Organization
      Episodic Prior Knowledge
      Semantic Prior Knowledge
      Procedural Prior Knowledge
      Conditional Prior Knowledge
      Prior Knowledge, and Don't You Forget It!

USING PRIOR KNOWLEDGE TO LEARN
   Imagery
   Mnemonics
      Rhymes
      Letter and Sentence Mnemonics
      Peg Mnemonics
      Stories
      Keyword Mnemonics
   Metaphors and Analogies
   Principles in Practice 6.3

CONCLUSION

Chapter Summary

Introduction: Understanding

- From a cognitive perspective, understanding means that a student can use information to solve problems and as a basis for further learning. The information can be facts, concepts, procedures, and so on.

- The information-processing view of learning is a cognitive model based on a computer metaphor. The model attempts to portray the way that learners transform information from the environment into cognitive codes and store them for retrieval and later use.

The Model of Human Information Processing: Structures

- The model includes structures and processes, as depicted in Figure 6–1. Tracing the flow of information through the structures gives us a first glance at the operations of the human cognitive mechanism.
- There are three major memory stores in the human cognitive mechanism. The sensory register holds information briefly as it arrives from the environment. The short-term store (STS) is working memory. The information in a learner's consciousness resides in short-term store for a relatively short period unless the information is processed further. The long-term store (LTS) holds a learner's prior knowledge.
- Information that resides in each of the three memory stores differs because the stores have different capacities, codes, permanence, sources, and modes of loss.

The Model of Human Information Processing: Processes

- Attention is the process that moves information from the sensory register to short-term store. Attention can operate selectively, as when a student consciously directs his or her concentration to some stimulus information. Attention can also operate automatically, as when some stimulus causes a learner to focus on that information without conscious effort.
- Encoding is the process of converting a message from the environment into a cognitive code. Encoding is "work" done in short-term store that allows information to be stored for later use. Information can be maintained through rote processing or elaboration by relating it to the learner's prior knowledge.
- Retrieval is the process that transfers information from long-term store to short-term store. This process brings prior knowledge to bear on new information from the environment. Retrieval can be influenced by the way in which it is encoded. If the process of retrieval yields new inferences, the process is called reconstructive retrieval.
- Cognitive processes can, with sufficient practice, occur automatically. Many of the processes of a skilled reader, for example, are automatic. Once automaticity has been achieved, processing can occur without cost to the limited capacity of short-term store.

Prior Knowledge

- Facts and concepts that make up a learner's prior knowledge can be organized as episodes (episodic knowledge) or as general "knowledge of the world" (semantic knowledge). Procedural prior knowledge is the knowledge of how to do things; how to use facts and concepts, for example. Conditional prior knowledge is knowledge of when and under what conditions facts, concepts, and procedures should be used.

Using Prior Knowledge to Learn

- Imagery is the capacity to generate cognitive codes, "mental pictures or sounds," which can be used for other purposes. Imagery is the basis for many types of elaborative encoding, including the use of mnemonic devices.
- Mnemonics are processing techniques that make information we wish to retain more memorable. Mnemonic devices include the use of visual images, stories, and rhymes.
- Metaphors and analogies are also useful in helping learners to integrate their prior knowledge with the information they have been asked to learn. Most often, metaphors and analogies are supplied by a teacher to help the student comprehend new information.

Key Terms

information processing	maintenance rehearsal
environment	elaborative rehearsal
receptors	retrieval
sensory register	encoding specificity
elaboration	prior knowledge
response generator	mental images
effectors	schema
executive control	procedural knowledge
Atkinson and Shiffrin model	metacognition
short-term store (STS)	mnemonic devices
long-term store (LTS)	mnemonics
episodic memories	rhymes
semantic memories	acronym
selective attention	acrostic
automatic attention	peg mnemonics
encoding	story technique

Teacher Chronicle Summaries

Teacher Chronicle 6.1: Knot Understanding (pp. 210–211)

By watching a student master the intricacies of string figures, a teacher learns something about the nature of learning itself. The student learns how to make the string figures by reading and rereading the instructions to understand how the strings work. The teacher, learning differently, makes the figure step-by-step with the directions in front of him. Three years later the student recalls many of the figures while the teacher is at a loss without the instructions in front of him.

Teacher Chronicle 6.2: Now I See! (pp. 220–221)

After teaching a unit on the human body, a teacher realizes his students haven't mastered the material on the eye. The teacher decides to approach the subject from a different angle. Instead of just telling them the information, he involves the students in discovering how the eye works. Their interest is heightened and mastery greatly improves.

Teacher Chronicle 6.3: Warming Up with Polliwogs (p. 231)

An elementary school teacher taps into her students' prior knowledge to help them better understand a story about polliwogs.

Possible Answers to Principles in Practice

Principles in Practice 6.1

1. How did the knowledge that Keith stored in LTS affect his STS capacity?

When we speak of Keith's mechanical aptitude, it means that he has mechanical knowledge in LTS. His ability to imagine how things should be put together allowed him to envision string figures in the abstract; therefore, Keith does not have to expend all of his STS capacity on figuring out the manipulation of the string.

2. Why was the teacher more confident in Keith's ability to recall the figures than his or her own?

The teacher realized that Keith's ability to generate a cognitive representation of the figures was superior. The teacher had to work back and forth between the written instructions and manipulation of the string. The teacher's cognitive effort was focused on physical manipulation, while Keith's effort was focused on creating a lasting representation.

3. How could Keith's knowledge be used to help other students learn string figures?

If Keith could describe some of the cognitive processes he uses to construct his mental representations of string figures, other students could attempt to use the same kinds of processes. Not all of the students will be able to follow Keith's instructions—the teacher was unable to—but some of Keith's classmates might find the processes useful.

Principles in Practice 6.2

1. Why do "experiments" attract students' attention so readily?

Students process information more actively when they see something demonstrated rather than just described. Experiments are more concrete than descriptions, making it easier to follow the steps of a procedure.

2. Is elaborative encoding more likely when the content to be learned is presented before or after some kind of "active" experience (such as the pupil experiment)?

By engaging students in an active experience before content, the appropriate LTS knowledge is accessed and students have a context for understanding the material to be learned. An active experience that is presented after content can also be effective in helping students to analyze their observations.

3. What kinds of learning activities best activate the retrieval of prior knowledge?

All sorts of activities can be used to activate prior knowledge: demonstration experiments, discussions, advance readings, questions, etc. The key is to facilitate the retrieval of students' experiences.

Principles in Practice 6.3

1. What would have happened if the teacher had introduced the story with, "This story is called . . ." and then began reading?

The students may have spent their effort in trying to determine why the teacher was reading the story instead of attending to the information conveyed in the story.

2. What could the teacher have done with the discussion and the story to enhance metacognition?

Enhancing metacognition requires that students become aware of their own cognitive processing. Thus, the teacher in Chronicle 6.3 might have introduced questions during the discussion or interwoven questions with the reading. These questions should address the processes or reasoning the students used.

3. What role do images play in animating a discussion?

Images are cognitive representations, but they are also concrete representations. Generating and manipulating images is a form of elaborative processing, or active learning. Generating images is a way to encourage thinking which contributes to an animated discussion.

CNN Connection to Issues in Educational Psychology

What did you have for lunch last Wednesday? What was the name of your first grade teacher? Questions like these are asked in the first video segment which explores why we remember some things but not others. The second segment looks at recent research exploring the memory capabilities of infants. A revealing research method suggests that human memory may develop far earlier than once thought.

Activities and Exercises

In-Class Activities

1. As a demonstration of the relationship between automaticity and capacity, find an accomplished juggler (there may be one among your students). Have the juggler begin juggling three balls. Ask students to notice the ease and grace of the juggling, pointing out the juggler's smooth rhythm. After a few moments ask the juggler questions. Begin by asking the juggler's name and then increase the amount of concentration necessary to answer the subsequent questions. For example, ask increasingly difficult math problems or questions such as, "How many *i*'s are in the word *Mississippi*?" Finish the demonstration by asking the juggler to start at 1,582,693 and count backward by thirteen. Observe and discuss what happens to the juggler's rhythm.
2. Working in small groups, have students brainstorm mnemonic devices for key terms listed at the end of the chapter. Encourage students to generate different types of mnemonic devices.

Teacher Interviews

Have each student ask a teacher to describe observable behaviors that allow him or her to infer various kinds of cognitive activities.

Have each student interview a teacher regarding instructions that he or she uses to encourage thinking in students.

Have each student interview a teacher regarding how he or she attempts to direct students to attend selectively to some material and how that teacher then fosters automatic processing.

Have each student interview a teacher regarding his or her use of drill and practice to achieve automaticity.

Have each student ask a teacher to distinguish between knowledge of what things are and knowledge of how to do things based on his or her own experiences.

Have each student interview a writing teacher regarding his or her use of imagery to support writing activities.

Have each student interview a foreign language teacher regarding the use of the keyword and other methods for memorizing foreign language vocabulary.

Field Observations

Have students read the passage on page 227 to several friends and document their interpretations. Have students interview the listeners to determine what information they retrieved as they listened to the passage.

Have students observe a class to discover other ways in which teachers encourage metacognition.

Have students observe language arts classes, documenting how metaphors and analogies in reading material are interpreted in class discussions.

Journal Entries

Have students reflect on various kinds of images that they generate as they read a novel and compare those images to those they generate when they learn from a text. Also, have them reflect on the stories that teachers have told them and whether these stories were effectively or ineffectively used.

Have students write on the reflections suggested in the text.

Have students reflect on the ways in which a teacher can use unusual behavior to teach material effectively.

Have students identify some key concepts or factual information that they anticipate teaching, speculating on the kinds of instructions they might give to their students to help them generate images of the key points.

Discussion Topics (based on Lecture Notes)

Have students discuss the meaning of the teacher's comments (p. 208).

Have pairs of students compare their study tactics and note the differences.

Have students in small groups identify information they would present in their classes and track the flow of that information through the various structures of the human cognitive mechanism.

Ask students to recall other types of elaborative rehearsal they used to learn information.

Ask students to share their experiences of their first "driving" lesson in Driver Education.

In discussion groups, have students identify several key elements of a concept and then generate a story that they could use in a classroom situation to aid them in remembering the information.

Application Scenarios

Present the following scenarios to students:

- Ernesto is clearly the best writer in your seventh-grade English class, and ought to be a cinch to win the City Oratory Contest. In fact, Ernesto has already written his speech, and it is excellent. The only problem is that the rules for the Oratory Contest specify that the contestant must recite his or her five-minute speech from memory. Ernesto's memory skills are as poor as his writing skills are excellent. The topic of the speech is "Citizenship in the 21st Century." Ernesto describes how the skills he learns in school will help make him a better citizen when he becomes an adult. Using your knowledge of mnemonic techniques, devise a specific strategy to help Ernesto remember his speech.

- You have introduced the Memory Game to your first-grade class, and they love it. They are not very good at it though. Can you use your knowledge of the flow of information through the information-processing model to design metacognitive strategies to help them play the game better? You might want to focus on the possible roles of selective and automatic attention, maintenance and elaborative rehearsal, and organization of input information in general.

Chapter 15 Casebook Previews

See Around the World.

See Beginning Each Day as a Learning Experience.

See Improvisation and Aesthetic Appreciation.

See Writers' Tea.

See Responsibility Education.

See Coup D'Etat in the Classroom.

See Writing Success in Science.

Teaching Anecdotes

Tell the story of the junior high science teacher who, convinced that the key to understanding a subject is the ability to understand and use a subject-appropriate vocabulary, hit upon a fun way for her students to learn new vocabulary: she had them write jokes. Extra credit was given for jokes and jokes regularly appeared on tests.

Ask students why joke writing would help in remembering subject-linked vocabulary. (See p. 209.)

Tell the story of the third-grade student who is fascinated by large machines. One morning a road crew began drilling and digging outside the school to replace a water main. The usually attentive student could not concentrate. The teacher was puzzled until he saw the student staring out of the window during free time.

Ask your students what they think the teacher did when he saw that the machines were the explanation for the student's unusual inattentiveness. (See p. 223.)

Tell your students about the kindergarten teacher who began each math session with a game. She would look over the class and ask certain students to stand up, choosing the students by a particular attribute: patterns in seating, initials, colors of clothing, eyes, hair, type of shoes, etc. The other students had to guess why the students were standing.

Ask your students why this game would help young students with mathematics. (See p. 224.)

Tell the story about the teacher who begins a review lesson with the question, "Who can remember what we were doing when we talked about ellipses?" Ask your students why this might be an effective retrieval method for some students. (See p. 233.)

Tell the story of the preschool teacher who uses the peg-word method to teach children their telephone numbers; also, the high school teacher who encourages students to use number peg words as an aid to remembering the order of species along a phylogenetic scale. For double-digit numbers, the images are combined. For example, twelve is a "bun-shoe"; twenty-one is "shoe-bun." The visual image for twelve is a foot wearing a kaiser roll. The visual image for twenty-one is a shoe inside a sliced roll, described as a shoe sandwich. (See p. 243.)

Transparencies

For transparencies to use with this chapter, see the Transparency Guides on page 213 and page 219.

Teaching Resources

Suggested Readings

Anderson, J. R. (1985). *Cognitive psychology and its implications* (2nd ed.). San Francisco: W. H. Freeman.

Gagné, R. M., & Driscoll, M. P. (1988). *Essentials of learning for instruction* (2nd ed.). Englewood Cliffs, NJ: Prentice-Hall.

Klatzky, R. L. (1980). *Human memory: Structures and processes* (2nd ed.). San Francisco: W. H. Freeman.

Schunk, D. H. (1991). *Learning theories: An educational perspective.* New York: Merrill.

Films, Videocassettes, Audiocassettes

- *Teaching Reading as Thinking,* 30 min. This video combines extensive research with practical experience to offer teachers this three-step approach:

  Before Reading—help students bring purpose, prior knowledge, and focus to assignments.

  During Reading—keep students involved and accountable for reading.

  After Reading—ensure that students apply reading and go back to the text.

  Teachers observe an exceptional teacher in action as she guides an elementary school class through all three steps. The manual also contains learning activities that encourage teachers to contribute their own classroom practices to the training.

- *Tactics for Thinking,* video. This training program introduces teachers to twenty-two instructional techniques that help students become better thinkers through concentration, memorization, and comparing and contrasting. The complete package contains a 250-page trainer's manual and 8-hour video presentations.

- *Teaching Skillful Thinking*, video. Four videotapes in this training program summarize research on thinking skills, show how teachers can demonstrate these skills to their students, and how several schools are using the program to improve student achievement.
- *Teaching Thinking in Elementary Schools*, audio. A complete framework for how to teach thinking in elementary schools with this set of audiotapes.
- *Analyzing Approaches to Teaching Thinking*, audio. This tape, by Ron Brandt and David Perkins, serves as an outline for choosing a successful program. It includes three examples of thinking skills programs that work.
- *Planning a Thinking Skills Program*, audio. This tape by Barry Beyer discusses which thinking skills can be most readily taught and how to incorporate them into your current curriculum.
- *The Development of Children's Thinking and Teaching in the River Edge, New Jersey, Schools*, audio. Esther Fusco and John Barell discuss the important "why-to" information you need about adapting instruction to children's cognitive development.

These seven productions are available through Association for Supervision and Curriculum Development, 125 North West Street, Alexandria, VA 22314-2798. Or call (703) 549-9110.

- *Memory: Fabric of the Mind*. This program looks at the various areas that brain researchers are now exploring: If long-term memory is a kind of permanent pattern on the fabric of the mind, what structural changes occur in the brain? Are different types of memory located in different areas of the brain? Are specific memories stored in separate places? What is the process of forgetting? Is it possible to improve memory? Available through: Films for the Humanities & Sciences, Inc., P.O. Box 2052, Princeton, NJ 08543. Or call 1-800-257-5126 (in NJ, 609-452-1128). CC-1738.
- *The Brain, Mind and Behavior, Program 5—Learning and Memory*, 60 min., color. How do we remember? Why do we forget? This program looks at theories about brain organization and activities at the synapse and the hippocampus to help unravel the mystery of memory. Available through WNET-TV, 356 West 58th Street, New York, NY 10019.

Test Questions

Test Questions 6.1–6.123

Study Guide

Assign Chapter 6 of the *Study Guide*.

7
Models for Learning

Chapter Objectives

1. General Objective

Recognizes imitative behavior as a form of vicarious learning (pp. 254–257).

SPECIFIC BEHAVIORS

1.01 Identifies a model's behavior as a stimulus.
1.02 Illustrates how perceived characteristics serve as stimulus properties.
1.03 Identifies models as influencing standards of behavior.
1.04 Differentiates what observers learn from the behaviors they perform.

2. General Objective

Applies Bandura's capabilities to observational learning (pp. 257–260).

SPECIFIC BEHAVIORS

2.01 Shows how the symbolizing capability contributes to reasoning and judgment.
2.02 Shows how the forethought capability contributes to goal setting.
2.03 Shows how the vicarious capability contributes to attitudes, values, and behaviors.
2.04 Shows how the self-regulatory capability contributes to self-evaluation.
2.05 Shows how the self-reflective capability contributes to a sense of self-efficacy.
2.06 Explains how the capabilities contribute to classroom learning.

3. General Objective

Understands the interrelationship among personal factors, behavior, and the environment (pp. 260–263).

SPECIFIC BEHAVIORS

3.01 Defines the roles of reciprocal determinism.
3.02 Explains how personal factors influence behavior.
3.03 Explains how behavior influences personal factors.
3.04 Explains how personal factors influence the environment.
3.05 Explains how the environment influences personal factors.
3.06 Explains how behavior influences the environment.
3.07 Explains how the environment influences behavior.

4. General Objective

Analyzes observational learning outcomes and processes (pp. 263–273).

SPECIFIC BEHAVIORS

4.01 Illustrates the observational learning effect.
4.02 Illustrates the inhibitory effect.
4.03 Illustrates the disinhibitory effect.
4.04 Illustrates the response facilitation effect.
4.05 Illustrates the environmental enhancement effect.
4.06 Illustrates the arousal effect.
4.07 Characterizes the attention process and its influences.
4.08 Characterizes retention processes.
4.09 Characterizes production processes.
4.10 Characterizes motivation processes.
4.11 Distinguishes direct, self-, and vicarious reinforcement.

5. General Objective

Judges the effectiveness of models (pp. 273–276).

SPECIFIC BEHAVIORS

5.01 Explains the effects of observers' perceptions of similarity.
5.02 Explains the effects of observers' perceptions of competence.
5.03 Explains the effects of peer models.

6. *General Objective*

Understands the development of a sense of self-efficacy (pp. 276–280).

SPECIFIC BEHAVIORS

6.01 Gives examples of performance outcomes that influence self-efficacy.

6.02 Gives examples of vicarious experiences that influence self-efficacy.

6.03 Gives examples of verbal persuasion that influence self-efficacy.

6.04 Gives examples of physiological states that influence self-efficacy.

6.05 Explains the relationship between outcome expectations and expectancy expectations.

6.06 Infers the relationship between goal-setting and self-efficacy.

7. *General Objective*

Understands the factors that influence the teacher's effectiveness as a model (pp. 280–282).

SPECIFIC BEHAVIORS

7.01 Explains defined competence as part of the teacher's role.

7.02 Explains the implications of perceived similarity of a teacher.

7.03 Explains teachers as "coping" models.

Focus Questions

- What is the difference between learning and performing?
- How do students learn by observing others learn?
- How do human capabilities influence the way in which students learn?
- How do personal factors, environment, and behavior influence each other?
- What processes are involved when one person learns by observing another person?
- How do a learner's perceptions determine who is and is not a role model?
- What do students learn about themselves by observing others?

Chapter Outline

INTRODUCTION: MODELS AND OBSERVERS

TEACHER CHRONICLE 7.1: WIZARD WEEK: IN THE BAG

LEARNING AND PERFORMANCE

CAPABILITIES OF LEARNERS
Symbolizing Capability
Forethought Capability
Vicarious Capability
Self-regulatory Capability
Self-reflective Capability

RECIPROCAL DETERMINISM
Personal Factors and Behavior
Personal Factors and Environment
Behavior and Environment
Principles in Practice 7.1

TEACHER CHRONICLE 7.2: JUGGLING

OBSERVATIONAL LEARNING
Modeling Outcomes
    Observational Learning Effects
    Inhibitory and Disinhibitory Effects
    Response Facilitation Effects
    Environmental Enhancement Effects
    Arousal Effects

OBSERVATIONAL LEARNING PROCESSES
Attention
    Properties of the Observed
    Properties of the Observer
Retention
Production
Motivation
Principles in Practice 7.2

TEACHER CHRONICLE 7.3: MAY I HAVE YOUR ATTENTION, PLEASE?

MODEL EFFECTIVENESS
Perceived Similarity
Perceived Competence
Peer Models

SELF-EFFICACY
Goal Setting

TEACHERS AS MODELS
Principles in Practice 7.3

CONCLUSION

Chapter Summary

Introduction: Models and Observers

- In social cognitive theory, observers learn by observing the behavior of other people (models) in their social environment.

Learning and Performance

- Learning is a cognitive phenomenon; performance is behavior. Observational learning need not be the result of performance.

Capabilities of Learners

- The ability to create symbols is one of the cognitive capabilities that learners have. It refers to the ability humans have to form a mental representation of modeled events.
- The forethought capability allows us to anticipate the results of certain courses of action. Forethought allows a student to decide whether a behavior he or she has learned should or should not be performed.
- The vicarious capability allows us to learn from others in our social environment. It is not necessary that learners perform a behavior in order to learn it. The assumption of vicarious capability clearly differentiates the social cognitive perspective from operant conditioning theory.
- The self-regulatory capability permits humans to use internal standards or criteria to regulate their own actions. It is an important reason why learning is distinguished from performance. An observer may learn to behave in a particular way but choose not to perform the behavior because it does not meet his or her internal standards.
- Information processing-theory labels the self-reflective capability *metacognition*. It is the capability humans have to analyze their own actions and thought processes. Self-reflection serves an evaluative function that leads to changes in one's thinking and behavior.

Reciprocal Determinism

- Personal factors include a person's cognitive, affective, and social characteristics. Personal factors and behavior interact with each other to produce learning outcomes. A person's thoughts influence his or her behavior. One's experience or behaviors influence how one thinks about himself or herself.
- One's personal characteristics cause other people in the environment to react in various ways. Those environmental reactions influence how a person views himself or herself.
- Behavior operates on the environment; it produces certain kinds of consequences. The consequences supplied by the environment influence future behavior.

Observational Learning

- Models can produce a variety of effects in an observer. They can teach behaviors, strengthen or weaken inhibitions, cue behaviors, highlight objects or aspects of the environment, or arouse emotions.
- When we acquire behaviors by observing models, we use the following cognitive processes in sequence: attention, retention, production, and motivation.

Model Effectiveness

- Perceived similarity is the observer's perception of similarity between him- or herself and a model. If an observer perceives a model to be similar to him- or herself, the model is more likely to have an effect on the observer's learning and/or performance.
- Perceived competence refers to the observer's perception of how competent a model is. Competence can be displayed by either a mastery model or a coping model. Modeling effects are more likely when a model is perceived as being competent.
- Peer models are those who share the same status as an observer. Peer models are, by definition, more likely to be perceived as similar to an observer. In a classroom, peer modeling is a form of peer tutoring.

Self-efficacy

- A person's sense of self-efficacy is a belief that he or she can successfully complete a certain kind of task. A student's beliefs about his or her abilities influences the goals he or she sets. A student's goals reflect his or her motivation.

Teachers as Models

- Teachers are in a unique position to function as models. Using their knowledge of the characteristics that have been shown to influence model effectiveness as a guide, teachers are encouraged to reflect on those qualities that might influence their students' perceptions.

Key Terms

social cognitive theory	disinhibitory effects
observer	response facilitation effects
model	environmental enhancement effects
learning	
performance	arousal effects
symbolize	attention
forethought	retention
self-regulation	production
self-reflection	motivation
sense of self-efficacy	direct reinforcement
reciprocal determinism	self-reinforcement
modeling	vicarious reinforcement
observational learning effects	perceived similarity
	perceived competence
inhibitory effects	peer models

Teacher Chronicle Summaries

Teacher Chronicle 7.1: Wizard Week: In the Bag (pp. 255–256)

To introduce Science Wizard Week, a junior high school teacher stabs a bag full of water with a pencil to get her students' attention. By tracing the steps she went through in designing the experiment, the teacher shows her students the process they will use as they find, practice, and demonstrate their own experiments.

Teacher Chronicle 7.2: Juggling (pp. 262–263)

A high school student awes his peers with his juggling skills. His demonstration inspires his teacher to use juggling as a reward if everyone in the class keeps up with his or her work.

Teacher Chronicle 7.3: May I Have Your Attention, Please? (pp. 272–273)

A sixth-grade teacher takes her class to an assembly on drug and alcohol awareness. The class pays little attention to the first speaker, a man dressed in a three-piece suit with an obviously well-prepared speech. But the students are excited and ready to listen to the next speaker, a professional baseball player.

Possible Answers to Principles in Practice

Principles in Practice 7.1

1. *What did the students learn about* selecting *experiments for their own Wizard Week presentations from the teacher's demonstration?*

They learned that they could consult different resources to find an experiment that interested them. They also found out that they should try the experiment at home before presenting it to the class.

2. *Describe how Carey's cognitive capabilities (i.e., symbolizing, forethought, etc.) influenced her learning during the demonstration.*

Carey was able to anticipate the outcome of poking the water-filled bag with a pencil. Although the result Carey anticipated did not occur, her attention increased. The unanticipated outcome made an impression, forcing Carey to reflect on what she observed.

3. *Describe how personal factors, behavior, and environmental events might have interacted during the remainder of Wizard Week, either from the teacher's or a student's point of view.*

From the teacher's point of view, watching students present experiments provides the teacher with considerable reinforcement, thus encouraging the teacher to use the activity with future classes. From a student's point of view,

his or her presentation abilities and behaviors were either greeted positively or negatively by the teacher and other students (the environment).

Principles in Practice 7.2

1. *During that first class, Charlie's juggling did not result in modeled performance. What did the other students learn?*

Although the students did not model Charlie's performance they learned that juggling attracts positive attention from classmates and from the teacher. Chronicle 7.2 implies that students also experienced vicarious reinforcement as they watched Charlie. Vicarious reinforcement would account for the eagerness with which the class embraced the idea of juggling lessons.

2. *Using the processes of observational learning as an aid, speculate on how the students in Teacher Chronicle 7.2 became jugglers.*

The juggling attracted the students' attention. They learned about the relevant aspects of juggling. The lessons gave them an opportunity to think about the act of juggling and to practice juggling skills. Because the lessons were sanctioned by the teacher, juggling was considered appropriate. With practice, the students became jugglers. Finally, the act of juggling brought self-reinforcement through a sense of accomplishment and, perhaps, direct reinforcement from family and friends.

3. *What other modeled behaviors, besides juggling, might you use for the same purpose as the teacher in Teacher Chronicle 7.2?*

Other party skills such as magic tricks, making balloon animals, or balancing feats may be used as modeling behaviors. One way to determine what students would be interested in learning would be to ask them with the help of a reinforcement menu and to use their selections according to the Premack principle.

Principles in Practice 7.3

1. *If you had been given responsibility for the assembly, would you have changed the order of the speakers? Why?*

The baseball players' perceived image could be used to capture the attention of the students. Once captured, the baseball player could increase the status of the drug and alcohol expert through a laudatory introduction, thus increasing the likelihood that students would listen to the expert's important message.

2. *How might a teacher use the sources of efficacy expectations to create a class project called, "You Bet I Can"?*

The teacher could begin by having students identify a special skill they possess. Each student can present their strength and share with the rest of the class how he or she acquired the skill. The teacher might also learn some new skills from students, thus becoming a coping model.

3. *How do you plan to maximize your effectiveness as a model for your students?*

The plans should account for the perceptions which influence a model's effectiveness. Regardless of the teacher's current status, Chapter 7 suggests that coping models are effective. By learning something with the students, a teacher is more likely to be perceived as a coping model.

CNN Connection to Issues in Educational Psychology

There are no CNN video segments for this chapter.

Activities and Exercises

In-Class Activities

1. Conduct a mock trial. Assign several students to form a team of prosecutors, several others to form a team of defenders, and an odd number of students—up to nine students—to sit as justices. A teenager who is charged with assault and battery is on trial. The defense will argue that the teenager committed the offense after viewing a popular movie star display similar aggression in a film; therefore, the defendant should be judged leniently. The prosecution seeks the harshest penalty allowed. In this trial, the only evidence admissible are the assumptions, explanations, and psychological research associated with Bandura's social cognitive theory. The justices will be responsible for keeping the arguments in the case admissible and, based on the arguments presented, decide the case.
2. Charge students with the responsibility for matching student teaching candidates with mentor teachers. To make these assignments, have the students establish criteria based on social cognitive theory.

Teacher Interviews

Have each student interview a teacher regarding the onset of "mob" behavior in the classroom.

Have each student interview a teacher about students who learn but do not perform.

Have each student interview a teacher regarding poor instructional decisions that he or she made that were caused by faulty information.

Have each student talk with a junior high or high school teacher regarding his or her efforts to encourage students to use their best judgment in various social situations.

Have each student interview a teacher regarding how he or she establishes the criteria for socially acceptable behavior in the classroom.

Have each student interview a teacher regarding the way that teacher establishes peer-tutoring pairs in his or her classroom.

Have each student interview a teacher regarding the problems that students with either unrealistically high or unrealistically low goals experience.

Have each student interview a teacher recognized for his or her enthusiasm, asking the teacher how he or she uses this enthusiasm to motivate students.

Field Observations

Have students identify students in a class who are different from most of their classmates, either in terms of some exceptionality or because they are members of a microculture. Have them observe patterns of interaction among classmates; paying particular attention to whether or not exceptional and minority students participate in those interactions.

Have students observe various kinds of classes—for example, physical education classes, foreign language classes, elementary math classes—documenting the various kinds of observational learning effects that occur.

Have students observe other students in a classroom and document the various properties of modeled actions.

Have your students observe students who are attempting to memorize a speech or a series of physical actions, documenting these students' behaviors and inferring their cognitive processes.

Have students observe teachers who display characteristics of a coping model and teachers who display the characteristics of a mastery model, documenting the differences in terms of classroom atmosphere and students' attitudes.

Have students observe other students in a classroom, identifying the behaviors and attitudes of those students who display a strong sense of self-efficacy. Then have them compare those behaviors and attitudes with those of students who seem to have a weaker sense of self-efficacy.

Journal Entries

Have students reflect on teachers who influenced them greatly, describing their impressions of those teachers.

Have students compare their motivation to carry out plans of action that were of their own design with their motivation to carry out plans that were designed by others.

Have students reflect on those instances when their own performances exceeded the requirements of the assignments.

Have students reflect on episodes from their schooling when response facilitation occurred, noting who among their classmates usually initiated such effects, and what the characteristics of the initiaters were.

Have students reflect on their heroes and heroines and the ways in which they were unique, identifying the reasons why they selected these people to emulate.

Have students consider the types of teaching behaviors that they might be capable of and that they consider acceptable, determining how their criteria of acceptability and judgments of capability will influence their teaching style.

Have students consider those practicing teachers whom they've had in class and consider to be more or less competent, listing factors that influenced their judgments of their competence.

Have students reflect on the kinds of decisions they might make that require them to rely on their "gut feelings." Have them start by reflecting on how their gut feelings influence decisions they make as they research and write papers.

Have students reflect on how outcome expectations and efficacy expectations might influence their own motivation, addressing the question, How will they use these insights to enhance their own students' motivations in the future?

Discussion Topics (based on Lecture Notes)

Ask students to compare the motivational implications of this view versus those of operant conditioning.

Ask students to compare the reciprocal determinism of social cognitive theory with the constructivism that underlies Piaget's theory of development.

Ask students to consider what role a teacher's enthusiasm plays in reducing response facilitation effects.

Have students discuss how teachers fulfill the various roles connected with modeling outcomes.

Have your students discuss Piaget's stages in terms of symbolic capability.

Ask students to consider the difference between response facilitation effects and the recognition of a model as being similar.

Ask students to discuss those teachers in their experience who were "charismatic." Was part of their charisma attributable to their status as competent models?

Application Scenarios

Present the following scenarios to students:

- Jeffrey always manages to be the last person in your fourth-grade class to complete his assignments. When you decide to monitor his performance on a book report, you find that he ends up running out of room consistently on his page, so he has to start over several times. Can you think of a few goals that Jeffrey might adopt and ways for him to meet those goals?
- Lydia loves to sing, but she does so very softly. You listen carefully and discover that she has a very nice voice. Can you help Lydia learn to sing louder? How could you encourage her to help other shy children learn to sing louder as well?
- For the last day of school, you promise your ninth-grade class that you will bring in a special guest.

Whom should you bring in for them: a famous local politician, a successful business person, or a local sports hero? What messages would you want your local celebrity to convey to your students?

Chapter 15 Casebook Previews

Teaching Anecdotes

Tell the story about the first-grade teacher who read picture books to her students every day. Many of the books dealt with families and brothers and sisters who were making mistakes, getting lost, living in the city, and having celebrations. After each story, the teacher led a discussion about the book and how it related to the children. All of the books, however, had animal, not human characters.

Ask your students why reading animal stories would be effective with this age group. Would similar stories work with students in high school (e.g., *Watership Down* and *The Hobbit*)? (See p. 258.)

Tell your students about the student who cannot seem to accept praise. She does *A* work, extra credit projects, and helps other students, but when it comes to accepting teacher praise for her efforts, she shrugs her shoulders and says, "Yeah, but it's no big deal."

Ask your students what this girl's sense of self-efficacy might be like and how the teacher might find ways to increase the student's sense of self-worth. Why did the girl feel this way about herself in the first place? (See p. 261.)

Tell the story of the second-grade teacher whose students were interested in the Persian Gulf War and concerned about its effect upon them. Each day news articles were brought from home and the war was discussed in the classroom. One day, several students brought in toy tanks, ships, and planes.

Have students address the following questions: Should the teacher have allowed the students to play with the toys whenever they liked? Should she have allowed them to play with the toys but discussed how real weapons are used to kill real people? Should she not have permitted the students to bring these toys to her classroom? (See p. 266.)

Tell the story about the first-year teacher who watched her second graders play school one day during an inside recess. Three students went to the chalkboard and became the "teacher."

"Now, boys and girls, it's time to gather 'round the carpet," one mimicked.

"How can you tell *isn't* is a compound word?"

"Make sure you put your name on the top!"

Ask your students how they interpret the children's imitations. (See p. 269.)

Tell your students about the English teacher who is perceived to be a most effective teacher by her students and the greater community. Although she demands a great deal of her students, she is always fair with them. When asked by a local newspaper reporter why she is so successful, she replied, "The answer is really quite simple: I love literature. I enjoy sharing what I have learned with students. Every so often, I find a kindred spirit among my students; someone who has the same passion that I do. That is when I really teach."

Ask your students why this teacher is not only seen as effective, but, in fact, is very successful in teaching her subject. (See p. 280.)

Transparencies

For transparencies to use with this chapter, see the Transparency Guides on page 260 and page 279.

Teaching Resources

Suggested Readings

Bandura, A. (1977). *Social learning theory.* Englewood Cliffs, NJ: Prentice-Hall.

Bandura, A. (1986). *Social foundations of thought and action.* Englewood Cliffs, NJ: Prentice-Hall.

Bandura, A., & Walters, R. H. (1963). *Social learning and personality development.* New York: Holt, Rinehart & Winston.

Schunk, D. H. (1987). Peer models and children's behavioral change. *Review of Educational Research, 57,* 149–174.

Films, Videocassettes, Audiocassettes

- *Head of the Class,* video, 14 min., color. Why are Japanese students so much more goal-oriented than Americans? Who motivates them? How? This story aroused tremendous interest when it was broadcast on *60 Minutes.* It shows three- and four-year-olds doing homework for hours each day to polish their skills so that they will get into the best kindergarten. Mothers overseeing (driving, Americans would say) their children so that they will do more and better. The goal of the learning process is to gain admission to college, which assumes a job commensurate with the exclusivity of the college. Education ends with the posting of one's name on a list of the admitted. CC-1684

- *Mastery Learning by Tom Guskey,* audio. Find out why mastery learning is building a successful track record for improving student achievement. Get an overview of the most widely used approaches. 612-20348c2

- *Improving the Quality of Student Thinking,* video. A videotaped interview with leading educators and scenes from classrooms explain twelve ways to bring higher-order thinking to every class including:

  Explicitly state that improving thinking is the goal of a particular lesson.

  Use broad, open-ended questions to jump start a discussion.

  Ensure that students process information, not just memorize it.

  Use "wait time" and other techniques to ignite the thinking process in students.

- *What Human Beings Do When They Behave Intelligently,* audio. Arthur Costa tells how to know when your thinking skills program is working by using this tape's list of twelve characteristics that indicate growth in student thinking abilities.

- *Critical Thinking in Elementary School,* audio. This tape, by Richard Paul, tells how to revise lesson plans in reading, social studies, and science to emphasize critical thinking.

These five productions are available through Association for Supervision and Curriculum Development, 125 North West Street, Alexandria, VA 22314-2798. Or call (703) 549-9110.

Test Questions

Test Questions 7.1–7.94

Study Guide

Assign Chapter 7 of the *Study Guide.*

8
Motivations

Chapter Objectives

1. General Objective

Understands motivation in terms of goals and means devised to attain those goals (pp. 286–291).

SPECIFIC BEHAVIORS
1.01 Gives examples of shared goals and divergent behaviors.
1.02 Gives examples of divergent goals and shared behaviors.
1.03 Distinguishes intrinsic and extrinsic goals.
1.04 Characterizes intrinsic goals.
1.05 Characterizes extrinsic goals.
1.06 Explains the importance of matching teaching to students' motivation.

2. General Objective

Recognizes the sources of intrinsic motivation (pp. 291–298).

SPECIFIC BEHAVIORS
2.01 Identifies the elements of curiosity that motivate students.
2.02 Illustrates the role of novelty, complexity, and/or incongruity in generating curiosity.
2.03 Identifies the elements of achievement that motivate students.
2.04 Shows how need to achieve is reflected in student behavior.
2.05 Identifies the elements of self-efficacy that motivate students.
2.06 Shows self-observation as contributing to expectations for self-efficacy.
2.07 Shows observation of others as contributing to expectations for self-efficacy.
2.08 Shows encouragement as contributing to expectations for self-efficacy.
2.09 Shows emotional arousal as contributing to expectations for self-efficacy.

2.10 Infers the relationship between sources of intrinsic motivation and the use of extrinsic reward.
2.11 Illustrates the undermining effect.

3. General Objective

Applies the conditions for achievement motivation identified in the ARCS model (pp. 298–304).

SPECIFIC BEHAVIORS
3.01 Predicts grade-appropriate teaching actions that will attract students' attention.
3.02 Predicts grade-appropriate teaching actions that will maintain students' attention.
3.03 Relates the attention condition to curiosity.
3.04 Predicts grade-appropriate teaching actions that will establish relevance.
3.05 Relates the relevance condition to students' goals.
3.06 Predicts grade-appropriate teaching actions that contribute to students' confidence.
3.07 Relates the condition of confidence to self-efficacy.
3.08 Predicts grade-appropriate teaching actions that contribute to students' satisfaction.
3.09 Relates the condition of satisfaction to reinforcement and need to achieve.

4. General Objective

Understands Maslow's hierarchy of needs as a way of identifying students' goals (pp. 304–307).

SPECIFIC BEHAVIORS
4.01 Gives examples of physical needs.
4.02 Distinguishes deficiency needs from growth needs.
4.03 Discusses basic needs for self-actualization.
4.04 Explains the implications of the hierarchy of needs for parenting.
4.05 Explains the implications of the hierarchy of needs for teaching.
4.06 Infers good choices and bad choices.

5. General Objective

Understands need to achieve as an explanation of student motivation (pp. 307–310).

SPECIFIC BEHAVIORS
5.01 Explains achievement motivation as a conflict of emotions.
5.02 Explains approach behavior as hope for success.
5.03 Explains avoidance behavior as fear of failure.
5.04 Predicts approach behavior on the basis of need achievement, probability of success, and incentive value.
5.05 Relates probability of success to incentive value.
5.06 Predicts avoidance behavior on the basis of motive to avoid failure, probability of failure, and incentive value.
5.07 Predicts achievement motivation on the basis of tendency to approach with intentions of success and tendency to avoid failure.
5.08 Explains the motivational state called fear of success.
5.09 Relates to achievement motivation to social interaction with peers and parents.

6. General Objective

Applies students' attributions of success or failure to identify student motivation (pp. 310–314).

SPECIFIC BEHAVIORS
6.01 Distinguishes the causal dimensions by which attributions can be defined.
6.02 Differentiates the endpoints of the locus of control dimension.
6.03 Differentiates the endpoints of the stability dimension.
6.04 Differentiates the endpoints of the controllability dimension.
6.05 Classifies the causation of ability attributions.
6.06 Relates students' attributions to self-image.
6.07 Classifies the causation of effort attributions.
6.08 Classifies the causation of task difficulty attributions.
6.09 Classifies the causation of luck attributions.
6.10 Relates students' achievement levels to attributions.
6.11 Predicts the condition of learned helplessness.

7. General Objective

Proposes classroom plans for enhancing motivation (pp. 314–317).

SPECIFIC BEHAVIORS
7.01 Designs student activities to enhance an internal locus of control.
7.02 Devises a procedure that enables students to set realistic goals.
7.03 Distinguishes between learning and performance goals.
7.04 Designs change programs which account for the attributional styles of students' culture.
7.05 Explains the relationship between labeling and attributions.

Focus Questions

- Why do students differ in their pursuits of academic achievement?
- What internal and external factors influence motivation?
- What are the sources of motivation?
- How might teachers inadvertently undermine students' motivation?
- What conditions have to exist if students are to be motivated toward achievement?
- How do the needs of each student explain differences in individual motivation?
- What can teachers learn from students' perceptions of their successes and their failures?

Chapter Outline

INTRODUCTION: GOALS

TEACHER CHRONICLE 8.1: CURIOUSER AND CURIOUSER

SOURCES OF MOTIVATION
Intrinsic Versus Extrinsic Goals
Intrinsic Motivation: A Closer Look
 Curiosity
 Achievement
 Self-efficacy

THE UNDERMINING EFFECT
Principles in Practice 8.1

TEACHER CHRONICLE 8.2: GOLDEN OPPORTUNITIES

THE ARCS MODEL
Attention
Relevance
Confidence
Satisfaction
Principles in Practice 8.2

TEACHER CHRONICLE 8.3: REACHING LISA

MASLOW'S HIERARCHY OF NEEDS

THE NEED TO ACHIEVE
Approach and Avoidance
 Fear of Success

ATTRIBUTION THEORY
    Learned Helplessness
    Attribution Training
        Cross-Cultural Evidence
    Principles in Practice 8.3

CONCLUSION

Chapter Summary

Introduction: Goals

- All students are motivated, but not all students may be motivated to do the things that teachers ask of them. Furthermore, students may share a goal, but use different means to achieve that goal. Understanding a student's goals and the means he or she uses to attain that goal is critical if a teacher is to be effective.

Sources of Motivation

- Some students work toward a goal because they wish to satisfy some personal need. Such students are intrinsically motivated. Other students work toward a goal in order to obtain rewards from the environment or people in that environment. Such students are extrinsically motivated.
- Intrinsic motivation is an internal state that leads to action toward a goal. The state may be triggered by stimuli from the environment, but action is taken for reasons internal to the learner. Curiosity is an example of such a reason.

The Undermining Effect

- The undermining effect results from using external incentives to encourage work toward a goal that is already intrinsically important to a student. By using external rewards to encourage a student who doesn't need encouraging, that student's intrinsic goals can be compromised. Teachers should guard against this effect.

The ARCS Model

- Attention is one of four conditions that contributes to student motivation. In order for students to work effectively on some academic task, they must attend to the task. There are a variety of useful ways to attract a learner's attention or interest.
- Relevance is the second condition in the ARCS model. Relevance means establishing some reason, which the student finds compelling, for working toward a particular goal. Relevance of content can be established in a variety of ways; it is not necessarily confined to preparing the student for "life after the classroom."

- A learner who believes himself or herself to be capable of performing well on assigned tasks has developed a sense of confidence. This aspect of the ARCS model is similar to Bandura's notion of self-efficacy.
- Satisfaction is the condition that accompanies the successful completion of a task. A student who successfully completes one task will be motivated to work on similar tasks.

Maslow's Hierarchy of Needs

- Maslow's hierarchy proceeds from basic physiological needs to psychological needs for self-actualization. The needs that are lower in the hierarchy are called deficiency needs; those that are higher are growth needs. The needs of one level must be met before the needs at the next higher level can effectively motivate behavior.

The Need to Achieve

- The approach and avoidance theory of behavior equates motivation and emotions. Approach behavior is motivated by a hope for success. Avoidance behavior is motivated by a fear of failure. Both the hope for success and the fear of failure are present when a student encounters an achievement-related task. The resultant achievement motivation is a function of both emotions. Some researchers have investigated how another emotion, the fear of success, motivates avoidance as well.

Attribution Theory

- Attribution theory classifies the reasons that students give for success or failure to determine their motivation. The reasons (or attributions) can reflect differences in locus of control, stability, and controllability. The major attributions are ability, effort, task difficulty, and luck.
- A student who attributes consistent failure to factors not under his or her control shows signs of a serious condition called learned helplessness.
- Personality characteristics related to poor motivation can be changed. Motivational change is reflected in changed attributions. Some programs focus on changing a student's locus of control from external to internal so that the student perceives his or her own efforts as making a difference. Other approaches deal with attributional problems by teaching goal-setting skills. Students who are effective at setting goals are less likely to "set themselves up for failure."

Key Terms

intrinsic goals	curiosity
extrinsic goals	achievement

self-efficacy	need to achieve
undermining effect	approach behavior
attention	avoidance behavior
relevance	fear of success
confidence	attributions
satisfaction	locus of control
deficiency needs	stability
growth needs	controllability
self-actualization	learned helplessness
growth motivated	attribution training
good choices	learning goal
bad choices	performance goal

Teacher Chronicle Summaries

Teacher Chronicle 8.1: Curiouser and Curiouser (pp. 289–290)

A fourth-grade teacher has a gifted student, Lynne, who constantly asks questions about everything from the human body to how an author chooses facts to include in a book. However, Lynne is disorganized, late in completing her work, and irresponsible. The teacher, recognizing Lynne's varied interests, accommodates her learning style as best he can in the context of his class.

Teacher Chronicle 8.2: Golden Opportunities (pp. 297–298)

A student with a speech impediment rarely participates in class until a teacher allows him to take a different tangent during a writing lesson. When the student reads his story to the class, three things happen: the student feels successful, his peers gain a new appreciation of him, and his teacher understands him better.

Teacher Chronicle 8.3: Reaching Lisa (pp. 303–304)

Lisa, a new student to the school, is belligerent, distracts other students, doesn't pay attention, and constantly gets into trouble. Her teacher tries to understand her difficulties, attributing them to being in a new school. But the problems persist. After one incident, the teacher realizes that Lisa is being abused at home, and that she transfers schools frequently because her family moves to avoid prosecution.

Possible Answers to Principles in Practice

Principles in Practice 8.1

1. *How might the teacher use Lynne's curiosity to trigger the curiosity of other students?*

If the teacher rewards Lynne's curiosity with opportunities to pursue her interests, other students might see that curiosity can empower. If a student displays curiosity, maybe he or she can define his or her own tasks.

2. *What do Lynne's behaviors tell you about her need to achieve and her sense of self-efficacy?*

In Chronicle 8.1 we learn that Lynne is motivated by an intrinsic need to achieve. The confidence she displays in class, in a variety of situations, attests to a sense of self-efficacy when confronted with academic tasks.

3. *How would you have responded to Lynne's question about Leslie in* Bridge to Terabithia, *"Did she boil in her own blood?"*

If, as a teacher, you perceive Lynne's question to be at least partially motivated by curiosity, even though she may have been seeking an effect as well, then you might encourage Lynne to conduct some research in order to answer her own question. What you ask Lynne to do with her research depends on whether you seek to encourage or discourage such questions. It is hoped that if you, as a teacher, seek to discourage questions of the "boiling-in-blood" sort, you will take care not to undermine motivating curiosity.

Principles in Practice 8.2

1. *How do you think the brainstorming influenced the motivational conditions of the ARCS model?*

Generally, brainstorming allows students to use their own ideas, establishing the condition of relevance. If students' contributions to a brainstorming session are given credence, a sense of satisfaction and confidence is likely to arise. If the pace and quality of the ideas are appropriate, attention can be easily maintained. In Bronson's case, the brainstorming gave him an idea that allowed him to express himself humorously. Because humor is relevant to Bronson, he has confidence in his humor.

2. *What made the writing assignment relevant for Bronson? How might it be made relevant for other students?*

The teacher's decision to allow Bronson to follow his own ideas made the task relevant for Bronson. It is reasonable to assume that the same thing would be true for other students as well.

3. *How does relevance contribute to confidence, satisfaction, and attention? Which, in your opinion, is the most basic condition?*

If a student finds that a task or concept is relevant, the student can see that something can be done with the material. Relevance means that a student perceives a task with confidence. Confidence means that the task is likely to receive close attention and therefore will be pursued to completion, leading to a sense of accomplishment or satisfaction.

Principles in Practice 8.3

1. *On the basis of her behaviors in school, at which level of Maslow's hierarchy would you place Lisa? Why?*

Lisa is clearly classifiable as a deficiency-motivated student. Given what the teacher discovered about Lisa's home life, it is reasonable to assume that several low-level needs have gone unmet, including safety needs due to the abusive nature of her home.

2. Although it is not stated in Teacher Chronicle 8.3, do you think Lisa approached or avoided achievement-related tasks? Why?

Given what we learned about Lisa in the Chronicle 8.3 regarding both her academic and social behavior in the classroom, it seems unlikely that she would approach achievement-related tasks.

3. Had Lisa remained in school, how might the teacher have approached attribution training for her?

The first step might have been to verify a suspicion that she viewed herself as having little effect on the outcomes of events in her life. The teacher might have tried the origin–pawn approach developed by DeCharms.

CNN Connection to Issues in Educational Psychology

It's hard to break out of a stereotype. When you live in a ghetto and struggle for economic survival, no one expects you to be a dazzling success in the classroom. Most people won't think that you could take on education's toughest challenges. Students will see how two teachers succeed in getting students whom others didn't expect much of, to expect a lot—and get a lot—from themselves.

Activities and Exercises

In-Class Activities

1. Have students assume that they have been assigned to an ad hoc committee in charge of planning a districtwide in-service day on motivational techniques. The committee's job is to demonstrate ways of establishing each of the four elements of the ARCS model.
2. An educational testing firm has hired your students as consultants. The company wants to develop a paper-and-pencil test that will yield an attributional profile for each student who takes the test. As consultants, your students are asked to contribute rough drafts of items for the test. At a later stage in the development of the test, the results will be compared with other data to help determine the value of the test.

Teacher Interviews

Have each student interview a teacher regarding the judicious use of novelty in his or her classroom.

Have each student interview a teacher regarding the way in which he or she uses verbal encouragement.

Have students interview teachers at various grade levels regarding the undermining effect.

Have each student interview a teacher regarding the influence he or she has on some students and the care he or she must take in dealing with such students.

Have each student interview a teacher regarding the value he or she places on risk taking in the classroom.

Have each student interview a teacher regarding how he or she encourages students to become "good choosers."

Have each student interview a teacher regarding differences between students who have either an internal or external locus of control.

Have each student interview a teacher regarding the ways in which teachers encourage learned helplessness and how they might remedy it.

Have each student interview a teacher regarding his or her experiences with "late bloomers."

Have each student interview a teacher regarding the influence of informal labeling of a child's motivation on that child's success in school.

Field Observations

Have students observe various classrooms, documenting how teachers use curiosity to introduce lessons or maintain attention.

Have each student interview a student in another classroom to determine those areas in which that student feels a sense of self-efficacy.

Have students observe classrooms to determine whether each is an "emotionally safe environment," documenting the elements that contribute to such an environment.

Have each student gather information from a school district or interview an administrator regarding the referral system used in the district.

Have students observe children, especially older children, and parents in public situations, such as a restaurant or a shopping mall, documenting the nature of their interactions.

Have students observe a classroom in which students are engaged in a goal-setting activity, documenting decision-making processes of the students in the class.

Journal Entries

Have students reflect on those courses in college in which their goals and the professor's goals did not match, identifying the problems that they experienced in such courses.

Have students reflect on those teachers who made them want to "prove" themselves to them.

Have students reflect on some activity in which they engaged that was undermined by external rewards.

Have students reflect on their reactions to watching *Sesame Street*.

Have students reflect on the ways their needs were gratified in elementary and secondary school, identifying the needs that went unmet and the ways in which those unmet needs influenced their experiences in school.

Have students reflect on their own "good choices" and "bad choices."

Have students reflect on their experiences in school and the salient emotions they experienced.

Have students reflect on their experiences in school, commenting on the relevance of fear of success.

Have students reflect on those episodes that caused them to rationalize outcomes in a way that maintained their positive self-image.

Discussion Topics (based on Lecture Notes)

Ask students to discuss the motivational implications of the three theories of learning presented in Chapters 5, 6, and 7.

Ask students to discuss the parts peers and parents play in rewarding behavior. The discussion could be placed in the context of Erikson's psychosocial theory (Chapter 3).

Have students discuss the difference between a cognitive process and a cognitive state.

Have students discuss the relationship between Maslow's growth and deficiency needs and the emotions of hope of success and fear of failure.

Have your class discuss the value of attributional style as a tool for understanding individual students.

Have students discuss in small groups what their ideas for attribution training might be.

Application Scenarios

Present the following scenarios to students:

- Morgan is a quiet but good student in your fifth-grade art class. She likes to draw, but she is reluctant to let anyone else, including you, look at her drawings. You feel that her work is very good, and you feel that she could win the County Art Fair for her grade, if you could persuade her to enter. How can you convince Morgan to take a chance with her work, and let other people see it? What are the possible pitfalls?

- It is one week before graduation. All of your twelfth-grade English students have turned in their semester term papers, except Debbie. If she does not turn it in, she will not graduate. Furthermore, she is scheduled to graduate in the top 10 percent of her class. When you ask her about the paper, she avoids the topic. She talks about her boyfriend instead, and how they want to get married right after graduation. What motivational conflicts seem to be at work here, and how can you help the situation?

Chapter 15 Casebook Previews

See Please Sign This Contract.

See I Am Leo.

See Around the World.

See Science Is Only Real When You Do It.

See Gifted Achievers and Underachievers.

Teaching Anecdotes

Tell the story of the fourth-grade student who really wanted to be in the top reading group but was not willing to work on his reading enough to make the top group. His parents offered him extra TV time in exchange for extra reading. This arrangement worked for a while. His teacher praised him whenever he deserved it, hoping that praise might provide the extra push needed to get him moving. The boy made some progress but not enough to merit moving him into the top group. Then his parents "hired" him to read: they offered to pay him by the hour to read. Because it was near Christmas and the boy needed money, he agreed. He soon became hooked, reading far more than his parents expected him to do. The teacher acknowledged the tremendous growth he achieved in two months and moved him into the top group.

Ask your students what elements of motivation are in action here. (See p. 289.)

Tell your students about a sister and brother: the boy in second grade, the sister in eighth. Both were very academically oriented and always did their best in class. Both students, however, seemed unduly concerned about grades and did all they could to get *A*'s. Anything less meant failure to them. Upon meeting the father, one teacher made the connection: the father, a war veteran who did not attend college, was a successful businessperson. He made certain his kids did something educational every weekend: trips around the state to historical places, museum tours, rodeos, or travel out of state.

Ask your students what effects the father's desires might have had on his children. Was the childrens' needs to achieve internally or externally driven? (See p. 294.)

Tell your students about the teacher who used a system of plus and minus marks to monitor student behavior. The pluses were good, the minuses, bad. At the end of the week, the students with five pluses got a treat—ice cream or a piece of candy. The teacher had tried this before with sixth graders, but it had failed within a couple of weeks. Now as a first-grade teacher, she tried it again and it worked quite well.

Ask your students why the teachers system did not work effectively or for very long with sixth graders, but was very successful with first graders. (See p. 296.)

Teaching Anecdote: Tell your students about the teacher who had a student who continually interrupted class with trivial nonsense: questions that were not relevant to the topic being discussed, jokes, and vulgar remarks. The teacher tried many ways to get the student to control her outbursts, including detention, trips to the principal's office, counseling, time after school, and poor grades. Nothing seemed to have any effect on the girl's behavior in class. During one heated exchange after school, the teacher realized the student had no adults she really trusted. Her parents were divorced, her father never invited her over to his new apartment, and her mother often worked late at night, leaving the student home alone. When the teacher decided to base their relationship on mutual trust, the girl's behavior slowly changed.

Ask your students why this change in behavior might have happened. (See p. 306.)

Tell the story about the ninth-grade math student who always proclaimed ''I can't do that'' whenever his teacher introduced new material. Granted, he often did have a difficult time mastering the new material, especially when compared with his more math-oriented peers, but this negative comment was always his first reaction.

Ask your students what purpose the student's repeated negative comments served. Did they affect his success as a learner? (See p. 309.)

Transparencies

For transparencies to use with this Chapter, see the Transparency Guides on page 305 and page 309.

Teaching Resources

Suggested Readings

Ames, R., & Ames, C. (Eds.). (1989). *Research on motivation in education* (vol. 3). New York: Academic Press.

Gagne, R. M., & Driscoll, M. P. (1988). *Essentials of learning for instruction* (2nd edition). Englewood Cliffs, NJ: Prentice-Hall.

Geen, R., Arkin, R., & Beatty, W. (1984). *Human motivation*. Needham Heights, MA: Allyn & Bacon.

Keller, J. M. (1983). Motivational design of instruction. In C. M. Reigeluth (Ed.), *Instructional design theories and models: An overview of their current status*. Hillsdale, NJ: Erlbaum.

Stipek, D. J. (1988). *Motivation to learn: From theory to practice*. Englewood Cliffs, NJ: Prentice-Hall.

Weiner, B. (1980). *Human motivation*. New York: Holt, Rinehart & Winston.

Films, Videocassettes, Audiocassettes

- *Head of the Class*, video, 14 min., color. Why are Japanese students so much more goal-oriented than Americans? Who motivates them? How? This story aroused tremendous interest when it was broadcast on *60 Minutes*. It shows three- and four-year-olds doing homework for hours each day to polish their skills so that they will get into the best kindergarten. Mothers overseeing (driving, Americans would say) their children so that they will do more and better. The goal of the learning process is to gain admission to college, which assumes a job commensurate with the exclusivity of the college. Education ends with the posting of one's name on a list of the admitted. Available through Association for Supervision and Curriculum Development, 125 North West Street, Alexandria, VA 22314-2798. Or call (703) 549-9110. CC-1684.

- *Motivating Underachievers*, video, 28 min., color. This program explores the problem of underachieving children and examines why so many schools fail to deal with the problem effectively. Suggestions for teachers and parents to motivate underachievers are shown. Available through Films for the Humanities & Sciences, Inc., P.O. Box 2052, Princeton, NJ 08543. Or call 1-800-257-5126 (in NJ, 609-452-1128). CC-1592.

- *Motivation, Cognition, and Instruction: The Dynamic Interplay*, audio. Invited Symposium, Division C, AERA 1987 Annual Meeting, Washington DC. Two audio cassettes. Order from: Teach'em, Inc., 160 East Illinois Street, Chicago, IL 60611. Or call (800) 225-3775. RA7-15.04.

- *Mastery Learning*, audio. Find out why mastery learning is building a successful track record for improving student achievement. This tape by Tom Guskey gives an overview of the most widely used approaches. Available through Association for Supervision and Curriculum Development, 125 North West Street, Alexandria, VA 22314-2798. Or call (703) 549-9110.

- *A New Look at Motivation*, 16 mm 32 min., color. Studies of human behavior have shown that people act in certain ways to satisfy integral needs. Often, people with high needs for affiliation will perform very menial tasks cheerfully and effectively as long as they are not deprived of social interaction. This film teaches personnel and management that self-motivation based on individual social and environmental preference is the most lasting and effective form of motivation. The importance of an employee and his manager understanding each others' motivations, and designing jobs and tasks to fit each personality is shown. CRM Films, 2233 Faraday Avenue, Carlsbad, CA 92008. Or call (619) 431-9800.

Test Questions

Test Questions 8.1–8.121

Study Guide

Assign Chapter 8 of the *Study Guide*.

9
Outcome Decisions

Chapter Objectives

1. General Objective

Judges the utility of the approaches to specifying instructional goals and objectives (pp. 322–334).

SPECIFIC BEHAVIORS

1.01 Contrasts the elements of behavioral objectives.
1.02 Evaluates Mager's view of behavioral objectives.
1.03 Distinguishes evaluative statements from instructional goals.
1.04 Evaluates McAshan's goals approach to instructional objectives.
1.05 Distinguishes general objectives from specific behaviors.
1.06 Evaluates Gronlund-type instructional objectives.
1.07 Appraises the arguments for using instructional objectives.
1.08 Interprets the research on the use of instructional objectives.
1.09 Contrasts instructional and expressive objectives.

2. General Objective

Analyzes the variety of learned capabilities associated with learning from instruction, based on Gagné's outcomes (pp. 334–344).

SPECIFIC BEHAVIORS

2.01 Illustrates verbal information as a learned capability.
2.02 Distinguishes the hierarchical levels of intellectual skills.
2.03 Illustrates discriminations as a learned capability.
2.04 Illustrates concrete concepts as a learned capability.
2.05 Illustrates defined concepts as a learned capability.
2.06 Illustrates rules as a learned capability.
2.07 Illustrates higher-order rules as a learned capability.
2.08 Illustrates cognitive strategies as a learned capability.
2.09 Illustrates attitudes as a learned capability.
2.10 Illustrates motor skills as a learned capability.

3. General Objective

Uses the cognitive taxonomy to classify learning activities (pp. 344–346).

SPECIFIC BEHAVIORS

3.01 Gives examples of knowledge level objectives and activities.
3.02 Gives examples of comprehension level objectives and activities.
3.03 Gives examples of application level objectives and activities.
3.04 Gives examples of analysis level objectives and activities.
3.05 Gives examples of synthesis level objectives and activities.
3.06 Gives examples of evaluation level objectives and activities.

4. General Objective

Uses the affective taxonomy to classify learning activities (pp. 346–349).

SPECIFIC BEHAVIORS

4.01 Gives examples of receiving or attending level objectives and activities.
4.02 Gives examples of responding level objectives and activities.
4.03 Gives examples of valuing level objectives and activities.
4.04 Gives examples of organization level objectives and activities.
4.05 Gives examples of characterization level objectives and activities.

5. *General Objective*

Uses the psychomotor taxonomy to classify learning activities (pp. 349–351).

SPECIFIC BEHAVIORS

5.01 Gives examples of reflex movements and level objectives and activities.

5.02 Gives examples of basic/fundamental movements and level objectives and activities.

5.03 Gives examples of perceptual abilities and level objectives and activities.

5.04 Gives examples of physical abilities and level objectives and activities.

5.05 Gives examples of skilled movements and level objectives and activities.

5.06 Gives examples of nondiscursive communication and level objectives and activities.

Focus Questions

- What is the difference between a strategic decision and a tactical decision?
- How can the outcomes of instruction be specified?
- What do instructional objectives do for teachers and for students?
- What capabilities might students gain from instruction?
- How can the different areas and levels of outcomes be classified?
- What student behaviors allow teachers to infer that particular outcomes have been attained?

Chapter Outline

INTRODUCTION: STRATEGIC AND TACTICAL DECISIONS

TEACHER CHRONICLE 9.1: STUDENTS: THE MISSING INGREDIENT

INSTRUCTIONAL OBJECTIVES
   The Behavioral Approach
   The Goals Approach
      Goals
      Evaluative Statements
   The General Objectives–Specific Behaviors Approach

USING OBJECTIVES
   Cautions for Using Objectives
   Alternative Views
   Principles in Practice 9.1

TEACHER CHRONICLE 9.2: CONTENT OR PROCESS?

GAGNÉ'S OUTCOMES OF INSTRUCTION
   Verbal Information

Intellectual Skills
   Discriminations
   Concrete Concepts
   Defined Concepts
   Rules
   Higher-Order Rules
Cognitive Strategies
Attitudes
Motor Skills
Principles in Practice 9.2

TEACHER CHRONICLE 9.3: A HARD NUT TO CRACK

TAXONOMIES OF OUTCOMES
   The Cognitive Domain
      Level 1: Knowledge
      Level 2: Comprehension
      Level 3: Application
      Level 4: Analysis
      Level 5: Synthesis
      Level 6: Evaluation
   The Affective Domain
      Level 1: Receiving or Attending
      Level 2: Responding
      Level 3: Valuing
      Level 4: Organization
      Level 5: Characterization
   The Psychomotor Domain
      Level 1: Reflexive Movements
      Level 2: Basic/Fundamental Movements
      Level 3: Perceptual Abilities
      Level 4: Physical Abilities
      Level 5: Skilled Movements
      Level 6: Nondiscursive Communication
   Deciding on Objectives
   Principles in Practice 9.3

CONCLUSION

Chapter Summary

Introduction: Strategic and Tactical Decisions

- Strategic decisions result in plans. Tactical decisions are made as the plan is executed. Strategic decisions begin with the teacher determining the outcomes desired for his or her students.

Instructional Objectives

- Instructional objectives can be specified in a number of ways. Instructional objectives prepared as specified by Robert Mager are called behavioral objectives. Behavioral objectives include a statement of terminal behavior, the conditions of performance, and the criteria used to judge attainment of an objective.

- The goals approach specifies instructional objectives by combining a general goal with an evaluative statement. The general goal provides a context that can be helpful when discussing student progress with others, including parents. The evaluative statement specifies how goal attainment will be evaluated.
- This approach was developed by Gronlund to specify objectives. General objectives identify a domain of student performances. Specific behaviors are then prescribed under each general objective in order to allow for evaluation of the general objective.

Using Objectives

- Instructional objectives serve a planning function for teachers. They specify the content to be covered and provide a means of evaluating not just students' progress, but the teacher's instruction as well. It is not clear that learning is enhanced when students are provided with objectives; it depends on the circumstances under which the objectives are established. However, the confidence teachers gain from planning by objectives seems to be worth the effort, whether students ultimately see the objectives or not.
- Some critics argue that using instructional objectives "trivializes" learning because outcomes are predetermined. Eisner suggests that another type of objective, the expressive objective, can be used to focus on process rather than outcome. Expressive objectives specify the kinds of experiences a teacher desires students to have without regard for the outcomes of those experiences.

Gagné's Outcomes of Instruction

- Verbal information is information that allows students to communicate about an object, event, or certain relations. It is the first of the variety of learned outcomes that students may attain from instruction. Knowing the name of an object is an example of verbal information.
- Students can acquire intellectual skills at varying levels of complexity. Gagné identified a hierarchy of intellectual skills. These skills are, from simple to complex, discrimination, concrete concepts, defined concepts, rules, and higher-order rules.
- Students can learn how to regulate their own cognitive processes. This regulation affords the student control over his or her own learning. Cognitive strategies perform a metacognitive function.
- For Gagné, attitudes are an acquired internal state. A student's attitudes influence his or her choice of action.
- Motor skills are physical capabilities. Examples include riding a bike or dancing. Just because the most obvious aspect of motor skills is the physical

aspect of a behavior does not mean that affect and cognition play no role in acquiring motor capabilities.

Taxonomies of Outcomes

- Taxonomies are classifications of behaviors that can be used to specify instructional objectives. Bloom's taxonomy of behaviors in the cognitive domain, from simplest to most complex, consists of six levels: knowledge, comprehension, application, analysis, synthesis, and evaluation.
- The affective domain, as described by Krathwahl, is also organized by levels: receiving, responding, valuing, organization, and characterization.
- The psychomotor domain identifies behaviors that have a major physical component. As described by Harrow, the levels of the psychomotor domain are reflexive movements, basic/fundamental movements, perceptual abilities, physical abilities, skilled movements, and nondiscursive communication.
- Instructional objectives define the content students encounter in a classroom. There are multiple sources of those objectives. Whether objectives are determined by the teacher or prescribed for the teacher, the teacher must make decisions about how the objectives will be addressed in the classroom.

Key Terms

strategic decisions	intellectual skills
tactical decisions	discrimination
behavioral objectives	concrete concepts
goals approach	defined concepts
goal statements	rules
evaluative statements	higher-order rules
internal conditions of learning	attitude
	motor skills
external conditions of learning	taxonomy
	cognitive taxonomy
outcomes of learning	affective taxonomy
verbal information	psychomotor taxonomy

Teacher Chronicle Summaries

Teacher Chronicle 9.1: Students: The Missing Ingredient (pp. 324–325)

A teacher muses about planning lessons and how each lesson, when taught, becomes something more than a plan on paper when students become involved.

Teacher Chronicle 9.2: Content or Process? (p. 334)

A high school English teacher reads *The Old Man and the Sea* while on vacation. She wonders about how her students read. Is it the process or the content that involves them?

Teacher Chronicle 9.3: A Hard Nut to Crack

An elementary school teacher has a student with a poor self-concept, yet he has outstanding intellectual abilities. When his teacher praises his work, the student is unable to accept the praise. The teacher then creates a plan to help the student gain an improved sense of self-worth, a plan that reaps benefits as the year progresses.

Possible Answers to Principles in Practice

Principles in Practice 9.1

1. Which procedure for stating objectives do you prefer? Why?

Answers will vary, but reasons should be stated in terms of need to state goals, specify evaluative criteria, or attach goals to more specific behaviors. A preference for expressive objectives should be accompanied by evidence that the student realizes the need for evaluative judgments.

2. When should a teacher supply students with objectives?

A teacher could supply students with objectives when they need to perform several steps in completing a task. A teacher could also supply objectives when knowledge of expected outcomes would enhance motivation—even if an expressive objective is used to build anticipation.

3. How could expressive objectives and instructional objectives be integrated into one lesson plan?

An expressive objective could be used to define experiences; instructional objectives could specify the types of analysis, synthesis, or applications students will be asked to make based on the experiences.

Principles in Practice 9.2

1. How do Gagné's learned capabilities account for the teacher's reflections while at the beach?

The teacher has developed some cognitive strategies that help her organize her experiences in the classroom. The teacher has also developed certain intellectual skills such as rules about how classrooms work.

2. What capabilities are necessary for a student to understand Huck's dilemma over turning in Jim as an escaped slave in Huckleberry Finn*?*

Some of the higher intellectual skills are necessary, which means that lower skills must also be in place. In this case, a student must understand certain defined concepts such as slavery, laws, justice, and freedom. Certain cognitive strategies that allow for analysis must also be in place.

3. Would asking students to describe how they read help them develop cognitive strategies?

If students can be made to reflect on their own cognition, it is more likely that they will develop metacognitive awareness. Metacognition is an important element in developing the capability to use cognitive strategies.

Principles in Practice 9.3

1. At what level of the affective taxonomy would you place Adam's behavior as described at the end of Teacher Chronicle 9.3?

It could be argued that Adam had reached the level of valuing. His interest in his work and attendance, and his hesitancy to make negative comments about others indicate that Adam believes that certain values have worth. It could also be said that his behavior reflects the establishment of a value system—the organization level—although Chronicle 9.3 does not supply convincing, long-term evidence of this.

2. Identify a future affective objective for Adam.

If one assumes that Adam has reached the level of valuing, a future objective might reflect organization: The student will be able to determine a priority of beliefs or opinions regarding interaction with classmates.

3. Why should the attainment of affective objectives be accompanied by cognitive progress?

As one moves up the hierarchy of affective objectives, there is increased need to analyze and evaluate. These traits translate into enhanced cognitive attainment.

CNN Connection to Issues in Educational Psychology

There are no CNN video segments for this chapter.

Activities and Exercises

In-Class Activities

1. Have students work in small groups on ideas for a grant proposal to be submitted to a private foundation to fund a program to help and encourage parents to read to their young children. Have one member of the group be a children's librarian who is providing expertise regarding the selection of reading material. The job of your students is to supply a rationale for the program based on Gagné's hierarchy of intellectual skills.
2. Have your students assume that their district has to cut back on academic programs due to fiscal problems. One of the prime candidates for cuts is the dance component of the fine arts program. Using the taxonomy of psychomotor objectives, have your students advance the argument that the dance program fosters high-level thinking in a way no other program in the district can.

Teacher Interviews

Have each student interview a teacher regarding his or her use of Mager's criteria.

Have each student interview a teacher regarding the importance of confidence, asking the teacher if planning enhances his or her confidence.

Have each student interview a teacher of adult special ed regarding the importance of verbal information and the acquisition of "life skills."

Have each student interview a teacher regarding the approach he or she uses to facilitate independent learning.

Have each student interview a teacher regarding how he or she determines student attitudes.

Have students interview teachers and administrators to determine how textbooks are selected and content prescribed in various school districts.

Have students interview teachers at various grade levels, using the affective taxonomy to collect examples of activities from the teachers' classrooms.

Have students interview teachers regarding the freedom they have to interpret curricular prescriptions.

Field Observations

Have students collect statements of instructional goals and objectives from various teachers and identify general objectives, specific objectives, goals, and evaluative statements.

Have students observe classrooms in which expressive objectives are the basis for learning activities, determining how the teachers evaluate expressive objectives.

Have each student observe a lesson in a classroom, identifying episodes during which students learn verbal information as opposed to their gaining other kinds of capabilities.

Have students observe preschool or kindergarten classes in which students classify objects according to a category or set of categories, documenting how such activity contributes to the attainment of concrete concepts.

Have students observe lessons in various classrooms, identifying opportunities within lessons to encourage problem finding.

Have students collect tests constructed by classroom teachers and examine them for verbs listed in Table 9–2 (p. 347).

Have each student observe a classroom in which a teacher takes control of the curriculum by designing many of his or her own activities and another classroom in which the teacher seems to be "following a recipe" provided by curriculum specialists, documenting the level of students' enthusiasm in each classroom.

Journal Entries

Have students reflect on their own course work, and then imagine the kinds of concerns their students will have when they walk into your classrooms.

Have students reflect on those classes where their teachers used behavioral objectives, commenting on the ways in which the behavioral objectives contributed to their learning.

Have students compare Duell's results with their experiences if they received objectives in this class. If they did not, have them comment on the ways by which they determined important content.

Have students reflect on the external conditions of learning created by their teachers. What kinds of conditions led to a change in your cognitive states, that is, the internal conditions of your learning?

Have students identify concrete concepts that they have learned in school, commenting on how important these examples were to their understanding of concrete concepts.

Have students reflect on those teachers in their experience who managed classes with a gesture, or a look, or by positioning themselves in certain areas of the class, noting the rules that they learned from these teachers.

Discussion Topics (based on Lecture Notes)

Have students discuss various ways of specifying objectives in order to determine instructional strengths and weaknesses.

In order to ensure that students understand the difference between verbal information and intellectual skills have them discuss the possibility of discriminating between types of rocks without knowing their geologic labels.

Have students discuss the importance of defined concepts in generating plans or theories. Students can be asked to determine how defined concepts can contribute to their theories of teaching.

Ask students to discuss the types of learning skills they anticipate teaching and the content areas in which those skills might be embedded.

Ask students to discuss how various motor activities also have cognitive and affective components. This discussion can serve as an introduction to the section on taxonomies of outcomes as well.

Have students, either individually or in small groups, generate additional examples for each level of the affective taxonomy.

Ask students, either individually or in small groups, to generate additional examples for each level of the psychomotor taxonomy.

Application Scenarios

Present the following scenario to students:

- Your ninth-grade civics class complains that all they do is learn list after list of pointless facts about the workings of government. How could you redesign your instructional objectives to make the class more interesting and practical and still retain the content that you want to teach?

Chapter 15 Casebook Previews

See Please Sign This Contract.

See Book Writings.

See Beginning Each Day as a Learning Experience.

See Improvisation and Aesthetic Appreciation or Coup D'Etat in the Classroom.

Teaching Anecdotes

Tell your students about the teacher who had problems keeping her math class focused when presenting new material. Many of the students squirmed in their seats, doodled, or passed notes. During her evaluation with a mentor teacher, she asked why this was so.

"Which kids do you call on when you're doing something new?"

"Oh! That's easy—Michelle, Marcus, Dugan, and Judith. They always pay attention and know the answers."

Ask your students why this approach might affect the interest of the other students in the class. (See p. 324.)

Tell the story of a school system that was switching from a grading system for primary school children to a progress report system that listed the specific skills the children had mastered and how they performed according to their own abilities.

Ask your students if they were teaching in this situation, how they would evaluate children and adjust to the new reporting system. (See p. 329.)

Tell your students about the teacher who used her lunch periods to evaluate her teaching in the morning periods, and spent the first thirty minutes after school reviewing her afternoon classes. She kept copies of lesson plans she had used and marked what worked, what didn't work, and what could have been improved on. She noted student responses, problems, and successes. She filed these for references for the following year.

Ask your students if they thought that when this teacher pulled the file the next year, she repeated the lessons as they were or used the previous lessons as a springboard for teaching the lessons anew. Ask them what they would do in a similar situation. (See p. 332.)

Tell your students about two teachers: one strictly followed the teacher's guide to her science book; the other created and shaped his lessons around the curriculum, gearing his experiments to the varying abilities of his students. Both teachers have students who believe each is "the best teacher in the school."

Ask your students why this might be so. (See p. 332.)

Tell your students about the American History teacher who loves the Civil War and because of the time spent on this topic, never carries his course in U.S. History up to the Persian Gulf War, as stated in the curriculum. After several parental and student complaints, the principal questioned the teacher about this problem.

"They'll get that material in World History next year," the teacher argues. "Besides, the Civil War is what I know best."

Ask your students if the teacher is justified in the way he or she follows the curriculum. (See p. 349.)

Transparencies

For transparencies to use with this chapter, see the Transparency Guides on page 335 and page 347.

Teaching Resources

Suggested Readings

Gagné, R. M. (1985). *The conditions of learning*. (4th ed.). New York: Holt, Rinehart & Winston.

Gagné, R. M., & Driscoll, M. P. (1988). *Essentials of learning for instruction*. Englewood Cliffs, NJ: Prentice-Hall.

Martin, B. L., & Briggs, L. J. (1986). *The affective and cognitive domains: Integration for instruction and research*. Englewood Cliffs, NJ: Educational Technology.

Schiever, S. W. (1991). *A comprehensive approach to teaching thinking*. Needham Heights, MA: Allyn & Bacon.

West, C. K., Farmer, J. A., & Wolff, P. M. (1991). *Instructional design: Implications from cognitive science*. Englewood Cliffs, NJ: Prentice-Hall.

Films, Videocassettes, Audiocassettes

- *Instructional Decisions for Long-Term Learning,* video. The program's three hours of videotape and eighty-page Leader's Guide help teachers plan lessons and make sound decisions in the classroom. Use the second 1-hour tape to show teachers how to structure lesson plans that get the students' attention, hold it, and deliver the new knowledge in ways that build retention. Videotaped sequences give the following tips for effective lesson planning: When—and when not—to tell the objectives of the lesson. Why not to ask, "Does everyone understand?" What kind of homework assignment produces the most learning?

  Tape three in this program demonstrates how teachers use active participation in the classroom to boost test scores and increase student retention of knowledge. The 30-minute video introduces you to teaching pairs, choral responses, and five other techniques for increasing student participation.

- *Teacher and School Effectiveness,* video. Featured educators: Ronald Edmonds, Michigan State University; Barak Rosenshine, University of Illinois; Peter Mortime, London Schools.

These two productions are available through Association for Supervision and Curriculum Development, 125 North West Street, Alexandria, VA 22314-2798. Or call (703) 549-9110.

- *Student-Centered Classroom, Secondary*, 16mm, 20 min., color. This film gives an overall view of what a student-centered classroom may look like when interaction, materials, and activities generate self-directed individualization and small group processes. Interaction is a language arts and reading program. Houghton Mifflin Company, Multimedia Division, 1 Beacon Street, Boston, MA 02107. HMC 1973.
- *Who Did What to Whom?: II. Recognizing Four Behavioral Principles in Action*, 16mm or videocassette, 20 min., color. Robert Mager is well known in the fields of education and business training for his excellent books on planning, thinking, and striving for objective-directed results. The program illustrates four of the basic principles of human behavior and consists of thirty-three short scenes of everyday interactions. Discussion time is provided after each scene to help viewers fully understand what occurred, the probability of it happening again, and how it could be changed to achieve a more positive result. Available through Research Press, Box 3177, Department R, Champaign, IL 61821. Or call (217) 352-3273.

Item No. 2113   16mm film   Item 21155 16mm film

Item No. 21141 VHS   Item 21151 VHS

Item No. 21142 Beta

Item No. 2114   3/4″

Item No. 2116   Additional Leader's Guide

Test Questions

Test Questions 9.1–9.102

Study Guide

Assign Chapter 9 of the *Study Guide*.

10
Instructional Models

Chapter Objectives

1. General Objective

Understands Gagné's events of instruction as a model for influencing the phases of learning (pp. 356–363).

SPECIFIC BEHAVIORS
1.01 Gives examples of gaining attention.
1.02 Gives examples of informing students of goals.
1.03 Gives examples of stimulating recall of prior knowledge.
1.04 Gives examples of presentation of stimulus material.
1.05 Gives examples of providing learning guidance.
1.06 Gives examples of eliciting performance.
1.07 Gives examples of providing feedback.
1.08 Gives examples of assessing performance.
1.09 Gives examples of enhancing retention and transfer.

2. General Objective

Distinguishes between the discovery learning and reception learning approaches to instruction (pp. 363–365).

SPECIFIC BEHAVIORS
2.01 Identifies instructional examples of discovery learning.
2.02 Identifies instructional examples of reception learning.
2.03 Specifies the conditions under which advance organizers support reception learning.

3. General Objective

Understands how transfer of learning can occur (pp. 365–369).

SPECIFIC BEHAVIORS
3.01 Summarizes vertical transfer.
3.02 Summarizes lateral transfer.
3.03 Distinguishes low-road and high-road transfer.
3.04 Explains forward-reaching and backward-reaching forms of high-road transfer.
3.05 Explains the relationship between transfer to metacognition.

4. General Objective

Interprets the utility of models for effective and direct instruction (pp. 369–375).

SPECIFIC BEHAVIORS
4.01 Explains Carroll's model of school learning.
4.02 Compares the elements of Carroll's model to the QAIT model.
4.03 Identifies the variables which influence effective instruction.
4.04 Characterizes Hunter's model as a prescription for direct instruction.
4.05 Gives examples of anticipatory set.
4.06 Gives examples of objective and purpose.
4.07 Gives examples of input.
4.08 Gives examples of modeling.
4.09 Gives examples of checking for understanding.
4.10 Gives examples of guided practice.
4.11 Gives examples of independent practice.

5. General Objective

Applies models for teaching thinking to instructional planning (pp. 375–382).

SPECIFIC BEHAVIORS
5.01 Generates a lesson using the general inductive model.
5.02 Generates a lesson using the concept attainment model.
5.03 Generates a lesson using the integrative model.
5.04 Generates a lesson using the general inquiry model.
5.05 Generates a lesson using the Suchman model of inquiry.
5.06 Generates a lesson using the general deductive model.

5.07   Generates a lesson using the interactive model.
5.08   Generates a lesson using the synectics model.

6. General Objective

Applies models for teaching affective outcomes to instructional planning (pp. 382–392).

SPECIFIC BEHAVIORS
6.01   Characterizes humanistic approaches to teaching.
6.02   Compares the characteristics of humanistic approaches to direct instruction approaches.
6.03   Generates a lesson using the exploration of feelings model.
6.04   Generates a lesson using the conflict resolution model.

Focus Questions

- Why do the conditions of instruction influence the outcomes of instruction?
- How do instructional events influence a student's cognitive processes?
- How can one instance of learning help or hinder another instance of learning?
- What are the important variables in effective teaching practice?
- What are the different ways of organizing a lesson to facilitate cognitive outcomes?
- What are the different ways of organizing a lesson to facilitate affective outcomes?

Chapter Outline

INTRODUCTION: PLANNING FOR ACTION

TEACHER CHRONICLE 10.1: WET BEHIND THE EARS

INSTRUCTION AND LEARNING
   Gagné's Instructional Events
      The Preparation Phases
      The Core Phases
      The Transfer Phases
   Discovery and Reception Learning
      Discovery Learning
      Reception Learning
         Advance Organizers

TRANSFER OF LEARNING
   Vertical and Lateral Transfer
      Low-Road and High-Road Transfer
   Principles in Practice 10.1

TEACHER CHRONICLE 10.2: WORD POWER

PLANNING DIRECT INSTRUCTION
   Carroll's Model of School Learning
   The QAIT Model
   Hunter's Model
      Research on Hunter's Model
   Principles in Practice 10.2

TEACHER CHRONICLE 10.3: A MAMMOTH UNDERTAKING

MODELS FOR TEACHING THINKING SKILLS
   Inductive Models
      The General Inductive Model
      The Concept Attainment Model
      The Integrative Model
   The General Inquiry Model
      The Suchman Model of Inquiry
   Deductive Models
      The General Deductive Model
         The Interactive Model
         The Synectics Model

INSTRUCTION FOR AFFECTIVE OUTCOMES
   Humanistic Education
      Nongraded Evaluation

MODELS FOR TEACHING AFFECTIVE OUTCOMES
   The Exploration of Feelings Model
   The Conflict Resolution Model
   Principles in Practice 10.3

CONCLUSION

Chapter Summary

Introduction: Planning for Action

- Determining outcomes are not the only strategic decisions that teachers have to make. They must also decide what approaches to instruction they will use if they are to accomplish these outcomes.

Instruction and Learning

- One way to view the connection between the teacher's instructional actions and the student's learning processes is by means of Gagné's instructional events, each of which supports the cognitive processes in a phase of learning.
- Instruction can facilitate either discovery learning or reception learning. Discovery learning is inductive. Students are presented with specifics and guided to general principles. Reception learning is deductive. Students are presented with general principles and guided to specific applications of these principles.

Both types of learning are meaningful only if students actively process information.

Transfer of Learning

- Transfer of learning means applying information learned in one situation to new situations. Previous learning can be transferred laterally or vertically, depending on the complexity of the new situation.

Planning Direct Instruction

- Carroll identifies variables that teachers should keep in mind when planning direct instruction. The variables concern the amount of time students require to master material.
- The QAIT model is also useful for planning direct instruction. The QAIT model focuses on those aspects of school learning that are under the teacher's control.
- Hunter's model specifies seven steps that should be included in every direct instruction lesson: anticipatory set, objective and purpose, input, modeling, checking for understanding, guided practice, and independent practice.

Models for Teaching Thinking Skills

- Models for teaching thinking provide step-by-step prescriptions to facilitate student thinking. Inductive models are those that begin with specific examples and move the student to an understanding of a general concept or principle.
- The general inquiry model and the Suchman inquiry model stress student participation in gathering information. Inquiry models can also be used to help students frame problems.
- Deductive models are those which start with general concepts and, through several steps, help students reason to specific instances or examples of the more inclusive idea.

Instruction for Affective Outcomes

- Humanistic education suggests approaches to teaching that allow students to make choices about what they will learn. The notion emphasizes affective outcomes so that students will learn to value learning for its own sake.

Models for Teaching Affective Outcomes

- Instructional models that focus on affective outcomes also facilitate thinking. The exploration of feelings model enables students to focus their thinking on the status of their own feelings.
- The conflict resolution model is an effective instructional model that helps students reason in situations where their opinions, beliefs, or feelings may run counter to those of other individuals or groups.

Key Terms

phases of learning	anticipatory set
preparation phases	objective and purpose
core phases	input
transfer phases	modeling
discovery learning	checking for understanding
reception learning	guided practice
advance organizers	independent practice
concrete advance	general inductive model
organizer	concept attainment model
transfer of learning	integrative model
vertical transfer	general deductive model
lateral transfer	interactive model
low-road transfer	synectics model
high-road transfer	humanistic education
direct instruction	

Teacher Chronicle Summaries

Teacher Chronicle 10.1: Wet Behind the Ears (pp. 359–360)

A student teacher plans and teaches a lesson on water to a fourth-grade class. Unfortunately, the lesson is scheduled just before lunch when the students' thoughts are on food rather than water. The lesson has its good and bad moments and the student teacher realizes that there is more to teaching a lesson than meets the eye.

Teacher Chronicle 10.2: Word Power (pp. 367–369)

A mentor teacher has a former student, who is now pursuing his secondary certification, drop by for a professional talk. Irving has been assigned to observe teachers in the English Department. Irving is puzzled by his observations of Mr. Blandworth's class, reputed to be a good one. He finds the class repetitive and boring. Then he observes another class, with many of the same students, that is exciting, engaging, and much more stimulating.

Teacher Chronicle 10.3: A Mammoth Undertaking (pp. 373–375)

A first-grade teacher leads a discussion about mammoths prior to reading a picture book about them. The teacher has several goals: for the children to have a literary experience, to create original art, and to learn to distinguish between what is real and what is imaginary in the story. In listening to student conversations the teacher learns how successful her lesson was on many different levels.

Possible Answers to Principles in Practice

Principles in Practice 10.1

1. According to the events of instruction model, which phases of learning were not supported by the student teacher?

From the account in Chronicle 10.1, it can be argued that the preparation phases were not supported. The students had little idea what the lesson was to be about, why they were covering the material, and had no opportunity to access prior knowledge. The material was presented in the lecture, but little guidance occurred. The worksheets elicited performance, but there is little evidence of feedback. The lesson self-destructed before the transfer phases could be addressed.

2. How should the student teacher have prepared the lesson in order to facilitate discovery learning?

The student teacher might have given students fresh water and salt water and encouraged them to conduct various tests to discover the differences between them. Students could be encouraged to discern differences in appearance, taste (if both were potable), and weight. They could be encouraged to find out how well various objects float in the two containers.

3. Why should lessons support the transfer of learning?

Unless lessons support the transfer phases of learning, it is unlikely that the material in one lesson can be used effectively as the basis for further lessons. It would be hard to build a true unit without transfer.

Principles in Practice 10.2

1. What elements of Carroll's and Slavin's models were missing from Mr. Blandworth's class?

Given that there was little or no effort to match instruction to the needs of students, it is difficult to argue that the Word Power lesson illustrated any of the elements of Carroll's or Slavin's models.

2. How would you plan a direct instruction lesson for the Word Power class?

Students could respond to this question by identifying the variables in Carroll's or Slavin's models and how their lesson will account for those variables. Another option for students would be to develop a lesson based on the seven steps in Hunter's model.

3. What sorts of topics do and do not lend themselves to direct instruction?

Lessons focused on the development of some skill or the application of concepts would most easily fit into Hunter's model. Discussions designed to elicit or clarify values or opinions, in a low consensus area, would not easily fit into a model like Hunter's.

Principles in Practice 10.3

1. Which model for teaching thinking best characterizes the events in Teacher Chronicle 10.3?

Although a case could be made for several of the mod-

els, because of the objectives of the lesson, the strongest case can be made for the concept attainment model.

2. Without using the story, what model for teaching thinking would you have used to encourage students to explore the difference between reality and fantasy?

Student answers should provide rationales for selections. Given the caveat to encourage exploration, one of the inquiry models would be a good candidate.

3. What elements of humanistic education did you observe in the lesson from the Chronicle?

In the discussion of the story, students were encouraged to choose a position and given an opportunity to justify why they believed as they did.

CNN Connection to Issues in Educational Psychology

"Hell Week" in Japan is a week-long period in the spring when high school students take their university entrance exams. There are endless hours of rote memorization required to pass the tests. If students fail the tests and don't gain entrance to a university, their futures can be devastated. This segment takes an in-depth look at the Japanese system to discover what works well, and what may not.

Activities and Exercises

In-Class Activities

1. Have several students prepare a brief lesson on Gagné's instructional events model. Each student should be assigned to teach the lesson according to a different model for teaching thinking. Have the students present their lessons to the class. Follow the lessons with a discussion of which model best fits the material to be learned.
2. Have students role-play parent–teacher conferences. The two parents should take the position that some of the values and beliefs expressed in their child's classroom during the "exploration of feelings" and "conflict resolution" sessions are in opposition to the values they are trying to instill in their child. The teacher must defend his or her use of these models for teaching affective outcomes.

Teacher Interviews

Have each student interview a teacher regarding his or her opinion of discovery and reception approaches to learning.

Have each student interview a teacher regarding his or her students' mindsets when problem solving.

Have each student interview a teacher regarding those aspects of teaching that are under his or her control and those that are alterable.

Have each student interview a teacher whose teaching has been evaluated on the basis of Hunter's model.

Have each student interview a teacher regarding his or her use of nonexamples.

Have each student interview a teacher regarding how his or her students respond to lessons that focus on other people's emotions.

Field Observations

Have students observe various classrooms, documenting the ways in which teachers gain student's attention.

Have students observe various classrooms to discover methods teachers use when functioning as advanced organizers.

Have students observe classrooms and document instances of transfer, classifying these instances as vertical, lateral, near, or far transfer.

Have your students observe students in a classroom with Carroll's degree of learning model in mind, noting behaviors that lead them to the conclusion that a student has spent more or less than the time he or she needed to learn.

Have students talk with principals or curriculum supervisors regarding teacher evaluations.

Have students observe classes in which inductive approaches are used, documenting the steps used in inductive lessons.

Have each student observe a classroom in which the Suchman inquiry model is used or a classroom in which data are collected by means of yes/no questions, documenting the strengths and weaknesses of these data collection techniques.

Have each student observe a classroom in which the exploration of feelings or a similar affective-oriented model is implemented, documenting the nature of the interaction between the teacher and his or her students and among students themselves.

Journal Entries

Have students reflect on the themes they anticipate emphasizing in their classrooms in the future.

Have students reflect on those lessons about which they had either a good sense of their goals or a poor one, commenting on how each type of lesson influenced their motivation.

Have students reflect on examples of vertical transfer that they have experienced.

Have students reflect on their own experiences of low-road and high-road transfer, speculating on how they will use the experiences when teaching skills and concepts that require these types of transfer.

Have students reflect on their styles of learning, answering the following questions: Do you normally tend toward inductive or deductive thinking? Is your usual approach a function of how you were taught or the type of problems you normally think about?

Have students reflect on the deductive model of instruction, addressing the following questions: Does this model generally describe the way you were instructed in elementary and junior high school? Did you have a sense that your learning occurred in the phases described in the model? What is the advantage to having a sense of "phases" in your learning?

Have students identify the topics, concepts, or issues they've covered in class using the synectics model. Ask them to justify their selections.

Discussion Topic (based on Lecture Notes)

Have your class discuss specific methods for preparing students for learning.

Ask students to compare Gagné's events of instruction with Hunter's model.

Ask students to discuss their ideas for teaching a lesson on the formation known as an isthmus using the general inductive model in Table 10.1.

Have students discuss, in small groups, how they would use the concept attainment model to teach the concept of counterpoint or another concept of their choosing.

Have students discuss the use of the integrative model to teach a problem-solving lesson on the issue of overcrowded courts.

Have students discuss what specific steps they might take in using the general inquiry model.

Have students discuss the kinds of concepts, skills, or problems that can be usefully approached using the Suchman inquiry model.

Have students, working in small groups, take an earlier example such as the isthmus lesson or the question concerning ocean tides and design a lesson according to the interactive model.

Application Scenarios

Present the following scenarios to students:

- Your second-grade class doesn't see the purpose of the "small world" lesson in your social studies book. All of your students were born and raised in your little Midwestern town, as were all of their parents before them. They have little curiosity about the rest of the world because most of them expect to live in the same town for the rest of their lives. How can you use your knowledge of humanistic education to get through to them? What resistance would you expect from them? From their parents?
- Dava is taking your typing course, and she is doing poorly. She is a college preparatory student who understands the value of typing, but she just can't seem to get the hang of it. When you ask her, she

tells you that she is busy trying to think about where to put her fingers and where the next letter ought to be. Can you develop a program of low-road transfer to help students like Dava develop automatic skills?

Chapter 15 Casebook Previews

See Responsibility Education.

See Science Is Only Real When You Do It.

See Beginning Each Day as a Learning Experience.

See Improvisation and Aesthetic Appreciation.

See Gifted Achievers and Underachievers.

See Writing Success in Science.

Teaching Anecdotes

Tell your students about the kindergarten teacher who had each of her children pick an object from a box each day and describe it. In the box, she had a collection of "junk" that she had gathered—everything from old records to nuts and bolts. After each child had described the object, the teacher asked him or her how the object might be used. At first, the children's guesses ranged far afield from the actual use of the objects. But as they became more skilled in describing, they also began to realize the functional attributes of the objects.

Ask your students why the teacher took the time to do this exercise and what value it might have had for the children. (See p. 363.)

Tell your students about two high school students in English class. Reading was difficult for the first student, but he worked every night on his assignments and did well. The second student, for whom English had always been a "breeze," soon found herself struggling in the same class. Although her IQ was much higher than her fellow student's, she received lower grades for the first quarter of the year.

Ask your students what might account for the difference in performance. Which student might retain new material for longer periods of time—the first or the second? (See p. 370.)

Tell your students about the high school that began using a computer system to access various data bases. By using a computer students' research time was cut from weeks to days, and the computer searched for and located far more sources than the students previously had access to. Instead of being inundated with the amount of material, most students found the extra data helpful. Many students began using the computers during lunch and free periods with no specific assignment due, but rather to discover more on topics that interested them individually.

Ask your students why this might have happened. (See p. 371.)

Tell your students about the fourth-grade teacher who paired students and then gave each pair a rock, a ball of clay, a paper clip, a bottle cap, and a pan of water. The students were to predict which objects would sink and which would float. After experimenting with the objects, the students were to use the material they had been studying about water displacement to get all of the objects to float.

Ask your students how this project might combine inductive and deductive thinking skills. (The final solution was to mold a boat from the clay and place the other objects inside.) (See p. 377.)

Tell your students about the teacher who describes her approach to teaching this way, "If I can make the students feel comfortable and enjoy being here, I can teach them anything."

Ask your students if this is an appropriate way to approach teaching. Why or why not? How would they respond to such a teacher? Ask them if this might be the way they feel as teachers themselves. (See p. 385.)

Transparencies

For transparencies to use with this chapter, see the Transparency Guides on page 362, page 376, and page 377.

Teaching Resources

Suggested Readings

Eggen, D. P., & Kauchak, P. D. (1988). *Strategies for teachers.* Englewood Cliffs, NJ: Prentice-Hall.

Gagné, R. M. (1985). *The conditions of learning* (4th ed.). New York: Holt, Rinehart & Winston.

Gagné, R. M., & Driscoll, M. P. (1988). *Essentials of learning for instruction* (2nd ed.). Englewood Cliffs, NJ: Prentice-Hall.

Gunter, M. A., Estes, T. H., & Schwab, J. H. (1990). *Instruction: A models approach.* Needham Heights, MA: Allyn & Bacon.

Films, Videocassettes, Audiocassettes

- *Student-Centered Classroom, Secondary,* 16mm, 20 min., color. This film gives an overall view of what a student-centered classroom may look like when interaction, materials, and activities generate self-directed individualization and small group process. Interaction is a language arts and reading program. Houghton Mifflin Co., Multimedia Division, 1 Beacon Street, Boston, MA 02107. HMC 1973.
- *Who Did What to Whom?: II. Recognizing Four Behavioral Principles in Action,* 16mm or videocassette, 20 min., color. Robert Mager is well known in the fields of education and business training for his excellent books on planning, thinking, and striving for objective-directed results. The program illustrates four of the basic principles of human behavior and consists of thirty-three short scenes of everyday

interactions. Discussion time is provided after each scene to help viewers fully understand what occurred, the probability of it happening again, and how it could be changed to achieve a more positive result. Available through Research Press, Box 3177, Department R, Champaign, IL 61821. Or call (217) 352-3273.

Item No. 2113   16mm film   Item 21155 16mm film

Item No. 21141 VHS   Item 21151 VHS

Item No. 21142 Beta

Item No. 2114   3/4"

Item No. 2116   Additional Leader's Guide

- *Improving the Quality of Student Thinking*, video. Videotaped interview with leading educators and scenes from classrooms explain twelve ways to bring higher-order thinking to every class:

Explicitly state that improving thinking is the goal of a particular lesson.

Use broad, open-ended questions to jump start a discussion.

Ensure that students process information, not just memorize it.

Use "wait time" and other techniques to ignite the thinking process in students.

And seven other useful tips. Available through Association for Supervision and Curriculum Development, 125 North West Street, Alexandria, VA 22314-2798. Or call (703) 549-9110.

- *Student Self-Concept and Standards*, color, 27 min. Joe Michel of Richfield Senior High School in Richfield, Minnesota, demonstrates how he contributes to student self-concept through such teaching techniques as establishing and maintaining high standards, encouraging inquisitive learning, individualizing instruction through small group tasks, and most of all, humanistic teaching. Available through Successful Teaching Practices Series, EBEC 1982. Encyclopaedia Britannica Educational Corporation, 310 South Michigan Avenue, Chicago, IL 60604.

Test Questions

Test Questions 10.1–10.110

Study Guide

Assign Chapter 10 of the *Study Guide*.

11

Instructional Tactics

Chapter Objectives

1. General Objective

Understands the implications of tactical decisions (pp. 396–401).

SPECIFIC BEHAVIORS

1.01 Infers the relationship between a tactical repertoire and effectiveness of instruction.
1.02 Distinguishes instructional tactics from management tactics.
1.03 Explains the "problem of the match."
1.04 Defends the notion that tactical decisions are hypotheses.

2. General Objective

Recognizes the benefits and liabilities of instructional tactics employed with large groups (pp. 401–407).

SPECIFIC BEHAVIORS

2.01 Identifies the utility of lecture as a tactic.
2.02 Uses the research on lecturing to judge the teaching skills necessary for effectiveness.
2.03 Differentiates between lecture and explanation.
2.04 Characterizes effective explanation.
2.05 Identifies the utility of questioning as a tactic.
2.06 Explains the stages of questioning (structure, solicitation, reaction).
2.07 Distinguishes types of questions based on instructional purpose.
2.08 Identifies wait-times (I and II) in terms of solicitation and reaction.
2.09 Illustrates the effects of varying wait-time I.
2.10 Illustrates the effects of varying wait-time II.
2.11 Identifies the roles of seatwork and homework in direct instruction.
2.12 Uses the research on seatwork and homework to formulate instructional hypotheses.

3. General Objective

Recognizes the benefits and liabilities of instructional tactics employed with small groups (pp. 407–414).

SPECIFIC BEHAVIORS

3.01 Identifies the utility of small group discussion.
3.02 Relates the use of small group discussion to the degree of consensus in the content area.
3.03 Explains how small group discussion can contribute to attitude change.
3.04 Breaks down leading a discussion into its component skills.
3.05 Identifies the tactics of cooperative learning.
3.06 Identifies the cognitive and motivational aspects of team learning.
3.07 Explains the use of student teams-achievement division (STAD).
3.08 Explains the use of teams-games-tournaments (TGT).

4. General Objective

Recognizes the benefits and liabilities of individualized instruction tactics (pp. 414–419).

SPECIFIC BEHAVIORS

4.01 Differentiates between the forms of individualized instruction.
4.02 Relates mastery learning to Carroll's model of school learning.
4.03 Identifies the managerial elements of the mastery learning tactic.
4.04 Characterizes programmed instructional materials.
4.05 Relates the use of programmed materials to Keller's PSI.
4.06 Explains the use of team-assisted instruction (TAI).

5. General Objective

Recognizes the benefits and liabilities of peer tutoring tactics (pp. 419–420).

SPECIFIC BEHAVIORS

5.01 Infers the modeling effects associated with peer tutoring.
5.02 Explains the cognitive and affective effects of peer tutoring.

5.03 Differentiates same-age and cross-age tutoring.

5.04 Identifies the guidelines for establishing and activating tutoring dyads.

6. General Objective

Recognizes the benefits and liabilities of computer-assisted instruction (CAI) tactics (pp. 420–423).

SPECIFIC BEHAVIORS

6.01 Differentiates between various CAI applications.

6.02 Selects grade-appropriate tutorial programs.

6.03 Selects grade-appropriate drill-and-practice programs.

6.04 Selects grade-appropriate simulation programs.

7. General Objective

Understands the administrative and instructional requirements of teaching exceptional students (pp. 423–433).

SPECIFIC BEHAVIORS

7.01 Paraphrases the requirements of PL 94-142 in relation to mainstreaming.

7.02 Explains least restrictive environment.

7.03 Generalizes tactical decisions from the guidelines for the regular education teacher working with exceptional students.

7.04 Explains individualized education program (IEP).

7.05 Explains due process.

7.06 Predicts the adaptive tactics required for mainstreaming.

Focus Questions

- Why should teachers use multiple tactics rather than using their "best" tactic exclusively?
- Why do so many teachers lecture?
- What factors influence the effectiveness of a teacher's questions?
- Under what conditions is it advantageous for students to work in small groups?
- How can a teacher instruct thirty individuals, all at the same time?
- What tactical decisions are required when teaching exceptional students?

Chapter Outline

INTRODUCTION: MANAGEMENT AND INSTRUCTION

TEACHER CHRONICLE 11.1: TRY, TRY AGAIN

LARGE GROUP INSTRUCTION
Lecture
Explanation

Questioning
Structure
Solicitation
Reaction
Seatwork
Homework

SMALL GROUP INSTRUCTION
Discussion Groups
High Consensus Versus Low Consensus
Values and Beliefs
Intervening in Small Group Discussions
Cooperative Learning in Teams
Student Teams-Achievement Divisions (STAD)
Teams-Games-Tournaments (TGT)
Principles in Practice 11.1

TEACHER CHRONICLE 11.2: SEEING THE LIGHT

INDIVIDUALLY ORIENTED TACTICS
Individualized Instruction
The Mastery Approach
Programmed Instruction
Personalized System of Instruction (PSI)
Team-assisted Instruction
Evaluation of Individualized Instruction
Peer Tutoring
Computers and Instruction
Tutorials
Drill and Practice
Simulations
Principles in Practice 11.2

TEACHER CHRONICLE 11.3: NO EXCEPTIONS TO THE RULE

TEACHING EXCEPTIONAL STUDENTS
Least Restrictive Environment
Adapting to Exceptional Students
Individualized Education Program
Due Process
The Traveling Notebook
Principles in Practice 11.3

CONCLUSION

Chapter Summary

Introduction: Management and Instruction

- Tactics can be classified according to two functions: instruction and management. Instruction involves helping students learn the material presented to them. Management involves the actions taken to connect students and the material to be learned. The focus of this chapter is instructional tactics.

Large Group Instruction

- Lecture is the most common large group tactic because it is a very efficient way of presenting information. It works at least as well as other methods when information needs to be organized in a particular fashion for a particular group of students. Lecture also provides an opportunity for the teacher to model communication skills and to demonstrate enthusiasm for the topic.
- Explanations are more focused than lectures. Effective teachers provide explanations that are more responsive to student needs than teachers who are less effective. Effective explanations tend to provide a context or framework for students. Although explanations are often part of a lecture, explanations can be initiated by student questions as well.
- Questioning, as a tactic, can be thought of as occurring in three stages. Structure sets the stage for the questions to follow. Solicitation refers to the types of questions that are asked. Reaction is the teacher's response to a student's answer. Generally, increased wait-time is associated with increased achievement. However, there are times, such as during drill-and-practice sessions, when longer wait-times are counterproductive.
- Seatwork refers to work completed independently by the student. Although independent practice is helpful, too much reliance on the tactic has been shown to compound the problems of low-achieving students. Seatwork is most effective when it is used in balance with other tactics. Homework is considered a special example of seatwork, the difference being that teachers are unable to monitor homework in the same way they monitor seatwork.

Small Group Instruction

- Small group discussions are best suited to topics on which there is a low level of consensus. This tactic has also been shown to be an effective way of changing attitudes and beliefs. If the tactic is selected in order to give students a chance to explore their own ideas, it is important not to intervene in the discussion unless there are signs that the group is getting off-task.
- Cooperative team learning calls for the formation of small groups that function as a team, not a group of individuals. The team members become responsible for other team members' mastering of material. The student teams-achievement divisions (STAD) procedure and the teams-games-tournaments (TGT) procedure are variations on the theme of group responsibility for individual performance.

Individually Oriented Tactics

- Individualized instruction refers to students working at their own pace with materials selected to meet their individual needs. The mastery approach, programmed instruction, Keller's personalized system of instruction, and team-assisted instruction are individualized procedures that allow students to work according to their individual needs in various ways.
- Peer tutoring involves arranging for one student to help another student learn material. The tactic enhances the performance of both the tutored student and the tutor. In a same-age tutoring situation, the tutor tends to be perceived as superior; researchers suggest that cross-age tutoring is a more effective way to use the tactic.
- Computer-assisted instruction (CAI) is a way of individualizing learning in a classroom. CAI programs can serve three basic functions—as tutorials, for drill-and-practice exercises, and as simulations. Simulations allow the student to experience ideas and relationships that might otherwise be too expensive or too dangerous to pursue.

Teaching Exceptional Students

- When teaching exceptional students, there are several legislated actions that must be undertaken (according to Public Law 94-142). To meet the requirements of the first, least restrictive environment, students must be taught in environments that approximate, as closely as possible, the regular classroom. The practical result is that exceptional students are mainstreamed whenever possible.
- Exceptional students require an individualized education program (IEP). An IEP is determined at a conference involving teachers, parents, a school official, and when possible, the student. The purpose of the conference is to plan a series of goals and a time-line for the exceptional student to attain those goals.
- Due process is the element of PL 94-142 that requires schools to establish procedures that guard the confidentiality of both parents and students. Due process gives parents the right to see records and to challenge placements or an IEP.
- The traveling notebook is a device for enhancing the communication among the professionals and the parents of an exceptional student. Because exceptional students may be working with several teachers and/or therapists, as well as parents at home, it is important for everyone working with the child to know what others are experiencing. The traveling notebook serves as a collective "diary." It contains the notes, observations, comments, and so on of everyone involved in the student's education. In this way, everyone is kept informed.

Key Terms

management tactics
instructional tactics
lecture
explanation
questioning
wait-time I
wait-time II
seatwork
team learning
student teams-achievement divisions (STAD)
teams-games-tournaments (TGT)
mastery approach
programmed instruction

personalized system of instruction (PSI)
team-assisted instruction (TAI)
peer tutoring
computer-assisted instruction (CAI)
tutorial programs
drill-and-practice programs
simulation programs
least restrictive environment
individualized education program (IEP)
due process
traveling notebook

Teacher Chronicle Summaries

Teacher Chronicle 11.1: Try, Try Again (pp. 399–401)

An elementary school teacher tries riddle writing with a class. The lesson is a complete failure. Later in the year, however, he tries writing riddles again after a visit to a nature center. This time the lesson succeeds beyond his highest expectations. The teacher, in reflecting on the failure and then success of the same idea, learns something about his students and his teaching.

Teacher Chronicle 11.2: Seeing the Light (pp. 413–414)

After assessing her class's knowledge of electricity, a middle school science teacher uses a lab set-up to teach electricity. In cooperative groups the students work at their own pace and help one another learn the concepts.

Teacher Chronicle 11.3: No Exceptions to the Rule (pp. 422–423)

A student with cerebral palsy is mainstreamed into a seventh-grade science class. The student, with the help of a full-time aide and his peers, covers the material presented. The teacher, in praising the class for its efforts to help the boy, comes to realize something more about herself as an educator.

Possible Answers to Principles in Practice

Principles in Practice 11.1

1. How did the unsuccessful and successful attempts at riddle writing differ in terms of question structuring?

The successful attempt provided a context for the task that was absent in the first attempt. The context included the elements of the task of riddle writing.

2. Would small group discussion have been more effective? Why or why not?

It could be argued that small group discussion might have recaptured some of the brainstorming that occurred spontaneously on the bus ride back from the field trip. Small groups could have served to provide feedback to first drafts of riddles, thus avoiding embarrassment of reading poor riddles before the entire class and decreasing motivation.

3. How do large and small group tactics differ with regard to the types of outcomes they foster?

Following the guidelines presented in the text, large group tactics tend to work best when there is a need to organize information. Small group tactics work best when alternatives need to be explored.

Principles in Practice 11.2

1. What form did peer tutoring take during the electricity experiments?

The same-age tutoring that took place in the lab occurred because students began asking each other questions informally. The more capable students, working at the more advanced stations, were often consulted. An important characteristic of the peer interaction was that it was not initiated by the teacher.

2. What was the advantage of having different kinds of apparatuses (e.g., circuit boards, computer graphics, etc.) available for students?

Because students began helping each other, the probability that someone knowledgeable about a particular apparatus could tutor someone needing help. Using different tactics increases the probability of matching learning styles.

3. Should the lab pairs have been formed on some basis other than or in addition to prior knowledge of electricity?

Whatever rationale students supply for their answer, the answer should reflect an awareness that this question is an empirical one. It needs to be answered in a classroom.

Principles in Practice 11.3

1. Given the activities of the science class, what adaptations might have been necessary for a blind student?

A blind student may need extra practice working with the equipment for labs. Perhaps arrangements would have been necessary to accommodate a Seeing Eye dog or to provide an audio description of some of the objects observed on field trips.

2. What questions would you have asked Louise, Tony's aide, before he was mainstreamed?

The questions should be attempts to specify Tony's disabilities, for example, how much extra time should be allowed for Tony to respond to oral questions? Receiving specific information about disabilities allows for adaptation so that the disabilities do not become handicaps.

3. If you were the teacher, what would you have told another teacher who was about to receive Tony as a mainstreamed student?

An important aspect of Tony's experience in the class was that he responded well to working with other students. One might want to discuss with the new teacher how cooperative pairs changed. The need to accommodate Tony's need to communicate through Louise should also be mentioned.

CNN Connection to Issues in Educational Psychology

Today's students have the advantage of living in a multimedia age. One of the most exciting new opportunities for learning comes from the computer and its newly forged links with laserdisc technology. In fact, the current revolution in technology can mean a whole new lease on learning for students with disabilities. As students will see in the segments that follow—the challenge lies in making teachers aware of up-to-the-minute technology and in training them to use it to every student's best advantage.

Activities and Exercises

In-Class Activities

1. Have students engage in small group discussion to describe exemplary use of the small group tactics discussed in the chapter. Assign other students to monitor the discussion and to take notes regarding their inclinations to intervene in the discussion. After the small group has finished, have the monitor share his or her notes with the group.

2. Have students generate questions which could be used in a teams-games-tournament approach to cooperative learning. The questions can be based on the key terms of the chapter. If desired, one or two rounds of a tournament could be conducted in class, followed by a discussion of the logistics of the approach.

Teacher Interviews

Have each student interview a teacher recognized for being effective, asking him or her to comment on the importance of having a variety of tactics at his or her disposal.

Have each student interview a teacher regarding the importance of "reading" his or her students.

Have students interview teachers regarding the rewarding nature of the "light bulbs" of understanding.

Have each student interview a teacher regarding the use of questioning in a review session, asking the teacher how wait-time relates to the amount of enthusiasm generated during such sessions.

Have students interview teachers regarding motivation as it is revealed by students' seatwork.

Have each student interview a teacher who uses small group discussion as a way of exploring and clarifying values and beliefs.

Have each student interview a teacher regarding his or her methods of avoiding the "ask the expert" syndrome.

Have each student interview a teacher regarding the use of team learning, asking the teacher to comment on the differences between small group discussion and cooperative learning in teams.

Have each student interview a teacher who uses a mastery approach to the management of the classroom and of learning activities.

Have each student interview a teacher who uses cooperative team learning regarding the issues that arise in parent–teacher conferences.

Have students interview special education teachers regarding the practical implications of PL 94-142.

Have each student interview a teacher, asking that teacher to comment on Maniet-Bellermann's guidelines by comparing them with his or her experiences with LD students.

Have each student interview a teacher who uses the traveling notebook about its usefulness and limitations.

Field Observations

Have each student observe an effective lecturer, documenting the theatrical qualities of his or her presentation.

Have students observe questioning sessions in classrooms, documenting the level of questions used by the teacher and the level of students' responses.

Have each student observe questioning sessions in classrooms documenting wait-time I and wait-time II and the level of students' responses.

Have students collect examples of seatwork exercises performed by students in elementary, junior high, and high school classrooms.

Have students observe teachers assigning homework, documenting how well the students are prepared to work independently.

Have students observe and document small group discussions in a variety of classrooms with the following questions in mind: What motivational differences do you notice? To what extent can those motivational differences be attributed to the presence or lack of controversy in the discussions?

Have students observe classrooms in which individualized instruction occurs, identifying differences in motivation among students in such classrooms.

Have students observe cross-age and same-age tutoring in classrooms, documenting differences in attitudes of the tutors and the tutored students.

Have each student observe a classroom in which CAI drill and practice is used for remediation, documenting his or her impressions of the advantages and disadvantages of this technique.

Have students collect IEP forms from various schools and interview principals or supervisors regarding their roles in IEP conferences.

Journal Entries

Have students reflect on the instructional tactics used by particularly effective teachers they have had in school, identifying the ways in which these instructional tactics contributed to the teachers' effective teaching styles.

Have students reflect on their own experiences with lecturers, addressing the question, What are the characteristics of poor lecturers and those of effective lecturers?

Have students reflect on the seatwork they did as students, addressing the question, What were your reactions to teachers who monitored seatwork and who gave you individual attention during seatwork periods?

Have students reflect on small group discussions in which they have participated, answering the following questions: Which discussions stand out in your mind as having fostered high-level thinking on your part? What were the characteristics of those discussion groups? What questions or issues guided the discussions?

Have students reflect on those teachers who made them feel important as individuals in their classes, commenting on the techniques these teachers used to accomplish this.

Discussion Topics (based on Lecture Notes)

Have students discuss the distinction between management and instructional tactics based on their experiences as students in classrooms and their experiences observing other teachers in classrooms.

Have students discuss the issue of matching levels of questions to desired outcomes. Have students use Gagné's learned capabilities (Chapter 9) as a basis for identifying desired outcomes.

Have students discuss guidelines they might use to set up small group discussions; in particular, ask the students to generate guidelines that might prevent a student from monopolizing a discussion.

Have students "brainstorm" ways of adapting classroom lessons involving students with varying disabilities.

Application Scenarios

Present the following scenarios to students:

- Your eleventh-grade English class has decided that you lecture too much, and they want a break from the constant talk. You suggest they explore group learning, and they seem eager to do so. Your students represent a wide range of ability levels, and some of the students frankly couldn't be less interested in American literature. How can you best match their desire for group work with the characteristics of the class?

- Arthur has quit coming to your chemistry class, even though he is your best student. You corner him in the hall, and he admits that he cannot bring himself to come to class anymore. It seems that he asked Mary, one of the brightest girls in school, to go to the prom with him, and she turned him down flat. You realize that Arthur will soon get over his crushing defeat in love, but meanwhile you don't want him to get into trouble or fall behind. Arthur is a whiz with computers. Suggest a way that you can work with Arthur to help him develop an individualized approach to chemistry instruction until he feels confident enough to return to class.

Chapter 15 Casebook Previews

See Around the World.
See Gifted Achievers and Underachievers.
See Science Is Only Real When You Do It.
See Writers' Tea.
See Taking Control.

Teaching Anecdotes

Tell your students the story of the high school science teacher who only lectured about science to his students. Each lecture revolved around a specific part of a specific chapter. There were 180 days in the school year and 180 files in his cabinet. Each morning, he pulled that day's file and lectured from it. Many of his students liked his classes and received A's, yet over the years he was there, a number of students did poorly in his class and never mastered the scientific concepts that he was teaching.

Ask your students why the lecture approach might have worked well with some students but failed with others. (See p. 401.)

Tell your students about the junior high teacher who carried a small stack of index cards with her as she walked around her room during small group discussions. Each card in the stack contained a question or comment, such as, "Are you talking about fact or opinion?" or "Go back to the original question." Her stack of cards also included blank cards on which she wrote specific questions pertinent to a specific discussion. As the teacher monitored the various discussion groups, she would periodically show one of the cards to a group member. She took care to vary the people in the group to whom she showed the cards.

Ask your students to evaluate this approach to monitoring small group discussions. (See p. 410.)

Tell your students about the fifth-grade student who regularly refused to do his written work in class. When the teacher gave him comprehension questions in reading, the student could answer the questions perfectly; but when he wrote anything down, it was sloppy and far less than what he was capable of doing. The teacher became increasingly frustrated with the student, and their relationship became a battle of wills. One day the teacher overheard the student telling a story to one of his friends in another class—the very story he had read that day. His retelling was accurate, and it was clear that he understood what he was reading. The next day the teacher asked the boy to retell the story to another student before completing his written assignment.

Ask your students why this approach might have worked with this student and if the effects are likely to be short term or long term. (See p. 419.)

Tell your students about the second-grade student who was having great difficulty learning the distinction between long and short vowel sounds. Her teacher had taught numerous lessons to the entire class and to the student's reading group. The teacher had also given the student individual help. None of these tactics created the understanding the teacher desired for the student. One day, in the computer lab, the girl chose a program on long vowel sounds. The program generated a graphic presentation of a clown who juggled one ball for every sound correctly identified. The program captivated the student. Within two weeks, the student passed a vowel mastery test with 100 percent accuracy.

Ask your students why the computer program might have enabled the student to master the critical distinction when the other tactics failed. (See p. 420.)

Tell your students about the first-grade teacher who was assigned five mainstreamed students for an hour of reading instruction. The students had been diagnosed as mentally retarded. The teacher, who had no training in teaching mentally retarded children, was willing to work with mainstreamed students. Prior to the mainstreaming, the teacher's reading program had focused exclusively on reading and writing. After several weeks of working with the mainstreamed students, the teacher moved away from her written word approach and began teaching by reading poems, rhymes, stories, and by having students take dictation as classmates told their own stories. She found that her new approach helped not only the mainstreamed students participate, but also discovered that other students expanded their language use and adapted to the printed word more easily.

Ask your students to explain the results of the teacher's "experiment." (See p. 424.)

Transparencies

For transparencies to use with this chapter, see the Transparency Guide on page 405.

Teaching Resources

Suggested Readings

Hollingsworth, P. M., & Hoover, K. H. (1991). *Elementary teaching methods.* Needham Heights, MA: Allyn & Bacon.

Johnson, D. W., & Johnson, R. T. (1991). *Learning together and alone: Cooperative, competitive and individualistic learning* (3rd ed.). Needham Heights, MA: Allyn & Bacon.

Kauchak, D. P., & Eggen, P. D. (1989). *Learning and teaching: Research-based methods.* Needham Heights, MA: Allyn & Bacon.

Levine, J. M. (1989). *Secondary instruction: A manual for classroom teaching.* Needham Heights, MA: Allyn & Bacon.

Rosenshine, B. V., & Stevens, R. J. (1986). "Teaching functions." In M. C. Wittrock (Ed.), *Third handbook of research on teaching.* Chicago: Rand McNally.

Films, Videocassettes, Audiocassettes

- *Instructional Decisions for Long-Term Learning,* video. The program's three hours of videotape and eighty-page Leader's Guide help teachers plan lessons and make sound decisions in the classroom. Use the second one-hour tape to show teachers how to structure lesson plans that get the students' attention, hold it, and deliver the new knowledge in ways that build retention. Videotaped sequences give the following tips for effective lesson planning:

  When—and when not—to tell the objectives of the lesson.

  Why not to ask, "Does everyone understand?"

  What kind of homework assignment produces the most learning?

  Tape 3 in this program demonstrates how teachers use active participation in the classroom to boost test scores and increase student retention of knowledge. The thirty-minute video introduces you to teaching pairs, choral responses, and five other techniques for increasing student participation.

- Video Library of Teaching Episodes, a set of ten videos:

  Episode 1: *Kindergarten Math* (readiness skills)

  Episode 2: *3rd Grade Math* (symmetry)

  Episode 3: *2nd Grade Math* (ways to make 10)

  Episode 4: *3rd Grade Classroom Art* (rules and procedures)

  Episode 5: *4th-6th Grade General Studies* (rules and procedures)

Episode 6: *7th Grade Social Studies* (crimes of commission and omission)

Episode 7: *8th Grade Social Studies* (4th and 6th Amendments)

Episode 8: *9th Grade English* (rules and procedures through letter writing)

Episode 9: *10th Grade Biology* (RNA/DNA transfer)

Episode 10: *12th Grade History* (student debate of Malthus essay)

- *Teaching Mathematics Effectively,* video. Eight actual classroom episodes in this thirty-minute videotape demonstrate to you and your staff the most effective way to structure a math lesson.

   Beginning Activities: Get students to review and check homework or to conduct mental computation exercises.

   Development: Introduce students to the new problems, give them controlled practice, and then assess their comprehension with appropriate questions.

   Seatwork: Increase and sustain involvement and make students accountable for their work through well-timed alerts.

   Homework: Help students retain the new skills.

- *Teacher and School Effectiveness,* video. Featured educators: Ronald Edmonds, Michigan State University; Barak Rosenshine, University of Illinois; Peter Mortime, London Schools.
- *Effective Teaching for Higher Achievement,* video. The following effective teaching strategies are demonstrated in two hours of videotape: increasing academic learning time; managing student behavior; six functions of effective teaching, daily review, structure presentation, guided practice, feedback, periodic review.

These five productions are available through Association for Supervision and Curriculum Development, 125 North West Street, Alexandria, VA 22314-2798. Or call (703) 549-9110.

- *In Pursuit of the Expert Pedagogue,* 50 min. David C. Berliner and his colleagues in a University of Arizona research project try to understand the nature of expertise in pedagogy. Their strategy is to find and study expert and experienced teachers and to compare them with ordinary or novice teachers in order to discover how they differ in their behavior and their approaches to tasks. Early findings indicate that among the most important differences is problem-solving ability, which expert teachers share with experts in such other fields as chess or physics. Available through AERA Videotape Sales, P.O. Box 19700, Washington DC 20036.

Test Questions

Test Questions 11.1–11.95

Study Guide

Assign Chapter 11 of the *Study Guide*.

12

Classroom Management, Discipline, and Communication

Chapter Objectives

1. General Objective

Distinguishes classroom management from discipline (pp. 439–442).

SPECIFIC BEHAVIORS
1.01 Illustrates management tactics as "primers" for instruction.
1.03 Identifies management to be a function of communication.
1.04 Relates degree of classroom organization, disciplinary problems, and active instruction to management tactics.

2. General Objective

Applies management skills that actively engage students in instructional tasks (pp. 442–457).

SPECIFIC BEHAVIORS
2.01 Explains the effects of giving clear instructions.
2.02 Explains the effects of beginning a lesson.
2.03 Explains the effects of maintaining attention.
2.04 Explains the effects of pacing.
2.05 Explains the effects of using seatwork effectively.
2.06 Explains the effects of summarizing.
2.07 Explains the effects of providing useful feedback and evaluation.
2.08 Explains the effects of making smooth transitions.

3. General Objective

Recognizes discipline tactics as ways of establishing standards of acceptable behavior and responding to unacceptable behavior (pp. 457–468).

SPECIFIC BEHAVIORS
3.01 Illustrates the ripple effect.
3.02 Illustrates withitness.
3.03 Illustrates overlapping.

3.04 Explains the operant conditioning basis of behavior modification.
3.05 Illustrates the rules-ignores-praise (RIP) approach to behavior modification.
3.06 Illustrates the rules-reward-punishment (RRP) approach to behavior modification.
3.07 Illustrates the contingency management approach to behavior modification.
3.08 Illustrates the contracting approach to behavior modification.
3.09 Characterizes Ginott's sane messages approach to classroom discipline.
3.10 Illustrates the use of "I-messages."
3.11 Illustrates the classroom communication characteristic of Canter's assertive discipline approach.

4. General Objective

Understands communication of teacher expectations and the effects of those expectations (pp. 468–472).

SPECIFIC BEHAVIORS
4.01 Identifies the Pygmalion effect.
4.02 Differentiates the Pygmalion effect from other expectancy effects.
4.03 Relates the communication of expectancies to the characteristics of students.

5. General Objective

Recognizes the social environments necessary for the effective operation of goal structures (pp. 472–477).

SPECIFIC BEHAVIORS
5.01 Differentiates the management tactics of cooperative, competitive, and individualistic goal structures.
5.02 Identifies the effects of cooperative goal structures.
5.03 Identifies the effects of competitive goal structures.
5.04 Identifies the effects of individual goal structures.

Focus Questions

- What is the difference between discipline and classroom management?
- How does classroom communication contribute to management?
- What tactics encourage active learning in students?
- How should a teacher approach discipline problems?
- How can problem behaviors be changed?
- How are teacher expectations related to management and discipline?
- How should rewards best be administered in a classroom?

Chapter Outline

INTRODUCTION: EXPERIENCE AND ORGANIZATION

TEACHER CHRONICLE 12.1: SHARPENING THE FOCUS

MANAGEMENT SKILLS
  Giving Clear Instructions
    Precise Directions
    Creative Delivery
    Student Involvement
  Beginning a Lesson
    Opening Cue
    Remove Outside Distractions
  Maintaining Attention
    Seating
    Recognizing Students
    Encourage Student Interaction
  Pacing
  Using Seatwork Effectively
  Summarizing
  Providing Useful Feedback and Evaluation
  Making Smooth Transitions
  Principles in Practice 12.1

TEACHER CHRONICLE 12.2: BOOK IT, RANDY!

DISCIPLINE
  Dynamics of Discipline
    The Ripple Effect
    Withitness
    Overlapping
  Skinner Revisited: Applied Behavior Analysis
    Catch 'em Being Good
    Rules-Ignore-Praise (RIP)
    Rules-Reward-Punishment (RRP)
    Contingency Management
    Contracting
  Sane Messages

Assertive Discipline
Principles in Practice 12.2

TEACHER CHRONICLE 12.3: ROOM FOR IMPROVEMENT

EXPECTATIONS AND COMMUNICATION
  Teacher Expectancies
    Qualifications of Teacher Expectancies
  Classroom Goal Structures
    Cooperative Goal Structure
    Competitive Goal Structure
    Individual Goal Structure
  Principles in Practice 12.3

CONCLUSION

Chapter Summary

Introduction: Experience and Organization

- It is necessary to make the distinction between classroom management and discipline. Classroom management refers to organizing learning experiences that minimize behavior problems. Discipline requires dealing with the behavior problems that have arisen.

Management Skills

- If you are to engage students in a learning activity, you must give them precise directions so that they know clearly what is expected of them. Creative delivery that involves students helps ensure on-task behavior.
- Provide cues that signal the beginning of a learning activity to help establish attention. It is helpful also to remove distractions so that when a lesson begins, students can focus on the important information.
- One way of helping students maintain their attention on a learning activity is to recognize and encourage their contributions. The seating arrangement in a classroom can also influence students' ability to pay attention.
- Pacing refers to the tempo of a lesson. It can be affected if the teacher makes a disorganized presentation. Pacing can also be disrupted by a lack of other management skills; the result is problem behavior that distracts students from the task at hand.
- Managing seatwork requires the careful monitoring of students. Before a teacher can redirect a student's attention or help the student solve a problem that is slowing his or her progress, the teacher must be aware of each student's in-class activity.
- Summarizing is useful to students because it helps them organize the information they have learned. If students understand how what they've learned

is organized, they are better able to fit new content in with the old. Summarizing at the end of a lesson is recommended at all grade levels.

- Feedback gives students information about the correctness of their responses and offers them an opportunity to correct mistakes. Feedback is not the same as reinforcement; what should be reinforced are students' efforts.
- Transitions are made when moving from one activity to the next. If transitions are not smooth, students are more likely to get off task. When students are off task, problem behaviors arise.

Discipline

- The Kounin approach to discipline emphasizes group skills. The ripple effect refers to the consequences that correcting one student's behavior has on the behavior of others. In order to effectively discipline, teachers need to be aware of all student activity; they need to cultivate "withitness." In addition to observational skills, teachers need to develop the skill to direct one activity while monitoring others. This skill is called overlapping.
- Applied behavior analysis involves analyzing problem behaviors and prescribing some kind of remedy for them. Remedies include the catch 'em being good approach, rules-ignore-praise (RIP), rules reward-punishment (RRP), contingency management, and contracting.
- *Sane messages* is Haim Ginott's term for the way in which a teacher should speak to students who present discipline problems. Central to the notion of sane messages are "I-messages." When presenting an I-message, the teacher speaks about his or her feelings regarding a classroom situation rather than attributing the situation to a student's negative characteristics.
- Assertive discipline is an approach that emphasizes clear and unambiguous statements. Rules are established and are enforced. Teachers communicate through promises not threats.

Expectations and Communication

- Teachers communicate their expectations to students through differential treatment. The Pygmalion effect refers to the influence that a teacher's expectations may have on student behavior. Expectations can have more influence in one situation than another. Nonetheless, it is important for teachers to be aware that they may be communicating expectations in the ways that they treat students.
- Classroom goal structures establish the conditions under which students are rewarded for attaining goals. Three types of classroom goal structures are cooperative, competitive, and individual.

Key Terms

on-task behavior
action zones
pacing
transitions
ripple effect
withitness
overlapping
applied behavior analysis
catch 'em being good
rules-ignore-praise (RIP)
rules-reward-punishment (RRP)
contingency management
contracting

sane messages
I-messages
assertive discipline
Pygmalion effect
classroom goal structures
cooperative goal structure
competitive goal structure
individual goal structure

Teacher Chronicle Summaries

Teacher Chronicle 12.1: Sharpening the Focus (pp. 441–442)

A sixth-grade teacher, team-teaching social studies for the first time, plans and teaches a unit on the Mayans. In observing her partner, as well as reflecting on her own lessons, the teacher learns about cutting down on discipline problems by making sure that every student has plenty to do for the entire class period.

Teacher Chronicle 12.2: Book It, Randy (pp. 455–457)

An elementary school teacher lists a disruptive student's positive and negative behaviors in an effort to understand the boy and work with him better. Realizing that the student misbehaved when he needed to be active, she devises a plan to channel his activeness in a positive direction.

Teacher Chronicle 12.3: Room for Improvement (p. 468)

An elementary school teacher, preparing his room at the beginning of the school year, ponders what the year will bring, wonders who are the people behind the names on his class list, and reflects on the multiple interactions soon to come.

Possible Answers to Principles in Practice

Principles in Practice 12.1

1. In which management skill areas did the second teacher experience difficulties?

Primarily, the second teacher failed to give clear instructions. Also, more difficulties were caused by the lack of a clear direction to the lesson and some problems with pacing, which were due to a miscalculation of what students would accomplish.

2. *How did a lack of clear instructions from the second teacher influence pacing and seatwork?*

Because students were not sure of what they were to do or how they were to do it, they had to keep asking procedural questions. This held up the momentum of the lesson and caused confusion with the worksheets. As a consequence, on-task behavior was relatively low during the seatwork portion of the lesson.

3. *How should the management skills examined here be used as you select material for your class?*

One way in which the management skills could be used to select materials is to consider the instructional tactics by which the materials could best be delivered. After determining the instructional tactics, a teacher could consider the management skills that should support instruction.

Principles in Practice 12.2

1. *Given Randy's interests, what other disciplinary solutions seem worth trying?*

The teacher could consult the list he or she constructed to find some other rewards, while ignoring undesirable behavior. Another solution is contracting with Randy—perhaps opportunities to read aloud would be reinforcing to him. Randy might also respond well to the establishment of rules.

2. *Why did the teacher's initial reprimands prove ineffective with Randy?*

As a form of punishment, the reprimands informed Randy of inappropriate behavior, but the lack of reinforcement did not inform him of appropriate behavior. As a consequence he learned what not to do, but not what he should do instead.

3. *What approach to class rules do you plan to use in your classroom? Why?*

Whatever approach the students choose, their answers should reflect a rationale. From this chapter, rationales could come from RIP or RRP approaches. It will be interesting to note if students refer back to Lickona's model discussed in Chapter 4.

Principles in Practice 12.3

1. *To what extent do you think the teacher in Teacher Chronicle 12.3 will use cooperative, competitive, and individual goal structures?*

Given the teacher's comment concerning peer interaction, it seems that the teacher might emphasize a cooperative goal structure.

2. *How do you imagine teacher expectancy operates in the classroom described in Chronicle 12.3?*

The teacher predicts that some students will thrive in his or her classroom, while others will need more structure than this teacher anticipates supplying. It seems that the teacher will attempt to modify the environment for those needing structure rather than simply expecting less of those students in his or her class.

3. *What do you want to know about your students before they enter your classroom? What do you not want to know?*

The answers here should indicate that students are aware that what the teacher expects of a particular student can sometimes be a negative message to the student. The response to the second question should especially indicate that sensibility.

CNN Connection to Issues in Educational Psychology

Learning to deal properly with the unpredictable aspects of student behavior in the classroom can be an intimidating prospect for many teachers. Experienced teachers can tell you that the best way to do it is to prevent problems from happening in the first place. As students will see in the segments that follow, good classroom management requires teachers to be much more than disciplinarians.

Activities and Exercises

In-Class Activities

1. Have your students role-play representatives to the district's professional evaluation committee. They are charged with developing criteria for the evaluation of teachers based on the management skills formulated by Jones and Jones and discussed in this chapter. Additionally, the committee is to develop a checklist questionnaire that administrators could use as they observe teachers working in classrooms.
2. Have your class assume that they are faculty members in the same building. As the principal, you call a faculty meeting during one of the in-service days just prior to the opening of the school year. Explain to your faculty that one of the reasons disciplinary problems occur at the beginning of the year is because students must learn a new form of discipline with each new teacher. Therefore, there will be a schoolwide policy for discipline. Tell your faculty that the purpose of today's meeting is to debate which of the several approaches described in the chapter should serve as the basis for the new policy.

Teacher Interviews

Have each student interview a veteran teacher regarding the classroom management benefits of organized teaching.

Have students interview teachers regarding the ways in which they prepare their classrooms for teaching.

Have students interview teachers regarding the seating arrangements they use, asking the teachers to explain the advantages and disadvantages of their arrangements.

Have each student interview a teacher regarding how he or she judges the pace of a lesson, and the techniques he or she uses to break up lengthy periods of instruction.

Ask a fellow teacher to attend a lecture as a consultant. Use the teacher to generate a plan for turning classroom summaries into journalistic role playing.

Have each student interview a junior high or high school teacher regarding his or her tactics for establishing student focus.

Have each student interview a teacher to determine how he or she deals with the "squeaky wheel syndrome."

Have students interview teachers at various levels regarding the practice of ignoring undesirable behavior.

Have students interview teachers regarding their experiences relevant to the Pygmalion effect.

Have students interview teachers regarding the finding that teachers interact most frequently with students for whom they have high expectations.

Field Observations

Have each student observe a teacher delivering a lesson, identifying the elements of the teacher's actions that reflect active teaching.

Have each student observe a classroom, documenting episodes of student uncertainty and correlating those episodes with the frequency of disruptive behavior in that classroom.

Have students observe teachers in classrooms, documenting the methods they use to deliver instructions.

Have students observe teachers as they introduce an activity, documenting the sequence in which they provide directions and provide motivation.

Have students observe several classrooms, documenting the action zones in each classroom and correlating differences in action zones with other classroom dynamics.

Have students observe the listening behavior of teachers and students in a classroom, documenting the classroom atmosphere and level of motivation.

Have students observe feedback delivered by teachers, identifying episodes in which student effort was reinforced.

Have students observe classrooms and document the extent to which their students exhibit the "packing-up syndrome." Have them try to identify the management tactics in classrooms where the syndrome occurs to a greater or lesser extent.

Have each student observe a class early in the year when the teacher is attempting to establish classroom rules.

Have students collect and compare contracts from a number of teachers.

Have each student observe a teacher who uses the assertive discipline approach, documenting the comments made by the teacher as he or she implements assertive discipline.

Have each student observe a multicultural classroom, documenting the extent to which he or she observes low- or high-differential treatment in that classroom.

Have students observe a number of classrooms, identifying the types of goal structures operating in each of them.

Journal Entries

Have students reflect on those teachers from their experiences who did or did not engage their attention and imagination. Have them reflect on teacher's actions that led them to their evaluations.

Have students reflect on phrases they might use that could serve to signal the beginning of a lesson and also provide a bit of humor or whimsy in the classroom. Have them consider a metaphor that you might use to manage the classroom; for example, the classroom might become a ship with various functions labeled with nautical terms. If this metaphor were used, the opening cue might be, "Welcome Aboard!"

Have students recall their own experiences in classes where classmates were recognized in either highly predictable or unpredictable ways. Have them comment on the ways in which the degree of predictability influenced their attention and motivation.

If a videotape of one of your classes is available, have students view it, commenting on your performance in class based on the questions listed in the text.

Have students reflect on their own seatwork experiences, identifying the conditions under which they reacted to it more or less seriously.

Have students reflect on their own experiences in school, commenting on the extent to which grades motivated them, and their ability to understand the motivation of students whose views of grades differ from their own.

Have students reflect on episodes from their own schooling that demonstrate the ripple effect.

Have students reflect on their experiences as junior high school students identifying those episodes from their own experiences that would support the contention that the "catch 'em being good" approach is laughable.

Have students reflect on any classroom experiences they had operating in a token economy. Ask them to consider how the token economy influenced their behavior in that class.

Have each student reflect on a teacher who attacked his or her self-image or the self-image of a classmate. Have the student consider how such attacks influenced his or her perception of the teacher.

Have students reflect on teachers from their experiences who made threats, but did not keep promises, documenting their own perceptions of such teachers and the ways in which these perceptions influenced their attitudes toward that class.

Have students reflect on the expectancies some of their teachers communicated to them as students, indicating how those expectancies were communicated and the effects they had on the students' attitudes.

Have students reflect on those activities for which they had either a sense of obligation or lacked one, trying to reconstruct the conditions that lead to their feelings.

Discussion Topics (based on Lecture Notes)

Ask students to discuss, in small groups, the actions of teachers who effectively demonstrated the eight skills listed on page 442.

Ask students to discuss the verbal responses of their teachers. Have them identify effective and ineffective verbal responses.

Ask students to discuss how various management skills are interrelated.

Ask students, in small groups, to identify various disruptive situations and to construct sane messages that address those situations.

Ask students to discuss the phenomenon of early impressions from the teacher's and the student's points of view.

Ask students to discuss, in small groups, their own experiences in classrooms containing "haves" and "have nots."

Ask students to discuss how a competitive goal structure might be focused on effort rather than on ability.

Application Scenarios

Present the following scenarios to students:

- The last period of the day is your biggest headache. Roberto and Maria are "going together" again, which is fifth-grade talk for holding hands in the back of the room and giggling. Leon insists that he should be allowed to answer each and every question you ask, and he punctuates that desire by standing up and waving his arm wildly when you ask a question. Anton and Debi are totally lost, and they look like they don't care. This class needs a whole new makeover, from top to bottom. Where do you start? What do you do?

- After many years of teaching kindergarten, you have volunteered to teach a group of migrant farmworkers so that they can pass their citizenship tests. Frankly, these students intimidate you. They are so eager and polite, but most of them speak very poor English. You don't want to treat them like children, but you want to make sure that they understand what you are trying to teach them. How would you devise a plan to make sure that you can teach this class effectively?

Chapter 15 Casebook Previews

See Bringing the Real World into the Classroom.

See Beginning Each Day as a Learning Experience.

See Writers' Tea.

See Science Is Only Real When You Do It.

See Responsibility Education.

See Please Sign This Contract.

Teaching Anecdotes

Tell your students about the teacher who used a spot-check method to get feedback from his students whenever he finished explaining an assignment. The teacher would call on six students: two students who he knew would respond correctly, two on whom he wanted to check to see if they understood the lesson, and two who needed encouragement if they were to participate. No matter how clearly the procedure was explained, one student continually asked, "But can I try it this way?"

Ask your students why such spot-checking might be successful and how they might handle the "questioning" student. (See p. 443.)

Tell your students about the high school teacher who always allows his kids to choose their own seats. He had but one rule: "If your grades drop, you get an assigned seat."

Ask your students why this approach might have worked for some students and not for others. How effective would this approach be with younger students as compared with older students? (See p. 446.)

Tell your students about the high school math teacher who had students design their own tests. Each test had fifty items. To obtain the fifty items, the teacher had each student write ten problems and their solutions. The teacher collected the problems and selected those to be included on the exam.

Ask your students how this technique aided the teacher in identifying problems, how it helped involve students more directly in their learning, and how it served as an effective evaluative tool. (See p. 452.)

Tell your students about the teacher who had a reputation for having eyes in the back of her head, especially when it came to cheating. Whenever she caught anyone cheating, she didn't make a show of it in front of the other students; rather, she wrote a note on the student's paper indicating what she had observed. Within each of her classes, the incidence of cheating dropped as the year progressed and the students realized her powers of observation.

Ask your students to tell about teachers from their own schooling who possessed "withitness" and why they were perceived that way. (See p. 457.)

Tell your students about the second-grade teacher who had one of her best friend's daughters in class. Because the teacher already knew the student well, the teacher had high expectations for the child. In addition, the teacher did not want to disappoint her friend in terms of her daughter's accomplishments that year. Therefore, the teacher gave the student extra responsibilities and extra attention, in some cases "bending the rules" for the student. One day the teacher overheard the student say, "I wish my mom and our teacher did not like each other. Then maybe she would treat me the same as everyone else."

Ask your students how the teacher should resolve this situation. (See p. 472.)

Transparencies

For transparencies to use with this chapter, see the Transparency Guides on page 447 and page 464.

Teaching Resources

Suggested Readings

Bauer, A. M., & Sapona, R. H. (1991). *Managing classrooms to facilitate learning*. Needham Heights, MA: Allyn & Bacon.

Emmer, E. T., Evertson, C. M., Sanford, J. P., Clements, B. S., & Worsham, M. E. (1989). *Classroom management for secondary teachers*. Englewood Cliffs, NJ: Prentice-Hall.

Evertson, C. M., Emmer, E. T., Clements, B. S., Sanford, J. P., and Worsham, M. E. (1989). *Classroom management for elementary teachers*. Englewood Cliffs, NJ: Prentice-Hall.

Jones, V. F., & Jones, L. S. (1990). *Comprehensive classroom management*. Needham Heights, MA: Allyn & Bacon.

Kounin, J. S. (1970). *Discipline and group management in classrooms*. New York: Holt, Rinehart & Winston.

Films, Videocassettes, Audiocassettes

- *Classroom Management: A Proactive Approach to Creating an Effective Learning Environment*, 60 min. This video shows how K–12 teachers can minimize behavior problems and maximize learning with a three-stage management plan: planning, implementing, and maintaining.

- *Strategies for Improving Classroom Management Skills*, audio. With these two audiocassettes, you discover dozens of practical tips for the classroom.

These two productions are available through Association for Supervision and Curriculum Development, 125 North West Street, Alexandria, VA 22314-2798. Or call (703) 549-9110.

- *Good Old-Fashioned Discipline*, video, 28 min., color. Are schools to be the repository for everyone below a certain age, or should those who disrupt classes and prevent others from learning be barred? This Phil Donohue program features a heated discussion between Deputy Undersecretary of Education Gary Bauer, author of a government report on the issue of escalating school violence; Joe Clark, outspoken principle who expelled one-tenth of his high school student body in an antiviolence campaign; proponents of other, innovative solutions, and critics of the expulsion policy. Available through: Films for the Humanities and Sciences, Inc., P.O. Box 2052, Princeton, NJ 08543. CC-1584.

- *Basic Training in Lee Canter's Assertive Discipline Behavior Management*. Topics include: a discussion of assertive, nonassertive, and hostile teachers; overcoming roadblocks to assertiveness; determining the behavior needed from students; setting limits in the classroom; using positive reinforcement; and how to establish a schoolwide discipline plan. Six thirty-minute videocassettes. Manuals, resource materials and instructor's guide. Filmstrip Package: 1131. 122 color filmstrips with audiocassettes. Plus same material as video package. Lee Canter & Assoc., Inc., P.O. Box 2113, Department MK, Santa Monica, CA 90406. Or call 1-800-262-4347 (in CA call 213-295-3221).

Test Questions

Test Questions 12.1–12.110

Study Guide

Assign Chapter 12 of the *Study Guide*.

13
Using Classroom Data

Chapter Objectives

General Objective

Understands the uses to which classroom evaluation can be put (pp. 482–490).

SPECIFIC BEHAVIORS

1.01 Infers how evaluation is an integral part of instruction and management.
1.02 Differentiates the terms *evaluation, measurement,* and *test*.
1.03 Gives examples of qualitative and quantitative measurement.
1.04 Differentiates the various uses of evaluative judgments.
1.05 Explains placement evaluation.
1.06 Explains formative evaluation.
1.07 Explains summative evaluation.
1.08 Explains diagnostic evaluation.
1.09 Identifies classroom observations as a source of evaluative data.

2. General Objective

Recognizes the properties of measurement that yield confident judgments (pp. 490–495).

SPECIFIC BEHAVIORS

2.01 Identifies the properties of reliable measurement.
2.02 Illustrates the test-retest method of estimating reliability.
2.03 Illustrates the alternate forms method of estimating reliability.
2.04 Illustrates the internal consistency method of estimating reliability.
2.05 Identifies reliable measurement as a necessary, but not sufficient, condition for evaluation.
2.06 Identifies the properties of valid measurement.
2.07 Illustrates judgments of content validity.
2.08 Illustrates judgments of criterion-related validity.

2.09 Illustrates judgments of construct validity.
2.10 Relates judgments of validity to the purpose of an evaluation.

3. General Objective

Applies guidelines for constructing reliable and valid classroom tests (pp. 495–508).

SPECIFIC BEHAVIORS

3.01 Identifies the four general steps in constructing classroom tests.
3.02 Uses a table of specifications according to a seven-step procedure to construct a test.
3.03 Differentiates selected response and constructed response items.
3.04 Explains binary choice items.
3.05 Prepares binary choice items.
3.06 Explains matching items.
3.07 Prepares matching items.
3.08 Explains multiple choice items.
3.09 Prepares multiple choice items.
3.10 Explains short answer items.
3.11 Prepares short answer items.
3.12 Explains essay items.
3.13 Prepares essay items.
3.14 Demonstrates scoring procedures for the various item types.
3.15 Prepares and uses item analyses.
3.16 Demonstrates observation as a source of evaluative data.

4. General Objective

Recognizes the implications of establishing a grading system (pp. 508–516).

SPECIFIC BEHAVIORS

4.01 Establishes a comparative basis for grading.
4.02 Distinguishes absolute and relative grading.
4.03 Selects among achievement, effort, and improvement as criteria for grading.
4.04 Selects between letter grades and pass/fail grades.

4.05 Identifies the utility of letters to parents as an alternative to assigning grades.

4.06 Identifies the utility of checklists as an alternative to assigning grades.

4.07 Identifies the utility of parent–teacher conferences as an alternative to assigning grades.

4.08 Illustrates the dos and don'ts of parent–teacher conferences.

4.09 Identifies the relationship between grading standards and performance.

4.10 Illustrates recommendations for classroom evaluation.

Focus Questions

- How does evaluation differ from measurement?
- For what purposes are classroom evaluations used?
- What determines the quality and, therefore, the usefulness of evaluative judgments?
- How do teachers construct useful classroom tests?
- How can a teacher tell if a test item is useful or not useful?
- How should a teacher determine grades?

Chapter Outline

INTRODUCTION: EVALUATION, MEASUREMENT, AND TESTS

TEACHER CHRONICLE 13.1: TEST TIME

CLASSROOM EVALUATION
Purposes of Evaluation
  Placement Evaluation
  Formative Evaluation
  Summative Evaluation
  Diagnostic Evaluation
Techniques of Evaluation

UTILITY OF EVALUATIVE INFORMATION
Reliability
  Estimating Reliability
    Test-Retest
    Alternate Forms
    Internal Consistency
Validity
  Content Validity
  Criterion-related Validity
  Construct Validity
  Summary of Reliability and Validity
Principles in Practice 13.1

TEACHER CHRONICLE 13.2: THE VERDICT, PLEASE

CONSTRUCTING CLASSROOM TESTS
Table of Specifications

ITEM TYPES
Binary Choice Items
  Guidelines for Writing Binary Choice Items
Matching Items
  Guidelines for Writing Matching Items
Multiple Choice Items
  Guidelines for Writing Multiple Choice Items
Short Answer Items
  Guidelines for Writing Short Answer Items
Essay Items
  Guidelines for Writing and Grading Essay Items

ITEM ANALYSIS
Indices of Item Difficulty and Discrimination

PITFALLS IN TESTING
Nontest Evaluation Techniques
  Checklists
  Anecdotal Records
  Rating Scales
Principles in Practice 13.2

TEACHER CHRONICLE 13.3: WHAT DID YOU GET ON YOUR REPORT CARD?

GRADING
The Grading System
Achievement or Effort?
  Pass/Fail Grading
Alternatives to Grading
  Contract Grading
A Summary of Grading Procedures
  Research on Grading
  Considerations for Testing and Grading
Principles in Practice 13.3

CONCLUSION

Chapter Summary

Introduction: Evaluation, Measurement, and Tests

- Evaluation is a process of gathering, analyzing, and interpreting data in order to make judgments. Measurement is a process of describing students' characteristics numerically. Tests are instruments of measurement.

Classroom Evaluation

- Classroom evaluation can be used to place students in the most appropriate learning situation (placement). Classroom evaluation can be used to modify instructional practice (formative evaluation) or to make judgments about the outcomes of instruction (summative evaluation). It can also be used to identify strengths and weaknesses (diagnostic evaluation).

- Evaluation occurs in the classroom in a variety of ways, including teacher-generated tests. In addition to tests, teachers evaluate papers, worksheets, speeches, recitations, and other student products and performances. Teachers also evaluate students informally through observation.

Utility of Evaluative Information

- To be useful, the data from tests and other measurements must be reliable, that is, the results of the test must be consistent. A teacher can rely on the data from a reliable test because they are stable.
- A valid test is one that measures what it is supposed to measure. Because tests serve different purposes, there are different kinds of validity: content, criterion-related, and construct validity.

Constructing Classroom Tests

- A table of specifications is a blueprint for test construction. It allows a teacher to match test items to instructional objectives both in terms of content and in terms of what students should be able to do with the content.

Item Types

- Classroom tests can be constructed with various types of items. Binary choice items require students to select one of two alternatives. True/false items are an example.
- Matching items require students to select a response that matches a premise. Examples include matching causes with effects and matching definitions with concepts.
- Multiple choice items consist of a *stem*, which can be a question, statement, or scenario; alternatives; and distractors. Students must select the correct answer from the set of alternatives.
- Short answer items require students to construct a response rather than select from supplied alternatives. An example of a short-answer item is a fill-in-the-blank question.
- Essay items require the student to construct a written response. Essays can require either long (extended) or short (restricted) answers.

Item Analysis

- Item analysis is a way of determining the extent to which an item contributes to the overall purpose of a multiple choice test. Item analysis yields an index of difficulty that defines the number of students who select the correct answer. Item analysis also yields an index of discrimination that identifies the extent to which a particular item contributes to students' overall performances on a test.

Pitfalls in Testing

- There are a number of pitfalls that need to be guarded against. Some of those pitfalls can be avoided by using measurement instruments other than tests. Those instruments include checklists, anecdotal records, and rating scales, all of which help make observation more systematic.

Grading

- Grading systems can be based on absolute standards of quality of performance or can be based on student performance relative to that of other students. No matter what kind of grading system is used, some basis for comparison of grades is required.
- Many teachers assign grades based on evaluation of both achievement and effort. Guidelines suggest that grades be based on achievement only. This does not mean a teacher cannot evaluate effort separately.
- Evaluations of classroom work do not have to take the traditional form of grades. Evaluative judgments can be presented in a number of ways. Additionally, students can contract for grades, thus, participating in the establishment of criteria used to assign grades.
- Grading is typically a summative judgment. It is important that the grade be determined on the basis of reliable and valid data. It is also important to keep in mind that the way grades are determined and assigned can influence both student effort and performance.

Key Terms

evaluation	table of specifications
measurement	selected response items
test	constructed response items
placement evaluation	binary choice items
formative evaluation	matching items
summative evaluation	multiple choice items
diagnostic evaluation	short answer items
reliability	essay items
test-retest	index of item difficulty
alternate forms	index of discrimination
internal consistency	checklist
validity	rating scales
content validity	absolute standard
criterion-related validity	relative standard
construct validity	

Teacher Chronicle Summaries

Teacher Chronicle 13.1: Test Time (pp. 485–486)

Two teachers discuss creating tests. The first teacher, relatively new to teaching, is frustrated by her students' poor performance on a recent test. The second teacher, a veteran with twenty-five years experience, gives advice on how to create an interesting, but still valid, test.

Teacher Chronicle 13.2: The Verdict, Please (pp. 494–495)

Imagining himself as judge, jury, and attorney, a teacher reflects on a student who has not passed the school-mandated timed test for math. The teacher reflects on the decisions he made regarding the student.

Teacher Chronicle 13.3: What Did You Get on Your Report Card? (pp. 507–508)

When report cards are passed out, a teacher listens to and watches her students' reactions to their grades. These reactions vary from excitement and pleasure to anxiety. The teacher wonders, too, what his "report card," his end of the year evaluation, will be.

Possible Answers to Principles in Practice

Principles in Practice 13.1

1. Identify the various purposes that the science teacher had in mind when she evaluated students.

The discussion in Chronicle 13.1 indicates that the teacher is interested in gaining information about students for both formative and summative purposes. In addition to purely evaluative purposes, the teacher also hopes students will learn from her tests.

2. What other steps could the science teacher have taken to enhance reliability and validity?

In addition to the effect of increasing the sample of behavior through multiple evaluations, the teacher could have had other science teachers judge the content of her tests. (Students will learn about the table of specifications in the next section.)

3. How will you be able to ensure the reliability and validity of the observations you will make (rather than the tests you will use) in your classroom?

No teacher can ever be 100 percent sure of the reliability and validity of his or her tests. The best a teacher can do is to take steps to ensure consistency in measurement and appropriateness of evaluative exercises. (Answering this question will access prior knowledge that students can use in studying guidelines.)

Principles in Practice 13.2

1. What kind of test items might the teacher in Teacher Chronicle 13.2 have used to make the judgment he or she was required to make?

The teacher could, and should, use a variety of item types to measure Brett's ability to accurately solve computation problems. A point students should remember is that the conditions under which tests are taken also influence the nature of the tasks students must perform. In this case, the time limit caused problems for the student.

2. Why should teachers use a variety of item types?

Teachers should use a variety of item types to enhance the reliability of a test. Writing a variety of items should increase the sample of behavior elicited by a test. Another reason is to enhance the validity. If a student performs poorly on multiple choice tests because such items cause anxiety, then a test comprising only multiple choice items will measure that student's anxiety as well as knowledge. A variety of item types increases the chance that a student's performance is a function of what he or she knows.

3. What outcomes that will not be easily measured by tests do you desire for your future students?

The students' answers to this question should serve to remind them that not all of the outcomes they will seek for their students will be measurable by paper-and-pencil tests.

Principles in Practice 13.3

1. How would the reactions of the students in Teacher Chronicle 13.3 have changed if they had received pass/fail reports?

The students probably would have been less concerned with parental reactions if they had received pass/fail reports. The students might have been more open to reflecting on the work that yielded their passing or failing.

2. Why didn't the students discuss the teacher's comments as much as the grades?

As is the case with much of the evaluation that occurs in schools, the emphasis is on summative evaluation, the "bottom-line." Letter grades reduce the work of an entire unit to one mark. Reading one mark makes it easy to judge the quality of a student's performance.

3. Speculate on the "speech" you will make to your students just before they receive grades from you for the first time.

The speech will depend on the type of grading system the students will use. Their comments should indicate not only the kinds of evaluative judgments that are reflected in the grades, but also the kinds of judgments not reflected in the grades they are about to report.

CNN Connection to Issues in Educational Psychology

Does multiple choice testing provide a good measure of students' reasoning capabilities? Should essay questions be used at some grade levels? Should calculators be allowed? Not surprisingly, as national concern over education increases, the ability to accurately measure results becomes critical. The following segments will demonstrate how the nation's standardized testing practices are being criticized—students will hear experts discuss the problems of race and gender bias, whether standardized tests accurately assess student ability, and reforms and solutions that offer promise.

Activities and Exercises

In-Class Activities

1. Group students according to their anticipated area and/or level of certification. Either supply or have students generate an abbreviated table of specifications. Have students bring their tables of specification to an item writing workshop held during a class session.

2. Have your students assume that they have been approached by the director of a summer camp who wishes to send evaluations home to parents. The parents are interested in receiving information regarding their child's level of social and emotional maturity. Have your students assist the camp director in developing nontest evaluation techniques.

Teacher Interviews

Have students interview teachers regarding their views of the ways in which evaluation functions in a classroom.

Have each student interview a teacher regarding how he or she "reads" the facial gestures and the body language of his or her students.

Have each student interview a teacher regarding the "pool" of possible items for a particular exam.

Have each student discuss with a teacher how he or she uses tests for formative and summative purposes.

Have each student interview a teacher who uses binary choice items on his or her tests, in particular, asking the teacher how he or she copes with guessing as a potential problem.

Have each student interview a teacher who uses short answer items, in particular, asking the teacher to share any tips they have learned in grading short answer items.

Have each student interview a teacher regarding his or her methods of controlling the halo effect.

Have each student discuss with a teacher the desirability of convergent evidence in making evaluative judgments.

Have each student ask a teacher who keeps anecdotal records to comment on how the anecdotal records help him or her better understand students.

Have students interview teachers regarding the advisability of separating achievement and effort in evaluation.

Have students interview teachers who use pass/fail grading in their class, asking them to comment on its advantages and disadvantages.

Have each student discuss with a teacher his or her comments on the recommendations listed in the text (p. 513).

Field Observations

Have students collect the criteria used by several school districts to place students in special programs.

Have each student obtain the policy of a local school district regarding the use of tests, and examine the policy to determine how reliability and validity of tests influence evaluative judgments.

Have each student observe a teacher who uses a table of specifications to construct a test, comparing the teacher's procedures with the seven-step process.

Have each student observe a classroom session in which the results of a test are being reviewed, documenting the results of the review in terms of improving the quality of the test.

Have each student observe a classroom in which the teacher uses a checklist for evaluative purposes. The students should obtain a copy of the checklist and complete it during the course of a lesson, comparing his or her checklist with the teacher's after the lesson.

Have each student arrange to attend an in-service on evaluation, comparing the recommendations presented in this chapter with those presented at the in-service.

Journal Entries

Have each student recall an episode from his or her schooling in which a teacher changed the activities of a class based on the results of a test or a quiz. The students should discuss how well or poorly the teacher made the shift.

Have students assume that they must interpret the results of an unreliable test, considering what the test might be measuring in addition to the content it covers.

Have students reflect on their experiences when taking a test designed to predict their future performances. In particular, have them reflect on the differences between taking a final exam for a course and the experience of taking the SAT exam.

Have students reflect on their experiences responding to selected-response items and constructed-response items, concentrating on the demands each item type placed on them.

Have students reflect on their experiences with multiple choice tests, and the strategies they've used in responding to multiple choice questions.

Have students reflect on the advisability of using a table of specifications for two purposes: as a way of constructing a reliable test, and as a tool for planning instruction.

Have students reflect on the tendency to view all quantitative data as rigorous. Given the discussion in this chapter, argue for the importance of a healthy skepticism of test results.

Have each student reflect on the ways in which grades affected him or her as a student, marshalling arguments for or against grading practices based on these experiences.

Have each student reflect on his or her experiences in a course graded competitively and in a course that took into account improvement, commenting on the ways in which those grading practices influenced his or her attitude and motivation.

Have each student reflect on the curvilinear relationship between standards and performance, matching the relationship with his or her experience.

Discussion Topics (based on Lecture Notes)

Ask students to discuss how a single test is sometimes used for multiple evaluation purposes.

Ask students to discuss the assumptions that must be in place in order to estimate reliability by means of alternate forms of a test. The chief assumption is that the same question can be asked equally well in at least two different ways.

Ask students to discuss how a table of specifications could be used for formative purposes.

Ask students to discuss the conditions under which a low or a high index of item difficulty would be desirable.

Ask students to discuss why systematic observation is preferable to relying on one's impressions concerning attitudes, work habit, and the like.

Ask students to discuss assignments and tests that not only measured their knowledge but enhanced their learning.

Application Scenarios

Present the following scenarios to students:

- You are totally perplexed by the performance of your eighth-grade business math class. You have had them for most of a semester and by now you know who your stronger and weaker students are. On your last test, though, which counts for a quarter of the semester grade, your stronger students did very poorly, and your weaker students did better than they have in the past. What can you say about this test? How should you count it? If you keep it, are you penalizing your better students? If you throw it out, are you penalizing your poorer students?

- The superintendent announces that there will be a

systemwide test for selected grades, including third grade (which you happen to teach). This test will be a curriculum-driven minimum competency test, and any student who falls below a certain score will have to take summer school to learn basic skills. How would this type of testing affect the way you teach? Should you alter your teaching to make sure your class is able to pass the test? Should you teach as you have always done, and hope that your students can pass the test based on what you have always thought was important to teach?

Chapter 15 Casebook Previews

See Writers' Tea.

See Bringing the Real World into the Classroom.

See Around the World.

See Book Writing.

See Responsibility Education.

See Writing Success in Science.

Teaching Anecdotes

Tell your students about the school district that used only the results of an IQ test to place students in their gifted program. A neighboring school district placed students using the results of IQ tests, peer recommendations, teacher observations, and parental evaluations.

Ask your students why a student admitted to the first district's gifted program might be denied entry into the gifted program of the second district. (See p. 486.)

Tell your students about the fourth-grade student who did well when responding verbally to reading comprehension questions but rarely completed a written assignment. The teacher often adapted lessons so that the student could respond verbally to comprehension questions. However, the teacher held the student responsible for completing all other kinds of written assignments.

Ask your students why the teacher made this adaptation, taking into account the teacher's purpose in evaluating reading comprehension. (See p. 489.)

Tell your students about the two pupils of equal ability in a senior history class. One student hated the class, especially the weekly multiple choice tests. The other student loved the class and looked forward to the weekly tests. The first student performed poorly on the tests; the second excelled.

Ask your students what might account for the differences in performance and attitude. (See p. 499.)

Tell your students about a school district that has ungraded elementary schools, but graded junior high and high schools. An alarming percentage of students in the district experience difficulties making the transition from elementary school to junior high.

Ask your students how differences in grading might contribute to these difficulties. (See p. 508.)

Tell your students about the school district that did not give grades but issued a progress report centered on a checklist with fifty items, ranging from academic progress to social interactions. Each report also included three sections for written comments by teachers.

Ask your students why this checklist system might or might not benefit students, parents, and teachers. (See p. 511.)

Transparencies

For transparencies to use with this chapter, see the Transparency Guides on page 506 and page 514.

Teaching Resources

Suggested Readings

Carey, L. M. (1988). *Measuring and evaluating school learning.* Needham Heights, MA: Allyn & Bacon.

Cole, N. S. (1981). Bias in testing. *American Psychologist, 36,* 1067–1077.

Ebel, R. L., & Frisbie, D. A. (1991). *Essentials of educational measurement* (5th ed.). Englewood Cliffs, NJ: Prentice-Hall.

Green, B. F. (1981). A primer of testing. *American Psychologist, 36,* 1001–1011.

Gronlund, N. E. (1988). *How to construct achievement tests* (4th ed.). Needham Heights, MA: Allyn & Bacon.

Films, Videocassettes, Audiocassettes

- *Norm-Referenced Tests: Uses and Misuses,* video, 30 min. Origins and nature of norm-referenced standardized achievement tests are discussed. Inappropriate uses of tests and how they can lead to unsound educational decisions are shown.
- *Criterion-Referenced Measurement: Today's Alternative to Traditional Testing,* video, 30 min. Viewers learn what they are, how they are constructed and how they are used.

These two videos are available through IOX, 5420 McConnel Avenue, Los Angeles, CA 90066-7028.

- *Four Keys to Classroom Testing,* audiovisual. This is an audiovisual instructional package that covers planning, constructing, assembling, and scoring teacher-made tests. It is well organized and can be used as the basis of a course, several class meetings, or independent or small group work. The package contains a guide for each of the four major sections, and also includes transparency masters, film strips, and accompanying audiocassettes. Available through the Educational Testing Service, Princeton, NJ.

Test Questions

Test Questions 13.1–13.119

Study Guide

Assign Chapter 13 of the *Study Guide.*

14
Using Standardized Test Data

Chapter Objectives

1. General Objective

Judges the utility of standardized tests (pp. 520–530).

SPECIFIC BEHAVIORS
1.01 Argues the necessity of understanding standardized test results.
1.02 Contrasts the purposes of norm-referenced and criterion-referenced evaluation.
1.03 Explains the importance of a norm group.
1.04 Justifies the assumption underlying the normal distribution.
1.05 Compares achievement, aptitude, and diagnostic standardized tests.

2. General Objective

Understands the properties of distributions of test scores (pp. 530–541).

SPECIFIC BEHAVIORS
2.01 Identifies a distribution.
2.02 Explains the property of central tendency.
2.03 Explains the property of dispersion.
2.04 Interprets the mean of a distribution.
2.05 Interprets the median of a distribution.
2.06 Interprets the mode of a distribution.
2.07 Interprets the range of a distribution.
2.08 Defends the conceptual definition of a standard deviation.
2.09 Interprets the standard deviation of a distribution.
2.10 Explains the standard deviation as a ruler applied to the normal distribution.

3. General Objective

Uses standardized scores to make evaluative judgments (pp. 541–548).

SPECIFIC BEHAVIORS
3.01 Interprets Z scores.
3.02 Interprets IQ scores.
3.03 Interprets percentile ranks.
3.04 Interprets T scores.
3.05 Interprets equivalence scores.

4. General Objective

Understands concerns for the use and the future of standardized testing (pp. 548–550).

SPECIFIC BEHAVIORS
4.01 Explains how the assumption that a test measures the same characteristics of all examinees can be interpreted as test bias.
4.02 Explains differential prediction as a form of test bias.
4.03 Explains how selection criteria can contribute to test bias.
4.04 Explains conditions of administration as contributing to test bias.
4.05 Relates the characteristics of standardized testing to test anxiety.
4.06 Infers how test bias influences reliability and validity.

5. General Objective

Recognizes the practical implications of trends in standardized testing (pp. 550–555).

SPECIFIC BEHAVIORS
5.01 Identifies the issues that influence the use of scores on minimum competency tests.
5.02 Infers the problems associated with measurement-driven instruction.
5.03 Identifies the conditions under which measurement-driven instruction can be beneficial.
5.04 Illustrates efforts to overcome the problems associated with measurement-driven instruction.
5.05 Identifies the implications of computerized adaptive testing.
5.06 Infers the relationship between standardized testing and labels.

Focus Questions

- Why do educators need standardized test results?
- Why is there so much negative public opinion concerning testing?
- What is a norm group and how does it influence standardized test results?
- What is the basis of all standardized test scores?
- How should teachers interpret standardized test scores for themselves, for students, and for parents?
- How should legitimate concerns over standardized tests govern their use?
- What form will standardized testing take in the near future?

Chapter Outline

INTRODUCTION: PROFESSIONAL JUDGMENTS

TEACHER CHRONICLE 14.1: TEST ANXIETY

NORM-REFERENCED AND CRITERION-REFERENCED MEASUREMENT

TYPES OF STANDARDIZED TESTS
  Achievement Tests
  Aptitude Tests
  Diagnostic Tests
  Comparing People and Numbers
  Principles in Practice 14.1

TEACHER CHRONICLE 14.2: STATISTICS?!?

STANDARDIZED TEST SCORES
  Properties of Distributions
    Measures of Central Tendency
      Mode
      Median
      Mean
    Measures of Dispersion
      Standard Deviation
  The Normal Distribution
    Standard Deviation and the Normal Distribution
    Z Scores
    IQ Scores
    Percentile Rank
    Deriving Standardized Scores
    Stanine Scores
    Equivalent Scores
  Principles in Practice 14.2

TEACHER CHRONICLE 14.3: SETTLING THE SCORE

ISSUES IN STANDARDIZED TESTING
  Test Bias
    Bias and Anxiety

Minimum Competency Testing
  Measurement-driven Instruction
Computerized Adaptive Testing
Principles in Practice 14.3

CONCLUSION

Chapter Summary

Introduction: Professional Judgments

- Teachers are required to make professional judgments. Some of the information on which judgments that are critical to students' futures are made comes from standardized tests.

Norm-referenced and Criterion-referenced Measurement

- Tests are forms of measurement. All measurement is based on comparison. Norm-referenced tests compare students with other students who took the same test (fellow members of the norm group). Criterion-referenced tests compare students' performances to a set of external criteria.

Types of Standardized Tests

- Standardized tests are tests that are administered to and norm-referenced on a large number of people. The scores from standardized tests are based on the performances of the people who took the test. The results of standardized tests can be used for several different purposes.
- Achievement tests are standardized tests designed to measure what students have learned.
- Aptitude tests are standardized tests designed to measure students' potential or aptitude. An aptitude test may measure potential narrowly—as in the case of a specific job, or broadly—as in the case of general academic potential.
- Tests designed to measure specific strengths and weaknesses for the purpose of making decisions about a student's learning program are called diagnostic tests.
- Standardized test results are numerical descriptions of a student's performance. It is important to keep in mind that the measurement of a student's performance is not the student—tests indicate, but do not define, what a student might accomplish.

Standardized Test Scores

- Standardized test scores are numerical comparisons of students' performances on a standardized test. The scores are based on statistics that describe the distribution of test scores.
- All distribution of test scores have two basic proper-

ties. *Central tendency* indicates where the middle of a distribution of a score is. A distribution's *dispersion* refers to how similar or different the scores are from one another.

- The normal distribution is a theoretical distribution that accurately describes many of the characteristics important to educators. It is the basis for many standardized test scores.

Issues in Standardized Testing

- Test bias occurs when a group of students is placed at a disadvantage when a test is administered, scored, or interpreted. Possible test bias must be considered when using the results of standardized tests to make decisions about students.
- Minimum competency tests are used to certify students in some way. A test that must be taken and passed in order to graduate from high school is one example of a minimum competency test. A danger to guard against with minimum competency tests is the possibility that these "high-stakes" tests may drive instruction.
- Computerized adaptive testing requires the use of sophisticated computer programs that present test items based on the abilities and skills of the test-taker. By tailoring test questions to the ability of a student, new and perhaps more useful evaluative information can be gained.

Key Terms

criterion-referenced	range
norm-referenced	standard deviation
standardized tests	Z score
achievement tests	percentile rank
aptitude tests	T score
diagnostic tests	stanine
central tendency	test bias
dispersion	measurement-driven instruction
mode	curriculum-based assessment
median	computerized adaptive testing
mean	

Teacher Chronicle Summaries

Teacher Chronicle 14.1: Test Anxiety (p. 523)

A teacher questions the importance of the results of a standardized IQ test concerning a student in her class, a student with a below average IQ on the test, but who is performing above average in class.

Teacher Chronicle 14.2: Statistics ?!? (p. 530)

A teacher recalls a disastrous parent–teacher conference when she failed to adequately explain standardized test scores.

Teacher Chronicle 14.3: Settling the Score (pp. 547–548)

While meeting with the principal, a teacher goes over recent math test scores used in placing students in ability groups. The teacher has a concern about one student, Heidi, who she feels would not benefit from the fast-track math class although Heidi's test scores would place her in that class.

Possible Answers to Principles in Practice

Principles in Practice 14.1

1. How might the teacher help Carrie's mother focus on Carrie's achievement in the classroom?

The teacher should explain the difference between criterion-referenced judgments and norm-referenced judgments. Carrie's achievement in the classroom documents the work Carrie has done in the class, not how she compares with other students from other schools.

2. Why does the mother place more importance on the standardized test results than the teacher?

Standardized tests are usually high-stakes tests. The mother knows that such tests are competitions. The teacher is more concerned with the progress Carrie makes in class. Because standardized tests may or may not reflect the work Carrie has done in class, the teacher places less emphasis on standardized test results.

3. How will you "balance" the classroom achievement and standardized test results of your students?

The students' answers to the question should indicate that they understand the difference between criterion-referenced and norm-referenced tests. Furthermore, their answers should reflect an understanding that the classroom achievement data and standardized achievement data are, properly, used for different kinds of judgments.

Principles in Practice 14.2

1. How should the teacher have used norm group information in the conference with Mr. Longley?

The teacher should have explained that information about the norm group identifies the students with whom Dan was being compared.

2. How do stanines differ from grade equivalent scores?

Stanines represent a range or band of scores. Grade equivalent scores do not connote a range. Because stanines represent relatively large groups within a distribution, relatively small differences between students are not perceived as significant.

3. How will you communicate standardized test results without giving statistics lessons to parents?

The students' answers here should focus on what norm-referenced measurement is, what a norm group means, and how standardized test scores communicate something different than class grades. Parents should be made aware of what tests are used for.

Principles in Practice 14.3

1. In what sense did the principal's "stanine score" criterion disadvantage Heidi?

Using an overall math score did not take into account the possibility that within the area of math, a student's abilities might vary considerably. In Heidi's case, she attained a high stanine in computation through sheer hard work. Her weakness was in math reasoning which would have put her at a disadvantage if she had been placed in advanced math.

2. How did the achievement test help in making the placement decision concerning Heidi?

Once the teacher and principal sat down to analyze Heidi's performance on the achievement test, they were able to see the discrepancy between her computation skills and her reasoning skills. The standardized test provided evidence of strength and of weakness.

3. How might computerized adaptive testing aid placement decisions such as the one made in Teacher Chronicle 14.3?

Because computerized adaptive testing accounts for the ability level of students, strengths and weaknesses can be more effectively probed by the test. If tests are being used for placement decisions, then the more complete the tests are, the more information would be available to make a decision.

CNN Connection to Issues in Educational Psychology

What are the criteria that define a good teacher, and who decides whether individual teachers are meeting them? At the heart of the current national concern about education are the educators themselves—teachers. The video segment explores these questions and takes an in-depth look at teachers in action.

Activities and Exercises

In-Class Activities

1. Using the quiz show format described under In-Class Activities in Chapter 5 of this Instructor's Section, have students develop review questions from the key terms list at the end of the chapter. If desired, the questions could include some sample

distributions so that contestants could be asked to calculate descriptive statistics.

2. Based on whatever instructional model they choose, have students develop a minilesson designed to reduce test anxiety. Have the students present them to each other in small groups. Following the minilessons, have the groups critique the lessons based on the discussion in the chapter.

Teacher Interviews

Have students interview teachers regarding the nature of professional judgments and the degree of public scrutiny that accompanies such judgments.

Have students interview teachers regarding their views on the growing professionalism in teaching, asking their opinions of the efforts of the National Board for Professional Teaching Standards and the opportunity teachers will have to become board certified.

Have each student interview a teacher regarding the interpretation of standardized test results during parent–teacher conferences.

Have each student interview a teacher regarding the advantages of reporting standardized test scores as bands or ranges or scores during parent–teacher conferences.

Have students interview teachers concerning the interpretation of grade equivalent scores, asking them to share their experiences with these scores.

Have students interview teachers concerning their experiences with test bias.

Have each student interview a teacher regarding political pressure and test performance, asking the teacher to contrast these concerns with Popham's criteria.

Have each student discuss with a practicing teacher how one balances the need for norm-referenced evaluation and the need to understand students as individuals.

Field Observations

Have students interview teachers and administrators in a school district, gathering their perceptions of how standardized achievement tests are used in the district.

Have students contact the central office of a school district and arrange to interview administrators concerning the use of individual, school, and districtwide profiles based on standardized test results.

Have students check with the local school district concerning their policy on minimum competency tests.

Journal Entries

Imagine that you were a teacher in the 1940s. Also imagine that your principal informed you that you would be grading on the curve. Your instructions from the principal included the following: "You will have exactly the same number of A's and

F's, the same number of *B*'s and *D*'s, 50 percent of your class will receive the grade *C*."

Reflect on the assumptions you would have had to make in order to carry out your principal's instructions.

Have students reflect on the three statistics that are indexes of central tendency, noting the conditions under which each index might be useful for a teacher.

Have students reflect on why the mean is the best index to use as a reference point.

Have students reflect on why is it possible to convert from IQ scores to percentile ranks.

Have students reflect on their experiences of anxiety in relation to standardized tests considering how these experiences will help them counsel future students who experience test anxiety.

Have students reflect on computerized adaptive testing and the kinds of information it might supply them in the future, considering how they will use computerized adaptive testing for instructional planning and for evaluation.

Discussion Topics (based on Lecture Notes)

As a way of introducing aptitude tests, ask students to share their stereotypes of aptitude tests.

Have students create their own standardized score by supplying a definition of a derived score.

Have students form small groups. Have them imagine that they have been placed on a task force by a school district and charged with generating a plan for implementing computer-based testing. Ask each group to generate a list of five recommendations.

Application Scenarios

Present the following scenarios to students:

- You recommend Ann for the fourth-grade gifted and talented science program. The coordinator of the program turns down Ann, arguing that her IQ scores and Standardized Achievement Test scores in science are just below the cut-off for entry. You know that Ann is quite interested in science and is motivated to do well. What should you do? Should you seek to get her into the program, or should you acquiesce to the coordinator, who insists that placing children in a program where they do not belong does more harm than good?

- You have several children with mild learning disabilities in your third-grade classroom, and they have been struggling to keep up all year. Your principal informs you that you can purchase two new computers and a limited amount of software for second semester. What can you do to help your learning disabled students? Can you justify helping them exclusively, when the rest of the class could benefit from new software as well? Is there a compromise that you can reach?

Chapter 15 Casebook Previews

See I Am Leo.

See Responsibility Education.

See Please Sign This Contract.

See Bringing the Real World into the Classroom.

See Writers' Tea.

Teaching Anecdotes

Tell your students the story of the school that had fallen below the city and state average on spelling as measured by a standardized test. At a faculty meeting, the reading specialist suggested that one of the school's goals for the following year would be to concentrate on spelling.

Ask your students if such a concentration will influence future test results. (See p. 526.)

Tell your students about the sixth-grade student who performed poorly on written tests but was outstanding in large and small group discussions. His teacher requested that the school psychologist administer a diagnostic test, which showed that the student was dyslexic.

Ask your students why this learning problem was not diagnosed earlier and how the test result might be used to improve the student's performance on written tests. (See p. 528.)

Tell your students about the junior high social studies curriculum committee charged with revising the district's social studies program. When several members of the committee complained that elementary students coming to the junior high were poorly prepared, it was brought to their attention that the district's sixth graders performed two years above grade level on their most recent standardized tests. The committee members scoffed and replied, "But they don't know what we want them to know before coming to seventh grade."

Ask your students where the problem might lie: in the test, in the elementary social studies curriculum, or in a mismatch between the elementary and the junior high curricula. (See p. 544.)

Tell your students about the teacher who had had two poor evaluations and was scheduled for a third evaluation. In each previous evaluation, the principal had cited the poor performance of the teacher's class on standardized tests as a major problem that had to be corrected. The teacher, determined to keep his job, decided to "teach to the test" the entire year. He geared his instruction to the material he thought would most likely be on the test.

Ask your students how professional this action was and if such test-driven instruction might actually improve student performance on tests or their ability to learn. (See p. 549.)

Tell your students about the first-grade student who had just begun to read. However, when she took a standardized reading test, she scored at a level that indicated that she needed remedial instruction. Her teacher, realizing the difference between her classroom performance and the test results, had her retested two months later. The results showed a dramatic gain in reading skill.

Ask your students what this story might reveal about testing young children. Ask them how a teacher's classroom evaluations might be taken into account in interpreting test results. (See p. 552.)

Transparencies

For transparencies to use with this chapter, see the Transparency Guides on page 535 and page 540.

Teaching Resources

Suggested Readings

Archibald, D., & Newman, F. (1988). *Beyond standardized testing: Authentic academic achievement in the secondary school.* Reston, VA: NASSP.

Cole, N. S. (1981). Bias in testing. *American Psychologist, 36,* 1067–1077.

Ebel, R. L., & Frisbie, D. A. (1991). *Essentials of educational measurement.* Needham Heights, MA: Allyn & Bacon.

Green, B. F. (1981). A primer of testing. *American Psychologist, 36,* 1001–1011.

Gronlund, N. E., & Linn, R. L. (1990). *Measurement and evaluation in teaching* (6th ed.). New York: Macmillan.

Films, Videocassettes, Audiocassettes

- *Making Sense Out of Standardized Test Scores,* video, 30 min. Interpretation of test scores that students earn on standardized tests: percentiles, grade-equivalents, and scale scores.
- *Norm-Referenced Tests: Uses and Misuses,* video, 30 min. Origins and nature of norm-referenced standardized achievement tests are discussed. Inappropriate uses of tests and how that can lead to unsound educational decisions are shown.
- *Criterion-Referenced Measurement: Today's Alternative to Traditional Testing,* video, 30 min. Viewers learn what they are, how they are constructed, and how they are used.

These three videos are available through IOX, 5420 McConnel Avenue, Los Angeles, CA 90066-7028.

Test Questions

Test Questions 14.1–14.104

Study Guide

Assign Chapter 14 of the *Study Guide.*

15

Casebook of Successful Teaching

Films, Videocassettes, Audiocassettes

- *Failures Before Kindergarten*, 28 min., color. There is intense debate going on over the screening of preschool children to determine whether they are ready for admission to kindergarten. This specially adapted Phil Donahue program discusses the pros and cons of assessing the educational readiness of such young children. Are some children being stigmatized as failures before they even start school? What are the criteria for evaluating a child's readiness for kindergarten? Panelists on the program include Sue Bredekamp, director of the National Association for the Education of Young Children and Madeline Duncan, a teacher who kept back an entire first-grade class. CE-2169.

- *The First Years: What to Expect*, video, 19 min., color. This video examines the critical parent–child relationship in the first five years; the effects in adolescence of traits learned in early childhood and the relationship between emotions and cognitive development.

- *The Developing Child: The Crucial Early Years*, video, 26 min., color. This program deals with ways in which mental growth can be assisted in normal infants and young children. As infants learn to control their environment, they are learning to learn—a task in which parents can provide help by encouraging learning without creating stressful conditioning.

- *Gifted Adolescents and Suicide*, video, 26 min. A Phil Donahue program about intelligent, accomplished, but emotionally immature, isolated, and vulnerable adolescents. Points out how to recognize pressures on gifted teens.

- *Telling Teens About Sex*, 28 min., color. Do today's teenagers know all about sex? Phil Donahue's audience of teenagers tells a panel of sex educators what they really know and what they would like to know. CC-1234.

- *Telling Teens About AIDS*, 52 min., color. Helping teachers and parents to confront the issue of AIDS with respect to their own children and speaking directly to teenagers, this program shows, without moralizing, how one seemingly innocent liaison can lead to death. Former NBA star Julius Erving is the host. CC-1688.

- *Preventing Teen Pregnancy*, 28 min., color. This program recommends sex education beginning in the preteens, sexual abstinence by teenagers, and education about contraceptives. CC-1438.

These seven productions are available through Films for the Humanities and Sciences, Inc., P.O. Box 2052, Princeton, NJ 08543.

- *Early Childhood Education: Classroom Management-Curriculum Organization*. See an exceptional early childhood classroom in action. A forty-minute video brings you the sights and sounds of a highly individualized approach to teaching K–1 children. Available through Association for Supervision and Curriculum Development, 125 North West Street, Alexandria, VA 22314-2798. Or call (703) 549-9110.

- *The Skillstreaming Video: How to Teach Students Prosocial Skills*, video, 26 min., color. Illustrates an innovative approach for teaching students the skills they need for coping with typical social and personal problems. Available through Research Press, Box 3177, Department K, Champaign, IL 61821. Or call (217) 352-3273.

Transparency Guide

Guide to *Teacher Magazine Reader*

In an effort to provide relevant, up-to-the-minute information on issues relating to education, Allyn & Bacon is piloting a special supplement in conjunction with *Teacher Magazine*—an exclusive selection of previously published articles. A copy of this supplement, *Teacher Magazine Reader: Focus on Teacher Education*, is packaged with every new copy of *Educational Psychology and Classroom Practice: A Partnership* ordered from Allyn & Bacon, and your students will receive their free readers when they purchase new texts from their bookstores. Your Allyn & Bacon representative will be happy to answer any questions you may have about this special limited offer.

This issue of *Teacher Magazine Reader* contains four articles we hope you and your students will enjoy. A summary of each article follows, along with suggestions for appropriate tie-ins to *Educational Psychology and Classroom Practice: A Partnership*.

FRIENDLY PERSUASION

Correspondence between a prospective teacher, Clare Fox; and her mentor teacher, Margaret Metzger, beginning in 1984 to the present is featured in this article.

The excerpted letters trace Clare's struggles in deciding to teach, adjusting to her first teaching position, leaving teaching after two years, and then—largely through Metzger's intervention—returning to teaching with renewed vision and commitment. As Clare's inspiring mentor, Metzger supplies candid and heartfelt observations of the teacher's mission in the face of the realities of teaching.

We suggest that you have your students read this article in conjunction with Chapter 1, Reflection and Teaching; and Chapter 15, Casebook of Successful Teaching.

THE *ABC*S OF CARING

This article presents a report on the success of a child development experiment in six San Ramon Valley, California, elementary schools that replaced traditional classroom approaches with methods designed to teach children the social values and skills needed for cooperative learning, group responsibility, and ethical problem solving.

The article explains how classroom organization, classroom management techniques, curriculum changes, and teaching strategies in this experiment foster group cooperation, democratic decision making, care and concern for others, and student responsibility for the quality of classroom life. An interclass buddy system, cross-age teaming, moral orientation modeling, special teacher training, and a vision of the future are among the elements that led to this experiment's success.

We recommend that you have your students read this article in conjunction with Chapter 3, Personal and Interpersonal Growth; Chapter 8, Motivations; Chapter 9, Outcome Decisions; and Chapter 12, Classroom Management, Discipline, and Communication.

BATTLE OVER MULTICULTURAL EDUCATION

A news summary from *Education Week* on controversies surrounding the development of multicultural curricula and teaching approaches is examined in this article.

Quoting experts, reformers, and critics, this article reviews the underlying assumptions and beliefs of both mainstream and multicultural approaches. This comparison is supported by examples from the growing bodies of criticism concerning both views. The article points out, for example, the racial and historical distortions often found in mainstream curricula, and also the inadequacies of the multicultural curricula that have been developed to date. The lack of agreement over the goals of multicultural education and the best way to implement them, the article concludes, points to a need for more study and greater understanding of this complex issue.

We suggest that you have your students read this article in conjunction with Chapter 4, Developmental Diversity; and Chapter 14, Using Standardized Test Data.

FROM STUDENT TO TEACHER

This article consists of a one-page list of riveting statistics about school systems, teachers, and the students they will teach.

This list includes data on at-risk students, racial/ethnic populations, enrollments at all grade levels, numbers of school districts, teacher preparation and job preferences, expenditures per pupil, and much more. Your students may be surprised to learn, for example, that there are 2.4 million public school teachers in the United States, that only 14 percent of beginning teachers plan to teach in culturally diverse schools, that only 12 percent of students are in bilingual education classes, or that 4 in 10 Native American students do not finish school.

The information on this list will be most useful to your students in conjunction with Chapter 1, Reflection and Teaching; Chapter 7, Models for Behavior; and Chapter 15, Casebook of Successful Teaching.

Educational Psychology and Classroom Practice: A Partnership

R. R. McCown
Duquesne University

Peter Roop
Appleton Area School District, Appleton, Wisconsin

Allyn and Bacon
Boston   London   Toronto   Sydney   Tokyo   Singapore

Series Editor: Sean Wakely
Executive Editor: Mylan Jaixen
Developmental Editors: Alicia Reilly and Carol L. Chernaik
Cover Administrator: Linda Dickinson
Composition Buyer: Linda Cox
Manufacturing Buyer: Megan Cochran
Editorial-Production Service: Proof Positive/Farrowlyne
  Associates, Inc.
Photo Researcher: Laurel Anderson/Photosynthesis
Cover Designer: Susan Slovinsky

McCown, R. R., 1952–
  Educational psychology and classroom practice :
  a partnership / R. R. McCown, Peter Roop.
    p. cm.
  Includes index.
  ISBN 0-205-13144-1
  1. Educational psychology.   2. Teaching.   I. Roop, Peter.
II. Title.
LB1051.M396   1992
370.15—dc20   91-37152
                                                   CIP

Copyright ©1992 by Allyn and Bacon
A division of Simon & Schuster, Inc.
160 Gould Street
Needham Heights, Massachusetts 02194

Printed in the United States of America

10 9 8 7 6 5 4 3 2 1   96 95 94 93 92 91

ISBN: 0-205-13144-1

Photo credits

1 p. 3: Mark Lunenberg/Picture Group, p. 4: Richard Hutchings/ Info Edit, p. 7: David Pratt/Positive Images, p. 11: Connie Roop, p. 13: Mary Kate Denny/PhotoEdit, p. 20: Lawrence Migdale/ Photo Researchers Inc., p. 22: Connie Roop, p. 34: Collections of the Library of Congress 2 p. 41: Jim Stratford/Black Star, p. 45: Bob Daemmrich Photography, p. 47: Margot Granitsas/Photo Researchers Inc., p. 59: Richard Palsey/Stock · Boston, p. 67: Tony Freeman/PhotoEdit, p. 75: Bob Daemmrich/Stock · Boston 3 p. 85: Tom Stack, p. 88: Bob Daemmrich Photography, p. 90: Elizabeth Crews/The Image Works, p. 91: Alan Carey/The Image Works p. 93: Ted Cordingley, p. 108: Jerry Howard/Positive Images, p. 113: Bob Daemmrich Photography, p. 114: John DeWaele/Stock · Boston, p. 115: Bob Daemmrich Photography 4 p. 129: Frank Pedrick/The Image Works, p. 132: Kevin Horan/Stock · Boston, p. 140: Mary Kate Denny/PhotoEdit, p. 145: Bachmann/The ImageWorks, p. 148: Tony Freeman/PhotoEdit, p. 153: Paul Conklin/ PhotoEdit 5 p. 171: Dag Sundberg/The Image Bank, p. 182: Doug Menuez/Stock · Boston, p. 185: Bob Daemmrich/The Image Works, p. 190: Dorfman, p. 200: Karen Kasmauski/Wheeler Pictures 6 p. 207: Michael G. Borum/The Image Bank, p. 212: Bob Daemmrich Photography, p. 214: Tony Freeman/PhotoEdit, p. 222: Tony Freeman/PhotoEdit, p. 224: Don Klumpp/The Image Bank, p. 232: Lawrence Migdale/Stock · Boston, p. 235: Paul Rezendes/Positive Images 7 p. 253: Bob Daemmrich Photography, p. 267: Richard Hutchings/Info Edit, p. 275: The Image Works, p. 281: John Ficara/Woodfin Camp & Associates 8 p. 287: Tony Freeman/PhotoEdit, p. 294: Charles Gupton/Stock · Boston, p. 300: Richard Hutchings/Info Edit, p. 306: Will and Deni MacIntyre, p. 312: Tony Freeman 9 p. 323: Tom Sobolik/Black Star, p. 328: Elizabeth Crews/The Image Works, p. 329: Matthew McVay/Stock · Boston, p. 341: Jerry Howard/Positive Images, p. 345: Michael Melford/The Image Bank, p. 348: Tony Freeman/ PhotoEdit, p. 350: Bob Daemmrich Photography 10 p. 357: Rick Friedman/Black Star, p. 358: Jeffrey W. Myers/Stock · Boston, p. 364: Peter Yates/Picture Group, p. 385: Brad Bower/Picture Group, p. 388: Jeff Reinking/Picture Group 11 p. 397: Kenneth Murray/Photo Researchers Inc., p. 406: Peter Menzel/Stock · Boston, p. 408: Frank Siteman/The Picture Cube, p. 411: Elizabeth Crews/The Image Works, p. 415: Wally McNamee/Woodfin Camp & Associates, p. 418: Bob Daemmrich Photography, p. 419: James Wilson/Woodfin Camp & Associates, p. 420: David Kennedy/ TexaStock 12 p. 439: Tony Freeman/PhotoEdit, p. 440: Michael Melford/The Image Bank, p. 444: Steve Dunwell/The Image Bank, p. 446: Cary Wolinsky/Stock · Boston, p. 449: Jerry Howard/ Positive Images, p. 458: Luis Castañeda/The Image Bank, p. 459: David Kennedy/TexaStock, p. 461: Don and Pat Valenti/f/Stop Pictures 13 p. 483: Frank Siteman, p. 486: Bob Daemmrich Photography, p. 489: Jerry Howard/Positive Images, p. 510: Bob Daemmrich Photography, p. 512: Jacques Chenet/Woodfin Camp & Associates 14 p. 521: Bob Daemmrich Photography, p. 524: Bob Daemmrich/Stock · Boston, p. 528: Mark Antman/The Image Works, p. 552: Janeart Ltd./The Image Bank 15 p. 559: Mel Digiagiacomo/The Image Bank, p. 562: Nancy Pierce/Black Star, p. 567: Richard Hutchings/Info Edit, p. 570: Alan Becker/The Image Bank, p. 573: Rhoda Sidney/PhotoEdit, p. 581: Walter Bibikow/The Image Bank

Contents

3   Personal and Interpersonal Growth   84

4 Developmental Diversity 128

5 Environment and Behavior 170

6 Cognition: Codes of Understanding 206

9 Outcome Decisions 322

10 Instructional Models 356

14   Using Standardized Test Data   520

15   Casebook of Successful Teaching

Preface

In the near future you will be facing your first class of students. Their learning, their behavior, and their development will be your responsibility. How will you ensure that each student maximizes his or her potential? How will you plan effective lessons? How will you handle discipline? How will you maintain your enthusiasm for teaching?

Our book, the result of a unique partnership between an educational psychologist and a classroom teacher, will help you answer these and other questions as you begin and continue your professional life as a teacher. Our collaboration joins two knowledge bases: the principles of educational psychology and the maxims of classroom practice. Lee Shulman calls ideas generated from formal, scientific theories and research *principles*. Ideas generated from practical classroom experience he calls *maxims*. In order to use the principles of educational psychology, it is imperative that you see how these principles are translated into action in real classrooms. The principles presented are based on the most relevant psychological theories and research. The maxims of classroom practice are based on the experiences and reflections of master teachers across North America. By uniting both perspectives in this book, we provide a firm base from which you can explore and develop creative classroom practice.

You have been much in our thoughts as we wrote this book. We have imagined you listening to a lecture on reinforcement and wondering, "How will I build self-confidence in my future students?" We have seen you discussing classroom management techniques and thinking, "How am I going to keep thirty students interested in my teaching?" We have thought about you observing adolescents at the mall and wondering, "Will they like me?" We have imagined you watching high schoolers interact at a fast-food restaurant and thinking, "If I were their teacher, would they respect me?"

Your doubts, your questions, your recollections are fundamental to learning educational psychology. Bring your memories of former teachers, your feelings as an elementary and secondary student, your beliefs about the tenets of good teaching to your reading of this book. Add what you know and believe to what we have written.

You are reading this book because you anticipate teaching your own students someday. The goals you set are the goals you hope they will attain. You can become a partner in their learning, but it is they who must master the subject matter. Our goal in writing this book is to make a difference in your teaching career just as you want to make a difference in the lives of the students you will teach.

Becoming a teacher is no easy task. The transformation from student to teacher occurs as you integrate classroom experience with your knowledge of how students learn and behave.

In this book we have tried to teach, but it is difficult to teach you without seeing your face. Because we can't interact directly with you, our words will be a resource, nothing more. The teaching will come from your instructor. The learning will come from you. We hope our book facilitates both.

FEATURES OF THE BOOK

This book and its features are designed to help you learn and use what you will learn in your teaching career. Part I, Chapter 1, focuses on the *Teacher as Learner*. Effective teachers are not those who reach a level of mastery and are content to stay at that level for the remainder of their careers. A master teacher is one who continually seeks new ideas, tests them in the classroom, and reflects on the results in order to improve their practice. Chapter 1 features the "Diary of a Day." It is an account of decisions, actions, and reflections made by one of the coauthors while teaching his students on St. Patrick's Day, 1989. It is a story of real teaching and, as such, provides a practical context for the remainder of the book.

Part II, Chapters 2–8, describes *Students as Learners*. Chapters 2, 3, and 4 address the developmental characteristics of students. Chapters 5, 6, 7, and 8 describe the ways in which students learn and how they are motivated to learn. Part III, Chapters 9–14, describes the *Teacher as Decision-Maker*. Chapters 9 and 10 focus on planning decisions. Chapters 11 and 12 address the tactical decisions required for instruction and for classroom management. Chapters 13 and 14 examine evaluative decisions.

Part IV, Chapter 15, refers to the *Teacher as Researcher* and presents the "Casebook of Successful Teaching"—real cases of teaching in which master teachers identify problems, test possible solutions, and reflect on the results of their "experiments." The Casebook includes accounts written by teachers from across the country and across grade levels.

Part I (Chapter 1) and Part IV (Chapter 15) differ in organization from Parts II and III (Chapters 2–14). In each of the latter chapters the following features are provided:

- A chapter opening that consists of the **Focus Questions, Chapter Outline,** and **Chapter Overview.** The Focus Questions help orient you to the conceptual and applied material described in the chapter. These questions, and the Chapter Outline and Chapter Overview, build expectations for what is to come.
- Another feature of these chapters is the **Teacher Chronicles,** true stories from the lives of teachers. Teacher Chronicles provide a practical context for the discussion of the principles of educational psychology that follows. After the principles are examined, another feature, **Principles in Practice,** appears. This feature identifies key principles of educational psychology and applies them to the events described in the preceding Teacher Chronicle.
- Each chapter in Parts II and III also contains a **Running Glossary of Key Terms** in the chapter's margins; a news feature related to the

subject matter of the chapter, **Issues in Educational Psychology;** and a commentary by a successful teacher called **Profiles in Successful Practice.**

- At the end of each chapter, a **Chapter Summary** briefly recounts important concepts, a page-referenced list of **Key Terms** helps you locate the concepts that appear in the chapter, and a **Suggested Readings** list offers you access to supplemental material. Additionally, a feature called **Reflections: Building Your Theory of Teaching** presents opportunities to reflect on teaching situations taken from real classrooms and to formulate ideas about the way in which you might deal with similar situations.

AN INVITATION

Teaching is a continual search for improvement. Our search for improving this teaching tool in future editions includes seeking new accounts of classroom practice for our **Casebook of Successful Teaching.** As you enter the profession, we invite you to contribute cases based on your classroom experiences that may help those who will follow you into the profession. Send cases or ideas for teacher chronicles to

McCown & Roop: A Partnership
Allyn and Bacon, Publishers
160 Gould Street
Needham Heights, MA 02194

In addition to case or chronicle material, we would especially appreciate receiving any comments that might help us improve the text in its next edition. The enhancement of the teaching profession requires that its members actively participate in the preparation of their future colleagues.

ACKNOWLEDGMENTS

There is no question about where to begin the pleasurable task of thanking those who contributed to this book. Our families deserve top billing. The McCowns—Nona, Christopher, and Sara—and the Roops—Connie, Sterling, and Heidi—deserve more thanks than we can express here. They listened to us, shared ideas, prodded, cajoled, understood, and kept things in perspective when they threatened to get out of whack. Without their love, their spirits, and their gifts of time, these words would not have made it into print.

Special thanks go to the classroom teachers and educational psychologists who served as our advisory editors: Marcy Driscoll, Florida State University; Mark Grabe, University of North Dakota; Pamela Maniet-Bellermann, Columbia Grammar and Preparatory School, New York, New York; Raymond Miller, University of Oklahoma; Sarah Peterson, Northern Illinois University; Connie Roop, Appleton Area School District (Wisconsin); Dorothy Sawyer, Gladstone School District (Oregon); and Neil Schwartz, California State University-Chico. Their contributions of literature reviews, cases, essays, and reactions to early outlines and drafts proved invaluable. Thanks also to Mark Resetar of Regent University for his review of the development literature.

The following educators shared not only their enthusiasm for teaching, but their commitment to bringing new teachers into the profession by writing cases/profiles based on their teaching experiences. Their voices throughout the book ring true because they know students, value teaching, and continually challenge themselves to develop professionally: Scott Niquette, Sue Misheff, Dianne Bauman, Nancy Gorrell, Linda Wygoda, Nanci Maes, Jean Sunde Peterson, Faye McCollum, William D. Smyth, Carol Jago, Barbara Vinson, Patricia Woodward, Gerald Walker, Betsy Young, Charles Bowen, Paula Williams, Sandy Wiley, and Terri Fields.

Peter's friends and colleagues over the past ten years—Charlie Lynch, Barb Walstrom, Donna Van Airsdale, Jackie Booher, Janet Schuda, Jean Wallace, and Judy DeShaney, all of Appleton—deserve special recognition for sharing their years of insight into teaching and helping him grow as a professional. Peter thanks especially Tom Loveall, his principal, the person who brought him into education and supported, understood, and had faith in his teaching.

The following educators, in late night talks and compelling conversations, contributed to this book in ways that they will never know, but that are appreciated tremendously: Martha Hemwall, Gary Finman, Martha Turner, Nan Luedtke, John Morgans, Bob Goldsmith, Tony Manna, Joan Glazer, Jill May, Richard Van Dongen, Katy Gould-Anderson, Laura Burrow, and Larry Madrigal.

Students, too numerous to mention individually here, also aided in the development of this book. We thank the 1988–1989 third and fourth graders at McKinley School who are the real stars of Chapter 1. Peter Roop's 1989–1990 first-grade class deserves special mention, for they truly taught him more about teaching than he ever knew before. Thanks also to Peter's other students at McKinley who have been his tireless teachers for over a decade. Their parents, too, deserve thanks for their active participation in their children's schooling and support for Peter's teaching.

We thank the two hundred aspiring teachers at Duquesne University—and instructors Dan Moore and Ann Derewicz—who used earlier drafts of the book and who offered sound criticism of the text. Their enthusiasm, their concerns, and their curiosity not only fed Rick's joy in teaching, but gave us a clearer image of our audience. We thank particularly Judy Zaharko, Ellen Cavanaugh, and Deborah D'Amico. Catherine Perich, Susan Simcik, and Arthur Victor, Jr., worked tirelessly to help secure case material.

We also say thanks to Rick's colleagues in the School of Education at Duquesne who offered advice when asked, references and books when sought, and a kind word when needed. They suffered through his obsessive periods, which were frequent and long lasting, with understanding and good humor. They are not only good colleagues, they are friends. A special thanks to those who read and argued and listened patiently, even when they had heard more than they ever wanted to hear: Derek Whordley, Bill Casile, Peg Ford, Bill Barone, Susan Munson, and Kathy Gosnell; and to Joe Maola and Frank Ribich for taking up the slack. We acknowledge also the support given this project by the administration of the School of Education and the university, particularly the sabbatical year awarded to Rick, without which the first draft of the book would not have been completed.

We are grateful to the family and friends who not only supported our efforts in a hundred other ways, but gave us meals, phones, use of a computer, a postal drop, or a quiet place to work during crucial periods in the book's development: Marge and Bob Betzer, Dorothy Roop Hart, Cam and John Maurice, Maxine and Terry McCown, Bonnie and Murray D. Nelson, and Jane and Brad Nelson. Thanks to Murray B. Nelson for identifying master teachers. And to Mike McGregor for engaging us in an informed discussion of teaching using the case method, great pizza, and a spirited singing of the old songs.

Writing the manuscript was the most rewarding part of the work; the innumerable tasks required to turn a manuscript into a book are not always so enjoyable. We are indebted to many people who undertook those tasks. For their word processing, we thank Joanne Gunn, Nancy Hartwig, and Nancy Provil; for word processing and permissions, Carol Brooks; for permissions, Elizabeth Ford Burkhart; for outline coordination, Bernie Elk; for permissions and yeoman's work on the references, Nancy J. Kress. Special thanks to our colleagues Tom Hancock for writing evaluation items, and to Gary Shank, who wrote the *Study Guide,* contributed thoughts and useful criticism, and lent his spirit to this enterprise.

We are grateful to those who provided developmental reviews of earlier versions of the manuscript:

Fintan Kavanagh
Marywood College

Janice Fauske
Weber State College

David S. Hill
Keene State College

Richard Purnell
University of Rhode Island

Richard Craig
Towson State University

Kay Alderman
University of Akron

Raymond B. Miller
University of Oklahoma

Barry J. Wilson
University of Northern Iowa

Peter R. Denner
Idaho State University

Michelle Comeaux
Gustavus Adolphus College

Mark Grabe
University of North Dakota

Neil H. Schwartz
California State University-Chico

Sarah Peterson
Northern Illinois University

Marcy Driscoll
Florida State University

Their hard work made us work harder and certainly better than we would have without it.

The people of Allyn and Bacon have made their house our house. Thanks to Leslie Kroft Wardrop for directing us to the door; to Ray Short for opening that door and making us feel welcome; to Beth Brooks for making us feel comfortable in a new place; to Bill Barke for showing us his favorite baseball hat and, along with Mylan Jaixen, for arranging our stay. Our stay has been filled with activity thanks to the hard work of Sean Wakely, Alicia Reilly, and Carol Chernaik. But at the Allyn and Bacon house, the people don't just tell you where to go, they keep you company along the journey. It's good company to keep.

Final notes of thanks from Peter to the Appleton Area School District who saw his potential as an educator and helped him develop it, and to Ken

Sager, whose questions opened Peter's eyes to teaching. A final note from Rick to Don Cunningham (whose marginalia were more instructive than the writing they addressed, and who unscrewed our heads many times in hopes that we might get them back on the right way): *Erin Go Bragh.*

We end with a deep bow to the Children of Goat Skin; they know who they are and that they are members of the partnership.

Educational Psychology and Classroom Practice: A Partnership

1

Reflection and Teaching

Chapter Overview

A master teacher is one who has experiences and learns from them. Through reflection each turns experience into expertise. This chapter examines what master teachers learn and shows how one master teacher uses his knowledge in the classroom. Novice teachers can use the experience of masters as a source of teaching ideas. Another source of ideas is the knowledge base called educational psychology. The chapter discusses how the classroom experiences of master teachers and the principles of educational psychology can be used by aspiring teachers as they prepare to enter the profession. ■

teaching The practice or
profession of a teacher.

Chap. Obj. 1
Test Ques. 1.1–1.10

Focus Questions: What is a theory;
how does an *intuitive* theory differ
from a *scientific* theory? What are the
differences between novice and expert
teachers?

INTRODUCTION: EXPERT THEORIES

This book is organized around the scientific theories and research that make up educational psychology. However, make no mistake, this is a book about teaching.

Teaching—the practice or profession of a teacher—is a complicated business. There are students of every description to reach. There are prescribed curricula to deliver, tests to administer and interpret, disciplinary problems to solve, and administrative plans to implement. There are students, parents, principals, colleagues, and school boards to please. Then there is you, the teacher. Statistics suggest that almost 50 percent of the people enrolled in education classes will not be teaching in five years.

The desire to teach, to make a difference in the lives of students, is a noble one, but desire alone is not a sufficient foundation on which to build a teaching career. In order to teach well, to develop as a professional, you must build an understanding of teaching, your own teaching. You must build a personal theory of teaching.

The word *theory* brings to mind laboratories, test tubes, white coats, and the instruments of precise measurement and rigorous control, the paraphernalia of the formal sciences. Scientific theories describe, explain, and predict phenomena. They are jargon-laden and formal, accessible only to those who share the theorist's training and vocabulary. When we think of "scientific theories" we think of Einstein, Skinner, Piaget.

The teacher who strives to be a successful professional will develop a personal theory of teaching that blends classroom experience with educational psychology.

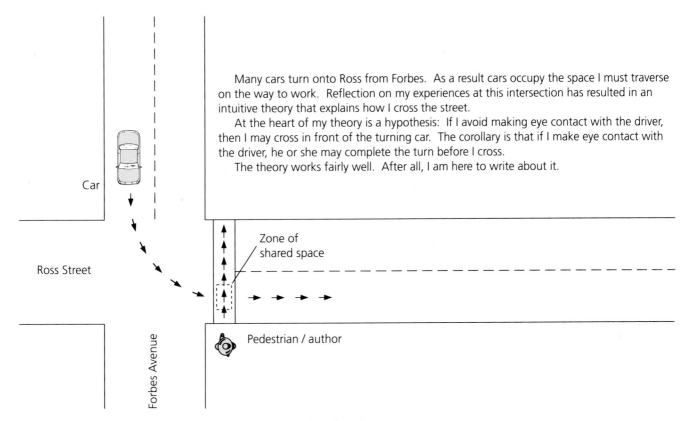

Many cars turn onto Ross from Forbes. As a result cars occupy the space I must traverse on the way to work. Reflection on my experiences at this intersection has resulted in an intuitive theory that explains how I cross the street.

At the heart of my theory is a hypothesis: If I avoid making eye contact with the driver, then I may cross in front of the turning car. The corollary is that if I make eye contact with the driver, he or she may complete the turn before I cross.

The theory works fairly well. After all, I am here to write about it.

Car

Ross Street

Forbes Avenue

Zone of
shared space

Pedestrian / author

■ **Figure 1–1** *The Intersection of Ross Street and Forbes Avenue*

However, because **theory** *can* be defined as a set of concepts and ideas that describes, explains, and predicts a phenomenon, it is incorrect to say that Einstein and Piaget are the only theorists. Everyone has theories. These less formal, or "intuitive," theories come out of one's practical experience. Intuitive theories are understandings that people have of everyday events, including the clinical practice of teaching. Without them it would be impossible to get through the day.

Intuitive theories do not come from scientifically controlled experiments but from practical experience—with all the constraints, limitations, and "contaminating" factors that operate in real-life situations. Like scientific theories, intuitive theories afford description, explanation, and prediction. With experience, our descriptions become more complete, our explanations more plausible, and our predictions more accurate. (For example, consider the daily phenomenon of crossing the street. Figure 1–1 presents McCown's intuitive theory of crossing a street in downtown Pittsburgh.)

Teachers, whether they are crusty veterans or shiny neophytes, use intuitive theories to instruct. A veteran's theory may more adequately describe, more completely explain, and more accurately predict instructional phenomena than that of the neophyte, but both are able to generate ideas about how to teach a particular group of students on a particular day.

> **theory** A set of concepts and principles that describes, explains, and predicts phenomena.

Lecture Note: This is a natural association; theories are the product of science. Ask students to identify several theories they know. Theories in this scientific sense are those of Einstein, B. F. Skinner, and Jean Piaget.

Journal Entry: After they read about crossing the street, ask students to identify some everyday experiences about which they have intuitive theories.

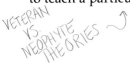

VETERAN VS. NEOPHYTE THEORIES

Chapter 15 Casebook Preview: Each classroom experiment in the casebook reinforces aspects of the case author's intuitive theory of teaching. Have students identify aspects of intuitive theory in one case.

Lecture Note: Berliner's 1986 paper (referenced in the text) was entitled "In Pursuit of the Expert Pedagogue." In one comparison, Berliner had novices, postulates (people entering teaching as a result of a midcareer shift), and experts view a slide of a classroom. The novices' and postulants' reports were very literal. One postulant reported seeing "a blonde-haired boy at the table, looking at papers." A novice reported seeing "a room of students sitting at tables." Viewing the same slide, experts' reports were more inferential. One expert said, "It's a hands-on activity of some type. Group work with a male and female of maybe late junior high school age." A second expert said, "It's a group of students maybe doing small-group discussion on a project."

Lecture Note: This sentence could be written on the board for students to ponder prior to class.

Connection: Point out that student learning, development, and motivation is the focus of Chapters 2–8 (Part II). Teacher influence, while discussed in various places in Part II, is the focus of Chapters 9–14 (Part III).

Transparency: This figure is duplicated in the acetate transparency package. See T-1 Construction of a Theory of Teaching.

Learning to Read Classrooms

What are the hallmarks of teaching expertise? Research has identified several characteristics that experts possess to a greater extent than do novices (Berliner, 1986). Experts classify problems and make inferences quickly. They are opportunistic, flexible, confident, and clear. They have efficient routines. All of these characteristics suggest that expert teachers are able to "read" their classrooms fluently. In other words, they interpret classroom events and student behavior less literally than novices do.

Consider briefly the following sentence: The roabian smapped the crin with rulk. Even though we don't know about roabians, smapping, or rulk, our knowledge of sentence structure allows us to conclude what was smapped (the crin), how it was smapped (with rulk), and who did the smapping (the roabian). But this is as far as our knowledge will take us. We can read the sentence literally, but we can't infer much about its meaning. The *prior knowledge* which experts bring to situations allows them to perceive not just literally, but inferentially. There are many studies to support the notion that expert teachers are expert "readers" of behavior in classrooms (e.g., Swanson, O'Connor, & Cooney, 1990).

Educational psychology, based on scientifically collected evidence, helps aspiring teachers learn the vocabulary and syntax of the classroom. It explains how students develop, how they learn, what their needs and motivations are. Educational psychology also explains how teachers influence student development, learning, and motivation.

So, both classroom experience (the experiments teachers conduct in their classrooms) and educational psychology (a way of reading classroom events) are the raw materials necessary for the construction of a theory of teaching. **Reflection,** a thoughtful consideration of these raw materials, is essential to this theory building. (See Figure 1–2.)

This text, which will examine what educational psychologists have learned and present accounts of classroom experiences, will provide you with additional material necessary to construct a theory of teaching.

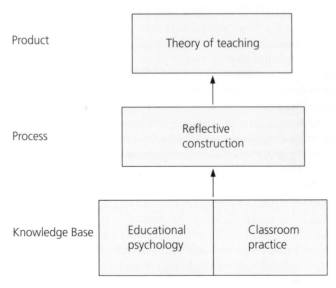

■ **Figure 1–2** *Construction of a Theory of Teaching*

The Diary of a Day

To begin, we present Peter Roop's autobiographical account of a teacher's day, March 17, 1989. His classroom is not identical to any other classroom. His students do not represent a random sample of all students at all grades. No teacher's classroom does.

Peter performs the teaching functions that every teacher must perform in order to be effective. The way in which he does so reflects his knowledge of himself, his students, his curricula—his theory of teaching. As you read Peter's account, pay close attention to Peter's thoughts and actions. Read his diary to discover the problems he identifies and the decisions he makes, his attitude toward children and toward the profession of teaching, and the routines he uses to motivate and manage. Read to see what inferences you can make about Peter's ideas of how instruction works.

You may not agree with Peter's ideas and attitudes. You may reject some of his decisions. You may not execute the functions of teaching in the same way Peter does, but your job will be similar in many ways.

Chap. Obj. 2
Test Ques. 1.11–1.13; 1.24–1.26; 1.29–1.30

Focus Question: What does a day of teaching look and feel like?

The mix of ideas, experiences, and innovative approaches that teachers and students share make every classroom unique.

Friday, March 17, 1989*

This is the diary of one teaching day. Like most days it was ordinary in many ways and extraordinary in many others. At the day's end, I left school exhausted yet with a smile on my face. If anyone had asked why I was smiling, I would have told that person that I have the best job in the world.

Getting to School

I am never away from teaching even though I am away from the classroom and the children. I find myself thinking about teaching early in the morning and late at night. Why did I say that to Eileen? Did I hurt her feelings or did she understand I was teasing her? Should I put Andre on the checklist to help control his behavior or has he shown enough improvement that that step will not be necessary? Should I ask my principal to help speed up the order for new math books? Will the kids be excited because it is Pizza Day?

Often my day begins in the middle of the night when I wake up and consciously confront a problem that my subconscious has been wrestling with. Midnight solutions can prove to be the best ones.

My first "teaching" thoughts in the morning are about my schedule, especially the morning reading groups. Some of my plans need further thought. Should I work on the "coding machine" project before trying it with the reading group? Or should I have the group read the directions and then do it? I choose the former course, hoping to find the right mixture of reading and following directions, increasing the involvement of all in the group.

I remind myself to tell Mrs. Paterson, another teacher in my unit, that Andre's parents are out of town for the week. Has she noticed any behavior changes? I didn't say anything to her earlier to avoid coloring her judgment. I have been disappointed in his behavior in social studies class. Yesterday, I told him that I was going to move him away from Charles. I know he'll be waiting to see if I forgot. I'll just leave a note on his desk as a reminder that I haven't forgotten!

I must also tell Andre that the one-day ban on his being in the "fort" has been lifted. He was being punished for climbing over a bus seat while returning to school from a field trip. My first reaction was that I wouldn't allow him to go on the next field trip. Upon reflection I realized that this was not an immediate punishment, the kind that works best with him. Personal reminder to myself to think through a situation before reacting; to make the punishment fit the crime more closely and be more immediate.

The "forts." Should I let them stay up or take them down? Have they outlived their usefulness or do they still fulfill their builders' needs, especially Andre's. The "forts" grew spontaneously one Monday morning when Andre wanted to work behind a movable storage cabinet.

"Yes," I had told him, "you can if you complete all of your reading work."

Behind the cabinet, cut off from the rest of the class by choice, he finished all of his assignments, without a single reminder, for the first time since January. That evening I thought, if it works, stick with it. So we both got

See Chapter 12
Connection: Relevant to active instruction, Chapter 12

See Chapter 13
Connection: Relevant to halo effect, Chapter 13

See Chapter 5
Connection: Relevant to time-out, Chapter 5

See Chapter 5
Connection: Relevant to contingency contracting, Chapter 5

---

*The marginal notes indicate where educational psychology principles and concepts relevant to the events of Peter's teaching day will be examined. Thus, each marginal note identifies a link between teaching practice and scientific theory.

what we wanted: Andre got his privacy and I was able to get off his case about finishing his work.

Next, Marti and Judy wanted to build their own "fort" under a table. I agreed. Being strong-minded individuals, they often quarreled with each other. This might be a fine opportunity to have them work together. "Yes, you can build a fort, but you must get along. The first fight means the closing of the fort." "And," I added, "you must finish your work."

For two weeks now the forts have operated with success. I'll let them stay up.

By now I have finished showering and am awake. Time for my morning walk, a good time to sort through the day and the weeks ahead. While walking I wonder how to tie together the new units on Wisconsin history. What speakers can we get in to talk with the kids?

Connection: Relevant to model effectiveness, Chapter 7
See Chapter 7

It snowed last night. The new snow will be helpful with my glacier unit. I can use fresh snow to make "glaciers" and snowballs to make "kettle holes" in sand. Will the kids be excited with the new snowfall and less attentive?

Some mornings on the way to school I listen to National Public Radio; on others, rock and roll claims my attention. Some mornings, however, I ride in silence, reviewing my plans; acting out, even rehearsing how I will introduce a lesson; reviewing previously taught material; deciding how I will resolve a playground situation. This morning I do all three, catching a report on Saul Bellow's new book, listening to "Satisfaction" by the Rolling Stones, and then mentally rehearsing the introduction to teaching the coding machine in reading.

See Chapter 4
Connection: Relevant to distractibility, Chapter 4

At School

At school, I stop by the office to say good morning to Sara, the secretary. Next I scan my mail, sorting it out in order of importance: The overdue books list goes on top as a reminder to my homeroom to return their books, the newsletter from the math department is next (remember to read parts during recess), a phone message third, summer school handouts last. I wonder who, if anyone, I'll recommend for summer reading or math sessions.

See Chapter 10
Connection: Relevant to anticipatory set, Chapter 10

I make one decision immediately upon unlocking and entering my room: The mobiles must come down. For three weeks I have learned to dodge them as I move around the classroom. I have enjoyed the twisting, turning mobiles but they are a distraction now. I wonder if the kids see them anymore or if they are just a part of the environment that passes unnoticed.

See Chapter 13
Connection: Relevant to diagnostic evaluation, Chapter 13

I glance across the room at the new bulletin board called "Weird, Wacky, Wonderful Words," a project from art class. Each student took one word and then designed it to reflect that word. Sterling's picture *FISH* stands out among the others, his lines clear, precise, his coloring sharp and distinct. Each letter is made from different kinds of fish: tuna, trout, mackerel, and rainbow fish. I wonder how long before the novelty wears off and this project, like the mobiles, fades into the background.

I outline the homeroom's schedule on the side board: March 17, CA (Communicative Arts), Recess, CA, Lunch, Math, Recess, Silent Reading, Social Studies. Next I write the schedule for my CA class, trying to see if I can remember all of my plans without looking at my lesson plans. I forget to add the regular Friday spelling bee.

Connection: Relevant to planning, Chapter 9
See Chapter 9

About fifteen minutes before the bell rings, the four unit teachers meet in the hall to discuss any major scheduling changes for the day, reminding each other of the events for the next week so that we can include them in our plans. We discuss the snowstorm in progress and how the children will probably react. We tell a few stories about the children, express concerns for Heidi's behavior, comment on Roy's success with keyboarding, ask how Sterling is doing in his new reading group.

"Boy, did I get my comeuppance yesterday," I tell them. "During Guidance, Mrs. Bradbury was talking with the children about expressing anger. She told them that it can become bottled up and has to be released somehow. For example, she said, some people write letters, which they never intend to send, to the people with whom they are angry in order to let off steam without hurting someone's feelings. One of the students piped up, 'Mr. Roop does that.' During a letter-writing unit I had told them how I sometimes vent my anger toward tardy editors this way. Seeing me sitting at my desk and writing, Cathy chimed in, 'Well, I hope he's writing a letter now.' It took me a moment to realize what she meant and then I laughed. She had been bothered by my grumpiness yesterday morning and in her own way let me know. The rest of my day went much better, thanks to Cathy."

"You don't mean you grump at your students, Mr. Roop?" teased Connie, one of the other unit teachers.

"Well, only this once," I replied.

All four of us had a chuckle at that, knowing full well that personal feelings enter the classroom and have an impact on the children.

The bell's ringing brought us back to the moment at hand as the kids came bubbling down the hallway.

Homeroom

We usually greet the students in the hall as they take off coats and boots. This gives us a relaxed way to begin the day together. We listen to stories, collect homework, and chat.

Jon, repeating an often-played joke, taps me on the shoulder opposite from where he is standing, hoping that I'll look the wrong way and not at him. This way of saying hello, which started after some racial name calling at Jon's expense occurred on the playground, has been going on for a month now. It has established a special link between us, especially at a time when Jon was vulnerable and hurting. Now it goes on just for fun.

Drew bounces down the hall, calling "How's your day so far, Mr. Roop?" From an easily distracted, overly boisterous student, Drew has learned to channel more of his energy into his schoolwork and, while not yet a scholar, he has made real academic progress, gaining confidence in his abilities. His cheerfulness brightens even the gloomiest of days, although I know things have sometimes been hard since his parents divorced.

Once in homeroom, the greetings and story tellings continue. A group of kids gather around my desk, eagerly awaiting their turn to tell what is most important to them this morning. I not only enjoy hearing these tales, but know that unless the kids have appropriate opportunity to express themselves, they won't be able to fully concentrate later on their work.

"Look Mr. Roop. I have my overdue book," exclaims Judy. "Can I take it to the library?"

"Yes, but don't give it to anyone but Mrs. Newbery so she can check you off her list." I wonder if Judy has her Ritalin today. Yesterday she didn't. I didn't understand that until about midmorning when I realized that she was

See Chapter 12
Connection: Relevant to classroom communication, Chapter 12

Connection: Relevant to peer relations, Chapter 3
See Chapter 3

Connection: Relevant to distractibility, Chapter 4
See Chapter 4

Connection: Relevant to belonging needs, Chapter 8
See Chapter 8

See Chapter 4
Connection: Relevant to hyperactivity, Chapter 4

Peter Roop uses his innovative "cool stool" to gain the attention of his class.

having trouble sitting down and doing her work. I'll ask her about the medication in a private moment.

"Guess what?" Heidi bubbles. "I got locked in the bathroom this morning. I went to the bathroom and shut the door and it locked. Then it wouldn't open. My mom sent for the neighbor who slid a screwdriver under the door. I took off the handle but it still wouldn't open. Then I took off the lock and could see through the hole. But the door still wouldn't unlock. Then my neighbor told me to take off the hinges. I did the top hinge first but the bottom one was stuck. Finally it came loose and the door fell in on top of me."

"Heidi, that's a great story. Why don't you write it down?" I suggested.

"I wish we were writing in our journals now so that I could."

Good insight, Heidi, I thought. We had put aside journal writing while working on writing and illustrating stories for the first graders.

"That's okay," I said. "Write it down anyway. You can skip a spelling page or two to get it done." Beaming, Heidi whirled away to get organized for the day.

While I listen to stories, concerns, and messages, the rest of the class prepares for their morning lessons, organizes their materials, and talks with their friends. There is a special buzz each morning as they catch up with each other's activities. Allowing them this opportunity cuts down on the need for such exchanges later on.

"Time to go over the schedule," I announce, sitting on my "cool stool," a tall stool that serves as a collection place for papers, a spot for reading aloud, a focal point in the room, a privileged seat for filmstrips, among other purposes. I have had a "cool stool" since my first days of teaching and, while

See Chapter 8
Connection: Relevant to intrinsic motivation, Chapter 8

many other things have changed, a cool stool, "the coolest stool in the school," has always served as my signal for attention.

Most of the conversations stop and the students' attention is focused on me. This combination of verbal instructions and my sitting on the stool clues them into the beginning of the school day. Our "official" day has started this way since school began. It has proven to be a quick way of getting everyone's attention.

See Chapter 5
Connection: Relevant to discriminative stimulus, Chapter 5

I go over the daily schedule and take attendance. Michelle, today's leader, leads us in the "Pledge of Allegiance." I dismiss my homeroom students to CA, saying, as I do each day, "Have a good morning." I give the attendance slip to the class leader to take to the office.

This beginning of the day usually takes less than ten minutes. I consider this time well spent—I get caught up in the excitement of locked bathroom doors, piano recitals, birthdays. It is a sharing time and a time to learn more about each child's life away from school.

⌒ Communicative Arts

At the beginning of the year, all of the desks in the room are in the traditional rows, but after the first week I let my homeroom students regroup them as they wish. This regrouping goes on throughout the year. In one group, there are eight desks. In another, five. Two students sit by themselves by choice. Other smaller groups of two and three form around the room.

See Chapter 12
Connection: Relevant to classroom communication, Chapter 12

I watch with interest the different groupings and pairings; they reflect friendships and difficulties. I respect the ebb and flow of my children's personal interactions. By allowing them to regroup in this way, I can contribute to their learning. It is a small thing in practice but gives them a little ownership in the room. Right now all of the large groups have a mixture of students of different ages, but each group is of the same sex.

See Chapter 3
Connection: Relevant to interpersonal development, Chapter 3

Students coming into my room for different subjects can pick where and with whom they want to sit. My only restriction is that I can move someone who falls behind, is not attentive, or talks too much in class. This arrangement works for me and my students; it allows them to take more responsibility for their behavior and make more choices within the structure of the room. After all, whose classroom is it really? I give them some leeway and choices in return for their cooperation.

See Chapter 8
Connection: Relevant to choosing, Chapter 8

From my perch on the stool, I go over this morning's CA schedule, explaining the various activities briefly. This allows me to head off many questions and provides a reference point for those students who are not tuned in entirely to the classroom routine. They can refer to the CA schedule on the board as we move through the morning. I also put up a schedule for my math, social studies, and science classes.

See Chapter 8
Connection: Relevant to expectations, Chapter 8

Our first activity is our weekly visit to the school library to return books and check out new material. Students who are already reading long books and are not in need of more use this as a study hall time. They take unfinished work along to do in the library while I am helping students select books. This week's study hall time can be used for finishing a spelling lesson, completing reading assignments, silent reading, or working on their stories for the first graders.

I treasure the book selection time. It is a special pleasure to link a reader with the right book. It doesn't happen every time or even most of the time, but because I know these students well our success rate is high.

Brad asks if he can get all nonfiction this week. Glancing at the three books in his hands, I see that they are all about Greek myths and legends. He rarely shows this much enthusiasm for reading so I modify my rule that at least two of the four books a student checks out be fiction. The four-book rule often undergoes on-the-spot revision, especially when one of the kids is on a reading binge.

See Chapter 11
Connection: Relevant to problem of the match, Chapter 11

Jani is next, wanting me to help her find "a good book." Knowing full well that she has enjoyed Jamie Gilson's books, I steer her toward Lois Lowry's *Anastasia* series. Cathy and Marti back me up with their enthusiasm for *Anastasia*, but Jani is reluctant.

See Chapter 8
Connection: Relevant to relevance, Chapter 8

"Well, let's walk and talk and see what we can find," I suggest.

Meanwhile, I am trying to keep an eye on everyone else's activities. Andre is peering around a curtain watching another group view a slide show about an upcoming camping trip. My first reaction is to pull Andre back, but because he is also working on his spelling I let him continue after making him aware that I know what he is doing. If "privileges" such as this keep him working when he stubbornly refused to work a month ago, then my intuition says to go with it.

Book selection and rejection continues for another ten minutes or so before I round everyone up to go back to the room. Every teacher's approach to movement in the hall varies. I usually walk about midpoint alongside the "line," such as it is. If no other classes are walking down the hall, the line spreads out, losing its structure. If others are coming, we walk in a more orderly fashion to avoid clogging up the hallway.

See Chapter 12
See Chapter 5
Connection: Relevant to overlapping, Chapter 12
Connection: Relevant to contingencies, Chapter 5

Talking is in whispers because we must pass other classes.

Once back in the room everyone has a seat as I perch on the cool stool for our daily read aloud. Like many other teachers do, I make reading aloud a cornerstone of my morning. The books I choose are sometimes ones the kids

A teacher's personal interest in a subject area, such as literature, can influence students' appreciation of the material.

can read on their own; at other times I choose books that would be a challenge for most of them. I want to spark their interest in a variety of authors, set a model for reading aloud, entice them to challenge themselves on other books, and provide a relaxing time for listening. This time is for reading aloud only; no interruptions are allowed (unless there is a fire alarm, they remind me).

At the beginning of the read aloud one of the children provides a brief recap of the story so far. I've observed that some of the students go into minute detail about the story, recalling just about everything; others give a simple outline of the major events. Each book seems to involve different children at different points.

During sharing time, after the reading, the children link the literature to their own lives, finding connections that are primarily personal, but that provide a response to the book. I believe this personal response is essential in reading. This is also a time for oral feedback, giving those students who find written responses more difficult a chance to express themselves.

↺ Gym: Unexpected Time

At 9:15, it is time for gym class. It usually takes about five minutes for the kids to get their shoes out of the cupboard, put them on, and line up to go to the gym. We also wait for three students to join us from their learning disabilities class. On Fridays, I teach the gym class myself, using an outline prepared by the gym teacher.

In gym, we are just finishing a dance unit, a unit that most of the students face with giggles and even some "I don't want to go to gym" statements. This time of year the boy–girl thing begins, especially with fourth graders. One of those things you come to realize after working with two age levels over the years is that there really is quite a difference between third and fourth graders. Boy–girl noticing in the springtime is one of those things that makes the differences clear.

Just before leaving for gym, I asked my kids if they knew who the best dancer in school was. After a few wild guesses, I told them that Mr. Betzer, the principal, was an expert, dancing two or three times a week, sometimes in contests. They were impressed and I think this also helped get the unit off on the right foot.

This Friday was to be my day to teach dance. Before leaving the room, I asked who would like to demonstrate certain dances. A forest of hands rose quickly and I selected several students for three dances. Michelle wanted to show the "Grapevine"; Judy was jumping to demonstrate "Celebration"; Stephen was eager to show off "Seven Jumps."

When we reached the gym, Mr. Wallace said that he would be taking my class along with a class of second-graders. We've used this arrangement before, allowing my class to help teach the younger students. I stayed a few minutes to watch them get started before heading for the phone to call a guest speaker. Such unexpected "free" time helps out tremendously in an already overcrowded day.

The phone is free so I place my call to my friend Elmer Franz. Elmer is a paper-making expert who demonstrates his skills around the country. He is an enthusiastic presenter who works wonderfully with kids.

Elmer charges a fee for his presentation. We've planned to use some of our unit money from a recent all-school candy sale to pay him. I said that I would check with Mr. Betzer first, however, and see if I could get him to

See Chapter 7
Connection: Relevant to teacher as model, Chapter 7

See Chapter 6
Connection: Relevant to prior knowledge, Chapter 6

See Chapter 11
Connection: Relevant to mainstreaming, Chapter 11

See Chapter 3
Connection: Relevant to social development, Chapter 3

See Chapter 8
Connection: Relevant to curiosity as motivation, Chapter 8

Connection: Relevant to peer tutoring, Chapter 11
See Chapter 11

See Chapter 7
Connection: Relevant to model effectiveness, Chapter 7

sponsor the workshop, saving our candy money to purchase multiple copies of books or classroom materials.

After making my call, I still have some ten minutes before I have to pick up the kids from gym so I decide to prepare the "coding machine" for the *Rhymes and Reasons* reading group. My main objective for the coding machine lesson is to teach students to carefully read directions and follow them exactly. This is a follow-up to a lesson on giving directions.

I always try to practice a project ahead of time before doing it with the students. Often I find many shortcuts and avoid unforeseen pitfalls. I later make note of student ideas that solve problems or work better for the rest of the class and incorporate them into the project as well.

I get the ruler, paper, pencil, and scissors I need and sit down with the book to begin making a coding machine. There are only six steps, but by the time I get to the second step I realize that this is going to be more complicated than I originally thought. Step 2 involves measuring with a ruler to one-half inch, something students should all be able to do, but that I know will cause some difficulties for many of them.

See Chapter 13
Connection: Relevant to formative evaluation, Chapter 13

I glance at the clock and see that it is time to scoot down and pick the kids up. I usually go down one or two minutes early to watch the lesson wrap-up and see what they're doing. This morning they're finishing a dance that requires coordinating movements with a partner to clap hands together, then switch to another partner. I join in, getting a few laughs as I try to catch up with the clapping movements. The bell rings and off we go for recess. Some kids go outside; others follow me to an upstairs classroom.

Recess

Other kids from different classes drift into the room. Kim and Stephen want help finding out the answer to Mrs. Paterson's "Question of the Day," a trivia question that she puts up each morning and that the kids have all day to answer. Today's question is, "What is the salary of the governor of Wisconsin?" This question is related to the part of the Wisconsin unit Mrs. Paterson is teaching. I enjoy these questions almost as much as the kids do.

See Chapter 7
Connection: Relevant to teacher as model, Chapter 7

There is a core group of about ten kids who always try to answer the questions each day. Kim and Stephen are two of the most avid searchers. Sometimes these two come right up and ask me for the answer. Other times they try to trick me into answering it. Usually I make them work for the answer, either by giving them a wrong answer that is somehow connected to the right answer or by sending them off to the library, as I do today, to find the answer. It's all a game in many ways, but a game in which several of the students actively use their research skills regularly.

See Chapter 7
Connection: Relevant to self-efficacy, Chapter 7

I leave them searching for salary in order to get back to the coding machine. In the meantime, Heidi and Abby, close friends, are now standing at my desk.

See Chapter 6
Connection: Relevant to problem solving, Chapter 6

"What's this?" Abby asks.

"That's a coding machine we're going to be making after recess," I tell them. "I'm trying it out ahead of time."

Then I get an idea.

"How would you two like to learn to make it and then teach the others in your group?"

Connection: Relevant to cooperative learning, Chapter 11
See Chapter 11

"Great," Heidi says, and we move the book and the materials to a table.

I explain to them what I have done and tell them that it looks as if measuring will be the biggest problem. They get out their rulers and begin measuring the paper themselves. They do so well that I know that it won't present any major roadblocks for the rest of the kids. I grab about ten rulers from my desk and bring them and the necessary paper to the table.

The Coding Machine

Soon the bell rings and recess is over. I stand in the hall as the kids come trooping up the stairs. The other three unit teachers are there too. Sue and I quickly discuss her keyboarding plans and I tell her about the coding machine project.

"Could my students join yours?" she asks. "I had planned to have them finish their other work, but I had also promised them a project this week, too."

"No problem," I tell her. "We'll just open the double doors and I'll teach both classes. My kids can share their books with yours as we go along. Maybe working in pairs will help."

So now instead of a small group activity back on the carpet I'll be teaching to forty kids.

I stand in the center of the two classes and wait without saying a word until everyone is settled.

See Chapter 11
Connection: Relevant to large and small group instruction, Chapter 11

"We've been studying secret codes and messages, and today we're making a secret coding machine. Making the machine is not difficult, but you will have to listen very closely to the directions. I have never made one before, but Heidi and Abby have been helping me get started. You can ask them for any help you might need if I can't help you immediately. You'll need a pencil, your scissors, and a ruler."

Knowing that there will be an immediate outcry of "I don't have a ruler with me," I tell them, "Don't worry about rulers. I have plenty and we can share them."

See Chapter 12
Connection: Relevant to management skills, Chapter 12

"If you listen carefully and follow the directions, this should be easy," I tell them. I sure hope it is, I think to myself.

We quickly pass out two sheets of paper to everyone.

"First, you'll need to turn one sheet of paper sideways so that the long side is toward the front of your desk. We're going to measure down one and one-half inches and draw a line."

I walk around checking to see if everyone is following so far. Only one boy had his paper the wrong way and I show him the right way. Heidi and Abby help those in their group who need help so I can turn my attention to the large group. To my surprise this measuring step has not proven difficult at all. Almost all of the students got it right away; those who didn't quickly figured it out with a little extra help from a neighbor.

"Now for the next step," I say. "We're going to write all the letters of the alphabet on the line you've just drawn. Use the blue lines already on the paper to mark off the place for each letter."

They quickly begin, but before long Craig calls out, "My paper only has twenty-four blue lines."

I walk over to see and he's right. "What if I draw in two more lines," he suggests and I agree that that is the solution. We use his idea on everyone's papers because each sheet has only twenty-four lines. An unforeseen problem, but one quickly and easily resolved through Craig's insight. This is a good, positive perk for Craig because he is often getting in trouble for not paying attention during lessons. I'm happy to give him a spot in the limelight.

"Next we're going to cut two slots on either end of the paper. Each slot should be about two-inches long." I show on my drawing where the slots will be placed and demonstrate on my paper how to make the cuts for the slots. This step takes a little time but soon everyone is ready for the next one. No one cut the slots vertically so I'm pleased.

See Chapter 7
Connection: Relevant to self-efficacy, Chapter 7

"Next we're going to cut off two strips about one-inch wide from the bottom."

Drew raises his hand. "Mr. Roop, why don't we use the paper cutter. It'll be more even."

See Chapter 10
Connection: Relevant to guided practice, Chapter 10

"If you want to cut your paper, go ahead," I tell them. "Or I can cut the paper with the paper cutter."

Most want me to cut their papers so Drew goes to get the paper cutter.

The first batch of papers brought to me I put in order, alphabets opposite the blade. I trim these and hand them back. The next batch of papers are ready, the top sheet with the alphabet opposite the blade. I chop again and hand these back.

There is an immediate chorus of groans.

"You cut off my alphabet," Marie says.

"Mine, too," Lee adds.

They were right. Instead of checking to see if all the papers were oriented correctly I had only checked the top sheet, thereby chopping off seven alphabets.

"Oops, guys," I say. "Guess what? I didn't look before I chopped. I'm sorry if I ruined your alphabets."

"That's okay," Craig said and quickly went back to work to get caught up. Within three minutes the "chopped" group had caught up with the others and we were ready to proceed.

Seeing me goof-up is good for the kids. I do it often enough and they know it is not a big deal if I make a mistake. I want them to realize that everyone makes mistakes, even teachers, and that everyone can learn from them. Sometimes I make mistakes on purpose just to see who will catch me. I've learned that when students see you trying to cover up mistakes they lose respect for you.

"I'll check the papers this time," Heidi says before handing them to me to chop. "Just to see if they're in the right order," she adds with a smile. The papers are in the right position, I chop them correctly, and we're on to the next step.

See Chapter 7
Connection: Relevant to coping models, Chapter 7

"Take your two strips of paper and tape them together so that at least two of the blue lines overlap." I hold up two strips to demonstrate. "After they're taped, start on the first blue line and write the alphabet twice, A to Z, then A to Z again." I help with taping and watch as they write their letters.

See Chapter 12
Connection: Relevant to transitions, Chapter 12

"We're almost done," I say. "Now slip your long alphabet sheet through the two slots like this. It should slide back and forth easily."

Everyone quickly completes this step before I ask them, "What do you notice about your alphabets?"

Anne's hand shoots up and I call on her. "That you match them up and slide the paper so they don't match."

"Right. Now how could this help us make a secret code?"

Connection: Relevant to logico-mathematical experience, Chapter 2
See Chapter 2

There is no immediate response to this. They slide their papers back and forth trying to discover the answer. Then Drew blurts out, "If you don't match the letters exactly you can write a mixed-up message with one set of letters and figure it out with the others."

"Right," I tell him and then demonstrate with an example on the board.

Most seem to catch on right away, but the puzzled looks on some faces tell me that I need to show them another example.

"Give me a word," I tell Andre, one of the puzzled ones.

"*Fish*," he says, and I show how to find it using the code. He grins when he sees how it works and immediately turns to show his neighbor.

See Chapter 2
Connection: Relevant to concrete operations, Chapter 2

I look at the clock and realize that we are already fifteen minutes past the time when we were to be finished. The keyboarders aren't back so we play with the coding machines until their return.

Now that the exercise has been completed, we quickly close the double doors between the rooms so that we can finish up the morning's activities. Spelling was next on my schedule.

This week I am trying something different with spelling. Instead of assigning a particular page to be worked on at a specific time, I assign the spelling pages on Monday after giving a pretest on the week's words. It is up to each student to make certain that his or her work is completed by Friday so that we can correct the pages in class before the posttest. My objectives are to allow students more responsibility for the way in which they use their time as well as to help them learn to meet specific deadlines.

See Chapter 7
Connection: Relevant to self-regulatory capability, Chapter 7

The experiment was a disaster. When I asked who had completed the four pages, only half of the class raised their hands. I let them know in no uncertain terms that I was disappointed that they could not handle this responsibility. I paused to let my message sink in, scanning the room to emphasize my point.

"Now, we'll go through the first two pages and correct them," I said, still speaking sternly. I didn't want the whole exercise to be wasted. (Within several weeks, however, we hit our stride and everyone was ready for correcting by Friday. I do need to remember that it takes time to establish a new routine.)

Connection: Relevant to successive approximations, Chapter 5
See Chapter 5

Spelling Bee

We usually end our Friday mornings with a spelling bee. This Friday we planned two spelling bees, one using the names of the states; the other, a regular bee.

Participation in the spelling bee is optional. There is a core group of eight children who always join in. I am usually surprised by the others who choose to participate. Sometimes even the marginal spellers join us, challenging themselves to see how far they can get against the "regulars."

Connection: Relevant to choosing needs, Chapter 8
See Chapter 8

Only half of the class chooses to take part in the "states' names" bee. Cathy and Ernesto were ready to burst because they had been practicing all week for this spelling contest. Many of the children missed *Colorado*, *Connecticut*, and *Georgia* in the first round. Ernesto, one of the most avid spellers, took over and shared one of his spelling secrets.

Connection: Relevant to mnemonics, Chapter 6
See Chapter 6

"Just think *COLOR*-ado for Colorado, or *CONNECT*-icut for Connecticut," he explained. Several others chimed in with their versions for remembering different states. Cathy's method was the most interesting. She had practiced the names of the states by writing them down at home. When she was unsure of a word in a spelling bee, she "wrote" it invisibly on her leg. Using this method she rarely missed a word she had practiced.

Connection: Relevant to rehearsal, Chapter 6
See Chapter 6

The contest ended with Cathy beating Ernesto by spelling *Massachusetts.* We still had time for a regular bee. Almost the entire class participated in the bee, which was interrupted at the end of class with five students still up.

Lunch

At 11:25, I dismiss my CA class to return to their homerooms. Then my homeroom class comes in; they put their books and supply boxes away, and get out their math materials for the afternoon math class. This is a time for a lot of chatter; they discuss their mornings, talk with me, see who will be sitting with whom at lunch. At 11:30, I dismiss them for lunch.

I follow them into the hall as do the other teachers. We continue our various conversations, answer questions, and watch to make sure that there is not too much fooling around.

Lunch is the time each day when I can read through the avalanche of papers that reaches each of us every day. Today my mailbox holds memos on fire drills; ways to improve spelling (seems appropriate today); and new classes to be offered through our Teacher Academy, a new staff development program. I read through them on my way back to the room.

Dave, the TAG teacher (Talented and Gifted program) stops by to talk and to let me know that Julio has been accepted into the program, but two other students we suggested did not make it.

"We'll look at Jake and Christopher again at the end of the year," Dave tells me. "They might get placed next year. They are strong candidates."

"Should I write down anecdotes about their classroom insights?"

"That would be great because then we'd have additional material to work with."

Dave leaves and I think about what his job must be like, trying all sorts of new things every week with a group of highly motivated and intelligent kids. I wonder if I'd be successful teaching in the TAG program. Jack's giggle brings me back to the real world of my room, and my thoughts quickly refocus on the challenging, yet wonderful conglomeration of "my kids."

"You finished yet, Mr. Roop?" Jack calls out.

"Sure, Jack. Now let's hit the computer."

I follow him to the learning disabled (LD) room and he boots up the "Oregon Trail" program. Earlier in the day I'd promised to play this computer game with him. It is interesting watching him as he bangs through the portions of the program that require any reading. He has memorized certain portions and goes directly to the easiest parts. We play for about ten minutes when the bell rings. He beats me of course.

"Don't worry, Mr. Roop," he consoles me, "you'll do better next time."

He writes the date of our rematch on the computer calendar and I hustle out into the hall to meet the first wave of returning students.

I greet the kids and they greet me as we walk down the hall to our room. There is a good deal of joking; I answer four questions about school work and deal with the usual after lunch "behavior" complaints.

Each complaint must be dealt with fairly. I try to get all sides of the story, then mete out punishment where and when it is called for. Often it is enough to listen to the complaint and follow through by talking with the others involved. Some situations require other steps, including isolation from fellow students for a time, a loss of recess, a loss of class privileges, a visit to the principal, or parental involvement if the problem is a major or continuing one.

Connection: Relevant to placement evaluation, Chapter 14
See Chapter 14

Connection: Relevant to observational data, Chapter 13
See Chapter 13

See Chapter 4
Connection: Relevant to exceptionality, Chapter 4

See Chapter 11
Connection: Relevant to CAI-simulations, Chapter 11

See Chapter 12
Connection: Relevant to discipline, Chapter 12

The conversation never seems to stop but flows steadily. This conversational interchange is important to my teaching. It allows me the opportunity to pick up clues about the children, what interests them at the moment or what bothers them, what they are excited about or bored with. Similarly, they pick up clues to my mood, getting feedback about their ideas or problems. For some of these students it might be the one chance during the day when they talk with an adult who listens and responds to them directly.

See Chapter 8
Connection: Relevant to deficiency needs, Chapter 8

Many children do not have adequate time at home for conversation, do not have friends come over, do not have siblings with whom to talk. Children need opportunities to interact, to quarrel if need be, to exchange feelings. Too often they are told what to do and how to do it, or simply pass the time watching TV. Communication in these situations is all in one direction, with the children taking passive roles.

Homeroom

When we reach the room the conversations continue as the children gather their materials for the afternoon classes. Most will not return to my room until the end of the day so they must gather everything they will need for math, silent reading, and social studies or science. While they are preparing, I quickly scan the room to see if anyone is absent.

See Chapter 2
Connection: Relevant to bilingualism, Chapter 2

One whose presence is always noteworthy is Lee, a Hmong refugee from Laos, one of the hardest working students in the entire unit. We've been together for two years and I have learned a lot from him. He has grown greatly in confidence, language skill, and math ability. He has a wonderful

As Peter Roop has demonstrated with Lee, a relationship that is based on mutual trust, support, and encouragement can enable a nonnative speaker to gain command of a new language and thrive socially in school.

sense of humor. It has been intriguing watching him gain command of English, as only Hmong is spoken at home. He reads both languages fluently and often helps his parents translate English material into his native language.

Math

After the initial rush has slowed, I sit on my stool. I quickly review the afternoon's schedule, "Math, Unit Meeting, Recess, Silent Reading, and Social Studies. We will be back in homeroom at 3:05 to clean up and get ready for the weekend. See you later."

The students who remain in homeroom for math shift desks as they choose. Just as with my reading class, I allow the children to sit where they wish as long as it doesn't interfere with their work.

The rest of my math class waits at the door until I invite them in. When I do, they pick their spots. Today, Luis wishes to move because Jack was bugging him yesterday.

Connection: Relevant to assertive discipline, Chapter 12
See Chapter 12

"Sure," I say and Luis moves next to Albert.

I go to Jack to talk with him about why Luis is moving. It is clear from his face that he understands all too well.

See Chapter 12
Connection: Relevant to individualized instruction, Chapter 12

Division has been a challenge for these kids because many have not yet learned all of their multiplication facts. My class is of "lower" ability students who have difficulty with reading. This class has only twenty-two students in it, down from the original twenty-nine. Five have moved to a faster paced class with individualization. All but two of my students work in a paced group. Those two are individualized and work about a chapter ahead of the others.

See Chapter 7
Connection: Relevant to perceived similarity, Chapter 7

One of the individualized students, Laura, knows her facts and is a capable math student. She is self-motivated, grasps new concepts quickly, and is quite good at working on her own. Rather than move her on to the faster class, I decided to keep her in my class. Her self-motivation sets an excellent example for the others, who have difficulty concentrating on their work. Also, she and I discussed moving her into another math class, and she decided to stay in my room.

See Chapter 7
Connection: Relevant to vicarious capability, Chapter 7

The second individualized student, Tiffany, is struggling. She is determined to succeed, however. At the beginning of the year she seemed to have little confidence in her ability to do math. She was last to finish her work, had many incorrect answers, and had difficulties understanding new material. Yet she worked hard all of the first semester and when she asked if she could work on her own, I allowed her to. I decided that since she took the initiative and asked, I would give it a try.

See Chapter 12
Connection: Relevant to individual goal structures, Chapter 12

Individualization began a month ago. Both students began on the same page, and, although Tiffany is now several pages behind Laura, she has shown a determination that I had not expected. She has proven to herself that she can accept challenges and, with lots of hard work, accomplish her goals.

It is interesting to note that no other student has asked to work on his or her own. Some I know like the comfort of working in a group with a single focus and pace. Others are not self-motivated enough and need the guidance and daily instruction from me.

Connection: Relevant to seatwork, Chapter 12
See Chapter 12

Many of the kids need constant monitoring to keep them on task; many need to learn better work habits and to complete their assignments within a

Peter Roop uses a variety of teaching techniques depending on the classes' response. In this math class, he combines group instruction with individualized attention.

given period of time. It is interesting to note how far they have come this year in these areas. Mrs. Paterson, who teaches them reading, and I have both focused on many of the same study skills. The extra attention we've given to these areas, along with the students' natural growth and development, have resulted in measurable progress. The majority of the class completes work on time, sticks with assignments with fewer interruptions, and remembers to finish work at home if necessary. These tasks were all quite difficult for this class when the year began.

See Chapter 11
Connection: Relevant to adaptive instruction, Chapter 11

There are twelve boys and ten girls in class. Three are LD students who have been mainstreamed for math. I meet with their LD teacher periodically to discuss their progress; we both feel that they are doing quite well in my class due to, we think, their hard work, their drive to master math, and quite possibly their desire not to be in an LD program for math or reading.

See Chapter 8
Connection: Relevant to ARCS model, Chapter 8

I begin this class by saying, "Yesterday I was bragging about all of you." This gets their attention immediately. "I was bragging about how quickly you've caught onto division with remainders."

"Oh, that's easy," Jack blurts out.

"Well, it was easy because you all paid attention and worked hard to understand it. In fact, Mrs. Paterson wants you to come teach her fourth-graders how to divide with remainders."

"I'll go," shouts Andre.

We all laugh knowing that he would do anything to get out of his own math work even if it means teaching math to someone else.

See Chapter 11
Connection: Relevant to guided practice, Chapter 11

I begin the lesson by reviewing what we covered yesterday, putting problems on the board, doing examples myself, and having students do several on the board for demonstration. I continue the review with a worksheet that has twenty problems on it. I often use worksheets with these children when we begin new material because many of them have difficulty copying problems from a book. When I introduce new material, my goal is understanding leading to mastery. Because we use worksheets, the students are able to concentrate more on the concepts taught than on transposing problems from book to paper. With another group I would use a different approach, one more suited to their needs.

I demonstrate the first worksheet problem on the board and we discuss it. While the children work on the next problem, I walk around the room and look for immediate difficulties.

See Chapter 6
Connection: Relevant to cognitive effort, Chapter 6

I then go around the room and ask for answers to the problems. I call on each child who raises his or her hand and on some who don't. I get a variety of answers.

As we discuss the problem further, I pick up such comments as "Oh, I see" and "But how can you subtract that?" I respond immediately. I am very pleased at the end of class when those who got the answer smile, and those who didn't understand where and how they went wrong. The best moment of all is when someone says, "Oh, now I get it!"

Before class started, I had decided to try something that worked well with last year's fourth-grade math class. That class also had difficulty mastering long division so I broke the problems down to the three smallest steps: Divide, Multiply, and Subtract.

See Chapter 6
Connection: Relevant to comprehension, Chapter 6

"Divide, Multiply, Subtract, Divide, Multiply, Subtract." We repeated it so many times that it became almost a chant. I blocked off the top part of one of my tall blackboards and wrote

See Chapter 9
Connection: Relevant to task analysis, Chapter 9

<u>D</u>ivide

<u>M</u>ultiply

<u>S</u>ubtract

in large block letters with a sample problem alongside. We had this reminder directly in front of us for constant referral.

I sense that now is the time to use this approach with these students. I ask them to tell what steps they took to get their answers.

See Chapter 6
Connection: Relevant to problem analysis, Chapter 6

"We divided," Ira says.

"Is that all?" I ask, leading him on.

He pauses, "No, we also multiplied."

"Anything else?" I ask.

Four hands shoot up as they catch on.

Ira looks puzzled and I wait for him to answer. Waiting for a student to answer is a game that must be played with great skill. It is something that comes from getting to know each student and how they respond. I know that Ira is eager to answer but rarely raises his hand. His answers are almost always correct, and I call on him frequently when others are stuck. Now he is stuck. He knows he should grasp the answer, but is becoming flustered by the others raising their hands, eager to share. More hands go up, but I still wait, trying to judge when it will be best to ask someone else.

See Chapter 12
Connection: Relevant to wait time, Chapter 12

Why do I wait?

Do I want him to complete the whole process?

Yes.

Do I want him to learn to trust his judgment?

Yes.

Do I want him to succeed?

Yes.

The waiting continues. Waiting time varies according to the child, and the amount of frustration read on his or her face. Reading the face is hard, at best, but the payoff is usually worth the wait.

Ira shakes his head and I know that it is time to ask another student.

I choose Andre. His hand isn't raised, but I want to pull him into the discussion. He has difficulty mastering new material unless his full attention is directed toward the material.

See Chapter 11
Connection: Relevant to questioning, Chapter 11

"I think you subtract," he answers hesitantly after glancing at the model problem on the board.

"You're right," I tell him. "Excellent!"

See Chapter 5
Connection: Relevant to reinforcement, Chapter 5

"Who can tell us all three steps?" I now ask, knowing that I will pick someone who grasps it. By doing so, I reinforce the pattern.

"Luis."

"Divide, multiply, subtract."

"Camey."

"Divide, multiply, subtract."

See Chapter 6
Connection: Relevant to maintenance rehearsal, Chapter 6

I bounce around asking each one who raises a hand, allowing each a chance at success.

"Divide, multiply, subtract. Divide, multiply, subtract." It becomes a chant with even the more reluctant students joining in now.

"One more time," I say, judging that I am about to lose them to silliness.

"Divide, multiply, subtract," they shout.

Then I hop up onto the top of Camey's desk.

Their immediate reaction is one of surprise, which is just what I wanted. Now that they have the steps memorized, I want to link them to something visual, in addition to the writing on the board. Jumping onto the desk wasn't planned but it seemed the right thing to do. I knew that they would be a while settling down again, but felt the impact would be worth the excitement.

"Now, Andre, tell me the steps once again."

He has a big grin on his face; I'm sure that I'm doing something he would love to do.

"You divide, multiply, then subtract," he calls out.

I write the three steps in huge letters and then put a problem beside it.

"Ira, how should I work this?"

Connection: Relevant to self-reinforcement, Chapter 7
See Chapter 7

"First you divide, see how many sixes will go into twenty-three without going over twenty-three." He takes me through step by step, all correctly, and is beaming when we are finished.

See Chapter 12
Connection: Relevant to classroom dynamics and discipline, Chapter 12

One of the difficulties with this class is that we are learning together when to let go and when to pull back; we are still learning our limits. Each class is different and responds differently to subject matter and teaching approaches. For example, with my CA class we can range far off the topic, knowing full well that when it is time to return, we can quickly regroup, settle down, and refocus our attention. I like to have fun with this class while teaching, but have to closely monitor it because at times I do lose them and most don't get back to the subject at hand.

See Chapter 11
See Chapter 6
Connection: Relevant to seatwork, Chapter 11
Connection: Relevant to retrieval cues, Chapter 6

We do the next four problems on the worksheet in the same way that we did the first problem. I watch to see which students are using the model. Most are and I'm pleased. They can repeat the steps, they have a model to which to turn if they are stuck, and I have provided an unusual link to their memories by standing on the desk. I know that I can refer to this throughout the rest of the year and it will get a response: Either they will remember the exact steps or they will look up at the board.

By doing five examples, I get immediate feedback as to who understands the concept, who is about to grasp it, and who is having difficulty with the concept. Problem 2 had about 50 percent right, 50 percent incorrect. Problem 3 had about 60 percent correct. With each problem the percentage correct improves.

After working through five problems I say, "Now, everyone do Problem 6 and I'll come around. I'll give you the go-ahead if you have it right."

Sometimes we need do only three demonstration problems; sometimes we do up to ten. If a number of kids have caught on and a number have not, we break up into two groups. One continues the assignments on its own; the rest meet to go over more problems. Some children do most of the work in these small groups; others drift in or out depending on whether they understand or not.

I roam the room, helping those having difficulties, answering questions, providing feedback, boosting confidence, giving the go-ahead. Often, I will offer extra help to any student who seems to need it.

Before everyone is working quietly, I decide to provide an extra incentive for completing fifteen of the twenty problems by the time class is over. I usually don't give candy or treats; instead I rely on praise—the squeeze of a shoulder or other signs of reward. But in this case, they seem to be so close to mastering the new material and feel so positive that I say, "I'll give everyone who finishes up to Problem Fifteen by the time class is over a piece of candy."

The response is immediate. Heads pop down, pencils flash.

I concentrate on working with Andre. We go through each step several times, then I have him show me. He refers constantly to the board; he needs this reinforcement. With enough repetition, I hope he will remember the steps in order.

Unit Meeting

All but three children finish the fifteen problems by the time we go for our weekly unit meeting at 1:00. Most have done all twenty. I tell the three who are not finished that they can work during recess if they wish. They want to. Oh, what they won't do for a piece of candy!

I wonder if this assessment is correct. Is it the candy or is it the idea of a reward? Would a penny have worked? Or additional recess time? I'll try it and see another time.

I dismiss the class and we go together down to the "Reading Pit," the usual place for our unit meetings. We meet once a week with the entire unit, all 108 children and 4 teachers, to discuss problems, show pets, discuss field trips, celebrate birthdays.

My first order of business is to remind the students about overdue books and discuss why books need to be returned on time. "You all know how it feels to want a book and not be able to find it, even after several weeks. This is why you should get your books back so that others can check them out."

We next celebrate reading awards for our "Read"ch for the Stars reading incentive program. We began this program two years ago to promote reading. Its goals are progressively harder the longer a student participates; it is surprising the number of students who continue to voluntarily participate in the program. At our unit meetings we acknowledge their efforts in front of the entire group. Six awards are given today.

See Chapter 13
Connection: Relevant to formative evaluation, Chapter 13

See Chapter 5
Connection: Relevant to positive reinforcement, Chapter 5

See Chapter 11
Connection: Relevant to reciprocal teaching, Chapter 11

See Chapter 5
Connection: Relevant to operant analysis, Chapter 5

See Chapter 8
Connection: Relevant to extrinsic motivation, Chapter 8

Since it is St. Patrick's Day we have a discussion about who St. Patrick was, why green is the St. Patrick's Day color, and what other colors symbolize holidays. This is an open-ended discussion with several children contributing and others asking questions. Sometimes these "topical" discussions go on for ten or fifteen minutes depending on the children's interest.

Sharing is an important part of every unit meeting. Today, Stephen has a special tadpole to share. He brings his pet up to the front of the group and tells us where he got the tadpole and how he feeds it. He also tells the group that the tadpole came from Africa and is specially bred, that it has sides through which you can see.

We promote this type of sharing, encouraging the children to bring things so that they have the experience of speaking before a large group and answering a variety of questions. Because most of the children have always been in units at McKinley, speaking in front of large groups becomes a natural thing for them to do. We want them to be prepared to answer questions in front of groups; most become quite adept at this during the time they are with us.

I kick Tyler out of the meeting because he has interrupted twice by talking with his neighbor. I will talk with him later in my room. This is the way that discipline is usually handled for these meetings; those who can't sit and participate are removed and talked with and/or punished later so as not to further interrupt the meeting.

Recess

We finish the unit meeting in time for recess. We dismiss the unit to go get their coats. Tyler is waiting for me. This is not his first time in being kicked out of a unit meeting and he already knows the consequences. He has a book in his hand.

"What was so important that you had to interrupt the meeting?"

He says nothing, staring at me.

I wait. He waits. I wait until he replies, "Nothing."

"Do you know why we don't want you to interrupt?" I ask, trying a different approach.

"Because the other kids can't hear," he says.

"Right. Now take your book and sit in the hall. You can silent read until recess is over."

He glares at me but obeys. He is a hard child to work with. Most of my contact with him involves discipline. I try to modify this contact at times by kidding him in the halls, but he is unresponsive to this tack. I'll have to try something else, I guess.

Marti approaches with a question, "Can I stay in to work on my windows for my fort?"

"Sure," I answer. "Will you help Tiffany if she has any questions?"

"Okay," she replies. I wonder if Tiffany will understand the math better with help from Marti. Many times it works out well when kids teach kids because they can explain things in their own terms. For some children this provides a "breakthrough" in understanding something difficult. I try to encourage this situation whenever possible.

I usually play outside during the afternoon recess. It gives me the opportunity to step outside my role as teacher and to just play. The fresh air is good

See Chapter 5
Connection: Relevant to practice effects, Chapter 5

See Chapter 5
Connection: Relevant to time-out, Chapter 5

See Chapter 12
Connection: Relevant to I-messages, Chapter 12

See Chapter 11
Connection: Relevant to peer tutoring, Chapter 11

for me, too, and playing outside seems to make the rest of the afternoon go more quickly. (When I'm on recess duty, I do not play at all. The responsibility is too great not to keep a roving eye on all the playground areas, watching for fights, accidents, rough situations.)

Another reason why I find myself outside in the afternoon involves my other responsibilities. This year, the aides have had recess duty. We have had problems with children who do not respect the aides enough. These kids seem to think that because the aides are not teachers that they can't enforce the school rules. We have had several discussions with our unit kids and seemed to have straightened them out about this. Still, it has proven helpful to have me outside at times during recess to bolster authority if need be.

See Chapter 12
Connection: Relevant to withitness, Chapter 12

Today the wind is too strong for football. I decide to stay inside and work on my lesson plan for Monday. After jotting down some follow-up ideas for Monday's lessons, I join Susan, Connie, and Jane who are talking in the hall.

See Chapter 9
Connection: Relevant to planning, Chapter 9

"Any way can we switch to something other than social studies?" Connie asks.

"Why don't you take the entire unit for storytelling or something?" Jane suggests teasingly.

"After all, it is Friday," Susan adds.

We all know, however, that we are under a tight time restriction for our social studies units. In order to finish the required material by the end of April and to do it properly we have to teach it today.

See Chapter 9
Connection: Relevant to curricular objectives, Chapter 9

Silent Reading

The bell rings and the kids return, still talking among themselves as they go back to their classrooms. They go immediately to their desks and take out their library books for silent reading.

We have silent reading and milk after the afternoon recess in order to settle them down. This is a routine which rarely varies. Our morning is so crowded that we are unable to have a regular silent reading then. In the afternoon, teachers read with the students or provide some extra instruction for particular children.

See Chapter 4
Connection: Relevant to physical characteristics, Chapter 4

I assign daily monitors to watch that kids are reading. The monitoring structure is something agreed on at the beginning of the year. By giving them responsibility for monitoring themselves, I let them have a little more control in the room. There are two monitors and each keeps a list of names of kids not reading or who talk. At the end of silent reading, I compare the lists, and if a name is on both lists, that student has to remain five minutes after school. I don't listen to excuses but make them report to me to discuss things.

See Chapter 12
Connection: Relevant to classroom rules, Chapter 12

Social Studies

At 2:10, we move for social studies. This quarter social studies has been set up by homeroom groupings, to provide a more heterogeneous grouping than we have in math or reading. Both third and fourth graders cover the same material this year, Wisconsin history, the regular fourth-grade curriculum area.

Today we are doing map activities to learn the five geographic regions of Wisconsin. The activity requires the children to follow specific instructions

Connection: Relevant to social characteristics, Chapter 4
See Chapter 4

Connection: Relevant to heterogeneous groups, Chapter 11
See Chapter 11

and locate places on the map, connecting them with black watercolor markers to outline the regions on plastic-coated maps.

I begin the lesson with a review of what we have covered before. "Who can name the four states that border Wisconsin?"

See Chapter 10
Connection: Relevant to events of instruction, Chapter 10

A dozen hands shoot up. Most of the children have learned these states because we have repeated them each day of our session.

Next I ask, "What are two kinds of borders we share with other states?"

I call on Wendy mostly because she has such an eager look on her face.

"Political and natural borders."

"Right. Now who can tell us the difference between natural and political borders."

Only a few hands are raised this time. I call on Marti because I am interested in hearing how she defines them.

"A political border is set up by a government. A natural border is something natural like a river or a lake shared with another state."

See Chapter 5
Connection: Relevant to verbal praise, Chapter 5

"Wow! Marti that was wonderful. You gave the best definition of a political border that any of the groups has given so far. I wish I could have explained it that well myself."

Marti is beaming as we turn to the maps.

There is a buzz of excitement as the maps are handed around. I watch as the students point things out to their neighbors, spotting Appleton, Madison, and other cities. I let them look their maps over for several minutes before refocusing their attention.

Connection: Relevant to prior knowledge, Chapter 13
See Chapter 13

"Who can tell one thing they saw on their map?"

I go around the room getting their responses until about ten have answered.

Then I pull a trick.

"I will pay $5.00 to anyone who can find this town in ten seconds."

Every eye is focused on me and every ear listening.

See Chapter 8
Connection: Relevant to attention, Chapter 8

I write the word *Unity* on the board. I know that Unity is a tiny town in the central part of the state and know that no one will be able to find it unless that person is extremely lucky. I watch the clock while listening to their comments.

"Oh, wow!"

"Where is it?"

"How can we ever find it?"

"Here it is!"

My heart jumps, but I quickly see that he is pointing to the southern part of the state.

"Time's up."

"That's impossible," Luke comments. "How can we ever find a city in ten seconds?"

"Before I show you, is there anyone who knows what I'm going to tell you?"

Far in the back of the room Hank raises his hand. Knowing that Hank is a geography fan, I call on him.

"By using the grid numbers and letters."

There are several "Oh, yeahs" as Hank has reminded them of something they have heard before.

See Chapter 6
Connection: Relevant to cued recall, Chapter 6

I draw a grid pattern on the board with A–D on the top and 1–4 along the side. "If Unity was at A-3, how many think they could find it?"

Most hands rocket up. I then tell them the coordinates of the real Unity. I glance at the clock to see how long before somebody finds it. It takes almost thirty seconds but then just about everyone finds it.

We practice several more towns, as first I give the coordinates, and then the kids do.

"Now that we've warmed up, we are going to find the five regions of the state."

I write the five regions on the board for reference and the order in which we will outline them on the maps. Then I pull down the large wall map of Wisconsin and sketch the regions with my finger, giving the kids an idea of the regions we will be marking. Then we turn to specific regions and show them how to mark them on their maps.

There is a pleasant buzz throughout the entire activity as the children find the cities and outline the regions. They show each other places they have discovered and help one another locate the cities we are spotting.

I enjoy this kind of teaching activity. There is a structure provided by the maps themselves, but a great deal of latitude in how we use them. I try to be open enough to begin another course of action if the situation warrants it. I will plan a similar lesson for Monday because this one was so positive and everyone became actively involved.

See Chapter 12
Connection: Relevant to seatwork, Chapter 12

There are not many times during the day when I can sit back and just observe. This map activity provided me with that opportunity because I could give the instructions and then watch as they were followed. This procedure gave me a chance to observe the children as they helped each other, to spot kids having difficulty and watch how they resolved it without me stepping in, to watch individuals make connections as they participated in activity. These types of observations go on continually, but rarely do I sit back and just watch them without getting involved in the action myself. I should do more of this type of observation, I tell myself.

We had only one problem during the period and it wasn't really a problem. Gary, an LD student, put one of the marking pens into his mouth while he was working on his map. He wound up with a black mouth from the pen. My initial reaction was to scold him, but I held back. After I told him what his mouth looked like, he looked puzzled, then smiled, and hopped up to look in my closet mirror.

See Chapter 10
Connection: Relevant to characteristics of learners, Chapter 10

"I'm a clown now," he laughed, "with black makeup on." Gary flashed a huge smile at all of us in the room and left.

By using a little humor, we were able to take a potentially negative situation and have fun with it.

While the kids resumed their work, I thought about a friend with whom I had recently taken a writing class. One of our assignments was to write a personal essay. Merrill's essay was about her son who has a learning disability and how she has come to grips with this difficulty. I thought of Gary and his family and how they are all cooperating in trying to help him build other strengths to compensate for his learning problems. By watching Gary and trying to imagine his mother's reaction when he came home with a black mouth, I sensed a little what Merrill must feel.

See Chapter 4
Connection: Relevant to learning disabilities, Chapter 4

At three we stopped and began cleaning the maps. I had the students bring the maps to a back table for me to inspect before they left the class. Only a few of the maps needed another swipe with a damp towel before they passed inspection.

⌒ The Day's End

The last ten minutes of each day are spent reviewing the highlights of the day, getting homework together, picking up the room, cleaning the boards, handing out notes for home, and putting the chairs on the desks so that the floors can be swept that night.

I wait until the children settle down and then call on three students for the highlights of their day.

"Beating you on the computer," Jack chortled.

"Wearing green clothes all day," Camey said.

"Making the coding machine," Andre added.

See Chapter 5
Connection: Relevant to reinforcement menu, Chapter 5

The leader for the day passes out the notes for home. There is a noisy bustle as they put up their chairs. I dismiss them a minute early to get their coats on. I stay in the hall to say good-bye to the kids after the bell rings, chatting, teasing, and answering a few more questions. Other kids from other units stop by on their way out of the building, as do some of the other teachers.

Connection: Relevant to lesson planning, Chapter 9
See Chapter 9

We chat about each other's weekend plans before we say good-bye. I return to my room to finish writing my lesson plans.

See Chapter 5
Connection: Relevant to appetitive consequences, Chapter 5

On my way out I call Roy's aunt for our biweekly checkup on his progress. This progress report call every two weeks has been good for Roy. He gets praise at home when it is due and encouragement when he falls behind. He senses the positive cooperation between his aunt and myself. There has been a noticeable improvement in his interest in school since we began these calls.

This teaching day, St. Patrick's Day, 1989 is over at McKinley School, though it is difficult to say when a day is really "over." Jack will tell a lot of people how he beat me on the computer. Several parents will learn that I chopped off the coding machines' alphabets. The $5.00 lost in rural Wisconsin will linger in some students' minds. I just hope "Divide! Multiply! Subtract!" fares as well. I wonder if I'll see vestiges of today's problem on the board next year.

All in all, a good teaching day. As I pull into my driveway, I wonder, "What kind of day did my own children have at their schools? Do their teachers feel as good as I do?" I sure hope so.

⌒ ⌒ ⌒ ⌒ ⌒ ⌒ ⌒ ⌒ ⌒ ⌒ ⌒ ⌒ ⌒ ⌒ ⌒ ⌒

Chap. Obj. 3
Test Ques. 1.14–1.23; 1.31–1.42

Focus Question: How does teaching experience contribute to teaching expertise?

EXPERIENCE AND EXPERTISE

The "Diary of a Day" is a report of an expert teacher's typical teaching day. We see him handle each situation and then move on with the day's agenda. The day runs smoothly, even though unexpected events occur. Peter moves through the day without becoming agitated or uncomfortable; he always seems to be in control, even when he makes mistakes. By the end of the day, we see that his students have made instructional progress. They made progress despite the many distractions that confronted him. He kept them on task and made it look easy. Ease and grace are hallmarks of expert performance.

If you have ever seen Steffi Graf execute a top-spin lob, or Stephen Jay Gould lecture, you know that experts make it look easy. They make it look so easy that you become caught up in the performance without questioning the work, the practice, the experience which preceded the performance. It is only after you have observed an expert performance, analyzed it, and tried to do it yourself that you can see how hard it is.

Peter Roop's talents may not seem extraordinary the way Michael Jordan's abilities seem extraordinary, but *could* you have done everything Peter did? Suppose you had been a substitute teacher for Peter that day. Suppose that you—without the benefit of Peter's teaching experience, his knowledge and understanding of students—had started teaching the coding machine project and chopped off the alphabets of many of the students in the class. What would have happened?

Field Observation: Have students observe and report on expert performances of classroom teachers. As an alternative, they could report on unnamed professors they have for courses. Other alternatives include the expert performances of athletes, movie actors, musicians, a mother or father, etc.

A St. Patrick's Day Analysis

A close reading of Peter's "Diary" will reveal the themes and techniques that Peter, as an experienced teacher, feels are important to stress in the classroom.

Themes

Peter has special interests that become themes in his teaching. For example, Peter places importance on self-regulation. He wants his students to develop a sense of responsibility for their work. The forts were a result of Peter's effort to find a way for Andre to do his work without having to be constantly prodded. The spelling contests allowed students to choose whether or not to participate. Notice also that journal writing is a regular feature in Peter's classroom. Although journal writing was not scheduled for that Friday, Peter was quick to take advantage of Heidi's enthusiasm for telling the story of the locked bathroom door by encouraging her to present it in written form.

Reading for enjoyment is another theme of Peter's teaching approach. He reads to his students, takes a very active role in helping students select reading material in the library, and has developed a literature program for all of the students in the unit. Clearly, Peter has special interests, and those interests influence his behavior as a teacher.

Lecture Note: Ask students to identify the themes used by particularly effective teachers they have had.

Flexibility

In addition to self-regulation, highlighting the importance Peter places on his approach to the forts provides insight into another aspect of his teaching expertise, his flexibility. This flexibility allows him to take advantage of situations as they arise. The forts were Andre's idea. Peter used Andre's interest, and later Marti and Judy's interest in a joint fort, to achieve certain goals.

He again demonstrated his flexibility in the way that he handled the change in the keyboarding schedule that doubled the class size for the coding machine lesson. Later, when Heidi and Abby expressed interest in the coding machines prior to the lesson, he tested some of his expectations about the lesson by observing them. At the same time he realizes that, during the lesson, he would be able to use Heidi and Abby as peer tutors. He always seems to be looking for ways to use unanticipated student behavior, especially enthusiastic behavior, to bring about positive outcomes.

Connection: Enthusiastic behavior can be explained in terms of intrinsic motivation. The undermining effect, discussed in Chapter 8, is pertinent here.

Issues in Educational Psychology

CNN™ This box relates to Segment 1 of the CNN videotape. See the Instructor's Section for a summary.

ELEVATING TEACHING STANDARDS

In 1987, the National Board for Professional Teaching Standards was founded. Unlike state licensing boards, which vary in their certification requirements, certification by the National Board represents "standards for measuring excellence rather than minimum competency," according to James Hunt, Jr., in a *Teacher Magazine* article. Hunt is the organization's chairperson and a former governor of North Carolina.

The first teacher assessments are scheduled to begin in 1993. The assessments cover over thirty fields, including English, math, science, art, foreign languages, and special education. The fields are divided into five categories, from early childhood to young adulthood.

Teachers with a bachelor's degree and three years experience in a primary or secondary school may apply for certification. The National Education Association (NEA) objected to these requirements, stating that certification should be granted only to those teachers who have a state license and have graduated from an accredited teacher education program. The American Association of Colleges for Teacher Education, with over 700 members, joined the NEA in urging the Board to reevaluate its certification policy.

Proponents of licensing and teacher education don't agree with observers such as Denis Doyle, a senior research fellow at the Hudson Institute. "Most good teachers," said Doyle in a *Teacher Magazine* article, "learn how to teach on the job, working at the elbow of an accomplished master teacher."

Whether or not the policy is altered, the Board faces other major challenges, such as teacher acceptance of its program. Although certification is voluntary, not all teachers are enamored of the idea. "I don't know who would want to go through this assessment, especially when all that matters is the opinion of your building supervisor at the local level," Angie Rinaldo, a Colorado social studies teacher, told the *Chronicle of Higher Education.*

In the same article, James Kelly, Board president, observed that "it is taking a little longer than I thought it would for the mission of the National Board—what it is and what it isn't—to be clearly understood."

What concerns most teachers are the assessments themselves. Rather than taking standard written tests, teachers' evaluations will be based on how they perform in classroom situations. Initial assessments may include videotaping a class while the teacher works with students rather than the traditional in-class observation. Other evaluation methods may include having the teacher's critique taped. Portfolios of both a teacher's and students' work may also be included in the process. Assessment standards are currently being developed by independent concerns, such as the Educational Testing Service and the Far West Laboratory for Education Research and Development.

Concerns have been raised about the assessors' ability to remain objective. Stephen Klein, a senior research scientist at the Rand Corporation, voiced his concern in the *Chronicle,* saying that "age, race, how a person is dressed—all these can influence an evaluation when the people who do the grading can see the person being graded."

The National Board still has obstacles to overcome, from teacher acceptance tc the form that the assessment procedures take. But the Board's purpose—to raise teaching standards and the status of teachers—is an idea whose time has come.

SOURCES: Watkins, Beverly T. "Teaching-Standards Board Foresees a Battle for Recognition, Acceptance." *Chronicle of Higher Education 36* (July 11, 1990): A14. "Forging a Profession." *Teacher Magazine* 1, no. 1 (September/October 1989): 12–16. "Wait a Minute. . . ." *Teacher Magazine* 1, no. 6 (March 1990): 16–18. "National Board Update." *Teacher Magazine* 2, no. 8 (May/June 1991): 17.

1. What do you think you would learn if you were a student teacher supervised by Peter Roop? Which of your weaknesses might be strengthened and which strengths reinforced?
2. Do you think that many of the situations in Peter Roop's day could be measured by tests? If so, which ones and how?

Planning, the Basis of Spontaneity

Peter's teaching is also based on planning. His effective planning allows him to be flexible and spontaneous. It frees him from worries about content so that he is able to concentrate on his students during the teaching day. He can focus on individual students, make mistakes, tolerate jokes at his expense—all because his careful preparation of the content he is teaching allows him also to focus on the people in his classroom.

Learning Students

The diary reveals another aspect of Peter's expertise, his belief that knowing and understanding students is a key to teaching well. He talks with the students. He listens to their stories and jokes. He builds time into his schedule to allow students to communicate informally with each other and with him.

Peter's efforts to understand his students allow him to "read" their behavior, individually and collectively. His observations allow him to judge how far he can go in joking with his math class without losing control. He reads Ira's hesitation in answering a question, balancing the benefit of Ira's coming up with the answer on his own against the liability of embarrassing him in front of his peers. He uses his judgment in determining how long he can wait before calling on someone else.

Peter can tell by reading the behavior of his students whether or not a particular course of action is working. Peter's attempts to teach long division, his practice of allowing students to chat at the beginning of a day, his challenge during the map-reading session in social studies, are all experiments of a sort. Peter attempts to bring about an outcome by establishing, through his own behavior, a set of conditions. Some of his experiments are planned efforts, the use of journal writing, for example. Other experiments—such as his decision to let Heidi and Abby work on the coding machines—are executed spontaneously in response to unanticipated events. In either case, Peter is experimenting; he is making decisions, then reading student behavior in order to evaluate the quality of those decisions.

Chapter 15 Casebook Preview/Field Observation: Generally, the classroom experiments in the casebook were planned in response to problems the teacher faced. Students might be asked to interview practicing teachers in order to identify examples of "spontaneous experiments."

Routines and Hypotheses

Peter has developed instructional routines that signal the end of one activity and the beginning of another. For example, when Peter sits on the "cool stool," his students know that they are to focus their attention on him and what he is about to say. Surely the "cool stool" did not work its magic on the first day of school. Routines develop when teachers experiment with ideas to solve problems. Peter needed a way to signal the beginning of large group activities. He tested hypotheses until he hit on the "cool stool" idea. He experienced some success, correcting and refining his use of the stool until it served its intended function with his class. Routines become established by testing hypotheses generated to help the teacher function effectively.

Every effective teacher must find ways to begin lessons, but not every teacher can use the "cool stool." Consider the high school physics teacher who, as soon as the bell rings, claps her hands, shouts "OK, let's go!", and then asks a question and answers it herself. She does this for every class, every day. The routine causes confusion in her students for the first week or so, but soon students enter the room and quickly get out their notebooks and pencils in an attempt to "beat the teacher."

Connection: Routines are discussed under management skills in Chapter 13.

Lecture Note: A junior high or high school teacher must begin activities—he or she must start anew six or seven times each day. It is unlikely, however, that a high school teacher will be able to use Peter's routine. Some high school teachers use a stool to signal attention, but it is not called a "cool stool."

You too will have to develop routines that serve necessary functions. Doing so is a problem you will have to use your own experiences to solve.

Using Expert Performance

Lecture Note: The Teacher Chronicles and the Casebook provide students with accounts of expert performance. (See also the Teaching Anecdote annotations in the AIE.)

Field Observation/Journal Entry: Have students observe expert classroom teachers throughout the course. If, as Glaser says, observing expert performance provides the novice with a temporary theory, such observations are a source of hypotheses: ideas of what actions to take when one has little or no personal experience. Have students keep a journal of teaching hypotheses.

Chap. Obj. 3
Test Ques. 1.27–1.28; 1.43–1.56

Focus Question: What should aspiring teachers do about their lack of classroom experience?

Huberman (1985) identified various problems faced by first-year teachers, including discipline, motivation, materials, and student differences. He asked experienced teachers how long it took them to solve the problems. A majority of the experienced teachers judged that developing workable solutions for several of the problems required no less than five-years experience.

Huberman's research might seem depressing: five years! Maybe that's why so many teachers drop out of teaching in the first five years. Novice teachers don't have the experience necessary to solve the problems they face in the classroom every day. It sounds like the old catch-22: You can't do the job well without experience, but you first need to do the job to gain experience.

Solutions to the problems faced by first-year teachers do exist. If other teachers have solved the problems, why not try their solutions? Their solutions may not always work, but their solutions provide hypotheses to test. The solutions of others can be the experiments that provide experience. If a teacher doesn't have experience, why not use someone else's?

Glaser (1987) suggested that the performance of experts can supply novices with a way of thinking about their practice, a temporary theory or framework. Using an expert's performance as the basis for an intuitive theory is a way for novices to gain the kind of experience that leads to expertise. (See Figure 1–3.)

SCIENTIFIC PRINCIPLES AND THE ART OF TEACHING

William James was the greatest psychologist of his day. His *Principles of Psychology,* published in 1890, was lauded as "a work of genius such as is rare in any language and in any country." James has been called the "Father of American Psychology."

It is highly significant that James, an eminent theorist, selected educators to be one of his first audiences. James had much to say about the classroom use of psychological theory. He warned teachers that the scientific theories of psychology, while helpful to teachers, are not recipes for effective teaching.

William James, the "Father of American Psychology," stressed the importance of a creative mind in applying scientific theories to the art of teaching.

> Psychology is a science, and teaching is an art; and sciences never generate arts directly out of themselves. An intermediary inventive mind must make the application, by using its originality.
>
> A science only lays down lines within which the rules of the art must fall, laws which the follower of the art must not transgress; but what particular thing he [or she] shall positively do within those lines is left exclusively to his [or her] own genius (1959, pp. 23–24).

The laws of science differ from the laws of society. Laws passed by governments are optional; we can obey them or ignore them. If we choose not to obey, we may be punished, but we can break them.

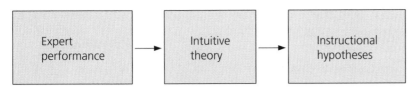

■ **Figure 1–3** *Developing Instructional Hypotheses*

Scientific laws are inflexible; we have no choice but to obey them. Suppose a woman jumps from the top of the Sears Tower in Chicago. The scientific law of gravity leaves her little choice: She will fall swiftly to the ground, most likely to her death. However, should she choose to equip herself with a parachute, she could foil the law of gravity by exploiting other laws of physics.

The idea that scientific laws or principles can and should be exploited is consistent with James's advice to teachers in 1892. Science identifies the boundaries within which art must fall, but these boundaries are more or less constraining depending on the creativity and innovation of the artist. The innovator pushes back the boundaries through exploitation of scientific principles.

Which psychological principles operate in classrooms, and how does a teacher, with little or no experience, exploit them? Educational psychology can show you *what* principles to exploit. Accounts of expert teaching show you *how* to do the exploiting.

We conclude this chapter by discussing the organization of this book—describing how principles of educational psychology and accounts of teaching are linked in subsequent chapters.

ORGANIZATION OF THE BOOK

Chap. Obj. 4
Test Ques. 1.57–1.71

Assign Chapter 1 of the *Study Guide*.

Focus Question: How will this book help an aspiring teacher develop professionally?

The book is organized into four parts. Part I (Chapter 1) has focused on the *Teacher as Learner*. Part II (Chapters 2–8) provides information about *Students as Learners:* the development of students, their ways of learning, and the factors that motivate their behavior. Part II will help you learn to "read" the students you will teach.

Part III (Chapters 9–14) examines the *Teacher as Decision-Maker:* your instructional planning, your interaction with students, and your evaluation of their progress.

Part IV (Chapter 15), *Teacher as Researcher,* presents classroom experiments of practicing teachers. You will see how hypotheses are tested in real classrooms by real teachers working with real students.

The most important part of the book is not listed in the Contents: what you already know about teaching. You know a great deal about teaching even if you have never taught. You have observed—at close range and for considerable lengths of time—a lot of teachers. If your K–12 schooling was of the usual sort, you have observed roughly seventy-five teachers operate in their classrooms. Granted, your frame of reference was that of a student rather than as an aspiring teacher. However, reflecting on the actions of your former

Profiles in Successful Practice

SCOTT NIQUETTE

McKINLEY ELEMENTARY SCHOOL

APPLETON, WISCONSIN

"I wonder what having a classroom of my own will be like?" This question frequently crossed my mind throughout my college and student-teaching days. The answer is that my first year was difficult. Nonetheless, it represented the realization of a long-time dream.

As I went through college, I made notes on procedures that would make me an effective teacher. My college education provided me a sound understanding of teaching. I acquired the basic tools I needed to become a successful instructor. However, when I finally became a full-time teacher after I graduated from college, I encountered many problems that my notebooks could not answer. Yes, I learned it is best to be well prepared for lessons, but what happens if the film projector blows or the well-planned lesson ends fifteen minutes before the end of class? These spontaneous educational situations were by far my most difficult experiences in student teaching. At the same time, these experiences opened my eyes to a more encompassing picture of education. Keeping a journal of daily routines, building a good rapport with the students, and simply trying new and different ideas despite fear of failure were among the most productive practices I took from student teaching.

Although practice teaching taught me a great deal about education, children, and myself, substitute teaching taught me about the fine skills of classroom management and spontaneous instruction. For example, I will never forget the penny a student threw at me in my very first subbing experience. I remember thinking to myself, "Should I ignore it? Should I send him to the principal's office?" I decided instead not to make a big deal out of it and responded, "If you want to throw money at me, throw dollar bills—they do not hurt as much, and I can buy more pizza too!" I found that showing students a willingness to work with them and providing appropriate positive reinforcement for work well done went much further than threats and screaming. When you are in front of a class, the children challenge you to be yourself. You have the choice of being a boring facilitator of information or an enthusiastic professional who ignites a love for learning within his or her students.

Before my first day as a school staff member, I recall being very anxious about my career's beginning. Substitute teaching in the classroom of a twenty-year veteran of the profession was one thing, but starting a program and establishing expectations of your own was another. "Did I plan enough?" "Are the kids going to respond to me in a respectful way?" "Will I make a good impression?" These and other questions ran through my mind. I believe that my first year has been successful because I followed through on the educational philosophy that I've nurtured since college, worked and shared ideas with professional colleagues, and continued to grow along with my students. For instance, before the students enter my classroom, I try to create a warm and positive learning environment that will best stimulate student growth. Structuring and planning lessons around students' interests and presenting the lessons in a motivating manner have proven effective. I find great joy in learning along with students. They are, in their own ways, also teachers. It is amazing what a person can learn from children—their perceptions can be very unique. Although I am still learning and modifying effective classroom techniques, I have found being firm and consistent to be the keys to control. Letting the students know your expectations, holding them accountable for their actions, and providing choices for them and the opportunity to cooperate with each other have been very effective.

Overall, this first year of full-time teaching has been quite positive. Knowing that I have touched students and provided them with some of the tools they will use throughout their lives is a very moving and satisfying experience.

teachers from your present vantage point can be instructive. How many times have you thought of a former teacher and said to yourself one of two things: "I will never teach like (fill in the name of a former teacher)," or "I hope I can teach like (fill in the name of a former teacher)."

Reflecting on past classroom experiences will make your job of comprehending and applying educational psychology easier.

Questions, Chronicles, Principles, and Reflections

The features described here apply to all remaining chapters but exclude the casebook (Chapter 15).

Each chapter begins with *Focus Questions.* The Focus Questions provide a context for the chapter. They invite you to reflect on what you already know.

Each chapter contains stories of teachers and students in action. These stories, called *Teacher Chronicles,* are based on the experiences of practicing teachers. The Teacher Chronicles cover teaching experiences ranging from kindergarten to Grade 12.

The Teacher Chronicles allow you to "view" performances—both successful and unsuccessful—of master teachers, to "hear" the questions these teachers ask themselves, to vicariously "experience" teachers teaching.

The Teacher Chronicles are written in the voice of a composite teacher, allowing the reader to share the experiences of master teachers across grade levels. As you listen to this voice, think about the most effective teachers you have had. They are part of the voice. If you can turn your experience into expertise, you will be adding your voice to theirs.

The *Principles in Practice* features, found at the end of each major topic section in the chapter, summarize educational psychology principles and relate them to the preceding Teacher Chronicle.

At the end of each chapter, there is a section called *Reflections: Building Your Theory of Teaching,* designed to help you build, through reflection, your intuitive theory of teaching.

Lecture Note: Remind students that the experiences they have had in classrooms, their current beliefs about and intuitive theory of teaching, their educational values, and their knowledge of self are sources of prior knowledge; that their prior knowledge is critical to any learning situation. In order to make new information, ideas, and concepts meaningful, people must integrate the new material with what they already know (i.e., their prior knowledge). In order to judge the practical utility of a psychological principle, they must make a judgment on the basis of what they know and believe. In order to apply a psychological principle, they must first understand the principle and then judge its utility. The Principles in Practice features will be helpful in this regard.

Lecture Note: Review the Contents with students, pointing out the function of the various features.

Chapter Summary

Introduction: Expert Theories
The chapter begins by distinguishing intuitive theories from scientific theories. Intuitive theories are the understandings that people have of everyday events, including the clinical practice of teaching.

Learning to Read Classrooms
Berliner identifies characteristics that distinguish experts from novices. Expert teachers have intuitive theories that allow them to "read" classrooms better than novices. Educational psychology, a source of scientific theories, can help the novice learn how to read behavior in classrooms.

The Diary of a Day
This account demonstrates the way Peter Roop carried out the functions of teaching in his classroom on March 17, 1989. The diary does not define the

way that all teachers should teach, but it does demonstrate the functions all teachers must fulfill. The marginal comments accompanying the diary indicate that the principles of educational psychology address the events that occur in real classrooms.

Experience and Expertise
Teaching experience is necessary for the development of teaching expertise, but experience does not guarantee expertise.

A St. Patrick's Day Analysis
The analysis of Peter Roop's teaching day yielded the presence of several themes. Peter allows his special interests to be part of, and therefore, enthuse his teaching. Other characteristics of his approach include flexibility, which is afforded by careful planning, and the belief that he must know his students as individuals in order to teach them effectively. Finally, Peter's testing of hypotheses has led to the development of effective classroom routines.

Using Expert Performance
New teachers lack the experience necessary to develop solutions to the problems they will most certainly face in their first classroom. A strategy for overcoming the lack of experience is to use the performances of experienced (and, better yet, expert) teachers as a guide to one's own performance. The solution of an expert teacher may not work as a model for every new teacher, but it will provide a hypothesis that can be tested. Testing hypotheses is a way to build the experience that leads to expertise.

Scientific Principles and the Art of Teaching
Science provides us with knowledge of the principles that govern phenomena. Art is the exploitation of those principles for some purpose. Educational psychology informs us about the principles that govern behavior in classrooms. Teachers who test these principles in their own classrooms can learn to exploit them for positive outcomes.

Organization of the Book
The book is organized into four parts: I. Teacher as Learner (the content of the present chapter); II. Students as Learners; III. Teacher as Decision-Maker; and IV. Teacher as Researcher. Chapters in the second and third parts contain features designed to relate theory to practice and to build a theory of teaching through reflection.

Reflections: Building Your Theory of Teaching

1.1 Thinking back on your own school experiences, describe a teacher you would wish to model. Describe a teacher you would not use as a model for your own teaching.

1.2 Recalling Peter's routines from the "Diary of a Day," select one, identifying the function served by that routine. Using your intuitive theory, generate a hypothesis that you could test in a classroom you imagine to be yours.

Key Terms

teaching (p. 4)   educational psychology (p. 6)
theory (p. 5)   reflection (p. 6)

Suggested Readings

Freedman, S. G. (1990). *Small victories.* New York: Harper & Row.

Kidder, J. T. (1989). *Among schoolchildren.* Boston: Houghton-Mifflin.

Marquis, D. M., & Sachs, R. (1990). *I am a teacher.* New York: Simon & Schuster.

Palonsky, S. (1985). *900 shows a year.* New York: McGraw.

Raphael, R. (1985). *The teacher's voice: A sense of who we are.* Portsmouth, NH: Heinemann.

Rubin, L. J. (1985). *Artistry in teaching.* New York: Random House.

Shulman, L. S. (1986). Those who understand: Knowledge growth in teaching. *Educational Researcher, 15*, 2, 4–14.

References

Glaser, R. (1987). On the nature of expertise. *Proceedings of the In Memorium: Herman Ebbinghaus Symposium.* Amsterdam, The Netherlands: Elsevier-North Holland Publishers.

Hanninen, G. (1985). Do experts exist in gifted education? Unpublished manuscript, University of Arizona, College of Education, Tucson.

Housner, C. D., & Griffey, D. C. (1985). Teacher cognition: Differences in planning and interactive decision-making between experienced and inexperienced teachers. *Research Quarterly for Exercise and Sport, 56,* 45–53.

Huberman, M. (1985). What knowledge is of most worth to teachers? Knowledge-use perspective. *Teaching and Teacher Education, 1,* 251–262.

Kagan, D. (1988). Teaching as clinical problem solving: A critical examination of the analogy and its implications. *Review of Educational Research, 58,* 482–505.

Leinhardt, G., & Greeno, J. D. (1986). The cognitive skill of teaching. *Journal of Educational Psychology, 78,* 75–95.

Smith, L. C., & Geoffrey, W. (1968). *The complexities of an urban classroom.* New York: Holt, Rinehart & Winston.

Swanson, H. L., O'Connor, J. E., & Cooney, J. B. (1990). An information processing analysis of expert and novice teachers' problem solving. *American Educational Research Journal, 27,* (3), 533–556.

2
Cognitive and Linguistic Development

Chapter Overview

This chapter, the first of three on human development, is devoted to cognitive development. (The terms *intellectual, cognitive,* and *mental* will be used in this chapter interchangeably.) Personal and social development are addressed in Chapter 3. Chapter 4 examines the diversity of development.

After considering the nature of developmental change, the chapter examines Piaget's view of cognitive development, introducing not only the stages of development, but also the experiences and mental processes that are associated with them. The chapter also explores useful variations of Piaget's ideas.

Because many classroom experiences depend on language, and teachers must understand the cognitive and linguistic capabilities of their students, the chapter concludes with a section on language development as it relates to cognition. ▪

INTRODUCTION: THE NATURE OF HUMAN DEVELOPMENT

How will you know if your students are capable of doing what you will ask them to do? How will you help them to progress toward realizing their potential? **Developmental psychology,** in its various aspects, is the study of how humans grow toward their potential and of the capabilities that accompany that growth. **Cognitive development theory** attempts to describe how humans gain more and more useful knowledge of their world. **Social development theory** addresses the way in which humans become capable of dealing with other people. **Personal development theory** attempts to explain how one's views of oneself change over the course of the human life span.

Theoretical descriptions of development are based on observations of change. For example, suppose that a girl is unable to swim in June. If we observe, in August, that the same girl can swim competently, we have observed a change. Why did the change occur? Was the girl physically capable of swimming in June, but unable to because she did not know how? Was she physically incapable of swimming in June, but matured enough over the summer to be able to swim in August? Is this a matter of sufficient development or of learning?

Development theories differ from learning theories in that development focuses on human capabilities, while learning focuses on the use of those capabilities. This difference has obvious implications for teaching. If we understand the capabilities students bring to our classrooms, we can do a better job of helping them to use those capabilities, that is, to learn. Attempting to teach reading to a child who is not ready can create problems for both teacher and student. The frustration of trying to learn something of which one is incapable can create negative attitudes toward learning. Imagine, for example, trying to learn most card games before you were capable of reading numbers.

The most influential view of cognitive development is that of Jean Piaget, whose early observations as a biologist influenced the views he developed as a psychologist. The following story is based on actual studies Piaget conducted as a biologist.

Jean Piaget: A Curious Biologist

A curious young biologist moves mollusks that lived in calm water, as did their "ancestors," to a turbulent shore. The descendants of the transplanted mollusks, finding themselves in need of a better foothold on the rocks, adapt to their new environment by growing shorter shells to enhance their foothold. The biologist observes this adaptation and theorizes, "Mollusks can accommodate the environment by changing themselves."

Watching his three children at play, Piaget ponders how children adapt to their environment, how they acquire knowledge of the world, and how their knowledge changes as they grow. The difference between humans and snails, he muses, is that humans can make use of their intellect to adapt to environmental changes. A person's intellectual progress is a matter of constructing increasingly adaptive knowledge of his or her environment.

The biologist, now recognized as a psychologist, writes, *"By what means does the human mind go from a state of less sufficient knowledge to a state of higher knowledge?"* (Piaget, 1970, pp. 12–13)

---

developmental psychology The study of how humans grow toward their potential and of the capabilities that accompany that growth.

cognitive development theory The theory that a person develops thinking and problem-solving abilities through gradual, orderly changes.

social development theory The theory that a person changes over time in dealing with other people.

personal development theory The theory that an individual's personality changes over the course of time.

Lecture Note: The same point can be made using the example of a student's improvement in algebra. Advancement from concrete logic to abstract reasoning could be previewed here as well.

Journal Entry: Have students describe something that they've learned easily and something that was difficult to learn. Was the difficulty due to development or learning?

Teaching Anecdote: Tell a story of the teacher who, during summer vacation, took classes in mime and karate. While he found them both challenging, he began dreading karate class. He just couldn't seem to coordinate his body movements and became increasingly frustrated. The mime class, although equally demanding physically, intrigued him and he became proficient enough to teach mime to his students in the fall. After reflecting on the difference between the two classes, the teacher felt he better understood his students' frustration in learning new concepts and skills.

Ask students how this experience made the teacher more effective.

Piaget began publishing his studies of early cognitive development in the 1920s (e.g., 1926, 1928, 1930). He continued to publish his studies and theories on the development of knowledge in children for over sixty years. During that period his theories inspired and dominated the field of cognitive development. Much of what we know today about how children and adolescents develop cognitively we know because of Piaget's work.

MAGNETS

Recess duty often affords opportunities that I don't have during the hectic pace of the day to talk with colleagues. I was pleased that my recess duty time was the same as Diane's; it gave me a chance to catch up on new things that were happening in her room. She seemed pleased at my interest because it gave her a chance to bounce ideas off me.

"How's Pat doing in third-grade math?" Diane asked one morning. She had taught Pat two years earlier.

"He's struggling," I said. "One day I can present a skill like regrouping, give examples, and he can work them with my help. I think he understands. Then the next day when we review, it is as if he never saw the stuff before."

"Do you think he's ready to do what you are asking him to do?" she asked. "I remember what a struggle he had with reading."

"In some ways he seems ready and in others not so ready. He just doesn't seem to grasp the abstractness of numbers. He doesn't understand, *really* understand, how numbers work."

"Have you tried giving him manipulatives for math: hands-on materials? I wish I could have him back for something that's working with my first graders now. It might have been perfect for him then."

"What's that?" I asked.

"I watched several of my students struggling trying to match letters with sounds. They would diligently write the letter and then try to tell me the sound it made. But they weren't making the connections I wanted them to make. The written letters held no meaning for them. So I bought a magnetized alphabet. They play with the letters; they invent words with them; they move the letters all over the board."

"What does that accomplish?" I asked. "It sounds more like play than learning."

"They're learning while they're playing. By handling the letters, saying them out loud, putting them together and mixing them up, they are making a mental connection between letters and sounds. The children who are ready are moving to paper and pencil tasks a lot more easily than before."

"How might that help Pat with math?"

"Well, if he has a number of objects on his desk and he moves them around to solve a problem, he might get it in his head that numbers represent objects."

"You mean if I give him concrete objects to manipulate, he'll be better able to understand what numbers represent?"

"I would guess so. Why not try it?"

BASIC PIAGETIAN CONCEPTS

maturation The emergence of genetically determined changes that establish the limits of human development at the particular stages of growth.

active experience The process of either manipulating objects in one's environment or reorganizing one's thought patterns based on experience.

social interaction The process of gaining experience with people in one's environment and transmitting ideas among them.

Chap. Obj. 1–2
Test Ques. 2.1–2.61

Focus Questions: What factors influence intellectual development? How do students mentally organize their experiences in an adaptive way?

Field Observation: Have students observe children in a playground, noting the age levels at which they play different games.

Piaget viewed human development as something that progresses gradually along a continuum. Applying his views in a classroom setting, you would not expect to see drastic changes in the capabilities of students occur overnight. You may see relatively sudden changes in specific behaviors, but general intellectual capabilities would change more slowly. For example, a student may arrive in your class and announce, "Hey, you know those conversion problems we worked on yesterday? I didn't understand how to do them in class, but while I was doing my homework, it just all-of-a-sudden clicked." The overnight improvement may reflect the assimilation of a new concept, but it does not necessarily mean that the student is now capable of more advanced mathematical thinking. Cognitive development occurs over time and is influenced by a number of factors, which we will discuss in the following sections.

Influences on Cognitive Development

Cognitive development is influenced by four factors: (a) maturation, (b) active experience, (c) social interaction, and (d) equilibration (cf. Piaget, 1961; Wadsworth, 1984).

Maturation

Some people mature more quickly than others. Two children of identical ages may differ in size, athletic skill, reasoning ability, intelligence, and emotional reactions. Differences in the rate of maturation lead to the differences—physical and psychological—you will see among the students in your classroom. Piaget assumed that maturation is tied to genetic inheritance. **Maturation** or "the unfolding of inherited potential" (Wadsworth, 1984, p. 29) establishes the limits of human development throughout the stages of growth. By identifying maturation as a critical factor, Piaget acknowledges the role heredity plays in cognitive development. Maybe part of Pat's problem, in Teacher Chronicle 2.1, was that he hadn't matured to the point that he could do what the teacher asked of him.

Active Experience

Active experience refers to either manipulating objects in one's environment or reorganizing one's thought patterns. An adolescent can figure out the parts of a carburetor by handling one—turning it over, and peering into it. By thinking about the carburetor, the adolescent can also think about its function in a new way. For Piaget, actively manipulating an object and actively thinking about it are important ways through which humans develop knowledge about their world.

Social Interaction

Journal Entry: Have students discuss the extent to which they have talked with children at various age levels, noting the "level" at which they talk when addressing children of various ages.

Social interaction focuses on the experiences we have with the people in our environment, and includes an exchange of ideas with them. An infant may actively experience his or her mother by touching and gazing intently into the mother's face. Knowing the mother's face as an object is a different kind of knowledge than that derived from the conversations the mother and child will have as the child grows older.

School provides an ideal environment for exchanging ideas and observations about new experiences.

Consider further: A girl plays with, pets, and feeds her dog. She also has discussions with her parents about the concept of "loyalty," which remind her of her experiences with the dog. Here it is through social interaction with her parents, not through petting the dog, that the girl gains her knowledge of loyalty. School is incredibly important to students' cognitive development because it provides them with opportunities for active experience and a rich source of social interaction for exchanging ideas about that experience.

Equilibration

Equilibration regulates other influences on cognitive development and governs how people organize knowledge to adapt to their environment. If maturation sets limits on the types of active experience and social interaction of which a child is capable, how are these factors brought together? What causes a child to seek experience and interaction? How are new experiences integrated with what the child already knows, resulting in new knowledge? How is the child's level of maturation, experience with objects, and interaction with people coordinated to influence cognitive development? The answer to all of these questions, according to Piaget, is equilibration.

Connection: Equilibration is discussed in relation to accommodation and assimilation later in this section.

Intellectual Organization and Adaptation

Remember those poor transplanted mollusks? They had to develop biological solutions to the problems posed by a change in their environment. Humans have to deal with their environment too, but they have something in addition to biology at their disposal. They have cognition. Humans "grow" cognitive

schemata Mental networks
for organizing concepts and
information.

Chapter 15 Casebook Preview: See
Responsibility Education.

structures that help them deal with their environment in two ways. First, they allow people to organize the environment. Second, cognitive structures can change as they adapt to the environment (Wadsworth, 1984).

Organization

Organization is the human tendency to arrange experiences, thoughts, and behaviors into a coherent system. People use their intellect to make sense of their environment and to form mental representations of it. For example, anyone who plays a guitar has formed a mental representation of the behaviors involved in holding the guitar, fingering the fret board with one hand, strumming or plucking the strings with the other hand, and translating musical notes or chords into physical actions.

Schemata

The tendency to organize concepts and information yields cognitive structures known as **schemata.** Schemata form a "filing cabinet" within which are organized objects, events, actions, and abstractions. Each individual schema acts as a file folder. One schema contains the thought patterns used to recognize a mother's face. There is a schema for riding a bike, for serving a tennis ball, for experiences that produce anxiety. Any set of objects or experiences or actions that is classified consistently forms a schema (Wadsworth, 1984).

Schemata, structural counterparts of concepts, enable you to differentiate between stimuli and to generalize across stimuli. Figure 2–1 is an example of generalization. Would you classify all of the objects in Figure 2–1 in the same way? There is considerable variation among the objects, yet we recognize them all as belonging to the same class of objects. Your capability to generalize and to differentiate increases as schemata increase in number and as the criteria provided by schemata become more refined. For example, young children raised in a city will typically classify the first cow they see as a dog.

Adults have developed more schemata than children, more file folders into which stimuli can be placed. Not only the number, but the nature of the file folders changes as children gain experience with the environment and interact with other people. Indeed, the schemata of an infant are less "men-

Lecture Note: Remind students that
schemata change continually as a person gains experience with his or her
environment. When a child uses the
"dog" schema to understand the experience of seeing a cow he or she is
actively constructing meaning. Once
interpreted, the new item becomes
part of the schema that was used to
interpret it.

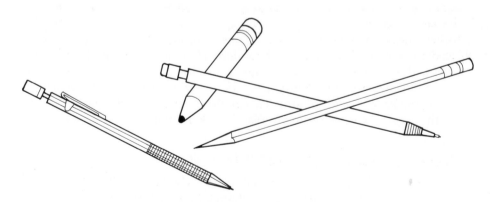

■ **Figure 2–1** *Are All of These Objects Members of the Same Category?*

Manipulatives can give students concrete, "hands-on" experience, helping them master subjects such as reading and math.

Lecture Note: An additional example of schema development: An infant is born with the reflex to grasp objects placed in his or her hand. If you have ever placed your finger in the palm of the infant's hand, for example, you have observed that the infant will automatically grasp your finger. Infants also are born with the reflex to suck. They have a schema for grasping and a schema for sucking. After some experience grasping some objects and sucking other objects, the infant begins to grasp an object and then move the object to his or her mouth. The grasping schema and the sucking schema become coordinated. We can conceive of a new schema that provides for the coordinated reflexes, enabling the infant to grasp a bottle of milk, move the bottle to its mouth, and suck the bottle to get nourishment.

Chapter 15 Casebook Preview: See Coup D'Etat in the Classroom.

tal" than they are reflexive; they are associated primarily with motor activity (Wadsworth, 1984).

As infants develop, they gain more and varied experiences with their environment. Organizing these experiences leads to new and more sophisticated schemata. The reflexive schemata of their early infancy become more "mentalistic."

The first graders in Teacher Chronicle 2.1 organized their manipulation of magnets into schemata that helped them move to paper and pencil tasks. A junior high student may organize his or her experiences in a math class into an algebraic rule.

The nature of schemata at various points along the continuum of intellectual development will be examined as stages of cognitive development. First, we must examine the basic processes by which schemata are changed.

Adaptation

Adaptation requires that schemata grow and change in response to the environment. Suppose, for example, that Ms. Florio requires her seventh-grade class to produce an oral history of the *Challenger* Space Shuttle disaster. Because her students have never used interviews to research a topic, they will

assimilation   In Piaget's
theory, a process whereby
new experiences with the
environment are incorporated
into existing cognitive
structures.

accommodation   In Piaget's
theory, a process of modifying
existing cognitive structures
or creating additional ones as
a result of some new
experience.

Connection: See Teacher Chronicle
11.1: Try, Try Again.

Lecture Note: Emphasize that instruction is often an attempt to develop new
ways to understand and interact with
the environment. Assimilation contributes to cognitive development by providing greater experience and thereby
strengthening an existing schema.
Changing the ways in which we understand our environment requires
accommodation.

Connection: See Teacher Chronicle
2.3: Cracking the Code.

need to adapt their current schemata in order to complete the assignment. Assimilation and accommodation are the processes that alter schemata (Piaget, 1952).

Assimilation and Accommodation

Assimilation and accommodation occur together. Gallagher and Reid (1981) view these processes as part of the general attempt made by an individual to adapt to various experiences with the environment.

Assimilation is a process through which new experiences with the environment are incorporated into existing schemata. Fitting the new experience into an existing schema builds the cognitive structure, but it does not change the schema's essential nature. For example, people who eat frog legs for the first time often comment that frog legs taste like chicken. They have organized their perceptions of taste according to their previous experiences. Therefore, having eaten chicken a great deal, they have a cognitive representation, their "taste of chicken" schema that allows them to understand the new experience of eating frog legs. Thus, they perceive the experience of eating frog legs as similar to that of eating chicken.

The ability to assimilate information increases our sense that we understand our experiences. Mistakes can occur when we change the nature of the experience in order to preserve our current way of understanding the environment. When a high school science student calls a colloid a solution, he or she is assimilating the new experience incorrectly into an existing schema. The process of assimilation can be the line of least resistance. The current state of our intelligence is the current state of our schemata. If we can fit our experiences into ways of understanding that already exist, the job of understanding the environment is less complex. Much of what happens in schools, however, is designed to change students' cognitive schemata.

While assimilation allows for the growth of schemata, it does not account for their modification. **Accommodation** is the process of modifying existing schemata or creating additional schemata as a result of experiences that cannot be easily assimilated. In such situations, a person's schema is forced to change in order to fit the new stimuli. Pat, in Teacher Chronicle 2.1, had trouble with new math concepts because the tasks that he was performing in class did not lead to modification of his "number concept" schema. Assimilation accounts for quantitative change; accommodation accounts for qualitative change. Together, they account for intellectual adaptation (cf. Piaget & Inhelder, 1958).

Piaget viewed assimilation and accommodation as complementary processes, not mutually exclusive ones. A high school student who has learned to use one word-processing program may be required to learn a different one. The requirements of the new program, such as new underlining or pagination commands, may require changes—accommodation—in the student's existing word-processing schema.

What about experiences that cannot be assimilated or accommodated very well? If a student experiences an event that is so unfamiliar that it cannot be filtered through existing schemata, then neither assimilation nor any subsequent accommodation will occur. For example, if a teacher were to begin writing meaningless symbols on a chalkboard, students may respond by trying to make sense out of the symbols. If they are unsuccessful in making sense out of them, they will probably stop trying to organize the information.

There is no adaptive advantage for them in doing so, so they simply ignore this strange new aspect of the environment.

Equilibration

Equilibration was discussed earlier as coordinating maturation and experience. One way in which this coordinating function is fulfilled is by balancing accommodation and assimilation. Assimilation and accommodation are necessary for cognitive development. The relative amounts of accommodation and assimilation that occur are of equal importance. A balance between these processes is as necessary as the processes themselves. Equilibration is the self-regulating process through which people balance new experiences with what they already know.

The students in Teacher Chronicle 2.1 assimilated the magnet letters into their existing schemata for "letter forms." When they started writing letters themselves, the new task required accommodation. Success in the classroom was a product of a coordination of the two processes. Gallagher and Reid (1981) describe equilibration as a self-regulator mechanism that is necessary to ensure that the developing student is interacting efficiently with his or her environment.

If new stimulus information does not fit into our existing schema then **disequilibrium** exists. Changing our existing schema to accommodate the new information is a way of achieving equilibrium. Our continual attempt to achieve a state of equilibrium is what leads to adaptive changes in our cognitive organization.

Experience and Knowledge

The experiences that people assimilate and/or accommodate influence the kinds of knowledge they construct. Experience can be divided into two types: physical experience and logico-mathematical experience.

Physical Experience

In Piaget's view, **physical experience** is any encounter with the environment in which a learner perceives and forms a mental representation of the physical properties of objects. Piaget often referred to the act of forming a mental representation as *abstraction*. The physical properties of objects are those aspects that can be seen, heard, touched, smelled, tasted. (The students in Teacher Chronicle 2.1, for example, constructed knowledge about the shape, size, and color of magnet letters.)

When a child listens to a clarinet and a trumpet he or she forms different mental representations of each of their sounds. The student may prefer the trumpet saying, "I like the clearer, stronger sound the trumpet makes. The clarinet sounds too gushy to me." The physical experience of the sounds gave the child an idea, a mental abstraction, of the sounds, which is reflected in the child's description.

The process of constructing knowledge based on physical experience is called **empirical abstraction.** Empirical means "of or relating to observation and experience." The knowledge gained through physical experience is called *exogenous knowledge* because it has as its source an external object. The essential characteristic of physical experience is the abstraction of the physical properties of environmental objects encountered. For example, by eating ap-

disequilibrium A state of cognitive imbalance that exists when new stimulus information does not fit into existing schemata.

physical experience In Piaget's theory, any encounter with the environment in which a learner perceives and forms a mental representation of the physical properties of objects.

empirical abstraction The process of constructing knowledge based on concrete physical experience.

Connection: See Teacher Chronicle 2.1: Magnets.

Connection: See Teacher Chronicle 2.1: Magnets.

Lecture Note: Further analysis of Teacher Chronicle 2.1: By moving the letters around the board they also discovered that the letters "stuck" to the board; they abstracted the magnetic property of the objects they were handling. Other physical qualities of the letters were probably abstracted as well. Perhaps one of the students stuck a letter in his or her mouth and formed an idea of how magnet letters taste.

Journal Entry: Have students think about an accident they nearly had, commenting on what they learned from their experiences.

logico-mathematical experience An internal experience that occurs when a person's pattern of thought is brought to a higher level through his or her own thought processes.
reflexive abstraction The generation of new knowledge by one's own thought processes.
constructivist theory Piaget's view of human cognition in which he sees all knowledge as being constructed by the individual through various experiences.

Lecture Note: Another example of a logico-mathematical experience would be discovering, while reading Shakespeare, that *anon* means "now," "immediately," or "even as we speak."

Journal Entry: Have students reflect on how they will account for differences between their perceptions and those of their students when they have their own classrooms.

ples, playing the oboe, and cultivating flowers, one comes to know that apples look "shiny," that oboes sound "reedy," and that roses smell "sweet."

Logico-mathematical Experience

A person's thought processes abstract knowledge from a **logico-mathematical experience,** which occurs anytime someone reorganizes his or her patterns of thought to a higher level. For example, while pondering apples falling from a tree, Newton is said to have formulated the notion of gravity. His experience, which led to this new way of thinking, was logico-mathematical. His invention was not due to an empirical abstraction of the properties of the apples. It did not matter if they were red or rotten or shiny. It was his thinking, a reorganization of thought, that led to a new idea.

Logico-mathematical experience generates new knowledge by a process referred to as **reflexive abstraction.** Reflexive, using Piaget's definition, means "turned back on itself." Thus, in reflexive abstraction one is thinking about one's thoughts. Because logico-mathematical experience is internal, the knowledge it yields is referred to as *endogenous knowledge.*

Empirical abstraction and reflexive abstraction differ with regard to their sources of knowledge. They also differ in that empirical abstraction requires some object in the environment. Reflexive abstraction can be triggered by something in the environment—such as a falling apple—but it is also possible for reflexive abstraction to occur in the absence of concrete objects. When reflexive abstraction occurs independently of any source of exogenous knowledge it is called *reflected abstraction.* We will further examine the distinction between types of abstraction when we turn our attention to a discussion of the stages of cognitive development.

Our examination of Piaget's theory of cognitive development, up to this point, has emphasized the "cognitive." The basic concepts presented in this section underscore his **constructivist theory**—his view of human cognition that holds that all knowledge is constructed by the individual through various experiences. Experiences are not simply things that happen to a person. The person contributes to the nature of the experience. The schemata that a person uses to understand an experience influences the knowledge gained from that experience. If you were to attend a performance of *Swan Lake* with a professional ballerina, your experience would differ from hers. The ballerina would filter the performance through her extensive set of "ballet" schemata, while you would filter your experience of the performance through a different, and presumably less-sophisticated, schema. You both "construct," but what you bring away from the performance is different from what the ballerina brings away.

Piaget's constructivist view of cognition begins with the raw materials of experiences and schemata. The process of assimilation enlarges schemata by adding experiences; accommodation modifies schemata to fit experiences. Both processes do their work under the supervision of equilibration so that the proper balance between experiences and schemata is maintained. The outcome of this construction is schemata that have been changed by experiences. By examining the changes in schemata that result from experience, we change the focus of our examination of Piaget's theory, shifting our emphasis from "cognitive" to "development."

Principles in Practice 2.1

Principles . . .

1. Students organize their experiences into knowledge structures called schemata.
2. Assimilation and accommodation are the processes by which experience becomes knowledge.
3. Experience of some kind is necessary for cognitive change to occur.

. . . in Practice

In Teacher Chronicle 2.1 the first graders did not seem to have the necessary schemata for letter-sound correspondence. The teacher's use of magnetized alphabets provided students with the right experiences to construct this knowledge.

1. What types of experiences, other than the manipulation of magnets, might have helped the first graders build appropriate schemata?
2. How did the magnets allow assimilation and subsequent accommodation to occur?
3. What about Pat, now a third grader? What sort of experiences could the teacher set up to help him understand the concept of numbers?

READY OR NOT?

Teacher
Chronicle
2.2

Be prepared, this will happen to you! One afternoon as I was scurrying to close the window, corral runaway pencils, and grab my coat to go pick up my son, an irate mother appeared in my doorway. She stepped into the room and pulled the door closed behind her. She looked loaded for bear.

"Why isn't Paul reading yet? His twin sister is reading, but he isn't. What is this I heard about your reading program? Aren't you using the right books?" All of this came out in one big rush.

My immediate reaction was to tell her that I was on my way out the door and that we'd have to talk later. I knew this would not be a good idea so I bit my tongue and offered her a chair instead.

We sat down and I told her how I perceived Paul.

"He is having difficulty learning how to read because he isn't ready to learn to read."

"Oh, really? Well, his sister is. And she's doing multiplication and division in math."

"I understand that, but Paul isn't ready for that kind of thinking yet. For example, today when we were learning new vocabulary words, he got stuck on the letter *L*. He couldn't tell me what sound it made until he started at the beginning of the alphabet and then said each letter until he reached *L*. I watched his eyes track the letters as he moved down the alphabet. He doesn't understand the link between letters and sounds yet."

"This is important before he can read?"

"It is critical. Until he understands this, he won't be able to read, no matter how much I push him." Then I asked a question of her. "How did he like kindergarten last year?"

"He hated it. Whenever they worked he got up and moved around. The teacher kept putting him in a chair in the corner."

"So he probably missed out on some important prereading skills?"

"Yes, I guess so. He probably missed out on other things, too."

"I'm sure he did," I said. "You know, I really like Paul. He has a wonderful vocabulary and contributes a great deal to group activities and discussions."

I'd really caught her off guard. "Yes," I continued, "he is quite confident with the spoken language and uses words many other children don't know yet. Has he had lots of experiences?"

She paused and said, "Yes, we take all of the kids to car shows. They go to Grandpa's farm on the weekends."

"That explains then why he knows so much about tractors. He told us all about them in his reading group this morning: how big they are, how fast they go, and what they sound like. He even told us he wanted to drive one to the beach." We had a good laugh imagining Paul behind the wheel of a tractor.

The conversation continued. I discussed Paul's strengths and weaknesses, relating many of the latter to his not being ready to translate printed symbols into words he knew.

"I suggest that you read to Paul every night. Have him sit with you and as you read, point out the words to him. This will help him see the connection between the sounds you are saying and the words on the page. Before long, he will be able to point to some of the words himself."

By the time Paul's mother left I had an ally, not an enemy. I had helped her understand that Paul would learn to read, but at his own pace. As I left the building, I wondered when that time would come.

■ ■

Chap. Obj. 3
Test Ques. 2.62–2.99

Focus Questions: How does a student's mental representation of his or her environment change as he or she develops?

Teaching Anecdote: Tell a story of the junior high math teacher who switched to teaching at the first-grade level. She learned that junior high and primary *(continued)*

PIAGET'S STAGES OF COGNITIVE DEVELOPMENT

Piaget's account of the processes, experiences, and structures involved in cognition describes how people come to know about their world. The experiences we have and the schemata we use to construct knowledge from those experiences change as we grow. Not only does a seventh grader know about more things than the second grader, the seventh grader knows in a different way. The seventh grader has developed cognitive capabilities that are not yet in the repertoire of the second grader.

In this section, we will focus on the capabilities of students who have reached different levels of cognitive development. All teachers need to know what the cognitive capabilities of their students are. Teachers of young students need to know the capabilities of older children in order to understand the direction that their students' development should be taking. Teachers of

Table 2–1 *Summary of Piaget's Stages of Cognitive Development*

Stages	Approximate Ages	Nature of Schemata*
Sensorimotor	0–2	Sensations and motor actions
Preoperations	2–7	Illogical operations; symbolic representations; egocentric; self-centered
Concrete operations	7–11	Logical, reversible operations; decentered; object-bound
Formal operations	11–Adult	Abstract—not bound to concrete objects

SOURCE: From *Piaget's Theory of Cognitive Development* (2nd ed., p. 29) by B. J. Wadsworth, 1979, New York: Longman. Copyright 1979 by Longman Publishing Group. Adapted by permission of the Longman Publishing Groups.

* It is important to remember that the stages are cumulative. The adaptive characteristics of earlier stages are present in later ones.

ordinality In Piaget's theory of cognitive development, the concept of a fixed sequence or order of stages.

grade students have very different understandings of the concept of time. The first graders, while knowing the words *hour* and *half hour,* had no concrete understanding of what those lengths of time meant. They were constantly asking when recess would begin. The frequent interruptions decreased when the teacher compared one "half hour" with the amount of time it took the students to watch a popular TV program.

Ask students to explain/verify the teacher's experience.

Transparency: This table is duplicated in the acetate transparency package. See T-2 Summary of Piaget's Stages of Cognitive Development.

Lecture Note: Emphasize that the names of the stages describe the nature of the schemata at each stage. For example, the schemata of the typical fourth grader allow the child to perform concrete operations. The schemata of an infant allow sensorimotor activity.

older students need to understand the capabilities that their students developed earlier. The development of new capabilities does not erase earlier ones. Additionally, not all behaviors reflect a student's highest level of functioning. Any experienced teacher can tell you that just because a student is capable of complex reasoning, doesn't mean the student will always reason in that way.

Piaget formulated stages of cognitive development, identifying the type of schemata people use and the age at which they use them to organize and interact with their environment. Piaget's stages are summarized in Table 2–1.

We will examine the specific nature of the cognitive capabilities of children and adolescents at each stage shortly. But before describing each stage, it is useful to examine Piaget's views of developmental change in general. Piaget (1952) saw development as a process of successive, qualitative changes in children's schemata. The changes that children undergo at each stage derive logically and inevitably from the cognitive structures of preceding stages. New structures do not replace prior structures. Rather, they incorporate prior schemata, resulting in the qualitative change.

Describing and Interpreting Cognitive Change

Piaget divided cognitive development into four broad, cumulative stages. Each new stage in development builds on and becomes integrated with previous stages.

In a general way, the fact should be emphasized that behavior patterns characteristic of the different stages do not succeed each other in a linear way (those of a given stage disappearing at the time when those of the following one take form) but in the manner of the layers of a pyramid (upright or upside down), the new behavior patterns simply being added to the old ones to complete, correct or combine with them. (Piaget, 1952, p. 329)

The concept of a fixed sequence or order of stages is called **ordinality.** According to Piaget, every child must pass through the stages of development in the same order. The age at which a child passes through the stages depends on his or her experience and hereditary potential (cf. Piaget, 1963).

Piaget's theory of development starts with *innate reflexes*. He assumes that children are born with certain reflexes that allow them to interact with the environment. By using the reflex intelligence to interact with the environment, the infant adapts. Adapting to the environment leads to changes in the internal organization of the innate reflexes. Some are strengthened and some are transformed into new forms of intelligence.

Piaget was also hesitant to place age descriptions on the developmental stages, lest they be viewed as a prescription for cognitive development. For example, the sensorimotor stage is identified with the approximate ages of from birth to two years. If a three-year-old child has not "graduated" from this stage, the child should not be diagnosed as developmentally retarded. It is inappropriate to ask, "How quickly should a child move from one stage to the next?" or, "What can be done to get a child to move faster through the stages?" Piaget never viewed his stage theory of cognitive development as a race course. Thus, teachers must understand that the rate of development ranges widely among children. What does not vary in Piaget's theory is ordinality, the order of the stages through which children develop.

The Stages: Hallmarks of Change

Sensorimotor Stage

The knowledge gained by the infant at the **sensorimotor stage** is obtained through physical experience with the environment. The infant uses his or her senses to experience the environment, and his or her physical or motor actions to interact with it. The reflexes that newborns use to build schemata are the starting point for cognitive development. The intellectual changes that occur during the sensorimotor period are quite dramatic.

The two hallmarks of the sensorimotor stage most significant for teachers are *object permanence* and *imitation*.

Object Permanence

When the child understands that an object can continue to exist whether or not he or she perceives it, **object permanence** has been achieved. Before the onset of object permanence, hiding an object from the child will also remove that object from the child's mind. It is, quite literally, out of sight, out of mind. Consider, as an example, an infant who is shown a red rubber ball and who begins to reach for the ball to grasp it. As the child begins to reach for the ball, an adult covers the ball with a blanket. If the child then stops reaching for the ball and turns his or her attention elsewhere, the indication is that object permanence has not yet been achieved. If, on the other hand, the child persists in reaching for the ball now hidden by the blanket, uncovers the ball, and grasps it, that is evidence of object permanence.

Object permanence is an important foundation for later development. The concept that objects have an existence that is separate from the child and permanent enables the child to conceive of objects and actions that are not in their immediate environment.

Imitation

Imitation, the capability to copy behaviors, begins with behaviors that are already part of the child's repertoire. For example, very young children can open and close their hands; their behavior is related to the grasping reflex. If a parent, playing with the child, begins opening and closing his or her hand, the child will likely imitate the behavior. The adult's action prompts the child to perform the same action. Many of the "games" that parents and infants play are forms of imitation.

Imitation continues to become more complicated as the child's repertoire of behaviors increases. Toward the end of the sensorimotor stage, toddlers begin to display novel behaviors in an effort to "be like a fire fighter" or to "be like an airplane" or to "be like a monkey." This is called *deferred imitation*. Pretending to be something or somebody does not require prompting. A little girl does not need to see a plane overhead in order to spread her arms, race around the yard, and make a "jet noise." A little boy does not need to see his mother brushing her hair before combing his teddy bear's head. The pretending and dramatic play-acting that preschool, kindergarten, and primary-grade teachers see in students have their roots in deferred imitation.

Acquiring the capabilities of object permanence and imitation prepares the child for symbolic thinking, a hallmark of the next developmental stage. However, because students develop the capacity for symbolic thinking does not mean they no longer need to handle objects and observe models. The need for tangible objects, models, analogies, and concrete examples never disappears. Remember that Paul in Teacher Chronicle 2.2 missed a lot of manipulative work with the alphabet in kindergarten. Without that physical experience, he had difficulty with reading. Students always need examples of the increasingly complex and abstract ideas that they are asked to learn.

Preoperations Stage

Piaget uses the term **operations** to refer to actions based on logical thinking. The actions of a child at the preoperations stage are based on thought, but the actions do not always seem logical from an adult perspective. Thus, the child's thinking is considered prelogical or **preoperational,** because illogical thinking does not prevent youngsters from mentally representing or symbolizing. Preschoolers can easily pretend that a wooden building block is a car or a baby in a carriage or a piece of cheese. Symbolizing of this kind is based on imitation. This capability to replace one object with another or to use words to talk about actions and experiences is called *symbolic representation*. It is a hallmark of the preoperations stage.

Symbolic Representation

Symbolic representation is the process whereby children learn to create their own symbols and to use existing symbol systems to represent and operate on the environment. The most important symbol system is language, which grows tremendously during the preoperations stage. Children's vocabularies increase several thousand percent. The complexity of their grammatical constructions also increases dramatically. From a developmental point of view, using language enhances the capability to think about objects that are not present. (We will examine these changes in more detail in the section on "Language Development" at the end of the chapter.)

In Teacher Chronicle 2.2, Paul's capability to use language to symbolize the tractor allowed him to describe it in great detail. The ability to describe the tractor, however, does not mean he could think logically. For example, he thought he could use the tractor to drive his family to the beach.

operations Term used by Piaget to refer to actions based on logical thinking.
preoperational According to Piaget, the stage at which children learn to mentally represent things.
symbolic representation The process whereby children learn to create their own symbols and to use existing symbol systems to represent and operate on the environment.

Field Observation: Have students observe young toddlers, perhaps in a day-care center, trying to distinguish *imitation* from *deferred imitation.*

Teaching Anecdote: Tell the story of the kindergarten teacher who built a tepee in her classroom as a place for silent reading. After reading a story about Native Americans and buffalo, children began an elaborate game, which they played intensely for weeks. They became Native American parents and children, hunters and horses, buffalo and bears. Ask students whether they see this as imitation or deferred imitation.

Connection: See Teacher Chronicle 2.2: Ready or Not?

Lecture Note: Inform students that one of the reasons for the Teacher Chronicles in the text is to provide them with concrete examples to read and reflect on.

Connection: See Teacher Chronicle 6.1: Knot Understanding.

Connection: See Teacher Chronicle 2.2: Ready or Not?

Field Observation: Have students administer conservation tasks to preschool students.

Chapter 15 Casebook Preview: See I Am Leo.

Lecture Note: Additional example: Picture a family on a long drive. The preoperational child in the backseat is listening through earphones to a song. (One lyric is, "Jeremiah was a bullfrog. . . .") Egocentrically, the child asks a parent in the front seat, "What did that singer say Jeremiah was?"

The other hallmarks of the preoperations stage are cognitive characteristics that prevent logical thinking: perceptual centration, irreversibility, and egocentrism.

Perceptual Centration

Preoperational children tend to focus their attention on only one aspect of an object or problem. This tendency to perceive an object in a very narrow way is termed **perceptual centration.** Piaget discovered perceptual centration (and other cognitive characteristics) by having children respond to problems he called **conservation tasks.**

The classic conservation task required children to judge the amounts of water in different containers. Starting with two identical beakers containing the same amounts of water, Piaget emptied the water from one beaker into a tall, slender, graduated cylinder. When asked to judge whether the cylinder or the beaker contained the most water, preoperational children consistently answer, "the tallest one." Their perceptions focus or center on the height of the liquid in the containers to the exclusion of width, circumference, or volume. Preoperational children who roll balls of clay into long "snakes" will judge the snakes to contain more clay than the balls. In perceiving these figures, children center on one salient feature of the two shapes, their length.

Irreversibility

Irreversibility refers to a person's inability to mentally reverse actions. The preoperational child may see the water being poured back and forth between the short beaker and the tall cylinder, but the child cannot perform the operation "mentally." A second grader, who is preoperational, may know that $4 + 2 = 6$, but may be unable to solve the subtraction problem $6 - 2 = ?$.

Egocentrism

The term *egocentrism* is not used derogatorily in Piaget's theory, but merely as descriptive of the way children think. **Egocentrism,** as Piaget describes it, refers to children's assumptions that everyone's experience of the world is the same as their own, and that they are, quite literally, the center of everything. For example, consider the case of a young girl seated at the dinner table who feels called on to "translate" her parents' conversation for them.

Father: Would you please pass the potatoes.
Child: Mommy, Daddy wants you to pass the potatoes.
Mother: Here, do you need the salt and pepper?
Child: Daddy, Mommy wants to know if you need the salt and pepper.
Father: Yes, please.
Child: Mommy, Daddy wants the salt and pepper.

Another form of egocentrism can be seen in what Piaget labeled **collective monologue,** the phenomenon of children talking in groups without having a conversation. One child may be talking about the colors in his painting; another child may be asking whether or not there is applesauce for a snack; and a third child may be arguing for a game of tag when playground time comes. Each child addresses the others, but no one responds. Very little linguistic interaction occurs, owing to the egocentric nature of each child's language. (We will see this form of egocentrism mentioned briefly again when we examine language development.)

When preoperational children develop the capabilities to create and use symbols—symbolic representation—adults begin to consider them "thinkers." However, teachers need to remember that preoperational thinking is not logical. A child who insists that one, and only one, perspective is correct, who talks but doesn't listen, who monopolizes social situations, who "refuses" to consider all aspects of a problem, may not be a troublemaker, but merely at the preoperations stage.

Concrete Operations

Concrete operations is the first stage of operational or logical thought, in which schemata allow students to realize that there is stability in the physical world and that reasoning about the physical world can proceed logically. Because the logical schemata are still new at this stage, students can best use them when considering objects and events that are concrete. Many educators refer to the concrete operations stage as the "hands-on" period of cognitive development. Although the child can reason, his or her ability to reason is limited to tangible objects and direct experiences.

Concrete operational thought is distinct from preoperational thought. Rules of logic, rather than one's perceptual experience, govern thinking at this stage. Two hallmarks of concrete operational thought are *reversibility* and *decentration*. They contribute to the other hallmarks of the stage: *conservation* and *multiple classification*.

Reversibility and Decentration

Reversibility is the ability to mentally reverse events, such as the steps in the amount-of-water problem. Students at this stage can imagine the results of pouring the water back and forth between containers of different shapes and

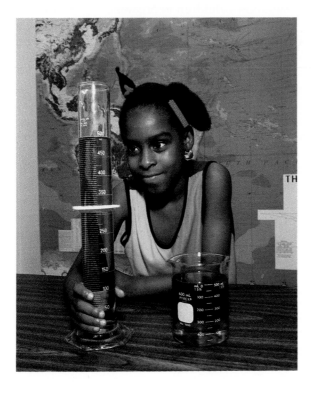

Children in the concrete operations stage of development are able to understand the principles of conservation and reversibility.

Teaching Anecdote: Tell the story of the first-grade teacher who could not understand why Myra, a bright student, was having difficulty learning to read. She was also very demanding of attention. Myra had appropriate language skills, but couldn't sit still or concentrate for longer than five minutes. In her teacher's words, "She's driving me crazy." Myra was falling behind her classmates. When the teacher checked Myra's birth date, she understood the problem. Myra had turned six only three days before school started; she was nearly a year younger than the majority of her classmates. Why would Myra's age make such a difference in her ability to learn how to read?

Teacher Interview: Have students interview elementary teachers to collect hypotheses for hands-on activities, analyzing them for developmental appropriateness.

Connection: See Teacher Chronicle
2.2: Ready or Not?

decentration The ability to consider more than one aspect of an object or problem at a time.
conservation The ability to recognize that properties do not change because form changes.
multiple classification A reasoning skill that allows children to organize objects according to more than one characteristic.
formal operations According to Piaget, the stage of development in which the abilities to reason abstractly and to coordinate a number of variables are acquired.

Lecture Note: An additional example: Roll the ball of clay into a long, skinny "snake." The length of the rod compensates for its thinness. The shortness of the ball of clay is compensated for by its fatness.

Lecture Note: As an additional illustration, the operational child may be able to classify animals into separate groups of carnivores and herbivores and still be able to classify both carnivores and herbivores as belonging to another group called mammals.

sizes. Paul's twin sister in Teacher Chronicle 2.2 had learned product/quotient families. Given the numbers 12 and 6, she could supply the answer "2" as the number that when multiplied by 6 yields the product of 12 *and* that when divided into 12 yields the quotient of 6. Paul's sister's ability to reverse the mathematical operations indicates that she is at the concrete operations stage.

Decentration is the ability to consider more than one aspect of an object or problem. Identifying product/quotient families requires that the student think about a number in two different ways: as a multiplier and as a divisor. Students capable of concrete operations can solve problems that have more elements and that are significantly more complex, which preoperational students cannot.

Conservation

Together, reversibility and decentration allow concrete operational students to successfully perform conservation tasks that stymied preoperational students. **Conservation** is the ability to recognize that properties do not change because form changes. Take the water problem. By applying logic, operational students understand that the amount of water does not change even though the shape does.

Children who successfully perform conservation tasks also understand that when transformations of objects occur, the objects maintain their basic characteristics. For example, a lump of bread dough is transformed into a loaf of bread by baking it. Operational students recognize a lump of dough and a loaf of bread as being essentially the same, whereas preoperational children would see them as two different things.

Multiple Classification

Reversibility and decentration are also the basis for **multiple classification,** an important reasoning skill that allows children to organize objects according to more than one characteristic. Suppose a student is presented with several cardboard cutouts in shapes of circles, squares, and triangles. The cutouts also vary in terms of color and size: red, yellow, and blue; small, medium, and large. A preoperational child will likely classify the objects by using one of the dimensions. The child at the concrete operations stage can use more than one dimension to classify. The preoperational child may form a group of yellow objects. The operational child may form groups of large yellow triangles, medium yellow triangles, small yellow triangles, large blue triangles, and so forth, indicating a more developed classification scheme.

Although concrete operations is the beginning of logical reasoning, it is not "pure" reasoning. Students in primary- through middle-school grades don't sit around in pure contemplation, inventing philosophies. They need to see things, touch things, experiment with things. They can reason when given concrete objects and experiences to reason with, but abstract reasoning doesn't occur until the final stage of cognitive development—formal operations.

Formal Operations

Formal operations—the final stage in Piaget's theory—begins roughly around eleven or twelve years of age and continues into and throughout adulthood. *Abstract reasoning* is the hallmark of the formal operations stage.

Children who exhibit characteristics of Piaget's formal operations stage tend to approach problems in a systematic way. They generate hypotheses and then test them by manipulation, one factor or variable at a time.

Abstract Reasoning

Abstract reasoning is the ability to think logically about intangibles. Students who reach the stage of formal operations can begin to deal with possibilities. They can think in terms of an hypothesis: If X then Y. They can see beyond the here and now. They can verbalize the mental rules they use in solving problems. The logical operations of the concrete operations stage can be performed outside the presence of concrete objects, themselves.

For example, imagine you are standing directly in front of a chair. As you look at the chair, there is a lamp to the right of it, a table to the left of it, and a rug behind it. You are then asked to imagine yourself standing in a new position so that the chair is behind the table. Given this condition, where is the lamp? A concrete operational student would have trouble with this problem, unless he or she could stand in proximity to the objects or symbolize them on paper. Being able to reason through this problem in the abstract is a hallmark of formal operations. (If you are having problems working out this problem do not fear for your stage of cognitive development. As Piaget noted, the ability to operate formally in one situation does not guarantee that the person operates formally in all situations.)

Inhelder and Piaget (1968) created a reasoning problem that illustrated the difference between concrete operational students and those in the formal operational stage. To solve the problem, students were supplied with objects that could be used to test a principle of physics, that the length of the pendulum influences its speed (see Figure 2–2).

The length of the pendulum could be shortened or lengthened; the weight at the end of the pendulum could be changed so that it was lighter or heavier. The height from which the pendulum is released could be changed and the force with which the pendulum was pushed could be changed. Given these

Chapter 15 Casebook Preview: See Science Is Only Real When You Do It.

Lecture Note: Inform students that when the authors wrote this example they were standing before a real chair, a real lamp, a real table, and a real rug.

■ **Figure 2–2** *Objects Used in the Pendulum Test*

Lecture Note: Additional detail from the Inhelder and Piaget Study: A fifteen-year-old student selected one weight to test with a long string and a short string. Next, the student selected a second weight and tested the second weight with a long and a short string. Finally, the fifteen year old selected a third weight and tested it with a long and a short string. After these operations, the student concluded that "it's the length of the string that makes it go faster and slower; the weight doesn't play any role."

A ten-year-old student presented with the same problem and the same apparatus began by varying simultaneously the weight and the impetus and then the weight, the impetus, and the length. Finally, the youngster varied the impetus, the weight, and the elevation.

The fifteen year old displays the characteristics of formal operations, approaching the problem in a systematic fashion by generating hypotheses and manipulating one factor to test each hypothesis. The concrete operational student fails to use abstract reasoning to identify rules governing the situation.

Chap. Obj. 4
Test Ques. 2.100–2.110

Focus Question: Can cognitive development be accelerated?

elements, students were asked which of these factors influenced the speed at which a pendulum swung.

Their findings indicated that a student who is formally operational approaches the problem in a very systematic fashion, generating and testing various hypotheses. To illustrate, a formal operational student might choose one weight and one length, and push the pendulum at constant force, while varying the height from which the pendulum is released. Discovering that the height does not influence speed, the student then proceeds to manipulate other factors one at a time in an effort to eliminate possible solutions to the problem. A concrete operational student is likely to approach this task in a much less systematic way.

THE PIAGETIAN THEME AND SOME VARIATIONS

Piaget's theory tells us how students understand and interact with their environment. The most obvious lesson for teachers is that children at different stages of cognitive development think differently, but there is a more important lesson. Teachers must never forget that they think differently than do the children and adolescents they are teaching. This is true even when their students have reached the stage of formal operations. Did you ever have a teacher in high school like the one described by a thirty-seven-year-old physician at her twentieth high school reunion?

> Do you remember old Mr. Benzine [not his real name, of course] from our advanced Chem class? He was brilliant. I'm convinced he knew more chemistry than most of my professors in college, but he couldn't teach his way out of a paper bag. The trouble was that Mr. Benzine could never figure out why we didn't catch on to some of the stuff in his class. It was incomprehensible to him that we didn't immediately understand every single concept. It was all in his head, but he couldn't put it in ours.

décalage Gaps in the experience of individuals that affect development within and between stages.

Piaget's stages are an attempt to paint human cognitive development in broad strokes. An individual student's thinking does not progress in neat, unambiguous steps according to a precise timetable. There are gaps in the experiences of every individual that affect development within and between the stages, which Piaget called **décalage.** Students do not "advance" from one stage to the next overnight. Exit from one stage and entrance into another is a tentative affair. Even those students who seem to be firmly established in a stage may exhibit discouraging "regressions." The fifteen-year-old student who reasoned so well on the pendulum problem may have trouble trying to critically analyze a poem because of gaps in his or her experiences. Décalage is a reminder that there are differences between the way a stage is characterized in theory and the thinking processes of any individual passing through that stage.

Teacher Interview: Have students interview teachers regarding their experiences and observations of developmental gaps.

Nevertheless, Piaget's theory gives teachers a way of characterizing individuals' thinking. To put that knowledge to use, teachers must do two things. First, they must provide their students with numerous opportunities to work with objects and symbols. Second, they must watch and listen closely as each student attempts to construct meaning. Recall the teacher's conversation with Paul's mother in Teacher Chronicle 2.2. By attending closely to Paul's contributions in a reading group, the teacher learned some important things about Paul's thinking.

Connection: See Teacher Chronicle 2.2: Ready or Not?

It is hard to overestimate Piaget's influence. Thousands of studies delving into his theory have been published. Scholars who investigate the implications of his ideas have formed national and international academic societies. Some of their research goes to the heart of Piaget's basic philosophical assumptions, some to the methods he used to observe children, and some to ways in which teachers might usefully characterize their students' thinking. We will look briefly at variations on Piaget's theory that bear on the last of these research concerns.

Zone of Proximal Development

Thinking back to the basic concepts that underlie Piaget's theory, you may recall that one of the major influences on cognitive development is social interaction. Social interaction provides opportunities for the transmission of the ideas, concepts, and symbol systems important to a culture. Through experiences with people—not just talking with them—children acquire knowledge of rules and laws, values and beliefs, ethics and morals (cf. Wadsworth, 1984). Even though Piaget acknowledges the influence of social inter-

Chapter 15 Casebook Preview: See Science Is Only Real When You Do It.

zone of proximal development
In Vygotsky's theory, an area in which a child who has trouble solving a problem alone can succeed with help from someone more knowledgeable.
information processing A theory of learning that relies on an analogy between the human mind and the computer to explain processing, storage, and retrieval of knowledge.
attention The process used to focus on one or more aspects of the environment.

Connection: Relevant to cross-age tutoring as discussed in Chapter 11.

Connection: See Teacher Chronicle 2.2: Ready or Not?

Connection: See Diary of a Day, Chapter 1, math class, the decision to move Tiffany away from Laura.

Lecture Note: Applying Vygotsky's notion does not alter the Piagetian implications that students need experiences and close scrutiny by their teachers.

Connection: Examined in more detail in the information-processing view of learning in Chapter 6.

action, his description of developing schemata, that is, stages, emphasizes the interaction with objects in the environment.

Vygotsky explained, in a more direct way than Piaget's social interaction concept was able to, how interaction with teachers can influence children's cognitive development (1978, 1986). Vygotsky believed that social interaction does more than simply transmit ideas. In his view, people provide guidance and support for children as they attempt new and more complicated tasks. People are the essence of Vygotsky's zone of proximal development concept. The **zone of proximal development** refers to an area in which a child has trouble solving a problem alone, but can succeed with help from someone more knowledgeable (cf. Wertsch, 1986). If cognitive development proceeds gradually, it makes sense that at any given time, a student is on the verge of a cognitive "breakthrough." We can think of a student's zone of proximal development, therefore, as the area of potential breakthroughs. In Teacher Chronicle 2.2, the teacher and Paul's mother discussed Paul's readiness for reading. The teacher was trying to find "the key" that would enable Paul to translate written symbols into words that were already part of his speaking vocabulary. The teacher sensed that "translation" was part of Paul's zone of proximal development; that's why the teacher encouraged Paul's mom to read aloud books for the beginning reader, giving him as much individual attention as possible.

Vygotsky suggests that students should be pushed to the edge of their capabilities, but that someone should be there to help and encourage them. Although the teacher is the most obvious candidate in the classroom, he or she is not the only person who can encourage breakthroughs. Another student who has recently made the same breakthrough might be the one who can most effectively communicate the necessary knowledge. Vygotsky's zone of proximal development suggests a more "aggressive" approach than Piaget's notion of social interaction. The difference is between guided discovery and "pure" discovery. In either case, a teacher needs to have a clear picture of his or her student's capabilities.

Information-processing Capabilities

Information processing is a theoretical perspective that has been derived not from the work of one individual, but from a school of thought. Researchers who contribute to information-processing theory are interested in techniques of human cognition, how people *code*, *store*, and *retrieve* information for later use. Their approach comes from the application of a computer metaphor to human thinking. When used as a theory of learning, information-processing concepts can be applied to issues of cognitive development, questioning how information-processing capabilities change as humans grow.

Attention

Attention, the process used to focus on one or more aspects of the environment, changes as the child gets older (Flavell, 1985). When a teacher notices a student looking out a window and says, "Will you *please* pay attention to me?" the teacher is asking that student to focus on what the teacher is saying to the exclusion of the activity outside. Flavell has identified four ways in which attention changes as children get older.

First, the ability to *control* attention increases with age. Control refers to the length of time a child can attend to a stimulus—sometimes referred to as the attention span—and the ability to concentrate. The attention span increases because the child also becomes less distractible. If every new sound, sight, or smell pulls the child's mind away from the task at hand, his or her attentional control is poor.

Second, the ability to *match task demands* increases with age. This proposition is similar to Piaget's concept of multiple classification. Suppose, for example, that a map-reading problem requires a student to focus on both the location and the elevation of a place as it relates to a river. An older child is better able than a younger child to attend to the location and elevation variables.

Third, the ability to *plan* attention increases with age. Older students are better able to determine what is important. They can interpret cues that tell what is important and, therefore, where they should direct their attention. Thinking back to the "Diary of a Day" in the first chapter, as an example, older students are more likely than younger students to attend to statements made from the "cool stool" in Peter Roop's classroom.

Fourth, the ability to *monitor* attention increases with age. Increases in attentional control, task matching, and planning enable students to better monitor themselves and to notice when they need to pay more or less attention. For example, older students are more likely than younger students to notice that they are daydreaming instead of focusing on the teacher's comments.

Memory and Metacognition

In Piaget's scheme, the processes of assimilation and accommodation account for cognitive change. In information-processing theory, memory processes are key. As we will see in Chapter 6, there are processes that transfer information among three memory structures. One of those memory structures, **short-term store,** holds the information a person is "working on" at any point in time—the information residing in a person's consciousness. An important characteristic of short-term store is its limited capacity. A person can only deal with a limited amount of information at any given moment. If you have ever tried to listen to a group of students each asking you a question at the same time, you know what limited capacity means.

Robbie Case has studied cognitive development by investigating changes in children's capacity to store information (1980, 1984, 1986). As children develop, they can solve problems that are increasingly complex. Case attributes improvement in problem solving to qualitative rather than quantitative changes in memory capacity. The total amount of "space" available in memory does not simply increase as children grow; what changes is how the space is used.

The space available in memory can function as either **operating space,** where the necessary operations are executed, or **storage space,** where additional information is stored (Case, 1984). Young children who are just learning to solve particular kinds of problems must use all of their capacity to execute the required operations. As they gain experience with the problems, the operation used requires less and less capacity. **Automaticity** is the point where an operation can be executed without conscious effort. Recall once

Field Observation: Have students observe children of various ages in school, church, at a concert, etc.

Connection: See Diary of a Day, Chapter 1.

Connection: Short-term store is examined in detail in Chapter 6.

Lecture Note: Make the following point to help students grasp the concept "operating space": In order to solve problems, students must carry out mental operations. The more complex the problem is, the greater the number of operations required to solve it.

Lecture Note: An example relating automatically to operating space: Think about the difference between a child who "knows" multiplication tables and a child who has not yet mastered multiplication facts. When each child encounters the problem, "9×3," the former responds "27" automatically, without effort. The child who is unable to respond automatically must use memory capacity to carry out mental calculations to get the answer. Automaticity reduces the amount of operating space necessary to solve problems. When operating space is reduced, storage space increases.

metacognition Knowledge about thinking and the capability to monitor one's own cognitive processing, such as thinking, learning, and remembering.

Connection: See Teacher Chronicle 2.2: Ready or Not?

Connection: See Diary of a Day, Chapter 1, math class.

Lecture Note: Remind students that they oversimplify the problem. They tend to focus on the length of a rod of clay to the exclusion of its narrow width. They calculate the amount of water by observing height in a container, but forget about the diameter of the container.

Connection: See Teacher Chronicle 2.2: Ready or Not?

Connection: Examined in relation to information-processing view of learning in Chapter 6.

Chapter 15 Casebook Preview: See Writers' Tea.

Journal Entry: As a way of reflecting on their own thinking processes, have students reflect on the shortcuts they *(continued)*

more Paul and his sister in Teacher Chronicle 2.2. Paul's memory capacity had to be devoted entirely to searching for letter–sound correspondences. His sister paired sounds to letters automatically, allowing her to perform the additional operations necessary for reading.

By practicing operations to the point of automaticity, students can increase their efficiency. A second way to do so is to discover shortcuts. Most students look for ways to simplify the steps they must take in order to solve a problem. Older students are better at finding shortcuts than are younger students. They discover more efficient ways of processing information, but they keep the necessary steps in mind. For example, the fourth step in solving a problem may require that three previously calculated subtotals be summed before proceeding to the next step. After working several problems like this, an older student may discover that the answer required in Step 4 can be accurately calculated through a single multiplication. The older student is better able to keep track of the elements in a problem. This monitoring capability, which we encountered in discussing "attention," also plays a role in memory. Younger students often overlook crucial steps. They oversimplify problems (Case, 1985). (Recall the difficulty younger students have with conservation problems.)

In addition to automaticity and the discovery of shortcuts, biological maturation of the brain contributes to "operational efficiency" (Case, 1984). The biology of the brain is a factor over which a teacher has no control, but the use of automaticity and of shortcuts suggest some instructional hypotheses that a teacher can test.

If a student in your class is having difficulty solving a certain kind of problem, the first step—this should sound familiar—is to observe the student carefully. You need to determine if the problem is a lack of automaticity in some critical operation, oversimplification of the task, or both. The cure for a lack of automaticity is practice, but the right kind of practice. Paul in Teacher Chronicle 2.2 seems to need practice in matching sounds to letters. But is that the right diagnosis of his difficulty? Would a more careful observation suggest that Paul doesn't yet recognize the letters? Careful observation is necessary lest the teacher prescribe the wrong kind of practice.

If the problem seems to be one of oversimplification of the task, a different approach is suggested. After determining what the student is leaving out, emphasize the missing step or steps by demonstrating how the oversimplification doesn't work. Then demonstrate a set of operations that accomplishes the task. Finally, break down the task into discrete steps and have the student practice each one. When dealing with increasingly complex problems, the student must monitor his or her progress while moving through the steps.

Metacognition is the capability to monitor one's own cognitive processing. It is, simply, one's knowledge about thinking. As students develop, they become more aware of their own thought processes and how they work (Meichenbaum, 1985). For example, after listening to a set of instructions, older students were more capable of judging how well they understood the instructions (Markman, 1979). Younger students can be taught explicitly to apply knowledge of their own thinking in a particular situation, but they tend not to apply metacognitive knowledge learned in one situation to other situations (Forrest-Pressley, MacKinnon, & Waller, 1985). The ability to think about one's own thinking is related to the planning of attention (see Flavell, 1985), to the attainment of automaticity, and to discovering valid shortcuts. As students develop knowledge about their world by experiencing objects and people and by solving problems, they also develop knowledge about themselves.

"discovered" and the shortcuts they were given by their teachers, commenting on whether it is better to discover or be given shortcuts.

Principles in Practice 2.2

Principles . . .

1. Schemata influence experiences at one stage and are the basis for the next stage.
2. The stages of cognitive development are a basis for characterizing a student's thinking.
3. Cognitive development is not uniform across all areas.

. . . in Practice

In Teacher Chronicle 2.2, Paul's mother equates cognitive development with age alone. The teacher points out the differences in experiences between her two children. Both have good vocabularies, but Paul missed some chances to develop the symbolic representations necessary to support the complex operations of reading. The teacher is not concerned with Paul's overall capabilities, and feels he will be able to read once he constructs the necessary schemata.

1. How will Paul's experiences at car shows and on his grandfather's farm contribute to logical thinking?
2. In terms of Piaget's stages, is Paul at a different stage of development than his sister?
3. Assuming that Paul's mother is capable of abstract reasoning, why did she misunderstand her son's reading problem?

CRACKING THE CODE

While teaching, I am constantly seeking clues from my students, weighing their reactions, looking for puzzled faces, seeking signs of Eureka! and finding frustration levels. Only minutes into a lesson, it becomes clear who is grasping new material, who is struggling to understand, and who is being overwhelmed.

One day I introduced secret codes to my seven-year-old students. I planned an easy message, one which I felt most of the children would be able to crack. My only worry was Ernesto, a Spanish-speaking boy who was new to the class. I had heard him read, listening to him struggle as he tried to pronounce certain English words. He also had difficulty putting words in correct order in English. We made a game out of my correcting him when he said, "I don't want nothing." Whenever he said it, I would hold my empty

Teacher
Chronicle
2.3

SCHOOL OF EDUCATION
CURRICULUM LABORATORY
UM-DEARBORN

hands out. He sensed the difference, but just did not seem able to say consistently, "I don't want anything." I made a mental note to watch him closely for signs of frustration as we were doing the codes.

I wrote this secret message on the board:

19 26 10 10 2   25 18 9 7 19 23 26 2
20 22 12 9 20 22   4 26 8 19 18 13 20 7 12 13

"We can't read it," Eric said. "It isn't letters."

"It's just bunches of numbers all mixed up," Heidi said.

"What can you tell me about the numbers?" I asked.

"They're all mixed up."

"They are not in order."

"They don't add up to anything."

"Do you see anything the same?" I asked next.

"Yes, some numbers are up twice."

"What else do you see?" I glanced at Ernesto whose knitted eyebrows signaled a look of intense concentration.

"You are not counting by twos or threes or fives."

"The highest number is 26."

"Hmm, that's interesting. What else do you know that has 26?"

"Twenty-six desks in our room?"

"Twenty-six rooms in the school?"

"Twenty-six books in Jeremy's desk?" A knowing giggle went round the room.

"Twenty-six letters in the alphabet," chipped in Ernesto.

There was a buzz of excitement. "Yeah, there are 26 letters in the alphabet."

"It's the alphabet in numbers."

"What do you now see about the numbers?"

The answers come quickly now. "They're in groups."

Eric almost bounces out of his seat. "They are words written in numbers."

"Right," I answer. "Now how can we figure out what they mean?"

Immediately, Carlene says, "A must be 1. B must be 2."

"Let's try it and see."

They each take pencil and paper and begin figuring out the code. Quickly, it becomes obvious that we're on the wrong track.

By their reasoning, 19 26 10 10 2 would mean "szjjb."

"What if A is 26?" Ernesto asks, looking at me for a clue to whether or not he is right. I try not to smile and give it away, but I can't hold it back.

"A is 26," he shouts.

A flurry of pencils scratch across the paper.

Ernesto calls out, "19 26 10 10 2 means 'Happy.' " The entire class turns to look at him as a big smile spreads across his face.

I needn't have worried about Ernesto. This exercise is a piece of cake for him.

Eric quickly finishes what he is writing.

"Ernesto's right," he says, looking at his neighbor with new respect.

Shannon, who is normally quiet, calls out next, "25 18 9 7 19 23 22 means 'Birthday.' "

Within minutes the entire message is translated, "Happy Birthday, George Washington."

For the rest of the day they wrote their work in code, and it was my turn to play translator.

■■■

LANGUAGE DEVELOPMENT

Language accounts for much of the communication that occurs in classrooms. Teachers and students talk. Words, phrases, sentences are written on the board. Textbooks are read. But not all communication is done in a spoken language. Students raise their hands, furrow their brows, slump in their chairs. Teachers raise their fingers to their lips, lift their eyebrows, and shake their heads at slumping students. A language comprises symbols, sounds, meanings, and rules that govern the possible interrelationships. Language is also arbitrary. Why do we call a cow a cow? Why do we associate the letter *R* with the sound "errrr" instead of "sssss"? Why do you recognize those sounds even though they are ink marks on a page? How do children become capable of using language to communicate?

Let's briefly review three theoretical perspectives on the development of the language in order to derive a useful description of language development. Because the material is important for its instructional implications, we will also look at research on bilingualism and at the linguistic differences associated with social class.

Chap. Obj. 5, 6
Test Ques. 2.111–2.142

Focus Questions: In what ways are language and cognition related and unrelated? How do students, with varying capabilities, come to communicate competently?

Field Observation: Have students collect ten examples of nonverbal communication while observing both teachers and students.

Spoken language is the primary form of communication used in the classroom.

Theories of Language Development

The Innatist Theory

Noam Chomsky is the major proponent of the **innatist theory,** which postulates that humans have an innate ability to acquire language; they are genetically preprogrammed for it. All normally developing children acquire language. Chomsky takes this as evidence of an innate **language acquisition device (LAD),** which is not a physical structure in the brain; it is a metaphor referring to a neurological predisposition to learn language (Chomsky, 1968, 1975). The environment in which children grow up does not affect whether or not they will learn language, but simply which language. The rate at which language develops from the onset may vary, but the environment will not change its course. As long as a child is exposed to language, the inborn tendencies will be activated.

Chomsky (1968, 1975) also maintains that language and thought are separate. Language develops in the same way in virtually all children despite the fact that they differ in cognitive skills. Supporting Chomsky's separation of language and thought, Pratelli-Palnerini (1980) contends that the structures governing each are radically different. Otherwise, how can we account for the evidence that severely retarded children often have relatively advanced linguistic abilities even though their other intellectual abilities are extremely limited?

Chomsky's innatist position derives from his linguistic theory called **transformational grammar,** in which he sets out the rules people use to transform written or spoken words into meaning (Chomsky, 1965). Chomsky proposed that language exists on two levels: deep structure and surface structure. The **deep structure** is the abstract meaning of an utterance. The **surface structure** is the actual utterance.

In Teacher Chronicle 2.3, Ernesto said, "I don't want nothing" when he meant, "I don't want anything." Both Ernesto and the teacher meant the same thing, but they used different surface structures to express the same deep structure. Not so incidentally, the correct phrase in Spanish is *"No quiero nada,"* which means literally "I don't want nothing." Ernesto used a surface structure that was "correct" Spanish, but not "correct" English.

Think about how a child's cultural background contributes to his or her repertoire of surface structures. Think also about the possibility that a teacher forms overall impressions on the basis of the surface structures that a student uses to communicate his or her meanings. Chomsky's transformational view of language has implications for our examination of dialect in the classroom.

The Cognitivist Theory

Throughout his career Piaget maintained that language acquisition cannot take place until cognitive development has paved the way for it (1967). **Cognitivist theory** asserts that children develop knowledge of the world and *then* "map" this knowledge onto language categories and relations. From this viewpoint, language development depends on cognitive development, but not vice versa.

This is not to say that language is unimportant. Piaget believed that language is important for communication, but communication is not of itself the acquisition of knowledge. Language often accompanies an experience with-

---

innatist theory Chomsky's theory that humans have an innate ability to acquire language and are genetically preprogrammed for it.

language acquisition device (LAD) Chomsky's term for a human neurological predisposition to learn language.

transformational grammar A grammar that generates the deep structures of language and converts these to surface structures by means of transformations.

deep structure The essential meaning of a sentence that underlies its written or spoken form; its abstract meaning.

surface structure The grammatical features of a sentence; the actual utterance itself.

cognitivist theory Piaget's theory that children develop knowledge of the world then "map" this knowledge onto language categories and relations.

Lecture Note: Have students discuss how language and thought are different.

Lecture Note: As an example, consider the two sentences that follow (from Hetherington & Parke, 1975).

1. Mary threw the ball.
2. The ball was thrown by Mary.

Both sentences have the same deep structure or meaning, but their surface structures differ.

Connection: See Teacher Chronicle 2.3: Cracking the Code.

out influencing it. Consider the following linguistic event involving Jenny and Chris, two preschoolers:

Jenny: They wiggle sideways when they kiss.
Chris: (Vaguely) What?
Jenny: My bunny slippers, they are brown and red and sort of yellow and white and they have eyes and ears and these noses that wiggle sideways when they kiss.
Chris: I have a piece of sugar in a red piece of paper. I'm gonna eat it but maybe it's for a horse.
Jenny: We bought them, my mommy did. We couldn't find the old ones; these are like the old ones. They were not in the trunk.
Chris: Can't eat the piece of sugar not unless you take the paper off. (Stone & Church, 1957, p. 146)

Jenny and Chris appear to be having a conversation. Each pauses after speaking to allow the other to speak, but their statements bear little relationship to one another. Their remarks focus on what each is doing by himself or herself. This "linguistic event" is an example of the collective monologue discussed earlier in the chapter.

The Social Contextual Theory

social contextual theory
Vygotsky's notion that language influences cognitive development.

Vygotsky is the primary proponent of the **social contextual theory** of language development, which states that social interaction influences both language and cognitive development (1962, 1978). You will recall that Vygotsky's *zone of proximal development* suggests that social interaction can help students make cognitive breakthroughs. Since much of that interaction occurs through language, it follows that language does influence cognitive development.

Vygotsky proposed that language and thought are separate and independent of each other until a child is approximately two years of age. He viewed Piaget's sensorimotor stage and the early acquisition of rudimentary language skills as separate accomplishments. According to Vygotsky, after two years of age, language and thought become interrelated.

As children begin to understand language, they use language to reason. Language provides labels for the objects and events that children think about. These labels become pointers or containers for generalizations about objects and events. For example, a child can "point out" one object in the environment by using the word *window* and another with the word *cat*. A child can also form the generalization that *cats like to sit by windows*. In this way, words become a crucial element for abstract conceptual development.

Vygotsky's view is supported by research indicating that children sometimes invent their own linguistic forms to help themselves grasp concepts (Karmiloff-Smith, 1979a). For example, we know a young connoisseur of apple juice who refers to apples as *juice balls*. Older children and adults also invent linguistic forms to help them understand new concepts. Have you ever heard someone trying to describe something they are unfamiliar with as a
_____ *thing*? Consider the young man who once asked an auto mechanic about the *gas-intake thing*, meaning the carburetor.

Additional research by Karmiloff-Smith (1979b) indicates that children can take linguistic information from a sentence and make meanings that extend beyond the information in the sentence. A student who reads about

Field Observations: Have students listen to and document preschool "conversations."

Lecture Note: The "conversation" is reminiscent of a comment attributed to the humorist, Fran Lebowitz, "The opposite of talking is not listening. The opposite of talking is waiting to talk again."

Connection: See Vygotsky's zone of proximal development discussed earlier in this chapter.

Lecture Note: Ask students to speculate about the inferential abilities of good versus poor readers.

Lecture Note: Ask students to discuss if there is a "grammar" of communication between people and their pets.

"transplanting forty-foot oak trees" might begin thinking about deforestation. Such research findings show the interconnectiveness of language and cognitive growth.

Hallmarks of Language Development

The theoretical perspectives that we have reviewed address the relationship between language and cognitive development. Regardless of its role in cognitive development, language is a tool of communication. Understanding the developmental hallmarks of that tool will be useful to those who seek to communicate with children.

Linguists, those who study the structure and function of language, identify the **grammar** of a language as a system of implicit rules which relate sounds to meaning (Clark & Clark, 1977). Grammatical rules operate on three major elements of language. The first is **phonology,** the sounds of a language and the structure of those sounds. The second is **syntax,** the way the words of language form sentences. The third is **semantics,** the meaning underlying words and sentences. There is one other element of language, pragmatics. **Pragmatics** refers to the contexts in which language is used and the way language can be used to create contexts. A linguist who focuses on pragmatics studies intonation, gestures, the conventions by which conversations occur, the meanings of pauses, the intention of a writer or speaker, and the like.

The most dramatic language developmental changes occur before a child reaches school age. The early stages of language development are presented in Table 2–2 (LeFrancois, 1991).

■ **Table 2–2** *The Stages of Grammatical Development*

Stage*	Middle of Age Range (years)	Grammatical Capabilities
Sounds	less than 1	Phonological experimentation; crying, cooing, babbling
Holophrases	1	Single words carrying sentential meaning; inflections
Telegraphic utterances	1½	Two-word "sentences"; key word modified; declarations, questions, imperatives, and negatives used
Short sentences	2–2½	Real sentences, subjects and predicates; tense changes
Complex sentences	3–4	New elements and clauses embedded; use of parts of speech in various ways
Adultlike structures	4	Structural distinctions made

SOURCE: From *Psychology for Teaching* (7th ed., p. 169) by G. R. LeFrancois, 1991, Belmont, CA: Wadsworth. Copyright 1991 by Wadsworth. Adapted with permission.

*The descriptors are relative. Remember the developmental changes outlined in this table occur before most children enter school.

The stages of grammatical development reflect changes in phonology, syntax, semantics, and pragmatics. Grammatical development occurs rapidly. This is especially true of phonology—the sounds of a language. The vast majority of English-speaking children can properly pronounce most of the sounds of their language by the time they reach school. The speech sounds that take the longest to develop are *s, z, v, th,* and *zh* (Rathus, 1988). The "lisping" quality in the speech of children in the primary grades can be traced to the lack of development of these sounds. Let's look briefly at some hallmarks of development in the other areas of language, especially those pertinent to school-age children.

Syntax

According to Wood (1981), children are using "adultlike" sentences by approximately age four. However, these are very basic forms: simple declarations and questions. Although early elementary-age children tend to use simple syntax when they speak, they are capable of understanding more complicated forms, such as the passive voice. For example, they are more likely to say, "Mary threw the ball," but they can understand, "The ball was thrown by Mary." The complexity of the forms they produce increases as they form compounds, learn to use conjunctions, add relative clauses, and master tenses. It is important that elementary school teachers recognize that students can understand forms that they do not use yet. When thinking about syntactic development, the rule of thumb is that comprehension precedes production (cf. Clark & Clark, 1977).

Connection: In Diary of a Day, Chapter 1, Peter Roop read aloud books that were more difficult than those students read on their own.

Field Observation: Have students document the sentence constructions of children of various ages. Have them give children a complex sentence and ask the children to repeat it in order to observe changes in syntax that the children make.

Semantics

One aspect of semantics is vocabulary. A child begins to use his or her first words around the time of the first birthday. Once the child learns to use words, a single word is often used to communicate a variety of messages. This is called holophrasic speech. For example, *milk* can mean "I want milk," "The milk is all gone," "That is milk," or "The milk fell" (Bates, O'Connell, & Shore, 1987; Snyder, Bates, & Bretherton, 1981). It takes approximately three to four months for the first 10 words to appear. Once the child has acquired approximately 10 words, he or she adds another word to the vocabulary every few days. A typical eighteen-month-old child has a vocabulary of approximately 40 to 50 words. The average twenty-four-month-old child knows approximately 300 words and by age six, a child may know upwards of 14,000 words (Carey, 1977; Templine, 1957). Reading and other language-based activities that occur in the early grades may contribute to the roughly 5,000 additional words the child gains by age eleven (cf. Berger, 1986).

Aside from the development of a vocabulary, a hallmark of semantic development is the capability to understand complex language functions. For example, many children and some adolescents have difficulty with metaphors, similes, sarcasm, and facetious remarks. Teachers who like to joke and kid with students must be careful when speaking with those whose semantics do not embrace these complex structures.

Teaching Anecdote: Tell the story of the high school English teacher who, when asked for the four-thousandth time, "How long does the paper have to be?" responded sarcastically, "The paper must be 4.23 pages long." He felt bad the next day when an anxious student asked, "How do you figure out how long .23 of a page is?"

Pragmatics

Pragmatic development occurs as a child becomes capable of using his or her grammatical competence to communicate in a variety of contexts. A collective monologue may contain grammatically correct language, but it is not communication. By adolescence, students have learned the conventions of con-

bilingualism Able to speak two languages fluently.
metalinguistic awareness Knowledge about language and the ability to think about one's own knowledge of language.
bilingual education An instructional program for students who are taught basic subject matter in their native language while the second language is being acquired.

Journal Entry: Ask students to reflect on a teacher (or other adult) who influenced their use of language as a child or adolescent. Have them reflect also on the time when they wrote their first poems (or used poetic language). What was the social context? Had they fallen "in love" for the first time?

Lecture Note: Ask any bilingual students in class to describe what it is like to grow up bilingual.

Lecture Note: Ask students whether they think learning number systems other than base 10 increases "meta-mathematical" awareness.

Connection: See Teacher Chronicle 2.3: Cracking the Code.

versation and can use them to gain information. The conversations in the halls of a junior high school are filled with snatches of conversations such as the following. "I can't believe he said that about her. Can you?" "I thought you liked Debbie. How come you didn't walk home with her yesterday?" "Don't you think he's the biggest jerk in school?"

Using language to gain information is just one aspect of pragmatic development. Language can also be used poetically, persuasively, humorously, artistically, tactfully. The language experiences provided by teachers influence pragmatic development throughout a student's career.

Language Differences

The demographics of schools are changing. In 1982, one in ten children in American schools was Hispanic. Projections suggest that, within a generation, a quarter of the students will be Hispanic, an increase of 150 percent. Over 15 percent will be African-Americans. One-half of the students in American schools will be Caucasian, a 33 percent decrease (Pallas, Natriello, & McDill, 1989). The cultural and linguistic heritages mixed together in classrooms spotlight two sources of language differences: bilingualism and dialect.

Bilingualism

Bilingualism is a term used to refer to people who can speak fluently in two different languages. Ianco-Worrell (1972) compared young children who were bilinguals (in Afrikaans and English) to monolinguals (in either Afrikaans or English). The children who were bilingual were better able to identify the semantic relationship between two terms presented together. Monolinguals tended only to observe the phonological relationship.

Feldman and Shen (1971) compared four- to six-year-old bilingual Mexican-Americans with peers of the same age and same socioeconomic status. The bilinguals performed significantly better than their monolingual counterparts in judging consistencies in various objects, switching common names of objects, and demonstrating an ability to place objects according to relations (e.g., on, top, in, under). Taken together, these studies suggest that bilingual children enjoy an advantage over monolingual children in a number of specific cognitive tasks.

Bialystok and Ryan (1985) argue that bilingual children are able to "step back" and reflect on the structure and function of language better than monolingual students are. Being fluent in more than one language seems to give them a broader perspective. This ability to think about their own knowledge of language is called **metalinguistic awareness.** (Metalinguistic awareness is metacognition, but applied strictly to language.) For example, bilinguals tend to have a better understanding of the arbitrary nature of linguistic labels. Ernesto, in Teacher Chronicle 2.3, was able to decipher the number code more quickly than his monolingual peers. Perhaps his experience with two languages increased his awareness that the letters and words are merely symbols and that the key to understanding them is finding the underlying code.

Assuming that English is the primary language of instruction in a school, what happens to students who come with little or no knowledge of it? Such students need to become bilingual and are, therefore, candidates for bilingual education. A student involved in **bilingual education** is taught some basic subject matter in his or her native language while the second language is

Issues in Educational Psychology

CNN™ This box relates to Segment 2 of the CNN videotape. See the Instructor's Section for a summary.

BILINGUALISM: YESTERDAY, TODAY, AND TOMORROW

The issue of bilingualism versus immersion is a complex one. Politics has played a part in it. History has played another. National pride and cultural identity factor in as well.

During the Carter administration, programs that employed native languages while teaching English mastery were favored. The Reagan administration, which followed Carter's, withheld its support for bilingual programs. The administration favored changing the Bilingual Education Act to allow English-immersion programs in America's public schools. In 1983, the act was amended to permit 25 percent of federal funding for English immersion.

Proponents of an English only program point to waves of immigrants who flooded America in the late 1800s and early 1900s and the way in which they adjusted to their adopted country. In a *New York Times Magazine* article that chronicled the controversy surrounding billingualism, a passage from Irving Howe's *A Margin of Hope* documented the predominant attitude of yesterday's immigrants. "The educational institutions of the city were still under the sway of a unified culture, that dominant 'Americanism' which some ethnic subcultures may have challenged a little, but which prudence and ambition persuaded

them to submit to." In the New York of the 1920s, as the child of Jews who had immigrated to the United States, Howe wanted to become an American.

Today, among immigrant groups, many Hispanics seem to resist assimilation. Raul Yzaguirre, who leads the National Council of La Raza, a Hispanic umbrella group, says that one reason for treating today's immigrants differently is the "critical mass," the large Hispanic population that exists in parts of the United States. Yzaguirre believes that billingualism speaks to a problem that arose, in part, from America's expansion into areas of the Southwest that were the domain of Spain and, later, Mexico. "The U.S. came to them. They didn't come to the U.S. So the idea of coming to a new country and having to adapt to it is not part of the mentality of many Hispanics," he says. Having witnessed billingualism over a number of years, Yzaguirre firmly believes that "it works."

Like Irving Howe, Hispanic author Richard Rodriguez wrote about his school days. In *Hunger of Memory* he wrote with pride about his ability to successfully use English in school for the first time. "The belief, the calming assurance that I belonged in public, had at last taken hold. It would have pleased me to have my teachers speak to me in Spanish, but I would have delayed having to learn the language of public society."

Opponents of bilingualism fear the cultural fragmentation that the

rise of other languages, especially Spanish, can cause. Proponents see bilingualism as a way to include all the disparate groups that make up this country. They favor a polycultural society within which each ethnic group is accorded respect.

As the arguments swirl around billingualism, the passions become more heated. It is worth noting that a report in the *Education Digest* observed that "the results [of a recent study] still favor strong bilingual programs over partial bilingual instruction or English-immersion programs." But reshaping the United States culturally and linguistically are also key aspects of what will be an ongoing debate.

SOURCES: Bernstein, Richard. "U.S. Schools: A War of Words." *New York Times Magazine* (October 14, 1990): 34. Monagle, Katie. "One Language or Two?" *Scholastic Update* (Teacher's Edition) 123, issue 8 (January 11, 1991): 13. Miller, Julie A. "Native-Language Instruction Found to Aid L.E.P.'s." *Education Week* 10, issue 9 (October 31, 1991): 1, 23. "Washington News: Bilingual Education." *Education Digest* (January 1991): 63–64.

1. What problems would you anticipate a Spanish-speaking student having in an English immersion class?
2. Reflecting on Richard Rodriguez's school experience, consider whether thinking and language are different from the perspectives of Chomsky and Piaget.

being acquired. After reviewing numerous studies of bilingual education, Willig (1985) concluded that children learn best when some subjects are taught in one language and other subjects are taught in the second language. How should this bilingual mix be achieved? More specifically, how should the second language be acquired?

One way to achieve bilingual balance would be to provide the child with initial exposure to the second language and then gradually increase the amount of second-language instruction he or she receives until balance is achieved. Another approach, referred to in research literature as **language immersion,** recommends starting instruction exclusively in the second language—in order to achieve competence quickly—and then reducing the amount of second-language instruction to achieve balance (see Figure 2–3).

Immersion programs work best when they are begun very early in a child's schooling. Young children learn a second language quite easily (cf. Lenneberg, 1967; McLaughlin, 1984). In addition, it makes sense from a curriculum standpoint. The social and experiential emphasis in kindergarten lends itself to language learning. Furthermore, a child who is taught in his or her native language for several years and then switched to an immersion program will likely suffer from the necessary disruption in the curricular sequence.

In many instances, the first year of immersion programs are just that, total immersion in the new language. A small amount of instruction in the native language occurs in the second year, increasing in subsequent years until the desired bilingual balance is achieved. Immersion programs in French are very common in Canada, as are Spanish immersion programs in some parts of the United States (LeFrancois, 1991).

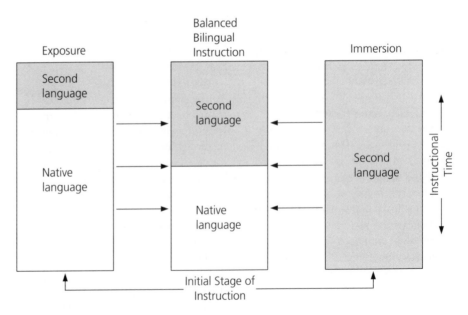

■ **Figure 2–3** *Two Approaches to Balanced Bilingual Instruction*

Two approaches may be used in teaching students who speak English as a second language: bilingual mix (teaching some subject matter in a student's first language, and others in English) and language immersion.

Genesee (1985) reports that participants in immersion programs in the United States learn to understand and produce the new language quickly and proficiently (in both oral and written form). Additionally, the academic performance of immersion students compares well with that of students in monolingual programs in math, science, and social studies.

The positive effects found by Genesee might be attributable to the student population that was studied. The native language of most U.S. students is English, the primary school language. The second language acquired through immersion in this study was a minority language. What are the effects of immersion when the native language of a student is a minority language, as in the case of an Hispanic child in the United States or a French-speaking child in Canada?

There is a greater possibility of negative outcomes from immersion when the child's second language is the school's primary language. For example, in the United States a child whose first language is Spanish is surrounded by a society that operates primarily in English. Schools support and encourage English. Society imbues English with greater value (Landry, 1987). If the child has learned a nonstandard dialect at home, his or her problems learning a second language will be compounded (cf. Carey, 1987). All of these conditions conspire against successful immersion.

In most cases, you will use one language when you teach a lesson to a group of students. Even if you plan to teach a foreign language, you may choose an immersion approach for your class. The point is, if the students you teach in one language are learning another, the conditions of their second-language learning will likely influence how they communicate in your classroom. Bilingualism, whether it is acquired from birth or through second-language learning in school, will contribute to the variability of communication skills in your classroom.

Connection: See Teacher Chronicle 2.3: Cracking the Code.

Lecture Note: Language differences and dialect differences may be accompanied by cultural differences, which are examined in Chapter 4.

dialect A variation of a language spoken by a particular ethnic, regional, or social group.

restricted language codes Linguistic codes associated with short, simple, grammatically uncomplicated sentences.

elaborated language codes Linguistic codes associated with sentences that are long, descriptive, and grammatically complex.

Field Observation: Have students interview elementary, middle, and high school students from schools in different socioeconomic neighborhoods to discover different "codes," i.e., phrases, connotations, etc.

Lecture Note: For emphasis, ask students to speculate on the possibility that Bernstein inferred restricted codes because he did not share the context of those speakers.

Lecture Note: Ask students if they or any of their friends use different dialects at home and at school. Ask them to compare their speech in the dorm, fraternity or sorority house, or even in small group discussions with the speech they use to recite in larger groups with a professor or instructor present.

Dialect

A **dialect** is a distinctive version of a language or a variation within a language. The differences between dialects may be in pronunciation, "yard" in the Midwest is "yahd" in New England; grammar, "I be going" in one neighborhood is "I am going" in another; or vocabulary, "gum band" in Pittsburgh is "rubber band" anywhere else. There are other ways in which dialects differ and factors other than location that define dialect groups. People who share dialects often share an ethnic heritage or social and economic backgrounds.

Bernstein (1971) did a classic comparison of the dialects used by working-class families and upper income families in England.

Through his observations, Bernstein identified what he called restricted and elaborated language codes. **Restricted language codes** are associated with short, simple, and grammatically uncomplicated sentences, which are usually devoted to actions and things. The meaning expressed in restricted codes is often implicit; much of it cannot be understood unless you know its context. Bernstein also concluded that restricted language codes have a strong correlation with parenting styles. Restricted codes are characteristic of authoritarian, power-centered families, or neglecting, ignoring families. Language is used in these contexts for the purpose of control, motivating action, and for rigid classifications. In such families, questions are rarely asked. Bernstein concluded that children from this type of language environment are "behind" when they enter school and that their deficit grows as they continue through school.

According to Bernstein, **elaborated language codes,** most often found in middle- and upper-class, educated families, are associated with sentences that are longer, more descriptive, and more grammatically complicated. Speech is explicit; meaning is clearly conveyed in the words used. Parents who exhibit elaborated codes tend to socialize their children. Speech is used for communication and discussion when children are asked to comply with parental wishes, not as an element of control. Those who exhibit elaborated language codes use language to describe the invisible as well as the visible world. Representational thought and imagery are supported by these codes.

When Bernstein discusses language as it relates to parenting style, his use of the terms *restricted* and *elaborated* has been viewed by some researchers as reflecting a bias toward certain groups of people. Critics point out that Bernstein concluded that one characteristic of restricted codes is that meaning is "contextually bound." Presumably, if one knows the context, the meaning of restricted-code utterances is clear. Perhaps Bernstein did not share the contexts of the speakers he heard. Perhaps you will not share the contexts of some of the students you will teach.

Furthermore, as we pointed out in our earlier examination of transformational grammar, meaning—deep structure—can be expressed in a number of different forms—surface structures. Dialect differences are reflected in surface structures, not in deep structures. Dialects differ in the transformational rules that map surface structures onto meaning. Unless one knows the transformational rules of a particular dialect, he or she will have difficulty making meaning. Bernstein may have been listening to a dialect (or possibly more than one dialect) with which he was unfamiliar.

It is important to remember that, with regard to deep structure, all dialects create meanings (cf. Edwards, 1979). Teachers should respect the cognitive abilities of students who speak in nonstandard dialects, but that does not mean that a teacher should accept nonstandard dialect.

Profiles in Successful Practice

PAM MANIET-BELLERMANN

COLUMBIA GRAMMAR AND PREPARATORY SCHOOL

NEW YORK, NEW YORK

Three messages have been on the walls of every classroom in which I have taught for the past fifteen years. One is in the form of a poster showing ten runners ready to burst from their blocks at the sound of a gun. The caption reads: "You have failed only if you have failed to try."

The other two messages are on homemade signs. The words have faded over the years, but their meanings are clear. One reads: "SUCCESS Lies Not in *BEING* the Best, But in *DOING* Your Best." The other reads: "THINK POSITIVE!"

These messages have been my mottoes; and I teach them to my students.

I am very privileged to be a teacher. Teaching is not easy. There is so much to be done and so little time to do it in! But teaching is the profession that allows me to make a genuine difference. The teachers I remember were either so bad that I could never forget them, or especially memorable because they reached out to me in some unique way. I remember very little about the others. When I decided to become a teacher, I knew I wanted to be the type of teacher a child remembered because I, too, had reached out in some special way.

Becoming that kind of teacher has been the hardest thing I ever attempted in my life; and my efforts are far from over. In fact, those efforts will never end if I am to be that teacher who makes a difference for the better in my students' lives.

As a young teacher straight out of college, the most important thing I had to learn was that I did not have all the answers. I was ready to tackle the world and felt prepared to set young minds afire with all the ideas and knowledge I had acquired. I had a lot of education, but very few answers. Realizing this was painful.

I was full of good ideas, but quickly found that they did not always work with every child. When I encountered difficulties, I tended to panic. I often saw suggestions as criticisms and sometimes even blamed the students for my shortcomings. It was easy to come up with reasons why a child was not learning: The homelife was terrible. Past schooling had been awful. The child was learning disabled, and so on. Many of these things were true, but they were not the only reasons why the students were not learning. I simply had been unable to reach them.

Learning to reach and teach each child demanded that I did not see myself as the focal point of the teaching process but that I saw the child as the center. It demanded that I did not force the child to submit to me, but that I submitted to him or her.

Each child is the product of countless and immeasurable influences, whether they be biological, social, economic, or political. To teach each child, therefore, to truly broadcast to him or her on a frequency that the child understands and absorbs, meant learning first from the child before he or she could learn from me. I had to learn who the child was. I could not come with preconceived notions about the student and what he or she was capable of. I had to listen and reflect on the many confusing and contradictory messages the child gave and gear my efforts to these often subtle, often quite unsatisfactory signals. I had to be prepared to realize that the understanding I have of the student today will be invalid tomorrow, next week, next month, or next year. If life changes for all of us, it never changes so rapidly as it does for a child.

It is often said that students must trust us and have confidence in us if we are to be successful teachers. I rather think that it is the other way around. As a teacher, I have to trust that my students will want to be an essential force in the learning process, that they will want to grow and master their environment, and that they will give me all sorts of clues as to how I might help them reach the limits of their potential.

If I listen to them and respect them, I might someday become the teacher who did indeed make a difference.

The physician who addresses a professional meeting of the AMA speaks in one way. When she addresses her children she speaks in a different way. The language she uses on the basketball court is different still. She can shift her codes to suit the situation. What of the child who knows only a nonstandard dialect? Unless that child learns standard English dialect, those situations which call for it are likely to remain out of bounds.

Principles in Practice 2.3

Principles . . .
1. Language is a tool of communication and an aid to (abstract) thought.
2. Basic grammatical capabilities are acquired by the time children reach school age; pragmatic development continues indefinitely.
3. Linguistic diversity can affect communication.

. . . in Practice
In Teacher Chronicle 2.3, Ernesto had difficulty with pronunciation, phonological fluency, and grammar. Thus, his success with the code task surprised everyone, including the teacher. Perhaps his bilingualism enhanced a metalinguistic awareness of the role symbols play in all languages, even a "new" dialect that formed words from numbers.

1. If Ernesto's metalinguistic awareness helped him think effectively about the code, why didn't that awareness prove as effective when he attempted to read or communicate?
2. Re-reading the utterances of the students, what do you understand the "speaking-in-class" rules to be in this classroom?
3. How much do you imagine other students in this class talk to Ernesto? What is his "social" position in this class?

CONCLUSION

Assign Chapter 2 of the *Study Guide*.

In this chapter, we have looked at patterns of cognitive development and the development of language. To the extent that Piaget was correct in documenting the parts that language and cognition play in providing a picture of the mental makeup of our students, we can use his notion of cognitive development and the various hallmarks of language acquisition to identify the capabilities of our students. Instructionally, we are in a position to make judgments about the types of activities we should expect of individual students.

Research on cognitive and linguistic development tells us three things quite clearly.

1. Our students are likely to think very differently from the way that we think.
2. Our students are likely to use different forms to communicate than we use.

3. There will be diversity in the thinking and communication among our students.

Instruction then becomes a matter of finding appropriate ways to communicate ideas, rules, and desires and of providing developmentally appropriate educational experiences.

Chapter Summary

Introduction: The Nature of Human Development
Jean Piaget: A Curious Biologist
The study of human development involves assessing the capabilities we possess as we grow into and develop our potential. There are several areas of human development that have been identified for the purpose of study: cognitive development, personal development, and social development. This chapter has focused on cognitive capabilities and the related area of language development.

The most influential cognitive theorist is Jean Piaget, who began his studies of early cognitive development in the 1920s.

Basic Piagetian Concepts
Influences on Cognitive Development
Piaget's theory of cognitive development is based on basic assumptions about the factors that influence cognitive development: maturation, that is, genetically determined growth; active experience with objects in the environment; social interaction with people in the environment; and equilibration, that is, the regulation of other factors.

Intellectual Organization and Adaptation
Piaget viewed cognitive development as being governed by the same principles that determined biological development. The human tendency to organize the environment yields schemata or knowledge structures. The tendency to adapt to the environment is played out through the processes of assimilation and accommodation. These processes allow one to modify schemata. Equilibration provides a balance between assimilation and accommodation in order to maintain schemata that yield to adaptive interaction with the environment.

Experience and Knowledge
Two types of experience allow us to construct knowledge. Using the first, physical experience, we observe and manipulate objects in the environment to construct knowledge of the physical properties of objects. Using the second, the logico-mathematical experience—thinking about one's thoughts—we can build new knowledge. Both types of experience are important for cognitive development.

Piaget's Stages of Cognitive Development
Describing and Interpreting Cognitive Change
Piaget viewed cognitive development as being gradual. He established stages as hallmarks along the continuum of cognitive development. The order of these stages is universal; each person passes through them in the same way. The rate at which development proceeds varies considerably from person to person.

The Stages: Hallmarks of Change
The stages of cognitive development define critical characteristics of the schemata possessed at each stage. Later stages include the characteristics of earlier ones. The first stage of development, the sensorimotor stage, is characterized by sensations and motor actions. The second stage, preoperations, is characterized by symbolic representation. The third stage, concrete operations, is characterized by schemata that allow logical operations. The fourth stage, formal operations, introduces the capability of abstract reasoning.

The Piagetian Theme and Some Variations
Zone of Proximal Development

Piaget's view of cognitive development provides us with a definition of the ways in which children think. Teachers who wish to carefully identify children's capabilities must carefully observe each child. One variation on the Piagetian theme is Vygotsky's zone of proximal development, a notion that suggests that teachers look for and support areas of imminent "breakthroughs."

Information-processing Capabilities

Another variation on Piaget's theme comes from information-processing theory. Information processing helps teachers to focus on how a student attends to his or her environment, uses his or her limited memory capacity, and monitors his or her own cognitive activity (metacognition).

Language Development
Theories of Language Development

Innatist, cognitivist, and social contextualist views of language development define the relationship between language and cognition. The innatist view suggests that a person's utterances do not reflect his or her cognitive capability. Cognitivist theory suggests that cognitive development must precede language. Social contextualist theory suggests that after two years of age, language and cognition are interrelated. In all cases, the relationship between language and cognition is not a simple one. Students who speak well are not necessarily more advanced.

Hallmarks of Language Development

A language is a set of grammatical rules covering phonology (sounds), syntax (putting words together to communicate ideas), and semantics (the meanings of words and sentences). In addition, language development involves pragmatics (the use of language in various contexts). Grammatical development occurs rapidly. Children can use relatively complex structures by the time they reach school. Pragmatic development continues indefinitely.

Language Differences

Language differences contribute to the variation in classroom communications. Demographic trends suggest that bilingual education is likely to increase. Students who are immersed in a second language will respond differently to instruction based on whether the second language is the school's majority or minority language. Dialects should be recognized as legitimate forms of language. The use of a nonstandard dialect does not indicate substandard cognitive capabilities.

Reflections: Building Your Theory of Teaching

2.1 Suppose you have decided to set up a cooperative project in your classroom. The purpose of the project is to discover a principle (i.e., some discipline's key concept). You want each group to produce something that documents the process of discovery.
  1. Identify a principle—of government, science, interpersonal relations, art, math, fiction-writing, and so on—that you would like to teach in the future. (You may, for example, want your students to discover the value of their own ideas, the necessity of compromise in democratic government, or the utility of carbon dating.)
  2. What materials, facts, rules for discussion, and so on will you provide to your class?
  3. What are the specifications for the answer that each group will submit?

2.2 Suppose you are participating in a districtwide study on nontraditional evaluation procedures. An advisory committee has been formed for each grade level. The study begins by gathering evidence on each student's zone of proximal development. One source of evidence will be a parent questionnaire; another source will be a teacher questionnaire. Suggest items that you think should be included on each of the questionnaires for your grade level.

2.3 The students in one or more of your classes are using two major dialects. You have determined that it is important for your students to be able to "shift codes," both from nonstandard to standard dialect and (to increase interpersonal understanding) from standard to nonstandard dialect. What actions will you take to accomplish code shifting?

Key Terms

developmental psychology (p. 42)

cognitive development theory (p. 42)

social development theory (p. 42)

personal development theory (p. 42)

maturation (p. 44)

active experience (p. 44)

social interaction (p. 44)

equilibration (p. 45)

schemata (p. 46)

assimilation (p. 48)

accommodation (p. 48)

disequilibrium (p. 49)

physical experience (p. 49)

empirical abstraction (p. 49)

logico-mathematical experience (p. 50)

reflexive abstraction (p. 50)

constructivist theory (p. 50)

ordinality (p. 53)

sensorimotor stage (p. 54)

object permanence (p. 54)

imitation (p. 54)

operations (p. 55)

preoperational (p. 55)

symbolic representation (p. 55)

perceptual centration (p. 56)

conservation tasks (p. 56)

irreversibility (p. 56)

egocentrism (p. 56)

collective monologue (p. 56)

concrete operations (p. 57)

reversibility (p. 57)

decentration (p. 58)

conservation (p. 58)

multiple classification (p. 58)

formal operations (p. 58)

abstract reasoning (p. 59)

décalage (p. 61)

zone of proximal development (p. 62)

information processing (p. 62)

attention (p. 62)

short-term store (p. 63)

operating space (p. 63)

storage space (p. 63)

automaticity (p. 63)

metacognition (p. 64)

innatist theory (p. 68)

language acquisition device (LAD) (p. 68)

transformational grammar (p. 68)

deep structure (p. 68)

surface structure (p. 68)

cognitivist theory (p. 68)

social contextual theory (p. 69)

grammar (p. 70)

phonology (p. 70)

syntax (p. 70)

semantics (p. 70)

pragmatics (p. 70)

bilingualism (p. 72)

metalinguistic awareness (p. 72)

bilingual education (p. 72)

language immersion (p. 74)

dialect (p. 76)

restricted language codes (p. 76)

elaborated language codes (p. 76)

Suggested Readings

Anderson, P. S., & Lapp, D. (1988). *Language skills in elementary education* (4th ed.). New York: Macmillan.

Case, R. (1984). The process of stage transition: A neo-Piagetian view. In R. J. Sternberg (ed.), *Mechanisms of cognitive development.* New York: W. H. Freeman.

Cazden, C. B. (1988). *Classroom discourse: The language of teaching and learning.* Portsmouth, NH: Heinemann.

Flavell, J. H. (1985). *Cognitive development* (2nd ed.). Englewood Cliffs, NJ: Prentice-Hall.

Piaget, J., & Inhelder, B. (1969). *The psychology of the child.* New York: Basic Books.

Vygotsky, L. S. (1986). *Thought and language.* Cambridge, MA: MIT Press.

Wadsworth, B. J. (1978). *Piaget for the classroom teacher.* New York: Longman.

Wadsworth, B. J. (1989). *Piaget's theory of cognitive and affective development* (4th ed.). New York: Longman.

References

Bates, E., O'Connell, B., & Shore, C. (1987). Language and communication in infancy. In J. D. Osofsky (Ed.), *Handbook of infant development* (2nd ed.). New York: Wiley.

Berger, K. S. (1986). *The developing person through childhood and adolescence* (2nd ed.). New York: Worth.

Bernstein, B. (1971). *Language and disadvantage.* London: Wauld.

Bialystok, E., & Ryan, E. (1985). Toward a definition of metalinguistic skill. *Merrill Palmer Quarterly, 31,* 235–252.

Carey, S. (1977). The child as ward learner. In M. Halle, J. Bresnan, & G. A. Miller (Eds.), *Linguistic theory and psychological reality.* Cambridge, MA: MIT Press.

Carey, S. (1987). Additive bilingualism, schooling, and special education: A minority group perspective. *Canadian Journal for Exceptional Children, 3,* 109—114.

Case, R. (1980). Intellectual development: A systematic reinterpretation. In F. Farley & N. J. Gordon (Eds.), *Psychology and education: The state of the union.* Berkeley, CA: McCutchan.

Case, R. (1984). The process of stage transition: A neo-Piagetian view. In R. J. Sternberg (Ed.), *Mechanisms of cognitive development.* New York: W. H. Freeman.

Chomsky, N. (1965). *Aspects of a theory of syntax.* Cambridge, MA: MIT Press.

Chomsky, N. (1968). *Language and the mind.* New York: Harcourt Brace Jovanovich.

Chomsky, N. (1975). *Reflections on language.* New York: Pantheon Books.

Clark, H. H., & Clark, E. V. (1977). *Psychology and language.* New York: Harcourt Brace Jovanovich.

Edwards, J. R. (1979). *Language and disadvantage.* London: Wauld.

Feldman. C., & Shen, M. (1971). Same-language-related cognitive advantages of bilingual five-year-olds. *Journal of Genetic Psychology, 118,* 235–244.

Flavell, J. H. (1985). *Cognitive development* (2nd ed.). Englewood Cliffs, NJ: Prentice-Hall.

Forrest-Pressley, D. L., MacKinnon, E., & Waller, T. G. (Eds.). (1985). *Metacognition, cognition, and human performance.* New York: Academic Press.

Gallagher, J., & Reid, D. (1981). *The learning theory of Piaget and Inhelder.* Monterey, CA: Brooks/Cole.

Genesee, F. (1985). Second language learning through immersion: A review of U.S. programs. *Review of Educational Research, 55,* 541–561.

Hetherington, E. M., & Parke, R. D. (1975). *Child psychology: A contemporary viewpoint.* New York: McGraw-Hill.

Ianco-Worrall, A. (1972). Bilingualism and cognitive development. *Child Development, 43,* 1390–1400.

Inhelder, B., & Piaget, J. (1958). *The growth of logical thinking from childhood to adolescence* (A. Parsons and S. Seagrin, Trans.). New York: Basic Books.

Karmiloff-Smith, A. (1979a). A functional approach to child language: A study of determiners and reference. In *Cambridge Studies in Linguistics* (No. 24). Cambridge, England: Cambridge University Press.

Karmiloff-Smith, A. (1979b). Language development after five. In P. Fletcher & M. Garman (Eds.), *Language acquisition.* Cambridge, England: Cambridge University Press.

Landry, R. (1987). Reading comprehension in first and second languages of immersion and Francophone students. *Canadian Journal for Exceptional Children, 3,* 103–108.

Lefrancois, G. R. (1991). *Psychology for teaching* (7th ed.). Belmont, CA: Wadsworth.

Lenneberg, E. H. (1967). *Biological foundations of language.* New York: John Wiley.

Markman. E. M. (1979). Realizing that you don't understand: Elementary school children's awareness of inconsistencies. *Child Development, 50,* 643–655.

McLaughlin, B. (1984). *Second-language acquisition in childhood: Vol. 1. Preschool children* (2nd ed.). Hillsdale, NJ: Erlbaum.

Meichenbaum, D. (1985). *Stress inoculation training.* New York: Pergamon.

Pallas, A. M., Natriello, G., & McDill, E. L. (1989). The changing nature of the disadvantaged population: Current dimensions and future trends. *Educational Researcher, 18,* 16–22.

Piaget, J. (1926). *The language and thought of the child* (M. Worden, Trans.). New York: Harcourt, Brace.

Piaget, J. (1928). *Judgment and reasoning in the child* (M. Worden, Trans.). New York: Harcourt, Brace & World.

Piaget, J. (1930). *The child's conception of physical causality* (M. Worden, Trans.). New York: Harcourt, Brace & World.

Piaget, J. (1952). *The origins of intelligence in children* (M. Cook, Trans.). New York: International Universities Press.

Piaget, J. (1961). The genetic approach to the psychology of thought. *Journal of Educational Psychology, 52,* 275–281.

Piaget, J. (1963). Problems of the social psychology of childhood (T. Brown and M. Gubety,

Trans. Manuscript). (Originally published in G. Gurvitch [Ed.] *Traite de Sociologie* [pp. 229–254]. Paris: Press Universitaires de France).

Piaget, J. (1967). *Biologie et connaissance.* Paris: Galliward.

Piaget, J. (1970). *Genetic epistemology.* New York: Columbia University Press.

Piaget, J. (1977). Problems in equilibration. In M. Appel & L. Goldberg (Eds.), *Topics in cognitive development: Vol. 1, Equilibration: Theory, research and application* (pp. 3–13). New York: Plenum Press.

Piaget, J. (1980). *Experiments in contradiction/Jean Piaget* (Derek Coltman, Trans.). Chicago: University of Chicago Press.

Piaget, J., & Inhelder, B. (1969). *The psychology of the child.* New York: Basic Books.

Pratelli-Palnerini, M. (1980). *Language and learning.* Cambridge: Harvard University Press.

Rathus, S. A. (1988). *Understanding child development.* New York: Holt, Rinehart & Winston.

Snyder, L., Bates, E., & Bretherton, I. (1981). Content and context in early lexical development. *Journal of Child Language, 8,* 565–582.

Stone, J. L., & Church, J. (1957). *Childhood and adolescence: A psychology of the growing person.* New York: Random House.

Templin, M. C. (1957). Certain language skills in children: Their development and interrelationships. *University of Minnesota Institute of Child Welfare Monograph, 26.*

Vygotsky, L. S. (1962). *Thought and language.* Cambridge, MA: MIT Press.

Vygotsky, L. S. (1978). *Mind in society: The development of higher mental processes.* Cambridge, MA: Harvard University Press.

Vygotsky, L. S. (1986). *Thought and language.* Cambridge, MA: MIT Press.

Wadsworth, B. J. (1984). *Piaget's theory of cognitive development: An introduction for students of psychology and education* (3rd ed.). New York: Longman.

Wertsch, J. (1986). *Mind in context: A Vygotskian approach.* Paper presented at the annual meeting of the American Educational Research Association, San Francisco.

Willig, A. C. (1985). A meta-analysis of selected studies on the effectiveness of bilingual education. *Review of Education Research, 55,* 269–317.

Wood, B. S. (1981). *Children and communication: Verbal and nonverbal language development* (2nd ed.). Englewood Cliffs, NJ: Prentice-Hall.

3
Personal and Interpersonal Growth

Chapter Overview

This chapter examines the developmental capabilities that allow students to interact with other people and to form a sense of themselves as they relate to those people. We begin with an examination of Erikson's theory of personality development—his eight stages and the crisis of development that is crucial to each stage. The resolution of each crisis depends on social experiences. We will also discuss several theories of moral judgment and moral behavior, including Kohlberg's and Gilligan's. The section on moral development culminates with a model for moral education. The final section of the chapter provides composite descriptions of students' physical, social/emotional, and cognitive capabilities at various grade levels. ■

INTRODUCTION: SELF AND OTHERS

Teachers understand intuitively that it is important for students to think well of themselves, to have a positive rather than a negative self-concept. **Self-concept** is a generic term that refers to an overall judgment that we make about ourselves. Much of what we learn about ourselves comes from our interactions with others. Conversely, the interactions we have with other people are influenced heavily by our self-concept.

We begin this chapter's examination of personal and interpersonal development with a discussion of Erikson's theory of psychosocial development.

Connection: Learning about self from others is also examined in relation to Bandura's concept of self-efficacy in Chapter 7.

Teacher Chronicle 3.1

A CHANCE TO CHAT

My teaching day usually ends when the last bell rings. My final official assignment is to stand outside my door as the students hastily grab their books (well, most of them do) and head for home or to their after-school jobs. I enjoy catching snatches of conversations I am normally not privy to.

"Hey, Mark, did you get the car for this Friday? I need a ride to the basketball game."

"Yeah, I finally got up a *B* in physics so my mom said it was okay to use the car. I'm going to have to bust a gut to keep it 'cause we've got a monster test next week."

"Do you think Mary will come to the mall tomorrow?"

"I hope so. She's always so funny. Remember her imitation of Mr. Rodgers?"

"Did you know that Juan is going out with Sarah this weekend?" Diane asked her close friend Katherine.

"You mean he's given up on Ellen?"

And on and on. The conversations seem to echo in the hall even after the last locker door slams and the kids have disappeared. Today only Mary Clearman is still digging in her locker. She glanced up at me when the others had gone. Her expression told me that she wanted to talk.

"Ms. Bianchi, do you mind if I ask you something personal?"

"Depends on what it is, Mary."

"Can I ask you something about boys?"

"Fire away," I told her. "I'll tell you as much as I've ever been able to figure out about them."

She looked away. "Do you have to be big in the chest for boys to ask you out?" she whispered.

"What makes you think that?"

"Well, I have some boys, you know, as friends. We kid around at the mall and stuff. But none of them ever asks me out or anything. They ask out other girls who have more than I do. I thought maybe that was the reason."

"Mary, your measurements shouldn't have anything to do with whether a boy asks you out or not. They should like you for who you are, not for your appearance. I know lots of kids who think your sense of humor is terrific."

She looked at me as if she didn't believe me. "Really?"

"Yes. And I know Margie appreciates your friendship, even if she spends so much time at work and doesn't have as much time to be with you as she used to."

I could see other unasked questions in her eyes, but knew she was not ready to ask those.

"Mary, may I make a suggestion?"

"Sure, Ms. Bianchi."

"You told me about your friends, you know, the boys. Is there one of them you like more than the others?"

She blushed slightly. "Yeah, Sean. He's really neat."

"Well, why don't you ask him to the movies or something? See what happens."

"I couldn't do that, he would laugh at me."

"Are you sure?" I asked.

She hesitated and then a big smile spread across her face.

"Margie has to work tomorrow afternoon and we were going to meet Sean and his friends. I think I'll call Sean and see if he would like to meet me before the others come."

She grabbed her books, dashed to the door, and turned around before leaving to say, "Thanks, Ms. B. Talking with you makes my day."

"See you Monday," I said to her disappearing back. I know she didn't hear me say, "Mary, talking with you makes my day, too."

psychosocial development According to Erikson, the process whereby relationships with others influence one's search for his or her own identity.

A THEORY OF PSYCHOSOCIAL DEVELOPMENT

Erik Erikson was born in Germany. He was an uninspired student who dropped out before graduating from high school. He spent several years exploring Europe and its art schools. At age twenty-five he met Sigmund Freud in Vienna. Freud was impressed with the young wanderer and invited him to study psychoanalysis. Erikson completed his studies with Freud about the time the Nazis acceded to power in Germany. Erikson came to the United States to escape Nazism.

The experiences Erikson had after coming to the United States caused him to reflect on Freud's ideas of psychoanalysis. Erikson wondered about Freud's decision to stay in Vienna and limit his clinical practice to a small group of individuals who were not representative of the general population. Because Freud had based his psychoanalytic theory on his clinical observations, Erikson reasoned that Freud's theory might be missing something—an account of how social and cultural factors influence behavior. Erikson decided to formulate a new theory based on psychoanalytic principles, which he considered sound, but to take into account social and cultural factors.

The label **psychosocial development** reflects Erikson's emphasis on how relationships with others influence one's search for his or her identity. By virtue of our cultural traditions, teachers occupy a potentially important position in the lives of young people. Teachers not only establish relationships

Chap. Obj. 1–3
Test Ques. 3.1–3.49

Focus Questions: How does a student's sense of self contribute to his or her relationships with others? What are the possible outcomes of a student's search for identity?

Lecture Note: While in the United States, Erikson taught at several universities and started a private practice as a psychoanalyst. He provided psychotherapy to soldiers during World War II.

Teacher Interview: Have each student interview a practicing teacher regarding his or her efforts to establish a classroom atmosphere that enhances interpersonal relationships.

Teaching Anecdote: Tell the story of the high-ability student who shows off her intelligence every chance she gets, always getting a perfect score in math and A's on essays in English. The student's labs always work. Instead of accepting success, she finds opportunities to call attention to how well she performs.

Ask your students why this student persists even in the face of resentment from her classmates.

The relationships students build with their peers and with teachers contribute to their individual personality development and sense of identity.

with students, but also influence the environment in which relationships between students are established. Erikson's theory gives us a way of understanding how the relationships young people build influence their sense of identity.

The Stages of Psychosocial Development

Erikson's theory of psychosocial development focuses on the tasks our culture sets before an individual at various points along the continuum of development. The eight stages postulated in Erikson's theory are summarized in Table 3–1.

Erikson's stage theory describes and explains the development of the human personality. Basic to the theory is the **epigenetic principle** that, when applied to personality, suggests that one's personality develops in parts. The parts of the human personality emerge at different times and later combine into a whole. Consider the physical development of a human fetus. The various human organs appear at different points during the gestation period. There are "critical periods" during the course of this gestation when particular organs or structures begin to function. The biological growth of the fetus follows the epigenetic principle.

Using the epigenetic principle as a framework, Erikson viewed psychosocial growth as consisting of **critical periods** when the "parts" of the individual's personality developed. It is these critical periods that define Erikson's eight stages of psychosocial development. Each stage identifies the emergence of a part of an individual's personality.

Each stage in Erikson's framework is structured as a **dichotomy** (e.g., trust versus mistrust, intimacy versus isolation), indicating the positive and negative consequences for each stage. Each dichotomy defines a **develop-**

■ Table 3–1 *Erickson's Eight Stages of Psychosocial Development*

Stages	Approximate Age	Important Event	Description
1. Basic trust vs. basic mistrust	Birth to 12–18 months	Feeding	The infant must form a first loving, trusting relationship with the caregiver, or develop a sense of mistrust.
2. Autonomy vs. shame/doubt	18 months to 3 years	Toilet training	The child's energies are directed toward the development of physical skills, including walking, grasping, and sphincter control. The child learns control but may develop shame and doubt if not handled well.
3. Initiative vs. guilt	3 to 6 years	Independence	The child continues to become more assertive and to take more initiative, but may be too forceful, leading to guilt feelings.
4. Industry vs. inferiority	6 to 12 years	School	The child must deal with demands to learn new skills or risk a sense of inferiority, failure, and incompetence.
5. Identity vs. role confusion	Adolescence	Peer relationships	The teenager must achieve a sense of identity in occupation, sex roles, politics, and religion.
6. Intimacy vs. isolation	Young adulthood	Love relationships	The young adult must develop intimate relationships or suffer feelings of isolation.
7. Generativity vs. stagnation	Middle adulthood	Parenting	Each adult must find some way to satisfy and support the next generation.
8. Ego integrity vs. despair	Late adulthood	Reflection on and acceptance of one's life	The culmination is a sense of acceptance of oneself as one is and of feeling fulfilled.

SOURCE: From *Psychology* (4th ed., p. 350) by L. A. Lefton, 1991, Needham Heights, MA: Allyn & Bacon. Copyright 1991 by Allyn & Bacon. Reprinted by permission.

mental crisis, a psychosocial issue that will be resolved in either a positive or negative way. The resolution of each developmental crisis will have a lasting effect on the person's view of himself or herself and of society in general. What follows are brief descriptions of the developmental crises associated with the different stages in Erikson's theory.

Journal Entry: Have each student reflect on those periods of growing up when he or she felt intensely focused on some aspect of his or her personality and how it was perceived by others, especially peers.

Lecture Note: Erikson shared Piaget's hesitancy to define stages of cognitive development in terms of exact ages. The ages associated with the eight stages of psychosocial development should be interpreted as averages.

Stage 1: Trust Versus Mistrust (birth–18 months)

If the interactions infants have with the other people in their environment are positive, then the infant will learn that people in their environment can be trusted. According to Erikson (1963), an outcome of trust is the result of "consistency, continuity, and sameness of experience." If the constancy of interaction between the infant and others meets the basic needs of the infant, then trust is developed. If, however, the interactions lack in warmth and caring and the basic needs of the infant go unsatisfied, the developmental crisis is resolved in a negative way. The infant will learn to mistrust those around him or her.

Stage 2: Autonomy Versus Shame and Doubt (18 months–3 years)

The developmental crisis at this stage occurs as the child enters toddlerhood. It is important for the toddler to explore his or her environment in an effort to establish some independence from parents. The toddler, who is now less dependent on others, seeks to develop a sense of independence and freedom through such exploration. If the child is encouraged to discover what is inside the book on the shelf, if his or her attempts to dress are uninterrupted, if the mess made while pouring cereal is tolerated, the crisis will more likely be resolved in the direction of **autonomy,** a sense of independence. If the toddler's exploration and attempts to be independent are discouraged, he or she will likely feel ashamed of these efforts, and develop doubts about his or her ability to deal with the environment. A parent or care-giver who is unable to allow the toddler to make mistakes, to persist, and to make further mistakes, manifests the kinds of interactions that lead to a negative resolution of the developmental crisis at this stage.

The issue of "autonomy" is crucial to Erikson's Stage 2. This child is attempting to assert independence by dressing herself.

initiative The quality of undertaking, planning, and attacking a new task. Initiative versus guilt characterizes Stage 3 of Erikson's theory of psychosocial development.

Children in Erikson's Stage 3 are typically very active, taking initiative as they try to operate physically and cognitively on their environment.

Stage 3: Initiative Versus Guilt (3–6 years)

During this stage, children are attempting to develop a sense of initiative, that they are operators on the environment. According to Erikson, **initiative** "adds to autonomy the quality of undertaking, planning, and attacking a task for the sake of being active and on the move" (1963, p. 225). The child's imaginative play often allows the child to imitate adults in performing various tasks. If you have ever seen a child pretend to read or "fix" a clock or "nurse" the family dog, you have seen evidence of the child's attempt to undertake grown-up tasks. It is during this period that children typically learn to identify and imitate same-sex models. Exploration in play during this period is as important as it was during the previous stage. Given the increased linguistic abilities of preschool children, their explorations often take the form of questions to adults. If their interactions and explorations during play are encouraged, if their questions are recognized and answered sincerely, positive resolution of the developmental crisis is more likely. If the child's efforts to explore or his or her questions are treated as a nuisance, the child may feel guilty about "getting in the way."

Stage 4: Industry Versus Inferiority (6–12 years)

As the child enters school and advances through the elementary grades, the developmental crisis focuses on the child's ability to win recognition through performance. The notion that elementary students need generous encouragement and praise for their accomplishments is consistent with Erikson's view of psychosocial development at this stage. Those of us in education have often recognized the importance of early success in school. The child who is en-

Teacher Interview: Have each student interview a preschool teacher regarding the kinds of physical activity and linguistic experimentation he or she observes students taking part in.

Journal Entry: Have students reflect on teachers they have had who either listened to them and made them feel important or who seemed disinterested in them or their problems.

Chapter 15 Casebook Preview: See I Am Leo.

Connection: This is related to the concept of self-efficacy, which will be discussed under Bandura's social cognitive theory in Chapter 7.

industry   An eagerness to produce. Industry versus inferiority typifies Stage 4 of Erikson's theory of psychosocial development.

identity   A sense of well-being, a feeling of knowing where one is going, and an inner assuredness of anticipated recognition from those who count. Identity versus role diffusion characterizes Stage 5 of Erikson's theory of psychosocial development.

identity diffusion   The negative outcome of Stage 5 of Erikson's theory of psychosocial development, whereby an adolescent is unable to develop a clear sense of self.

intimacy   The state of having a close psychological relationship with another person. Intimacy versus isolation is Stage 6 of Erikson's theory of psychosocial development.

isolation   Failure to establish a close psychological relationship with another person leads to this feeling of being alone. The negative outcome of Stage 6 of Erikson's theory of psychosocial development.

generativity   A sense of concern for future generations, expressed through childbearing or concern about creating a better world. Generativity versus stagnation marks Stage 7 of Erikson's theory of psychosocial development.

stagnation   The feeling that one's life is at a dead end. This is the unsuccessful resolution of Stage 7 of Erikson's theory of psychosocial development.

Lecture Note: Emphasize that the period of adolescence has been described by Erikson as a search for personal identity and independence.

couraged to complete tasks and who receives praise for his or her performance is likely to develop a sense of **industry,** an eagerness to produce. If the child does not experience success—if his or her efforts are treated as unworthy and intrusive—the child will develop a sense of inferiority.

Stage 5: Identity Versus Role Diffusion (adolescence)

The developmental crisis of adolescence centers on the youth's attempt to discover his or her identity—to identify those things about himself or herself that are unique. For Erikson, **identity** "is experienced merely as a sense of psychosocial well-being . . . a feeling of being at home in one's body, a sense of 'knowing where one is going,' and an inner assuredness of anticipated recognition from those who count" (1968, p. 165). An important aspect of an adolescent's sense of identity is his or her choice of occupation (Marcia, 1980). Reflect on the groups or "cliques" from your own high school. Did not most members of any particular clique share similar aspirations about careers, if not about identical occupations?

Another important contributor to the adolescent's sense of identity is his or her emerging sexuality (Marcia, 1980). Adolescence is the period of puberty, dramatic physical maturation, and an increase in relationships with those of the opposite sex. If the nature of the adolescent's interactions support the sense of who he or she is, the resolution of the developmental crisis is positive. A positive resolution instills a sense of self-confidence and stability; whether fulfilling the roles of friend, child, student, leader, boyfriend or girlfriend, the adolescent feels at ease. Negative experiences that do not allow a student to integrate his or her various social roles into a unitary, stable view of self lead to a sense of diffusion. The adolescent who feels "torn apart" by what he or she perceives as inconsistent expectations exhibits **identity diffusion.**

Stage 6: Intimacy Versus Isolation (young adulthood)

The young adult's personality—stemming from his or her sense of self—is influenced by efforts to establish an **intimacy,** a close psychosocial relationship, with another person. Typically, this is the period when a young adult who has just finished his or her education or training strikes out on his or her own to begin work and establish a life away from the childhood family. Among young adults, the need for intimate relationships can be seen at any number of places: work, health clubs, singles bars, church functions, athletic teams, recreation groups. Many young adults who are interviewing for jobs in a new town take into account the town's "supply" of eligible partners. Failure to establish a close relationship with another leads to a sense of **isolation,** a feeling of being alone.

Stage 7: Generativity Versus Stagnation (young adulthood–middle age)

Erikson identifies **generativity** as a concern for future generations. Childbearing and nurturing occupy the thoughts and feelings of people at this stage in the life span. Many people who decide against having a family and raising children are concerned with questions about their role regarding future generations. The classic career versus family decision reflects the developmental crisis that epitomizes this stage. Unsuccessful resolution leads to a sense of **stagnation,** the feeling that one's life is at a "dead end."

Stage 8: Integrity Versus Despair (later adulthood–old age)

According to Erikson, **integrity** is a sense of understanding how one fits into one's culture and accepting that one's place is unique and unalterable. An inability to accept one's sense of self at this stage leads to despair—the feeling that time is too short and that alternate roads to integrity are no longer open.

This summary of Erikson's stages has highlighted the dichotomies that make up each developmental crisis. Although each dichotomy describes well the nature of the crisis to be resolved, it is a mistake to assume that each crisis will be resolved in favor of either the positive or negative qualities of the dichotomy. A student's personality contains positive and negative qualities. Positive resolution of any developmental crisis simply means that the positive quality of that stage is present to a greater degree than the negative quality.

Identity: A Closer Look

The phrase "identity crisis" has become part of our everyday language. It suggests junior high and high school students struggling with questions about themselves, their relationships with peers, their future. We chalk up much of their behavior to their attempt to "find themselves." How does that search for a sense of self work?

From the preschool years through high school, the resolutions of developmental crises, culminating with the developmental crisis of adolescence, contribute to a student's sense of identity. Identity is the positive resolution of the developmental crisis of adolescence. Negative resolution of crises,

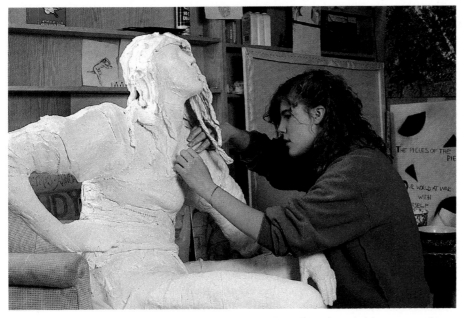

Individuals nurture and display personal identity through such activities as art, dance, debate, and public speaking.

Journal Entry: Have students reflect on groups in their high schools whose members saw themselves as wanting to be members of some kind of profession—even if they were unsure of the specific profession they would pursue. Have them consider if there were other groups made up of people who aspired to practice a trade, and whether some of those groups were even labeled with reference to a future occupation.

Field Observation: Have students interview working adults, making comparisons between those who are active in community activities and those who are not.

Field Observation: Have students interview grandparents or other senior citizens regarding their sense of integrity.

Lecture Note: As an example, the stage of industry versus inferiority. A student who resolves this developmental crisis will generally feel competent. This does mean, however, that the student will feel equally competent in all areas.

Lecture Note: Remind students that Erikson understood identity as one end of a continuum; role diffusion is located at the other end.

Lecture Note: A person is more likely to make sound life-style decisions if he or she has resolved earlier crises in a positive way.

Journal Entry: Have each student reflect on his or her own life-style decisions, and whether the decisions have met the demands of others in his or her social environment.

Teaching Anecdote: Tell the story of the student who did so well in high school math that she was accepted at a local community college to continue math in her senior year. The student had done well in other courses, and had a job and a car. Yet after graduation, she decided to remain at the community college rather than attend one of the universities to which she had won acceptance. "I don't think I'll be able to make the grade," she said. "I'm really not that good."

Ask your students why she might have felt this way and what a teacher or counselor could have done to encourage her to realize her potential.

either before or during adolescence, contributes to role diffusion. What was playful in childhood becomes serious business during adolescence. The choices and decisions made by an adolescent increasingly define who that young person is and what he or she will become.

If we reflect on the stages leading up to adolescence, we see that the resolution of all the crises contribute, in one way or another, to one's sense of self. A child who comes to adolescence having developed trust in others, independence, initiative, and a desire to tackle problems is well on the road to successfully resolving the identity versus role diffusion crisis.

If earlier development has produced an adolescent who feels guilty, who lacks a sense of competence, who is self-doubting, decisions about identity may be very difficult to make. Negative resolution at this stage results in confusion about where one fits into the social fabric.

Consider Mary's situation in Teacher Chronicle 3.1. Her doubts about whether boys found her attractive caused her enough concern to ask her teacher for advice. Mary's confusion about how she fits into the boy–girl network is, no doubt, a major issue for her; other adolescent issues are more pervasive in the ways that they affect behavior. Consider an adolescent who is torn between two sets of values: one at home, another in his or her peer group. Suppose the parents have assumed, since their child was born, that he or she would attend an Ivy League college. Suppose also that the adolescent's peer group disdains academic achievement, extracurricular activities, and the mores of the "social establishment." What "life-style" decisions can the adolescent make that would satisfy both sets of social demands?

The urgency of such decisions can overwhelm some young adolescents. They enter a state Erikson called psychosocial moratorium, rather than deal with life-style decisions they are not prepared to make. A **psychosocial moratorium** is a suspension of any decisions that commit the adolescent to a certain occupational or social role. The adolescent "buys time." Recall Erikson's own late adolescence and young adulthood. Not knowing what career he wanted to pursue, he spent a considerable period of time wandering around Europe. A psychosocial moratorium can be a positive developmental step, as it was in Erikson's case. A moratorium period that is used to gain new experiences, to taste adventure, is likely to contribute to sound decisions when the moratorium ends.

A young person who is unable to commit to decisions and who is unable to postpone decisions by declaring a psychosocial moratorium may seek another solution to the developmental crisis—a solution that Erikson called a **negative identity.**

> The loss of a sense of identity is often expressed in a scornful and snobbish hostility toward the roles offered as proper and desirable in one's family or immediate community. Any aspect of the required role, or all of it—be it masculinity or femininity, nationality or class membership—can become the main focus of the young person's acid disdain. (1968, pp. 172–173)

Young people who adopt a negative identity are often those who "rebel" against authority—parents and teachers. Take, for example, the adolescent who thwarts parental desires for academic excellence by abandoning any pretense of working hard in school. As the parents become more demanding—because their child is "throwing away" the opportunity to attend a good college—the negative identity course becomes more and more clear to the adolescent. The adolescent's thoughts might run along the following lines:

"If they want me to do well in school, I won't study. If they want me to join extracurricular activities to enhance my chances for college, I will drop out of all activities. If they don't like my friends, I'll spend all of my time with them. I might even run away and join a commune, that'll shake 'em up."

Negative identity in the face of confusion about one's identity affords decisive action for the young person. It is simply a matter of determining what parents, teachers, a priest, or counselor think should be done and then doing the opposite.

Identity Types or Statuses

James Marcia's work on the different types of identity—called **identity statuses**—is among the best known work derived from Erikson's own. Marcia was interested in conducting empirical research based on Erikson's theory. During interviews with male adolescents, Marcia explored concerns and opinions regarding occupational choice, sexuality, religion, and personal value systems (1967). As a result of his analysis of these interviews, Marcia proposed four identity statuses:

1. Identity diffusion types
2. Moratorium types
3. Identity achievement types
4. Foreclosure types

Identity diffusion types are adolescents who avoid thinking about life-style decisions. Typically, they are disorganized; they act impulsively; they are not goal oriented. They often avoid commitment to schoolwork or to interpersonal relationships.

Moratorium types have given thought to identity issues but have not arrived at any conclusive decisions. Their relationships are often intense, but usually short lived. They seem distracted a good deal of the time. It is not unusual for moratorium types to "try on" a negative identity for a short time before adopting the status of identity achievement.

Identity achievement types have made life-style decisions, although not in all areas. For example, a young woman might decide, against the advice of her parents, to pursue a medical career. The same young woman may still be confused about sexuality, but she is determined about her occupational choice. The decisions made by identity achievement types are their own; they have not simply followed the advice of parents, teachers, or counselors. Identity achievement types may not have "all the answers," but they have made some decisions that give their development direction.

Foreclosure types avoid crises by simply accepting the decisions made by others as their own. Often, the decisions they accept were made by their parents. It is typical of foreclosure types to make—or perhaps more appropriately, adopt—their decisions early. With no decisions to make, the crises of identity are averted.

Interpreting Erikson's Theory

A teacher who is knowledgeable about developmental crises will be alert to the kinds of "emotional baggage" students might carry into the classroom.

identity statuses Different types of identity, as identified by Marcia.
identity diffusion types According to Marcia, adolescents who avoid thinking about life-style decisions and are unable to develop a clear sense of self.
moratorium types According to Marcia, adolescents who have given thought to identity issues but have not arrived at any conclusive decisions.
identity achievement types According to Marcia, adolescents who have made life-style decisions, although not in all areas.
foreclosure types According to Marcia, adolescents who simply accept the decisions made by others for them. These decisions are often made by their parents.

Chapter 15 Casebook Preview: See Gifted Achievers and Underachievers.

Lecture Note: State that the theme of psychosocial development is coming to know oneself in relation to other people.

Lecture Note: Identity achievement types are reasonably "healthy." Should a serious setback occur to any one of them that prevents that person from pursuing chosen goals, he or she may experience a crisis, but his or her experience has included committing to a decision. Such an experience augers well for success the second time around.

Imagine that a fifth-grade teacher learns through a parent conference that one of her students never receives encouragement at home, that the child is viewed as a "bother." The teacher might then observe the child carefully for a sense of inferiority, hypothesizing that the child needs to experience success and to receive praise to offset that effect.

Connection: Gilligan's theory of moral development will be examined in detail in the next section in this chapter.

Some research suggests the use of caution when interpreting a student's psychosocial well-being in terms of Erikson's stages. One caveat is that Erikson's stages are better descriptions of personality development in males than in females. During the industry versus inferiority period, for example, females appear to be concerned not only with achievement but with interpersonal relationships as well (cf. Marcia, 1980). Gilligan (1982) suggests that during adolescence, young women deal with the crisis of intimacy as well as with the crisis of identity.

Another caveat to keep in mind when making judgments based on Erikson's stages is that the crises that begin in toddlerhood and continue through the preschool, elementary, and middle-school years are quite similar. The crises of autonomy, initiative, and industry all stress the need for independence and encouragement. Classroom tasks that allow students to succeed and that result in recognition for accomplishment are as critical for sixth graders who are working through the crisis of industry as for preschoolers who are working through the crisis of initiative.

Principles in Practice 3.1

Principles . . .

1. A student's personality is influenced by his or her social experiences.
2. Positive resolution of a developmental crisis does not ensure that all areas of psychosocial experience will be equally positive.
3. The development of personality culminates, during the school years, in the crisis of identity and the adoption of an identity status.

. . . in Practice

The after-school conversation in Teacher Chronicle 3.1 suggests that Mary is working through the crisis of identity. She is concerned about her appearance because she thinks it might have something to do with the direction that her social life with boys is going in. Ms. Bianchi, her teacher, is sympathetic to Mary's concerns; she helps Mary talk through her feelings. She also tries to encourage Mary by focusing on her positive qualities. Ms. Bianchi's suggestion that Mary call Sean presents her with a social task that offers a high probability of success. Such success will contribute to the positive resolution of Mary's crisis of identity.

1. What other suggestions would you make to Mary that might contribute to a positive resolution of her identity crisis?
2. Based on what you've learned about Mary in Teacher Chronicle 3.1, what areas do you see as being strengths and weaknesses in her personality?
3. What would be the advantage of inviting Mary for another after-school chat, but this time to talk about her career goals?

THE FIRE DRILL

Every so often something happens that makes it clear to me how differently children and adults perceive the world. Usually the incident is funny, but sometimes it has serious overtones.

Most young children willingly do what "teacher" asks them to do: clean up their desks, bring back library books, raise their hands when they ask questions, sit down during work time, and so on. Many times they take such directions literally and do exactly as they are told.

One day I was in the faculty lounge at recess. The topic of conversation was the fire drill that had taken place earlier that morning. I walked in to the lounge just as the art teacher said, "Wouldn't you know? There we all were up to our elbows in clay, when the blasted fire alarm goes off."

Those of us who witnessed the thirty mud-armed kids chuckled.

"Yeah," chimed in Mr. Robertson, a fifth-grade teacher. "We were taking an end-of-the-semester spelling test, you know the real biggie before I calculate my spelling grades. We had reached the midway point when the alarm went off. I tried to get the kids refocused when we got back, but it was hopeless. We'll try again tomorrow."

Mrs. Stein, a second-grade teacher, shook her head. "I wish we knew ahead of time when we're going to have the drills. It would save a lot of hassle. I had the craziest thing happen in my class." She had everyone's attention. Her strictness was legendary and whenever anything crazy happened in her room it was worth hearing about.

"You know how my kids must raise their hands if they want to get out of their desks." We nodded, knowing this all too well. "We were doing our reading work and everyone was busy when the alarm went off. I went to the door and the children lined up."

"Quietly, I bet," I said. Everyone laughed.

"Yes, quietly. Well, when I got outside I counted to see if everyone had come. Three children hadn't. I counted heads again. Three students were still missing. I knew no one was absent and no one was in the bathroom, so I had Mrs. Bazemore watch my class while I went to find them."

"You mean, you went back into the burning building?" Mr. Robertson asked in mock dismay.

"I sure did. I had to find them. And I did. There they were, sitting at their desks, tears in their eyes. When I asked why they hadn't come with the rest of us, Stephen Shepherd said, "You told us never to get out of our desks during reading without raising our hands and asking. We got mixed up when you left, so we sat back down. You weren't here, so we couldn't ask you.""

"I didn't mean when there is a fire drill. You don't have to ask my permission then."

She laughed. "You can teach children for one hundred years and never really understand them."

Everyone laughed at this pronouncement and then scattered as the recess bell rang.

Chap. Obj. 4
Test Ques. 3.50–3.75

Focus Question: How does moral decision making change as a student develops?

Connection: Teacher Chronicle 3.2: The Fire Drill.

Field Observation: Have students interview children of varying ages using Piaget's stories.

Lecture Note: Incidentally, Piaget was just as reluctant to attach ages to his levels of moral judgments as he was to his stages of cognitive development.

Lecture Note: The alternate label—moral realism—comes from the young child's perception that rules are "real," that they exist in a literal form.

moral judgments Judgments about right or wrong.
morality of constraint According to Piaget, a type of moral thinking made by children under ten years of age; rules come from some external authority and strictly define what is right and wrong.
morality of cooperation According to Piaget, a type of moral thinking made by older children; rules provide general guidelines but should not be followed blindly without considering the context.

Erikson's framework gives us a way of looking at interpersonal relationships. If we are to relate effectively with other people in our environment, we must make judgments about what is right and what is wrong. These judgments change with age. A student may behave in one way at age six and in a very different way at age sixteen. In both instances, the student may consider himself or herself as behaving in the "right" way. It is hard to imagine a fire drill in a high school causing problems similar to those related in Teacher Chronicle 3.2. In this section we will examine moral development. We begin by examining how judgments of right and wrong change as people grow.

Piaget's Framework of Moral Reasoning

Piaget loved to observe children as they reacted to their environment. As a way of eliciting certain reactions, he made up the following pair of stories and asked children of different ages to discuss them.

> There was a little boy called Julian. His father had gone out and Julian thought it would be fun to play with father's ink-pot. First he played with the pen, and then he made a little blot on the table cloth.
>
> A little boy who was called Augustus once noticed his father's ink-pot was empty. One day that his father was away he thought of filling the ink-pot so as to help his father, and so that he should find it full when he came home. But while he was opening the ink-bottle he made a big blot on the table cloth. (1948, p. 118)

Piaget questioned children about these stories. "Who was the naughtiest?" "Were Julian and Augustus equally guilty?" Piaget began to formulate a description of how **moral judgments**—judgments about right and wrong—develop based on the variety of responses children of different ages gave and the consistency of the responses among children of similar ages.

Piaget concluded that there are general types of moral thinking. The first type—**morality of constraint**—describes judgments made by children up to approximately age ten. The second type of moral thinking—**morality of cooperation**—refers to the moral judgments of older children.

Morality of Constraint

Morality of constraint is sometimes referred to as *moral realism*. Rules define what is right and what is wrong and come from some external authority. Because these rules are established by authoritative people—those who know—the rules should be obeyed. For students in early elementary grades, rules are sacred. There is no allowance made by the young realist for the context in which events occur. The intention of a person, for example, is not taken into account when judgments of right and wrong are made. Furthermore, the seriousness of a "crime" is determined by its consequences (cf. Lickona, 1976; Piaget, 1965).

Augustus made a bigger blot on the table cloth than did Julian. Therefore, Augustus was more "guilty" than Julian.

Morality of Cooperation

Older children practice the morality of cooperation, alternatively called *moral relativism* or *moral flexibility*. The older child is a relativist; rules are not "carved in stone." A hallmark of cognitive development is decentration. As applied to moral judgments, it is evident in older children's awareness that others may not share their perceptions of rules. Rules, as older children understand them, provide general guidelines. It is inappropriate to follow rules blindly without considering the context in which they are applied. Rules should be obeyed not just because some "authority" has established them, but because they guard against violation of the rights of others. A person who with good intentions causes an injury or damage is not as culpable as a person who with premeditation commits an act of wrong (cf. Lickona, 1976; Piaget, 1965).

Older children who apply the morality of cooperation judge Julian to be more guilty than Augustus, who was attempting to do something nice for his father when he stained the table cloth.

preconventional morality
Rules of conduct of children (birth–9 years) who do not yet understand the conventions of society. This is Level 1 of Kohlberg's theory of moral reasoning.

Connection: Consider morality of co-operation in connection with Lickona's model of moral education discussed later in this chapter.

Kohlberg's Stages of Moral Reasoning

Laurence Kohlberg, during his graduate studies, became fascinated with Piaget's views on moral development. He followed Piaget's lead in using stories as a vehicle for investigating moral reasoning. Kohlberg wanted to apply his Piagetian-informed ideas on moral thinking to all ages, through adulthood. As a consequence, Kohlberg's "stories" were more elaborate and afforded a deeper analysis of an interpreter's reasoning. The stories Kohlberg created have become well known as "moral dilemmas." The following is a classic example that has been used by Kohlberg and others in research on stages of moral reasoning.

Lecture Note: In much the same way that Marcia expanded Erikson's views of identity, Kohlberg expanded Piaget's views of moral judgment.

Journal Entry: Have students respond to Kohlberg's dilemma.

> In Europe a woman was near death from cancer. One drug might save her, a form of radium a druggist in the same town had recently discovered. The druggist was charging $2,000, ten times what the drug cost him to make. The sick woman's husband, Heinz, went to everyone he knew to borrow the money, but he could only get together about half of what it cost. He told the druggist that his wife was dying and asked him to sell it cheaper or let him pay later, but the druggist said "No." The husband got desperate and broke into the man's store to steal the drug for his wife. Should the husband have done that? Why?
> (Kohlberg, 1969, p. 376)

By classifying the reasoning his subjects used to respond to this and other moral dilemmas, Kohlberg formulated six stages of moral reasoning. Kohlberg's stages are divided into three levels: preconventional morality, conventional morality, and postconventional morality. Each level subsumes two stages. The levels and stages are presented in Table 3–2.

Preconventional Morality (birth–9 years)

Preconventional morality refers to judgments made before children understand the conventions of society. Children at this level base their reasoning on two basic ideas: first, one should avoid punishment; and second, good behavior yields some kind of benefit.

Stage 1: The Punishment–Obedience Level

The child behaves in order to avoid punishment. Bad behavior is behavior that is punished; good behavior, therefore, is behavior that is rewarded. The children in Teacher Chronicle 3.2 who remained in their seats did so because authority, the teacher, deemed the act of leaving one's seat without raising

Connection: Teacher Chronicle 3.2: The Fire Drill.

■ Table 3–2   *Kohlberg's Stages of Moral Development*

Levels/Stages

Level I—Preconventional
  Stage 1: Obedience and punishment orientation
  Stage 2: Naively egoistic orientation

Level II—Conventional
  Stage 3: Good-boy orientation
  Stage 4: Authority-and-social-order maintaining orientation

Level III—Postconventional
  Stage 5: Contractual-legalistic orientation
  Stage 6: Conscience or principle orientation

SOURCE: From *Psychology* (4th ed., p. 326) by L. A. Lefton, 1991, Needham Heights, MA: Allyn & Bacon. Copyright 1991 by Allyn & Bacon. Adapted by permission.

one's hand punishable. Consider the moral dilemma Heinz faced and the question, "Should Heinz have stolen the drug?" A typical Stage 1 answer is, "No, he could get arrested for stealing."

Stage 2: The Instrumental Exchange Orientation

This stage represents the beginnings of social reciprocity; the thinking here is "you scratch my back and I'll scratch yours." The moral judgments that children make at this stage are very pragmatic. They will do good to another person if they expect the other person to reciprocate or return the favor. In response to the Heinz question, a typical Stage 2 response is, "He shouldn't steal the drug and the druggist should be nicer to Heinz."

Conventional Morality (9 years–young adulthood)

Conventional morality refers to judgments based on the rules or conventions of society; behaviors that maintain the social order are considered good behaviors. The reasoning at this level is based on a desire to impress others. Peer relationships become very important during this period.

Stage 3: The Interpersonal Conformity Orientation

Reasoning about morality focuses on the expectations of other people, particularly the expectations of people in authority and peers. This stage is sometimes called the "good-boy/nice-girl" orientation. In order to create and maintain good relations with other people, it is important to conform to their expectations of good behavior. By being nice or good, approval from others is likely. A typical Stage 3 response to the Heinz question is, "If Heinz is honest, other people will be proud of him."

Stage 4: The Law-and-Order Orientation

The conventions of society have been established so that society can function. Laws are necessary and, therefore, good. The moral person is one who follows the laws of a society without questioning them. A typical Stage 4 response to the Heinz question is, "Stealing is against the law. If everybody ignored the laws, our whole society might fall apart."

Postconventional Morality (adulthood)

Postconventional morality is typified by judgments that recognize the societal need for mutual agreement and the application of consistent principles in making judgments. Through careful thought and reflection, the postconventional thinker arrives at a self-determined set of principles or morality.

Stage 5: The Prior Rights and Social Contract Orientation
At this stage, laws are open to evaluation. A law is good if it protects the rights of individuals. Laws should not be obeyed simply because they are laws, but because there is mutual agreement between the individual and society that these laws guarantee a person's rights. A typical answer to the Heinz question is, "Sometimes laws have to be disregarded, for example, when a person's life depends on breaking the law."

Stage 6: The Universal Ethical Principles Orientation
The principles that determine moral behavior are self-chosen; they unify a person's beliefs about equality, justice, ethics. If a person arrives at a set of principles, the principles serve as guidelines for appropriate behavior. A typical Stage 6 response to the Heinz question is, "An appropriate decision must take into account all of the factors in the situation. Sometimes, it is morally right to steal."

Criticisms of Kohlberg's Theory

Kohlberg's theory is a landmark in the scientific literature on moral development. A good scientific theory is one that generates new research. In this regard, Kohlberg's theory has proven very successful. Much of the research done in response to Kohlberg's theory has raised questions about the theory's utility. A discussion of some of those questions follows.

The Question of Stages
Kohlberg (1971) shared Piaget's view about the ordinality of stages; that is, Kohlberg held that all people progress through the stages of moral development in sequence. There is evidence, however, that calls into question Kohlberg's assumption of ordinality. For example, Holstein (1976) found that responses to moral situations did not consistently and unambiguously place subjects at a particular stage. Holstein also found that females and males differed systematically in their judgments. Other researchers have found that the level or stage that a person's moral reasoning is found to be at is dependent on the particular moral dilemma that the person responds to (e.g., Fishkin, Keniston, & MacKinnon, 1973).

Although Kohlberg assumed ordinality, he did not assume that all people arrived at Stage 6—the universal ethical principles orientation. After others began to question the validity of his stages, Kohlberg went back and reexamined some of his original data (Colby & Kohlberg, 1984) and subsequently discounted the sixth stage in his theory (see also, Kohlberg, 1978).

The Question of Generalizability—Gilligan's Theory
For Kohlberg, moral development culminates in the recognition of individual rights and individually generated ethical principles. It is not surprising that Kohlberg, having grown up in a Western culture, would emphasize the Western value of individualism. The question is whether Kohlberg's stages would

postconventional morality
Rules of conduct of adults who recognize the societal need for mutual agreement and the application of consistent principles in making judgments. This is Level 3 of Kohlberg's theory of moral reasoning.

Lecture Note: Ask students to consider whether the attainment of formal operations is necessary to postconventional moral judgments.

Lecture Note: The laws of a society are still considered to important in maintaining social order, however, the laws themselves are open to evaluation.

Lecture Note: The principles are not a "recipe" which, if followed, ensures moral behavior.

Lecture Note: This is also true of good intuitive theories of teaching that generate hypotheses to be tested in the classroom.

Lecture Note: Ask students to speculate about why a person's moral reasoning might change depending on the particular dilemma he or she is considering.

Lecture Note: Upon reanalysis of the data—collected from subjects in their twenties—it was found that less than 15 percent of the subjects could be classified as having achieved Stage 5. None of the subjects exhibited Stage 6 reasoning.

Connection: The value "individualism" compared to "groupism" is examined in greater detail in the discussion of cultural differences in Chapter 4.

Lecture Note: Emphasize the difference between hypothetical dilemmas and real situations. Gilligan collected data from pregnant women who had been referred to a counseling clinic and who were struggling with an abortion decision.

Connection: The emphasis on differences in values is discussed further in the discussion of cultural differences in Chapter 4.

Lecture Note: Ask students how the transitions in Gilligan's theory integrate affect and cognition.

Journal Entry: Have students reflect on the ways that Kohlberg's and Gilligan's theories differ with regard to their values, noting the set of values that best reflects their own views.

Connection: Teacher Chronicle 3.2: The Fire Drill.

apply to cultures that prize the good of the group or of the family more highly than the good of the individual. Attempts to apply Kohlberg's scheme to other cultures have met with mixed results (e.g., Hwang, 1986; Vasudev & Hummel, 1987).

Another question of generalizability refers to gender differences (Gilligan, 1982; Holstein, 1976). Kohlberg developed his stages based on a longitudinal study of males. In other studies classifying males and females according to Kohlberg's stages, a disproportionate number of women have been placed in Stage 3 as compared with Stage 4. One explanation is that females are generally more empathetic and compassionate toward others and more sensitive to social relationships than males (Gilligan, 1977; Holstein, 1976). Based on these and other studies, Gilligan has developed a stage model of moral development.

Brabeck (1986) has compared Kohlberg's view on moral development with Gilligan's. Brabeck labels Kohlberg's theory a "morality of justice" that stresses rights, fairness, rules, and legalities. Gilligan's theory, by way of comparison, is called a "morality of care and responsibility." This theory stresses relationships, care, harmony, compassion, and self-sacrifice. Some have called Gilligan's model a theory of female moral development, but such generalizing across groups is always a risky business.

Perhaps a better way to think about Gilligan's theory is that it stresses different values than Kohlberg's. Support for this view comes from a study by Walker, deVries, and Trevethan (1987). These researchers asked children and adults to describe personal experiences that involved some kind of moral conflict. The descriptions indicated that some subjects valued justice while others valued caring, but were not tied to the gender of the subject.

Gilligan's theory, presented in Table 3–3, comprises three levels and two transitions. The first level of Gilligan's theory, **individual survival,** identifies selfishness as its primary concern. The transition from individual survival to self-sacrifice and social conformity leads to the realization that caring for others rather than just caring for oneself is "good." Gilligan's second level, **self-sacrifice and social conformity,** is similar to Kohlberg's Stage 3. Brabeck (1986) identifies the second level as "the conventional view of women as caretakers and protectors" (p. 70). The transition from the second to the third level involves a growing realization that in order to care for others, one must also take care of oneself. Note the different motives for self-care in this second transition as opposed to the motives in the first transition. The third level of Gilligan's theory is the **morality of nonviolence.** The ethic of this third level is the equality of self and others. It is wrong to serve oneself at the expense of others.

Gilligan's theory presents us with a different set of values to consider. It is not confined to moral reasoning (i.e., cognitive judgments of right and wrong, but stresses affect (i.e., feelings, attitudes, emotions).

The Question of Applicability

Very often, teachers need to reason with a student about the student's classroom conduct. If a teacher knows how a student reasons when confronted with a decision about what's right and what's wrong, the teacher can encourage the child to make a change in behavior in terms he or she will best understand. Consider, for example, the children in Teacher Chronicle 3.2 who decided to remain in their seats during the fire drill. These children reasoned that breaking classroom rules was wrong. If classroom rules are

Stages
1 Individual Survival
1A* From Selfishness to Responsibility
2 Self-sacrifice and Social conformity
2A* From Goodness to Truth
3 Morality of Nonviolence

SOURCE: From "Moral Orientation: Alternative Perspectives of Men and Women" by M. Brabeck, 1986, in *Psychological Foundations of Moral Education and Character Development: An Integrated Theory of Moral Development* (p. 71) by R. T. Knowles and G. F. McLean (eds.), Lanham, MD: University Press of America. Copyright 1986 by University Press of America. Adapted with permission.

*Marks a transition stage.

central to students' decisions of what is right and wrong, a simple reference to classroom rules by the teacher is likely to be effective. With older students, a teacher might use the approval of parents or peers to encourage appropriate behavior.

Direct attempts by teachers to facilitate moral development in students have resulted primarily in group discussions of moral dilemmas. Moral dilemmas can be of the type used by Kohlberg in his research: hypothetical situations that require a judgment about what is the correct or incorrect action to take in that hypothetical situation. There can also be real-life situations in the classroom or school (e.g., Reimer, Paolitto, & Hersh, 1983). Real-life dilemmas can deal with episodes of aggressive behavior, cheating on tests, copying homework, abusing rules, and so on.

Whether the dilemmas used for discussion are hypothetical or come from real life, one technique used to enhance moral reasoning is called plus-one matching (Lockwood, 1978). In using this technique, the teacher determines a student's stage of moral development and then presents conflicting views that are consistent with the next higher stage. The goal of plus-one matching is to create some disequilibrium in the student so that he or she is encouraged to entertain other points of view on the issue under discussion. Keep in mind that discussions of moral dilemmas are likely to be free flowing. Unexpected ideas are often introduced. As you might imagine, the problems with using plus-one matching involve accurately placing a student's stage of moral development, and spontaneously generating counterarguments that derive from the next higher stage.

While Kohlberg's framework informs us about how children think, we must remember that there is more to moral development than cognition. Peters (1977) characterizes Kohlberg's theory as cognitive, with little or no attention paid to affective feelings and attitudes. Peters argues that any attempt to facilitate moral development should address not only how to think, but how to feel as well. Among the attitudes that accompany sound moral decisions, Peters places "caring for others" at the top (1977). Gilligan's framework introduces affect into the mix and certainly emphasizes caring as an important element of morality. Even so, the question is whether a student's reasoning and his or her attitudes are applied consistently in all situations that require a moral judgment.

Lecture Note: Emphasize that the way a student reasons in response to a hypothetical dilemma may or may not be the way the student will behave in real-life situations. Ask students to explain why that is the case.

Lecture Note: Remind students of Holstein's study (1976) that found that responses to moral dilemmas did not consistently or unambiguously place students at a particular stage.

Lecture Note: For example, a student may be able to recite a "moral creed," reason at a high level through a hypothetical moral dilemma, and show compassion for the plight of a friend. But are these attitudes and reasoning processes always demonstrated in situations requiring moral decisions. Does moral behavior in one instance guarantee moral behavior in all instances?

Teaching Anecdote: Tell the story of the Honor Council president who cheated to get a passing grade in English. Without a good grade he would have failed the semester and lost his position on the council. After he was caught, he told his fellow council members why he cheated. "I knew that one way or the other—either failing or getting caught cheating—I would be off the council."

Ask your students if they think the other Honor Council members "accepted" the president's explanation.

Journal Entry: Have students reflect on any students in their high schools who felt they were under tremendous pressure from home and who took "shortcuts" in order to maintain grades.

Chap. Obj. 5
Test Ques. 3.76–3.86

Focus Question: What classroom processes influence moral judgments, feelings, and behavior?

Lecture Note: The model has also been called an "integrative model of the moral agent." (The moral agent is a person; each student is a moral agent.)

In a classic study, Hartshorne and May (1930) found that, for many children, moral behavior is situation specific. Children who are generally honest and trustworthy will, under certain circumstances, cheat, especially if the stakes are high enough. Lickona (1976) concluded that, "variations in the situation produce variations in moral behavior" (p. 15). Lickona added, however, that there is evidence to suggest that some children are more morally "integrated" or consistent than others. What appears to be needed is educational practice that does not rely solely on reasoning exercises, but that integrates cognition, affect, and behavior.

AN INTEGRATIVE VIEW OF MORAL DEVELOPMENT

The Council for Research in Values and Philosophy, a group of scholars concerned with the moral dimension of education, share a view of moral development—an **integrative model** that combines cognition, affect, and behavior. The integrative view postulates moral development as occurring along two dimensions, vertical and horizontal. The **vertical dimension** refers to growth as an increased ability to coordinate the perspectives and needs of others, to discriminate values that advance the human condition from values that do not, to make principled decisions, and to be aware of one's moral weaknesses (Ryan & Lickona, 1987). Vertical growth is the kind described by Kohlberg and Gilligan as advancement to higher levels of cognition and affect.

The **horizontal dimension** of moral growth refers to the application of a person's moral reasoning and affective capacities to an increasingly wider range of real-life situations. Horizontal growth requires that a person not only think and feel, but also act in accordance with their cognitive and affective capacities. Suppose that a business executive reasons that laws must be determined through agreement and, at the same time, protect the rights of individuals (Stage 5 in Kohlberg). Suppose further, that our executive decides to eliminate a company policy of job sharing without consulting employees. The lack of consistency between the executive's moral capacity to reason and actions taken reveals weak horizontal development. (Note that the notion of horizontal development could be used to explain the classic Hartshorne and May findings: good intentions do not always mean moral actions.)

An integrative model of moral education (sometimes called character education, emphasizing a concern with issues beyond moral reasoning) requires that attention be paid to vertical growth issues: reasoning, clarifying values, pursuing moral principles. It means also that students should use their thinking and feelings in a wide variety of ways, that is, that they pay attention to horizontal development.

Thomas Lickona presents an integrative model of moral education in *Character Development in the Schools and Beyond* (Ryan + McLean, 1987). The model is based on his work with elementary teachers, but as you will see in the discussion that follows, the model speaks to classrooms at all levels.

Lickona's Model of Moral Education

Lickona's model specifies four processes that need to operate in classrooms if teachers are to influence the developing character of their students: (a) building self-esteem and social community, (b) encouraging cooperative learning

Issues in Educational Psychology

CNN™ This box relates to Segment 3 of the CNN videotape. See the Instructor's Section for a summary.

TEACHING VALUES IN THE 90S

Have students lost their moral compass in an America where instant gratification is promoted and violence is glamorized? How does a public school teacher impart moral values without raising issues of religion? Can democracy survive without teaching values to guide its citizens? The answers to these questions pose formidable challenges for American education.

In an article for *Teacher Magazine*, Robert Coles and his associate, Louis Genevie, described the findings of a national student survey Coles directed in late 1989. Five thousand children from the fourth to twelfth grades were asked a series of questions concerning belief in God, cheating in school, teenage abortion, and how students decide between right and wrong. Only 16 percent relied on religion in making value judgments. Another 11 percent were essentially rudderless "with no clear-cut form of moral logic or reasoning to help them decide." The balance of students relied on self-interest, community standards, or what they felt worked.

Practicality and popularity seem to be closely linked in young people's moral reasoning. One student tried "to stick by the rules: If you break them, the next thing you know, you're in trouble." Although she had her own opinions at times, her judgments in class were made after "checking on how the people next to me are deciding."

Neither Coles nor Genevie wants to see religion and organized prayer return to public schools. They believe strongly in the separation of church and state, but point out that "when religion was removed from the schools, nothing came along to take its place, and teachers were stripped of the moral authority they once had."

As teachers themselves, Coles and Genevie stress that students should be told what is expected of them morally. Writers such as Leo Tolstoy and Robert Frost offer teachers a nonreligious authority on which to base morality.

Lessons in morality also come from outside the classroom. In "Teaching Values by Example," *Education Digest* presented the views of community leaders who decry the role models American society presents to students. A North Dakota educator stressed that "every day, adults demonstrate to children how to celebrate success and how to cope with failure. Happy events, sad events, and all things in between are commemorated by drinking. Drugs are simply an extension of the nation's love affair with alcohol."

An editor for a major newspaper lamented that gambling offers youngsters "the glitter of instant gratification." Violence in the media, noted a Massachusetts educator, is "a glamorous, always successful, always rewarded way to solve problems, and never do they show the tragedy of it."

It's not just individuals who suffer when there is a moral vacuum. As a democratic society loses its shared values, democracy itself is threatened. Amy Gutmann, a political philosophy professor at Princeton and director of the Center for Human Values, combines the conservative emphasis on morality and the liberal focus on personal choice to make a convincing argument. "In order to have a valuable set of choices in life, one has to have certain virtues of character." Ideally, Gutmann sees education combining these priorities so that values form a foundation on which students can make informed choices.

In the 90s, teachers have to educate the whole student, both intellectually and morally, or risk getting only half the job done.

SOURCES: Gutmann, Amy. "Mass Culture: Drowning in a Sea of Irrelevance—Educating for [Multiple] Choice." *New Perspectives Quarterly* 7, issue 4 (Fall 1990): 48–52. Billings, Jessica C. "Teaching Values by Example." *Education Digest* 56, issue 4 (December 1990): 66–68. Coles, Robert, and Louis Genevie. "The Moral Life of America's Schoolchildren." *Teacher Magazine* 1, no. 6 (March 1990): 39–49.

1. How might Erikson's theory of psychosocial development enable teachers to encourage enhanced moral reasoning in students?
2. How does Lickona's model for moral education address Amy Gutmann's concerns about teaching students to "make informed choices"?

Transparency: This figure is duplicated in the acetate transparency package. See T-4 Lickona's Model of Moral Education.

Lecture Note: The processes in Figure 3–1 overlap because if any one process is to operate well, the other processes must be involved as well.

Connection: What is involved in knowing a person as an individual rather than in a stereotypic way is discussed in Chapter 4.

Teacher Interview: Have each student interview a teacher regarding the practices described here.

Teaching Anecdote: Starratt (1987) reports a small group exercise in which each student writes his or her name at the top of a sheet of paper. The paper is passed to the next student who writes something likable about the student named on the page. The page continues around the circle until each student has named something likable about every other student in the group. Students can be encouraged to place their own sheet in their locker or on a wall at home. Some teachers display the sheets on the walls of their classrooms. Others have their class return to the sheets to elaborate on earlier comments. Another variation is to have students write affirming notes to parents, while the teacher asks parents to write affirming letters back to their children.

Ask students to explain why this technique has proved effective.

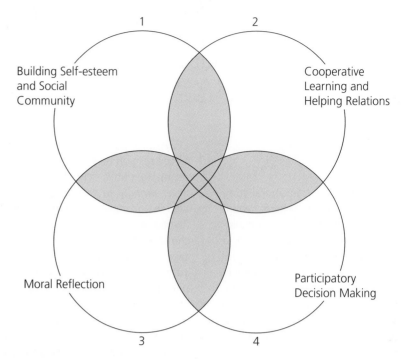

■ **Figure 3–1** *Lickona's Model of Moral Education*

Source: From "Character Development in the Elementary School Classroom" by T. Lickona, 1987, in *Character Development in Schools and Beyond* (p. 183) by K. Ryan and G. McLean (eds.), New York: Praeger Publishers. Copyright 1987 by Praeger Publishers. Reprinted by permission of Greenwood Publishing Group.

and helping relations, (c) eliciting moral reflection, and (d) effecting participatory decision making (see Figure 3–1). Keep in mind that Lickona's model is aimed at both vertical and horizontal development.

Building Self-esteem and Social Community

This process involves building a child's **self-esteem,** a sense of competence and mastery, in the social community of the classroom. This process also requires that students come to know each other as individuals, respect and care about each other, and feel that they are members of and accountable to the group.

Self-esteem can be fostered in the classroom in a number of ways. Lickona reports a third-grade teacher's practice of learning something special about each student at the beginning of the school year. The teacher asks each student to tell her of an award, a skill, something he or she is proud of. In the teacher's words, "I then make this something important to me. I stress to the child how important it is to me and it's something just the two of us share" (p. 185). The teacher values each student and each student tends to value himself or herself more highly.

One sixth-grade teacher who felt that too many of her students viewed themselves negatively decided to write a note to each child. In each note, the teacher mentioned a characteristic in the student that she admired. The notes also invited the students to write back to the teacher, telling her about characteristics they admired in themselves. The teacher reported that following the note exchange, the students displayed the characteristics identified as positive more frequently in the class. This kind of affirmation exercise has also been reported as effective in a high school classroom (Starratt, 1987).

Any sort of public effort to share personal feelings and perceptions can contribute to a sense of community. In developing this sense of community, it is important that each student feel that he or she is being listened to with respect.

Cooperative Learning and Helping Relations

The spirit of cooperation and the skills to realize that spirit are essential to adult living (Wynne, 1987). Cooperative learning, students learning from and with each other, can be fostered in classrooms at any grade level. (Cooperative learning will be discussed in more detail in Chapter 11.)

One third-grade teacher, teaching a unit on measurement, assigned pairs of children to collect physical measurements. The children were given the tasks of measuring the length of their jumps on a sidewalk, how far they could spread their feet, how high they could reach on the building, and so on. The teacher suggested that when one partner jumped or reached, the other partner should mark the effort. The teacher reported that children enjoyed the active nature of the exercise and the active nature of the interaction with their partners.

Establishing cooperation and helping as an integral part of one's classroom is not always "sweetness and light." In many cases, children who have not been in highly cooperative classrooms before will unintentionally subvert cooperative efforts by reverting to the skills required in classrooms emphasizing individual effort and achievement. One way of making cooperation easier for students is to help children learn to support each other socially. One fifth-grade teacher, attempting to establish cooperative learning, instituted a daily "appreciation time." At the end of the day each student could speak about something that another student did that day that the speaker appreciated. "Appreciation time" became the favorite classroom activity. Such acknowledgments allowed students to value helpfulness and thoughtfulness; it also gave students practice in delivering and receiving compliments.

Moral Reflection

The third process in Lickona's model is **moral reflection,** which focuses on the cognitive aspects of moral development. It might involve reading, thinking, debate, and/or discussion.

A fifth-grade teacher in New York City organizes her whole social studies curriculum around the theme of the Middle Ages. The classroom is turned into a Scriptorium, enabling students to approximate the experience of monks. They work on artistic ornamentation and calligraphy in the manuscripts they produce, which requires slow, painstaking effort. These efforts give the students "a great sense of achievement and appreciation of the artist monk" (Frey, 1983, p. 33). The medieval theme is carried through in the historical fiction that the students read. Reading and discussing good literature—which engages the mind and the heart—can go far beyond a contrived moral dilemma in eliciting moral reflection.

A teacher who attempts to pursue goals of moral education must be alert to the real-life moral situations that arise in every classroom. Lickona tells

moral reflection A process in Lickona's model that focuses on consideration of the cognitive aspects of moral development.

Lecture Note: Lickona argues that a sense of social community will seem rather "thin" in classrooms where sharing occurs only during scheduled sessions with the rest of the time devoted to individual work.

Lecture Note: Additionally, the children, while laughing and relaxed, remained focused on the measurement tasks. They began quite naturally helping one another when one student or a pair of students experienced difficulty. In a number of instances, pairs would disagree, recheck and compare, and resolve inconsistencies between the "teams," which is what the pairs became.

Field Observation: Have each student observe a cooperative classroom and try to identify student behaviors designed to subvert cooperative efforts.

Chapter 15 Casebook Preview: See Science Is Only Real When You Do It.

Lecture Note: As examples of raw material for reflection, consider literature, Kohlbergian dilemmas, or first-hand experiences. Moral reflection incorporates the moral reasoning addressed by Kohlberg, but Lickona suggests that the process be carried out so that affect is also involved.

Chapter 15 Casebook Preview: See Improvisation and Aesthetic Appreciation.

participatory decision making
A process in Lickona's model that holds students accountable for decisions that influence the quality of classroom life.

Through shared participation in educational activities, students develop motor coordination and learn how to work cooperatively.

the story of a second-grade teacher whose class was incubating chicken eggs. One day, the teacher suggested that it might be instructive to open one egg each week as a way of studying embryonic development. Later that day, one of her students objected to the suggestion because it seemed cruel to him. The teacher saw the opportunity to engage the class in meaningful moral reflection. The class discussed the merit of the objection; alternative, though less satisfying ways of finding out about chick embryos; and even questions about whether the embryos were really live chickens. Here was a moral dilemma that required reasoning, a clarification of feelings, and ultimately, action.

Participatory Decision Making

Teacher Interview: Have each student interview a practicing teacher regarding his or her efforts to incorporate participatory decision making.

The fourth process in Lickona's model of moral education is **participatory decision making,** which holds students accountable for decisions that influence the quality of classroom life. This process is not simply a matter of having students participate in defining classroom rules; it is also a matter of establishing a sense of responsibility and genuine participation in the welfare of the classroom community. The process, when practiced well, yields a set of norms that guides students' behavior.

If students have participated in establishing class rules, the sense of collective responsibility will facilitate the development of norms. Suppose that a class meets to discuss some problems: too much noise during seatwork, too little help during cleanup, and so on. These problems are not treated as isolated issues and the students involved in them are not "singled out" for special attention. The issues are considered by the class as a whole. The theft of one student's lunch money needs to be solved by the whole class. Helping a transfer student make friends and figure out the school's routine is a problem the class has to solve. In effect, the teacher can ask students to identify problems that they would like others in the class help them solve.

To make his point, Lickona relates the experiences of a young substitute teacher. She was asked to take over a class of a teacher who found the children incorrigible and had taken a six-week mental health leave. The substitute was greeted with an announcement from the class that they were the worst class in the school. The substitute immediately brought the class together to decide what rules were needed and why they were necessary. The discussion went on for some time and ended with consensus on one last student-generated rule: "Care about each other" (Lickona, 1987, p. 200).

The meetings continued on a daily basis. Caring for each other became the class ethic. When the substitute left at the end of six weeks, the students asked her to "teach" the returning regular how these class meetings worked. The substitute advised the regular teacher that the class meetings had had a wonderful effect on the class. The regular chose not to continue the meetings and, by all accounts, the class reclaimed its dubious reputation.

Journal Entry: Have students reflect on the "worst" classes they were in during elementary, junior high, and high school, and the ways in which they differed.

The four processes of Lickona's model are not effective in isolation. If the classroom sense of community is weak, it will be difficult to generate the kind of discussion and debate that makes useful reflection possible. If students do not participate in establishing the rules and norms of their community, it is less likely that a truly cooperative environment will develop. The Likona model has been applied successfully in a variety of classrooms. But its application requires a teacher who believes deeply in the value of moral education, a teacher who will persist through rocky beginnings and find a way to develop the sensitivity necessary to help students find character.

Lecture Note: Ask students to share their impressions of former teachers who would meet these criteria.

Principles in Practice 3.2

Principles . . .
1. As moral reasoning develops so does the capability to account for complex and multiple viewpoints.
2. Moral development must be understood within the context of values.
3. The processes of moral education integrate cognition, affect, and behavior.

. . . in Practice
In Teacher Chronicle 3.2, the children who decided to remain in their seats during the fire drill were preconventional thinkers. They took the rules of their classroom very literally. It also seems that they feared that they would

be punished if they broke the rules. Clearly, the children experienced strong feelings as they considered whether they should leave their seats for the fire drill. It is interesting to speculate on the social/moral atmosphere of their classroom in terms of Lickona's processes of moral education. It seems likely that the children in Mrs. Stein's class neither participated in deciding class rules nor met regularly to discuss class problems.

1. Would participatory decision making have helped the children put the "stay-seated" rule in context?
2. How could the fire-drill episode be used to address values with the students in Teacher Chronicle 3.2?
3. If you were to take over Mrs. Stein's class, how would you implement Lickona's processes without losing the discipline she instilled in her students?

Teacher Chronicle 3.3

Looks Can Deceive

I was pleased to see William Lavender's name on my class list. I had taught both of his older sisters in my social studies class and looked forward to teaching William. I had noticed him around school and, while he seemed like a typical seventh grader, his clean-cut appearance and handsome looks indicated to me that he must be a model student, too.

This impression carried over through the first weeks of school. He seemed attentive in class, asked questions, and did average work on his tests. But by the end of the second quarter, I realized something about William, something that happens every so often with students, something I don't quite understand. I discovered that I didn't like William at all.

I pride myself on being able to reach most kids, even the ones who try to make me dislike them on purpose to get my attention. Yet every so often I get a student that I just don't like, period. I know as a teacher that I shouldn't dislike any student. Disliking other adults is OK; disliking a student doesn't fit my self-image as a professional. Yet it happens. When it does, I try to keep it hidden from the student.

William did nothing to antagonize me. He did not argue with me or disrupt the class. He had never been sent to the office in his life. He had many friends, was a star on the swimming team, and was a member of the Student Council. He didn't swear (at least so that I heard him) and seemed to enjoy his role as a model student. Yet there it lurked, day after day, this feeling that I didn't like William.

One day, I went for a long walk after school and tried to sort out my feelings about William. After all, I wasn't being fair to him. As I walked, I tried to figure out what it was about him that I disliked. Was it his good looks or excellent behavior? Was it his high academic achievement or the high esteem in which his peers held him? Was it that he was just too nice, too perfect? I couldn't come up with an answer that satisfied me, but I did realize that I was reacting to the external person, not the real William underneath the facade.

One day that facade cracked and I caught a glimpse of the William behind it, a William who I rather liked. It was close to Christmas and we had just had a two-foot-deep snowfall. School didn't close, but getting around presented challenges. When I called for the homework assignments the day after the snowfall, William was the only student who didn't have his ready to be turned in. This was a first and I was surprised. He didn't offer any explanation for not having done the work, but accepted the zero for the assignment with a resigned look. There goes his *A* average. I did not think I would ever see that average slip. When he didn't come up to negotiate with me about the zero after school the way any other kid would have done, I began to wonder if something was wrong.

The next day I made a point to ask William to see me after school. He nodded with the same resigned look I had seen the day before. When everyone had left, he approached my desk.

"William, is something bothering you?" I asked. "I haven't seen you act this way before."

"No, nothing's wrong," he kept his eyes down, looking at a spot on the floor.

"Well, you know that zero on the assignment the other day will ruin your *A* average. You've never missed an assignment before."

"I know."

Dragging the words out of him was like pulling up a sequoia stump. "Could you tell me why you missed the assignment?"

He hesitated, then finally looked at me. "You know that big snow we had a couple of days ago?"

I nodded.

"Well, you see, I'm supposed to shovel Mr. Walker's sidewalk for him. He has a bad heart and my family's known him for years and I've always cleaned his sidewalks for him."

"He used to run Walker's Service Station at the corner of Memorial and Parkway."

"Right. Well, I went over to David's house after school during the snowstorm and completely forgot about Mr. Walker. He had to go to the store and began shoveling his driveway. He had a heart attack doing it. We spent the night at the hospital with him and so I didn't do my work."

Tears welled up in William's eyes.

"How is he doing?" I asked.

"He's okay now. But it was close."

"And you think that it is your fault that he had the heart attack."

He nodded.

"William, you don't know that. He could have had a heart attack just standing up after he'd been sitting down. You can't blame yourself."

"But he wouldn't have been shoveling if I had remembered to come do it for him."

"William, we all forget things. Your life is especially busy with all of the school things you do. Certainly Mr. Walker won't blame you."

"You don't think so?"

"William, he's a dear friend of your family's. I'm sure he's appreciated all the shoveling you've done for him more than he can tell you. Why don't you skip that assignment for tonight's homework and go see Mr. Walker. He needs you more than any old homework does."

He hesitated. "Don't worry," I said. "You'll still get an *A*."

stereotype A commonly held impression, either favorable or unfavorable, about the characteristics of a particular group.

Chap. Obj. 6
Test Ques. 3.87–3.109

Focus Questions: How are the various areas of development—social, cognitive, physical—related to each other? How does knowledge of the development of the "typical student" help us understand individuals?

Lecture Note: As an introduction to this section, point out that in Chapter 2, and to this point in this chapter, we have examined a variety of developmental theories. The theories provided descriptions of students, but descriptions separated into the areas of thinking, language use, view of self, and social—including moral—interaction. No one theory combines these areas into a composite of developmental capabilities, but the students in your classroom will be exactly such a composite. Therefore, in this final section of the chapter, we will step back from the separate areas in order to consider an overall picture.

Connection: Teacher Chronicle 3.3: Looks Can Deceive.

Lecture Note: Ask students to comment on the ways in which they have used stereotypic knowledge in dealing with people.

Field Observation: Have students observe primary-grade classes, noting the differences in physical size among students and whether those differences are associated with patterns of social interaction.

On the way out, I noticed that William's shoulders had lost much of their droop. I smiled to myself. "He's not such a bad kid after all. You hardly know him."

The next day William gave me a thumbs-up sign as he entered the room. "Mr. Walker goes home today," he whispered as he passed me.

"You know, William," I said to myself. "I'd like to have a friend like you when I'm too old to shovel my walks."

GRADE-LEVEL CHARACTERISTICS

Groups and Individuals

Consider William in Teacher Chronicle 3.3. When he walked into class he was, in the teacher's mind, a stereotype. A **stereotype** is the impression one has of a person based on that person's group. He turned out to be different from the stereotype the teacher held. If we look closely enough, all students turn out to be different from our stereotypes of them. Knowing what is typical of a group of students does not inform a teacher about the unique qualities that each individual brings into the classroom. Nevertheless, knowledge of what is "typical" is helpful.

Stereotypes provide developmental reference points in much the same way averages or norms identify what is typical. For example, even as we speak of an "average fourth grader," we know that there is no such individual. However, having the "average fourth grader" in mind gives us a reference point against which we can "measure" the characteristics unique to a particular individual.

Key Capabilities in the Primary Grades (K–3)

Physical

The child's rapid growth rate, typical of the preschool years, slows by the time he or she reaches first grade.* Growth during this general period of development is rather smooth. Bodily changes are characterized by a decrease in body fat and an increase in bone and muscle. This change means an increase in coordination and agility; a change that occurs more rapidly in males than in females. There are considerable differences in size among primary-grade students. If some of these size differences are due to poor nutrition or to hormonal deficiencies, the deficiencies can be overcome. Children are capable of catch-up growth, if slow growth has not been severe or prolonged up to this point.

Children in the primary grades have lots of physical energy. They have attained fairly good control of their large muscles and are beginning to develop control of fine motor skills. Their energy and muscular control seek physical outlets; therefore, providing opportunities for physical activity is important in the primary grades. Their new-found physical competence

---

*The physical characteristics, unless otherwise indicated, are based on descriptions provided by Seifert and Hoffnung (1987).

In the primary grades, children gain independence from their families and begin to form friendships. Their activities are more interactive than the parallel play that is typical of very young children.

sometimes causes primary-graders to be overconfident. There are more accidents in the primary grades because children "overstep" their capabilities. Their physical independence can try the patience of parents and teachers.

Social/Emotional

During the preschool years, children begin to develop peer relationships. Most primary graders have one or two best friends, but these friendships change quickly. Most of their social development comes about through play situations. Even in kindergarten, a major emphasis of the year is to prepare the child socially for school.

By the primary grades, children typically have developed through a series of stages that represent levels of sociability (Parten, 1932; Rubin, et al., 1976–1978). Their play has progressed from solitary or parallel to play that's more socially interactive. When children begin to play, they play in close proximity but with little awareness of each other. Older primary students engage in a common play activity and communicate with each other. Primary-grade students consciously work in groups to accomplish some activity. Roles are often taken or assigned.

The primary grades offer the child a number of challenges: achieving in school, establishing new peer relationships, and developing a new independence from family. In their new role, primary graders just begin developing a sense of themselves. Primary graders typically are eager to please their teachers—they seek their praise and are sensitive to criticism.

Cognitive

We discussed the cognitive level of primary graders when we examined Piaget's theory of cognitive development. It is important to point out here that

Field Observation: Have students observe children of varying ages at play in the neighborhood or on a school playground.

Connection: See the discussion of Piaget's theory of cognitive development and the stages of linguistic development in Chapter 2.

Connection: See the examination of moral development earlier in this chapter.

sex role stereotypes
Commonly held expectations about the roles of each sex.

primary-graders typically have developed their language abilities significantly. Most first-graders learn to read and to write; their ability to understand language is fairly well developed. Although understanding language requires the use of symbols, communication with primary-grade students needs to be concrete rather than abstract. Students at this level tend to interpret things literally, including any classroom rules that you may establish. Primary graders tend to be very aware of rules; they are eager to call your attention to any violation of the rules that may occur.

Developmental Issue: Sex Roles

Primary-grade children typically have acquired knowledge about society's expectation of the roles of each sex (Wynn & Fletcher, 1987), that is, of society's **sex role stereotypes.**

Journal Entry: Have students reflect on their acquisition of sex role stereotypes.

Parents have "taught" their children behaviors that are appropriate for boys and for girls before these children reach the primary grades. One way parents "teach" is through the toys they give their children. Parents tend to provide their children with "gender-appropriate" toys (Sidorowicz & Lunney, 1980). Parents also interact with their children in ways that communicate their aspirations for their children. Parents encourage achievement, independence, competition, and control of emotions in boys. Daughters are encouraged to be warm, dependent, and nurturing (Block, 1983).

Other children reinforce sex role stereotypes. Sex role stereotypes are often reflected in cooperative play. Preschoolers are likely to praise and to join in their peers' sex-appropriate behavior and to criticize what they perceive as sex-inappropriate behavior (Fagot, 1977; Langlois & Downs, 1980; Shepher-Look, 1982).

By the time children enter the primary grades, they already have learned sex role stereotypes from their parents and from gender appropriate toys.

Primary-grade students are well versed in the language of sex role stereotypes. Whether these stereotypes will continue to be reinforced or not depends, in part, on teachers' responses to student behavior. For example, sex role stereotypes suggest that girls are more likely to request assistance than boys. A teacher who wishes to combat stereotypes will take care to provide assistance to girls only when it is truly needed. Responding to requests from a female student who is quite capable of completing a task on her own reinforces dependence.

Lecture Note: A teacher who encourages the boys of a primary-grade classroom to be sensitive to the needs of others provides another example of an effort to counter sex role stereotypes.

Key Capabilities in the Intermediate Grades (4–6)

Physical

The physical variations in size and body shape that began to appear in the primary grades continue in Grades 4–6. Stereotypes associated with size and shape become more pronounced. A student who wears glasses may be viewed as a "nerd" or as an "egghead." A child with large ears may be called "Dumbo" or "clown." Some children in intermediate grades are considerably smaller than their classmates. Very small children look younger and may be treated as if they are by teachers and friends.

Children who suffer from obesity—at least one out of ten in the United States (Bray, 1976)—encounter problems with stereotyping. Reactions to children's obesity may occur unconsciously, but they are real nonetheless. Children and adults respond negatively to obese children. This negative reaction begins in kindergarten and increases as children get older (cf. Brenner & Hinsdale, 1978; Lerner & Schroeder, 1971). Children with the "wrong" looks tend to be excluded from certain peer groups that develop during this period.

Field Observation: Have students interview intermediate-grade children regarding the reactions of other children to their physical appearance.

Although these boys are approximately the same age, they are at various stages of physical development. Whether a child experiences early or late maturation can be a source of social and emotional stress.

Children with the "wrong" looks may also blame themselves for their exclusion (Seifert & Hoffnung, 1987). Obese children exhibit more problem behaviors, have lower self-esteem, and are more depressed than nonobese peers (Banis et al., 1988; Strauss et al., 1985).

Athletic activity becomes more important during the intermediate grades. Children who are not motivated to do well in academic tasks may show motivation when involved in athletics. Children begin to play team sports at this age. These activities provide opportunities for cooperation and competition. A child may show a preference for either cooperation or competition at this point.

Social/Emotional

Lecture Note: Ask students to describe their own memories of social groups in elementary school. How were those social groups defined?

Some of the physical characteristics described earlier have obvious social and emotional effects because intermediate-grade students are typically concerned about their status within groups. This is true socially and academically. During this period, students become more focused on their own capabilities or inabilities. Differences between the learning skills of students become more pronounced. Peer relations are also stronger; peers begin to replace adults as the major source of influence. The peer groups that typically form at this level of development vary in membership and behavior according to the age mixture and the gender of the groups (Seifert & Hoffnung, 1987).

Popularity or unpopularity exerts a strong influence on the development of peer groups and whether or not children join them. Popular children tend to associate with other popular children. As a group, they possess socially desirable qualities, including self-confidence. Unpopular children establish peer groups less often than popular children. Unpopular children are more aggressive and selfish.

Cognitive

Connection: See the sections on Piaget's stages of preoperations and concrete operations.

Chapter 15 Case Preview: See Responsibility Education.

Most intermediate-grade students have the ability to solve problems by reasoning them through. At this stage, however, abstract thought is not yet common. When objects can be seen and manipulated as part of the problem-solving process, solutions are most easily reached. Differences in cognitive styles—including learning disabilities—also become apparent during the intermediate grades.

Developmental Issue: Growth Spurt Begins

Toward the end of the intermediate grades, the **growth spurt,** a dramatic increase in height and weight that signals the onset of puberty, begins (cf. Dusek, 1987). Because girls mature more quickly than boys, girls tend to be taller and heavier than their fifth- and sixth-grade classmates. Because of the variability in physical maturation in girls and boys, some students appear quite mature while others do not. Because appearance is an important aspect of social and emotional experience, the wide-ranging differences can cause problems for students in these grades.

Teacher Interview: Have students interview an intermediate-grade teacher regarding the social implications of student appearance.

Teachers in the intermediate grades need to be aware of the social implications of appearance and to offer reassurance to students who feel "funny" about themselves. Students can experience uneasiness about themselves either because they have experienced sudden growth or because they haven't. Students need to know that the rates of physical maturation range widely; that the social and emotional discomforts that accompany the growth spurt are temporary. The implications of the growth spurt in the intermediate grades carries over to the junior high grades.

Key Capabilities in Junior High School Grades (7–9)

Physical

Seventh graders have just recently or will shortly enter **puberty,** the time of physical change during which individuals become sexually mature. The pubertal sequence for girls involves the budding of the breasts, the growth spurt already mentioned, the appearance of pubic hair, and menarche—the beginning of menstruation. The pubertal sequence for boys is enlargement of the testes, the appearance of pubic hair, growth of the penis, and the growth spurt. (Figure 3–2 maps the pubertal development.)

Journal Entry: Have students reflect on their thoughts and feelings as they entered puberty.

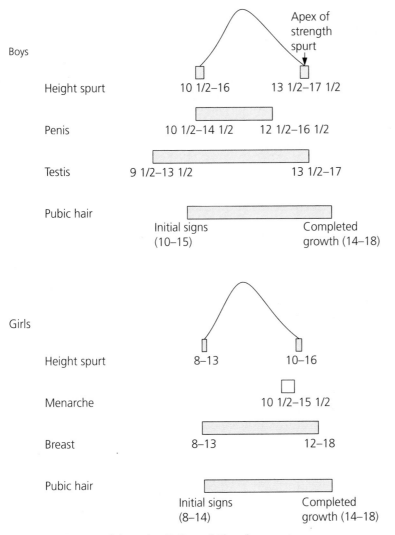

■ **Figure 3–2** *Range of Ages for Pubertal Development*

Source: From *Child Development* (2nd ed., p. 175) by L. E. Berk, 1991, Needham Heights, MA: Allyn & Bacon. Copyright 1991 by Allyn & Bacon. Adapted by permission. (Where a bar appears, the left end indicates initial signs; the right end, completed growth.)

Social/Emotional

The key task for adolescents is to develop a sense of their own identity. Junior high school students find themselves in the midst of a process of becoming a person separate and independent from others. Forming one's identity involves the selection of some behaviors that have developed in childhood and the discarding of others (see Erikson, 1975). Peer friendships become increasingly important during this period of development. There is also a trend toward a greater mutuality of friendships. Loyalty to friends increases as does intimacy (Douvan & Adelson, 1966; Douvan & Gold, 1966).

Mutuality involves an understanding of how different people can cooperate for mutual benefit. The other primary aspect of friendship that develops during this period is intimacy or feelings of closeness. Intimacy manifests itself in three aspects: self-revelation, confidence, and exclusivity. The experience of self-revelation involves finding a friend with whom you feel comfortable discussing your problems openly. You develop confidence in sharing and keeping secrets with friends. This mutual trust leads to a sense of the exclusivity of the relationship.

In recent years, the number of adolescents who experience family stress has increased. Family stress is introduced by divorce, remarriage, or single parenthood. At a time when the adolescent is struggling to develop a sense of identity, turmoil within the family can make the task more difficult. Peers, who become increasingly important during the elementary grades, take on an even greater role for the adolescent. Small and close-knit cliques and larger and less intimate groups are an important part of the young adolescent's social environment.

Teacher Interview: Have each student interview a junior high school teacher regarding his or her understanding of social characteristics and how they influence his or her teaching.

Cognitive

According to Piaget, this is the period when students become capable of formal operational thought. However, teachers should be aware that many junior high students do not yet reason abstractly. Indeed, some are just entering the stage of concrete operations. Evaluating the level of cognitive development of ninth-graders, Epstein (1980) found that roughly 32 percent were just entering concrete operations, 43 percent were well into concrete operations, 15 percent were entering formal operations, and only 9 percent were judged to be well within the stage of formal operations. Obviously, there is great variability among the cognitive capabilities of junior high students.

Developmental Issue: Early and Late Maturation

Most girls complete their growth spurt around the seventh grade. The growth spurt for boys is usually not completed before the eighth or ninth grade (Tanner, 1978a, 1978b). Within each sex, there is a wide variation in maturation rates. Early maturing girls, therefore, can be as much as four or five years ahead of late maturing boys. (Refer back to Figure 3–2 to verify this.)

In junior high, early maturing males are the better athletes; they are more confident; they inspire higher expectations from teachers and parents; and they are more attractive to females. Early maturing males are the most popular boys in junior high. It is likely that William, in Teacher Chronicle 3.3, matured early in junior high.

The same cannot be said for early maturing females. Early maturing females are so much different from their age peers that they are often branded as "the odd woman out" (Lefton, 1991). Early maturing females are not likely

Connection: Teacher Chronicle 3.3: Looks Can Deceive.

to be popular or be chosen as class leaders. Their appearance outstrips their social skills. Late maturing females are more in the mainstream—when compared with all junior high students, male and female. Late maturing females are more confident and socially assured, and more likely to be chosen as leaders. Socially, late maturing females are similar to early maturing males.

Late maturing males are on the other end of the continuum from early maturing females. A late maturing male is the "odd man out." Late maturing males are more likely to act out as a way of gaining attention. They are not likely to be popular or chosen as class leaders.

Teachers need to be aware that much of the behavior they see in junior high students can be traced to where they "fit in" with their classmates. Peers are very important to adolescents. The need to belong to their "social community" is a driving force. Junior high teachers would be well advised to consider using Lickona's process for building self-esteem and social community.

Another tactic is for teachers to encourage, whenever possible, participation in athletics. Athletic activity during junior high can counter many of the negative feelings that occur during this period (cf. Kirshnit, Richards, & Ham, 1988). Fortunately, many athletic activities at the junior high level still operate on a "voluntary participation" rather than a "selection by tryout" basis. Counseling athletic activity, while assuring the student that physical differences will decrease, is a strategy that a junior high teacher might find use for.

Key Capabilities in the High School Grades (10–12)

Physical

By the eleventh grade, most students have reached physical maturity; virtually all have attained puberty. Females have typically grown to their full height. Some males, however, may continue to grow after graduation. Sexual maturity is attained in the high school grades, a physical fact that influences many other aspects of the high school experience, including social relations.

Social/Emotional

Dunphy (1963) surveyed males and females from thirteen to twenty-one. The subjects were studied at beaches, social clubs, parties, on street corners, and inside their homes. They were questioned about their friendships and other peer relationships. The research indicated two types of peer groups.

The first type of peer group is the **clique,** a close-knit group of two or more people who share intimately purposes and activities. The clique is not only intensely inclusive of its members, it is intensely exclusive of those who do not share the interests of the clique. The second type of peer group, the **crowd,** is a less cohesive group, numbering between fifteen and thirty people. Crowds are typically informal associations of between two and four cliques.

The clique is like a family; it provides the high school student a social environment within which he or she feels comfortable and safe. Cliques generally meet during the school week. Crowds usually gather on the weekends at parties or dances (Seifert & Hoffnung, 1987).

High school peer groups differ from junior high groups in important ways. Junior high peer groups are more likely to be same-sex cliques. The cliques of junior high tend not to interact with one another.

clique A narrow, exclusive group of peers who share interests, purposes, and activities.
crowd A larger, less cohesive group of peers who have something in common.

Teaching Anecdote: Tell the story about the fifth-grade girl who towered above her classmates. Although she was well-liked, her physical development set her off from the rest of the fifth and sixth graders. She felt awkward and uncomfortable. Her teacher began to see a slip in her work and attitude. Then a long-term substitute teacher—a very tall woman—came into the building. One day the girl stopped by to see her and they chatted. Soon the student came by every afternoon for a talk. Her grades picked up and the smile returned to her face.

Ask your students why the contact with the teacher seemed to help.

Teacher Interview: Have each student interview a junior high school teacher to find out how physical differences influence peer relations.

Lecture Note: Ask students to describe cliques and crowds to which they belonged.

SUE MISHEFF
MALONE COLLEGE
CANTON, OHIO

I have always known that I would be a teacher. I suppose that the reason for this almost innate sense of mine is partially due to nature and partially to nurture. I haven't settled that debate yet. But what I do know is that I define myself as a teacher, in spite of the role that I might be engaged in at any given moment.

As a former classroom teacher and reading specialist, I've had the joy of being able to share in the lives of some very special learners. Now, as a teacher educator, I am continuing to grow in this on-going process of teaching and learning. Whatever the age of my students, I never tire of being a participant in their discoveries and changes.

If someone were to write a "teacher's epitaph" for me, I would want it to say, "She listened." As a teacher, the single most important activity for me is to listen *to* my students rather than listen *for* prescribed answers. In a world of technology and "smart bombs," the human communication aspects of education are ever more crucial. A classroom that is student-centered will always be more conducive to the educational process than one whose student–teacher interaction is dependent on materials or instructional approaches. Student-centeredness is at the heart of trends toward literature-based curricula or whole language classrooms. What else are these approaches but attempts to get teachers to pay attention to the needs and interests of their students?

We know from research in response to reading programs that conditions intrinsic to the learner, all part of the subjective nature of reading, are integral to reader engagement and understanding. This appears to be true in both narrative and expository text, so that when a student finds personal meaning in a lesson, that becomes the key to sustained and continuing learning, the springboard for knowledge development. No number of workbook pages or computer programs or creative bulletin boards can substitute for the subjective response.

Emerson told us that "[o]ur chief want in life is somebody who will make us do what we can." That's how I see teaching—helping other people become what they can be as I strive to do the same.

In high school, male and female cliques interact with each other. For example, a group of two or three boys will arrange to meet a group of two or three girls at a local shopping mall. This is how opposite-sex relationships begin. Because of the numbers of people involved, the meeting of cliques, rather than individuals, provides a social "safety net." The initial contacts between opposite-sex cliques can lead to the formation of new heterosexual cliques. Dual-sex cliques and crowds provide the first opportunities for serious intimate relationships between individuals.

The natural evolution from same-sex cliques to individual opposite-sex relationships seems to be encouraged by parents, teachers, and students themselves (Newman, 1982). The social influence of peer groups includes the pressure to conform to an expectation of opposite-sex relationships. The judgments adolescents make are clearly influenced by peer opinion.

The cliques and crowds that exist in high school are likely to be defined in terms of the futures their members see for themselves. For example, a clique that includes a student who intends to apply to college is not likely to include a member who intends to enter the unskilled labor market after high school. As they become more focused on their lives after graduation, high schoolers seek out peers who have similar plans and interests.

Developmental Issue: Social Pressure and Anxiety

Sexually mature eleventh-graders have evolved socially from same-sex cliques to opposite-sex cliques to dating relationships among individuals. The pressures of more intimate relationships, along with anxiety about the future, increases the emotional stress that high school students experience. It is not uncommon for teenagers to experience symptoms of depression. In fact, depression is the most common type of emotional disorder during the period of late adolescence. Common symptoms include crying, statements of low self-worth, fatigue, and difficulty concentrating (Winer, 1980). Females tend to experience depression to a greater extent than males. Rutter (1980) speculates that females in late adolescence sometimes come to the conclusion that they have little control over significant aspects of their lives. If this explanation is accepted as true, it leads to a type of depressed state called **learned helplessness** (cf. Seligman, 1975), in which the student who experiences it feels that no matter what he or she does, these acts cannot influence important life events. Efforts to make things better always end in failure. After repeated failures, the student has come to the conclusion that he or she is helpless.

The symptoms of learned helplessness or other forms of depression are serious. High school teachers cannot afford to ignore them. Depressive symptoms include threatening or attempting suicide. Recent research on teenage suicide indicates that it is the third leading cause of death among adolescents. Suicide rates in 1960 were 8.2 percent for males and 2.2 for female per 100,000 adolescent deaths. Twenty years later the rate had climbed to 20.2 percent for males and 4.3 percent for females.

Suicidal students, those who threaten or attempt suicide, are likely to give many clues. It is critical that teachers recognize these clues. Suicidal symptoms include the following:

- Mention of suicide (80% of suicidal people discuss their intentions)
- Significant changes in eating or sleeping habits
- Loss of interest in prized possessions
- Significant changes in school grades
- Constant restlessness or hyperactivity
- Loss of interest in friends

Every teacher should know what referral process for suicidal students is available in his or her school district. Teachers should also mentally rehearse what actions can be taken from various locations in the school in an emergency situation. In the event that you discover that one of your students is suicidal, it is critical that you remain with the student. Suicidal individuals remain suicidal for limited periods of time. *Do not leave the student alone!* (cf. Bell, 1980; Meyer & Salmon, 1988).

learned helplessness A depressed state in which a person feels that no matter what he or she does, these acts cannot influence important life events.
suicidal students Students who threaten or attempt suicide.

Connection: See Marcia's identity types and statuses discussed earlier in this chapter.

Teacher Interview: Have each student interview a high school teacher regarding the behaviors he or she has observed in depressed students.

Principles in Practice 3.3

Principles . . .

1. Stereotypes provide reference points for understanding individuals.
2. Physical, social and cognitive characteristics interact to influence a student's behavior.
3. The complexity of the factors that interact during adolescence puts older students at risk psychologically.

. . . in Practice

In Teacher Chronicle 3.3, we saw how stereotyping a student can lead to erroneous conclusions about that student. But we also saw that the teacher looked for answers when questions about the student's behavior arose. William turned out to be different from his teacher's initial impression. Getting to know William as an individual enabled the teacher to better understand the student's problems and to offer some help as William crossed some rough psychological territory.

1. Will this teacher limit him- or herself to a first impression the next time a student like William comes to class?
2. How do physical differences come into play in William's social circle?
3. Why do social and moral problems seem so much more traumatic for high school students than for elementary school students?

Assign Chapter 3 of the Study Guide.

CONCLUSION

Human beings have a natural tendency to want to know why events happen as they do. Teachers are inquiring human beings. When they see a student behave in a particular fashion, it is natural for them to ascribe a reason to the behavior they have observed. Teachers, and other inquiring people, tend to seek explanations regardless of how much they may know about a particular student.

If a teacher knows little about a student's personal background, he or she may rely on stereotypic knowledge to explain the student's behavior. If a teacher knows a great deal about the personal history of a student, the teacher can explain the student's behavior on the basis of this idiosyncratic knowledge. Although we are aware of the danger of explaining behavior on the basis of stereotypic knowledge, it is important to acknowledge this very human tendency.

We are often advised to avoid stereotyping. But sometimes the only knowledge we have about a student is stereotypic knowledge. Using this knowledge as the basis of a behavioral observation is not the same thing as "stereotyping a child." Teachers, because of the nature of their task, must explain what they see in the students who are before them. If stereotypic or normative knowledge is the only knowledge on which a teacher can base an explanation, then stereotypic knowledge should be used.

Whatever the basis, our explanations of the way our students behave are our guides in our interactions with them, socially and academically. Unless we test these explanations—our hypotheses of interaction—we will not learn the best ways to reach each and every student.

To find out the best way to "connect" with each unique individual, we must often consult our stereotypes. As we leave the normative or stereotypic descriptions of Chapters 2 and 3 for those that are idiosyncratic in Chapter 4, keep in mind that both types of knowledge are necessary if we are to find ways of connecting with our students. And, after all, our inquiring minds want to know.

Chapter Summary

A Theory of Psychosocial Development
The Stages of Psychosocial Development
Erikson proposes eight stages of psychosocial development. Each stage's developmental crisis is identified as a dichotomy of qualities, positive and negative. If the social experiences during that period are generally positive, positive qualities result. If experiences are generally negative, the crisis is resolved negatively.

Identity: A Closer Look
Erikson's Stage 5—identity versus role diffusion—can be resolved in ways other than the positive and negative qualities of the dichotomy. One additional resolution is to enter a state called psychosocial moratorium, which is really no resolution at all, but rather a postponement of life-style decisions. Another resolution is to adopt a negative identity, rebellion against authority.

Identity Types or Statuses
James Marcia extended Erikson's work as it applied to adolescents' search for identity. He identified four identity statuses. Identity diffusion types are confused, disorganized, and avoid commitment. Moratorium types (not to be confused with Erikson's psychosocial moratorium) have given a great deal of thought to identity issues, but have not yet arrived at any conclusions. Identity achievement types are those adolescents who have made life-style decisions on their own. Foreclosure types do not experience a crisis of identity; they simply adopt decisions made for them by others.

Interpreting Erikson's Theory
If a teacher uses Erikson's theory to make decisions about a student's psychosocial needs, he or she should keep in mind the evidence that suggests that Erikson's framework is a better description of males than of females. There is also a good bit of overlap in the stages—crises that begin in toddlerhood and continue through the middle school years are quite similar.

Moral Development
Piaget's Framework of Moral Reasoning
Piaget distinguishes between the moral reasoning of younger and older children. Younger children follow the morality of constraint; they follow rules without question. Older children, who follow the morality of cooperation, take into account the context of behaviors in order to judge whether an action is right or wrong.

Kohlberg's Stages of Moral Reasoning
Kohlberg based his framework on Piaget's views. Kohlberg identified stages of moral reasoning that exist at three levels. At the first level, preconventional morality, reasoning about right and wrong is based on the idea that correct behavior is that which avoids punishment and yields some kind of reward. The second level, conventional morality, is based on respect for authority and a desire to impress others. The third level is postconventional morality. The reasoning at this level recognizes the need for societal agreement and the consistent application of moral principles.

An Integrative View of Moral Development
Lickona's Model of Moral Education
Lickona identified four overlapping processes that should occur in classrooms where moral education is addressed. The first process focuses on building healthy self-esteem through social support and a sense of belonging to the community of the classroom. The second process operates to establish cooperative learning; the emphasis is on students learning to help each other. The third process, moral reflection, is similar to Kohlberg's—and more similar to Gilligan's—moral reasoning. The final process encourages participatory decision making on questions of behavior in the community of the classroom.

Grade-Level Characteristics
Groups and Individuals
These composites of the developmental capabilities of students at various grade levels provide reference points for identifying the uniqueness of individuals. The physical, social/emotional, and cognitive characteristics of primary, intermediate, junior high, and high school students contribute to critical developmental issues at each level. The issues include sex role stereotypes, the growth spurt, early and late maturation, and social pressure and anxiety.

Key Capabilities in the Primary Grades (K–3)
Primary students differ from one another considerably in size; as a group they seek outlets for their abundance of physical energy. Peer relationships are being formed, but friendships change often and quickly. Cognitively, students are generally preoperational; some students may begin to display concrete operations late in the primary grades. Although their language skills are fairly well developed, their comprehension is very literal.

Developmental Issue: Sex Roles
Primary-grade children have learned sex role stereotypes. Typically, boys have been encouraged to achieve, be independent, compete, and control their emotions. Girls have been encouraged to be warm, dependent, and nurturing. Sex role stereotypes can be combated by encouraging nonstereotypic behaviors in both female and male students.

Key Capabilities in the Intermediate Grades (4–6)
Students' diversity in physical size and appearance can have pronounced social effects in the intermediate grades, including name calling. Athletic activity can be a useful way of encouraging motivation. Status within a group is an important aspect of social interaction. Cognitively, students are becoming more logical in their thinking, moving from preoperations to concrete operations.

Developmental Issue: Growth Spurt Begins
Toward the end of the intermediate grades, rapid physical changes—typical of the growth spurt—are evident. This time of change can make many students feel uncomfortable with their bodies and, in turn, uncomfortable in their interactions with peers.

Key Capabilities in Junior High School Grades (7–9)
Junior high students have recently or will soon begin experiencing the physical and emotional changes that are part of puberty. Close friendships with other individuals and within a small group become important. Close-knit peer relations are especially important when students experience family stress. Although Piaget's age estimates suggest that junior high students are becoming formally operational, a large percentage of these students are still concrete operational.

Developmental Issue: Early and Late Maturation
The onset of puberty and the growth spurt during the junior high years produces differences between students who mature early and those who mature later. Females as a group mature earlier than males; females who mature early are very different from most peers. The same is true of late-maturing males. Owing to the importance of "fitting in" during junior high, these two groups suffer more social and emotional stress that other students.

Key Capabilities in the High School Grades (10–12)
Although physical growth may continue past graduation, especially for males, virtually all high school students have become sexually mature. Cliques and crowds, which include members of both sexes, provide the social context for the development of close, opposite-sex relationships. It is important to remember that many high school students will still be concrete operational.

Developmental Issue: Social Pressure and Anxiety
The development of intimate relationships, questions about one's future, and other pressures increase the emotional stress experienced by high school students. It is not uncommon for teenagers to experience symptoms of depression. If serious depression results, the possibility of suicide cannot be ignored. A suicidal student must never be left alone.

Reflections: Building Your Theory of Teaching

3.1 We often hear the call to "teach the whole child." We have tried to understand the development of children by dividing the child's growth into areas of development, which we examine closely. From this analysis comes grade-level descriptions, an attempt to provide reliable composites. Reflect on whether the practice of teaching children requires the same separation–analysis–reintegration. Do we really, during any one lesson or interaction, teach the "whole" student?

3.2 Suppose that you have a student who exhibits a negative identity. Suppose further that this student disrupts the class with inappropriate behavior. How might you approach the problem of controlling the student's behavior without validating the label "troublemaker"?

3.3 Identify the crisis of psychosocial development that corresponds most closely to the grade level you intend to teach. Use Lickona's model of moral education to design instructional experiences that will contribute to a positive resolution of the developmental crisis.

Key Terms

self-concept (p. 86)
psychosocial development (p. 87)
epigenetic principle (p. 88)
critical periods (p. 88)
dichotomy (p. 88)
developmental crisis (p. 88)
autonomy (p. 90)
initiative (p. 91)
industry (p. 92)
identity (p. 92)
identity diffusion (p. 92)
intimacy (p. 92)
isolation (p. 92)
generativity (p. 92)
stagnation (p. 92)
integrity (p. 93)
psychosocial moratorium (p. 94)
negative identity (p. 94)
identity statuses (p. 95)

identity diffusion types (p. 95)
moratorium types (p. 95)
identity achievement types (p. 95)
foreclosure types (p. 95)
moral judgments (p. 98)
morality of constraint (p. 98)
morality of cooperation (p. 98)
preconventional morality (p. 99)
conventional morality (p. 100)
postconventional morality (p. 101)
individual survival (p. 102)
self-sacrifice and social conformity (p. 102)
morality of nonviolence (p. 102)
integrative model (p. 104)
vertical dimension (p. 104)
horizontal dimension (p. 104)
self-esteem (p. 106)

moral reflection (p. 107)
participatory decision making (p. 108)
stereotype (p. 112)
sex role stereotypes (p. 114)
growth spurt (p. 116)
puberty (p. 117)
clique (p. 119)
crowd (p. 119)
learned helplessness (p. 121)
suicidal students (p. 121)

Suggested Readings

Erikson, E. H. (1963). *Childhood and society* (2nd ed.). New York: Norton.

Erikson, E. H. (1968). *Identity: Youth and crisis.* New York: Norton.

Gilligan, C. (1982). Why should a woman be more like a man? *Psychology Today,* June, 68–77.

Knowles, R. T. (1986). The acting person as a moral agent. In R. T. Knowles & G. F. McLean (eds.). *Psychological foundations of moral educational and character development.* Lanham, MD: University Press of America.

Lickona, T. (1985). *Raising good children.* New York: Bantam Books.

Lickona, T. (1987). Character development in the elementary school classroom. In K. Ryan & G. F. McLean (eds.), *Character development in schools and beyond.* New York: Praeger.

References

Banis, H. T., Varni, J. W., Wallander, J. L., Korsch, B. M., Jay, S. M., Adler, R., Garcia-Temple, E., & Negrete, V. (1988). Psychological and social adjustment of obese children and their families. *Child: Care, Health and Development, 14,* 157–173.

Bell, R. (1980). *Changing bodies, changing lives: A book for teens on sex and relationships.* New York: Random House.

Block, J. (1983). Differential premises arising from differential socialization of the sexes: Some conjectures. *Child Development, 54,* 1335–1354.

Brabeck, M. (1986). Moral orientation: Alternative perspectives of men and women. In R. T. Knowles & G. F. McLean (Eds.), *Psychological foundations of moral education and character development: An integrated theory of moral development.* Lanham, MD: University Press of America.

Bray, G. (1976). The obese patient. In *Major problems in internal medicine* (Vol. 9). Philadelphia: Saunders.

Brenner, D., & Hinsdale, G. (1978). Body build stereotypes and self-identification in three age groups of females. *Adolescence, 13,* 551–561.

Colby, C., & Kohlberg, L. (1984). Invariant sequence and internal inconsistency in moral judgment stages. In W. Kurtines & J. Gewirtz (Eds.), *Morality, moral behavior, and moral development.* New York: Wiley-Interscience.

Douvan, E., & Adelson, J. (1966). *The adolescent experience.* New York: Wiley.

Douvan, E., & Gold, H. (1966). Modal patterns in American adolescence. In M. L. Hoffman & L. W. Hoffman (Eds.), *Review of developmental research* (Vol. 2). New York: Russell Sage.

Dunphy, D. C. (1963). The social structure of urban adolescent peer groups. *Sociometry, 26,* 230–246.

Dusek, J. B. (1987). *Adolescent development and behavior.* Englewood Cliffs, NJ: Prentice-Hall.

Ellerod F. E., & McLean, G. F. (Eds.). (1986). *Act and agent: Philosophical foundations for moral education and character development.* Washington: University Press of America.

Epstein, C. (1980). Brain growth and cognitive functioning. In *The emerging adolescent: Characteristics and implications.* Columbus, OH: NMSA.

Erikson, E. (1963). *Childhood and society* (2nd ed.). New York: Norton.

Erikson, E. (1968). *Identity, youth and crisis.* New York: Norton.

Fagot, B. I. (1977). Consequences of moderate cross-gender behavior in preschool children. *Child Development, 48,* 902–907.

Fishkin, J., Keniston, K., & MacKinnon, C. (1973). Moral reasoning and political ideology. *Journal of Personality and Social Psychology, 27,* 109–119.

Frey, G. (1983). The Middle Ages: The social studies core of the fifth grade. *Moral Education Forum* (Summer 1983), 30–34.

Gilligan, C. (1977). In a different voice: Women's conceptions of self and of morality. *Harvard Educational Review, 47,* 481–517.

Gilligan, C. (1982). *In a different voice.* Cambridge: Harvard University Press.

Hartshorne, H., & May, M. A. (1930). *Studies in deceit.* New York: Macmillan.

Holstein, B. (1976). Irreversible, stepwise sequence in the development of moral judgment: A longitudinal study of males and females. *Child Development, 47,* 51–61.

Hwang, K. (1986). A psychological perspective of Chinese inter-personal morality. In M. H. Bond (Ed.), *The psychology of the Chinese people.* New York: Oxford University Press.

Kirshnit, C. E., Richards, M. H., & Ham, M. (1988, August). *Athletic participation and body-image during early adolescence.* Paper presented at the 96th Annual Convention of the American Psychological Association, Atlanta, GA.

Knowles, R. T., & McLean, G. F. (Eds.). (1986). *Psychological foundations of moral education and character development: An integrated theory of moral development.* Lanham, MD: University Press of America.

Kohlberg, L. (1969). Stage and sequence: The cognitive-developmental approach to socialization. In D. A. Goslin (Ed.), *Handbook of socialization theory and research.* Chicago: Rand McNally.

Kohlberg, L. (1971). From is to ought: How to commit the naturalistic fallacy and get away with it in the study of moral development. In T. Mischel (Ed.), *Cognitive psychology and epistemologies* (pp. 151–235). New York: Academic Press.

Kohlberg, L. (1978). Revisions in the theory and practice of moral development. *Moral Development: New Directions for Child Development, 10,* (No. 2) 83–88.

Langlois, J. H., & Downs, A. C. (1980). Mothers, fathers, and peers as socialization agents of sex-typed play behaviors in young children. *Child Development, 51,* 1237–1247.

Lefton, L. A. (1991). *Psychology* (4th ed.). Needham Heights, MA: Allyn & Bacon.

Lerner, R. M., & Schroeder, C. (1971). Physique identification, preference, and aversion in kindergarten children. *Developmental Psychology, 5,* 538.

Lickona, T. (Ed.). (1976). *Moral development and behavior: Theory, research and social issues.* New York: Holt, Rinehart & Winston.

Lickona, T. (1987). Character development in the elementary school classroom. In K. Ryan & G. McLean (Eds.), *Character development in schools and beyond.* New York: Praeger.

Marcia, J. E. (1967). Ego identity status: Relationship to change in self-esteem, "general adjustment," and authoritarianism. *Journal of Personality, 35* (1), 119–133.

Marcia, J. E. (1980). Ego identity development. In J. Adelson (Ed.), *The handbook of adolescent psychology.* New York: Wiley.

Meyer, R. G., & Salmon, P. (1988). *Abnormal psychology* (2nd ed.). Boston: Allyn & Bacon.

Newman, P. (1982). The peer group. In B. Wolman (Ed.), *Handbook of developmental psychology.* Englewood Cliffs, NJ: Prentice-Hall.

Parten, M. B. (1932). Social participation among preschool children. *Journal of Abnormal and Social Psychology, 27,* 243–269.

Peters, R. (1977, August 19–26). *The place of Kohlberg's theory in moral education.* Paper presented at the First International Conference on Moral Development and Moral Education, Leicester, England.

Piaget, J. (1948). *The moral judgment of the child* (M. Cabain, Trans.). Glencoe, IL: Free Press.

Piaget, J. (1965). *The moral judgment of the child.* New York: Free Press.

Reimer, R. H., Paolitto, D. P., & Hersh, R. H. (1983). *Promoting moral growth: From Piaget to Kohlberg* (2nd ed.). New York: Longman.

Ruben, K., Maioni, T., & Hornung, M. (1976). Free play behaviors in middle and lower class preschools: Parten and Piaget revisited. *Child Development, 47,* 414–419.

Ruben, K., Watson, K., & Jambor, T. (1978). Free play behaviors in preschool and kindergarten children. *Child Development, 49,* 534–536.

Rutter, M. (1980). *Changing youth in a changing society: Patterns of adolescent development and disorder.* Cambridge, MA: Harvard University Press.

Ryan, K., & McLean, G. F. (Eds.). (1987) *Character development in schools and beyond.* New York: Praeger.

Seifert, K. L., & Hoffnung, R. J. (1987). *Child and adolescent development.* Boston, MA: Houghton Mifflin.

Seligman, M. E. P. (1975). *Helplessness: On depression, development, and death.* San Francisco: W. H. Freeman.

Shepherd-Look, D. (1982). Sex differentiation and the development of sex roles. In B. Wolman (Ed.), *Handbook of developmental psychology.* Englewood Cliffs, NJ: Prentice-Hall.

Sidorowicz, L. S., & Lunney, G. S. (1980). Baby X revisited. *Sex Roles, 6,* 67–73.

Starrat, R. J. (1987). Moral education in the high school classroom. In K. Ryan & G. McLean (Eds.), *Character development in schools and beyond.* New York: Praeger.

Strauss, C. C., Smith, K., Frame, C., & Forchand, R. (1985). Personal and interpersonal characteristics associated with childhood obesity. *Journal of Pediatric Psychology, 10,* 337–343.

Tanner, J. (1978a). *Education and physical growth* (2nd ed.). London: Hadder & Stoughton.

Tanner, J. (1978b). *Fetus into man: Physical growth from conception to maturity.* Cambridge, MA: Harvard University Press.

Vasudev, J., & Hummel, R. C. (1987). Moral stage sequence and principled reasoning in an Indian sample. *Human Development, 30,* 105–118.

Walker, L. J. DeVries, B., & Trevethan, S. D. (1987). Moral stages and moral orientations in real-life and hypothetical dilemmas. *Child Development, 58,* 842–858.

Weiner, B. (1980). *Human motivation.* New York: Holt, Rinehart & Winston.

Wynn, E. A. (1987). Students and schools. In K. Ryan & G. McLean (Eds.), *Character development in schools and beyond.* New York: Praeger.

Wynn, R. L., & Fletcher, C. (1987). Sex role development and early educational experiences. In D. B. Carter (Ed.), *Current conceptions of sex roles and sex typing.* New York: Praeger.

4

Developmental Diversity

Chapter Overview

The two previous chapters have described what is true of students as part of a general population at various periods of development. In this chapter, we examine how students as individuals differ from one another. There are a number of ways to think about the differences among students. One is to consider the student's capacity to learn, his or her intelligence—or intelligences. Another is to consider the student's individual learning style. In addition to intellectual differences, students also have different attitudes, beliefs, and values that reflect their cultural backgrounds. Finally, there are the different types of mental and physical conditions that make students exceptional. To understand students as learners, it is necessary to know how students resemble one another in a group and the ways that they are unique. ■

INTRODUCTION: SEEING THE INDIVIDUALS IN A GROUP

It is critical to understand the difference between a group and an individual. Much of what we know about social, emotional, and cognitive development has been learned by studying the thoughts, feelings, and actions of groups of children at particular developmental stages. In the last two chapters, we have examined the similarities among students at the same developmental stages. We know, for example, the intellectual capabilities of a group of concrete operational students. We also know the personal concerns of a group of students wrestling with the industry-versus-inferiority crisis.

Effective teachers know a lot about the characteristics of the groups to which their students belong, but they also know their students as individuals. By coming to know individual students, teachers can accommodate learning styles; make specific decisions about learning activities, effective reinforcements, and motivation; and make those critical personal connections that can mean the difference between a year of growth and a year of stagnation for the student.

Here are a master teacher's comments on the necessity of knowing students as individuals:

> The very first bell of the very first day of the year rings. In every classroom in my school and around the city, teachers are watching students and students are studying teachers.
>
> Calling the roll, I begin to match names with the students. I start getting a sense of who they are. I see the gamut of emotions on their faces and in their actions. Anxiety, eagerness, uncertainty, confidence, friendliness, silliness, shyness, boisterousness are all out there before me.
>
> I know also that there are differences in intelligence, motivation, interests, habits, learning styles there before me. I perceive a broad outline of the class. Yet within this outline I must fill in the details of every individual. And I only have 180 days in which to do it.

To fill in the outline with details of individuals, it is necessary to understand the ways in which students can differ. In this chapter, we will examine the sources of differences among individuals. The first such source is part of almost every cumulative record of every student—intelligence.

Connection: See A St. Patrick's Day Analysis, Chapter 1.

Lecture Note: An interesting "analysis" of cumulative records is given in *Among Schoolchildren* by Tracy Kidder, p. 8.

Teacher Chronicle 4.1

AREN'T I SMART?

As I scanned my fifth-hour class list, the dreaded name leaped out: Louis Chambers. Rumors of his talent for disruption had reached me long before I met him. He was supposedly a master at interrupting a lesson, starting fights, failing tests, and being obnoxious. I knew of several instances where the police had checked up on his "extracurricular" activities. Last year I had a student who had lost a fight with him; it took two weeks for the black eye to fade away. I knew Louis was "street smart," but was he any other kind of smart? I wondered if he might indeed be bright, but not letting on. I'd seen this with other tough students.

I reached for his records to see if I could glean some helpful information. I didn't want his past reputation to influence my working with him, so I decided to look for something positive in his folder. A quick scan revealed nothing but a recognition award for an art project in eighth grade. Well that's a start, I thought. Tonight I would take a longer look.

I wasn't quite sure how, but I was determined to find a way to teach him. I decided right off the bat that I'd have to establish who the boss was in my room. And I hoped it would be me.

Louis entered the room determined to exceed his reputation. As I called the roll, I received the appropriate "Here" following each name. But not with Louis. When I called his name, there was a long pause. I called again and he answered "Yeah." I decided not to force the issue at this point, so I just reminded the entire class after I had finished that when I called roll everyone was to answer, "Here." Looking at Louis, I guaranteed them that it would save time and hassles.

Louis replied to my comments with an obscenity muttered in a tone of voice just loud enough to hear. I chose to ignore his remark, aiming for a way to win him to my side rather than be at odds with him all year. I didn't want to establish a negative pattern on the first day.

Louis obviously did. On the way to sharpening his pencil, he knocked Paula's books onto the floor. When I mispronounced someone's name, he was the first to laugh. He did everything he could to attract the attention of his buddies.

The in-class assignment that day was to sketch a favorite environment. Because we would soon be studying environments around the world, I wanted a way to assess the students' ideas of what elements made up an environment. As I roamed the room watching them sketch, I kept an eye on Louis. For some reason, however, he was giving his entire attention to his drawing. It was as if he had entered a different place. He even sketched right through the bell.

"Louis," I said cautiously, half expecting this to be another of his ploys, "the bell rang."

"Oh, yeah," he said looking up. "I got to hurry to hassle the English teacher." He looked like he wanted to say something to me but changed his mind and left the room quickly.

That night, as I skimmed through the sketches, I was more than pleased with Louis's. He had chosen to draw a coral reef. He had all of the elements in place: a variety of corals, a number of fish of differing shapes and sizes, a moray eel peering out of a hole, a diver drifting past overhead. What struck me was his handling of details; not only was the moray eel lurking, it had its eye on a nearby fish. The snorkeling diver had a look of wonder on his face, the fanlike coral seemed to be waving in the water. His drawing was the best of the class by far.

The next day I made a point of pulling Louis aside and asking if he had ever taken drawing lessons.

"Nah," he answered. "My mom wouldn't pay for them and I couldn't steal 'em. I just learned on my own. You like my reef picture?"

"It was exceptional," I said. "That's why I asked about art lessons." Then I had an idea. "Louis, when is your free period?"

"Seventh hour."

"What would you think if I set things up so that you could draw in here while I have another class? I really need some pictures on the walls to jazz up the room. Your reef picture done in a larger size would be perfect."

intelligence A personal capacity to learn, often measured by one's ability to deal with abstractions and to solve problems.

Chap. Obj. 1–2
Test Ques. 4.1–4.29

Focus Questions: What is intelligence and how does it contribute to differences among students? Can students be intelligent in different ways?

Teacher Interview: Have each student interview a teacher or curriculum supervisor to find out the criteria for entrance into instructional programs for exceptional students, including those who are gifted and talented.

Connection: IQ tests are examined in greater detail in Chapter 14.

He looked at me as if I were trying to set him up for something. Then he smiled, "Sure thing, then I can get out of study hall." I swear he almost said thanks when he left the room.

VARIETIES OF INTELLIGENCE

The term **intelligence,** generally defined as a personal capacity to learn, is probably the one piece of educational jargon most used in everyday language. As teachers, we learn about the intelligence level of students. Intelligence is measured in schools periodically and is included on most permanent records of students. Indeed, in many school districts the measured intelligence of a child is used in concert with other information to make instructional decisions concerning a student's future.

The measurement of intelligence yields an index called an intelligence quotient (IQ). A person's IQ is typically represented by a single number. For example, someone with an IQ of 102 is considered to be of average intelligence; an IQ of 120 is considered to be above average. In and out of educational circles, when we talk about a person's intelligence, we usually think of it as a unitary thing that can be reflected in a single number. Incidentally, while we usually talk about IQ as a single value, it is more accurate to speak of the probable range of a person's IQ. The measurement of intelligence will be discussed in Chapter 14. In this section, we will examine the meaning of the term *intelligence* rather than its measurement.

NOT TRUE (RANGE)

Students' varied personal backgrounds and experiences influence greatly their intelligences and abilities. It is critical that teachers be able to recognize and accommodate diverse learning styles.

There has been a long and animated debate among psychologists as to the meaning of the term *intelligence*. Intelligence is a **construct,** an idea devised by a theorist in order to explain something else. Intelligence, for example, has been used to explain why some students graduate from law school and others can't finish high school; why some students complete tasks with ease and others struggle; why some students succeed and others fail. It is a measure of differences among students. Some psychologists suggest that there is a general overriding mental ability that can be referred to as a person's intelligence. Others take the view that intelligence is not a unitary thing. Rather, there are many intelligences. One psychologist argues that "all intelligent people know what intelligence is—it is the thing the other guy lacks!" (McNemar, 1964) We will examine briefly several influential views of the construct called intelligence.

A teacher who is conversant with this construct can do two things. One, the teacher can critically interpret the results of IQ tests. Two, the teacher can usefully identify ways in which students differ from one another. Being able to do both is important to teachers, but our focus in this chapter is on the latter. Interpreting IQ tests will be discussed in the chapters on evaluation.

Piaget's Dynamic View

In Piaget's view, a person's intelligence is **dynamic,** that is, it changes as a person's interaction with his or her environment changes. Recall Piaget's stages of cognitive development as discussed in Chapter 2. Each stage defines a person's intelligence. According to Piaget, an infant organizes his or her environment into sensorimotor schemata; he or she is using sensorimotor intelligence to understand the environment. As the infant accommodates and assimilates new experiences, he or she constructs new types of cognitive structures, called preoperational schemata. Development proceeds through concrete operational schemata and formal operational schemata. The type of schemata a person uses defines the type of intelligence a person has. Because schemata change throughout the course of a person's cognitive development, a person's intelligence is dynamic. Cognitive development can be thought of as the development of new forms of intelligence.

For Piaget, individual differences in intelligence are more qualitative than quantitative. It makes little sense to say that a first grader is less intelligent than a ninth grader. Rather, the two students have different kinds of intelligences. If they are typical, the first grader has preoperational intelligence; the ninth grader has either concrete or formal operational intelligence.

Wechsler's Global View

David Wechsler made his fame as a developer of IQ tests. Although he died in 1981, one of the most respected IQ tests for children remains the Wechsler Intelligence Scale for Children-Revised (the abbreviation, WISC-R, is pronounced "wisk, r"). From his investigations in measuring intelligence, he developed a **global view** of the construct of intelligence: "Intelligence is the aggregate or global capacity of the individual to act purposefully, to think rationally, and to deal effectively with the environment" (1958, p. 7). Because Wechsler viewed people's intelligence as an overall ability to deal with the world around them, he argued against summing the parts to estimate the whole.

construct   A complex idea devised by a theorist from a synthesis of simpler ideas.
dynamic   Marked by continuous change.
global view   Wechsler's view of people's intelligence as an overall ability to deal with the world around them.

Lecture Note: Have students discuss the differences between constructs and measurements, generally, and intelligence and IQ in particular. See also *Mismeasure of Man* by Stephen J. Gould, p. 24.

Teaching Anecdote: Tell the story of Marshall who was an excellent reader but struggled with math. He enjoyed problem solving when writing a story or working on the structure of a research paper. He couldn't seem to grasp mathematical problem solving. He grew increasingly frustrated with what he called "the absoluteness of math." Everything seemed so black and white, right or wrong, there didn't seem to be a place for his kind of creativity in math class.

Connection: Interpretation of the results of IQ tests (and other standardized tests is the focus of Chapter 14.

Connection: See Piaget's stages of cognitive development and his construct of schemata, Chapter 2.

Lecture Note: Ask students to argue for and against Wechsler's global view of intelligence.

Guilford's Multifactor View

three faces of intellect
Guilford's model of intelligence, which organizes intellectual capabilities along three dimensions: operations, products, and content.

Chapter 15 Casebook Preview: See Writers' Tea.

Lecture Note: Ask students to identify examples of operations from their own school experiences.

While Wechsler focused his efforts on defining intelligence as a single entity, Guilford worked to establish a definition of intelligence that recognized the whole range of factors composing it. Guilford sought some way of organizing appropriate factors into a framework. The result of his efforts was the **three faces of intellect** model, which organized intellectual capabilities along three dimensions or "faces" (Guilford, 1967; see also 1980, 1985). The model is structured around five kinds of operations, four kinds of content, and six kinds of products (see Figure 4-1). The 5 × 4 × 6 configuration yields 120 separate factors.

Operation

The first dimension in Guilford's model describes the type of operation a person performs. Guilford's use of the term *operation* differs from Piaget's use of it (presented in Chapter 2). In Guilford's model, an operation is a kind of intellectual activity or process.

1. **Cognition** is the operation that refers to knowing, being aware, discovering.
2. **Memory** is the process of remembering, retrieving previously stored information.
3. **Divergent production** is the generation of multiple responses, solutions, hypotheses.
4. **Convergent production** involves arriving at the one correct solution to a problem.
5. **Evaluation** is the process of making judgments.

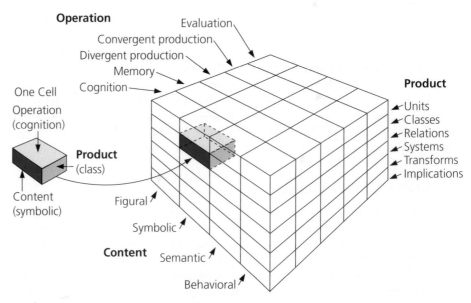

■ **Figure 4–1** *Guilford's Three Faces of Intellect Model*

SOURCE: From *Psychology* (4th ed., p. 271) by L. A. Lefton, 1991, Needham Heights, MA: Allyn & Bacon. Copyright 1991 by Allyn & Bacon. Reprinted by permission.

Content

The second dimension in Guilford's model is the content of the operation. *Content* refers to the nature of the information being operated on.

1. Figural content refers to images, objects, or other concrete information.
2. Symbolic content refers to abstract systems of codes, such as numbers.
3. Semantic content is meaning derived, for example, from words.
4. Behavioral content is information derived from human behavior and interaction, such as a person's mood.

Connection: Behavioral content is pertinent to the idea of "reading students" in Chapter 1.

Product

When a person operates on some kind of content, a *product* results. The information that defines the content is transformed through processing.

1. Units are single, independent items of information.
2. Classes are sets of items that share properties.
3. Relations are connections between items.
4. Systems are ways of organizing information.
5. Transforms are changes in information.
6. Implications are predictions, interpolations, or extrapolations from information.

An Interim Report on Intelligence Theories

Which of these theories of intelligence is correct? Perhaps all of them are correct in a limited way, but the important question for teachers is, What do these theories suggest about educational practice? (That is, are there hypotheses to be tested in one's classroom?)

Piaget's dynamic view suggests that there are dangers in thinking about intelligence as some intellectual "substance"—such as the ability to reason abstractly—which students should acquire in greater and greater quantities as they proceed through school. To use only one yardstick to measure intelligent behavior is to deny the differences in cognitive capabilities that exist among students at different stages of intellectual development.

Wechsler's global view, derived as it was from concerns about testing the construct, suggests that a test of spatial ability, a test of mathematical computation, or a test of verbal reasoning may tell us very little about a student's overall ability to deal with the world. Intelligence, from the global view, is more than the sum of its parts.

Guilford's three faces of intellect model identifies five different kinds of intellectual operations. In most classrooms, students have many opportunities to engage in cognition, memory, and convergent thinking. Practice abounds in the use of language skills, math skills, and motor skills. There tends to be less emphasis, however, on divergent production and evaluation.

Divergent thinking is often referred to by another name, *creativity*. Creative thinking generates ideas and solutions that go beyond the usual, the conventional, the average. Unless students are given opportunities to think in unusual ways, and are encouraged to do so, they may not develop their creative potential. It is reasonable to assume that students who are classified as gifted and talented would thrive in classrooms where divergent thinking

Journal Entry: Have students generate some teaching hypotheses consistent with the three theories examined up to this point, comparing and contrasting the hypotheses.

Field Observation/Teacher Interview: Have each student observe a lesson or interview a practicing teacher regarding the types of operations stressed in classrooms.

Teaching Anecdote: Tell the story of Roy, an attentive, alert student. He contributed to every discussion, often adding a divergent perspective. When the class performed lab assignments, Roy always managed to add a new "twist" to the assignment. At first, this tendency to go beyond the assigned task annoyed the teacher until she realized that Roy was expressing his creativity. What might have happened had the teacher insisted that Roy's labs strictly follow the lab sheet?

Lecture Note: Have students discuss their school experiences that encouraged divergent thinking.

is expected and encouraged. Educators should ask themselves why the drop-out rate for adolescents identified as gifted is often higher than that of the general school population (McMann & Oliver, 1988).

Having looked at some long-established views of the construct of intelligence, we will next examine a final view of intelligence, a relative new-comer—Sternberg's triarchic theory of intelligence.

Connection: Teacher Chronicle 4.1: Aren't I Smart?

Sternberg's Triarchic Theory of Intelligence

Ask a hundred people on the street, "How can you tell if a person is intelligent?" and the vast majority of them will tell you to look at school performance. Louis, introduced in Teacher Chronicle 4.1, does not have a good record of school performance, but there are hints that he is intelligent. Academic performance and intelligence are so often linked that it is easy to forget that students can display their intelligence in a variety of ways outside the school environment. One view of intelligence that recognizes this fact is Sternberg's triarchic theory (1985, 1986).

Sternberg's theory comprises three parts or subtheories. Each subtheory addresses a different kind of (or perhaps a different aspect of) intelligence (see Figure 4-2).

Experiential intelligence
Ability to formulate new ideas and combine unrelated facts. A test measures experiential intelligence if it assesses a person's ability to deal with novel tasks in an automatic manner. Such a task might involve remembering all words containing the letter *T* in a paragraph.

Contextual intelligence
Ability to adapt to a changing environment and ability to shape one's world to optimize opportunities. Contextual subtheory deals with an individual's ability to use intelligence to prepare for problem solving in specific situations.

Componential intelligence
Ability to think abstractly and process information. A person's ability to determine what tasks need to be done. Tasks that can be used to measure the elements of the componential subtheory are analogies, vocabulary, and syllogisms.

■ **Figure 4–2** *Sternberg's Triarchic Theory of Intelligence*
SOURCE: From *Psychology* (4th ed., p. 272) by L. A. Lefton, 1991, Needham Heights, MA: Allyn & Bacon. Copyright 1991 by Allyn & Bacon. Reprinted by permission.

The Experiential Subtheory

The **experiential subtheory** describes a person's capacity to deal with novel tasks or new ideas. Think about a class that encounters chemical equations for the first time. In the beginning, work on the equations is slow and halting. With practice, however, the students become more proficient. With enough experience, they can solve novel equations very efficiently.

The Contextual Subtheory

The **contextual subtheory** defines intelligence that is reflected in one's ability to adapt to one's environment, select one's environment, or shape one's environment in order to optimize one's opportunities. In order to measure this type of intelligence it would be necessary to test the quality of one's existence within his or her environment.

Sternberg (1986) provides a cross-cultural example to illustrate what he means by contextual intelligence and why he feels that the measurement of intelligence must be sensitive to context.

Suppose an intelligence test developed in North America were used to assess the intelligence of an African Pygmy. The types of intelligence tapped by North American tests is not likely to be the type of intelligence that allows the African Pygmy to survive and flourish in his or her everyday environment. While the North American tests used in this situation might measure something, it is not contextual intelligence. The test would serve little purpose unless, of course, the Pygmy had as a goal adapting to North American culture.

Consider the example of a special education teacher who undertook to instruct her students on how to tell time. One of her students, who had great difficulty learning to read his watch, spent part of each day in a work program away from the school. Because the student had to catch a bus back to school each day, it was important that he keep track of the time. Every day, the teacher half expected that the student would miss his ride back to school but he never did. One day, while chatting with the director of the work program, she mentioned that she was surprised by this. The teacher discovered that at work the student wore a watch (something he never did at school) that did not function. Whenever the student needed to know the time he would look at his watch and then say to someone, "Excuse me, but my watch doesn't seem to be working. Could you tell me the time please?" His practice of putting on a nonfunctional watch on arriving at the work program was an adaptation to his new environment, and a rather ingenious one at that.

Ingenious adaptations are made by students—and adults in the workforce—who can't read; by model students who develop their own methods of organizing assignments; and by students who find shortcuts or loopholes in order to avoid classroom work.

The Componential Subtheory

The **componential subtheory** identifies the mental components of what we call intelligent behavior. Componential intelligence refers to a person's ability to reason abstractly and to determine the kind and sequence of operations required for a task or problem. Componential intelligence is the type usually measured on IQ tests. A student who possesses a high degree of componential intelligence is likely to perform academic tasks well.

experiential subtheory Part of Sternberg's theory of intelligence, describing a person's capacity to deal with novel tasks or new ideas and to combine unrelated facts.
contextual subtheory Part of Sternberg's theory of intelligence, relating to one's ability to adapt to a changing environment and to shape one's world in order to optimize one's opportunities.
componential subtheory Part of Sternberg's theory of intelligence, referring to a person's ability to reason abstractly, process information, and to determine the kind and sequence of operations required for a task or problem.

Lecture Note: Ask students to share their own "ingenious ways of adapting" to classrooms. Did they find ways to "beat the system"?

learning styles Differences in the ways that students think, reason, and learn.

Teacher Interview: Have students ask teachers to identify their creative students by using these questions and then interview the creative students.

Chap. Obj. 3
Test Ques. 4.30–4.37

Focus Question: Why do students approach learning tasks differently?

Chapter 15 Casebook Preview: See Science Is Only Real When You Do It.

Journal Entry: Have students recall former classmates and try to categorize them.

To summarize, in Sternberg's triarchic view of intelligence, the differences among students are not due simply to presence or absence of one general ability. Intelligence manifests itself in a number of ways. Consider the many examples of people who did not perform well in school, but who later demonstrated conceptual insight, creativity, and even genius. Thomas Edison and Albert Einstein come easily to mind.

Does insightful creation or invention require experience with tasks and problems in the environment? Does the nature of insight depend on the type of experiences a person has had with his or her environment? What of students who possess high levels of contextual intelligence but who have academic problems? Are they more likely to become creative problem-solvers?

Sternberg's triarchic view describes differences among the individuals in our classrooms. The three elements of contextual intelligence that he describes offer additional dimensions along which students can differ. Thinking about types of intelligence—rather than intelligence—we have a basis for examining the diversity students display in what they think, reason, and learn. Researchers have labeled such differences **learning styles.**

LEARNING STYLES

Psychologists have been studying differences in the ways that students learn for several decades. Some students work better than others when tasks are highly structured. Some can study effectively with the stereo blaring; others need quiet. Some students learn well from one particular teacher, while others in the same class learn very little. By identifying students' learning styles, we can understand diversity in classrooms, and select particular instructional methods and techniques to accommodate it.

Students have different learning styles just as they have different personalities. Indeed, one way of approaching the question of learning styles is to first consider personality types. Carl Jung, in his correspondence with Sigmund Freud, postulated personality types (1960/1926). In the book *People Types and Tiger Stripes* (Lawrence, 1982), Jung's personality types were organized into four bipolar pairs:

1. Extrovert–Introvert. A person who is outgoing and vivacious is classified as an extrovert. An introvert does not share his or her feelings freely.
2. Sensory–Intuitive. Sensory types rely on the evidence of their senses. A person who relies on "gut feelings" is classified as intuitive.
3. Thinker–Feeler. A thinker is one who relies on logic more often than emotion. A person who responds emotionally to situations is classified as a feeler.
4. Judger–Perceiver. A person who takes time to evaluate various aspects of a situation is classified as a judger. A perceiver acts on unanalyzed events.

Meinke (1987) investigated the relationship between personality types and learning styles among first-year college students who were education majors. Meinke found that the greatest learning-style differences were between judgers and perceivers.

Personality types influence what people prefer to do and how they prefer to do it. Taken one step further, these preferences apply not only to how students prefer to learn, but also how teachers prefer to teach. It is a good idea for teachers to analyze their own preferences for teaching, what we could call in the present context their teaching style. In addition, teachers who understand the learning preferences or styles of their students can compare them with their own teaching styles. Such an approach allows a teacher to anticipate and take steps to avoid the interpersonal conflict that has been shown to occur when individual learning and teaching styles differ (Barger & Hoover, 1984).

There are other ways in which the learning styles of students differ. Guilford's three faces of intellect model distinguishes between convergent and divergent production (1967). Whether students are convergent or divergent thinkers will have important effects on their emerging learning styles. **Convergent thinkers** tend to react to instructional materials in conventional ways. **Divergent thinkers** tend to respond in unconventional or idiosyncratic ways. We tend to think of divergent thinkers as being more creative in their responses to instructional tasks and materials. If a teacher decides to encourage one style or the other—in order to "balance" a student's operational approach, for instance—instructional tasks can be designed to encourage either conventional or unconventional thinking.

Kagan (1964a, 1964b) distinguished between impulsive or reflective styles of learning. **Impulsive** students tend to answer questions quickly; **reflective** students take their time, preferring to evaluate alternative answers. Reflective students are more concerned with being accurate than with being fast. An impulsive learning style indicates a "perceiver" personality; a "judger" personality is more likely to have a reflective learning style. Kagan also distinguished between analytic and thematic styles. **Thematic** students tend to seek the patterns of a whole; **analytic** students take greater note of detail.

If reflective students give themselves more time to consider a problem or situation, a question arises: Do they reflect in order to discover details or to discover an overall pattern? Zelniker and Jeffrey (1976) found that reflective students are better at analyzing details. Impulsive students perform better on tasks requiring more global interpretations.

What should you do about the differences in learning styles that students will bring to your classroom? First, be aware that they exist; that they are important contributors to the diversity you will encounter. Second, analyze how students respond to various learning tasks you give them. For example, during class discussions or reviews, notice which students respond to questions immediately and which students prefer to think about the answers. Are the answers of a particular student conventional or innovative? Take note also of the questions students tend to ask. Are the questions thematic or analytic in nature? In general, the tasks your students perform provide more than just ways of collecting scores for the grade book; they are opportunities for you to learn about your students. Third, allow for learning-style differences by planning a variety of learning activities. As you plan, keep in mind your own teaching preferences. If a teacher's plans reflect only the most preferred activity, some students' learning styles will never be accommodated. (The importance of building a repertoire of teaching techniques will be addressed in Chapter 11.)

convergent thinkers People who tend to react to instructional materials in conventional ways.
divergent thinkers People who tend to respond to instructional materials in unconventional or idiosyncratic ways. Such thinkers are often creative.
impulsive Learning style characterized by quick actions.
reflective Learning style characterized by quiet thought or contemplation.
thematic Learning style that seeks patterns of a whole.
analytic Learning style that gives greater emphasis to analysis of details.

Journal Entry: Have students reflect on their own teaching styles. What are their current preferences? Who influenced those preferences? Their favorite teachers? Their least favorite teachers?

Connection: The importance of varying instructional tactics is examined in Chapter 11.

Field Observation: Have students observe other students in a classroom, trying to identify impulsive, reflective, thematic, and analytic thinkers.

Students often express their individuality through in-class and extracurricular activities.

Connection: See the discussion of instructional tactics in Chapter 11.

Many teachers do not attempt to match their instructional practices with the learning styles of their students (Smith & Renzulli, 1984). It is not clear whether this happens because these teachers are unaware of style differences, because they do not assess style, or because they do not plan activities with learning styles in mind. Research suggests, however, that taking the time to determine learning styles and then using that information in planning is worth the effort. In one study, for example, a survey was used to first determine and then match learning styles to teaching styles. Matching learning and teaching styles resulted in positive changes in student achievement, motivation, discipline, and interest in that subject matter (Smith & Renzulli, 1984; see also Schmeck, 1989).

Journal Entry: Have each student design a survey of learning styles for use in your classroom.

Principles in Practice 4.1

Principles . . .

1. Intelligent behavior involves adapting to one's environment.
2. One source of differences among students is the type of intelligences they exhibit in classrooms.
3. Students' learning styles influence their classroom performance.

. . . in Practice

Louis, in Teacher Chronicle 4.1, seems to deserve his reputation as an effective disrupter of classrooms. In the first meeting of the class, he attempted to provoke the teacher several times. Even at the end of the episode, when the teacher recognized his talent, Louis didn't accept the offer with a simple "thanks." He acknowledged the offer to do the artwork, but added a little twist consistent with his reputation. He used his street-smarts in school to the point that he hid other kinds of intelligences he might have possessed. The teacher's initial assignment happened to uncover one of Louis's other intelligences, the teacher lost no time in trying to capitalize on this discovery.

1. Do some students adapt to their environments better or just differently than others do? How has Louis adapted?
2. In what ways is Louis intelligent?
3. Would suggesting to Louis that he "draw a picture" depicting the content of a history lesson be a good test of his learning style?

Teacher
Chronicle
4.2

GRANDMA TALES

Kevin was a storyteller. He loved to tell about his older brother the basketball star, his Native-American tribe, his aunt (with whom he lived), children around school, and recent trips. Kevin's reading was weak and his written work was a constant struggle, compared with that of other students in his English class. He was unable to organize his thoughts on paper. Storytelling was his only outstanding skill. He was on the verge of failing my English class. He got no help at home. There seemed to be no way to head off an *F* at report card time.

Kevin's Native-American background was based on a strong oral tradition, that is obvious now, in retrospect. I could kick myself for not seeing it sooner. He could tell stories that captivated his listeners, stories with solid beginnings, intriguing middles, and powerful endings. Kevin could tell stories, but he had not yet equated storytelling with story writing.

We were discussing tall tales in preparation for a writing assignment. We went around the room sharing the tales I had given as a preparatory reading assignment: Paul Bunyan, Captain Stormalong, Pecos Bill, and Joe Magarac.

About halfway through the sharing, Amy noted, "You know, there aren't any tall tales about women."

Kevin piped up, "Have you ever heard about the time Grandma made the Great Lakes?" There was a glint in his eye that I read as a stalling tactic. I knew he hadn't read the assignment and was trying to throw me off the track by spinning some story.

And spin he did.

"Many years ago, where the Great Lakes are now, there was an open prairie. Grandma came along, saw this prairie, and decided to make her garden there. She reached inside her leather pouch and took out the five seeds: the long green bean seed, the fat pumpkin seed, the flat squash seed, the hard maize seed, and the round eye of a potato. Then she took her hoe and began to dig the right hole for each seed: A long skinny hole for the green bean, a fat hole for the pumpkin, a flat hole for the squash, a hole in granite for the hard corn seed, and a potato-shaped hole for the potato. It only took her one day to dig the five holes. She took all the dirt she dug and threw it to the east where she made mountains. Then, just as she got ready to drop in the seeds, along came this huge thunder storm. It rained and rained for more days than Grandma could count (although she could count as high as she wanted to, she just didn't want to). She stayed under her hoe to keep dry. Well, finally it stopped raining and Grandma looked out. The five holes she had dug were filled to the brim with water. And that's how Grandma made the five Great Lakes."

An appreciative silence followed Kevin's story. I was just as amazed as the kids were at what Kevin had told us. I didn't dare ask if he made it all up, but Amy did.

"Is that a story the Menominees tell?"

Kevin shook his head. "I just made it up," he beamed.

"Do you know any other Grandma tales?" Brent called out.

"I could tell you about the time Grandma made the Earth from an old basketball," Kevin said.

I was just going to say "Go ahead" when the bell rang. This was the kind of class I hated to see end. We might never capture the same moment again.

The kids hopped up and left. I heard the group around Kevin asking, "Did Grandma make the Atlantic Ocean?"

"Oh, sure, but it took her a little longer than to make the Pacific because the ground is harder there."

Soon they drifted out of my hearing range. I sat at my desk pondering what had just happened and wondering how I could turn it to Kevin's advantage. The following day, I asked him if he told stories at home.

"Oh, sure. We tell stories all of the time. My aunt says that telling stories to the whole family is much better than reading."

"Why?"

"She says because when you tell a story, everyone gets to be part of it. But when you read a story, only one person hears it."

"How would you like to tape-record your stories so that you could share them at school and at home too?"

He jumped at the chance and for the rest of the year he tape-recorded stories and then wrote them with the help of a friend.

At the end of the semester, when Kevin got a *B* in English, I laughed thinking, "Grandma helped Kevin pass English. Now that's a real tall tale!"

▪ ▪

CULTURES AND VALUES

Not all of the students in your classroom will come from the same cultural background. There will be religious, economic, and ethnic differences that account for different **values,** which are beliefs and attitudes that define norms of appropriate behavior. The parenting (or child-rearing) practice of your students' families will vary. Cognitively, socially, and morally, your students will have been influenced by their cultural backgrounds.

Western nations, such as the United States and Canada, are multicultural societies; they comprise a shared national culture and many subcultures. The larger shared culture is called the **macroculture,** representing the core values of a society. Because public schools are a product of the macroculture, schools tend to emphasize core values. The smaller subcultures are called microcultures (Banks, 1989), which share many, but not all of the core values (see Figure 4-3). **Microcultures** comprise groups of people who share a set of

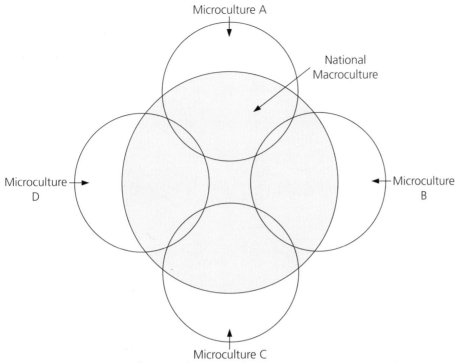

Microculture A

National
Macroculture

Microculture
D

Microculture
B

Microculture C

■ **Figure 4–3** *Macroculture and Microcultures*

SOURCE: From *Multicultural Education: Issues and Perspectives* (p. 11) by J. A. Banks and C. A. McGee Banks, 1989, Needham Heights, MA: Allyn & Bacon. Copyright 1989 by Allyn & Bacon. Reprinted by permission.

multicultural education
Educational goals and methods that increase students' understanding of cultural diversity.

Transparency: This figure is duplicated in the acetate transparency package. See T-5 Macroculture and Microcultures.

values, knowledge, skills, symbols, and perspectives. (As we will see in the final section of this chapter, people who are in some ways exceptional form a microculture.) **Multicultural education** is an effort to increase educational equity for students whose values, skills, perspectives, and so on have been formed outside the mainstream macroculture.

For teachers, the term *cultural differences* is best understood as differences between the macroculture of the school and the microcultures of students in their classrooms. How are cultural differences represented in a classroom?

The most obvious microcultural differences a teacher sees are those of skin color, facial features, dialects (see Chapter 2), and other "surface clues." Microcultures are not defined by ethnicity alone, however. Some religious groups, made up of people from a variety of ethnic backgrounds, also define a microculture. People from similar economic backgrounds, regardless of ethnic heritage, often share a set of values.

Cultural differences are represented in the values students bring to the classroom. In Figure 4-4, we see that an individual can be a member of many different microcultural groups. For example, a student may have certain values because he or she is deaf, other values because he or she is a member of a Unitarian church, still others because everyone in his or her family must work to pay the bills. Thus, one student brings into a classroom values that represent several microcultures.

It is more difficult to observe differences in values than differences in ethnicity; but understanding differences in values is critical to a teacher's

Journal Entry: Have students reflect on their experiences of how cultural differences influence, positively or negatively, educational equity.

Teaching Anecdote: Tell the story of the student whose parents would not allow him to exchange valentine cards at school. His teacher, not wanting him to feel left out, devised a unit that included Valentine's Day letters, but revolved around the workings of a post office. Activities such as making stamps and mailing and delivering letters kept him involved, but did not require that he exchange valentines. Note how the teacher respected the parents' wishes without disrupting a traditional activity.

Lecture Note: Have students identify specific values that are shared by people from different ethnic groups.

Teacher Interview: Have each student interview a teacher regarding the teacher's knowledge of his or her students' values and skills, observing the teacher's effectiveness in the classroom.

Transparency: This figure is duplicated in the acetate transparency package. See T-6 The Individual and Microcultures.

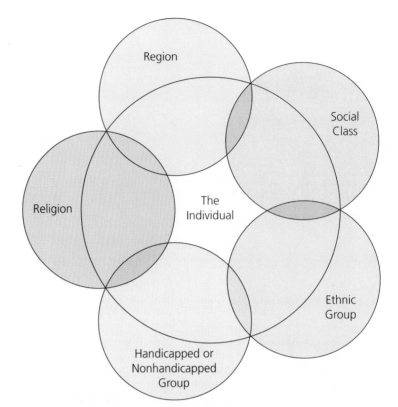

■ **Figure 4–4** *The Individual and Microcultures*

SOURCE: From *Multiethnic Education: Theory and Practice* (2nd ed., p. 79) by J. A. Banks, 1988, Needham Heights, MA: Allyn & Bacon. Copyright 1988 by Allyn & Bacon. Reprinted by permission.

success. Knowing the values and skills a student possesses tells a teacher much more about how that student is likely to learn, make friends, interpret social messages, and approach school work than knowing that student's ethnicity. Much research has been done on cultural differences; that which is the most useful for teachers investigates conflicts between values.

Achievement-related Value Conflicts

Journal Entry: Have each student reflect on whether his or her upbringing engendered the values of individualism or groupism.

Chapter 15 Casebook Preview: See Bringing the Real World into the Classroom.

Connection: Teacher Chronicle 4.2: Grandma Tales.

One of the most dominant core (macroculture) values in the United States is **individualism** (Banks, 1989), the idea that success is gained through the hard work and ingenuity of the individual. In Asian countries, one of the most dominant core values is **groupism,** the idea that the welfare of the group is more important than that of the individual (Butterfield, 1982; Reischauer, 1981). For example, it is common practice for families in the United States to expect their elderly relatives to live independently or in senior citizen homes. Such a practice is viewed with much disdain in Asian countries (and in other macrocultures or U.S. microcultures that value groupism).

Schools in the United States stress individual achievement over achievement of the group. The help provided by one student to another is usually viewed as a form of remediation. True cooperative learning, evaluating stu-

A primary goal of multicultural education is to increase equity for all students. Teachers must realize that achieving this goal involves their recognition of the microcultures that constitute the macroculture of the school.

dents' work on a cooperative product, is rare. When students with group-centered values encounter the individualism of school, problems can arise. As you recall, in Teacher Chronicle 4.2, Kevin's microculture valued storytelling because it brought the family together. Story writing was perceived as an individual activity.

Students from the lower economic classes are more likely to have had experiences that caused them to rely on family and friends. Likewise, they are more likely to have been called on to help keep the family running smoothly, for instance, by caring for younger siblings. Reliance on and support for the group is important in this microculture; cooperation is necessary. Children from lower-class families tend to value the group and to be less competitive than children from middle-class families (cf. Pepitone, 1985). Middle-class children tend to value individualism; they learn best when in competition with others (Kagan et al., 1985; Wheeler, 1977).

The important point here is not the comparison of economic classes, but the mismatch that occurs when the school's emphasis on individualism and some children's group orientation clash (cf. Boykin, 1986). One way a teacher can reduce the conflict of individualism and groupism is to stress cooperative learning from time to time. This technique gives group-oriented students school experiences that are more compatible with their backgrounds. (Cooperative learning techniques are discussed in Chapter 11.)

Another source of value conflict is time orientation. Schools, by nature, reward performance after some period of time has passed, whether it be the end of a class period, a day, a week, or the end of the year. Slavin (1988) argues that students raised in middle-class homes are more likely to have had experiences that prepare them for the delayed gratification pattern they are

Connection: See the discussion of cooperative learning in Chapter 11.

Lecture Note: Ask students if anyone has traveled to a foreign country and experienced a sense of punctuality different from their own.

Field Observation/Teacher Interview: Have students observe other students in a classroom or interview a teacher regarding his or her use of student-selected activities.

likely to encounter in school. Students who are less oriented toward the future may require greater assistance in managing their own time, especially on class assignments or projects that extend over a period of at least a week.

Some microcultures value what can be called *expressive affect* (cf. Boykin, 1983). Following Boykin, expressive affect implies an integration of feeling, thinking, and action in a way that makes it difficult for learners to engage in an activity they do not feel is interesting or challenging. Students who hold this value have learned that it is important to pursue their own interests, to make their own decisions about what is worth doing and what isn't. Such students may find themselves in conflict with a teacher who provides no options for students to complete assigned tasks. For the teacher's part, this value may be interpreted as a "lack of respect" for the teacher's authority. To avoid this conflict, Boykin suggests that students be given as many opportunities as possible to select their own learning activities. Providing an opportunity to choose from among a variety of activities each day allows students to put their personal "stamps of approval" on learning activities.

As implied by this discussion, values influence a student's motivation. Is motivation solely the student's responsibility? the teacher's responsibility? Differences in how motivation is valued by different microcultures were investigated by comparing Chinese, Chinese-American, and Caucasian-American mothers' beliefs concerning their children's math performances (Hess, Chih-Mei, & McDevitt, 1987). Chinese mothers were more likely to attribute failure to a lack of effort than Chinese-American mothers who were, in turn, more likely to cite lack of effort than were Caucasian-American mothers. The differences are consistent with cultural values placed on effort and talent. Talent is valued highly in most Western macrocultures. Chinese people value effort more highly than talent. The results of this study are explained by a Chinese proverb cited by Hess et al. (1987, p. 180): "Will is the teacher of study and talent is the follower of study. If a person has no talent, it is possible. But if a person has no will, it is not worth talking about study."

Communication-related Value Conflicts

Field Observation: Have students observe nonverbal communication in or out of classrooms to see if microcultural differences exist.

The values learned from one's upbringing are lessons for living. They include not only the way one should approach achievement-related tasks, but how one should communicate, verbally and nonverbally, with others. In Hispanic culture, for example, encouragement is communicated through close proximity, occasional touching, and smiling (Triandis, 1986). A teacher who expects Asian students to make direct eye contact may make these students uncomfortable (cf. Yao, 1988). A student raised in an Arab microculture may stand so close to an American teacher that the teacher feels uncomfortable (cf. Hall, 1966). Everyone expects social interactions to occur according to "lessons" each person has learned. When there are differences in the lessons that the student and the teacher have learned, the teacher is likely to lower his or her judgment of the student's ability.

Lecture Note: Have students consider if cultural differences in communication can best be understood as "non-shared contexts" (see the discussion of Bernstein's restricted codes in Chapter 2).

Consider the findings of a study that compared the interactions of school counselors with students who were culturally similar or dissimilar (Erickson & Schultz, 1982). In conversation, the culturally dissimilar students did not acknowledge the individual counselor's comments; the culturally similar students did. The acknowledgment difference was due to differences in values; the culturally dissimilar students did not want to interrupt the counselor. The counselors interpreted the lack of acknowledgment as a lack of understanding. Counselors repeated their messages several times, simplifying them each time. After the conversations, the counselors judged the culturally dissimilar students as less bright than students who were culturally similar to themselves. The culturally dissimilar students reported that the counselors made them feel stupid. Neither the students nor the counselors seemed to understand the subtle cultural differences that affected their judgments of each other.

If cultural differences can lead to judgments of low ability, the instruction received by students whose cultural values are not shared by the teacher may suffer. Chun (1987–1988) reports a difference in the quality of instruction offered to low-performing students when compared with high-performing students. Teachers had lower expectations for those in the low-performing groups. When questioning low-performing students, teachers tended to wait a shorter time for answers than they did when they questioned high-performing students. Low-performing students received greater criticism and less attention. Chun also reports that teachers more often failed to provide proper feedback to low-performing students. Chun concludes that low-performing students fail because teachers expect them to and because effective means for helping students identified as low performers are lacking.

Where do students learn cultural values? The family is a critical source of "value lessons." We conclude our discussion of cultural differences by looking at parenting practices.

Parenting Styles

Clark (1983) provides further evidence that a student's values are more important as cultural differences than is ethnicity. He examined the differences in family life between African-American children who succeed in school and those who fail. Clark lived with the families in order to study their interactions, aspirations, expectations, and values. Clark concluded that parents' behaviors, including the environment that they provide, their direct interaction and involvement with their children and their children's schools, and their expectations of and aspirations for their children, determined the degree of success the children achieved.

High-achieving children tended to come from homes where parents were frequently in contact with the schools; were emotionally calm with the children, providing firm, consistent monitoring and enforcement of rules; and deferred to their children's knowledge in intellectual matters. Low-achieving students tended to come from homes where parents were in emotional conflict with their children; had less explicit achievement-centered rules and norms; were less liberal with nurturance and support; and did not defer to the children in intellectual matters. These were not the only differences that the families of high- and low-achieving students exhibited, but these differences do suggest different sets of values.

Another researcher, Diana Baumrind, has studied parenting styles extensively (1967, 1973). Baumrind identifies three styles parents use in providing discipline for their children. Parents using the first style identified by Baumrind, the **authoritative style,** are firm, demanding, and controlling in developmentally appropriate ways. They are loving, responsive, involved, communicative, and consistent in disciplining their children. Authoritative

authoritative style Parenting style that mixes firm guidance with love and respect.

Teaching Anecdote: Tell the story of two teachers discussing a child who had become a discipline problem. The first teacher complained, "She just doesn't seem to want to cooperate. She's always talking and refuses to do assignments in class."

"I know," the second teacher said. "When she is near her friends, you might as well forget teaching her."

Just then, the student walked by. The teachers stopped talking as she passed. When she rounded the corner, the second teacher asked, "Do you think we're too harsh because she doesn't speak English very well?"

Ask your students if they have ever had to "overcome" negative first impressions they've formed of people who were somehow different from themselves.

Journal Entry: Have students reflect on the parenting styles they experienced growing up and the amount and nature of the care-giver contact they had with their teachers.

authoritarian style
Parenting style through which parents strictly enforce their authority over their children and tend to be unresponsive to their children's needs and interests.

permissive-indulgent style
Parenting style where parents do not exhibit much control over their children's behavior.

Parenting styles can have a profound impact on a child's academic success. Children whose parents use the authoritative style of discipline tend to be high achievers.

parents possess a willingness to listen and respond to their children's needs and interests. (Note that authoritative parents and the parents of high-achieving students in Clark's study share similar characteristics.)

The second parenting style Baumrind identifies is the **authoritarian style;** the parents are controlling, but in less appropriate ways; they tend to be rejecting; unresponsive to their children's needs and interests; less involved in their activities; and more adult centered than child centered. The children of authoritarian parents tend as a group to be more withdrawn and to experience greater difficulty in trusting others. They are also more likely to be low achievers in school. (Again, note the similarity of characteristics between these parents and those of low-achieving students in Clark's study.)

The third type of parenting style identified by Baumrind, the **permissive-indulgent style,** involves parents who are undemanding, but warm and loving; do not exhibit much control over their children's behavior; and tend to use little discipline and do not establish rules of conduct. When questioned about their own parenting abilities, permissive-indulgent parents express doubts. As a consequence, their attempts at discipline tend to be infrequent

Lecture Note: In addition to the conclusion they draw from Clark's study of African-American families, have students note that parenting styles—and the values that these styles engender—are more important than ethnicity.

and inconsistent. The children of permissive-indulgent parents tend to exhibit little self-reliance and to exhibit low levels of achievement in school, especially among the male children.

The behaviors of students, of teachers, and of parents reflect cultural values. A conflict of values, like the mismatch between learning and teaching styles, is another place where teachers may find an explanation of poor student performance.

Principles in Practice 4.2

Principles . . .
1. Cultural differences are reflected in differences in values.
2. A student's values provide guidelines for behavior.
3. Differences between the values held by a teacher and those of a student can create instructional problems.

. . . in Practice
Kevin, in Teacher Chronicle 4.2, had difficulties with writing assignments. His difficulties were puzzling to the teacher because Kevin was a very creative storyteller. The problem stemmed from a conflict of values so subtle that it took the teacher quite some time to understand Kevin's hesitancy to work on writing assignments. Once the teacher understood how much value Kevin's family placed on storytelling, and how little value was placed on writing, the teacher was able to adapt writing exercises to better fit Kevin's cultural background.

1. In what other instructional situations might the teacher need to account for Kevin's cultural background?
2. What should be the thrust of the teacher's message to Kevin's parents at the next parent–teacher conference?
3. How might a teacher find out about the communication values in order to enhance students' participation in classroom interactions?

LOST AND FOUND

We were working on reading color-coded maps. I had just finished explaining how to identify areas on a cross-section map of a mining area when I saw the look on Nick's face. Reading Nick's face was like reading one of the maps; he had taken a wrong turn and was lost. I knew I had to steer him back on the right track. But first we had to find where he made the wrong turn. It meant backtracking with him.

While the other students worked on a map assignment using the color codes, I pulled up a chair and sat beside Nick.

Teacher
Chronicle
4.3

exceptional students
Students with mental,
emotional, or physical
conditions that create special
educational needs.

"Feeling sort of lost?" I asked.

"Yeah," he said, grinning as he caught the joke. "I just don't see what you mean about the key and the colors."

"Let's look at the key first," I suggested. "What does it say here?" I asked, pointing to the word beside the dark brown key.

"That's coal."

"And this?" pointing to a medium brown key.

"That's oil. That's water," he said touching the light brown key. "And that's just rock," pointing to the reddish-brown key. "There's gold." This was the yellowish-brown key.

"Great," I said. "Now let's trace the outlines of the areas on the map." He carefully outlined one section with his finger.

"Is that coal or oil or what?" I asked.

"Coal?" I could hear the question in his voice.

"Right. Now outline this one and tell me what it is."

He traced the lens-shaped pool of underground water.

"Oil?"

"No. How can you tell what it is?"

He glanced at the key. "By looking at the key."

"Right," I said, taking his fingers and placing one on the water symbol and one on the pool of water. "See the connection?"

"Yes, I guess. That's water?"

"Good, you've got it now," I told him, thinking that he was on the right track now. I should have listened more closely to the question marks at the end of his answers.

I went around spot-checking other students, answering questions, helping here and there. Soon Nick was at my side, a look of intense frustration on his face.

"Still stuck?" I asked.

He nodded.

"I'll be there in a minute," I said. It was more than ten minutes before I could get back to him and by then he was almost in tears. He had clearly reached his frustration limit. I decided to call it quits for the day. So had he.

"Can I take it home and work with my mom?" he asked.

"Great idea," I said. "Then we can talk about it tomorrow."

When Nick came in the next day, he had a grin he could have tripped over. His work was complete and accurate.

"How did you do it?" I asked.

"I told my mom what letter each color started with and then we wrote the letters on the key. Then I wrote them on the map. Then I could read it. And guess what, I'm color blind."

How could I have missed that?

■ ■

Chap. Obj. 5
Test Ques. 4.70–4.99

Focus Questions: How is a disability distinguished from a handicap? What is exceptionality in general and what forms does it take in students?

EXCEPTIONAL STUDENTS

Exceptional students, who are impaired by mental retardation, learning disabilities, emotional/behavioral disorders, communication disorders, hearing loss, visual impairment, physical disabilities, or giftedness, require special instruction and services to reach their full potential (Hallahan & Kauffman, 1991). Recent figures indicate that 10 percent of school-age children are handicapped to such an extent that they need special instruction or services. An additional 3 percent to 5 percent require special attention as a result of giftedness (U.S. Department of Education, 1989).

Formal recognition of the special needs of exceptional students came in the form of legislation passed by the U.S. Congress in 1975. **Public Law 94-142** is the "Education for All Handicapped Children Act." A key phrase in the legislation refers to a **least restrictive environment,** an instructional environment that is as similar to the regular classroom as possible. It is from PL 94-142 that the practice of **mainstreaming,** the inclusion of students with special needs in regular classroom instruction, began. Mainstreaming is one way to meet the requirements of the least restrictive environment. PL 94-142 also requires that instruction be designed to meet the needs of each exceptional student. The plan for instructing an exceptional student is called an **individualized education program (IEP).** (The instructional implications of PL 94-142 will be examined in greater detail in Chapter 11. Our purpose in this section is to examine the characteristics that are shared by students who are exceptional.)

Most types of exceptionality stem from a disability. The terms *disability* and *handicap* are often used interchangeably, not only in everyday language, but in the more formal language of legislation as well. Even so, the terms are distinctive, and the distinction is an important one for teachers to understand. "A **disability** is an inability to do something, a diminished capacity to perform in a specific way. A **handicap,** on the other hand, is a disadvantage imposed on an individual. A disability may or may not be a handicap, depending on the circumstances" (Hallahan & Kauffman, 1991, p. 6, boldface added). Nick, in Teacher Chronicle 4.3, had a visual disability; he was unable to discriminate colors. The map assignment handicapped him because it required him to do something he was incapable of doing. Once the map was labeled with letters, he no longer had to rely on the map's colors and the handicap disappeared.

In your classroom, you will encounter students who are disabled in some way. As you read about the disabilities in the text that follows, keep in mind that they may or may not be handicaps, depending on the requirements you impose in your classroom. Keep in mind also that you can't always judge an exceptional student by his or her disability.

Stephen W. Hawking is arguably one of the most creative and productive individuals of the twentieth century. Hawking is the Lucasian Professor of Mathematics at Cambridge University, a post once held by Sir Issac Newton. Hawking suffers from amyotrophic lateral sclerosis (a.k.a. ALS or Lou Gehrig's disease), a disease that attacks the central nervous system. For several years, only one of Hawking's students was able to understand his speech and served as translator. In 1985, after Hawking caught pneumonia, he had an operation that eliminated entirely his ability to speak. He now uses a communications program and a speech synthesizer with a small personal computer mounted on his wheelchair to communicate. He is cared for by a team of nurses. As you will see, Hawking may not fit well into the characteristics of the group to which the label "gifted and talented" is applied, but he is without question an individual possessed of extraordinary gifts and talents.

Teaching Anecdote: Tell the story of John, a high school student with multiple sclerosis who is confined to a wheelchair. His science teacher planned a snowshoeing field trip at a local nature center. A special van transported John to the nature center. John was placed on a sled and pulled by several friends who took turns.

Does this approach to the activity meet the least restrictive environment clause of PL 94-142?

Connection: Instructional tactics pertinent to teaching exceptional students are discussed in Chapter 11.

Connection: Teacher Chronicle 4.3: Lost and Found.

Lecture Note: The preface of Hawking's book, *A Brief History of Time*, discusses how Hawking has adapted to some of his disabilities so that they are not handicaps. (Recommend the book as a helpful resource for those teaching secondary science.)

mental retardation
Significantly subaverage intellectual functioning, usually present at birth, resulting in or associated with impairments in adaptive behavior and manifested during the developmental period.

learning disabilities
Disorders in cognitive processing that impede the learning of people who are not mentally retarded or emotionally disturbed.

Field Observation: Have students observe teachers in living skills programs for mentally retarded adults or visit community living arrangements.

Connection: See Sternberg's triarchic theory of intelligence earlier in this chapter.

Lecture Note: Note the dangers of stereotyping through the use of labels. Derogatory terms such as *imbecile*, *moron*, and *idiot* were once clinical classifications.

Mental Retardation

The AAMR (American Association on Mental Retardation) provides the most widely accepted definition of mental retardation. "**Mental retardation** refers to significantly subaverage intellectual functioning resulting in or associated with impairments in adaptive behavior and manifested during the developmental period" (Grossman, 1983, p. 11, boldface added). At one time, mental retardation was determined solely on the basis of scores on intelligence tests. The AAMR definition includes an additional criterion, adaptive behavior.

Adaptive behavior refers to a variety of skills—sensory motor, communication, self-help, learning, socialization, living, and vocational skills, among them. Adaptive skills change as children develop. Sensory motor, communication, self-help, and socialization skills are important in early childhood. Adaptive behavior in middle childhood and early adolescence requires skills for learning and for interpersonal interaction. Late adolescence and adulthood requires living and vocational skills.

A junior high student may perform very poorly on intelligence tests and on school tasks, but be able to cope with the requirements of public transportation, a paper route, and peer relations. According to the AAMR definition, the student does not qualify as mentally retarded; his or her adaptive behavior is not significantly impaired. In terms of Sternberg's triarchic theory of intelligence, this student exhibits low componential intelligence, but high, or at least adequate, contextual intelligence.

Mental retardation is not an all-or-none phenomenon. The AAMR system of classification lists four levels of mental retardation: mild, moderate, severe, and profound.

Instruction for mildly (sometimes called educable) and moderately (sometimes called trainable) retarded students focuses on developing readiness skills in the early elementary grades. Readiness skills include sitting still, following directions, discriminating sounds and visual stimuli, self-help (for example, dressing, using the restroom), and working cooperatively with peers. Instruction in later elementary grades addresses "functional academics." Mildly and moderately retarded students are taught to read ads in the newspaper, the telephone book, labels at the supermarket rather than social studies or fiction. The purpose of such a reading program is to allow them to function independently. Junior high and high school instruction encourages the development of community living and vocational skills (Epstein, Polloway, Patton, & Foley, 1989).

The major instructional goal for severely and profoundly retarded students is independent behavior. Practical skills, such as eating, dressing, and personal hygiene, are emphasized. In order to live as independently as possible, instruction is based in the community rather than in the classroom whenever possible. Simulated grocery shopping in the classroom may be used to prepare for a trip to the store, but severely and profoundly retarded students need instruction in the actual setting where they may one day function independently.

Learning Disabilities

Learning disabilities is a generic term referring to a disorder in cognitive processing. It emerged as a field of study for educational researchers in the early 1960s. Since that time, eleven different definitions of learning disabili-

Under Public Law 94-142, teachers are required to provide exceptional students with the least restrictive environment and an individualized education program that will bring out personal aptitudes and talents.

ties have, at one time or another, been embraced by a significant number of researchers (Hammill, 1990). At present, the most popular definition is the one endorsed by the U.S. government:

> "Specific learning disability" means a disorder in one or more of the basic psychological processes involved in understanding or in using language, spoken or written, which may manifest itself in an imperfect ability to listen, think, speak, read, write, spell, or do mathematical calculations. The term includes such conditions as perceptual handicaps, brain injury, minimal brain dysfunction, dyslexia, and developmental aphasia. The term does not include children who have learning problems which are primarily the result of visual, hearing, or motor handicaps, of mental retardation, of emotional disturbance, or of environmental, cultural, or economic disadvantage (*Federal Register,* 1977, p. 65083)

Nearly half of all handicapped children are identified as learning disabled (U.S. Department of Education, 1989), making it important that teachers know the "official" definition of the term. It is even more important for teachers to know what learning disabled students are like, how they see themselves, and how they understand their disabilities. What follows is an excerpt from a remarkable book (the cover of which is shown in Figure 4-5). Notice who the book's authors are. Pam Maniet-Bellermann (nee Maniet) is a learning disabilities teacher. One of her classes wanted to give students just entering an LD program the benefit of its own experience and put together a book documenting that experience.*

Connection: The basic psychological processes referred to in the definition are cognitive processes, which will be examined as part of the information-processing view of learning in Chapter 6.

"L.D." Does NOT Mean Learning Dumd! is available from Upward Bound Press, 29 Jefferson Avenue, Bayville, NY 11709. A guide for parents and teachers that accompanies the book is also available. Text excerpted by permission of the publisher.

Lecture Note: Have students discuss how they might use *"L.D." Does NOT Mean Learning Dumd!* to build social understanding in their classrooms.

■ **Figure 4–5** *Cover of "L.D." Does NOT Mean Learning Dumd!*

SOURCE: *"L.D." Does NOT Mean Learning Dumd!* by Miss Maniet's Class, 1985, Bayville, NY: Upward Bound Press. Copyright 1985 by Upward Bound Press. Reprinted by permission.

What IS a Learning Disability?

A person with a "disability" has difficulty doing things that most people can do easily. A person with a "visual" disability may not be able to see well or at all. A person who has a "hearing" disability may be deaf or able to hear only a few sounds. "Physically" disabled people may have trouble using their arms, legs, and other parts of their body. The "learning" disabled person has difficulty with learning. "Mentally" disabled or retarded people also have trouble with learning but having a learning disability is not the same as being retarded. Sometimes people have called us retarded or dumb and that makes us feel bad because we know they just don't understand us! AND when we have so much trouble learning something, we get mad at ourselves and begin to feel like we ARE dumb! Miss Maniet has to remind us many, many times that we are not dumb. We've needed alot of convincing!!

She explains it like this. . . . Every person has what is called an IQ. IQ tells how intelligent or smart a person is. Some people are smarter and some aren't as smart. Most people fall right in the middle. They have "average" intelligence. People who are smarter have above average intelligence. People who are retarded have below average intelligence. Most learning disabled people have average or above average intelligence!

You're probably wondering . . . IF A PERSON WITH A L.D. PROBLEM HAS AVERAGE OR ABOVE AVERAGE INTELLIGENCE, THEN WHY DO THEY HAVE TROUBLE LEARNING????

Our brain has to control every part of our body. One part controls your eyes, another controls your legs, another tells your heart to beat, and so on. The brain sends messages to each part telling it what to do. Just to write your name many parts of the brain have to work at the same time. Sometimes when the brain sends messages, these messages get jumbled or confused and give the wrong message and that part doesn't know what it is to do.

When you are trying to learn something and the messages keep getting stuck or confused then you have a problem or a learning disability.

So even though you know your name and how to spell it, you may not remember how to write the letters that make up your name. Another thing—L.D. people can see and hear just as well as most people but WHAT they see or hear may not be the same as you or everyone else.

If that sounds confusing, you're right—it is!! That's what makes learning disabilities so hard to understand. To help you understand we have many examples of what we mean coming up in the [text that follows].

Lecture Note: Have students compare the L.D. students' view of intelligence with the theories of intelligence examined earlier in this chapter.

More About Learning Disabilities

Most people experience a "temporary" disability at one time or another, like a broken leg, finger, or arm. Or maybe you've had an eye patched so you couldn't see or have had drops put in your ears so you couldn't hear well. People who aren't L.D. sometimes have difficulties that L.D. people experience all the time.

For example—did you ever go crazy trying to remember someone's name, an address, or even your own phone number? Think of how frustrated you've become trying to put something together following directions that are confusing!!!! These times can make you angry and upset with yourself. These are experiences that L.D. people may have trouble with everyday! That's what makes L.D. people different from other people. We have many problems like these most of the time rather than sometimes!

Difficulties That L.D. People Might Have

Even though our vision is usually normal, sometimes our mind "sees" something different from what our eyes see. Some examples: We might see "but" instead of "put," "mose" instead of "nose," "6" becomes "9."

We may read and write words backwards or upside down: "was" becomes "saw," "107" becomes "701," "spot" becomes "pots," "sung" becomes "snug."

SOMETIMESALLTHELETTERSAREJUMBLEDTOGETHER.
or
THEW ORD SARE NOTSP ACED COR RECT LY.
Sometimes it's hard ^{to} Writ^e ^{o}n the $_{Lines.}$

Copying words and designs and cutting with scissors are hard when your fingers don't do what you want them to. Coloring within the lines is hard too!

We spell wrds xatle az tha snd to us! "Girl" becomes "gril," "house" becomes "howc." We like to add extra letters when we spell or leave out the letters we don't hear.

Our hearing is usually normal but sometimes we don't hear the endings or beginnings of words, or we hear a different word altogether! Instead of "Go to bed" we hear "the goat is read," "but" - "bat" - "bet" - "bit" all sound the same to us.

or

We hear too much!! Even soft sounds can seem loud to us and make it hard to concentrate. Hearing a clock ticking or water dripping can keep us from being able to finish our math. Or we hear everybody but the person who is talking to us.

We often have a hard time paying attention because noises and movements distract us. People think we are not paying attention when we don't follow directions. Actually we are paying attention too much!!

We get directions confused easily and become lost even in places we know. We forget what's "left" and "right," "up" and "down," "under" and "over."

Changes in our routine can also confuse us. This confusion can blow our whole day!

Sometimes we say and do things without thinking first. We often move too quickly and end up running into furniture or people!!

A lot of times we have difficulty sitting on our chairs. We feel like we need to jump and move around even when it's time to sit still. Our mind just keeps jumping and our body wants to too!

One day we know something, the next day we forget it. Remembering things like the days of the week, spelling words, or math facts are hard for us. But, some days we remember very well.

At times we know what we want to say but just can't get it out. It's that way when we write. Our mind and our hands just don't cooperate! Our mind thinks "animal" but our mouth says "maminal."

Sometimes we can do a math problem in our head, but, when we have to write it, we can't! We can add and multiply, but not subtract or divide.

Emotional/Behavioral Disorders

Emotional/behavioral disorder (E/BD) is a handicapping condition that has proven difficult to define in a way that has been widely accepted. Despite the lack of a generally accepted formal definition, E/BD students are easily noticed in a classroom (Hallahan & Kauffman, 1991). Through advanced statistical analyses, researchers have identified patterns or dimensions of disordered behavior (e.g., Achenbach, 1985; Quay, 1986; Quay & Peterson, 1987).

One broad category of disordered behavior is **externalizing;** that is, acting out against others. Acting out in the form of classroom disruption, showing off, fights, and/or temper tantrums, is a particular kind of externalizing, called *conduct disorder.* Experienced teachers recognize that these behaviors occur in normal students as well as in E/BD students, the difference being that E/BD students cry, scream, and fight much more impulsively and with much greater frequency. Acting out that occurs in the company of others is called *socialized aggression.* The aggressive, illegal, and disrespectful behavior of gangs is an example.

Another broad category of disordered behavior is **internalizing;** that is, behavior that reflects emotional problems, such as depression or debilitating anxiety. More specific types of internalizing are immature behavior and withdrawn behavior. Students who exhibit immaturity tend to have shorter attention spans, are easily distracted, and answer questions impulsively. Immature students also tend to be physically lethargic. Behaviors symptomatic of withdrawal include embarrassment, self-consciousness, sadness, and anxiety.

Although withdrawn behavior and immature behavior are causes for concern in classrooms, the most serious forms of internalizing behavior are autism and schizophrenia. Autism is a condition characterized by an inability to respond or communicate effectively with other people. Autistic children attach themselves to certain objects or have peculiar interests. Schizophrenic children suffer from delusions or hallucinations. Their thinking is disordered to the point that they may believe that they are under the control of unknown forces or voices. The emotions they display are often inappropriate (Hallahan & Kauffman, 1991).

Communication Disorders

Communication disorders fall into two major categories: speech disorders and language disorders (American Speech-Language-Hearing Association, 1982).

A speech disorder is a voice problem. Sounds are sometimes omitted, substituted, added, or distorted. Voice quality problems, such as abnormal pitch, loudness, or quality, also fall into the category of speech disorder. A lack of fluency in the flow of verbal expression—stuttering—is another form of speech disorder. Stuttering can begin in childhood and persist into adulthood. However, stuttering is chiefly a childhood disorder. With the help of a speech therapist, most children stop stuttering by the end of adolescence.

Language disorders are problems in using symbol systems to communicate, resulting in difficulty in understanding or generating messages. Language disorders may involve phonological impairment (see Chapter 2); they may also be experienced by students who use a nonvocal system of symbols such as American Sign Language (ASL). Children who experience commu-

emotional/behavioral disorder (E/BD) A handicapping condition in which people have difficulty controlling their feelings and behavior.
externalizing A type of behavior disorder characterized by acting out against others.
internalizing A type of behavior disorder that reflects emotional problems, such as depression or debilitating anxiety.
communication disorders Speech (voice) and language (symbols) disorders.

Teacher Interview: Have each student interview a teacher regarding the behaviors and attitudes of E/BD students. The student should ask how the teacher approaches his or her interactions with the students and write a definition of E/BD based on the interview.

Lecture Note: Describe autistic savants (e.g., the Dustin Hoffman character in the movie *Rain Man*) as autistic people who have a remarkable mental capability. For example, such individuals play complicated piano pieces from memory after hearing the piece once, do complicated mathematical calculations, and so on.

Lecture Note: Ask if any of your students underwent speech therapy for stuttering when they were children. Ask these students to share their experiences, discussing their therapy and the effect that stuttering had on their social lives.

Connection: See the discussion of language development in Chapter 2.

Lecture Note: Bring someone to your class who knows ASL. Ask the guest to interpret your remarks and then discuss the grammar of ASL to demonstrate that it is a complete language.

hearing impairment A weakness in hearing, ranging from being hard of hearing to being deaf.

visual impairment A weakness in vision, ranging from being able to read print to having to use braille or audiotapes.

nication disorders do not necessarily experience other types of challenges, though it is quite possible that they will experience other types of disorders, including cerebral palsy, mental retardation, and learning disabilities.

As we shall see, other types of disabilities can affect a student's ability to communicate. Communication is basic to social interaction and to our intuitive judgments of a student's general intellectual ability. It is important to remember that although a student's ability to send and receive messages may be impaired, that impairment does not necessarily mean that the student's intellect is also impaired.

Hearing Impairment

There is a continuum of hearing impairment. **Hearing impairment** includes students who, on one end of the continuum, are hard of hearing and, on the other end, are deaf. Students who are hard of hearing can, with the aid of special amplification devices, use their sense of hearing to good advantage. Deaf children must be instructed through other senses. Hearing impairment often results in some type of communication disorder. A student's ability to understand language is often taken intuitively as a sign of intellectual ability. Because a hearing-impaired child may have difficulty speaking or understanding speech, he or she is often assumed to have below average intelligence. Language deficits are not deficits in intellectual ability.

Hearing-impaired students must learn special communication techniques. In addition to auditory training, which helps hearing-impaired students make use of whatever hearing they possess, the techniques include speechreading, fingerspelling, and true sign languages. Speechreading is a more accurate name for what most people call lipreading. Hearing-impaired students use not only visual cues from the speakers' mouths, but cues associated with the message that are not part of oral speech. Fingerspelling (shown in Figure 4-6, p. 160) is different from sign language. Fingerspelling translates spoken English into a form that is conveyed through manual signs.

A true sign language, such as ASL, has its own grammar and, contrary to the opinion of many, can be used to convey abstract ideas (Sacks, 1989). Those who communicate primarily with ASL use fingerspelling only occasionally to communicate words such as proper nouns. The communication techniques used by the hearing-impaired makes it difficult for non-hearing-impaired people to join a conversation among hearing-impaired people, and vice versa. Because communication plays a critical role in social interaction, deaf people socialize with those who share their disability to a greater extent than people in other exceptional categories (Hallahan & Kauffman, 1991).

Visual Impairment

Legal definitions of **visual impairment** specify a person's acuity and field of vision. A legally blind person is one whose acuity is 20/200 or less. (A visually impaired person with 20/200 vision sees at 20 feet what a person with normal vision sees at 200.) Field of vision refers to the width, measured in angles, of a person's peripheral vision.

Educators define visual impairment in terms of the method of reading instruction a visually impaired student requires. A low-vision child is able to read print; a blind child must use braille or audiotapes. Low-vision students

Lecture Note: Stress the extent to which judgments of intellectual ability are based on use of language. Ask students to recall their impressions of people that were sometimes based on very brief samples of speech.

Lecture Note: Have students carry out a simple conversation using fingerspelling. Have them start with, "Where are you going after class?" Allow them five minutes to carry on the conversations and then have them share their feelings about the experience.

Field Observation: Have each student interview a blind person about his or her learning experiences while growing up.

Issues in Educational Psychology

CNN™ This box relates to Segment 4 of the CNN videotape. See the Instructor's Section for a summary.

GALLAUDET UNIVERSITY

In March 1988, Elizabeth A. Zinser became the flash point for student anger at Gallaudet University in Washington, D.C. Dedicated to educating the deaf, Gallaudet had never had a deaf person as its president. Two of the three candidates the board of trustees had considered that winter were deaf. Zinser was not. To the students, Zinser's appointment as president represented the will of the hearing majority. They felt cheated. They wanted a role model. "Deaf President Now" became their battle slogan.

The students blocked the university's gates. They boycotted classes. They won the support of faculty as well as presidential aspirants George Bush, Michael Dukakis, and Jesse Jackson. But the board of trustees remained adamant. So did the students. Jackson summed up their stand-off. "The problem is not that the students do not hear. The problem is that the hearing world does not listen," he said.

The fight over who would be the university president was symbolic of a centuries-old struggle. It wasn't until the 1700s that a French priest matched sign language with the written word. At Gallaudet, signing had been forbidden for decades. In the 1960s, scholars finally acknowledged signing as a language with its own syntax and grammar.

After a week of protests, the students won. Irving King Jordan, one of the two original deaf candidates and the dean of Gallaudet's College of Arts and Sciences, was selected as president.

Rolling Stone magazine documented those hectic days and their aftermath, including Jordan's inauguration the following October. In the article Jordan described his fear that supporting the students might have meant his termination as dean. He ultimately recognized that the students' actions were more than a protest: they were "a revolution, a move towards social change." Jordan characterized the events that led to his selection "as a dynamic shift in consciousness. The world, and deaf people themselves, think about deafness differently than they did before."

John Limnidis, a sophomore and member of the Gallaudet football team, expressed his frustrations as a deaf person in the same article. "I want to be equal. Why do deaf people have to be treated lower than hearing people? Deafness is not a handicap. It's a culture, a language."

Limnidis is not alone. Jerry Covell, who was also interviewed, spoke while a candidate for homecoming king that fall. He exhorted fellow students to keep the spirit of their protest alive. "Last spring we revolted, and the world listened! For the first time in their lives, people across the world saw we could talk and argue. . . . Friends, we mustn't let the revolution end here."

The revolution did spread beyond Gallaudet. In an interview with the *Chronicle of Higher Education,* Jordan stressed the positive impact the controversy had on children in schools for the deaf around the country. He noted that their "self-concept and expectations of themselves have changed dramatically." Jordan met deaf students who wanted to run for the Congress, and even the presidency.

It is leaders such as Jordan who embody the aspirations of deaf people everywhere, especially students. At his inauguration, he told enthusiastic students that "we showed the world that the only thing deaf people can't do is hear."

SOURCES: Karlen, Neal. "Louder Than Words." *Rolling Stone,* issue 548 (March 23, 1989): 133–140. DeLoughry, Thomas J. "Gallaudet's President Is a Symbol of His Students' Pride." *Chronicle of Higher Education* 35, issue 26 (March 8, 1989): A3. "The Indomitable Word." *Commonweal* 116, issue 22 (December 15, 1989): 691–692.

1. How would Sternberg's triarchic theory of intelligence support Jordan's statement that "we showed the world that the only thing deaf people can't do is hear"?

2. What do the events at Gallaudet University and the advice of the learning disabled students in this chapter suggest about the values and microcultures of these two groups?

physical disabilities
Disorders of the skeleton, joints, and muscles, or health conditions that interfere with students' educational performances.

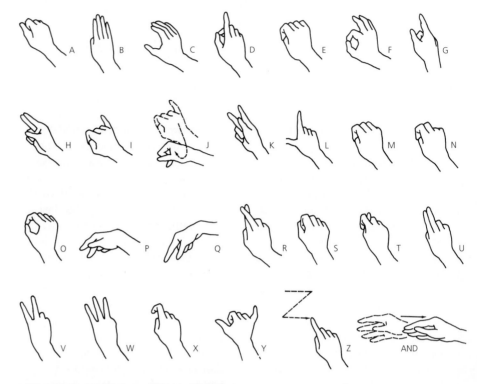

■ **Figure 4–6** *Fingerspelling Alphabet*

SOURCE: *Exceptional Children* (5th ed., p. 284) by D. P. Hallahan and J. M. Kauffman, 1991, Englewood Cliffs, NJ: Prentice Hall. Copyright 1991 by Prentice Hall. Reprinted by permission.

usually use magnification devices or require large print books. Improved technology has made it possible to teach visually impaired students in regular classrooms. (In addition to devices that enlarge viewing material or vocalize printed matter, visually impaired students often require the use of aids, such as guide dogs or sensor devices, to move about.)

Physical Disabilities

Physical disabilities include disorders of the skeleton, joints, and muscles, or health conditions that interfere with students' educational performances. Some physical disabilities, such as cerebral palsy, spina bifida, and epilepsy, are due to neurological impairments. Cerebral palsy is not a disease in the proper sense of the word. It is neither contagious, remissive (relief from symptoms), nor progressive (although poor treatment can cause complications). It is a syndrome that includes motor and/or psychological dysfunctions, seizures, behavior disorders, or any combination of symptoms due to brain damage.

Spina bifida is a failure of the spinal column to properly close during prenatal development. As a result, unprotected nerve fibers in the spinal cord cause paralysis or dysfunction below the point of the defect. Spina bifida leaves children susceptible to infection in the linings of the brain or spinal cord (e.g., meningitis) and to injuries such as burns, fractures, and lacerations due to lack of sensation in the lower extremities. Despite these problems, most students with spina bifida have the stamina to participate in school activities for an entire day.

Epilepsy is a condition that, periodically, causes abnormal amounts of electrical activity in the brain, resulting in seizures. Seizures vary in duration, frequency, and intensity. Some seizures last only a few seconds; others may last for several minutes. Some epileptic children have seizures every few minutes, others have them only about once a year. The most intensive seizures involve major convulsions, which can be frightening to the unsuspecting observer. Minor seizures, a common indicator of which is rapid eye blinks, sometimes go unnoticed.

Skeletal/muscular disabilities, such as muscular dystrophy and arthritis, can limit a student's movement and, as a result, his or her participation in some school activities. Other disabilities caused by health problems can also limit participation in school activities. Perhaps no health-related disability has been so readily turned into a handicap as acquired immune deficiency syndrome (AIDS). The devastating nature of the disease and its epidemic proportions (Church, Allen, & Stiehm, 1986) have made it difficult for children who have contracted it to interact normally with their peers. AIDS is transmitted through intimate sexual contact with infected partners, through blood transfusions from those who are infected, or from using contaminated hypodermic needles. It is not transmitted through casual social contact. Sex education to help adolescents prevent infection is helping to curb the spread of the disease. Programs to educate classmates of infected students and to help alleviate social stigmas and enhance social interactions are also available.*

Lecture Note: Bring in a nurse, paramedic, or other medical professional to discuss first aid for epileptic seizures. Printed first aid guidelines are available from the Epilepsy Foundation of America.

Gifted and Talented

Gifted and talented students are able to meet academic challenges better than the vast majority of their peers in any number of areas. Renzulli (1982) distinguishes between academic giftedness and "creative/productive" giftedness. Students who are academically gifted are able to learn quickly and easily. They generally score well on tests of intelligence, aptitude, and achievement. Creatively and productively gifted students tend to solve problems in new and effective ways. Interestingly, academically gifted students tend, as a group, not to be any more or less successful in later life than the general student population, whereas creatively gifted students are more likely to achieve later success.

In one of the largest psychological research projects ever undertaken, Terman and associates (1925, 1947, 1959) began following the lives of 1,528 gifted males and females. Terman's subjects all have intelligence scores that rank them in the top 1 percent of the population. This continuing study, which began a lifetime ago, will not be completed for another generation. (It is scheduled to continue until the year 2010.)

Field Observation/Teacher Interview: Have each student visit a gifted and talented class or interview a teacher about the way he or she interacts with gifted and talented students.

*The American Red Cross has several publications available. Contact your local Red Cross Office or write AIDS Education Office, 1730 D St. NW, Washington, DC 20006. Useful information is also available by writing for the *NEA AIDS Booklet*, NEA Communications, 1201 16th ST. NW, Washington, DC 20036.

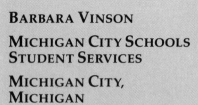

Profiles in Successful Practice

BARBARA VINSON

MICHIGAN CITY SCHOOLS
STUDENT SERVICES

MICHIGAN CITY,
MICHIGAN

What does wide-ranging student diversity mean for us as teachers? To me, it means prejudice must be left outside the classroom. The teacher is there to educate all the children—those who are eager and teacher-pleasers and those who seem to thwart everything a teacher tries to do for them. Children know when they are accepted for themselves. They respond to the teacher who sets standards and expects them to meet those standards, as long as it is done with respect and caring for the child. Some teachers who children describe as "tough" and who give them much homework are also the teachers whom they name as their favorites. These teachers make learning exciting. They encourage children to experience learning actively rather than having them sit quietly at their desks. These teachers treat all children with respect and fairness. They build students' self-esteem and self-confidence by making it possible for them to experience success rather than intimidation and ridicule. Teachers are under pressure to meet the demands of curriculum and state requirements, but must be careful not to lose the child in the process.

The teachers whom I remember fondly and who had great impact on my development are those who not only taught me the required subjects, but also how to care for others. It was those teachers who taught me important qualities necessary for a teacher. While in high school, I became involved in the exploratory teacher program for students considering the teaching profession. I was fortunate to work with Geraldine Lynn who was teaching mentally handicapped children at that time. She later was named the Indiana Federation Council for Exceptional Children Teacher of the Year for her contribution to the teaching profession. I was also honored to be a recipient of the IFCEC Teacher of the Year award.

I have taught mentally handicapped, emotionally handicapped, physically handicapped, and learning disabled children from preschool through sixth grade. I have also been involved in a program to educate young parents in the care and stimulation of infants at-risk to facilitate their readiness for school. My most recent position was that of a learning disability resource teacher. My program was structured to meet the needs of the individual students. My students brought with them different learning problems, but all had feelings of low self-esteem brought on by years of failure and frustration. My main goal was to emphasize their strengths to set them up for success so that they gained the self-confidence needed to motivate

and reawaken a desire to learn. I also worked with their regular education teachers to help them understand the children and work with them in the classroom. We worked as a team to create a positive learning environment for the children we taught.

I am now completing a doctorate in school psychology. As a school psychologist, I assess children's intellectual ability, academic achievement, social skills, self-help skills, physical and motor development, and personality and emotional development. I also consult with teachers, parents, administrators, school counselors, school nurses, therapists, and community agencies to meet the needs of children. As a school psychologist, I continue to regard myself as a teacher. Working with others, I teach them about testing, what it does and does not tell us. I teach about child development and what can be expected of children at different stages. I also continue to work with children, individually and in groups, to help them understand themselves. Teaching continues to be an exciting, sometimes frustrating, but rewarding profession. The many backgrounds, beliefs, and abilities of the children we teach can add to the frustration, but it also increases the excitement and reward as we meet the challenges they bring and watch the progress they make on their way to adulthood.

The Terman study has thus far determined that gifted children tend to be larger, stronger, and healthier than normal children. As a group, they often walk earlier as infants and are more athletic as adolescents. It is important to note that nongifted siblings of gifted children are also physically larger and more healthy than the population in general. The Terman study has also found that gifted students are more emotionally stable than their peers. They experience lower rates of delinquency, drug problems, emotional problems, and in later life, divorce. The health and emotional stability of the subjects in the study may be due to the selection criteria used by teachers who recommend students as subjects.

Just as there are normal students who do not achieve to their potential, so are there underachieving gifted students. School work that does not challenge gifted students is considered a major reason for underachievement (Hallahan & Kauffman, 1991). Gifted underachievers often have negative attitudes toward school and toward themselves (Delisle, 1982; Ribich, Barone, & Agostino, 1991). One approach to working with underachieving gifted students involves (a) observing carefully their performances and behaviors in various instructional situations; (b) sharing those observations and hypothesized causes for underachievement with the students; and (c) developing a partnership with the students (and their parents, if possible) aimed at solving the problem (Whitmore, 1986).

Lecture Note: Ask students who were in classes with underachieving gifted and talented students to share their impressions and experiences.

Chapter 15 Casebook Preview: See Gifted Achievers and Underachievers.

Principles in Practice 4.3

Principles . . .

1. Disabilities may or may not be handicaps in a classroom.
2. Learning disabilities, the most frequently encountered disabilities, affect each student's sense of self.
3. Disabilities that affect a student's ability to communicate do not necessarily reflect intellectual impairment.

. . . in Practice

Nick, in Teacher Chronicle 4.3, has a disability—he is color blind. The teacher, unaware of Nick's disability, assigned a map-reading task that did not take his disability into account. Thus, in the context of the map-reading task, Nick's disability became a handicap. As he worked on the task in class, Nick became confused, frustrated, and embarrassed. After the map was labeled so that having to discriminate colors became unnecessary, he was able to complete the task.

In the future, the teacher, who is now aware of Nick's disability, will be able to adapt tasks involving color discrimination so that Nick will not be handicapped by them.

1. What other undetected disabilities might exist in this or other classes?
2. Why are learning disabilities especially likely to become handicaps?
3. Why should teachers be aware of disabilities that cause problems with communication?

Assign Chapter 4 of the *Study Guide*.

CONCLUSION

As teachers, we need to know before we meet any class of students what to expect of them and from them. Theories of development provide us with such expectations. They tell us about third graders, sixth graders, ninth graders. Knowing what is "typical" of the average sixth grader will allow us to more easily recognize what is exceptional or atypical. Every group of students is, inevitably, diverse. Theories give us a starting point for knowing what our classes are like. By testing theoretical descriptions against our observations of the individuals whom we teach, we move from knowing our classes as a group to understanding each person in them.

Piaget, Erikson, Kohlberg, Baumrind, Sternberg, and others suggest that students share certain characteristics. If this were not true, we would not recognize any of our friends or acquaintances when we read, for instance, Sternberg's triarchic view of intelligence. But we do. The cognitive capabilities and moral decisions described by Piaget, Kohlberg, and Gilligan would not be supported by research. But they are. There are aspects of cognitive, psychosocial, and moral development that are common to all people. Human development is predictable. We can state with confidence that high school students are concerned with peer relationships. For high school teachers that is a useful piece of knowledge. Knowledge of the groups we teach is always helpful, if we understand its limits.

Every student is exceptional in some way. Elizabeth may be like George in terms of cognitive ability. Elizabeth may be similar to Leticia in terms of cultural background and moral judgments. She may experience problems with opposite-sex relationships similar to those Linda has experienced. But if we mix George's cognition, Leticia's culture and morals, and Linda's social life, we get someone who is different from all three. We get Elizabeth.

We shall examine human learning and motivation in the next four chapters. As we do so, keep in mind that psychological theories allow us to see those characteristics and abilities that students have in common and those that make each student unique.

Chapter Summary

Introduction: Seeing the Individuals in a Group

Knowledge about the developmental groups that students belong to is important for teachers. It is also important, however, for teachers to know each student as an individual. Knowledge of individuals helps teachers make sound decisions.

Varieties of Intelligence

Piaget's Dynamic View

According to Piaget, intelligence changes as a person adapts to his or her environment. The modes of adaptation change as a student develops intellectually. Because ways of adapting change (see Piaget's stages in Chapter 2), so does intelligence. In Piaget's view, intelligence is dynamic, not static.

Wechsler's Global View

Wechsler views intelligence as a general or global capacity that allows the individual to deal effectively with his or her environment. This global capacity is not simply the sum of several subscales on an intelligence test.

Guilford's Multifactor View

Guilford viewed intelligence as comprising a whole range of factors. His three faces of intellect model combines five kinds of operations, four kinds of content, and six kinds of products to yield 120 separate factors.

An Interim Report on Intelligence Theories

Piaget's, Wechsler's, and Guilford's views of intelligence focus on different aspects of intelligent behavior. Piaget warns against using just one "yardstick" to judge intelligence. Wechsler warns that intelligence is more than the sum of its parts. Guilford warns against ignoring divergent operations.

Sternberg's Triarchic Theory of Intelligence

Sternberg's theory of intelligence is made up of three subtheories. The experiential subtheory describes a person's capacity to handle new ideas and situations. The contextual subtheory describes one's ability to adapt to his or her environment. The componential subtheory describes the mental components of intelligent behavior.

Learning Styles

Learning styles are the ways students prefer to learn. Personality types have been used to determine learning styles. The personality type approach suggests that teaching styles also exist. This discovery raises questions about the ways learning and teaching styles match up. Learning styles have been identified along the dimensions of convergent-divergent thinking, impulsive-reflective thinking, and thematic-analytic thinking.

Cultures and Values

Achievement-related Value Conflicts

Different macro- and microcultures have different values. If students have values about achievement-related behavior that differ from the values reflected in a classroom, problems can occur. One source for an achievement-related value conflict is the value placed on individualism in most schools and the value of groupism held by students from some microcultures.

Communication-related Value Conflicts

The value systems of certain microcultures include the "rules" of social interaction. When the cultural background of a teacher and a student are different, misunderstandings can result.

Parenting Styles

The family acts as a significant source of values for students. Parents communicate what is and is not valued by the way they raise their children. Certain parenting behaviors are associated with high and low achievement in their children. As is the case with other cultural influences, it is the values that the parents communicate, not their ethnic background, that is significant.

Exceptional Students

Mental Retardation
Mental retardation is a condition within which intellectual functioning and adaptive behavior are significantly subaverage.

Learning Disabilities
A learning disability is a disorder of one or more of the psychological processes involved in general language use, reasoning, or computation. Learning disabilities are distinct from mental retardation, physical disabilities, and emotional disorders.

Emotional/Behavioral Disorders
E/BD students can display externalizing behavior or acting out in ways that disturb or injure others. Another category of disordered behavior is internalizing behavior, which refers to the emotional problems that may result in anxiety or depression. In the extreme, internalizing can manifest itself as autism or schizophrenia.

Communication Disorders
Communication disorders are of two major types: speech disorders, which refers to some type of voice problem (e.g., stuttering); and language disorders, which make it difficult to understand or generate messages.

Hearing Impairment
Students who are hearing-impaired may be able to hear with the use of special amplification devices (the hard of hearing), or may have to learn special communication techniques (deaf students). Because of the special nature of communication among deaf people, they tend to socialize more with other deaf people.

Visual Impairment
Visual impairment can be defined legally or educationally. Educators define the degree of visual impairment in terms of the type of reading instruction required.

Physical Disabilities
Physical disabilities include skeletal, joint, muscle, or health problems that interfere with students' performances. Depending on the disability and its severity, seizures may result. Teachers should know first aid for seizures.

Gifted and Talented
Gifted and talented students are able to meet educational challenges better than most students. A distinction has been drawn between those who are gifted academically and those whose gifts allow them to be creative and productive in nonacademic ways. Just because gifted students are able to outperform most students does not mean they always do.

Reflections: Building Your Theory of Teaching

4.1 Select a topic appropriate to the grade level and content area you will teach. Generate some questions to ask your students to determine their learning styles. What types of answers would you anticipate from students of the varying learning styles?

4.2 Design a project that will enable students to (a) recognize microcultural differences within their class, and (b) anticipate the types of misunderstandings that might result from those differences.

4.3 A new student, Jenny Washington, will be mainstreamed into your class next week. She has cerebral palsy and is confined to a wheelchair. A speech impairment makes it difficult for her to communicate. Even so, she is quite intelligent. Indeed, a former teacher claims that Jenny is gifted, but her communication difficulties prevent her from being so labeled. How will you prepare your classroom and your students to prevent Jenny's disability from becoming a handicap?

Key Terms

intelligence (p. 132)
construct (p. 133)
dynamic (p. 133)
global view (p. 133)
three faces of intellect (p. 134)
experiential subtheory (p. 137)
contextual subtheory (p. 137)
componential subtheory (p. 137)
learning styles (p. 138)
convergent thinkers (p. 139)
divergent thinkers (p. 139)
impulsive (p. 139)
reflective (p. 139)
thematic (p. 139)
analytic (p. 139)
values (p. 142)

macroculture (p. 142)
microcultures (p. 142)
multicultural education (p. 143)
individualism (p. 144)
groupism (p. 144)
authoritative style (p. 147)
authoritarian style (p. 148)
permissive-indulgent style (p. 148)
exceptional students (p. 150)
Public Law 94-142 (p. 151)
least restrictive environment (p. 151)
mainstreaming (p. 151)
individualized education program (IEP) (p. 151)
disability (p. 151)

handicap (p. 151)
mental retardation (p. 152)
learning disabilities (p. 152)
emotional/behavioral disorder (E/BD) (p. 157)
externalizing (p. 157)
internalizing (p. 157)
communication disorders (p. 157)
hearing impairment (p. 158)
visual impairment (p. 158)
physical disabilities (p. 160)
gifted and talented students (p. 161)

Suggested Readings

Banks, J. A., & McGee Banks, C. A. (Eds.). (1989). *Multicultural education: Issues and perspectives.* Needham Heights, MA: Allyn & Bacon.

Baron J. B., & Sternberg, R. J. (Eds.). (1987). *Teaching thinking skills.* New York: W. H. Freeman.

Hallahan, D. P., & Kauffman, J. M. (1991). *Exceptional children: Introduction to special education.* Englewood Cliffs, NJ: Prentice Hall.

Sternberg, R. J. (1985). *Beyond IQ: A triarchic theory of human intelligence.* New York: Cambridge University Press.

References

Achenbach, T. M. (1985). *Assessment and taxonomy of child and adolescent psychopathology.* Beverly Hills, CA: Sage Publications.

American Speech-Language-Hearing Association. (1982). Definitions: Communicative disorders and variations. *ASHA, 24,* 942–950.

Banks, J. A. (1988). *Multiethnic education: Theory and practice* (2nd ed.). Boston: Allyn & Bacon.

Banks, J. A., & Banks, C. A. (1989). *Multicultural Education: Issues and Perspectives.* Boston: Allyn & Bacon.

Barger, R. R., & Hoover, R. L. (1984). Psychological type and the matching of cognitive styles. *Theory into Practice, 23,* 56–63.

Baumrind, D. (1967). Childcare practices anteceding three patterns of preschool behavior. *Genetic Psychology Monographs, 75,* 43–88.

Baumrind, D. (1973). The development of instrument competence through socialization. In A. Pick (Ed.), *Minnesota Symposium on Child Psychology* (Vol. 7, pp. 3–46). Minneapolis: University of Minnesota Press.

Boykin, A. W. (1986). The triple quandry and the schooling of Afro-American children. In U. Neisser (Ed.), *The school achievement of minority children.* Hillsdale, NJ: Erlbaum.

Butterfield, F. (1982). *China: Alive in the bitter sea.* New York: Bantam Books.

Chun, E. W. (1987–1988). Sorting black students for success and failure: The inequity of ability grouping and tracking. *Urban League Review, 11* (1–2).

Church, J. A., Allen, J. R., & Stiehm, E. R. (1986). New scarlet letter(s), pediatric AIDS. *Pediatrics, 77,* 423–427.

Clark, R. E. (1983). Reconsidering research on learning from media. *Review of Educational Research, 53,* 445–459.

Delisle, J. (1982). Learning to underachieve. *Roeper Review, 4*, 16–18.

Epstein, M. H., Polloway, E. A., Patton, J. R., & Foley, R. (1989). Mild retardation: Student characteristics and services. *Education and Training in Mental Retardation, 24*(1), 7–16.

Grossman, H. (1983). *Classification in mental retardation.* Washington, DC: American Association on Mental Deficiency.

Guilford, J. P. (1967). *The nature of human intelligence.* New York: McGraw-Hill.

Guilford, J. P. (1980). Fluid and crystallized intelligences: Two fanciful concepts. *Psychological Bulletin, 88*, 406–412.

Guilford, J. P. (1985). The structure-of-intellect model. In B. B. Wolman (Ed.), *Handbook of intelligence.* New York: Wiley.

Hall, E. T. (1966). *The hidden dimension.* Garden City, NY: Doubleday.

Hallahan, D. P., & Kauffman, J. M. (1991). *Exceptional children: Introduction to special education* (5th ed.). Englewood Cliffs, NJ: Prentice-Hall.

Hess, R., Chih-Mei, C., & McDevitt, T. M. (1987). Cultural variation in family beliefs about children's performance in mathematics: Comparisons among People's Republic of China, Chinese-American, and Caucasian-American families. *Journal of Educational Psychology, 79*, 179–188.

Jung, C. G. (1960). *The structure and dynamics of the psyche: Collected works* (Vol. 8). Princeton, NJ: Princeton University Press. (Originally published in German, 1926)

Kagan, J. (1964a). *Developmental studies of reflection and analysis.* Cambridge, MA: Harvard University Press.

Kagan, J. (1964b). Impulsive and reflective children. In J. D. Krumbolz (Ed.), *Learning and the educational process.* Chicago: Rand McNally.

Kagan, S., Zahn, G. L., Widamin, K. F., Schwartzwald, J., & Tyrrell, G. (1985). Classroom structural bias: Impact of cooperative and competitive classroom structures on cooperative and competitive individuals and groups. In R. E. Slavin et al. (Eds.), *Learning to cooperate, cooperating to learn.* New York: Plenum Press.

McNemar, Q. (1964). Lost our intelligence? Why? *American Psychologist, 19* (17), 871–883.

Meinke, D. L. (1987). *Personality typologies and their relationship with learning styles.* A paper presented at the Annual Meeting of the American Psychological Association, New York.

Pepitone, E. A. (1985). Children in cooperation and competitions: Antecedents and consequences of self-orientation. In R. E. Slavin, S. Sharan, S. Kagan, R. Hertz-Lazarowitz, C. Webb, & R. Schmuck (Eds.), *Learning to cooperate, cooperating to learn.* New York: Plenum Press.

Quay, H. C. (1986). Classification. In H. C. Quay & J. S. Werry (Eds.), *Psychopathological disorders of childhood* (3rd ed.). New York: Wiley.

Quay, H. C., & Peterson, D. R. (1987). *Manual for the Revised Behavior Problem Checklist.* Unpublished manuscript.

Reischauer, E. O. (1981). *The Japanese.* Cambridge, MA: Harvard University Press.

Renzulli, J. (1982). Dear Mr. and Mrs. Copernicus: We regret to inform you. . . . *Gifted Child Quarterly, 26*, 11–14.

Ribich, F., Barone, W., & Agostino, V. R. (1991, February). A semantically different: Perspectives on underachieving gifted students. Presented at EERA, Boston.

Sacks, O. W. (1989). *Seeing voices: A journey into the world of the deaf.* Berkeley: University of California Press.

Schmeck, R. R. (Ed.). (1989). *Learning strategies and learning styles.* New York: Plenum Press.

Slavin, R. (1988). Cooperative learning: A best evidence synthesis. In R. E. Slavin (Ed.), *School and classroom organization.* Hillsdale, NJ: Erlbaum.

Smith, L. H., & Renzulli, J. S. (1984). Learning style preferences: A practical approach for classroom teachers. *Theory into Practice, 23*, 44–50.

Sternberg, R. (1985). *Beyond IQ: A triarchic theory of human intelligence.* New York: Cambridge University Press.

Sternberg, R. (1986). *Intelligence applied: Understanding and increasing your own intellectual skills.* New York: Harcourt Brace Jovanovich.

Terman, L. M., assisted by others. (1925). Mental and physical traits of a thousand gifted children. In L. M. Terman (Ed.), *Genetic studies of genius* (Vol. 1). Stanford, CA: Stanford University Press.

Terman, L. M., & Olden, M. H. (1947). The gifted child grows up. In L. M. Terman. (Ed.), *Genetic studies of genius* (Vol. 4). Stanford, CA: Stanford University Press.

Terman, L., & Olden, M. H. (1959). The gifted group at mid-life. In L. M. Terman (Ed.), *Genetic studies of genius* (Vol. 5). Stanford, CA: Stanford University Press.

Triandis, H. C. (1986). Toward pluralism in education. In S. Modgil, G. K. Verma, K. Mallick, & C. Modgil (Eds.), *Multicultural education: The interminable debate*. London: Falmer.

U. S. Department of Education. (1989). *Eleventh annual report to Congress of the implementation of the Education of the Handicapped Act*. Washington, DC: U. S. Government Printing Office.

Wechsler, D. (1958). *The measurement and appraisal of adult intelligence* (4th ed.). Baltimore, MD: Williams & Wilkins.

Wheeler, R. (1977, April). *Predisposition toward cooperation and competition: Cooperative and competitive classroom effects*. Paper presented at the annual convention of the American Psychological Association, San Francisco.

Yao, E. L. (1988). Working effectively with Asian immigrant parents. *Phi Delta Kappan, 70,* (3), 223–225.

Zelniker, T., & Jeffrey, W. E. (1976). Reflective and impulsive children: Strategies of information processing underlying differences in problem solving. *Monographs of the Society for Research in Child Development, 41* (5, Serial No. 168).

5
Environment and Behavior

Chapter Overview

Chapters 2 through 4 described aspects of student development. We continue our examination of Students as Learners in Chapters 5 through 8, focusing on how students learn and what motivates them to do so. This chapter presents a behaviorist approach to the subject of how students learn. Behaviorism emphasizes the role that the environment plays in determining behavior. The environment provides stimuli that elicit responses; it also provides consequences to those responses. The way in which stimuli and consequences are arranged influences what and how well a person learns. Consequences of behavior also influence motivation. ∎

INTRODUCTION: BEHAVIORISM

When your first group of students walks into your classroom on your first day as a certified teacher, they will respond to you and to the classroom you have prepared for them. When you present a lesson, administer a test, lead a discussion, monitor study hall, ask and answer questions, review a test, organize a lunch line, or referee a scuffle in the hall, students will respond to you. How will they respond? Will they do what you ask of them? Will they ignore you? Will they defy you? Let's examine the principles of behaviorism as they apply to human learning and see if they provide answers to these questions.

Behaviorism focuses on the observable aspects of the environment in-stead of on mental or cognitive processes. According to the behaviorist view of learning, the environment provides stimulation and the learner responds to that stimulation. The response changes the environment in ways that increase or decrease the likelihood of the same response in the future. Imag-ine, for example, that a student encounters discussion questions at the end of an assigned chapter. The student responds to the questions by taking notes from the chapter in order to answer the questions. On the chapter test, the end-of-chapter questions appear in modified form as essay items. As a con-sequence of the notes taken from the chapter, the student earns the highest possible score on the essays. For all remaining reading assignments, the stu-dent makes notes based on the discussion questions. Such a view of how people learn can be applied in the classroom.

The behaviorist view offers hypotheses for classroom management and suggests ways to prevent and resolve discipline problems. (Incidentally, class-room management, as we will see in Chapter 12, is much more than student discipline. It involves managing the learning activities of students as well.) Behaviorism is the view that most clearly defines, for educators, the abso-lutely crucial concept of reinforcement. *Reinforcement* refers to consequences of responses that establish and maintain desirable behavior. The high score on the essays served as reinforcement of the note-taking response.

The term *behavior*, when used in everyday conversation, comprises an immense body of activities. From the behaviorist point of view, the term *behavior* includes only observable behaviors. We can think of behavior as outcomes produced by environmental conditions. By applying this view to learning, we can understand how learners determine whether a particular behavior in a particular situation is appropriate or inappropriate. Take, for example, an eighth-grade student who responds to a question from a fellow student by saying, "Oh, Dahellwiddit." That response may be appropriate and even expected when offered at the lunch table when the student is sur-rounded by peers, but inappropriate when the question is asked of the stu-dent in a classroom by the geometry teacher. The appropriateness of behaviors is judged within the context of the environment in which they are displayed.

The interaction of environment and behavior is a strong determinant of the appropriateness of a behavior. Think back to Peter Roop's behavior in the classroom and on the playground. He did things on the playground that he did not do in the classroom. And the same is true of his students. When students learn what behaviors are and are not acceptable in the classroom, classroom discipline has been established. Even within a classroom, the en-vironment or circumstances vary. Under certain conditions it may be acceptable to toss an eraser at a teacher, under other circumstances it will not be. Depending on the environmental conditions established by the teacher, tossing an eraser at the teacher may earn a smile and a chuckle or it may earn scorn, detention, or even suspension.

Environmental events can come to control the behavior of those who find themselves in that environment. An important question for any teacher, but especially novice teachers, to ask is, How do I establish and maintain control of my students' behavior? Behaviorism provides answers to that question by offering hypotheses for classroom management.

B. F. Skinner's theory of operant conditioning is the predominant behavioristic view of learning.

Origins of Operant Conditioning

Skinner became interested in questions of behavior and environment by reading the work of Ivan Pavlov, who won a Nobel Prize in 1904. Pavlov's conditioning experiments are classics in the history of psychology. Pavlov studied how a dog's salivation reflex might be conditioned, that is, brought under control of the environment. Pavlov's procedure began by simply presenting food to the dog. The dog salivated. The food is an **unconditioned stimulus (US),** a stimulus that automatically elicits a response. Salivation is an **unconditioned response (UR),** an automatic reflex. Reflexes do not need to be learned or conditioned; they occur automatically in the presence of particular stimuli. People flinch when they see they are about to be hit. As youngsters, we played a game called "pokes." The game began with one child trying to elicit an unconditioned response from another. The first child would flip his hand near the face of the second (US). If the second child flinched—a natural reflex or unconditioned response—the first child would shout "Flinch!" Then came the pokes (actual punches to the upper arm of the flincher) followed by a series of "gives," "no gives," "wipe offs," and "rebounds" that perpetuated the hitting, sometimes for an entire afternoon if you couldn't think of anything else to do.

In the case of Pavlov's experiments, the trick was not to get the dog to exhibit a reflex, salivate in the presence of food. The trick was to get the dog to salivate predictably before the food was presented. Pavlov conditioned the dog to salivate to a tone, a stimulus that does not normally elicit salivation. The tone is the **conditioned stimulus (CS),** a stimulus that is paired with an unconditional stimulus. The tone preceded slightly the presentation of food. After several pairings of the conditioned stimulus (tone) with the unconditioned stimulus (food), the tone elicited salivation. Salivation elicited by the previously neutral tone is a **conditioned response (CR),** a response to a conditioned stimulus. Figure 5–1 illustrates how Pavlovian conditioning works.

The reflexes elicited by stimuli (unconditioned responses) are responses to the environment. Skinner (1938) called the reflexes with which Pavlov worked **respondent behavior.** For this reason, Pavlovian conditioning is sometimes called **respondent conditioning.**

Skinner, after carefully analyzing Pavlov's work, became interested in behaviors that were not simply elicited reflexes, but that operated on the environment to produce consequences. Skinner called behavior that operates on the environment **operant behavior.** Consider a student who raises his or her hand during a classroom discussion. If we examine the situation from the student's point of view, the student responded to some stimulus by raising

unconditioned stimulus (US) In classical conditioning, a stimulus that automatically elicits a response. For example, in Pavlov's experiments, food produced the response of salivation in a dog.

unconditioned response (UR) In classical conditioning, an automatic reflex. For example, people flinch when they see they are about to be hit.

conditioned stimulus (CS) In classical conditioning, a stimulus that is paired with an unconditioned stimulus and eventually produces a response when presented alone.

conditioned response (CR) In respondent conditioning, a learned response to a conditioned stimulus.

respondent behavior Skinner's term for the reflexes with which Pavlov worked.

respondent conditioning Pavlovian conditioning.

operant behavior According to Skinner, behavior that is not a simple reflex to a stimulus but rather a response that operates on the environment.

B. F. Skinner explored behaviors that operated on the environment to produce consequences or responses.

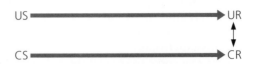

■ **Figure 5–1** *Elements of Respondent Conditioning*

Source: From *Educational Psychology: Mastering Principles and Applications* (p. 208) by J. T. Gibson and L. A. Chandler, 1988, Needham Heights, MA: Allyn & Bacon. Copyright 1988 by Allyn & Bacon. Adapted by permission.

his or her hand. The student's response leads to an environmental consequence: the teacher acknowledges the student. In this example, the student's hand raising is called operant behavior. Through **operant conditioning**—learning through responses and consequences—the student has learned how and when to raise his or her hand during classroom discussions. Because operant behavior is the type most often encountered in classrooms, our examination of behavior and environment will concentrate on operant conditioning.

Assumptions of Operant Conditioning

Several assumptions underlie Skinner's view of learning. These assumptions guide the methods used by researchers and the types of conclusions that can be drawn from investigations of operant behavior. The assumptions are as follows (adapted from Bell-Gredler, 1986):

1. Learning is defined as changes in behavior that are functionally related to changes in the environment.
2. Describing lawful relations requires definitions of the observable and carefully controlled conditions.
3. The essential nature of the interaction between an organism and its environment is the same for all species.
4. The individual is the appropriate source of data about behavior.

The first assumption is the basis of the behaviorist's focus on the observable aspects of behavior and the environment in which behavior occurs. The second, third, and fourth assumptions are basic to Skinner's approach to the scientific study of behavior. Building a science of behavior is no easy task. The complexity of behavior requires precise description and highly controlled conditions. Scientifically speaking, the best way to control conditions is to use experimental methods. Experiments are scientifically clean when extraneous factors that might influence their results are eliminated. Scientists who are searching for cause-and-effect relationships use experiments as a way of controlling possible causes. The early work in operant-behavior studies was done with rats; later work, with pigeons. The experimental environments of rats and pigeons can be more completely controlled than the environments of humans. Many of the functional relationships between aspects of the envi-

Lecture Note: Note the distinction between observable behavior and inferences based on observation. You can observe a student working on the same math problem for twenty minutes, erasing figures, rewriting the problem, and scratching his or her head. You can infer from the behaviors that the student is having difficulty with the problem.

Lecture Note: Ask students how they would design an experiment to determine whether instructional method A or instructional method B was better. After they list ways of controlling or eliminating contaminating factors, ask them to what extent the experimental situation resembles a real classroom.

ronment and the behaviors of rats and pigeons have strong parallels to human behavior as observed in uncontrolled settings (cf. Skinner, 1969). (We will look at some examples later in the chapter.)

This last assumption serves as a scientific basis for what Skinner calls the "experimental analysis of behavior." He uses the phrase to distinguish his research program from any philosophical approach to science (1974). In a 1950 article entitled "Are Theories of Learning Really Necessary?" Skinner argues that theories of learning get in the way of collecting hard facts about behavior change. He denies that what he does should be called a theory at all. Rather, it is empirically based, an experimental analysis of behavior.

The practical implications of the assumption about the way behavior affects the environment and Skinner's concern for the empirical are critical for those of us who use a behaviorist approach to teaching. The principles of operant conditioning provide us with the conceptual tools to analyze behavior in a classroom. If we encounter inappropriate behavior, **operant analysis** helps us generate hypotheses about what environmental changes might be necessary to change problem behavior. Teaching is a matter of trying ideas, of testing hypotheses. It is an empirical endeavor. In order to use operant conditioning, we must learn how to analyze the interaction between environments and behavior patterns.

> **operant analysis**   Analysis of the interaction between environments and behavior patterns.

Field Observation: Have students record, in strictly behavioral terms, inappropriate student behaviors and antecedent and consequent events.

CALL IN THE REINFORCEMENTS

Teacher
Chronicle
5.1

Rodney was a handful in the classroom. If he could disrupt a lesson, he did. If he could hit someone, he did. If he could avoid work, he did. If he could cause trouble on the playground, he did.

Nothing in my bag of tricks seemed to work in my attempts to "manage" his behavior. Not only did I want to control his outbursts and problems with others, I wanted him to eventually internalize some control over his own behavior.

One day I discovered Rodney's desire to play football at recess. Not only did he want to play, he wanted to be the one to take the football out to the playground. At times, his need to take the ball superceded his wish to play. Once I finally "saw" his desire to have the ball, I used it in the classroom to effect a change in his behavior preceding recess. Together we decided that he could take the ball on those days when he was nice to others. For several weeks he took the ball on good days and couldn't play with it on bad days. Each morning he checked with me to see how he'd done, although he already knew ahead of time whether the ball would be his. Then a day came when he was good and forgot all about the ball as a reward. For the next two days, he behaved himself without needing the ball. After that, his behavior backslid and the football became necessary again—but only for the rest of the week. Unfortunately, we had a spell of rotten weather; with recess inside his behavior deteriorated. But as the weather got better, the football once again became an important tool for eliciting appropriate behavior.

discriminative stimulus   A
stimulus that is present
consistently when a response
is reinforced.
behavioral control
Reinforcement of behavior in
the presence of a particular
stimulus, when the stimulus
acquires the ability to control
the behavior.

Chap. Obj. 2
Test Ques. 5.29–5.52

Focus Question: How does the environment control what is learned?

Lecture Note: As a mnemonic, use Antecedent event, Behavior, Consequent event: ABC.

COMPONENTS OF LEARNING

Skinner (1953) identified three components of learning: (a) the discriminative stimulus, (b) the response, and (c) the reinforcing stimulus. A general model of Skinnerian learning can be described as follows:

$$(S^{\mathrm{D}})—(R)—(S^{\mathrm{Reinf}})$$

It is important to understand that this model indicates a series of events that are elements of a larger whole. That's what analysis is: breaking down a larger whole into its component parts. If you think about chemical analysis, the analyst is given a compound and asked to identify the elements that constitute the compound. Using the operant analysis of behavior, we can understand learning by identifying the three elements present in every learning episode.

Keep in mind that the elements must fit together if the model is to be useful in analyzing classroom behavior and generating hypotheses. A behavior or response (R) occurs in the presence of an environmental stimulus (S^{D}). As a consequence of response, a reinforcing stimulus (S^{Reinf}) is delivered. The addition of the reinforcing stimulus changes the environment.

Discriminative Stimuli

The notion of a discriminative stimulus depends on the presence of reinforcement. Because a **discriminative stimulus** is any stimulus that is present consistently when a response is reinforced, it becomes a kind of "signal" that certain behaviors will be reinforced. If a response is not reinforced, then a discriminative stimulus doesn't exist. The best way to discuss the discriminative stimulus is under the general concept of behavioral control.

Behavioral control is affected when a behavior is reinforced in the presence of a particular stimulus and that stimulus acquires the ability to "control" the behavior. Suppose a teacher begins a discussion session in a science class by walking around her desk and sitting on the edge nearest the students. She smiles and says, "Okay, let's see if we can figure out the material in Chapter 6 together." She then asks a question about the material. A student raises his hand, is called on, and answers the question. The teacher praises the student's response. The teacher's pattern of positive reactions is consistent for all students who respond, even when a student's answer is not what it should be. For instance, a teacher may ask the class how an airplane is able to fly. If a student responds, "By going real fast," the teacher may reinforce the attempt by saying, "Speed is a very important part of the answer. Your answer shows me that you are thinking. Keep it up, Sharon. Now, Sharon has identified speed as an important reason why airplanes can fly. What are some of the other reasons?"

Lecture Note: Ask students if they recall any "signals" used by their teachers.

The teacher's question, her smile, and her position on the desk are all aspects of the stimulus situation present during reinforcement of student responses. Asking the question, smiling, and being seated on the desk are potential "signals" to participate in the discussion. Students may participate in future discussions even when the teacher is not seated on the desk, but the probability of "participation behavior" is enhanced by the presence of the additional discriminative stimulus.

Now, further suppose that the same teacher is in the habit of pacing quickly up and down the rows while asking drill-and-practice questions in a rapid-fire manner. The questions during drill-and-practice are factual questions. Quick recall is sought, but student responses are not praised or elaborated on in the way they are during discussions. The teacher's smile is gone.

If reinforcement is delivered when the teacher is seated and smiling, but not while she paces stonefaced, the nature of the class participation will be different. Students will learn to discriminate between questions asked while she is seated and smiling, and questions asked while she is pacing. The students may volunteer less frequently in the latter instance, forcing the teacher to call on students who have not raised their hands. (This may be precisely what the teacher wants to have happen.) A cognitive interpretation of this example might ascribe the differences in behavior to a mental process called discrimination; operant behavior analysts refer to this behavior as coming under the control of a discriminative stimulus. The focus is on behavior that is observable.

Recall Rodney's behavior in Teacher Chronicle 5.1. His social responses to classmates were appropriate on nice days but were less appropriate during periods of inclement weather. Reinforcement, allowing Rodney to take the football out for recess, was available only on days when the weather allowed the children to go out for recess. Nice weather was a discriminative stimulus.

Behavioral control operates in classrooms with greater frequency than one might imagine. Teachers are largely responsible for the environment in which students respond; they are a source of discriminative stimuli. If discriminative stimuli are "signals," remember that students of all ages are enthusiastic readers of the signals that teachers emit. A teacher may even be sending signals to students that he or she is unaware of. We have all heard stories about the strange and seemingly irrelevant aspects of a teacher's behavior that students pass on to their parents. Any of those signals can gain control of student behavior. An entire junior high health class once decided that quizzes always came the day after the teacher wore a particular blue dress. (Lest you doubt the ability of students to identify discriminative stimuli, think back to your days in junior high and high school and the time you spent analyzing; critiquing; and, in many cases, making fun of the dress, mannerisms, and behavior of some of your teachers.)

Reinforcing Stimuli

Discriminative stimuli can exist only when a reinforcing stimulus follows the learner's response. In the Skinnerian model of learning, the **reinforcing stimulus** is a consequence of the response that increases the probability of that response occurring in the future. The use of reinforcement is the most important management skill a teacher can possess. Understanding reinforcement and its effects are matters of making distinctions. For example, it is important to draw the distinction between primary reinforcers and conditioned reinforcers.

Primary Reinforcers and Conditioned Reinforcers

A **primary reinforcer** is something that is basic to biological functioning. Food, water, shelter, and sexual contact are reinforcers that are positive con-

reinforcing stimulus A pleasurable consequence that maintains or increases the probability of that behavior occurring in the future.
primary reinforcer An element, such as food, water, or shelter, that satisfies a basic need.

Connection: See Teacher Chronicle 5.1: Call in the Reinforcements.

Lecture Note: Superstitious behavior can be understood in terms of the behavioral control gained by discriminative stimuli. Janet Evans, winner of three gold medals in swimming during the 1988 Olympics, has a superstitious mother. Her mother wore her lucky yellow blouse to Janet's first race. Janet, as the broadcasters say, captured the gold. The stimulus of a race lead to the mother's selection of a yellow blouse. Her selection was followed by a reinforcing stimulus, Janet's victory. Janet's mother wore the same blouse to the rest of Janet's races.

Connection: Types of consequences, including positive and negative reinforcement and punishment, are examined in the next section.

Chapter 15 Casebook Preview: Around the World.

Teaching Anecdote: Tell the story of the teacher who used a secret code to manage Jeff who loved to tickle, poke, grab, and shove other students. Only the teacher and Jeff knew the code. The code worked this way: Whenever Jeff bothered someone, the teacher pulled on her left ear, a signal for him to stop. Whenever she "caught him being good," she pulled on her right ear. Why would such signals work with Jeff?

Journal Entry: Have students reflect on the types of reinforcing stimuli they can deliver in a classroom. Have them analyze their own interpersonal strengths and weaknesses. Not every teacher can communicate praise by laying a hand on a student's shoulder.

Lecture Note: With regard to the reinforcing nature of manipulating one's environment, ask students if they have ever sat down at a computer and run a simulation program, only to be surprised when looking up at a clock at the amount of time that had passed.

tributors to human functioning. Negative contributors can also be primary reinforcers: a hard blow to the head, extreme heat or extreme cold, poison, electric shock. In most classroom situations, teachers do not use primary reinforcers as consequences of student behaviors. Rodney's football did not fulfill a basic biological need, but it did serve as a conditioned reinforcer.

A **conditioned reinforcer** is a neutral object, gesture, and so on that acquires the power to reinforce behavior as a result of being paired with one or more primary reinforcers. Perhaps the most ubiquitous conditioned reinforcer for humans is money. Pieces of paper, authorized as legal tender, have become associated with many of the necessities of existence. The potency of money as a reinforcer is extraordinary. Consider all of the behaviors people engage in to receive it in sufficient quantities. The key to potency of a conditioned reinforcer is whether it can make an appropriate pairing for the learner in question. Money doesn't possess reinforcing qualities for a pigeon; nor does U.S. currency have reinforcing qualities for someone living in the far reaches of Tibet.

Some conditioned reinforcers are social in nature. A gesture of affection, a word of praise, a hand placed on a shoulder, a handshake, a physical threat, or a verbal reprimand are examples. Can you recall from your own childhood a teacher or other adult who could comfort you with a smile, or one whose look ignited terror in your youthful chest?

Evidence suggests that both primary and conditioned reinforcers can be used effectively in instructional settings (cf. Rachlin, 1991). Working to remedy the behavior problems of an autistic child, Wolf, Risley, and Mees (1964) used small bits of food to train the child to wear his glasses. The researchers also report success in using this form of primary reinforcement in speech training. However, most of the reinforcements used in classrooms are conditioned reinforcers. In a study of changes in behavioral preferences, statements of approval by a teacher in a physical education class yielded an increase in the positive statements students made about themselves (Ludwig & Maehr, 1967).

A conditioned reinforcer that becomes associated with more than one primary reinforcer is called a **generalized reinforcer** (Skinner, 1953). Money, again, is an example. We make the distinction between primary and conditioned reinforcers, and identify some conditioned reinforcers as generalized in an effort to address the question: What is a reinforcing stimulus? This question is crucial for teachers; it is one that each teacher must answer for himself or herself. Furthermore, it is a question that each teacher must answer for each student; not every student is motivated by a good grade or a kind word. (Remember, the individual is the appropriate data source.)

The distinctions we make among various kinds of reinforcement act as guidelines for those who practice the art of teaching. These distinctions are sources of ideas, grist for the hypothesis mill. Skinner (1987) proposed the simple idea that many reinforcers offer learners the opportunity to manipulate the environment successfully. What is the attraction of video games? Why do people bowl or play billiards? Why do people enjoy hobbies such as painting or gardening? Why do people engage in behaviors "just for the fun of it"? (Nye, 1979, p. 38) Perhaps because these activities allow them to manipulate their environments.

Think about educational computer programs. Once, on a visit to St. Anthony's School, a school for the mentally disabled, we watched a five-year-old boy work steadily for thirty minutes without once shifting his gaze from the computer screen. He was working on a program that helped develop letter recognition skills, including the spelling of his own name. His teacher was delighted because one of his problems was a short attention span. She had never been able to hold his attention for longer than four minutes; in most cases, she would lose his attention after about thirty seconds. His intense concentration on the keyboard as he made a response, his smiling and nodding as he looked at the screen to see what his responses had wrought provided convincing evidence that manipulating one's environment is a powerful reinforcer.

The components of learning described in this section are what Skinner (1969) called the contingencies of reinforcement. In order to understand—and thereby control—the acquisition, retention, or loss of any behavior, we must know (a) the behavior itself, (b) the conditions surrounding the occurrence of the behavior, and (c) the reinforcer responsible for the acquisition and maintenance of the behavior. Reinforcement is contingent on behavior. In your classroom, you will reinforce certain student behaviors, but not others. The behaviors that bring about reinforcement can be controlled by discriminative stimuli, which, in turn, are established only in the presence of reinforcement. The components of learning are interrelated; their interactions are the contingencies of reinforcement.

Another way to view the contingencies that influence behavior is to ask: What's the deal? What will happen if behavior X is exhibited? What will happen if behavior Y is exhibited? In the next section, we will examine consequences of behavior. Understanding these consequences is an important part of operant conditioning theory. Teachers spend their days providing the consequences of student behavior.

Field Observation: Have students observe behavior in classrooms, in a workplace, or among children on a playground to determine the contingencies of reinforcement.

Principles in Practice 5.1

Principles . . .
1. Discriminative stimuli can control behavior.
2. Reinforcing stimuli increase the likelihood of a response in the same or similar circumstances in the future.
3. The components of learning are interrelated.

. . . in Practice
The teacher in Teacher Chronicle 5.1 looked for ways to improve Rodney's interaction with other students in the class. When the teacher noticed that Rodney wanted to take the football out for recess, taking the ball out was made contingent on socially acceptable behavior. Allowing Rodney to take the ball out served as a reinforcing stimulus for his social behavior.

The episode also shows that the weather was a discriminative stimulus. The reinforcement was only available during nice weather, when students took recess out-of-doors.

1. What other aspects of this situation might serve as discriminative stimuli?
2. Are there other potential reinforcers the teacher might have tried to improve Rodney's behavior?
3. Why should a teacher attend to discriminative stimuli when testing possible reinforcers?

JUST IN CASE

Leticia hated school. She spent a terrible year in the first grade at another school; on some days, she had to be dragged to school. At the beginning of her year with me, she frequently complained of stomachaches and headaches. After I had to take her to the principal's office and have her mom come to get her, I realized that something had to be done to convince Leticia that she could feel comfortable at school. I tried being extra nice to her, reassuring her at those moments when she seemed to lack confidence, building her up at every opportunity. After a time, this approach worked and I saw an improvement in her schoolwork as well as in her attitude.

Then things regressed and we had the stomachaches all over again. I consulted the school nurse for suggestions. We had her evaluated by the school psychologist. There seemed to be no physical or real mental problems. She just had a fear of teachers.

I got frustrated and grumped at her one day. She burst into tears. I expected a long phone call that night, but to my surprise I did not hear from her mom. The next day Leticia came to school but kept her distance from me. I decided to try something new. I kept a log of when she seemed upset or when she had a stomachache. After two weeks, I saw a pattern emerging. Her unhappy moods came right before recess or, if we didn't have recess, about midmorning. I called her mother and asked if she snacked during the midmorning on weekends. "Yes," her mother said. "It always seems to re-energize her."

"How about sending a snack to school that she can have at recess?" I asked. "I won't make any big deal out of it but she can hang back and have it before she goes outside." We tried this the next day. Leticia did not complain of a stomachache that morning. The midmorning snack continued to work each day thereafter. Whether it was actually the food or her feeling that she was somehow getting something extra, I don't know. Either way, the solution worked.

Chap. Obj. 3
Test Ques. 5.53–5.75

Focus Question: How does behavior operate on the environment?

law of effect Thorndike's law of learning, which states that any action that produces a satisfying consequence will be repeated in a similar situation. An action followed by an unfavorable consequence is less likely to be repeated.

CONSEQUENCES OF BEHAVIOR

The distinction between primary reinforcers and conditioned reinforcers partially defines reinforcement. In order to use it in a classroom, teachers must understand that reinforcement is not the only consequence of a response. In this section we will examine four kinds of consequences: positive reinforcement, negative reinforcement, and two types of punishment.

Related to the ideas of reinforcement and punishment is E. L. Thorndike's **law of effect** (1913, p. 4):

When a modifiable connection between a single situation and a response is made and is accompanied by a satisfying state of affairs, that connection's strength is increased. When made and accompanied by an annoying state of affairs, its strength is decreased.

The "states of affairs" in Thorndike's law of effect are consequences of behaviors. Some consequences increase the likelihood of behavior; others decrease it. In order to define the various kinds of consequences and to understand their effects on behavior, we will discuss the 2 × 2 matrix in Figure 5–2, which indicates the four types of consequences that can follow the response a learner makes in a particular stimulus situation.

Consider first, the dimensions that form the matrix in Figure 5–2. The horizontal dimension on the top of the matrix is "Desirability of Consequence." Desirability is in the eye of the learner. This is a crucial point for teachers who seek to manage their classrooms well, one to which we will return in this and other chapters. A desirable consequence is something for which the learner has an appetite. An undesirable consequence is something the learner does not want.

The vertical dimension of the matrix is "Change in Stimulus." The consequence of a response changes the stimulus situation. The situation is changed either by the addition of something new to the original stimulus or by the removal of some aspect of the stimulus that was originally present. In Leticia's case, discussed in Teacher Chronicle 5.2, a snack was added to her situation.

Here is a "shorthand version" of Figure 5–2.

- Desirability of Consequence: Behavioral consequences can be desirable or undesirable.
- Change in Stimulus: Consequences can add something new to the situation or take something away.
- The four cells of the matrix: Adding something desired by the learner as a consequence of behavior is called **positive reinforcement.** Adding something undesirable is called **punishment.** Removing something desirable, another type of punishment, is called **time-out.** Removing something undesirable is called **negative reinforcement.**

Connection: The examples include a story that introduces the section on the Premack principle later in this chapter.

Teaching Anecdote: Tell the story of a teacher who kept putting a disruptive boy out in the hall. She figured that he would miss participating in class and would control his behavior. She didn't realize that he provoked her when he was bored and wanted stimulation. He loved going to the hall, seeing the activity near the office, and talking with everyone who passed by. When the teacher discovered this attraction, she turned the tables. She began using the hallway as a reward when he cooperated in class.

Connection: See Teacher Chronicle 5.2: Just in Case.

Transparency: This figure is duplicated in the acetate transparency package. See T-7 Types of Consequences.

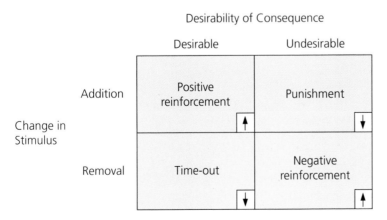

■ **Figure 5–2** *Types of Consequences*

SOURCE: From *Behavior Modification: Principles, Issues, and Applications* (p. 112) by W. E. Craighead, A. E. Kaydin, and M. J. Mahoney, 1976, Boston: Houghton Mifflin. Copyright 1976 by Houghton Mifflin. Adapted by permission.

Chapter 15 Casebook Preview: See Taking Control.

The following examples are presented to illustrate more clearly the four types of consequences and their effects. (If we have exaggerated these examples a little, we've done so to make the types of consequences more memorable.)

Positive Reinforcement

Imagine that you are taking a summer course. You are sitting in a steamy, hot classroom, when the instructor says, "Okay, let's take a ten-minute break." You bound from the room and dash to the soda machine down the hall. You plunk in coins and push a button in order to get something to quench your burning thirst. The stimuli here include the hot classroom, your thirst, and the soda machine. Your responses in this situation are to deposit money in the machine and press a button. Now, as a consequence of your response, imagine that the soda of your choice (how about an ice-cold diet drink?) drops with a satisfying clunk into the dispensing bin at the bottom of the machine. You reach for the can and feel the condensation on the cold aluminum. The can hisses as you pop the top. You take a long drink of the cold liquid. As you finish that first satisfying drink from the can, you give voice to your refreshment, "Ahhhh . . . ." As a consequence of plying the machine with quarters, you've received something desirable. The can of soda is added to the stimulus situation. This is an example of positive reinforcement.

Lecture Note: Emphasize that a consequence is not positive reinforcement until and unless the probability of the response increases.

If, a week from now, you find yourself in that stifling classroom as the instructor calls a ten-minute break, what will be your response? Because depositing money in the soda machine has led in the past to the addition of a desirable stimulus, you will likely engage in the same behavior. Positive reinforcement is a consequence that increases the probability that the behav-

Positive reinforcement by a teacher, such as praise and encouragement, can be a strong motivational force in learning.

ior will occur in the same or similar stimulus situations. (The upward-pointed arrow in the positive reinforcement cell of the matrix indicates that the probability of the response is increased.)

Punishment

Let's consider the cell to the right of positive reinforcement in Figure 5–2. In this cell, as with positive reinforcement, something is added to the stimulus situation as a consequence of a response. The difference is that the learner finds this consequence undesirable. The addition of an undesirable consequence is labeled "punishment." Let's return to your thirst in the classroom and examine the effects of this kind of punishment.

The instructor announces a ten-minute break; you dig for quarters as you stride to the soda machine. You respond to the stimulus in the same way as described in the previous example. This time, instead of being rewarded with something you want, you receive a can that is warm to the touch from the machine. You open the can to discover that it is only half filled. You take a sip anyway, but what you taste is just thick, sweet syrup. Someone forgot to add the carbonated water. You have not had your thirst quenched; rather, you are now anxious to get the taste out of your mouth. The addition to your stimulus situation in this case is undesirable; the consequence is an instance of punishment.

Because you've received warm syrup as a consequence of inserting coins in the soda machine, the probability that you will repeat your response (inserting coins in the machine) has been decreased. The next time you are hot and thirsty, you may use the soda machine again, reasoning that the warm syrup was a fluke. But the probability that you will has decreased. Suppose that you receive a can of syrup a second time, a third time, a fourth. The probability of inserting coins in the machine decreases after each instance. Eventually, you will stop feeding your money to the machine. You might even begin to behave other ways: You might stake out the machine to see if the responses of other thirsty learners receive the same consequence or you might call the vending company. Do you think you might try going to a different machine?

Time-Out

The two types of consequences represented in the bottom half of the matrix in Figure 5–2 occur when something is removed from the stimulus situation as the result of a response. The lower left cell is a kind of punishment called time-out, which occurs when a response is followed by the removal of a desirable stimulus instead of the addition of an undesirable one.

Suppose you find yourself back in that stifling summer classroom, but this time you have placed a small fan on your desk. The fan blows a pleasant, cooling breeze on your grateful countenance. The instructor has prefaced his presentation by saying, "I am going to speak about a critical concept for the next twenty minutes or so. I want you to think along with me. Please follow my remarks closely. I do not want you to take notes. If you try to write down everything I say, you will miss some of the important ideas I am discussing."

As the instructor begins, you listen dutifully but can't help jotting down a few notes from time to time. As you write in your notebook, the instructor walks over to your desk and turns off your fan. The fan, a desirable aspect of

Teaching Anecdote: Tell the story of Lawrence who tried to do everything he could to provoke a strong negative reaction from his teacher. Whenever he broke a rule, the teacher would yell at him, move his desk, or send him to the office. Whenever she tried persuading, rather than coercing, Lawrence would find a way to anger her. At conference time, the teacher gained an insight when his mother said, "If you ever have any problems with him, feel free to wallop him. That's what we do at home all the time."

Was Lawrence consciously trying to make his teacher angry or was he simply displaying behaviors he had learned at home?

Chapter 15 Casebook Preview: Gifted Achievers and Underachievers.

Lecture Note: Discuss what it means when the probability of a response is decreased in terms of motivation.

Issues in Educational Psychology

CNN™ This box relates to Segment 5 of the CNN videotape. See the Instructor's Section for a summary.

CORPORAL PUNISHMENT: AN ANACHRONISM IN THE '90S?

Sharon Pratt Dixon, Mayor of Washington, D.C., touched off a firestorm recently with a suggestion that teachers be given the right to use corporal punishment in the city's public schools. In an interview for NBC television, the mayor stressed that teachers "need to have the authority to instill standards and values and discipline in young people, especially in a society where so many women are working and trying to rear children alone."

The *Washington Post* reported that Dixon's endorsement of "spanking young people" triggered heated opposition. Educators, community leaders, politicians, and students voiced their concerns. William Simons, president of the Washington Teachers Union, stressed that in our litigious society, teachers wouldn't want the responsibility that goes with corporal punishment. More importantly, Simons didn't agree that hitting students was a way to handle problems. "Violence begets violence, and I consider corporal punishment as a form of violence that doesn't solve anything," he said.

Representative Major Owens (D-NY), in the meantime, has put together a bill to withhold federal funding from school districts that rely on corporal punishment. Echo-ing Simons, Owens emphasized that "one thing the children of Washington don't need is more violence. Their lives are full of violence."

In recent years corporal punishment as a disciplinary tactic in the schools has been losing ground nationwide. Nat Hentoff, writing in the *Washington Post* a full year before Dixon's remarks, sparked headlines with an article he did on the subject. Hentoff noted that in 1972 a psychologist from California began a newsletter devoted to eliminating school beatings. Hentoff also cited the National Parent Teachers Association stand against corporal punishment. But his most passionate argument against this form of discipline focused on the case of a first-grade boy in upstate New York who was "belted three times in one day" at school for minor infractions. The boy's father, who worked in law enforcement, had "frightening pictures of the damage done to the child." A judge's hands were tied because New York State law then allowed corporal punishment "short of deadly force."

In a *Washington Post* column, William Raspberry, commenting on Dixon's suggestion, recalled that in the rural Mississippi of the 1940s spankings at home and in school were a normal part of child rearing. He offered the opinion that being spanked in school did no harm to some children, "and probably did some good."

Raspberry stressed, however, that other children—those who failed a test or were too slow in class—were spanked "not because their deportment was significantly worse but because the teachers didn't like them." He wrote that as children he and his classmates understood that difference and the harm these spankings caused. "They humiliated their victims, confirmed them in their belief that they were stupid (or bad) and made them hate school."

Perhaps the city's students have captured the essence of the debate. One seventh grader noted that corporal punishment "would make you not come to school." A classmate put it even more strongly saying that "some children go to school to get away from abuse. A lot of kids would say, 'I go through that at home. Why go to school?' "

SOURCES: Hentoff, Nat. "Civilizing America's Schools." *Washington Post* 113 (March 10, 1990): A25, col. 1. French, Mary Anne. "Let Teachers Spank, Dixon Urges." *Washington Post* 114 (April 10, 1991): A1, col. 3. Gaines-Carter, Patrice, and Kenneth J. Cooper. "District's Mayor Taken to Task on Student Spanking." *Washington Post* 114 (April 11, 1991): C1, col. 5. Raspberry, William. "School Spanking: It Hurts." *Washington Post* 114 (April 12, 1991): A19, col. 2.

1. Why, according to Skinner's theories, is corporal punishment an ineffective method to deal with misbehavior?
2. Analyze Raspberry's statements concerning spanking in school from a behavioral learning perspective.

Time-out can be an effective method of decreasing the occurrence of undesirable behavior. Typically, the misbehaving student is separated from the rest of the classroom.

your stimulus situation, is removed when you look down to make notes. After several such episodes, the time-out consequence yields a decrease in your note-taking behavior.

Time-out is a form of punishment because its effect is to decrease the probability of the response that precedes it. The term *time-out* originally applied to the educational practice of separating a disruptive student from the rest of his or her classmates. Many times, the misbehaving student was put out in the hall or, in some classrooms, the "time-out" corner. The rationale for this practice is that if the child misbehaves to receive the attention of the teacher and/or other students, separating the troublemaker from his or her audience removes a desirable aspect of the environment, namely, the attention of others.

Teacher Interview: Have each student interview a teacher who uses time-out as a consequence to find out if the procedure works with all students, and if there is a pattern related to each student's desire for attention.

Negative Reinforcement

The final type of consequence is represented by the bottom right cell of the matrix. Negative reinforcement is often mistakenly thought to be a type of punishment, but it is distinct from both punishment and time-out. Negative reinforcement increases the probability of the response it follows. As can be seen in the matrix, types of punishment have the effect of decreasing that probability.

Once again you find yourself in that summer classroom. This time you encounter a set of circumstances that render the heat and your thirst trivial. This time, the instructor surprises the class with the most dreaded of classroom tortures: a pop-quiz.

"There are ten problems on the quiz," says the instructor as he passes them out. "We have been studying this type of problem for the last week. They have been addressed in the three chapters assigned last Thursday.

Lecture Note: The word *negative* has connotations that suggest punishment, but it is important to remember that negative reinforcement increases, rather than decreases, behavior.

Therefore, I expect each person to work these problems with practiced efficiency. In order to evaluate your efficiency, I will monitor your work closely. As you work, do not be surprised when I appear at your shoulder. Remember, practiced efficiency is what I expect to see from each and every one of you."

And practiced efficiency is what you want to show the instructor as he arrives to scrutinize your work. "The quicker I can demonstrate that I know how to work these problems," you think to yourself, "the quicker he will leave me alone."

Although this may be an extreme example, people are negatively reinforced with surprising frequency. Consider real schools and classrooms, workplaces and homes. Think of your own experiences in such environments. How many behaviors have you exhibited in order to escape or avoid undesirable stimuli? How many things have you done to keep a boss, a parent, or a teacher off your back? Negative reinforcement is sometimes called "escape conditioning" (see Sulzer-Azaroff, 1977). Skinner (1987) has long argued that our culture, in general, relies too heavily on negative reinforcement, when positive reinforcement is a better solution. As teachers, anytime we try to motivate by threat, we use negative reinforcement.

Although negative reinforcement is distinct from either type of punishment, it does have something in common with both. Three cells of the matrix rely on aversive control of behavior. **Aversive control** involves consequences that the learner finds undesirable. Punishment adds an undesirable aspect to the stimulus situation as a consequence of a response. Time-out removes a desirable aspect; such removal is undesirable. Finally, negative reinforcement works only if something undesirable is present initially in the stimulus situation, so that it can be removed in order to increase behavior. Positive reinforcement, which Skinner asserts is the best consequence to use to change behavior, is the only type of consequence that does not rely on aversive control. Think about Leticia in Teacher Chronicle 5.2. Were some of her problems in school the product of aversive control?

Before we move on, it will be helpful to note that reinforcement, both positive and negative, increases behavior. Punishment decreases behavior. Thus, a consequence is not reinforcement *until and unless* it increases the likelihood of a behavior. Conversely, a consequence is not punishment or time-out until and unless it decreases the likelihood of a behavior. Yelling at a student is not punishment until and unless the behavior that prompted the yelling decreases. We will examine this point in some detail later in the chapter. Keep it in mind as you consider how the consequences of behavior contribute to the behavioral contingencies that operate in classrooms.

CONTINGENCIES

The contingencies that operate in a classroom are determined by the behaviors emitted and the consequences provided by the environment. The **contingencies** of a classroom are the rules, the rewards, the punishments, the standards for academic performance; in short, the answer to the question, "What's the deal in this class?" When you begin a course you want to know the contingencies: What do I have to do to get an *A*? How many tests are

Field Observation: Have students take note of the differences in atmosphere of a classroom whose teacher relies heavily on threat and one in which the teacher relies more on positive reinforcement.

Connection: See the section on the Premack principle.

Chap. Obj. 4
Test Ques. 5.76–5.92

Focus Question: Why do some behaviors persist while others cease?

Journal Entry: Have students reflect on a classroom they enjoyed and one which they didn't enjoy. Have them identify the differences in terms of the contingencies that operated in each room.

there? Are the tests multiple choice or essay? Are there any papers? Is attendance taken? Do papers, if any, have to be typed? How long do they have to be?

Consequences of behavior are contingent on changes in behavior. As we saw in the last section, the nature of the consequences that follow a response influences the type of behavior change that occurs. For example, positive and negative reinforcement increase behavior while punishment and time-out decrease behavior. The frequency of consequences also plays an important role. In practice, the consequences do not always occur uniformly. Not every child who raises his or her hand to participate is called on. Not every smile from the teacher serves to reinforce; not every misbehavior is reprimanded. A student doesn't have to make the correct response to every item on every test to be rewarded with an *A*. How then does the frequency of reinforcement influence behavioral change?

Schedules of Reinforcement

Reinforcement can be delivered on a continuous or intermittent schedule. **Continuous reinforcement** is delivered after each and every response. **Intermittent reinforcement** is contingent not on each response, but on some schedule or combination of schedules (cf. Ferster & Skinner, 1957). There are two types of schedules of intermittent reinforcement: interval schedules and ratio schedules. Interval schedules are based on time. Reinforcement is available only after a certain interval of time has elapsed. Ratio schedules are based on the number of responses exhibited by the learner. Note that interval schedules are controlled from the environment; ratio schedules are controlled by the learner's behaviors (Skinner, 1953).

In addition to conditions of time and number, schedules of reinforcement are defined by the consistency with which reinforcement is delivered. Fixed schedules, whether they are interval or ratio, deliver reinforcement at a constant rate. Variable schedules deliver reinforcement at an unpredictable rate. Figure 5–3 identifies four schedules of reinforcement: fixed interval, variable interval, fixed ratio, and variable ratio.

Fixed Interval Schedules

A **fixed interval schedule** provides reinforcement for a correct response only after a certain period of time has passed. Classrooms are full of fixed interval schedules: the weekly spelling test on Friday, the unit test every six weeks, Friday afternoon films. All are schedules in which reinforcement is available only after a fixed period of time has passed.

Consider a high school math class in which the teacher gives a quiz every Friday. The reinforcement—a good grade on the quiz—is available to students only by taking the quiz. The behavior that will lead to reinforcement is studying. Judy is a typical student in the class. Let's follow her studying behavior throughout the week. Little studying occurs early in the week. Monday night is a wash-out; the math quiz seems as if it is a geological epoch away. On Tuesday night, Judy has fleeting thoughts about studying math, but not much studying for the quiz gets done. By Wednesday, Judy sees the clouds of Friday's quiz gathering on the horizon. Judy glances at the chapter that will be covered on Friday. On Thursday night, the storm is full-blown. The quiz

continuous reinforcement Reinforcement delivered after every correct response.
intermittent reinforcement Reinforcement delivered after correct responses on some, but not all, occasions, depending on some schedule or combination of schedules.
fixed interval schedule A schedule that provides reinforcement for a correct response only after a fixed period of time has passed.

Chapter 15 Casebook Preview: See Science Is Only Real When You Do It.

Lecture Note: Piecework is an example of a ratio schedule.

Journal Entry: Have students reflect on their experiences in classes in which they were given pop quizzes and those in which tests were given according to a predictable schedule.

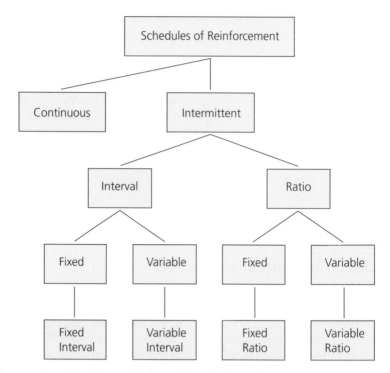

■ **Figure 5–3** *Schedules of Intermittent Reinforcement*

is imminent. In order to do well tomorrow, Judy sits down to work the example problems and reread sections of text when she runs into problems. She does the bulk of her math work for the week on Thursday night. Friday dawns and with it the availability of reinforcement.

The graph depicted in Figure 5–4 records Judy's cumulative studying behavior over several weeks. The scallop shape of the response rate is characteristic of behavior that is reinforced on a fixed interval schedule.

The length of a fixed interval can be relatively brief or relatively long and still yield the scalloped response rate. Think of the time axis in Figure 5–4 as representing semesters. Do you find the scallop rate descriptive of your own studying patterns? If you do, then you know something about "cramming." By the way, Ferster and Skinner (1957) recorded the same scallop shape when they observed rat behavior on a fixed interval schedule.

Variable Interval Schedules

A **variable interval schedule** yields a more uniform rate of response than a fixed interval schedule. If the day of Judy's weekly math quiz were unpredictable, Judy would study a little each day, rather than cramming on Thursday night. But then, it wouldn't be a weekly quiz, strictly speaking. Judy may have a quiz on Tuesday one week, Monday the next week, Thursday the week after. On average, the quizzes would occur once a week, but Judy could have a quiz two days in a row and then not have another for two weeks. Overall, the amount of studying might be the same under both fixed and variable interval schedules, the difference being whether the studying is massed (as on a fixed schedule) or uniformly distributed (as on a variable schedule).

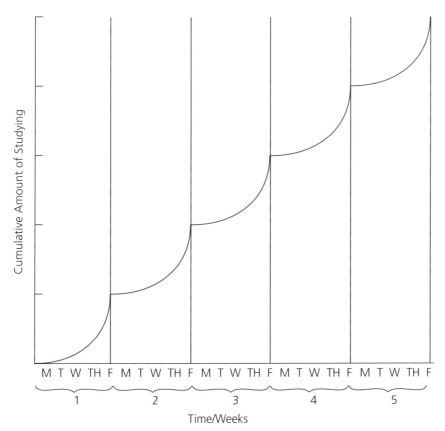

■ Figure 5–4 *Cumulative Responses Under a Fixed Interval Schedule*
SOURCE: From *Theories of Learning* (5th ed., p. 180) by G. H. Bower and E. R. Hilgard, 1981, Englewood Cliffs, NJ: Prentice-Hall. Copyright 1981 by Prentice-Hall. Adapted by permission.

fixed ratio schedule A schedule of reinforcement for a predetermined, fixed number of responses regardless of how long it takes to produce them.

Fixed Ratio Schedules

A **fixed ratio schedule** provides reinforcement for a consistent number of responses regardless of how long it takes to produce these responses. A child working on a computer program that requires five correct responses before allowing the child to advance to a new screen is working on a fixed ratio schedule. As in the case of a fixed interval schedule, a fixed ratio schedule can yield an uneven rate of response. Immediately after a reinforcement is delivered, the rate of response slows. It's as if the learner has taken a break to savor the reinforcement just received. Gradually, the rate of response increases.

In a fixed ratio schedule, each response brings the learner closer to reinforcement. As reinforcement gets closer, the rate of response increases. The uneven pattern of response is evident when the reinforcement to response ratio is high (e.g., one reinforcement for every seven responses, a ratio of 1:7). When the ratio is low, say, 1:100 or 1:500, a more stable response rate results (Skinner & Ferster, 1957). A low ratio of reinforcement to response means that each single response is less instrumental in bringing about a reinforcer. A stable response rate occurs when the reinforcement to response

variable ratio schedule   A schedule of reinforcement in which the number of desired responses varies from trial to trial.

The classic example of a variable ratio schedule of reinforcement is the slot machine, which "pays off" intermittently.

means that each single response is less instrumental in bringing about a reinforcer. A stable response rate occurs when the reinforcement to response ratio is low because the learner is conditioned to respond many times without reinforcement. This is important for teachers to understand. One of the things we hope for our students is that, as they develop, they become less dependent on external reinforcement. A high ratio of reinforcement is usually necessary when we seek to initiate a change in behavior. As learning progresses, the need for reinforcement lessens. Decreasing the frequency of reinforcements is called stretching the ratio (cf. Bell-Gredler, 1986).

Variable Ratio Schedules

Connection: Stretching the ratio is pertinent to the discussion of extrinsic and intrinsic motivation in Chapter 8.

A **variable ratio schedule** of reinforcement provides reinforcement after a varying number of desired responses are produced. This type of schedule is similar to a variable interval schedule; but reinforcement is contingent on the number of responses rather than on the time interval between reinforcements.

One high school teacher wanted to use extensive practice to teach math concepts in her remedial classes. She faced a major problem in encouraging her students, who were not highly motivated, to complete homework. She used a variable ratio schedule to solve her problem. For each homework assignment a student completed with at least 90 percent accuracy, he or she got some number of chances to spin the "wheel of fortitude." (Some assignments were worth more spins than others.) The wheel contained each student's name. If the student's name came up on one of his or her spins, the student won points that could be used to "buy" certain privileges. The teacher found that homework performance improved dramatically, and consequently, so did test scores. The teacher's scheme is an example of a variable ratio schedule because the number of spins that lead to winning varied. (There are other behavioral techniques at work in this example as well. We will encounter them shortly.)

If this classroom example sounds like a variation on a casino game, it is because variable ratio schedules underlie many games of chance. Slot machines, for example, pay off with a certain probability, albeit a very low probability. The more times you play a slot machine, the more likely you are to win. Veteran slot machine players persist in playing for long periods. Furthermore, their rate of response is very consistent.

A few years ago, one of the authors of this text had occasion to fly frequently to the West Coast, usually with a layover at McCarron Airport in Las Vegas, where the slot machines in the terminal taught him a lot about the effects of variable ratio schedules. He observed passengers leaving planes and literally running to play the slot machines. After observing this behavior several times, he walked over to ask some questions of one of the players.

"Excuse me. I've noticed that you play these slot machines with a flair."

"Yes," said the player without taking her eyes off the machine, "it's my rhythm. It's important to get a rhythm going on the slots. That way you can get more pulls per minute. The more pulls, the better you do." She said all this without losing a beat. "When I'm really in my rhythm, nothing bothers me. It's the rhythm that pays off, not the machine."

"How do you decide that it is time to stop playing a particular slot machine?" he asked.

"That's the hardest thing," said the player, still playing. "Every losing pull gets you closer to a payoff on that machine. The worst thing in the world is to walk away from a machine and have someone step in and win after just a couple of pulls. The longer you go without a jackpot, the closer every pull seems to get you. But you still have to stay in your rhythm; that's the best way to win."

Intermittent reinforcement, with sufficiently long intervals or ratios, can be a powerful controller of behavior. Setting up an environment and providing appropriate consequences is part of the teacher's job. The other part of the job is determining what responses should be reinforced.

Field Observation: Have students observe a token economy, paying attention to the effects of intermittent reinforcement.

Principles in Practice 5.2

Principles . . .
1. The consequences of behavior can increase or decrease the likelihood of that behavior being continued.
2. Positive reinforcement is superior to aversive control.
3. The schedule of reinforcement influences the rate of behavior.

. . . in Practice
For Leticia, in Teacher Chronicle 5.2, school was the site of a number of undesirable situations. There is no reason to doubt the authenticity of her

discomforts. Whether or not she actually experienced physical pain is almost beside the point, by reporting a stomachache or a headache she was able to leave the classroom. The teacher reported that using praise as a positive reinforcer temporarily improved her attitude toward school. Finally, noticing that Leticia's discomfort came at the same time each day as if on schedule, the teacher arranged for Leticia to have a midmorning snack, something she did at home on weekends. The snack worked. Whether it was the food itself or the sympathetic attention that she received, Leticia no longer found ways to avoid or escape the classroom. She no longer found the classroom situation to be aversive.

1. What are some possible explanations for the failure of the teacher's praise as a permanent solution to Leticia's discomfort?
2. What other actions might the teacher take to provide positive reinforcement for Leticia?
3. Assuming that it would be medically safe, what would be the advantage of "weaning" Leticia from her snacks?

Teacher
Chronicle
5.3

GETTING TO KNOW YOU

Every year I try to get to know my students as well as possible and as soon as possible. One method I use is to have the students complete an "interest inventory" sheet that lists such things as favorite foods, hobbies, family members, and pets. I fill in details in this profile as the year progresses. Getting to know the students as individuals helps me in making decisions that have an impact on them.

For example, Marlene was an exceptional reader. Previously, she had been held up to the other students as a model they should emulate. She obviously disliked being placed on a pedestal. She almost felt burdened because she read so well, as if she were different and therefore not part of the class. She rarely smiled. The other kids tolerated her but didn't really become involved with her in the classroom or on the playground. Her ability set her so far apart that she was isolated even in a crowded room.

How then could I challenge her and keep her interested in reading? More importantly, how could I do this and at the same time put a smile on her face?

I decided to set aside a certain shelf on the bookcase for her books. I filled the shelf with a variety of books at and above her reading level, and I then invited her to select her reading material from the shelf. She was thrilled by having her own shelf and the independence to select her own books.

Yet I did not want her to feel left out of the other activities in the room. In talking with her, I realized that she wanted to join the reading group, "but not all the time," as she put it. This suggestion proved an ideal solution. She decided each day whether she would read on her own or be part of the group. The class would discuss ahead of time the day's reading and she could choose whether or not to join the group. Eventually, she learned to combine individual reading and group activities almost every day. She benefited as did the other children because she became an excellent role model for individual reading. She contributed a great deal to group discussions and activities; she helped others in the group get over difficulties. Most importantly, her involvement helped break down some of the barriers between herself and the other children. Within a month, she was giggling with the rest of them and became one of the best shadow tag players at recess.

shaping The process of reinforcing responses that are successively more similar to the ultimate desired behavior. **successive approximations** Behaviors that, over time, come closer and closer to some complex action.

CHANGING BEHAVIORS

Chap. Obj. 4
Test Ques. 5.93–5.117

Focus Question: How can reinforcement be used to change behavior?

Chapter 15 Casebook Preview: See Student of the Week.

Teachers want students to be able to do things they weren't able to do before they had instruction. Sometimes teachers want students to eliminate certain behaviors from their repertoire. How do teachers effect changes in student behavior? In this section, we will consider several behavioristic techniques that teachers might employ.

Teachers have certain goals in terms of the behaviors they want their students to adopt. These goals are somewhat like holes on a golf course. A golfer rarely makes a hole in one. Instead, the golfer starts by taking his or her best shot with a driver. The object of the initial shot is to get as close to the green as possible so that the next shot will carry to the general vicinity of the hole. As the golfer gets closer and closer to the hole, he or she needs to be more precise in selecting the clubs to use and the shots to make. So it is in a classroom. The behaviors that the teachers set as their goals cannot be reached with one shot. Teachers must choose their environmental clubs and make their shots with increasing finesse, until they reach their goal, the change in students' behavior that they wish to effect.

Shaping

Chapter 15 Casebook Preview: See Taking Control.

The process of reinforcing successive approximations to a target behavior is called **shaping** (Reynolds, 1968; Skinner, 1954, 1963b). **Successive approximations** are behaviors that, over time, come closer and closer to some complex action. The first approximation of a forehand stroke in tennis is to grip the racket correctly.

Lecture Note: Using small steps to successively approximate complex behaviors increases the likelihood of success and, therefore, reinforcement.

Shaping behavior can be accomplished in a number of ways with a wide variety of behaviors. By simply paying attention to a little boy on the school playground, adding social reinforcement to the child's environment, a teacher shapes his play on the jungle gym, encouraging him at various stages of proximity to the jungle gym, touching, climbing, and finally extensive climbing—the target behavior (Harris, Wolf, & Baer, 1967). Skinner (1958) discussed shaping academic behaviors by using teaching machines, before the days of instructional computing. The presentation of material—either on audiotape, on a video monitor, or in a book—is called programmed instruction. Skinner prescribes programs that provide reinforcement of correct responses and that gradually increase in difficulty. Small steps, or frames, that proceed from simple to complex help to ensure that students respond correctly and are reinforced as often as possible.

Teacher Interview: Have students interview a teacher to find out how complex behaviors are broken down so that they can be successively approximated.

Shaping is necessary because many of the behaviors we desire of students are complex. If we waited for students to learn multiplication on their own or

fading The gradual withdrawal of a discriminative stimulus while the behavior continues to be reinforced.

speak French spontaneously before reinforcing learning behaviors, we might wait a very long time. So, teachers have to take an active role in modifying behavior. In Teacher Chronicle 5.3, the teacher had to take steps to shape Marlene's participation in the reading group.

Sulzer-Arazoff and Mayer (1986) have researched a variety of behavior modification techniques. Many of these techniques involve changing the contingencies of reinforcement as responses move closer and closer to the target behavior, stretching a ratio or interval, for example. Making desirable behavior less dependent on a reinforcing stimulus is one approach to achieving permanent changes in behavior. Another approach is to work with the discriminative stimulus.

Fading

Recall that discriminative stimuli can exert a measure of control over behavior. Suppose a student named Heidi has learned to stay on task whenever the teacher, Mr. Sterling, is walking around the room monitoring students. The monitoring aspect of Heidi's environment has come to control her seatwork behavior. Mr. Sterling is happy with Heidi's effort, but he also wants her to work effectively on her own.

Terrace (1963a, 1963b) conducted studies with pigeons that led to an approach called fading. **Fading** is the gradual withdrawal of a discriminative stimulus while the behavior continues to be reinforced. Mr. Sterling could use fading to make Heidi's seatwork behavior less dependent on his own behavior. Here's how he might do it.

Mr. Sterling knows that Heidi stays on task whenever he walks around the room monitoring students' work. Because she is working well, she is getting good marks on her papers. Mr. Sterling begins the fading procedure by spending less time next to Heidi's desk as he strolls around the room. As he continues, from day to day, to decrease his proximity to Heidi, he checks her work carefully to ensure that she is still earning good marks. He makes sure he reinforces Heidi's good work with laudatory comments on her papers or with verbal praise. He continues fading the discriminative stimulus. Occasionally he leaves the room for brief periods of time. While he is slowly removing the discriminative stimulus, he continues to reinforce Heidi's efficient seatwork.

If you think about it, teachers are in the business of making themselves unnecessary elements in their students' environment. Fading is an approach that helps achieve that end.

Teaching Anecdote: Tell the story of the teacher who used bear-shaped note paper to send her first graders' weekly reports home. Good notes were written on the front and notes about negative behavior on the back. The teacher decided to stop writing the notes at midyear but did not tell the students. Much to her surprise, only two students asked why they weren't getting their bears anymore. Why didn't more students ask about the notes?

Chapter 15 Casebook Preview: See Writers' Tea.

Connection: See the discussion of the "ripple effect" in the context of classroom management in Chapter 12.

Eliminating Behaviors

Behavior can also be effectively shaped by using various schedules of reinforcement and altering discriminative stimuli while maintaining reinforcement. However, in order to successively approximate desirable behavior, it is sometimes necessary to eliminate undesirable behavior. Mr. Sterling can't shape Heidi's seatwork if she is always out of her seat.

Earlier in this chapter we examined punishment. Its effect on behavior is to reduce the likelihood of a reoccurrence of the behavior it follows. If one student is hitting another student, the hitting is certainly a behavior that should decrease, and fast. If a toddler is about to probe an electrical outlet with a paper clip, punishment may be the best consequence to use. Punishment can stop behavior immediately; it can enhance discrimination by informing the learner of inappropriate behavior; it can be instructive to other learners (Azrin & Holz, 1966). The disadvantage of punishment is that it is a form of aversive control. Punishment may stop an undesirable response, but it doesn't encourage a desirable response in its place. Punishment can result in maladaptive side effects as well.

A psychology teacher, in order to demonstrate the problem of side effects, once asked his students to choose a behavior he exhibited frequently. Without informing the teacher of their decision, the students chose the teacher's habit of stroking his chin. After the behavior was chosen, the teacher handed out five squirt guns to students seated in the front of the room. The squirters were instructed to do nothing for a period of fifteen minutes while the teacher presented a bogus lecture; after that, for the next fifteen minutes, they were to shoot the teacher whenever he demonstrated the chosen behavior. The other students were to keep records of how many times the teacher engaged in the chosen behavior during that first fifteen minutes. Soon, the squirters began shooting the teacher each time he touched his chin with his hand. After only three minutes, the squirting stopped. There was no need to continue using the punishment because the teacher had stopped touching his chin. He had stopped almost every other behavior as well. He delivered the last twelve minutes of his bogus lecture with his face shoved into a corner—not the most adaptive of behaviors for a lecturer.

Elimination of behaviors can also be accomplished with a procedure called response cost, which is closely related to time-out (see Figure 5–2). Both procedures involve removing something desirable as a consequence of a response, the difference being that **response cost** is the withdrawal of *specified amounts* of reinforcers to reduce or eliminate some behavior (Weiner, 1969). For example, a child earns one dollar each week for taking out the trash. The child's mother is frustrated because she can't get the child to empty the wastebasket in the basement before he takes out the trash. The mother may try a response cost procedure, fining the child a dime each time he forgets to empty the basement wastebasket.

The procedure for eliminating behaviors that has shown the best results is **extinction,** a procedure by which a behavior that has been reinforced consistently is no longer reinforced. A parent who has decided after two weeks of interrupted sleep to ignore the crying of an infant is attempting to extinguish the baby's crying. Extinction has been demonstrated to eliminate effectively a wide variety of behaviors. In addition to crying, extinction has worked with tantrums, disruptive classroom behavior, aggression, and study avoidance (cf. Sulzer & Mayer, 1972). Extinction works best, as do other techniques for eliminating behaviors, when it is used in combination with reinforcement procedures to increase alternative, desirable behaviors.

The rapidity with which extinction works depends largely on the schedule of reinforcement that established the behavior. If the reinforcement has been continuous, extinction occurs very quickly. Behaviors reinforced through intermittent schedules of reinforcement resist extinction. The lower the ratio of reinforcement to response, or the longer the interval, the more resistant to extinction the reinforced behavior is. Consider an assembly line worker whose job it is to connect a "sproinger" to the "kintchel valve." The worker is able to make the connection quickly and then send the assembly down the line. An automatic counter keeps track of the number of connections completed. A bell in the counter sounds and a seven-minute break is awarded each time the worker completes one thousand connections, a low ratio of reinforcement to response. What would happen if the bell broke?

response cost A procedure that involves removing a specified amount of something desirable in order to reduce or eliminate some undesirable behavior.
extinction The gradual disappearance of a learned response by withdrawing the reinforcement.

Journal Entry: Have students reflect on classes in which their behavior was not very "adaptive." What contingencies operated in those situations?

Lecture Note: As an additional example, use the situation in which a teacher awards five points for completed homework assignments, but subtracts points for inaccuracy.

Teacher Interview: Have each student observe or interview a teacher regarding the types of behaviors that can and cannot safely be ignored.

Lecture Note: Ask students about the implications of a parent's insisting that a child eat green beans before being excused from the table and then after a twenty-minute "test of wills" allows the child to leave the table without having eaten the beans.

Chapter 15 Casebook Preview: See Bringing the Real World into the Classroom.

Field Observation: Have students observe a token economy or interview teachers who use this approach. Have them ask if the teachers have plans for stretching the ratio or fading.

Would the worker keep working or stop? What if the ratio were higher, say 1:200? What if the bell broke for a worker who was being reinforced continuously?

Token Economies

In a **token economy,** students earn objects (e.g., poker chips, marbles, stickers) that can be redeemed for reinforcers. Each reinforcer has a "price." After the requisite number of tokens has been earned through correct responses, the reinforcer is obtained. In many respects, token economies are fixed ratio schedules. The fixed ratio is different for each reinforcer: a dinosaur pencil may cost seven tokens while thirty minutes of free time on the computer may cost twenty-four. For a particular reinforcement, however, the ratio of responses to reinforcer is fixed.

Token economies have been shown to work in a variety of settings, including with patients in mental hospitals (cf. Ayllon & Azrin, 1968). In a remedial classroom, a token economy was used effectively to help students stay on task and to ask questions (Wolf, Giles, & Hall, 1968). Bushell, Wrobel, and Michaelis (1968) demonstrated the effective use of a token economy with children in a regular classroom, who, as a result of their participation in a token economy, increased their attention to task instructions and became more quiet.

Token economies differ from simple token collection systems, such as the ones set up by libraries to encourage children to participate in summer reading programs. Typically, children are awarded a star or a point or a sticker—which are displayed on a chart—for reading a certain type or number of books. After the children have completed the requirements of the program, they receive a certificate and have their names posted at the library. Similar systems are used in many classrooms: behavior charts, reading charts, multiplication charts, as examples. In such systems, unlike the true token economies, collecting stars or checks does not allow the student to choose a reinforcer. True token economies allow the learner some choice in determining reinforcement. In a token economy, the tokens acquire the status of conditioned reinforcer. As we saw in a previous section, conditioned reinforcers can, of themselves, be powerful motivators of behavior.

Lecture Note: Ask the class a question such as, "How many of you expect to teach in elementary schools?" After students have raised their hands, ask them to explain why they responded to your question by raising their hands. Use the demonstration as an example of rule-governed behavior.

Journal Entry: Have students reflect on teachers they had whose actions did not match their words. How effective were such teachers?

Rule-governed Behavior

The contingencies, or the "rules," that students learn and that come to govern their behavior can be learned by responding in an environment. Behavior that is controlled by rules is called **rule-governed behavior.** When students enter school, they must learn what the rules are. After spending several years in school, however, many of the "rules" are givens. Much of the behavior expected by teachers is rule-governed behavior (cf. Rachlin, 1991).

Without implying disrespect, the work of the teacher is, in some ways, the same as the work of an animal trainer. Both attempt to bring about certain behaviors on the part of a subject by controlling the reinforcement contingencies. In another respect, the work of the teacher and the trainer differ significantly. A teacher can talk to his or her students. The only language available to the animal trainer is the behavior of the animal and the delivery or removal of reinforcement or the use of punishment. The teacher can tell his or her students what the contingencies in the classroom environment are. To be sure, the teacher's actions must match his or her words if the contingencies are to govern behavior in the long run, but the business of prescribing the behaviors that will bring about particular consequences can be done much more efficiently by the teacher than by the animal trainer. It isn't always necessary for learners to respond and experience the consequences themselves. Learners, human learners anyway, can be told what the contingencies of a learning situation are.

If the squirters had told our chin-stroking psychology teacher that a water pistol barrage would follow chin stroking, chances are that our teacher would have fared better. The squirters were successful in eliminating chin stroking, but maladaptive behaviors replaced chin stroking. Had the teacher been told the rules of the situation, he would not have ended up in the corner. Once he knew the rules, being squirted would have served to remind him that his behavior was inappropriate. The chin stroking would still have decreased, but with less confusion and fewer maladaptive behaviors.

Many everyday behaviors are prescribed. Rules tell us how to operate a computer, how to conduct ourselves at a school assembly, how to write a check. You don't have to be punished to know that robbing a corner drugstore is inappropriate behavior. Rules inform us on that score. So, all you have to do in your classroom is tell your students what the rules are, right? Wrong.

We can tell students what the rules are, but knowing the rules and following the rules are two different things. Following rules is something a person does—a kind of behavior. Rule-following behavior, like any behavior, can be influenced by the consequences of the behavior.

Recall the last time you traveled by car on an interstate highway. Rules exist for driving on that highway, the speed limit, for example. No matter what the posted speed limit on the interstate was, most drivers on the road disregarded it, didn't they? Maybe you were one of the drivers who chose not to follow the rule. Why did you do that? You know why speed limits exist. Why were you speeding? And why will you probably speed again? Because, assuming that you were not caught, the consequences of exceeding the speed limit do not discourage speeding.

But, maybe you were caught. Were you pulled over by a state trooper? Did your heart pound with anxiety as the trooper approached your car? Did you wonder aloud if you had enough cash to pay the ticket you were about to receive? Such consequences will influence your rule-following behavior the next time you drive on an interstate highway.

The idea of rule-governed behavior accounts for the fact that behavior can be influenced by verbal advice, suggestions, and instructions. Rules also include generalizations that have developed as the result of consequences experienced by others. The stories, maxims, proverbs, and laws of a culture provide rules that prescribe behavior (Skinner, 1969).

It is important to remember that rules can be followed or ignored. Whether or not your students follow the rules you establish in your classroom is determined by the consequences they experience. So, remember the old teaching maxim: practice what you preach. If you follow that rule, your consequences will be desirable ones.

Knowing the effects of various types of behavioral contingencies is helpful in generating hypotheses about classroom management. It is one thing to know that positive reinforcement increases the probability of a response. It is another matter to know what, specifically, acts as a reinforcer and what does not. The last section of the chapter addresses a question asked continually by teachers: What do I use for reinforcement?

Lecture Note: Emphasize that learning rules involves more than being told what the rules are. It is a matter of experiencing the consequences of following or not following the rules.

PREMACK PRINCIPLE

What follows is a true story. The names have been changed to protect the recalcitrant.

Our actors are a sixth-grade boy—call him Neil, and a teacher—call him Mr. Snow. It is just after lunch. English class has started. Mr. Snow is handing back the tests that the students took the day before. He is not happy.

"I am sick and tired of you people not doing the assigned readings." He hands back some tests, shaking his head in disgust. "The scores on this test were atrocious. If you don't know what *atrocious* means, look it up in the dictionary. You'll find a picture of your test there." A few more tests, more disgust. "What's with you people? When I assign a story, you are to read it. Nobody read this story." Mr. Snow arrives at Neil's desk and pauses as he continues. "Nobody read this story with the exception of one person." He hands back Neil's test and says loudly, "Good work, Neil. I'm proud of you." Turning to the rest of the class, Mr. Snow says, "Neil got a 96 percent on the test; the next highest grade was 45 percent. Now what's the difference between you people and Neil? Think about it, think about it a lot, because you are going to take this test again tomorrow."

Mr. Snow finishes returning the tests and walks to the front of the room. "Okay, now let's review this test with the story in front of us." The students, including Neil, start opening their books to the assigned story. "Neil, you can put your book away. You don't have to waste your time going over this again, you've already done this work. You are excused to go to the library for the remainder of the period. You don't need to come to class tomorrow, either. The rest of the class will be tested on material you've already mastered."

Neil gathers his books, stands up, and walks past the other desks toward the door. He notices the faces of his classmates, especially the faces of Larry, Devin, and Charlie—the "guys." They are not happy.

"Good work, Neil," Mr. Snow says again as Neil reaches the door. "Enjoy the time off."

For the next two weeks, Neil suffers unending abuse from the "guys" for doing well on the test.

"Honest, you guys," says Neil for the twentieth time, "I didn't read that story. I just got lucky on the test. It was matching and true–false. I just guessed lucky and you guys didn't. Honest. Come on, give me a break."

"Shurrr, Neil." Neil is not happy.

Perhaps Mr. Snow thought he was reinforcing Neil while sending a message to the other people in the class. He said a lot of good things about Neil. He heaped praise on Neil. Verbal praise is a positive reinforcer. Right? Therefore, Mr. Snow was delivering positive reinforcement ensuring that Neil will work hard in English class. Right? Shurrr.

This story illustrates an important point: A teacher's action is not positive reinforcement because the teacher thinks it is. The "punishment" a teacher dishes out is only punishment if behavior decreases.

Effective reinforcement by a teacher must meet two requirements. First, the consequence must be desirable for the learner. We cannot assume that verbal praise is always desirable, nor candy, nor free time, nor high grades. As you recall, one of the basic assumptions of operant conditioning is that the individual is the appropriate source of information about learning. Individuals differ in what they find desirable and undesirable. Some people love

Profiles in Successful Practice

DIANNE M. BAUMAN

ST. THOMAS MORE SCHOOL

PITTSBURGH, PENNSYLVANIA

I teach a high-sixth grade, low-seventh grade reading class (22 students). I knew that I would have to be on my toes to keep the interest of such a diverse group. I have begun some of my lessons by running into class wearing my jogging suit and a bronze medal, while the theme from *Chariots of Fire* played in the background. My entrance caught their attention. The students' reading lessons at the time were about sports figures; they were eager to bring in their own trophies and medals to share with the rest of the class. It seemed that from that point on, I had created an environment in which they were much more willing to learn.

Another activity I have used is having students read "how to" books and then bring in homemade projects based on their readings. Their projects have included ecology boxes, stationery, and doll houses. The students are proud of the accomplishments, and we display them in the main hall of the school so other students can enjoy them as well.

I have also asked students to complete a unique kind of book report: a hanging mobile! I am usually amazed at the creativity they display in these assignments. One little boy read the mystery, *Ten Little Indians*. His "report" consisted of a bow from which he suspended each of the characters from the story. Parents have called to say that their children are genuinely interested in reading projects such as these, and that it's nice to see them excited about their education for a change!

English grammar can be taught in a multisensory way. For example, my sixth graders were experiencing difficulties with complex sentences. They could not understand that a main clause stood alone, and that a subordinating clause needed a conjunction to connect it with the main clause. So, I made signs that read "main clause" and "conjunction" and "subordinating clause." I chose three students and made up an elaborate story about the "main clause" being so independent, and so on. The story became a comedy with the students as the role players, although I was leading it in the direction I wanted it to go. I made each student a part of the sentence, giving each one a comical identity. Through the hilarity, the students were able to learn and enjoy English grammar.

All ages benefit from experience rather than lecture. In the elementary years, the subjects taught are more readily learned and accepted when creative activity accompanies the lesson. Hands-on teaching also creates a classroom with fewer behavior problems. After eleven years of teaching, I have found that to keep the juices of creativity flowing, I have had to vary my strategies.

Before I started teaching, I was an interpreter for the deaf, working in the Pittsburgh elementary and secondary school system. I became aware that students need to "experience" education, not just read it from a book. This approach to teaching requires creativity, stamina, and consistency, but in the long run, students benefit from it greatly. And so do you.

to spend time working in the yard; some people spend money so others will work in their yards for them.

Second, the teacher must be comfortable with the consequences he or she uses. There are any number of potential positive reinforcers. Many are tangible and obvious; an equal number are more subtle: a smile, a nod, a casual comment (Nye, 1979). Some teachers can reinforce students by laying a hand on a shoulder; some can't. Some can reinforce with a smile and a wink; others can't. Still others can joke with students, while colleagues are uncomfortable trying to be clever. The particular action that a teacher takes to reinforce or punish will work its intended effect only if the teacher can perform the action convincingly. Effective social reinforcement, for example, requires rapport between student and teacher. In addition to the personal rapport a teacher

Field Observation: Have students observe a classroom in which the teacher enjoys a good rapport with his or her students. Find out how he or she reinforces desirable behavior.

Premack principle A preferred behavior can be used to reinforce a less preferred behavior. The less preferred behavior would come first: for example, a child must eat his or her vegetables before having dessert.

does or does not enjoy with students, there is the matter of the particular classroom environment and the group of students with whom the teacher is working. In some schools, a teacher may be able to use a trip to the computer lab as a reward. In other schools, the school's structure and rules may not permit him or her to do so. Knowing one's interpersonal strengths and weaknesses, knowing what can and cannot be used as reinforcement in a particular classroom, allows the teacher to make realistic choices among reinforcers.

David Premack (1959, 1965) reviewed the conditions under which positive reinforcement influences behavior. His analysis yielded what is known as the **Premack principle:** A high-probability behavior can be used to reinforce a low-probability behavior.

What is a high-probability behavior? If you were given the opportunity to choose between playing a game of chess or jogging a mile, which activity would you choose? The activity you choose is your high-probability behavior. The Premack principle goes by another name, "Grandma's rule." The name comes from the contingency millions of grandmothers have used to get kids to eat vegetables, "Eat your green beans and then you may have some cake." Given a choice, most kids would choose to eat cake rather than green beans. The high-probability behavior—eating cake—is used to increase the incidence of the low-probability behavior—eating green beans.

When considering the Premack principle, we must keep in mind that we are thinking in relative terms. Does a high-probability behavior have a high enough probability to reinforce a low-probability behavior? Are there some behaviors with such a low probability that nothing could serve to reinforce them? Staying with the food motif, a person, whom we know well, is given a choice of eating liver (no onions) or okra. Of the two choices, our well-known eater would choose to eat the okra. Eating okra is the high-probability behavior, not because okra is highly desirable, but because liver causes our eater to gag. Under such conditions, Grandma is ill-advised to say, "Eat your liver and you may have some okra."

Connection: See Diary of a Day, Chapter 1.

Perhaps you have observed a classroom in which the teacher says something like, "Okay, we are going to have ten minutes of free time now so that

Privileges such as extra free reading time can be earned by successful performance on a less popular task.

we will be ready to concentrate on those verb conjugations during language arts." Assuming that using free time is a high-probability behavior, such an attempt misses the point of the Premack principle because the high-probability behavior is not used to reinforce verb conjugation, a low-probability behavior. You may recall Peter Roop's practice of allowing his students to chat for a few minutes before starting the day's activities. Peter does not miss the point, however, because he does not link free time and later work.

The Premack principle does not change what Skinner tells us about contingent reinforcement. Rather, Premack increases our chances of selecting effective reinforcers. How do you select a reinforcer that will be effective for a particular student? Why not ask? Restaurants give their customers menus from which to choose. A reinforcement menu can be used to determine what students would like to receive as a consequence of their behaviors. Once you have identified high-probability behaviors, you can use those behaviors to reinforce other behaviors you desire for your student. One way to strike a deal is to negotiate a contract. We will see some examples of contingency contracts and other management techniques in Chapter 12.

Journal Entry: Have students reflect on situations in which they had a choice of reinforcers and how that choice influenced their behavior.

Connection: See the discussion of contracting in Chapter 12.

Principles in Practice 5.3

Principles . . .
1. Modifying behavior takes time.
2. Presenting contingencies to learners increases changes in behavior.
3. A high-probability behavior can be used to reinforce a low-probability behavior (the Premack principle).

. . . in Practice
Marlene, in Teacher Chronicle 5.3, did not enjoy an easy-going relationship with her classmates. The teacher tried a solution that, over a period of time, improved her social interaction. An important aspect of Marlene's problem was that she participated in designing a solution. By discussing the situation with Marlene, the teacher was able to make the contingencies very clear to her. Marlene realized that she had some control over her environment through her own behavior. The solution also allowed Marlene to make some choices that, in turn, allowed the teacher to discover higher and lower probability behaviors.

1. Would a token economy have induced Marlene to participate in reading groups more quickly? Would a token economy have been preferable to the solution devised?
2. Do you think Marlene felt empowered by the solution? Do you think that empowerment made a difference?
3. What other items would you put on a reinforcement menu for Marlene to choose from?

CONCLUSION

Assign Chapter 5 of the *Study Guide*.

This chapter has given us one view of how students learn. The operant perspective, which dominated the chapter, emphasizes those aspects of behavior that fall under instructional rules of discipline and classroom management.

Connection: See the discussions of motivation in Chapter 8 and of classroom management and discipline in Chapter 12.

(We will see the operant perspective again when we consider motivation in Chapter 8 and classroom management in Chapter 13.)

Let's reflect briefly on what the operant perspective does for us as teachers. The psychology of B. F. Skinner shows us a way to observe the environment and the behavior of a learner. It provides the tools necessary to perform an operant analysis of behavior, which we as teachers must do in our own classrooms. We must decide what behaviors to change and how to change them. We must test the effectiveness of various consequences with the individuals whose behavior we are attempting to change. Teaching is an empirical endeavor, not a theoretical one.

The classroom situations considered in this chapter focused on behaviors that teachers can see students displaying. There are other views of learning that focus on behavior that cannot be observed directly, but only inferred from other behavior. Chapter 6 presents the information-processing theory of learning. In that chapter, we will consider how students understand the content they encounter, how they retain that understanding, and how they use it to solve problems.

Chapter Summary

Introduction: Behaviorism
Origins of Operant Conditioning
Operant conditioning is a behavioristic view of human learning. This explanation of learning relies on the observable environment and observable behaviors. Skinner's operant model of learning came from his study of Pavlov's work with behaviors that were reflexes to environmental stimuli. Skinner's theories address behaviors that lead to environmental consequences, and thus operate on the environment.

Assumptions of Operant Conditioning
The assumptions underlying operant conditioning are consistent with the principles of behaviorism. They address the necessity for careful control and observation of behaviors and the environments in which behaviors occur. Most important, from a teaching standpoint, is the assumption that the individual is the appropriate data source about behavior.

Components of Learning
Discriminative Stimuli
Discriminative stimuli are aspects of the environment that are dependent on the presence of reinforcement. Such stimuli can control behavior. The behaviors that teachers use to accompany reinforcement are potential signals of appropriate behaviors for students. Discriminative stimuli can also control superstitious behavior.

Reinforcing Stimuli
Reinforcing stimuli are consequences that follow a behavior and that serve to increase the likelihood of that behavior. Reinforcement, either positive or negative, is not the only kind of consequence. Forms of punishment may also follow behaviors. Punishment decreases the likelihood of reoccurrence of a behavior.

Primary Reinforcers and Conditioned Reinforcers
Primary reinforcers meet some basic need, such as food, water, or shelter. Conditioned reinforcers are, of themselves, neutral. They can become associated with primary reinforcers to such an extent that they influence behavior. Examples include money, grades, and other forms of recognition.

Consequences of Behavior
Positive Reinforcement
Positive reinforcement is the addition of something desirable to the stimulus situation as a consequence of some response. The effect of positive reinforcement is to increase the likelihood that the behavior will reoccur. A consequence cannot be judged to be a positive reinforcement unless the probability of reoccurrence increases.

Punishment
Punishment is the addition of something undesirable to the stimulus situation as a consequence of a response. The effect of punishment is to decrease the likelihood that the behavior will reoccur. A consequence cannot be judged to be punishment unless the probability of reoccurrence decreases.

Time-Out
Time-out is the removal of something the learner finds desirable as a consequence of a response. The effect of time-out is to decrease the likelihood that the behavior will reoccur. A consequence cannot be judged to be time-out unless the probability of reoccurrence decreases.

Negative Reinforcement
Negative reinforcement is the removal from the stimulus situation of something the learner finds undesirable as a consequence of some response. The effect of negative reinforcement is to increase the likelihood that the behavior will reoccur in the future. A consequence cannot be judged to be negative reinforcement unless the probability of reoccurrence increases.

Contingencies
Schedules of Reinforcement
Reinforcement can be delivered intermittently on schedules that are variable or fixed. Schedules of reinforcement can also define contingencies in terms of number of responses or the period of time between responses. There are four types of intermittent reinforcement: variable interval, fixed interval, variable ratio, and fixed ratio.

Changing Behaviors
Shaping
Shaping is the use of reinforcement, preferably positive reinforcement, to encourage successively closer approximations of some target behavior. Because many of the behaviors teachers desire for their students are complex, behaviors must be shaped.

Fading
Fading is the gradual withdrawal of discriminative stimuli while continuing to reinforce the response. Fading is a procedure teachers use when they wish to make student behavior less dependent on themselves or other aspects of the student's environment.

Eliminating Behaviors
Punishment is one way to decrease undesirable behaviors, but it can also lead to new, maladaptive behaviors. Response cost is a procedure by which a specified amount of reinforcers is removed to reduce or eliminate behaviors. Extinction, another procedure for eliminating behavior, is the removal of all reinforcement. The effectiveness of extinction depends on the schedule of reinforcement in place when extinction is begun.

Token Economies
In a token economy, students earn objects (or tokens) as the result of appropriate behavior. The tokens can then be used to "buy" reinforcers. The reinforcers may include free time in the library, computer use, or something as simple as a pencil. In a token economy, the token acquires the status of a generalized reinforcer.

Rule-governed Behavior
Behavior prescribed by rules as appropriate or inappropriate is called rule-governed behavior. In a classroom, rules can be established, but the rules will only govern behavior if the consequences of following or violating the rules are delivered consistently.

Premack Principle
The Premack principle states that a high-probability behavior can be used to reinforce a low-probability behavior. In practical application, if a teacher can find out what behaviors students prefer, those behaviors can be used to increase behaviors that the students find less preferable. One way to use the Premack principle is to establish a contract for student behavior.

Reflections: Building Your Theory of Teaching

5.1 Think about teachers you had in school with whom you interacted well. Analyze their behaviors, determining which behaviors were reinforcing to you and your classmates. Which of these teacher behaviors would you add to your repertoire of reinforcing behaviors?

5.2 Suppose Judy has just moved to Massachusetts from Laramie. She is naturally apprehensive about her new school; her new classmates; and the customs of speech and dress in New England, which she thinks might differ from those she grew up with in Wyoming. Judy brings these apprehensive feelings into the classroom on her first day. Reflect on how you, as the teacher of her class, might help Judy adapt to her new environment.

5.3 The productivity in a factory suffered because of a massive amount of worker tardiness. In order to solve the problem, a token economy was started. Tokens, which could be exchanged for a small amount of money, were given to workers who arrived at work on time. As a result, the amount of tardiness fell from roughly 10 percent to 2 percent and remained there.

The company had, prior to the token reinforcement program, awarded an annual bonus of $40 to workers who were consistently punctual. Under the new program, a worker who earned all the tokens available would wind up with a cash incentive of approximately $40. The annual bonus did not work. The token economy did. What classroom hypotheses does this study suggest? (The findings reported here are from a study by Herman, deMontes, Dominquez, Montes, & Hopkins, 1973.)

Key Terms

behaviorism (p. 172)
unconditioned stimulus (US) (p. 173)
unconditioned response (UR) (p. 173)
conditioned stimulus (CS) (p. 173)
conditioned response (CR) (p. 173)
respondent behavior (p. 173)
respondent conditioning (p. 173)
operant behavior (p. 173)
operant conditioning (p. 174)
operant analysis (p. 175)
discriminative stimulus (p. 176)

behavioral control (p. 176)
reinforcing stimulus (p. 177)
primary reinforcer (p. 177)
conditioned reinforcer (p. 178)
generalized reinforcer (p. 178)
law of effect (p. 180)
positive reinforcement (p. 181)
punishment (p. 181)
time-out (p. 181)
negative reinforcement (p. 181)
aversive control (p. 186)
contingencies (p. 186)
continuous reinforcement (p. 187)
intermittent reinforcement (p. 187)

fixed interval schedule (p. 187)
variable interval schedule (p. 188)
fixed ratio schedule (p. 189)
variable ratio schedule (p. 190)
shaping (p. 193)
successive approximations (p. 193)
fading (p. 194)
response cost (p. 195)
extinction (p. 195)
token economy (p. 196)
rule-governed behavior (p. 196)
Premack principle (p. 200)

Suggested Readings

Nye, R. D. (1979). *What is B. F. Skinner really saying?* Englewood Cliffs, NJ: Prentice-Hall.

Rachlin, H. (1991). *Introduction to modern behaviorism* (3rd ed.). New York: W. H. Freeman.

Skinner, B. F. (1948). *Walden two.* New York: Macmillan.

Skinner, B. F. (1974). *About behaviorism.* New York: Knopf.

Skinner, B. F. (1987). Whatever happened to psychology as the science of behavior? *American Psychologist, 42,* 780–786.

References

Ayllon, T., & Azrin, N. H. (1968). *The token economy*. New York: Appleton-Century-Crofts.

Azrin, N. H., & Holz, W. C. (1966). Punishment. In W. K. Honig (Ed.), *Operant behavior: Areas of research and application* (pp. 380–447). New York: Appleton-Century-Crofts.

Bell-Gredler, M. E. (1986). *Learning and instruction*. New York: Macmillan.

Bushell, D., Wrobel, P., & Michaelis, M. (1968). Applying "group" contingencies to the classroom.

Ferster, C. B., & Skinner, B. F. (1957). *Schedules of reinforcement*. New York: Appleton-Century-Crofts.

Harris, F. R., Wolf, M. M., & Baer, D. M. (1967). Effects of adult social reinforcement in child behavior. In S. W. Bijou & D. M. Baer (Eds.), *Child development: Readings in experimental analysis*. New York: Appleton-Century-Crofts.

Herman, J. A., deMontes, A. J., Dominiquez, B., Montes, F., & Hopkins, B. L. (1973). Effects of bonuses for punctuality on the tardiness of industrial workers. *Journal of Applied Behavioral Analysis, 6*, 563–570.

Hess, R., Chih-Mei, C., & McDevitt, T. M. (1987). Cultural variation in family beliefs about children's performance in mathematics: Comparisons among People's Republic of China, Chinese-American, and Caucasian-American families. *Journal of Educational Psychology, 79*, 179–188.

Ludwig, P. J., & Maehr, M. L. (1967). Changes in self-concepts in stated behavioral preferences. *Child Development, 38*, 453–469.

Nye, R. D. (1979). *What is B. F. Skinner really saying?* Englewood Cliffs, NJ: Prentice-Hall.

Premack, D. (1959). Toward empirical behavior laws: I. Positive reinforcement. *Psychological Review, 66*, 219–233.

Premack, D. (1965). Reinforcement theory. In D. Levine (Ed.), *Nebraska Symposium on Motivation* (Vol. 13, pp. 123–180). Lincoln: University of Nebraska Press.

Rachlin, H. (1991). *Introduction to modern behaviorism* (3rd ed). New York: W. H. Freeman.

Reynolds, G. S. (1968). *A primer of operant conditioning*. Glenview, IL: Scott, Foresman.

Skinner, B. F. (1938). *The behavior of organisms: An experimental analysis*. New York: Appleton-Century-Crofts.

Skinner, B. F. (1950). Are theories of learning necessary? *Psychology Review, 57*, 193–216.

Skinner, B. F. (1953). *Science and human behavior*. New York: Macmillan.

Skinner, B. F. (1954). The science of learning and the art of teaching. *Harvard Educational Review, 24*, 86–97.

Skinner, B. F. (1958). Teaching machines. *Science, 128*, 969–977.

Skinner, B. F. (1963). Operant behavior. *American Psychologist, 18*, 503–515.

Skinner, B. F. (1969). *Contingencies of reinforcement*. New Jersey: Prentice-Hall.

Skinner, B. F. (1974). *About behaviorism*. New York: Random House.

Skinner, B. F. (1987). *Upon further reflection*. Englewood Cliffs, NJ: Prentice-Hall.

Sulzer, B., & Mayer, G. R. (1972). *Behavior modification procedures for school personnel*. New York: Holt, Rinehart & Winston.

Sulzer-Azaroff, B., & Mayer, G. R. (1977). *Applying behavior-analysis procedures with children and youth*. New York: Holt, Rinehart & Winston.

Sulzer-Azaroff, B., & Mayer, G. R. (1986). *Achieving educational excellence*. New York: Holt, Rinehart & Winston.

Terrace, H. (1963a). Discrimination learning with and without learning. *Journal of Experimental Analysis of Behavior, 6*, 1–27.

Terrace, H. (1963b). Errorless transfer of a discrimination across two continua. *Journal of Experimental Analysis of Behavior, 6*, 223–232.

Weiner, H. (1969). Controlling human fixed-interval's performance. *Journal of Experimental Analysis of Behavior, 12*, 349–373.

Wolf, M. M., Giles, D. K., & Hall, V. R. (1968). Experiments with token reinforcement in a remedial classroom. *Behavioral Research and Therapy, 6*, 51–64.

Wolf, M. M., Risley, T. R., & Mees, H. L. (1964). Application of operant conditioning procedures to the behavior problems of an autistic child. *Behavior Research and Therapy, 1*, 305–312.

6
Cognition: Codes of Understanding

Chapter Overview

This chapter examines the information-processing view of learning, which is, unlike operant conditioning, a cognitive theory. It explains learning in terms of mental structures and processes that cannot be directly observed, but only inferred. The major structures of the model of human information-processing are called memory stores. Among the ways that these structures differ is in their storage capacity and the nature of the information they store. Information moves from store to store by means of other cognitive processes. The ways in which students process new information are heavily influenced by the prior knowledge students bring to learning situations. This chapter concludes with a detailed discussion of the ways teachers can help students integrate prior knowledge with new material they are learning. ■

INTRODUCTION: UNDERSTANDING

A high school teacher walked into her advanced placement physics class and said, "What I'm about to write on the board is the most important formula in physics. Learn the formula!" She turned to the board and wrote

$$E = mc^2$$

Turning back to the class, she waited for her students to write the formula. Then she said, "E is energy, m is mass, c is a constant which, in this case, is the speed of light. Remember the definitions!" She wrote on the board

$$E = \text{energy}$$
$$m = \text{mass}$$
$$c = \text{constant (speed of light)}$$

"Now," she said, "here's what it means." She paused to make sure every student was paying attention. "The energy available in any object is equal to the mass of the object times the square of the speed of light." She repeated the sentence as she wrote it on the board. When the students had finished writing in their notebooks, she said, "That means the amount of energy available from the objects in this room is enormous. Does that make sense?" All of the students nodded earnestly.

One student even blurted out, "Yeah, because the speed of light is a large number, energy will be large." Several students voiced their agreement amidst more confirming nods.

"So, everyone understands the formula, right?" She walked slowly around the desk, sat on the front edge, and, in a very quiet voice said, "That's good, very good. I'm impressed, I really am. I learned that formula when I was a senior in high school and I have remembered it all these years. But I must tell you, I still don't understand it."

What does it mean to "understand"? Royer and Feldman (1984) draw a useful distinction between *understanding* as we use the term in an everyday sense and *understanding* as it is used by cognitive psychologists. The everyday sense of the word conveys a subjective experience of empathy or comprehension. If a friend tells you about his or her disappointment and anger at not being accepted in a graduate program, you might say, "I understand how you feel." When you use "understand" in this sense, you mean that you can empathize with your friend's emotional state.

Consider the use of the word *understanding* to denote comprehension. For example, "For best results, squeeze tube from bottom." After reading the sentence, you probably have a sense of what it means. However, consider this sentence, "The trip was delayed because the bottle broke" (Bransford & McCarrell, 1974). This sentence most likely leaves you with a sense of uncertainty. The words are familiar but you are not sure what they mean. As a message, the sentence is difficult to decipher. When the physics teacher asked her students if they understood Einstein's formula, they had a sense that they followed her message, so they responded affirmatively to her query. Teachers must monitor students' understanding to know when their students do and do not understand the material. It is, perhaps, the most important kind of feedback a teacher can receive from students. Is asking them for their subjective sense of comprehension ("Do you understand?") the best way to monitor their understanding? The students said they understood Einstein's formula, but did they?

Understanding—from a Cognitive Perspective

From a cognitive perspective, understanding is the most important outcome of learning. When students have acquired information in a way that allows them to solve problems or serves as a foundation for mastering additional material, this important learning outcome—understanding—has been achieved (cf. Royer & Feldman, 1984).

From a cognitive perspective, understanding the concept of *percentages* means more than being able to say that "percentage is computed by dividing the smaller number by the larger number." The student who truly understands percentages should be able to use this knowledge to solve problems. What we are considering is the question of the degree of difficulty of the problems proposed. How difficult or complex must the problems be to qualify as tests of understanding? Does the student who is able to work the prepared problems at the end of a textbook chapter understand the chapter's material? Must the student demonstrate knowledge of percentages on a tax return before one concludes that the student understands?

Cognitive understanding can also serve as the foundation for continued learning. The concepts and information that students understand become part of their accumulated knowledge and experience; they bring this with them to school and can use it to make sense out of new information. Recall the sentence, "The trip was delayed because the bottle broke." It is difficult to make sense of this sentence without existing, or prior, knowledge. But suppose you had just read a passage about a ship launching. This passage would have activated your prior knowledge about the events that take place when a ship is launched. The sentence beginning, "The trip was delayed . . ." could now be considered in a different, more informed context. Integrating information that students are to learn with their prior knowledge is a crucial instructional task.

Information Processing

Information processing, the cognitive theory underlying this chapter, is based on a computer model of how humans process information. The advent of the widespread use of computers coincided with the growth of psychological research. Psychologists were among the first to use computers to help them in their work (particularly in conducting statistical analyses). These psychologists became knowledgeable about the ways in which computers processed information; they began to theorize that humans processed information in an analogous way (Hunt, 1971). Human information-processing models borrow heavily from the vocabulary of the computer using terms such as *input, output, storage systems, capacity, encoding, retrieval,* and *executive control.*

Much of the information encountered in classrooms is coded information. Making sense out of written or spoken information is a matter of using a linguistic code. Using numerals and symbols to define and solve mathematical problems requires another code. Making sense of information from the environment requires students to represent that information cognitively. How do students transform messages from their teachers and textbooks into

information processing A theory of learning that relies on an analogy between the human mind and the computer to explain processing, storage, and retrieval of knowledge.

Chapter 15 Casebook Preview: See Around the World.

Connection: Transfer of learning is discussed in detail in Chapter 10.

Lecture Note: Sherlock Holmes once used the analogy of "storing items in an attic" to describe human cognition. Ask students why the computer metaphor is better.

Teaching Anecdote: Tell the story of the junior high science teacher who, convinced that the key to understanding a subject is the ability to understand and use a subject-appropriate vocabulary, hit upon a fun way for her students to learn new vocabulary: she had them write jokes. Extra credit was given for jokes and jokes regularly appeared on tests.

Ask students why joke writing would help in remembering subject-linked vocabulary.

Lecture Note: Emphasize the fact that no student who enters a classroom is devoid of knowledge. Students come to a class knowing a great many things. What students know and do not know is an important determiner of the success you will have as an instructor. From an information-processing point of view, the question a teacher needs to ask is, "What should students do with what they know?"

Lecture Note: Have pairs of students compare their study tactics and note the differences.

cognitive codes that can be stored and then retrieved for later use? How do students learn the codes? And once learned, how do they use the codes to comprehend new information, understand concepts, and use skillfully what they have learned? The information-processing view assumes that certain types of mental structures form a mechanism by which information is acquired, comprehended, stored, and retrieved for later use.

As you read the remainder of this chapter, remind yourself from time to time of the distinction between "theme" and "variations." Information-processing theory is a general description and explanation of how humans understand, remember, and learn. As such, the theory is a theme. Themes have variations, however. For example, we will examine the process of encoding—how humans interpret signals from the environment. Everyone encodes information, but not everyone encodes in precisely the same way. The process of encoding is the theme, the different ways of encoding are variations on that theme. Keeping this relationship in mind, we will be able to use the information-processing view of learning to define workable classroom hypotheses.

Teacher
Chronicle
6.1

KNOT UNDERSTANDING

Ownership. When does knowledge become a student's for keeps? When do they "own" the information, the procedure you wish them to know? Is it after constant repetition, or is it when they understand how something "works"?

Once I was teaching Keith how to do string figures. Keith was a hands-on kind of kid. He could fix clocks, take apart a TV and reassemble it, or open a locked desk with a paper clip. When I needed help one Saturday fixing the broken chain on my bike, I called on Keith.

I had been learning string figures to use in teaching a unit on Eskimo storytelling. I had "learned" the "Cat's Cradle" and "Jacob's Ladder" the night before. My learning technique involved reading the directions and following them until mastering the string figure. Then I taught them to the class the next day. Of all of the students, Keith became the most intrigued. He begged me to teach him string figures.

I went home and learned the "Sunset." But I couldn't do all of the complicated steps without having the book open before me. I brought the book to class and watched Keith as he learned the new figure. While I had read the instructions and tried the process immediately, he read and reread the directions without using the string at all. But when he did pick up the string he could immediately make the figure.

When I asked him how he learned the difficult "Sunset" so fast, he looked at me with a puzzled expression and said, "I see how the strings work. Then I can do it." He understood; he "saw" in his mind how the strings interacted and therefore quickly mastered new figures. I did not "understand" how the string worked but was simply following the pattern in the book. As the figures got more complicated, he mastered them much more quickly than I did. Even in sixth grade, three years after we'd made the string figures, Keith was still able to make all of the ones we'd learned together.

Now, ten years later, I tried to make the string figures again. My fingers remembered the "Cat's Cradle," but I could not recall how to make "Jacob's Ladder." And I'd certainly need the book again for the "Sunset." I'd be willing to bet that if I called up Keith now he'd be able to make just about any of the figures we had learned together. He owned the information. He had really learned it.

■ ■

THE MODEL OF HUMAN INFORMATION PROCESSING: STRUCTURES

Chap. Obj. 2
Test Ques. 6.11–6.44

Suppose you went to a museum where you could see an exhibit depicting the workings of a student's mind. Keeping in mind the distinction between physical description and psychological description, what would such an exhibit look like?

Let's call this imaginary exhibit SMART. Imagine that a museum guide is describing the exhibit.

"SMART," says the guide, "is an acronym that stands for the Student's Mind: Analogical Representations for Teachers. The exhibit is based on the knowledge cognitive psychologists have provided us with about how people process information. The Student's Mind is hard to describe because it's so abstract. When you look at the exhibit from the outside, the only thing you see is the vaguely tunnellike entrance. Once you step inside the Student's Mind, however, you see representations of mental structures and processes.

The mental structures are represented by boxes, a box for short-term memory, a box for long-term memory, and so forth. In addition, there are arrows and other lights that flash in various patterns to indicate how the mental processes work, how information moves through the Student's Mind, and how information changes as different mental structures come into play. What we have tried to do is create a structural representation of the information cognitive psychologists have given us about the working of a student's mind."

Figure 6–1 (p. 213) is a flowchart illustrating the human information-processing system—the cognitive mechanism by which information from the environment is perceived, understood, and retained. Most information-processing models can be traced to Atkinson and Shiffrin (1968). (This is true of the flowchart in Figure 6–1 adapted from Gagné and Driscoll, 1988.)

Focus Question: Why do students learn and remember some concepts more easily than others?

Connection: We refer here to the museum of modern instruction discussed as an organizational metaphor in the Instructor's Section.

Overview of the Model

The Model in Figure 6–1, which we will refer to a number of times as we move through the chapter, depicts storage structures, support structures, cognitive processes, control (metacognitive) processes, and neural connections. In this chapter, we will focus primarily on the storage structures and cognitive processes.

First, let's follow the flow of information through the various structures, listing and defining the important components. Later, we will pause to look more closely at how information is transformed and how it is transferred from one structure to another.

Connection: Metacognition was described in the discussion of "cognitive development" in Chapter 2.

By using techniques such as visual aids, students can learn and master diverse skills.

environment The source of input into the human information-processing system.

receptors Sensory systems that allow humans to see, hear, smell, taste, and feel.

sensory register Component of the memory system where sensory information is stored for a brief time.

elaboration The process of extending meaning by connecting new information with knowledge already in long-term store.

response generator Mental process that converts cognitive activity into messages for physical activity.

effectors Physical systems that produce the response made by the learner (e.g., the muscles that are used to speak if the response is to speak).

executive control Monitoring the use of various processes in order to transform, store, and retrieve information.

- The **environment** is the source of input into the information-processing system. Stimulus information from the environment impinges on the learner's receptors.
- The **receptors** are those sensory systems that allow humans to see, hear, smell, taste, and feel. They are the physical connection between the organism and the environment.
- Information from the receptors enters the **sensory register,** where stimuli are stored for a brief moment.
- From the sensory register, information that receives the learner's attention moves into the short-term store (STS).
- Information that reaches the short-term store (STS) meets one of four fates: it is lost; it is maintained in STS; it triggers the response generator; or it is transferred, by means of **elaboration,** to long-term store.
- Information reaching long-term store (LTS) can remain in LTS, reenter STS through the process of retrieval, or trigger the response generator.
- Triggered by STS or LTS information, the response generator transmits neural messages that activate effectors. The **response generator** is a "conversion box," converting cognitive activity into messages for physical activity.
- The **effectors** are the systems that produce the response made by the learner (e.g., if the response is to speak, the muscles that are used to speak serve as effectors). The effectors are the physical means by which the learner operates on the environment.
- **Executive control** monitors the flow of information through the system. It governs the use of various processes in order to transform information, store information, retrieve information. The monitoring and governing functions are executed by means of control processes.

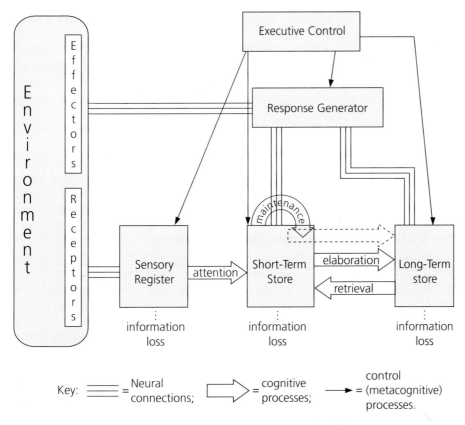

Transparency: This figure is duplicated in the acetate transparency package. See T-8 The Human Information-
processing Model.

■ Figure 6–1 *The Human Information-processing Model*
Source: From *Essentials of Learning for Instruction* (2nd ed., p. 13) by R. M. Gagné and
M. P. Driscoll, 1988, Englewood Cliffs, NJ: Prentice-Hall. Copyright 1988 by Prentice-Hall.
Adapted by permission.

Following the trail of information takes us from the environment (stimulus input), through the cognitive mechanism of the learner, and finally back
to the environment (response output). Behaviorists focus exclusively on the
stimulus, response, and associated environmental changes. Information-
processing theorists focus primarily on what goes on inside the learner—the
cognitive mechanism—to investigate learning processes.

Memory Structures

In this section we focus on the three memory structures in the human information-processing system: sensory register, short-term store (STS), and long-
term store (LTS). Waugh and Norman (1965) were among the first theorists
to suggest that there are different types of memory functions, which they
called primary memory and secondary memory. The structures in Figure 6–1
were identified by Atkinson and Shiffrin (1968). The **Atkinson and Shiffrin
model** of information processing, an extension of Waugh and Norman's notion, has undergone many modifications since it was first introduced, but its

Lecture Note: Have students in small
groups identify information they
would present in their classes and
track the flow of that information
through the various structures of the
human cognitive mechanism.

Teacher Interview: Have each student
ask a teacher to describe observable
behaviors that allow him or her to infer
various kinds of cognitive activities.

Chapter 15 Casebook Preview: Beginning Each Day as a Learning
Experience.

Lecture Note: Remind students that in order to learn it is necessary to remember information but that memorization is not always the learning goal.

essential structures—sensory register, short-term store, and long-term store—have remained intact.

All three of the structures store information. The three stores are complementary; they operate together to produce learning. In order to understand how the stores work in concert, it is necessary to examine them separately. It is important that a teacher appreciate the instruments that produce coordinated cognitive activity.

Sensory Register

The sensory register is the memory structure most closely connected to the information in the learner's environment. The sensory register stores information in a form that is very close to the physical stimulus, a literal copy of the input. For example, when you are listening to a friend speak, the information in your sensory register takes the form of sounds not words. You turn those sounds into words at a later stage of processing.

Lecture Note: Use the following example: Perhaps this has happened to you. Someone says something to you and you respond saying, "I'm sorry. I didn't quite understand what you said. Could you say it again?" But before the person repeats the message you understand what he or she said. This experience is not possible without the sensory register.

The information in the sensory register is not very durable. Information can reside in the sensory register for something on the order of one-half of a second (Houston, 1986); it decays quickly unless further processing takes place. Sperling (1960) presented visual stimuli using a tachistoscope, an instrument that displays stimuli for very short periods. Sperling flashed letters on a screen for fifty milliseconds (one-twentieth of a second). Subjects in his experiment were then asked to report what letters were on the screen. Subjects relied on an "afterimage," which seemed to remain on the screen after the letters were turned off. Sperling (1960, 1963) concluded that a temporally limited sensory store existed for visual information. He reasoned that the purpose of the sensory store was to keep information available just long enough for some of it to be selected for additional processing. Darwin,

Information from the environment enters the sensory register where it may be transferred to short-term store. If we are to remember this information, it must be meaningfully integrated with prior knowledge from long-term store.

Issues in Educational Psychology

CNN™ This box relates to Segment 6 of the CNN videotape. See the Instructor's Section for a summary.

MEMORIES

Members of disciplines as different as history and medicine agree that we remember the various occurrences that touch our lives selectively. We choose to remember some events while we filter out those that no longer successfully work for us in the present.

David Thelen, a professor of History at Indiana University at Bloomington and editor of the *Journal of American History,* wrote about the role selectivity played in the memories of John Brown's children. In the *Chronicle of Higher Education,* Thelen reported that "Brown's children told ever-changing stories about what they had done (and not done) during their father's raid on Harper's Ferry to free the slaves." Citing a colleague's work in the *Journal of American History,* Thelen wrote that for Brown's heirs "their reconstructions reflect typical processes by which families reshape their memories in order to establish their identities amid changing circumstances."

As a cardiologist and poet, John Stone has a unique perspective on how memory works in our daily lives. In an article in the *New York Times Magazine,* Stone pointed out that poets hope that the world will remember their words, and frequently, we do find ourselves reciting a few lines from some long-ago memorized poem. Stone asks, How do we remember?

In literary terms, the answer may lie in the dramatic impact the writer's words have had on our minds. Stone recalled the words of poet and essayist E. B. White, whose line "'which not to look upon would be like death . . .' arrests us with its unexpectedness, its directness (just as death might)—and we remember."

Stone related a common practice among medical students who rely on mnemonic devices to remember vast amounts of factual material. "The first letters of words of an unrelated phrase jog into recall the associated material," he explained. Outlandish and risqué devices have the best chance of being remembered, for example, "Never Lower Tillie's Pants; Grand-Mother Might Come Home." The "n" in "Never" recalled the navicular bone in the wrist, while "Grand-Mother" represented the multangular.

"Every powerful emotion" is a factor in memory. Whenever he attended a funeral, Stone flashed back to the day when his paternal grandmother was buried and the then-small boy witnessed his father crying at the death of his mother. Any emotion—anger, happiness, envy, or love—can provoke memories of similar feelings from our past.

The opposite of memory is forgetting and Stone pointed out that the two are balanced, "part of a long biochemical and emotional equilibrium." He emphasized that forgetting can be equally important in our daily struggles.

Are humans unique in how they remember? Do we alone filter out data as time goes by? It seems that whales, mammals like ourselves, may employ mnemonic devices in their songs. *Mother Earth News* reported that two biologists from the World Wildlife Fund discovered a "common trait" in over 35 percent of the hundreds of whale songs they analyzed. These basic rhyming sounds weigh heavily in these songs, but whales apparently rely on pitch and organization to remember as well. Throughout the singing season, the songs evolve, becoming totally different. Apparently the whales, like humans, listen to each other, learning and adapting what they need to remember as part of their aquatic world.

SOURCES: Thelen, David. "A New Approach to Understanding Human Memory Offers a Solution to the Crisis in the Study of History." *Chronicle of Higher Education* 36, issue 4 (September 27, 1989): B1, B3. Stone, John. "A Pointillist Painting." *New York Times Magazine,* part 2 (October 8, 1989): 60. "Bits and Pieces: Rhyming Whales." *Mother Earth News,* issue 119 (September 1989): 128.

1. Why might feelings of "anger, happiness, envy, or love" help lock memories in long-term store?
2. What poems or phrases, such as E. B. White's "which not to look upon would be like death," have you memorized and what "triggers" bring them forth?

Turvey, and Crowder (1972) replicated Sperling's findings using auditory stimuli. Taken together, the studies support the idea that the sensory register operates similarly for information from all kinds of receptors.

Although the sensory register holds information in an "undeveloped" state for only the briefest period, its capacity is quite large. A lot of information from the environment enters the sensory register. At any time, there is an incredible amount of information available for a learner to process. A student sitting in a classroom receives sensory information from the teacher, a neighbor's whisper, the chalkboard, the bulletin board, the ticking of the clock, the aroma from the cafeteria, the buzz in the lights, the breeze from the window, the clouds rolling by, the graffiti on his or her desk. All of that information enters the student's sensory register, but not all of it is being noticed by the student. It is only the information that is noticed that moves on to short-term store.

Short-Term Store (STS)

Ms. Wilson describes a homework assignment to her class. Ben raises his hand and asks whether answers may be printed or if cursive writing is required. Meanwhile, John watches a spider in the corner; he does not know what Ms. Wilson has said. Auditory information has entered Ben and John's respective sensory registers. From the students' behavior, we can infer that the auditory stimuli coming from Ms. Wilson have found their way into Ben's STS, but not into John's STS.

In some versions of the information-processing model, **short-term store (STS)** is called *working memory* (cf. Bell-Gredler, 1986); STS is where the learner works on the information from the environment. It is in STS that physical signals are converted into meaning; sounds become spoken words, visual patterns on a page become written words. Remember, in Teacher Chronicle 6.1, how Keith was able to convert written instructions into string figures through intensive study?

As we have already discovered, information from the environment arrives in STS through the sensory register. The knowledge that allows us to make sense of sensory input is stored in LTS. The most important "work" done in STS is the integration of information from the environment with the knowledge stored in LTS. STS is a busy place; it is where what students know comes together with the information they are to learn. (This is a critical theme for those of us who teach; we will see the theme in several guises throughout the chapter.)

Another reason why STS is such a busy place is that it has a limited capacity. If you have ever had thirty students all asking you questions at the same time, you know what limited capacity means. In his classic article, Miller (1956) identified the capacity of STS at about seven pieces of information. Pieces of information are known technically as "chunks." *Chunks* may not sound much like a scientific term, but it is a good descriptor. What follows is a row of numbers, fifteen pieces of information—DON'T LOOK YET. Study the digits for about ten seconds and then cover the list with your hand. Here are the fifteen digits you will be asked to remember in order:

1 4 9 1 6 2 5 3 6 4 9 6 4 8 1

Now, with the list covered, see how many of the digits you can remember in order. (By the way, if you cheated and looked ahead at the digits, try this little experiment with a friend by reading the numbers to him or her.)

Lecture Note: The making of meaning occurs in STS. It is in STS that information from the environment is brought together with prior knowledge, that is, information from long-term store. Refer students to the flow of information depicted in Figure 6–1.

Connection: Teacher Chronicle 6.1: Knot Understanding.

Lecture Note: Write this list of numbers on the board prior to having students read the chapter. Have them record the results of their attempts at memorization and ask them to speculate on explanations for their performances. Have them compare their explanations with the explanation in the text.

If you tried to process each digit separately, you were taxing the limit of your STS. As a result, you probably did not recall all of the digits. If you grouped the digits into two- or three-digit numbers (e.g., 149, 162, etc.), you probably recalled more of the information. Grouping the digits into numbers is an example of chunking (Miller, 1956; Simon, 1974). When the digits are chunked, the number of pieces of information to remember is reduced. The amount of information per se has not changed, but the limited capacity of STS has been used more efficiently.

An item of information in STS can last for approximately twenty to thirty seconds (Miller, 1956; Peterson & Peterson, 1959). Items may not last that long if they are displaced by new information arriving from the sensory register. Have you ever tried to take verbatim notes during a lecture? As you will see, there are a number of reasons why this isn't a good way to learn. In the context of STS, the problem with transcribing is that it taxes capacity. Unless you are a very fast writer, you are working on the new information that the lecturer is presenting while attempting to remember old information long enough to write it down on paper. We have all tried this kind of note taking at one time or another and most of us gave it up about the time we realized that we had very little idea of what the lecturer was trying to convey.

Items in STS can be maintained for longer than thirty seconds if they are rehearsed (Anderson & Craik, 1974). Rehearsing information in order to maintain it in STS has a positive side effect. Rehearsal can lead to the transfer of information from STS to LTS. Transfer is not guaranteed but the longer information is rehearsed the more likely it will be transformed to LTS (cf. Atkinson & Shiffrin, 1971; Jacoby & Bartz, 1972).

Long-Term Store (LTS)

Long-term store is considered to be the permanent store of the human information-processing system (Leahy & Harris, 1989). **Long-term store (LTS)** houses many different kinds of information: episodes that you have experienced in childhood, facts, abstract rules that allow you to understand language, strategies for solving problems, smells, sounds, tastes, feelings, and visual images. There is information in LTS that you may not know is there.

"How many windows were in the house or apartment in which you were raised?" Our guess is that no one has ever asked you for that information. Therefore you have never retrieved it from your LTS. The number of windows is not the kind of information you use everyday, but let us see if we can find the information somewhere in the recesses of your LTS.

First, picture in your mind the house or apartment that you grew up in. Do you have the place in mind? If it had multiple stories, concentrate on the main floor. Now, imagine that you are inside your childhood home. Picture yourself just inside the front door. As you stand there, turn to your right. Now begin walking around the main floor. If there is a wall, follow it to an opening. If there are doors, open them and proceed slowly. Walk through all of the rooms on that floor and look out each window, keeping track of the number of windows you encounter.

How many windows are there?

Long-term store contains much of what we learned and much that we never made a conscious effort to learn. As learners we bring the contents of our long-term stores to school with us. Our experiences are represented there. Our knowledge is represented there. We call that knowledge and experience prior knowledge. (The instructional significance of prior knowledge is such that we will devote an entire section of this chapter to it.)

long-term store (LTS) A component of memory whereby large amounts of information can be stored permanently.

Lecture Note: Another way to memorize the fifteen digits is to reduce them to one piece of information. The fifteen digits, in order, are the squares of the numbers 1–9 ($1 \times 1 = 1$, $2 \times 2 = 4$, etc.). Discuss this alternative memorization device with your students.

Field Observation: Have students observe junior high or high school students taking notes in a classroom.

Lecture Note: I once knew a person who loved to recite multiplication tables while someone was attempting to rehearse a telephone number. Use this as an example of one way to displace information from other people's STS.

Lecture Note: Ask students to recall facts, such as the capitals of Missouri, South Dakota, Oregon, or New Hampshire.

Journal Entry: Have students reflect on various kinds of images that they generate as they read a novel and compare those images to those they generate when they learn from a text. Also, have them reflect on the stories that teachers have told them and whether these stories were effectively or ineffectively used.

episodic memories Long-term memories associated with specific personal experiences, including the time and place they occurred.
semantic memories Long-term memories of facts and general knowledge, but not including the time and place they were learned.

The different kinds of information stored in LTS can be thought of as either episodic memories or semantic memories (Tulving, 1972). **Episodic memories** are those associated with a particular time and place or those connected with "events." The memory you have of a phone call you made this morning, the breakfast you ate, the birthday gift you received when you were twelve years old would all be episodic memories. Semantic memories differ in nature from memories of specific episodes. **Semantic memories** make up one's "general knowledge," for example, that "*i* comes before *e*, except after *c*" and that "what goes up must come down." When and where did you learn those rules? Most of us know rules but have forgotten the exact circumstances in which we acquired them. Such information is stored semantically in LTS.

Recently, some cognitive theorists have suggested a need for additional classifications of information in LTS. Brewer (1986) suggests that the memory of the movie you saw on a first date differs considerably from the memory of learning a list of fifteen digits, yet both are episodic. Brewer establishes an elaborate taxonomy of information stored in LTS, including four types of input: ego-self (personal experiences), visual-spatial (objects and places), visual-temporal (events and actions), and semantic. In addition, Brewer's taxonomy identifies two forms of representation and two conditions of acquisition.

Tulving's distinction and Brewer's taxonomy, taken together identify a variety of codes used to represent information in LTS. It seems reasonable that some information in LTS is coded in more than one way. What kind of information is "the number of windows in your childhood home"? A visual-spatial code seems likely, but couldn't a case be made for a semantic code as well?

Instructionally, the trick is to find a code—not *the* code—that allows a student to access information needed for a particular task. How well did our instructions to "walk mentally around your childhood home" work? Is there a different set of instructions that would allow you to retrieve the same information? LTS codes provide clues for helping learners use their stored experiences. Remember, the primary instructional principle of the information-processing view of learning is to integrate environmental information with information already in LTS (prior knowledge). Failure to integrate is failure to understand.

Imagine that you are listening to two people speaking in a foreign language. It sounds as if these speakers are talking very fast. You can't tell where one word stops and the next word begins. Their conversation is just a string of sounds. Why is that?

You can hear the sounds they emit, but no matter how hard you concentrate, you can't make words and meanings out of the sounds because you do not have the knowledge of the speakers' language in your LTS. Integration is impossible and, therefore, so is comprehension.

Teacher Interview: Have each student interview a teacher regarding instructions that he or she uses to encourage thinking in students.

Summary of Structures

To summarize this examination of memory structures, we can consider each of the three stores with respect to five properties: capacity, code, permanence, source, and loss. Each property is defined as follows:

Capacity—the amount of information that can be held in a store

Code—the way in which information is mentally represented in a store

Table 6–1   *Summary of Memory Structures*

Transparency: This table is duplicated in the acetate transparency package. See T-9 Summary of Memory Structures.

Properties	Structures		
	Sensory Register	Short-Term Store	Long-Term Store
Capacity	Large	Small	Large
Code	Literal copy of physical stimulus	Dual code -verbal -visual	Episodic semantic
Permanence	0.5 seconds	20–30 seconds	Permanent
Source	Environment	Environment and prior knowledge	Effective encodings from STS
Loss	Decay	Displacement or decay	Irretrievability

Permanence—the length of time information can reside in a store

Source—the origin of the information that resides in a store

Loss—the way(s) in which information is lost from a store

Understanding the functions of the three memory stores is necessary if information processing theory is to yield hypotheses of practice. (Table 6-1 is a shorthand description of sensory register, STS, and LTS.) In this section, we have seen how information flows through the stores, how each store functions, and what the nature of the information in each store is. In the next section we shift our attention to the cognitive processes that transform messages into codes and yield understanding (the process arrows in Figure 6–1).

Principles in Practice 6.1

Principles . . .
1. Information is transformed as it moves through the memory stores.
2. Short-term store is consciousness—the store where cognitive work is done.
3. Information enters STS from the environment—through sensory register, and from long-term store.

Lecture Note: Ask students in groups to identify topics they anticipate teaching in their own classrooms and how they conceptualize the topics. Using Figure 6–1 and Table 6–1, ask each to describe from a student's point of view how he or she might process the information that allows him or her to conceptualize the topics that will be taught.

. . . in Practice
Keith, in Teacher Chronicle 6.1, had a talent for using his hands. It showed up in this episode in his ability to make string figures. He was able to translate written instructions into actual string figures much more efficiently than his teacher. Keith created his cognitive "picture"—a string figure without using string. The teacher had to use the string while reading the instructions. The two used their STS capacities differently. It took Keith a long time to "work" on the written information from the environment, but once he had created a cognitive representation in STS, he was able to store it in LTS. His ability to generate a useful representation in STS was the product of paying

close attention to material from the environment and using the "mechanical knowledge or aptitude" that was stored in LTS. Keith's processing of the information was more cognitively, if not physically, active than the teacher's and for that reason more efficient—the information was more integrated, more memorable.

1. How did the knowledge that Keith stored in LTS affect his STS capacity?
2. Why was the teacher more confident in Keith's ability to recall the figures than his or her own?
3. How could Keith's knowledge be used to help other students learn string figures?

Teacher
Chronicle
6.2

Now I See!

Day after day, I present new information to my students: how to identify a bird of prey by its body shape; what a contraction is; how to fold a piece of paper into eight squares.

One year while teaching a unit on the human body, I discussed the eye and how it worked. First, we discussed the parts of the eye. Then I handed out a picture of the eye and had the students label it: cornea, pupil, iris. I taught them tricks to remember the parts: going to the "cornea," all pupils have "pupils," don't pick your "iris." I told them how the pupil expands and contracts, how the eye "sees" upside down, and how the brain reverses the image. I presented lots of information.

At test time, however, while many of the students could identify the various parts of the eye, many missed the basic concepts of how the eye works.

I was frustrated. I had presented the curriculum. Most of the students had seemed to be paying attention. Why didn't they learn this? I asked myself, as I looked over tests a second time.

On my way out that night, I noticed a sign taped onto one of the other teacher's doors.

Tell Me, I Forget.
Show Me, I Remember.
Involve Me, I Understand.
—Chinese proverb

The words rattled through my head on the way home. I had *told* the students about the eye and they had forgotten. I had *shown* them and they had remembered the parts of the eye. But had I *involved* them?

I made new plans that night.

The next day, as soon as everyone was settled, I walked to the window and closed the curtain.

"All right," Mark said. "A filmstrip."

"Where's the projector?" Brian asked, looking around the room.

"I want everyone to get a partner," I said, crossing the room to the light switch. There was a shuffling of chairs and a flurry of conversations. "Now look into your partner's eyes." This brought on a round of giggles.

"Now I wish I had picked Marci as my partner," Brian said.

Marci made a face at Brian.

"On the count of three, I'm going to turn off the lights. I want you to watch what happens to your partner's pupils."

"What's a pupil?" Tim asked.

A chorus of groans went around the room.

"It's the black dot in the middle of your eye," Sam told him.

"One. Two. Three." I hit the switch. The room darkened.

"Wow!"

"Cool!"

"Did you see that?"

"What do you think will happen when I turn the lights back on?" I asked.

"Our pupils will get smaller," Sara said.

"They'll contract," Susie pointed out, looking in my direction.

"Super answers," I encouraged. "Susie gave us the science word for what will happen. What word describes what just happened to your pupils?"

"They expanded," Adam said.

"Right. Now one, two, three." I switched on the lights.

Another round of exclamations burst forth.

"Can you do that again?" Corey asked.

"Sure. On the count of three." I had connected!

After five rounds of lights on, lights off, Tim said with surprise in his voice, "Now I see how the pupil works."

"Would this work on my cat?" Marci asked.

"Try it tonight and see," I suggested.

"What about my dog's eyes?" Maren asked.

"Try it."

I had them. They were involved. They were learning. I had found a way. The material wasn't any easier, it was the same stuff. But I had found a way to make it easier for them to understand. I had eased their learning. And for the rest of the year, whenever we had a filmstrip, we did a pupil check.

▪ ▪

THE MODEL OF HUMAN INFORMATION PROCESSING: PROCESSES

Chap. Obj. 3
Test Ques. 6.45–6.81

As information is transferred through the various memory structures, it undergoes a transformation. This transformation is accomplished by cognitive processes. Understanding the student's cognitive processes is important to a teacher. In educational circles, "active learning" is desired. By *active learning* we mean that the learner is engaged in transforming the information from the environment into a meaningful cognitive representation. In Teacher Chronicle 6.2, the teacher found a way to make the students' processing of the lesson's content more active.

Focus Questions: How can I help my students comprehend, retain, and apply what they learn? Why are students more actively engaged in learning at some times than at others?

Chapter 15 Casebook Preview: Improvisation and Aesthetic Appreciation.

Attention

Ms. Kelly turns from the board where she has just written several trigonometric functions. She notices that Gary is gazing out the window in the direction of the parking lot. She is surprised because Gary usually pays close attention in this class.

Connection: Teacher Chronicle 6.2: Now I See!

Active learning is effective because students can transform an abstract concept, such as static electricity, into a meaningful cognitive representation. The information can then be transferred to short-term store.

"Gary! Will you please direct your attention to the board?"

Gary is startled. "Huh? Oh, I'm sorry Ms. Kelly. I thought I heard my girlfriend calling me."

Ms. Kelly smiles. "Well, the cosine is calling you also. And as you will learn, the cosine has a very jealous nature."

In the information-processing model, attention is a process. When we speak of a student focusing, directing, or altering his or her attention, our emphasis is on the cognitive activity involved.

Sensory register has a large capacity. Short-term store has a limited capacity. Not all the information represented in sensory register can fit into STS. Attention determines which information is transferred to STS and which information is not. What causes a learner to attend to information?

Attention can be engaged selectively or automatically. **Selective attention** is under the control of the learner. Learners have the ability to orient their cognitive effort toward a particular source of information in the environment. A student in a classroom can make a conscious effort to attend to the speech and actions of the teacher. A student can also direct his or her attention to other information available in the classroom environment.

Imagine that you are at a wedding reception or some other gathering. There are twelve groups of people in the room. Each group, consisting of between three and six people, is carrying on its own conversation. You have, through no fault of your own, become entangled in a group where a man is talking about his mail-order business and the unlimited future for an enterprising person such as yourself. As it happens, you are not the least bit interested in the mail-order industry. But courtesy requires that you at least look at the man, and, from time to time, nod as he speaks. You are allocating just enough attention to the man so that you can nod, but you are not really following what he is saying. Rather, you are listening to a conversation that is occurring in the group adjacent to yours. A woman in the adjacent group is describing her recent trip to Australia where she saw a great white shark while diving near the Great Barrier Reef. You are giving her story your selective attention.

You selectively attend to the shark story at the expense of the future of the mail-order business. Should the gentleman standing right in front of you ask you to estimate the cost-effectiveness of catalog marketing, you will be at a loss for an answer. The reason is that selective attention, the "gatekeeper" of STS, uses up some of the limited capacity available in STS. Attending to some aspects of the environment precludes the processing of other information.

You continue your nodding at the mail-order business while attending to the shark when, three groups over, you hear someone mention your name. Suddenly, the great white shark joins the mail-order business as you strain to hear what is being said in that faraway group. The switch of attention, a cognitive phenomenon, is almost a physical sensation. You can almost feel your ear growing in the direction of your name.

Why did you hear your name spoken? You have no idea what was said just prior to the mention of your name, but suddenly, you hear the conversation quite clearly. The explanation is **automatic attention**—processing information without effort.

The conversation occurring three groups away has been entering your sensory register. (Remember, sensory register has a large capacity.) Prior to the mention of your name, you were not attending to that conversation. Therefore, the conversation did not enter your STS. The mention of your name automatically drew your attention. The conversation thus became part of the information in your STS, part of your consciousness. Information is transferred from sensory register to STS by means of the process of attention, which can occur in either a selective or an automatic fashion.

Controlling, or at least guiding, the attention of students is something teachers attempt every hour of every school day. Reflect on the teachers that you have had who were adept at keeping your attention focused on the content of the class. Reflect on those teachers who could direct your attention to themselves, but not to the material you were supposed to learn. Reflect on those teachers who did not control your attention at all.

Early studies of attention led to several notions of how attention works (cf. Broadbent, 1957; Deutsch & Deutsch, 1963; Kahneman, 1973; Norman, 1968; Triesman, 1970). Although the views of attention differ slightly in their portrayal of the process, they all acknowledge that attention is a limited resource. Grabe (1986), taking into account these early studies of attention and recognizing the selective and the automatic modes of operation, sought to identify the instructional implications of attention. Effective learning de-

automatic attention The process of attention that occurs without effort.

Lecture Note: At this point, it would be helpful to remind students that cognitive processes, for example, attention, transfer information from one memory store to other stores; in this case, from sensory register to short-term store.

Lecture Note: Ask students if they've had experiences similar to the "great white shark" discussion.

Teaching Anecdote: Tell the story of the third-grade student who is fascinated by large machines. One morning a road crew began drilling and digging outside the school to replace a water main. The usually attentive student could not concentrate. The teacher was puzzled until he saw the student staring out of the window during free time.

Ask your students what they think the teacher did when he saw that the machines were the explanation for the student's unusual inattentiveness.

Journal Entry: Have students write on the reflections suggested in the text.

pends on the learner's ability to selectively attend to specific portions of sensory input while automatically processing other information. Grabe's view is that the teacher's task is to help students focus on the critical features of the instructional environment while fostering the development of automatic processing. Fostering automaticity of attention helps the learner in several ways. It is important to our understanding of attention. It also underlies other processes as well. We will examine the notion of automaticity in greater detail after discussing, in turn, encoding and retrieval.

Encoding

To *encode* means to convert a message into a code. In information-processing theory, **encoding** is the process of converting a message from the environment to a cognitive code so that the information can be stored and later remembered (Kulhavy, Schwartz, & Peterson, 1986). *Encoding* is a general term, a theme with variations. Information can be encoded in many different ways: one student may attempt to encode the periodic table of elements by rote memorization; another may attempt to find patterns that allow elements to be categorized.

We noted earlier that short-term store is sometimes called working memory. Encoding is one kind of "work" done in STS, and, from an instructional perspective, it is the most important. Making codes—constructing cognitive representations—is the primary business of the human cognitive mechanism. This is the work we want our students to do in our classrooms. The codes learners create in STS allow them to say they understand or do not understand the material that has been presented to them. The codes also allow students to perform tasks of varying complexity.

Teachers can use visual aids, categorization of ideas, and rote memorization to facilitate the process of encoding.

Maintenance and elaboration are two variations on the encoding theme (Craik & Watkins, 1973; Woodward, Bjork, & Jongeward, 1973). We will turn our attention to these two processes, already identified in the information-processing model in Figure 6–1.

Maintenance Rehearsal

Maintenance and elaboration are the two "process" arrows that originate in STS. **Maintenance rehearsal** keeps information available in STS by keeping the information "activated." Repeating a telephone number over and over to maintain the information long enough to dial it, is maintenance rehearsal. With enough rehearsal, it is possible to transfer the information to LTS. You've probably stored a lot of information in LTS simply because of repetition. Do you remember the telephone number of a high school friend whom you have not called in a while? An old address? Through sheer repetition—maintenance rehearsal—the information may have been stored in LTS.

Maintenance rehearsal is a type of encoding that could be called "brute force" learning. Repeating information doesn't guarantee that information will be stored permanently, but it can lead to permanent storage. Information stored in this way, however, may not be all that meaningful.

Memory does not equal understanding. A child we know grew up listening to his father say grace before every family meal. He was told to listen carefully to the prayer and to say it silently with his father because someday it would be his turn to say grace. His father, like most fathers, mumbled the prayer very quickly. One evening, when the child was about twelve, the father turned to the child and said, "Rick, it's your turn to say grace." The child was stricken with anxiety, not because he was afraid of saying the prayer, but because he realized, at that moment, that he did not "know" the prayer. All he knew were the sounds he had heard his father mumble thousands of times. At that fateful meal, Rick bowed his head and mumbled as quickly as he could the following:

Blesso lor our knees I guess,
Blessoby the handover lor, . . .

Rick completed the remaining four lines of sounds he had stored in his LTS, ending with the only word in the prayer he was sure of, *Amen*. He looked at his father expecting to see displeasure at the obviously feeble effort. His father was beaming. "You said that as well as I do. Pass the potatoes."

Maintenance rehearsal, or rote memorization, is helpful or necessary in many situations, both in and out of the classroom. However, the learning outcomes we seek for students are outcomes of understanding, and maintenance rehearsal does not guarantee understanding. Understanding is best achieved through another type of encoding, elaborative rehearsal.

Elaborative Rehearsal

Elaborative rehearsal is a type of encoding that relates new information to information already stored. This stimulus information becomes transformed because the learner elaborates it in some way (cf. Bell-Gredler, 1986). A student, after reading a description of a concept, might generate an example of that concept. The teacher in Teacher Chronicle 6.2 provided the students with experiences, encouraging them to observe changes in the pupil. The "experiment" allowed the students to elaborate the information the teacher wanted

maintenance rehearsal Rote memorization, which does not guarantee understanding.
elaborative rehearsal A type of encoding that relates new information to information already in long-term store.

Lecture Note: Remind students that maintenance rehearsal works best at keeping information available in short-term memory.

Lecture Note: Make the point that rote memorization can allow a student to respond to a particular situation or question, but it doesn't guarantee that the student will understand what he or she has memorized.

Lecture Note: The nature of the cognitive representation is transformed as information is transferred from one memory store to another.

Connection: Teacher Chronicle 6.2: Now I See!

Connection: Teacher Chronicle 6.1: Knot Understanding.

retrieval The process that transfers information from long-term store to short-term store.

them to learn. A student might create a mental picture of stimulus information, as Keith did in Teacher Chronicle 6.1. Stimulus information might be supplemented with additional information that aids recall, for example, learning to spell *arithmetic* by memorizing the sentence, "*a* rat *in* the *house* may *eat* the *ice* cream."

Do you recall learning the names of the Great Lakes? Perhaps your teacher wrote the names of the lakes on the chalkboard:

Huron

Ontario

Michigan

Erie

Superior

Having written the names, the teacher might have asked the class to repeat the names several times, erased the names, and continued the drill-and-practice session by having each student recite the names. These sessions may have occurred every day for a week. The encoding technique being used here is a form of maintenance rehearsal.

Elaborative rehearsal would have called for a different approach to encoding the information. Your teacher, after writing the names on the board, may have asked the class to look closely at the names. "Did anyone in the class notice anything about the names of the Great Lakes? Don't answer aloud, but does anyone notice something about the first letters of each lake? Look at the first letters and see if they form a word. What is the word?"

Using the word *HOMES* to store the names of the Great Lakes is a form of elaborative rehearsal.

Lecture Note: Ask students to recall other types of elaborative rehearsal they used to learn information.

Connection: Mnemonic devices are discussed in greater detail later in this chapter.

Lecture Note: Elaborative rehearsal may take more effort than maintenance at the point of encoding, but in the long run it is a more efficient learning tactic.

Whether you, as a teacher, decide to use maintenance rehearsal or elaborative rehearsal in the classroom has important implications for the way students will encode information effectively. The teacher who asks students to continually repeat information puts an additional burden on him- or herself. Drill and practice can be boring. Using maintenance rehearsal as an instructional technique makes it hard to maintain a high level of attention in the classroom. It is easier to keep students interested and on task if they are transforming information rather than merely repeating it.

Another implication of your choice relates to students' cognitive efforts. Both maintenance and elaboration require STS capacity, but the student who elaborates is "doing more" with information than the student who merely maintains. Maintenance rehearsal occurs in STS. Maintenance rehearsal *may* cause information to be transferred to LTS, but the encoding itself is an STS activity. Elaboration requires the use of knowledge in LTS. In order to integrate stimulus information with prior knowledge, prior knowledge must be transferred from LTS to STS.

Retrieval

Retrieval is the process that transfers information from LTS to STS. Murdock (1974) defines *retrieval* as the utilization of stored information. In order for information stored in LTS to be used by the learner, it must be brought into working memory. How is information stored in LTS brought to bear on stimulus information being encoded in STS? And, what can a teacher do to facilitate retrieval?

Retrieval is closely connected to encoding. The nature of the code constructed by the learner influences the ease with which information can be retrieved. **Encoding specificity** is connection between encoding and retrieval (Flexser & Tulving, 1978; Tulving & Thomson, 1973). According to the principle of encoding specificity, information present at the time of encoding can serve as an effective retrieval cue. Recall the teacher who used the word *HOMES* to help students elaboratively encode the names of the Great Lakes. At some later time, the teacher will be able to use *HOMES* as an effective retrieval cue. The cue—*HOMES*—is specific to the encoding of the names of the Great Lakes.

Another connection between encoding and retrieval is evidenced by the nature of the codes created during elaborative encoding. The prior knowledge a learner retrieves in order to make sense of incoming information influences the comprehension of the stimulus. Consider the following examples (see Anderson & Ortony, 1975):

1. The container held the apples.
2. The container held the cola.

Compare your interpretation of the meaning of the word *container* in the first sentence with its meaning in the sentence that follows. Your interpretations differ because your prior knowledge of apples and cola influence your encoding of the information. If you had to describe the kind of container referred to in the first sentence, you would probably describe a basket. Your prior knowledge about apples leads you to infer *basket* rather than *bottle*. The inference, which becomes part of the encoded representation of the stimulus information, serves as an effective retrieval cue (Till, 1977). There is theoretical debate about whether the inference occurs at the time when stimulus information is encoded or at the time when the information is retrieved (Anderson, Pichert, Goetz, Shallert, Stevens, & Trollip, 1976; Bransford, 1979). If inferences are added at the time of encoding, the process is called *construction* (e.g., Bransford, Barclay & Franks, 1972). If inferences are made at the time of retrieval, the process is called *reconstruction* (e.g., Spiro, 1977). Both construction and reconstruction probably influence learning. For practical purposes, it is clear that the learner can infer meanings that are not explicitly presented from previously learned information.

Reconstructive Retrieval

Although cues, such as the *HOMES* cue, can make retrieval very efficient, some information in LTS is not so readily available. Earlier in this chapter you were asked to retrieve "the number of windows in your childhood home." The cues we provided to help you retrieve that information were not memory tricks (again, the *HOMES* cue), or something you inferred (for example, that "apples are contained in baskets"). Instead, we suggested that you create a visual image of your home, which helped you to reconstruct the information you were asked to retrieve.

Retrieval of this sort can be viewed as a type of problem solving. The learner uses logic, retrieval cues, and prior knowledge to reconstruct information (Lindsay & Norman, 1977). Reconstructive retrieval is highly sensitive to the particular knowledge and experiences stored in a learner's LTS. To demonstrate, read the following passage (see Anderson, 1977).

Rocky slowly got up from the mat, planning his escape. He hesitated a moment and thought. Things were not going well. What bothered him

encoding specificity   The connection between encoding and retrieval whereby information present at the time of encoding can serve as an effective retrieval cue.

Lecture Note: Recall the parts of the eye discussed in Teacher Chronicle 6.2: Now I See! An effective retrieval cue for those students might be the remark, "Don't pick your (iris)."

Lecture Note: Inferential comprehension is an important milestone in the development of fluent reading.

Chapter 15 Casebook Preview: See Writers' Tea.

Field Observation: Have students read this passage to several friends and document their interpretations. Have students interview the listeners to determine what information they retrieved as they listened to the passage.

most was being held, especially since the charge against him had been weak. He considered his present situation. The lock that held him was strong but he thought he could break it. He knew, however, that his timing would have to be perfect. Rocky was aware that it was because of his early roughness that he had been penalized so severely—much too severely from his point of view. The situation was becoming frustrating; the pressure had been grinding on him for too long. He was being ridden unmercifully. Rocky was getting angry now. He felt he was ready to make his move. He knew that his success or failure would depend on what he did in the next few seconds.

What prior knowledge from your LTS does this story lead you to retrieve? Did you retrieve some things you know about jails and prisoners? Perhaps you were reminded of a classic James Cagney movie. Or, did you retrieve some things you know about wrestling?

Instructionally, when you help students solve the problem of accessing information you help them make sense of the material they are to learn, facilitating the process of retrieval. The knowledge students retrieve from LTS influences their understanding.

Connection: The importance of prior knowledge is discussed later in this chapter.

Automaticity

Lecture Note: Ask students to share their experiences of their first "driving" lessons in Driver Education.

Remember when you first learned to drive a car? You concentrated intently on the task. You thought about the position of your hands on the steering wheel (ten o'clock and two o'clock). You checked your rearview mirror and the speedometer every few seconds. If the car you learned to drive had a standard transmission, you had to focus on using the clutch to change gears.

When you first learned to drive all of your consciousness was occupied by the task at hand. Your STS capacity was so filled with driving the car, you couldn't talk to anyone. As you gained driving experience, you found the task of driving required less concentration. You could carry on a conversation with your passenger or listen to a newscast or sing along with the radio. Now, with enough experience, driving requires so little of your working memory that you are sometimes surprised, even dismayed, at how little concentration it required. Have you ever been driving and suddenly wondered what happened to last several blocks or miles? You can't remember passing places you know you had to pass. You don't remember the traffic lights. You weren't paying attention! Were there pedestrians? Small animals? What happened back there?

Nothing happened, nothing serious, anyway. You were simply processing information automatically. To be sure, a great deal of cognitive processing was going on, but you did not have to expend any conscious effort. The development of automaticity allows a learner to perform cognitive tasks without any cost in capacity. This is a crucial point for a teacher.

Chapter 15 Casebook Preview: See Responsibility Education.

Earlier in the chapter, we focused on two modes of operation: selective attention and automatic attention. Recall Grabe's (1986) suggestion that the teacher's job is to direct selective attention—conscious cognitive effort—while developing automaticity. Encoding and retrieval can occur automatically as well. Automaticity in processing is something we desire for our students. Bloom called automaticity "the hands and feet of genius" (1986).

He argued that automatization of basic skills—not simply mastery—would be a desirable objective in the primary grades.

Picture two students reading aloud. One is a skilled reader; one is a poor reader. How do their performances differ? The poor reader stumbles over words and uses little inflection to signify a deep understanding of the material. He or she expends a great deal of effort to "sound out" difficult or unfamiliar words. The poor reader has to devote much of his or her cognitive capacity to the task of word recognition and pronunciation, leaving little capacity for the business of constructing meaning.

In reading, and other content areas, component skills must be learned to the point of automaticity if learners are to be considered truly skilled or fluent (LaBerge & Samuels, 1974). LaBerge and Samuels propose three stages in the development of automaticity in reading.

Stage 1. Inaccuracy—words are not accurately recognized.
Stage 2. Accuracy—words are recognized, but only with effort.
Stage 3. Automaticity—words are recognized without great cognitive effort; reading proceeds automatically.

If automaticity can be developed through practice, it follows that a teacher must choose carefully the cognitive tasks students practice. It is possible for automaticity training to yield strange results. In a study on the development of automatic attention, Shiffrin and Schneider (1977) trained subjects to attend to target letters. For example, a subject might be instructed to attend to the letter *A* whenever it appeared. Their procedure was to present, for a very brief period, slides containing two symbols (see Figure 6–2).

Teacher Interview: Have each student interview a teacher regarding his or her use of drill and practice to achieve automaticity.

Lecture Note: Read aloud a passage in a halting manner, sounding out the words. The purpose of the demonstration is to show how cognitive capacity is taken up by sounding out the words rather than focusing on their meaning.

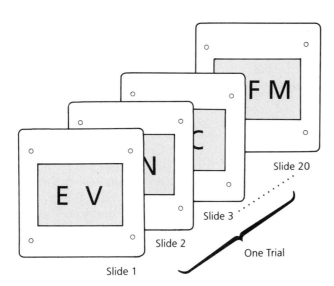

■ **Figure 6–2** *Example of the Type of Slides Used by Shiffrin and Schneider (1977)*

SOURCE: From "Controlled and Automatic Human Information Processing: II. Perceptual Learning, Automatic Attending, and a General Theory" by R. M. Shiffrin and W. Schneider, 1977, *Psychological Review, 84* (2), pp. 127–190. Copyright 1977 by the American Psychological Association. Adapted by permission.

The slides were presented in succession. Each trial consisted of a viewing of a series of slides. If the subject saw their target letter on any one of the slides in the series, they were to press a button indicating the presence of the target. If their target was not present, they were to press a second button. After considerable practice, subjects would view twenty slides, presented one at a time. The total time taken to display twenty slides was four seconds. Recognizing target letters in a series of twenty slides, in succession, in four seconds and signaling that recognition is a tough task; indeed, it's impossible, unless attention is drawn automatically to the target letter. Subjects in Shiffrin and Schneider's experiment became so proficient at their task that they performed the target identification with over 90 percent accuracy. Furthermore, subjects began carrying on conversations with each other as they watched the slides go by in rapid succession. By the time the training ended, subjects performed the task without effort. So, what were the strange results of the study?

Subjects in the study would come to lab in the afternoon and perform the target identification. After a session of identifying *A*'s, subjects found it difficult to read for a period of time. They reported opening a textbook in order to study only to have all the *A*'s on the page "leap out at them." Moral: Be careful what you practice, it may become automatic.

Lecture Note: Ask students to comment on any bad study habits they may have developed.

Principles in Practice 6.2

Principles . . .
1. Attention can occur selectively or automatically (as can other cognitive processes).
2. Elaborative processing, which is a more active form of encoding, is superior to rote processing.
3. Retrieval is influenced by one's prior knowledge.

. . . in Practice
The students in Teacher Chronicle 6.2 did not respond well to the teacher's first attempt to teach the parts of the eye. The memory tricks helped them remember the names of the parts of the eye, but did not help them understand how those parts functioned. The teacher tested the hypothesis that students actively involved in "discovering" some of the functions of the eye would better understand them. The students found the "experiment" to be interesting and fun, which is to say, it drew their attention automatically. Their encoding during the experiment was of an elaborative nature; they related the part called the pupil to the function that they saw operate.

1. Why do "experiments" attract students' attention so readily?
2. Is elaborative encoding more likely when the content to be learned is presented before or after some kind of "active" experience (such as the pupil experiment)?
3. What kinds of learning activities best activate the retrieval of prior knowledge?

Teacher
Chronicle
6.3

WARMING UP WITH POLLIWOGS

"What is a polliwog?" I ask the entire class, which is sitting on the carpet in front of me. Only two hands go up, Krystle's and Paul's. I call on Krystle.

"They come from water," she answers.

"They're baby frogs," Paul adds.

By this time more hands shoot up as more students make connections between what they know about polliwogs and what they've just heard Krystle and Paul say.

"They live in that swampy water behind the new house."

"I catch them at Grandpa's."

"They are really tadpoles."

I go around the classroom until everyone who wants to speak has a chance. I'm not fishing for a polliwog definition, but trying to get the students thinking "polliwog."

The discussion continues.

"They change into frogs," Paul says. "Once I kept one on our table and it grew its legs."

"Gross," Amanda says, grimacing. "How could you eat?"

"My dad kept saying he was going to eat the frog legs when they got big enough."

Todd is wiggling in anticipation. "I ate frog legs once." All eyes swivel to him. "They tasted a little like chicken."

"Yuck, I would never eat frog legs," Kathy said, sticking out her tongue.

"Remember the caterpillars in Mrs. Roger's room last year and how they became butterflies," Sam says excitedly. He hadn't participated yet but the wheels in his head have been spinning.

"That reminds me of the *Very Hungry Caterpillar*," Todd says. "Remember the book where the caterpillar eats all that good stuff and spins his, ah . . ."

"Cocoon," Sam replies.

"Yeah, his cocoon and then he turns into a butterfly."

"That's a really neat book," Kathy adds. "Can we read it again this year?"

"Sure," I answer. "I have it right on the shelf. But first we're going to read *Patrick's Polliwogs*." I chose this moment to work into the story, my goal in the first place.

PRIOR KNOWLEDGE

Chap. Obj. 4
Test Ques. 6.82–6.100

Focus Question: Why do students enjoy sharing their own experiences?

prior knowledge Knowledge that has already been acquired.

Prior knowledge—knowledge that has already been acquired— influences the quality and quantity of what students learn. The teacher's task is to help students integrate what they know with what they are to learn. Information that enters STS from the sensory register encounters prior knowledge as it enters STS from LTS (see Figure 6–1). Integration does not take place in a random fashion. Prior knowledge must be in some way compatible with the new information.

Prior knowledge is an important part of what students bring to a learning situation. Their knowledge of insects, for example, will enhance their encounters with butterflies.

Lecture Note: Recalling the formula for computing the hypotenuse for a triangle would not be very helpful in interpreting the meter of a poem.

Human beings intuitively understand that prior knowledge is useful in understanding new information. Recall a time in high school when you were listening to a teacher's explanation of some concept. If its meaning somehow eluded you, what did you do? You probably knitted your brow, raised your hand, and said something to this effect, "I don't understand what you are talking about. Could you give me another example?"

Translated into the language of information-processing theory, your comment might go as follows:

> I can perceive the sounds you are providing to my sensory register and am able to turn them into words in my STS. The meaning of your words, however, does not allow me to integrate your message with my prior knowledge. Perhaps a different example would activate information that will help me construct a meaningful representation of your message.

Connection: Teacher Chronicle 6.3: Warming Up with Polliwogs.

As a teacher you want your instructional messages to make sense to your students. If they are to do so, you must find ways to tap your students' prior knowledge, connecting the information you want them to learn with what they already know. In Teacher Chronicle 6.3, the teacher allowed the students to retrieve prior knowledge about the ways animals go through stages of development. In the sections that follow, we will examine ways that teachers can put students' prior knowledge to good use. Let's examine the organization of prior knowledge before we look at those ways of integrating environmental information with prior knowledge.

Organization

Prior knowledge is organized in the following ways: as episodic prior knowledge, semantic prior knowledge, procedural prior knowledge, and conditional prior knowledge.

Episodic Prior Knowledge

Episodic information tends to be stored in the form of **mental images** which we usually think of as visual representations, but which can be "verbal" images as well (Paivio, 1971, 1975, 1978). Consider the following sentence: "Although we know that the blue whale is considered the largest living animal, the sight of a blue whale's tail breaking the water's surface is stupifying." It is easy to create a visual representation of this information, but we can also create a verbal image. A verbal representation might include the speaker's recognition of the difference between possessing intellectual knowledge of a subject—in this case, the blue whale—and knowledge based on experience— a blue whale sighting. Indeed, it is likely that a reader would encode the sentence visually and verbally, "It was a whale of a tail" (see Schwanenflugel & Shoben, 1983).

The organization of these images is based on the temporal and spatial relationships of events. Family gatherings or class reunions often include a period of reminiscing, sitting around with friends or family and talking about old times. Descriptions of events trigger mental images. A parent describes the old train set that was placed under the Christmas tree every year; you retrieve your image of the train. Your memory of the train set is connected to other events stored as images. Perhaps you recall the time when a young cousin starting chewing on the train while saying, "Choo-choo. Choo-choo." You remember laughing about it.

As evidence of the time and space relationships around which episodic information is organized, imagine yourself in the following situation:

You are taking a multiple-choice test. You have gone through the exam, completing all of the items that you are sure of. Now you are contemplating an item that has two plausible alternatives: *A* and *C*. You ponder the alternatives, knowing that you read the pertinent information somewhere in the text. You try to recall exactly what you read. You can't seem to remember what you read, but you do know that it was located on the upper left-hand part of the page.

Why is it that you remember the location of the information, but not the information itself? You search LTS in an attempt to find the specific information you need. What you recall is the location of the information you seek, but not its content. Because the information is stored episodically, it is natural for the spatial nature of the information to be retrieved (see Rothkopf, 1970).

Many episodic experiences follow a pattern (e.g., one family dinner is very much like other family dinners). Because many events fit into the same pattern, the distinctiveness of each specific instance is lost. A departure from the pattern can make one episode very distinctive and, therefore, easily remembered. Those of us who are old enough, remember in vivid detail where we were and what we were doing when we heard that President John F. Kennedy was assassinated. What were you doing when you heard that the *Challenger* crew had perished in an explosion?

Semantic Prior Knowledge

As a rule, we structure the memory of our experiences around certain patterns. These stored patterns tend to subsume the details of those experiences. We can remember the general pattern, but we lose the autobiographical tags of these events. Each general pattern of experience is stored in LTS as a knowledge structure called a schema (plural: schemata). (We use the term here in much the same way that Piaget used it. For a review of Piaget's theory,

Teaching Anecdote: Tell the story about the teacher who begins a review lesson with the question, "Who can remember what we were doing when we talked about ellipses?" Ask your students why this might be an effective retrieval method for some students.

Lecture Note: Ask students to recall times when they reminisced with friends or family. Ask them to identify some of the images that were elicited by those reminiscences.

Journal Entry: Have students reflect on the ways in which a teacher can use unusual behavior to teach material effectively.

Connection: See Piaget's definition of *schema* in Chapter 2.

see Chapter 2.) Concepts that we acquire as the result of various instructional experiences are stored in this way as well. Richard C. Anderson (1977) provides a clear description.

> A **schema** represents generic knowledge; that is, it represents what is believed to be generally true of a class of things, events, or situations. A schema is conceived to contain a slot or a place holder for each component. For instance, a Face schema includes slots for a mouth, nose, eyes, and ears. (p. 2, boldface added)

Take as an example an event schema. A person who has had considerable experience dining in fine restaurants knows that there are several courses to the meal, that soup precedes an entrée, that certain wines go with certain foods. Such knowledge is stored in the "fancy restaurant" schema (see Anderson, 1977; Schank & Abelson, 1975, 1977). If that person were to go to a fine restaurant and find on the menu "Hot Dogs en Brouchette," he or she would be surprised. The dinner-goer's expectations, in the form of slots in the fancy restaurant schema, would be violated.

Now imagine that one of your students has been assigned some reading material. The meaning that the student constructs will be based on the schema he or she uses to make the material meaningful. Sir Frederick Bartlett (1932) conducted a now classic study of the influence of prior knowledge on learning from text. He asked subjects to read an Indian folktale, "The War of the Ghosts."

The story did not match the experience of Bartlett's subjects (cf. Baddeley, 1990). When Bartlett asked his subjects to recall the story, their versions contained many distortions. The distortions were consistent. Subjects tended to make the story shorter and to change the details of the story so that it was more consistent with their own schemata. For example, many people who were asked to recall the story, remembered that two young men went down to a river to fish. In the story, they went down to river to hunt seals. Learners construct meaning by integrating new information into prior knowledge even when prior knowledge leads to distortions of new information.

Procedural Prior Knowledge

Prior knowledge that includes knowledge of how to do things is called **procedural knowledge.** Procedural prior knowledge is thought to be stored as a series of stimulus–response pairings. Assume that you have procedural knowledge of how to ride a bike. It is difficult to explain the procedure verbally and yet it is easy to demonstrate it. It is also difficult to engage in the correct bike-riding responses unless a bike is part of the stimulus situation. If you doubt this, put down your book and try to display "bike-riding" behavior without a bike.

The stimulus–response pairings stored as part of prior knowledge allow learners to respond to certain stimuli automatically. You jump into water and start to swim (if swimming procedures are stored). Procedural knowledge is acquired through practice. With enough practice, the appropriate responses are stored permanently and can be retrieved automatically, without conscious effort. (This is the reason there is a direct connection between LTS and the response generator in Figure 6–1).

Conditional Prior Knowledge

Prior knowledge also includes knowledge of when and how to use certain schemata and/or procedural knowledge. A student may have the procedural knowledge that allows him or her to read fluently. But there may be some reading tasks that required a text to be skimmed rather than read closely. Conditional knowledge allows a student to match procedures and semantic knowledge to the task at hand (Schunk, 1991).

This kind of "regulation" of knowledge and processes is referred to as **metacognition,** which means, literally, cognition about cognition (Flavell, 1985). In the information-processing model examined at the beginning of the chapter, control processes are labeled as "metacognitive" (see Figure 6–1). One metacognitive function is the application of conditional knowledge. For example, the students in Teacher Chronicle 6.2 who decided to conduct the pupil contraction and dilation "experiment" on their pets were learning how to use a procedure at home that they had just learned in class. Another function of metacognition is to monitor and evaluate thinking processes. A student who is metacognitively aware is one who questions his or her comprehension of ideas; who makes decisions about how to study based not only on the material to be learned, but also on his or her own cognitive strengths and weaknesses.

Instructionally, metacognition can be referred to as "learning how to learn." A teacher interested in encouraging metacognition might have students read a humorous story or a set of instructions, or listen to a lecture at

> **metacognition** Knowledge about thinking and the capability to monitor one's own cognitive processing, such as thinking, learning, and remembering.

Chapter 15 Casebook Preview: See Writers' Tea.

Connection: Teacher Chronicle 6.2: Now I See!

Field Observation: Have students observe a class to discover other ways in which teachers encourage metacognition.

Students who are metacognitively aware can think critically and reflectively about what they know and the ways in which they learn.

mnemonic devices
Techniques for remembering
that may connect new
information with prior
knowledge.

Chapter 15 Casebook Preview: See
Writers' Tea.

Chap. Obj. 5
Test Ques. 6.101–6.120

Focus Questions: How should I use
what my students already know to enhance their learning? How can I make
my students better learners?

Chapter 15 Casebook Preview: See
Writing Success in Science.

Connection: Teacher Chronicle 6.3:
Warming Up with Polliwogs.

the planetarium or a political debate. A discussion of purposes for listening or reading might follow (e.g., enjoyment, specific directions, concepts, decision making). If students can distinguish between reading for enjoyment and reading for the purpose of making a decision, then these different concepts can be applied to other learning situations from which students will derive further benefit (Schunk, 1991).

Prior Knowledge, and Don't You Forget It!

The prior knowledge learners bring to a learning situation influences their understanding of new information. Indeed, part of the understanding constructed by a student is due to his or her prior knowledge (Rumelhart, 1980). Tobias (1982) argues that students' prior knowledge is the most important factor in determining the outcome of any instructional situation. Tobias suggests further that we should worry less about ability or other individual differences and concentrate on discovering methods of instruction that will best tap the learner's prior knowledge, capitalizing on the knowledge that a student brings to the lessons you are teaching. Keep in mind this quote at the beginning of a book by Ausubel, Novak, and Hanesian (1978).

> If I had to reduce all of educational psychology to but one principle, I would say this: The most important single factor influencing learning is what the learner already knows. Ascertain this and teach him [or her] accordingly.

USING PRIOR KNOWLEDGE TO LEARN

The approach that a teacher uses to help bridge the gap between the material we want students to learn and their prior knowledge depends on the use to which this new material will be put. Are students simply supposed to remember the information so that it can be used for other purposes later? Are they supposed to create concepts, solve problems, apply a procedure, make judgments? The "higher level" outcomes are the ones most teachers aspire to in their classrooms, and they should. In many cases, however, students must be able to remember information before they can pursue loftier goals. Thus, using prior knowledge to aid memory is an important application of information-processing theory. (We will examine a hierarchy of cognitive learning outcomes in Chapter 9 of this book.)

Imagery

Imagery can be considered a form of elaborative encoding. Mental images are mental pictures, sounds, smells, and so on. Mental images can be retrieved; for example, we may retrieve an episodic memory in the form of an image from long-term store. The "count your windows" example allowed you to conjure a mental image. We can also construct images during encoding to help us remember information better. In the next section, we will examine mnemonic devices. Many **mnemonic devices** sometimes called memory techniques, aids, or even tricks, make use of the imagery capability of human beings.

There is ample evidence to suggest that images, and the mental processing of those images, can be applied profitably in instructional situations. Images aid in encoding information in a way that increases the likelihood that the information will be retained for a long period of time (see Corbett,

1977). Usually, when we think of this image-generation capability, we think in terms of images developed by students (Bower, 1972; Paivio, 1971). Although the generation of images by students is a more active form of processing, evidence suggests that images provided by a teacher can also be beneficial (Wollen & Lowry, 1974). Consider how pictures (visual images) are used to help students understand the material they are being asked to learn. Consider also the possibility that students are, at the same time, generating their own images. When using images for instructional purposes, it is important to keep in mind the distinction between interactive and noninteractive images.

Let's suppose, for example, that a teacher begins a history lesson on the War of the Roses (the actual event, not the movie). Some children may create an image to represent this war on their own. They may start with two visual symbols, a gun—representing war—and a rose. The gun pictured separately from the rose would be a noninteractive image of those two symbols. One interactive image could have the rose sticking out of the barrel of the gun; the two portions of the image are connected—they interact in some way. The image doesn't always have to be static. A student who generates an interactive image for the War of the Roses might, for example, picture a rose being blown to bits by gunfire from a rifle (Houston, 1986). Creating or providing images for students is a way of making the connection between the material to be learned and the students' prior knowledge. Most of the research on the use of imagery as a memory aid have dealt with fairly simple stimuli. Even so, there exists compelling evidence that interactive imagery is more beneficial as a retention aid than separation imagery, and that both of these types of imagery seem to work better than no imagery at all.

The ability to generate images develops along with other cognitive abilities. Reese (1977) reviewed studies of the conditions under which imagery proved useful as a strategy for learning and remembering information. The research reviewed by Reese suggests that young children can benefit from images provided by a teacher for use during learning, but that they cannot readily generate of their own. As children develop, they become more effective in generating their own images than in using those provided by a teacher. The more cognitively advanced students become the more likely it will be that images introduced by an instructor will interfere with the tendency to generate images on their own. As instructors, we should remember the general principle derived from the information-processing model: the more active the student is in processing information, the more likely it is that the student will retain and elaborate on that information. (As an example of a more complex image generated by a student, consider the drawing in Figure 6–3.)

The image depicted in Figure 6–3 was suggested by a student at Southern Illinois University. This image was generated by the student in an effort to understand and retain the information about the civil rights movement in the United States. Certain symbols used in the image represent obstacles to be overcome (bricks in a wall). Key figures in the civil rights movement are depicted in the image (Rosa Parks, Justice Marshall). Using this type of processing technique—imagery generation—proved to be very helpful to the student in question. When the student was asked how he used this image in his history course, he replied that this was his review sheet. He knew there would be an essay question on his upcoming history exam covering the civil rights movement. The image was his attempt to integrate the information into

Teacher Interview: Have each student interview a writing teacher regarding his or her use of imagery to support writing activities.

Lecture Note: Ask students what images they can recall creating as they learned various facts or concepts.

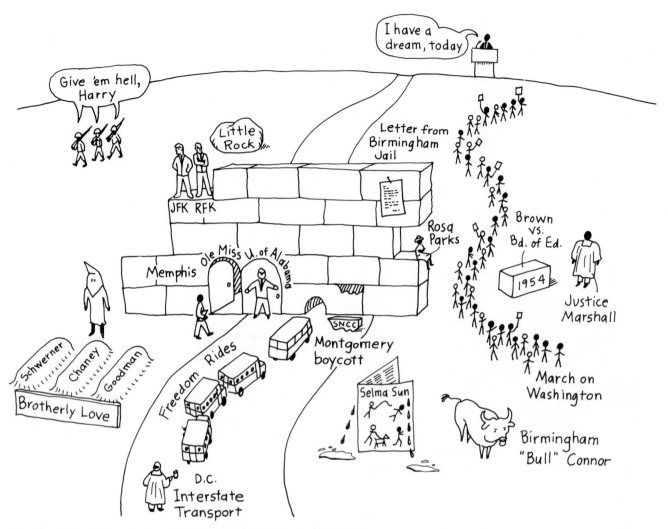

■ **Figure 6–3** *A Facsimile of the Civil Rights "Review Sheet"*

a meaningful whole and to remind himself of some of the key points in the struggle for civil rights. The student indicated that with this image in mind, it would be an easy matter to write the essay of five hundred words expected on the history exam. In fact, the student wondered aloud if his "review sheet" might not be a bit too elaborate for the purposes of the test. Although the image in Figure 6–3 contains no striking or unusual characteristics, it is a rather unusual way of organizing information.

Another distinction that has been investigated in relation to the human capability to produce imagery is the distinction between bizarre and nonbizarre images. Bizarre images are often strange and unusual pictures. Good examples of bizarre images come from political cartoons, such as the one reproduced in Figure 6–4.

This cartoon by Billy Ireland was published on Mother's Day in 1932, perhaps the darkest year of the Depression. The concrete image of the cartoon

Lecture Note: Ask students to share any bizarre images they have used or generated to help them remember information.

makes the abstract conditions of the Depression quite real in our minds. Looking back at Figure 6–3, we can see in the student's review sheet many of the devices used by political cartoonists. The Billy Ireland cartoon is perhaps closer to what we might consider a bizarre image because there are distortions of objects as we know them. Whether or not a bizarre image is effective as a learning aid seems to be related to the type of material to be learned. If a student, for example, is asked to remember that the word *piano* is to be paired with the word *cigar*, the use of bizarre images does not appear to be particularly helpful (Wollen, Weber, & Lowry, 1972).

You might want to give your students practice in developing their own mental images. Have them invent a logo or image for an imaginary company. Provide them with a description of the type of company it is, the product or service that it offers, and the ways in which the company is unique. Assign them the task of creating an image that communicates this information about the company, one that will be memorable to potential customers. Your instructions in this task could also include some advice on the effect of interactivity and bizarreness on the generation and retention of visual images.

Journal Entry: Have students identify some key concepts or factual information that they anticipate teaching, speculating on the kinds of instructions they might give to their students to help them generate images of the key points.

■ **Figure 6–4** *An Example of Bizarreness in Imagery (Cartoon by Billy Ireland)*

Source: From *The Thurber Album* (p. 343) by J. Thurber, 1952, New York: Simon & Schuster. Copyright 1952 by Simon & Schuster. Reprinted by permission.

Profiles in Successful Practice

DOROTHY SAWYER

GLADSTONE HIGH SCHOOL

GLADSTONE, OREGON

I have never been able to think of myself as a teacher or to describe myself as one. Finally I know why.

Some people are called into the profession to teach. They are called to *impart* knowledge—to add knowledge to students' minds. I respect what they do very much; for a long time I tried to do the same. It was only when I began to heed my instincts that I realized I was called to educate: to *bring forth* what is already present in students' minds.

My highest priority now is to acknowledge the existence of each student. In practice, I try to use each student's name at least once a class period. Much of the time I fail to do that, but it remains my daily goal. I stand at the door and greet students by name as they come in. Sometimes I shake their hands; sometimes I use that opportunity to hand them a paper or a book. I always use their names when they speak in class discussion, and I thank them for their contributions. I want each person in my class to feel valued and important. I want the students to know that I love them.

At first, I loved the "good" students. Then, I learned to love the clean and neat ones who didn't cause me any problems. Next, I learned to love the ones who tried hard. Finally, I learned to love the ones who weren't students at all; who didn't brush their teeth or bathe; who were abusing drugs and alcohol. Some days I can love all my students lavishly. Other days my love gives up, and I have to start over again the next morning.

I am learning to be very careful about what I say to students individually and as a class. I hope that some of the things I've said have been mercifully erased from their minds. Last summer I made some tapes with my eighty-year-old parents. They talked about their parents and what they learned from them, about almost sixty years of marriage, and about school. They couldn't recall the names of some of the shopkeepers and bankers in the farm town where they grew up, but the teachers' names they remembered with ease. And they repeated to me, word for word, the loving and painful things that teachers had said to them over seventy years ago. Words that they remembered for over seventy years. I had to say to myself, "Self, watch your mouth!" When I asked my parents what teachers did to make school positive for them, they both said, "The way they respected us." I want to respect my students that way.

I devote energy to planning and creating activities for learning. I try to invite student participation rather

mnemonics Techniques that help us to organize or elaborate information we wish to retain.

Mnemonics

Mnemonics are techniques that help us to organize or elaborate information we wish to retain. Mnemonics work by relating well-known or familiar information to the new information to be learned (Houston, 1986; Norman, 1969). Although we think of mnemonics as procedures that help improve one's memory, the word *mnemonics* also refers to the art of memory, which served an important function for the ancient Greeks. The art was taught to Greek scholars as a technique to help them remember long speeches. The mnemonic method used familiar locations as a way of organizing material. We will examine an example of this method of loci shortly.

Unlike the general capability of imagery, mnemonic devices have been demonstrated to be useful for students of all ages, including preschool students (Levin, 1985; McCormick & Levin, 1987).

than mandate it. I prefer to say, "I invite you to try . . .," or "Would you please join me in . . .?" rather than, "What I want you to do is. . . ." The classroom atmosphere is usually more serious when I am able to do the same work the students are doing. I try to have more than one activity prepared so students are free to choose one they will enjoy. These activities should decrease my ownership in the product and increase the students' ownership. I work on activities in which I talk very little, but which give each student an opportunity to say something during the discussion. Usually I vary the format of each class session so that it does not become routine.

I will try anything to make the material more personal for the students, to reduce tension and fear so that they will take a chance and participate in class. I want students to recognize and point out connections and relationships. I encourage them to do so. And then I have to take some risks myself. There is much stress in students' school and personal lives. Part of what I try to do is reduce classroom stress as much as possible and help them cope with what is left. So I offer prearranged late work and test retakes within reason. I emphasize that no one has ever made a school-work mistake that can't be corrected. I talk to them about my own academic struggles and my failures with time management and people-relations.

I try to keep the classroom life vital and the goals high. Backward and forward . . . that's how I would like to know my subject matter. But no teacher can be fully prepared for two or three language arts assignments and one social studies class. "Fully prepared" is some sort of distant destination that no real teacher ever reaches because the job assignments themselves make full preparation impossible. If I'm not secure in my preparation, and often I'm not, I say, "I haven't tried this yet. Let's see what we can do."

I was called to teach and I answered. Awkwardly at first, until I accepted and honored my own gifts and style. I've celebrated and rejoiced. I've raged and wept. I've been honored and unappreciated. I've questioned my sanity. I feel rested in the fall. I'm ready to drop from exhaustion in the spring. All my projects are incomplete. So many books unread. So many notes unfiled. So many poems unwritten. But I've never been bored. Not once. I've never been bored.

Rhymes

Many mnemonic devices make use of sound patterns or **rhymes.** Consider many of the memory aids you learned as a child: "Thirty days hath September, April, June, and November. . . ." "*I* before *E*, except after *C*." The rhyming pattern makes it easier to remember. Most people learn the alphabet by reciting it in a sing-song manner. If you silently sing the alphabet song to yourself, you will discover that the song makes use of rhyme.

Letter and Sentence Mnemonics

A second type of mnemonic makes use of letters or sentences. The memory device we used to encode the names of the Great Lakes (HOMES) is an example of an **acronym** or a first-letter mnemonic. Another example is ROYGBIV (pronounced as a name, Roy G. Biv). This name stands for the

Lecture Note: As a way of introducing the use of rhyme, ask students, "What comes after Q in the alphabet?" Give them a few seconds and then ask how many of them started singing the "alphabet song" to themselves.

rhymes Words that are identical to others in their terminal sound.
acronym A word formed from the initial letters of a group of words (e.g., NASA).

colors of the spectrum of visible light: red, orange, yellow, green, blue, indigo, and violet. A technique very similar to the acronym is the acrostic.

An **acrostic** is a mnemonic that uses a sentence as a memory cue for information. One acrostic mnemonic is a sentence that helps in remembering the nine planets in order: Men Very Easily Make Jugs Serve Useful New Purposes. The acronym ROYGBIV can be turned into the acrostic, "Richard Of York Gave Battle in Vain." In this case, the acrostic itself carries information about Richard of York.

Paivio's dual-coding hypothesis holds that we are able to encode information in both verbal and visual ways. Consistent with this theory is the fact that it is possible for students to add visual imagery to the rhyming, letter, and sentence mnemonics. For example, a student may imagine Big Bird from "Sesame Street" singing the *ABC* song. Recalling the names of the Great Lakes might be enhanced by imagining five homes situated on a lake. The acronym for the colors of the spectrum might be used with the image of a rainbow. Although rhyming and letter mnemonics usually serve their purposes without the added imagery, many mnemonic devices make direct use of visual imagery.

Peg Mnemonics

Peg mnemonics are mnemonic devices that make use of visual imagery. Peg mnemonics are organizational in nature. The learner uses known information as organizational pegs from which to "hang" new information. Some peg mnemonics require that the learner first learn the pegs and then use the pegs to remember additional information. One peg mnemonic is the method of loci mentioned earlier. (Loci is from the Latin word *locus* which means "place.") The pegs used in the method of loci are familiar locations. For example, a student can be asked to remember the route he or she takes when walking home from school and to identify several distinctive landmarks along the route. With the well-known locations serving as pegs, new information can then be imaged and mentally stored. Suppose you wanted your students to learn the thirteen original colonies and the order in which they were established. The method of loci could be used to remember the names of the colonies. By placing the colonies along a familiar route, they could be recalled by mentally walking the route.

The use of imagery comes into play when imagining the familiar route home. The new information to be learned—in this case, the names and order of establishment of the thirteen colonies—requires the use of imagery as well. For example, images representing the colonies of New York, Pennsylvania, and the other eleven colonies would be required. Because the colony of New York was chartered prior to Pennsylvania, a landmark near school would be used for "storing" New York and location nearer home for Pennsylvania. Our "colonist" may be a student who leaves the school grounds and encounters a crossing guard adjacent to the school. As the crossing guard holds up the stop sign, the student imagines that the crossing guard is the Statue of Liberty. (The example presumes that the Statue of Liberty is effective as an image or symbol of New York.) After the student passes the crossing guard on the way home, he or she might a imagine a lamppost as a huge pencil, a reminder of Pennsylvania. A filling station could be used as a mnemonic for Philadelphia, which is associated with Pennsylvania.

A more direct application of the method of loci, as it was used by the Greeks, would be to store images that represent topics for an informational speech. The images would be stored in various locations around the the student's home or even in the classroom in which the speech will be delivered.

Another peg mnemonic is called the peg-word method. The peg words are learned by the student for use in a variety of situations requiring sequential recall. Note that the peg words make use of rhyme.

One is a bun.

Two is a shoe.

Three is a tree.

Four is a door.

Five is a hive.

Six is sticks.

Seven is Heaven.

Eight is a gate.

Nine is a line.

Ten is a hen.

With the exception of *Heaven*, the peg words are concrete. All of the peg words, however, can be easily imaged. By integrating new material with the familiar peg words, the new information can be more easily recalled. The value of this peg-word mnemonic is in remembering information in a particular sequence. The key to using this mnemonic is to learn the peg words themselves so that they can be recalled automatically. Learning the list is quite easy. The rhyme scheme takes advantage of the principle of encoding specificity. Thus, "door" is an effective cue for the number "four."

Stories

Another mnemonic technique that helps in recalling ordered information is the **story technique,** which combines the elements to be remembered in their correct order in a brief story. Suppose you wanted students to remember the order of the elements in a simple declarative sentence: subject, verb, object. "His best subjects in school were verbal. He hated using his hands to make objects."

An ever shorter "story" is as follows: "The subject verbed the object."

Using the word *verb* as a verb is a bit whimsical, but the elements serve their defined function. The passive voice might be illustrated this way as well: "The object was verbed by the subject."

Memory experts who present mnemonic techniques in business seminars or to the general public tout the story technique as a good way of remembering a list of chores or errands. For example, "The post office forgot to mail its mortgage payment. So, the banker cashed a check, bought some lighter fluid, torched the place, and brought home the charred bricks for the cookout." If nothing else, the technique adds a bit of spice to the drudgery of going to the post office, the bank, and to the store to buy lawn torches, lighter fluid, and charcoal briquettes.

Teaching Anecdote: Tell the story of the preschool teacher who uses the peg-word method to teach children their telephone numbers; also, the high school teacher who encourages students to use number peg words as an aid in remembering the order of species along a phylogenetic scale. For double-digit numbers, the images are combined. For example, twelve is a "bun-shoe"; twenty-one is "shoe-bun." The visual image for twelve is a foot wearing a kaiser roll. The visual image for twenty-one is a shoe inside a sliced roll, described as a shoe sandwich.

Lecture Note: In discussion groups, have students identify several key elements of a concept and then generate a story that they could use in a classroom situation to aid them in remembering the information.

Keyword Mnemonics

Most mnemonics have been in use for quite a long time. The final mnemonic discussed here is of recent vintage. The keyword method was developed specifically for learning foreign language vocabulary (Atkinson, 1975; Atkinson & Raugh, 1975). The keyword method requires first that a known word be chosen from the learner's first language. The chosen word must sound similar to part of the foreign language word to be learned. The Spanish word for letter is *carta*. The English word *cart* becomes the keyword. The German word for newspaper is *zeitung*. The last syllable is similar to the English word *tongue*.

The second step is to generate a visual image combining the keyword and the meaning of the foreign word. To remember the word *zeitung*, the student might use an interactive image of a person reading a newspaper with his or her tongue sticking out. Or a more bizarre image—giving the newspaper a tongue of its own—might be generated. What image would you create to remember the Spanish word *carta*?

The keyword method has been used in other content areas, to aid the memory in absorbing data about U.S. presidents—concerning chronology, biography, and statistical information—for example (Levin, Dretzke, McCormick, Scruggs, McGivern, & Mastropieri, 1983; McCormick & Levin, 1987). The keyword method has also been demonstrated to be an effective learning technique for students with low reading ability and for learning-disabled students (see Goin, Peters, & Levin, 1986; Peters & Levin, 1986).

Because we have examined several mnemonic techniques that make use of imagery, it is important to keep in mind Reese's findings (1977). Self-generated imagery is difficult for younger students to produce. If teachers provide appropriate images for younger students, the mnemonic devices examined here can be used profitably (Pressley, Levin, & Delaney, 1982).

Metaphors and Analogies

A central proposition of the information-processing view of learning is that learning is enhanced when new information is integrated with prior knowledge. The techniques discussed in the "Prior Knowledge" section provide ways for students to integrate what they already know with the information they have been asked to learn. When you help students retrieve prior knowledge, you make it easier for them to comprehend and retain new information. From a cognitive perspective, this is an important instructional job. In addition to using imagery techniques and mnemonic devices, we can help students make the connections between new information and prior knowledge by using metaphors, analogies, and examples.

Houser (1987) identifies the role of analogy and metaphor by using an example. "When the teacher . . . says that the sun is the mother of the earth, the metaphor is intended to present an immediate object that the student would otherwise not associate with the sun and the earth, but which informs the student of something important about their relationship" (p. 272).

Royer and Cable (1976) have demonstrated that when learners are presented with concrete analogies, their retention of abstract information improves significantly. In their study, subjects read an abstract passage about the flow of heat or the conduction of electricity. Some readers were provided

Lecture Note: Suggest that your students might consider using the keyword mnemonic as a way of remembering new vocabulary in the course. Ask them to think of a keyword that was new to them and, then, together in class generate a keyword mnemonic to help remember that piece of information.

Teacher Interview: Have each student interview a foreign language teacher regarding the use of the keyword and other methods for memorizing foreign language vocabulary.

Lecture Note: Make the point that if mnemonic devices, especially the keyword method, are effective with low-ability students, it may be especially appropriate to use them. The success with mnemonic devices may produce more than just memory; it may produce a feeling of accomplishment that is especially helpful for low-achieving students.

Field Observation: Have students observe language arts classes documenting how metaphors and analogies in reading material are interpreted in class discussions.

Connection: See the example of the museum exhibit labeled "SMART" used earlier in this chapter.

with a relevant physical analogy: the molecular structure of the conductor was presented as a tinker toy structure. In this way a connection was made between the students' knowledge of tinker toys and the new information about the way that heat or electricity is conducted through a solid object.

The connections between prior knowledge and new information can be made by the students (through use of imagery or mnemonic devices) or by the teacher (through the use of examples, metaphors, or analogies). In either case, the integration yields lasting and organized representations that can then be retrieved and used for other learning tasks. The instructional goal of integration is not simply the retention of the new information; its purpose is to make the new information available so that it enhances additional learning in the future. As teachers, we want the information we teach today to aid our students' learning tomorrow.

Chapter 15 Casebook Preview: See Coup D'Etat in the Classroom.

Principles in Practice 6.3

Principles . . .
1. Prior knowledge influences the quantity and quality of learning.
2. Learning how to learn requires learning how to use prior knowledge.
3. Imagery and mnemonic techniques activate prior knowledge.

. . . in Practice
The students in Teacher Chronicle 6.3 responded well to the opportunity to talk about their experiences and knowledge as they related to polliwogs. The discussion allowed them access to appropriate prior knowledge. Research on prior knowledge suggests that the students will comprehend a story better and remember it longer because of the discussion they had about that story. The episode in Teacher Chronicle 6.3 does not tell us how the teacher intends to use the polliwog story later. When the story is used again, students will recall not only the story but also the context created by the discussion. Not incidentally, their opportunity to share prior knowledge generated enthusiasm among the students.

1. What would have happened if the teacher had introduced the story with, "This story is called . . ." and then began reading?
2. What could the teacher have done with the discussion and the story to enhance metacognition?
3. What role do images play in animating a discussion?

CONCLUSION

Assign Chapter 6 of the *Study Guide*.

Chap. Obj. 6
Test Ques. 6.121–6.123

We have examined the cognitive mechanism of students in this chapter. An understanding of how students process information gives us some clues about how we might facilitate their cognitive work. The phrase "facilitation of learning" carries overtones of "easing" and "easy."

For a teacher, it is important to distinguish between "easy learning" and "ease of learning." When we use the phrase "easy learning" we often mean that content has been simplified. Simplifying content is one way to reduce the effort students must make in order to acquire it. But simplifying content does the students a disservice. The question is, How can teachers ease learning their students must do without simplifying content?

The answer from the cognitive point of view is that we should help students integrate new information with prior knowledge. We have examined several ways of accomplishing the integration. Easing the burden of the student means making learning more efficient, not less complex.

If we can ease our students' burdens, we increase the likelihood that they will persist in the tasks we assign them. Easing the cognitive burden of the student is the motivational part of our job. We are supposed to encourage students in their pursuit of academic goals.

The two learning perspectives examined thus far have motivational overtones. The behavioristic view of learning focuses on how environmental consequences influence the likelihood of future behavior. The cognitive view presented in this chapter focuses on how prior knowledge can be used to increase attention, relevance, and understanding. Chapter 7 deals with the social cognitive view of learning, which is based on the work of Albert Bandura. Bandura began his investigations of learning by looking at the role other people play in the environment of the learner. Some have called Bandura's work a theory of imitation or observational learning. In addition to describing how people learn by observing others in their social environment, Bandura has also investigated the reasons why people observe and imitate others. Much of what people learn by observing others influences their views of themselves and their ability to regulate their own learning.

Chapter Summary

Introduction: Understanding
Understanding—from a Cognitive Perspective
From a cognitive perspective, understanding means that a student can use information to solve problems and as a basis for further learning. The information can be facts, concepts, procedures, and so on.

Information Processing
The information-processing view of learning is a cognitive model based on a computer metaphor. The model attempts to portray the way that learners transform information from the environment into cognitive codes and store them for retrieval and later use.

The Model of Human Information Processing: Structures
Overview of the Model
The model includes structures and processes, as depicted in Figure 6–1. Tracing the flow of information through the structures gives us a first glance at the operations of the human cognitive mechanism.

Memory Structures
There are three major memory stores in the human cognitive mechanism. The sensory register holds information briefly as it arrives from the environment. The short-term store (STS) is working memory. The information in a learner's consciousness resides in short-term store for a relatively short period unless the information is processed further. The long-term store (LTS) holds a learner's prior knowledge.

Summary of Structures
Information that resides in each of the three memory stores differs because the stores have different capacities, codes, permanence, sources, and modes of loss.

The Model of Human Information Processing: Processes
Attention
Attention is the process that moves information from the sensory register to short-term store. Attention can operate selectively, as when a student consciously directs his or her concentration to some stimulus information. Attention can also operate automatically, as when some stimulus causes a learner to focus on that information without conscious effort.

Encoding
Encoding is the process of converting a message from the environment into a cognitive code. Encoding is "work" done in short-term store that allows information to be stored for later use. Information can be maintained through rote processing or elaboration by relating it to the learner's prior knowledge.

Retrieval
Retrieval is the process that transfers information from long-term store to short-term store. This process brings prior knowledge to bear on new information from the environment. Retrieval can be influenced by the way in which it is encoded. If the process of retrieval yields new inferences, the process is called reconstructive retrieval.

Automaticity
Cognitive processes can, with sufficient practice, occur automatically. Many of the processes of a skilled reader, for example, are automatic. Once automaticity has been achieved, processing can occur without cost to the limited capacity of short-term store.

Prior Knowledge
Organization
Facts and concepts that make up a learner's prior knowledge can be organized as episodes (episodic knowledge) or as general "knowledge of the world" (semantic knowledge). Procedural prior knowledge is the knowledge of how to do things; how to use facts and concepts, for example. Conditional prior knowledge is knowledge of when and under what conditions facts, concepts, and procedures should be used.

Using Prior Knowledge to Learn

Imagery

Imagery is the capacity to generate cognitive codes, "mental pictures or sounds," which can be used for other purposes. Imagery is the basis for many types of elaborative encoding, including the use of mnemonic devices.

Mnemonics

Mnemonics are processing techniques that make information we wish to retain more memorable. Mnemonic devices include the use of visual images, stories, and rhymes.

Metaphors and Analogies

Metaphors and analogies are also useful in helping learners to integrate their prior knowledge with the information they have been asked to learn. Most often, metaphors and analogies are supplied by a teacher to help the student comprehend new information.

Reflections: Building Your Theory of Teaching

6.1 Identify a specific problem that a student might experience. As examples, a student might be having difficulty writing a persuasive essay, reading a scientific table or map, or interpreting a passage of music. After you've defined the student's problem, speculate on what processing difficulties might be contributing to the problem.

6.2 Reflect on ways in which your own teachers helped you use your prior knowledge to learn new material. Select a topic you will someday teach in your own classroom. How might you use your former teachers' effective techniques in your own classroom? From an information processing perspective, why do you expect that those techniques will work?

6.3 Imagine that you have given your students mnemonic devices to help them remember critical information. A month later, your principal informs you that he or she has received a letter from one of your student's parents. The letter complains that you are teaching that student nothing but how to remember arbitrary information. How would you use the principle of automaticity to answer the parent's concern?

Key Terms

information processing (p. 209)
environment (p. 212)
receptors (p. 212)
sensory register (p. 212)
elaboration (p. 212)
response generator (p. 212)
effectors (p. 212)
executive control (p. 212)
Atkinson and Shiffrin model (p. 213)
short-term store (STS) (p. 216)
long-term store (LTS) (p. 217)
episodic memories (p. 218)

semantic memories (p. 218)
selective attention (p. 222)
automatic attention (p. 223)
encoding (p. 224)
maintenance rehearsal (p. 225)
elaborative rehearsal (p. 225)
retrieval (p. 226)
encoding specificity (p. 227)
prior knowledge (p. 231)
mental images (p. 233)
schema (p. 234)
procedural knowledge (p. 234)
metacognition (p. 235)

mnemonic devices (p. 236)
mnemonics (p. 240)
rhymes (p. 241)
acronym (p. 241)
acrostic (p. 242)
peg mnemonics (p. 242)
story technique (p. 243)

Suggested Readings

Anderson, J. R. (1985). *Cognitive psychology and its implications* (2nd ed.). San Francisco: W. H. Freeman.

Gagné, R. M., & Driscoll, M. P. (1988). *Essentials of learning for instruction* (2nd ed.). Englewood Cliffs, NJ: Prentice-Hall.

Klatzy, R. L. (1980). *Human memory: Structures and processes* (2nd ed.). San Francisco: W. H. Freeman.

Schunk, D. H. (1991). *Learning theories: An educational perspective.* New York: Merrill.

References

Anderson, C. M. B., & Craik, F. I. M. (1974). The effect of a concurrent task on recall from primary memory. *Journal of Verbal Learning and Verbal Behavior, 13,* 107–113.

Anderson, R. C. (1977). Schema-directed processes in language comprehension. In A. Lesgold, J. Pelligreno, S. Fokkema, & R. Glaser (Eds.), *Cognitive psychology and instruction.* New York: Plenum Press.

Anderson, R. C., & Ortony, A. (1975). On putting apples into bottles: A problem of polysemy. *Cognitive Psychology, 7,* 167–180.

Anderson, R. C., Pichert, J. W., Goetz, E. T., Schallert, D. L., Stevens, K. V., & Trollip, S. R. (1976). Instantiation of general terms. *Journal of Verbal Learning and Behavior, 15,* 667–679.

Atkinson, R. C. (1975). Mnemotechnics in second-language learning. *American Psychologist, 30,* 821–828.

Atkinson, R. C., & Raugh, M. R. (1975). An application of the mnemonic keyword method to the acquisition of a Russian vocabulary. *Journal of Experimental Psychology: Human Learning and Memory, 104,* 126–133.

Atkinson, R. C., & Shiffrin, R. M. (1968). Human memory: A proposed system and its control processes. In K. Spence & J. Spence (Eds.), *The psychology of learning and motivation* (Vol. 2.). New York: Academic Press.

Atkinson, R. C., & Shiffrin, R. M. (1971, August). The control of short-term memory. *Scientific American,* pp. 82–90.

Ausubel, D. P., Novak, J. D., & Hanesian, H. (1978). *Educational psychology: A cognitive view* (2nd ed.). New York: Holt, Rinehart & Winston.

Baddeley, A. (1990). *Human memory: Theory and practice.* Needham Heights, MA: Allyn & Bacon.

Bartlett, F. (1932). *Remembering: A study in experimental and social psychology.* London: Cambridge University Press.

Bell-Gredler, M. E. (1986). *Learning and instruction.* New York: Macmillan

Bower, G. H. (1972). Mental imagery and associative learning. In L. W. Gregg (Ed.), *Cognition in learning and memory.* New York: Wiley.

Bransford, J. D. (1979). *Human cognition: Learning, understanding, and remembering.* Belmont, CA: Wadsworth.

Bransford, J. D., Barclay, J. R., & Franks, J. J. (1972). Sentence memory: A constructive versus interpretive approach. *Cognitive Psychology, 3,* 193–209.

Bransford, J. D., & McCarrell, N. S. (1974). A sketch of a cognitive approach to comprehension: Some thoughts about understanding what it means to comprehend. In W. B. Weiner & D. S. Palermo (Eds.), *Cognition and the symbolic processes.* Hillsdale, NJ: Erlbaum.

Brewer, W. F. (1986). What is autobiographical memory? In D. C. Rubin (Ed.), *Autobiographical memory* (pp. 25–49). Cambridge: Cambridge University Press.

Broadbent, D. F. (1975). A mechanical model for human attention and immediate memory. *Psychology Review, 64,* 205–215.

Corbett, A. T. (1977). Retrieval dynamics for rote and visual image mnemonics. *Journal of Verbal Learning and Verbal Behavior, 16,* 233–246.

Craik, F. I. M., & Watkins, M. J. (1973). The role of rehearsal in short-term memory. *Journal of Verbal Learning and Verbal Behavior, 12,* 599–607.

Darwin, C. J., Turvey, M. T., & Crowder, R. G. (1972). The auditory analog of the Sperling partial report procedure: Evidence for brief auditory storage. *Cognitive Psychology, 3,* 225–267.

Deutch, J. A., & Deutch, D. (1963). Attention: Some theoretical considerations. *Psychology Review, 70,* 80–90.

Flavell, J. H. (1985). *Cognitive development* (2nd ed.). Englewood Cliffs, NJ: Prentice-Hall.

Flexer, A. J., & Tulving, E. (1978). Retrieval independence in recognition and recall. *Psychological Review, 85,* 153–171.

Gagné, R. M., & Driscoll, M. P. (1988). *Essentials of learning for instruction* (2nd ed.). Englewood Cliffs, NJ: Prentice-Hall.

Goin, M. T., Peters, E. E., & Levin, J. R. (1986). *Effects of pictorial mnemonic strategies on the reading performance of students classified as learning disabled.* Paper presented at the annual meeting of the Council for Exceptional Children, New Orleans.

Grabe, M. (1986). Attentional processes in education. In G. D. Phye & T. Andre (Eds.), *Cognitive classroom learning: Understanding, thinking and problem solving.* New York: Academic Press.

Housner, N. (1987). Toward a Peircean semiotic theory of learning. *American Journal of Semiotics, 5* (2), 251–274.

Houston, J. P. (1986). *Fundamentals of learning and memory* (3rd ed.). New York: Harcourt Brace Jovanovich.

Hunt, E. B. (1971). What kind of computer is man? *Cognitive Psychology, 2,* 57–98.

Jacoby, L. L. & Bartz, W. H. (1972). Rehearsal and transfer to LTS. *Journal of Verbal Learning and Verbal Behavior, 11,* 561–565.

Kahneman, D. (1973). *Attention and effort.* Englewood Cliffs, NJ: Prentice-Hall.

Kulhavy, R. W., Schwartz, N. H., & Peterson, S. (1986). Working memory: The encoding process. In G. D. Phye & T. Andre (Eds.), *Cognitive classroom learning.* New York: Academic Press.

LaBerge, D., & Samuels, S. J. (1974). Toward a theory of automatic information processing in reading. *Cognitive Psychology, 6,* 293–323.

Leahy, T. H., & Harris, R. J. (1989). *Human learning* (2nd ed.). Englewood Cliffs, NJ: Prentice-Hall.

Levin, J. R. (1985). Educational applications of mnemonic pictures: Possibilities beyond your wildest imagination. In A. A. Sheikh (Ed.), *Imagery in the educational process.* Farmingdale, NY: Baywood.

Levin, J. R., Dretzke, B. J., McCormick, C. B., Scruggs, T. E., McGivern, S., & Mastropieri, M. (1983). Learning via mnemonic pictures: Analy-

sis of the presidential process. *Educational Communication and Technology Journal, 31,* 161–173.

Lindsay, P. H., & Norman, D. A. (1977). *Human information processing: An introduction to psychology* (2nd ed.). New York: Academic Press.

McCormick, C. B., & Levin, J. R. (1987). Mnemonic prose-learning strategies. In M. Pressely & M. McDaniel (Eds.), *Imaginary and related mnemonic processes.* New York: Springer-Verlag.

Miller, G. A. (1956). The magical number seven, plus or minus two: Some limits on our capacity for processing information. *Psychological Review, 63,* 81–97.

Murdock, B. B. (1974). *Human memory: Theory and data.* New York: Wiley.

Norman, D. A. (1968). Toward a theory of memory and attention. *Psychological Review, 75,* 522–536.

Paivio, A. (1971). *Imagery and verbal processes.* New York: Holt, Rinehart & Winston.

Paivio, A. (1975). Coding distinctions and repetition effects in memory. In G. H. Bower (Ed.), *The psychology of learning and motivation* (Vol. 9). New York: Academic Press.

Paivio, A. (1978). Dual coding: Theoretical issues and empirical evidence. In J. M. Scandura & C. J. Brainard (Eds.), *Structural/process models of complex human behavior.* Leyden, The Netherlands: Sijthoff & Nordhoff.

Peters, E. E., & Levin, J. R. (1986). Effects of a mnemonic imagery strategy on good and poor reader's prose recall. *Reading Research Quarterly, 21,* 179–192.

Peterson, L. R., & Peterson, M. J. (1959). Short-term retention of individual verbal items. *Journal of Experimental Psychology, 58,* 193–198.

Pressley, M., Levin, J., & Delaney, H. D. (1982). The mnemonic keyword method. *Review of Research in Education, 52,* 61–91.

Reese, H. W. (1977). Imagery and associative memory. In R. V. Kail & J. W. Hagen (Eds.), *Perspectives on the development of memory and cognition.* Hillsdale, NJ: Erlbaum.

Royer, J. M., & Cable, G. W. (1976). Illustrations, analogies, and facilitative transfer in prose learning. *Journal of Educational Psychology, 68,* 205–209.

Royer, J. M., & Feldman, R. S. (1984). *Educational psychology: Applications and theory.* New York: Alfred A. Knopf.

Rumelhart, D. E. (1980). Schemata: The building blocks of cognition. In R. Spiro, B. C. Bruce, &

W. F. Brewer (Eds.), *Theoretical issues in reading comprehension.* Hillsdale, NJ: Erlbaum.

Schank, R. C., & Abelson, R. P. (1977). *Scripts, plans, goals, and understanding.* Hillsdale, NJ: Erlbaum.

Schunk, D. H. (1991). *Learning theories: An educational perspective.* New York: Macmillan.

Schwanenflugel, P. J., & Shoben, E. J. (1983). Differential context effects in the comprehension of abstract and concrete verbal materials. *Journal of Experimental Psychology, 9,* 82–102.

Shiffrin, R. M., & Schneider, W. (1977). Controlled and automatic human information processing: Perceptual learning, automatic attending, and a general theory. *Psychological Review, 84,* 127–190.

Simon, H. A. (1974). How big is a chunk? *Science, 183,* 482–488.

Sperling, G. A. (1960). The information available in brief visual presentations. *Psychological Monographs, 74* (No. 498).

Sperling, G. A. (1963). Model for visual memory tasks. *Human Factors, 5,* 19–31.

Spiro, R. J. (1977). Remembering information from text: Theoretical and empirical issues concerning the state of schema reconstruction hypothesis. In R. C. Anderson, R. J. Spiro, & W. E. Montague (Eds.), *Schooling and the acquisition of knowledge.* Hillsdale, NJ: Erlbaum.

Till, R. E. (1977). Sentence memory prompted with inferential recall cues. *Journal of Experimental Psychology: Human Learning and Memory, 3,* 129–141.

Tobias, S. (1982). When do instructional methods make a difference? *Educational Researcher, 11*(4), 4–10.

Treisman, A. M. (1970). Contextual cues in selective listening. *Quarterly Journal of Experimental Psychology, 12,* 242–248.

Tulving, E. (1972). Episodic and semantic memory. In E. Tulving & W. Donaldson (Eds.), *Organization of memory.* New York: Academic Press.

Tulving, E., & Thompson, D. M. (1973). Encoding specificity and retrieval processes in episodic memory. *Psychological Review, 80,* 352–373.

Waugh, N. C., & Norman, D. A. (1965). Primary memory. *Psychological Review, 72,* 89–104.

Wollen, K. A., & Lowry, D. H. (1974). Conditions that determine effectiveness of picture-mediated paired-associated learning. *Journal of Experimental Psychology, 102,* 181–183.

Wollen, K. A., Weber, A., & Lowry, D. H. (1972). Bizarreness versus interaction of mental images as determinants of learning. *Cognitive Psychology, 2,* 518–523.

Woodward, A. E., Bjork, R. A., & Jongeward, R. H. (1973). Recall and recognition as a function of primary rehearsal. *Journal of Verbal Learning and Verbal Behavior, 12,* 608–617.

7

Models for Learning

Chapter Overview

This section of the book, on learning and motivation, began with an examination of environmental effects on behavior—operant conditioning (Chapter 5). Next, we examined how cognitive processes operate on information, the information-processing model (Chapter 6). The theoretical perspective that we examine in this chapter focuses on how information from models in the environment is processed to influence an observer's learning and performance. We also focus on the cognitive capabilities that allow observers to learn through the observation of others. We then move on to a consideration of the outcomes that can result from observing a model and the processes that produce those outcomes. Finally, we discuss the characteristics that make models more or less effective with an eye toward how teachers can become more effective role models for their students. ■

social cognitive theory   A learning theory, originated by Bandura, that draws on both cognitive and behavioral perspectives. According to the theory, people learn by observing the behavior of others in their social environment.

observer   The learner is the observer, according to Bandura.

model   The behavior of another person, which acts as a stimulus to learning, according to Bandura.

Chap. Obj. 1
Test Ques. 7.1–7.7

Lecture Note: Point out that social cognitive theory is a hybrid.

Lecture Note: Ask students to identify behaviors that they learned by observing others.

Journal Entry: Have students reflect on teachers who influenced them greatly, describing their impressions of those teachers.

Teacher Interview: Have each student interview a teacher regarding the onset of "mob" behavior in the classroom.

The theoretical perspective that we will examine in this chapter is that of social cognitive theory. It's major proponent, Albert Bandura, takes a broad view of learning. Bandura's **social cognitive theory** stresses both central concepts of operant conditioning (the environment and reinforcement) and a central concept of information processing (cognitive processes).

Social cognitive theory has its origins in Bandura's early research on the phenomenon of observational learning (imitation). His investigations were partially motivated by a dissatisfaction with the operant-conditioning explanation of learning. Operant conditioning holds that a student learns by doing. Bandura felt that much of what humans learn they learn by watching what other people do.

In his early work (1962, 1965, 1971a, 1971b), Bandura investigated a number of variables that influence the outcomes of observational learning. In all of these studies, the learner is an **observer.** The stimulus is the behavior of another person, acting as a **model.** Bandura studied the effects of age, sex, and the perceived status and perceived similarity of the model. (An observer's perceptions of a model have important instructional implications; we will examine those implications later in the chapter.) In addition to investigating the perceived characteristics of the model, Bandura also investigated the type of behavior that the model displayed, including displays of skills unknown to the observer, hostile and aggressive behaviors, and standards of reward that the model accepted.

In a series of classic investigations known as the "bobo doll" studies, children who observed models kick and punch a large inflatable doll (the bobo doll) demonstrated this aggressive behavior more often than children who did not observe such behavior (e.g., Bandura, Ross, & Ross, 1963; Bandura & Walters, 1963). Another early finding suggested that observers tend to imitate the types of moral standards exhibited by a model. If an observer sees a model behave in questionable way, the observer is more likely to lower his or her standards of appropriate behavior.

To illustrate, picture yourself at a banquet or wedding reception, some kind of gathering where each table has a floral centerpiece. As the festivities wind down, a few people wonder aloud if it would be appropriate to take a centerpiece home. Conversations about the flowers take place at a number of tables. These discussions end with someone saying, "Well, if we don't take them home with us, they'll just be thrown out." Finally, one of the guests picks up a centerpiece and leaves. No one stops or even questions the flower-toting guest. A model is born. The observers, even some who initially questioned the "correctness" of taking the centerpieces, imitate the model.

Another example of a model influencing an observer's standards of appropriate behavior might be found in the old cliche, "Everybody cheats on income tax." A recent government report indicated that one out of every thirteen Americans fails to pay income tax. How many of us have observed people in our immediate social environment model questionable behavior when it comes to the issue of reporting and paying income tax?

Observational learning is not limited to aggression or questionable moral behavior; not all models beat up bobo dolls or cheat on their income tax. Many positive outcomes can be gained by observing models. In order for teachers to find and use models to their advantage, they must first understand the cognitive capabilities that allow students to learn, not by doing, but by observing.

WIZARD WEEK: IN THE BAG

Teacher
Chronicle
7.1

It was the start of "Wizard Week," when each student would select, demonstrate, and explain a scientific experiment. Dressed in a long, white lab coat, I stood in front of my sixth-hour science class, water-filled plastic bag in one hand and a newly sharpened pencil in the other. I certainly had everyone's attention as I prepared to jab the bag with the pencil.

"Don't," Carey begged. She was in the front row. Other students in the front made ready to move if I was to be so rash as to pop the bag.

"What do you think will happen when I stab the bag?" I asked.

Hands popped up all over the room.

"The bag will explode."

"We'll get drowned."

"You'll ruin my new shirt and my Mom will kill me."

"Are you sure it will pop?" I asked.

"Yeah!" No room for disagreement.

I jabbed the bag. The pencil passed harmlessly through the bag and not a drop of water dripped out.

Carey sagged with relief. (Inside I did too. Sometimes this experiment doesn't work the way it is supposed to.)

"Awesome!"

"Neat!"

They were clearly impressed, even astonished.

"How did you do that?" Eric asked.

"Is it magic?" Tami wanted to know.

"No," I said, "It's science. And tonight I want you to try this at home."

"No way," John exclaimed. "My dad would hit the ceiling if it didn't work right."

"John has a point. Sometimes experiments don't work out the way they are planned to. That's something you'll discover this week as you work on your own experiments." Still holding the bag, I watched them glance around. Lots of head nodding was a good sign. I had them hooked.

"Now let me tell you what I did to get ready for this water-in-bag experiment. First, I looked through these books to find an experiment I wanted to try. Then, I got my materials together and practiced the experiment at home to see if there were any unexpected problems. As I experimented I also planned how I was going to explain it to you. Finally, I demonstrated the experiment to you. Before you start looking through the books for your experiment, let me tell you why the bag did not pop as you expected it to."

I held the bag high over my head. "The molecular bonds between the atoms in this kind of plastic are very long. When they are pushed apart by the sharp pencil they don't blow out like a balloon. Instead they pull closer together to stop the leak."

"Is that like car tires that don't blow out?" Brad asked.

"Great connection, Brad. That's exactly how car tires are designed nowadays. Long ago, when I was growing up, the tires used to blow out like an exploding balloon. Now if they are punctured, the molecules in the rubber pull in on each other. Now you can get books and begin looking for your own experiments."

■ ■

LEARNING AND PERFORMANCE

Bandura raised a key point with his research in the early 1960s: Learners need not experience punishment or reinforcement in order to learn what is and is not appropriate behavior in a given situation. Much human learning can be done vicariously, by observing another person responding in a situation. From Bandura's point of view, learners need not be behavers; they can be observers.

Bandura's early studies examined how the consequences of a model's behavior affected imitation by the observer. Behaviors that are rewarded instead of punished or ignored lead to a higher degree of imitation by the observer. How many of the students in Teacher Chronicle 7.1 do you think will demonstrate the plastic bag experiment to family or friends? Would they be as likely to experiment in front of friends and family if the teacher had tried repeatedly to insert the pencil and wound up being soaked each time? (Even if the teacher had failed miserably, the students may have tried the experiment out of curiosity, but probably in private and not in front of people as the teacher/model did.) Bandura also examined the effects that various levels of motivation had on an observer's imitation of modeled behavior. In an interesting manipulation, Bandura demonstrated that regardless of whether the model's behavior is rewarded or punished, the observer's imitative performance increases in the presence of a reward. Bandura rewarded observers for imitating behavior for which the model was punished in order to see if the observer *could* imitate unrewarded behavior. In interpreting Bandura's findings, Bower and Hilgard (1981) stated, "Thus it was found that the observer had learned the 'bad guy's' responses, even though he did not perform them until the incentive to do so was offered" (p. 463).

Bandura's research provides a basis for distinguishing **learning**—becoming capable—from **performance**—exhibiting a capability. In this respect, the social cognitive perspective differs from the operant-conditioning perspective. Operant-conditioning theory says that learning is behavior; social cognitive theory separates what observers learn from the behaviors they perform.

Bandura enlisted the concept of cognitive processes to explain how observers can learn without performing. As we will begin to see, the social cognitive theory of learning is a hybrid of behaviorist and cognitivist notions. The processes that Bandura postulated to explain observational learning are cognitive processes of the type found in information-processing theory (see Chapter 6).

Bandura's research has been truly programmatic. His research moved from issues of model effectiveness, reward of model, and reward of observer, to consideration of the ways in which an observer's personal factors influence learning and performance. Understanding the role that an observer's perceptions of a model or of himself or herself play in the learning process will make us more aware of issues of student motivation. Social cognitive theory is not only a hybrid of behaviorist and cognitivist learning theories, it bridges the gap between issues of learning and issues of motivation.

As Bandura has pointed out, the technological age has provided observers with a multitude of models in a variety of communicative contexts. We observe models in our homes, in our churches, in our classrooms, in malls, and on television and other media. The behaviors that we observe and their consequences teach us a great many things about ourselves. Because learners have certain capabilities, they can extract from their observations many kinds of information. In discussing the assumptions underlying social cognitive theory, let's first of all consider the capabilities of observers.

CAPABILITIES OF LEARNERS

Bandura's definition of social cognitive theory includes the social aspect of the environment and the cognitive processes of the learner. The theory assumes the following capabilities: symbolizing capability, forethought capability, vicarious capability, self-regulatory capability, and self-reflective capability. Let's look at each of these capabilities in turn.

Symbolizing Capability

People use symbols in virtually every aspect of their lives, as a way to adapt to and alter their environment. From the information-processing perspective, the cognitive process is a mental activity that transforms the environment into some kind of cognitive representation. This perspective is shared by Bandura's social cognitive theory as well. Humans **symbolize,** or process symbols, that help us to transform our experiences into internal or cognitive codes. These codes serve as guides to future action. Humans can cognitively play out scenarios of action by using prior knowledge and their power to symbolize. Playing out scenarios releases humans from the need to attempt each possible course of action. Testing ideas symbolically saves people from many mistakes. The teacher in Teacher Chronicle 7.1 played out the scenario of the plastic bag and pencil experiment and decided the demonstration would work.

Using symbols also helps people communicate with one another across great distances and even across time. Technological advances have taken advantage of this use of symbols. Essentially, the use of symbols assumes that people's behavior is based on thought. Behavior based on thought, however, does not mean that thoughts and the consequent behavior will always be rational. Rationality depends on the skills of the learner. The individual may not have fully developed the ability to reason, which is at the foundation of rationality. (We will see later in this chapter that social cognitive theory accounts for many of the cognitive developmental characteristics that we discussed earlier in Chapter 2.)

Even if an individual is capable of sound reasoning—of logical reasoning—that individual will make mistakes because of faulty information. We may reason possible outcomes based on inadequate knowledge of a situation, inadequate interpretation of events, or failure to consider all of the possible consequences of a particular choice of action. Suppose, for example, that a

symbolize To form mental representations of modeled events.

Lecture Note: Ask students to compare present-day teachers with teachers of the past in terms of differences in the amount of competition between themselves and other models that they might have experienced.

Chap. Obj. 2
Test Ques. 7.13–7.27

Focus Questions: How do students learn by observing others learn? How do human capabilities influence the way in which students learn?

Connection: Teacher Chronicle 7.1: Wizard Week: In the Bag.

Connection: See the section on cognitive development in Chapter 2.

teacher assigns a student extra homework because she was not paying attention in math class. The teacher takes the action because the student was unable to answer questions about the addition problems on the board. Two days later, the school nurse, in the course of a visual screening, informs the teacher that the child has poor eyesight. Symbolizing capability accounts not only for accomplishment, but also for poor judgment and even irrational behavior.

Forethought Capability

Human beings do not simply react to their immediate environment, but are guided by their past experiences as well. Using knowledge of the past, humans are capable of **forethought,** of anticipating the future. They can consider possible courses of action and anticipate the outcomes of those actions. People set goals for themselves and plan for what Bandura calls "cognized" futures, planned courses of action. Anticipating that one's goals will be met by following these plans provides the motivation to do so. The capability of forethought—the capability to plan, to carry out intentions, to achieve a purpose—is based firmly in symbolic activity.

We often use a metaphor or an analogy to represent our past experiences and imagine future events. Using these symbolic representations, we plan possible courses of action. For example, viewing one's job as "war" leads one to think about colleagues and/or competitors as either friends or foes. Our course of action would likely be a "militant" one. Viewing the job as a "public educational campaign" would lead to a different course of action. Our cognized futures can have a strong causal effect on our present action. A student might focus great effort on athletic training or academic study because he or she envisions a college scholarship. Our capability to think ahead, to imagine the future, serves as an impetus for present action.

Vicarious Capability

The social cognitive point of view assumes that learning can be a vicarious as well as a direct experience. By observing other people's behaviors and the consequences of those behaviors, we can learn what courses of action are and are not effective. Such observations allow us to build up our own store of knowledge and then to use our symbolizing capability to plan courses of action. The vicarious capability affords us a major advantage. Because we can learn by watching others make mistakes or succeed, we do not have to learn everything by trial and error. We do not have to spend as much time "acquiring" experience.

Many skills and much knowledge in our culture could not be transmitted very efficiently without vicarious learning. What would happen if everyone had to learn to drive a car by means of trial and error, that is, through selective reinforcement of the correct responses? What would happen if students of medicine had to learn the techniques of surgery in a trial-and-error fashion? Indeed, what would happen if aspiring teachers had no models from which to learn? Many complex skills could not be mastered at all were it not for the use of modeling. Children who had no models of linguistic behavior in their environments would be hard-pressed to develop the linguistic skills necessary to communicate with fellow members of their society.

The technology of communication has increased the symbolic environments from which humans, children and adults, learn vicariously. We learn not only ways of behaving, but also patterns of thought, life-styles, values, and attitudes from television, film, and print media. We are able to learn from symbolic environments because we possess the vicarious capability.

Self-regulatory Capability

Bandura assumes that humans do not behave solely in order to please others in their environment, that they also behave in ways that please themselves. To this end, they develop a technique of **self-regulation,** by applying a set of internal standards and evaluative reactions to their own behavior. Through evaluative self-reactions, they are able to detect discrepancies between their performance and their internal standards of behavior. By taking particular actions, and evaluating those actions against personal standards of performance, they are able to adjust their behavior. Although behavior is undoubtedly influenced by others in one's environment, Bandura assumes that self-produced influences also play a role. For example, junior high and high school students are under immense social pressure to "follow the crowd," but not every adolescent bows to peer pressure.

Self-reflective Capability

Humans are capable of thinking about their own experiences and reflecting on their own thought processes. (We discussed this ability, metacognition, in Chapter 6.) For Bandura, **self-reflection** leads to self-knowledge, that is, knowledge about our effectiveness under certain circumstances and, more generally, knowledge about our ability to adapt to our environment. Humans gain an understanding of themselves. Beyond that, they evaluate and, on the basis of that evaluation, alter their own thought processes and enhance their future actions.

The self-reflective capability, however, does not guarantee that future actions will always produce positive consequences. If we operate on faulty or mistaken beliefs, such beliefs can lead to erroneous thought, and therefore, erroneous action. Suppose, for example, that a teacher believed that fear is the only effective way to motivate students. Such a teacher might reflect on the methods he or she used to make students fearful: Were my threats taken seriously? Was the exam sufficiently difficult to scare them into studying harder? Could I have gotten Elizabeth suspended for her inadequate reading of the assignment? Our fear-monger is capable of self-reflection, but reflecting on ways to motivate solely through aversive control will not lead to sound instructional decisions.

Self-reflection leads to evaluative judgments about our own thought and action capabilities. Central among these judgments of self, is a **sense of self-efficacy,** a human being's judgment about his or her ability to deal effectively with tasks he or she faces (Bandura, 1986). Self-efficacy is an important concept in social cognitive theory and it is important to teachers. The sense that students develop about their ability to perform tasks influences their motivation and, ultimately, their learning performance. Several sources of information contribute to our self-judgments of efficacy. We will look at those variables later in this chapter.

self-regulation The act of applying an internal set of standards and criteria to regulate one's own behavior.
self-reflection The act of thinking about one's own experiences and reflecting upon one's own thought processes.
sense of self-efficacy A human being's judgment about his or her ability to deal effectively with tasks that need to be faced.

Connection: Reflect on the learning of values in various microcultures as discussed in Chapter 4.

Journal Entry: Have students reflect on those instances when their own performances exceeded the requirements of the assignments.

Teacher Interview: Have each student talk with a junior high or high school teacher regarding his or her efforts to encourage students to use their best judgment in various social situations.

Chapter 15 Casebook Preview: See Improvisation and Aesthetic Appreciation.

Connection: See the discussion of metacognition in Chapter 6.

Lecture Note: Emphasize that self-reflection does not ensure self-correction.

Chapter 15 Casebook Preview: See I Am Leo.

The human ability to use and generate symbols along with the ability of forethought, to cognize futures, allows us to set goals and plan courses of action. Because we can symbolize and anticipate, we are able to learn by observing others. We gather information about ourselves through direct experience and through vicarious experience. Our self-knowledge includes the set of internal standards by which we judge the effectiveness of our own thought and action and thereby regulate our own behavior. Self-regulation of behavior is one source of information that influences our all-important sense of self-efficacy. The capabilities reviewed here are clearly cognitive in nature and interrelated. For Bandura, these capabilities are a major part of what the observer contributes to learning outcomes. The capabilities of the learner are but one reason why humans learn and behave as they do.

RECIPROCAL DETERMINISM

The capabilities that Bandura ascribes to humans reveal his assumption that cognition plays a major role in determining behavior. The capabilities, which produce beliefs, values, and expectations, are subsumed into a category that Bandura called *personal factors*. Noncognitive characteristics, learner's size, sex, physical attractiveness, race, and social skills, are included in the category as well. Personal factors interact with the environment and with behavior to influence learning and performance. Both behavior and environment are modifiable. Each controls the other, to some extent. The three-way relationship that exists among personal factors, environment, and behavior is called **reciprocal determinism.** Bandura (1986) described the reciprocal interactions (depicted in Figure 7–1) as follows:

> In the social cognitive view people are neither driven by inner forces nor automatically shaped and controlled by external stimuli. Rather, human functioning is explained in terms of a model of triadic reciprocality in which behavior, cognitive and other personal factors, and environmental events all operate as interacting determinants of each other. (p. 18)

We will examine the reciprocal interactions by focusing, in turn, on the three sides of the triangle in Figure 7–1.

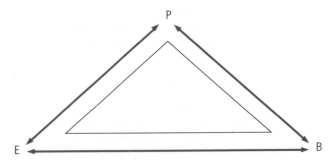

■ **Figure 7–1**   *The Relationships of Reciprocal Determinism*
SOURCE: From *Learning and Instruction* (p. 240) by M. E. Bell-Gredler, 1986, New York: Macmillan. Copyright 1986 by Macmillan. Adapted by permission.

Personal Factors and Behavior

To describe the interrelations, let's start from the top of the triangle with the personal factors at the apex. The personal-factors category influences and is influenced by behavior and environment. Personal factors, such as cognition, a sense of self-efficacy, attitudes, appearance, and demeanor, influence behavior by means of the capabilities discussed earlier ($P{\rightarrow}B$). Carey (a student in Teacher Chronicle 7.1), because of her learning capabilities, can imagine herself doing the bag-and-pencil experiment. She is likely to try the experiment at home. Even if the experiment fails, she will likely persist because she has seen it done and believes herself capable of performing the experiment. Carey's personal factors influence her behavior.

Behavior also influences personal factors ($B{\rightarrow}P$). If Carey succeeds in carrying out an experiment of her own during "Wizard Week," her success will translate into an enhanced sense of self-efficacy. Personal factors influence a learner's behavior. The behavior, once evaluated, influences personal factors.

Personal Factors and Environment

In addition to cognition, other personal factors, such as physical characteristics, size, sex, and social attributes, influence (or activate) the reactions from the environment ($P{\rightarrow}E$). A friend of ours, who is confined to a wheelchair, tells us that many of the people she encounters in her daily travels ignore her presence. It is unusual for people she sees everyday to make eye contact or nod a casual acknowledgment as they pass in the halls where she works. She tells the story of how she was heading to the parking lot one day with her ambulatory office partner. Another employee said hello to the office partner and chatted about office matters for a couple of minutes. Not once during the chat did the employee acknowledge our friend's presence with a word or look. The environment responds to the personal factors one displays to the environment.

The social environment provides us with feedback that influences personal factors, such as thoughts and attitudes ($E{\rightarrow}P$). Once activated by personal factors, differential social treatments from the environment influence personal factors. The environment informs an individual's perception of self, including a sense of self-efficacy that grows out of various social situations.

Behavior and Environment

Behavior operates on the environment to produce certain consequences ($B{\rightarrow}E$). For example, the teacher in Teacher Chronicle 7.1 changed the classroom environment by beginning the class dressed in a white lab coat, with a water-filled bag and a sharp pencil poised in dangerous proximity to one another.

Environmental consequences influence the likelihood that a behavior will occur in similar environmental situations ($E{\rightarrow}B$). Given the students' responses to the demonstration, it is likely that the teacher will use the demonstration to introduce other Wizard Weeks.

Now that we have examined the assumptions of human capabilities and reciprocal determinism that underlie social cognitive theory, we will move on

Teaching Anecdote: Tell your students about the student who cannot seem to accept praise. She does *A* work, extra credit projects, and helps other students, but when it comes to accepting her teacher's praise for her efforts, she shrugs her shoulders and says, "Yeah, but it's no big deal."

Ask your students what this girl's sense of self-efficacy might be like and how the teacher might find ways to increase the student's sense of self-worth. Why does the girl feel this way about herself in the first place?

Connection: Teacher Chronicle 7.1: Wizard Week: In the Bag.

Field Observation: Have students identify students in a class who are different from most of their classmates, either in terms of some exceptionality or because they are members of a microculture. Have them observe patterns of interaction among classmates; paying particular attention to whether or not exceptional and minority students participate in those interactions.

Connection: Teacher Chronicle 7.1: Wizard Week: In the Bag.

Lecture Note: Emphasize that this element of reciprocal determinism derives from operant conditioning theory.

to a discussion of the processes that underlie observational learning. We will be concerned with the ways in which an observer learns vicariously through the actions of a model, and with the variables that influence the effectiveness of a model. After we look at the processes of observational learning and the variables that influence model effectiveness, we will focus on the major product of self-regulation, namely, self-efficacy.

Principles in Practice 7.1

Principles . . .

1. A student can learn behavior that may or may not be performed.
2. Students possess cognitive capabilities that allow them to learn vicariously.
3. Learning is the result of reciprocal interactions among personal factors, behavior, and environmental events.

. . . in Practice

The students in Teacher Chronicle 7.1 learned behavior by watching their teacher. On the evening after the demonstration some of them presumably performed what they had learned, using the teacher as their model. The students used their cognitive capabilities to learn vicariously from the model and thus became capable of performing the behavior. The students learned more than the overt behavior—sticking a pencil through a plastic bag filled with water. They saw how the teacher's demonstration was received by others. And, they were given the opportunity to anticipate the experiments they would soon demonstrate to their peers.

1. What did the students learn about *selecting* experiments for their own Wizard Week presentations from the teacher's demonstration?
2. Describe how Carey's cognitive capabilities (i.e., symbolizing, forethought, etc.) influenced her learning during the demonstration.
3. Describe how personal factors, behavior, and environmental events might have interacted during the remainder of Wizard Week, either from the teacher's or a student's point of view.

Teacher
Chronicle
7.2

JUGGLING

It was the end of Christmas vacation. A new year was underway. The anticipation we had all felt as we approached the holiday had vanished. Now it was back to the grind with the long haul until "Spring Break" looming ahead of us.

As I walked down the hall, I saw a group of kids clustered around Charlie as he juggled three balls. The red, green, and yellow balls cascaded through the air. Appreciative "oohs" and "ahs" followed the flight of the balls. The kids were clearly impressed with Charlie's performance.

modeling Learning by
observing the behavior of
others.

As I paused to watch, I remembered my junior high physics teacher teaching us how to juggle. I could almost feel the balls in my hands. Something clicked. I had an idea. I would offer to teach juggling on Fridays as a reward for good work. Charlie was in my first-hour class, the "squirrelliest" class I had all day. I discussed my idea with the class to see if such a reward would provide any incentive.

"Get those juggling balls for Christmas?" I asked Charlie, after taking the roll.

"Yes, it's something I've always wanted to learn."

"Anyone else want to learn how to juggle?" I asked.

Almost every hand went up.

"Why?" I asked.

"It looks like fun," Jamie added.

"I could show off to my little sister," Sandy said.

"You could really impress girls," Richard chipped in. A swirl of laughter followed his comment.

"Charlie, can I borrow those for a second?"

He handed me the balls. I rolled them in my hands, watching the class as I did so. They looked like they wondered if I could do it. I did, too!

The moment seemed right and I tossed the first ball up, and the second, and the third. Round and round they went. Red, green, yellow. Red, green, yellow.

"Great job."

"Wow."

"Super!"

I understood how Charlie felt as I showed off in front of the class.

"Well, folks," I said, struggling to juggle and talk at the same time, "what if we set aside time on Fridays to learn how to juggle. If everyone keeps up with their work, we'll have juggling lessons at the end of each week. Charlie and I will teach." I caught the balls dramatically to emphasize the point.

"Great idea," Tom said, almost leaping out of his chair.

And so that's what we did. By spring break, my class clowns were all jugglers.

OBSERVATIONAL LEARNING

Modeling is a generic term in social cognitive theory (Bandura, 1986) that refers to psychological changes (e.g., changes in thought, action, attitude, emotion) that can occur when a learner observes one or more models (cf. Rosenthal & Bandura, 1987; Schunk, 1991). Modeling produces a variety of effects or outcomes.

Because teachers are potential models for all students, it is important that they understand the outcomes of modeling. The effects of observational learning are central among them. After a brief description of these and other possible outcomes, we will focus on the processes that result in observational learning outcomes.

Chap. Obj. 4
Test Ques. 7.36–7.63

Focus Question: What processes are involved when one person learns by observing another person?

Connection: Teacher Chronicle 7.2: Juggling.

Field Observation: Have students observe various kinds of classes—for example, physical education classes, foreign language classes, elementary math classes—documenting the various kinds of observational learning effects that occur.

Connection: Teacher Chronicle 7.2: Juggling.

Journal Entry: Have students reflect on episodes from their schooling when response facilitation occurred, noting who among their classmates usually initiated such effects, and what the characteristics of the initiators were.

Modeling Outcomes

Too often theorists and clinicians use the term *modeling* as a synonym for *imitation*. Modeling involves more than just mimicking the behaviors of a model; the acquisition of new behaviors is just one type of change brought about through modeling. The teacher in Teacher Chronicle 7.2 used modeling to establish more than just a troupe of jugglers.

Bandura (1986) has identified five categories of modeling outcomes: observational learning effects, inhibitory and disinhibitory effects, response facilitation effects, environmental enhancement effects, and arousal effects. A teacher who understands the distinctions between these outcomes can use modeling as an effective classroom tool.

Observational Learning Effects

Observational learning effects involve the acquisition of cognitive and behavioral patterns that, prior to modeling, had a zero probability of occurring. A model may teach an observer new behavioral skills, such as juggling, or cognitive competencies, such as long division. An observer may learn new standards of socially acceptable behavior or rules for generating such behavior. The observational learning effect includes new ways of organizing existing component skills. For example, when a student learns to pronounce a new word, he or she is learning to combine previously known sounds in a new way.

Inhibitory and Disinhibitory Effects

Inhibitory effects strengthen previously learned inhibitions. By observing a model, an observer acquires information about the feasibility and probable consequences of modeled actions, and in this way learns restraint. For example, an observer may know how to whistle loudly. By observing the consequences of whistling in the classroom for a model who does so, the observer learns not to engage in that behavior. His or her whistling behavior is inhibited, but only in situations that are the same or similar to the model's situation. In this example, the observer will refrain from whistling in the classroom, but not on the way home from school.

Disinhibitory effects occur when a behavior already known by the observer but infrequently performed increases as a result of observing a model. If, in our whistling example, the model had received reinforcement or, at least, had not experienced discouraging consequences as a result of whistling in the classroom, our observer's whistling behavior would be disinhibited. The observer would be more likely to whistle as a result of observing the model. In Teacher Chronicle 7.2, we saw the teacher's juggling behavior disinhibited.

Response Facilitation Effects

Response facilitation effects serve as social prompts for previously learned behavior. Bandura refers to response facilitation as "exemplification" (1986). Response facilitation effects are similar to disinhibitory effects. Both result in previously learned behavior being performed as a result of observing a model. The difference is that response facilitation increases behaviors not by lifting inhibitions, but by introducing behavior inducements. Often the simple observation of a model's behavior is sufficient inducement for the observer to engage in the same type of behavior. Take, as an example, applauding in the middle of a speech given at a school assembly. If one students begins applauding, other students will likely join in. The modeled behavior "cues" a known response by the learner. Bandura (1986) uses the example of one person looking up at the sky. Once one person looks up, others will imitate the behavior and look up too.

Meaningful classroom behavior can also be facilitated or exemplified by models. Research has shown that models can activate altruistic behavior, conversation, discussion, questioning, and brainstorming (cf. Bandura, 1986). Schunk (1991) presents, as an example of response facilitation, a new display in a classroom. If the display causes one student, upon entering the room, to examine it closely, a group is likely to form around it. If the group begins discussing the display, other students will join the group even though they do not know why their schoolmates have gathered.

Environmental Enhancement Effects

Environmental enhancement effects direct an observer's attention to certain aspects or objects in the model's environment. If a model's behavior includes the use of certain objects, an observer will focus more on those objects than on other objects in the model's environment. As a result of having their attention thus directed, observers are more likely to select the objects used by the model than other objects. This result holds true even if the observer uses the object in a different way or for a different purpose than does the model. In Teacher Chronicle 7.2, the other students observed Charlie juggle the red, yellow, and green balls. It is easy to imagine another student picking, say, the red ball and tossing it, squeezing it, or bouncing it off the floor.

Arousal Effects

Arousal effects are changes in an observer's emotional level caused by a model's expressed emotion. Although an emotional model may cause an observer's emotions to be aroused, the observer may not display the same emotion that the model does. Recall or imagine a situation in which you observed two angry people arguing in public, perhaps in a store or in a restaurant. As you observed the argument, you probably felt a surge of emotion, but the emotion you felt might not have been anger. It is more likely that you felt embarrassed by this public display. If the argument appeared to be on the brink of becoming an altercation, you might have felt anxiety or fear.

Positive emotions can also be aroused by models. The enjoyment that Charlie and the teacher modeled as they juggled was translated into excitement by the other students when they realized they, too, would have a chance to juggle.

To summarize, modeling can result in cognitive, affect, and/or motor outcomes. Depending on the context and consequences of modeled actions. Observational learning effects occur when a model serves as an "instructor" or "training demonstrator." Inhibitory or disinhibitory effects occur when a model plays a role analogous to that of either a "subject" in a research study or a "test pilot." Response facilitation effects occur when a model serves as a "prompter" who cues certain behaviors. Environmental enhancement effects occur when the model serves as a "prop handler" or "tour guide" who highlights certain objects or aspects of the environment. Arousal effects occur when the model serves as a "cheerleader," a cheerleader not confined to

environmental enhancement effects Consequences of modeling that direct an observer's attention to certain aspects or objects in the model's environment.
arousal effects Consequences of modeling that change an observer's physical and psychological reactions caused by the model's expressed emotions and actions.

Lecture Note: Ask students to consider what role a teacher's enthusiasm plays in reducing response facilitation effects.

Connection: Teacher Chronicle 7.2: Juggling.

Connection: Teacher Chronicle 7.2: Juggling.

Lecture Note: Emphasize in class that modeling or observational learning leads to more than just the modeling of observable behaviors.

Students choose whether or not to attend to a lesson or modeled event by considering the properties of the model (the teacher), the modeled behavior (the material), and their own knowledge bases.

Lecture Note: Have students discuss how teachers fulfill the various roles connected with modeling outcomes.

Teaching Anecdote: Tell the story of the second-grade teacher whose students were interested in the Persian Gulf War and concerned about its effect upon them. Each day news articles were brought from home and the war was discussed in the classroom. One day, several students brought in toy tanks, ships, and planes.

Have students address the following questions: Should the teacher have allowed the students to play with the toys whenever they liked? Should she have allowed them to play with the toys but discussed how real weapons are used to kill real people? Should she not have permitted the students to bring these toys to her classroom?

Journal Entry: Have students reflect on their heroes and heroines and the ways in which they were unique, identifying the reasons why they selected these people to emulate.

whipping up enthusiasm, but all emotions. Depending on the emotion, a model who causes arousal effects might be called a (dare we say it?) "fearleader"?

The outcomes examined here occur in classrooms because students observe and learn from models. Some of the models that affect classroom learning and performance are internal. These internal models include the teacher, classmates, and fictional characters and historical figures encountered in assigned readings. Other models—such as television, movie, sports, and rock stars, cartoon characters, parents, religious leaders, people in the news—are external. Any model, no matter who or what it is, is capable of causing one or more of modeling outcomes.

If a teacher is to use modeling as an effective tool, he or she must understand modeling outcomes. Teachers who understand the various kinds of information that models can convey, understand the roles a model can play. Armed with such knowledge, teachers can select models to play the role or roles students need to observe. However, just because a teacher selects models that students need to observe does not ensure that students will accept those models as their own. Knowledge of modeling outcomes is necessary, but not sufficient. Teachers need to know about the effects models can have, but they must also understand that it is the observers who must process the information conveyed by these models.

Observational Learning Processes

Bandura characterizes observational learning as an information-processing activity of the type examined in Chapter 6. Information from modeled events is transformed into symbolic representations that serve to guide future action. There are four processes that operate as observers learn from models: attention, retention, production, and motivation (see Figure 7–2).

Attention governs the aspects of the modeled event that learners observe or fail to observe. **Retention** converts modeled events into cognitive representations. **Production** allows the observer to organize his or her observations so that he or she may perform the modeled behavior. **Motivation** determines the likelihood that observational learning is turned into performance. Let us examine each process in turn.

Attention

Unless people pay attention to modeled events, they cannot learn much from them. This conclusion is consistent with the attention process as it is understood in the information-processing model. Attentional processes in observational learning allow the observer to determine which aspects of the modeled events are relevant and which are irrelevant. Selectively attending to aspects of the modeled event is a crucial subfunction in observational learning. There are a number of factors that influence the observer's selectivity. Some are properties of the model and the modeled behaviors; others are properties of the observer.

Properties of the Observed

The quality and quantity of observational learning can be effected by the *salience* of modeled actions or the extent to which these actions stand out from other aspects of the environment. In a classroom filled with potential models, one classmate may behave in highly conspicuous manner. The conspicuous model may jump up on his or her desk and sing the "Star Spangled Banner." Such an event would likely be considered salient.

Relevance—the extent to which relevant and irrelevant behaviors can be discriminated—is another property of modeled events that influences the attention process. Suppose an observer is watching a professional tennis player on television. The observer may attend not only to the position of the racket prior to the swing and to the footwork of the professional player, but

> **attention** The ability to observe modeled behavior.
> **retention** The capacity to remember modeled behavior.
> **production** The act of producing the modeled behavior.
> **motivation** The desire to produce the modeled behavior.

Field Observation: Have students observe other students in a classroom and document the various properties of modeled actions.

Lecture Note: Ask students to consider how the observer's prior knowledge influences his or her judgment of what is and is not relevant.

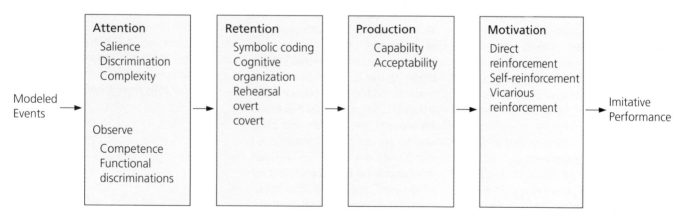

■ **Figure 7–2** *The Four Processes of Observational Learning*

SOURCE: From *Social Foundations of Thought and Action: A Social Cognitive Theory* (p. 52) by A. Bandura, 1986, Englewood Cliffs, NJ: Prentice-Hall. Copyright 1986 by Prentice-Hall. Adapted by permission.

Issues in Educational Psychology

MUSIC WITH A TWIST

Do the lyrics in heavy metal music debase human existence? Does rap merely reflect the bleak reality musicians see in the world? Depending on their starting points—socioeconomic status, age, and race—a number of people might answer these questions in very different ways.

For the heavy metal band, Judas Priest, music "is a friend that gives great pleasure and enjoyment and helps them through hard times," according to Rob Halford, the band's spokesperson and one of its chief songwriters. Halford was quoted in an interview with *Billboard,* commenting on an unsuccessful lawsuit against the band that alleged Judas Priest's music influenced two young Nevada men to commit suicide.

The two men had listened to the band's albums during an afternoon of drinking and drug taking. Lyrics such as, "He couldn't take anymore/ Keep the world with all its sin/It's not fit for living in," blared from the stereo. The lyrics portrayed the band's view of the world; they also reflected the despair of two young men who had been abused emotionally and physically as children. But pointing to heavy metal as the sole culprit in their deaths denies the influences society brought to bear on these young men. When children are made to believe they are worth-less at an early age, substance abuse and inflammatory lyrics only contribute to emotional distress or something worse.

If heavy metal is viewed as artistic expression, then how is rap music viewed? The band 2 Live Crew touched off a major dispute in Florida with lyrics many saw as obscene—devoid of any artistic merit.

Scholastic Update pointed out that 2 Live Crew's leader, Luther Campbell, defended the group's album *As Nasty As They Wanna Be* by saying that it used the kind of language that "comes out of the mouths of men in locker rooms. It's just exaggerated talk about sex, bragging, and being macho. It is meant to be funny, not taken seriously." He reportedly views 2 Live Crew's overtly sexual lyrics in the same vein as the comedy of black cultural icons Richard Pryor and Redd Foxx. Campbell states that "we wanted to be known as the Eddie Murphys of rap."

As a black woman, Michele Moody-Adams, assistant professor of Philosophy at the University of Rochester, disputed Cambell's assertions. "2 Live Crew's music doesn't speak to the history of black people. It supports the myth that black men are sexually irresponsible and black women are fair game." She stressed that 2 Live Crew's lyrics are "dangerous not only for black people but for all people." She asked how dehumanizing women can be defended.

In fact, the lyrics, while offensive to both blacks and whites, reflect the anger and desperation of young blacks in urban areas. Perhaps these lyrics simply complete a circle. Bred out of despair, the lyrics release and feed the anger that seethes in black youth. Although rap music may well contribute to acts of sexual and violent misconduct, as in the case of heavy metal music, it cannot bear the sole responsibility for society's problems.

SOURCES: Will, George F. "Why Poverty is a Public-Health Problem." *Boston Sunday Globe* (June 23, 1991): A29, col. 3. Billard, Mary. "Heavy Metal Goes on Trial." *Rolling Stone,* issue 582/583 (July 12, 1990): 83–88. Bessman, Jim. "Judas Priest Defending Metal's Faith." *Billboard* (November 3, 1990): 46. Hardy, James Earl. "Rapping Nasty." *Scholastic Update* (Teacher's Edition) 123, issue 2 (September 21, 1990).

1. How might the suicides attributed to the music of Judas Priest be explained using social cognitive theory?
2. From the social cognitive point of view would you expect positive messages in rap music to be equally as powerful as negative ones? Why or why not?

may also attend to the particular tennis clothing worn by that player. Attending to the position of the racket and the footwork of the player are relevant aspects of the model's behavior; such attending will allow the observer to better imitate the model's tennis stroke. Imitating the model's style of dress may occur as a function of observation, but the style of dress is irrelevant for imitating the model's tennis stroke.

An observer's attention can also be influenced also by the *complexity* of the modeled events. Complex modeling requires that the observer acquire the rules for generating behavior rather than simply imitating the behavior itself. If an observer is to learn chess by observing a model, he or she must watch how the various pieces are moved and, from those moves, abstract the rules that govern each piece. If the observer is to acquire some level of competence, he or she must also abstract the strategies and tactics that govern a series of moves.

The salience, relevance, and complexity of modeled events affect an observer's attention. But remember that a basic assumption of social learning theory is reciprocal determinism: aspects of the environment and personal factors determine each other. In terms of attention, this means that what is salient, relevant, and complex about a modeled event is influenced by the personal factors an observer brings to the modeled event.

Properties of the Observer

The attentional process can be influenced by properties of the observer, in addition to properties of the model's behavior. An experienced chess player will attend to different aspects of a televised chess match than will a chess novice. The complexity of the modeled event is better appreciated by the expert observer because the expert observer has a knowledge base that allows him or her to make more crucial discriminations of the actions taking place. Similarly, a chess master's cognitive competencies and prior knowledge influence what he or she sees as salient and relevant in the modeled activity. The cognitive competencies of the observer, therefore, influence the perception of the modeled events.

Observers make a determination of the functional value of modeled events. An observer who expects to function in an environment similar to that of the model will pay closer attention to the behavior of the model than an observer who does not expect to function in such an environment. A junior high student who studies ballet may watch both ballet and gymnastics on television. The student will perceive the salience, understand the complexity, and make better discriminations of relevant and irrelevant behaviors of the ballet dancers than those of the gymnasts.

There is a developmental effect in observational learning that is associated with attentional processes. Bandura (1986) reports that young children cannot attend well to modeled events for long periods of time. Furthermore, they do not easily distinguish relevant aspects of modeled behavior from irrelevant aspects. Rather it seems that salience is the most important factor, even though the most salient aspect of a modeled event may not be the most relevant. As children mature, they develop a more extensive knowledge base and are better able to make use of various memory strategies. Maturation influences the capacity for observational learning. As children develop cognitively, they get better at symbolically representing vicarious experiences.

Connection: See the sections on prior knowledge in Chapter 6.

Teaching Anecdote: Tell the story about the first-year teacher who watched her second graders play school one day during an inside recess. Three students went to the chalkboard and became the "teacher."

"Now, boys and girls, it's time to gather 'round the carpet," one mimicked.

"How can you tell *isn't* is a compound word?"

"Make sure you put your name on the top!"

Ask your students how they interpret the children's imitations.

Lecture Note: Have your students discuss Piaget's stages in terms of symbolic capability.

Retention

Retention processes include symbolic coding, organization of what has received attention, and rehearsal. In order for the observer to form and retain a cognitive representation of the modeled behavior, it is necessary that he or she code and store observations. The cognitive representation that results is the basis for further action by the observer.

In order to perform a modeled behavior, a student must form an accurate cognitive version of the model's behavior—what Bandura refers to as symbolic coding and organization. Retaining the information requires more than simply coding and organizing a model's behavior, however. Some sort of rehearsal is necessary if the observer is to perform. Bandura refers to two types of rehearsal: cognitive rehearsal and enactive rehearsal, also known as *covert* and *overt* rehearsal (Morsund, 1976). Overt rehearsal is of the type that most of us think of as "practicing." It usually involves a physical action. Imagine, for example, the prospective dancers who arrive at an audition for a Broadway show. Typically, the choreographer of the show brings the hopefuls out onto the stage and demonstrates a series of dance steps. Those auditioning are given the opportunity to briefly rehearse the dance steps in an overt fashion, that is, to actually do them. After being shown the steps, the auditioners go into the wings to await their turn to perform the steps for the director of the show. As the dancers wait in the wings for their opportunity to perform, they practice the dance steps. Because there is insufficient room in the wings for them to perform the series of steps fully, they tend to abbreviate their actions.

In some cases, you can even see an auditioner sitting quietly, perhaps with his or her eyes closed, and "dancing" to themselves. This is covert rehearsal. We have all heard or read of Olympic athletes, especially gymnasts or figure skaters, who must perform a prescribed program of action, engage in a kind of covert rehearsal called imaginary practice (Bower & Hilgard, 1981). Reports by Olympic athletes indicate the effectiveness of such covert rehearsal. Greg Louganis, a gold-medal-winning diver, "choreographs" his dives to music. The music is not played aloud, but covertly, in his head. After much covert and overt practice, the music becomes part of his symbolic code. The dive can be covertly rehearsed by mentally playing the musical accompaniment. More formal evidence also exists to suggest that covert rehearsal is an effective way to improve actual performance (see Corbin, 1972; Feltz & Landers, 1983).

Production

After the observer attends to and retains modeled behaviors, he or she is ready to produce the behaviors. Production processes are influenced most immediately by the observer's physical capabilities. Later, production is influenced by the self-observation and self-feedback associated with the performance.

The cognitive component of production processes can be thought of as decisions that the observer must make. The first of these is whether or not he or she is physically capable of producing the modeled behavior. The second decision is whether or not producing the modeled behavior is socially acceptable.

Suppose you read about a teacher with an unusual way of energizing her students at the beginning of class. From time to time she dons a cape and

Field Observation: Have your students observe students who are attempting to memorize a speech or a series of physical actions, documenting these students' behaviors and inferring their cognitive processes.

Teacher Interview: Have each student interview a teacher regarding how he or she establishes the criteria for socially acceptable behavior in the classroom.

runs into the classroom to the taped strains of a trumpet fanfare. As she reaches the front of the classroom, the taped music switches to a rock tune. She invites the class to stand and dance with her. After a minute or so of dancing, the music fades, she removes her cape and begins the day's lesson.

What would you do with this modeled event? Would you imitate the behaviors? You have two decisions to make. Am I capable of producing the modeled behaviors? If so, do I judge the behaviors to be acceptable? In order to make those decisions, you need to consult your knowledge of self. Having observed and judged your own past behavior, you can anticipate the consequences of modeling the caped dancer. The decision of capability is more than simply determining whether or not you are physically capable of the modeled behaviors. The question, Is this behavior acceptable? means deciding if you can bring yourself to display such behaviors. What if you tried the cape-and-music gambit and it led not to energy, but to embarrassment? Devastating embarrassment. Credibility-destroying embarrassment. The point is that decisions of capability spill over into decisions of acceptability.

Motivation

Motivation is the last component of Bandura's observational learning model. Motivational processes include three kinds of reinforcement: direct reinforcement, self-reinforcement, and vicarious reinforcement.

Direct reinforcement is provided by the external environment. If the production decisions are positive, the observer performs the modeled behavior. The observer's behavior yields an environmental consequence: direct reinforcement. If the students in Teacher Chronicle 7.2 learn to juggle and perform the behavior for others, they receive direct reinforcement just as Charlie did.

Self-reinforcement is derived from the observer's evaluation of his or her own performance independent of environmental consequences. The caped teacher may perform her musical lesson staging simply because she enjoys it or because she feels competent doing it. Jugglers do not always need an audience—a source of direct reinforcement—to perform. Juggling is performed in solitude when the juggler finds reinforcement in the act itself.

Vicarious reinforcement is derived from viewing a model engaged in the behavior. Vicarious reinforcement explains why one of your authors stays up until 3 A.M. to watch Humphrey Bogart movies. Your author is neither capable nor particularly desirous of producing the behaviors he observes, but he does derive vicarious pleasure from watching Bogie perform them over and over again.

If students learn behaviors by observing others in their social environment, and if through the processes of observational learning, they come to decisions about their capabilities and their efficacy in performing behaviors that they have learned, an important instructional question arises. What makes an effective model? Furthermore, how can we, as teachers, provide and serve as effective models for our students?

If we consider the questions developmentally, the most obvious candidates for potential models change as children change—as they grow older. For very young children, prominent adults in their social environment have an advantage as potential models. As children grow older, the influence of significant adults in their environment decreases. As children enter the intermediate elementary grades and proceed through junior high school and high school, the importance of peers increases.

direct reinforcement Using direct consequences from the external environment to strengthen a desired behavior.
self-reinforcement Using consequences that come from within to strengthen a desired behavior.
vicarious reinforcement Using consequences derived from viewing a model engaged in a desired behavior to strengthen that behavior.

Journal Entry: Have student's consider the types of teaching behaviors that they might be capable of and that they consider acceptable, determining how their criteria of acceptability and judgments of capability will influence their teaching styles.

Connection: Teacher Chronicle 7.2: Juggling.

Lecture Note: Ask students what activities they use to "pass the time," for example, playing video games or solitaire.

Connection: Consider Erickson's theory of psychosocial development discussed in Chapter 3.

Principles in Practice 7.2

Principles . . .

1. Modeled behavior can result in a variety of outcomes.
2. The observer's capabilities and prior knowledge influence outcomes.
3. Modeling is a source of motivation.

. . . in Practice

The teacher in Teacher Chronicle 7.2 was looking for a long-term motivator. He saw his students reactions to the juggling Charlie modeled for them. The teacher reasoned that juggling lessons could be used as reinforcement; the students observed the reinforcement Charlie received for his performance and anticipated receiving such reinforcement themselves. Thus, the teacher embarked on a program of observational learning in order to motivate students to do their academic work.

1. During that first class, Charlie's juggling did not result in modeled performance. What did the other students learn?
2. Using the processes of observational learning as an aid, speculate on how the students in Teacher Chronicle 7.2 became jugglers.
3. What other modeled behaviors, besides juggling, might you use for the same purpose as the teacher in Teacher Chronicle 7.2?

**Teacher
Chronicle
7.3**

MAY I HAVE YOUR ATTENTION, PLEASE?

"May I have your attention, please?" The buzz in the room died out and all eyes turned toward the intercom speaker. "You may now bring your class to the auditorium for the special assembly on drug and alcohol awareness," cheeped a squeaky voice over the intercom.

"Andy is the line leader today," I said, watching my sixth graders close their books.

"I hope this guy is better than the last speaker we had," moaned Connie. "He was so boring."

"Yeah, I almost fell asleep," Maren said in support.

"But we get to get out of class!" Gary exclaimed.

I gave them my semiserious teacher look saying, "I'm not all that bad, am I?"

He smiled, "Nah."

We trooped into the auditorium and took our assigned seats. My kids whispered as they waited for the other classes to trickle in. Mrs. Samuelson, the principal, sat on stage. Looking around, I spotted two men sitting conspicuously alone in the front row.

I sympathized with the students. Too often these "educational" assemblies were anything but a learning experience.

As soon as everyone was settled, Mrs. Samuelson began, "Good morning, boys and girls. Today we are privileged to have two speakers here to talk with us about drugs and alcohol. Our first speaker, Mr. Peck, is the director of the District Alcohol and Drug Abuse Program. Mr. Peck has taught high school, and has a masters degree in counseling. Today, he will share with us his knowledge about the dangers of alcohol and drugs. Let's give a big welcome to Mr. Peck."

The kids are well versed in the ritual. They applauded on cue. Mr. Peck stood up and took the mike from Mrs. Samuelson. He was impeccably dressed in a three-piece suit. He looked like the voice of authority.

"Thank you, friends at Macintosh School. It is a pleasure for me to be here. . . ." He launched into his well-prepared presentation.

After five minutes, I sensed that my kids' attention was wavering. I watched for signs of boredom that indicate trouble. Andy seemed antsy and I caught his eye. He settled down for the time being. There was no arguing with Mr. Peck's message. Yet I (like the kids) was glad when he began to wind it up. "Thank you again boys and girls for having me here. Now I would like to introduce my friend Don Mattingly of the New York Yankees."

A jolt passed through the audience.

"Is it really Mattingly?" I heard Andy almost shout.

Mattingly stood up and the entire auditorium exploded in applause. No matter what he told them, I thought, they'd hang on to his every word.

▪▪

MODEL EFFECTIVENESS

Teachers who know the processes and outcomes of observational learning are better able to decide when and under what conditions models might prove useful. But, as we saw in Teacher Chronicle 7.3, not all models are equally effective. In order to select the right model, a teacher must know what makes a model more or less effective. In general, effectiveness depends on the perceptions of the observer; model effectiveness is in the eye of the beholder. We will now examine two types of observer perceptions, similarity and competence, and ways in which those perceptions relate to peer modeling.

Perceived Similarity

Perceived similarity is an observer's perception of similarity between himself or herself and the model. As is the case with other characteristics of a model, it is the observer's perception that influences the model's effectiveness.

Rosenkrans (1967) showed children a film of a model playing a war game. The children were then led to believe that they were similar or dissimilar in background to the model. The high-similarity condition produced more modeled behaviors than the low-similarity condition. Rosenkrans's study supports the notion that models who are perceived by observers to be similar to themselves are more effective models.

Schunk (1987), in reviewing the literature on model effectiveness, recognizes that when it comes to the question of how many models are needed, more is better. Studies have shown that multiple models increase the likelihood that observers will perform the model behavior. (This is a form of response facilitation, which we examined earlier.) But why should an increased number of models increase response facilitation effects? Schunk reasons that increasing the number of models increases the likelihood that observers will see themselves as being similar to at least one of the models.

perceived similarity An observer's perception of similarity between himself or herself and the model.

Chap. Obj. 5
Test Ques. 7.64–7.72

Focus Question: How do a learner's perceptions determine who is and is not a role model?

Connection: Teacher Chronicle 7.3: May I Have Your Attention, Please?

Lecture Note: Remind students of the importance of conformity in adolescent relations.

Lecture Note: Ask students to consider the difference between response facilitation effects and the recognition of a model as being similar.

Connection: See sex role stereotypes in Chapter 3.

Journal Entry: Have students consider those practicing teachers whom they've had in class and consider to be more or less competent, listing factors that influenced their judgments of their teachers' competence.

Field Observation: Have students observe teachers who display characteristics of a coping model and teachers who display the characteristics of a mastery model, documenting the differences in terms of classroom atmosphere and students' attitudes.

Spence (1984) reviewed research to determine what influence the sex of the models had on the research findings. Spence concluded that the sex of the model seems to affect performance more than it does learning. Children learn behaviors from models of both sexes; they also judge the sex-appropriateness of those behaviors. Some behaviors are considered appropriate for both sexes; others are judged more appropriate for members of one sex or the other. The tendency to initiate behaviors performed by same-sex models can be attributed to perceived similarity.

Perceived similarity is an important element of model effectiveness. If an observer sees himself or herself as being similar to the model, and then observes the model succeeding in a particular situation, the observer is more likely to infer self-efficacy. If an observer views someone whom he or she perceives as being similar to him- or herself, and that person is successful, the observer is likely to say to him- or herself, "If he (she) can do it, I can do it."

Perceived Competence

Perceived competence is an observer's evaluation of how expert a model is. Simon, Ditrichs, and Speckhart (1975) found that children are more likely to follow the behavior of models they perceived as being competent than they are to follow models they perceive as being less than competent in the displayed skill. This is especially true when they are learning a novel response.

A model who masters a situation is perceived as being competent. However, this competency can itself be perceived in at least two different ways. Suppose that a teacher brings in two published novelists to talk about creative writing. The first novelist reads a scene from his latest book and discusses his characters' motivations and their symbolic meanings. The second novelist brings in marked-up copies of her first five drafts of a scene and describes the frustrations involved in getting from the rough draft to the published version. Both models have mastered the skill of creative writing. The first novelist presents his mastery as an accomplished fact; he can be called a *mastery model*. The second novelist demonstrates how she overcomes problems on her way to mastery; she can be called a *coping model* (cf. Schunk, 1991).

When learners are fearful about a particular situation, they are more likely to improve their performances and gain self-confidence when they observe coping models rather than mastery models. Coping models initially demonstrate the typical fears and deficiencies of the observers. A model who copes with a situation rather than mastering it instantly may be a model who helps observers enhance their sense of self-efficacy (Schunk, Hanson, & Cox, 1987).

There is one other aspect of perceived competence that merits mention here. Perceived competence can be influenced by an observer's perception of a model's social status. One attains high social status by distinguishing her- or himself from others in a field of endeavor. A well-known political figure has been elected ahead of others. A well-known movie actor has been cast in more leading roles than other actors. A professional athlete has been selected over other athletes. If a model has high social status, he or she is often given credit for competence outside his or her area of expertise. We buy breakfast cereals because they are endorsed by athletes, not nutritionists. In Teacher Chronicle 7.3, the baseball player, who knew less about drug abuse than the other speaker, was the more effective model.

A teacher who is judged by students to be "a really great teacher" has attained high status within the school community. The teacher may have attained that status because he or she is a recognized authority in a particular academic field or is recognized as a competent leader of intellectual development. Nevertheless, "really great teachers" are often asked to give advice in areas outside their training and expertise.

Peer Models

Peer models are people who are from the same social environment as the observer. In a classroom, students who model behavior for other students are peer models. The literature on peer modeling suggests that classroom peers can help in training social skills, enhancing self-efficacy, and remedying deficiencies in a variety of skill areas (Schunk, 1987). In another study of the effects of peer models, Gresham (1981) examined the acquisition of social skills in physically disabled children. Disabled children who observed peer models engaging in a variety of social interactions showed enhanced social skills.

The effectiveness of coping models is reinforced when coping models are the observer's peers. Peer models who must cope with difficult or stressful situations can enhance the self-efficacy of observers. It is not surprising that peer models who can enhance the self-efficacy of observers under stressful or difficult conditions are effective in situations that require remedial instruction.

What is called *peer modeling* when seen from a social cognitive point of view becomes *peer tutoring* when put into practice in a classroom. The teacher who uses peer tutoring in his or her classroom should do so with an eye

peer models Models who are from the same social environment.

Connection: Teacher Chronicle 7.3: May I Have Your Attention, Please?

Chapter 15 Casebook Preview: See Science Is Real.

Teacher Interview: Have each student interview a teacher regarding the way that teacher establishes peer-tutoring pairs in his or her classroom.

Peer models or tutors can be effective in fostering cognitive and social skills. As one student helps the other, they both learn more about the computer, and on a less conscious level, they increase their feelings of self-efficacy.

toward model effectiveness. A student chosen to tutor another student is a potential model; the student to be helped, the observer. Social cognitive theory holds that the observer's perceptions of the model determine the model's effectiveness.

Generally, research evidence suggests that peer tutoring works. Such evidence can be explained in terms of perceived similarity—a model who is a peer is likely to be perceived as being similar by the observer. There are several practical advantages to peer tutoring, for instance, it allows a teacher to make more efficient use of time. (In Chapter 11 of the book, we will examine the instructional implications of peer tutoring more closely.)

Although peer tutoring has the "built-in" advantage of perceived similarity, the evidence on peer modeling suggests that coping models benefit observers as well. Finding a good match between students in terms of competence provides a reasonable basis for forming peer-tutoring pairs in the classroom.

SELF-EFFICACY

Chap. Obj. 6
Test Ques. 7.73–7.88

Focus Question: What do students learn about themselves by observing others?

Chapter 15 Casebook Preview: See Responsibility Education.

Lecture Note: Ask students to consider the competent model who is perceived as dissimilar in terms of how a teacher should establish peer-tutoring pairs.

In Chapter 6, we mentioned the importance of learning to learn, how developing the metacognitive awareness and abilities of students will help them to better monitor their own learning activities. Bandura postulates the existence of a self-regulating system within the learner, which permits the learner to observe and evaluate his or her own performance. The judgments that the learner makes by means of self-evaluation influence his or her belief that he or she is capable of learning. Learning to learn is an outcome of instruction. To the extent that observational learning occurs in classrooms—and it occurs a great deal—self-efficacy is also an outcome of classroom instruction.

Bandura (e.g., 1977, 1982, 1986) suggests four possible sources by which students can gain information relevant to their sense of self-efficacy: outcome of performance, vicarious experience, verbal persuasion, and physiological states.

The first source of information about self-efficacy is the outcome of performance. Successful performance on a given task enhances one's sense of self-efficacy.

A second source of efficacy information is vicarious experience. Students who observe models who attain success can use those observations to determine their own efficacy. If the role model attains success, the student will make judgments about the similarity between himself or herself and the model. The observer, seeing that the model has successfully completed the task, will also infer competence. If the competent model is perceived as being similar to the observer, the observer's sense of efficacy will be enhanced. If, however, the competent model is seen as being dissimilar, the observer may attribute the model's success to those qualities that he or she does not possess.

A third source of information that can influence self-efficacy is what Bandura refers to as verbal persuasion. Other people in the learner's social environment—peers, teachers, parents—can persuade the learner verbally that they are capable of success at a particular task. Verbal persuasion by others is a substitute for the self-evaluation that occurs normally in observational learning. Verbal persuasion can occur internally as well, taking the form of what might be called a "self-delivered pep talk."

Profiles in Successful Practice

NANCY GORRELL

MORRISTOWN HIGH SCHOOL

MORRISTOWN, NEW JERSEY

Teaching for me is a means of creative self-expression. I consider myself a "teaching/artist," and as such, I am engaged with my students in the appreciation and love of learning, literature, and writing. As a writer, I am able to model for my students, to share my own work, to write with my students, and to learn with them. I am as much a part of their creations as they are part of mine. I share with them the evolution of a poem, for example, and ask for their criticisms. Conversely, they seek and respect my comments.

My classroom is a laboratory of experimentation. I continually test new ideas and strategies. My students are my partners in what I view as a joyous journey of learning. After a lesson, I ask my students to evaluate the strategy to see if it worked. I engage their imaginations to help make the next lesson better. My writing classes are taught using a workshop format. I favor hands-on lessons, individual and group participation, shared writings, and peer editing and critiquing. I rarely lecture, but rather, I teach inductively, by modeling or demonstrating activities so learning can be self-discovery.

I strive for an exciting and inspiring educational environment. Too often learning is segmented; isolated skills are developed with little satisfaction to the student. My lessons are all planned around the synthesis of the critical and affective realms. When reading a literary work, my students will take objective tests, write critical essays of evaluation, but then they will often have a creative project—something that allows them to respond to their feelings and imaginations. Each year, I strive to develop some project that will make my students feel special.

I believe that education should not be confined to the four walls of the classroom. Students should be given every opportunity to act as "professionals," writing, interacting, or performing for "real" audiences. The project ideas that interest me not only expand my students' knowledge and appreciation, but also help to develop their self-esteem and interpersonal skills as well. For example, in 1975, my creative writing students visited a senior citizens' center to read poetry. The seniors liked it so much, they returned to our high school to share their own writings. Much was gained academically and humanistically. Currently, I have developed an award-winning project called "Poem Pals." Students from one school exchange poetry with students from a school in another state or district. Presently, my creative writing classes are writing poetry books that will be catalogued and shelved permanently in our library. The students are thrilled that future classes will read their books and be able to find their names in the card catalog. They are also engaging in a peer-editing project with another creative writing class in Flagstaff, Arizona. In pen pal fashion, students exchange their poetry and stories with an anonymous peer for criticism and feedback. The students are learning not only how to improve their writing by giving and receiving criticism in a professional way, but they are also learning about another culture. My students have learned about other ethnic groups, in particular, Native Americans. Their horizons have certainly broadened.

I believe in providing the freedom and structure necessary to meet all the learning styles and needs of various students. Thus, all my lessons are highly structured and directed toward teaching sequential skills. Yet, I always allow for freedom for those students who have a creative idea and want to diverge. I strive to maintain the highest degree of excellence; I want my students to succeed. Many have won awards. Yet, I do not believe in fostering a competitive atmosphere within the classroom. I believe students should be "free to fail" for how else will they learn? In my writing classes, there is no "failure," only unlimited time to write and rewrite to strive for the unattainable—perfection.

Teaching's rewards are limitless. Some are small: seeing a student with a negative attitude toward poetry suddenly take a liking to it, for example. Some are more dramatic: having a student who wins a second-place national Scholastic Writing Award for a short story certainly qualifies as such. But most rewards come from the daily struggles and joys of the interaction of teacher and student. Teaching is a nurturing profession. The rewards come from planting the seeds and from seeing the seedlings blossom.

Journal Entry: Have students reflect on the kinds of decisions they might make that require them to rely on their "gut feelings." Have them start by reflecting on how their gut feelings influence decisions they make as they research and write papers.

Field Observation: Have students observe other students in a classroom, identifying the behaviors and attitudes of those students who display a strong sense of self-efficacy. Then have them compare those behaviors and attitudes with those of students who seem to have a weaker sense of self-efficacy.

Journal Entry: Have students reflect on how outcome expectations and efficacy expectations might influence their own motivation, addressing the question, How will they use these insights to enhance their own students' motivations in the future?

Connection: See the discussion of classroom reward structures in Chapter 8.

Chapter 15 Casebook Preview: See Please Sign This Contract.

Physiological states provide a last source of information about self-efficacy. Bandura refers to the "gut feelings" that convince a learner that he or she can or cannot achieve a goal. By taking into account factors such as perceived ability of the model and of self, the difficulty of the task, the amount of effort that needs to be expended, and aids to performance, students may experience physical sensations of increased alertness or excitement.

Teachers must try to provide the type of information that will enhance students' sense of self-efficacy. For example, suppose you were to respond to a sense of difficulty in your class by saying, "I don't understand why you people can't do this; the class last year had no problems." Such a response would require students either to perceive themselves as dissimilar to last year's class or to perceive themselves as less capable.

The degree to which a sense of self-efficacy has been developed is an outcome of observational learning. As there is with all learning and motivation issues, the relationship between self-efficacy and motivation is a strong one. Bandura (1977) argues that students with a sense of high self-efficacy will produce greater effort and persist longer in a task than students with a sense of low self-efficacy.

Motivational overtones are also seen in the relationship between self-efficacy and choice of activity. Bandura argues that self-efficacy influences a student's choice of activity. Students with low self-efficacy in a particular area take measures to avoid tasks in that area. On the other hand, students with high-efficacy expectations toward a particular task tend to approach that task eagerly.

Self-efficacy involves a belief that one can produce some behavior regardless of whether one actually can or cannot produce that behavior. Bandura (1977) proposes that the concept of self-efficacy is an indicator of both performance and achievement. He states that "individuals can believe that a particular course of action will produce certain outcomes, but if they entertain serious doubts about whether they can perform the necessary activities, such information does not influence their behavior" (p. 193).

Therefore, outcome expectations and efficacy expectations must be met before a person will enact a behavior that leads to an anticipated outcome (see Figure 7–3). Efficacy expectations, which are predictions of how effective or competent one will be in his or her performance, differ from outcome expectations. Outcome expectations refer to a person's predictions about the likelihood that a given behavior will lead to particular consequences. In this sense, outcome expectations are the judgments that observers make about the functional value of modeled behaviors.

As we will discover in Chapter 8, the learner's expectations are important determiners of motivation, especially in classroom achievement situations. Goal setting is an important component of the self-regulation system, and therefore, an important determiner of a student's sense of self-efficacy.

Bandura (1977, 1986) suggests that when individuals set goals, they determine a desired standard against which they compare internally their present levels of performance. Bandura suggests further that delaying self-reward until goals are met increases the likelihood that individuals will sustain their efforts until the goals are attained. Bandura's observations have led to additional research on the practice of goal setting and its influence on the individual student's sense of self-efficacy.

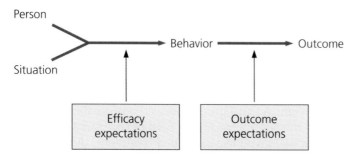

■ **Figure 7–3** *The Relationship Between Efficacy Expectations, Outcome Expectations, and Behavior*

SOURCE: From *Social Learning Theory* (p. 79) by A. Bandura, 1977, Englewood Cliffs, NJ: Prentice-Hall. Copyright 1977 by Prentice-Hall. Adapted by permission.

Transparency: This figure is duplicated in the acetate transparency package. See T-11 The Relationship Between Efficacy Expectations, Outcome Expectations, and Behavior.

Goal Setting

Learners who are good at regulating their own learning activities are likely to set more realistic goals for themselves. Positive efficacy expectations motivate students to achieve. It is important to remember, however, that a sense of self-efficacy results from gathering information from the environment and from one's own performance. Because so much information must be gathered and interpreted, there is a possibility that mistakes will be made. Setting unrealistically high goals, for example, would be the result of erroneous beliefs or inaccurate observation of models. The same could be said for setting unrealistically low goals. Locke, Shaw, Saari, and Latham (1981) identify the properties of goals as being important to the goal-setting process. They note that setting goals using specific standards of performance is better than setting nonexplicit or general goals for improving performance. Additionally, assuming that one is capable of performing the goal, setting more difficult goals tends to lead to better performance.

Goals can be long range or short range. Short-range goals are called *proximal* goals. Long-range goals are referred in social cognitive literature as *distal* goals. Schunk and Gaa (1981) argue that it is better to set proximal goals than distal goals for improving self-motivation and performance. They suggest that the result is especially important for young children who may not be capable of cognitively representing distal goals. They also maintain that learners who set proximal goals may be promoting self-efficacy; as they observe their progress toward these goals, the quality of their performance increases. Successful performance helps children maintain their motivation and enhance their sense of self-efficacy.

The evaluation of one's own performance is part of the self-regulation system. Evaluation can be made in terms of the internal standards that are part of the self-regulation system. In a social environment, however, it is difficult for students to escape the reality of social comparison. Ruble, Boggiano, Feldman, and Loebl (1980) provided a developmental analysis of the role of social comparison in self-evaluation. They found that very young children make little use of comparative information when performing evaluations of their own performance. However, by the fourth grade, students utilize social information in evaluating their own competence. This use of social information, according to Bandura, can have a vicarious influence on self-efficacy.

Teacher Interview: Have each student interview a teacher regarding the problems that students with either unrealistically high or unrealistically low goals experience.

Lecture Note: Ask students to consider how progress toward proximal goals relates to intermittent reinforcement, as discussed in Chapter 5.

Lecture Note: Ask students to consider whether these findings can be explained using Piaget's stages of cognitive development.

Additional research on the relationship between goal setting, social comparison, and self-efficacy was undertaken by Schunk (1983). Schunk compared the effects of social comparative information against proximal goal setting. Four groups of children were studied. The first group was given comparative information about problems solved by other children in a division-skills program. A second group pursued a goal of a set number of problems in each session. A third group received both of the treatments. A fourth group served as the control, receiving neither treatment.

The third group, given the combined treatment, demonstrated the highest perceived self-efficacy and achieved the highest skill level. These results indicate that the combined use of social comparison information and an internal standard leads to higher levels of self-efficacy.

TEACHERS AS MODELS

Social cognitive theory provides us with an explanation of how observers learn from models. As instructional leaders, teachers are in a unique position to choose models for their students and to serve as models themselves. As we learned earlier in this chapter, the perceived competence of a person influences their effectiveness as a potential model. When students walk into a classroom, the teacher is in a position of defined competence. What the teacher does with that status influences his or her ability to model behaviors for the students. Although social cognitive theory tells us that perceived competence makes for an effective model, it is important that we realize that our defined status of authority will not maintain our effectiveness. Students may attend to us initially because we are teachers. But unless we can maintain our status as competent models, students will soon stop attending to our behaviors. If the attention process is not supported by the model in the environment, then the retention, production, and motivation processes of observational learning will not occur.

We are often told as teachers that we should model enthusiasm for the content we are going to teach. If teachers are not enthusiastic, then neither will the students be enthusiastic. But think back to your own elementary school and high school experiences. Weren't there teachers in your classrooms who seemed to be enthusiastic and yet who attracted little of your attention? One explanation is that their competence was mitigated by a lack of perceived similarity. One of the authors of this text can recall a high school teacher who displayed competence, but was perceived by his students as being so dissimilar that he was not an effective model. It was not unusual for this teacher, who taught chemistry, to walk into the class and exclaim that he did not understand why we did so poorly on our tests. Our reaction as observers in this situation was that this particular teacher was absolutely correct in his reaction to us. He simply could not understand that we did not understand the material. Because he was so dissimilar from us as students, his enthusiasm for the content was not enough to make him an effective teacher. Did you ever have a teacher like that?

If we assume that as teachers we must serve as models, we must find ways of "connecting" with students. In Chapter 6, when we considered connections, we examined ways of connecting the content we teach to students'

Chap. Obj. 7
Test Ques. 7.89–7.94

Teaching Anecdote: Tell your students about the English teacher who is perceived to be a most effective teacher by her students and the greater community. Although she demands a great deal of her students, she is always fair with them. When asked by a local newspaper reporter why she is so successful, she replied, "The answer is really quite simple: I love literature. I enjoy sharing what I have learned with students. Every so often, I find a kindred spirit among my students; someone who has the same passion that I do. That is when I really teach."

Ask your students why this teacher is not only seen as effective but, in fact, is very successful in teaching her subject.

Lecture Note: Ask students to discuss those teachers in their experience who were "charismatic." Was part of their charisma attributable to their status as competent models?

Teacher Interview: Have each student interview a teacher recognized for his or her enthusiasm, asking the teacher how he or she uses this enthusiasm to motivate students.

An exemplary model teacher exhibits enthusiasm for the subject matter and connects with students on a personal level.

prior knowledge. Social cognitive theory requires that we look for ways to connect ourselves with our students. How can we be an effective model for Monica? for Jamal? Whether the outcome we seek for our students is discipline or understanding or self-efficacy, making connections remains an important part of the job.

Reflecting on our own characteristics as models is one way of pursuing avenues of connection. If our students experience difficulties, we can set ourselves up as coping models. If we show ourselves to have or have had difficulties with material, and then provide examples of how we mastered the material in the face of those difficulties, we are more likely to be perceived as similar—and competent—by our students, and therefore, more likely to serve as effective models.

Principles in Practice 7.3

Principles . . .
1. A model's effectiveness is determined by an observer's perceptions of the model's characteristics.
2. A sense of self-efficacy is built from multiple scores of information.
3. Teachers are in a unique position to be effective models.

. . . in Practice
The students in Teacher Chronicle 7.3 were not very attentive to the first speaker at the assembly on drug and alcohol abuse. However, when a famous

baseball player was introduced, the students reacted, not only by paying attention but also with emotion. The students' perceptions of the two speakers influenced the extent of their attention and, subsequently, what they learned from each speaker.

1. If you had been given responsibility for the assembly, would you have changed the order of the speakers? Why?
2. How might a teacher use the sources of efficacy expectations to create a class project called, "You Bet I Can"?
3. How do you plan to maximize your effectiveness as a model for your students?

Assign Chapter 7 of the *Study Guide*.

CONCLUSION

In Chapters 5, 6, and 7, we have examined three theories of how people learn: operant-conditioning theory, information-processing theory, and social cognitive theory. The three provide us with ways of addressing important instructional outcomes. Viewing learning from the operant-conditioning point of view gives us clues as to how students learn appropriate behavior. The information-processing model of learning explains how students acquire an understanding of information and concepts. From an instructional perspective, information processing provides us with clues as to how best to present information we want students to acquire. Social cognitive theory points us toward a different, and yet equally important, instructional outcome—the self-regulation of a learner, and more specifically, the learner's sense of self-efficacy.

If we are to effectively present information and concepts for our students to acquire, we must learn to manage behavior in our classrooms. Attaining the cognitive objectives—the content goals—we have for students is only part of our job, however. In addition to classroom management and discipline, which allow us to teach content, it is important that our students leave our classrooms with a sense that they are capable of performing tasks that will be required of them in the future. Possessing confidence in one's own abilities is a function of motivation. Reinforcement theory has clear motivational overtones. We can influence the way in which students will behave by manipulating the environmental consequences of their behavior. If we can engage students' prior knowledge, we can make information meaningful to them. Meaningful learning leads to higher achievement success. Success in the classroom leads to higher motivation. A sense of self-efficacy gives the students confidence that the tasks placed before them can be accomplished. It leads to more persistent behavior. A sense of self-efficacy also motivates students to pursue goals and gives them the ability to derive reinforcement not only from the environment but, most importantly, from themselves.

Learning and motivation go together. If students are not motivated, their teachers will find it extremely difficult to guide their learning. Motivation, which is supplied by the environment, leads to a reliance on people and incentives that are external to the student. Intrinsic motivation is a product, at least in part, of a sense of self-efficacy.

In Chapter 8, we will look at the final piece of the puzzle. The theories of motivation presented in that chapter will provide clues about the needs and expectations that learners bring into our classrooms.

Chapter Summary

Introduction: Models and Observers
In social cognitive theory, observers learn by observing the behavior of other people (models) in their social environment.

Learning and Performance
Learning is a cognitive phenomenon; performance is behavior. Observational learning need not be the result of performance.

Capabilities of Learners
Symbolizing Capability
The ability to create symbols is one of the cognitive capabilities that learners have. It refers to the ability humans have to form a mental representation of modeled events.

Forethought Capability
The forethought capability allows us to anticipate the results of certain courses of action. Forethought allows a student to decide whether a behavior he or she has learned should or should not be performed.

Vicarious Capability
The vicarious capability allows us to learn from others in our social environment. It is not necessary that learners perform a behavior in order to learn it. The assumption of vicarious capability clearly differentiates the social cognitive perspective from operant conditioning theory.

Self-regulatory Capability
The self-regulatory capability permits humans to use internal standards or criteria to regulate their own actions. It is an important reason why learning is distinguished from performance. An observer may learn to behave in a particular way but choose not to perform the behavior because it does not meet his or her internal standards.

Self-reflective Capability
Information processing-theory labels the self-reflective capability *metacognition*. It is the capability humans have to analyze their own actions and thought processes. Self-reflection serves an evaluative function that leads to changes in one's thinking and behavior.

Reciprocal Determinism
Personal Factors and Behavior
Personal factors include a person's cognitive, affective, and social characteristics. Personal factors and behavior interact with each other to produce learning outcomes. A person's thoughts influence his or her behavior. One's experience or behaviors influence how one thinks about himself or herself.

Personal Factors and Environment
One's personal characteristics cause other people in the environment to react in various ways. Those environmental reactions influence how a person views himself or herself.

Behavior and Environment
Behavior operates on the environment; it produces certain kinds of consequences. The consequences supplied by the environment influence future behavior.

Observational Learning
Modeling Outcomes
Models can produce a variety of effects in an observer. They can teach behaviors, strengthen or weaken inhibitions, cue behaviors, highlight objects or aspects of the environment, or arouse emotions.

Observational Learning Processes
When we acquire behaviors by observing models, we use the following cognitive processes in sequence: attention, retention, production, and motivation.

Model Effectiveness
Perceived Similarity
Perceived similarity is the observer's perception of similarity between him- or herself and a model. If an observer perceives a model to be similar to himself or herself, the model is more likely to have an effect on the observer's learning and/or performance.

Perceived Competence

Perceived competence refers to the observer's perception of how competent a model is. Competence can be displayed by either a mastery model or a coping model. Modeling effects are more likely when a model is perceived as being competent.

Peer Models

Peer models are those who share the same status as an observer. Peer models are, by definition, more likely to be perceived as similar to an observer. In a classroom, peer modeling is a form of peer tutoring.

Self-efficacy
Goal Setting

A person's sense of self-efficacy is a belief that he or she can successfully complete a certain kind of task.

A student's beliefs about his or her abilities influences the goals he or she sets. A student's goals reflects his or her motivation.

Teachers as Models

Teachers are in a unique position to function as models. Using their knowledge of the characteristics that have been shown to influence model effectiveness as a guide, teachers are encouraged to reflect on those qualities that might influence their students' perceptions.

Reflections: Building Your Theory of Teaching

7.1 Who were your role models in elementary, junior high, and high school? Which of their actions or behaviors did you learn and/or perform? What attracted you to those models?

7.2 Imagine you are teaching a lesson on your favorite topic, something that you explore whenever you have a chance. As you are teaching the lesson, how will you model enthusiasm for the topic?

7.3 Many of the skills we teach our students are skills we have long ago mastered. Therefore, we sometimes forget how hard it is for our students to acquire those skills. Choose a skill that you had difficulty with as a student. Describe how you would attempt to act as a coping model for a student who is trying to learn that skill.

Key Terms

social cognitive theory (p. 254)
observer (p. 254)
model (p. 254)
learning (p. 256)
performance (p. 256)
symbolize (p. 257)
forethought (p. 258)
self-regulation (p. 259)
self-reflection (p. 259)
sense of self-efficacy (p. 259)
reciprocal determinism (p. 260)

modeling (p. 263)
observational learning effects (p. 264)
inhibitory effects (p. 264)
disinhibitory effects (p. 264)
response facilitation effects (p. 264)
environmental enhancement effects (p. 265)
arousal effects (p. 265)
attention (p. 267)

retention (p. 267)
production (p. 267)
motivation (p. 267)
direct reinforcement (p. 271)
self-reinforcement (p. 271)
vicarious reinforcement (p. 271)
perceived similarity (p. 273)
perceived competence (p. 274)
peer models (p. 275)

Suggested Readings

Bandura, A. (1977). *Social learning theory.* Englewood Cliffs, NJ: Prentice-Hall.

Bandura, A. (1986). *Social foundations of thought and action.* Englewood Cliffs, NJ: Prentice-Hall.

Bandura, A., & Walters, R. H. (1963). *Social learning and personality development*. New York: Holt, Rinehart & Winston.

Schunk, D. H. (1987). Peer models and children's behavioral change. *Review of Educational Research, 57*, 149–174.

References

Bandura, A. (1962). Social learning through imitation. In N. R. Jones (Ed.), *Nebraska Symposium in Motivation*. Lincoln: University of Nebraska Press.

Bandura, A. (1965). Influence of models' reinforcement contingencies on the acquisition of imitative response. *Journal of Personality and Social Psychology, 1*, 589–595.

Bandura, A. (1969). *Principles of behavior modification*. New York: Holt, Rinehart & Winston.

Bandura, A. (1971a). *Psychological modeling: Conflicting theories*. Chicago, IL: Aldine-Atherton.

Bandura, A. (1971b). Vicarious and self-reinforcement processes. In R. Glaser (Ed.), *The nature of reinforcement* (pp. 228–278). New York: Academic Press.

Bandura, A. (1977). *Social learning theory*. Englewood Cliffs, NJ: Prentice-Hall.

Bandura, A. (1982). Self-efficacy mechanisms in human agency. *American Psychologist, 37*, 122–147.

Bandura, A. (1986). *Social foundations of thought and action*. Englewood Cliffs, NJ: Prentice-Hall.

Bandura, A., Ross, D., & Ross, S. A. (1963). Vicarious reinforcement and imitative learning. *Journal of Abnormal and Social Psychology, 67*, 601–607.

Bandura, A., & Walters, R. (1963). *Social learning and personality development*. New York: Holt, Rinehart & Winston.

Bower, G. H., & Hilgard, E. R. (1981). *Theories of learning* (5th ed.). Englewood Cliffs, NJ: Prentice-Hall.

Corbin, C. (1972). Mental practice. In W. Morgan (Ed.). *Ergogenic aids and muscular performance* (pp. 93–118). New York: Academic Press.

Feltz, D. L., & Landers, D. M. (1983). Effects of mental practice on motor skill learning and performance: A meta-analysis. *Journal of Sport Psychology, 5*, 25–57.

Gresham, F. (1981). Social skills training with handicapped children: A review. *Review of Educational Research, 51*, 139–176.

Locke, E. A., Shaw, K. N., Saari, L. M., & Latham, G. P. (1981). Goal setting and task performance: 1969–1980. *Psychology Bulletin, 90*, 125–152.

Morsund, J. P. (1976). *Learning and the learner*. Belmont, CA: Wadsworth.

Rosenkrans, M. A. (1967). Imitation in children as a function of perceived similarity to a social model and vicarious reinforcement. *Journal of Personality and Social Psychology, 7*, 301–315.

Rosenthal, T. L., & Bandura, A. (1978). Psychological modeling: Theory and practice. In S. L. Garfield & A. E. Bergin (Eds.), *Handbook of psychotherapy and behavioral change: An empirical analysis* (2nd ed, pp. 621–658). New York: Wiley.

Ruble, D. N., Boggiano, A. K., Feldman, N. S., & Loebl, J. H. (1980). Developmental analysis of the role of social comparison in self-evaluation. *Developmental Psychology, 16*, 105–115.

Schunk, D. H. (1983). Developing children's self-efficacy and skills: The roles of social comparative information and goal setting. *Contemporary Educational Psychology, 8*, 76–86.

Schunk, D. H. (1987). Peer models and children's behavioral change. *Review of Educational Research, 57*, 149–174.

Schunk, D. H. (1991). *Learning theories: An educational perspective*. New York: Macmillan.

Schunk, D. H., & Gaa, J. P. (1981). Goal-setting influence on learning and self-evaluation. *Journal of Classroom Interaction, 16*(2), 38–44.

Schunk, D. H., Hanson, A. R., & Cox, P. D. (1987). Peer-model attributes and children's achievement behaviors. *Journal of Educational Psychology, 79*, 54–61.

Simon, S., Ditricks, R., & Speckhart, L. (1975). Students in observational paired-associate learning: Informational, social, and individual difference variables. *Journal of Experimental Child Psychology, 20*, 81–104.

Spence, J. T. (1984). Gender identity and its implications for concepts of masculinity and femininity. In T. B. Sonderegger (Ed.), *Nebraska Symposium on Motivation* (Vol. 32). Lincoln, NB: University of Nebraska Press.

8

Motivations

Chapter Overview

In this chapter, we examine student motivation. Every student has goals and hence motivation. The question is, Do a student's goals match the goals of the teacher? Motivation can come from various sources. Motivation that derives from within the student is intrinsic motivation. Motivation that comes from outside the student—from the teacher, for example—is extrinsic motivation. In addition to considering the distinction between intrinsic and extrinsic sources of motivation, we discuss the preconditions for student motivation as contained in the ARCS model. In the last section of the chapter, we examine how various theories of motivation can be used to determine a student's motivational state and, when appropriate, how that state might be improved. ▪

INTRODUCTION: GOALS

Focus Question: Why do students differ in their pursuits of academic achievement?

Are you reading this chapter now because your instructor told you to do so? Are you reading it because you have a quiz at the end of the week? Are you reading this chapter because you want to understand why students behave as they do? Are you reading this chapter because you will be a student teacher next year and you're worried about how you will motivate your students? What motivates you to do what you're doing right now? What motivates you to do well in school?

What motivates you to put off reading a chapter that has been assigned?

What is it that drives the information-processing system? Why do we allocate cognitive effort to transform information by means of a number of processes (described in Chapter 6)? Is it because a reward is likely, some sort of positive reinforcement (discussed in Chapter 5)? Are we motivated to read because of the promise of a reward, a behavior we've learned from observing others (discussed in Chapter 7)?

Lecture Note: Ask students to discuss the motivational implications of the three theories of learning presented in Chapters 5, 6, and 7.

Lisa and Carla's histories are well known in their school. Both students stand out in the minds of the faculty. Carla is a model student. She always does what she is told. When a volunteer is needed, she often offers her help. She even volunteers for extracurricular work. She enjoys spending time with teachers in and out of class. She answers questions enthusiastically. She participates in discussions. She is the darling of the teachers' lounge. When teachers discuss Carla, one comment is heard over and over again, "I wish I had thirty more just like her."

Now consider Lisa. She is at least as well known as Carla in school, but Lisa is known as a lost cause. Lisa hasn't completed a homework assignment all year. All she contributes to class discussions are crude jokes or insults. She resents being asked questions in class and often makes her resentments known to the teacher, sometimes in a confrontational way. Lisa is discussed in the teachers' lounge as well, but no one wants another Lisa.

What is the difference between Lisa and Carla? How should a teacher view these two students in order to maintain motivation in one case and to establish motivation in the other?

Connection: See the discussion of instructional objectives in Chapter 9.

As a teacher, you have motives for doing what you do. Your students have motives too. Peoples' motives are reflected in their goals. As a teacher, you have certain goals for your students, which you can communicate to them in a variety of ways. Setting behavioral objectives, which we will discuss in Chapter 9 of this book, provides you with a number of ways to communicate these goals to your students. You may communicate your goals verbally at the beginning of a lesson: "Our goals for today are to understand the procedures for long division and to correctly complete ten long division problems." Once you have communicated those goals to your students, do your goals become their goals?

Suppose your goal is for students to become proficient at long division, quadratic equations, keyboarding, library research, dissection, editing, or some other skill appropriate to your anticipated class. As you begin the skill lesson, picture the sorts of behaviors that Carla and Lisa, your model student and your troublemaker, will display. Carla is a very attentive to your presentation/demonstration. Lisa pays no attention to you, looks everywhere but at you, knocks a neighbor's pencil off the desk, and asks, "Why do we have to learn this junk?"

What are the goals of your model student and your troublemaker? Do their goals match your goals? In this case, let's assume the answer is "no." Neither Carla nor Lisa shares your goal. In fact, let's assume that Carla and Lisa share the same goal: to gain your attention.

When you discuss these students with your colleagues in the teachers' lounge, what do you say about them, that one is motivated and the other is not? Most people would say "yes." As a teacher, you know better.

In fact, both students are motivated by the same goal, but their motivation is channeled into different behaviors. Carla, the model student, enjoys recognition from her teachers and has found that working diligently in class and producing her best efforts gain that recognition. Lisa, the lost cause, is motivated by the same goal. Because of her past history, however, she has learned that academic effort is not an effective way to gain the recognition of her teachers. Perhaps she has learned that not doing assignments gets her teachers' attention. Perhaps her teachers call her in after school to ask her about problems that she's having with her homework. Perhaps her attempts to contribute to discussions have met only with criticism. Therefore, she chose a different route to her goal of teacher recognition. The alternate route was to tell jokes or to demonstrate her wit through insults. The recognition she gains is negative, but it is not an indictment of her intellect.

Just as students may use different behaviors to achieve the same goal, similar behaviors may be routes to different goals. The goals students bring to the classroom are important because they help explain the behavior they display in the classroom. Nevertheless, it is our job to be aware and make use of what motivates our students to achieve academically.

Teaching Anecdote: Tell the story of the fourth-grade student who really wanted to be in the top reading group but was not willing to work on his reading enough to make the top group. His parents offered him extra TV time in exchange for extra reading. This arrangement worked for a while. His teacher praised him whenever he deserved it, hoping that praise might provide the extra push needed to get him moving. The boy made some progress but not enough to merit moving him into the top group. Then his parents "hired" him to read: they offered to pay him by the hour to read. Because it was near Christmas and the boy needed money, he agreed. He soon became hooked, reading far more than his parents expected him to do. The teacher acknowledged the tremendous growth he achieved in two months and moved him into the top reading group.

Ask your students what elements of motivation are in action here.

CURIOUSER AND CURIOUSER

"Will everyone who is reading *Bridge to Terabithia* meet at the back table now?" I asked my fourth graders. When we were all settled I looked around the group. No Lynne.

"Lynne, it's time for your reading group."

She looked up from the book she was reading. It wasn't *Bridge to Terabithia*, but I could guess what it was: *101 Answers to Questions About the Human Body*.

"Did you know that our bodies are 98 percent water?" she said sitting down. "Why would lightning kill people like Leslie in the book if she's mostly water? Did she boil in her own blood?"

Great way to launch into a discussion of Leslie's death, the pivotal point of the story.

Lynne was one of the most consistently curious students I have ever had. In reading, she asked unusual questions. How did the author know this? How much of this story really happened and how much did the author make up? Does the author use a word processor or write the story out in cursive? She even looked up information about settings in encyclopedias and compared their descriptions to descriptions in books.

Teacher
Chronicle
8.1

In math, she wanted to solve real problems from situations in her life. How many squares on her block? How many worms lived in her yard? How many hairs on her arm?

In science, she related almost everything to her curiosity about the human body. She could rattle off the names of bones, identify an organ and tell its location, tell you how many miles of blood vessels were in your body, draw a diagram of a hair.

She wanted to be a doctor when she grew up.

I tried to provide as many outlets for her investigations as possible. Her desk looked like something out of a mad scientist's lab. I never knew what I would find on it or in it: a mold collection made from old pieces of bread from the lunchroom, a bagful of squirming worms, a disemboweled clock.

I made a great many accommodations to her curiosity when it came to schoolwork. I did not want to deter her and thus tried to link her handwriting to topics of interest, her math to the most recent numerical investigations, her science to the human body. She was disorganized, always late getting somewhere, scatterbrained in so many ways. Yet I envied her that driving curiosity.

What motivated Lynne's curiosity? Was it a need to know; a need to understand how things worked, what they were made of? Why was she curious in so many areas?

Someday I imagine that Lynne's dream of becoming a doctor will come true. Or who knows. . . .

SOURCES OF MOTIVATION

In order to generate a practical hypothesis for improving student motivation in your classroom, it is important to understand the goals of your students and how they match or fail to match with your own goals. Where do goals come from? What is the source of motivation for academic achievement?

Intrinsic Versus Extrinsic Goals

Academic goals have been categorized as either intrinsic or extrinsic (Maehr, 1983). **Intrinsic goals,** which the student has internalized, can be task related. For example, a student may find that *Silas Marner* is worth reading simply for its own sake. Some students perform extra lab assignments in science class because they have discovered something of value in the task. When asked why they do the extra work, such students say something such as, "I don't know, I just like to do labs." Intrinsic goals may be ego related; a student who challenges himself or herself may go "over and above" the requirements of an assignment.

Extrinsic goals, which are external to the student, are often social. A student may work hard in the classroom in order to please parents, teachers, or friends. An extrinsic goal may involve rewards. Academic achievement may mean, for the student, an increase in his or her allowance, the recognition of being on the honor roll, or the respect of teachers for attaining good grades. If you recall our discussion of operant-conditioning theory (Chapter 5), extrinsic goals should ring a bell. Desirable consequences of behavior increase the likelihood of that behavior. If a student finds being on the honor roll desirable, the student will continue to work toward that goal.

There is an important reason for understanding the distinction between extrinsic and intrinsic goals: a teacher who understands the distinction will be better able to determine whether student goals match teacher goals.

A professor, who has researched motivation in children, identified the problem of mismatched goals in her own college classroom. She had assumed intrinsic motivation in her students, but discovered that they were extrinsically motivated. What follows is her description of the mismatch.

> In an effort to orient students' attention toward the joy of learning about child psychology, I did not give grades for class participation or papers. I found very quickly that my own goals were initially incompatible with the students'. Rather than studying to understand child development, they studied to get good grades in their other classes and came to my class unprepared!
>
> While it is important for the teacher to understand each student's goals, teachers do not necessarily need to change their practices to be compatible with the student. The student's goals can usually be changed to be more compatible with the teacher's. This, nevertheless, requires a good understanding of "where the student is coming from" and, as I found with my college students, changing students' goals sometimes requires a significant amount of resocialization. (Stipek, 1988, pp. 11–12)

curiosity An eager desire to know caused by stimuli that are novel, complex, or strange.

Journal Entry: Have students reflect on those courses in college in which their goals and the professor's goals did not match, identifying the problems that they experienced in such courses.

Intrinsic Motivation: A Closer Look

In our examination of various learning theories, we have devoted a significant amount of attention to environmental (or external) causes of behavior. More specifically, we have described the role of reinforcement from an operant perspective, and the roles of direct and vicarious reinforcement from a social cognitive perspective. In this section, we will focus on intrinsic motivation.

Gagné and Driscoll (1988) have identified three sources of intrinsic motivation: curiosity, achievement, and self-efficacy. Let's look briefly at each in turn.

Curiosity

Curiosity is a knowledge state caused by stimuli that are novel, complex, or in some way incongruous (Berlyne, 1965). Intuitively, we recognize that curiosity is a strong source of motivation. Consider the following example of arousing curiosity in a classroom context:

Field Observation: Have students observe various classrooms, documenting how teachers use curiosity to introduce lessons or maintain attention.

> "Before we begin the next science chapter," the teacher said, "I'd like to tell you a story. Then," she added with a slight smile, "I'll ask you a question."
>
> The sixth graders looked at their teacher expectantly.
>
> "A man was out driving his car," the teacher began, "when he noticed something quite unusual. A truck stopped in the middle of a block and the truck driver got out with a baseball bat in his hands. He walked back to the center of the truck and suddenly hit the side several times with the bat. Then he got back in and drove on."
>
> Several children who had been somewhat indifferent when the teacher started now looked at her raptly.

Issues in Educational Psychology

CNN™ This box relates to Segment 8 of the CNN videotape. See the Instructor's Section for a summary.

MEXICAN-AMERICAN STUDENTS BEATING THE ODDS

In the '60s, Garfield High School in East Los Angeles was little more than a day-care center. Students worked at grade-school levels. Gangs staked out their turf on the school's grounds. Garfield's accreditation was threatened. Hope was in short supply for impoverished Mexican-American students from the barrios.

Teachers like Jaime Escalante helped break that cycle in the '70s. As an immigrant, Escalante knew firsthand the type of jobs Latinos could expect. When he came to the United States, he had to work as a busboy and then a cook to support his wife and two sons. But Escalante, whose parents were teachers, had gained national recognition in his native Bolivia as a teacher himself. Attending the university in La Paz, he was granted an emergency teaching credential in the late 1940s at a time when Bolivia was experiencing political turmoil. Escalante emigrated in 1963 when military and economic problems once again threatened his country.

Determination has been the key to Escalante's success. After graduating from Pasadena City College, Escalante worked for the Burroughs Corporation testing computers while studying for his California teaching certification.

Escalante, who inspired the film *Stand and Deliver,* was equally determined to help his new students.

But miracles were in short supply during his first year at Garfield. When the final math exams were completed, the grades weren't what he expected. "I thought, what am I doing wrong? Either the kids are an empty set, or the teacher is a bonehead," Escalante said in an interview with the *Los Angeles Times.* He renewed his efforts, focusing on areas which seemed to give students the most difficulty. He formulated new material and tried new teaching ideas.

Currently, Escalante keeps his teaching materials in color-coded files. He has refined his classroom tactics to grab the attention and the imagination of his students. For example, in the course of praising the Mexican heritage of new students, he reminds them that it was the Mayan Indians who formulated the concept of "zero."

Students have to answer math questions to get into the classroom. If they fall asleep, Escalante bops them with a red velvet pillow. The students have become willing partners with Escalante, responding to rock music warm-ups as they clap and beat their desks in rhythm.

Jokes, magic tricks, sports equipment, and posters of Albert Einstein and leading athletes are all part of Escalante's classroom tools. "A good teacher has to attract kids, make their life easy, not complicated. I entertain them. At the same time, I get 100 percent out of them," Escalante stressed, when he spoke with the *Los Angeles Times.*

Escalante expects his students to succeed and works to make them

believe in themselves. "I'll make a deal with you. I'll teach you math, and that's your language. With that you're going to make it. You're going to go to college and sit in the front row, not in the back, because you're going to know more than anybody," said Escalante, in a *New York Times* profile.

The students have become as determined as Escalante. Since 1978, hundreds of Garfield students have taken the Educational Testing Service's Advanced Placement calculus exam to earn college credits (nationally, fewer than 2 percent of U.S. high school students even take this rigorous exam). In 1990, 71 percent of the Garfield students who took the calculus test passed.

Today, Garfield's accreditation is no longer threatened. Its students are leading the way out of the barrios of East Los Angeles.

SOURCES: Woo, Elaine. "Teachers at the Head of Their Class." *Los Angeles Times* 107, sec. 1 (July 29, 1988): 1, col. 1. LaBrecque, Ron. "Something More Than Calculus." *New York Times* 138 (November 6, 1988): 20. Mathews, Jay. "Inner-City School Program Wins Federal Support." *Washington Post* 112 (June 25, 1989): A12, col. 2. "Acclaimed Instructor Uses Magic to Motivate Other Teachers." *New York Times* 138 (August 2, 1989): B7, B9. Mathews, Jay. "The Teacher's New Formula." *Washington Post* 113 (August 6, 1990): B1, col. 3.

1. How would the theories of motivation examined in this chapter explain the turnaround that Escalante's students made?
2. In what specific way can you envision Escalante enhancing intrinsic motivation?

"As the man in the car followed the truck," she continued, "he saw the truck again stop after about three blocks and again the driver got out, beat his truck a few times with the bat, returned to his seat, and drove off."

Every eye in the room was now riveted on the teacher.

"Once more," the teacher went on, "the man in the car followed the truck and, sure enough, in another three blocks it stopped, the driver got out and banged away with his bat."

The teacher paused and glanced around the room. Satisfied that she had the class's attention she continued. "The man in the car," she said, "was fascinated. He followed the truck for almost two miles trying to figure out what the truck driver was doing. Finally he gave up."

The teacher again paused, scanning the intent faces in front of her.

"The next time the truck stopped," she went on, "the man jumped out of his car, ran over to the truck driver, and said, 'Sir forgive me for bothering you. But I've been following you for almost two miles. Why on earth do you drive exactly three blocks, get out with a baseball bat, and hit your truck a few times?' The truck driver said, 'It's really very simple. I've got a two-ton truck and inside I've got three tons of canaries. So I've got to keep one ton of them in the air at all times.'"

A few of the students looked puzzled, some seemed skeptical, and several laughed. As the teacher waited, the laughter gradually spread until the entire class was smiling.

"Now," she said, "let me give you a question."

Looking pointedly at the class, she said, "Was the truck driver stupid?"

There was a sudden silence as the children pondered the query.

"Yes," a sandy-haired boy said suddenly. "He still had three tons in his truck."

The teacher remained silent watching her students. Then a bright-eyed girl in the corner of the room raised her hand shyly.

"Beth."

"He really wasn't stupid," the girl said, "because if one ton was flying around inside the truck, they wouldn't add any weight."

With this the teacher smiled and walked to the board. She then began a lesson on the principle of air support. (Rubin, 1985, pp. 129–130)

Using novelty, as the teacher in our example did, is one way of creating the knowledge state we call curiosity. Curiosity—a form of novelty or complexity or incongruity—is a source of motivation. Consider what would happen, however, if the teacher telling the story of the canaries were to use such a story to begin every lesson. Would the novelty of such incongruous stories wear off? If so, would she be less likely to engage her students' curiosity? Curiosity, as a source of motivation, has a somewhat limited use in the classroom. Not everything we say as teachers, not every task we assign, can arouse the curiosity of students. Other sources of motivation are required. One such source is called the need to achieve.

Achievement

As a source of motivation, **achievement** can be thought of as a need, something intrinsic to the learner, which can manifest itself as an attitude of competitiveness (e.g., McClelland, 1965). Competitiveness born of an intrin-

achievement Something that has been attempted and completed successfully by personal effort and abilities and satisfies some intrinsic need.

Teacher Interview: Have each student interview a teacher regarding the judicious use of novelty in his or her classroom.

Students with a high need to achieve tend to be academically competitive.

sic need to achieve does not presuppose a need to compete against other people; rather, it is a competition against some standard of excellence. For example, a student with a high need to achieve may turn in a book report on time and neatly typed. In addition to the timeliness and neatness with which the assignment is done, the student might provide illustrations, a glossary, a table of contents—features not required by the teacher. The extra work does not earn extra credit but satisfies some internal need to achieve a standard of excellence.

Students with a high need to achieve often persist for long periods in pursuit of an unattained goal. For one, an invention, perfected after many months, may be the result. For another, a publication based on a journal of thoughts and observations painstakingly made, may be realized. In all of its manifestations, the need to achieve yields performance. Students use performance to test their competence. They perform over long periods of time in order to see the outcome of their performance. Successful completion is an outcome that satisfies and feeds the need to achieve.

Self-efficacy

When students observe their own successful completion of academic tasks, they develop a belief in their ability to continue to do so—a belief we call **self-efficacy** (Bandura, 1977). A student's belief about his or her own ability to perform successfully influences his or her motivation. From experience, a student may learn that he or she is able or unable to perform well under certain conditions. For example, the student may classify him- or herself as a good or poor test-taker. Perhaps through experiences on standardized or multiple-choice tests in class, the student has come to consider him- or herself capable or incapable of performing well on such tests. The belief in the ability to perform under those conditions represents a sense of self-efficacy. A student may develop expectations of self-efficacy from a number of sources.

The first source of self-efficacy is simple self-observation. Past success leads you to expect you will succeed in the future on similar tasks, such success enhances your sense of self-efficacy.

A second source of self-efficacy is the observation of others. When you observe others whom you perceive to be similar to yourself, you attend to their behavior; you view yourself as being capable of achieving the same outcome they do. You say to yourself, "If that person can do it, I can do it."

Connection: See the discussion of "perceived similarity" in social cognitive theory (Chapter 7).

A third source of self-efficacy is encouragement, usually in the form of verbal praise. Verbal encouragement may come from a teacher who says, "I know that you have the ability to accomplish this particular task and I'm confident that you will be able to perform well." Verbal encouragement can also come from one's self, an internal pep talk.

A fourth source of expectation for self-efficacy is emotional arousal. Some kind of emotional event can spur your determination to attain a particular outcome. Perhaps you have experienced, in your own academic career, a teacher who expressed doubt in your abilities to do well in school. As a result of your indignence at the doubt expressed by the teacher, you set out to prove to him or her, to others, and to yourself that you are indeed capable of attaining what they thought was, for you, unattainable. If a student has expectations of efficacy, if a student believes he or she is capable of accomplishing a particular goal, the belief will serve as motivation. The same is true even in cases where there are many obstacles to success. Consider some of the extraordinary efforts expended by individuals in order to overcome physical or intellectual challenges. Stephen Hawking, mentioned in Chapter 4, comes to mind again.

Teacher Interview: Have each student interview a teacher regarding the way in which he or she uses verbal encouragement.

Journal Entry: Have students reflect on those teachers who made them want to "prove" themselves to them.

Some of your students will be physically, emotionally, or psychologically challenged in some way. When such students overcome obstacles and succeed in attaining the goals they've set, they can be assumed to harbor expectations of efficacy. Learners who persist, learners who believe in their abilities under certain conditions, and learners who exert an extraordinary amount of effort in pursuit of a particular academic goal are motivated by their sense of self-efficacy. They use their capabilities in a focused way. We often speak of a student's ability or inability to concentrate on a task. The student who is unable to concentrate for an extended period of time on a particular task is assumed to be unmotivated. The mental effort that a student exerts after an academic goal can be an index of that student's motivation.

Chapter 15 Casebook Preview: See I Am Leo.

We have seen in earlier chapters, particularly in Chapter 5, how the environment influences a learner's behavior. If our goal is to produce students who have attained the academic objectives set for them and who are also intrinsically motivated, then we face something of a dilemma as classroom teachers. In Teacher Chronicle 8.1, the teacher wanted to let Lynne's intrinsic curiosity drive her intellectual progress, but as a result she was also faced with Lynne's disorganization. We must, as teachers, set up the environment for our students. Included in that environment are various forms of external reward, praise, and encouragement. We use extrinsic motivation as a way to manage our classrooms. Our goal, however, is to produce students who are motivated intrinsically. As teachers, we are extrinsic to our students. How can we behave in ways that will lead students to motivate themselves? The answer is, of course, very carefully. Let's consider some evidence that has been collected on what is called the undermining effect (Deci, 1971, 1975; Morgan, 1984).

Connection: Teacher Chronicle 8.1: Curiouser and Curiouser.

Chap. Obj. 2
Test Ques. 8.27–8.29

Focus Question: How might teachers inadvertently undermine students' motivation?

Teaching Anecdote: Tell your students about the teacher who used a system of plus and minus marks to monitor student behavior. The pluses were good, the minuses, bad. At the end of the week, the students with five pluses got a treat—ice cream or a piece of candy. The teacher had tried this system before with sixth graders, but it had failed within a couple of weeks. Now as a first-grade teacher, she tried it again and it worked quite well.

Ask your students why the teacher's system did not work effectively or for very long with sixth graders, but was very successful with first graders.

Journal Entry: Have students reflect on some activity in which they engaged that was undermined by external rewards.

Teacher Interview: Have students interview teachers at various grade levels regarding the undermining effect.

Connection: See Diary of a Day, Chapter 1, and the analysis of the diary.

THE UNDERMINING EFFECT

The **undermining effect** is the result that extrinsic reward can have on behavior that is intrinsically motivated. For example, a student who begins reading biographies of World War II figures and who brings those biographies to the attention of a parent or teacher may find the parent or teacher delighted with the student's new found interest. As a function of their delight, the parent or teacher tells the student that for every new World War II biography read, he or she will receive some sort of reward—either free time in the classroom to pursue the hobby of reading or release from a household chore or some more tangible reward. According to Deci and other researchers, the establishment of external rewards may serve to undermine the student's intrinsic motivation. The student may begin to perceive his or her reading behavior as being caused not by some internal curiosity about the figures in World War II, not by some need to understand the events of that war and not because of some expectation that he or she may have an ability to understand these personalities. Rather, the student may begin to suspect that his or her reading behavior is being caused by the rewards delivered from external sources—the parent or the teacher.

It is tempting for a teacher to encourage academic pursuits, especially in a student who has not demonstrated a keen interest in reading or writing or other cognitive activities. However, teachers should take care in identifying those areas in which students require motivation from external sources and to allow intrinsically motivated behavior to flourish on its own terms. The undermining effect appears to operate at all ages. The intrinsic motivation of young children is especially susceptible to being undermined by extrinsic rewards (see Gottfried, 1983; Lepper, Greene, & Nisbett, 1973; Sarafino, 1984).

We have learned from other chapters that reinforcement is a powerful teaching tool. Research about the sources of motivation suggests that teachers should not reinforce student behavior indiscriminately. To reinforce effectively, a teacher needs to know students' goals and their intrinsic motivations. In Chapter 1, "knowledge of one's students" was identified as a hallmark of a master teacher. Part of the reason is that such knowledge helps a teacher to decide when to provide extrinsic motivation and when to allow the intrinsic motivation of a learner to determine classroom activity.

Principles in Practice 8.1

Principles . . .
1. Curiosity is an internal motivational state, but it can be triggered by external events.
2. Achievement is a need for some students, a source of self-efficacy for others.
3. Indiscriminate reinforcement can decrease intrinsic motivation.

. . . in Practice
Lynne, in Teacher Chronicle 8.1, is easily classified as intrinsically motivated. The teacher did not have to trigger her curiosity or enhance her sense of self-efficacy. The problem was staying out of the way of those positive motivations, allowing Lynne to "follow a different drummer," while marching in

the midst of twenty-five other students whose progress the teacher was also responsible for.

1. How might the teacher use Lynne's curiosity to trigger the curiosity of other students?
2. What do Lynne's behaviors tell you about her need to achieve and her sense of self-efficacy?
3. How would you have responded to Lynne's question about Leslie in *Bridge to Terabithia*, "Did she boil in her own blood?"

GOLDEN OPPORTUNITIES

Golden opportunities to reach a student appear at the most unexpected times. These moments provide the best teaching of the day.

Take Bronson, for example. He was a tall boy, much larger than his peers, who had a minor speech impediment. Bronson rarely participated in class because it embarrassed him when I couldn't understand him or when the other students couldn't. He was a good reader who did above-average work when he applied himself. He had a super sense of humor, which I tried to tap whenever possible. By doing so, I gave him a chance to express himself orally. Often, I was able to get some insights into how much he had learned from his responses.

The board was covered with the results of a brainstorming session that the class had just completed. Lists of words filled the board, connected by a web of lines linking one idea to another. We had been prewriting for a story-writing session and had listed everything we knew about listening to and following directions: order, obey, read, write, learn, goof-up, skip, and so on.

Everyone was intensely punching their computer keyboards except Bronson. Bronson had his hand up. He had been following our brainstorming, but had not contributed to it.

I went to his desk.

"Does it have to be something you make or can it be what happens to food or something after it is made?" he asked me.

"What are you thinking?" I asked.

"About what I do when I am served broccoli."

"You eat it, don't you?"

"No, I hate broccoli. Can I write about how to get rid of broccoli?"

Now I had to make a decision. My goal had been to have the class learn about following directions. If Bronson wrote about the steps necessary in getting rid of unwanted broccoli, he would be accomplishing the same objective, albeit from a different perspective.

"Sure," I told him. "Remind me to tell you later how my sisters and I got rid of our spinach."

He smiled at me, grabbed his pencil, and began to write.

As I walked around helping, I also thought about Bronson's idea. If the kids developed an interest in his writing about getting rid of broccoli, then I could use that idea for another story starter.

Every time Bronson looked up it seemed that he would explode with excitement.

"What would happen," I asked, setting up Bronson, "if you made something you didn't like and wanted to get rid of it so that your mother wouldn't know? What if Bronson did not like broccoli?"

Everyone shifted around to look at Bronson, who was grinning like a jack-o'-lantern. Normally, he did not like to be the focus of attention, but I had obviously made a connection with him, allowing him the freedom to go in a different direction from the others.

In his clearest and best voice he began sharing his directions.

"'What to Do When Your Mother Serves You Broccoli.' First, you look at it and say, 'Yuck, broccoli again.' This is to trick her into thinking you feel the same way about it as you always have so that she suspects nothing. Then, you cut the broccoli up into ten small pieces and spread them around on your plate. You hide two of the small pieces under the mashed potatoes. You chew up three pieces of the broccoli and then spit them into your napkin. Make sure you have a paper napkin. Now, you spill two pieces on the floor and clean them up with your napkin. Throw the napkin away immediately and get a clean one. This time, chew three pieces and spit them into your new napkin and put this in your pocket to get rid of later. Point out to your mother that you have eaten all of your broccoli, but are too full to finish your mashed potatoes. Remember the hidden broccoli under the potatoes and don't eat them. Offer to clear the table even if it isn't your job so that you can throw out the hidden broccoli. And that's how to get rid of your broccoli without eating it."

By the time Bronson finished, everyone was laughing. We had all understood every word he said, which was a confidence builder for him. He was enjoying very positive attention from his peers instead of holding back. He had written much more than he usually did on an assigned topic. Bronson benefited from all of this.

"Can I write about getting rid of meatloaf?" Paul asked.

"What about getting rid of cooked carrots?" Kelly asked.

"Let me tell you how to get rid of gross asparagus," Denise blurted.

"Let me tell you how to get rid of your yucky sister," Mike said.

"It's just about lunch time," I said. "When we come back this afternoon, we will talk more and write a story."

I looked around sternly and said, "Now if anybody has any broccoli they don't want, make sure to give it to Bronson. He knows what to do with it." They all laughed and looked at Bronson.

And on that note, the bell rang and off they went buzzing to lunch with Bronson in the middle of a crowd. I ate my lunch feeling pretty good. I had not only completed my lesson goals and had fun while they learned, but had found a new link with Bronson as a student. The expression of his face when he left made my whole day. This afternoon, I would tell them about my spinach experience, a ready-made lead-in for this afternoon's lesson. If only every lesson went as well!

■ ■

Chap. Obj. 3
Test Ques. 8.30–8.47

Focus Question: What conditions have to exist if students are to be motivated toward achievement?

THE ARCS MODEL

Let's take a look at some of the conditions that should exist if achievement motivation is to exist within a student. The conditions can be referred to by the acronym ARCS. ARCS is a general model of motivation that was developed by Keller (1983, 1984) and described by Gagné and Driscoll (1988). There are four elements in this model of motivation, representing conditions that must exist in order that a learner be motivated: Attention, Relevance, Confidence, and Satisfaction (ARCS).

Attention

We've examined the term *attention* as part of our discussion of information-processing and social cognitive theories. In those discussions, attention referred to a process. In the ARCS model, **attention** is a state or condition of the learner. A student in the classroom is either attending or not attending to the achievement-related stimuli. In the ARCS model attention is a necessary condition for motivation.

One of the things that new teachers worry most about is their ability to gain their students' attention. Obviously, in order to teach a student, you must first gain his or her attention. It's possible to study many different attention-getting devices by observing teachers in the field. Some teachers will clap their hands or make some sudden noise that will automatically get the attention of students. Other teachers will engage in a particular routine that signals to students that it's time for them to pay attention (for example, Peter Roop's use of the "cool stool," noted in Chapter 1).

If we want a student to learn the pronunciation of a single word, *calligraphy,* for example, we only need attract their attention for a moment. However, attention, in the context of student motivation, is something that must be sustained over long periods of time. In fact, maintaining attention is even more important than attracting it.

Consider the children's program, "Sesame Street," which is designed not only to capture, but also to sustain attention. Lesser (1974) attributes the program's attention-sustaining ability to humor, incongruity, and encouragement of viewer anticipation. This anticipation comes in the form of known characters, such as Big Bird, Oscar the Grouch, Grover, Bert and Ernie, and the Count. Viewers come to know these character personalities and anticipate their actions. When they see Oscar the Grouch emerge from his residence, a garbage can, viewers anticipate the kind of comments Oscar will make. In order to satisfy their curiosity, in order to determine whether their anticipations are correct, viewers listen to Oscar the Grouch to see what he has to say.

Perhaps you are a fan of a particular soap opera on television. If so, you know the personality characteristics of the soap opera characters quite well. You can, therefore, predict the types of behaviors they are likely to display. Your attention to their activities is sustained because you are curious to see if their personalities will influence events in unexpected ways.

The attention condition in the ARCS model appeals to a particular kind of learner interest. It is the interest that people have in events that make them curious.

Relevance

Relevance, the second condition in the ARCS model requires the engagement of learner interest; that is the learner must perceive that the content of the material presented is important enough to do something with.

Beginning teachers are often advised to make their lessons relevant to students' lives by relating the lesson to the experiences of students. One way

attention A state or condition of the learner necessary for motivation; the first condition of the ARCS model.
relevance The engagement of the learner's interests; the second condition of the ARCS model.

Connection: See discussions of information processing theory (Chapter 6) and social cognitive theory (Chapter 7).

Lecture Note: Have students discuss the difference between a cognitive process and a cognitive state.

Connection: See Diary of a Day, Chapter 1.

Chapter 15 Casebook Preview: See Around the World.

Journal Entry: Have students reflect on their reactions to watching "Sesame Street."

Connection: Teacher Chronicle 8.2: Golden Opportunities.

to demonstrate the relevance of material is to convince students that the material will enable them to achieve an instructional goal. For example, in Teacher Chronicle 8.2, the teacher might have demonstrated how brainstorming makes story writing easier. This would be an effective approach for students who view instructional goals as important, for either intrinsic or extrinsic reasons.

For some students, lessons can be made relevant by the use of humor or by the use of the unexpected. Recall the teacher who told the story about a truckload of canaries. The story itself is relevant for some students, not because it illustrates the principle of air support, but because it is funny. They can take the story home and entertain their parents with it. The entertainment value of the story makes it relevant for the student who fancies himself or herself a storyteller. For a student with story-telling goals, the story establishes a condition of motivation. Other students may find the information relevant because it provides a unique example of a scientific principle.

Suppose you were teaching the five senses and the lesson for the day was on the eyes. You might use the same procedures as the teacher who had students observe the dilation and contraction of their classmates' pupils. The experiment left the students with a desire to try the same test with their pets. Instilling a desire to do something with the information may indicate either an intrinsic or extrinsic motivation on the part of the student. Some students

Lecture Note: Emphasize that relevance for the student is determined by the student's goals.

Classroom activities that engage students actively—such as this exercise in negotiation— make subject matter more relevant to the students' lives.

may wish to do something with the information in order to please parents or to please the teacher or to get good grades. Other students may wish to do something with the information for their own pleasure.

Suppose that you were going to teach a lesson about the Solar System. Part of your job is to teach the students about the dimension and properties of the Sun. The size of the Sun, for example, could be communicated in any number of ways.

It could simply be communicated by a number. The Sun's diameter is 864 thousand miles; it weighs 330 thousand times as much as Earth, and it's mean distance from the Earth is 92.9 million miles. Each square centimeter of the Sun's surface radiates 1,500 calories of energy per second. Unless your students are studying for an imminent appearance on the game show "Jeopardy," these numbers may hold little relevance for them. Suppose, however, that in communicating the dimensions of the Sun, you were to provide the appropriate numbers and then describe the size of the Sun in the following terms.

The Sun could be hollowed out so that half of it were hollow. We could place Earth with the Moon still orbiting around it in the hollow half. At the turn of the century, Sir James Genes calculated that if he could remove matter the size of a pinhead from the core of the Sun, and place that bit of matter on the Earth, the heat from that pinhead of matter would kill a human being ninety-four miles away. Describing the dimensions of the Sun in these terms rather than in those that are solely numeric may, for some students, prove relevant to their interests and, therefore, motivate them to attend to the rest of the lesson.

Information may be deemed relevant by some students simply because it is uttered by a particular teacher. For students whose motivational orientation is to please the teacher, the simple utterance of information by the teacher is enough reason for them to learn it.

The notion of relevance takes us back to the importance of goals in considering the motivation of students. If you understand what goals students bring with them to your classroom, then you are better able to present information in a way that will be relevant to them.

Confidence

Confidence is a student's belief that he or she can perform competently in a particular learning situation. Learners are motivated when they believe that they can be successful in learning new material and in performing new tasks. The notion of confidence is similar to that of self-efficacy.

Confidence contributes to achievement. Studies have shown that confident learners are more able to attain goals than learners who are not confident in their own abilities (Bandura, 1977; Jones, 1977). When students have successful learning experiences, they infer that they can perform effectively. Such success builds confidence and enhances expectations of efficacy.

Satisfaction

Satisfaction occurs when a learning task is successfully completed. Successful completion of a task also leads to some type of reinforcement. It may lead to

confidence A belief that one can perform competently in a particular learning situation; the third condition of the ARCS model.
satisfaction A result of the learning task being successfully completed; the fourth condition of the ARCS model.

Lecture Note: Remind students that making a connection with prior knowledge—in this example, by means of concrete imagery—enhances not only retention of the information, but makes that information "relevant."

Teacher Interview: Have each student interview a teacher regarding the influence he or she has on some students and the care he or she must take in dealing with such students.

Connection: See the notion of self-efficacy discussed in Chapter 7.

Lecture Note: Emphasize the relationship between the condition of satisfaction and the notion of reinforcement (Chapter 6), and the motivation process (Chapter 7).

an extrinsic reward, such as a good grade, teacher praise, or parental encouragement. It may lead also to intrinsic reinforcement. The condition of satisfaction is met when a student fulfills his or her need to achieve.

In summary, the ARCS model identifies four conditions that must be met within the learner if motivation is to exist. Although these conditions should exist within the learning situation in your classroom, it is important to keep in mind that many of these conditions may arise from earlier events in your students' experiences. Now that we have discussed the importance of goals to student motivation, made the distinction between intrinsic and extrinsic motivation, and looked at the four conditions of motivation that must exist in a classroom situation, we turn our attention to three theoretical views of human motivation.

Lecture Note: Have your class discuss how important it is to know a student's background when attempting to understand a student's motivation.

As was true in our discussion of the different theories of learning, looking at three perspectives on motivation will allow us to address slightly different questions. All of the questions focus on how we can provide the circumstances necessary for student achievement.

The first theoretical perspective we will examine is Maslow's hierarchy of needs. Maslow's theory will give us an understanding of what requirements must be met if students are to be prepared to pursue learning. The second theoretical perspective is McClelland's theory of need achievement. In this discussion, we will focus specifically on academic tasks and how students approach or avoid those tasks. The third theoretical perspective is Bernard Weiner's attribution theory. Attribution theory will tell us something about how students perceive their successes and their failures and what those perceptions mean in terms of future motivation.

Principles in Practice 8.2

Principles . . .
1. Creating the conditions for attention, relevance, confidence, and satisfaction contributes to student motivation.
2. Relevance can be established in a variety of ways.
3. The conditions of the ARCS model contribute to one another.

. . . in Practice
In Teacher Chronicle 8.2, the teacher found an opportunity to encourage Bronson, who was embarrassed by his speech impediment, to read his own composition aloud. The teacher, knowing Bronson's sense of humor, allowed him to follow a humorous approach to the writing assignment. Writing about hiding broccoli gave Bronson a chance to use his humor, something about himself in which he had confidence.

1. How do you think brainstorming influenced the motivational conditions of the ARCS model?
2. What made the writing assignment relevant for Bronson? How might it be made relevant for other students?
3. How does relevance contribute to confidence, satisfaction, and attention? Which, in your opinion, is the most basic condition?

REACHING LISA

Losing a student is the hardest part of teaching for me.

With Lisa, I should have recognized the signs early in the first weeks of school. She called me "Teacher" whenever she wanted my attention. She was aggressive in the classroom, bothered other students, made distracting noises, and fiddled with things when she should have been paying attention. She often missed a good portion of my instruction because of these distractions.

She got into trouble on the playground right away. Rules held little meaning for her. Her physical aggressiveness led other students to frequently complain about it. She usually responded, "Sorry. I didn't mean to do it." She blamed her problems on anything or anyone but herself. "I didn't know the rule. In my old school we didn't have that rule. But Shawn did it before I did."

In class, she always tried to top everyone else's story. If we talked about boats, her father had the fastest boat on the lake. If we discussed dinosaurs, her father found one bigger than a bus. If we talked about a place, her father had already traveled there.

At first, I saw her behavior as the result of attempts to become assimilated to the new school, new teachers, new friends. Lisa had been in three schools the previous year. Perhaps this explained her calling me "Teacher." Why learn the teacher's name if you aren't going to be there long anyway? Her aggressive behavior might have been an attempt to reach out and feel that she belonged to the group. I often talked with her about being the new student and how she could make friends by following the rules in games. I felt that once the newness of this school wore off, she would begin to feel part of the whole.

Yet as the year progressed, Lisa's attitude and problems worsened. She became so annoying to those seated near her that I often had to separate her from the rest of the class, although this did not improve her behavior.

She and I set up a system that allowed her to stamp her daily work with dinosaurs if she finished it on time. She also had a dinosaur sheet that she could stamp each day if she had a good day. At the end of the week, if she had a stamp for each day, she could collect a reward of extra free time and a note of praise to take home. This system worked for a few weeks, but then she lost interest in it. The notes home seemed to mean nothing to her. Nothing seemed to motivate her to succeed academically or socially.

I realized that Lisa must have had some unknown needs that I had to meet before we could overcome her other problems. It occurred to me that Lisa's problems might reflect an abusive situation at home. Once when I sent a note home about her lying to me after she took something from a student's desk, I got a note from her father saying, "You will not have any more problems."

The next week she took something else. When she saw me writing another note home, she cried and begged me not to send it. When I asked why, she said, "My dad spanks me and sends me to my room."

I did not send the note. The following day I talked with the school social worker. She knew the family from one of Lisa's previous schools. She then visited Lisa's current home and confirmed that Lisa had been beaten, not spanked. The next time we discussed Lisa, she said that Lisa's mother told her that Lisa's dad had been beaten as a child.

I began to realize that Lisa's frequent school changes were probably linked to her abusive family situation. When the heat got too great from the school, the family moved.

We set up several conferences with both parents, but Lisa's dad came only once. We arranged counseling, but her dad quit after the first session. We closely monitored Lisa's appearance for evidence of physical abuse.

All year I tried to gain Lisa's trust, to motivate her to learn, to teach her how to get along with others, to provide a sanctuary for her at school, and to be a positive role model. I wanted her to gain a sense of self-worth. But it was frustrating knowing that unless her needs for love and approval from her father were met, she was doomed to failure.

One day Lisa did not show up at school. When I called home, there was no answer. Then a note came requesting that her records be sent to a new school in another state.

And so the cycle continued.

I often wonder what Lisa is doing today. I wonder how she will treat her children. And I wonder if I made any difference.

Chap. Obj. 4
Test Ques. 8.48–8.71

Focus Question: How do the needs of each student explain differences in individual motivation?

Connection: Teacher Chronicle 8.3: Reaching Lisa.

MASLOW'S HIERARCHY OF NEEDS

Human beings need things. They need water to drink; they need food to eat. Human beings need shelter and love. They need to feel safe, both physically and psychologically. Part of being human is the need to feel good about oneself. Part of being human is the need to understand the world around oneself. Different people have different needs; their needs vary in degree. For some, the need for shelter is more important than for others. For some, the need for food motivates them more than others. Within a given individual needs change as well. The desire to eat an apple may be greater for a person at 11:00 A.M. than it is at 7:00 P.M., just after finishing a four-course dinner.

The concept of human needs is basic to the theory formulated by Abraham Maslow (1943, 1954), known as Maslow's hierarchy of needs (see Figure 8–1). At the lower levels of the hierarchy are basic needs that humans require for physical and psychological well-being called **deficiency needs.**

Deficiency needs must be, at least, partially satisfied before a person can be motivated to pursue satisfaction of higher level needs. These higher level needs that, when satisfied, enable the human being to grow psychologically are called **growth needs.**

As an example of how the hierarchy of needs explains motivation, consider Lisa in Teacher Chronicle 8.3. As the year progressed, the teacher suspected an unhealthy, abusive home environment. Any student who comes to class from such an abusive or neglectful environment has unfulfilled basic needs. Given his or her life circumstances, that student may not feel very safe. If a student has an unfulfilled need as basic as safety, it will be very difficult for that student to focus on higher order needs, such as the need to understand. Parents play an obviously important role in satisfying the deficiency and growth needs of their children.

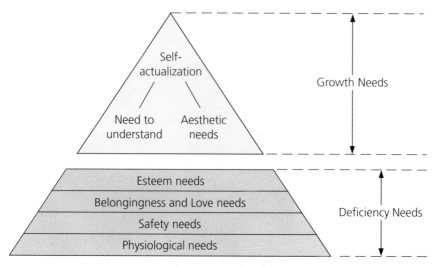

self-actualization According to Maslow, the realization of personal potential.

Transparency: This figure is duplicated in the acetate transparency package. See T-12 Maslow's Hierarchy of Needs.

■ **Figure 8–1** *Maslow's Hierarchy of Needs*
SOURCE: From *Psychology* (4th ed., p. 406) by L. A. Lefton, 1991, Needham Heights, MA: Allyn & Bacon. Copyright 1991 by Allyn & Bacon. Reprinted by permission.

Nystul (1984) discusses the role of parenting in bringing about self-actualization in the child. Nystul sees **self-actualization** as a natural process that occurs once the child's basic needs have been met. Thus, parents who wish their children to become self-actualized need to help their children satisfy their more basic needs of health, safety, belonging, love, and self-esteem. Sappinton makes a similar conclusion regarding adult learners (1984).

Sappinton argues that teachers of adult learners must also help those learners satisfy basic needs before expecting that the learners will be motivated to understand and to grow in other ways. Sappinton discussed the need to establish an emotionally safe learning environment. Using terms familiar from our discussion of operant conditioning (Chapter 5), an "emotionally safe environment" can be conceived as one of positive reinforcement rather than aversive control. Aversive control fosters escape and avoidance responses in students. The learner finds positive reinforcement to be a desirable consequence. Establishing a safe environment enables students to address constructively any fears they may bring to the learning situation. It also allows learners to take risks in the classroom, to participate more fully, and, thereby, to grow psychologically.

Schultz (1976) made several observations about the broad implications of Maslow's hierarchy of needs. The gratification of growth needs, being less necessary for survival, can be postponed longer than the gratification of deficiency needs. There are more preconditions to the gratification of growth needs than there are to the gratification of deficiency needs. Growth needs also require better external conditions than deficiency needs do.

These observations provide some guidelines for teachers who wish to use Maslow's theory as a way of identifying problems in students who appear to be unmotivated. Remember that by *unmotivated* we mean students who are motivated by goals other than academic achievement and who take nonacademic routes to their goals.

Consider a student who lacks motivation for academic work. Observe that student and, starting at the bottom of the hierarchy, ask yourself some ques-

Field Observation: Have students observe classrooms to determine whether each is an "emotionally safe environment," documenting the elements that contribute to such an environment.

Teacher Interview: Have each student interview a teacher regarding the value he or she places on risk taking in the classroom.

Teachers and parents play an important role in fulfilling a child's deficiency needs. Once these basic needs are met, the student can become self-actualized.

Connection: See Lickona's model of moral education in Chapter 3.

Teaching Anecdote: Tell your students about the teacher who had a student who continually interrupted class with trivial nonsense: questions that were not relevant to the topic being discussed, jokes, and vulgar remarks. The teacher tried many ways to get the student to control her outbursts, including detention, trips to the principal's office, counseling, time after school, and poor grades. Nothing seemed to have any effect on the girl's behavior in class. During one heated exchange after school, the teacher realized the student had no adults she really trusted. Her parents were divorced, her father never invited her over to his new apartment, and her mother often worked late at night, leaving the student home alone. When the teacher decided to base their relationship on mutual trust, the girl's behavior slowly changed.

Ask your students why this change in behavior might have happened.

Journal Entry: Have students reflect on the ways their needs were gratified in elementary and secondary school, identifying the needs that went unmet and the ways in which those unmet needs influenced their experiences in school.

tions. Are the student's physiological needs being met? Is the student receiving adequate food and shelter? If physiological needs have been met, what about the safety of that student? Does the student feel physically safe at home and in school? An interview with the student might give you some clues about the student's feelings of safety. If your interview with the student convinces you that he or she does feel safe at home and at school, the hierarchy suggests that you ought next be concerned about this student's need to belong to a group and to feel loved. In this regard, you can think about Lickona's model of moral education (examined in Chapter 3). Observing this student's social interactions can give you some clues about the extent to which his or her need to belong and need to be loved have been gratified.

If the student appears to have a normal relationship with peers, if he or she is not a social isolate, if the student exhibits a sense of community in the family and at school, and if the student seems to feel loved, then the next set of questions to ask should address the student's self-esteem and his or her sense of efficacy. You may want to assign tasks that you feel sure the student could perform successfully in order to gauge the student's views of his or her abilities. Finding out what the student's expectations of efficacy are could give you some clues about self-esteem, especially as it relates to academic work.

As Arkes and Garske (1977) point out, the failure to gratify a need results in a related form of dysfunction or disturbance. When using the hierarchy of needs to gauge the type of problem an unmotivated student may have, you should look for a type of dysfunction that is consistent with a particular deficiency need.

If your observations reveal a dysfunction related to deficiency needs, some kind of action is necessary. For example, safety, belongingness, and esteem needs might be gratified in a classroom that operates on the basis of Lickona's model (1987). But, for the most part, teachers can exert influence only at school, as was the case with Lisa in Teacher Chronicle 8.3. If problems related to deficiency needs cannot be met at school, a teacher must seek outside help. Lisa's teacher contacted the school social worker. One of the first things a new teacher should do is learn the school district's "referral system." Find out what student services and other professional help are available for students.

A student whose deficiency needs have been met is said to be **growth motivated.** Growth-motivated students have a need to understand and to know. They also have aesthetic needs. A student in physics may appreciate the beauty inherent in the phenomena of astronomy, for example. Another student may appreciate equally the rhythm of a sonnet or the elegance of a mathematical formula. Growth-motivated students tend to seek a tension that they find pleasurable, usually in the form of a challenge. Learners who attempt independent studies, for example, seek to solve problems of their own devising.

It is important to note here that students who are growth motivated tend to be self-directed. These students take the responsibility to satisfy their need to know and understand and their aesthetic needs. Recalling the earlier distinction between intrinsic and extrinsic motivation, we can see that growth-motivated students tend to rely more on intrinsic rewards than extrinsic rewards. Teachers who work with such students should provide them with opportunities to pursue self-directed learning and take care not to undermine their intrinsic motivation with unnecessary extrinsic rewards.

One final aspect of Maslow's theory of motivation is helpful to teachers. Maslow distinguishes between good choices and bad choices. **Good choices** are choices that yield a challenge for the learner; **bad choices** are choices that do not. A student who makes bad choices is a student who has not satisfied all of his or her deficiency needs. A growth-motivated person has had his or her deficiency needs met, and therefore seeks the challenge of meeting growth needs. The implication is that as you set up learning situations for your students, it is important that your students see the learning situation as being supportive of good choices. If students perceive your classroom as threatening, they are likely to play it safe. They will not take risks academically; they will not seek out the challenge. From Maslow's perspective, therefore, the best classrooms are those that maximize the opportunities for growth by reducing the possibilities for failure and embarrassment. Risk-taking behavior, in an academic sense, is to be encouraged.

THE NEED TO ACHIEVE

Motivation can be thought of as part of a person's overall personality. Henry Murray (1938) defined *need to achieve* as a personality characteristic. The **need to achieve** is a desire or tendency to overcome obstacles and to accomplish some difficult task through the exercise and use of some power.

growth motivated Motivated to understand and to know; occurs after the deficiency needs have been met, according to Maslow.

good choices Choices that yield a challenge for the learner, according to Maslow's theory of motivation.

bad choices Choices that do not yield a challenge for the learner, according to Maslow's theory of motivation.

need to achieve A person's desire or tendency to overcome obstacles and to accomplish some difficult task through the exercise and use of some power.

Connection: Teacher Chronicle 8.3: Reaching Lisa.

Field Observation: Have each student gather information from a school district or interview an administrator regarding the referral system used in the district.

Lecture Note: Emphasize that many of the problems encountered by growth-motivated students are problems they have devised themselves. The tension created by such problems is created by the student and is hence pleasurable.

Journal Entry: Have students reflect on their own "good choices" and "bad choices."

Teacher Interview: Have each student interview a teacher regarding how he or she encourages students to become "good choosers."

Chap. Obj. 5
Test Ques. 8.72–8.92

Murray developed a way to measure the need to achieve, as well as other personality characteristics. His measurement device is called the Thematic Apperception Test (TAT). The TAT is a projective technique. People are shown pictures depicting a particular state of events. They are then asked to describe what set of events led to the conditions depicted in the picture and how the events will be resolved. The TAT is called a projective technique because each subject's stories are assumed to be projections of his or her state of mind. If, for example, a subject were to tell a story that emphasized the theme of achievement, one might assume the need to achieve is part of the storyteller's personality.

The level of the need to achieve that students project gives us an index of the amount of "risk-taking behavior" that they are capable of and, to some extent, the types of goals that motivate them. In a classic study, McClelland (1958) asked children to play a ring-toss game. The children were allowed to choose the distance from which they would toss a ring over a peg. McClelland found that "high-need achievers" preferred to toss the ring from a medium distance. "Low-need achievers" tended to choose a distance either very near or very far from the ring. The interpretation that McClelland offered was that high-need achievers stand in the middle distances because the probability of success is estimated to be around 50 percent. This probability of success balances the probability with the value of winning, and maximizes the challenge of the game. A child who stands very near to the peg increases the probability of success, but such a success is easily won and does not present much of a challenge. When a child chooses to stand very far from the peg, he or she decreases the probability of success to such a point that the goal of tossing the ring onto the peg is not likely to be achieved very often. Success from a great distance is more a matter of luck than a matter of achievement.

If we interpret McClelland's study in terms of academic goals, the children high in need to achieve appear to set goals for themselves that are at once challenging and realistic.

Atkinson and Litwin (1960) followed McClelland's classic ring-toss study with one of their own. The Atkinson and Litwin study introduced another variable in addition to the need to achieve—anxiety. Atkinson and Litwin were interested in seeing how one's need to achieve and one's level of anxiety might interact to influence behavior. The results of their research led Atkinson (1964) to view achievement motivation as a conflict of emotions.

Approach and Avoidance

As Atkinson saw it, the conflict of emotions was between the hope for success and the fear of failure. The hope of success has come to be known as **approach behavior;** the fear of failure as **avoidance behavior.**

Approach behavior (the hope for success) is a function of three factors: the *need to achieve,* the *probability of success,* and the *incentive for success.*

The probability of success and the incentive value of success are closely related. As the probability of success decreases, the incentive value of success increases. If the probability of succeeding on a particular task is equal to .5 (a 50–50 chance), then the incentive value of success is equal to .5. If the probability of success is high, for example, .9, then the incentive value for success is low, in this case, .1. A high probability of success means the task is easy. Accomplishing it does not carry a great deal of incentive value. Atkinson has described the incentive value for success as "pride in accomplishment." There is little pride in accomplishing an easy task because of the high probability of success. Conversely, a difficult task, once accomplished, produces a feeling of great pride. Receiving a grade of *A* in an easy course leads to a different sense of accomplishment than receiving a grade of *A* in a difficult course.

Avoidance behavior (the fear of failure) is determined in a similar manner except that the motivation and incentive reflect negative emotions. If the motive to succeed is "pride in accomplishment," then the motive to avoid failure can be conceptualized as "shame."

A student faced with the prospect of achieving a task has two kinds of feelings based on his or her experience with similar tasks: hope for success and fear of failure. The tendency to approach an achievement-related goal with the intention of success is a positive one. The tendency to avoid failure, on the other hand, is negative.

Atkinson used a formula to estimate the tendency of a person to either approach or to avoid an achievement-oriented activity. The formula that defines that relationship is as follows:

$$Ta = Ts - Taf$$

The tendency to approach or avoid an achievement-related activity (*Ta*) is determined by our tendency to approach with the intention of success (*Ts*) minus our tendency to avoid failure (*Taf*). The resulting *Ta* is an index of our achievement motivation for a particular task. Table 8–1 provides the resultant achievement motivation for various combinations of the "hope for success" and the "fear of failure."

Just as Maslow's view of motivation indicates that a healthier student is growth motivated rather than deficiency motivated, the need-to-achieve literature suggests that the more "healthy situation" is that of a student who is motivated by hope of success to a greater extent than he or she is by fear of failure.

Fear of Success

Atkinson's investigations of approach and avoidance in achievement-related tasks led other researchers to identify various types of motivations in students. Matina Horner studied a motivational state she called fear of success

■ **Table 8–1** *Levels of Approach and Avoidance and Resultant Achievement Motivation*

Hope of Success (Approach)	Fear of Failure (Avoidance)	Achievement Motivation
High	Low	High
High	High	Intermediate
Low	Low	Intermediate
Low	High	Low

SOURCE: From *Human Motivation* (p. 197) by B. Weiner, 1980, New York: Holt, Rinehart & Winston. Copyright 1980 by Holt, Rinehart & Winston. Adapted by permission.

fear of success A state that leads to the avoidance of achievement-related activities.
attributions The explanations, reasons, or excuses that students give for their own successes or failures.
locus of control According to the attribution theory of motivation, the perception of where the cause of success or failure lies—either within oneself or outside of oneself.
stability According to the attribution theory of motivation, the perception that an attributed cause may be something that is consistent or inconsistent across situations.

Field Observation: Have students observe children, especially older children, and parents in public situations, such as a restaurant or a shopping mall, documenting the nature of their interactions.

Chapter 15 Casebook Preview: See Science Is Only Real When You Do It.

Chap. Obj. 6–7
Test Ques. 8.93–8.121

Focus Question: What can teachers learn from students' perceptions of their successes and their failures?

Lecture Note: Ask students to think about classmates who exhibited either an internal or an external locus of control.

(1968, 1970; see also Tresemer 1974, 1977). A **fear of success,** which leads to the avoidance of achievement-related activities, is most often seen in competitive situations. Horner's studies attracted a great deal of popular attention in the 1970s, just as women were entering the work force in increasing numbers. Horner was intrigued by the possibility that as a result of "abandoning" traditional female roles and competing with men for jobs, they would begin to exhibit a fear-of-success orientation. In your own classroom, you may find that some of your students exhibit a fear-of-success orientation, for various reasons. Perhaps most typically, students avoid success because they fear disapproval from their peers.

Weiner (1980) suggests that many adolescents who are referred to counseling because of academic problems may have a fear of success. Adolescents, who are experiencing conflict with their parents, respond to the parents' demands for academic achievement by avoiding success. They cannot or will not meet these parental demands. Avoiding success is a form of retaliation, earning low grades is a way of thwarting parents' desires.

As we mentioned earlier, the need to achieve is a personality characteristic. As such, achievement motivation is a factor in social attraction and interaction. Teevan, Diffenderfer, and Greenfeld (1986) investigated social interactions and perceived social status among fifth graders. They found that fifth graders who had a high need to achieve were perceived to be more socially attractive by their peers. High-need achievers also seemed to interact with their peers to a greater degree than low-need achievers. The results imply that students who possess a high need to achieve tend to be more socially skilled than students with a low need to achieve.

One way to evaluate success or failure in achievement-oriented activities is to ask students to explain why a particular outcome occurred. Why, for example, did they do well on a test or why did they perform poorly? Looking at motivation from this perspective requires an understanding of attribution theory.

ATTRIBUTION THEORY

The explanations, reasons, or excuses that students give for succeeding or failing at tasks are called **attributions.** Understanding the reasons, or attributions, a student gives for succeeding or failing is one way of identifying the type of motivation that governs a student's behavior. For example, a student who says, "I got a good grade on the test because it was easy" is attributing his or her success to the test rather than to his or her effort or ability.

Weiner's attribution theory of motivation is based on three dimensions of attributions: locus of control, stability, and controllability (1980, 1986). The first dimension is **locus of control,** that is, the location of the cause of success or failure. A student may cite, as the cause for his or her success or failure, something that is internal or something that is external. For example, attributing success on a test to one's effort is an internal attribution.

The second dimension is called stability. **Stability** refers to the observation that an attributed cause may be something that is consistent or inconsistent across situations. Effort is an unstable attribution because a student might exert much effort in studying for a history exam and little or no effort in preparing for a math exam.

The third dimension in Weiner's formulation is **controllability,** that is, whether a perceived cause of success or failure is under the student's control. From the point of view of a student, effort is a controllable attribution; the difficulty level of a test it is not. Therefore, depending on the reasons given for success or failure, the situation may or may not have been under the student's control. (Table 8–2 provides a taxonomy of the attributions of success and failure.)

No matter what reason is given for success or failure, a central assumption of attribution theory is that students will seek in their reasoning to maintain a positive self-image. If a student performs well on a standardized achievement test, that student will most likely attribute success on the test to his or her own ability. The locus of control is internal. If a student performs poorly on such a test, that student will likely attribute the failure on the test to some external factor, such as the difficulty of the test or poor instruction by a teacher, or to something that is uncontrollable, such as illness during the test.

Several studies have been conducted during which one group of subjects is told that they have succeeded on a task, and a second group is told they have failed (when, in fact, the success rate of both groups is equal). The people who are told they've failed tend to attribute their failure to bad luck; those who are told they've succeeded tend to attribute their success to skill or intelligence or ability. In either case, group members sought to maintain a positive self-image (Frieze & Weiner, 1971; Kukla, 1972; see also Aronson, 1972).

Research with students suggests that they provide four major reasons for success or failure: ability, effort, task difficulty, and luck. These four reasons can be best understood when matched with Weiner's two dimensions of

controllability According to the attribution theory of motivation, the perception of whether a cause of success or failure is under the student's control.

Lecture Note: Ask students to consider the relationship between controllability and Maslow's need for a sense of belongingness.

Journal Entry: Have students reflect on those episodes that caused them to rationalize outcomes in a way that maintained their positive self-image.

■ **Table 8–2** *Causal Dimensions and Perceived Causes**

Casual Dimensions			
Locus of Control	Controllability	Stability	Perceived Causes (Categories of Attributions)
Internal	Controllable	Stable Unstable	Stable effort of self Unstable effort of self
	Uncontrollable	Stable Unstable	Ability of self Fatigue, mood, skill fluctuation in self
External	Controllable	Stable Unstable	Stable effort of others Unstable effort of others
	Uncontrollable	Stable Unstable	Ability of others; task difficulty Fatigue, mood, skill fluctuation in others; luck

SOURCE: From *A Dimensional Analysis of the Perceived Causes of Success and Failure* (p. 21) by R. M. Rosenbaum (unpublished doctoral dissertation).

*Assumes external cause is controllable.

Students who plan their actions have a greater chance of successfully meeting their goals.

Teacher Interview: Have each student interview a teacher regarding differences between students who have either an internal or an external locus of control.

Chapter 15 Casebook Preview: See Gifted Achievers and Underachievers.

Lecture Note: Have your class discuss the value of attributional style as a tool for understanding individual students.

attributions: locus of control (internal or external) and stability (stable or unstable).

Table 8–3 arrays the four major reasons—ability, effort, task difficulty, and luck—on the two dimensions of locus of control and stability. Think for a moment about students with whom you went to school. Try to identify at least one student who would probably use the attributions provided in Table 8–3.

Of all of the dimensions identified by Weiner as underlying attribution theory, perhaps the most important for educators is locus of control. A major difference between high achievers and low achievers is that low achievers tend to attribute their failure to lack of ability (internal). They also, incidentally, tend to attribute their successes to luck (external). High achievers, on the other hand, attribute failure to lack of effort (internal). This attribution leads them to try harder on subsequent occasions.

Let's take a close look at the difference between high and low achievers and the reasons they give for failure on academic tasks. Low achievers who attribute their failure to lack of ability demonstrate an internal locus of control. High achievers who attribute their failure to lack of effort also reflect an internal locus of control. The difference between them, however, is on the dimension of stability. Ability, as an attribution, is a stable reason for failure. Ability is a characteristic that does not change quickly, or to any great degree. Effort, on the other hand, is an unstable attribution. Effort can change quite rapidly, and explains why high achievers who attribute failure to lack of effort tend to try harder on the next occasion.

An ability attribution for failure provides the learner with a negative self-perception. They have failed and the reason they have failed is that they lack ability. Ability is something that is internal to them. Furthermore, it is stable and not likely to change.

■ **Table 8–3** *Causal Dimensions and Major Attributions*

Primary Casual Dimensions		Success Attributions		Failure Attributions
Locus of Control	Stability			
Internal	Stable	"I'm smart."	←Ability→	"I'm dumb."
	Unstable	"I tried."	←Effort→	"I didn't try."
External	Stable	"That was easy."	←Task difficulty→	"That was hard."
	Unstable	"I was lucky."	←Luck→	"I was unlucky."

SOURCE: From *Human Motivation* (pp. 345–346) by B. Weiner, 1980, New York: Holt, Rinehart & Winston. Copyright 1980 by Holt, Rinehart & Winston. Adapted by permission.

Learned Helplessness

A student who fails consistently and attributes these failures to causes that are not under his or her control can develop a serious motivation problem called **learned helplessness** (Dweck, 1975; Seligman & Meier; 1967). A student who has a learned-helplessness orientation feels that nothing he or she does matters. He or she tends to attribute failures to reasons that are internal and stable. For example, "I do not succeed because I am dumb. Therefore, nothing I do will improve my situation. I will always fail."

Learned helplessness as a condition can also arise from teacher-mandated consequences that are inconsistent and therefore unpredictable. In such situations, the students cannot predict what sorts of behavior will bring about a particular consequence, such as positive reinforcement or punishment. The environment operates on the students rather than the students being instrumental in bringing about changes in the environment. Perceiving themselves as being unable to alter events by their behavior, students develop low expectations, which cause deficits in future learning as well as motivational and emotional disturbances (Seligman, 1975).

Looking at learned helplessness from the perspective of attribution theory, Fincham, Diener, and Hokoda (1987) identified fifth graders as falling into one of two groups: those exhibiting the characteristics of learned helplessness, and those who were mastery oriented. The two groups were found to be relatively stable. They tended to differ in their responses to stimuli and tended to reflect depressive symptoms in the expected direction.

Children who fall into the learned helplessness group are often perceived as unmotivated. Landman (1987) studied 164 children who had been referred to a school problems clinic. As a result of evaluations at the clinic, the primary cause of difficulty for 80 of the 164 children was identified as a lack of motivation. When the 80 "unmotivated" children were compared with the 84 who were perceived as "motivated," it was found that the unmotivated children were farther behind academically and received less remedial help in school.

Learning to be helpless can not only influence a student's perception of himself or herself, his or her self-efficacy and sense of self-esteem, but can also influence the instructional treatment he or she receives in schools.

learned helplessness A depressed state when a person feels that no matter what he or she does, it will have no influence on important life events.

Teacher Interview: Have each student interview a teacher regarding the ways in which teachers encourage learned helplessness and how they might remedy it.

Lecture Note: Ask students to consider how the results of Landman's study might be explained in terms of "the squeaky wheel getting the grease."

attribution training
Attempting to change the student's style of explaining his or her own successes or failures.

In recent years we have heard more and more about the tragic phenomenon of depressed children. We are alarmed by suicide rates among adolescents. Many of these children have been identified as clinically depressed. Learned helplessness is a form of depression. Attribution theory may give us a way to identify motivation problems that could become quite serious in their consequences, but does it provide us any way of trying to remediate these motivational problems in children?

Attribution Training

Teacher Interview: Have each student interview a teacher regarding his or her experiences with "late bloomers."

Motivation-related personality characteristics can be altered. Changes can be seen when students are given specialized training in areas in which they excel. A student who is provided special vocational training in an area of ability tends to do better in that area than in the general academic environment. There are also children who are late bloomers. They do not do well early in their academic careers, but, for a variety of reasons, begin to improve their performances. These kinds of changes lead to successful experiences in instructional settings.

Chapter 15 Casebook Preview: See I Am Leo.

But not every student who is experiencing motivational problems can be referred to a special instructional situation. Programs that address achievement motivation and the attributions without changing instructional settings have been developed. For example, Alschuler (1973) identified several programs designed to help students who were at risk of dropping out of school. The programs described by Alschuler focused on the use of self-paced materials: games and activities that were intended to enhance the student's sense of personal responsibility for success and failure. In effect, they are **attribution training,** attempting to change the attributional style of the student.

Lecture Note: Have students discuss in small groups what their ideas for attribution training might be.

DeCharms's work (1976, 1980) is among the best known examples of attribution training. In his attributional training program, DeCharms used the analogy of origins and pawns. The program focused on treating the students as origins rather than pawns. *Origins* are people who are masters of their own fate; those who exhibit an internal locus of control. *Pawns* are people who do not exert a control over the events in their environment but, rather, are controlled by them. Pawns have an external locus of control. Children in the DeCharms program were trained to become origins. They were taught to plan their actions, starting with the establishment of realistic goals—goals that are neither so difficult that they preclude successful completion, nor so easy that success in completing them would be perceived as meaningless. (Recall the Atkinson and Litwin study.)

Field Observation: Have students observe a classroom in which students are engaged in a goal-setting activity, documenting the decision-making processes of the students in the class.

What DeCharms demonstrated was that one way to combat the problem of the pawn syndrome or the characteristics of learned helplessness is to teach children how to set realistic goals. Greer and Withered (1987) suggest a concerted effort by parents, teachers, and students to seek opportunities for success, change attributions from external to internal reasons, and learn to use feedback in a positive manner. The keys to the success of these programs seem to be the establishment of adaptive goal-setting behavior; learning the difference between realistic and unrealistic goals; and, having established these goals, planning actions that will lead to their attainment. Attributional training programs that implement these suggestions have been found to be successful. For example, students trained in DeCharms's program attended school more regularly than those who did not participate in origins and

Profiles in Successful Practice

WILLIAM D. SMYTH

CHARLESTON SCHOOL FOR THE ACADEMICALLY TALENTED

CHARLESTON, SOUTH CAROLINA

I want my elementary class to become an extended family. I start building my family by making home visits early in the fall. I call every parent and arrange a time to drop by. Parents often ask me to come to dinner. I enjoy this because it enables me to get to know a child's whole family—parents, siblings, and even pets. I see where he lives. I find out what's important to her. I get a sense of the family's values. I get to see the child in relation to everyone around him or her, and each student begins to see me as a member of the family. Right from the beginning, we're a team. We're one unit working toward one goal: to develop a well-rounded person complete in all dimensions.

I like preparing our room every morning. I like pulling up blinds, straightening desks or maybe rearranging them, watering the plants, and laying out all the materials I will need for the day. I like writing the day's activities on the board. Sometimes I'll write a "teaser" beside each event to whet everyone's appetite for that part of the day. When the bell rings, I stand by the door and greet my students by name, welcoming them to their "other home." I think that's important.

We like to sing songs together. We like to start with a patriotic song, such as "America the Beautiful." Then we sing some of our theme songs, "4–A Is the Best" or "Great and Smart," for example. We wrote these theme songs using old tunes and then putting new lyrics to them. Usually we end with "Weave Us Together." That song and "What Would I Do Without My Music" are our favorites. Singing together around the piano helps us see ourselves as one big family.

Home is not one place, it is wherever family goes together. On warm days, we go outside to do some of our work. We write in our journals. We talk about art. We do science experiments. We play our review games in a campfire area we constructed near a nature trail. Field trips—extended classroom experiences, as we like to call them—get us away from school. It would be fun to take one each week. There are islands to explore and beaches to comb. There are new exhibits at the museum and plays and concerts in town. Going on a trip broadens our knowledge about the world and widens our horizons, together. We learn about new places and we learn about each other. Caring, sharing, being responsible for, and helping each other can't always be taught in our classroom. Sometimes we need a bigger home, we are, after all, a big family.

---

pawns training. Participants in the DeCharms's program were also more likely than untrained students to graduate from high school.

Elliott and Dweck (1988) make an important distinction between performance goals and learning goals. A **learning goal** is a goal through which a student seeks to increase his or her competence; it reflects a challenge-seeking, mastery-oriented response to failure, regardless of the student's ability. A **performance goal** is a goal through which a student seeks to gain favorable judgment of his or her competence or to avoid negative judgment. Performance goals lead to challenge avoidance and learned helplessness when perceived ability is low. When perceived ability is high, a student who sets performance goals tends to avoid taking risks.

learning goal An aim of students who place primary emphasis on increasing competence.
performance goal An aim of students who place primary emphasis on gaining recognition from others.

Connection: See the section on learning disabilities in Chapter 4.

It is important for teachers to encourage students, no matter what their ability levels, to identify learning goals rather than performance goals. In their study, Elliott and Dweck observed elements of learned helplessness, deterioration of learning strategies, and failure attributions for students who were perceived to be of low ability and who operated under performance-goal conditions rather than under learning-goal conditions.

Learning goals lead to the improvement of competence and improvement in ability. Smith (1986) discussed techniques and strategies that teachers might use to help the development of positive self-concepts in learning-disabled children. She suggests that learning-disabled children should be praised sincerely and honestly for any task successfully completed. Learning needs to be structured and anxiety reduced in the classroom. Teachers should communicate their expectations for success by concentrating on each student's strengths, that is, by identifying goals for individual learners. Smith also suggests that by encouraging an internal locus of control, we can avoid the undermining of whatever intrinsic motivation students bring to the learning situation.

Cross-Cultural Evidence

In an effort to determine whether attributions as defined by Weiner and others exist across cultures, Little (1987) investigated the attributions of 140 school children from Sri Lanka and 149 children from England. The attributional dimensions of locus of control, stability, and controllability were present, but there were differences in the frequency with which certain attributions were used.

Weiner's attribution theory identifies "luck" as a major attribution. Little, in interviewing children from Sri Lanka, found that luck was not a frequent attribution; however, "karma" was a prevalent attribution for the Sri Lankan children. Little suggested that attribution theory should be used along classification dimensions that are consistent with the culture of the subject rather than with the culture of the researcher.

Watkins and Astilla (1984) found the three dimensions of attribution theory—locus of control, stability, and controllability—to be useful in identifying differences between male and female children in the Philippines. Their study demonstrated that, for females, attributions that are external and uncontrollable led to the adoption of rote learning approaches. Watkins and Astilla suggest that the rote learning approach was taken because of fear of failure. Males tended to attribute along the internal end of the locus of control dimension. This attributional style led to an emphasis on internalizing and approaches to study that led to high achievement.

These studies suggest that cultural background might influence attributions. If a teacher uses a child's attributions to gauge his or her motivation, cultural differences need to be taken into account. These studies indicate macrocultural differences (see Chapter 4). But isn't it possible that the microcultural differences in a classroom might also affect a teacher's judgment of student motivation?

Connection: See the discussion of cultural differences in Chapter 4.

Teacher Interview: Have each student interview a teacher regarding the influence of informal labeling of a child's motivation on that child's success in school.

Palmer (1983) reviewed attribution theory and its implications for labeling. The review concludes that a relationship exists between informal labeling and attributional processes. When the teacher uses labels without checking carefully to see if the labels fit the attributional styles of students a problem develops. Attributions, not the presence or absence of formal labels, are the critical variables. Attribution training has been shown to affect the motivation and performance of educationally at-risk children and of retarded adults. Participation of students, their parents, their peers, and teaching and counseling professionals in such programs may reduce the use of informal labels.

Principles in Practice 8.3

Principles . . .

1. Deficiency needs must be met before growth needs can be gratified.
2. Emotions, such as fear of failure and hope for success, influence achievement motivation.
3. The reasons students give for their successes and failures are indicative of their motivation.

. . . in Practice

Lisa, in Teacher Chronicle 8.3, got off to a bad start from which she never recovered. Her behavior, both academically and socially, remained a source for concern for the teacher throughout her time in the class. It became apparent to the teacher that Lisa came from an abusive home. This observation was confirmed by the social worker. Lisa had some basic needs—deficiency needs—that were going unmet. The confirmation that her home was dysfunctional coincided with Lisa's being moved, once again, to a different school.

1. On the basis of her behaviors in school, at which level of Maslow's hierarchy would you place Lisa? Why?
2. Although not stated in Teacher Chronicle 8.3, do you think Lisa approached or avoided achievement-related tasks? Why?
3. Had Lisa remained in school, how might the teacher have approached attribution training for her?

CONCLUSION

Assign Chapter 8 of the *Study Guide*.

The theories of motivation examined in this chapter—Maslow's hierarchy of needs, the theory of achievement motivation, and Weiner's attribution theory—provide teachers with clues about students' goals. Their goals may involve satisfying the need for belongingness or love. Their goals may be to approach success or to avoid failure. Their goal may be to maintain a positive self-image by blaming their failures on external reasons. No matter what the goals of students are, it's important to keep in mind that those goals determine how students approach the instructional tasks you set before them.

All students are motivated. The question is, are they motivated to accomplish the instructional tasks set out for them? Students' goals give us some answers to that question. The theories examined in this chapter give us clues that will help us recognize students' goals.

This chapter brings us to the end of Part II of the book, Students as Learners. We have examined various aspects of student development, learning, and motivation. Now that we have considered the nature of the students you will teach, let's consider, in Part III (Chapters 9–14), some of the decisions you will need to make in order to teach them well.

Chapter Summary

Introduction: Goals

All students are motivated, but not all students may be motivated to do the things that teachers ask of them. Furthermore, students may share a goal, but use different means to achieve that goal. Understanding a student's goals and the means he or she uses to attain that goal is critical if a teacher is to be effective.

Sources of Motivation

Intrinsic Versus Extrinsic Goals

Some students work toward a goal because they wish to satisfy some personal need. Such students are intrinsically motivated. Other students work toward a goal in order to obtain rewards from the environment or people in that environment. Such students are extrinsically motivated.

Intrinsic Motivation: A Closer Look

Intrinsic motivation is an internal state that leads to action toward a goal. The state may be triggered by stimuli from the environment, but action is taken for reasons internal to the learner. Curiosity is an example of such a reason.

The Undermining Effect

The undermining effect results from using external incentives to encourage work toward a goal that is already intrinsically important to a student. By using external rewards to encourage a student who doesn't need encouraging, that student's intrinsic goals can be compromised. Teachers should guard against this effect.

The ARCS Model

Attention

Attention is one of four conditions that contributes to student motivation. In order for students to work effectively on some academic task, they must attend to the task. There are a variety of useful ways to attract a learner's attention or interest.

Relevance

Relevance is the second condition in the ARCS model. Relevance means establishing some reason, which the student finds compelling, for working toward a particular goal. Relevance of content can be established in a variety of ways; it is not necessarily confined to preparing the student for "life after the classroom."

Confidence

A learner who believes himself or herself to be capable of performing well on assigned tasks has developed a sense of confidence. This aspect of the ARCS model is similar to Bandura's notion of self-efficacy.

Satisfaction

Satisfaction is the condition that accompanies the successful completion of a task. A student who successfully completes one task will be motivated to work on similar tasks.

Maslow's Hierarchy of Needs

Maslow's hierarchy proceeds from basic physiological needs to psychological needs for self-actualization. The needs that are lower in the hierarchy are called deficiency needs; those that are higher are growth needs. The needs of one level must be met before the needs at the next higher level can effectively motivate behavior.

The Need to Achieve

Approach and Avoidance

The approach and avoidance theory of behavior equates motivation and emotions. Approach behavior is motivated by a hope for success. Avoidance behavior is motivated by a fear of failure. Both the hope for success and the fear of failure are present when a student encounters an achievement-related task. The resultant achievement motivation is a function of both emotions. Some researchers have investigated how another emotion, the fear of success, motivates avoidance as well.

Attribution Theory

Attribution theory classifies the reasons that students give for success or failure to determine their motivation. The reasons (or attributions) can reflect differences in locus of control, stability, and controllability. The major attributions are ability, effort, task difficulty, and luck.

Learned Helplessness
A student who attributes consistent failure to factors not under his or her control shows signs of a serious condition called learned helplessness.

Attribution Training
Personality characteristics related to poor motivation can be changed. Motivational change is reflected in changed attributions. Some programs focus on changing a student's locus of control from external to internal so that the student perceives his or her own efforts as making a difference. Other approaches deal with attributional problems by teaching goal-setting skills. Students who are effective at setting goals are less likely to "set themselves up for failure."

Reflections: Building Your Theory of Teaching

8.1 Imagine that you are teaching a class of thirty-two students (at a grade level appropriate to your certification). You notice rapid improvement in the performance and attitude of several students in the class. Design a discussion, a questionnaire, a writing assignment, an interview, or some other evaluative exercise that will allow you to account for their change in motivation.

8.2 Suppose you were hosting a talk show for National Public Radio. The show's topic is: Do schools meet the needs of students? The guests on the show are a prisoner from a federal penitentiary, a Nobel Prize winner in economics, and a retired teacher who taught the other two guests as students in junior high.

What questions would you ask the teacher about the needs—fulfilled and unfulfilled—that the other two guests brought to the classroom in junior high school?

8.3 A female student stops by after school for a chat. She has experienced much success in school. Her success has triggered high expectations from peers, parents, and teachers. She says to you, "No matter how hard I work or how difficult the challenge, my parents, relatives, other teachers, and even my friends always say, 'I never had any doubt that you would succeed.' I know they mean well, but it's really frustrating. It's like they just dismiss my effort because I've always done well in school."

How would you classify her attributions and how would you respond to her assertions?

Key Terms

intrinsic goals (p. 290)
extrinsic goals (p. 290)
curiosity (p. 291)
achievement (p. 293)
self-efficacy (p. 294)
undermining effect (p. 296)
attention (p. 299)
relevance (p. 299)
confidence (p. 301)
satisfaction (p. 301)
deficiency needs (p. 304)
growth needs (p. 304)

self-actualization (p. 305)
growth motivated (p. 307)
good choices (p. 307)
bad choices (p. 307)
need to achieve (p. 307)
approach behavior (p. 308)
avoidance behavior (p. 308)
fear of success (p. 310)
attributions (p. 310)
locus of control (p. 310)
stability (p. 310)
controllability (p. 311)

learned helplessness (p. 313)
attribution training (p. 314)
learning goal (p. 315)
performance goal (p. 315)

Suggested Readings

Ames, R., & Ames, C. (Eds.). (1989). *Research on motivation in education* (vol. 3). New York: Academic Press.

Gagné, R. M., & Driscoll, M. P. (1988). *Essentials of learning for instruction* (2nd edition). Englewood Cliffs, NJ: Prentice-Hall.

Geen, R., Arkin, R., & Beatty, W. (1984). *Human motivation.* Needham Heights, MA: Allyn & Bacon.

Keller, J. M. (1983). Motivational design of instruction. In C. M. Reigeluth (Ed.), *Instructional design theories and models: An overview of their current status.* Hillsdale, NJ: Erlbaum.

Stipek, D. J. (1988). *Motivation to learn: From theory to practice.* Englewood Cliffs, NJ: Prentice-Hall.

Weiner, B. (1980). *Human motivation.* New York: Holt, Rinehart & Winston.

References

Alschuler, A. S. (1973). *Developing achievement motivation in adolescents.* Englewood Cliffs, NJ: Educational Technology Publications.

Arkes, H. R., & Garske, J. P. (1977). *Psychological theories of motivation.* Monterey, CA: Brooks/Cole.

Aronson, E. (1972). *The social animal.* San Francisco: W. H. Freeman.

Atkinson, J. W. (1964). *An introduction to motivation.* Princeton, NJ: Van Nostrand.

Atkinson, J. W., & Litwin, G. H. (1960). Achievement motive and test anxiety conceived as motive to approach success.

Bandura, A. (1977). *Social learning theory.* Englewood Cliffs, NJ: Prentice-Hall.

Berlyne, D. E. (1965). Curiosity and education. In J. D. Krumbolz (Ed.), *Learning and the educational process.* Chicago: Rand McNally.

DeCharms, R. (1976). *Enhancing motivation.* New York: Irvington.

DeCharms, R. (1980). The origins of competence and achievement motivation in personal causation. In L. J. Fyans, Jr. (Ed.), *Achievement motivation.* New York: Plenum Press.

Deci, E. (1971). Effects of externally mediated rewards on intrinsic motivation. *Journal of Personality and Social Psychology, 18,* 105–115.

Dweck, C. (1975). The role of expectations and attributions in the alleviation of learned helplessness. *Journal of Personality and Social Psychology, 31,* 674–685.

Elliott, E. S., & Dweck, C. S. (1988). Goals: An approach to motivation and achievement. *Journal of Personality and Social Psychology, 54*(1), 5–12.

Fincham, F. D., Diener, C. I., & Hokoda, A. (1987). Attributional style and learned helplessness: Relationship to the use of causal schemata and depressive symptoms in children. *British Journal of Social Psychology, 26*(1), 1–7.

Frieze, I., & Weiner, B. (1971). Cue utilization and attributional judgments for success and failure. *Journal of Personality, 39,* 91–109.

Gagné, R. M., & Driscoll, M. P. (1988). *Essentials of learning for instruction* (2nd ed.). Englewood Cliffs, NJ: Prentice-Hall.

Gottfried, A. E. (1983). Intrinsic motivation in young children. *Young Children, 39*(1), 64–73.

Greer, J. G., & Withered, C. E. (1987). Learned helplessness and the elementary student: Implications for counselors. *Elementary School Guidance and Counseling, 22*(2), 157–164.

Horner, M. S. (1968). *Sex differences in achievement motivation and performance in competitive and noncompetitive situations.* Unpublished doctoral dissertation, University of Michigan.

Horner, M. S. (1970). Femininity and successful achievement: A basic inconsistency. In J. M. Bardwich, E. Douvan, M. S. Horner, & D. Guttman (Eds.), *Feminine personality and conflict.* Belmont, CA: Brooks/Cole.

Jones, R. A. (1977). *Self-fulfilling prophesies: Social psychological, and psychological effects of expectancies.* New York: Halsted Press.

Keller, J. M. (1983). Motivational design of instruction. In C. M. Reigeluth (Ed.), *Instructional-design theories and models: An overview of their current status.* Hillsdale, NJ: Erlbaum.

Keller, J. M. (1984). The use of the ARCS model of motivation in teacher training. In K. Shaw (Ed.), *Aspects of educational technology: XVII. Staff development and career updating.* New York: Nichols.

Kukla, A. (1972). Foundations of an attributional theory of performance. *Psychological Review, 79,* 454–470.

Landman, G. B. (1987). An evaluation of the effects of being regarded as "unmotivated": Developmental and behavioral disorders [Special issue]. *Clinical Pediatrics, 26*(5), 271–274.

Lepper, M. R., Greene, D., & Nisbett, R. E. (1973). Undermining children's intrinsic interest with extrinsic rewards: A test of the overjustification hypothesis. *Journal of Personality and Social Psychology, 28*, 129–137.

Lesser, G. S. (1974). *Children and television.* New York: Random House.

Lickona, T. (1987). Character development in the elementary school classroom. In K. Ryan & G. F. McLean (Eds.), *Character development in schools and beyond.* New York: Praeger.

Little, A. (1987). Attributions in a cross-cultural context. *Genetic, Social, and Genetal Psychology Monographs, 113*(1), 61–79.

Maehr, M. (1983). On doing well in science: Why Johnny no longer excels; why Sara never did. In S. Paris, G. Olson, & H. Stevenson (Eds.), *Learning and motivation in the classroom* (pp. 179–210). Hillsdale, NJ: Erlbaum.

Maslow, A. H. (1943). A theory of human motivation. *Psychological Review, 50*, 370–396.

Maslow, A. H. (1954). *Motivation and personality.* New York: Harper & Row.

McClelland, D. C. (1958). Risk taking in children with high and low need for achievement. In J. W. Atkinson (Ed.), *Motives in fantasy, action, and society.* Princeton: Van Nostrand.

McClelland, D. C. (1965). Toward a theory of motive acquisition. *American Psychologist, 20*, 321–333.

Morgan, M. (1984). Reward-induced decrements and increments in intrinsic motivation. *Review of Educational Research, 54*, 5–30.

Murray, H. et al. (1938). *Explorations in personality: A clinical and experimental study of fifty men of college age.* New York: Oxford University Press.

Nystul, M. S. (1984). Positive parenting leads to self-actualizing children. *Individual Psychology Journal of Adlerian Theory, Research and Practice, 40,* (2), 177–183.

Palmer, D. J. (1983). An attributional perspective on labeling. *Exceptional Children, 49*(5), 423–429.

Rubin, L. J. (1985). *Artistry in teaching.* New York: Random House.

Sappington, T. E. (1984). Creating learning environments conductive to change: The role of fear/safety in the adult learning process. *Innovative Higher Education, 9*(1), 19–29.

Sarafino, E. (1984). Intrinsic motivation and delay of gratification in preschoolers: The variables of reward salience and length of expected delay. *British Journal of Developmental Psychology, 2*(2), 149–156.

Schultz, (1976). *Theories of personality.* Monterey, CA: Brooks/Cole.

Seligman, M. E. P. (1975). *Helplessness: On depression, development, and death.* San Francisco: W. H. Freeman.

Seligman, M. E. P., & Meier, S. F. (1967). Failure to escape traumatic shock. *Journal of Experimental Psychology, 74*, 1–9.

Smith, G. B. (1986). Self-concept and the learning disabled child. *Journal of Reading, Writing, and Learning Disabilities International, 2*(3), 237–241.

Stipek, D. (1988). *Motivation to learn: From theory to practice.* Englewood Cliffs, NJ: Prentice-Hall.

Teevan, R. C., Diffenderfer, D., & Greenfield, N. (1986). Need for achievement and sociometric status. *Psychological Reports, 58*(2), 446.

Tresemer, D. (1974). Fear of success: Popular but unproven. *Psychology Today, 7*(10), 82–85.

Tresemer, D. (1977). *Fear of success.* New York: Plenum Press.

Watkins, D., & Astilla, E. (1984). The dimensionality, antecedents, and study method correlates of the causal attribution of Filipino children. *Journal of Social Psychology, 124*(2), 191–199.

Weiner, B. (1980). The role of affect in rational (attributional) approaches to human motivation. *Educational Researcher, 9*, 4–11.

9
Outcome Decisions

Chapter Overview

Educational psychology is the study of the thoughts and actions that constitute teaching and learning. In Part II (Chapters 2–8) of this book, we concentrated on the thoughts and actions of students. In the remaining chapters, we turn our attention to teachers. Instruction is the essence of the teacher's job. When people think of teaching, they think of instruction. *Instruction* is a broad term, however. It accounts for great variety of decisions and activity. In Part III (Chapters 9–14), we will examine the types of decisions and the types of activity that constitute teaching.

In this chapter, we focus on decisions about the outcomes that teachers desire for their students. The ways in which outcomes can be specified are examined in the section on instructional objectives. The variety of outcomes from instruction are discussed in terms of Gagné's learned capabilities. Finally, outcomes are considered across the cognitive, affective, and psychomotor domains of behavior. ■

Focus Question: What is the difference between a strategic decision and a tactical decision?

Teaching Anecdote: Tell your students about the teacher who had problems keeping her math class focused when presenting new material. Many of the students squirmed in their seats, doodled, or passed notes. During her evaluation by a mentor teacher, she asked why this was so.

"Which kids do you call on when you're doing something new?"

"Oh! That's easy—Michelle, Marcus, Dugan, and Judith. They always pay attention and know the answers."

Ask your students why this approach might affect the interest of the other students in the class.

Journal Entry: Have students reflect on their own course work, and then imagine the kinds of concerns their students will have when they walk into your classroom.

INTRODUCTION: STRATEGIC AND TACTICAL DECISIONS

Teachers are called on to make hundreds of decisions each day, in and out of the classroom. The decisions that a teacher makes influence everything from the content presented to students to the posters on the walls to the types of notebooks students may use. Some decisions have larger effects on a student's experience than others, but even the smallest decisions eliminate some possibilities and open the door to others. Because of the sheer number of decisions teachers make, their cumulative effect is enormous. A teacher constructs the character of his or her classroom by the decisions he or she makes. Learning to make good decisions—to exercise sound judgment—is central to effective teaching.

Some decisions, once made, set the course for later decisions. One way to think about teaching decisions is to distinguish between those decisions that define a general plan or approach—**strategic decisions**—and those decisions that are made while carrying out the plan—**tactical decisions.** In this chapter and in Chapter 10, we focus on strategic decisions: the plans teachers make before they face their students in a classroom.

Reflect on courses you have taken in college. When you walk into the first class in a course, what are the first things you want to know? Are there tests, a term paper, both? If there are tests, what kind of tests are they? Multiple choice? Essay? You want to know what is required of you as a learner because the information will influence decisions you make in your approach to the subject matter. If you will be taking multiple choice tests exclusively, you will probably pay particular attention to terms and definitions. If essays are required, you will approach the material differently. Once you determine what you will be expected to do, you make plans to meet those expectations. You want to know where you are going so that you can plan the best way to get there.

As a teacher, you will make strategic decisions about where your students are going and how they will get there. Teachers want students to acquire new behaviors and new skills, to learn rules and concepts, and to regulate their own learning. Teachers want students to develop positive attitudes toward themselves, toward others, and toward the subject matter they learn. Strategic decisions begin with outcomes, the destinations teachers select for students. The outcomes of instruction are myriad; they are as broad as the range of human behavior itself.

Teacher Chronicle 9.1

STUDENTS: THE MISSING INGREDIENT

Students are the missing ingredient in any lesson plan. No matter how well prepared, well organized, and well thought-out my lesson is, usually it does not proceed in the way that I envisioned it. I have my materials. I have created an engaging lesson. I have super follow-up activities. None of this preparation is a guarantee that the lesson will click with the students. The lesson may appear to be terrific on paper, but until students get involved, it is often impossible to predict what the exact outcome will be.

This unpredictability is frustrating, but it also provides me an opportunity to learn as I reflect on the success or failure of a lesson. Did I match my material to my students? Was the time frame too short or too long? Did I presume that the students knew more about the subject than they actually did? If so, how do I find out just where they are? Did the entire lesson fail or just parts of it? If parts weren't successful, why not? Was the practice part too hard, too easy? Was the content brand new, a review, or somewhere in between? If I were to teach this same lesson to a different class, would it be a flop or a success?

There are also those lessons that for some unexplained, never-duplicated reasons develop a life of their own. Those are the moments when the kids are intrigued, their minds speed along, and they really learn something new. The room is alive with a buzz. At these times, I want to run down the hall and pull people into the room and say, "Hey, look at this!"

These are the moments that I enjoy sharing with the teachers next door or down the hall. "You wouldn't believe what happened when we began weighing ourselves in math. Mark suggested we compare ourselves to a *Tyrannosaurus rex* and we did!" Or, "This morning, the music teacher had to send a runner to my room to remind us that we are already ten minutes late for music. We were so involved in long vowel sounds that we did not pay attention to the time!" Or when someone says, "Why do we have to go home now? I want to continue to work on this project."

These are the lessons that I wish I could bottle and save so that I might open them another time and add their "flavor" to those lessons that don't have much magic. These are lessons that invigorate me, totally involve the kids, and remind me that this is the best profession in the world.

How can I achieve a high moment in each lesson? Can I adjust to the fact that every lesson won't reach the mountain top? Am I able to prepare a lesson that aims high, yet is flexible enough to allow for contingencies along the way: an intriguing student observation that leads everyone forward, an unexpected turn that slows everything down, a complication that brings the entire lesson to a halt?

I have no set formula for planning my lessons. I do, however, keep certain elements in mind when I plan. A major point to keep in mind is that it is necessary to adapt the lesson to fit individual interests, skills, and needs. If I am teaching the formation of the letter *p*, I plan my lesson so that those who need review get only that, those who need extended practice get that, and those who are struggling with the letter's circle shape get direct instruction in how to form it.

One critical element is to allow for student-generated options. Doing so is often tricky because I have to make quick decisions about whether or not to go off on an unexpected tangent. Is Mark really interested in how a computer works? Will explaining the rise and fall of tides lead the lesson forward? Will a discussion of the origins of the names of months really help the students learn to spell them?

Such side trips are most successful when I have a sure idea of where the class is going and feel that the side trip will help us get there. Sometimes it means letting those who are inclined to do so take the sideroad, while the rest of us stick to the main highway. It may mean avoiding a detour now and taking one later, either individually or as a class. When I understand what my objectives are, I am able to make such decisions more easily.

Issues in Educational Psychology

SCHOOL-BASED HOME RULE

Since the mid-1800s American public education has been in a process of transformation. Where once members of the local community had much more direct control over schools, today administrators run the schools. But changes in how local schools are governed—from the inner cities to the suburbs—are taking place.

Memphis is a city of contrasts. Sleek buildings dominate its skyline; poverty dominates its streets. Among the country's top 100 metropolitan areas, Memphis has the distinction of being the poorest.

Poverty, gang violence, and drugs all took a front-row seat in the Memphis inner-city schools. To help break that cycle of despair, Memphis inaugurated a school-based management program. Seven local councils, made up of principals, teachers, parents, community members, and nonvoting students, are working to create a climate of hope in each of their schools. The councils have been able to foster "a learning environment where teachers and parents are empowered to make major differences without the encumbrances of a heavy central office," Reverend Maurice Dickerson told *NEA Today*. Dickerson chairs the Vance Junior High School council.

Have the councils worked? Rosetta Peterson chairs Vance's Social Studies Department. In the same article, Peterson noted that "in the past, we got the spillover from the violent life in the projects in school, and it stayed in school. Now students can come in and feel comfortable talking about what's going on outside."

Because of the councils, principals have had to change their decision-making processes. They can no longer arbitrarily dictate how major issues should be decided. Vance principal Dorothy Evans told *NEA Today* that she has "a problem with shared decision making when it means getting consensus on something I know will work. I get impatient with discussions."

Memphis isn't the only place where the traditional top-down approach has been altered. *NEA Today* also profiled Appleton, Wisconsin. The local school board and the Appleton Education Association reached an agreement on shared decision making. Each of the twenty-two schools have some consultative mechanism to shoulder the responsibility for the school's management structure. The AEA president has become a part of the superintendent's management team.

Seven standing committees at Einstein Junior High School decide on the budget, school-year calendar, schedule, student programs, and staff development. Teachers, parents, and business leaders on Appleton East High School's Futures Committee hope "to set up broad 'houses' or career paths for students in science and technology, health and human services, and the humanities," according to committee coordinator Jane Azzi.

In addition to taking on leadership roles in Appleton's schools, teachers are also coordinating the district community relations, ESL, and wellness programs. Teachers now work the number of hours it takes to get the job done, just like any other professionals.

In Illinois, the legislature sidestepped ensconced Chicago educators and created local school councils on which parents were to hold the majority of seats. The plan was placed in limbo when the council election process was ruled unconstitutional by the state Supreme Court. Other states have already passed or are considering bills to empower parents to take a more active role in the management of local schools.

In the next century, if central administrators continue to surrender control, the administration of America's schools may be back in the hands of local communities.

SOURCES: Lytle, Vicky. "Memphis in Motion." *NEA Today* 9, no. 9 (May/June 1991): 10–11. Weiss, Stefanie. "Innovation: 'We Changed How We Do Business'." *NEA Today* 9, no. 8 (April 1991): 17. Snider, William. "Power Sharing." *Teacher Magazine* 2, no. 5 (February 1991): 12–13.

1. How will the movement toward school-based management influence the selection of instructional objectives?
2. Assume that school-based management will be used in your school. How will you use Gagné's learned capabilities and taxonomies to plan content?

INSTRUCTIONAL OBJECTIVES

Determining outcomes is one of the tasks that teachers perform as they organize themselves for instruction. Outcomes can be defined generally as goals, or more specifically as objectives. Instructional objectives can be specified in one of several ways. Because specifying objectives is a critical part of planning (Berliner, 1985; Rosenshine & Stevens, 1986), we will examine briefly three approaches to specifying objectives that have been developed: the behavioral approach, the goals approach, and the general objectives–specific behaviors approach.

The Behavioral Approach

Robert Mager's view of instructional objectives has influenced the way in which a generation of teachers has gone about preparing its instructional objectives (Mager, 1962). Instructional objectives prepared according to Mager's view are sometimes called behavioral objectives.

Behavioral objectives are a form of instructional technology that came from the operant-conditioning view of learning. Operant conditioning's emphasis on observable behavior gave educators a way of specifying what outcomes to expect of their students. Behavioral objectives also provided a way to monitor teacher accountability with regard to the outcomes of their instruction. Skinner (1968) said, "The first step in designing instruction is to define the terminal behavior. What is the student to do as the result of having been taught?" A behavioral objective tells the teacher, and others, what students should be able to do as a result of instruction.

Mager (1962) identified instructional objectives as statements that specify outcomes as opposed to procedures or processes. According to Mager, instructional objectives should contain three elements: (a) a statement of the terminal behavior, (b) the conditions under which the terminal behavior will be demonstrated or exhibited, and (c) the criteria by which attainment of the objective will be judged.

Thus, according to Mager, the objective should contain the performance, the condition, and the criteria. Consider the following examples and identify in each the three elements of a behavioral objective.

> Example A: Using a daily newspaper, students will correctly identify the opening and closing prices of twenty issues on the New York Stock Exchange.
>
> Example B: Given an unmarked sky chart, students will correctly identify at least seven constellations.
>
> Example C: Using their own library research, students will, in essay form, distinguish the postwar economies that developed in Japan and in the United States.
>
> Example D: After viewing slides of Impressionist paintings, students will compose a sonnet that matches the paintings in style.

Some of the criteria in the objectives are implied. Some of the terminal behaviors are more easily evaluated than others. For example, it would be easier for a teacher to judge that a student has attained the objective in Example B than the objective in Example D. Even so, what is common among all of the objectives is that specific actions or behaviors are stated.

behavioral objectives
According to Mager, statements about what students should be able to do as a result of instruction, the conditions of their performance, and the criteria used to judge attainment of the objectives.

Chap. Obj. 1
Test Ques. 9.1–9.23

Focus Question: How can the outcomes of instruction be specified?

Chapter 15 Casebook Preview: See Please Sign This Contract.

Lecture Note: Emphasize the connection of behavioral objectives to operant conditioning by discussing shaping as a way of approximating instructional outcomes.

Lecture Note: As a result of their using behavioral objectives, teachers have been held more accountable for the achievements of their students.

Teacher Interview: Have each student interview a teacher regarding his or her use of Mager's criteria.

Journal Entry: Have students reflect on those classes in which their teachers used behavioral objectives, commenting on the ways in which the behavioral objectives contributed to their learning.

By setting behavioral objectives, teachers are able to monitor the degrees to which their instruction is successful. For example, the extent to which this child has mastered a sky-chart indicates the effectiveness of the lesson on the solar system.

The Goals Approach

McAshan (1974) suggested that the behavioral objectives should also allow a teacher to determine if students have attained the objective. Behavioral objectives as described by Mager do not reflect the broader outcomes desired by a teacher, but rather are statements of how to evaluate students. In McAshan's view, instructional objectives should include, in addition to evaluative statements, the teacher's instructional goals. For this reason, McAshan's approach to preparing instructional objectives is called the goals approach (Eggen & Kauchak, 1988).

Goals

McAshan's **goals approach** to instructional objectives calls for combining the evaluative statements, which are behavioral objectives, with a goal. A goal is a statement of the outcomes a teacher desires for his or her students. Goals are stated in general terms. The following are examples of educational goals provided by Eggen and Kauchak (1988).

1. For first graders to know the vowels.
2. For eighth-grade science students to understand Newton's second law.
3. Freshman literature students will understand the difference between a novel and a short story.
4. Fifth graders will understand the difference between similes and metaphors. (p. 75)

Teachers make the decisions that determine the character of their classrooms—whether or not they will be positive learning environments.

Consider the difference between behavioral objectives and goal statements. Behavioral objectives describe actions that students will perform when they attain the objective. Goal statements, on the other hand, do not specify observable behavior. Judgments of whether students "know" or "understand" require more than observation. They require inference. In order to infer that a student has understood, however, a teacher must observe behavior.

Goal statements provide a general framework of outcomes. When we examined professional growth in Chapter 1, we noted that having an instructional theme, whether it be to instill the joy of reading, to encourage independent thinking, or to appreciate natural beauty, is a characteristic of master teachers. The instructional themes fostered by a teacher are more easily stated as goals rather than as specific objectives. Goal statements contain verbs such as *understand, know, appreciate, recognize* (in the sense "be aware of" or "be sensitive to"). Goal statements are also helpful in discussing a student's academic progress with his or her parents in a nontechnical way. In order for goal statements to contribute to effective planning, however, they need to be combined with evaluative statements.

Evaluative Statements

Evaluative statements specify an observable student behavior that a teacher can use to judge whether or not a student has attained an objective. In Mager's scheme, an evaluative statement is a complete objective (performance, condition, and criteria). According to McAshan, it specifies how a goal will be evaluated. Consider the following examples of instructional objectives that were prepared according to the goals approach.

[Example A:] For biology students to know the parts of a cell so that, when given a slide of the cell showing ten parts, the student will label seven.

[Example B:] For art students to understand perspective so that, when given a photograph of a landscape, the student will draw it using three-point perspective.

[Example C:] For physics students to know the second law of thermodynamics so that, without aids, the student will state the law verbatim as stated in class.

[Example D:] Language arts students will know the concept adverb so that, when given ten sentences, the student will underline all the adverbs. (Eggen & Kauchak, 1988, p. 77)

The General Objectives–Specific Behaviors Approach

Gronlund (1985) distinguishes among types of objectives in terms of level of generality or specificity. The first level of objective is called a general instructional objective. A general instructional objective identifies an intended outcome of instruction, and states it in general terms so that it encompasses a domain of student performances. Gronlund's general objectives are similar to the goal statements in McAshan's approach.

In order to evaluate general objectives, they need to be further defined by specific behaviors. A specific behavior identifies an intended outcome of instruction and is stated in terms of specific and observable student performance.

Gronlund's approach to the preparation of instructional objectives is similar to the goals approach. One difference is in the form in which the objectives are stated. Gronlund-type objectives are illustrated in the examples that follow:

General objective: Knows basic concepts in chemistry.
Specific behaviors:

1. Defines terms in his or her own terms.
2. Identifies examples of concepts.
3. Distinguishes between closely related concepts.

General objective: Understands solutions to problems.
Specific behaviors:

1. States law that applies to problem.
2. Identifies relevant variables.
3. Selects data from given information.
4. Computes solution.
5. Describes meaning of solution in his or her own words.
6. Describes relationship between solution and "real-world" example. (Eggen & Kauchak, 1988, p. 83)

Let's summarize the three approaches to instructional objectives. Mager's approach yields statements that specify performance, the conditions of the

Field Observation: Have students collect statements of instructional goals and objectives from various teachers and identify general objectives, specific objectives, goals, and evaluative statements.

performance, and the criteria by which the performance will be judged. Mager's behavioral objectives, as we will see in Chapter 13, facilitate evaluation. McAshan's goals approach is an expansion of Mager's behavioral objectives. The goals approach includes, in addition to evaluation statements, statements of instructional intent. Gronlund's approach combines statements of instructional intent with specific objectives.

All of the approaches specify performance, but Gronlund's does not specify performance conditions or criteria by which performance is judged—a major difference. Gronlund recommends that the objectives should avoid specifying subject matter topics. In the two examples presented earlier, the only mention of subject matter is the specification that it be "chemistry." Chemistry is a very broad field. No specific topic within chemistry—such as atomic weight or oxidation reactions—is included in objectives that strictly follow Gronlund's approach.

The three approaches examined here suggest ways in which instructional objectives can be prepared. In practice, the approaches are often combined. You will generate some of your own objectives for your students. You will select others from curriculum guides that accompany texts and from those required by state departments of education and your school district. Many curriculum guides present objectives in a format that resembles Gronlund's approach. A consistent modification of Gronlund's approach is often made, however. They present a general objective followed by statements that specify subject matter. Following this pattern, a curriculum guide for chemistry might include an entry similar to the following:

1. General objective: Demonstrate knowledge of acids and bases. The student will

    1.01. Define the term *ions.*

    1.02. Identify common acidic solutions.

    1.03. Distinguish between an acid and a base.

    1.04. Demonstrate a litmus test (etc.).

USING OBJECTIVES

Statements of objectives can provide the teacher with a basis to plan, to teach, and to evaluate. As for students, statements of instructional objectives help them determine what sorts of behaviors will and will not be rewarded. In this sense, instructional objectives can provide motivation and guidelines for self-regulation (see Gagné & Driscoll, 1988).

In general, the advantage of using instructional objectives is that they provide the teacher with a plan of action. Davies (1976) calls the use of instructional objectives "anticipatory decision making" (p. 5). Specifying objectives helps the teacher plan outcomes. Although it is possible to be organized without the use of objectives, such objectives give a clear direction for instructional activities. Kubiszyn and Borich (1984) suggest that without objectives, teachers often do not know where they are going and so do not know when they arrive at their destination.

Greeno (1976) agrees that instructional objectives specify the tasks that students are expected to perform during instruction. How well a student understands the material identified in an instructional objective can be inferred from the student's behavior on the task. The use of objectives can direct the teacher's attention to the components of the instructional task and therefore help the teacher design and evaluate curricular materials. Instructional objectives can also serve the teacher's need to evaluate student performance. Gronlund (1985) states that "the key to effective evaluation of pupil learning is to relate the evaluation procedures as directly as possible to the intended learning outcomes. This is easiest to accomplish if the general instructional objectives and specific learning outcomes have been clearly stated in terms of pupil performance" (p. 47).

Instructional objectives also provide teachers with guidelines for judging the adequacy of their own instruction. If instructional objectives provide clear statements of the behaviors students will perform, teachers may gather evidence that can improve their own instruction by measuring their students' actual behavior against the projected or "ideal" behavior (Popham & Baker, 1970).

Cautions for Using Objectives

It seems to make sense that teachers can approach systematically the job of determining outcomes by using instructional objectives. It is widely accepted that planning through objectives makes the teaching-learning process productive and efficient. However, Zahorik (1970) examined the effect of planning by objectives on teaching. He suggests that it tends to make a teacher's thinking rigid and puts him or her on a track that is nearly "derail proof." "Once a teacher decides what outcomes he or she wants from the lesson and how he or she will achieve them, the teacher sets out to produce those outcomes regardless of what pupils introduce into the teaching learning situation" (pp. 149–150). Not all teachers would agree with Zahorik, however. In Teacher Chronicle 9.1, the teacher credits objectives with allowing a class to take "side trips" without getting "sidetracked" from the desired outcome.

Duchastel and Merrill (1973) reviewed studies that investigated the effects of behavioral objectives on learning. The studies they reviewed were placed into two categories: type of learning and learner characteristics. They found that the availability of objectives facilitated learning in some instances, but not in others. No significant relationship was found between objectives and types of learning, defined in most studies as knowledge of facts. Conflicting evidence was found when learner characteristics were applied. Their review raises doubt about whether communicating objectives to students has a facilitative effect on learning.

Duell (1978) conducted two studies using college students in educational psychology classes. Results indicated that the use of behavioral objectives does produce greater learning. However, learning is enhanced if the objectives identify for students information that they had not already classified as important or as likely to be tested.

In sum, the research on instructional objectives is mixed at best. The use of instructional objectives for planning has an intuitive appeal. Such objectives would certainly seem to provide a way to be organized in the classroom. Yet, as we have seen, the research does not entirely support the supposed effectiveness of objectives.

The question a teacher might ask him- or herself is whether the confidence that is gained from planning by objectives is worth the effort. Many practicing teachers think so. In an informal survey of experienced teachers, we found that the majority of teachers plan by stating objectives in one form or another. Interestingly, of those who plan by objectives, only about one half of them communicated the objectives to their students.

Alternative Views

Elliot Eisner (1971) distinguishes two types of objectives in education—instructional objectives and expressive objectives. Eisner's version of the instructional objective is similar to the behavioral objective that we examined earlier (e.g., Mager). Instructional objectives specify the particular behavior that a student will demonstrate. The student's demonstration of the behavior is taken as evidence that learning has occurred.

Expressive objectives are quite different from instructional objectives. An expressive objective describes not the behavior the student will demonstrate but rather the type of instructional activity the student will encounter. An expressive objective may describe the particular situation in which children are to work or a task that they may undertake. An expressive objective does not, however, specify what students are to learn from the instructional encounter. "An expressive objective is evocative rather than prescriptive" (p. 99). Some examples of expressive objectives are as follows:

1. To view the film *A Clockwork Orange* and discuss reactions and impressions
2. To construct an ecological collage
3. To visit the animal shelter at the humane society

The use of instructional or expressive objectives, according to Eisner, can provide the teacher with a plan for instruction. Expressive objectives, even though they do not include a specific plan for evaluating the behavior of students, still provide the teacher with a plan for instructional activity.

Chapter 15 Casebook Preview: See Book Writing.

Field Observation: Have students observe classrooms in which expressive objectives are the basis for learning activities, determining how the teachers evaluate expressive objectives.

Principles in Practice 9.1

Principles . . .
1. Objectives specify instructional outcomes.
2. The effects of communicating objectives to students are unclear.
3. Objectives benefit teachers by providing an instructional plan.

. . . in Practice
In Teacher Chronicle 9.1, the teacher reflected on planning instructional outcomes so that students' contributions can be accommodated. The teacher finds objectives useful as a planning tool, but takes the view that a teacher's plans should not be executed without allowing students to take a lesson in unanticipated directions. Objectives allow the teacher flexibility in the sense that a clear idea of an instructional outcome allows a class to wander from "the main highway" while still heading in the right direction.

1. Which procedure for stating objectives do you prefer? Why?
2. When should a teacher supply students with objectives?
3. How could expressive objectives and instructional objectives be integrated into one lesson plan?

CONTENT OR PROCESS?

Over spring break I was reading Hemingway's *The Old Man and the Sea*, a book I read every year on visits to the shore. The old man hooked the fish and . . . I read along, my eyes taking in each word. After reading three more pages, I realized that I could not remember what it was I'd read. My mind had been elsewhere. To an outside observer I was "reading"; my eyes were indeed seeing the words, but I was not thinking about what I was reading.

My reading interrupted, I let my mind wander still further. Why did I read *The Old Man and the Sea* only at the beach? Was I linking the sea and the book? Would the book mean the same thing to me if I read it back in the Midwest?

My thoughts jumped to how I read a book. Do I make mental pictures? I've heard that others do so when they read. No, not really. Do I simply plow through to get the story line first, only occasionally pausing to reread an enjoyable phrase or sentence? Yes, that's the tack I take. How do my students read? I've never really thought about that. Do their thoughts wander as mine did then? If so, how often does this happen and to whom? I thought of my Advanced Placement English class reading *Huckleberry Finn* just before break. By all appearances when they read silently in class, they seem intent upon the task. But how were they going about that task? What capabilities allowed them to make pictures, if that's what they did? How do they become capable of locating an aesthetically pleasing phrase? Who was wandering with Huck and Jim and who was just wandering?

Before turning back to my book, I made a mental note to rethink the way that I test those students. I usually ask them to tell me about the content of a novel. Maybe what I should do is ask them about how they read and not just what they read.

GAGNÉ'S OUTCOMES OF INSTRUCTION

Chap. Obj. 2
Test Ques. 9.35–9.67

Focus Questions: What capabilities might students gain from instruction? How can the different areas and levels of outcomes be classified?

Lecture Note: Inform your class that from Gagné's point of view it is important to think about instructional outcomes as capabilities gained by each student.

Robert Gagné views capabilities acquired by students as the outcomes of learning. Students do not learn "history" per se; they become capable of talking about historical events; they become capable of making historically significant discriminations, using concepts developed by historians and generating and applying rules pertinent to historical issues; they become capable of approaching problems that their study of historical events makes them aware of; they acquire an internal state that increases their affinity for historical information. In some cases—for example, when they collect historical artifacts from a field site—they become capable of new motor skills. Teachers do not open students' heads and pour in the content they teach.

According to Gagné and Driscoll (1988), "The *purpose* [italics in original] of learning is the establishment of internal states or capabilities" (p. 83). These internal states and capabilities are the outcomes of learning. The outcomes of a student's learning are influenced by the conditions under which the learning takes place (see Figure 9–1).

Learning begins with the stimulation that the student encounters from his or her environment: the events of instruction. The events of instruction

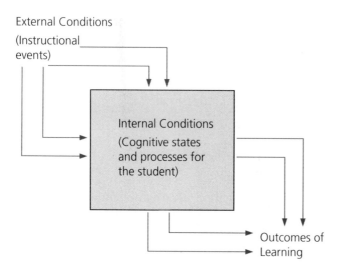

External Conditions (Instructional events)

Internal Conditions (Cognitive states and processes for the student)

Outcomes of Learning

■ **Figure 9–1** *Influences on the Outcomes of Learning*

SOURCE: From *Learning and Instruction: Theory into Practice* (p. 121) by M. E. Bell-Gredler, 1986, New York: Macmillan. Copyright 1986 by Macmillan. Adapted by permission.

Transparency: This figure is duplicated in the acetate transparency package. See T-14 Influences on the Outcomes of Learning.

internal conditions of learning The cognitive states and processes with which the student operates on stimuli.
external conditions of learning The events of instruction.
outcomes of learning Capabilities acquired by the student resulting from the interaction of external and internal conditions of learning.
verbal information According to Gagné, learned capabilities that enable children to communicate about objects, events, or certain relationships.

(which we will discuss further in Chapter 10) interact with the cognitive states that the student brings to the classroom and the cognitive processes that the student uses to understand the stimuli from the environment. The cognitive states and processes with which the student operates on stimuli are the **internal conditions of learning.** The events of instruction are the **external conditions of learning.** The interaction of these external and internal conditions of learning produces the **outcomes of learning.**

Gagné views learning outcomes as being diverse. Learning accounts for all of the attitudes, values, skills, and knowledge acquired by human beings. When people learn, they become capable of a variety of behaviors. The outcomes of learning experiences are called *capabilities* (Gagné, 1977, 1985; Gagné & Driscoll, 1988). According to Gagné, there are five types of learned capabilities:

1. Verbal information
2. Intellectual skills
3. Cognitive strategies
4. Attitudes
5. Motor skills

When we plan instruction, we make decisions about outcomes—strategic decisions. Gagné's learned capabilities remind us that instruction can produce different types of results. Sound instructional planning, therefore, requires a working knowledge of the outcomes of learning.

Verbal Information

Verbal information is one capability that makes communication possible. When a student states that Herman Melville wrote *Moby Dick,* he or she is declaring some knowledge. The declaration provides evidence that the student has acquired some verbal information. Being able to make declarations about the environment enables us to communicate. For example, a young

Journal Entry: Have students reflect on the external conditions of learning created by their teachers, addressing the question, What kinds of conditions led to a change in your cognitive states, that is, the internal conditions of your learning?

Lecture Note: Inform students that they can use the acronym VICAM to remember Gagné's five learned capabilities.

intellectual skills According to Gagné, learned capabilities that include making discriminations, identifying and classifying concepts, and applying and generating rules.

Field Observation: Have each student observe a lesson in a classroom, identifying episodes during which students learn verbal information as opposed to their gaining other kinds of capabilities.

Connection: Transfer of learning is described in detail in Chapter 11.

Teacher Interview: Have each student interview a teacher of adult special ed students regarding the importance of verbal information and the acquisition of "life skills."

child begins asking questions about his or her environment in order to communicate about the environment. The endless chain of questions which parents often hear is the child's search for verbal information.

"What's that Daddy?"

"A tree."

"Mommy, what's that?"

"A car."

"What's that?"

"An airplane."

"What's that?"

"A giraffe."

Acquiring verbal information enables the child to communicate. Gagné and Driscoll (1988) identify as units of verbal information names, facts, principles, and generalizations. A child may be able to state that the name of the household cat is "Meatball." A student may be able to state that the capital of Missouri is Jefferson City, that chefs prepare food in restaurants, or that a particular poem is an example of a rondeau or haiku. But, just because a student is able to make a particular statement of fact does not mean that he or she fully understands the implications of the statement. For example, because a student can identify a poem as a rondeau does not mean that he or she can tell a good rondeau from a poor one.

By its nature the learning outcome that we call "verbal information" allows us to make statements. We know "that something is called X." The acquisition of verbal information serves other functions for the learner as well. One function is as a prerequisite for further learning. Verbal information is the conduit for what is known as the transfer of learning. When teachers set out to teach a new unit they often begin with vocabulary for the students to learn. Learning the relevant vocabulary words gives the students and the teacher the verbal information that will allow them to communicate about the topic. For example, in teaching a unit on geology, it is helpful that students begin by learning the meaning of terms such as *igneous, metamorphic,* and *sedimentary.*

Another function of verbal information is that it provides labels that allow us to operate in everyday situations. Preschool students are often quizzed on their home phone numbers and on emergency phone numbers. A child might be taught that when shopping with his or her parents that should he or she become lost, he or she should wait by the *elevator*. In Great Britain, the child would be advised to wait next to the *lift*. The terms are different but they both serve the function of labels.

Verbal information also serves as a basis for thinking or as a vehicle for thought (Gagné & Driscoll, 1988). Because he or she possesses verbal information about car engines, a mechanic is able to hypothesize about the causes of various engine problems.

Intellectual Skills

If we can consider verbal information as knowing "what," we can consider intellectual skill as knowing "how." **Intellectual skills** include making discriminations, identifying and classifying concepts, and applying and generating rules. If we can state that a particular poem is a rondeau, we evidence verbal information. If we know how to arrive at that determination, we evidence intellectual skill.

Intellectual skills are not necessarily more complex than verbal information, just different. Intellectual skills can be ordered in terms of complexity (see Table 9–1). In examining intellectual skills, we will proceed from the simplest of intellectual skills to the most complex.

Discriminations

The simplest kind of intellectual skill is the knowledge of how to make discriminations. **Discrimination** is the ability to distinguish between two or more stimuli. A human being must be able to discriminate one feature of the environment from another. In Chapter 7, we saw the importance of discriminating between a model's relevant and irrelevant behaviors. Young children must learn to discriminate between adults who are parents and adults who are not parents.

The capability to discriminate requires experience. A baby may learn that the red object rolls and the yellow object rattles. The baby may also learn that the white cylindrical object yields milk but the blue cylindrical object, mother's antique vase, is not to be touched. As children enter school, they are still acquiring the ability to discriminate. In school, a great deal of their discrimination learning revolves around symbols. Children must learn to discriminate between the letter *T* and the letter *F*, and between the numeral 5 and the numeral 3. As children proceed through school, the discriminations they are required to make become finer and finer. Consider the junior high school student who learns the difference between the pronunciation of the French *R* and the English *R*.

Discrimination is a simple intellectual skill. It requires that the learner of whatever age be able to discriminate features in the environment. An infant may be able to discriminate between a stuffed toy and a pull toy without knowing that the stuffed toy is a bear and that the pull toy is a dog. Having verbal information that sedimentary, metamorphic, and igneous rocks differ from one another serves as a prerequisite for further learning. Having the intellectual skill to discriminate among sedimentary, metamorphic, and igneous rocks also serves that purpose.

> **discrimination**
> Distinguishing between and responding differently to two or more stimuli.

Lecture Note: Inform students that skills can be thought of in terms of a hierarchy. Hierarchies will come into play later in this chapter when we discuss disciplined taxonomies.

Connection: See the discussion of relevance in terms of modeling (Chapter 7), and also the discussion of relevance as part of the ARCS model (Chapter 8).

Lecture Note: Ask a student who has learned French to demonstrate the French *R* and describe any difficulties he or she had in initially producing it.

Lecture Note: In order to ensure that students understand the difference between verbal information and intellectual skills have them discuss the possibility of discriminating between types of rocks without knowing their geologic labels.

■ **Table 9–1**   *Categories of Intellectual Skills*

Intellectual Skill	Example of Performance Based on the Capability
Discrimination	Distinguishing printed *p*'s from *q*'s
Concrete concept	Identifying the spatial relation "below"
Defined concept	Classifying a "city" by using a definition
Rule	Applying the rule for finding the area of a triangle to specific examples
Higher-order rule	Generating a rule for predicting rainfall in a particular location

SOURCE: From *Essentials of Learning for Instruction* (p. 61) by R. M. Gagné and M. P. Driscoll, 1988, Englewood Cliffs, NJ: Prentice-Hall. Copyright 1988 by Prentice-Hall. Adapted by permission.

Concrete Concepts

After the child has developed the skill to discriminate horses, cows, sheep, and dogs, the child is ready then to learn the concept "dog." **Concrete concepts** refer to objects, events, and relations that can be observed or experienced.

"Dog" is a concrete concept. It is an object, something that can be pointed to in the environment. Humans acquire concrete concepts by making appropriate discriminations in a number of instances; in this case, acquiring knowledge of the critical features that make an animal a dog but not a horse. If you consider the wide range of features included in the concept "dog," you can see that although the concept may be concrete, it is not necessarily simple. For example, a Chihuahua and the Newfoundland are both instances of the concept "dog."

Concrete concepts are not only objects or classes of object features, they can also be events. A student may learn, for example, that one sound is produced by a violin and a different quality of sound is produced by a piano. A child will also learn the critical features that distinguish parades from the lines of people entering a ride at Walt Disney World.

Concrete concepts include the spatial relations among objects. Take, for example, the concepts of "above" and "below." A child will learn through experience that the red light is above the green light on a traffic signal. Other relational concrete concepts include the concepts of up, down, higher, lower, near, and far. The successful acquisition of concrete concepts allows students to identify entire classes of objects, events, or relations and point them out in the environment. Keep in mind the difference between the outcome of verbal information and that of intellectual skill. Just because a student can point out an example of a concept in his or her environment does not mean he or she is able to name the concept. In order to communicate about the concept, some verbal information is necessary.

Defined Concepts

Among the many concepts that we expect our students to acquire are **defined concepts**—concepts that cannot be pointed out in the environment the way that concrete concepts can and, thus, must be defined. Take as an example the concept "information." There are many instances of information in our environment and many sources of information as well, but "information" itself is not a concrete object, event, or relation.

Students who have acquired defined concepts are able to use them in an abstract fashion. To understand the defined concept "liberty" is to have acquired it. The student cannot point to "liberty" in the environment. However, the student can learn to use the notion of liberty to discuss the Constitution.

Concrete concepts can acquire the properties of defined concepts. A child who first learns the concept "dog" by seeing concrete instances in the environment may later become capable of defining the concept in abstract terms. The student who can define a dog as a mammalian quadruped with a carnivorous diet has provided a definition for the concept "dog." Although a student may have acquired a defined concept, it is not necessarily the case that the student no longer uses his or her concrete concept. Indeed, in many instances, students have stored in memory both a concrete and a defined concept.

---

concrete concepts
Abstractions based on objects, events, people, and relations that can be observed.

defined concepts
Abstractions that cannot be observed in the environment but must be defined (e.g., *liberty*).

Journal Entry: Have students identify concrete concepts that they have learned in school, commenting on how important these examples were to their understanding of concrete concepts.

Field Observation: Have students observe preschool or kindergarten classes in which students classify objects according to a category or set of categories, documenting how such activity contributes to the attainment of concrete concepts.

Lecture Note: Have students discuss the importance of defined concepts in generating plans or theories. Students can be asked to determine how defined concepts can contribute to their theories of teaching.

Lecture Note: Ask students how many of them learned the definition of certain concepts for purposes of taking a test without really understanding the nature of those concepts.

Rules

Next in order of complexity is an intellectual skill called rules. Normally, we think of a rule as a verbal statement such as "*i* before *e* except after *c*." As a learned capability, this rule allows us to spell correctly the word *receive*. **Rules** allow learners to use symbols. Typically, the symbols used in school are linguistic and mathematical. There are other symbols that operate in a classroom, however. For example, consider the signals that a teacher's body language or facial expressions provide. Students learn these symbols because they have acquired rules.

Students learn the rules of grammar, the rules of decoding words, the rules of algebraic manipulation, and the rules of verb conjugation. A learner who acquires rules is able to understand and to interact with his or her environment in generalized ways. In a classroom, for example, a student may be told that his or her name should appear always in the upper right-hand corner of the paper. As a type of intellectual skill, the rule-governed behavior is the student's ability to remember to put his or her name in the upper right-hand corner of all papers.

A student who acquires concrete and defined concepts can, as a result, acquire rules, allowing him or her to respond to a class of events. Thus, knowing Strunk and White's (1979) rule that "a participial phrase at the beginning of a sentence must refer to the grammatical subject" saves us from writing a sentence such as the following: "Being in a dilapidated condition, I was able to buy the house very cheap" (p. 14). Knowing the rule also helps us to respond to sentences that we read and that we have never before seen.

Higher-Order Rules

The final type of intellectual skill is called higher-order rules. **Higher-order rules** are formed by combining two or more rules, which allows a student to solve problems. The characteristics of higher-order rules are the same as the characteristics of rules. The only difference is that higher-order rules are more complex.

In the case of mathematics, the application of higher-order rules is easily seen. For example, in order to solve a long-division problem, a student must use rules of "multiplication," "subtraction," and "simple division." Although the use of higher-order rules in solving problems is more obvious in mathematics than in some other disciplines, it is assumed that students solve problems in other content areas as well by generating higher-order rules (Gagné & Driscoll, 1988). When a student attempts to apply the economic principle of "supply and demand," he or she is generating a higher-order rule.

In summary, intellectual skills vary in complexity and can be ordered according to that complexity. Learning simple intellectual skills, such as discrimination, allows the learner to acquire more complex capabilities, such as concepts. (We will return to this theme after examining the remaining outcomes in Gagné's scheme. Using one type of learning to facilitate another type of learning will be discussed in the section on "Transfer of Learning" in Chapter 10.)

Cognitive Strategies

Gagné uses the term *cognitive strategies* to identify the capability to internally organize skills that regulate and monitor the use of concepts and rules

rules The ways phenomena work. As a learned capability, rules allow learners to use symbols.

higher-order rules Rules formed by combining two or more rules, thus allowing students to solve problems. As a learned capability, they are the most complex type of intellectual skill.

Journal Entry: Have students reflect on those teachers in their experience who managed classes with a gesture or a look, or by positioning themselves in certain areas of the class, noting the rules that they learned from these teachers.

Connection: See the discussion of the transfer of learning in Chapter 10.

Connection: See Figure 6–1.

(Gagné, 1985). In the information-processing model (Chapter 6), "cognitive strategies" are represented by the executive control function. As students acquire the various capabilities discussed in this chapter, they become more adept at regulating the cognitive processes by which they attend, encode, and retrieve information, and solve problems. Gagné (1985, p. 138) states (italics in original) that

> in other words, they learn *how* to learn, *how* to remember, and *how* to carry out the reflective and analytic thought that leads to more learning. It is apparent as individuals continue to learn that they become increasingly capable of *self-instruction* or even what may be called *independent learning*. This is because learners acquire increasingly effective strategies to regulate their own internal processes. This new function of control over internal cognitive processes is what distinguishes [cognitive strategies] from the intellectual skills.

Teacher Interview: Have each student interview a teacher regarding the approach he or she uses to facilitate independent learning.

Connection: Teacher Chronicle 9.2: Content or Process?

Cognitive strategies serve a metacognitive function; they enable students to organize and monitor the cognitive processes they use to represent the environment. The teacher, in Teacher Chronicle 9.2, was able to reflect on his or her cognitive processing while reading Hemingway. When a learner acquires a cognitive strategy, he or she acquires a way of approaching problems.

For example, a high school student who is facing a unit test on John Steinbeck's work may develop a cognitive strategy in order to study effectively for the exam. The student determines as precisely as possible what is expected of him or her. With the exam expectations in mind, the student adopts the following approach:

1. Review the vocabulary list handed out at the beginning of the unit
2. Reread the synopsis written as one of the assignments in the unit
3. Answer the textbook discussion questions at the end of each of Steinbeck's stories to discover where weaknesses lie
4. After discovering deficiencies, rereads part or all of a particular Steinbeck story

Gagné incorporated a distinction made by Bruner (1971), which distinguished between problem solving and problem finding, into his discussion of cognitive capabilities. The student who is preparing for the unit exam on John Steinbeck may be presented with several problems by his or her teacher. One problem may be to compare and contrast the symbolism in *The Red Pony* with the symbolism in *Cannery Row*. While looking for similarities and differences between the use of symbols in the two stories, the student may discover something about Steinbeck's use of dialogue that opens up a new line of analysis. In this way, the student has found a problem. The problem was not supplied from the external environment but was generated internally by using his or her cognitive processes.

Field Observation: Have students observe lessons in various classrooms, identifying opportunities within lessons to encourage problem finding.

Researchers have investigated whether the cognitive strategies that develop as learners acquire intellectual skills can be taught. Such studies constitute a research literature called "learning strategy research."

Pressley, Borkowski, and O'Sullivan (1984) recommended that more attention be given to metacognition or the learner's awareness of his or her own thinking process. Metacognitive awareness seems to play a critical role in the

Students who exhibit the finely developed motor skills necessary to cut and reorganize paper into recognizable shapes are demonstrating cognitive skills as well.

attitude According to Gagné, a learned capability that influences a person's choice of personal action.

learner's ability to develop self-instruction skills and skillfully transfer learning strategies. According to Derry and Murphy (1986), educators should take a two-part approach to teaching learning strategies. First, they should devote the beginning of each school year to the training of students' learning skills. Second, the use of strategies should be imbedded within the content curriculum, so that this use calls attention to how the strategies can be applied to other content areas.

Attitudes

An **attitude** is an acquired internal state that influences a student's choice of personal action (Gagné, 1985; Gagné & Driscoll, 1988). We acquire attitudes toward any number of things. The things toward which we acquire attitudes are called *attitude targets*. For example, a student may acquire an attitude toward teachers (the target) that influences his or her behavior in a certain way when in their presence.

Students acquire attitudes that influence other social behavior. Often such attitudes are instilled at an early age and, in many cases, they are learned at home. For example, a student may have acquired an attitude toward people of a different creed or race. This attitude influences the student's behavior toward people who are different.

In general, attitudes are evidenced in the actions that a learner chooses. The learner who chooses to watch a National Geographic special over MTV programming is exhibiting an attitude. But the simple observation of one choice may not provide us with sufficient information to judge what the

Lecture Note: Ask students to discuss the types of learning skills they anticipate teaching and the content areas in which those skills might be embedded.

Connection: See the discussion of values and cultural differences in Chapter 4.

Teacher Interview: Have each student interview a teacher regarding how he or she determines student attitudes.

attitude is. Is the student's attitude toward the topic covered on the National Geographic special positive or is his or her attitude toward the rock videos negative? Because the attitudes learned by students predispose them to certain actions, attitudes ring with motivational overtones. Before inferring whether a learner is predisposed toward the National Geographic special or away from rock videos, observe whether the learner chooses to volunteer time or money to the World Wildlife Foundation, or some other activity that indicates interest in environmental or ecological issues.

Motor Skills

The final type of learning capability that Gagné discusses is motor skills. **Motor skills** are physical capabilities, such as the ability to ride a bike, or to use a computer keyboard, that require a set of organized motor acts.

When we think about motor skills, we are forced to consider the distinctions between the cognitive, the affective, and the psychomotor domains of behavior. For example, we tend to think exclusively of motor skills when we think about riding a bike. However, there are also cognitive and affective components involved in riding a bicycle. In an earlier chapter, we asked you to put down the book and to imagine riding a bicycle. Although it was probably difficult to "mentally ride the bike," you nevertheless retrieved a cognitive representation of riding a bicycle. One's predisposition toward bike riding—whether one likes or dislikes it—is indicative of the affective aspect of bicycle riding. Just because a complex behavior—such as executing a pas de deux in *Swan Lake*—requires motor skills, we should remember that the motor capabilities rarely develop in the absence of affect or cognition.

Principles in Practice 9.2

Principles . . .

1. Through instruction, students acquire learned capabilities.
2. Intellectual skills are hierarchical.
3. Cognitive strategies are a type of capability that, once acquired, allows the student to regulate cognitive processes.

. . . in Practice

In Teacher Chronicle 9.2, the teacher, pondering the cognitive processes involved in reading, recognized that certain capabilities are required for one to be able to read. What are those capabilities? How are those capabilities used? Gagné's view of the outcomes of instruction answers those questions.

1. How do Gagné's learned capabilities account for the teacher's reflections while at the beach?
2. What capabilities are necessary for a student to understand Huck's dilemma over turning in Jim as an escaped slave in *Huckleberry Finn*?
3. Would asking students to describe how they read help them develop cognitive strategies?

A HARD NUT TO CRACK

Adam had been diagnosed at age four as having learning problems. He had been in an early childhood class and had received special instruction in speech, social skills, and listening. His kindergarten year was not a positive experience and he began first grade saying, "I hate school. School is dumb."

Adam rarely smiled. He laughed at things no one else thought funny. He made ridiculous comments, and he shot down other kids whenever he had a chance. He was continually tardy. He tried to blame problems and mistakes on others. "You didn't tell us to do that." "You didn't talk loud enough for me to hear." "Mark said we didn't have to write that down."

His academic work was uneven. One day he could read like a wiz kid and the next it was as if he had never seen a book before. In math, he rarely finished his work without a great deal of prodding. He had to be continually reminded to finish his work before moving on to another task.

Adam was going to be a hard nut to crack. Yet many times he surprised me with insights that showed me he was a good thinker. "If you put all the bikes together, I wonder if they would stretch around the school." or "I saw a hawk yesterday. You know you can tell a bird of prey by the sharp outline of its wings?" or "Why does the sun stay on the other side of the world while we're asleep?" Adam asked interesting questions. Nonetheless, his attitude toward school remained abysmal.

I came to realize that Adam did not think very much of himself. We were writing in our journals at the end of the day. Adam grumbled about writing in his journal and told me he had nothing to write about. I remembered that he had been late this morning because he had locked his bike to his sister's and thought he had lost the key. As it turned out, he hadn't lost the key, his sister had it all the time.

"Why not write about how it felt when you thought you lost your bike key," I suggested.

He grumbled some more, but went ahead. Much to my surprise (and his!) he got involved and actually stayed after school to finish his entry. It was his longest journal entry ever.

"Adam, this is wonderful. Look how much you wrote. You really told me how it felt when you thought the key was lost. I especially like the part when you looked on the ground for the key."

What surprised me most was his reaction to my remarks. His eyes were downcast, he shrugged his shoulders, and he quickly put the journal away. Most kids would have lit up like a Roman candle at such praise.

I thought about Adam and how he could not accept praise. I decided that I needed to identify some attitudinal objectives and to work on those as hard, if not harder, than the cognitive objectives I had established for the whole class. To help Adam attain a sense of self-worth, I decided to go after only the positive with him and see what happened. But first, I had to convince him that my praise really meant something.

The next morning when Adam was on time I teased him good-naturedly. "Well, look," I said. "We have a new boy in class. You can have Adam's old seat, he rarely uses it at this time of day." He looked at me with a puzzled look, but the hint of a grin crossed his face. I had taken a chance by teasing him, but it worked.

Instead of saying something when he made a silly comment, I ignored it. When he was first to answer a question, I praised him. He looked away, but raised his hand again later. When it was time to write in our journals, I praised him again for the nice work he had done the day before.

"It wasn't any good," he told me. But that day he filled another page in his journal.

I kept working on his attitude in this way. Ever so slowly, I convinced Adam that he was good in many things. He was no longer tardy. He frequently caught himself when beginning a negative comment about someone else. He finished work with improved accuracy.

It was clear that, for the first time, Adam had begun to believe in himself. He didn't need praise as much. And he accepted gracefully the praise he got. "I don't know what you did," his mother said on the phone toward the end of the year. "Adam is like a new kid. I don't have to be after him so much. He's smiling when he leaves for school."

TAXONOMIES OF OUTCOMES

Instructional outcomes are the things students become capable of doing, thinking and, as was the case in Teacher Chronicle 9.3, feeling. In theory, determining instructional outcomes is a matter of planning the things students will do and the content they will encounter. In practice, the material you present to your students will be, to a large extent, determined for you. Governmental agencies, such as the state department of education, will prescribe content. Your school district will prescribe content. Your department may prescribe content. The textbook selection committee, through its choice of texts, prescribes content. But, what will you have your students do with the content you present?

One way educators think about the question is through taxonomies. A **taxonomy** is a classification system. Educational taxonomies have been developed for the cognitive, affective, and psychomotor domains of behavior (see Bloom, 1968; Krathwahl, Bloom, & Mosia, 1967; Harrow, 1972, respectively). Many of the curriculum guides you will see are organized around these taxonomies.

The Cognitive Domain

Bloom's **cognitive taxonomy** consists of six levels, which progress from simple to complex. Gagné's intellectual skills also progress from simple to complex. Being able to use intellectual skills, as well as verbal information and cognitive strategies, allows students to perform certain kinds of tasks. The examples given at each level specify a behavior a student might be asked to perform.

According to Bloom's cognitive taxonomy, essay writing can involve analysis, synthesis, and evaluation.

Level 1: Knowledge

Knowledge objectives involve the recall of specifics and universals, methods and processes, patterns and structures. The focus of these objectives is remembering. For example: List the twelve cranial nerves.

Level 2: Comprehension

Comprehension objectives represent the lowest level of understanding. At this level, the learner can know what is being communicated and make use of the idea without relating it to other ideas or seeing its fullest implications. For example: Discriminate between cognitivist and behaviorist theories of learning.

Level 3: Application

Application objectives require students to use information that they have learned in new situations. The information can be general ideas, rules, methods, principles, or theories that must be remembered and then applied. For example: Use the appropriate formula to solve problems of volume.

Level 4: Analysis

Analysis objectives require that students identify elements embedded in a whole. For example: Identify the logical fallacies in a political speech.

Level 5: Synthesis

Synthesis objectives put elements together to form a new whole. For example: Design a unique scientific experiment.

JEAN SUNDE PETERSON

NATIONAL CENTER FOR
GIFTED AND TALENTED

IOWA CITY, IOWA

As a high school English teacher, I used novels as an excuse to teach history, geography, theology, philosophy, psychology, art, music, and current events. We did not discuss the content of the novels much, but rather used class time for pertinent background to enhance the *experience* of the novels. My students wrote their reactions to their reading in journals, thereby giving each student a chance to "be heard" and responded to. They were lauded for insights and independent thought. They wrote analyses in more formal papers. We studied the vocabulary of the novels. *before* reading them. At the sophomore level, my students had a semester of intensive writing, followed by this course on the novel, which included seven challenging novels. Many reported that it was the first time they had managed a "big book"; they felt affirmed in their ability to think on their own. They also matured greatly in writing skill.

I made many presentations at conferences on the teaching technique used in the novels class and also on a vocabulary-teaching technique I developed, in which words were taught and learned by context, not by definition, in "verbal immersion," with the same contexts appearing on weekly tests. In this way we were able to familiarize students—even below-average students—with approximately nine hundred words per year.

In gifted education I have built a program that has options for gifted students in many areas of interest, including science, mathematics, art, futuristics, global issues, music appreciation, career exploration, exotic languages, and creative thinking. An affective dimension, recognizing shared and unique social and emotional needs among adolescents, is another aspect of the program. I believe it important not to assume that all gifted children have the same intellectual needs and that academic challenge is *all* they need.

I credit my mother, my early experience with Sunday School teaching, and 4-H leadership training with directing me toward teaching. I was hooked by the thrill of interacting with "audiences" and by the satisfaction of helping individuals. I was always interested in how people

---

affective taxonomy
Krathwahl's classification of behavior in the affective domain. It is organized by levels: receiving, responding, valuing, organization, and characterization.

Field Observation: Have students collect tests constructed by classroom teachers and examine the tests for the verbs listed in Table 9–2.

Lecture Note: Have students, either individually or in small groups, generate additional examples for each level of the affective taxonomy.

Level 6: Evaluation

Evaluation objectives involve judgments based on criteria of value or worth. For example: Using the four principles of music appreciation, validate Beethoven's Fifth Symphony as a masterpiece.

The level of the cognitive taxonomy identifies the level of complexity. The higher the taxonomic level, the more complex the learning involved.

The taxonomy can be used to determine learning outcomes by making judgments of the appropriate level of learning required of students. For example, in the cognitive domain, the teacher must decide whether students should be required to know, to apply, or to evaluate the material. As an exercise, consider how various learned capabilities come into play at each taxonomic level. Table 9–2 organizes the language of behavioral objectives around the levels of the cognitive taxonomy (Tuckman, 1988).

The Affective Domain

There are five levels in Krathwahl's **affective taxonomy,** including capabilities defined by Gagné as attitudes, that allow the learner to experience a variety of internal states as described in the text that follows.

think and function; I have always been hypersensitive to interpersonal nuances. I also wanted to continue to learn. Teaching offered an arena where I could put all of these to use and meet personal needs as well. I have never felt I should have chosen another profession. Nor am I tempted to become an administrator. Teaching is the "highest calling" in education.

Prospective teachers should assess whether they are process or product oriented. If they can enjoy "process" and people, and if they can manage a good level of organization when they need to, they can probably find great satisfaction in teaching, watching the growth of students in their care. Teaching is a process profession; the most satisfied teachers are those who can "enjoy the trip" without being overly concerned about "destination."

I would recommend that teachers seek out positive colleagues in the teachers' lounge. I would also recommend that they offer active support to new teachers, all of whom need it. Teachers need to take good care of themselves and to maintain balance in their lives. And they need to stay alive throughout their careers by "nourishing" themselves through continued professional development. If they sense stagnation in their methodology or content, they should pursue sources that will infuse new energy into their teaching. They should even model risk taking in trying new courses, new approaches, and new learning experiences for themselves. And they should beware of negative self-talk.

We need to entice our best and brightest students into the profession, because we need their creativ-

ity and intellect to develop even better strategies for meeting the complex educational needs of our society. Those who are inspired and satisfied should not hesitate to promote teaching as a career option to students who want a generative, people-centered, satisfying life.

A teacher is the "resident intellect" for all students in the classroom and is sometimes the only intellectual role model for even gifted children. It is important for the teacher to affirm the brightest, from whom many teachers withhold affirmation because they think these students have "so much." As many bright students have poignantly told me, that acknowledgment can be the difference in making school a positive experience.

Level 1: Receiving or Attending

Receiving or attending objectives require that the learner be sensitive to or aware of certain stimuli. These objectives include a willingness to receive or selectively respond to stimuli. An example would be a willingness to listen to a guest speaker.

Chapter 15 Casebook Preview: See Beginning Each Day as a Learning Experience.

■ **Table 9–2** *A Selected List of Verbs for Writing Cognitive Objectives*

Knowledge	define / describe / identify / label / list
Comprehension	convert / defend / distinguish / estimate / explain
Application	change / compute / demonstrate / discover / manipulate
Analysis	diagram / differentiate / discriminate / distinguish / identify
Synthesis	categorize / combine / compile / compose / create
Evaluation	appraise / compare / conclude / criticize / describe

SOURCE: From *Testing for Teachers* (2nd ed., p. 17) by B. W. Tuckman, 1988, Orlando, FL: Harcourt Brace Jovanovich. Copyright 1988 by Harcourt Brace Jovanovich. Reprinted by permission.

Transparency: This table is duplicated in the acetate transparency package. See T-15 A Selected List of Verbs for Writing Cognitive Objectives.

A child who is willing to receive new information and respond to it when necessary demonstrates characteristics of the affective domain.

Connection: Teacher Chronicle 9.3: A Hard Nut to Crack.

Level 2: Responding

Responding objectives specify that the learner be motivated to learn. The category includes acquiescence in responding, a willingness to respond, and finding satisfaction in response. For example, Adam, in Teacher Chronicle 9.3, eventually exhibited a willingness to write in his journal when asked by the teacher.

Level 3: Valuing

Valuing objectives specify that the learner comes to be perceived as holding a value, that a behavior has worth. The category includes acceptance of a value, preference for a value, and commitment to a value. A student who chooses, because of a committed belief, to participate in a protest march is an example.

Level 4: Organization

The organization category of objectives describes the beginnings of a value system. As ideas, opinions, and beliefs become internalized, the learner gives some of them priority over others, thus, conceptualizing values and organizing a value system.

Teacher Interview: Have students interview teachers at various grade levels, using the affective taxonomy to collect examples of activities from the teachers' classrooms.

Level 5: Characterization

Characterization objectives specify that behavior consistently reflects values that are organized into some kind of system. Learners at this level "practice what they preach" and believe deeply in these values.

The Psychomotor Domain

Harrow's **psychomotor taxonomy** of objectives, which includes six levels, can be used to specify psychomotor objectives in areas of physical education, dance, theater, and motor development therapies for exceptional students. The higher levels of the taxonomy are the organized acts that Gagné calls motor skills.

Level 1: Reflex Movements

These reflex movements are involuntary; they are either present at birth or develop as the learner matures. The sucking reflex in infants is an example.

Level 2: Basic/Fundamental Movements

Basic movements are components of more complex actions. An example is a gripping movement of the hand that is part of a forehand stroke in tennis.

Level 3: Perceptual Abilities

Perceptual abilities allow input from the environment to be transmitted to the brain so that motor messages can be sent out to appropriate muscle groups. An example is the ability to feel that one is too close to a hot surface.

Level 4: Physical Abilities

These physical abilities are the characteristics of a person that, assuming proper development, allow efficient movement. An example is the ability to walk reasonable distances, indicating normal endurance.

Level 5: Skilled Movements

Skilled movements, whether simple or complex, must be learned. The ability to do word processing is an example.

Level 6: Nondiscursive Communication

Nondiscursive communication is nonverbal communication. Everyday examples include gestures and facial expressions. Expressive examples are mime and ballet.

Deciding on Objectives

The business of translating general outcomes into specific objectives that guide instruction is an important part of the classroom teacher's job. No matter what blue-ribbon panels, state departments of education, or school districts determines curricular objectives, it is still the classroom teacher who translates goals and objectives into instruction.

Brophy (1982) argues that the curricula developed by a school district are either reduced or distorted by teachers. Teachers reduce school district curricula because of demands on instructional time brought about by yearly additions to an original plan. Distortions of curricula occur, in part, because of this reduction. Teachers operate within time constraints. They are forced to provide brief or vague explanations for some of the content prescribed by the district. School boards and other administrators, commercial publishers, and even federal and state agencies establish educational objectives and prepare curricular materials. It is ultimately the teacher, however, who adapts the curriculum according to his or her own educational beliefs.

psychomotor taxonomy Harrow's classification of behavior in the psychomotor domain. The levels are reflexive movements, basic/fundamental movements, perceptual abilities, physical abilities, skilled movements, and nondiscursive communication.

Chapter 15 Casebook Preview: See Improvisation and Aesthetic Appreciation or Coup D'Etat in the Classroom.

Lecture Note: Ask students, either individually or in small groups, to generate additional examples for each level of the psychomotor taxonomy.

Teaching Anecdote: Tell your students about the American History teacher who loves the Civil War and because of the time spent on this topic, never carries his course in U.S. History up to the Persian Gulf War, as stated in the curriculum. After several parental and student complaints, the principal questioned the teacher about this problem.

"They'll get that material in World History next year," the teacher argues. "Besides, the Civil War is what I know best."

Ask your students if the teacher is justified in the way he or she follows the curriculum.

Even though many curricular decisions are made by local school boards, educational administrators, taxpayers, and parents, it is the teacher who decides the most effective way to teach the material.

Teacher Interview: Have students interview teachers regarding the freedom they have to interpret curricular prescriptions.

Field Observation: Have each student observe a classroom in which a teacher takes control of the curriculum by designing many of his or her own activities and another classroom in which the teacher seems to be "following a recipe" provided by curriculum specialists, documenting the level of students' enthusiasm in each classroom.

Decisions about what to teach in schools are shared by local school boards, educational administrators and teachers, taxpayers, parents, and students. Sometimes curriculum committees adopt plans developed outside the community and marketed for wide use. In most cases, local educators are free to exercise their professional judgment regarding site-specific curriculum decisions (Saylor, Alexander, & Lewis, 1981).

Teachers are given the responsibility to lead students through a curricular maze. By the end of the year, a student should be able to use certain skills, know certain facts, apply certain concepts, and evaluate certain materials. A good number of the learning outcomes that students are to attain have been prescribed for the teacher by external sources.

The outcome information provided by those who put together lists of educational objectives, such as those from the National Assessment of Educational Progress; the objectives of the various taxonomies presented earlier; and the curricular objectives set by state education departments and local school districts define what students should be able to do. The task of determining outcomes for a particular course, units within that course, and lessons within those units must be determined by the teacher. Using the prescriptions for content coverage, the teacher's job becomes one of planning the trip through the content of a course. A science teacher, for example, is given the assignment to teach seventh-grade science. Along with that assignment comes a set of curricular materials including text books. These materials will define to some extent the learning outcomes students will attain in that class. Even though the materials may define the content to be covered, the teacher must still make decisions about what students should do with these materials.

Principles in Practice 9.3

Principles . . .
1. Taxonomies classify behaviors in a hierarchical fashion.
2. The behaviors defined by taxonomic levels can be used to specify objectives.
3. Because the domains of behavior—cognitive, affective, and psycho-motor—are not mutually exclusive, the behaviors specified in the three domains are interrelated.

. . . in Practice
Adam, in Teacher Chronicle 9.3, was known around school as a trouble-maker. After the journal-writing episode, the teacher hypothesized that Adam had a very low opinion of himself. To test the hypothesis, the teacher decided to focus some effort on affective objectives in an effort to enhance Adam's self-esteem. The careful combination of ignoring undesirable behavior and judiciously reinforcing positive behavior paid dividends not only in the attainment of affective objectives, but cognitive objectives as well.

1. At what level of the affective taxonomy would you place Adam's behavior as described at the end of Teacher Chronicle 9.3?
2. Identify a future affective objective for Adam.
3. Why should the attainment of affective objectives be accompanied by cognitive progress?

CONCLUSION

Assign Chapter 9 of the *Study Guide*.

In this chapter, we have discussed how teachers can determine what learning outcomes to set for their students. By making those strategic decisions, teachers answer the question: What do I want my students to be able to do? In Chapter 10, we will look at another aspect of planning instruction. Having determined the outcomes of learning for students, the next issue concerns how the teacher can best facilitate those outcomes. What actions should a teacher take in order to guide students toward the goals that have been set for them?

If the outcomes obtained by students are the ends of instruction, the actions taken by teachers are the means to that end.

Chapter Summary

Introduction: Strategic and Tactical Decisions

Strategic decisions result in plans. Tactical decisions are made as the plan is executed. Strategic decisions begin with the teacher determining the outcomes desired for his or her students.

Instructional Objectives
The Behavioral Approach

Instructional objectives can be specified in a number of ways. Instructional objectives prepared as specified by Robert Mager are called behavioral objectives. Behavioral objectives include a statement of terminal behavior, the conditions of performance, and the criteria used to judge attainment of an objective.

The Goals Approach

The goals approach specifies instructional objectives by combining a general goal with an evaluative statement. The general goal provides a context that can be helpful when discussing student progress with others, including parents. The evaluative statement specifies how goal attainment will be evaluated.

The General Objectives–Specific Behaviors Approach

This approach was developed by Gronlund to specify objectives. General objectives identify a domain of student performances. Specific behaviors are then prescribed under each general objective in order to allow for evaluation of the general objective.

Using Objectives
Cautions for Using Objectives

Instructional objectives serve a planning function for teachers. They specify the content to be covered and provide a means of evaluating not just students' progress, but the teacher's instruction as well. It is not clear that learning is enhanced when students are provided with objectives; it depends on the circumstances under which the objectives are estab-

lished. However, the confidence teachers gain from planning by objectives seems to be worth the effort, whether students ultimately see the objectives or not.

Alternative Views

Some critics argue that using instructional objectives "trivializes" learning because outcomes are predetermined. Eisner suggests that another type of objective, the expressive objective, can be used to focus on process rather than outcome. Expressive objectives specify the kinds of experiences a teacher desires students to have without regard for the outcomes of those experiences.

Gagné's Outcomes of Instruction
Verbal Information

Verbal information is information that allows students to communicate about an object, event, or certain relations. It is the first of the variety of learned outcomes that students may attain from instruction. Knowing the name of an object is an example of verbal information.

Intellectual Skills

Students can acquire intellectual skills at varying levels of complexity. Gagné identified a hierarchy of intellectual skills. These skills are, from simple to complex, discrimination, concrete concepts, defined concepts, rules, and higher-order rules.

Cognitive Strategies

Students can learn how to regulate their own cognitive processes. This regulation affords the student control over his or her own learning. Cognitive strategies perform a metacognitive function.

Attitudes

For Gagné, attitudes are an acquired internal state. A student's attitudes influence his or her choice of action.

Motor Skills

Motor skills are physical capabilities. Examples include riding a bike or dancing. Just because the most obvious aspect of motor skills is the physical aspect of a behavior does not mean that affect and cognition play no role in acquiring motor capabilities.

Taxonomies of Outcomes
The Cognitive Domain

Taxonomies are classifications of behaviors that can be used to specify instructional objectives. Bloom's taxonomy of behaviors in the cognitive domain, from simplest to most complex, consists of six levels: knowledge, comprehension, application, analysis, synthesis, and evaluation.

The Affective Domain

The affective domain, as described by Krathwahl, is also organized by levels: receiving, responding, valuing, organization, and characterization.

The Psychomotor Domain

The psychomotor domain identifies behaviors that have a major physical component. As described by Harrow, the levels of the psychomotor domain are reflexive movements, basic/fundamental movements, perceptual abilities, physical abilities, skilled movements, and nondiscursive communication.

Deciding on Objectives

Instructional objectives define the content students encounter in a classroom. There are multiple sources of those objectives. Whether objectives are determined by the teacher or prescribed for the teacher, the teacher must make decisions about how the objectives will be addressed in the classroom.

Reflections: Building Your Theory of Teaching

9.1 Imagine that you are going to a school as a substitute teacher tomorrow. In what form do you hope to find the instructional objectives (behavioral, goals, or general objectives/specific behaviors)? Why?

9.2 Identify a unit you expect to teach. What intellectual skills will students need to acquire in order to master the topic? How would you facilitate the development of cognitive strategies while teaching this unit?

9.3 Using the cognitive taxonomy, set objectives for the intellectual skills and cognitive strategies specified in Reflection 9.2. Using the affective and, if appropriate, the psychomotor taxonomies, specify other objectives you would like to see students attain during the unit of instruction.

Key Terms

strategic decisions (p. 324)
tactical decisions (p. 324)
behavioral objectives (p. 327)
goals approach (p. 328)
goal statements (p. 329)
evaluative statements (p. 329)
internal conditions of learning (p. 335)
external conditions of learning (p. 335)
outcomes of learning (p. 335)
verbal information (p. 335)
intellectual skills (p. 336)
discrimination (p. 337)
concrete concepts (p. 338)
defined concepts (p. 338)
rules (p. 339)
higher-order rules (p. 339)
attitude (p. 341)
motor skills (p. 342)
taxonomy (p. 344)
cognitive taxonomy (p. 344)
affective taxonomy (p. 346)
psychomotor taxonomy (p. 349)

Suggested Readings

Gagné, R. M. (1985). *The conditions of learning* (4th ed.). New York: Holt, Rinehart & Winston.

Gagné, R. M., & Driscoll, M. P. (1988). *Essentials of learning for instruction.* Englewood Cliffs, NJ: Prentice-Hall.

Martin, B. L., & Briggs, L. J. (1986). *The affective and cognitive domains: Integration for instruction and research.* Englewood Cliffs, NJ: Educational Technology.

Schiever, S. W. (1991). *A comprehensive approach to teaching thinking.* Needham Heights, MA: Allyn & Bacon.

West, C. K., Farmer, J. A., & Wolff, P. M. (1991). *Instructional design: Implications from cognitive science.* Englewood Cliffs, NJ: Prentice-Hall.

References

Berliner, D. (1985, April). *Effective teaching.* Paper presented at the meeting of the Florida Educational Research and Development Council, Pensacola, FL.

Bloom, B. S. (1968). Learning for mastery. *Evaluation Comment, 1*(2).

Brophy, J. (1982). Classroom management and learning. *American Education, 18,* 20–23.

Bruner, J. S. (1979). *The relevance of education.* New York: Norton.

Davies, I. K. (1976). *Objectives in curriculum design.* London: McGraw-Hill.

Derry, S. J., & Murphy, D. A. (1986). Designing systems that train learning ability: From theory to practice. *Review of Educational Research, 56,* 1–39.

Duchastel, P. C., & Merril, P. F. (1973). The effects of behavioral objectives on learning: A review of empirical studies. *Review of Educational Research, 43*(1), 53–69.

Duell, O. K. (1978). Overt and covert use of objectives of different cognitive levels. *Contemporary Educational Psychology, 3,* 239–245.

Eggen, P. D., & Kauchak, D. P. (1988). *Strategies for teachers: Teaching content and thinking skills* (2nd ed.). Englewood Cliffs, NJ: Prentice-Hall.

Eisner, E. W. (1971). Instructional and expressive educational objectives. In M. D. Merril (Ed.), *Instructional design: Readings.* Englewood Cliffs, NJ: Prentice-Hall.

Gagné, R. M. (1977). *The conditions of learning* (3rd ed.). New York: Holt, Rinehart & Winston.

Gagné, R. M. (1985). *The conditions of learning* (4th ed.). New York: Holt, Rinehart & Winston.

Gagné, R. M., & Driscoll, M. P. (1988). *Essentials of learning for instruction* (2nd ed.). Englewood Cliffs, NJ: Prentice-Hall.

Greeno, J. G. (1976). Cognitive objectives of instruction: Theory of knowledge for solving problems and answering questions. In D. Klahr (Ed.), *Cognition and instruction.* Hillsdale, NJ: Erlbaum.

Gronlund, N. E. (1985). *Measurement and evaluation in teaching* (5th ed.). New York: Macmillan.

Harrow, A. J. (1972). *A taxonomy of the psychomotor domain: A guide for developing behavioral objectives.* New York: McKay.

Krathwahl, D. R., Bloom, B. S., & Masia, B. B. (1967). *Taxonomy of educational objectives: The classification of educational goals: Handbook II. Affective domain.* New York: David McKay Company.

Kubiszyn, T., & Borich, G. (1984). *Educational testing and measurement: Classroom applications and practice.* Glenview, IL: Scott, Foresman.

Mager, R. (1962). *Preparing instructional objectives* (2nd ed.). Palo Alto, CA: Fearon.

McAshan, H. (1974). *The goals approach to performance objectives.* Philadelphia, PA: Saunders.

Popham, W. J., & Baker, E. L. (1970). *Establishing instructional goals.* Englewood Cliffs, NJ: Prentice-Hall.

Pressley, M., Borkowski, J. G., & O'Sullivan, J. T. (1984). Memory strategy instruction is made of this: Metamemory and durable strategy use. *Educational Psychologist, 9*(2), 94–107.

Rosenshine, B. V., & Stevens, R. (1986). Teaching functions. In M. C. Wittrock (Ed.), *Handbook of research on teaching* (3rd ed.). New York: Macmillan.

Saylor, J. G., Alexander, W. M., & Lewis, A. J. (1981). *Curriculum planning for better teaching and learning* (4th ed.). New York: Holt, Rinehart & Winston.

Skinner, B. F. (1968). *The technology of teaching.* New York: Appleton-Century-Crofts.

Strunk, W., Jr., & White, E. B. (1979). *The elements of style* (3rd ed.). New York: Macmillan.

Tuckman, B. W. (1988). *Testing for teachers* (2nd ed.). Orlando, FL: Harcourt Brace Jovanovich.

Zahorik, J. A. (1970). The effects of planning on teaching. *Elementary School Journal, 71*(3), 143–151.

10
Instructional Models

Chapter Overview

This chapter focuses on the instructional approaches a teacher might use to bring about desired outcomes. The relationship between instruction and learning is considered in the context of Gagné's instructional events, discovery learning, and reception learning. Transfer of learning is also examined to provide an understanding of the way in which students can apply material learned to one situation to new situations. Models that address issues of planning and presenting direct instruction lessons, the instructional form typically used in the classroom, are considered. The current emphasis in education is on the teaching of thinking skills. The chapter addresses this issue through an examination of models of instruction. ■

INTRODUCTION: PLANNING FOR ACTION

If we are to initiate sound instructional planning we must have a clear idea of the outcomes we desire for our students. Familiarity with Gagné's learned capabilities, examined in the last chapter, will help us understand these outcomes. Being able to discriminate intellectual skills from verbal information is crucial to our planning. Our capability to discriminate among types of outcomes helps us understand the cognitive processes (the internal conditions of learning) that are required to achieve the various learning outcomes. Our knowledge of the variety of learned capabilities does not ensure, however, that our students will achieve them. We must determine the instructional events (the external conditions of learning) that will support the necessary cognitive processes.

Teachers spend most of their instructional planning time in the following ways: allocating time to various learning activities; studying and reviewing content to be taught; organizing daily, weekly, and term schedules; attending to administrative requirements; and assisting substitute teachers (Clark & Peterson, 1986; McCutcheon, 1980). Much of this planning is done to implement the plans and wishes of educational administrators, school boards, and state departments of education.

Many of the decisions made about instructional outcomes are determined by the school district or the state department of education. Educational administration plays a large role in prescribing the curricula taught in schools. As the agent of implementation, however, the teacher wields a great deal of power. It is the teacher who determines how much time will be allotted to the various prescribed outcomes, how the outcomes themselves will be interpreted, what supplemental materials to use, and how those materials will be used. Teachers, especially effective teachers, put their own "twist" on the material they present. In this way, teachers pursue instructional outcomes

Lecture Note: Refer students to Figure 9.1 in order to remind them of the internal and external conditions of learning.

Lecture Note: Though the amount of prescribed curriculum will vary depending on the district and school where your students teach, emphasize the point that once the door is closed, the teacher controls much of what happens to the curriculum in the classroom.

Inspiring and effective teachers are those who bring a personal flair or interest to prescribed curricula.

that are important to them. If you recall our discussion in Chapter 1, you'll remember that one of the hallmarks of a master teacher is that his or her actions reflect a personal theme. The theme produces learning outcomes. It is emphasized in a variety of ways over a variety of content areas. The outcomes are ends; the models for instruction examined in this chapter are the means to those ends.

Journal Entry: Have students reflect on the themes they anticipate emphasizing in their classrooms in the future.

Teacher
Chronicle
10.1

WET BEHIND THE EARS

I laugh to myself when I think back to the first time I ever had to create a two-week unit for fourth graders and teach it to them. I was student teaching and had met my reading group under the eye of my supervising teacher, Mrs. Stone. After working with a small group and observing Mrs. Stone teach large groups for a week, we both felt it was time for me to plan, teach, and evaluate a unit over a period of time. We had just finished the science unit on rocks and the next one was on the water cycle. As Mrs. Stone said, "It's time for you to get your feet wet." Laughing, I added, "I'll either sink or swim with this unit."

I spent the weekend at the public library with the curriculum guide, and at my university education resource center. I quickly realized that most of the material about the water cycle was way over my students' heads. I decided to read the material and gear it to their level. After creating an outline of the most pertinent points, I began making instructional materials for the initial lesson.

My primary objective the first day was to explain the differences between fresh water and salt water. I decided to do this by discussing water and the places where we find it. I thought this should take about fifteen minutes of the thirty-minute science slot. Next, I would give the class a worksheet reviewing what I had covered. We would split up into small groups to complete the worksheet cooperatively. After ten minutes, we'd get back together to review the worksheet as a final evaluation of what had been learned. This would take up the final five minutes. By late Sunday evening I was all set.

Science was the last subject covered before lunch. As I worked with my reading group, my thoughts drifted to the water lesson. Did I have enough material? Would they like my teaching? Would I have any behavior problems?

Then, Mrs. Stone announced, "Boys and girls, today we will begin a new unit in science. You will be studying water." She told the children that I would be the teacher for the unit. "I hope that you give your new teacher the same respect and attention that you always give me." I hoped so, too.

My moment had come. I walked to the front of the class as Mrs. Stone went to her desk to observe. I glanced at the clock. Exactly thirty-five minutes before the lunch bell, thirty of which were mine.

I launched immediately into my lecture about water, where we found water, and what the differences between fresh water and salt water were.

When I finished I asked, "Does anybody have a question?" No hands went up. I looked at the clock. Twice. It had only taken five minutes. I hoped that the worksheet would take a lot longer than I had planned.

At least no one had been disruptive, although I noticed that several students were getting restless.

"Now, we're going to break up into small groups with five in each group." They immediately began grouping themselves. Pandemonium erupted as they jockeyed to be with friends. Four kids stood looking forlorn; no one had invited them into a group. I looked at Mrs. Stone for help, but her eyes were on the papers she was correcting.

"Now, children," I almost shouted, "sit down in your groups so I can see who still needs to find a group." I placed the remaining students in one group or another. A quick look at the clock showed me that this had taken up five minutes. Good, I thought.

"When's lunch?" Mark asked, after they had settled down.

"In twenty-five minutes," I replied, wishing that it were in five minutes.

"I'm hungry," Luis complained.

"Me, too," Teresa moaned.

The class let out a chorus of groans.

"Before we can go to lunch," I told them, "we must do this worksheet. David, you're the leader today. Would you please pass five papers out to each group?"

After David had dropped the stack twice, each child finally had the worksheet. "First I want you to work on the paper alone. When you are finished filling in the blanks, then you can share your answers with someone in your group. Any questions?"

Abdul raised his hand. "What if you can't read all the words?"

"I will be coming around helping. Just raise your hand and I'll come to you."

For the next ten minutes I scrambled around the room answering questions. I was so busy that I lost track of the time. Mrs. Stone raised her voice above the din and said, "Time to put the papers away and get ready for lunch."

Like magic, the kids returned to their desks and began quietly lining up for lunch. Mrs. Stone handed out lunch tickets; I collapsed in a chair just as the bell rang.

What a disaster! I thought to myself. All my plans had failed. I was organized and I tried to teach and evaluate, but it had all gotten so jumbled together. How did Mrs. Stone ever keep everything going so smoothly? Maybe I should go into business for myself. At least there I can control what happens.

Mrs. Stone smiled and said, "Nice job. We can talk about it after school. They're like a bunch of hungry sharks just before lunch, aren't they?"

I nodded, pleased with the compliment and wondering if they'd be barracudas tomorrow.

■ ■

Chap. Obj. 1–2
Test Ques. 10.1–10.26

Focus Questions: Why do the conditions of instruction influence the outcomes of instruction? How do instructional events influence a student's cognitive processes?

Connection: Teacher Chronicle 10.1: Wet Behind the Ears.

INSTRUCTION AND LEARNING

Instruction and learning are two sides of the same coin. Teachers instruct, but instruction is meaningless unless students learn from it. A teacher who claims to have taught when students do not learn is like a salesperson who claims to have made a sale even though the customer did not buy anything.

The teacher's actions should engage the learner. Consider the student teacher in Teacher Chronicle 10.1 who so intently planned his or her actions. Just because actions are carefully planned is no guarantee that those actions will lead to student learning. The instructional models that we will now examine were developed to help teachers take actions that help learners effectively process the information they are asked to learn.

Gagné's Instructional Events

In Chapter 9, we examined Gagné's outcomes of learning. In this chapter, we examine his instructional model to understand the connection between the instructional actions of a teacher and the learning processes of students.

Figure 10–1 identifies the learning processes that typically occur in classroom learning situations and the instructional events (external conditions) that support those processes. (These processes should remind you of the information-processing model described in Chapter 6.) The processes define **phases of learning** (Bell-Gredler, 1986; Gagné, 1977). Each instructional event supports the student's cognitive processes in each phase of learning. The order of the external events are typical of a lesson; the order of events may change, however, depending on the particular lesson one teaches.

The Preparation Phases

According to Bell-Gredler (1986), the first three phases of learning—gaining attention, informing the student, and stimulating prior knowledge—are **preparation phases.** The first instructional event is gaining attention. If the teacher is successful in gaining the student's attention, the student apprehends or becomes aware of the relevant stimuli in the classroom.

The second event is informing the student of the goals or objectives of the lesson. If the student knows what he or she is expected to do, the student can make appropriate decisions throughout the course of the lesson. When you orient the student toward the goal of the lesson, you activate the student's motivation. For example, if students know that they will be expected to write a summary at the end of a lecture, they will process information differently than if they expect that they will have to define terms introduced during the lesson. A student who knows what he or she is supposed to do is more likely to do so. Have you ever procrastinated on a task because you were not quite sure what you were supposed to do? Building expectancies for a student activates his or her motivation.

The third event is stimulating recall of prior knowledge. By encouraging the student to retrieve prior knowledge appropriate to the goals of the lesson, you will enhance the student's acquisition and retention of material to be learned. Considered together, the first three instructional events function to prepare the student for learning.

The Core Phases

The next four phases (4–7) in Figure 10–1—the acquisition and performance phases—are the essence of what most people call classroom learning, and are referred to as the **core phases** by Bell-Gredler (1986). The fourth instructional event in a typical lesson is the presentation of stimulus material. The teacher's presentation helps the student to perceive selectively the important stimuli in the situation. By focusing on just the important elements, the student is

phases of learning The elements of an episode of learning.

preparation phases Used by Bell-Gredler to describe Gagné's first three phases of learning: (1) gaining the student's attention, (2) informing the student of the goals or objectives of the lesson, and (3) stimulating the recall of prior knowledge.

core phases Used by Bell-Gredler to describe Gagné's second four phases of learning: (4) presenting stimulus material, (5) providing learning guidance, (6) eliciting performance, and (7) providing feedback.

Connection: See the model of the human cognitive mechanism presented in Chapter 6.

Lecture Note: Inform students that they may think about Gagné's instructional events as being descriptive of an episode of learning.

Field Observation: Have students observe various classrooms, documenting the ways in which teachers gain students' attention.

Journal Entry: Have students reflect on those lessons about which they had either a good sense of their goals or a poor one, commenting on how each type of lesson influenced their motivation.

Connection: See the section on prior knowledge in Chapter 6.

Lecture Note: Have your class discuss specific methods for preparing students for learning.

Connection: See the discussion of selective attention in Chapter 6.

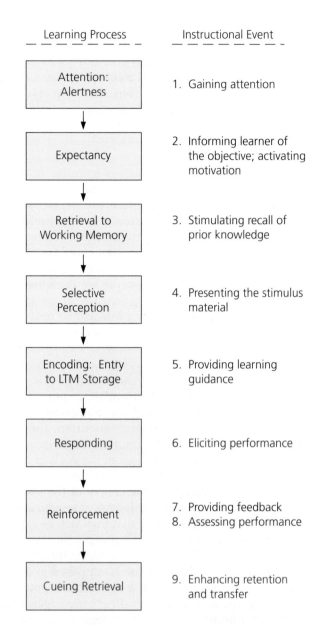

■ **Figure 10–1** *Gagné's Instructional Events and Learning Processes*

SOURCE: From *Essentials of Learning for Instruction* (2nd ed., p. 128) by R. M. Gagné and M. P. Driscoll, 1988, Englewood Cliffs, NJ: Prentice-Hall. Copyright 1988 by Prentice-Hall. Reprinted by permission.

better able to store the elements in short-term store. (Recall that STS has a limited storage capacity.)

The fifth instructional event is providing learning guidance. The teacher's actions during this phase of learning support the student's attempt to create a mental representation of the stimulus information that can be stored in long-term memory. In terms of the information-processing model examined in Chapter 6, the student attempts to make the stimulus information meaningful. Meaningful information is more easily stored and is retained longer.

The sixth event is referred to as eliciting performance. The teacher helps the student retrieve the information needed to make an appropriate response. For example, if a student has encoded the process of long division as "divide, multiply, subtract"—as in Peter Roop's Diary of a Day—the teacher might ask students to recite the steps just prior to working a problem.

The seventh event of instruction is providing feedback. This feedback supplied by the teacher is the basis for reinforcement. The type of reinforcement depends, of course, on the nature of the feedback supplied. Feedback functions to confirm the student's expectations about the goal of the lesson.

The Transfer Phases

The final two events of instruction, called the **transfer phases** by Bell-Gredler, support the cognitive processes necessary for transfer of learning. The eighth event, assessing performance, requires that the teacher give the student opportunities to use what he or she has learned. Recall that Gagné views the outcomes of learning as capabilities. If a student is truly capable of making a discrimination or applying a rule, he or she should be able to use the new capability in a variety of situations. Assessment allows students to "test his or her wings" and allows teachers to determine if learning is limited to the circumstances in which the initial learning took place.

The ninth event is enhancing retention and transfer. Actions that enhance retention and transfer encourage the student to retrieve the learned information in new situations. A student who can generalize beyond the instructional context in which information was learned has developed an elaborate encoding of the information and more retrieval cues for using the information in the future.

Discovery and Reception Learning

Consider the core phases of instruction. What material should be presented? guidance given? performance elicited? feedback provided? The answers to these questions depend on whether a teacher decides to facilitate learning through discovery or through reception.

Discovery Learning

Discovery learning occurs when students are presented with problem situations that require them to discover the essential concepts of the subject matter (Bruner, 1960). Bruner advocates learning through discovery because it encourages active learning. A teacher who uses a discovery learning approach to instruction presents examples or problems and then encourages students to examine and think about them with a goal of formulating a general principle. For example, the student teacher in Teacher Chronicle 10.1 might have given students equal amounts of fresh water and salt water and encouraged them to "experiment with containers to find out the differences between the two"—differences in appearance, taste (if both were potable), and weight. They could be encouraged to find out how well various objects float in the two containers. By "experimenting," the students would discover the essential properties, rather than being told what they are.

Discovery learning encourages students to actively use their intuition, imagination, and creativity. Because the approach starts with the specific and then moves to the general, it encourages inductive thinking. (Later in this chapter, we will examine a model for teaching inductive thinking.)

transfer phases Used by Bell-Gredler to describe Gagné's final two phases of learning: (8) assessing performance and (9) enhancing retention and transfer.

discovery learning Bruner's approach to teaching, in which students are presented with specific examples and use these examples to form general principles. Discovery learning is inductive.

Connection: See Diary of a Day, Chapter 1.

Chapter 15 Casebook Preview: See Responsibility Education.

Connection: Methods of classroom evaluation are discussed in Chapter 13.

Teaching Anecdote: Tell your students about the kindergarten teacher who had each of her children pick an object from a box each day and describe it. In the box, she had a collection of "junk" that she had gathered—everything from old records to nuts and bolts. After each child had described the object, the teacher asked him or her how the object might be used. At first, the children's guesses ranged far afield from the actual use of the object. But as they became more skilled in describing, they also began to realize the functional attributes of the objects.

Ask your students why the teacher took the time to do this exercise and what value it might have had for the children.

Connection: Teacher Chronicle 10.1: Wet Behind the Ears.

Connection: Inductive models are described later in this chapter.

By using nonconventional instructional actions, this teacher is actively engaging her students in the concept of nonstereoscopic vision.

Reception Learning

Ausubel, like Bruner, believes that meaningful learning occurs when students actively process the information they are asked to learn. Unlike Bruner, Ausubel believes that knowledge is best acquired through reception rather than discovery. **Reception learning** occurs when students receive the essential principles or concepts and are then shown how to apply them in specific instances.

For Ausubel, active processing of information on the part of students occurs when the ideas presented by teachers are well organized and clearly focused. In order to present effectively, teachers must carefully organize, sequence, and explain the material so that students can efficiently process it. The kind of instruction that leads to reception learning is called expository teaching. (*Exposition* means explanation.) An essential element of expository teaching is the advance organizer.

Advance Organizers

An **advance organizer** is information presented prior to learning that assists in understanding new information (Ausubel, Novak, & Hanesian, 1978). Suppose that a teacher is lecturing about Buddhism. For an advance organizer, the teacher could ask students to read a passage about the relationship between Christianity and Buddhism (see Ausubel & Youssef, 1963). Advance organizers are thought to provide a context for unfamiliar target information by activating prior knowledge.

Continuing research on "abstract" advance organizers has led Ausubel et al. (1978) to conclude that abstract organizers can enhance the learning of target material if two conditions are met. The first condition is that the target information must be a unitary topic or a related set of ideas. It would be inadvisable, for example, to write a statement subsuming a topic such as an "introduction to teaching." The wide ranging set of ideas covered by this topic would require a subsuming statement so general as to be useless. An obvious way to meet this condition, however, would be to break down the broad topic into constituent unitary topics. Thus, abstract advance organizers could be used.

The second condition for effective use of abstract advance organizers is that the organizing statement must account for the prior knowledge of the learner. (One reason advance organizers are written at a general level is that a general statement can more easily "activate" the prior knowledge of multiple learners.) If the organizer is unrelated to a learner's prior knowledge, the advance organizer becomes an additional piece of information to be learned rather than an aid to understanding the target information.

Although considerable evidence has been amassed that shows that advance organizers are beneficial, a number of researchers have found it difficult to replicate or accept Ausubel's findings (cf. Cunningham, 1972). The problem lies in interpreting Ausubel's criteria for what is or is not an advance organizer. Richard Mayer, wrestling with the problem, began to study a different type of advance organizer, a "concrete" advance organizer (Mayer, 1975, 1976; Mayer & Bromage, 1980). A **concrete advance organizer** is a statement or representation that provides a concrete rather than abstract overview of the target material students will encounter. As an example, suppose you were going to teach a unit on human digestion. Assuming that your students have prior knowledge of the major parts of the digestive system, you could use a plastic model of the human digestive system to introduce them to the unit. As you discuss the various phases of digestion, you could identify the digestive organs involved using this model.

Advance organizers, whether abstract or concrete, can be used to introduce new information for which little or no appropriate prior knowledge exists (cf. Joyce & Weil, 1986; Tessmer & Driscoll, 1986). Mayer (1987) has identified three conditions under which advance organizers are most likely to work. Advance organizers are more effective when (a) they are used before learning unfamiliar text, (b) they are used to enhance creative problem solving, and (c) they are concrete rather than abstract.

Advance organizers enable learners to integrate new information and prior knowledge. In order to integrate new and old knowledge, the learner must actively encode the new and retrieve the old (see Chapter 6). It is, in this way, that expository teaching makes reception learning active. Expository teaching leads to deductive thinking. (A step-by-step model for teaching deductive thinking will be presented later in the chapter.)

Whether material is learned through reception or through discovery, it is important that students be able to use what they have learned, not only in the circumstances in which learning occurred, but in new situations as well.

TRANSFER OF LEARNING

Transfer of learning refers to the influence that learning something in one situation has on learning in other situations. We hope, for example, that the problems our students learn to solve on Monday will help them solve new problems on Tuesday, on Friday, and next year. What follows is a discussion of a variety of transfer effects.

concrete advance organizer A statement or representation that provides a concrete rather than abstract overview of the target material students will encounter.
transfer of learning The application of knowledge acquired in one situation to other situations.

Field Observation: Have students observe various classrooms to discover methods teachers use when functioning as advanced organizers.

Lecture Note: Emphasize that the key to effective expository teaching is activating the learner's prior knowledge.

Connection: Deductive models are described in detail later in this chapter.

Chap. Obj. 3
Test Ques. 10.27–10.37

Focus Question: How can one instance of learning help or hinder another instance of learning?

Vertical and Lateral Transfer

Journal Entry: Have students reflect on examples of vertical transfer that they have experienced.

Field Observation: Have students observe classrooms and document instances of transfer, classifying these instances as vertical, lateral, near, or far transfer.

Journal Entry: Have students reflect on their own experiences of low-road and high-road transfer, speculating on how they will use the experiences when teaching skills and concepts that require these types of transfer.

Chapter 15 Casebook Preview: See Writing Success in Science.

Teacher Interview: Have each student interview a teacher regarding his or her students' mind-sets when problem solving.

Gagné (1985) defines two types of transfer, vertical and lateral (see also Royer, 1979). When complex skills are more easily learned because of simple skills that were acquired earlier, **vertical transfer** has occurred. A good example is the acquisition of intellectual skills—learning discriminations facilitate the learning of concepts. Therefore, one outcome of acquiring the discrimination capability is to facilitate the acquisition of concepts. Likewise, the acquisition of concepts results in easier acquisition of rules.

Lateral transfer is the generalization of knowledge or skill to a new situation—one that is different from the original situation in which the knowledge or skill was acquired. However, the new situation is not more complex. Lateral transfer is promoted when students are given novel tasks that require the use of what has been previously learned. For example, a student who has finished studying a spelling list might be given a word search task containing the spelling words.

Vertical or lateral transfer can be distinguished further as either near or far transfer. *Near transfer* refers to situations in which acquired skills are applied in new ways that are very similar to the original learning situation; *far transfer* occurs when the skill is applied in situations that are quite far removed from the original learning situation. For example, learning to type on a manual typewriter might facilitate using a computer keyboard. The situations are quite similar and would be referred to as near transfer. Learning typing might also facilitate the use of a stenographic machine. However, the situations are quite different and, if facilitation occurs, would be an example of far transfer.

Low-Road and High-Road Transfer

Salomon and Perkins (1989) have suggested another way of looking at transfer: low-road transfer and high-road transfer. **Low-road transfer** is the "spontaneous automatic transfer of highly practiced skills with little need for reflective thinking" (p. 118). Low-road transfer involves a great deal of practice to attain the automaticity of skills required. Salomon and Perkins use the example of driving a truck after one has learned to drive a car.

High-road transfer involves "the explicit conscious formulation of abstraction in one situation that allows making a connection to another" (p. 118). High-road transfer can occur in a forward-reaching sense when a general principle is so well learned that it suggests itself spontaneously in a new situation. It can occur in a backward-reaching sense when a need arises in a new situation that causes the learner to look back at past experiences for a potential solution. In either case, high-road transfer depends on mindful abstraction. The learner must deliberately use a principle acquired in one context in a new context.

Generating the abstraction and making a decision to use that abstraction in a new way requires the learner to think about his or her own thinking—metacognition. Brown (1988) investigated whether preschool children can learn a principle on the basis of one or two examples and if so, whether or not the ability to abstract a principle was affected by the ability to explain why a concept is an instance of a rule. The results indicated that preschool children are able to form "mind-sets" that aid them in looking for analogous solutions to problems. The effect was both rapid and quite dramatic. The results indicated that the effect was facilitated by the elaborations and explanations the students were asked to make. The conclusion is that reflection about one's cognitive activity is important. Metacognition plays a role.

Principles in Practice 10.1

Principles . . .

1. External events of instruction support internal learning processes.
2. Instruction can facilitate either discovery or reception learning.
3. Transfer occurs in a variety of ways.

. . . in Practice

In Teacher Chronicle 10.1, the student teacher prepared diligently for his or her first lesson. The teacher spent hours in the library gathering and creating materials. When the time came for the lesson to begin, the student teacher followed the plan for instruction faithfully. The problem was that the instructional events did not facilitate meaningful learning for the students. The student teacher's actions did not support internal learning processes. The student teacher, so intent on executing planned actions, forgot to instruct.

1. According to the events of instruction model, which phases of learning were not supported by the student teacher?
2. How should the student teacher have prepared the lesson in order to facilitate discovery learning?
3. Why should lessons support the transfer of learning?

WORD POWER

Teacher
Chronicle
10.2

As a mentor teacher, I often have other teachers drop in and discuss teaching situations they have observed. I enjoy these sessions because they are informal sharings of perceptions or misperceptions. One afternoon Irving stopped in. He was a former student and I knew him to be intelligent and sensitive. He was clearly puzzled by his recent observations of a supposedly good class.

Irving, who was pursuing his secondary certification, had been assigned to observe the teachers in the English Department. During his two weeks at the school, he observed the same students in two different classes.

"My first observation was in Mr. Blandworth's class, 'Word Power,'" Irving began. "The class was in its fourth week when I began to sit in. I was immediately puzzled by how the students took their seats, filling them from the back right corner toward the front left corner. Two students, obviously good friends, noticed me and came over to talk.

"Hi, I'm Julie, and this is Karen. You're not another student teacher, are you?" Julie asked.

"No," I said, "I'm not a student teacher. I'm just here to observe."

"That's too bad," said Julie. "I hope you survive."

The bell rang and several students scrambled to find seats. Two students headed for the last seat in the third row. One plopped his books on the desk just ahead of the other student, who turned with resignation and proceeded to a seat in the first row of the class.

As Mr. Blandworth arranged his teaching materials, the students took out their workbooks. They all turned to the same page. In each of the three workbooks that I could see, I noticed that only the first few and last few items on that page were completed.

Mr. Blandworth said, "Yesterday, we completed the words on page 36. Your homework for today was page 37. Let's get started." He turned to the student seated at the first desk in the far-left corner of the classroom and said, "Tania, please begin."

Tania began reciting. She pronounced the first word on the workbook page, gave a definition of the word, and described its etymology. After Tania had finished, Mr. Blandworth said, "OK, very good. Any questions? No? Carlos, you're next, go ahead." Carlos began the same drill. As Carlos recited, I watched the other students in the classroom. Most of the students were counting those seated in front of them. After completing their counting, they worked furiously in their workbooks.

The recitations proceeded in order down the first row, through the second and third rows. After a student completed his or her recitation, Mr. Blandworth would ask if there were any questions. There never were. Julie and Karen were seated in the fourth row. Julie was in front of Karen. Both were working with their dictionaries and workbooks. I suddenly realized that most students had come to class without completing their homework.

Mr. Blandworth sat behind his desk, his eyes on his materials. I glanced back at those students seated in the first row. As other students recited, these students completed the blank entries in their own workbooks by writing down what their fellow students recited. They had found a very effective way of avoiding homework.

Julie was about to recite. She closed her dictionary quietly, and waited for Mr. Blandworth to say "Next." When he did, Julie announced her word. "*Impropriety*," she said, and began defining the word.

I was immediately distracted by Karen's response. Her head had popped up and her eyes widened in disbelief. She quickly counted down the page, opened her dictionary, and desperately flipped through the pages.

Mr. Blandworth said, "OK, any questions? Good. Next."

Karen hesitated, looking hard at the next word in the list, *crepe de chine*.

Several seconds had passed when Mr. Blandworth looked up and said "Who's next?"

Karen raised her hand and said sheepishly, "I am."

"OK, let's get going," he said, "we have to get through the rest of this list by the end of the period."

Karen swallowed hard, cleared her throat, and said, "Creepy dee chine" (the last rhyming with "pine"). A few students giggled.

Mr. Blandworth looked at Karen and said, "You didn't complete your homework for today, did you?"

"Well," said Karen, "not all of it. I did everything except for numbers 26 through 33."

"That's not good enough," said Mr. Blandworth. "You know what happens when you do not complete your homework in this class. I'll record that as an *F* for the day, unless you turn in a one thousand-word essay using every word in the list within one week."

He continued, "Since Karen can't help us, who can?" Several hands went into the air. Mr. Blandworth called on one, the student recited, and then Mr. Blandworth said "OK. Next word, number 27." After the last student in the last row had recited, there were still four words left in the list. Mr. Blandworth called upon Tania again to continue the recitations. At this point, I understood why the students in the first row had completed, prior to class, the first several and the last several items in the list.

Mr. Blandworth's wristwatch alarm rang. He said, "It's important for you to do your work every day. That's how you build a vocabulary. Let's not have any more episodes of incomplete work. For tomorrow, I want you to complete page 38 and be prepared to share your work. That will be all for today." The bell rang five seconds after Mr. Blandworth completed his charge. I glanced at Karen who seemed crushed.

I watched Mr. Blandworth's second-period students file in. They repeated the same routines as the first-period students. For the remainder of the week I witnessed nothing other than the activities I had observed in the very first class. I was relieved when this tedium ended and I could go to Ms. Estefan's class. No matter what she taught, nothing could be as dull as Word Power.

Many of the students in Ms. Estefan's class were also students in Mr. Blandworth's classes. It was like stepping onto a different planet. Their reactions in class were entirely different.

Ms. Estefan first lectured on "The Tradition of Humor in American Literature." Everyone participated in a lively discussion comparing and contrasting the works of James Thurber and Fran Lebowitz. Karen was particularly involved, displaying her strong vocabulary. The discussion turned into a closely argued but good-natured debate. The following day the class worked in small groups on an assignment to construct a list of five sentences unrelated to one another. "Each sentence is to sound funny without being funny," she said. She handled the confused looks and questions of her students with ease. I was surprised at their willing involvement once they understood what was asked of them. In Mr. Blandworth's class these same enthusiastic students had been like the walking dead. The rest of the week continued with lots of sharing, personal insights, and intellectual challenges."

Irving finished his story and looked at me. "I hope I never become a Blandworth," he said.

I smiled and said, "Irving, I don't think you have to worry."

■ ■

PLANNING DIRECT INSTRUCTION

The term *direct instruction* was coined by Rosenshine (1979).

> **Direct instruction** refers to academically focused, teacher-directed classrooms using sequenced and structured materials. It refers to teaching activities where goals are clear to students, time allocated for instruction is sufficient and continuous, coverage of content is extensive, performance of students is monitored, . . . and feedback to students is imme-

Chap. Obj. 4
Test Ques. 10.38–10.68

Focus Question: What are the important variables in effective teaching practice?

Connection: Teacher Chronicle 10.2: Word Power.

Lecture Note: Emphasize that Carroll's model and Slavin's QAIT model should be kept in mind when planning; they do not prescribe the events of a lesson.

Teaching Anecdote: Tell your students about two high school students in English class. Reading was difficult for the first student, but he worked every night on his assignments and did well. The second student, for whom English had always been a "breeze," soon found herself struggling in the same class. Although her IQ was much higher than her fellow student's, she received lower grades for the first quarter of the year.

Ask your students what might account for the difference in performance. Which student might retain new material for longer periods of time—the first or the second?

Field Observation: Have your students observe students in a classroom with Carroll's degree of learning model in mind, noting behaviors that lead them to the conclusion that a student has spent more or less than the time he or she needed to learn.

diate and academically oriented. In direct instruction, the teacher controls instructional goals, chooses materials appropriate for the student's ability, and paces the instructional episode. (p. 38, boldface added)

Think about the extent to which the two classrooms in Teacher Chronicle 10.2 were teacher centered. Direct instruction may be teacher centered, but it does not mean that students are not involved. Rosenshine views direct instruction as occurring in a "convivial atmosphere." Direct instruction has more recently been referred to as *explicit instruction* (Rosenshine, 1986).

Models for direct instruction appeal to many educators who value the rational sequence of actions they propose. They appeal to their intuitive sense of what a lesson ought to look like. Two models that can be used to plan direct instruction are examined below. Carroll's model of school learning and Slavin's QAIT model do not tell teachers how to present a lesson; they merely identify variables that teachers should take into account as they formulate their instructional strategies.

Carroll's Model of School Learning

Carroll identifies five classes of variables thought to account for differences among students in school achievement.

1. Aptitude. Aptitude in Carroll's model is viewed as the amount of time required by a student to learn a task as defined by a particular criterion.
2. Opportunity to learn. Opportunity to learn is the amount of time allowed for learning a particular task.
3. Perseverance. Perseverance is the amount of time a student willingly spends on the task.
4. Quality of instruction. If optimal, the quality of instruction reduces the amount of time a student needs to learn a task to a criterion.
5. Ability to understand instruction. The ability to understand instruction includes a student's readiness to learn. For example, a very bright student is not ready to learn percentages until he or she has acquired skill in understanding and working with proportions. If ability to understand instruction is lacking in students, the time needed for learning is increased.

Carroll's model emphasizes time as an important variable in learning. Carroll expressed the degree of a student's learning as a ratio of time spent to time needed.

$$\text{Degree of Learning} = \text{Time Spent/Time Needed}$$

The Carroll model has attracted considerable research attention since its publication. John Carroll was asked to address the convention of the American Educational Research Association in 1988, on the occasion of the twenty-fifth anniversary of the publication of his model. That address was published in 1989. In his address, Carroll reflected on his model and its impact in education. He concluded that "all or most of its components have been amply confirmed as influential in school learning, although it has not always been possible to say exactly how they are effective or how they can be controlled or manipulated" (pp. 29–30). Carroll proposed that future work on the model emphasize to a greater degree "equality of opportunity for all students, not necessarily equality of attainment" (p. 30). Equality of opportunity in Carroll's view means providing many different appropriate ways for students to learn.

The QAIT Model

In much of the research on individual differences in achievement, the focus has been on differences in ability among students. Bloom (1976) argued that attention should be shifted away from the individual differences among learners toward more alterable variables present in a learning situation. Slavin's QAIT model (1987) focuses on the alterable elements that were identified in Carroll's model of school learning. (QAIT is an acronym that stands for Quality, Appropriateness, Incentive, and Time.) By identifying the alterable elements in Carroll's model, Slavin's view of effective instruction addresses those aspects of instruction that teachers can more easily control.

Quality of instruction refers to the ways that teachers present information or skills. Slavin sees quality of instruction as dependent on the quality of curricular materials and the presentation of the lesson itself. Quality of instruction can be viewed as the degree to which instructional actions ease the learning of students. (Recall our discussion of "ease of learning" in Chapter 7.)

Appropriateness of instruction refers to the match between instructional activities and students' levels of readiness. At an appropriate level of instruction the particular lesson presented proves neither too easy nor too difficult for students.

Incentive refers to motivation. It is the degree to which students approach, as opposed to avoid, the tasks presented in a lesson.

Time, in the QAIT model, corresponds to Carroll's notion of time needed. Enough time must be spent on the material to enable students to learn.

One important characteristic of the QAIT model, according to Slavin, is that each element in the model is necessary in order for instruction to be effective. Slavin (1988) says, "Effective instruction is not just good teaching." A teacher may present content very well, but if students are not ready to learn the content, if they lack motivation, or if the time allowed to learn the material is insufficient, the lesson will fail. Although all elements of the QAIT model must be present if effective instruction is to occur, quality of instruction is perhaps the most critical. If students are ready to learn, if they are motivated, and if they are given sufficient time, low-quality instruction alone will prove fatal to the success of a lesson.

Hunter's Model

Carroll's model and the QAIT model identify variables that should be kept in mind as teachers plan direct instruction. Hunter's model prescribes what a direct instruction lesson should look like.

Hunter's model (1982, 1984) is probably the most widely recognized model for direct instruction. Hunter identifies seven elements that constitute an effective lesson.

1. **Anticipatory set** refers to a mind-set that leaves students curious about the remainder of the lesson. Their curiosity leads them to spec-

Teacher Interview: Have each student interview a teacher regarding those aspects of teaching that are under his or her control and those that are alterable.

Lecture Note: The point here is that the teacher's job is to ease learning without making learning easier.

Teaching Anecdote: Tell your students about the high school that began using a computer system to access various data bases. By using a computer students' research time was cut from weeks to days, and the computer searched for and located far more sources than the students previously had access to. Instead of being inundated with the amount of material, most students found the extra data helpful. Many students began using the computers during lunch and free periods with no specific assignment due, but rather to discover more on topics that interested them individually.

Ask your students why this change might have happened.

Chapter 15 Casebook Preview: See Science Is Only Real When You Do It.

Lecture Note: Using their observations of classrooms, ask students to discuss how the elements of the QAIT model interact.

Teacher Interview: Have each student interview a teacher whose teaching has been evaluated on the basis of Hunter's model.

objective and purpose The point at which students are provided explicitly with the objective or purpose of the lesson; the second element of Hunter's model of direct instruction.
input The presentation of new material in a well-organized and logical sequence; the third element of Hunter's model of direct instruction.
modeling The use of frequent examples in a lesson to clarify meanings; the fourth element of Hunter's model of direct instruction.
checking for understanding The evaluation of students' comprehension and understanding by means of oral or written questions; the fifth element of Hunter's model of direct instruction.
guided practice The provision of immediate feedback in the classroom after students answer questions and solve problems as a means of allowing them to check their own understanding; the sixth element of Hunter's model of direct instruction.
independent practice The tactic of encouraging students to answer questions and solve problems on their own. Immediate feedback is helpful and may occur after students have completed a homework assignment; the seventh element of Hunter's model of direct instruction.

Lecture Note: Ask students to compare Gagné's events of instruction with Hunter's model.

Field Observation: Have students talk with principals or curriculum supervisors regarding teacher evaluations.

ulate about or anticipate what is to come. This is the part of a lesson through which the teacher captures the attention of the student. (A good example of anticipatory set is the story about a truck load of canaries that you read in Chapter 8.)

2. **Objective and purpose,** the second element in Hunter's model, provides students explicitly with the objectives or purpose of the lesson. By informing the students of what you expect them to be able to do, you are building on the anticipatory set.

3. **Input** is the presentation of new material. Input, as an element of an effective lesson, requires that information be well organized and presented in a logical sequence. Hunter suggests that input can be made effective by presenting information in a verbal and a visual manner. (This practice exploits the dual-coding capabilities discussed in Chapter 6.)

4. **Modeling** means that you should use frequent examples in the lesson to clarify meanings. Hunter refers to the modeling phase of a lesson as "modeling what you mean." When the objective of the lesson is to attain a skill, modeling serves the same purpose as Bandura's observational learning. If the objective of the lesson is to attain a concept or acquire verbal information, modeling calls for the use of examples or analogies or metaphors.

5. **Checking for understanding** is the evaluation of students' comprehension and understanding by means of questions asked orally or on a written quiz. Students may be asked also to provide an example of the material on their own.

6. **Guided practice** begins the process of transfer by presenting students with a few problems or questions to answer on their own. Their practice in answering such questions is guided by immediate feedback in the classroom. This feedback gives students a way of checking their own understanding and receiving help on any aspect of the lesson that they may have misunderstood.

7. **Independent practice** encourages students to answer questions or work problems on their own. Providing immediate feedback after independent practice is particularly helpful. However, feedback may occur after students have completed a homework assignment, another form of independent practice.

Research on Hunter's Model

Stallings and Krasavage (1986) studied the effectiveness of Hunter's model as it was used in elementary grades. Teachers were taught the Hunter model as part of an in-service project that included two years of supervised program implementation and a one-year maintenance follow-up period, during which teachers and administrators were to continue the project on their own. During the two implementation years, teachers increased their use of Hunter's principles; however, they decreased their use during the last year. The amount of time students spent engaged in tasks and achievement of those tasks increased during the two years of implementation. These too decreased during the last year.

Students from classrooms in which teachers implemented the Hunter model were compared with control students. During the last year, the control subjects showed greater achievement gains than did those students in the classrooms taught using the Hunter model. The research suggests that Hunter's model is effective in producing achievement gains. The research by Stallings and Krasavage indicates also that close monitoring of classroom practice may be required in order for the Hunter model to be fully implemented. Some educational administrators have taken research such as the Stallings and Krasavage study to mean that teachers should be required to submit plans and to document their lessons. New teachers should not be surprised if evaluations of their teaching are based, to some extent, on a model for direct instruction.

Principles in Practice 10.2

Principles . . .
1. Direct instruction is teacher centered.
2. In planning direct instruction, teachers must account for those variables that are under their control.
3. Hunter's model identifies the elements of a lesson presented by means of a direct instruction.

. . . in Practice
In Teacher Chronicle 10.2, we visited two classrooms. The first classroom presented lessons that were teacher centered. The teacher, however, did not use direct instruction. The second classroom, Ms. Estefan's, was much more lively and, incidentally, less teacher centered. The telling difference between the classes was each teacher's attitude and enthusiasm.

1. What elements of Carroll's and Slavin's models were missing from Mr. Blandworth's class?
2. How would you plan a direct instruction lesson for the Word Power class?
3. What sorts of topics do and do not lend themselves to direct instruction?

Teacher Chronicle 10.3

A MAMMOTH UNDERTAKING

"How do we know something is true?" I asked my first graders. "Do we have to do something like climb a mountain, discover a dinosaur, or explore the ocean to believe it can be done?"

"I have seen people in pictures at the top of the mountain, so they must have climbed there," Marcus answered.

"We have never seen a live dinosaur but we know they once existed," Michael said.

"How do we know that?" I asked.

"We've seen their bones in a museum, like when we went on the field trip."

I guided this discussion toward mammoths.

"Who remembers what we call those gigantic sheets of ice that once covered our area?" Because we had already been studying glaciers, I decided to capitalize on this "connection."

"Ice blankets?" Shana asked tentatively.

"Good guess. But there is another word," I prompted.

"Glassiers?" Emily half-asked, half-said.

"Close. Real close," I encouraged.

Marcus popped up, "Glaciers!" he shouted.

Brian joined in. "Remember how you told how tall the glaciers were? As high as fifty schools stacked one on top of the other. And later we went outside and climbed the snowhills behind the playground and pretended those were glaciers."

Heads nodded as they remembered the experience.

"What kind of animals do you think lived near the glaciers?"

"Polar bears," James said.

"Dinosaurs?" Michael, our resident dinosaur expert, asked.

The class laughed.

"Michael, that's a good thought. Let's think about that. Were dinosaurs near the glaciers?"

"No," Michael said, shaking his head. "They didn't like the cold and besides, they were all extinct then. Maybe mammoths?" he asked.

"Did they like ice and snow?"

"It must be mammoths," Barbi nodded her head knowingly. She hadn't said a word yet.

"What did they look like?" I asked.

"They were big like elephants," Teresa said.

"And all hairy," Ernesto said.

"They had huge tusks that curved up," Mark added.

"Are there mammoths living today?" I asked.

"No, they're all dead," Michael said.

"What is the word for that?" I asked.

"They're extinct," said Kelly.

"Like the dinosaurs," Sharon added.

"Sharon's right," I told them. "The dinosaurs were dead long before mammoths lived here."

"Mammoths lived here?" Katy asked.

"No way," Paul said. "There was no town here when the mammoths were here."

And so I let the discussion continue for several minutes while they discussed what they knew about mammoths.

I had two goals in mind when I planned this lesson. First, I wanted the children to experience a beautiful picture book and to create original art of their own. My second goal was to help them distinguish between what is real and what is imaginary. *Will's Mammoth* was the perfect book to use to accomplish these goals because the artwork is intriguing and the story line is alternately real and imaginary.

As I read the book, we discussed each picture. The artwork intrigued the students. Why did the mammoth have rainbow-colored tusks? Did real mammoths have such tusks? They decided that Will's mammoth was not real; the rainbow colors reminded us that this adventure was in Will's imagination.

I then had them create pictures of themselves on mammoths. While they were working, I listened in on an excellent discussion.

"Was Will's mammoth real?" Chris asked Michael.

"No," answered Michael. "It's a fiction book."

"Then why does he fall asleep with the flower the mammoth gave him?"

"He just imagines it."

"No, he doesn't," Chris said, hopping up to get the book.

The two poured over the book, going back and forth from the scene where the mammoth plucks the flower and gives it to Will to the final page illustrating Will asleep with the flower in his hand.

"See, he does have the flower so the mammoth was real," Chris argued.

"No way," Michael countered. "The flower is not real."

"Then how can he be holding it?"

"I don't know," Michael answered. He looked puzzled, not quite so certain about his sense of what is real and what is imaginary.

As a concluding activity, we discussed what we knew was real about mammoths and what we had created using our imaginations. We reread *Will's Mammoth*, focusing on what we had learned and discovered. Each child told something new he or she had learned about mammoths.

Although mammoths had disappeared long ago, that week they were very much alive in my room.

> **general inductive model**
> Method of lesson presentation that guides thinking from specific examples as a starting point to a general principle or pattern as an ending point.

MODELS FOR TEACHING THINKING SKILLS

Chap. Obj. 5
Test Ques. 10.69–10.90

Thinking skills are grouped into two broad categories: inductive and deductive. Inductive thinking requires that the student examine specific examples and, from those examples, reason to a general pattern. (Bruner's notion of learning through discovery is based on inductive thinking.) Deductive thinking involves seeing or observing general patterns and reasoning to a specific conclusion based on the patterns. (Ausubel's notion of reception learning is based on deductive thinking.)

What follows is a brief discussion of models used to instruct students on how to think. The models examined here are described in greater detail in Eggen and Kauchak's *Strategies for Teachers* (1988) or in Gunter, Estes, and Schwab's *Instruction: A Models Approach* (1990).

Inductive Models

Eggen and Kauchak identify three inductive models: the general inductive model, the concept attainment model, and the integrative model. Let's examine each in turn.

The General Inductive Model

Eggen and Kauchak advise using the **general inductive model** to develop several skills important to inductive thinking, including observation, comparison, and pattern recognition. Suppose you were in the midst of a geography unit covering land formations. You have finished teaching your class about islands and peninsulas and are about to introduce the formation known as an isthmus. Imagine how you might teach the lesson using the inductive model by translating its four phases into concrete instructional actions. (The four phases of the general inductive model are provided in Table 10–1.)

Working through this inductive model using the isthmus as an example provides us with an instance of using the model to teach a concept. The inductive model can be used to teach other content objectives as well, namely,

Focus Question: What are the different ways of organizing a lesson to facilitate cognitive outcomes?

Journal Entry: Have students reflect on their styles of learning, answering the following questions: Do you normally tend toward inductive or deductive thinking? Is your usual approach a function of how you were taught or the type of problems you normally think about?

Chapter 15 Casebook Preview: See Beginning Each Day as a Learning Experience.

Chapter 15 Casebook Preview: See Writing Success in Science.

Lecture Note: Ask students to discuss their ideas for teaching a lesson on the formation known as an isthmus using the general inductive model in Table 10.1.

Teacher Interview: Have each student interview a teacher regarding his or her use of nonexamples.

Transparency: This table is duplicated in the acetate transparency package. See T-17 The General Inductive Model.

■ **Table 10–1** *The General Inductive Model*

Phase 1: The Open-ended Model
Present examples of a concept or principle (or nonexample). Have students observe and describe an example. Present a second example (or nonexample). Have students observe and describe the second example. Have students compare examples and nonexamples.

Phase 2: The Convergent Phase
Provide prompts to students that encourage them to identify patterns in the examples.

Phase 3: Closure
Explicate the concept or principle by defining it explicitly.

Phase 4: The Application Phase
Apply the definition using additional examples.

SOURCE: From *Strategies for Teachers: Teaching Content and Thinking Skills* (2nd ed., pp. 112–113) by P. D. Eggen and D. P. Kauchak, 1988, Englewood Cliffs, NJ: Prentice-Hall. Copyright 1988 by Prentice-Hall. Adapted by permission.

rules and higher-order rules. Using Gagné's learned capabilities, we can identify two main differences between teaching a concept and teaching a rule or a higher-order rule. In terms of the inductive model, the first difference is in the use of nonexamples.

Using nonexamples is very important when teaching a concept, particularly when the concept being learned is closely related to other concepts. In this case, the concept of isthmus is closely related to the concepts of peninsula and island. Rules and higher-order rules are often taught without using nonexamples.

The second difference between teaching a concept and a rule or higher-order rule is in the application phase. In the case of a concept, the model prescribes that the teacher provide additional examples for students to analyze and then asks the students to supply their own examples. In the case of a rule or higher-order rule, students would make an application by asking for additional examples or by using the rule or higher-order rule to explain an observation. (Consider using the inductive model to teach the following rule: The most efficient volume-to-surface-area ratio is that of a sphere. Students who have learned the rule could apply it by explaining why soap bubbles are spherical.)

The Concept Attainment Model

The **concept attainment model** emphasizes inductive and deductive thinking. It is categorized as an inductive model because it requires that the student use inductive reasoning. It differs from the general inductive model in that deductive reasoning is also required. (The concept attainment model in Table 10–2 was first suggested by Joyce and Weil, 1972.)

As you examine the concept attainment model, imagine that you are teaching the concept of counterpoint in music. Counterpoint is the use of two or more melodies at the same point in a composition.

■ Table 10–2 *The Concept Attainment Model*

Phase 1: Presentation of Examples
Examples and nonexamples are displayed.

Phase 2: Analysis of Hypotheses
Students hypothesize a name for the concept exemplified in Phase 1. After
initial hypotheses are generated, another example and nonexample are
displayed. Initial hypotheses are evaluated. Some are discarded, and new
hypotheses are added to the list. The cycle of examples–analyzing hypotheses–
examples continues until all hypotheses but one are eliminated.

Phase 3: Closure
Students are asked to define explicitly the remaining concept hypotheses and
to identify the characteristics of the concept.

Phase 4: Application
Students apply the concept by classifying examples or by generating examples
of the concept.

SOURCE: From *Strategies for Teachers: Teaching Content and Thinking Skills* (2nd ed., pp. 134–135)
by P. D. Eggen and D. P. Kauchak, 1988, Englewood Cliffs, NJ: Prentice-Hall. Copyright 1988
by Prentice-Hall. Adapted by permission.

> **integrative model** Method of
> lesson presentation that
> combines inductive skills,
> deductive skills, and content
> in one model.

Transparency: This table is duplicated
in the acetate transparency package.
See T-18 The Concept Attainment
Model.

The concept attainment model is quite similar to the inductive model.
Looking back at Phase 2 of the concept attainment model, however, we can
see how deductive skills are introduced through the analysis of hypotheses.
At this point, it is helpful to note that the phases of the inductive models
discussed so far can be recycled indefinitely. During the recycling, various
prompts can be provided by the teacher as a way of guiding students toward
the attainment of the content goal.

The Integrative Model

Both the inductive model and the concept attainment model combine the
development of thinking skills with content goals. The inductive model relies
on inductive reasoning; the concept attainment model reinforces inductive
skills but focuses, in the analysis of the hypothesis phase, on deductive skills.
The **integrative model** combines inductive skills, deductive skills, and content in one model (Eggen & Kauchak, 1985). Eggen and Kauchak, in describing the integrative model, acknowledge the early works of Taba as the
foundation for the integrative model (1965, 1966, 1967).

As you consider the integrative model, imagine that students are given
information about the types of cases being tried in the local judicial system:
the backlog of cases, the number of judges required, the number of juries
required for civil and criminal cases in the jurisdiction, and the local court's
budget. Imagine also that students are charged with reducing the caseload of
the courts without increasing the budget. (The five phases of the integrative
model are given in Table 10–3.)

Phase 1 in the integrative model taps the descriptive abilities of the students and develops intellectual skills to that end. Phase 2 provides the opportunity to compare two pieces of information. Discrimination is a skill that is
developed here. It is in Phase 3 that the thinking requirements for the student

Lecture Note: Have students discuss,
in small groups, how they would use
the concept attainment model to teach
the concept of counterpoint or another
concept of their choosing.

Teaching Anecdote: Tell your students
about the fourth-grade teacher who
paired students and then gave each
pair a rock, a ball of clay, a paper clip,
a bottle cap, and a pan of water. The
students were to predict which objects
would sink and which would float. After experimenting with the objects, the
students were to use the material they
had been studying about water displacement to get all of the objects to
float.

Ask your students how this project might combine inductive and deductive thinking skills. (The final
solution was to mold a boat from the
clay and place the other objects inside.)

Lecture Note: Have students discuss
the use of the integrative model to
teach a problem-solving lesson on the
issue of overcrowded courts.

■ **Table 10–3** *The Integrative Model*

Phase 1: Describe
Information is presented to the students who are encouraged to describe the data.

Phase 2: Compare
Additional information is presented to the students who describe and compare the new information with the information presented in Phase 1. The comparisons may range from observing similarities and differences between the two pieces of information to summarizing a pattern that exists between or within the pieces of information.

Phase 3: Explain
Having identified similarities and differences in Phase 2, students are asked to explain why differences/similarities exist.

Phase 4: Hypothesize
Having explained observed similarities and differences to the satisfaction of the teacher, students are asked to generalize or abstract. Thinking more generally and more abstractly is encouraged by asking students to respond to a hypothetical situation that exceeds the data presented in Phases 1 and 2.

Phase 5: Generalize
This phase achieves closure by asking students to form one or more generalizations that describe the pattern or patterns that exist in the information.

SOURCE: From *Strategies for Teachers: Teaching Content and Thinking Skills* (2nd ed., pp. 168–169) by P. D. Eggen and D. P. Kauchak, 1988, Englewood Cliffs, NJ: Prentice-Hall. Copyright 1988 by Prentice-Hall. Adapted by permission.

shift from inductive to deductive. Phases 4 and 5 are extensions of the deductive activity initiated in Phase 3.

The General Inquiry Model

Field Observation: Have students observe classes in which inductive approaches are used, documenting the steps used in the inductive lessons.

Chapter 15 Casebook Preview: See Science Is Only Real When You Do It.

The development of thinking skills "culminate[s] in the ability to systematically perform inquiry tasks" (Eggen & Kauchak, 1988, p. 207). The inquiry model is designed to teach students a systematic process by which they can approach questions or problems. The inquiry model is a way of encouraging students to consider facts, to make observations, and to use the accumulated information to answer questions or solve problems. (Table 10–4 provides a description of the five phases of the inquiry model.)

Imagine that students are asked, "Why are there ocean tides?" The question about ocean tides is a form of closed inquiry because the teacher has a definite generalization or answer in mind. Open inquiry can lead to a number of different, but equally good, solutions. The general inquiry model can be used in either an open or a closed inquiry mode.

The Suchman Model of Inquiry

Lecture Note: Have students discuss what specific steps they might take in using the general inquiry model.

Use of the general inquiry model often presents problems of time and expense for the classroom teacher. Richard Suchman (1966a, 1966b) developed a specialized inquiry model that uses student questions as a substitute for

■ **Table 10–4** *The General Inquiry Model*

Phase 1: Question or Problem Presentation
The question or problem is simply presented to the students in either written or verbal form. The teacher determines that students understand the question itself and any concepts that may be embedded in the question or problem statement.

Phase 2: Hypothesis Generation
Once the question or problem has been understood and any clarification provided, students are encouraged to provide tentative answers to the question, that is, to generate hypotheses. After students have generated a number of hypotheses, the hypotheses are evaluated. The result of the evaluation is a set of hypotheses listed in order of priority for investigation.

Phase 3: Data Collection
The hypotheses that receive priority guide the collection of information. Depending on time and expense, the teacher determines whether data collection will be done individually, in small groups, or by the class as a whole.

Phase 4: Assessment of Hypothesis
The data gathered in Phase 3 is used to assess the hypothesis being tested. During this phase, the teacher takes care that students do not allow the hypothesis to influence interpretation of data.

Phase 5: Generalization
Closure of the lesson is achieved in this phase by accepting, rejecting, or changing the hypothesis in light of the interpretation of data.
    A second way to achieve closure is to generalize from the basic conclusions in Phase 4. Teachers should guide students toward accepting conclusions as tentative and encourage students to use generalized conclusions as the basis for new questions to guide further inquiry.

SOURCE: From *Strategies for Teachers: Teaching Content and Thinking Skills* (2nd ed., pp. 214–217) by P. D. Eggen and D. P. Kauchak, 1988, Englewood Cliffs, NJ: Prentice-Hall. Copyright 1988 by Prentice-Hall. Adapted by permission.

what are often resource intensive data-gathering procedures. In the general inquiry model, collecting the data used to test the hypothesis can be very time consuming. If extensive library research is required to collect needed information, for example, the testing of the hypothesis can go on for weeks. Although the acquisition of such data-collection skills can be beneficial, there are times when the teacher wishes to concentrate on the process of conducting an inquiry and doing so within a short period of time. The Suchman model provides advantages in this regard.

The major difference between the Suchman inquiry model and the general inquiry model is in the data-collection phase. Suchman developed a means for collecting information through student questioning. Using Suchman's inquiry technique, students may ask questions that meet two requirements. First, the question must be answerable with a "yes" or a "no." Second, the answer to the question must be observable. For example, a student would not receive an answer to the question, "Does this have anything to do with supply and demand?" The answer to that question is not observable. Other than the difference in the data-collection phase, the Suchman inquiry model looks very similar to the general inquiry model (see Table 10–4).

Field Observation: Have each student observe a classroom in which the Suchman inquiry model is used or a classroom in which data are collected by means of yes/no questions, documenting the strengths and weaknesses of these data collection techniques.

Lecture Note: Have students discuss the kinds of concepts, skills, or problems that can be usefully approached using the Suchman inquiry model.

Connection: The concepts, rules, and higher-order rules mentioned here refer to Gagné's learned capabilities discussed in Chapter 9.

Journal Entry: Have students reflect on the deductive model of instruction, addressing the following questions: Does this model generally describe the way you were instructed in elementary and high school? Did you have a sense that your learning occurred in the phases described in the model? What is the advantage to having a sense of "phases" in your learning?

Connection: See the section on prior knowledge in Chapter 6.

Deductive Models

The General Deductive Model

The **general deductive model** guides thinking from a general standpoint to specific instances as an ending point. Like the inductive model, the general deductive model is designed to teach concepts, rules, or higher-order rules. Like the inductive model, the deductive model relies on examples. Both models require a high level of involvement by the teacher. Let's use the isthmus lesson mentioned earlier to examine the general inductive model. (Note the differences between an isthmus lesson planned using the general inductive model in Table 10–1 and the same lesson organized according to the general deductive model in Table 10–5.)

The deductive model is used in situations similar to those in which the inductive model is used. The major differences are that the activities in Phases 3 and 4 of the deductive model are the reverse of those in the inductive model. Using the general deductive model, students are provided with the object of the lesson in the first phase. They are provided with the generalization or pattern and, throughout the lesson, are asked to generate specific instances.

The Interactive Model

The **interactive model** is so labeled in order to emphasize the interaction between teacher and students, students and the new content being learned, and prior knowledge and new information. The interactive model is used when the students' learning goal is to attain organized bodies of knowledge for the long term. All of the models reviewed here are interactive, as Eggen and Kauchak have emphasized. The discussion of schemata as structures of prior knowledge (see Chapter 6) points us toward the goal that guides the use of the interactive model. That goal is to enable students to form schemata or, in the words of Eggen and Kauchak, "to structure knowledge."

■ **Table 10–5** *The General Deductive Model*

Phase 1: Presentation of the Abstraction
In this phase, the teacher provides a definition of the concept or a generalized statement, such as an advance organizer. The new abstraction is related to previously learned information. The objectives of the lesson are also supplied.

Phase 2: Illustrations
The teacher provides examples of the abstraction defined in Phase 1. The examples (nonexamples) may serve as illustrations as well. The classification of an illustration as an example or a nonexample is explained. Students are asked to provide illustrations.

Phase 3: Application
As in the inductive model, students provide additional examples of a concept or apply the rule to a new situation.

Phase 4: Closure
Students are asked to restate the concept or rule learned in the lesson.

SOURCE: From *Strategies for Teachers: Teaching Content and Thinking Skills* (2nd ed., pp. 260–264) by P. D. Eggen and D. P. Kauchak, 1988, Englewood Cliffs, NJ: Prentice-Hall. Copyright 1988 by Prentice-Hall. Adapted by permission.

The phases of the interactive model are based on David Ausubel's theory of meaningful verbal learning (1963). We have already discussed what serves as Phase 1 of the interactive model, namely the presentation of an *advance organizer.*

The second phase of the interactive model is called progressive differentiation. *Progressive differentiation* is the term given by Ausubel to the process of breaking down general concepts or rules into more concrete subsets. Large bodies of information can usually be represented in the form of hierarchies. For example, living things can be classified into subsets called kingdoms. The kingdoms are animals, plants, monerans, fungi, and protists. Under each kingdom are more specific classifications.

  Kingdoms
    Phyla
      Classes
        Orders
          Families
            Genera
              Species

The third phase in the interactive model is referred to as *integrative reconciliation*, a term also coined by Ausubel. Progressive differentiation is an attempt to separate ideas. Integrative reconciliation is an explicit attempt, on the part of the teacher, to identify relationships among the ideas that have been broken out during progressive differentiation. The purpose of this phase in the interactive model is to help students organize the ideas discovered during differentiation into a coherent whole. From the teacher's perspective, integrative reconciliation means asking students questions or requiring students to perform tasks that encourage the student to integrate prior knowledge and the new information. From the point of view of the students, integrative reconciliation requires that they form relationships between ideas. If we were to apply Gagné's theory of learned capabilities to this model, we would think in terms of rules, higher-order rules, and cognitive strategies.

Lecture Note: Tell students about the junior high student who used the following "newspaper headline" as a mnemonic for the classification hierarchy: King Phylum Clanged Order, Family Genius Speaks.

The Synectics Model

The **synectics model** for instruction is designed to enhance creative thinking and problem solving. However, according to Gunter, Estes, and Schwab (1990), there is an element of the model the purpose of which "is to provoke the learner into projecting his or her consciousness into the object or idea under consideration in an effort to experience an emotional understanding that goes beyond the merely cognitive" (p. 121).

The term *synectics* means "understanding together that which is apparently different." When a learner is able to connect ideas or objects that are not normally thought of together, he or she is thinking creatively—conceptualizing new relationships. William Gordon (1961) developed the process called synectics. It was used originally by people in industry to develop new products. Gordon has developed materials for classroom use, specifically, for teaching creative thinking and writing (see Gunter et al., 1990).

The synectics model makes use of three kinds of analogy: direct analogy, personal analogy, and symbolic analogy. A direct analogy compares metaphorically two objects, concepts, or ideas. For example, students might be asked, "How is a book like a street?" "How is liberty like a tomato plant?"

Lecture Note: Have students, working in small groups, take an earlier example such as the isthmus lesson or the question concerning ocean tides and design a lesson according to the interactive model.

humanistic education An approach to instruction that emphasizes the development of students' attitudes, feelings, and independent learning.

Connection: See the section on prior knowledge in Chapter 6.

Chapter 15 Casebook Preview: See Improvisation and Aesthetic Appreciation.

Journal Entry: Have students identify the topics, concepts, or issues they've covered in class using the synectics model. Ask them to justify their selections.

Chap. Obj. 6
Test Ques. 10.91–10.102

Lecture Note: A point of interest, B. F. Skinner was presented the Humanist of the Year Award by the American Humanist Society in 1972.

"How is the scientific method like a kitchen?" A direct analogy, as used in the synectics model, uses analogy and metaphor as a way of engaging the student's prior knowledge (see Chapter 6).

A personal analogy uses imagery to invoke the student's feelings. Students are encouraged to imagine themselves as the object or as part of the problem under discussion. For example, "How would you feel if you were a dolphin trained to perform at a marine amusement park?" "How would you feel if you were a computer who fell victim to a 'virus'?" "Do plants like to be eaten?" "What is it like to be a seeing-eye dog?" The idea behind the use of a personal analogy is that the learner project his or her own knowledge, attitudes, values, and feelings onto the material being presented.

The symbolic analogy is also referred to in the synectics model as "compressed conflict" (Gunter et al., 1990). The conflict is created by juxtaposing descriptions that appear to be contradictory. To make sense of the contradiction, the student must use creative insight. The compressed conflict often takes the form of an oxymoron. Consider, for example, what students would have to do in order to make sense of "a poor little rich girl," "thundering silence," and "meekly vicious." By forcing together opposing descriptions or, for younger students, forcing together terms that "fight" with each other, students can gain a new viewpoint on the material of a lesson.

The process of synectics, developed by Gordon, is the basis for the model of instruction presented in Table 10–6.

INSTRUCTION FOR AFFECTIVE OUTCOMES

The approaches to instruction that we have emphasized in the chapter thus far reflect a concern with enhancing the skills and knowledge of students. The major focus has been on the attainment of cognitive outcomes. There is, however, another important category of outcomes, namely, the affective domain.

Humanistic Education

Approaches to instruction that emphasize affective outcomes fall into the category of **humanistic education,** which came into being as the result of a concern that behavioristic and cognitive approaches to learning failed to account for the feelings of students in regard to what they learned, with whom they learned, and under what conditions they learned. Proponents of the view employed the term *humanistic education* in order to call the attention of educators to the "human" side of learning. (Incidentally, many behaviorists and cognitivists resent the implication that only humanists are concerned with the human side of learning.)

Perhaps the most famous example of humanistic education was described in a book entitled *Summerhill* (Neill, 1960). *Summerhill* described an English school that was run on the basis of the principles of humanistic education. If you had been enrolled in a teacher education program in the early 1970s, it is likely you would have been assigned *Summerhill* as required reading. The headmaster of Summerhill described the philosophy of the school as follows: "The child is innately wise and realistic. If left to himself [or herself] without adult suggestion of any kind, he [or she] will develop as far he [or she] is capable of developing" (Neill, 1960, p. 4). At Summerhill, many of the deci-

■ **Table 10–6** *The Synectics Model*

Step 1: Describing the Topic
Select a topic to explore with your class, one related to the subject matter that you are teaching. The topics may be as varied as the concept of asynchrony in theoretical physics, the Treaty of Versailles, Louis in E. B. White's *Trumpet of the Swan,* or the butterfly stroke in swimming. Ask your students to describe the topic. Record their descriptions.

Step 2: Create Direct Analogies
Select a category, such as colors, machines, animals, plants, or movie stars. Have your students examine the descriptions generated in Step 1 so that they can describe how the topic described in Step 1 is like an item from the selected category. Have the students explain their choices.

Step 3: Describe Personal Analogies
Direct your students to select one of the direct analogies created in Step 2 and create a personal analogy. Students are asked to become the object and to describe how it feels and/or works. Record the words students use to describe their feelings.

Step 4: Identify Compressed Conflicts
Direct students while they create several compressed conflicts, using words from the personal analogies developed in Step 3. Students can be asked to pair words that "fight" with each other or to create word pairs that are charged with tension.

Step 5: Create a New Direct Analogy
Have students use one of the word pairs (a compressed conflict) to create another direct analogy. They create the new direct analogies by choosing objects that are described by the compressed conflicts.

Step 6: Reexamine the Original Topic
Return to the original topic you selected in Step 1 and explore it with your class. Have students generate some kind of product (painting, sketch, photograph, skit, essay, journal entry, dance, poem, etc.) based on the ideas generated in the synectics process. The product can focus either on the final analogy created in Step 5 or on ideas created throughout the entire process.

SOURCE: From *Instruction: A Models Approach* (pp. 122–125) by M. A. Gunter, T. H. Estes, and J. H. Schwab, 1990, Needham Heights, MA: Allyn & Bacon. Copyright 1990 by Allyn & Bacon. Adapted by permission.

sions about learning activities were made by the students themselves. For example, reading instruction was not initiated according to some prescribed curricular calendar; it was initiated for a particular student when, and only when, that student requested it.

Although not all programs of humanistic education are as student directed as the Summerhill program was, nonetheless, one of the hallmarks of humanistic education is that students make many of the decisions regarding their own instruction. Students are encouraged to find ways to direct their own learning and motivate themselves rather than be passive. Humanistic education can be thought of as a reaction against the conduit metaphor (Reddy, 1979). The *conduit metaphor* indicates that the nature of communication in a classroom starts with a sender—usually the teacher—moves through some communication channel, and is received by the student. By assuming

Connection: See the discussion of "good choosers" and "bad choosers" in Maslow's hierarchy of needs (Chapter 8).

Issues in Educational Psychology

CNN™ This box relates to Segment 10 of the CNN videotape. See the Instructor's Section for a summary.

EDUCATION IN JAPAN

Japan emerged from self-imposed isolation in the last century only to come face-to-face with an industrialized West. To compete successfully, the country needed to train a technological elite and a literate work force. In 1872, reformers established a national education system. Today, the Ministry of Education is the hub around which Japanese schools turn. It is the Ministry that establishes the curricula and approves all textbooks.

Japan's primary and secondary schools are viewed in the United States as a standard against which American schools are judged. But U.S. educators who have spent time in Japan, as well as the Japanese themselves, have observed flaws in this highly praised system. In Japanese schools, discipline isn't a problem, students are well behaved, and uniforms are common. But conformity is the rule by which teachers and students live.

Peggy Lukens teaches English in a Cincinnati high school. In her year teaching in Japan, she discovered the truth behind a number of myths regarding Japanese education. One of those myths concerns the amount of time Japanese students attend class. Lukens related in the *Education Digest* that there are a number of days when students don't have class. From early December to early April, her Japanese students had twenty-one school days with no formal classes, and recesses totalling another twenty days. Even with half-day classes on Saturday, her Japanese students had an equal number of weekly class periods as her American students.

In Japanese high schools, students become walking encyclopedias as they memorize a myriad of facts, from the names of the Chinese dynasties to the dates of the Napoleonic wars. Nina Hurwitz, who teaches history in a surburban New York high school, described Japanese classes for *Teacher Magazine*. Japanese teachers lecture with no interruptions, transmitting "an astounding volume of facts." But students have no time to engage in debate with so much material to cover. Hurwitz observed that "the authoritarian nature of the Japanese classroom gives young adults the impression that it is acceptable to receive information from a single source without question."

Vast knowledge is necessary to pass the university admission tests that are the sole source for acceptance in most schools. "Applicants must take the entrance exam at each university to which they apply," said Lukens. She emphasized that each spring students "zip from test to test and city to city—all within a week or so. No wonder the students collapse."

The result of this academic preparation is best summed up by Miki Kurosu, a manager at Nissan Motor Corporation. Kurosu told the *Los Angeles Times* that all his high school cramming "might have helped me in TV quiz shows, but not in academic pursuits."

According to critics, Japan's universities do little to generate academic excellence once students are enrolled. Undergraduates are left rudderless, taking courses haphazardly. Little is demanded of them. Universities turn out graduates who lack intellectual creativity. In the same *Times* article, Makoto Kikuchi, executive technical adviser to Sony Corporation, lamented the fact that "Japanese university students are like canned food. They're almost all alike."

The Ministry of Education has begun to implement some reforms. But it will take a national consensus among parents, students, teachers, and the Ministry before Japan's schools significantly alter their present course.

SOURCES: Watanabe, Teresa. "Cookie-Cutter Education." *Los Angeles Times* 109 (June 24, 1990): D1. Lukens, Peggy. "Probing the 'Myths' about Japanese Education." *Education Digest* 59, issue 9 (May 1989): 13–16. Hurwitz, Nina. "Turning Japanese." *Teacher Magazine* 1, no. 8 (May 1990).

1. If you were placed in charge of Japanese education, which of the instructional models in this chapter would you advocate the increased use of?

2. Based on Gagné's sequence of instructional events, how effective is the Japanese emphasis on lecturing in creating students who can think?

that students should be active rather than passive during classroom instruction, humanistic educators have taken an opposite tack from the one suggested by this metaphor. (Cognitive approaches to instruction also imply an active learner. An essential difference between cognitive approaches and affective approaches is in the origin of instructional decisions. For the former, decisions originate with the teacher.)

Humanistic education also emphasizes how important it is that students acquire values as part of their education (Combs, 1967; Glasser, 1969; Rogers, 1969). Student values must be inferred from their behavior: An honest student is not likely to cheat; a student who is respectful shares, is courteous, and respects the rights of others (cf. Davis, 1983). We can infer that a student values schoolwork if he or she follows directions, meets deadlines, and works hard. Humanistic educators attempt to model and, when possible, reinforce behaviors that reflect desirable values.

Nongraded Evaluation

Another characteristic of humanistically oriented classrooms is nongraded evaluation. The methods of formal evaluation, including standardized testing, that lead to letter grades are not viewed as desirable. Kirschenbaum, Simon, and Napier (1971) suggest that using written evaluations or no evaluations at all are more consistent with the goals of humanistic approaches to

Teaching Anecdote: Tell your students about the teacher who describes her approach to teaching in this way, "If I can make the students feel comfortable and enjoy being here, I can teach them anything."

Ask your students if this is an appropriate way to approach teaching. Why or why not? How would they respond to such a teacher? Ask them if this might be the way they feel as teachers themselves.

Connection: Classroom evaluation is discussed in detail in Chapter 13.

Visual aids in the classroom, such as a telescope, can actively involve students with the subject matter that is being taught.

Carol Jago

Santa Monica High School

Santa Monica, California

Coming from a family of teachers, I never wanted to be one. Almost by accident I found myself in the University of Southern California Education Department being asked, "Where would you like to student teach, Arcadia or Santa Monica?"

New to Los Angeles, I hesitantly replied, "I think Santa Monica is closer to where I'm staying." After one week in an eighth-grade classroom, I knew I could never leave. Fifteen years later, I thank heaven for that hasty decision.

For several years, my greatest contribution to education was enthusiasm. I was endlessly delighted by my students' ideas and work, and publishing the yearbook, newspaper, and literary magazine. Ah, the energy of youth! Fortuitous exposure to the UCLA Writing Project and the Poets in the Schools Program helped me to guide their sheer energy with sound pedagogical principles for the teaching of writing and literature. When I moved to the district high school in 1978, I continued advising the yearbook staff. I also became involved in the publishing of a great deal of student work in various forms.

I measure my accomplishments by how well I've been able to facilitate my students' success. Many of my remedial students had never before seen their writing in print. As an incentive, I make their stories, poems, and letters as public as possible, sending booklets to parents, administrators, the board of education, middle schools, and local papers. In this way, students see the purpose of correctness in writing; they feel that they have joined the literate community. I am proud of my students, and not only those who are admitted to Harvard and Yale. I'm proud of their confidence with literature, their honest and natural voices in writing, their understanding that language is powerful and that this power can be theirs.

Education can be seen as a simple transaction between the knower and the learner. The goods labeled "knowledge" are packaged and passed unmodified from one person to another. Tidy as this model may sound, in my experience it just doesn't work. For learning to be meaningful, it must be interactive. Teacher and students together must wrestle with text, discover what it means in their world, and create meaning for themselves. In this

Connection: See the section on the undermining effect in Chapter 6.

instruction than evaluation designed to "label" the quality or quantity of the student's performance.

The opposition to formal evaluation procedures among humanistically oriented educators is consistent with one final principle of humanistic approaches to instruction. That principle is that learning should be valued for its own sake. The reasoning behind the principle is that if students work continually toward a goal of obtaining a good grade, they are less likely to focus on the rewards of accomplishment itself. Humanistic educators point to the undermining effect (discussed in Chapter 6) as a rationale for avoiding graded performances. All educators, no matter what approach to instruction they favor, share the goal of developing a positive attitude toward learning in their students. Humanistic approaches to instruction simply emphasize the rewards of learning rather than the independent evaluation of that learning.

As a consequence of this approach students in humanistic classrooms frequently have opportunities to discover new information and to use the new information to solve problems independently. Simulations, field trips,

process, the teacher is primarily a catalyst, but she or he must also serve as a resource and manager of the time and space. The goal is to create an environment within which students learn how to learn.

Pleasure is a key ingredient in an interactive classroom: the pleasure of figuring out something for yourself, the pleasure of working with friends on a project, the pleasure of watching students perform *The Idylls of the King* encased in aluminum foil. I could fill a hope chest with the bed sheets that have been left behind from a decade of Caesar skits. Emotional responses to literature stay with us long after we've forgotten the characters' names. Learning that is attached to feeling lasts.

I want students to see their work in the classroom as real. Their essays are not meant to be practice for college; they are living, breathing pieces of writing. Their ideas may need sharing and refining, but they are no less valid for that.

In my opinion, an outstanding teacher is one who is also a lifelong learner and who has developed strategies for helping students become the same. To accomplish this, a teacher will need to read current research with an open mind, adapt new ideas to her students' needs, and listen. A teacher who listens carefully to the sounds of her classroom will know intuitively what tomorrow's lesson should be.

The rewards I find in teaching are many. The work is intellectually stimulating and endlessly fascinating. When I watch my students struggle together with a poem—matching wits, defending their views, finding meaning if not consensus—I feel that my classroom is a laboratory for the human experiment. I see growth.

Another reward is the knowledge that I am engaged in something worth doing, something that does make a difference. Very few professionals in other fields receive letters like this one from Roberto Ramirez.

Dear Miss Jago,

Out of all the teachers in my life you are the only one who didn't write a retard on me or didn't throw me out the class. You stirred up many thoughts and emotions. I have grone in this class.

The Nut,
Beto

I believe that I make a difference, that the brains God gave me are being used to help others find their way through the maze of modern life.

and role playing are features of humanistically oriented classrooms. Reflect on some of the cognitive models for instruction presented in this chapter. You can see that many of those models would fit easily into a humanistic approach to instruction. Because the humanistic approach focuses on the goal of valuing learning for its own sake, the ability to think metacognitively is especially important to it.

In sum, humanistic approaches to instruction attempt to

1. allow students to make decisions concerning their own learning activities.
2. emphasize the development of values by focusing on affective outcomes.
3. avoid formal evaluation techniques that utilize grades or other forms of labeling.
4. teach students how to think metacognitively so that they will value learning for its own sake.

Focus Question: What are the different ways of organizing a lesson to facilitate affective outcomes?

MODELS FOR TEACHING AFFECTIVE OUTCOMES

After reflecting on the principles of humanistic education and cognitively oriented models of instruction, we see that affective outcomes can be attained in a variety of ways. Even so, there are models for instruction that focus directly on affective outcomes. We conclude our examination of approaches to instruction by considering two such models.

The Exploration of Feelings Model

The exploration of feelings model and the conflict resolution model that follows were developed by Hilda Taba (1971). The models are related and often used in tandem in the classroom. The purpose of the exploration of feelings model is to enable students to understand the perspectives of others. To this end, it is necessary that they explore the feelings and perspectives that other people bring to bear on particular events, ideas, or issues. The exploration of feelings model uses as its basic information not only facts, ideas, and concepts, but also the emotions and behaviors of other people.

Teacher Interview: Have each student interview a teacher regarding how his or her students respond to lessons that focus on other people's emotions.

According to Gunter et al. (1990), the exploration of feelings model can be used across grade levels and content areas. Because the model focuses on

The different models of instruction a teacher uses can reflect his or her personality. For example, a teacher who employs the exploration of feelings model tends to be attuned to the emotions and behaviors of others, as well as to concepts and facts.

Step 1: Prepare List
List all facts pertinent to the already selected conflict. The key question answered by students in this step is, What happened? The focus is on what happened to people involved in the conflict. Students answers are recorded; they form the "data base" for the remaining steps.

Step 2: Draw Inferences
Students, after describing *what* happened in Step 1, are now asked to infer *how* the people involved in the conflict felt.

Step 3: Hypothesize About Feelings
Having identified the feelings of the people involved in the conflict, the next step is to hypothesize or speculate about the reasons *why* people felt as they did. This step can be carried out after each student describes how someone felt, or the step can be performed after all descriptions of feelings have been collected and recorded.

Step 4: Describe Similar Experiences
Students are asked to identify with the people in the conflict situation by recalling their own experiences, which may be similar. Students describe the situations and their feelings at the time, and offer reasons for why they felt as they did.

Step 5: Compare Feelings
Students are asked to determine if the feelings they experienced are similar or different from the feelings of the people in the conflict situation. After comparisons are made, the key question becomes, Are there any general conclusions that can be made concerning people who find themselves in situations similar to the conflict situation?

SOURCE: From *Instruction: A Models Approach* (pp. 188–191) by M. A. Gunter, T. H. Estes, and J. H. Schwab, 1990, Needham Heights, MA: Allyn & Bacon. Copyright 1990 by Allyn & Bacon. Adapted by permission.

affective outcomes, one might expect this model to enhance the atmosphere of a classroom. Gunter et al. argue that an open discussion of feelings within the class helps to bring individuals within that class closer together. This position is reminiscent of the "classroom as community" idea in Lickona's model of moral education (see Chapter 3). In such a classroom atmosphere, disruptive behavior is less likely to occur.

The steps in the exploration of feelings model are initiated after a conflict has been selected (see Table 10–7). The conflict can be a synopsis of an actual event, a hypothetical situation, or a conflict in literature or history.

The exploration of feelings model is designed to be used as a precursor for the resolution of conflict model. Hilda Taba argues that conflicts between people are best resolved when the people involved in the conflict are aware of and are sensitive to the feelings of others (1971; see also, Gunter et al., 1990). A teacher who uses the exploration of feelings model until his or her students are proficient at understanding the feelings of others, and communicating their understanding, helps these students become better prepared to resolve conflicts.

Field Observation: Have each student observe a classroom in which the exploration of feelings model or a similar affect-oriented model is implemented, documenting the nature of the interaction between the teacher and his or her students and among students themselves.

Lecture Note: Point out that the exploration of feelings model and the resolution of conflict model are often implemented in tandem.

Chapter 15 Casebook Preview: See Gifted Achievers and Underachievers.

The Conflict Resolution Model

The conflict resolution model is used in an effort to attain affective objectives with regard to empathy, cooperation, and interpersonal relations. The model is closely related, conceptually and procedurally, to the exploration of feelings model. Indeed, some authors present exploration and resolution as separate

■ **Table 10–8** *The Conflict Resolution Model*

Step 1: Prepare List
List all facts pertinent to the already selected conflict. (This step is identical to Step 1 in the exploration of feelings model.)

Step 2: Draw Inferences
Students, after describing *what* happened in Step 1, are now asked to infer *how* the people involved in the conflict felt. (This step is identical to Step 2 in the exploration of feelings model.)

Step 3: Propose Resolutions
Given the feelings attributed to people in the conflict situation, students propose and defend resolutions, which must be generated within the context of the feelings of the people in the conflict situation.

Step 4: Decide Best Solution
After possible solutions are presented, students decide which of the solutions is the best one and offer reasons for its selection.

Step 5: Describe Similar Situations
Students are asked to relate the selected solution to their own experience by describing a similar situation from their own experience. Students describe the situation and what happened to them in that situation. (This is similar but not identical to Step 4 in the exploration model.)

Step 6: Describe the Feelings of Others
Using the personal experience described in Step 5, students describe the feelings of the other people imagined to be involved in their personal experience.

Step 7: Evaluate Personal Situation
Students are asked to evaluate their handling of the situation described in Step 5. After providing reasons for their own actions, students are asked to speculate on why the other people in their personal situation might act as they did.

Step 8: Alternative Solutions
Students generate solutions to their personal situations other than the solution that occurred. Each alternative solution is evaluated by asking what the outcome of the conflict might have been if the alternative solution had been tried.

Step 9: Generalizations
Students are asked to generalize about how people handle situations similar to the original conflict situation and the similar personal situations. Students are also asked to explain why those typical reactions occur in such situations. (This is similar to Step 5 in the exploration of feelings model.)

SOURCE: From *Instruction: A Models Approach* (pp. 192–197) by M. A. Gunter, T. H. Estes, and J. H. Schwab, 1990, Needham Heights, MA: Allyn & Bacon. Copyright 1990 by Allyn & Bacon. Adapted by permission.

strategies that are part of the same model for instruction (cf. Gunter et al., 1990). We consider the models separately because the affective objectives attained by use of the exploration model are prerequisite to the objectives pursued through the use of the resolution model. (The steps in the conflict resolution model are listed in Table 10–8.)

Taba's models of exploration and resolution are presented here as affect-oriented models for instruction. Clearly, there are cognitive elements in these models just as there are affective elements present in the cognitive-oriented models examined earlier in this chapter. The degree to which cognitive and affective goals are sought is, and should be, a function not of the model used, but of the teacher who uses a particular model.

Lecture Note: Emphasizing this point affords another opportunity to identify the distinction among cognitive, affective, and psychomotor domains of behavior as being one of conceptual convenience.

Principles in Practice 10.3

Principles . . .

1. Inductive models for teaching thinking encourage students to "discover" essential concepts.
2. Deductive models for teaching thinking encourage students to generate specific examples and applications.
3. Humanistic education and affect-oriented instructional models encourage student choice.

. . . in Practice

In Teacher Chronicle 10.3, the teacher wanted students to distinguish between reality and fantasy. The teacher encouraged the students to discuss a story that combined the two elements. Not only did the teacher seek opinions from the students, but students were asked to justify their opinions. The models for thinking incorporate these elements in a variety of ways.

1. Which model for teaching thinking best characterizes the events in Teacher Chronicle 10.3?
2. Without using the story, what model for teaching thinking would you have used to encourage students to explore the difference between reality and fantasy?
3. What elements of humanistic education did you observe in the lesson from the Chronicle?

CONCLUSION

Assign Chapter 10 of the *Study Guide*.

Models for instruction are like blueprints. A blueprint provides a plan for that which will be built. Although the blueprint identifies what elements will be built and how those elements will relate to each other, it does not specify the techniques that will be used to construct the various elements of the building. Models for instruction provide us with the elements of a lesson and suggest the sequence in which those elements should occur. But, as Eggen and Kauchak (1988) point out, no model can be so prescriptive as to eliminate the professional judgments of teachers and remain an effective model for instruction.

In Chapter 9, we discussed one aspect of instructional planning: how we best determine the outcomes that we ask our students to pursue. In this chapter, we have examined another aspect of instructional planning: how we design the actions we take in while attempting to guide our students toward the outcomes we desire for them. When we decide on the instructional actions to take, we must do so with the instructional outcomes we desire in mind. The capabilities and the thinking skills we wish to engender in our students are not the only determinants of our instructional methods, however. The question, "How to teach?" must be answered within a context.

Models may provide the structure for our teaching efforts, but human beings—teachers and students—provide the context. Teaching is a highly personal activity. How we teach depends very much on who we are. Eggen and Kauchak have assumed, in presenting their models for instruction, that teachers will take some liberties with the models. They assume that teachers will adapt these models to better suit their own personalities in the classroom.

Each student responds differently to the instructional actions of a teacher. If our job is to facilitate the achievement of our students, we must make decisions about instructing them while keeping their individual characteristics in mind. We should follow the lead of Eggen and Kauchak in not setting up one model for instruction as superior to other models. There is no one best way to teach, and the effective teacher, responding to his or her own strengths or weaknesses, the characteristics of his or her students, and the instructional outcomes he or she desires, must be equipped with a supply of instructional behaviors. Finding one set of instructional actions and following it day after day leads to teaching that is so uninspired as to be worth nothing.

Having examined the types of strategic decisions teachers make as they plan for instruction, we will proceed to consider the nature of actual classroom interaction. In classrooms plans go awry; plans must be modified; plans work beyond our wildest expectations.

In Chapter 11, we will examine various types of instructional interactions. The models presented in this chapter are instructional strategies; the next chapter examines a repertoire of instructional tactics.

Chapter Summary

Introduction: Planning for Action
Determining outcomes are not the only strategic decisions that teachers have to make. They must also decide what approaches to instruction they will use if they are to accomplish the outcomes they've specified.

Instruction and Learning
Gagné's Instructional Events
One way to view the connection between the teacher's instructional actions and the student's learning processes is by means of Gagné's instructional

events, each of which supports the cognitive processes in a phase of learning.

Discovery and Reception Learning
Instruction can facilitate either discovery learning or reception learning. Discovery learning is inductive. Students are presented with specifics and guided to general principles. Reception learning is deductive. Students are presented with general principles and guided to specific applications of these principles. Both types of learning are meaningful only if students actively process information.

Transfer of Learning
Vertical and Lateral Transfer
Transfer of learning means applying information learned in one situation to new situations. Previous learning can be transferred laterally or vertically, depending on the complexity of the new situation.

Planning Direct Instruction
Carroll's Model of School Learning
Carroll identifies variables that teachers should keep in mind when planning direct instruction. The variables concern the amount of time students require to master material.

The QAIT Model
The QAIT model is also useful for planning direct instruction. The QAIT model focuses on those aspects of school learning that are under the teacher's control.

Hunter's Model
Hunter's model specifies seven steps that should be included in every direct instruction lesson: anticipatory set, objective and purpose, input, modeling, checking for understanding, guided practice, and independent practice.

Models for Teaching Thinking Skills
Inductive Models
Models for teaching thinking provide step-by-step prescriptions to facilitate student thinking. Inductive models are those that begin with specific examples and move the student to an understanding of a general concept or principle.

The General Inquiry Model
The general inquiry model and the Suchman inquiry model stress student participation in gathering information. Inquiry models can also be used to help students frame problems.

Deductive Models
Deductive models are those which start with general concepts and, through several steps, help students reason to specific instances or examples of the more inclusive idea.

Instruction for Affective Outcomes
Humanistic Education
Humanistic education suggests approaches to teaching that allow students to make choices about what they will learn. The notion emphasizes affective outcomes so that students will learn to value learning for its own sake.

Models for Teaching Affective Outcomes
The Exploration of Feelings Model
Instructional models that focus on affective outcomes also facilitate thinking. The exploration of feelings model enables students to focus their thinking on the status of their own feelings.

The Conflict Resolution Model
The conflict resolution model is an effective instructional model that helps students reason in situations where their opinions, beliefs, or feelings may run counter to those of other individuals or groups.

Reflections: Building Your Theory of Teaching

10.1 Suppose you were required to teach vocabulary lessons from a workbook. Begin your reflection by imagining that you used Mr. Blandworth's approach. Consider what sorts of cognitive outcomes you might expect from your students. Consider also what sorts of affective outcomes might be realized. After reflecting on Mr. Blandworth's approach, decide how you would choose to teach vocabulary skills. Assume that you are required to cover the material in a workbook assigned by the district.

10.2 The district's curriculum guide calls for lessons on pollution. Design a conflict situation around the pollution theme. Decide how you would use the exploration of feelings model and the conflict resolution model to teach the lessons on pollution.

10.3 As a substitute teacher, you are required to teach a lesson on the Constitution of the United States to eighth graders. Select appropriate cognitive objectives. Then select one of the models for teaching thinking skills and outline a lesson according to that model. After you see your lesson on paper, reflect on the match between your objectives and the model you selected.

Key Terms

Suggested Readings

Eggen, D. P., & Kauchak, P. D. (1988). *Strategies for teachers*. Englewood Cliffs, NJ: Prentice-Hall.

Gagné, R. M. (1985). *The conditions of learning* (4th ed.). New York: Holt, Rinehart & Winston.

Gagné, R. M., & Driscoll, M. P. (1988). *Essentials of learning for instruction* (2nd ed.). Englewood Cliffs, NJ: Prentice-Hall.

Gunter, M. A., Estes, T. H., and Schwab, J. H. (1990). *Instruction: A models approach*. Needham Heights, MA: Allyn & Bacon.

References

Ausubel, D. P. (1963). Is drill necessary? The mythology of incidental learning. *Bulletin, National Association of Secondary School Principals, 47*, 44–50.

Ausubel, D. P., Novak, J. D., & Hanesian, H. (1978). *Educational psychology: A cognitive view* (2nd ed.). New York: Holt, Rinehart & Winston.

Ausubel, D. P., & Youseff, M. (1963). Role of discriminability in meaningful parallel learning. *Journal of Educational Psychology, 54*, 331–336.

Bell-Gredler, M. E. (1986). *Learning and instruction: Theory into practice*. New York: Macmillan.

Bloom, B. S. (1976). *Human characteristics and school learning*. New York: McGraw-Hill.

Brown, A. L. (1988). Motivation to learn and understand: On taking charge of one's own learning. *Cognition and Instruction, 5*, 311–321.

Bruner, J. S. (1960). *The process of education*. New York: Vintage Books.

Carroll, J. B. (1989). The Carroll model: A 25-year retrospective and prospective view. *Educational Researcher, 18*, 26–31.

Clark, C. M., & Peterson, P. L. (1986). Teachers' thought processes. In M. Witrock (Ed.), *Handbook of research on teaching* (3rd ed.). New York: Macmillan.

Combs, A. W. (Ed.). (1967). *Humanizing education: The person in the process*. Washington, DC: Association for Supervision and Curriculum Development, National Education Association.

Cunningham, D. J. (1977). The retention of connected discourse: A review. *Review of Educational Research, 42*, 47–71.

Davies, G. A. (1985). *Educational psychology: Theory and practice*. Reading, MA: Addison-Wesley.

Eggen, P. D., & Kauchak, D. (1985). Thinking skills in the classrooms: Where do they fit? How can they be integrated? *Impact on Instructional Improvement, 19*(4), 11–18.

Eggen, P. D., & Kauchak, D. P. (1988). *Strategies for teachers: Teaching content and thinking skills* (2nd ed.). Englewood Cliffs, NJ:; Prentice-Hall.

Gagné, R. M. (1977). *The conditions of learning* (3rd ed.). New York: Holt, Rinehart & Winston.

Gagné, R. M. (1985). *The conditions of learning* (4th ed.). New York: Holt, Rinehart & Winston.

Glasser, W. (1969). *Schools without failure.* New York: Harper & Row.

Gordon, W. J. J. (1961). *Synectics: The development of creative capacity.* New York: Harper & Row.

Gunter, M. A., Estes, T. H., & Schwab, J. H. (1990). *Instruction: A models approach.* Needham Heights, MA: Allyn & Bacon.

Hunter, M. (1982). *Mastery teaching.* El Segundo, CA: TIP Publications.

Hunter, M. (1984). Knowing, teaching, and supervising. In P. Hosford (Ed.), *Using what we know about teaching.* Alexandria, VA: Association for Supervision and Curriculum Development.

Joyce, B., & Weil, M. (1972). *Models of learning.* Englewood Cliffs, NJ: Prentice-Hall.

Joyce, B., & Weil, M. (1986). *Models of teaching.* (3rd ed.). Englewood Cliffs, NJ: Prentice-Hall.

Kirschenbaum, H., Simon, S. B., & Napier, R. W. (1971). *Wad-Ja-Get? The grading game in American education.* New York: Hart Publishing.

Mayer, R. E. (1975). Information processing variables in learning to solve problems. *Review of Educational Research, 45,* 525–541.

Mayer, R. E. (1976). Some conditions of meaningful learning of computer programming: Advance organizers and subject control of frame sequencing. *Journal of Educational Psychology, 68,* 143–150.

Mayer, R. E. (1987). *Educational psychology: A cognitive approach.* Boston, MA: Little, Brown.

Mayer, R. E., & Bromage, B. K. (1980). Different recall protocols for technical texts due to advance organizers. *Journal of Educational Psychology, 72,* 209–225.

McCutcheon, G. (1980). How do elementary school teachers plan? The nature of planning and influence on it. *The Elementary School Journal, 81*(1), 4–23.

Neill, A. S. (1960). *Summerhill: A radical approach to child rearing.* New York: Hart.

Reddy, M. (1979). The conduit metaphor: A case of frame conflict in our language about language. In A. Ortony (Ed.). *Metaphor and thought.* New York: Cambridge University Press.

Rogers, C. (1969). *Freedom to learn.* Columbus, OH: Charles E. Merrill.

Rosenshine, B. (1979). Content, time, and direct instruction. In P. Perterson & H. Walberg (Eds.), *Research on teaching: Concepts, findings, and implications.* Berkeley, CA: McCutchan.

Rosenshine, B. (1986). Synthesis of research on explicit teaching. *Educational Leadership, 43*(7), 60–69.

Royer, J. M. (1979). Theories of the transfer of learning. *Educational Psychologist, 14,* 53–69.

Salomon, G., & Perkins, D. N. (1989). Rocky roads to transfer: Rethinking mechanisms of a neglected phenomenon. *Educational Psychologist, 24*(2), 113–142.

Slavin, R. (1987). Cooperative learning and the cooperative school. *Educational Leadership, 45,* 7–13.

Slavin, R. (1988). Cooperative learning: A best-evidence synthesis. In R. E. Slavin (Ed.), *School and classroom organization.* Hillsdale, NJ: Erlbaum.

Stallings, J., & Krasavage, E. M. (1986). Program implementation and student achievement in a four-year Madaline Hunter follow-through project. *Elementary School Journal, 87*(2), 117–138.

Suchman, R. (1966a). *Inquiry development program: Developing inquiry.* Chicago, IL: Science Research Associates.

Suchman, R. (1966b). *Teacher's guide: Inquiry development program in physical science.* Chicago, IL: Science Research Associates.

Taba, H. (1965). Techniques of in-service training. *Social Education, 29,* 44–60.

Taba, H. (1966). *Teaching strategies and cognitive functioning in elementary school children* (Project No. 2402). Washington, DC: USOE.

Taba, H. (1967). *Teachers' handbook to elementary social studies.* Reading, MA: Addison-Wesley.

Taba, H. (1971). *Hilda Taba Teaching Strategies Program.* Miami, FL: Institute for Staff Development.

Tessmer, M., & Driscoll, M. P. (1986). Effects of a diagrammatic display of concept definitions on classification performance. *Educational Communications and Technology Journal, 34,* 195–205.

11
Instructional Tactics

Chapter Overview

In the first two chapters of Part III (Chapters 9–10), we examined strategic decisions concerning anticipated outcomes and selected models for teaching. In this chapter and in Chapter 12, we will examine tactics that teachers use in the classroom to implement their plans. Tactics are divided into two kinds: instructional tactics and management tactics. We will focus on instructional tactics in this chapter and discuss management tactics in Chapter 12. Teachers use instructional tactics to help students with the material they are to learn. Making sound tactical decisions requires knowledge of the conditions under which each tactic works well. In this chapter we will examine large and small group tactics, tactics that can be used with individual students, and tactics involved in teaching exceptional students. ■

management tactics Specific
steps taken by a teacher to
establish and maintain a
connection between students
and instructional material.
instructional tactics Specific
steps taken by a teacher to
help students learn from
instructional materials.

Chap. Obj. 1
Test Ques. 11.1–11.6

Focus Question: Why should teachers
use multiple tactics rather than using
their "best" tactic exclusively?

Lecture Note: Have students discuss
the distinction between management
and instructional tactics based on
their experiences as students in classrooms and their experiences observing other teachers in classrooms.

Journal Entry: Have students reflect
on the instructional tactics used by
particularly effective teachers they
have had in school, identifying the
ways in which these instructional tactics contributed to the teachers' effective teaching styles.

Teacher Interview: Have each student
interview a teacher recognized for
being effective, asking him or her to
comment on the importance of having
a variety of tactics at his or her disposal.

INTRODUCTION: MANAGEMENT AND INSTRUCTION

One way to examine the elements of teaching is to consider how the elements function. Ellen Gagné (1985) distinguishes between instruction and management functions. Using her distinction yields the following concepts.

Management tactics are specific actions taken by a teacher to establish and maintain a connection between students and instructional material. For example, a teacher might establish class rules governing appropriate behavior during seatwork assignments. Management tactics are necessary but are not of themselves sufficient for effective teaching.

Instructional tactics are specific actions taken by a teacher to help students learn from instructional materials. For example, a teacher might choose to lecture on the principle of supply and demand and then assign problems to be solved cooperatively in small groups. In this chapter we will consider and reflect on instructional tactics. (Management tactics are the subject of Chapter 12.)

When people think about teaching, the types of activities that most likely come to mind are instructional in nature. The stereotypic image of teaching is that of the teacher in front of the class presenting information—lecturing. Lecturing is an instructional tactic. It is an action a teacher takes to help students learn material. Lecturing is not, however, the only kind of instructional tactic a teacher may choose.

Our examination of instructional tactics in this chapter (and of management tactics in Chapter 12) should not be taken as prescriptive. We report what educational researchers have found with regard to various instructional and management tactics so that you, as a teacher, can use the information to make decisions about when and under what circumstances a particular tactic may be effective in your classroom. What we offer, therefore, is a menu from which you can select the tactics that may become part of your repertoire of instructional actions.

It is worthwhile to have a variety of teaching tactics at your disposal. First, when you use a variety of tactics to attain strategic goals it is less likely that your classroom will be divided between a group of students who are "haves" and another group of "have nots." If a teacher presents information in the classroom in the same way every day, the students whose learning styles and personality characteristics match the instructional technique are likely to attain more than those students for whom the technique is not a good match. Using a variety of techniques increases your chances of matching the material you are presenting to the learning characteristics of your students. Second, it is much easier to hold students' interest when you vary your teaching approach. Rosenshine and Furst (1973) found that variety—along with clarity and enthusiasm—is important in maintaining student interest and attention; ultimately, it is instrumental in producing higher achievement. Not incidentally, teachers who use some variety are able to sustain a high level of interest in their careers as well.

Peterson and Clark (1978) found that effective teachers of social studies seem to have more tactics available for use when something goes awry in the classroom. Less effective teachers were aware that something was wrong but were not able to make changes, perhaps because they were less willing to do so or less able to try different tactics owing to insufficient repertoires.

As a by-product of our examination of instructional tactics, a number of teaching tactics will be made available to add to your repertoire. The more tactics at your disposal, the more likely it is that you will be able to make informed judgments about instructional tasks and the attainment of learning outcomes for each individual in your classroom.

Lecture Note: Emphasize that reading about various tactics is only the first step toward enhancing a repertoire of instructional tactics. Encourage students to reflect on each tactic discussed.

Teacher
Chronicle
11.1

TRY, TRY AGAIN

If only every lesson turned out as I had envisioned it. Before most classes begin, I run through the lesson in my head. Do I have my materials? Do I understand what it is I am teaching? What problems might crop up? How will my students react to this lesson? Do I have alternatives for expanding or contracting the lesson?

Nevertheless, even the best laid plans backfire. There are those times when, no matter how much planning I have done ahead of time, the whole lesson fails. In assessing the damage after such a disaster, it is not hard to pinpoint where I took a wrong turn. Sometimes, the time of day is the factor. It is difficult to command everyone's attention when teaching fractions at 2:45 in the afternoon. Getting everyone to concentrate on English as the smell of the pizza for lunch drifts down the hallway is also a challenge.

Most lessons that fail don't crash as badly as one language activity did. My students were writing questions, a difficult skill with which many of them had problems. One day, after reading a chapter in *Little House on the Prairie*, the students wrote five questions each. Some were good, some were bad, but the answers to them were so obvious that they presented no difficulty. I had wanted them to write thinking questions, questions that challenged the reader to make connections.

As I planned for the next day, I thought about how to accomplish my objective—teaching them how to write involving questions—from a different angle. After discarding several ideas, I hit upon riddles. Riddles use thinking questions. Kids love riddles. I'll teach question writing through riddle writing, I decided.

"Remember yesterday when we were writing questions?" I asked, beginning the lesson. "We're going to be writing a different kind of question today. How many of you like riddles?" All of their hands shot up. "Well, today we're going to write and illustrate our own riddles."

A ripple of excitement ran through the class. "First, let's read a few riddles and then we'll write our own."

"Why did the sheriff put the star in jail?" I asked.

"Because he broke the law."

"Because the star blew up."

"Because the sheriff was lonely."

"No," I said. "Because it was a shooting star."

This is going great, I thought. What a terrific idea! I should have realized that, because no one was getting the answer, a problem loomed ahead.

"Let's try another. Where do cows go on Saturday night?"

"Top of the barn."

"To the outfield."

"To the moo'vies."

"Right. To the moo'vies."

Sam looked puzzled. "I don't get it," he said. "A cow can't go to the movies."

I knew I had to explain, but before I could, Josh said, "Cows go moo, right?"

"Yes," Sam answered.

"Then they go to the moo'vies. Get it? Moo'vies."

Now Sam laughed. Another clue I should have picked up on, but I didn't.

"Let's read the riddles on the handout. After that, I want you to write a new riddle. You have to make it up. Make a good question and write the answer. Then we'll share them."

I walked around the room helping with spelling as they wrote their riddles. As I toured, I read several of their "riddles." Something seemed wrong. No one was writing anything that made any sense, or they were writing jokes they had already heard.

At riddle-sharing time I called on Ellie first.

"Why did the elephant eat a banana?" Ellie asked. Then answered, "Because he was in a hurry," without pausing.

Everyone laughed. I smiled, but did not find anything funny or original.

On and on it went in the same vein. Every riddle had a literal answer. And they weren't very funny, at least not to me. And the questions were mediocre. They were no closer to writing involving questions than they had been the day before. If anything, I had clouded the issue. But why had the lesson failed? They liked riddles so I knew the interest was there. They seemed to enjoy sharing them so the involvement was there. The lesson may have been a success to them; it wasn't to me.

"Forget riddle writing from now on," I told myself. "It is beyond their abilities."

Later in the year, I took my class to the nature center. In preparation for the field trip, we had been studying vocabulary words about the plants, animals, and environments they would see. *Burr, hybernation, chrysalis, den, camouflage, badger, groundhog, swamp, bog,* and *prairie* were a few of the words we discussed before heading off to the wilds. As a follow-up activity, I had planned to have each student illustrate his or her favorite part of the day, highlighting an animal or plant in its environment.

Near the end of the day, my group was discussing seeds with our guide. She held up a burr, explaining to the kids how it attached itself to our clothes or to the fur of an animal and hitchhiked to another location.

Out of the clear blue sky, Julie turned to me and said, "What is the coldest seed in the woods?"

"The ones left here in the winter," I said, thinking literally.

"No," she said, shaking her head at my ignorance, "it's the burr. Get it? Burrrrr."

"Now I get it," I laughed as my thoughts jumped back to the great riddle-writing day of disaster. Maybe it had not been such a failure after all. Maybe the seeds sown then were beginning to sprout.

On the bus ride back, Julie told her joke to anyone who would listen. I threw out my follow-up plans for the next day, deciding to give riddle writing one more chance. This time, however, I would limit our word choices to the vocabulary list. For practice, I would write a few riddles myself that night.

That evening I played around with the words on the list. I broke the words into syllables and found rhyming words. I turned each word over and over trying to find multiple meanings and synonyms. This time I wouldn't just share a few jokes and hope they understood the lesson. We would review the vocabulary list; we would brainstorm antonyms and synonyms; we would break the words apart for rhymes. We would write the answers first and then write the questions that set the reader up to get the answer.

The next day we did those things. We brainstormed; we played with the words; we turned them inside out and upside down. We laughed when they worked and examined them when they didn't.

"What do you call a monkey who eats chips? . . . A chip monkey."

"What appliance do you feel like when you are camouflaged? . . . A blender."

"What is the richest thing in the woods? . . . A crystal-is."

"What's the saddest part of a nature center field trip? . . . When it's time to leaf."

I was excited and felt that the lesson had been successful on several counts. First, we had reviewed the vocabulary and by looking at the words differently had come to a new understanding of many of the words. Second, the class had developed a different sense of how to ask questions. Third, I had engaged them completely and we had had fun.

Out of the ashes of the failed lesson a new lesson had arisen. I went home that day feeling like a phoenix.

■ ■

LARGE GROUP INSTRUCTION

The tactics described in this section are typically, but not necessarily, used when a teacher engages an entire class in the same instructional activity. The first tactic, lecture, is the tactic most people envision when they think about teaching.

Lecture

The **lecture,** a presentation usually given before a large group, is one action you can take to help students learn content. Your own experience will tell you that lecture or perhaps, more accurately, large group presentation is a tactic that is employed by most teachers most of the time.

Lecturing is also the instructional tactic that has received the most criticism. It is a well-established tradition among students to complain about lectures. Students maintain that lectures are boring, poorly organized, irrelevant, and redundant. However, such complaints are more properly directed at the lecturer rather than the lecture.

Despite the criticism that lecturing has attracted, it is a mainstay in the repertoire of instruction. The lecture remains in use because it is a practical tactic; it is efficient and flexible. Lecturing is efficient because one teacher can present material to many students at one time. The lecture is also flexible because a teacher can exercise a high degree of control. When circumstances in the classroom require a teacher to change his or her plans, the lecture is

Chap. Obj. 2
Test Ques. 11.7–11.39

Focus Questions: Why do so many teachers lecture? What factors influence the effectiveness of a teacher's questions?

Teaching Anecdote: Tell your students the story of the high school science teacher who only lectured about science to his students. Each lecture revolved around a specific part of a specific chapter. There were 180 days in the school year and 180 files in his cabinet. Each morning, he pulled that day's file and lectured from it. Many of his students liked his classes and received A's, yet over the years he was there, a number of students did poorly in his class and never mastered the scientific concepts that he was teaching.
    Ask your students why the lecture approach might have worked well with some students but failed with others.

Journal Entry: Have students reflect on their own experiences with lecturers, addressing the question, What are the characteristics of poor lecturers and those of effective lecturers?

Connection: See the material on reading student behavior in Chapter 1.

Teacher Interview: Have each student interview a teacher regarding the importance of "reading" his or her students.

Field Observation: Have each student observe an effective lecturer, documenting the theatrical qualities of his or her presentation.

Lecture Note: Rubin's (1985) *Artistry in Teaching* is a good source for examples of theatrical teaching.

easily adapted. Tactics that require the use of supplemental materials or equipment cannot be changed as quickly or easily. Unlike assigned readings, a lecture places the source of the material and the student in face-to-face interaction. If a student encounters an idea that is unclear in a textbook, the source of that information, the author, cannot respond to the student's difficulty. A lecturer, on the other hand, is able to "read" his or her audience directly. If a point being made in a lecture is unclear to students, the lecturer is more likely to detect each student's difficulty and thus offer immediate remediation. Although the practical advantages alone would guarantee the widespread use of the tactic, there also is research evidence that supports the use of lectures in the classroom. Lectures have been found to be at least as effective as other instructional tactics (cf. Gage & Berliner, 1988).

Lectures have been found to be superior to discussion methods in three areas: test scores, retention and higher-level thinking, and attitude and motivation (McKeachie & Kulik, 1975). McKeachie (1986) states that "effective lectures combined the talents of scholar, writer, producer, comedian, showman, and teacher in what they contribute to student learning" (p. 69). Lectures can be very efficient in delivering the content to students in the classroom. Moreover, use of lectures is one way to model communication before a large group for your students. From the teacher's point of view, the lecture is an opportunity to perform. If McKeachie is correct in his characterization of effective lectures, then effective lecturers have to display something of a theatrical bent. For the teacher who organizes material well and presents it clearly, lectures are the best opportunity he or she has to display knowledge of particular subject matter.

Not all tactics are equally effective for all outcomes. This is true of the lecture. Several conditions under which lecture is a "suitable" tactic have been identified (e.g., Bligh, 1972; McKeachie, 1967; McLeish, 1976; Verner & Dickinson, 1967). The evidence suggests that lecturing can be effective when material needs to be organized in a special way for a particular group. The lecture is an appropriate way to introduce a topic of study or a task. The lecture has also been shown to be effective when students' interest needs to be aroused.

Explanation

Teacher Interview: Have students interview teachers regarding the rewarding nature of the "light bulbs" of understanding.

The public may think of the teacher as being, first and foremost, a lecturer, but the teaching activity that captures the essence of teaching, for teachers, is explanation. It is by delivering successful explanations that teachers are rewarded with the "light bulbs" of understanding above their students' heads. Explanations are more focused than lectures. The purpose of **explanation** is to define, clarify, or provide an account of concepts, events, and relationships (cf. Gage & Berliner, 1988). Although lectures often include explanations, explanations are not always presented in the context of a lecture. For instance, an explanation could be triggered by a student's question about a concept from the previous night's reading assignment.

Connection: Teacher Chronicle 11.1: Try, Try Again.

The teacher who presents explanations effectively tends to be more responsive to the specific needs of the student and has a clearer idea of the student's misunderstanding. The explanation that such a teacher offers provides information that goes to the heart of the student's problem. Effective teachers also tend to provide a context or framework for the answers that their explanations provide (Duffy, Roehler, Meloth, & Vavrus, 1986). The brainstorming session in Teacher Chronicle 11.1 allowed the teacher to provide a context for riddles. Such explanations help students build cognitive representations or schemata (see Chapter 6). Thus, teachers should attempt to zero in on students' needs, help students make connections with prior knowledge, and use the occasion of the explanation to instruct students on how to use the information in other learning situations—an element of metacognitive awareness and transfer of learning.

> **questioning** The act of asking questions as a tactic of instruction.

Questioning

Questioning simply means that a teacher asks students questions, as a tactic of instruction. But what types of questions and under what conditions should they be asked?

Chapter 15 Casebook Preview: See Around the World.

Socrates taught Plato by asking questions. We can imagine Socrates seated on a marble bench resting while Plato paced back and forth contemplating the question addressed to him and formulating an answer. As we imagine the session continuing, we can picture Socrates leading Plato to higher and higher levels of thought by means of carefully wrought questions.

Consider another great teacher, Jaime Escalante, whose efforts to teach calculus to students from the barrio are portrayed in the movie, *Stand and Deliver*. Escalante uses the questioning tactic as drill and practice. He asks questions to help students learn the basic math facts that they will have to master in order to understand and use more advanced concepts.

In terms of Bloom's taxonomy of cognitive objectives (see Chapter 9), questions, such as those Plato pondered, can be used to teach objectives at the levels of analysis, synthesis, and evaluation. The drill and practice used by Escalante address objectives at the taxonomic levels of knowledge, comprehension, and application. In both cases, the questions asked by the teacher require the student not only to attend to the teacher, but also to formulate and deliver responses. The interactive nature of the questioning tactic is more likely to produce active than passive learners. The nature of the questions the teacher asks, the manner in which he or she elicits responses to questions, and the type of feedback or reaction to students' answers that he or she provides determine the types of outcomes that questioning will produce in a particular classroom situation.

Connection: See discussion on the taxonomy of cognitive objectives in Chapter 9.

Clark, Gage, Marx, Peterson, Staybrook, and Winnie (1979) identified stages of questioning as viewed by the teacher: *structure* (setting the stage for the questions that follow), *solicitation* (asking the questions), and *reaction* (responding to students' answers).

Field Observation: Have students observe questioning sessions in classrooms, documenting the level of questions used by the teacher and the level of students' responses.

Structure

Structure is established through lecture, explanation, assigned reading, or other activities. This stage "sets up" students, providing them with a background or structure to use when answering questions. Structure can be established by providing rules that govern the answers students give. For example, a teacher might prepare a class for a review session by saying, "I am going to ask you some practice questions similar to the ones that will be on the test Friday. As you know, Friday's test will require short essay answers. For today's review, I want you to give a brief answer followed by supporting evidence. Let's try the first review question. . . ." In Teacher Chronicle 11.1,

Connection: Teacher Chronicle 11.1: Try, Try Again.

Lecture Note: Have students discuss the issue of matching levels of questions to desired outcomes. Have students use Gagné's learned capabilities (Chapter 9) as a basis for identifying desired outcomes.

Field Observation: Have each student observe a questioning session in a classroom, documenting wait-time I and wait-time II and the level of students' responses.

Teacher Interview: Have each student interview a teacher regarding the use of questioning in a review session, asking the teacher how wait-time relates to the amount of enthusiasm generated during such sessions.

the students' initial attempts at providing riddles suffered because of a lack of structure. The students did not have sufficient background to respond to the teacher's request.

Solicitation

What types of questions should be asked during the solicitation phase? Should they be questions that rank high in Bloom's taxonomy, such as the questions of analysis, synthesis, and evaluation asked by Socrates? Or should they be low-level recognition and comprehension questions such as those Escalante used for drill and practice? High-level questions require more and more elaborate cognitive processing than low-level questions do. One complaint about current evaluative practices is that low-level questions tend to predominate; there is too much emphasis on facts and too little on creative problem solving.

Is Socrates better than Escalante? If we take into account the outcomes sought by these two tacticians, the answer is "no." Solicitation in a drill-and-practice mode necessitates low-level questions, nonetheless, Escalante accomplished what he set out to do. Certainly, educators ought to strive for high-level thinking in their students, but often analysis, synthesis, and evaluation must await the recognition, comprehension, and application of more basic information. The type of question asked during the solicitation phase of questioning depends, as do all tactical decisions, on the outcomes sought by the teacher (see Gall, 1984; Good, 1988; Stallings & Kaskowitz, 1975).

Reaction

Between solicitation (asking the question) and reaction (responding to the student's answer), there is the period of time, called **wait-time I,** when the student formulates his or her answer and delivers it (Rowe, 1974). The period of time between the student's answer and the teacher's reaction to that answer is called **wait-time II** (see Figure 11-1).

The routine a teacher uses to acknowledge or call on students affects the length of wait-time I. For example, if students in a classroom are allowed to respond spontaneously, without first being acknowledged by the teacher, wait-time I will be diminished. If students are required to raise their hands and be acknowledged before responding, the teacher can control the length of wait-time I, which has its advantages. Research has shown that lengthening wait-time to about three seconds (but no longer than three seconds) enhances student attention and yields longer, more complex student answers (e.g., Fagan, Hassler, & Szabo, 1981; Tobin & Capie, 1982).

Think about Socrates and Escalante. If Socrates had pressed Plato for quick answers to questions, what would have happened to Plato's answers? If Escalante, using questions for drill and practice, had waited and waited for a student to state a fact, what would have happened?

Tobin (1987) reviewed several studies and found that longer wait-times (approximately three seconds) are generally related to achievement. Nevertheless, the tactical decisions you make about solicitation and reaction must take into account the goals you are trying to achieve.

There are many classroom contexts in which shorter pauses between speakers can be justified. For example, when rote memorization or recall of facts is required, drill and practice activities might be conducted at a brisk pace using shorter wait-time. (Tobin, 1987, p. 91)

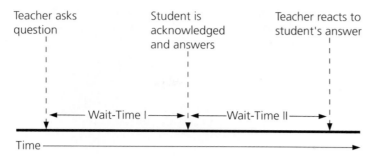

■ **Figure 11–1** *Wait-Times Associated with Questioning*

Transparency: This figure is duplicated in the acetate transparency package. See T-19 Wait-Times Associated with Questioning.

Seatwork

Seatwork refers to tasks a student completes independently while in the classroom. In many classrooms, seatwork constitutes a large proportion of the student's day. This is especially true in elementary school classrooms. Rosenshine (1980) estimates that elementary students spend between 50 percent and 70 percent of their time doing seatwork. One reason seatwork is so common in elementary classrooms is that elementary teachers tend to work with their students in groups. While the teacher is working with one group, the other students need to be occupied with a task that does not require the teacher's constant attention. In many instances, the most practical solution to this problem is seatwork.

Evertson, Enner, and Brophy (1980) documented the amount of time seventh- and eighth-grade math teachers devoted to lecture versus seatwork. The most effective math teachers divided class time between lecture and seatwork almost equally. Students of those teachers who were the least effective spent more than three times as long doing seatwork as they did learning from lectures or demonstrations. Heavy reliance on seatwork can compound the problem of low-achieving students (Anderson, Brubaker, Alleman-Brooks, & Duffy, 1985). Many low-achieving students lack the adequate motivation and confidence necessary for profitable independent work. Some of these students lack reading and other basic skills and have not developed the kinds of self-monitoring and organizational skills that would allow them to benefit from seatwork. For many of these students, simple completion of the assignments is the goal that guides their efforts on seatwork.

According to the direct instruction model (Chapter 10), independent practice should be preceded by guided practice (Hunter, 1984). If a student enters into independent practice without a clear notion of what the task is, or with a mistaken idea of how a skill is to be applied, the student will practice making errors (Gunter et al., 1990). Thus, in order to use seatwork effectively, students must know clearly what to do and how to do it.

Because seatwork does offer practical value, it is likely to stay in the repertoire of many teachers. When you find it necessary or desirable to use seatwork in your own classroom, there are several guidelines that can enhance its effectiveness.

If seatwork is to be a regular feature in your classroom, time should be spent early in the year establishing rules and procedures that will enable students to work independently. In formulating these general rules and pro-

Field Observation: Have students collect examples of seatwork exercises performed by students in elementary, junior high, and high school classrooms.

Teacher Interview: Have students interview teachers regarding motivation as it is revealed by students' seatwork.

Connection: See the discussion of the direct instruction model in Chapter 10.

Lecture Note: Ask someone with experience in British schools to comment on the use of seatwork in those schools.

When assigning seatwork, it is critical that the teacher explain the procedures for independent work and closely monitor students' work.

cedures, try to anticipate the many routine questions that might otherwise distract you while you are helping other students (cf. Brophy & Evertson, 1974).

Make yourself as available as possible to students during their practice sessions. Walk around the room and spot-check the progress of students so that you can readily intervene when a student is working poorly or incorrectly. Moving about the room while monitoring seatwork also sends a message to students that you are aware of their behavior and that you place some importance on the task at hand (Fisher, Berliner, Filby, Marliave, Cahen, & Dishaw, 1980).

If students, especially less motivated students, perceive seatwork as "just practice," they will be less likely to put forth their best efforts. Thus, evaluating seatwork and incorporating student performance on seatwork into any grades you assign is a good way of emphasizing the importance of independent work.

Journal Entry: Have students reflect on the seatwork they did as students, addressing the question, What were your reactions to teachers who monitored seatwork and who gave you individual attention during seatwork periods?

Homework

Homework is similar to seatwork; both can be used for independent practice by students. A number of studies have found a strong correlation between the amount of homework assigned and higher grades (e.g., Keith, 1982; Marshall, 1982; Wolf, 1979).

The guidelines that apply to seatwork also apply to homework. The obvious difference between homework and seatwork is the teacher's ability to monitor the performance of students. Although the teacher can suggest procedures and routines that will help students to more efficiently complete homework, the teacher is not readily available to answer students' questions as they arise. Preparing students in class for their homework assignments is, therefore, a critical element of the tactic. If students are confused or unclear about what they are to accomplish at home or how they are to accomplish it, they are less likely to derive benefits from homework.

As is the case with seatwork, it is recommended that homework be checked and that feedback, in the form of comments, be given to students. This way of evaluating homework has been shown to enhance achievement (Elawar & Corno, 1985).

Field Observation: Have students observe teachers assigning homework, documenting how well the students are prepared to work independently.

SMALL GROUP INSTRUCTION

Chap. Obj. 3
Test Ques. 11.40–11.57

Some learning outcomes are better suited to small group instruction than to large group tactics. We will examine two types of small group instruction—discussion and cooperative learning—in the sections that follow. In general, small group discussion tends to work well when the topics discussed are open to a number of possible interpretations; the tactic also works well when teaching critical thinking and problem solving, and when attempting to change attitudes. Cooperative learning in small groups makes use of learning teams and provides opportunities for group motivation.

Focus Question: Under what conditions is it advantageous for students to work in small groups?

Discussion Groups

A discussion group is a relatively small gathering that allows students to exchange information, opinions, attitudes, and so on. Small group discussion appears to be a better method to use when the desired outcomes are higher-level thinking skills or attitudes (McKeachie & Kulik, 1975). Small group discussion is helpful in fostering a student's ability to think critically (Gage & Berliner, 1988). In small group discussions, students interact with each other to a greater extent than in large group lectures. Exchanging information in small group discussion requires that students not only respond to general discussion questions, but also offer and support their opinions. A student's reasoning then becomes part of the content of the group's discussion.

Chapter 15 Casebook Preview: See Gifted Achievers and Underachievers.

If a student is to learn effectively in a discussion group, he or she must develop skills that are not necessary for learning in large groups or in a lecture situation. The environment of small group discussion encourages students not only to listen but also to respond to what they've heard. The ability to listen for the purpose of responding is different from the ability to listen effectively to a lecturer. Thus, students learn to think through problems as part of a group process rather than reaching certain conclusions by themselves.

Journal Entry: Have students reflect on small group discussions in which they have participated, answering the following questions: Which discussions stand out in your mind as having fostered high-level thinking on your part? What were the characteristics of those discussion groups? What questions or issues guided the discussions?

High Consensus Versus Low Consensus

In choosing small group discussion as a tactic, teachers are well advised to consider the particular learning objectives that their students are to attain. If the objectives come from a subject area in which there is high consensus,

Lecture Note: Ask students to share their own experiences from small group discussions. Have them characterize those experiences in which they did or did not listen to their classmates.

A perceptive teacher can alter his or her instructional tactics to fit the learning styles of the students. Some lessons are better suited to small group instruction where cooperative learning can be emphasized.

there already exists a high degree of agreement as to what is and is not important in that particular area. For example, using small group discussions to learn mathematical and scientific formulas might not prove beneficial. Subject areas that are not as well defined—social sciences, the arts, and literature—can provide interesting subject matter for give-and-take discussion. Consider, as an example, a small group discussion on the relative merits of the behaviorist versus the cognitivist view of learning.

Values and Beliefs

Evidence exists that suggests that small group discussion as a tactic can also lead to changes in attitude and behavior. Students who take a position in small group discussions are, in effect, making a public statement that implies a course of action on their part. A student may become convinced that capital punishment is wrong. If the student comes to that conclusion while listening to someone lecture, the conclusion is arrived at privately. Unless a discussion follows the lecture, the student is not required to take a stand. Arriving at the same conclusion within the context of a small group discussion, however, is more likely to require the student to make a personal statement to that effect. Gall and Gall (1976) reviewed studies that indicate that discussions change opinions and attitudes in myriad ways. Their review suggests that discussions can change attitudes in areas ranging from reactions toward mentally retarded persons to the use of orange juice and cod liver oil by mothers.

Students faced with the challenge of marshaling arguments in small group discussions must learn to reason and think critically about questions, issues, or problems. When identifying concepts or evidence that support a position, students are engaging in the learning process called discovery. Students engaged in small group discussions are not being provided with a reasoned presentation, rather they are providing the reasons themselves.

The tactic works not only in areas of low consensus, but also in areas of low consensus that are emotionally charged. For example, a discussion of legislation and court decisions that involve reproductive rights will most assuredly elicit opposing opinions from students. Many of the topics typically discussed in classrooms are noncontroversial in nature. Gage and Berliner (1988) suggest that controversial topics be addressed more often. Among the advantages of addressing a controversial topic in a small group discussion is the motivational effect that controversial discussions have. A discussion that requires one to take and defend a position against the positions of others forces students to find new information, to organize their thinking, and to engage in conflict resolution. In addition, such discussions require students to construct logical arguments that can withstand new information and the perspectives brought to the discussions by other students. Finally, discussions of controversial topics lead to a heightened understanding of one's self. Taking a position and maintaining that position in the face of conflicting opinion requires the student to examine his or her own position and the reasons for taking it more carefully.

Intervening in Small Group Discussions

For some teachers (your authors included), staying out of a discussion among students is one of the more difficult tactical elements of small group discussion. There is a natural tendency for teachers to respond to any difficulty that students are having. Even if you have some good ideas to contribute to the discussion, it would be well to keep them to yourself until after the group has had a chance to develop its own ideas. In this way, you can avoid what we might call the "ask the expert" syndrome. The question then becomes, How does one avoid interfering with student participation while, at the same time, attempting to foster interaction in a faltering discussion? When several small groups are discussing the same topic, you should monitor all of the groups, while asking a leading question here or reminding a group of the task there.

Gage and Berliner (1988) make suggestions about when to intervene in small group discussions. The first suggestion is to notice when and to what extent digressions are occurring in a group. Because you are monitoring several groups, it is important to check all groups frequently to see if one student is monopolizing the discussion. You will discover that it is possible to listen to several groups at one time and to focus your attention on the exchange in one particular group even though that group may be physically located across the room.

Another symptom that calls for intervention is lengthy pauses between student contributions to the discussion. Long pauses between contributions may be a sign that students are becoming confused or have forgotten the task at hand.

As you monitor the groups, it is important to attend to the meaning of the contributions as well. If a discussion proceeds very far along an avenue begun with a factual error, the usefulness of the discussion is compromised. Although it is better that students correct factual errors themselves, it is detrimental to allow a group to proceed very far on the basis of incorrect factual information. You will have to use your judgment about when to intervene in this type of situation, but it is important to note that early correction of factual errors saves a good deal of time.

When students have problems distinguishing values or opinions from facts, intervention is again called for. In a lively discussion, this type of

Field Observation: Have students observe and document small group discussions in a variety of classrooms with the following questions in mind: What motivational differences do you notice? To what extent can those motivational differences be attributed to the presence or lack of controversy in the discussions?

Teacher Interview: Have each student interview a teacher regarding his or her methods of avoiding the "ask the expert" syndrome.

Lecture Note: Have students discuss guidelines they might use to set up small group discussions; in particular, ask the students to generate guidelines that might prevent a student from monopolizing a discussion.

Teaching Anecdote: Tell your students about the junior high teacher who carried a small stack of index cards with her as she walked around her room during small group discussions. Each card in the stack contained a question or comment, such as "Are you talking about fact or opinion?" or "Go back to the original question." Her stack of cards also included blank cards on which she wrote specific questions pertinent to a specific discussion. As the teacher monitored the various discussion groups, she would periodically show one of the cards to a group member. She took care to vary the people in the group to whom she showed the cards.

Ask your students to evaluate this approach to monitoring small group discussions.

Chapter 15 Casebook Preview: See Science Is Only Real When You Do It.

Teacher Interview: Have each student interview a teacher regarding the use of team learning, asking the teacher to comment on the differences between small group discussion and cooperative learning in teams.

distinction may go unnoticed by several participants. Indeed, teachers themselves may have difficulty distinguishing values from fact, especially if the discussion at hand challenges positions that they have held over a long period of time. If you are in doubt about the ability of the group to distinguish values or opinions from fact, a short question, quickly inserted into the discussion, can alert the group. Simply saying something such as, "Is Rodney's statement an opinion or a fact?" may be sufficient.

Another signal related to the problem of incorrect factual information is the appearance of logical fallacies. If logical fallacies stated by one member of the group go undetected by other members, the validity of the discussion is damaged. Logical fallacies may include overgeneralization or reasoning that assumes conditions that may or may not be true. For example, a student may argue that because someone makes a lot of money, he or she is successful in his or her profession. Therefore, wealthy people are competent and poor people are incompetent.

Cooperative Learning in Teams

Earlier we noted that discussions best serve learning in subject areas of low consensus. This does not mean, however, that small groups cannot be employed in areas of high consensus, such as science and mathematics. Small group instruction in areas of high consensus and low consensus can occur if the objective is to learn as a team.

Team learning is an instructional tactic that calls for groups to be formed to facilitate student cooperation in attaining certain goals. There is increasing recognition of the fact that when students leave school and join the work force, they will be expected to perform jobs that will require them to work as part of a team. The team learning tactics that we will examine provide a classroom context in which a student's effort pays off if it contributes to the overall performance of his or her team.

Student Teams-Achievement Divisions (STAD)

One type of team that can be formed is referred to as **student teams-achievement divisions (STAD),** a cooperative learning method that employs a cycle of teaching tactics, consisting of lecture, cooperative study in small groups, and quiz (Slavin, 1987). Rewards are given to teams whose members show the greatest improvement over their own past performances, the "real-world" equivalent of increased productivity. STAD teams work best when each numbers four or five persons.

Each lesson using the STAD procedure begins with a lecture presentation of material, usually conducted over one or two class periods. During the team study phase, which lasts for one or two class periods, each team is provided with worksheets or other materials pertaining to the topic covered in the lecture. Each team is to make sure that all of its members master the material. In order to encourage real teamwork, a teacher can insist that team members work together on just one or two copies of the worksheets.

The team score is the total amount of improvement of each individual over his or her own past performances. A team score can be computed by adding together the number of improvement points earned by the team and dividing that number by the number of team members who took the test.

After team scores have been calculated, some reward or recognition should be delivered to any team that averaged two or more improvement

Cooperative learning tactics introduce students to the concept of teamwork as a learning tool and lessen the impact of competition in certain classroom situations.

points. Rewards are based not on the performance of the team compared with other teams, but with its own past performance.

Consider this STAD procedure for teaching math. After you have lectured on the objectives of a math lesson and teams have convened for team study, you might distribute worksheets containing math problems based on the lecture just presented. In this case, each student on the team should work each problem. Each student should compare his or her answer with those of teammates. If any member of the team has missed a problem, it is the responsibility of the other teammates to provide remediation. The STAD procedure emphasizes that team study is not complete until all members of the team have mastered the material. Student questions that arise during team study are to be addressed to teammates before the teacher is consulted. After team study is completed, the entire class is tested as individuals and then team scores are calculated.

Slavin also recommends that STAD teams be reconstituted every five or six weeks. When the teams are reconstituted, students who were on low-scoring teams have a chance to try again. This recommendation is similar to the idea of changing the membership of teams on a playground when one team has won a number of games in a row.

Teams-Games-Tournaments (TGT)

Another form of team learning is referred to as **teams-games-tournaments** or **TGT** (Slavin, 1987). As in the STAD procedure, the team is responsible for preparing each team member for competition. In TGT, a team comprises four or five members of varying ability levels. Once the mixed-ability teams are formed, team members leave their teams to compete as individuals in homog-

Lecture Note: Ask students to consider the sources of reinforcement available to students who are operating in a STAD arrangement.

enous three-person competition groups. Each team member competes against members of other teams in weekly tournaments. The competitive groups change each week, but the level of ability within groups remains constant. An individual's performance in the weekly tournament contributes to his or her team's score.

In each competition group, players take turns serving one of three functions: Reader, Challenger I, or Challenger II. The Reader on a particular turn reads the problem or question to the two challengers. The Reader attempts to solve the problem or answer the question. Challenger I can then choose to challenge the reader's answer by giving a different answer, or Challenger I may pass. Challenger II may challenge or pass. Challenger II then checks the correct answer to the problem or question using an answer sheet provided by the teacher. The roles are exchanged so that each student plays each role within a tournament. The score received by each player is his or her contribution to the team's total score for a particular tournament.

The three players who compete against each other in a group change each week. The winners in each group are moved to a higher-ability group for the next week's tournament. The low scorer in each group is moved to a lower-level group for the next week's tournament. In this way, each team member has an increased chance of contributing points to the team's overall performance.

Lecture Note: Have students compare the sources of reinforcement and motivation of the STAD procedure as compared with those of the teams-games-tournaments approach.

Principles in Practice 11.1

Principles . . .
1. Teachers should choose tactics with the outcomes they desire in mind.
2. Large group tactics are efficient ways of organizing content.
3. Small group instruction requires careful monitoring.

. . . in Practice
In Teacher Chronicle 11.1, the teacher was pursuing the goal of question writing. The teacher tried using riddle writing as a way to achieve this goal. The initial large group presentation failed. Later in the year, after students began playing with riddles during a field trip, the teacher again decided to try riddle writing. But this time, the teacher did not simply read the students some riddles in hopes that they would catch on by imitation. Rather, the teacher prepared the students for the task by identifying the elements of riddle writing. As a large group, they examined riddles using the identified elements. Now that the students understood the elements involved, the second attempt at riddle writing was successful.

1. How did the unsuccessful and successful attempts at riddle writing differ in terms of question structuring?
2. Would small group discussion have been more effective? Why or why not?
3. How do large and small group tactics differ with regard to the types of outcomes they foster?

SEEING THE LIGHT

We were beginning a unit on electricity and I wanted to assess the students' understanding. I listed twenty concepts related to electricity on the board and said, "Look over the list. Think about the concepts you already understand. If you don't know any of the words, write those down. I want to be able to match the experiments we will be doing with what you already know."

They wrote in their notebooks for about fifteen minutes and then we discussed concepts.

"I already know all of the words," said Karl, in a bored tone.

"Well, I can't even pronounce the third one," admitted Lisa.

"That's 'rheostat,'" Paul said.

"What does 'series' mean?" asked Lena.

"You'll find out tomorrow when I assign lab partners," I told them.

"I want to be with Karl," Michael said. "He already knows it all."

It was clear to me that some students had little knowledge of electricity, some had a moderate understanding, and some were electrical wizards. I took notes as the discussion continued. My plan was to enable students with little previous understanding to gain new knowledge while allowing those with a depth of understanding to explore more complicated investigations.

The following morning, I set up the different labs. For students at the lowest level, I set up the simplest experiments with open and closed circuits. For those at the next level, I set up experiments that involved connecting theories and parallel circuits. On the computer, I had a graphics program for making diagrams of electrical circuits. The most advanced students would use this program to create a working rheostat and demonstrate its operation for the entire class.

There was a buzz of excitement as I assigned groups and the students began their work. I roamed about the room listening in on conversations, questioning, prompting, and demonstrating. About halfway into the class, I was able to step back and let the dynamics of the situation take hold.

"Hey, Karl," Lisa asked. "How do you know when the circuit is closed?"

"Just a second," he replied. Turning to his partner he said, "Try attaching the blue wire to the red one while I help Lisa."

On his way back to his station, Karl stopped by to look in on what was happening on the computer. He looked and smiled, but he did not comment.

"Wow," yelled Lena. "My light came on!"

"See, you're not such a dimwit after all," Charlotte teased.

"Bruce, come here. Let me show you how the circuit works running side by side."

"That's 'parallel,'" Karl said without looking up from his rheostat.

"Myra, do you know which is positive and which is negative?" Abby asked. "I keep getting them mixed up."

"You just look for the plus sign for positive on the battery and the minus sign for negative."

Bells rang sporadically, lights flickered, the computer printer clattered, and conversations spun one into another. Suddenly the class bell rang for dismissal.

"Oh, I don't want to go," complained Sara. "I was just getting the hang of 'series.'"

"Can I do your experiment tomorrow?"

"Tomorrow, tomorrow," I said. "Everyone who wants to can 'switch' to another experiment."

They groaned. "Switch. . . ."

"I don't get it," Al said.

"It was another of her 'brilliant' jokes," Karl pointed out, before turning to me and adding, "I get a 'charge' of out this class."

"Now, Karl, I find that 'shocking.'"

"Now if I can only make our rheostat work," Karl said.

■ ■

Chap. Obj. 4–6
Test Ques. 11.58–11.80

Focus Question: How can a teacher instruct thirty individuals, all at the same time?

INDIVIDUALLY ORIENTED TACTICS

The instructional tactics used to teach an entire class—take lecture as an example—expose all students to the same material at the same pace. Small group tactics give students more opportunity to influence, if not control, the material that is covered, the rate of the coverage, and whether the coverage will be in depth or cursory. The dynamics of a discussion group exemplify this. Even so, the topics under discussion or the material covered through cooperative learning teams do not vary much from group to group.

We now turn our attention to tactics that are "individually oriented" in the sense that the individual student's learning needs determine specific content and the pace at which the content is covered. The teacher still makes instructional decisions, but the instructional agenda that is established is for individual students rather than for an entire class.

Individualized Instruction

Journal Entry: Have students reflect on those teachers who made them feel important as individuals in their classes, commenting on the techniques these teachers used to accomplish this.

Because each student brings unique experiences, abilities, attitudes, and social and emotional needs to the classroom, truly adaptive instruction would require that each student be taught in a different way. Taken to its logical conclusion, adaptive instruction would require that each student have his or her own teacher. Assigning one teacher to each student is obviously impractical, however. Equally impractical is the expectation that one teacher can provide an entirely different set of instructional experiences for each of thirty students in his or her class.

A more practical implementation of individualized instruction offers students the opportunity to work at their own pace with materials and activities best suited to their individual needs. Research on the achievement of students who receive exclusive one-to-one instruction from an adult tutor demonstrates the positive effect of individualized instruction (Bloom, 1984).

Chapter 15 Casebook Preview: See Writers' Tea.

Connection: See Diary of a Day in Chapter 1.

As a tactic used in a classroom, individualized instruction involves designing plans that help individuals reach instructional goals within the context of a large group. In the "Diary of a Day" (Chapter 1), there were several instances when Peter Roop allowed students to work on activities independently. The instructional activities in which they engaged were planned and monitored by Peter; they were not activities designed for the entire class. In

Individualized instruction involves determining a student's needs and selecting topics and activities that meet those and the needs of the other students in the classroom.

another example, although students in Teacher Chronicle 11.2 worked in pairs, the teacher initially assigned them to experiments that were geared to match their level of knowledge of electricity.

Connection: Teacher Chronicle 11.2: Seeing the Light.

The Mastery Approach

The **mastery approach** to instruction, based on Carroll's model of school learning (Chapter 10), provides one way to individualize instruction in an effort to help students master the material. As with other instructional approaches, when using the mastery approach, it is important to specify outcomes, facilitate motivation, and provide appropriate materials. What is unique to the mastery approach is that it facilitates the presentation of materials at rates appropriate to each student.

Connection: See the discussion of Carroll's model of school learning in Chapter 10.

Students involved in a program that uses this approach do not progress through the series of activities and materials at a uniform pace; therefore, keeping an accurate record of each student's progress is critical. Management of a mastery learning environment calls for more than just record keeping, however. Appropriate feedback and reinforcement must also be delivered in order to establish and maintain each student's progress.

A mastery approach assumes that the important difference among students is not what they are capable of learning, but rather the rate at which they are capable of learning. Typically, mastery instruction assumes that between 80 percent and 90 percent of the students will attain mastery of the assigned objectives. What will differ is how quickly each will attain the program's objectives and the materials and activities that these students will use to attain mastery. Some students may require more remediation than others; some students may need to read different materials due to differences in reading ability (Bloom, 1968).

Teacher Interview: Have each student interview a teacher who uses a mastery approach to the management of the classroom and of learning activities.

programmed instruction
Structured lessons that students work on individually, at their own pace, without the aid of a teacher. The lessons present material in small units and provide immediate feedback.

personalized system of instruction (PSI) A teaching program in which students work on programmed materials on an individual basis. When they pass the exam for a particular unit, they are allowed to advance to the next unit.

team-assisted instruction (TAI) A teaching tactic in which students work on programmed materials as members of a heterogeneous group. Rewards for completing the work accurately and quickly are given to the team as a whole.

Lecture Note: Ask students to compare programmed instruction with the concept of shaping discussed in Chapter 5.

Lecture Note: Emphasize that in the Keller plan lectures and demonstrations by the teacher are infrequent and, therefore, introduce a degree of novelty into the learning situation. This novelty may account for a portion of the motivational effect that the teacher presentations have, assuming, of course, that the lectures and demonstrations are effectively presented.

Teacher Interview: Have each student interview a teacher who uses cooperative team learning regarding the issues that arise in parent–teacher conferences.

Programmed Instruction

Programmed instruction is a more independent form of learning than is the mastery approach; it allows students to work with materials designed to help them obtain objectives on their own without the aid of a teacher. In practice, a teacher often provides instructional support for students using these programmed materials. However, the basic idea behind the programmed materials is that they be self-instructional.

Skills taught through the use of programmed materials are presented as a series of subskills. Small steps are more likely to yield success as the student works through the materials. This result is consistent with the behavioristic view of learning. Many computer programs that are designed to be self-instructional are forms of programmed instruction.

Personalized System of Instruction (PSI)

Keller's (1968) **personalized system of instruction (PSI)** incorporates programmed materials on an individual basis. PSI is known also as the Keller Plan. The Keller Plan begins with programmed materials. Students study the programmed materials independently and take an exam. If their performance on the exam meets a predetermined criterion, they are given new programmed materials for use in the next unit of study. If they do not pass the exam, they are directed back to specific parts of the programmed materials for further study. Students work with the programmed materials for a particular unit until they pass the exam. At that point, they are allowed to advance to the next unit. An interesting aspect of the Keller Plan is that lectures or demonstrations by the teacher are designed as rewards for those who demonstrate mastery of the programmed materials by successfully completing unit exams.

In general, the results of research on programmed instruction have proven disappointing (Bangert et al., 1983; Schoen, 1976). Total reliance on programmed materials appears to be in question. A survey of current classroom instructional tactics indicates that programmed materials are still used frequently, but programmed instruction is used more as a supplement to other tactics or for remediation than as the primary mode of instruction (Slavin, 1988). Among the problems that might account for the disappointing results of programmed instruction is the function of the teacher. The teacher who uses programmed instruction removes himself or herself as a source of information and becomes something resembling a clerk who records and documents exams. Some teachers are quite comfortable and even desirous of surrendering the role of "primary information source." What they must guard against is losing the role of motivator. It also seems likely that the exclusive use of programmed materials day after day would prove boring to students.

Team-assisted Instruction

The **team-assisted instruction (TAI)** approach prescribes that students work individually with programmed materials. However, students also belong to a mixed-ability group (see the discussion of STAD). As is the case in other cooperative group learning situations, the rewards for completing work accurately and quickly are given to the team as a whole. Although the assigned content provided to each student is in the form of programmed materials, his or her teammates are available to check work and to encourage and remediate. Because the team as a whole is rewarded for the work of individual

Issues in Educational Psychology

CNN™ This box relates to Segment 11 of the CNN videotape. See the Instructor's Section for a summary.

TECHNOLOGY ON THE UPSWING

A recent study conducted by the International Society for Technology in Education (ISTE) concluded that when students avail themselves of technology, their test scores, deductive skills, and the amount of material learned all increase. Funded by IBM, *Vision: TEST* (TEST is an acronym for Technology-Enriched Schools of Tomorrow) drew a number of conclusions: technology combined with training and a challenging curriculum will reduce absenteeism and dropout rates; active teacher participation is essential; teachers require training and encouragement to successfully introduce technology into the curriculum; and technology can help teachers significantly increase student learning.

Teacher training is at the heart of New York State's program to foster greater technology usage in the classroom. The Department of Education currently funds 111 technology centers to train teachers. Operating on college campuses, in schools and shopping centers, and even in buses, the centers offer teachers the opportunity to investigate different technologies. Typical equipment ranges from computers and modems to CD-ROMs and robots. The centers offer teachers extensive use of the equipment.

One of the most interesting and promising technologies shown at the centers is CD-ROM. Like audio compact discs, CD-ROMs (ROM is an acronym for read only memory) rely on a laser to access digitally coded material housed on a disc. With their large information storage capacity (over 600 megabytes), CD-ROMs offer students more than brief article summaries. Having selected articles from a computerized data base, students utilizing a computer's CD-ROM drive can view complete text and print out copies without the necessity of wading through library stacks.

At Queen Anne's County High School in Maryland, the library media center has captured the students' attention. Seventeen computers help to expedite card catalogue searches while 150 data bases including encyclopedias and periodical indexes, are stored on CD-ROMs. Students rely on the library's computers to do research, create graphics, and write homework assignments because of their speed and ease of use. As a media specialist at the high school, Patricia Cheek described to *Teacher Magazine* how valuable technology has become as an important part of the learning process. "Students are so used to instant reinforcement; they're really turned on by how fast computers can be."

Today's compact discs can also offer interactive multimedia presentations that allow students to view text and illustrations while listening to music or sound effects. Major players like the Microsoft Corporation and Tandy, as well as Philips and Sony, are gearing up to offer multimedia platforms to a broad base of businesses and consumers.

Microsoft and Tandy have agreed on specifications for computers, which use MS-DOS, to offer multimedia presentations. Philips and Sony have developed a standard for what's called the compact disc-interactive (CD-I). Aimed at consumers, CD-I will turn a television into an interactive multimedia platform with the use of a hand-held device. For manufacturers to succeed, however, applications have to be available. Developers are currently working on titles for both multimedia approaches.

As these platforms gain greater acceptance in society, more educational uses will be developed. Interactive multimedia may soon become a standard tool in the classroom.

SOURCES: Wolcott, Lisa. " 'T' to the Third Power." *Teacher Magazine* 2, no. 4 (January 1991): 38. Ladestro, Debra. "Information at Your Fingertips." *Teacher Magazine* 2, no. 7 (April 1991): 28–29. Kinnaman, D. "ISTE's Vision: TEST-More Support For Technology-Using Educators." *Technology & Learning* 11, issue 5 (February 1991): 31. Salpeter, Judy. "Beyond Videodiscs: Compact Discs in the Multimedia Classroom." *Technology & Learning* 11, issue 5 (February 1991): 32–40+.

1. How might the increased use of computers lead to improved individualization in teaching exceptional students?
2. How might the increased use of technology in the classroom cut down on management problems in large classes?

"players," it is to each individual's advantage to assist others on his or her team. The TAI approach allows teammates to become a source of motivation for individual students. Another advantage of TAI is that teammates can perform some of the clerical work that otherwise would be performed by the teacher. In studies of math classes, classes taught via TAI compared favorably to classes taught in a more traditional way (Good et al., 1983; Slavin, 1985).

Evaluation of Individualized Instruction

Generally, the research indicates that individualized approaches to instruction are not better than traditional approaches for elementary and secondary students (Bangert, Kulik, & Kulik, 1983). However, individualized approaches at the college level appear to be quite effective. One explanation offered is that the college student population is not as varied as the student populations of elementary and secondary schools. Elementary and secondary students who do not possess sufficiently high levels of self-motivation are less likely to attend college.

Because the student–teacher ratio in K–12 classrooms is typically high, any attempt to individualize instruction usually involves a lot of independent work on the part of the students. The teacher's time is consumed by planning, preparing, organizing, monitoring, and evaluating the progress of each student. Time consumed by the clerical aspect of individualized instruction is time lost to the design and implementation of other tactics. The trade-off of time is implicit in each and every tactical decision we make about our instruction.

In general classroom practice, individualized tactics are not used as often as lecture and discussion. (Think about the classrooms in which you were

Field Observation: Have students observe classrooms in which individualized instruction occurs, identifying differences in motivation among students in such classrooms.

Lecture Note: Have students investigate computer software for classroom record management.

Peer tutoring is highly effective in helping students learn assigned material. Studies have shown that peer tutoring can increase academic achievement for both the tutor and the student being tutored.

Computer-aided instruction is useful in providing tutorials, drill and practice, and simulations covering a variety of subjects.

taught.) However, individualizing instruction to even a modest degree introduces variety into the instructional environment.

Peer Tutoring

One way in which a teacher can free his or her time to deal with the problems of individual students is to engage students in the practice of tutoring each other, or **peer tutoring,** which occurs when one student is assigned to help another learn assigned material (see the discussion of peer modeling in Chapter 7). According to research, peer tutoring improves the academic performances and attitudes of both the student who tutors and the student who is tutored (Cohen, Kulik, & Kulik, 1982).

There are two basic types of peer tutoring, cross-age tutoring and same-age tutoring. There is little research to suggest what specific characteristics of the tutor and the tutored should be considered in forming groups. Nonetheless, this is the critical question to ask yourself when considering tutoring, especially in the case of same-age tutoring. Forming pairs of students of the same age is particularly difficult. When one classmate is appointed to tutor another classmate a relationship based on ability is implied. The student assigned to tutor is likely to be perceived by both students as superior. For

Teaching Anecdote: Tell your students about the fifth-grade student who regularly refused to do his written work in class. When the teacher gave him comprehension questions in reading, the student could answer the questions perfectly; but when he wrote anything down, it was sloppy and far less than what he was capable of doing. The teacher became increasingly frustrated with the student, and their relationship became a battle of wills. One day the teacher overheard the student telling a story to one of his friends in another class—the very story he had read that day. His retelling was accurate, and it was clear that he understood what he was reading. The next day the teacher asked the boy to retell the story to another student before completing his written assignment.

Ask your students why this approach might work with this student and if the effects are likely to be short term or long term.

Connection: See the section on peer modeling in Chapter 7.

Field Observation: Have students observe cross-age and same-age tutoring in classrooms, documenting differences in attitudes of the tutors and the tutored students.

Teaching Anecdote: Tell your students about the second-grade student who was having great difficulty learning the distinction between long and short vowel sounds. Her teacher had taught numerous lessons to the entire class and to the student's reading group. The teacher had also given the student individual help. None of these tactics created the understanding the teacher desired for the student. One day, in the computer lab, the girl chose a program on long vowel sounds. The program generated a graphic presentation of a clown who juggled one ball for every sound correctly identified. The program captivated the student. Within two weeks, the student passed a vowel mastery test with 100 percent accuracy.

Ask your students why the computer program might have enabled the student to master the critical distinction when the other tactics failed.

Lecture Note: Arrange a demonstration by a teacher who uses CAI in its various forms.

Lecture Note: Some of these disadvantages will be remedied by newer technology, such as multimedia and hypermedia programs.

this reason cross-age tutoring is more often recommended than same-age tutoring (Devin-Sheehan, Feldman, & Allen, 1976). Cross-age tutoring is more likely to be acceptable to the younger student who has been assigned an older tutor. Devin-Sheehan et al. recommend that the separation between the tutor and the student being tutored be two to three grade levels.

Computers and Instruction

Computer-assisted instruction (CAI) makes use of computer programs as primary or supplementary instructional materials. Computer programs can serve three basic functions. They can be used for tutorials, drill and practice, and simulations.

Tutorials

Tutorial programs present information to students. They function in a way that is similar to a teacher using a textbook. Better tutorial programs allow students opportunities to work with information and then evaluate their performances. A student who is able to put the evaluation function to good use will be better prepared to learn additional information. A good tutorial has several advantages over a book. It can provide immediate interactive feedback; it may include animated graphics; it can focus the attention of the student more carefully. Tutorials also have some disadvantages. A student may be able to move about more easily in a book and the computer screen may not be large enough to simultaneously display all of the information that the student needs.

Computer simulations are particularly useful for students who have been mainstreamed. The teacher can use simulations to create environments or circumstances that would not otherwise be accessible.

Profiles in Successful Practice

LINDA WYGODA

SAM HOUSTON HIGH SCHOOL

MOSS BLUFF, LOUISIANA

The integration of science with other content areas is central to my teaching philosophy. I enjoy motivating students through inquiry lab activities, creative writing assignments, writing journals, and role-playing simulations. Some of my science lessons incorporate music, math, history, literature, and art. I have found that student-centered lessons allow me to better know my students' experiences so that I can adjust and plan future class work. These types of lessons create a motivating environment that encourages students to think critically and relate science to other areas of their lives.

Today's high school students are often preoccupied with the demands of work, family, and peers. As teachers, we compete for their attention and must use creative methods and a variety of teaching techniques to satisfy the variety of learning styles that students bring to our classrooms. The teacher who has a broad background in the content area and who stays current in that area as well as in educational research is better able to adapt to the changing classroom environment. For example, one of the highlights of my career was my selection and participation in the Mt. St. Helens Workshop with thirty other science teachers from across the country. This opportunity to study a unique environmental feature with other teachers greatly rejuvenated my enthusiasm and creativity in the classroom.

Teaching is a most challenging and demanding profession because today's teachers do not just teach but are asked to perform numerous tasks: supervise playgrounds, monitor halls and restrooms, counsel students, participate on committees, sponsor clubs, order equipment, collect money, hold parent conferences, among others. I became a teacher because of my love of science and my desire to share that enthusiasm with others. I think that for all teachers one of our greatest thrills is the look of understanding in the face of a child struggling to learn.

Drill and Practice

Drill-and-practice programs provide repeated exercises and feedback on a designated objective. Drill and practice has a reputation of being boring for students. By working on a computer terminal, it is possible to tailor the type and amount of practice to a student's individual needs, thus heightening interest.

Simulations

Simulation programs approximate activities that cannot be done in the classroom because they are too expensive, dangerous, time consuming, or even unethical. Suppose a teacher wished to discuss the importance of rain forests and the effects of deforestation, not only in the particular locale of the rain forest, but on a global scale. It would be a difficult and expensive field trip. The effects of deforestation, however, can be modeled on a computer, trees can be cut down with a key stroke, and the effects of deforestation examined. A good simulation program should focus on the target phenomenon without letting extraneous information distract the student. A good simulation should also provide an accurate model of the actual phenomenon.

drill-and-practice programs Computer programs that provide repeated practice and immediate feedback on designated objectives.
simulation programs Computer programs that model real-life phenomena that cannot be done in the classroom in order to promote problem solving and motivate interest in the areas presented.

Field Observation: Have each student observe a classroom in which CAI drill and practice is used for remediation, documenting his or her impressions of the advantages and disadvantages of this technique.

Principles in Practice 11.2

Principles . . .

1. Individually oriented tactics match learning activities with student needs.
2. Individually oriented tactics relieve the teacher of the responsibility of being the sole source of instruction.
3. Individually oriented tasks allow the teacher time to observe and "troubleshoot."

. . . in Practice

In Teacher Chronicle 11.2, the teacher began by determining each student's level of knowledge about concepts of electricity. With this information in hand, the teacher assigned students, in pairs, to various lab stations, matching the level of the student's knowledge to the complexity of the assigned task. The teacher encouraged students to help each other. The class ended with students motivated to try new stations in subsequent classes.

1. What form did peer tutoring take during the electricity experiments?
2. What was the advantage of having different kinds of apparatuses (e.g., circuit boards, computer graphics, etc.) available for students?
3. Should the lab pairs have been formed on some basis other than or in addition to prior knowledge of electricity?

Teacher
Chronicle
11.3

NO EXCEPTIONS TO THE RULE

Mainstreaming exceptional students is one of the most intriguing and challenging aspects of teaching today. How do I meet the needs of a learning disabled student? a gifted child? someone with a hearing problem? How do I teach science to a boy with cerebral palsy or teach math to a mentally retarded girl? How do I adapt my tactics to fit each child? How do I find the match between ability and material? There are no easy answers to these questions. Each answer lies in meeting the individual needs of the student.

When Tony, who had cerebral palsy, was assigned to my science class, I knew there were challenges ahead for me, for Tony, and for the rest of the class. I had met Tony the year before because his EMR room was across the hall from my class. His teacher gave me a quick rundown on Tony. She told me that "Tony has great difficulty expressing himself, but Louise, his aide, can usually understand what he is saying and will tell you. He cannot control his hands well enough to write, so he'll have to dictate written work to Louise. He does like to learn and should do well in your class."

She failed to mention his spontaneous outbursts of moaning that frequently interrupted my lectures, his inability to use science equipment, or his social problems.

My mission was to teach him regular seventh-grade science. Knowing that Tony would have a full-time aide to help him, I made my main goal to involve him as much as possible and to adapt the lessons to fit his special needs. To do this I knew I would have to use my ingenuity as well as rely on help from his peers.

First, I established a rotation system for seating to ensure that all students would work with and help Tony individually. I also geared my lessons to large group as well as small group activities, again using a rotation system to make certain that Tony worked with everyone on a team. Arrangements were made to bring Tony on my regular field trips to the nature center, state museum, and the local limestone quarry.

From the beginning Tony put his heart into his work. I soon realized how difficult it must be for him with so much going on in his head, the understanding he was gaining of basic science, and his frustration at not being able to communicate as he wished to. But with Louise translating and writing for him and his group participation, he made great progress from the first day. I could see the strain of the effort to successfully stop a moaning outburst on his face. His eyes sparkled with pride when he turned in his leaf collection project. He nearly jumped out of his wheelchair when he got a *B* on his first report card.

One day in the first quarter when Tony was absent, I told the rest of the class how proud I was of them. "You have all been so helpful in working with Tony. No one has complained about being in his group or being his individual partner. If there was a grade for social acceptance, I would give you all an *A*! If we can all keep this up, Tony might even get an *A* before school's out."

Tony never got that grade, although his progress continued all year. Louise summed things up best at the end of the year when she told me, "You accomplished things with Tony that no one else has been able to do. Not even his special ed teacher has the rapport with him that you have. I've never seen him learn so much."

Tony wasn't the only one who learned a lot that year. I did, too. Kids really are more alike than they are different.

■■■

TEACHING EXCEPTIONAL STUDENTS

The implementation of the various instructional tactics examined in this chapter requires the teacher to make decisions regarding the specific needs of learners. In Chapter 4, we examined the characteristics of various groups of exceptional students. In this section, we will focus on the tactical requirements of teaching exceptional students. Most tactical decisions are made by the teacher; some of the adaptive actions that the teacher takes are mandated by law. Such actions include the instruction of students who have been identified as exceptional.

The instructional actions required for exceptional students are provided in the Education for All Handicapped Children Act of 1975, also known as Public Law 94-142. There are three major elements of PL 94-142 that teachers must consider when making instructional decisions for exceptional students: least restrictive environment, individualized education program (IEP), and due process.

Least Restrictive Environment

PL 94-142 has, at times, been called the mainstreaming law. *Mainstreaming* is the inclusion of exceptional students in regular classrooms. The least restric-

Chap. Obj. 7
Test Ques. 11.81–11.95

Focus Question: What tactical decisions are required when teaching exceptional students?

Connection: The characteristics of various exceptionalities are described in Chapter 4.

Teacher Interview: Have students interview special education teachers regarding the practical implications of PL 94-142.

least restrictive environment
An instructional environment that is as similar to the regular classroom as possible given the child's special needs.

tive environment element of PL 94-142 refers to the instructional placement of an exceptional student. **Least restrictive environment** means that a student should be educated in an environment that is as "normal" as possible. Mainstreaming, therefore, is the practice of placing exceptional children in what is considered the "normal" educational environment, that is, the regular classroom. Of all possible placements, the regular classroom is the least restrictive environment. Although PL 94-142 mandates placement in the least restrictive environment, it has not eliminated special classes, institutions, or a student's home as possible educational placements. When the regular classroom proves to be the least restrictive environment possible for a particular exceptional student, that student is mainstreamed.

Aside from the regular classroom as a placement, some exceptional students may find themselves working individually with a consulting or itinerant teacher for part of the school day. Exceptional students may also spend part of the school day in the regular classroom and part of the day in a resource room.

Adapting to Exceptional Students

Lecture Note: Have students "brainstorm" ways of adapting classroom lessons involving students with varying disabilities.

Pamela Maniet-Bellermann is the teacher whose students wrote *"L.D." Does NOT Mean Learning Dumd!* Maniet-Bellermann has herself published guidelines for the regular education teacher working with exceptional students (1986). Her general guidelines emphasize the abilities of students rather than their disabilities.

Teaching Anecdote: Tell your students about the first-grade teacher who was assigned five mainstreamed students for an hour of reading instruction. The students had been diagnosed as mentally retarded. The teacher, who had no training in teaching mentally retarded children, was willing to work with mainstreamed students. Prior to the mainstreaming, the teacher's reading program had focused exclusively on reading and writing. After several weeks of working with the mainstreamed students, the teacher moved away from her written word approach and began teaching by reading poems, rhymes, stories, and by having students take dictation as classmates told their own stories. She found that her new approach helped not only the mainstreamed students participate, but also discovered that other students expanded their language use and adapted to the printed word more easily.

Ask your students to explain the results of the teacher's "experiment."

Connection: *"L.D." Does NOT Mean Learning Dumd!* is excerpted in the learning disability section in Chapter 4.

1. Present material on tape for students who cannot read successfully. School volunteers, older students, or parents can be asked to make recordings of assigned material.
2. Allow students to tape-record answers if writing is difficult or their handwriting is illegible.
3. Provide lots of visual reminders (pictures, maps, charts, graphs) for students who have trouble listening or attending.
4. Present handouts that are clear, legible, and uncrowded. Blurred copies are very hard for the LD child to read.
5. Break directions and assignments into small steps. Completion of each step is an accomplishment—reward it.
6. Give tests orally if the child has trouble with reading, spelling, or writing. Testing which demonstrates what the student knows rather than language skills gives you a clearer picture of the student's abilities. The student demonstrates abilities, not disabilities.
7. Emphasize quality rather than quantity of writing.
8. Be consistent with directions, rules, discipline, and organization.
9. Arrange the class schedule so the exceptional student does not miss important activities when he or she goes to the resource room.
10. Dispense encouragement freely but fairly. If students make errors, help them find the correct answers, and then reward them.
11. Discover the exceptional student's strengths and special interests. Capitalize on them in the regular classroom.
12. Carefully establish routines so that the student does not become further handicapped by the confusion of unclear expectations.
13. Arrange desks, tables, and chairs so every person can be easily seen and every word easily heard. Remember, students with hearing deficits need to see your face as you speak.

14. If possible, schedule difficult subjects when there are no outside noises, such as a class at recess.
15. Provide carrels or screens—an "office"—for students who are easily distracted.
16. When checking students' work, check correct answers rather than incorrect answers. The student is still informed of mistakes, but sees his or her successes emphasized.
17. Allow the exceptional student to tape lectures or arrange for a classmate who writes neatly to use carbon paper. Either the carbon copy or a copy of the teacher's notes can be given to the exceptional student.
18. Correct deficient lighting, glare from windows, and light-blocking partitions. Small lighting problems can be big distractions for some exceptional students.
19. Fit the furniture to the child. Discomfort leads to distraction and restlessness.
20. Generally, become sensitive to the obstacles which prevent the exceptional student from exercising his or her abilities.

The practical implication of the least restrictive environment clause in PL 94-142 is that you will likely teach exceptional students no matter what your certification area. Use Maniet-Bellermann's guidelines as hypotheses to test if you find yourself teaching exceptional students. Indeed, some of the actions she suggests seem likely to benefit any student.

Individualized Education Program

The second element of PL 94-142 is the individualized education program. An **individualized education program (IEP)** is an instructional plan developed through a conference involving the exceptional student's teacher or teachers, parents, other school personnel, and, when appropriate, the student. It is at the IEP conference that a determination is made of the specific services required to assist the student. Although the formats for IEP's vary from state to state, most IEP's include a statement of the student's current level of academic, social, psychomotor, and self-help skills. The IEP also includes a statement of the long-term goals and short-term objectives for the student. In addition, the IEP contains a timeline for attaining goals, the environment in which the student will receive instruction, criteria for judging the attainment of goals and objectives, a justification for all decisions, and a list of the people who will execute the IEP (Heward & Orlansky, 1980). (See Figure 11-2.)

Due Process

The final element in PL 94-142 concerns **due process,** procedures that protect the rights of parents and students. The rights of students and parents include confidentiality. Schools must have established procedures that maintain the confidentiality of school records of exceptional students. Rights mandated by PL 94-142 also include forms of evaluation that do not discriminate against students who come from minority cultural backgrounds.

Parents have the right to see the records and, if they desire, to obtain an independent evaluation of their child. Parents are involved in the IEP confer-

individualized education program (IEP) An instructional plan tailored to the needs of an exceptional student.
due process A course of legal proceedings that protect the rights of parents and students.

Teacher Interview: Have each student interview a teacher, asking that teacher to comment on Maniet-Bellermann's guidelines by comparing them with his or her experiences with LD students.

Chapter 15 Casebook Preview: See Taking Control.

Field Observation: Have students collect IEP forms from various schools and interview principals or supervisors regarding their roles in IEP conferences.

Confidential Information — **INDIVIDUALIZED EDUCATION PROGRAM** — School Year 89-90 — SE 10

Name Kevin Doe DOB 1-9-84 School Curry Elementary Grade 1 (primary EMR)

Handicapping condition mild mental retardation/speech-language delay Date of IEP meeting 4-11-90 (M-D-Y) Notification to parent 4-6-90 (M-D-Y)

Initiation and anticipated duration of services 4-90 (M-Y) to 6-92 (M-Y) Eligibility/Triennial 4-1-93 (M-D-Y) Plan to be reviewed no later than 9-90 (M-Y)

Educational/Vocational Program

Special Education Services	Regular Education Services
self-contained EMR class	first grade homeroom
	art, music, lunch, fieldtrips with first grade
Total Amount Times/Wk. 5 Hrs./Day 3	Total Amount Times/Wk. 5 Hrs./Day 2

Related Services

Type	Amount
speech-language therapy	2 30 min./wk

Physical Education
Adapted Class Amount none
Regular Class Amount as scheduled for homeroom

Transportation
Special ______ Regular ✓

Current Level of Performance Orally spells his name but cannot write it without help (often gets letters in wrong sequence). Names sounds m, a, ē, r, s, f, d inconsistently. "Counts" to 14, but not always sequentially ("1, 2, 5, 8..."). Names numerals, but not consistently. Has one-to-one correspondence to 10. Knows only colors red and green. Difficulty with plurals. Does not consistently answer who, what, where, when questions. Impulsive in group. Imitates misbehavior and doesn't stop when asked. Usually falls asleep by 11:00 am.

Participants in Plan Development

Name	Title
Corine Doe	mother
Jessica Via	first grade teacher
Pat Hassie	teacher (EMR)
Dan Ruffner	principal

For High School Students ONLY (to be initially completed at 9th grade IEP meeting and reviewed annually).
This student is a candidate for: High School Diploma _____; Special Ed. Certificate _____; GED Equivalency Diploma _____.
Is the Minimum Competency Test to be administered this school year? Yes _____ No _____ If yes, attach addendum.

White: Confidential Folder Yellow: Parent Copy

INDIVIDUALIZED EDUCATION PROGRAM — School Year 89-90 — SE 10a

ANNUAL GOAL: The student Kevin Doe will: increase reading/language skills commensurate with ability

SHORT TERM OBJECTIVES	Grading Periods	PROGRESS REPORTS: COMMENTS
Objective: will name following sounds with 100% accuracy when presented randomly (2 trials): m, a, d, ē, f, r, s, i, t Beginning Skill Level: inconsistent on above Date Initiated 4-16-90	1. 2. 3. 4.	
Objective: will name color of object when presented with object and asked what color for red, blue, yellow, green, orange, black, brown (100% accuracy, 2 trials) Beginning Skill Level: Knows only green and red Date Initiated 4-16-90	1. 2. 3. 4.	
Objective: will identify and name letters a-g with 100% accuracy on 2 trials. Beginning Skill Level: inconsistent on above Date Initiated 4-16-90	1. 2. 3. 4.	
Objective: will blend consonant-vowel-consonant words using sounds m, a, d, ē, f, r, s, i, t with 100% accuracy on 2 trials. Beginning Skill Level: no current skills Date Initiated 4-16-90	1. 2. 3. 4.	

Evaluation Procedures: Annual goals will be evaluated during the annual review. Short term objectives will be monitored at each nine week marking period. Beginning skill level indicates the student's performance prior to instruction.

Progress Key: No mark—Objective not initiated; P—Progressing on the Objective; D—Having difficulty with the objective (comment to describe difficulty); M—Objective mastered; M/R—Objective mastered, but needs review to maintain mastery

White: Confidential Folder Yellow: Parent Progress Report Pink: Teacher Working Copy Goldenrod: Parent Original

■ **Figure 11–2** *An Example of a Form Documenting an IEP*

SOURCE: From *Exceptional Children* (5th ed., p. 27) by D. P. Hallahan and J. M. Kauffman, 1991, Englewood Cliffs, NJ: Prentice Hall. Copyright 1991 by Prentice Hall. Reprinted by permission.

ence. The due process clause of PL 94-142 guarantees that parents may bring a representative to the IEP conference in order to ensure that the best interests of their child are served. Parents must receive written notice before any evaluation or change in placement is made. Parents also have the right to challenge the IEP developed for their child, including any placement.

A recent estimate suggests that between 11 percent and 12 percent of American schoolchildren participate in some kind of special education program (Gartner & Lipsky, 1987). Whether they have a formal diagnostic label or not, you will encounter exceptional students in your classroom. Teachers are required by PL 94-142 to provide certain kinds of instructional environments. Maniet-Bellermann's (1986) guidelines help us focus on the types of tactical decisions required when teaching exceptional students. Despite the legal requirements that teachers must follow when teaching exceptional children, it is important to recall that the advice of the LD students whose book is excerpted in Chapter 4. Exceptional students are more like their peers than they are different from them.

The Traveling Notebook

Exceptional students can listen to lectures, engage in small group discussions, and work on computers. Depending on a student's disability, physical or procedural adaptations may be necessary, but mainstreamed students will be exposed to the same tactics as regular students. One difference is the degree of coordination required among regular education and special education teachers, therapists or other educational specialists, and parents. Some of the coordination of instructional tactics needed to teach an exceptional student is taken care of through the IEP. However, an ongoing communication among professionals and parents is helpful to all involved in caring for and educating an exceptional student.

A **traveling notebook** documents the actions, decisions, and evaluations of the people who work with an exceptional student. It is a tool for establishing and maintaining the communication necessary for effective coordination (Hallahan & Kauffman, 1991). Figure 11-3 (pp. 428–432) presents excerpts from the traveling notebook of a preschool girl who has cerebral palsy.

traveling notebook A "collective diary" that documents the decisions and evaluations of the people who work with an exceptional student.

Lecture Note: Remind students of the distinction made in Chapter 4 between *disability* and *handicap*.

Teacher Interview: Have each student interview a teacher who uses the traveling notebook about its usefulness and limitations.

Principles in Practice 11.3

Principles . . .
1. Mainstreaming requires teachers to adapt classroom activities to the needs of exceptional students.
2. Individualized education programs are required for all exceptional students.
3. Because exceptional students may work with a number of education professionals, coordination among professionals and parents is important.

. . . in Practice
In Teacher Chronicle 11.3, the teacher used "regular" tactics to teach Tony along with his classmates. The major adaptation was to accommodate the aide who assisted Tony in communicating. Although special arrangements

were necessary so that Tony could participate in all activities in and out of the classroom, the teacher did alter the content of the course or lower academic criteria. The teacher expected the same standards of performance of Tony that were expected of the other students. The teacher helped everyone in the class understand that although Tony was exceptional, he was not an exception.

1. Given the activities of the science class, what adaptations might have been necessary for a blind student?
2. What questions would you have asked Louise, Tony's aide, before he was mainstreamed?
3. If you were the teacher, what would you have told another teacher who was about to receive Tony as a mainstreamed student?

The following short excerpts are taken at random from a notebook that accompanies two-year-old Lauren, who has cerebral palsy, back and forth to her special class for preschoolers. The notebook provides a convenient mode for an ongoing dialogue among her mother, Lyn; her teacher, Sara; her occupational therapist, Joan; and her speech therapist, Marti. As you can see from this representative sample, the communication is informal but very informative on a variety of items relating to Lauren.

Lyn,
 Lauren did _very_ well—We had several criers but—She played & worked very nicely. She responds so well to instruction—that's such a plus!
 She fed herself crackers & juice & did a good job. She was very vocal & enjoyed the other children too. She communicated c̄ me very well for the 1ˢᵗ day.
 Am pleased c̄ her first day.
 Sara

■ **Figure 11–3** *Excerpts from a Traveling Notebook*

SOURCE: From *Exceptional Children* (5th ed., pp. 472–476) by D. P. Hallahan and J. M. Kauffman, 1991, Englewood Cliffs, NJ: Prentice Hall. Copyright 1991 by Prentice Hall. Reprinted by permission.

Sara,   9/15

    Please note that towel, toothbrush/paste + clean clothes may be removed from bag today—WED. We witnessed an apparently significant moment in her oral communication: She'll try to say "all done" after a meal. The execution is imperfect, to say the least, but she gets an "A" for effort. Could you please reinforce this after snack? Just ask her, "What do you say after you finish your snack?"

                        Thanks,

                           Lyn

9/28

    Lauren had an esp. good day! She was jabbering a lot! Being very expressive ō her vocalness & jabbering. I know she said "yes" or an approximate thereof, several times when asked if she wanted something. She was so cute ō the animal sounds esp. pig & horse—she was really trying to make the sounds. It was the first time we had seen such a response. Still cruising a lot! She walked ō me around the room & in the gym. She used those consonant & vowel sounds: dadada, mama ma—her jabbering was just so different

& definitely progressive. I am sending her work card c̄ stickers home tomorrow for good working.

Several notes:

① Susie (VI) came today & evaluated Lauren. She will compile a report & be in touch with you and me. She seemed very pleased c̄ Lauren's performance.

② Marti (speech) will see Lauren tomorrow at 11 AM for evaluation. She'll be in touch afterwards.

③ Susie informed me about the addition to the IEP meeting on Mon. Oct. 4 at 10 AM here at Woodbrook.

How is the tape & cards working at home? I know you both are pleased c̄ her jabbering. She seems so ready to say "something" – we are very, very pleased. See you tomorrow.

Sara

9/29

Lauren was a bit fussy during O.T. today—she stopped fussing during fine motor reaching activities (peg board, block building) but wasn't too pleased with being handled on the ball. She did a great job with the peg board & readily used her left hand.

I want to bring in some different spoons next week to see if she can become more independent in scooping with a large handle spoon or a spoon that is curved

Joan

Joan —

Although Lauren would very much approve of your idea for making her more independant during feeding, we'd rather not initiate self-feeding with an adaptive spoon at this time. Here's why:

① When I feed Lauren or get her to grip a spoon and then guide her hand, I can slip the entire bowl of the spoon into her mouth and get her to close her lips on it. When Lauren uses a spoon without help, she turns it upside-down to lick it or inserts just the tip of it into her mouth and then sucks off the food...

② Lauren has always been encouraged to do things "normally". She never had a special cup or a "Tommy Tippee", for instance. Of course, it took a year of practice before she could drink well from a cup, and she still dribbles a little occasionally; but she's doing well now. We really prefer to give Lauren practice in using a regular spoon so that she doesn't get dependant on an adaptive utensil. I'd like to assure you that we appreciate your communication about sessions with Lauren and ideas for her therapy. Coordinating her school, home, and CRC programs is going to be a challenge, to say the least

Lyn

☺! Lauren walked all the way from the room to Gym & back—
She also walked up & down the full length of the gym!
Several other teachers saw her and were thrilled.
She fell maybe twice!
But picked herself right up—

Sara

3/2

Lauren had a great speech session! We were playing with some toys and she said "I want help" as plain as day. Later she said "I want crackers" and at the end of the session, she imitated "Cindy, let's go." Super!

Marti

CONCLUSION

Assign Chapter 11 of the *Study Guide*.

Through this chapter we have discussed the tactical decisions that go along with the instructional part of teaching (see E. Gagné, 1985). Choosing the tactics to use to bring our students into contact with content material is central to our success as teachers. But instructional decisions are critical only if such decisions make a difference. Imagine the futility of agonizing over a choice between team learning and peer tutoring when one half of your students sleeps through classes and the other half never listens to you. Instructional decisions, no matter how carefully reasoned, are rendered useless by a classroom full of disruptive students.

There is a set of decisions that we make about how our classrooms will be run and the rules that our students will be asked to follow. The decisions we make about the classroom environment in which our instructional efforts occur are management decisions. The management tactics examined in Chapter 12 support the instructional tactics discussed in this chapter.

Students will find it difficult to learn in situations in which they are unsure of what is expected of them. It will make little difference when you decide that students should learn in teams if you have not taught them to cooperate in your classroom.

Chapter Summary

Introduction: Management and Instruction
Tactics can be classified according to two functions: instruction and management. Instruction involves helping students learn the material presented to them. Management involves the actions taken to connect students and the material to be learned. The focus of this chapter is instructional tactics.

Large Group Instruction
Lecture
Lecture is the most common large group tactic because it is a very efficient way of presenting information. It works at least as well as other methods when information needs to be organized in a particular fashion for a particular group of students. Lecture also provides an opportunity for the teacher to model communication skills and to demonstrate enthusiasm for the topic.

Explanation
Explanations are more focused than lectures. Effective teachers provide explanations that are more responsive to student needs than teachers who are less effective. Effective explanations tend to provide a context or framework for students. Although explanations are often part of a lecture, explanations can be initiated by student questions as well.

Questioning
Questioning, as a tactic, can be thought of as occurring in three stages. Structure sets the stage for the questions to follow. Solicitation refers to the types of questions that are asked. Reaction is the teacher's response to a student's answer. Generally, increased wait-time is associated with increased achievement. However, there are times, such as during drill-and-

practice sessions, when longer wait-times are counterproductive.

Seatwork

Seatwork refers to work completed independently by the student. Although independent practice is helpful, too much reliance on the tactic has been shown to compound the problems of low-achieving students. Seatwork is most effective when it is used in balance with other tactics. Homework is considered a special example of seatwork, the difference being that teachers are unable to monitor homework in the same way they monitor seatwork.

Small Group Instruction
Discussion Groups

Small group discussions are best suited to topics on which there is a low level of consensus. This tactic has also been shown to be an effective way of changing attitudes and beliefs. If the tactic is selected in order to give students a chance to explore their own ideas, it is important not to intervene in the discussion unless there are signs that the group is getting off-task.

Cooperative Learning in Teams

Cooperative team learning calls for the formation of small groups that function as a team, not a group of individuals. The team members become responsible for other team members' mastering of material. The student teams-achievement divisions (STAD) procedure and the teams-games-tournaments (TGT) procedure are variations on the theme of group responsibility for individual performance.

Individually Oriented Tactics
Individualized Instruction

Individualized instruction refers to students working at their own pace with materials selected to meet their individual needs. The mastery approach, programmed instruction, Keller's personalized system of instruction, and team-assisted instruction are individualized procedures that allow students to work according to their individual needs in various ways.

Peer Tutoring

Peer tutoring involves arranging for one student to help another student learn material. The tactic enhances the performance of both the tutored student and the tutor. In a same-age tutoring situation, the tutor tends to be perceived as superior; researchers suggest that cross-age tutoring is a more effective way to use the tactic.

Computers and Instruction

Computer-assisted instruction (CAI) is a way of individualizing learning in a classroom. CAI programs can serve three basic functions—as tutorials, for drill-and-practice exercises, and as simulations. Simulations allow the student to experience ideas and relationships that might otherwise be too expensive or too dangerous to pursue.

Teaching Exceptional Students
Least Restrictive Environment

When teaching exceptional students, there are several legislated actions that must be undertaken (according to Public Law 94-142). To meet the requirements of the first, least restrictive environment, students must be taught in environments that approximate, as closely as possible, the regular classroom. The practical result is that exceptional students are mainstreamed whenever possible.

Individualized Education Program

Exceptional students require an individualized education program (IEP). An IEP is determined at a conference involving teachers, parents, a school official, and when possible, the student. The purpose of the conference is to plan a series of goals and a timeline for the exceptional student to attain those goals.

Due Process

Due process is the element of PL 94-142 that requires schools to establish procedures that guard the confidentiality of both parents and students. Due process gives parents the right to see records and to challenge placements or an IEP.

The Traveling Notebook

The traveling notebook is a device for enhancing the communication among the professionals and the parents of an exceptional student. Because exceptional students may be working with several teachers and/or therapists, as well as parents at home, it is important for everyone working with the child to know what others are experiencing. The traveling notebook serves as a collective "diary." It contains the notes, observations, comments, and so on of everyone involved in the student's education. In this way, everyone is kept informed.

Reflections: Building Your Theory of Teaching

11.1 Reflect on teachers you have had who were both good lecturers and good explainers. What made them good lecturers? Why were their explanations effective? What skills are required to explain subject matter effectively that are not required to lecture on it?

11.2 Think about a unit you anticipate teaching. First, without looking ahead, write two discussion questions that you would assign to small groups. Second, describe how you and your former classmates would have responded to the questions you just wrote.

11.3 What guidelines will you implement in your classroom to ensure that students from minority microcultures and exceptional students will feel comfortable contributing to group discussions or cooperative work?

Key Terms

management tactics (p. 398)
instructional tactics (p. 398)
lecture (p. 401)
explanation (p. 402)
questioning (p. 403)
wait-time I (p. 404)
wait-time II (p. 404)
seatwork (p. 405)
team learning (p. 410)
student teams-achievement divisions (STAD) (p. 410)
teams-games-tournaments (TGT) (p. 411)
mastery approach (p. 415)
programmed instruction (p. 416)
personalized system of instruction (PSI) (p. 416)
team-assisted instruction (TAI) (p. 416)
peer tutoring (p. 419)
computer-assisted instruction (CAI) (p. 420)
tutorial programs (p. 420)
drill-and-practice programs (p. 421)
simulation programs (p. 421)
least restrictive environment (p. 424)
individualized education program (IEP) (p. 425)
due process (p. 425)
traveling notebook (p. 427)

Suggested Readings

Hollingsworth, P. M. & Hoover, K. H. (1991). *Elementary teaching methods.* Needham Heights, MA: Allyn & Bacon.

Johnson, D. W. & Johnson, R. T. (1991). *Learning together and alone: Cooperative, competitive and individualistic learning* (3rd ed.).

Kauchak, D. P. & Eggen, P. D. (1989). *Learning and teaching: Research-based methods.* Needham Heights, MA: Allyn & Bacon.

Levine, J. M. (1989). *Secondary instruction: A manual for classroom teaching.* Needham Heights, MA: Allyn & Bacon.

Rosenshine, B. V. & Stevens, R. J. (1986). "Teaching functions." In M. C. Wittrock (Ed.), *Third handbook of research on teaching.* Chicago: Rand McNally.

Wittrock, M. C. (Ed.). (1986). *Third handbook of research on teaching.* Chicago: Rand McNally.

References

Anderson, L. M., Brubaker, N. L., Alleman-Brooks, J., & Duffy, G. G. (1985). A qualitative study of seatwork in first-grade classrooms. *Elementary School Journal, 86,* 123–140.

Bangert, R., Kulik, J., & Kulik, C. (1983). Individual systems of instruction in secondary schools. *Review of Educational Research, 53*(2), 143–158.

Bligh, D. A. (1972). *What's the use of lectures?* (2nd ed.) Harmondsworth, England: Penguin.

Bloom. B. S. (1968). Learning for mastery. *Evaluation Comment, 1*(2).

Bloom, B. S. (1984). The two sigma problem: The search for methods of group instruction as effective as one-to-one tutoring. *Educational Researcher, 13*(6), 4–16.

Brophy, J., & Evertson, C. (1974). *The Texas Teacher Effectiveness Project: Presentation of non-linear relationships and summary discussion* (Report No.

74–6). Austin: Research and Development Center for Teacher Education, University of Texas in Austin. (ERIC Document Reproduction Service No. ED 099 345)

Clark, C. M., Gage, N. L., Marx, R. W., Peterson, P. L., Staybrook, N. G., & Winne, P. H. (1979). A factorial experiment on teacher structuring, soliciting, and reacting. *Journal of Educational Psychology, 71*, 534–552.

Cohen, P. A., Kulik, J. A., & Kulik, C. C. (1982). Educational outcomes of tutoring: A meta-analysis of findings. *American Educational Research Journal, 19*, 237–248.

Devin-Sheehan, L., Feldman, R. S., & Allen, V. L. (1976). Research on children tutoring children: A critical review. *Review of Educational Research, 46*, 355–385.

Duffy, G. G., Roehler, L. R., Meloth, M. S., & Vavrus, L. G. (1986). Conceptualizing instructional explanation. *Teaching and Teacher Education, 2*, 197–214.

Elawar, M. C., & Corno, L. (1985). A factorial experiment in teachers' written feedback on student homework: Changing teacher behavior a little rather than a lot. *Journal of Educational Psychology, 77*, 162–173.

Evertson, C., Emmer, E., & Brophy, J. (1980). Predictors of effective teaching in junior high mathematics classrooms. *Journal of Research on Mathematics Education, II*, 167–178.

Fagan, E. R., Hassler, D. M., & Szabo, M. (1981). Evaluation of questioning strategies in language arts instruction. *Research in the Teaching of English, 15*, 267–273.

Fisher, C., Berliner, D., Filby, N., Marliave, R., Cahen, L., & Dishaw, M. (1980). Teaching behaviors, academic learning time, and student achievement: An overview. In C. Denham & A. Lieberman (Eds.), *Time to learn*. Washington, DC: National Institute of Education.

Gage, N. L., & Berliner, D. C. (1988). *Educational psychology*. Boston, MA: Houghton Mifflin.

Gagné, R. M. (1985). *The conditions of learning* (4th ed.). New York: Holt, Rinehart & Winston.

Gall, M. D. (1984). Synthesis of research on teachers' questioning. *Educational Leadership, 41*, 40–47.

Gall, M. D., & Gall, J. P. (1976). The discussion method. In N. L. Gage (Ed.), *The psychology of teaching methods: Seventy-fifth yearbook of the National Society for the Study of Education* (Pt. 1, pp. 166–216). Chicago, IL: University of Chicago Press.

Gartner, A., & Lipsky, D. K. (1987). Beyond special education: Toward a quality system for all students. *Harvard Educational Review, 57*, 367–395.

Good, T. L. (1988). Teacher expectations. In D. Berliner & B. Rosenshine (Eds.), *Talks to teachers*. New York: Random House.

Good, T. L., Grouws, D., & Ebmeier, H. (1983). *Active mathematics teaching*. New York: Longman.

Gunter, M. A., Estes, T. H., & Hasbrouck Schwab, J. (1990). *Instruction: A models approach*. Boston, MA: Allyn & Bacon.

Hallahan, D. Pl, & Kauffman, J. M. (1991). *Exceptional children: Introduction to special education* (5th 3d.). Englewood Cliffs, NJ: Prentice-Hall.

Heward, W., & Orlansky, M. (1980). *Exceptional children*. Columbus, OH: Charles E. Merrill.

Hunter, M. (1984). Knowing, teaching, and supervising. In P. Hosford (Ed.), *Using what we know about teaching*. Alexandria, VA: Association for Supervision and Curriculum Development.

Keith, T. Z. (1982). Time spent on homework and high school grades. A large-sample path analysis. *Journal of Education Psychology, 74*, 248–253.

Keller, F. S. (1968). "Good-bye teacher. . . ." *Journal of Applied Behavior Analysis, 1*, 79–88.

Maniet-Bellermann, P. J. (1986). *Mainstreaming children with learning disabilities: A guide to accompany "L.D." does not mean Learning Dumd!* Pittsburgh, PA: Upward Bound Press.

Marshall, P. M. (1982). *Homework and social facilitation theory in teaching elementary school mathematics*. Unpublished doctoral dissertation, Stanford University, Stanford, CA.

McKeachie, W. J. (1967). Research in teaching: The gap between theory and practice. In C. B. T. Lee (Ed.), *Improving college teaching*. Washington, DC: American Council on Education.

McKeachie, W. J. (1986). *Teaching tips: A guide book for the beginning college teacher*. Lexington, MA: D. C. Heath.

McKeachie, W. J., & Kulik, J. A. (1975). Effective college teaching. In F. N. Kerlinger (Ed.), *Review of research in education* (Vol. 3). Washington, DC: American Educational Research Association.

McLeish, J. (1976). The lecture method. In N. L. Gage (Ed.), *The psychology of teaching methods: Seventy-fifth yearbook of the National Society for the Study of Education*. Chicago, IL: University of Chicago Press.

Peterson, P. L., & Clark, C. M. (1978). Teachers' reports of their cognitive processes during teaching. *American Educational Research Journal, 15,* 555–565.

Rosenshine, B. (1980). How time is spent in elementary classrooms. In C. Denham & A. Lieberman (Eds.), *Time to learn.* Washington, DC: National Institute of Education.

Rosenshine, B., & Furst, N. (1973). The use of direct observation to study teaching. In R. Travers (Ed.), *Second handbook of research on teaching.* Chicago, IL: Rand McNally.

Rowe, M. B. (1974). Wait-time and rewards as instructional variables, their influence on language, logic, and fate control: Part one—Wait-time. *Journal of Research in Science Teaching, 11,* 81–94.

Schoen, H. L. (1976). Self-paced mathematics instruction: How effective has it been? *Arithmetic Teacher, 23,* 90–96.

Slavin, R. E. (1985). Team-Assisted Individualization: A cooperative learning solution for adaptive instruction in mathematics. In M. Wang & H. Walberg (Eds.), *Adapting instruction to individual difference,* Berkeley: McCutchan.

Slavin, R. (1987). Cooperative learning and the cooperative school. *Educational Leadership, 45,* 7–13.

Slavin, R. (1988). Cooperative learning: A best-evidence synthesis. In R. E. Slavin (Ed.), *School and classroom organization.* Hillsdale, NJ: Erlbaum.

Stallings, J. A., & Kaskowitz, D. H. (1975, April). *A study of follow-through implementation.* Paper presented at the annual meeting of the American Educational Research Association, Washington, DC.

Tobin, K. (1987). The role of wait-time in higher cognitive level learning. *Review of Educational Research, 57,* 69–95.

Tobin, K. G., & Capie, W. (1982). Relationships between classroom process variables and middle-school science achievement. *Journal of Educational Psychology, 74,* 441–454.

Verner, C., & Dickinson, G. (1967). The lecture: An analysis and review of research. *Adult Education, 17*(2), 85–100.

Wolf, R. M. (1979). Achievement in the United States. In H. J. Walberg (Ed.), *Educational environments and effects: Evaluation, policy, and productivity.* Berkeley, CA: McCutchan.

12

Classroom Management, Discipline, and Communication

Chapter Overview

The models for instruction investigated in Chapter 11 give us blueprints, general ideas, about how to structure a lesson. In this chapter we'll be talking more about lessons as well, with an eye toward the problem of keeping students engaged in lesson activities. This chapter also presents approaches teachers can use when dealing with discipline problems. Finally, we'll examine several types of goal structures to determine how and under what conditions students can be rewarded. Throughout the chapter, we will emphasize the importance of clear communications within the classroom. ∎

Focus Question: What is the difference between discipline and classroom management?

Lecture Note: Before assigning this chapter, ask students to write a brief reflection on the phrase, "classroom management." Compare your students' reactions to the results of the informal survey discussed in the chapter.

Teacher Interview: Have each student interview a veteran teacher regarding the classroom management benefits of organized teaching.

Field Observation: Have each student observe a teacher delivering a lesson, identifying the elements of the teacher's actions that reflect active teaching.

INTRODUCTION: EXPERIENCE AND ORGANIZATION

The terms *classroom management* and *discipline* are often used interchangeably by those outside the teaching profession. Even those who are preparing to teach often use the terms synonymously.

We asked aspiring and veteran teachers to reflect on what is meant by the phrase "classroom management." The vast majority of aspiring teachers answered that classroom management is discipline. One aspiring teacher wrote, "I'm scared to death of what will happen when I walk into my first classroom. What happens if I walk in there and they all turn on me?" Veteran teachers, on the other hand, rarely used the word *discipline* in their descriptions of classroom management. For the veteran teachers, classroom management meant organizing for instruction, finding and preparing materials for lessons, and planning the sequence of objectives. Essentially, their answers revolved around organization. The best way to establish discipline in the classroom, say the veterans, is to be organized in your instruction (see also Royer & Feldman 1984; Woolfolk, 1987).

Teachers who have little problem with discipline in their classrooms engage and maintain their students' attention. They are what has been called "active teachers." Good (1986) has summarized the instructional factors that are associated with active instruction.

> Teachers who present information accurately, pay attention to the meaning and conceptional development of content, look for signs of student comprehension and confusion, and provide successful practice opportunities appear to have more achievement gains than do teachers who are less active and who rely more upon seatwork and other activities. . . . In active teaching, the initial style may be inductive or deductive, student learning may be self-initiated or teacher-initiated (especially if thorough

Management of a classroom requires energy, planning, involvement, and discipline.

critique and synthesis activities follow student's learning attempts). Active teaching also connotes a broader philosophical base (it may occur in classrooms using a variety of organizational structures) and should become somewhat less direct as students become more mature and instructional goals more focused on affective and process outcomes (p. 59)

Active teachers engage students' minds. If students are busy working on tasks that interest them, they do not have to invent other ways of keeping themselves occupied. Those "other ways" are often the disruptive behaviors that novice teachers dread.

The tactics you select to prime students, engage their attention and concentration on instructional tasks, and maintain their efforts are the subject matter of this chapter. We will examine various tactics teachers should keep in mind when they are lecturing, questioning, and leading a small group. We will look at the ways in which a teacher communicates his or her ideas about discipline in the classroom, and how the general atmosphere of the classroom is established.

Journal Entry: Have students reflect on those teachers from their experiences who did or did not engage their attention and imagination. Have them reflect on teachers' actions that led them to their evaluations.

SHARPENING THE FOCUS

Teacher Chronicle 12.1

One year, I jointly taught a forty-five minute social studies period with Mabel, the teacher next door. I would teach the combined classes for two days and she would teach the other two days. When I wasn't teaching, I scheduled planning time in the room in case I was needed to help. I had just switched to sixth grade and so the extra planning time came in handy. There was also a bonus—watching Mabel teach. I rarely had the opportunity to watch another teacher in action.

Mabel taught the first two days and my turn followed. While Mabel taught, I watched how she managed the large group of sixty students. I studied her mixture of lecture and seatwork practice. I enjoyed her final wrap-up. I noted that she had extra material on hand that she did not get to.

During this class time, I prepared my first lesson: the Mayans of Mexico. I had raided the library for everything that was in any way connected with the Mayans—filmstrips, books, maps, and *National Geographic* articles. I pored over these materials, creating two worksheets for each day as well as a map project, and selecting a filmstrip for introductory information. I was prepared for anything.

My turn to teach came. Picking up cues from Mabel, I made sure that certain kids did not sit together, that I had the entire group's attention focused on me before I said a word, and that my teaching materials were close at hand when I needed them.

I showed the first filmstrip, an overview of Mayan culture. We had a lengthy discussion afterward, but I kept my eye on the clock. I had to cover all that I prepared and we were already behind schedule. I pushed on to the first worksheet, a multiple choice questionnaire about the filmstrip. I had planned to discuss the worksheet before moving on to the map exercise, but the students had barely finished it before the class was over. We didn't finish, in part, because the students kept asking the same questions over and over. I also had to spend a lot of time keeping several students focused on the assignment. I looked at the pile of material I had to cover tomorrow and wondered how we would ever do it.

The next day was a repeat of the first. We never even came close to covering everything.

After school, I dragged into Mabel's room. "How do you do it?" I asked. "You cover all of your material and only have a little left over at the end."

She laughed. "You look like you prepared enough stuff to teach for two weeks, not two days."

"But I saw that you had extra things left over after each lesson, so I made certain that I had enough for each day with some left over. I have enough left over for all of next week."

"Do you know why I have material left over?" she asked.

"You didn't get to it in time."

"That's part of it. But that material is there just in case I need it. Say the kids were all clicking and we had breezed through the first part of my lesson. What would have happened?"

"Well," I paused, thinking of the possible disaster that might have occurred if the kids weren't focused and occupied. "You would have had difficulty keeping them under control."

"Exactly. I know that if I always have plenty to involve them in, I cut my discipline problems down to almost nothing. You watch, when things are left hanging, even the best kids get in trouble."

"So you always have more to do than you really can reasonably accomplish?"

"Right. And now you do, too. You've got all of next week's lessons planned already. Now that you know what you want them to do, make sure they understand clearly what they are supposed to do. You won't get the kind of confusion that leads to problems."

Suddenly, I didn't feel quite so tired.

■ ■

Management Skills

Chap. Obj. 2
Test Ques. 12.6–12.41

Focus Questions: How does classroom communication contribute to management? What tactics encourage active learning in students?

Lecture Note: Ask students to discuss, in small groups, the actions of teachers who effectively demonstrated the eight skills listed here.

Chapter 15 Casebook Preview: See Bringing the Real World into the Classroom.

In Chapter 11, we defined management tactics as the specific actions taken by a teacher to establish and maintain a connection between students and instructional material. (Management tactics are necessary, but not sufficient for effective teaching.) Jones and Jones (1990, p. 255) identified eight classroom management skills that facilitate the active engagement of learners in the instructional task. The eight skills are as follows:

1. Giving clear instructions
2. Beginning a lesson
3. Maintaining attention
4. Pacing
5. Using seatwork effectively
6. Summarizing
7. Providing useful feedback and evaluation
8. Making smooth transitions

As we consider these skills, keep in mind that they will be used in the context of the instructional tactics examined in Chapter 11.

Giving Clear Instructions

A healthy proportion of disruptive behavior in classrooms occurs when students are unsure of what they are to do when assigned a particular task. Students who are unsure of how to ask for assistance or what further activity to engage in when a task is completed are more likely to display disruptive behavior than students who are well informed about what procedures to follow in completing a task and what actions to take after the task is completed (cf. Brophy & Evertson, 1976; Jones & Jones, 1990; Kounin, 1970). Giving clear instructions is one of the skills Jones and Jones identify as increasing the time students spend engaged with academic tasks, referred to as **on-task behavior.** By increasing on-task behavior, teachers reduce the amount of disruptive behavior in their classrooms.

Precise Directions

There are several steps that teachers can take to make sure their instructions are clear. First, they should make sure that directions to students are precise. These directions should include information about what students will be doing, the reason for doing it, how students can find help if it is needed, and what they should do when their work is completed. Students express their uncertainty about tasks in a number of disruptive ways. As an example, they might ask questions repeatedly about the task they have been assigned. Other forms of disruption might occur as expressions of boredom or acting out.

Providing precise directions tells students *what* they are to do. Clarity can be enhanced by describing *how well* students should perform also. Jones and Jones report that one teacher uses three labels to inform students of the desired quality of their work. The first label, "throw away," is for practice material, material that will not be handed in. The second label, "everyday learning," is applied to work that will be turned in and graded. This work, therefore, should be neatly done. The presentation does not have to be perfect, however; the main purpose of everyday learning work is to check the student's understanding of the material. The final label, "keepers," refers to work that the students may want to retain permanently or work that may be displayed somewhere.

Creative Delivery

When giving clear instructions, it is helpful to vary the way in which these instructions are communicated. When giving verbal instructions, the teacher can change tone of voice; the teacher may also choose to provide the instructions in a written form—on the chalk board, an overhead projector, or a handout, for example.

Student Involvement

One way to check if students understand your instructions is to ask them to paraphrase the directions they have received. As we saw in our discussion of the models for instruction, checking students' understanding of instructional content is an important part of active instruction. It is helpful to check students' understanding of the instructions to make sure they are engaged correctly in a task. No matter how clearly teachers present instructions to their students, and no matter how well students listen to those instructions, there will be times when students must ask questions about what they are to do. Applying Maslow's hierarchy of needs (Chapter 8) to this situation leads us

on-task behavior Student action pertaining to academic tasks in the classroom.

Field Observation: Have each student observe a classroom, documenting episodes of student uncertainty and correlating those episodes with the frequency of disruptive behavior in that classroom.

Lecture Note: Ask students how this way of introducing seatwork builds expectations and how the various labels might influence motivation.

Field Observation: Have students observe teachers in classrooms, documenting the methods they use to deliver instructions.

Teaching Anecdote: Tell your students about the teacher who used a spot-check method to get feedback from his students whenever he finished explaining an assignment. The teacher would call on six students: two students who he knew would respond correctly, two on whom he wanted to check to see if they understood the lesson, and two who needed encouragement if they were to participate. No matter how clearly the procedure was explained, one student continually asked, "But can I try it this way?"

Ask your students why such spot-checking might be successful and how they might handle the "questioning" student.

Connection: See models of instruction discussed in Chapter 11.

Connection: See Maslow's hierarchy of needs discussed in Chapter 8.

The teacher who presents his or her lectures with interest and animation will involve students and have no trouble maintaining their attention.

to suggest that student questions be accepted in a positive manner. If students' questions are accepted by the teacher, that acceptance contributes to the classroom atmosphere in which students work. If they find the teacher to be a willing helper, one who will support their efforts, the atmosphere in the classroom will seem safe. A safe atmosphere encourages risk taking by students who will now attempt to meet higher-level needs because the lower-level need of safety has been satisfied.

There are other ways to ensure that instructions are clear to students. After instructions are initially presented, they can be placed on a chalkboard or on a bulletin board so that students may refer to them. Students could be asked to write out the instructions before beginning the activity in order to ensure that they have understood the directions correctly. Another suggestion that Jones and Jones make is to engage students in listening or attention games that improve their listening skills. If students are experiencing some difficulty in following a complex set of instructions, teachers can break down the instructions into smaller units. Directions should always be given immediately prior to presenting the activity that the students are being asked to do. If a teacher provides a description of independent practice activities and then proceeds to tell a story designed to motivate the students, the effect of the directions may be decreased.

Beginning a Lesson

The easiest place in the lesson to "get the ball rolling" is at the beginning. A lesson that begins badly or that fails to capture the attention of students is not likely to turn into an exciting learning experience later in the class period (see Kounin, 1970).

Field Observation: Have students observe teachers as they introduce an activity, documenting the sequence in which they provide directions and motivation.

Connection: Kounin's dynamics of discipline are discussed later in this chapter.

Opening Cue

Jones and Jones provide several tips for beginning a lesson. Their first tip is to select or teach a "cue" that signals to the students that a lesson is about to begin. Using phrases such as "OK, we're just about ready to get started here so everyone pay attention" or "OK let's get ready to start" are so common that they tend to be ineffective in capturing students' attention. Jones and Jones report a method they have used successfully to signal students that a lesson is about to begin. Their method is to invent a phrase that will, for some period of time, serve as a cue for the entire class. Students are invited to generate the catch phrase that will be used to signal that a lesson is about to begin as a way of involving them in the management of their own class. One year, students in the Jones's classroom chose the catch phrases "boo" for October, "gobble gobble" for November, and "ho ho ho" for December.

The technique apparently works even if the students are themselves veteran teachers. Jones and Jones used a summer institute on classroom management to demonstrate the utility of a catch phrase. As the first step they recorded the time it took forty practicing teachers to attend to the instructor after the instructor said quietly, "May I please have your attention?" Averaging the time it took these teachers to respond over five separate requests, Jones and Jones estimated the delay to be nearly two minutes. The class of teachers was presented with this finding. It surprised them that it took nearly two minutes for them to respond to the instructor's request for their attention. The teachers developed their own catch phrase. The instructor then practiced using the phrase until the class could attend within ten seconds. Over the next two weeks of the summer institute, data were collected on the delay of attention after the instructor used the catch phrase. During the two-week follow-up period, the group never took more than ten seconds to become quiet and attentive.

Some signals can serve additional purposes, such as communicating the teacher's interest or enthusiasm to the students. For example, we know a teacher who always wears a sport coat to class, but never wears it while teaching. The sport coat is merely a prop. When the administrative details at the beginning of a period are complete, the instructor always removes his coat. On those occasions when he is wearing long sleeves, he rolls them up to indicate that he is ready to "get down to work."

The use of a verbal cue or some other signal, such as Peter Roop's "cool stool," must be followed by a waiting period. If the catch phrase or signal succeeds in directing students attention to the teacher, then the delay will be short. Jones and Jones suggest that it is important for the teacher not to begin until everyone in the classroom is paying attention, no matter what the delay. The effectiveness of the signal is diminished if the teacher begins the lesson before all students are paying attention.

Remove Outside Distractions

Many students are easily distracted. Before beginning a lesson, teachers should look around their classrooms and remove any potential distractions. For example, if there is noise coming from the hallway, the door should be closed. Indeed, such preparations can serve as additional signals that the lesson is about to begin.

The other tips for beginning a lesson that Jones and Jones discuss—presenting the goals of the lesson, relating the lesson material to previous

Journal Entry: Have students reflect on phrases they might use that could serve to signal the beginning of a lesson and also provide a bit of humor or whimsy in the classroom. Have them consider a metaphor that you might use to manage the classroom; for example, the classroom might become a ship with various functions labeled with nautical terms. If this metaphor were used, the opening cue might be, "Welcome Aboard!"

Connection: See Diary of a Day, Chapter 1.

Connection: See models for instruction discussed in Chapter 10.

Teacher Interview: Have students interview teachers regarding the ways in which they prepare their classrooms for teaching.

Chapter 15 Casebook Preview: See Beginning Each Day as a Learning Experience.

experience, or using a provocative question or story—are consistent with the models for instruction reviewed in Chapter 10, and with principles of attention and prior knowledge reviewed in Chapter 6.

Maintaining Attention

The time that students spend directly engaged in learning activities relates positively to their level of achievement (Fisher, Berliner, Filby, Marliave, Cahen, & Dishaw, 1980; Fisher, Filby, Marliave, Cahen, Dishaw, Moore, & Berliner, 1978). If students are to be engaged in instructional tasks, the teacher must develop strategies to help them maintain their attention during a lesson. Fisher et al. (1978) report that the amount of time students spend working directly on instructional tasks varies from less than 50 percent for some teachers to more than 90 percent for others.

Seating

Teaching Anecdote: Tell your students about the high school teacher who always allows his kids to choose their own seats. He had but one rule. "If your grades drop, you get an assigned seat."

Ask your students why this approach might have worked for some students and not for others. How effective would this approach be with younger students as compared with older students?

Jones and Jones suggest several ways in which teachers can arrange and manage students that will help maintain their attention during lessons. Two of their suggestions involve the seating arrangement in the classroom. The first suggestion is to arrange the classroom desks so that no student will have his or her back to the speaker. Typically, this results in a seating arrangement using rows, a circle, or ∪ shape. Figure 12–1 shows a seating arrangement

A seating arrangement that allows teachers and students to move freely is conducive to smooth transitions from one activity to another. If a classroom is cluttered or restrictive, students will spend less time on-task, which creates opportunities for disruptive behavior.

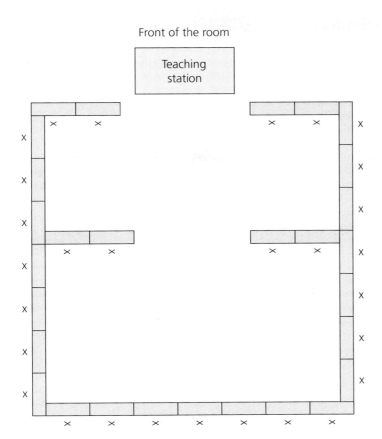

Front of the room

Teaching station

Teacher Interview: Have students interview teachers regarding the seating arrangements they use, asking the teachers to explain the advantages and disadvantages of their arrangements.

Field Observation: Have students observe several classrooms, documenting the action zones in each classroom and correlating differences in action zones with other classroom dynamics.

Transparency: This figure is duplicated in the acetate transparency package. See T-20 Classroom Seating Arrangement.

■ **Figure 12–1** *Classroom Seating Arrangement*

SOURCE: From *Comprehensive Classroom Management: Motivating and Managing Students* (3rd ed., p. 261) by V. F. Jones and L. S. Jones, 1990, Needham Heights, MA: Allyn & Bacon. Copyright 1990 by Allyn & Bacon. Adapted by permission.

that permits all students to face the speaker. (The arrangement also makes it easy for a teacher to monitor seatwork.)

Note that seating arrangements must be considered in conjunction with the location from which the teacher typically speaks. In our experience, we have found that a teacher who wanders around the room while speaking can sometimes walk behind students without distracting their attention. In those situations, there is a focal point to which the teacher often returns and from which he or she speaks most often.

The second suggestion that Jones and Jones make for maintaining attention is to use a seating arrangement that does not lead to differential treatment of students. Researchers investigating the pattern of interaction among teachers and students have discovered action zones. **Action zones** are those areas in a seating arrangement where teachers direct most of their attention. For most teachers, the action zone is the front of the classroom. Students who are not in the front of the classroom tend to contribute less to class discussions, are judged to be less attentive, and achieve at lower levels than students who are (Adams & Biddle, 1970; Daum, 1972; Delefes & Jackson, 1972; Schwebel & Cherlin, 1972). Daum (1972) demonstrated that low-ability students who are moved to an action zone improve their level of achievement. Coincidentally, high-achieving students who were placed farther from the teacher in the classroom do not suffer a decrease in achievement. As a way of maintaining the attention of all students, the seating arrangement is not simply a matter of arranging the desks, but also arranging the students who sit at those desks.

Recognizing Students

Lecture Note: Remind students of the various forms of team learning discussed in Chapter 11. Ask them to comment on the relationship between seating arrangement and the assignment of students to cooperative teams.

Connection: Teacher Chronicle 10.2: Word Power.

One way to avoid discriminating between those students who are seated in the action zone and those students who are seated outside of it is to develop an unpredictable pattern when calling on students to respond in class. Recall the Word Power class in which the routine of proceeding up and down the rows affected the on-task behavior of students in the classroom. Achieving unpredictability is as simple as calling on students in a random pattern. *Random* means that each and every student has an equal probability of being selected to answer a particular question. Although it would not be efficient to follow a table of random numbers or to select numbered Ping-Pong balls as in state lotteries, we can, with a bit of practice, approximate random selection. One helpful tip is to monitor the extent to which you call on low-achieving students. The tendency, for many teachers, is to call on high-achieving students more often (Brophy & Good, 1974; Cooper & Good, 1983). Another tip is to return occasionally to a student of whom one has recently asked a question. Such practices keep the students alert because they are unable to predict, with a great deal of accuracy, who will be called on for a particular question.

A more systematic approach, suggested by Jones and Jones, is to keep a tally sheet and mark it each time a student is called on. Jones and Jones suggest further that you inform students that you intend to call on each of them. If students understand your intentions, it is less likely that students who volunteer frequently will experience frustration if they are not called upon as often as they would like to be.

Journal Entry: Have students recall their own experiences in classes where classmates were recognized in either highly predictable or unpredictable ways. Have them comment on the ways in which the degree of predictability influenced their attention and motivation.

Connection: See the section on questioning in Chapter 11.

On a related matter, we offer the reminder that the question should be asked before calling on a student. When you ask the question prior to calling on a student and use an unpredictable pattern of selection, all students will tend to listen more carefully to the question. When a teacher selects a student before asking a question, the other students in the classroom are relieved from responsibility. Consider, "Ronald, what do we call a word that modifies a verb?" In this case, Ronald is on the spot, and the other students in the classroom are more likely to respond to the fact that they were not called on than to the question that was asked.

Encourage Student Interaction

Another way to maintain attention is to encourage students to interact with their classmates. One way to do this is to ask students if they agree with the answers that other students have provided. Keep in mind that it is helpful to avoid repeating the answers that students give to questions. Jones and Jones (1990) have observed that many teachers parrot nearly every answer that students give. Although this practice may ensure that all students hear the answers to questions, Jones and Jones view it as debilitating. A teacher who repeats each answer given by a student teaches the students that they do not have to speak clearly or loudly when answering. Students learn that the teacher is the only one who is required to hear the answer. They pay less attention to peers because they have learned that the teacher will provide the

Students who are actively involved in a stimulating learning activity are unlikely to misbehave. A student walk around the United States, for example, should be an invigorating lesson in geography.

answer. Finally, students learn that the teacher is the source of all information in the classroom. These effects, taken together, decrease the attention that students pay.

Students will listen carefully to their classmates' answers when they are encouraged to do so by the example of their teacher. If a teacher pays close attention to what a student says, he or she is modeling good listening behavior for students. A teacher can demonstrate careful listening to students by using those occasions when he or she does not clearly understand a student to ask that student to repeat what he or she has said. This practice indicates that the teacher is not only interested in what the student has to say, but that he or she desires to understand clearly the student's point of view.

Maintaining attention can be facilitated by a teacher who is animated. The animation in the teacher's voice and facial expression is indicative of a high level of energy for the topic being discussed. This demonstrated enthusiasm can be further enhanced by using more positive than negative verbal statements. Verbal reinforcement should be sincere. If every student response is followed by the teacher saying, "Oh, what an insightful answer!" students will learn that any response will receive verbal reinforcement, the reinforcing effect of verbal praise will be diminished.

It is important to keep in mind that the silences between utterances also communicate information to the students. The research on wait-time (discussed in Chapter 11) indicates that silence can give students an opportunity to think more clearly about the question at hand. Silence can also gain attention. Silences serve to separate verbally related thoughts from each other. When writing we can separate thoughts by using periods and paragraphs and sections. Silences in the classroom are the auditory equivalent, and can signal to students when an idea is important.

Field Observation: Have students observe the listening behavior of teachers and students in a classroom, documenting the classroom atmosphere and level of motivation.

Lecture Note: Ask students to discuss the verbal responses of their teachers. Have them identify effective and ineffective verbal responses.

Connection: See the section on questioning in Chapter 11.

pacing The tempo a teacher establishes while teaching.

Connection: Teacher Chronicle 12.1: Sharpening the Focus.

Journal Entry: If a videotape of one of your classes is available, have students view it, commenting on your performance in class based on the questions listed in the text.

Lecture Note: Ask students to identify the conditions under which hand signals might or might not be effective.

Pacing

Pacing refers to the tempo a teacher establishes while teaching. Pacing can be affected by other management skills. It was the major problem experienced by the teacher in Teacher Chronicle 12.1. The tempo with which we present our lessons is partially dictated by our teaching style. Some of us speak faster than others. Some are more likely to digress, telling a story or providing other examples. Some of us prefer rapid-fire drill and practice to a more leisurely seatwork assignment. But pacing is determined by more than just our own personal styles. It is determined by the way we organize our material and by our ability to observe our students' responses. As we reflect on our performances in the classroom, we will become more skilled at judging the appropriateness of our pacing. As you gain field experience or as you video-tape lessons in your teacher education program, ask others and yourself questions such as

Did I speak too quickly?

Did I exhibit enthusiasm?

Did I pace the lesson by modulating my voice?

Did I use silences effectively?

Did I repeat myself too often?

Asking students questions like these can also yield useful information about pacing. You may also ask students whether you are accurately picking up their cues when they do not understand, or if you provide sufficient time for them to complete seatwork. You can obtain this feedback after a lesson, in either an informal question-and-answer period, or through written evaluations. One high school teacher reported to Jones and Jones that he wanted to improve his pacing without interrupting the class and without spending time after the lesson reviewing the form of the lesson rather than its substance. The high school teacher taught his students several hand signals that they could use during the lesson to inform him of the appropriateness of his pacing—whether he was talking too much or repeating himself, talking too fast, or presenting material that they did not understand. In addition to being receptive to explicit feedback provided in this way, the teacher who looks for and interprets nonverbal cues from students can also improve his or her pacing.

Kounin (1970) found that teachers who were able to scan their rooms and to respond to problems effectively before they became serious had fewer discipline problems. For example, if a student appears restless—shifting in his or her seat, picking up and putting down pencils, playing with materials on the desk—the teacher can avoid disruptive behavior by simply recognizing the student's restlessness and asking him or her to offer an explanation. The teacher has another option. He or she can speculate on the cause of the disruption and adapt the lesson accordingly. Jones and Jones favor asking the student why he or she is having difficulty paying attention for two reasons. First, the student's answer provides the teacher with direct feedback on his or her pacing. Second, this approach encourages a student to share feelings because his or her observations and opinions are taken seriously by the teacher.

Pacing can be influenced by varying the style in which content is presented, breaking up activities into short segments, or providing a structured break period for lessons that last longer than thirty minutes. The use of films, videotapes, or other media also provide the teacher with an opportunity to change the class's pacing. (Using media also provides a sort of natural break after the film or videotape is completed and the equipment is attended to.)

Using Seatwork Effectively

We examined the use of seatwork as an instructional tactic in Chapter 11. In this chapter, we will consider seatwork as a management tactic. Seatwork takes up a major portion of the instructional day, especially in elementary school classrooms. Angus, Evans and Parkin (1975) found that elementary school students spend more than 50 percent of their time doing seatwork. Other studies (e.g., Fisher et al., 1978) indicate a high percentage of errors are made during seatwork. Because students learn best when they are successful, it is important that we structure seatwork effectively. Jones and Jones (1990) have several recommendations for enhancing seatwork activity and success.

Students should perceive seatwork as serving an important instructional function, such as diagnosis and prescription. What we want to communicate to our students is that we are using seatwork to identify any problems they may have and to prescribe the necessary remediation that may be needed. The process involves monitoring seatwork, recording the results of seatwork, and discussing it in periodic teacher–student conferences. If students understand that seatwork is a key to teacher evaluations and to their own instructional activities, they are more likely to take it seriously and less likely to act out during seatwork periods.

The recommendations for giving clear instructions apply here. Students should understand clearly what they are to do during the seatwork period, what they are to do when it is completed, and how they are to obtain assistance if needed.

Seatwork can be made more effective by pacing the tasks that students are working on privately in the same way that a lecture or a discussion can be paced. Items such as puzzles, cartoons, or even personalized questions on worksheets can be used to control the pace of seatwork.

The teacher can accomplish part of the monitoring function by moving around the room while students are working. Just as teachers have action zones when they are asking questions, they can also develop action zones when monitoring seatwork. One way to ensure that all students are monitored is to carry a clipboard and note when each student's work has been checked. An added result is that students may perceive such record keeping as an indication of the importance of their seatwork assignments.

If the teacher's attention is divided between a small group of students with whom he or she is working and the remainder of the class engaged in seatwork, one way to maintain the monitoring function is to assign a task to the small group. As the small group begins its task, the teacher can use this brief time to monitor the remaining students.

Because not all students can be monitored at the same moment, it is probable that some students will experience difficulties at any given time. One way to reduce this possibility is to work through several example problems prior to distributing the worksheets. By investing sufficient time before students begin to work on their own, problems can be minimized and on-task behavior can be maximized. Monitoring seatwork is a matter of continually scanning the room to discover if students are on or off task, providing

Teacher Interview: Have each student interview a teacher regarding how he or she judges the pace of a lesson, and the techniques he or she uses to break up lengthy periods of instruction.

Connection: See the section on seatwork as an instructional tactic in Chapter 11.

Journal Entry: Have students reflect on their own seatwork experiences, identifying the conditions under which they reacted to it more or less seriously.

Connection: See the section of giving clear instructions earlier in this chapter.

Lecture Note: Remind students that what is judged to be "on-task behavior" depends on the instructional context of seatwork. For example, if students were asked to reflect upon the relationship between two historical events, it would be inappropriate to expect them to write continuously.

quick remediation whenever necessary. Jones and Jones recommend that you keep your contact with individual students while monitoring seatwork relatively short, thirty seconds or less. Another procedure that can enhance the students' attention to seatwork is to periodically have students perform seatwork in small groups or even in dyads. Even in a situation where the seatwork will be judged in a competitive way, working in groups allows students to develop their answers cooperatively before submitting them in group competition.

Summarizing

Connection: See the observation at the day's end in the Diary of a Day, Chapter 1.

Providing students with summaries of what has been taught during a particular lesson or, in the case of primary grades, over the course of a day is a way of helping them organize information. By stepping back at the end of an instructional unit and putting the material into perspective, we facilitate the development of organized knowledge structures or schemata. Jones and Jones suggest several ways in which students can become actively involved in summarizing activities.

One way that students can be encouraged to provide their own summaries is to have them write, perhaps in a daily journal, one of the things that they have learned in the lesson or during the instructional day. Such an activity also provides the teacher with an opportunity to diagnose problems (for example, if a student has difficulty writing down something he or she has learned).

Teacher Interview: Ask a fellow teacher to attend a lecture as a consultant. Use the teacher to generate a plan for turning classroom summaries into journalistic role playing.

Role playing can also be used as a summary-generating device. For example, have students play the role of a reporter and provide a news summary of the learning events that occurred during the lesson. Jones and Jones provide a clever device for teachers to use. A teacher might say something like, "We go now to our classroom correspondent, Christopher Michael, who will report on the vandalism that destroyed a considerable amount of English tea in the Boston Harbor. Come in, Christopher." Another role-playing device that can serve to generate a summary is to have students create and act out a skit. Summaries can also be facilitated by asking students to create learning displays or to develop newspaper articles or schematic drawings indicating the key points in the lesson.

If student-centered activities or student-centered summarizing are not possible or desirable, the teacher can provide the summary. If such is the case, Jones and Jones recommend that review sessions be held frequently. Frequent reviews enhance the chances that the information will be retained and reinforce the concept that learning builds on previous learning. Used in this way, summarizing is an aid in developing metacognitive awareness. Frequent reviews also encourage students to synthesize the concepts from one lesson with information from another lesson.

Teaching Anecdote: Tell your students about the high school math teacher who had students design their own tests. Each test had fifty items. To obtain the fifty items, the teacher had each student write ten problems and their solutions. The teacher collected the problems and selected those to be included on the exam.

Ask your students how this technique aided the teacher in identifying problems, how it helped involve students more directly in their learning, and how it served as an effective evaluative tool.

Finally, tests can be used as summarizing tools. Going over a test after it has been completed provides students with feedback about the correctness or incorrectness of their responses. Such a review provides students who have made errors with an opportunity to correct those errors. It also acts as an additional presentation of important information from the unit.

Too often, the academic tasks we present to our students are perceived by them to be a set of unrelated hoops to jump through. By summarizing material we can show them how what they are doing relates to what they have been doing in past lessons, and what you hope to accomplish in upcoming class sessions.

Providing Useful Feedback and Evaluation

We review here recommendations for providing feedback during a lesson in the context of management skills that help students remain on task. (We will discuss evaluation in the classroom and the use of standardized tests to do so in Chapters 13 and 14.)

Feedback can occur during a lesson when students respond to questions or when they perform seatwork. When a teacher responds to a student's answer in class, he or she provides information about the correctness of the student's response. Informational feedback is not reinforcement (see Chapter 5). By providing knowledge of results, feedback can help students correct errors, but it does not ensure that the students will respond more frequently. What needs to be reinforced is the student's effort (Kulhavy, 1977; Phye & Andre, 1986). Although the effects of feedback and reinforcement are conceptually separate, it is possible for a teacher to provide feedback and reinforcement in one comment to a student. For example, if a student answers a verbal question incorrectly, a teacher could respond, "Your answer is based on an assumption that is questionable. But if, for the sake of argument, we accept the assumption, your answer indicates that you have given the issue a good deal of thought. Let's go back to that assumption for a minute." The trick here is to inform the student that he or she is incorrect while encouraging effort and without damaging his or her self-concept. (Later in this chapter, we will look at the work of Hiam Ginott. Ginott discusses what he calls sane messages, which pertain to the example given here.)

Jones and Jones recommend that students be asked to identify the reasons for their successes in the classroom. According to Bernard Weiner's attribution theory (Chapter 8), it is usually the case that low-achieving students view their successes as being due to luck or the ease of the test, that is, something external to themselves. You can encourage low-achieving students to identify factors that are under their control when they list factors that contributed to their success. Students who, through this exercise, establish a relationship between their own abilities and efforts and their successes may come to accept greater responsibility for their own actions.

Finally, Jones and Jones recommend that, as a form of feedback, grades be deemphasized. By themselves, grades provide the student with little useful information. A letter grade does not identify the specific areas in which the student needs to improve. This information comes from teacher–student conferences that outline the effort the student will have to make to improve specific skills. In addition to grades, teachers should provide some detailed comments that honestly identify weaknesses and provide suggestions for improvement in the content area. A student who is provided with some possible courses of actions is more likely to be more motivated to pursue content goals than one who is not. As Covington and Beery (1976) state, "Grades tend to motivate those students who least need it; that is, those who are already successful; while, perversely the very students who need motivating the most (poor students) are most put off and threatened by grades" (p. 116).

Making Smooth Transitions

A great deal of classroom time is spent in **transitions,** that is, moving from one activity to the next. Consider a junior high or high school, where students change classes approximately every forty to fifty minutes. Packing up from

---

transitions Movements from one classroom activity to the next.

Chapter 15 Casebook Preview: See Writers' Tea.

Connection: Teacher-made and standardized tests will be discussed in Chapters 13 and 14.

Field Observation: Have students observe feedback delivered by teachers, identifying episodes in which student effort was reinforced.

Connection: See the discussion of sane messages later in this chapter.

Connection: See the section on attribution theory in Chapter 8.

Journal Entry: Have students reflect on their own experiences in school, commenting on the extent to which grades motivated them, and their ability to understand the motivation of students whose views of grades differ from their own.

Teacher Interview: Have each student interview a junior high or high school teacher regarding his or her tactics for establishing student focus.

one class, moving into the hall, meeting friends, talking, stopping at the locker, and moving into the next class where materials are retrieved, notebooks are opened, and pencils are readied, are major transitions in themselves. Add to this, any change of focus or topic that may occur during a period. As you can see, the number of transitions experienced by junior high and high school students is significant. In elementary school, nearly 15 percent of classroom time is taken up with approximately thirty major transitions that occur each day in those classrooms (Gump, 1967; Rosenshine, 1980). A major difference between master teachers and less-skilled classroom managers is the way in which they handle transitions (Arlin 1979; Doyle, 1984). Because transitions are times when students are not engaged in an academic task, it is a time ripe with opportunity for disruptive behavior. Jones and Jones recommend several ways to reduce transition time and lessen the opportunity for disruptive behavior.

Physical arrangement of the classroom can influence the amount of time spent in transition from one activity to another. If desks are arranged so that students and teacher cannot easily move around the room, the probability of off-task behavior increases. If it is difficult for students to retrieve materials from the room—in order to begin a seatwork assignment, for example—the transition time from lecture or discussion to seatwork also increases. Furthermore, the physical arrangement of the classroom should enable students who need to retrieve or turn in materials at different times to do so without disturbing other students.

Jones and Jones also suggest that a daily schedule be posted for easy reference by the students and that any changes in the schedule be discussed each morning. Scheduling is especially important in elementary classrooms. Having materials prepared in advance—including possibly an outline of the lesson for the next period—or a film projector threaded and ready to switch on decreases the time that must be spent in transition. A teacher who must spend time preparing materials during class is inviting the students in the classroom to move off task.

Field Observation: Have students observe classrooms and document the extent to which their students exhibit the "packing-up syndrome." Have them try to identify the management tactics in classrooms where the syndrome occurs to a greater or lesser extent.

When you end one lesson, do not relinquish the student's attention until you have introduced or provided instructions for the following activity. The "packing-up syndrome" is common at all instructional levels. It is important to keep students focused through the end of one lesson and to give them on-task directions before packing up is permitted.

Another way of shortening transitions is to ask students to do any task that can be done by students. For example, if you can use a student to take attendance, hand out papers, or collect materials, you will have more time to engage in other tasks in preparation for a lesson, thus reducing the transition time. If you use students to perform administrative and logistical tasks, you will also have more time to monitor the classroom and attend to individual needs that students may have. For example, based on recommendations made by Jones and Jones, rather than having students raise their hands when they've completed seatwork so that you have to go and collect their papers, arrange the classroom so that, upon completion, students can turn in their completed work and pick up any materials they may need for follow-up activities. In this way, while students are taking care of the collection and distribution of assignments, you can monitor those still engaged in seatwork, helping them to solve any difficulties they may have.

Again, if you give clear instructions, you can decrease transition time. If students are given simple step-by-step directions, they can focus more easily on the tasks that must be completed during transition. Jones and Jones give the example of a teacher asking students to "get ready for lunch." Although this message alerts the students that an activity is upcoming, simple step-by-step directions may prove more efficient.

Just as students can be encouraged to generate summaries, students can also be encouraged to generate transition activities. A teacher might suggest that the class invent or generate a game in which groups compete against one another to complete transition tasks. Students can also be asked to develop transition activities themselves. By asking students how we might most easily get from reading groups into the daily spelling lesson, for example, the teacher focuses the students on the desirability of quick transitions.

Lecture Note: Ask students to discuss how various management skills are interrelated.

Principles in Practice 12.1

Principles . . .

1. On-task behavior reduces disruptive behavior.
2. The management skills identified by Jones and Jones keep students on task.
3. Management skills are interrelated.

. . . in Practice

In Teacher Chronicle 12.1, the second teacher had prepared a great deal of material, but was unable to get through the material during class time. The first teacher explained that she "overprepares," bringing material to class that she doesn't intend to use, so that students will always have something to work on. The first teacher also emphasized the students' need to have a clear understanding of what it is they are supposed to do. There is little advantage in preparing a great deal of material if students do not know what they are supposed to do with it.

1. In which management skill areas did the second teacher experience difficulties?
2. How did a lack of clear instructions from the second teacher influence pacing and seatwork?
3. How should the management skills examined here be used as you select material for your class?

BOOK IT, RANDY!

"Randy, sit down. Randy, stop interrupting, Randy, finish your work. Randy, you don't need to wash your hands again." Randy, Randy, Randy. . . . I felt if I said "Randy" one more time that day, I would explode. And it was only the first month of school. What was I going to do?

I sat down that night and listed Randy's negative and positive behaviors.

Negative	Positive
Interrupts	Likes to read
Aggressive on playground	Likes to help at clean up

Teacher
Chronicle
12.2

Negative	Positive
Always wants to wash his hands	Likes being line leader
Up and down from his desk	Likes praise, wants hugs
Complains about anyone sitting near him; those sitting near him complain about him	
Bothers people whenever he moves around the room	

Next, I wrote down how I responded when he misbehaved.

Interrupting	Reprimand; loss of recess
Aggressiveness	Reprimand; loss of recess
Handwashing	Reprimand; restricted to washing just before recess and lunch
Out of desk	Reprimand; loss of free time
Complaints about neighbors	Reprimand; sit by self
Bothering others	Reprimand; restricted to desk

I detected a definite pattern in my approach with Randy: first a reprimand and then punishment. These tactics clearly were not working.

Looking back over the list, I realized how few positive items I had written. Shouldn't the positive at least equal the negative? I asked myself. I decided to put Randy in situations in which the positive would begin to exceed the negative. I decided to start with a small task that could be easily accomplished and then expanded as he succeeded.

Looking back over the list, I saw that a lot of his bad behavior came when he was most active: handwashing, his apparent need to be up and down, playing at recess. What situation could I create that would play to his need for activity as well as to his strengths? I wondered. Looking at the list again, I linked reading, orderliness (the appeal of cleaning up), and his interest in being in charge. What activity might encompass these three things? It took me a whole weekend to hit upon the solution. I had been planning to organize my room library. Why not make Randy the room librarian?

I have always collected books for a room library, no matter what the age of the students I was teaching. I've purchased some books through book clubs and school book fairs; others, at rummage sales and used book stores. I've always let kids borrow whatever books they wanted, but had no way of keeping track of who had what. I had often thought of organizing the books, but had never really gotten around to doing it.

Randy took to being librarian like a bear takes to honey. He could get up whenever his work was finished and check returned books back in. If his hands got dirty, he had a reasonable excuse to wash them frequently. He could "boss" other kids around in a positive way, making sure they checked out books properly. He could straighten the books and organize them by title, thus practicing alphabetizing skills. After all, I wanted him to continue to learn.

Over time, I saw the decrease in the frequency of his interruptions that I had been looking for. Although he was by no means perfect in this area yet, I stopped feeling like a tape recorder repeating "Randy" over and over. All in all he seemed to have gained some control over his environment, which is really what he was asking for in the first place.

This year I wish I could say "Randy" a few times. My library is a mess without him.

▪▪▪

ripple effect The consequences that interacting with one student has on the behavior of other students in the class.
withitness According to Kounin, the teacher's ability to observe everything that happens in the classroom and to deal effectively with misbehavior.

DISCIPLINE

Chap. Obj. 3
Test Ques. 12.42–12.75

In the previous section, we presented data that suggest that aspiring teachers tend to equate discipline with management. A better way to conceive of discipline is as a by-product of sound management. The management tactics that we will examine in this section are not as directly connected to instructional activities as the skills of lesson staging, giving directions, or summarizing. Rather, the tactics examined here present ways to respond to problems and inform students of the rules defining acceptable and unacceptable behavior in your classroom.

Focus Questions: How should a teacher approach discipline problems? How can problem behaviors be changed?

Journal Entry: Have students reflect on episodes from their own schooling that demonstrate the ripple effect.

Chapter 15 Casebook Preview: See Science is Only Real When You Do It.

Dynamics of Discipline

Jacob Kounin (1970) has researched the dynamics of classroom discipline as much as any educational psychologist. Out of this research has come several key ideas, which we will now examine (Charles, 1985).

The Ripple Effect

A key concept of Kounin's approach to classroom discipline is called the ripple effect. When a teacher issues a reprimand designed to stop or suppress disruptive behavior to one student in the presence of classmates a **ripple effect** occurs—the reprimand influences the behavior not only of the disruptive student, but also of the other students who witness the reprimand. The effect of the reprimand ripples out from the disruptive student to other students in the classroom the way the ripples on a pond spread when a stone is tossed into the water. If the reprimand is to have a ripple effect, it must be clear.

Lecture Note: Ask students to consider how the perception of a teacher is related to both the ripple effect and to the teacher's potential as a model (the later discussed in Chapter 7).

Teaching Anecdote: Tell your students about the teacher who had a reputation for having eyes in the back of her head, especially when it came to cheating. Whenever she caught anyone cheating, she didn't make a show of it in front of the other students; rather, she wrote a note on the student's paper indicating what she had observed. Within each of her classes, the incidence of cheating dropped as the year progressed and the students realized her powers of observation.

Ask your students to tell about teachers from their own schooling who possessed "withitness" and why they were perceived that way.

Clarity is achieved when the reprimand specifies the behavior that was unacceptable, names the disruptive students, and provides reasons why the reprimand is being issued. Kounin (1970) investigated the extent to which the ripple effect occurs in classrooms. The ripple effect is most pronounced on the first day of school and tends to diminish as the year lengthens. The effect is also stronger in elementary school than it is in junior high or high school. At the junior high and high school levels, the ripple effect is quite dependent on the students' perceptions of the teacher. A teacher who is well liked by junior high and high school students can initiate a ripple effect. A teacher who is not held in high esteem by students has little chance of influencing other students through the reprimand of one disruptive student.

Withitness

Kounin coined the term *withitness* when the phrase "being with it," meaning being alert or aware, was popular. **Withitness** means the observational acuity

overlapping A teacher's ability to deal with more than one issue at the same time.

Punishment, such as detention, should be seen by students as the consequence of activities they should try to avoid.

to scan the classroom well. If a teacher is thought to have "eyes in the back of his or her head," he or she would qualify as a teacher possessing withitness. Teachers who possess withitness possess various skills. They have the ability to identify quickly and accurately the disruptive student(s) among a group. For example, suppose that two students in the back of the room are talking with each other during seatwork. Student A grabs a pencil from Student B's desk. Student B shouts out, "Hey, give me that back." A teacher who punishes Student B because he or she was the one who shouted rather than Student A who grabbed the pencil from the desk lacks the type of observational skill or scanning ability that Kounin described.

Teacher Interview: Have each student interview a teacher regarding his or her judgments of disruptive events, providing criteria for such judgments, as well as examples.

Another withitness skill is the ability to discriminate between the more serious and less serious forms of disruptive behavior. A teacher should be able to observe two simultaneously occurring disruptive events, judge which of the two is the more serious, and deal with the more serious problem first. Breaking up a scuffle between two students prior to reprimanding another student for being out of his seat at an inappropriate time is an example. Withitness is a quality that students are able to perceive in teachers. If they perceive that teachers are observant and can deal effectively with misbehavior, they are less likely to misbehave.

Overlapping

Classroom Observation: Have students observe teachers, documenting the extent to which the teachers' skills overlap.

Overlapping is the skill necessary to attend to two issues simultaneously. Consider the following illustration: A teacher, in the midst of monitoring seatwork, has stopped to help one student who is having difficulty with the task. While clarifying a crucial concept, the teacher spots a student who is being disruptive elsewhere in the classroom. In this situation, overlapping might consist of a quick verbal reprimand of the disruptive student while keeping track of the particular problem of the student being monitored. Not surprisingly, Kounin's research found that teachers who were adept at overlapping activities also exhibited withitness. Students who were engaged in seatwork and who perceived the teacher to be "with-it" are more likely to receive overlapping attention and, therefore, more likely to stay on task.

The ability to manage groups is central to Kounin's notions of discipline. The ability to deal with a large group of students by monitoring effectively all areas of the classroom—being able to take action quickly and efficiently in one area without losing the momentum of a lesson in another part of the classroom—is the type of skill that comes with experience. In order to gain the right type of experience, you should begin by modeling teachers who display what Kounin sees as the essential skills of group management. As you gain field experience, look for experienced teachers who can serve as effective models. Your model should be a teacher who can communicate his or her knowledge of classroom activities to the students. Your model must be able to overlap, that is, to deal with more than one issue at the same time. Choose as a model a teacher who can identify and correct behavior before misbehavior escalates. Try to find a teacher who can use the ripple effect as an effective means of communicating appropriate classroom behavior. If you

In a heated moment, a teacher who takes the time to listen to a student provides a cooling-off period and establishes a calmer atmosphere for dealing with the problem.

Lecture Note: Ask a student to serve as a confederate by asking an irrelevant question at a predetermined point in your lecture. Respond to the student's question and then stop the class. Ask the students to reflect on the loss of momentum in terms of their comprehension and motivation.

Connection: See operant conditioning discussed in Chapter 5.

Connection: Teacher Chronicle 12.2: Book It, Randy!

Teacher interview: Have each student interview a teacher to determine how he or she deals with the "squeaky wheel syndrome."

make your observations late in the school year, interview the teacher concerning his or her use of the ripple effect earlier in that year. Finally, find a model who can establish and maintain momentum during an instructional activity (cf. Kounin, 1970).

Skinner Revisited: Applied Behavior Analysis

It is useful to review Skinnerian concepts in the context of discipline. Neobehaviorists, those who have succeeded Skinner as proponents of operant conditioning, have applied the basic Skinnerian concepts to discipline in the form of **applied behavior analysis**—the analysis of behavior problems and the prescription of remedies (sometimes called behavior modification). The type of classroom behavior that might be modified is typically disruptive and undesirable. The natural human tendency is to respond to disruptive behavior or misbehavior by simply telling the student to stop. Skinner, you will recall, advocated the use of positive reinforcement over all other consequences. Punishment, while effective in decreasing the likelihood of the behavior, is not effective in encouraging desirable behavior, nor is negative reinforcement. Both punishment and negative reinforcement rely on aversive control. Consider the teacher's initial reaction in Teacher Chronicle 12.2. A negative approach to Randy's problems was not effective.

Catch 'em Being Good

The **catch 'em being good** approach is a response to discipline problems based on the principles of applied behavior analysis—a conscious effort to notice desirable behavior and reinforce it positively (Charles, 1981). It is a less formal approach to behavior change than those outlined in Chapter 5. It does, however, contain all of the elements of positive reinforcement in the true Skinnerian tradition.

Imagine the following situation in your own classroom. Students are working quietly in groups of two on an assignment you have given them. You are quietly monitoring their seatwork, walking around the room, and rather enjoying the students' progress. Here and there you offer a word of advice or ask a question to determine whether or not a student is experiencing difficulty. While speaking to one student, you notice that two students across the room have just started arguing. You address the students with a reprimand in an effort to get them back on task. You succeed in quelling the argument. The students settle into their work once more and you continue monitoring the class. Another disruption breaks out and again your attention is automatically drawn to it. You address the students causing the disruption in the presence of the other students.

What we have in this situation is an example of what we might call "the squeeky wheel syndrome," as in "the squeaky wheel gets the grease." Most people tend to ignore the behavior of others until it becomes disturbing. As long as students are behaving quietly and attending to their work, they do not attract our attention. The moment they begin to disrupt the quiet work atmosphere, we pay attention to them. The idea behind the "catch 'em being good" approach to behavior modification is not to ignore good behavior but to reinforce it.

Charles (1981) argues that the "catch 'em being good" approach is highly effective in the primary grades. He points out that through third grade, teachers need use little else in the way of behavior modification strategies. As students grow older and as the influence of their peers increase, the "catch 'em being good" approach to discipline loses its effectiveness. By junior high school, according to Charles, students find it laughable. Other forms of applied behavior analysis are needed.

Rules-Ignore-Praise (RIP)

The **rules-ignore-praise (RIP)** approach begins with the establishment of rules determined by the teacher or in collaboration with the students. (These rules should be very clear and understandable to students. The list of rules should be kept fairly short—perhaps six or seven rules—so that students can learn them quickly and keep them in mind easily.) Students who follow the rules are praised as often as possible. Misbehavior in the classroom is ignored. No consequence for misbehavior occurs, following Skinner's principle that positive reinforcement is the best way to bring about change in behavior.

If this sounds similar to the "catch 'em being good" approach to discipline, it will not surprise you that RIP works fairly well at the elementary school level, but not at the secondary school level (Charles, 1981).

Rules-Reward-Punishment (RRP)

The **rules-reward-punishment (RRP)** approach introduces limits and aversive consequences absent from the two previous approaches to behavior modification. As in the case of the RIP approach, RRP starts with the establishment of rules and emphasizes positive reinforcement for students who follow the rules. However, RRP does not ignore misbehavior. The rules that are established under the RRP approach include not only a statement of the rules, but also a statement of the consequences for breaking those rules.

rules-ignore-praise (RIP) An approach to classroom management in which the teacher praises as often as possible students who follow the rules. Misbehavior in the classroom is ignored.

rules-reward-punishment (RRP) An approach to classroom management in which the teacher praises students who follow the rules but does not ignore misbehavior.

Journal Entry: Have students reflect on their experiences as junior high school students, identifying those episodes from their own experiences that would support the contention that the "catch 'em being good" approach is laughable.

Teacher Interview: Have students interview teachers at various levels regarding the practice of ignoring undesirable behavior.

The rules-reward-punishment approach offers students choices. For example, this boy chose to return his library book on time. In effect, he chose to be rewarded.

Chapter 15 Casebook Preview: See Responsibility Education.

Field Observation: Have each student observe a class early in the year when the teacher is attempting to establish classroom rules.

Journal Entry: Have students reflect on any classroom experiences they had operating in a token economy. Ask them to consider how the token economy influenced their behavior in that class.

Connection: See the discussion of the Premack Principle in Chapter 5.

Connection: See intermittent reinforcement discussed in Chapter 5.

Students are informed that they have a choice to make. They can choose to abide by the established rules or not. Students are informed further, that if they choose to break a rule, they are also choosing to receive the prescribed punishment. Presenting the contingency in this way means that the teacher does not punish misbehavior, rather the students choose to punish themselves. Charles argues that the RRP approach is very effective with older students, especially if students have had a hand in establishing both the rules and the consequences of breaking the rules.

Contingency Management

Contingency management—often referred to as a token economy—involves the use of tangible reinforcers. The hallmark of this approach is the use of tokens that students earn for exhibiting desirable behaviors. The value of various desirable behaviors is determined in advance so that students know what the positive consequences of their appropriate behavior will be. In addition to earning tokens, students are given access to tangible goods that they may buy with their tokens. Prizes might include stickers, pencils, some forms of food, a book, magazine, drawing paper, crayons, or other objects that are desired by students in the class. It is important for teachers who use token economies to take care in keeping records so that tokens are distributed fairly and consistently. Using this approach also means that class time must be set aside for "shopping."

Tokens can also be used to purchase activities. A student who earns the sufficient number of tokens may purchase, for example, free time on the computer to play games. During shopping time, the teacher can issue a voucher for such activities. In essence, a token economy that "sells" activities is an application of the Premack principle described in Chapter 5. Students engage in task behaviors (presumably of low probability) that will eventually be rewarded with an opportunity to engage in "purchased" behaviors (presumably of higher probability).

Charles (1981) suggests that any teacher who chooses to implement a token economy explain clearly and completely to his or her principal, to parents, and to students how the token economy will work before it is implemented. It is necessary to use this approach to minimize disruptive behavior. Nothing is quite so disruptive as a token economy gone awry. Token economies have been successfully used in a variety of classroom situations at all grade levels, including classrooms containing students with severe mental disabilities.

Token economies delay the delivery of primary reinforcement following a desirable student behavior by using secondary reinforcement (tokens) as an immediate consequence of behavior. The effect is to lengthen, sometimes considerably, the time between the appropriate behavioral response and primary reinforcement. If we can instill in our students an ability to delay gratification for their efforts, we are providing them with an opportunity to learn that sustained effort can bring rewards.

Contracting

Contracting, which involves drawing up a contract between the teacher and the student, is another applied behavior analysis approach that can be used to teach students about the rewards of sustained effort. The teacher can specify, with or without negotiation, the behaviors required if a particular reward is to be earned. In addition to identifying the behaviors, the contract should include terms or conditions under which appropriate behaviors will be displayed. If a teacher were to use the contracting approach to decrease a student's out-of-seat behavior and increase the amount of seatwork the student completes, the contract should specify how much out-of-seat behavior will be tolerated and under what conditions it will be allowed, as well as the amount of seatwork that must be completed. For example, a teacher might require that 100 percent of seatwork be completed in fulfillment of the contract.

Contracts have been quite successful at junior high and high school levels; they can also be used with younger children. Many teachers who employ contracting use the contract itself to introduce variety into the learning situation (see Figures 12–2 through 12–4 for some examples).

Although considerable research has been amassed to demonstrate the effectiveness of behavior change programs, perhaps the informal comments

Field Observation: Have students collect and compare contracts from a number of teachers.

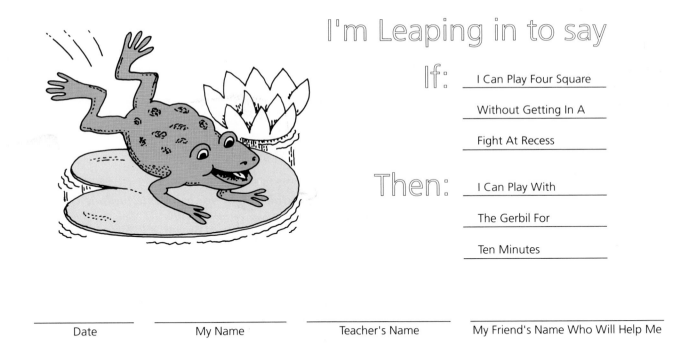

I'm Leaping in to say

If:
I Can Play Four Square
Without Getting In A
Fight At Recess

Then:
I Can Play With
The Gerbil For
Ten Minutes

_____ _____ _____ _____
Date   My Name   Teacher's Name   My Friend's Name Who Will Help Me

■ **Figure 12–2** *A Student Contract Appropriate for Primary Grades*
SOURCE: From *Comprehensive Classroom Management: Motivating and Managing Students* (3rd ed., p. 369) by V. F. Jones and L. S. Jones, 1990, Needham Heights, MA: Allyn & Bacon. Copyright 1990 by Allyn & Bacon. Adapted by permission.

Transparency: This figure is duplicated in the acetate transparency package. See T-21 A Student Contract Appropriate for Intermediate Grades.

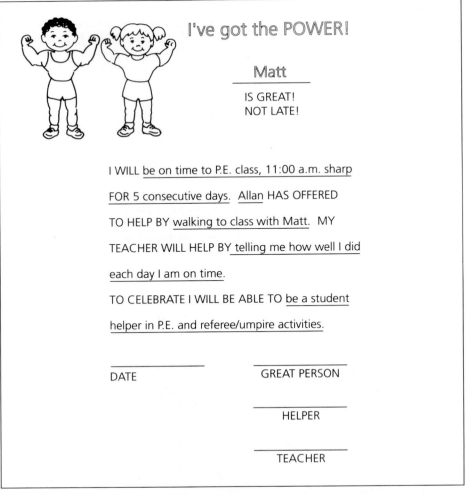

■ Figure 12–3   *A Student Contract Appropriate for Intermediate Grades*

Source: From *Comprehensive Classroom Management: Motivating and Managing Students* (3rd ed., p. 370) by V. F. Jones and L. S. Jones, 1990, Needham Heights, MA: Allyn & Bacon. Copyright 1990 by Allyn & Bacon. Adapted by permission.

Lecture Note: Remind students that operant conditioning provides a useful system for analyzing the effects of the environment on behavior.

of teachers provide the most telling evidence in its favor. As an exercise, you might find it instructive and enlightening to discuss behavior change programs with teachers who have implemented them in their own classrooms. As you complete your interview, ask the teacher what their plans for the future are. There is an excellent chance that the teacher will tell you that the results are highly encouraging and that applied behavior analysis has become embedded in his or her teaching style.

Sane Messages

Haim Ginott has written on issues relevant to classroom management in a way that reminds us that management is a channel of communication (1972). Ginott died in 1973 after having achieved a good deal of popular success. It is

Name of Student: Suzy Jones   Grade: 9th   Date:_____
School: Middle School   Contract Monitor*: Mrs. Smith
Reason for Contract: Demonstrates difficulty controlling anger with regard to peer interaction

---

Student Expectations for Responsible Behavior
1. Follow all classroom and school rules.
2. Expectations requiring additional instructions and clarification.
  A. When angry, Suzy is expected to remain in control by making responsible choices to handle her anger. This applies in the classroom so students can continue working and applies to unstructured time outside the classroom.

Student Choices

Responsible choices
(ways to meet expectations)
A. Ignore situation
B. Remove self from situation
C. Ask for five mnutes time out at desk
D. Do deep breathing or relaxation exercises at desk
E. Write down feelings until I can talk the situation over with teacher or counselor

Irresponsible choices
(choosing negative consequences)
A. Not doing work
B. Refusing to continue working
C. Distracting classmates from work
D. Yelling at peers or teachers
E. Running away
F. Fighting

Student Consequences

Consequences for Responsible Behavior at School:
A. Stay in class
B. Be with friends
C. Learn new things
D. Have a boyfriend
E. Feel good about my ability to control my anger
At Home:
If Suzy chooses to control her anger all week at school, she will earn an extra half-hour on the weekend to have private time with mother.

Consequences for Irresponsible Behavior

A. If the behavior occurs, Suzy will go to the office and fill out a Problem-Solving Worksheet; she must be able to control herself prior to returning to class.
B. If the behavior occurs during unstructured time, she will be expected to sit on the curb until end of free time and then will be expected to go to the office to fill out Problem-Solving Sheet.

Contract Monitor agrees to:
1. Consistently apply stated consequences for both responsible and irresponsible behavior.
2. Regularly review contract with student every three weeks.
3. Review contract at staffings as appropriate.

Contract Termination Criteria:
Contract will be terminated when student consistently makes responsible choices to deal with her anger for a three-week period.

Student Signature:_____   Date:_____
Contract Monitor Signature:_____   Date:_____
Parent Signature:_____   Date:_____

_____

*Staff member responsible for contract development, application, and review

■ **Figure 12–4**   *A Behavior Contract That Emphasizes Student Responsibility*

Source: From *Comprehensive Classroom Management: Motivating and Managing Students* (3rd ed., pp. 381–382) by V. F. Jones and L. S. Jones, 1990, Needham Heights, MA: Allyn & Bacon. Copyright 1990 by Allyn & Bacon. Adapted by permission.

sane messages According to Ginott, comments by a teacher that address a disruptive situation but do not attack the self-concept of the disruptive student.
I-messages Clear, nonaccusatory statements by a teacher that describe how he or she feels about a disruptive situation rather than attribute the situation to a student's negative characteristics.
assertive discipline An approach to classroom management that stresses the establishment and enforcement of rules. When there is an infraction of the rules, the teacher follows through with the consequences fairly and consistently. The teacher makes promises, not threats.

Lecture Note: Ask students, in small groups, to identify various disruptive situations and to construct sane messages that address those situations.

Journal Entry: Have each student reflect on a teacher who attacked his or her self-image or the self-image of a classmate. Have the student consider how such attacks influenced his or her perception of the teacher.

Lecture Note: Emphasize that the use of "I-messages" requires practice in order to achieve an effective tone. Ask students to identify instructional situations in which they would likely become angry and have them generate appropriate "I-messages."

a credit to his ideas that they are still discussed in the professional literature on classroom management, especially as management relates to discipline.

Ginott viewed discipline in the classroom as a series of small victories of communication. Chief among the issues relevant to communication is the use of what Ginott calls sane messages. **Sane messages** are comments by a teacher that address a disruptive situation but do not attack the self-concept of the disruptive student. Consider as an example of a sane message, "Talking must not occur during sustained silent reading." The message addresses the situation: students should not be talking during a time in class when talking is against the rules. However, the message does not attack the personalities of students who engaged in the disruptive talking. An insane message would do so. An example of an insane message in the same situation would be something like the following, "You are always thinking about yourself and never about anyone else. Your talking during silent reading is an example of what makes you so rude." In this example, the message not only indicates that the teacher is dissatisfied, but it attacks the student's self-image as well.

Another aspect of communication in the classroom involves the expression of anger. Teachers are in an intensely social situation for an extended period of time each day. They are responsible for the well-being of a large number of children. Because they are human, there will be times when they become angry in the classroom. When these situations occur, Ginott recommends the use of sane messages to communicate the anger.

Ginott also encouraged the use of what he called "**I-messages**," a way in which teachers can express feelings about situations that provoke anger, disappointment, or frustration. For example, a teacher may become angry with a student who talks during sustained silent reading, particularly at the end of a long, hard teaching day. Rather than directing this anger at the student's personality, Ginott's "I-message" approach suggests that the teacher communicate his or her anger along the following lines: "The class has established the rule that talking is forbidden during sustained silent reading. We have another rule in this class that if you have something to say, at any time, you should raise your hand. Because talking during sustained silent reading interrupts important work, and because it shows disrespect for the rules that we all worked on, I get angry."

Again, the "I-message" addresses the situation and communicates how the teacher feels, but the message avoids labeling the student as rude, inconsiderate, or otherwise unworthy.

Assertive Discipline

The approach to discipline called **assertive discipline,** developed by Canter and Canter (1976), makes use of several of the principles of applied behavior analysis, including the establishment of rules and consequences prior to the implementation of disciplinary actions. In addition to the establishment of rules, assertive discipline emphasizes that teachers follow through with consequences; that the consequences be delivered fairly but consistently. Assertive discipline also makes use of Ginott's notion of "I-messages," that the teacher speak to situations rather than personalities.

A communication that is characteristic of assertive discipline is a clear and succinct statement that identifies the problem and suggests a way of remedying it. Charles (1981) provides three examples of responses to fighting in the classroom. Of the three, the last is characteristic of the assertive approach.

Nonassertive: "Please try your very best to stop fighting."
Hostile: "You are acting like a disgusting savage again!"
Assertive: "We do not fight. Sit down until you cool off so we can talk about it."

Examining the three responses, we can see that the first expresses some dissatisfaction on the part of the teacher. The response does not help assert the authority of the teacher or suggest a remedy to the situation. Nor is it delivered in terms that are likely to influence the behavior of students who are engaged in fighting. The hostile response is aggressive, if not assertive, but it crosses the boundary of situation and attacks personality. The third response, an example of assertive discipline, provides a clear message about what the problem is and a clear message about how the problem will be solved.

Returning to the example of talking out during sustained silent reading, let's see how an assertive discipline approach might be used to verbally respond to the disruption.

The teacher upon hearing the talking out says, "Marsha, our rules do not tolerate talking out during sustained silent reading. You must not talk out again."

Marsha says, "But I need something."

The teacher responds, "That may be the case, but talking out during sustained silent reading is against the rules. If you have something to say, raise your hand and I will come to you."

"But, but, George is bothering me."

"If it happens again, raise your hand and I will come over. I'll keep an eye on things, but you may not talk out during sustained silent reading."

In this exchange, the teacher asserts the rule that is being broken and follows through by continuing to assert the rule. By reminding the student that she may speak to the teacher after raising her hand, the teacher also provides a remedy to the problem. To summarize, using the assertive discipline approach means that teachers make promises not threats.

Field Observation: Have each student observe a teacher who uses the assertive discipline approach, documenting the comments made by the teacher as he or she implements assertive discipline.

Journal Entry: Have students reflect on teachers from their experiences who made threats but did not keep promises, documenting their own perceptions of such teachers and the ways in which these perceptions influenced their attitudes toward that class.

Principles in Practice 12.2

Principles . . .
1. Sound discipline practices require careful observation and analysis.
2. Clear communication enhances disciplinary actions.
3. Discipline must be consistent to be effective.

. . . in Practice
In Teacher Chronicle 12.2, the teacher was having difficulty with Randy. Initially, the teacher was frustrated by the ineffectiveness of continuous reprimands. After reflecting on Randy's behaviors, the teacher decided to make

Randy the class librarian. The solution took into account the situations in which Randy misbehaved as well as Randy's interests.

1. Given Randy's interests, what other disciplinary solutions seem worth trying?
2. Why did the teacher's initial reprimands prove ineffective with Randy?
3. What approach to class rules do you plan to use in your classroom? Why?

Teacher Chronicle 12.3

ROOM FOR IMPROVEMENT

My room seems so empty when I walk in at the beginning of the school year—nothing on the walls, the bookcases covered with paper to keep off the summer dust, the desks in a jumble in one corner, my desk in another. I am reminded of Ichabod Crane's one room schoolhouse after Brom Bones plays his Halloween prank and changes everything around.

My first inclination is to begin arranging the desks. This is a ritual for me. However, I know that over the next three days I will move everything at least three more times before the kids come to class. Nonetheless, I move the desks, thinking as I do so how much easier it would be to sketch a floor plan on paper or on the board. I could sketch where my desk will be, which board I will be using the most and where I want their attention directed, where my activity table will be placed, where my big armchair for reading aloud will be. But there is something about physically moving furniture that helps me reenter the world of the classroom so I begin shoving furniture around.

I am satisfied with my first arrangement. For now. I sit down and think about the room. It really is a world. There is the immediate physicalness that is so apparent, that part of the environment that must be accepted but can also be improved. There are other, less tangible aspects of our world that become apparent only when the students arrive: my goals and expectations, what rewards I will use for motivation and reinforcement, interactions between the students and myself, and my teaching approaches.

Picking up a class roster I read down through the names: Ernesto, Paula, Raeanne, Todd, James, Meghan, Karl, Matt, Daniel. How will they fit into this world? Will my teaching style match their needs? Patrick, Jonathon, Clint, Melissa, Halley, Lida, Adam, Pam, Scott, Nick, Brad. Who will find this environment stimulating, engaging, demanding, and intriguing? Who will prefer another environment, less open, more controlled, less demanding?

It takes sunlight about eight minutes to reach earth, I thought. How long will it take me to reach some students? I wonder. And I only have three days to get ready for this world of human emotions, ideas, thoughts, problems, interests, feelings, growth, and developments.

Enough daydreaming. Hopping off my desk, I wonder, will a circular arrangement encourage more peer interaction? How will I arrange the desks tomorrow?

EXPECTATIONS AND COMMUNICATION

Everything a teacher says and does communicates something to students. The rules we establish and enforce in our classrooms communicate a message. The way in which rules are established—either by the teacher's fiat or through discussion and negotiation with students—tells our students something. In addition to the ways in which we establish and maintain discipline, we create a general atmosphere in our classroom, an atmosphere that the teacher in Teacher Chronicle 12.3 ponders. There is information exchanged when a teacher asks a question that goes beyond the question itself. The teacher's demeanor as he or she asks questions sends a message as well.

Classroom communication occurs through and is embedded in the interactions between a teacher and his or her students and among students. Indeed, some kinds of interactions can have the effect of stifling communication (Puro & Bloome, 1987). In a variety of ways, we send messages to our students. We tell a student, sometimes with a subtle glance, what we expect from him or her. The tactics we use to reinforce appropriate behavior, the behavior we dub "appropriate" and "inappropriate," and the reinforcements themselves tell our students something about how we perceive them. Classroom management is a matter of communication.

Teacher Expectancies

The **Pygmalion effect** refers to the influence that teachers' expectations have on the behavior of students. The term comes from the myth of a Greek sculptor, Pygmalion, whose expectations of a statue he worked on caused the statue to come to life. (George Bernard Shaw's *Pygmalion*, the story of the transformation of a cockney flower girl, Eliza Doolittle, into a refined lady of aristocratic demeanor, was the basis for the musical, *My Fair Lady*.)

The term *Pygmalion effect* was applied to teachers' expectations by Rosenthal and Jacobson (1968). Rosenthal and Jacobson measured the intelligence of children in the first through sixth grades in a school in San Francisco. The test, administered at the beginning of the school year, was not a widely used test of intelligence. It was designed to be administered to groups not to individuals. After the test was administered, the teachers of certain students were told that the test predicted substantial intellectual gains for those students in the coming year. In reality, the students identified as "potential achievers" performed no better or worse than other "average" children who took the test. At the end of the school year, the children took the group intelligence test a second time.

The results of the second test showed that the "potential achievers" showed significant gains in intelligence. The gains were attributed to the heightened expectations of the students' teachers. This result was labeled the "Pygmalion effect." These and similar results have also been referred to as *self-fulfilling prophecy* and the *teacher expectancy effect*, terms that are still used to identify any situation in which the communication of expectations by a teacher is thought to influence student behavior.

Rosenthal and Jacobson's study was intensely scrutinized. Additional research studies directed toward the effects of teacher expectations were also undertaken. Close inspection of Rosenthal and Jacobson's results showed that the self-fulfilling prophecy operated in the first and second grades, but not in

Pygmalion effect The influence that a teacher's expectations may have on the behavior of students. Also called the *teacher expectancy effect*.

Chap. Obj. 4–5
Test Ques. 12.76–12.110

Focus Questions: How are teacher expectations related to management and discipline? How should rewards best be administered in a classroom?

Connection: Teacher Chronicle 12.3: Room for Improvement.

Teacher Interview: Have students interview teachers regarding their experiences relevant to the Pygmalion effect.

Journal Entry: Have students reflect on the expectancies some of their teachers communicated to them as students, indicating how those expectancies were communicated and the effects they had on the students' attitudes.

Issues in Educational Psychology

CNN™ This box relates to Segment 12 of the CNN videotape. See Instructor's Section for a summary.

BRIDGING TEACHER–STUDENT BARRIERS

Although much of the responsibility for successful classroom communication belongs to the teacher, students can be the catalysts in forging a bond between a class and its teacher.

In *Teacher Magazine*, Suzanne Hershey talked about her first year as an English teacher. Working in a Washington, D.C., inner-city high school, Hershey's rapport with her classes went from bad to worse. Students told her that they hated white people. They drove her to distraction with their incessant gum chewing in class. One day Hershey wound up in a screaming match with a student while the rest of the class went out of control.

It was the student with whom Hershey had the screaming match who eventually helped her bridge the communication gap. The turning point came at a school dance when the student spied Hershey dancing—one of the few teachers to join in the fun. Running over to Hershey, the student began dancing, too. "I guess it was because I was a teacher trying to dance to go-go music—that made me a human being to her. That was the first step toward acceptance," noted Hershey.

As she gained acceptance, Hershey became a better teacher. "I gave up some of my old rules that weren't working. Rules such as 'no gum'. And I got serious about calling parents, holding detentions, tak-ing away points for rudeness, and making students stay after school and talk to me about what was going wrong."

Journal writing assignments gave Hershey a chance to get to know her students as individuals. The journals gave students a chance to show how creative they could be. Hershey wrote comments about their entries that encouraged the students. She even asked them to evaluate her each quarter. By the end of the year, students were praising Hershey for her commitment to them.

Even when teachers and students have established a good rapport, setbacks occur that can permanently sever their relationships. In the same issue of *Teacher Magazine*, Jacqueline Bernard talked about her first-year teaching experiences. Working with behaviorally disturbed students, Bernard had forged a good relationship with a student she described as "a streetwise kid in trouble." But the trust they built up was shattered when Bernard had to report the student for smoking. "For her, that was it," said Bernard. "I tried writing her a letter, but she threw it back in my face."

Can teachers and students ever understand each other? Some teachers describe communications with their students as if both sides are speaking at cross purposes. Clark Brown, who teaches college English, observed that "students think that teachers speak in code, that 'Please pass the salt' is a request for pepper." Brown observed that some of the best teachers are often those who manage "a Zen-like talent for eluding the conventional." These teachers get their points across without beating students over the head. Unconventional classroom approaches can allow students to learn for themselves, which, for Brown, is what "real learning" is all about.

Brown experienced mixed results when he offered students praise. One minority student gave Brown a hug to express his thanks for simple encouragement. Brown has had other minority students who couldn't accept praise for their good work. Success to them meant betrayal of their heritage.

"Learning and teaching are explorations, and explorations by their very nature carry us into the unknown," Brown observed. Perhaps that's why each teacher must find the approach that works best with each class in bridging the barrier between teacher and students.

SOURCES: " 'It Was a Testing Ground': An Interview with Suzanne Hershey." *Teacher Magazine* 1, no. 7 (April 1990): 34–35. " 'Here I Am—Instant Teacher': An Interview with Jacqueline Bernard." *Teacher Magazine* 1, no. 7 (April 1990): 44–45. Brown, Clark. "Great Teachers and the Art of the Unconventional." *Education Week* (June 12, 1991): 36.

1. Explain Hershey's gaining acceptance from her students in light of Kounin's concepts.
2. According to Jones and Jones, why would "eluding the conventional" enhance student attentiveness and hence learning?

the third through six grades. Some questioned the test used to measure IQ, arguing that better measures of IQ should have been used. Wineburg (1987), among others, pointed out that even the positive results in the first and second grades could not be construed as convincing evidence that negative expectations necessarily lead to low student performance.

Qualifications of Teacher Expectancies

The interest of researchers in teacher expectancy effects has remained high. The variety of ways in which expectancy has been studied has yielded some important qualifications regarding the influence a teacher's expectations have on student behavior. Raudenbush, reviewing the research literature on teacher expectancy in 1984, concluded that teacher expectancy has only a moderate effect on the IQ scores of students. Furthermore, the effect is likely to show up only in early primary grades and then, only if the expectancy is generated during the first two weeks of school. One explanation is that after two weeks, the teacher has observed and communicated with his or her students often enough to have formed a strong opinion of who is, and who is not, a "potential achiever."

If the effects of expectancy on the IQ of students have been less pronounced than initially thought after the Rosenthal and Jacobson study, the expectancy effects on other outcomes have not been. A substantial amount of research has shown that the expectancies of teachers are strongly associated with both positive and negative changes in classroom achievement and participation (Braun, 1976; Cooper, 1979; Rosenthal, 1987). Cooper's (1979) review of the expectancy literature concludes that teacher expectations support extant tendencies, but are not likely to produce dramatic changes in student behavior.

Lecture Note: Ask students to discuss the phenomenon of early impressions from the teacher's and the students' points of view.

There is evidence to suggest that teachers' expectations are communicated to students and that those expectations play some role in influencing student behavior in classrooms, even if that influence is less than Pygmalion-like. Marshall and Weinstein (1986) observed first-, third-, and fifth-grade classrooms. The students in those classrooms had judged their teachers as being one of two types: (a) teachers who treated high- and low-achieving students differently, or (b) teachers who did *not* treat high- and low-achieving students differently. Let's call the first type "high-differential treatment" teachers and the second type "low-differential treatment" teachers. In fifth-grade classrooms, there were more positive interactions between "low-differential treatment" teachers and students than between "high-differential treatment" teachers and students. Curiously, the pattern was reversed in first-grade classrooms. The analysis of observations made as part of the Marshall and Weinstein study was complicated by the infrequent occurrence of certain behaviors and range of teaching styles and social atmospheres that were observed within each of the classrooms. The authors conclude that their study demonstrates the complexity of the process by which expectations are communicated. Nevertheless, the possibility that fifth graders are better able to judge differential treatment than first graders are may lend more validity to one part of this study than to another. What this might indicate is that teachers should be aware of their treatment of high- and low-achieving students.

Field Observation: Have each student observe a multicultural classroom, documenting the extent to which he or she observes low- or high-differential treatment in that classroom.

As a follow-up to the earlier study, Weinstein, Marshall, Sharp, and Botkin (1987) explored the possibility that older children do, in fact, have a greater awareness of teacher expectations and of the relationship between that awareness and self-expectations. The findings suggested that first graders are less accurate than fifth graders in predicting teacher expectations. Fifth graders were more likely than first graders to describe themselves in ways consistent with teacher expectations. The tendency for self-description to match teacher expectancy occurs in the fifth grade regardless of whether the teacher treats high and low achievers differently or not.

The effect of expectancy on third- and sixth-grade students was investigated in Australia (Leder, 1987). Students were identified in two ways. First, they were identified as high or low achieving. Second, they were identified according to teacher expectations. The results showed that teachers tended to interact most *frequently* with high-achieving and high-expectancy students. The effect was most pronounced in sixth grade. However, teachers consistently spent more *total time* waiting for and interacting with low-achieving and low-expectancy students. Leder's findings suggest that the study of differential treatment by teachers needs to account for both the number of interactions and the amount of time spent in interactions. Does the greater number of interactions with high-achieving, high-expectancy students "balance out" the greater amount of time spent with their low-achieving, low-expectancy classmates? Being aware of both the amount of time spent in these interactions and the frequency of interaction will help us gauge the "fairness" of our interactions with students.

Is it important to balance our interactions, that is, to avoid differential treatment of students? Jussim (1986) suggests that self-fulfilling prophecies operate in a three-stage process. During the first stage, teachers develop expectations. In the second, teachers begin differential treatment based on those expectancies. In the third, students behave in expectancy-confirming ways. If we interact with students differently depending on our expectancies, we will enhance the performance of high-expectancy students, but at the expense of low-expectancy students. If we balance our interactions, we interrupt the process by which self-fulfilling prophecies come to fruition.

To the extent that we allow expectancies to be formed and communicated, we risk creating a classroom of "haves" and "have nots." If we are aware that expectancies can influence interactions in our classrooms, we can guard against differential treatment. The issue of teacher expectancies will be examined again in Chapter 13. As a preview to our discussion of teacher expectancies and classroom evaluation in Chapter 13, consider the study by Barowsky (1986). Eighteen mainstream teachers and eighteen special education teachers were asked to evaluate two written passages, each of which were equal in frequency of error. One passage was attributed to an exceptional student; the other was attributed to a mainstream student. The teachers—both mainstream and exceptional—perceived more errors in the passage "written" by the exceptional student.

Classroom Goal Structures

The patterns of communication in a classroom contribute to the atmosphere of the classroom and, ultimately, to the management tactics a teacher will use to bring students into contact with the content to be learned. The key, of course, is to find management tactics that establish an atmosphere that contributes to the motivation to achieve in your classroom.

The tactics employed to evaluate and reward student performance have been studied under the heading, **classroom goal structures** (e.g., Ames & Ames, 1984; Dweck, 1986; Michaels, 1977). The types of goal structures and the names of the structures vary slightly depending on the researcher using them. We will focus on the work of Johnson and Johnson (1987), who describe three types of reward or goal structures: cooperative, competitive, and individualistic. These structures reflect separate management tactics; they differ from one another in the way that learning is managed and evaluated.

Johnson and Johnson (1987) believe that it is essential for teachers to know what the reward structures are and how to establish the social environment necessary for each structure to operate effectively. The tactical decision is not simply one of selecting one of the structures and eliminating the others. Each reward structure is viewed as having a place. Therefore, the tactical decision involves determining the conditions under which the use of each structure is most appropriate. Let's look at each structure in turn.

Cooperative Goal Structure

In Chapter 11, we examined cooperative learning and several tactics for presenting material. In this chapter, we are concerned with the effects that a teacher's actions can have on a student's motivation. A true **cooperative goal structure** is present when the rewards are awarded to a group, not to individuals within the group, and when the performance that is rewarded is the performance of the group as a whole. If a group is given the task of presenting a play, the play is evaluated and rewards delivered as appropriate on that basis. One student cannot receive a higher grade for his or her contribution to the play than another student. In such instances, the individual is motivated not only to help himself or herself, but also out of a sense of obligation to the other members of the group.

Think back to your own high school experience. Perhaps you were in a group—the band, the cast or crew of a play, the French club, an athletic team, or on the school yearbook staff. The success of the product or performance depended on cooperation. If you contributed to such an effort, part of your motivation was likely a sense of obligation; you may have worked harder than you might have because you didn't want to let the other people down. To be sure, you invested time and effort in the group because the group was doing something you liked. But weren't there times when you went "above and beyond the call of duty"?

According to Johnson and Johnson (1987), cooperative goal structures are effective for several reasons:

1. Group work requires discussion, promotes the discovery process, and leads to a higher level of learning.
2. Discussion promotes diversity of ideas, opinions, and positions. In arguing for a position, explanations are sought, repeated, and—through repetition—clarified. Comprehension and retention are enhanced.
3. Members in the group provide feedback and, because it is a group project, encouragement for each other.

Competitive Goal Structure

In a cooperative goal structure, students attain the goal only if others also attain the same goal. In a **competitive goal structure,** students view attainment as possible only if other students do not attain the goal. By definition, competitive goal structures ensure that some students will be unsuccessful. When competitive situations are used frequently in a particular classroom, the students who win and the students who lose rarely change positions.

cooperative goal structure A classroom management tactic in which the rewards are given to the group, not to individuals within the group.
competitive goal structure A classroom management tactic in which students view attainment of goals as possible only if other students do not attain them.

Chapter 15 Casebook Preview: See Please Sign This Contract.

Connection: See the discussion of cooperative and team learning tactics in Chapter 11.

Journal Entry: Have students reflect on those activities for which they had either a sense of obligation or lacked one, trying to reconstruct the conditions that lead to their feelings.

Connection: See the section on inquiry models in Chapter 10.

NANCI MAES

RIVERVIEW ELEMENTARY SCHOOL

WAUTOMA, WISCONSIN

As a teacher, I must provide an atmosphere for growth and learning so effective that each child realizes his or her academic, social, and emotional potential. I must go beyond imparting basic facts and devote time to helping children develop intellectually, socially, and personally. I must create a positive attitude toward learning and help each child develop a good self-image. I must stress the positive by using much positive reinforcement. I must provide the motivation necessary to make school a welcome place to be. The children must feel they are liked and like what they are doing. They must be happy about themselves and their work. Each teacher, likewise, must have a good self-image, enjoy the work, and love children.

I must strive to actively engage all students so that they are very involved. I must provide a classroom atmosphere that promotes enthusiasm, with a high level of stimulating thought and interaction between teacher and students. I must allow my students freedom of imagination and not stifle their creativity. I must strive to individualize my instruction to meet the needs of all students, recognizing that each one is different. All groups of children should be kept heterogeneous to prevent a child from getting labeled or becoming "stuck" in one particular group. The longer children remain in relatively fixed groups the wider the communication gap between the groups becomes. Each child needs to be made to feel special and important.

I must strive to use many good public relations ideas and techniques. I must continue to get many community members involved in my classroom as speakers and demonstrators so as to bring about good public relations between home, school, and community. I must continue to open important lines of communication between parent and child and between school and home through weekly classroom reports.

There are many rewarding experiences in teaching. It is very difficult for me to select the most significant one. I guess I would have to say that the most rewarding is measuring the academic growth each child makes from September until June, and knowing that you are a major factor in this growth. I like to have the children print their names and draw pictures of themselves in September, and then save these and compare them with their printing and self-portraits in May. I like to tape-record the children's reading in September and then again in May and compare their abilities. I find it rewarding to look over the year's records, charts, and test scores to see how each child has progressed. I also like to compare a sample of the child's creative writing from September with one from May. Usually, the child goes from not being able to construct a sentence to using proper capitalization, punctuation, adjec-

---

Connection: See the section on the need to achieve in Chapter 8.

Those who are not successful are likely to be unsuccessful most of the time. The view of motivation based on need to achieve (see Chapter 8) predicts that students with a history of failure develop patterns of behavior designed to avoid failure.

In general, students who experience a classroom managed by means of a competitive goal structure tend to have low expectations, show little persistence on achievement-oriented tasks, and, as just indicated, avoid tasks if they have experienced little success at them (cf. Johnson & Johnson, 1987).

It may seem plausible that students who show improvement, even if they continue to lose competitions, might interpret this improvement as success. Ames and Ames (1984) collected data that suggest that students reward their

tives, and so on. I like to contrast the simple spelling lists the children began with in September with the more difficult words and dictation they can do at the end of the year. It's rewarding to keep a list of all the vocabulary words I introduced to the child over the school year and see how many he or she can recognize and read by the end of the year. I find it very rewarding to be able to feel responsible for the majority of this growth, and to realize that over a nine-month period I have been one of the most significant figures in these young children's lives—possibly one they will never forget.

Our concept of education often requires that we give repetitive, mechanical attention to basic facts and skills. Not enough time and effort is spent going beyond imparting facts. More time should be devoted to helping children develop intellectually, socially, and personally. The day-to-day curriculum should make a greater attempt to stress the positive and keep children motivated as they learn. I would like to change any emotionally flat, passive school atmosphere where there is no joy or laughter or emotion into an atmosphere alive with enthusiasm. Instead of walking into a classroom filled with students listening passively and doing seatwork, I'd like to see more classrooms with a high level of stimulating thought and interaction between teacher and students. I'd like to see fewer worksheets used and a wider range of teaching practices implemented. There should be more individualization of lessons, allowing students to take control of their learning. I feel there could be more "peer teaching." A student's classmates are an important resource in any classroom.

Teachers should shift from large-group teaching to small-group teaching and back again in different subject areas to give children opportunities to experience and function in both types of learning situations. I would eliminate all achievement and ability groupings because I feel that they limit the chance for children in lower groups to keep pace with their peers. Not enough periodic regrouping takes place; once children get labeled in a group, they become "stuck" there. Studies show that teachers actually use better teaching methods with high-achieving groups than with low-achieving groups. High-achieving students are expected to be the independent thinkers, leaders, and problem solvers; lower group children are too often expected to just be followers. Educators often teach high-achieving groups a different content than to lower groups, thus producing a big communication gap between them. I would like to see all groups of children kept heterogeneous. I would like to see more positive feedback given to all children to keep their self-esteem high.

I hope I never reach my goals, so that I will continually strive for new ways to teach and better ways to achieve success, creating new challenges for my students and myself.

own behaviors only if they win. Students who win a competition tend to think of their success as due to ability. When other students win, however, they attribute that success to luck. Competition fosters social comparisons along with attributions of ability. Contrast these attributions with those typical of cooperative goal structures. Cooperation fosters concern for the group. Success attributions focus on effort and lead to a mastery orientation (Ames & Ames, 1984).

Are there any classroom situations in which the competitive management of rewards is appropriate? Consider a spelling bee. In a spelling bee, there is only one winner. In order to attain the goal of winning the spelling bee, others must lose. Does this mean that spelling bees are inappropriate man-

Lecture Note: Ask students to identify the kinds of attributions that mastery-oriented students exhibit.

agement? Not necessarily. If a class spelling bee were conducted at the beginning of a spelling unit, the competition would highlight the differences among learners in terms of prior skill or ability. If the spelling bee were conducted at the end of the unit when all students have had a chance to master the list, the results would be more easily attributed to effort. At the end of the unit, more students have a chance of winning. Failure for any one student is less likely because all students have mastered the material or are approaching mastery. The outcome of the "game" or competition is more in doubt and therefore more fun. In sum, competitive goal structures can be used profitably if the competition is based on effort toward mastery rather than the ability levels students bring to the learning situation.

Individual Goal Structure

An **individual goal structure** provides rewards on the basis of an individual's performance, unaffected by the performance of other students. An individual is not a contributor to a group performance nor are rewards available to only one or a few "winners." An individual goal structure allows each student to "compete" against a criterion. If all students achieve the criterion, all students are rewarded.

Ames and Ames (1984) view individual goal structures as yielding effort attributions. The motivation under such conditions is likely to be, "If I try hard, I can do it." Ames and Ames found that students working to meet a criterion rather than competing against other students were more likely to monitor their work carefully. They are more likely to plan their actions. Overall, it can be said that they are employing greater metacognitive awareness as they work.

The goal structures used to manage classroom learning situations determine the motivational factors that can and cannot operate. The students' perceptions of what records are available are a function of the type of goal structure used in a particular episode of classroom learning. The goals that we place before our students are not simply statements of outcome, they define the types of evaluation we will use to judge and reward performance.

Principles in Practice 12.3

Principles . . .
1. Teachers tend to behave in ways consistent with their expectancies.
2. The way that students are rewarded and evaluated contributes to classroom atmosphere.
3. Classroom goal structures influence motivation.

. . . in Practice
In Teacher Chronicle 12.3, the teacher was pondering the nature of the classroom being prepared for the students who would soon arrive. The teacher realizes that much will depend on how the classroom is "set up." It is not only the physical aspect of the classroom that influences atmosphere, but the way the teacher establishes routines and reinforces and evaluates learning behavior. What the teacher expects from students, and how those expectan-

cies are communicated, and the extent to which the teacher's style matches the needs of students are critical to the establishment of an atmosphere that works for the students.

1. To what extent do you think the teacher in Teacher Chronicle 12.3 will use cooperative, competitive, and individual goal structures?
2. How do you imagine teacher expectancy operates in the classroom described in the Chronicle?
3. What do you want to know about your students before they enter your classroom? What do you not want to know?

CONCLUSION

Assign Chapter 12 of the *Study Guide*.

We use instructional tactics to present the content we want our students to learn (as discussed in Chapter 11). We communicate many other messages to our students as we establish the conditions for classroom tasks, establish and maintain discipline, and reward their efforts. The ways in which we manage learning in our classrooms contributes heavily to the attitudes and, therefore, motivations of our students.

We have examined instructional tactics and management tactics separately in order to deepen your understanding and appreciation of the tactical decisions required of teachers. Taken together, management and instructional tactics represent our efforts to help students learn what we want them to learn.

There is one more type of decision that teachers are required to make. After students have been engaged and given the opportunity to learn, we must make judgments about how successful their efforts and our efforts have been. Those judgments rest on evaluative decisions, which we will consider in Chapters 13 and 14.

Chapter Summary

Introduction: Experience and Organization

It is necessary to make the distinction between classroom management and discipline. Classroom management refers to organizing learning experiences that minimize behavior problems. Discipline requires dealing with the behavior problems that have arisen.

Management Skills
Giving Clear Instructions

If you are to engage students in a learning activity, you must give them precise directions so that they know clearly what is expected of them. Creative delivery that involves students helps ensure on-task behavior.

Beginning a Lesson
Provide cues that signal the beginning of a learning activity to help establish attention. It is helpful also to remove distractions so that when a lesson begins, students can focus on the important information.

Maintaining Attention
One way of helping students maintain their attention on a learning activity is to recognize and encourage their contributions. The seating arrangement in a classroom can also influence students' ability to pay attention.

Pacing
Pacing refers to the tempo of a lesson. It can be affected if the teacher makes a disorganized presentation. Pacing can also be disrupted by a lack of other management skills; the result is problem behavior that distracts students from the task at hand.

Using Seatwork Effectively
Managing seatwork requires the careful monitoring of students. Before a teacher can redirect a student's attention or help the student solve a problem that is slowing his or her progress, the teacher must be aware of each student's in-class activity.

Summarizing
Summarizing is useful to students because it helps them organize the information they have learned. If students understand how what they've learned is organized, they are better able to fit new content in with the old. Summarizing at the end of a lesson is recommended at all grade levels.

Providing Useful Feedback and Evaluation
Feedback gives students information about the correctness of their responses and offers them an opportunity to correct mistakes. Feedback is not the same as reinforcement; what should be reinforced are students' efforts.

Making Smooth Transitions
Transitions are made when moving from one activity to the next. If transitions are not smooth, students are more likely to get off task. When students are off task, problem behaviors arise.

Discipline
Dynamics of Discipline
The Kounin approach to discipline emphasizes group skills. The ripple effect refers to the consequences that correcting one student's behavior has on the behavior of others. In order to effectively discipline, teachers need to be aware of all student activity; they need to cultivate "withitness." In addition to observational skills, teachers need to develop the skill to direct one activity while monitoring others. This skill is called overlapping.

Skinner Revisited: Applied Behavior Analysis
Applied behavior analysis involves analyzing problem behaviors and prescribing some kind of remedy for them. Remedies include the catch 'em being good approach, rules-ignore-praise (RIP), rules-reward-punishment (RRP), contingency management, and contracting.

Sane Messages
Sane messages is Haim Ginott's term for the way in which a teacher should speak to students who present discipline problems. Central to the notion of sane messages are "I-messages." When presenting an I-message, the teacher speaks about his or her feelings regarding a classroom situation rather than attributing the situation to a student's negative characteristics.

Assertive Discipline
Assertive discipline is an approach that emphasizes clear and unambiguous statements. Rules are established and are enforced. Teachers communicate through promises not threats.

Expectations and Communication
Teacher Expectancies
Teachers communicate their expectations to students through differential treatment. The Pygmalion effect refers to the influence that a teacher's expectations may have on student behavior. Expectations can have more influence in one situation than another. Nonetheless, it is important for teachers to be aware that they may be communicating expectations in the ways that they treat students.

Classroom Goal Structures
Classroom goal structures establish the conditions under which students are rewarded for attaining goals. Three types of classroom goal structures are cooperative, competitive, and individual.

Reflections: Building Your Theory of Teaching

12.1 Sketch and describe narratively the physical arrangement of the space in which you expect to teach. Describe how your arrangement matches your management "style."

12.2 Invent some management routines you expect to test in your classroom. Invent a routine that prepares your students for a lesson, maintains their on-task behavior, and concludes a classroom activity.

12.3 Imagine a student who continually disrupts small group discussions by telling jokes. Prescribe a disciplinary approach for that student's behavior.

Key Terms

on-task behavior (p. 443)
action zones (p. 447)
pacing (p. 450)
transitions (p. 453)
ripple effect (p. 457)
withitness (p. 457)
overlapping (p. 458)
applied behavior analysis (p. 460)
catch 'em being good (p. 460)

rules-ignore-praise (RIP) (p. 461)
rules-reward-punishment (RRP) (p. 461)
contingency management (p. 462)
contracting (p. 462)
sane messages (p. 466)
I-messages (p. 466)
assertive discipline (p. 466)

Pygmalion effect (p. 469)
classroom goal structures (p. 472)
cooperative goal structure (p. 473)
competitive goal structure (p. 473)
individual goal structure (p. 476)

Suggested Readings

Baur, A. M., & Sapona, R. H. (1991). *Managing classrooms to facilitate learning.* Needham Heights, MA: Allyn & Bacon.

Emmer, E. T., Evertson, C. M., Sanford, J. P., Clements, B. S., & Worsham, M. E. (1989). *Classroom management for secondary teachers.* Englewood Cliffs, NJ: Prentice-Hall.

Evertson, C. M., Emmer, E. T., Clements, B. S., Sanford, J. P., & Worsham, M. E. (1989). *Classroom management for elementary teachers.* Englewood Cliffs, NJ: Prentice-Hall.

Jones, V. F., & Jones, L. S. (1990). *Comprehensive classroom management.* Needham Heights, MA: Allyn & Bacon.

Kounin, J. S. (1970). *Discipline and group management in classrooms.* New York: Holt, Rinehart & Winston.

References

Adams, R. S., & Biddle, B. J. (1970). *Realities of teaching: Explanations with videotape.* New York: Holt, Rinehart & Winston.

Ames, C., & Ames, R. (1984). Goal structures and motivation. *The Elementary School Journal, 85,* 39–52.

Angus, M. J., Evans, K. W., & Parkin, B. (1975). *An observational study of selected pupil and teacher behavior in open plan and conventional design classrooms* (Australian Open Area Project, Tech. Rep. No. 4). Perth: Educational Department of Western Australia.

Arlin, M. (1979). Teacher transitions can disrupt time flow in classrooms. *American Educational Research Journal, 16,* 42–56.

Barowsky, E. I. (1986). Effects of stereotypic expectations on evaluation of written English attributed to handicapped and non-handicapped students. *Psychological Reports, 59*(3), 1097–1098.

Braun, C. (1976). Teacher expectations: Sociopsychological dynamics. *Review of Educational Research, 46*(2), 185–213.

Brophy, J. E., & Evertson, C. (1976). *Learning from teaching: A developmental perspective*. Boston, MA: Allyn & Bacon.

Brophy, J. E., & Good, T. L. (1974). *Teacher-student relationships: Causes and consequences*. New York: Holt, Rinehart & Winston.

Canter, L., & Canter, M. (1976). *Assertive discipline: A take-charge approach for today's educator*. Los Angeles: Lee Canter and Associates.

Charles, C. M. (1981). *Building classroom discipline: From models to practice* (2nd ed.). New York: Longman.

Cooper, H. M. (1979). Statistically combining independent studies: A meta-analysis of sex differences in conformity research. *Journal of Personality and Social Psychology, 37*, 131–146.

Cooper, H. M., & Good, T. L. (1983). *Pygmalion grows up: Studies in the expectation communication process*. White Plains, NY: Longman.

Covington, M., & Beery, R. (1976). *Self-worth and school learning*. New York: Holt, Rinehart & Winston.

Daum, J. (1972). *Proxemics in the classroom: Speaker-subject distance and educational performance*. Paper presented at the annual meeting of the Southeastern Psychological Association.

Delefes, P., & Jackson, B. (1972). Teacher-pupil interaction as a function of location in the classroom. *Psychology in the Schools, 9*, 119–123.

Doyle, W. (1984). How order is achieved in classrooms: An interim report. *Journal of Curriculum Studies, 16*, 259–277.

Dweck, C. S. (1986). Motivational processes affecting learning. *American Psychologist, 41*, 1040–1047.

Fisher, C. W., Berliner, D. C., Filby, N. N., Marliave, R., Cahen, L. S., & Dishaw, M. M. (1980). Teaching behaviors, academic learning time, and student achievement: An overview. In C. Denham & A. Lieberman (Eds.), *Time to learn*. Washington, DC: National Institute of Education.

Fisher, C. W., Filby, N. N., Marliave, R., Cahen, L. S., Dishaw, M. M., Moore, J. E., & Berliner, D. C. (1978). *Teaching behaviors, academic learning time, and student achievement: Final report of phase III-B, Beginning Teacher Evaluation Study* (Tech. Report V-1). San Francisco: Far West Laboratory for Educational Research and Development.

Ginott, H. (1972). *Teacher and child*. New York: Macmillan.

Good, T. (1986). Recent classroom research: Implications for teacher education. In D. Smith (Ed.), *Essential knowledge for beginning educators*. Washington, DC: American Association of Colleges for Teacher Education.

Gump, P. (1967). *The classroom behavior setting: Its nature and relation to student behavior* (Report No. BR-5-0334). Washington, DC: Office of Education, Bureau of Research.

Johnson, D., & Johnson, R. (1987). *Learning together and alone: Cooperative, competitive, and individualistic learning* (2nd ed.). Englewood Cliffs, NJ: Prentice-Hall.

Jones, V. F., & Jones, L. S. (1990). *Comprehensive classroom management: Motivating and managing students* (3rd ed.). Needham Heights, MA: Allyn & Bacon.

Jussim, L. (1986). Self-fulfilling prophesies: A theoretical and integrative review. *Psychological Review, 93*(4), 429–445.

Kounin, J. (1970). *Discipline and group management in classrooms*. New York: Holt, Rinehart & Winston.

Kulhavy, R. W. (1977). Feedback in written instruction. *Review of Educational Research, 47*, 211–232.

Leder, G. C. (1987). Student achievement: A factor in classroom dynamics? *Exceptional Child, 34*(2), 133–141.

Marshall, H. H., & Weinstein, R. S. (1986). Classroom context of student-perceived differential teacher treatment. *Journal of Educational Psychology, 78*(6), 441–453.

Michaels, J. W. (1977). Classroom reward structures and academic performances. *Review of Educational Research, 47*, 87–98.

Phye, G. D., & Andre, T. (Eds.). (1986). *Cognitive classroom learning*. Orlando: Academic Press.

Puro, P., & Bloome, D. (1987). Understanding classroom communication. *Theory into Practice, 26*(1), 26–31.

Rosenshine, B. V. (1980). How time is spent in elementary classrooms. In C. Denham & A. Leiberman (Eds.), *Time to learn*. Washington, DC: National Institute of Education.

Rosenthal, R. (1987). Pygmalion effects: Existence, magnitude, and social importance. A reply to Wineburg. *Educational Researcher, 16*, 37–41.

Rosenthal, R., & Jacobson, L. (1968). *Pygmalion in the classroom*. New York: Holt, Rinehart & Winston.

Royer, J. M., & Feldman, R. S. (1984). *Educational psychology: Applications and theory.* New York: Alfred A. Knopf.

Schwebel, A. I., & Cherlin, D. L. (1972). Physical and social distancing in teacher-pupil relationships. *Journal of Educational Psychology, 63,* 543–550.

Weinstein, R., Marshall, H., Sharp, L., & Botkin, M. (1987). Pygmalion and the student: Age and classroom differences in children's awareness of teacher expectations. *Child Development, 58*(4), 1079–1093.

Wineburg, S. S. (1987). The self-fulfillment of the self-fulfilling prophecy: A critical appraisal. *Educational Researcher, 16,* 28–37.

Woolfolk, A. (1987). *Educational psychology* (3rd ed.). Englewood Cliffs, NJ: Prentice-Hall.

13
Using Classroom Data

Chapter Overview

The first two chapters in Part III (Chapters 9–10) were devoted to planning. The next two chapters in Part III (Chapters 11–12) were devoted to classroom interaction. This chapter and Chapter 14 are devoted to evaluation. In this chapter, we focus on evaluation that is initiated by the classroom teacher rather than those outside the classroom. Teachers need to be aware of the various purposes to which evaluation can be put. In order for evaluative data to be useful it must come from tests and measurements that are reliable and valid. Because the types of items that appear on classroom tests measure in different ways, we will examine guidelines for each type of item. Finally, we will also examine the ways in which scores on tests and other evaluative instruments can be used to determine grades. ∎

Introduction: Evaluation, Measurement, and Tests

evaluation The judgment of how well students are achieving by the process of gathering, analyzing, and interpreting information.
measurement The numerical description of students' characteristics.
test A procedure or an instrument designed to measure a sample of behavior.

Chap. Obj. 1
Test Ques. 13.1–13.7

Focus Question: How does evaluation differ from measurement?

Lecture Note: Remind students of the number of decisions made in the Diary of a Day, Chapter 1.

Lecture Note: Ask students to provide examples of judgments not based on measurement and examples of measurements not based on a test.

When people converse about classroom assessment, they use the terms *evaluation, measurement,* and *test* interchangeably. Although the terms are related, the decisions teachers must make require that they understand the terms as being distinct. To help understand the distinction, suppose a student gets 90 percent of the questions on a geography test correct. Does the student's score mean he or she knows geography well? Should means other than the test be used to determine the student's knowledge of geography? What judgment can be justified on the basis of the 90 percent score on the test?

Evaluation is the process of gathering, analyzing, and interpreting information in order to judge how well students are achieving. Evaluation enables the teacher to answer the question, "How good?" (Gronlund, 1985) For example, a teacher might judge "how good a student is in geography" or "how good the geography lessons were." Evaluation is the most general of the three terms; it subsumes the terms *measurement* and *test.* The key to understanding "evaluation" is to see that it is a process that yields judgments. Evaluative judgments range from decisions about what students' activities for the next seven minutes will be to those about placing students in reading groups or in special education programs. Measurement provides one basis for making evaluative judgments.

Measurement is the process of numerically describing a student's particular characteristics. Measurement answers the question, "How much?" (Gronlund, 1985) The geography test is a measurement because it shows "how much" of the information on the test was known by the student. Measurement is a quantitative description rather than a qualitative description or value judgment. One way to measure how much a student understands is to determine the number of test items the student answers correctly.

A **test** is a procedure or an instrument used for measuring a sample of behavior. Tests answer the question, "How well does a student perform when compared against other students or against performance standards?" (Gronlund, 1985) A score of 90 percent on the geography test might mean that the student performs better than one half of the class and is allowed to move on to the next unit because 90 percent correct is taken as a criterion of mastery. A test is one specific type of measurement; it is the most specific of the three terms.

To summarize, evaluation is a judgment. Some judgments are based on measurement. Some measurements are made by means of a test.

Consider the types of judgments you might make about students. Some of your evaluative judgments are based on measurements taken by you or by others. Some of those measurements are based on tests that you administer or that are administered by the school or district. If you make the judgment that one of your students should be referred to the principal for discipline, you have made an evaluation. The judgment may not be based on measurement (i.e., some collection of quantitative data), but it is a form of evaluation. One of the reasons for parent–teacher conferences is to allow teachers to communicate evaluative judgments that are not reflected in the reports on grades or standardized test scores or homework assignments or completed tests that are sent home for parents to see.

The way teachers evaluate is important, but of equal importance is the purpose for which evaluation is to be used. The technical issues of classroom evaluation must be understood in order to make sound decisions about students.

Lecture Note: The point that we should keep in mind is that the purpose for which evaluation is used is critical. Remind students to keep that point in mind as they learn the concepts of classroom evaluation.

Teacher
Chronicle
13.1

TEST TIME

I plopped down in a chair in the teachers' lounge and let out a long sigh. Amy Pearson, a friend and fellow science teacher, came over to join me.

"You look bushed," she said. "Good thing it's Friday."

I smiled at her concern. "Yes, it has been a long week. But it's not that so much as the disaster my kids made of the unit test I just gave them. I don't know if it's them, my teaching, or the test that's the problem."

I looked at Amy, a veteran of twenty-five years teaching experience, and asked, "Amy, how do you make up your tests? Your kids always complain about how hard your tests are, but they never complain that they aren't fair."

She laughed, "You know I really enjoy creating tests. Creating might seem a funny way to think of what one does in putting a test together, but test making is a creative thinking and writing process for me.

"For instance, when I create a test for my science classes, I want my test to be a fair representation of the material we have covered since the previous test, so I give multiple choice questions related to class lectures and lab experiments. I make sure some of my questions can be answered correctly in a number of ways."

"But don't the guidelines for making multiple choice tests say to have only one 'correct' response?" I interrupted.

"Yes, but in my experience I have found that students can often provide a good argument for a different answer being correct. I'm always pleased when this happens because it demonstrates that the student has thought carefully about the material being tested. In my view, the use of more than one correct answer on a multiple choice item is justified as long as the students understand clearly how the test works."

"Doesn't that screw them up? I mean the format interferes with the test."

"I give them practice tests to familiarize them with my format. It seems to me that the best way to make a test reliable is to eliminate the possibility that someone could miss an item they really know well. I like to encourage students to read the test questions carefully and really consider their responses. I want them to read through every possible answer first before deciding on a solution. My students have difficulty with this at the beginning of the school year, but most get to be quite adept at it by the end of the first quarter."

"Are your tests only multiple choice then?" I asked.

"No, I also ask at least one essay question that covers the material presented in the lab assignments. Because my labs are set up as small group activities, I know that sometimes most of the work is done by one person. In order to ensure that each student participates to the best of his or her ability, I make the essay question one that links things they should have learned."

"I also give extra credit for details covered in class or discovered in a close reading of the textbook. As a vocabulary extension and extra credit exercise, I also include jokes and riddles based on the terminology covered in the unit. The students enjoy these jokes, and over the years I have found that such wordplay actually enhances the growth of their scientific vocabulary."

"That's a great idea," I said. "You should write that up as a magazine article."

Amy laughed as the bell rang. "You know, I might just do that."

CLASSROOM EVALUATION

Chap. Obj. 1
Test Ques. 13.8–13.19

Focus Question: For what purposes are classroom evaluations used?

Teaching Anecdote: Tell your students about the school district that used only the results of an IQ test to place students in their gifted program. A neighboring school district placed students using the results of IQ tests, peer recommendations, teacher observations, and parental evaluations.

Ask your students why a student admitted to the first district's gifted program might be denied entry into the gifted program of the second district.

Natriello (1987) identifies four general functions of evaluation: certification, selection, direction, and motivation.

1. Certification assures that a student has achieved a level of competence. Many states now require that students perform at a level of minimum competency in order to attain promotion from grade to grade or to graduate from high school.
2. Selection refers to the evaluative procedures used to identify students who will enter or continue in educational or vocational programs. For example, a test might be used to determine whether a student should be considered for entry into a gifted program. The evaluation is also used to create tracks or ability grouping within a class. In some

At the secondary school level, the most common evaluation technique is the objective test. Testing can be used to determine placement, to monitor instruction, to evaluate performance at the end of a unit, and to identify learning difficulties during instruction.

instructional situations, evaluation is used to determine when a student should proceed to new or more complex material.

3. Direction involves the use of a test to guide or direct future instruction. Evaluation provides teachers with information on which to base feedback to students. Evaluation also enables the teacher to diagnose problems and to plan additional instruction. A student who performs poorly on a particular test may be required to undertake remedial activities before moving on to the next unit of instruction.

4. Motivation comes from the knowledge that students will be evaluated. Recall our earlier examination of extrinsic motivation in Chapter 8. In Teacher Chronicle 13.1, students who expect to take the veteran teacher's exams are probably motivated to study the material. A student's performance on a test can affect his or her self-image. Success in instructional situations can lead to a sense of self-efficacy. The reasons students give for succeeding or failing on evaluative tasks provide clues for understanding how they view themselves. (See Weiner's attribution theory, also in Chapter 8.)

The type of evaluation procedure used should depend on the purposes for which it is being conducted. It makes little sense for a classroom teacher to test simply for the sake of testing. A consideration of the purpose of an evaluative practice is critical in designing a procedure which puts it into effect. Evaluation procedures can be classified sequentially, as they occur in classroom instruction. These procedures are classified according to their purposes, whether they be used for placement or for formative, summative, or diagnostic purposes.

Purposes of Evaluation

Placement Evaluation

Placement evaluation is performed in order to determine the types of instructional experiences to which a student should be exposed. For example, evaluation at the beginning of instruction can be used to place a student within the instructional sequence. Determining what a student knows and does not know is one way of measuring "entering behavior." Evaluating students prior to instruction enables the teacher to make informed decisions about where instruction should begin for the class as a whole, for groups within that class, or for individual students. Placement evaluation also assists teachers who are making decisions about what type of instructional method would best suit a student. Does a student need remedial instruction? Would a student benefit most from an advanced placement class? Decisions about whether or not a student will be placed in a particular teacher's classroom are also made with the aid of a placement evaluation.

Formative Evaluation

Formative evaluation, which is used to monitor instruction, provides feedback to both the student and the teacher. It is used to "form" instruction, but not used in grading a student's performance. The models for direct instruction examined in Chapter 11 contain a component for checking the students' understanding of subject matter. Checking their understanding during a lesson is an example of formative evaluation. As a result of checking students' understanding, the teacher is better able to decide whether to proceed to the next objective in the lesson or to attempt to remedy any problems students

placement evaluation
Assessing the most appropriate learning situation in which to place the student.
formative evaluation
Monitoring instructional practices in order to judge progress and guide the content and pace of lessons.

Connection: See the discussion of extrinsic motivation in Chapter 8.

Connection: See the discussion of attribution theory in Chapter 8.

Teacher Interview: Have students interview teachers regarding their views of the ways in which evaluation functions in a classroom.

Field Observation: Have students collect the criteria used by several school districts to place students in special programs.

Connection: See the discussion of the models for direct instruction in Chapter 11.

Issues in Educational Psychology

CNN™ This box relates to Segment 13 of the CNN videotape. See the Instructor's Section for a summary.

A New Age in National Examinations

As commissioner of the Texas Higher Education Board, Kenneth Ashworth made a strong case for standardized testing. Writing in the *Education Digest,* Ashworth noted that during World War I "test developers claimed they could measure innate differences in mental acuity and aptitude" among Americans. Their claims seemed to offer to rich and poor alike an equal opportunity to prove their intelligence. But although testing initially offered access to college, noted Ashworth, through the years it has come to be "seen as a device to deny access."

Ashworth admitted that minority students have a higher failure rate on standardized tests. But he was adamant that "testing does not reveal any intrinsic deficiencies of individuals who happen to be from minority groups." All ethnic, racial, or sexual biases must be eliminated from tests to make them fair. Ashworth firmly stated that tests should "reveal only the relative deprivation of educational opportunities." Once biases have been removed, test results will show how well students have been educated. Ashworth stated his belief "that tests can be used to hold individuals accountable for leadership, teaching, or learning."

Like Ashworth, Marc Tucker believes in accountability. Interviewed by *Teacher Magazine,* Tucker stressed that "the burden cannot fall exclusively on the kids: it has to fall on the system." He offered support for "real rewards for school professionals who help those kids meet the standard, and consequences for those who don't."

Tucker knows what he's talking about. He was the principal author of *A Nation Prepared: Teachers for the 21st Century.* Today he heads the National Center on Education and the Economy (NCEE) in Rochester, New York. Along with the University of Pittsburgh's Learning Research and Development Center, plus ten to twenty school districts and state education systems, NCEE is working to develop "an examination system that will put a premium on thinking, problem solving, and a capacity to apply knowledge to real-world problems," according to Tucker.

Establishing a National Education Standards Board lies at the heart of the pilot program. Representing ten to twenty participating cities and states, the board will develop standards and model examinations. The exams may be modified on a state-by-state basis, but they would be linked to national standards.

Whether or not differing exams, textbooks, and local curricula can provide students with an education that meets national standards is currently being explored. Actual testing will probably consist of a formal examination, student portfolios, and long-range projects.

Besides writing essays, students would offer presentations of skills learned. Such unconventional assessments have already been used in some states, for example, South Carolina. The Rural Educational Alliance for Collaborative Humanities (REACH) program allowed students to explore the humanities as they researched the culture and history of their communities in South Carolina. In a statewide achievement fair, students presented historical profiles, skits about a local dialect, and a performance of gospel songs to show the link between the musical expression of one local community and East Africa.

Whatever the mix of formal examination and assessments, national standards will create greater equality among the country's school systems. Tucker has criticized the lower standards that are acceptable in the nation's inner-city schools. If the NCEE pilot program provides the basis for a national program, American students will be playing on a more level field.

Sources: Ashworth, Kenneth. "Standardized Testing: A Defense." *Education Digest* 56, issue 3 (November 1990): 40–42. Gursky, Daniel. "Ambitious Measures." *Teacher Magazine* 2, no. 7 (April 1991): 51–56. Barone, Thomas. "Assessment as Theater: Staging an Exposition." *Educational Leadership* 48, issue 5 (February 1991): 57–59.

1. Why might essays, student portfolios, and long-range projects be more effective ways of assessing student learning than a two-hour multiple choice exam?

2. What are the advantages and disadvantages of unconventional routes for evaluation as exemplifeid in the REACH program?

have with the current objective that may exist. Formative evaluation can also take the form of quizzes or other types of tests. The teacher may, for example, decide that additional reading assignments are necessary before proceeding with the original plan for instruction. The teacher may use oral questioning to make decisions about when to proceed. Formative evaluation can also be used when advising students on particular activities that will enhance their learning.

Summative Evaluation

Summative evaluation is the evaluation of a student's performance at the end of an instructional unit. It is most often used for the purpose of assigning grades. A final exam is an example of a summative evaluation procedure.

Diagnostic Evaluation

Diagnostic evaluation involves making judgments about what should happen to a student on a sequence of instructional activities. Such evaluations might be used to judge learning difficulties during instruction. Diagnostic evaluation may lead to a student being placed in a special education program. It may be used to formulate a specific instructional program or to make some sort of summary judgment of the student. Diagnostic evaluation illustrates how the various types of classroom evaluation overlap. We may give a test for what are, initially, summative purposes, but make formative judgments based on the results of that test.

Techniques of Evaluation

We evaluate in a variety of ways in classrooms. In a survey of elementary and secondary teachers, Gullickson (1985) discovered that the three most com-

summative evaluation
Judgments that follow an instructional unit and are most often used for the purpose of assigning grades.
diagnostic evaluation
Analyzing specific areas of strength and weakness for the purpose of making decisions about a student's learning program.

Journal Entry: Have each student recall an episode from his or her schooling in which a teacher changed the activities of a class based on the results of a test or a quiz. The student should discuss how well or poorly the teacher made the shift.

Lecture Note: Ask students to discuss how a single test is sometimes used for multiple evaluation purposes.

Chapter 15 Casebook Preview: See Writers' Tea.

Teaching Anecdote: Tell your students about the fourth-grade student who did well when responding verbally to reading comprehension questions but rarely completed a written assignment. The teacher often adapted lessons so that the student could respond verbally to comprehension questions. However, the teacher held the student responsible for completing all other kinds of written assignments.
   Ask your students why the teacher made this adaptation, taking into account the teacher's purpose in evaluating reading comprehension.

One of the purposes of diagnostic evaluation is to determine whether students belong in gifted or special education programs. Assessment of motor and cognitive skills may be accomplished by using written, oral, and physical tests.

mon evaluation techniques were (a) objective teacher-generated tests, (b) class discussion, and (c) papers or notebooks. In the survey, Gullickson determined that elementary teachers use a greater variety of techniques and tend to use "nontest" techniques, whereas secondary teachers place a major emphasis on objective tests. Clearly, however, the most commonly used evaluation procedure is the day-to-day observation of students in classes.

As we proceed through a lesson we watch the faces of our students. We collect data in the form of furrowed eyebrows, a smile, an affirming nod, a glazed stare or, heaven forbid, a rolling of eyes. Based on the observations we make of our students, we decide whether a lesson is going well or not. We determine whether to stick with the original plan or to implement "Plan B." We make on-the-spot diagnoses and alter our instructional actions accordingly.

The decisions we make based on our evaluation through observation involve drawing inferences. We infer from the affirming nod that a student understands the material we are presenting. We infer from a furrowed brow that the student requires an additional example or perhaps a different analogy. We must be careful when drawing inferences from such observations. Making inferences from behavioral observation can be tricky. A student who nods in affirmation may not truly understand the material we are presenting, but may have learned that nodding pleases teachers. If the student's goal is to be perceived as an attentive, hard-working student, the student's nodding behavior may be a means to that end. To increase the accuracy of our evaluative judgments, therefore, it is important that we understand the conditions that influence our observations.

If the form of our evaluation requires measurement—the collection of quantitative data—we must approach that form of evaluation with equal care. A student's test score is an index of his or her performance. Before using the results of that test for an evaluative purpose, we need to examine the conditions under which the student's performance occurred. We can be as wrong about the student's performance on a test as we are about the meaning of a student's affirming nod.

UTILITY OF EVALUATIVE INFORMATION

Whether we use quantitative tests or qualitative observations to make evaluative judgments, it is important that we have confidence in the evaluation procedures that we use. The extent to which we can be confident in tests or qualitative procedures rests on two properties of any evaluation procedure: reliability and validity.

Reliability

It is easier to understand the properties of evaluative procedures in terms of paper-and-pencil tests when we exclude qualitative evaluation, such as observing facial expressions. We will, therefore, examine reliability and validity as properties of tests. The properties, however, apply to all forms of measurement, including informal observation.

Reliability refers to the consistency of measurements, which can be judged either over time, across different forms of the same test, or within a test itself. If a test measures in a consistent fashion, then we can rely on the results of that test.

Let's consider an example. If you were to give a history test to a group of thirty students on Monday and give the same test to the same students on Wednesday, the students who scored well on Monday should also score well on Wednesday. The same holds true for students who scored poorly. Assume, in this example, that there is no change in the relative knowledge or abilities of the thirty students between Monday and Wednesday. If the test yields the same rank order of students on both administrations, it can be said to be consistent or reliable. An inconsistent test is unreliable. If the students who do well on Monday perform poorly on Wednesday, the test's reliability will be called into question. An unreliable test creates problems in interpreting results. We cannot be quite sure what exactly it is the test is measuring.

If the test proves to be reliable, if the results of the test are consistent across different times or forms, then we know that whatever characteristic the test is designed to measure, it is doing so in a consistent fashion. As we will see shortly, consistency—or reliability—is a necessary condition for confident interpretation results, but it is not sufficient of itself. It is also important to measure enough behavior so that consistency can be judged. Very short tests offer little opportunity to determine consistent performance. Therefore, one way to enhance reliability is to make sure tests are long enough. As we examine the ways in which reliability can be determined, think about the ways in which the length of a test (or the amount of observation) influences those estimates.

Estimating Reliability

Test-Retest

The reliability of a test can be estimated in one of three ways. The first method of estimating test reliability is called **test-retest**. The example previously examined in which students are tested on Monday and then retested on Wednesday illustrates the test-retest method of estimating reliability.

Alternate Forms

The consistency of a test can be measured not only by administering one test on two separate occasions, but by using different forms of the same test. Different forms of the same test are called **alternate forms** or parallel forms. They are designed to measure the same information but to do so using slightly different items. If two forms of one test yield a consistent ranking of students, the test is judged to be reliable. Inconsistent ranking means that the test is unreliable.

Internal Consistency

Internal consistency refers to how consistently items within a single test measure. Reliability estimates can be made using only one form of a test that is administered only once. To illustrate: Use a test of sixty items that can be divided into two subtests. Compare the ordering of students on the even items with that of the students on the odd items. By splitting the test in half and comparing the ordering on the split halves, an estimate of the test's reliability can be gained.

By way of restating, the three methods of obtaining reliability estimates for a test are the test-retest method, the alternate forms method, and the internal consistency or split-half method.

Journal Entry: Have students assume that they must interpret the results of an unreliable test, considering what the test might be measuring in addition to the content it covers.

Lecture Note: Emphasize that the discussion of various ways to determine reliability is presented in order to help students understand the nature of the property of tests referred to as "reliability."

Lecture Note: Remind students that reliability is estimated using the test-retest method by comparing the rank order of students.

Lecture Note: Ask students to discuss the assumptions that must be in place in order to estimate reliability by means of alternate forms of a test. The chief assumption is that the same question can be asked equally well in at least two different ways.

Lecture Note: Ask students to determine the assumptions that must be in place in order to estimate reliability by means of internal consistency. The chief assumption is that when a test is split in half, each half measures the same characteristics.

Lecture Note: Introduce the concept of validity by having students consider the following question: Does the test measure what it purports to measure?

Teacher Interview: Have each student interview a teacher regarding the "pool" of possible items for a particular exam.

Journal Entry: Have students reflect on their experiences when taking a test designed to predict their future performances. In particular, have them reflect on the differences between taking a final exam for a course and the experience of taking the SAT exam.

Connection: See the section on intelligence tests in Chapter 4.

Validity

We noted earlier that reliability is a necessary condition for the confident interpretation of test results, but not sufficient of itself. Before we can be wholly confident that the results of our tests mean what they appear to mean, we must be sure that the test possesses the property of validity as well as that of reliability. When we can provide a positive answer to the question, "Does the test measure consistently?" we can be sure of its reliability. The question we ask of tests when we want to judge their validity is, "Does the test measure what it purports to measure?" When the answer is "yes," when the test measures what it purports to measure, its **validity** is established. A test can be judged to be valid on the basis of content validity, criterion-related validity, or construct validity.

Content Validity

The **content validity** of a test is judged by determining whether the test provides a representative sample of possible tasks in the content domain being measured. For example, if a teacher has designed a test to measure his or her students' ability to use a dictionary, the test ought to represent all of the possible items that could be generated to measure dictionary use. If the test does not include a representative cross-sample of all of the items in that content domain, the test is judged to be invalid with respect to the content. Thus, one way for a teacher to enhance the validity of a test is to select items randomly from a large pool of possible items.

Criterion-related Validity

A second type of validity is called criterion-related validity. **Criterion-related validity** is important when the purpose of the test is to accurately predict performance, either at the present time or in the future. A test may be given, for example, in order to predict whether a student should be moved into a higher ability grouping for mathematics class. The test is used to predict the student's behavior; that is, the student's ability to behave in a different situation at the present time.

Other tests are administered in order to make predictions about future behavior. One example is the Scholastic Aptitude Test (SAT). The purpose of SATs is to predict whether the test-takers will perform well in college. Again, the type of validity we need to know about in this situation is criterion-related validity.

Construct Validity

A third type of validity is construct validity. We are interested in the **construct validity** of a test when its purpose is to measure some psychological trait or construct. Take, for example, the IQ tests discussed in Chapter 4. Intelligence is a construct. It is a concept that some theorist literally constructed as an explanation for certain observations. IQ tests are designed to measure the psychological characteristics we call intelligence. When we ask the question of validity—Does the test measure what it purports to measure?—about an intelligence test, we are asking whether the IQ test is a valid measure of intelligence. Does the IQ test measure intelligence or does it measure something else? The results of a valid test can be interpreted with confidence.

Summary of Reliability and Validity

In all three cases, validity is measured by matching the performances of students on the test in question with comparative data. For example, when we construct a test to measure students' knowledge of the Civil War, it should yield results that match well the results of other tests that measure the same area of knowledge. If it does, a basis exists for inferring that the test possesses content validity.

Criterion-related validity is measured by matching the performance on a predictive test with the performance on the criterion being predicted. For example, if a student performs well enough on a predictive test for placement in an advanced course of study, the test will be judged valid if the student performs well at that advanced level. In the case of the SAT, students' performances on tests are matched against performances in college in order to determine criterion-related validity.

When comparing any of the various ways that a construct such as intelligence is measured, if the performances across the various measurements are consistent, the construct validity of the initial test is assumed.

A reliable test can be counted on because it is consistent. A valid test can be counted on because it measures what it says it measures. It is possible for a test to be reliable without being valid. A test of grammar might rank order students in exactly the same way time after time. But if the test itself contains items that are incorrect, the results of that test will not be valid. Reliability is a prerequisite to validity; both are necessary if we are to use the results of the test with confidence.

Even if a test is judged to be both reliable and valid, the responsibility for using the results of that test still rests with the teacher or administrator who makes the evaluative judgments. Most of the problems that we hear about in educational testing arise from the misuse or misinterpretation of test results, that is, making evaluative judgments that are not warranted by a test (see Kubiszyn & Borich, 1987).

In the next section of the chapter, we examine some principles of test construction. A teacher who follows these principles will enhance the reliability and validity of the tests he or she constructs.

Field Observation: Have each student obtain the policy of a local school district regarding the use of tests, and examine the policy to determine how reliability and validity of tests influence evaluative judgments.

Principles in Practice 13.1

Principles . . .
1. Evaluation can be used for different purposes.
2. If test results are to be relied on, the test itself must provide the same measurement consistently.
3. Valid tests measure what they purport to measure.

. . . in Practice
In Teacher Chronicle 13.1, one of the teachers has a real interest in creating tests that the students will judge as being fair. Through the conversation, we learned that the twenty-five-year teaching veteran used a variety of measures to accomplish her purposes. This variety not only allowed her to evaluate various aspects of her students' performances, it enhanced the sample of

behavior she could judge as well. Increasing the sample of behavior allowed her to judge both reliability and validity. Perhaps it was the variety that led to the perception that her tests, while tough, were fair.

1. Identify the various purposes that the science teacher had in mind when she evaluated students.
2. What other steps could the science teacher have taken to enhance reliability and validity?
3. How will you be able to ensure the reliability and validity of the observations you will make (rather than the tests you will use) in your classroom?

Teacher
Chronicle
13.2

THE VERDICT, PLEASE

Sometimes, when I am assessing students, I feel like judge, jury, and attorney for the client all at once.

As the attorney I must present the evidence that establishes the success or failure of my client. As the judge, I must preside over the proceedings to make sure that as much admissible evidence as possible is brought to bear on the issues. Finally, as the jury, I have to weigh the evidence and decide just what grade to give—the degree of success as established by the laws.

"The court calls the case of *Evaluative Criteria vs. Brett Washburn*."

"Your Honor, it is clear from the fact that my client, Brett Washburn, fails every timed math test, that he is suffering from an extreme case of test anxiety. He obviously knows his math facts as seen by the evidence that he can do math computations on his daily work in class. You have witnessed this yourself, Your Honor."

"Yes, counselor, I have studied the evidence submitted. Your client clearly can do addition and subtraction based on his knowledge of the math facts."

Addressing the jury, the judge says, "Please keep in mind, however, that school laws require that the student be able to demonstrate competency on the weekly timed math tests. This he clearly has not been able to do."

The counselor speaks up again. "Please keep in mind, Your Honor, the evidence submitted by Brett's mother. She is well aware of his difficulty on the timed tests, but she, too, recognizes his ability to perform complicated computations on his homework."

"I am equally aware of that fact," the judge replies. "However, the procedure states that every student must be able to do 100 facts in five minutes. Can Brett do this?"

"He can do the 100 facts, Your Honor."

"But can he do them within the stipulated five minutes?"

"No, but given a longer time he gets 90 out of 100 correct."

"That evidence will be considered by the jury."

"I would also like to submit as evidence the fact that Brett is a diligent, hardworking math student determined to succeed. His daily work, attitude, and class participation bear this out."

"The jury will consider this too in its deliberations."

(The jury is out. Time passes. The jury reenters the courtroom.)

"Foreperson of the jury, has the jury marked the report card?"

"We have, Your Honor."

"Will the student, Brett Washburn, please come forward to receive his report card."

Brett comes up, takes his card, opens it, and looks for the timed test information.

"I passed," he shouts. Judge, jury, and attorney congratulate him.

In my chambers before the "trial," I had asked myself, "What was the purpose of the test?"

"To encourage students to learn the facts." I answered. Therefore, if Brett knew the facts, then he had fulfilled the purpose of the test. The problem is with the test, not Brett.

I do, however, wonder how he did the following year. Did he lose some of that test anxiety? Or did it come back full blown with that year's tests and teacher? Did I do him a disservice by not insisting that he "pass" within the given time? Or did I boost his confidence by weighing more than one piece of evidence and deciding in his favor?

The decision I made seemed right at the time. Like so many teaching decisions, we don't get to see the long-term effects. We can only act within a limited time and within the structure of the environment. I find it frustrating never knowing the long-range outcomes.

CONSTRUCTING CLASSROOM TESTS

To collect the appropriate evidence and to make sound judgments teachers must design reliable ways of making evaluations—as illustrated by the reverie in Teacher Chronicle 13.2. Tests designed by teachers are appropriate ways to collect evidence. To make sure that the evidence collected is reliable and valid, teachers should follow four steps in preparing classroom tests (Gronlund, 1985).

1. Will the test be used for formative or summative purposes? Is the test being administered in order to make diagnoses of learning difficulties? Asking these questions of *purpose* will influence the length of the test and the breadth of content it covers. The purpose of the test will also influence the type of items constructed.

2. Using a *table of specifications* to construct a test enhances the test's content validity. We will examine the table of specifications in more detail shortly.

3. The *item types* selected have to match the learning outcomes that are being measured. Because each item has certain advantages and limitations, we will devote a section of this chapter to an examination of item types.

4. *Items* may be generated from scratch, may come from published curricular materials, or may be a combination of the two. Published items may be edited in order to make them more appropriate.

Chap. Obj. 3
Test Ques. 13.43–13.53

Focus Question: How do teachers construct useful classroom tests?

Connection: Teacher Chronicle 13.2: The Verdict, Please.

Teacher Interview: Have each student discuss with a teacher how he or she uses tests for formative and summative purposes.

Chapter 15 Casebook Preview: See Bringing the Real World into the Classroom.

Table of Specifications

The **table of specifications,** an important tool for teachers to use when generating classroom tests, provides a systematic way of ensuring that tests represent the instructional content and objectives of the unit being evaluated. Generally, the table of specifications takes the form of a two-way grid with content areas listed vertically down the left and levels of skill listed across the top. (Table 13–1 is a table of specifications showing categories of cognitive outcomes, usually levels of the cognitive taxonomy, across the top and instructional objectives on the left.)

According to Kubiszyn and Borich (1987), using a table of specifications is a seven-step process.

1. Determine the category to which each instructional objective belongs.
2. Determine the number of test items that need to be constructed for each objective. Record that number in the cell corresponding to the category for the objectives.
3. Repeat Steps 1 and 2 until every objective has been classified and the number of items recorded. (The first two steps will ensure that the test reflects the relative weights of the topics in the unit being tested.)
4. Add the number of items for each instructional objective and place the sum in the total column for each objective.
5. Repeat Steps 1 through 4 for each topic, that is, each objective being evaluated on the test.

■ **Table 13–1** *A Table of Specifications for a Test on Subtraction Without Borrowing*

Content Outline	K	C	A	Percentage
1. Distinguishes addition and subtraction signs	1			4
2. Distinguishes addition problems from subtraction problems	2			8
3. Identifies correctly and incorrectly solved subtraction problems		4		16
4. Correctly solves single-digit subtraction problems			6	24
5. Correctly solves double-digit minus single-digit subtraction problems			6	24
6. Correctly solves double-digit problems that do not require borrowing			6	24
Total	3	4	18	25 items
Percentage	12	16	72	100

SOURCE: From *Educational Testing and Measurement: Classroom Application and Practice* (2nd ed., p. 65) by T. Kubiszyn and G. Borich, 1987, Glenview, IL: Scott, Foresman. Copyright 1987 by Scott, Foresman, and Company. Adapted by permission of HarperCollins Publishers.

Key: K = Knowledge; C = Comprehension; and A = Application.

6. Add the number of items in each category and place the number at the bottom of the table.
7. Determine the column percentage and the row percentage by dividing each total by the number of items in the total test.

Using a table of specifications is the best way to generate a valid test. Recall, however, that for a test to be valid, it must first be reliable. It is important to remember how reliability can be established. Reliability is enhanced when a test provides a representative sample of all of the items that could be asked (an item population). The table of specifications contributes to, but does not ensure, reliability in this way.

Reliability is more than a representative sample, it is also a product of matching the test to instructional actions. For example, if the objectives listed in Table 13–1 were generated prior to instruction, but not followed by the teacher during the unit, then a test developed on the basis of those objectives may prove unreliable. The test would measure something that was not taught. This is a problem of validity, but it shows that a test must be both reliable and valid before the measurement it provides can be confidently interpreted. In the case just noted, the results would be based on factors other than knowledge pertinent to the test items.

The table of specifications is just one tool that a teacher can use to enhance the reliability and validity of the tests he or she constructs. Constructing a test is a job which requires more than one tool, however. Specifying the content to be covered by the items is just one part of the process, producing those items themselves is another.

selected response items Test items that require students to make choices from among the optional responses provided. Selected response items require recognition of the correct answer.
constructed response items Test items that require students to provide each response. Constructed response items require recall.
binary choice items Test items that require students to select one of two alternatives (e.g., true/false items).

Field Observation: Have each student observe a teacher who uses a table of specifications to construct a test, comparing the teacher's procedures with the seven-step process.

Lecture Note: Ask students to discuss how a table of specifications could be used for formative purposes.

ITEM TYPES

All test items are either selected response items or constructed response items. **Selected response items** require examinees to make choices from among the optional responses provided. **Constructed response items** require the examinee to provide each response. A distinction can also be made in terms of the cognitive processes required of the examinee. Selected response items require recognition of the correct answer. Constructed response items require recall.

There are several item types within these two broad categories. The first three item types that we will examine—binary choice, matching, and multiple choice—are selected response items. The last two item types—short answer and essay—are constructed response items. Each item type has advantages and disadvantages. The type of item the teacher selects should depend on the instructional objectives he or she wants to measure (Popham, 1981). Let's examine the various types of items that teachers may generate or select as they construct a test.

Chap. Obj. 3
Test Ques. 13.54–13.83

Focus Question: How do teachers construct useful classroom tests?

Journal Entry: Have students reflect on their experiences responding to selected-response items and constructed-response items, concentrating on the demands each item type placed on them.

Binary Choice Items

Binary choice items include any selected response item that offers two optional answers from which to select. Examples include true/false items, yes/no items, and items that require the student to classify a statement as fact or opinion, or as a cause or effect.

Binary choice items offer a number of advantages. They are efficient in covering a great deal of material. Binary choice items are also useful in covering content topics that can be placed into two categories (for example, an item might ask the student to identify whether an essay question is either a selected or constructed response item). Binary choice items can measure some fairly high levels of learning if they are constructed properly. What is usually required in this case is a fairly complex question. Finally, binary choice items are easy to score. It takes very little of the teacher's time to correct a binary choice item test.

One disadvantage of binary choice items is that the items are subject to guessing. Constructing longer tests can solve this problem. A longer test will provide a better sample of the item population. In this sense, it is more difficult to guess the correct answers to forty binary choice items than to guess correctly on twenty items. Another disadvantage is that poorly written items tend to encourage rote memorization rather than a higher level of cognitive processing. While the disadvantages of binary choice items are widely recognized, Ebel and Frisbie (1986) argue that these disadvantages are myths. They argue that well-written binary choice items overcome these disadvantages.

Guidelines for Writing Binary Choice Items

The following guidelines for writing binary choice items have been culled from several sources (Carey, 1988; Cunningham, 1986; Ebel & Frisbie, 1986; Gronlund, 1985; Hopkins & Antes, 1985; Hopkins & Stanley, 1981; Nitko, 1983; Popham, 1981). (These sources were also used in putting together guidelines for writing matching items, multiple choice items, short answer items, and essay items.)

1. Items should not deal with trivialities, but should avoid broad general statements if they are to be judged true or false.
2. Avoid the use of negative statements, especially double negatives. Do not add the word *not* to make a statement false.
3. Avoid long, complex sentences that include two ideas in one statement unless the item measures cause and effect or if/then relationships.
4. If opinion is used, attribute it to some source unless the ability to identify the opinion is what is being measured specifically.
5. True statements and false statements should be approximately equal in length and in number.
6. Avoid specific determiners, such as always, never, all, or none, that give unintended clues.
7. Make false statements plausible to someone who does not know the correct answer.
8. Statements should be paraphrased, not lifted verbatim, from instructional material so that understanding is required.
9. Make sure the item is either definitely true or false to avoid ambiguity.
10. Avoid constructing a predictable pattern of correct answers. For example, true true, false false, true true, false false.
11. Do not create trick statements using petty wording.
12. Directions should specify the type of judgment to be made and how students are to record their answers.

Teacher Interview: Have each student interview a teacher who uses binary choice items on his or her tests, in particular, asking the teacher how he or she copes with guessing as a potential problem.

Lecture Note: Have students form small groups. Have each student generate an instructional objective and write a binary choice item to measure that objective. Have students exchange objectives and binary choice items and critique their classmates' work according to the guidelines listed in the text.

Good binary choice items should be conceptualized in pairs. Write positive and negative statements, but use only one item from the pair on the test. This practice increases the item pool from which the test is built and, hence, the test's reliability.

Matching Items

Matching items usually consist of two columns of words or phrases to be matched. Items on the left are called *premises*. Items on the right are called *responses*. Matching items are compact in form and are efficient for measuring associations. They are also easy to score.

The disadvantage of matching items is that they are restricted to material that can be associated based on simple relationships. Matching items are difficult to write because they require homogeneous material throughout the unit being tested. Matching items are susceptible to unintended clues. That is, it is easy to "read in" meanings in this format. Matching items also tend to focus on lower-level outcomes. Finally, it is difficult to construct an entire test solely from matching items. In short, matching items work well when they are appropriate for the learning outcome and when they are constructed properly. Otherwise they should be avoided.

Guidelines for Writing Matching Items

1. Use homogeneous material in a given exercise. A set of matching items must deal with the same material. It is difficult to write matching items across topics.
2. Use an uneven number of responses and premises, providing instructions that responses may be used once, more than once, or not at all to avoid giving away answers.
3. Keep the list of premises and responses brief.
4. List responses in a logical order. This means that if an examinee were to read only the response column, the responses, as a group, would make sense.
5. Indicate, in the test directions, the basis to be used for matching premises to responses.
6. Place all items for one matching exercise on the same page.
7. Label the premises with numbers and the responses with letters.

Multiple Choice Items

Multiple choice items consist of questions or incomplete sentences that are accompanied by three or more alternative responses, one of which can be selected as a correct or best answer. The question or statement in the multiple choice item is called the *stem*. The responses are called *alternatives*. Incorrect alternatives are called *distractors*.

An important advantage of multiple choice items is that they can measure a wide variety of outcomes, including higher-level outcomes. Multiple choice items are very flexible in this way; flexibility combats some of the shortcomings of other objective items. For example, multiple choice items avoid the problem of having more than one correct answer for a short answer item. They eliminate some of the guessing that can take place with binary choice items. They can cover a wider array of material than matching items and there is no need for the material covered on the test to be homogeneous.

matching items Test items that require students to select a response that matches a premise (e.g., matching definitions with terms).

multiple choice items Test items that consist of questions or incomplete statements that are accompanied by three or more alternative responses, one of which can be selected as a correct or best answer.

Lecture Note: Ask students why this practice should enhance a test's reliability.

Chapter 15 Casebook Preview: See Around the World.

Teaching Anecdote: Tell your students about two pupils of equal ability in a senior history class. One student hated the class, especially the weekly multiple choice tests. The other student loved the class and looked forward to the weekly tests. The first student performed poorly on the tests; the second excelled.

Ask your students what might account for the differences in performance and attitude.

Lecture Note: Have students form small groups. Have the students identify an instructional objective and write matching items to evaluate that objective. Have students exchange their work and critique their classmates' efforts based on the guidelines in the text.

Journal Entry: Have students reflect on their experiences with multiple choice tests, and the strategies they've used in responding to multiple choice questions.

Another advantage of multiple choice items is that if alternatives are well written, multiple choice items can facilitate diagnosis of learning errors. Multiple choice items are easy to score and they are relatively unaffected by response patterns.

One disadvantage of multiple choice items is that it is sometimes difficult to find plausible distractors.

Guidelines for Writing Multiple Choice Items

1. The stem of the item should be meaningful and present a clear problem without the student's having to look at the alternatives.
2. Include as much of the item as possible in the stem without providing irrelevant material.
3. Use negatively stated items only if necessary.
4. Make the alternatives grammatically consistent with the stem.
5. There should be only one correct, clearly best answer.
6. All distractors should be plausible.
7. Avoid verbal associations between the stem and the answer that give unintended clues.
8. The length of the correct alternative should not provide clues by being either significantly longer or shorter than the distractors.
9. Each alternative position (A, B, C, or D) should be the correct answer approximately an equal number of times. The correct answer position should be arranged randomly.
10. Avoid using "all of the above" and "none of the above" unless there are specific reasons for doing so.
11. Place alternatives in a vertical list.
12. Avoid requiring personal opinion.
13. Avoid wording that is taken verbatim from the text.
14. Avoid linking two or more items together, except when writing interpretive exercises. Items should be independent and not provide clues to other items.

Short Answer Items

Short answer items include incomplete statements, such as fill-in-the-blanks or direct questions, requiring a brief response. Short answer items can be answered with a word, a number, a phrase, a symbol, or the like. One advantage of using short answer items is that they require recall versus simple recognition. A second advantage is that short answer items reduce guessing to a minimum.

One disadvantage of short answer items is that such items are usually limited to lower-level outcomes because of the brevity required in the answer. A second disadvantage is that they are somewhat difficult to score. Difficulty in scoring arises from unanticipated answers that must be considered, poor handwriting, and interpretation of phrases used by students.

Guidelines for Writing Short Answer Items

1. The required answer should be brief and specific.
2. Avoid verbatim statements from the text.
3. Word the item as a direct question, if possible.
4. Provide the numerical unit desired where appropriate (for example, feet, pounds, kilometers).

5. If fill-in-the-blank items are used, do not use too many blanks.
6. A blank should be at the end of a question or a statement.
7. Omit the most important, not trivial, words in completion items.
8. Avoid unintended clues.
9. Prepare a scoring key with anticipated acceptable answers.
10. Provide sufficient answer space.

Essay Items

Essay items require students to construct written responses of varying lengths. *Restricted response essays* strictly limit response in terms of content and length. *Extended response essays* allow more latitude in the content of the responses and usually require longer answers.

Essay items can be used to measure very complex outcomes. Teachers often attempt to teach a higher level of thinking. Essay questions are appropriate ways to test the efficacy of such teaching. Essay items assess students' differing abilities to express their thoughts in writing.

Essay items present some disadvantages. Scoring can be unreliable due to the subjective nature of essay grading. One such problem in grading is called the halo effect. This effect occurs when a teacher's general impression of a student influences the way the essay is graded. Because the teacher knows the student by reputation or because other items on the test have been answered well, he or she may assume that the essay answers will be equally good. Scoring essays also consumes a great deal of the teacher's time. Finally, it may take students a great deal of time to answer each essay question, therefore, only a limited number of questions can be asked and only a limited sample of the material from the unit can be covered on a test.

Teacher Interview: Have each student interview a teacher regarding his or her methods of controlling the halo effect.

Guidelines for Writing and Grading Essay Items

When writing essay items:

1. Use essay questions only for outcomes not satisfactorily measured by objective items.
2. Phrase the question so that the task is clearly defined.
3. Provide approximate length expectations, point values, and time limits for each question.
4. Avoid optional questions unless there is a specific reason, for example, individualized instruction.
5. Ask a colleague to critique the questions.
6. Usually, having more short items is better than having a few long essay items.
7. Verify the question by writing a trial response.

Lecture Note: Have students form small groups. Ask the students to generate an instructional objective and an essay item to evaluate that objective. Have students exchange their work and critique their classmates' efforts based on the guidelines in the text.

When scoring essay items:

1. Prepare an outline of the answer as a scoring guide in advance.
2. Decide how to handle factors, such as spelling and grammar, that are irrelevant to learning outcomes.
3. Grade all answers to one question before going onto the next question (halo effect).
4. Grade answers anonymously (halo effect).
5. If the results are very important to the student, obtain a second opinion or reread the papers.

Journal Entry: Have students reflect on the guidelines for scoring essay items, commenting on how well these guidelines match their current view of the value of essay items.

> **index of item difficulty** An estimate of the difficulty of items on a multiple choice test.

Chap. Obj. 3
Test Ques. 13.84–13.89

Focus Question: How can a teacher tell if a test is useful or not useful?

Field Observation: Have each student observe a classroom session in which the results of a test are being reviewed, documenting the results of the review in terms of improving the quality of the test.

Lecture Note: Inform students that these steps are illustrated in the next section.

Lecture Note: Ask students to discuss the conditions under which a low or a high index of item difficulty would be desirable.

ITEM ANALYSIS

As you begin teaching and evaluating your students, you will accumulate test items of different types. You will be pleased with some of the items and displeased with others. A good test item is a prized possession for any teacher. Evaluating the item after tests are administered serves an important instructional function. Item analysis allows the teacher to determine whether an item functions in the way the teacher intends it to. By reviewing an item and your students' responses to it, you can determine whether the item is testing the intended objective, whether it measures at the appropriate level of difficulty, and whether it distinguishes between those who know the content and those who don't.

For multiple choice tests, item analysis also allows the teacher to determine whether the distractors work well or not. Analyzing items in class—reviewing the items on the test—is a way to provide students with feedback. Item analysis by means of in-class review also helps the teacher determine common student errors and difficulties. Item analysis can suggest the best way to revise curriculum, improve test items for future use, and improve the teacher's test writing skills, as well (Nitko, 1983). Once suitable tests have been developed, their reliability and validity can be improved by using item analysis procedures. Ebel and Frisbie (1991) suggest the six-step procedure that follows (see Figure 13–1):

Step 1. Arrange the test scores in order from the highest score to the lowest.

Step 2. Identify an upper and a lower group. The upper group is the highest-scoring 25 percent of the entire class; the lower group is the lowest-scoring 25 percent.

Step 3. For each item, count the number of upper-group students who chose each alternative. Repeat the count for the lower group.

Step 4. Record the counts for each item on a copy of the test.

Step 5. Add the two numbers (from the upper and lower groups) for the keyed response. Divide this sum by the number of students in both the upper and lower groups. Multiply this decimal value by 100 to form a percentage. This percentage is the *index of item difficulty.*

Step 6. For the keyed response, subtract the count of the lower group from that of the upper group and divide this number by the number of examinees in one of the groups. You can use the number in either group because both groups are the same size. The result is a decimal that is the *index of discrimination.*

Indices of Item Difficulty and Discrimination

The **index of item difficulty,** the result of Step 5 in the Ebel and Frisbie procedure, represents the proportion of students who answered the item correctly. Note that the Ebel and Frisbie procedure does not include all of the students who took the test, only the upper and lower groups. Therefore, the index of discrimination, as calculated here, is an estimate of the difficulty.

The **index of discrimination,** the result of Step 6 in the same procedure, is the extent to which an item differentiates students who do well on the entire test from those students who perform poorly overall. The discrimination index can vary between .00 and 1.00. The closer to 1.00, the better the item discriminates between those who did well from those who did poorly on the test. If the same number of students in both the upper and lower groups answer the item correctly, the discrimination index will be .00. If no one in one of the groups answers the item correctly, while every student in the other group answers correctly, the discrimination index will be 1.00.

index of discrimination An estimate of the extent to which an item differentiates students who do well on the entire test from those who perform poorly overall.

Unless the index of discrimination is exactly .00, it will be either negative or positive. If the number of correct answers from the upper group is less than the number of correct answers from the lower group, the index of discrimination will be negative. If more correct answers are made by the upper group, the index of discrimination will be positive.

In sum, a positive discrimination index means that those who performed well on the overall test answered the item correctly more often than those who performed poorly overall on the test. Positive discrimination indicates a good item; the item discriminates in the "right" direction. Negative discrim-

Lecture Note: Ask several students to paraphrase what it means to discriminate in the right or the wrong direction.

Item: What change in life expectancy (number of years a person is likely to live) has been occurring?
*a. It has been increasing (Upper=47/ Lower=24).
b. It has been declining due to rising rates of cancer and heart disease (Upper=0/Lower=10).
c. It has increased for young people but decreased for older people. (Upper=0/Lower=5).
d. It has remained quite stable (Upper=1/Lower=7).
Omits (Upper = 0/Lower = 2)
Total numbers of students in Upper and Lower groups (N) = 96
Upper Correct (UC) = 47 Lower Correct (LC) = 24

$$\textit{Index of Difficulty} = \frac{UC + LC}{N} = \frac{47 + 24}{96} = .74 \times 100 = 74\%$$

$$\textit{Index of Discrimination} = \frac{UC - LC}{(1/2)\,N} = \frac{47 - 24}{48} = .48$$

* Correct alternative.

■ **Figure 13–1** ***An Illustration of Item Analysis***

From: *Essentials of Educational Measurement* (5th ed., p. 226) by R. L. Ebel and D. A. Frisbie, 1991, Englewood Cliffs, NJ: Prentice Hall. Copyright 1991 by Prentice Hall. Adapted by permission.

Lecture Note: Have students, working in small groups, generate an item analysis that demonstrates a poor multiple choice item.

Chap. Obj. 4
Test Ques. 13.90–13.98

Teacher Interview: Have each student discuss with a teacher the desirability of convergent evidence in making evaluative judgments.

Journal Entry: Have students reflect on the advisability of using a table of specifications for two purposes: as a way of constructing a reliable test, and as a tool for planning instruction.

Journal Entry: Have students reflect on the tendency to view all quantitative data as rigorous. Given the discussion in this chapter, they should argue for the importance of a healthy skepticism of test results.

Lecture Note: Ask students to consider whether this finding is best explained with reference to the ways in which teachers formulate objectives or construct test items.

ination means that those who performed poorly overall on the test answered the item correctly more often than those who did well overall. Negative discrimination indicates a bad item; the item discriminates in the "wrong" direction. A .00 discrimination means the item does not differentiate at all those who did well on the test from those who did poorly.

PITFALLS IN TESTING

We have examined various item types and guidelines for constructing them. By following these guidelines and by using a table of specifications, you will avoid many of the problems commonly experienced by practicing teachers. Ebel and Frisbie (1991) have identified some common mistakes made by teachers when constructing and using tests. One problem is that teachers tend to rely too heavily on subjective judgments rather than on reliable and valid measurements.

The tendency is to rely on informal observations and the inferences that result from such observations when making evaluative statements. Observations yield necessary and highly useful data; measurements of the type examined in this chapter provide evidence of a very different kind. Any time that two sources of evidence converge toward the same conclusion, you can be more confident that the conclusion is correct. Similarly, if your observational inference diverges from test results, you have found a problem worthy of additional thought and investigation.

Too many teachers cause themselves problems by putting test preparation off until the last minute rather than planning ahead. Using a table of specifications is one way of ensuring that last minute test making does not yield a test weighted heavily toward the material at the end of the unit while ignoring material from the beginning of the unit.

Many teachers construct and administer tests that are simply too short. A test that is too short increases the likelihood that the items on the test will not be representative of the population of items that could be used to measure the domain. In other words, tests that are too short run the risk of being unreliable. Writing tests that are too short, putting off test preparation until the last minute, and relying on subjective judgments rather than specifying the objectives and the cognitive level at which items ought to be written, yield an overemphasis on trivial details to the exclusion of some of the more important principles or applications in the unit.

Failure to use the Ebel and Frisbie guidelines tends to yield items that are ambiguous and that tend to answer each other by providing unintentional clues. Many teachers, once they have the results in their hand, forget that all measurement, no matter how carefully designed, is prone to error and imprecision. Frequent testing is one way to combat this problem. The item analysis procedures reviewed earlier is another way to overcome problems. Failure to use item analysis yields tests that, over time, do not improve in quality.

Fleming and Chambers (1983) examined approximately 400 teacher-made tests and found that about 80 percent of the questions on those tests measured knowledge in terms, facts, rules, and principles. The figure was highest for junior high school teachers at approximately 94 percent versus approximately 60 percent for both elementary and high school teachers. Few of the questions examined by Flemming and Chambers were found to measure the ability to make applications.

Nontest Evaluation Techniques

Paper and pencil tests of the type described in the previous section are not the only ways to collect data. As we have suggested earlier, informal observation during instructional sessions is another way teachers collect a great deal of information about the performance of their students. The observation teachers perform is not only observation of intellectual development, but also physical, social, and emotional development. To be useful, observation should be systematic, objective, selective, unobtrusive, and carefully recorded.

Checklists

An observer can carefully document his or her observations in a classroom by using a checklist. A **checklist** is composed of a listing of the behaviors that the observer looks for. Checklists are best used for making yes/no, present/absent decisions about behaviors. Is a student on task? Does a student participate in small group discussion? Does the group divide labor on a cooperative project? Have students completed all of the steps in a procedure? The observer makes a yes/no decision. The behavior is either observed or it is not. If a behavior exists on a continuum of good to bad or some other scale, then a rating scale should be used instead of a checklist. Checklists serve their function best if they include specific, well-defined behaviors.

An example of a checklist from a physical fitness unit is presented in Figure 13–2. The checklist is used to evaluate students' development and the implementation of their personal exercise programs.

Anecdotal Records

Another way to record observational data is through anecdotal records. Anecdotal records are written descriptions of observed events. The use of anecdotal records has this advantage: any behavior can be recorded. In any case, the recorded observation should be focused on a simple description of what was observed, making sure that facts are kept separate from opinions. Using anecdotal records has several advantages. These records are made in a natural setting and can focus on something significant. Many teachers keep anecdotal records in the margins of their lesson plans or as "day notes." In the way of disadvantages, they are somewhat time consuming and are subject to personal bias or lack of objectivity (Kubiszyn & Borich, 1987; Popham, 1981).

Rating Scales

Rating scales are measurement instruments used to make judgments about some continuing behavior or product. Rating scales can be used to judge frequency of occurrence of some behavior, or the quality of some performance or product.

Rating scales that use numbers consist of a list of attributes that can be rated numerically from "excellent" to "poor" or from "satisfactory" to "unsatisfactory." The following item is an example from a rating scale on student characteristics:

Student is prompt.

1	2	3	4
Always	Usually	Seldom	Never

checklist A listing of the behaviors that an observer looks for in the classroom.
rating scales Measurement instruments used to judge frequency of occurrence of some behavior or the quality of some performance or product.

Chapter 15 Casebook Preview: See Book Writing.

Field Observation: Have each student observe a classroom in which the teacher uses a checklist for evaluative purposes. The student should obtain a copy of the checklist and complete it during the course of a lesson, comparing his or her checklist with the teacher's after the lesson.

Teacher Interview: Have each student ask a teacher who keeps anecdotal records to comment on how the anecdotal records help him or her better understand students.

Transparency: This figure is duplicated in the acetate transparency package. See T-22 A Sample Checklist.

Directions for completing the checklist: Place a plus (+) in front of each step completed satisfactorily. Place a minus (–) in front of each step completed unsatisfactorily. Place a zero (0) in front of a missing step.

_____1. Obtained doctor's advise about an
   exercise program.

_____2. Took baseline fitness test.

      _____a. pull-upes or arm-hangs

      _____b. sit-ups

      _____c. recovery index test

_____3. Established improvement goals.

_____4. Selected goal-appropriate exercises.

_____5. Established a weekly time schedule.

_____6. Included a journal of program use.

_____7. Included personal reactions
   regarding effectivemess, enjoyment,
   and need for program change.

■ **Figure 13–2** *A Sample Checklist*

From: *Essentials of Educational Measurement* (5th ed., p. 248) by R. L. Ebel and D. A. Frisbie, 1991, Englewood Cliffs, NJ: Prentice Hall. Copyright 1991 by Prentice Hall. Adapted by permission.

Rating scales can be used to evaluate products or performances as well. A rating scale might be used to help evaluate a student's public speaking performance. Items included on it could rate frequency of eye contact, level of enthusiasm, quality of persuasive language, and posture.

Many learning outcomes are measurable through these observational techniques. Such outcomes include skills such as speaking, writing, listening, oral reading, lab experiments, drawing, playing musical instruments, dancing, gymnastics, work skills, study skills, and social skills. Work habits, the way in which students use time and use equipment, are not easily measured by paper-and-pencil tests. Checklists, anecdotal records, and rating scales are good candidates for use in collecting such information. Other measurable outcomes in this category include social attitudes, scientific attitudes, interests, appreciations, relationships to peers, reaction to praise and criticism, and emotional stability (Gronlund, 1985).

Lecture Note: Ask students to discuss why systematic observation is preferable to relying on one's impressions concerning attitudes, work habits, and the like.

Principles in Practice 13.2

Principles . . .
1. A table of specifications helps teachers construct tests that match instructional objectives.
2. Matching items to the purpose of evaluation and conducting item analyses improve the quality of teacher-made tests.
3. Many of the evaluative judgments teachers make cannot be easily measured by tests.

. . . in Practice
In Teacher Chronicle 13.2, the teacher reflected on the nature of the judgments teachers must make and the nature of tests that provide data for those judgments. The case in Teacher Chronicle 13.2 points out that it is necessary for teachers to consider the conditions imposed by a test and the specific purpose for which a test is used when evaluating a student's performance. Because teachers influence the evidence through the creation of tests, and make judgments based on that evidence, it is important that they understand how tests should be constructed.

1. What kind of test items might the teacher in Teacher Chronicle 13.2 have used to make the judgment he or she was required to make?
2. Why should teachers use a variety of item types?
3. What outcomes that will not be easily measured by tests do you desire for your future students?

WHAT DID YOU GET ON YOUR REPORT CARD?

There is always a special buzz on report card day. You can see the anxiety on some faces, the look of relief on others. No matter how indifferent a student has been during the term, that indifference slides away when the report cards are about to be passed out.

I remind the students that their grades reflect what they have achieved in class. My comments about effort and attitude are on a separate sheet, enclosed with the report card. I remind them to discuss both the grades and my comments with their parents. After handing out report cards, I listen to the conversations.

"What'd you get in math?"

"Another C. My mom is going to kill me."

"Look, I got an A in gym. All right!"

"Too bad I blew that last social studies test. I had an A going into it. Now I got a B+."

"Yeah, but that paper I did for science brought my grade up to a B. Pizza party at home tonight for me!"

"What'd you get, Louis? Straight A's again?"

Teacher
Chronicle
13.3

Chap. Obj. 4
Test Ques. 13.99–13.119

Focus Question: How should a teacher determine grades?

Teaching Anecdote: Tell your students about a school district that has ungraded elementary schools, but graded junior high and high schools. An alarming percentage of students in the district experience difficulties making the transition from elementary school to junior high.

Ask your students how differences in grading might contribute to these difficulties.

Journal Entry: Have each student reflect on the ways in which grades affected him or her as a student, marshaling arguments for or against grading practices based on these experiences.

Chapter 15 Casebook Preview: Writing Success in Science.

Connection: The terms *criterion referenced* and *norm referenced* are addressed in greater detail in Chapter 14.

"Yeah, it gets boring after a while. Maybe you should try it sometimes."

"Yeah, but maybe you should learn to hit a baseball sometime, too. There's more to school than just grades."

Ain't that the truth, I laugh to myself. Then I stop, thinking I must pick up my end of the year evaluation in the office. I wonder what "grade" I will get.

■■■

GRADING

We use tests and observations of various sorts to collect evaluative data, which will be the basis of our judgments. One of the most important judgments we make as teachers are the grades that we assign to students.

Some schools or districts have and still experiment with nongraded instruction. Ebel and Frisbie (1986) argue that grades are important for students as a means by which to evaluate themselves. Grades are important for reporting progress to parents, to future teachers, and to potential employers. Grades also provide a basis for future educational decisions. Grades serve to motivate and reward students as well.

Those who criticize grades argue that they provide extrinsic but not intrinsic motivation. They argue that what students learn is more important than the grade they receive. Ebel and Frisbie, in reviewing these arguments, counter that rather than placing less importance on grades, educators should improve the way in which grades are assigned, making sure that they are accurate, valid, meaningful, and correctly interpreted.

The lack of clear definition of what a grade means is a major problem in grading. As a result, there is a good deal of variability in grading practices and procedures among teachers, courses, and schools. A second major problem is that grades are often awarded on the basis of insufficient relevant and objective evidence. Unsound evidence results in grades that are, from an evaluation standpoint, unreliable. We must establish the criteria that are used to assign grades in conjunction with a plan for evaluating students before the construction of tests occurs. If we follow the guidelines we develop for generating well-constructed tests, we lessen the impact that less-than-reliable grading has.

The Grading System

One of the decisions we must make about our grading system is about what our standard of comparison will be. Remember, all evaluative statements are made on a comparative basis. A student's performance is judged against some standard. That standard may be an absolute or relative one. An **absolute standard** is based on the amount of course content the student has learned; its criterion is the content. Students' grades are decided independent of one another. What they are subject to is called a criterion-referenced evaluation. The basis for the comparison is some external criterion of performance.

A **relative standard** is based on the student's performance vis-à-vis other students; it is referred to as norm-referenced grading. Relative or norm-referenced grading is decided not only on the basis of a student's performance, but on how well that student performed compared with all other students.

Profiles in Successful Practice

FAYE W. McCOLLUM

ROTHSCHILD JUNIOR HIGH SCHOOL

COLUMBUS, GEORGIA

A teacher, more than a person in any other profession, remains a part of a student's life forever. How many persons, for instance, remember the name or actions of their first-grade teachers? A teacher's influence, for better or worse, tends to persist because it becomes an integral part of everyday existence.

In today's world students have so many distractions that school must be made attractive and exciting to keep their full attention. A teacher must be able to entertain in order to compete with television, videos, and computer games while at the same time instilling essential concepts as part of his or her lessons.

Metaphorically, my classroom is a stage and my students are alternatively actors and audience. Each performance must be a success because at the end of class the curtain closes. No performances will be repeated. Every student must absorb carefully planned lessons during the allotted time. For this reason, the stage must accommodate the wide variety of props or tools necessary to facilitate achievement. Many of the plays include small laboratory set-ups that utilize films, computer programs, experiments, games, and hands-on activities designed to stimulate enthusiasm for investigative learning.

Students and teachers must look forward to class and expect illuminating surprises. The best opportunities to teach often occur as a result of a question, a news story, or an unusual event in the classroom or community. These occurrences can be integrated into previously planned objectives. Teachers must be flexible, compassionate, and willing to understand the complexities of today's society. Each day is different and must be treated as a new opportunity to nurture, stimulate, and challenge not only oneself but the future of education.

One hundred years from now no one will remember the fancy clothes I wear or the house I live in, but will remember me because I taught. In my opinion teaching is not only a profession and an art, it's an exciting opportunity to make a difference.

Either type of grading, absolute or relative, can be reported with traditional letter grades. Absolute grading can also be reported in percentages (Ebel & Frisbie, 1986). Recent trends in classroom practices indicate that most teachers use criterion-referenced grading. (In Chapter 14 we will examine further the distinction between criterion-referenced and norm-referenced evaluation in the context of standardized testing. Standardized testing yields results that are judged on a relative basis. That is, standardized tests are norm-referenced.)

Achievement or Effort?

Among the questions that teachers must answer for themselves are, Should grading be done on the basis of achievement? on the basis of effort? on the basis of the two in combination? There is a general agreement among measurement specialists that grades should simply reflect achievement. Effort, behavior, and other factors should be kept separate. But because they are kept separate does not mean that they are precluded from evaluation. Based on

Teacher Interview: Have students interview teachers regarding the advisability of separating achievement and effort in evaluation.

Providing immediate, constructive feedback can enhance a student's sense of self-efficacy and increase motivation.

Journal Entry: Have each student reflect on his or her experiences in a course graded competitively and in a course that took into account improvement, commenting on the ways in which those grading practices influenced his or her attitude and motivation.

attribution research and research on classroom goal structures, many educational psychologists recommend focusing on effort as part of a teacher's general evaluation. Nevertheless, the teacher, and anyone who has been assigned a grade by the teacher, should be clear about what it is that the grade reflects.

Some educators respond to the intuitive appeal of grading on the basis of achievement as related to a person's potential or aptitude. Grading in relation to aptitude takes into account the individual differences that exist among students. The specter of competition that exists even in criterion-referenced measurement makes grading in this way even more appealing. Hopkins and Stanley (1981) argue that this is not a good practice, however, simply because there is not a valid enough case for measuring aptitude.

A similar problem arises when we consider the advisability of grading on the basis of improvement. In order to grade on the basis of aptitude or improvement, it is necessary to have a valid starting point. Grading on the basis of improvement can be done as long as the teacher has available valid pre- and postmeasures of achievement. Even if measurements are taken before and after instruction, however, the scores reported for each student are problematic. The scores reported in a pre- and posttest design are called gain scores. Gain scores are unreliable for several reasons, not the least of which is that students can quickly catch on to the idea that they are being graded on improvement and make sure that they score low on a pretest.

Pass/Fail Grading

One approach to grading has been to assign grades of pass/fail to student performance rather than traditional letter grades. Hopkins and Antes (1985) have identified the advantages and disadvantages of using pass/fail grading.

One advantage of pass/fail grading is that students may experience less anxiety by eliminating some of the competition. The use of pass/fail grading may create an atmosphere that encourages more intellectual risk taking. Another advantage is that students may work toward fulfilling requirements with less pressure. Finally, the teacher and the student may work together to determine the criteria for a pass grade.

One disadvantage of using pass/fail grading is that the grades themselves provide less information for future teachers, for parents, and for the students. Another disadvantage is that students may do less work without the graduated criteria of letter grades. The students' effort may fall to the lowest acceptable or pass level. Students who fail in a pass/fail course may experience even greater pressure from such failure than students who fail in traditionally graded courses. Pass/fail grading also fails to provide information on the specific strengths and weaknesses of a student's work. As with other forms of grading, what constitutes a pass grade varies from instructor to instructor. Although this is true of traditional letter grades, the range of variation within the grade "pass" is, by definition, greater.

In some cases, a pass/fail system has been combined with the traditional letter grade system. In such cases, whether a student passes or fails depends on whether or not he or she is doing enough work to earn a traditional grade of *D*. The basis for the combined grading system leans heavily on the traditional grading system.

Teacher Interview: Have students interview teachers who use pass/fail grading in their class, asking them to comment on its advantages and disadvantages.

Alternatives to Grading

Hopkins and Stanley (1981) identify alternatives to grades, some of which can be used in addition to traditional grade reports. One alternative is letters to parents. The advantages of using this alternative is that letters allow the teacher to discuss the unique strengths and weaknesses of the students. Teachers can suggest specific ways that parents can help their children academically. Letters also open a line of communication between parents and teachers. Although it takes more time, Hopkins and Stanley consider the use of a letter an advantage to the teacher because it forces the teacher to think about the individual student's achievements. In addition to being time consuming, letters are also subjective. Depending on the letter-writing ability of the teacher, statements in a letter may be vague and may lack continuity year after year.

Checklists are another alternative to grades. The checklist provides statements and the teacher checks the statement that corresponds to the degree to which the student has achieved an objective or needs to improve in a subject area. Checklists are advantageous because they provide detailed information, are easy to understand, and can include information on behavior, effort, or other nonacademic characteristics. On the other hand, many statements and judgments are needed for each student if the checklist is to provide an accurate profile. Filling out such checklists can be time consuming—certainly a disadvantage.

Chapter 15 Casebook Preview: See Responsibility Education.

Teaching Anecdote: Tell your students about the school district that did not give grades but issued a progress report centered on a checklist with fifty items, ranging from academic progress to social interactions. Each report also included three sections for written comments by teachers.

Ask your students why this checklist system might or might not benefit students, parents, and teachers.

Open communication between parents and teachers can lead to mutual understanding of students' strengths and weaknesses. Communication is fostered by parent–teacher conferences, among other techniques.

A final alternative—one used in most cases in addition to grade reports—is the parent–teacher conference. These conferences offer the parents and the teacher a chance to sit down and discuss each student's progress and the instructional plan most suited to that student. Parents can provide pertinent information that will help the teacher to understand the student in his or her classroom. Parent–teacher conferences are time consuming; conferences alone do not provide a systematic record of student achievement. Nonetheless, most practicing teachers view these conferences as important. The first round of conferences for a new teacher usually arouse a considerable amount of anxiety.

Hopkins and Stanley (1981, p. 327) have provided a list of teacher dos and don'ts for parent conferences.

The dos of parent conferences:

1. Review the student's cumulative records prior to the conference.
2. Assemble samples of the student's work.
3. Use a structured outline to guide the conference.
4. List questions to ask parents and try to anticipate parents' questions.
5. Be professional and maintain a positive attitude.
6. Be willing to listen, be understanding, and encourage two-way communication.
7. Be honest. Begin by describing the pupil's strengths.
8. Accept some of the responsibility for any problems.
9. Conclude the conference with an overall summary.
10. Keep a succinct written record of the conference. List problems and suggestions with a copy for the parents.

Lecture Note: Have students role-play parent–teacher conferences. After the simulated conferences, have the "parents" critique the "teachers' " performances using the "dos" and "don'ts" list.

The don'ts of parent conferences:

1. Don't blame parents or put them on the defensive. Never argue.
2. Don't make derogatory comments about other teachers, other students, or the school.
3. Don't play amateur psychiatrist.
4. Don't discuss the conference with others, except other school personnel directly involved with the student.
5. Don't do all the talking; skilled professionals are good listeners.

Contract Grading

Taylor (1980) reviewed the literature on contract grading and concluded that students like it. Teachers who used contracts assigned more high grades than those who used conventional methods. In terms of student achievement, however, contract grading was no better than conventional grading. Contract grading appears to be best suited to very small classes or to independent studies. Written agreements should be used in order to avoid misunderstandings of the criteria by which students will be judged.

Connection: See the section on contracting in Chapter 12.

A Summary of Grading Procedures

Hopkins and Antes (1985) provide a good summary of sound grading procedures. They recommend the following:

Teacher Interview: Have each student discuss with a teacher his or her comments on the recommendations listed in the text.

- Collect information from a variety of sources, a number of tests, a number of different types of tests, and a number of evaluative procedures other than tests, including observation.
- Good grading requires that data be recorded in a systematic fashion. Maintenance of an up-to-date grade book qualifies here.
- The information collected should be quantified in some way, that is, given a numerical value. Value judgments, while important, should be saved until the final evaluation. Parent–teacher conferences are an ideal place to communicate such judgments.
- Weight the final evaluation more heavily on information collected near the end of a grading period so that the focus of the grade is on terminal performance.
- Grades should be based only on achievement data. Reports on other traits should be done separately.

Research on Grading

Natriello (1987) examined the impact that evaluation processes have on students. Natriello suggests that higher evaluative standards lead to more effort and to higher performance, but only if students view those standards as obtainable. The research also suggests that there is a relationship between evaluative standards and effort in performance such that students should be challenged but not frustrated in their efforts. The relationship can be described as a curvilinear relationship (see Figure 13–3). As evaluative standards increase so do effort and performance, but only up to a point. As standards continue to increase beyond a certain point, effort and performance decrease.

Natriello also reviewed research that compared norm-referenced evaluative standards with individually referenced standards, the issue being the merits of absolute versus relative grading. Natriello's review found mixed

Journal Entry: Have each student reflect on the curvilinear relationship between standards and performance, matching the relationship with his or her experience.

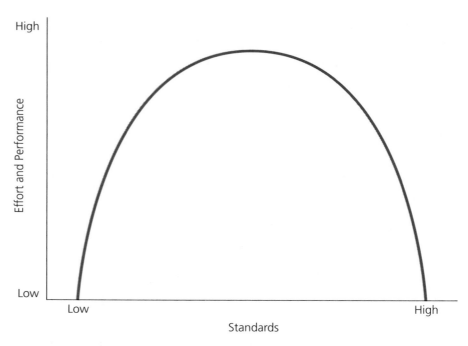

■ **Figure 13–3** *The Effects of Standards on Effort or Performance*

results, but more of the studies seemed to favor individually referenced grading. Focusing on the individual and using an absolute basis for comparison in deriving grades may be most beneficial to students whose initial performance is poor, who have low self-esteem, and who have an external locus of control. Self-referenced standards (comparison against self rather than against an absolute, and therefore an external, criterion) seem to work best for students with low self-esteem and an internal locus of control. Norm-referenced standards work best for students with high esteem. The results of the studies reviewed by Natriello suggest that teachers need to consider individual differences in grading.

Connection: See the section on attribution theory in Chapter 8.

Considerations for Testing and Grading

Because classroom evaluation affects students in so many ways, teachers should plan their evaluation procedures very carefully. Teachers who want to plan carefully must devote a sufficient amount of time to generating objectives that can then be placed in a table of specifications. Time is also needed to consider the cognitive level of each objective and to distribute items throughout the table of specifications so that there is representative coverage of the material that has been covered in the unit (Crooks, 1988).

Classroom evaluation should encourage the development of understanding, transfer of learning, and thinking skills that are necessary to deep rather than shallow learning. Models for instruction can be used to enhance both content goals and thinking skills; evaluation procedures can also serve those functions. If evaluation follows the objectives and if the objectives indicate to students that they will be required to engage in application, synthesis, or evaluation, the teacher increases the likelihood of higher-level learning.

Classroom evaluation should assist learning by providing useful feedback to students. A summative, norm-referenced evaluation that focuses on grades is not as useful in focusing a student's effort on weaknesses in content areas. It is the teacher's responsibility to provide some kind of summative evaluation of student performance. The teacher should bear in mind, however, that classroom evaluation procedures are the best way of providing formative evaluation. It is formative evaluation that leads to the remediation of student problems.

Lecture Note: Ask students to discuss assignments and tests that not only measured their knowledge but also enhanced their learning.

Evaluation procedures that provide effective feedback focused on the mastery of tasks should be used. Feedback that is provided as quickly as possible enhances the student's ability to improve. To be useful feedback must be specific. The teacher has to communicate standards. Feedback is a vehicle for enforcing those standards. The theory of need achievement, examined in Chapter 8, suggests that standards be high, but not so high that they cause frustration (see also Figure 13–3).

Connection: See the section on the need to achieve in Chapter 8.

Evaluation should be frequent enough to give students regular opportunities to practice skills and to receive feedback. Frequent evaluation does not mean that tests are given in every instance. Frequent evaluation can include discussions, recitation questions, and reviews.

Evaluation tasks should be appropriate for the goals being assessed. When generating measurement procedures in the classroom context, it is easy for teachers to get carried away with the task of writing ingenious questions. Sometimes, the questions themselves can become the focus of creative activity. It is possible for a teacher to become so interested in creating an ingenious item that he or she forgets the objective for which the item is being written.

Field Observation: Have each student arrange to attend an in-service on evaluation, comparing the recommendations presented in this chapter with those presented at the in-service.

Finally, evaluations should focus on important skills, knowledge, and attitudes. It is difficult to evaluate higher-level skills and attitudes, but they are among the most important outcomes of instruction. Efforts should be made to collect relevant information (Crooks, 1988).

Principles in Practice 13.3

Principles . . .
1. Most grading procedures are based on absolute standards established by the teacher.
2. Teachers should make it clear whether or not an assigned grade reflects only achievement.
3. The evaluative standards established by a teacher influence student effort and performance.

. . . in Practice
In Teacher Chronicle 13.3, the teacher listened to student comments about the grades they received on their report cards. Their conversations focused on the letter grade that was recorded. In only one instance did a student think about the work that earned the grade (the "blown" social studies test). Most of the comments centered on parents' reactions—the rewards and the punishments.

1. How would the reactions of the students in Teacher Chronicle 13.3 have changed if they had received pass/fail reports?

2. Why didn't the students discuss the teacher's comments as much as the grades?

3. Speculate on the "speech" you will make to your students just before they receive grades from you for the first time.

Assign Chapter 13 of the *Study Guide*.

CONCLUSION

In this chapter we have examined classroom evaluation based on data collected as part of your instructional program. There is another source of information that you will use to make decisions about students, however. You will be responsible for interpreting this information to parents. This additional evaluative information comes from . . . standardized tests.

There, we said it. Now relax. Standardized tests may be the most dreaded of educational topics, but they are not that hard to understand. When we understand standardized tests, we gain a better "fix" on our students. The better we know them, the better we teach them.

Chapter Summary

Introduction: Evaluation, Measurement, and Tests

Evaluation is a process of gathering, analyzing, and interpreting data in order to make judgments. Measurement is a process of describing students' characteristics numerically. Tests are instruments of measurement.

Classroom Evaluation
Purposes of Evaluation

Classroom evaluation can be used to place students in the most appropriate learning situation (placement). Classroom evaluation can be used to modify instructional practice (formative evaluation) or to make judgments about the outcomes of instruction (summative evaluation). It can also be used to identify strengths and weaknesses (diagnostic evaluation).

Techniques of Evaluation

Evaluation occurs in the classroom in a variety of ways, including teacher-generated tests. In addition to tests, teachers evaluate papers, worksheets, speeches, recitations, and other student products and performances. Teachers also evaluate students informally through observation.

Utility of Evaluative Information
Reliability

To be useful, the data from tests and other measurements must be reliable, that is, the results of the test must be consistent. A teacher can rely on the data from a reliable test because they are stable.

Validity

A valid test is one that measures what it is supposed to measure. Because tests serve different purposes, there are different kinds of validity: content, criterion-related, and construct validity.

Constructing Classroom Tests
Table of Specifications

A table of specifications is a blueprint for test construction. It allows a teacher to match test items to instructional objectives both in terms of content and in terms of what students should be able to do with the content.

Item Types
Binary Choice Items
Classroom tests can be constructed with various types of items. Binary choice items require students to select one of two alternatives. True/false items are an example.

Matching Items
Matching items require students to select a response that matches a premise. Examples include matching causes with effects and matching definitions with concepts.

Multiple Choice Items
Multiple choice items consist of a *stem,* which can be a question, statement, scenario; alternatives; and distractors. Students must select the correct answer from the set of alternatives.

Short Answer Items
Short answer items require students to construct a response rather than select from supplied alternatives. An example of a short-answer item is a fill-in-the-blank question.

Essay Items
Essay items require the student to construct a written response. Essays can require either long (extended) or short (restricted) answers.

Item Analysis
Indices of Item Difficulty and Discrimination
Item analysis is a way of determining the extent to which an item contributes to the overall purpose of a multiple choice test. Item analysis yields an index of difficulty that defines the number of students who select the correct answer. Item analysis also yields an index of discrimination that identifies the extent

to which a particular item contributes to students' overall performances on a test.

Pitfalls in Testing
Nontest Evaluation Techniques
There are a number of pitfalls that need to be guarded against. Some of those pitfalls can be avoided by using measurement instruments other than tests. Those instruments include checklists, anecdotal records, and rating scales, all of which help make observation more systematic.

Grading
The Grading System
Grading systems can be based on absolute standards of quality of performance or can be based on student performance relative to that of other students. No matter what kind of grading system is used, some basis for comparison of grades is required.

Achievement or Effort?
Many teachers assign grades based on evaluation of both achievement and effort. Guidelines suggest that grades be based on achievement only. This does not mean a teacher can not evaluate effort separately.

Alternatives to Grading
Evaluations of classroom work do not have to take the traditional form of grades. Evaluative judgments can be presented in a number of ways. Additionally, students can contract for grades, thus, participating in the establishment of criteria used to assign grades.

A Summary of Grading Procedures
Grading is typically a summative judgment. It is important that the grade be determined on the basis of reliable and valid data. It is also important to keep in mind that the way grades are determined and assigned can influence both student effort and performance.

Reflections: Building Your Theory of Teaching

13.1 You have assigned a high school class the following task: Design a test to evaluate applicants for the astronaut program. The test must be valid. Prepare a handout that identifies the steps that students should follow in order to complete the assignment.

13.2 Identify a specific objective you intend to teach. Decide how to test the attainment of the objective using an objective item, a short-answer item, and an essay item.

13.3 Prepare a letter to be sent home to parent(s) that explains your decisions about the grading system you intend to use in your classroom.

Key Terms

evaluation (p. 484)
measurement (p. 484)
test (p. 484)
placement evaluation (p. 487)
formative evaluation (p. 487)
summative evaluation (p. 489)
diagnostic evaluation (p. 489)
reliability (p. 490)
test-retest (p. 491)
alternate forms (p. 491)
internal consistency (p. 491)

validity (p. 492)
content validity (p. 492)
criterion-related validity (p. 492)
construct validity (p. 492)
table of specifications (p. 496)
selected response items (p. 497)
constructed response items (p. 497)
binary choice items (p. 497)
matching items (p. 499)

multiple choice items (p. 499)
short answer items (p. 500)
essay items (p. 501)
index of item difficulty (p. 502)
index of discrimination (p. 503)
checklist (p. 505)
rating scales (p. 505)
absolute standard (p. 508)
relative standard (p. 508)

Suggested Readings

Carey, L. M. (1988). *Measuring and evaluating school learning.* Needham Heights, MA: Allyn & Bacon.
Cole, N. S. (1981). Bias in testing. *American Psychologist, 36,* 1067–1077.
Ebel, R. L., & Frisbie, D. A. (1991). *Essentials of educational measurement* (5th ed.). Englewood Cliffs, NJ: Prentice-Hall.

Green, B. F. (1981). A primer of testing. *American Psychologist, 36,* 1001–1011.
Gronlund, N. E. (1988). *How to construct achievement tests* (4th ed.). Needham Heights, MA: Allyn & Bacon.

References

Carey, L. M. (1988). *Measuring and evaluating school learning.* Newton, MA: Allyn & Bacon.
Crooks, T. J. (1988). The impact of classroom evaluation practices on students. *Review of Educational Research, 48,* 438–481.
Cunningham, G. K. (1986). *Educational and psychological measurement.* New York: Macmillan.
Ebel, R. L., & Frisbie, D. A. (1986). *Essentials of educational measurement* (4th ed.). Englewood Cliffs, NJ: Prentice-Hall.
Ebel, R. L., & Frisbie, D. A. (1991). *Essentials of educational measurement* (5th ed.). Englewood Cliffs, NJ: Prentice-Hall.

Fleming, M., & Chambers, B. (1983). Teacher-made tests: Windows on the classroom. In W. E. Hathaway (Ed.), *Testing in the schools: New directions for testing and measurement: No. 19* (pp. 29–38). San Francisco: Jossey-Bass.
Gronlund, N. E. (1985). *Measurement and evaluation in teaching* (5th ed.). New York: Macmillan.
Gullickson, A. R. (1985). Student evaluation techniques and their relationship to grade and curriculum. *Journal of Educational Research, 79,* 96–100.

Hopkins, K. D., & Antes, R. L. (1985). *Classroom measurement and evaluation* (2nd ed.). Itasca, IL: F. E. Peacock.

Hopkins, K. D., & Stanley, J. C. (1981). *Educational and psychological measurement and evaluation* (6th ed.). Englewood Cliffs, NJ: Prentice-Hall.

Kubiszyn, T., & Borich, G. D. (1987). *Educational testing and measurement*. Glenview, IL: Scott, Foresman.

Natriello, G. (1987). The impact of evaluation processes on students. *Educational Psychologist, 22,* 155–175.

Nitko, A. J. (1983). *Educational tests and measurement: An introduction*. New York: Harcourt Brace Jovanovich.

Popham, W. J. (1981). *Modern educational measurement*. Englewood Cliffs, NJ: Prentice-Hall.

Taylor, R. P. (Ed.). (1980). *The computer in the school: Tutor, tool, tutee*. New York: Teachers College Press.

14
Using Standardized Test Data

INTRODUCTION: PROFESSIONAL JUDGMENTS

TEACHER CHRONICLE 14.1: TEST ANXIETY

Focus Questions
Why do educators need standardized test results? Why is there so much negative public opinion concerning testing?

NORM-REFERENCED AND CRITERION-REFERENCED MEASUREMENT

TYPES OF STANDARDIZED TESTS

Focus Question
What is a norm group and how does it influence standardized test results?

- Achievement Tests
- Aptitude Tests
- Diagnostic Tests
- Comparing People and Numbers
- **Principles in Practice 14.1**

TEACHER CHRONICLE 14.2: STATISTICS?!?

Focus Questions
What is the basis of all standardized test scores? How should teachers interpret standardized test scores for themselves, for students, and for parents?

STANDARDIZED TEST SCORES

- Properties of Distributions
- The Normal Distribution
- **Principles in Practice 14.2**

TEACHER CHRONICLE 14.3: SETTLING THE SCORE

ISSUES IN STANDARDIZED TESTING

Focus Questions
How should legitimate concerns over standardized tests govern their use? What form will standardized testing take in the near future?

- Test Bias
- Minimum Competency Testing
- Computerized Adaptive Testing
- **Principles in Practice 14.3**

CONCLUSION

Chapter Overview

Data obtained from classroom activity is critical for student evaluation, but there is another source of data that contributes to the decisions teachers make about students: standardized tests. Standardized tests compare students with other students so that the teacher can make judgments with regard to achievement or aptitude. The results of standardized tests are based on and presented as statistics—numerical descriptions of a group of scores. This chapter offers a brief explanation of the statistics on which standardized test results are based, and then presents various types of standardized scores. It concludes with an examination of issues that influence the interpretation of standardized test scores and instructional practices.

Introduction: Professional Judgments

Professionals are expected to make professional judgments. The public served by professionals has become increasingly more sophisticated, demanding greater accountability of and more information from those who make judgments affecting their lives. The general public is no longer willing to accept the opinions of these professionals in an uncritical manner—whether they are in the legal profession, the medical profession, or the teaching profession. The manner in which professionals in any field make judgments is being more closely scrutinized. Nowhere has this scrutiny been more intense than in the field of education.

As we saw in Chapter 13, teachers use tests of various kinds to make evaluative judgments about the abilities and the capabilities of students. The results of classroom tests are the grades and other evaluative statements we assign to our students and which stay with those students throughout their academic careers.

Teacher Interview: Have students interview teachers regarding the nature of professional judgments and the degree of public scrutiny that accompanies such judgments.

Connection: See the section on item types in Chapter 13.

The types of tests we will discuss in this chapter have implications for students' futures that are at least as important as grades. In many instances, the results on standardized tests can override in importance students' cumulative grades. In other cases, the scores on standardized tests can reinforce the judgments reflected by cumulative grades. The students' classroom teachers do not design standardized tests, but they are given the results and are asked to make instructional judgments based on those results. Teachers do not design standardized tests, but they are asked to interpret them. As you enter the teaching profession, you too will have the results of standardized tests available to you, to make your own instructional judgments, and to interpret for your students and for their parents. Understanding and interpreting the results of standardized tests is not an additional burden laid at the doorstep of the classroom teacher, rather, it is a hallmark of the growing sophistication of the profession that those who practice it are expected to understand the technical bases of their judgments.

Because most people have experienced, at one time or another, frustration or anxiety when taking a test, it is not surprising to discover a general negativism toward the entire enterprise of educational testing. Perhaps you, a person who will soon be joining the ranks of the profession, have your doubts about the utility of tests. It is important to remember that the difference between understanding testing as an educator and seeing it as a member of the general public is that as a teacher you are responsible for making evaluative judgments.

Lecture Note: Emphasize the point that professionals cannot afford uninformed opinions.

Critics within the profession have the responsibility to justify their judgments. If a teacher decides that a particular set of test results are of limited value, either in the diagnosis of educational problems or as the basis of educational judgments, it is incumbent upon that teacher to articulate his or her concerns. A professional must be able to explain in a competent manner why the results of a particular test should not be considered sound evidence of a student's ability or aptitude.

Everybody's a critic or can be if they so desire. Public critics can offer their opinions, professional critics must defend their opinions in a knowledgeable way. If we go to a movie and decide that, in our opinion, the movie is not a particularly fine example of cinematic art, we can voice that opinion. If Siskel and Ebert, professional movie critics, go to that same movie, and share our evaluation of the movie, their job is not done. Part of their responsibility is to articulate the reasons for their judgments. Indeed, their professional status derives from their ability to justify their judgments. Professionals do not simply make professional judgments; they have the knowledge and experience to justify their judgments. Perhaps you have doubts about the utility of standardized tests. Skepticism is healthy in a professional. Uninformed skepticism, however, is a luxury available only to members of the general public; it is not a luxury afforded those of us in the teaching profession.

Teacher Interview: Have students interview teachers regarding their views on the growing professionalism in teaching, asking their opinions of the efforts of the National Board for Professional Teaching Standards and the opportunity teachers will have to become board certified.

Teacher
Chronicle
14.1

TEST ANXIETY

As soon as I realized the phone call was from Mrs. Lynch, I knew what the call was about—Carrie's test scores. Gripping the pink telephone slip in my hand I headed for the phone and began dialing.

"Hello, Mrs. Lynch, I'm returning your call."

"Oh, thanks for calling back so soon. I really would like to know when the results of Carrie's standardized test come back and if I could have a conference with you then."

"No problem, Mrs. Lynch. They should be back before Christmas. I'll mark my calendar to give you a call when they come in. Anything else?" I asked.

"No, that's all. See you in December. Good-bye."

I hung up the phone, grumbling about standardized tests. Are they really worth the trouble? Teachers hate giving them. We lose tons of teaching time, kids get all uptight when they have to take them, they seem to create nothing but misunderstanding with parents, and they just get filed away. Only rarely does anyone refer to them except to get negative information. But I went ahead and marked my calendar for my conference on Carrie's test scores.

Walking back to my room I thought about Carrie. I knew her mother was worried because Carrie had only scored a 95 on her recent IQ test. I had tried to convince Mrs. Lynch that a 95 was an average IQ score, that the test was only one measurement tool, that actually Carrie was doing above average work in all of her subjects, and that I had a great deal of faith in her academic abilities. I had suggested to Mrs. Lynch that maybe Carrie had had an off day when she took the IQ test.

I had told her mother these things before, but she had remained unconvinced. "The IQ test said Carrie was below average and maybe she shouldn't be placed in the reading group she is in," was Mrs. Lynch's viewpoint.

I only hoped that Carrie did as well on the standardized test as I sensed she would. Then her mother might believe that Carrie was indeed very capable academically. If she didn't do so well. . . .

Opening my door, I wondered whether my feelings about testing were due not to the tests themselves, but the way some people use the results to make judgments about kids. I hoped I would be able to make Carrie's mother understand these feelings when I met with her in December.

criterion-referenced A grading system in which scores are compared to a set performance standard. Also called *absolute standard.*

norm-referenced A grading system in which the performance of one student is compared against the performances of others. Also called *relative standard.*

Chap. Obj. 1
Test Ques. 14.4–14.11

Focus Questions: Why do educators need to standardize test results? Why is there so much negative public opinion concerning testing?

Connection: Teacher Chronicle 14.1: Test Anxiety.

NORM-REFERENCED AND CRITERION-REFERENCED MEASUREMENT

In Chapter 13, we examined the ways by which teachers collect the data that allow them to evaluate their students' classroom performances. We learned in that chapter that all measurement is based on comparisons. There must be some basis for comparison before an evaluative judgment can be made. A student who receives a score of 37 on a test can be judged as having performed well or poorly only after the score is compared with some criterion. The criterion might be the number of points possible on the test, say 40, or the criterion might be the performance of other students who took that same test. A score of 37 might mean that the student has outperformed 20 percent of his or her classmates. If the basis of comparison is some external criterion, for example, "the student will score at least 90 percent correct to receive an *A*," then the test is being used to make what are called **criterion-referenced** judgments. If the basis of comparison is the performance of other students in the class, then the test is being used to make **norm-referenced** judgments (see Popham, 1981).

The labels "criterion referenced" and "norm referenced" refer to the manner in which test results are interpreted, not to actual tests. In practice, the two types of measurement are used for different purposes. Criterion-referenced tests measure specific domains of competency; they are sometimes referred to as domain referenced. Norm-referenced tests are interpreted in relation to other people, such as the standardized test Carrie's mother was worried about in Teacher Chronicle 14.1. The other people who take the test

Standardized tests can be used in making criterion- and norm-referenced judgments of students' performances.

are known collectively as the norm group. Norm-referenced tests are usually designed to be broader and more general in scope, and are typically more comprehensive than criterion-referenced tests.

The use to which the test will be put and the underlying basis for comparison used for a particular test determine whether a particular test is criterion referenced or norm referenced. Glaser (1963) argued for the use of criterion-referenced tests in classrooms in order to assess specific learning objectives rather than norm-referenced tests, which he felt were inappropriate. Before the use of instructional objectives became a common practice in classrooms, instructional evaluation was generally based on norm-referenced assumptions. In the old days, which you may not remember but which your authors can recall all too easily, teachers very often graded "on the curve."

The curve on which our early teachers graded, the famous bell-shaped curve, was also called the normal curve (see Figure 14–1). The old practice of grading on the curve was based on the assumption that any group of students represented a range of abilities: there would be a very few people in the class who would excel and there would be a very few people in the class who would fail. Most of the people in the class would perform somewhere in the middle. Looking at the distribution of grades along the bell-shaped curve in Figure 14–1, we can see how the assumption of fixed ability led to the assignment of grades according to the normal curve.

We recall high school science classes in which a teacher announced in the first session that he or she would be grading on the curve. As high school students, we were unaware of the practice of norm-referenced measurement and what it meant technically, but we had an intuitive notion of what it meant to grade on the curve—that only a few people would receive A's. It also meant that we would compete against each other. As soon as the teacher had announced that he would be grading on the curve, most of us began looking around at the classroom and counting the number of students whom we knew

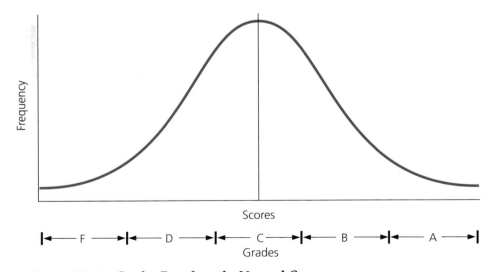

■ **Figure 14–1** *Grades Based on the Normal Curve*

to be good in science. Intuitively, we compared ourselves with a number of good students in order to determine the possibility that we might receive an *A* in the course. In this form of norm-referenced grading, the number of *A* grades was determined prior to instruction. (Incidentally, some of us in that class also looked around to see which of the other students would be receiving *F* grades and hoping that a sufficient number of *F* grades could be counted so that we might be excluded from that category.)

The use of norm-referenced measurement as a way of determining classroom performance and, therefore, grades is no longer a common practice. As we saw in the last chapter, grades are determined primarily on the basis of criterion-referenced measurements.

Although the above reminiscence suggests that norm-referenced measurement is generally an evil, while criterion-referenced measurement can be generally considered "good," we will see later in this chapter that norm-referenced measurement is a legitimately useful source of information in education.

Regardless of whether the purpose of measurement is to make judgments based on criteria or judgments based on a comparison with other people (i.e., a norm group), it is critical that the user of test information understand the purpose for which the test was designed. It is critical to compare the designed purpose of a test with its use.

TYPES OF STANDARDIZED TESTS

Standardized tests, which are norm referenced, are designed to enable the user of test data to make comparisons between one person who took that test and other members of the norm group. We can identify three types of standardized tests by the function each serves. Standardized tests can be used to measure achievement, aptitude, or to make diagnoses (see Gronlund, 1985; also Kubiszyn & Borich, 1987).

Achievement Tests

Achievement tests measure students' knowledge in various content areas. According to Gronlund (1985), standardized achievement tests are useful in five ways:

1. To evaluate general educational development in basic skill areas
2. To evaluate progress during the year or over years
3. To group students for instruction
4. To determine broad areas of strength and weakness
5. To compare achievement with aptitude

A recent trend among companies who design achievement tests is to provide, in addition to the norm-referenced data, criterion-referenced data. Criterion-referenced information is provided through the reporting of results by instructional objective or by specific skill area. Standardized test results may include criterion-referenced information, but they have been designed for other purposes. Because standardized achievement tests are norm referenced, their purpose is primarily for use in comparing a student's performance with those of other students. The number of items used to measure each skill area is usually quite small.

Issues in Educational Psychology

CNN™ This box relates to Segment 14 of the CNN videotape. See Instructor's Section for a summary.

TEACHER COMPETENCY

For fifty-four years the National Teacher Examination has been a factor in the lives of America's teachers. Thirty-seven states still require teachers to take the exam—with each state determining its own passing grade.

The Educational Testing Service is eliminating its old test in favor of a new exam that "more accurately assesses the candidate's abilities inside the classroom," according to NEA Vice President Robert Chase. Chase stressed in *NEA Today* that "our goal is to make sure the candidate can teach, not just pass tests."

The new exam will be phased in over a five-year period starting in the fall of 1992. In the same article, Gregory Anrig, ETS president, noted that "unlike the current written test given in several two-hour segments on a single day, our new test will evaluate teacher candidates at pivotal stages in their training."

After deciding to teach, students will be tested on basic skills in the first stage of the test. If weaknesses are detected, students will have time to remedy their problems. Offered by appointment, the test will employ computers to assess reading and math capabilities. Students will also be asked to write essays.

Once students have chosen their areas of concentration, they will be tested in the second stage on their familiarity with general teaching matter as well as their subject areas. They may also be tested on subject matter pedagogy. This stage will be administered when they have completed or are about to complete their undergraduate studies. Because this test is composed of modular sections, states will have the flexibility to select the test modules that best suit their needs. Students will benefit because they will be able to choose modules for states in which they may be considering teaching.

In the third stage, new teachers must work under classroom supervision. Having gained experience, they will be formally evaluated and interviewed, and possibly asked to submit a portfolio.

Although the new exam modernizes the assessment process, it still includes subjective on-site evaluations, which have long been a source of concern for teachers, especially those just out of college. For example, in Ohio, a controversy erupted two years ago when a Toledo teacher failed to have his contract renewed. Under the Toledo program, first-year teachers are assessed by other experienced teachers, who then make recommendations to a review board on whether contracts should be renewed.

In this case, there was a good chance that the teacher's complaint would have been upheld in court because the teacher enjoyed union job protection. Peer-review programs in other Ohio cities were also threatened by the possibility of court action. The state legislature subsequently added peer review to its list of fair labor practices, giving the program the imprimatur it needed to survive.

Teachers themselves are divided over the issue of peer review. The American Federation of Teachers endorses it. The National Education Association is against it. The Ohio Education Association (OEA) endorses peer review when school administrators determine contract renewals; nonetheless, it is interesting to note that the Columbus Education Association, the OEA's biggest local, took the opposing side in the Toledo controversy.

Even adminsitrators are torn. Some see peer review as an encroachment on their jobs. Others, such as Joseph Rutherford, who works for the Toledo Public Schools superintendent, hailed review as "the cornerstone of educational reform."

Even after the new National Teacher Examination comes on line, evaluations, and who does them, will continue to present problems.

SOURCES: Merina, Anita. "National Teacher Examination." *NEA Today* 9, issue 7 (March 1991): 3. Schmidt, Peter. "A Vote for Peer Review." *Teacher Magazine* 1, no. 8 (May 1990): 22. Bradley, Ann. "Who's in Charge Here?" *Teacher Magazine* 1, no. 5 (February 1990): 22–24.

1. How might performance-based norms be used to assess teacher competency?
2. How might both performance-based assessment and standardized competency tests contribute to the image of teaching as a profession?

Lecture Note: As a way of introducing aptitude tests, ask students to share their stereotypes of aptitude tests.

Connection: See the section on test bias later in this chapter.

Chapter 15 Casebook Preview: See I Am Leo.

Teaching Anecdote: Tell your students about the sixth-grade student who performed poorly on written tests but was outstanding in large and small group discussions. His teacher requested that the school psychologist administer a diagnostic test, which showed that the student was dyslexic.

Ask your students why they think this learning problem was not diagnosed earlier and how the test result might be used to improve the student's performance on written tests.

Aptitude Tests

Aptitude tests measure learned abilities based on a broader spectrum of in-school and out-of-school experiences. A common distinction between achievement and aptitude tests is that achievement tests measure what has been learned and aptitude tests measure learning potential. Gronlund suggests that it is too simplistic to make distinctions in this way. A better way to think about the distinction is that achievement tests measure what is learned from school activities and experiences.

Aptitude tests are usually shorter than achievement tests. They are less likely to be biased with respect to students of differing backgrounds. We will return to this issue later under the label cultural bias. Aptitude tests can be used before training because they are not designed to measure achievement. Aptitude tests are used to identify underachievers in combination with achievement tests.

Diagnostic Tests

Diagnostic tests can be used to identify learning difficulties by pinpointing student errors. Such tests do not identify the causes of such difficulties. They do, however, identify specific strengths and weaknesses. Having identified strengths and weaknesses by means of a diagnostic test, a teacher can then engage in careful observation and seek other information in search of the cause of a student's learning problem.

As all types of standardized tests are typically designed by people outside the school or classroom, it is important for a teacher to be cognizant of the purpose for which the test was designed. Appropriate use of standardized

Individualized testing is used to determine a student's personal strengths and those areas in which he or she needs to improve.

test results requires that teachers have an accurate perception of the nature of the tests administered. Teachers must know the types of evaluative judgments that are possible with a given test.

Comparing People and Numbers

The results of standardized tests are typically communicated in numbers. We will soon learn what the numbers from a standardized test mean. But before proceeding to an explanation of numerical information, an important caveat is in order. Data communicated in the form of numbers carry a curious and undeserved reputation as truth. Placing a number on an ability or characteristic imbues that characteristic with an aura of reality it may or may not deserve.

Take, for example, the characteristic we call intelligence. Intelligence is measured by IQ tests. We administer an IQ test to an individual, score the test, and give the individual a number. The number serves as an index of that individual's intelligence. In this way, a number becomes a label which we use to describe an aspect of that student. It becomes easy to compare people's numbers. Comparing the IQ numbers of two people would seem to tell us which person is more intelligent. The number, in a sense, tends to make us think of intelligence as a real thing that exists independently of any measurement. Once we have placed numbers on a characteristic or skill or performance, there is a tendency to construct additional meanings for that number. Standardized test results make it easy to compare people. Carrie's mother seemed obsessed with comparing her daughter's numbers with the numbers of others in the norm group. Using the results of standardized tests requires that we understand the difference between the characteristics of people and measurements of those characteristics. In the next section, we will look at the numbers that allow us to make sense out of test data.

Connection: Teacher Chronicle 14.1: Test Anxiety.

Principles in Practice 14.1

Principles . . .

1. Norm groups or external criteria can be used to make evaluative judgments.
2. Standardized tests are designed to allow different kinds of evaluative judgments.
3. Measurements of characteristics are not the characteristics themselves.

. . . in Practice

Carrie's mother, in Teacher Chronicle 14.2, seemed preoccupied with Carrie's scores on standardized tests. In her mother's eyes the fact that Carrie was meeting achievement criteria in classroom work did not counterbalance Carrie's performance on standardized tests. Neither did the mother perceive much of a distinction between achievement and aptitude tests. The teacher's task at the December meeting will be to help Carrie's mother understand the purpose of different kinds of tests and that there are other data that can be used to judge Carrie's abilities.

1. How might the teacher help Carrie's mother focus on Carrie's achievement in the classroom?
2. Why does the mother place more importance on the standardized test results than the teacher?
3. How will you "balance" the classroom achievement and standardized test results of your students?

- -

Teacher
Chronicle
14.2

STATISTICS?!?

"Statistics. Ugh! What good will they ever be for me?" How often have I heard student teachers say that when taking the required stats course. And how often do I wish I had really paid attention and understood statistics when I was taking them? How much more could I have understood about my students' performances on tests? How many embarrassing moments might I have spared myself at parent–teacher conferences?

Oh, how I remember my first conference with Mr. Longley, a former teacher. He had evidently stayed awake during stats class and he really knew what he was talking about.

"I see that Dan's stanine is 8 in reading and 5 in math. Is he really that poor in his daily work?"

"No, not really," I answered slowly, trying to grasp some meaning from the figures. "He's in the middle group. Doing the best in the group I might add."

"What about this 8 stanine in reading? Is he really that good?"

"Well, Mr. Longley, this result means that he should be in the top reading group, but I'm afraid that he just isn't reading that well and he would be overwhelmed in that group."

"What about here where it says that Dan's grade equivalent for all reading skills is 9.5 and he's only in fifth grade?"

"Well, Mr. Longley, that means that he could be reading at a ninth-grade level but since he's only in fifth grade he belongs there socially."

Mr. Longley looked at me for a long moment and then asked, "Do you know what you're talking about?"

- -

Chap. Obj. 2–3
Test Ques. 14.24–14.70

Focus Questions: What is the basis of all standardized test scores? How should teachers interpret standardized test scores for themselves, for students, and for parents?

STANDARDIZED TEST SCORES

The results of standardized tests are communicated in a variety of numerical ways. The numbers that provide teachers an understanding of test results are based on statistics.

For those of you who expect to be certified as secondary math teachers, the word *statistics* generates little anxiety. You may even have learned that statistics can be fun. For those of you in other certification areas, seeing the words *fun* and *statistics* in the same sentence may seem somewhat contradictory. If the term *statistics* does not produce anxiety, then what follows is probably a review for you. Even if this is the case, you may also find that statistics are used somewhat differently to communicate standardized test scores. If you are in the latter group, take a deep breath, it's not as bad as you think. Finally, keep in mind Teacher Chronicle 14.2; it will be your responsibility to help parents and students understand test scores.

Imagine that you are now nine weeks into your first teaching job. You feel that you are beginning to get a handle on the administrative routine in the school. You are starting to understand and communicate with your colleagues. The students in your classroom have settled into a good working rhythm. As you walk into the office to pick up your mail, you find yourself thinking about the progress you have made during those first nine weeks. You notice in your mailbox that there is an official looking memo from the superintendent of the school district (see Figure 14–2).

Connection: Teacher Chronicle 14.2: Statistics?!?

Interoffice Memo

A reminder to all school personnel, especially principals and classroom teachers:

Parent–teacher conferences will be scheduled in your school during the second week of November. In addition to discussing the grade reports that parents of your students will receive next week, parents have also been advised that they may discuss with you the results of the standardized achievement tests that were administered during the first week of school. The achievement tests provide us with important data concerning the academic levels of our students. It is important for parents to understand and appreciate the results of those tests. They have been advised that they may bring any questions they may have about the results of the tests to the conference. Therefore, you should be familiar not only with the classroom work of your students, but with their performances on the achievement tests.

■ **Figure 14–2** *A Memo Regarding Standardized Test Scores*

Teacher Interview: Have each student interview a teacher regarding the interpretation of standardized test results during parent–teacher conferences.

Connection: See the section on equivalent scores later in this chapter.

Lecture Note: As an introduction to the importance of both properties, central tendency and dispersion, you might use the following story: There once was a fellow who was laying down with his feet in the fireplace and his head on a block of ice. When asked how he felt, the fellow replied, "Overall, pretty good."

You finish reading the memo on the way to the teachers' lounge to grab a cup of coffee and to look over your lesson plans. Although the prospect of parent–teacher conferences is a bit daunting, you feel prepared to discuss and justify the grades you have assigned your students during the first grading period. The idea of discussing the results of standardized tests that you did not design and score, on the other hand, is a bit worrisome.

In the lounge, you ask a more senior colleague about the memo on the standardized achievement tests. Your colleague chuckles and tells the story of a parent who once came in wanting to know why her daughter in the second grade, who was reading at the fourth-grade level, wasn't in the fourth grade. You chuckle yourself and ask, as nonchalantly as possible, "What did you tell her?" The smile on your colleague's face fades as he says, "Well, you know, I told her that her daughter wasn't really ready socially for the fourth grade, even though she may be ready mentally." Somehow your colleague's explanation seems a bit thin, even though you're not sure why.

As we will discover, there are good reasons why that child should not be in the fourth grade—reasons that are based in the interpretation of statistics. Although the comment about social readiness may be accurate, an understanding of the nature of statistical results, and more importantly, the use to which they are put, will provide you with a more convincing argument to offer the parent of that second grader, and to your colleagues, as well.

Properties of Distributions

The results of standardized tests are based on a comparison between one test-taker and other test-takers. That comparison is based on an analysis of test scores. The scores made on a test form a distribution. Suppose, for example, you gave a test to your future class. Suppose, furthermore, that you were asked by your principal to describe your class's performance on a particular task. You might provide your principal with a statistic: a number that represents all of the scores in the distribution.

Every distribution of scores has two properties. One is called the central tendency. The **central tendency** of a distribution is a description of where the middle of the distribution is. For example, in describing the performance of your class to your principal, you might tell him or her what the average score for the class was. If there were 50 possible points on the test and the average performance of your students was 38, you might say to your principal, "The average was 38 out of a possible 50 points." The number 38 is a statistic. It is a number used to describe the other numbers in the distribution.

A second property of distributions is called **dispersion,** which is an indication of how similar or different the scores in the distribution are from one another. Your principal, having learned the average, or central tendency of the distribution, might inquire further about the performance of the class. If the principal were to ask you what was the lowest score and the highest score on the test, he or she would be inquiring about the dispersion of scores.

Let's examine three ways to measure the central tendency of a distribution and two ways to measure the dispersion of a distribution.

Measures of Central Tendency

Measures of central tendency are numerical descriptions of the average, or typical, value in a distribution. There are three different ways to measure the property of central tendency: mode, median, and mean. Each way of measuring the central tendency yields a statistic.

Mode

The first statistic that describes the typical value in the distribution of scores is the mode. The **mode** of a distribution is the most frequently occurring score.

Take a look at the list of test scores in Figure 14–3. Ten students took the test. The distribution of scores is called a frequency distribution because the frequency with which each score occurs in the distribution is available. (The score of 20 occurs twice in Figure 14–3.) The mode of this distribution of scores is 23 because the score of 23 was attained by more students than any other score.

mode The most frequently occurring score in a set of scores; one of the three measures of central tendency.

median The central score of a set of scores; the score that divides the set of scores into two equal halves; one of the three measures of central tendency.

Lecture Note: A mnemonic for the mode of a distribution is to imagine the frequency distribution graph. If the data in the graph were considered to be scoops of ice cream on top of a slice of pie, the highest point of the "à la mode" is the mode of the distribution.

Median

The median is the second index that can be used to identify the central tendency of a distribution of scores. The **median** of the distribution is that point along the distribution of scores that divides the set of scores into two equal halves. Half of the scores will be above the median; half of the scores, below. In Figure 14–3, the median is equal to 20.5; half of the scores in the distribution are above 20.5, and half of the scores are below.

Lecture Note: A mnemonic for the median is to remember that the median of a highway divides that highway in half.

Student Name	Score
Sara M.	20
George B.	23
Lyndon J.	18
Brenda W.	19
Lupe E.	23
Sean W.	21
Ruth V.	24
Denora T.	19
Samuel C.	23
Oscar H.	20

■ **Figure 14–3** ***A Hypothetical Distribution of Students' Scores***

Lecture Note: Ask a student in class to describe the procedure for calculating an average. Use the student's description to identify the scores in the distributions, the summation of the scores, and division by the number of scores in the distribution.

Mean

The third measure of central tendency is the mean. The **mean** of a distribution is its arithmetic average. If your notion of taking an average is to add scores and divide the sum by the total number of scores in the distribution, then you have the correct notion of a mean. By adding the ten scores in the distribution in Figure 14–3 and dividing the total sum by ten, we arrive at the index of central tendency called the mean, which in this case is 21.

The mean, median, and mode are three statistics; three numbers that describe a set of other numbers. Why do we need three ways of describing one property of a distribution? The answer is that each statistic provides a different type of information about a distribution. Consider, as illustration, the following story:

A young man sets out on his first task in a brand new job as a market researcher. His task is to go to a small community in western Pennsylvania to conduct market research. The company for which he works is interested in marketing its product in this community. Before attempting to sell the product, however, the company needs to have some information about the average income of the community.

The company's past experience with the product indicates that a community whose average income is less than $32,000 per family will not prove to be a profitable market. Therefore, the company is sending out the new market researcher in order to collect the information needed to make a marketing decision.

The young man arrives in the community and begins knocking on all the doors in town. As each door is opened, our young market researcher asks the following question, "How much money did your family make last year?" Every family in this community cheerfully answers our researcher's question (at least they do in this example).

The community is a very small one, consisting of only twenty families. The town grew up around a coal mine, which has long since been played out. The demise of the mine has left a very small population of families whose fortunes were tied to the mine's.

As our young researcher discovers the income level of each family, he enters it into a frequency distribution. The results of his efforts are given in Figure 14–4A, a bar graph illustrating the distribution of incomes in this small community. If we connect the top of each bar in the graph with a line and round out that line into a curve, we have a general picture of the distribution of scores.

After completing his survey, our young researcher retires to the local coffee shop on the main street of the town, one of the few storefronts in the square open for business. As he looks at the distribution of scores, he is very disappointed. He orders a cup of coffee and sips sadly. The proprietor of the coffee shop, sensing dismay, asks our young researcher what is troubling him. The researcher looks up from his coffee and speaks to the proprietor.

"Well, I've spent the entire day in this town, going from door to door trying to find out the incomes of each family. With some persistence and an unusual amount of charm, I have acquired the information I need. Here it is." Our young researcher shows the graph to the proprietor.

"Uh-huh," says the proprietor. "What does this mean?" Our young researcher explains to the proprietor that the company for which he works, had hoped to market their product in the community. He explains also that in order to successfully market the product, the average income in the commu-

A.

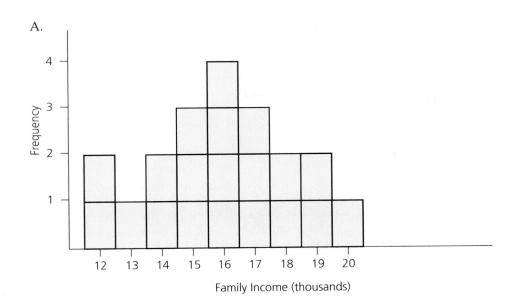

B.

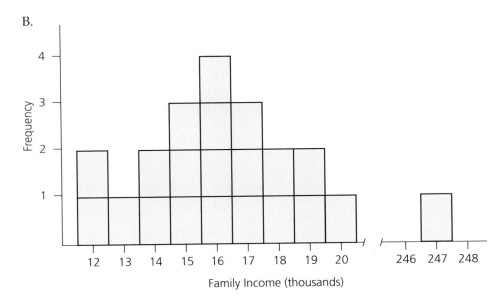

■ **Figure 14–4** *The Market Researcher's Initial Distribution of Income (A) and the Second Distribution (B)*

nity must be $32,000 or greater. "As you can see from my graph, the average income in this community is right around $16,000. That's why I'm so sad," says our young researcher. "You see, this was my first project. I had hoped to send back a report to my boss telling her that I had identified a potential market for our company. Instead, on my first report back to my home office, I have to tell my superiors that I have failed to discover a market for our product."

The proprietor fills the researcher's cup, and says, "Are you sure you got everybody in town?"

"Yes," says the young researcher. "I went to every house that I could find."

"Did you go up to the big house on the hill?" asked the proprietor, pointing out the window.

"What house on the hill?" asked our researcher.

"See up on top of that hill, there's a big house. It's hidden by the trees, but it's up there and it's beautiful."

"I didn't go up there," says our researcher. "I didn't know there was a house. Who lives there?"

"Well," said the proprietor, "this town was built around a coal mine. The family who owned the mine built a big house up there on the hill and planted trees around it. It gets pretty windy up on that hill in the wintertime. Anyway, the family in the big house made a lot of money from the coal mine by selling it just before the coal petered out. You should talk to that family."

Our young researcher, his energy restored, thanked the proprietor for the coffee and the information and headed up the hill to the mansion. He knocked on the front door, and asked to speak to a member of the family. A gentleman came to the door, and our young researcher said, "Excuse me sir, but I'm conducting a survey for my company, and we need to know how much money your family made last year." The gentleman, in the spirit of this community, says, "Why, certainly, I'd be glad to tell you. Our family made $247,000 last year."

The young researcher thanked the gentleman for his time, and on the way down the hill, entered the new score to his distribution of family incomes. The new distribution of scores, with the mansion family included, is given in Figure 14–4B. Looking at his new distribution, our young researcher recalculated the mean family income of this community and discovered that it exceeds the criterion income of $32,000. Happily, he sends a report to his boss, telling her that with his first market report, he has discovered a market for the company's product.

The company sends the product to this community to sell through its general store, and in a period of eighteen months sells in this community one item. The company's management is very disappointed in the performance of their product in this small community; the director of marketing calls in our young researcher and fires him on the spot.

Why did this misfortune occur?

It occurred because our young researcher used the wrong measure of central tendency in filing his report to the company. Let's compare the two distributions in Figure 14–4 (A and B). The distribution in Figure 14–4A is the distribution of incomes prior to the inclusion of the mansion family, which made $247,000. Figure 14–4B includes the mansion family. What is the mode of the distribution in Figure 14–4A? How does the mode in Figure 14–4A compare with the mode in Figure 14–4B? What is the median of the two distributions and how do they compare?

The modes of the two distributions and the medians of the two distributions are the same or very similar. As measures of central tendency, the mode and the median are not sensitive to extreme scores. What is the mean score in Figure 14–4B? As we discovered in the story, the mean score was $16,000. Adding in the new mansion family, whose income last year was $247,000, we find that the mean of the entire distribution changes dramatically. The mean, as a measure of central tendency, is sensitive to extreme scores.

What is the best measure of central tendency? To answer that question, one must know the use to which the statistic will be put. Using the median or mode as the index of central tendency of a distribution does not take into account the extreme scores. Comparing the two figures, we can see that comparing the median and mode as indices do not change even though the distributions differ.

In making the kind of norm-referenced comparisons that lead to standardized test scores, it is important to take into account all of the members of the norm group. For this reason, the mean is the preferred measure of central tendency in the reporting of standardized test scores. There is one other reason why the mean of a distribution is the preferred educational statistic. We'll discover this reason as we look at the second property of distributions, dispersion.

Measures of Dispersion

In the earlier example, your principal asked about the performance of your class. You described the distribution of scores by identifying the middle of the distribution, using the statistic we call the mean. The dispersion of that distribution was described by providing the principal with the lowest and the highest score. By subtracting the lowest score from the highest score, we are left with a statistic of dispersion called the range. The **range** is a relatively crude measure of dispersion, which, although it provides a quick estimate of the dispersion of scores, can be influenced considerably by extreme scores. The range does tell us much about how similar or dissimilar the majority of scores in a distribution are.

Consider, for example, the difference in the range of scores in Figure 14–4A compared with Figure 14–4B. The only difference between the scores in the two distributions is the one extremely high score in the distribution in Figure 14–4B. The range, then, tells us only about the difference between the two most extreme scores. If we want an index of dispersion that tells us something about all of the scores in a distribution, we need to use a statistic called the standard deviation.

Standard Deviation

Conceptually, a **standard deviation** is nothing more nor less than the average deviation score in a distribution. Let's examine how one calculates a standard deviation; not for the purpose of learning to do the calculation, but for the purpose of understanding how the standard deviation describes the dispersion of a distribution.

It is important to understand the statistic called a standard deviation because all standardized test scores are based on that statistic. Because your job will be to consume and interpret standardized scores, you need to understand the standard deviation.

Throughout the following discussion of the standard deviation, keep in mind that the standard deviation is an arithmetic average, that is, a mean. The formula for the mean can be written as follows:

$$\overline{X} = \frac{\Sigma X}{N}$$

range The difference between the highest and lowest scores in a set of scores.
standard deviation A statistic that expresses the variability in a distribution of scores.

Journal Entry: Have students reflect on the three statistics that are indexes of central tendency, noting the conditions under which each index might be useful for a teacher.

Chapter 15 Casebook Preview: See Responsibility Education.

Lecture Note: Ask students why the range tells us little about the majority of the scores in a distribution.

Lecture Note: To emphasize that the standard deviation is a form of average, place the formula for standard deviation on the board. Point out that at the heart of the formula is the calculation of an average (deviations are summed and then the sum of deviations is divided by the number of deviations in the distribution).

$\overline{X}$ (read "X-bar") stands for the mean. X in the formula refers to each score in the distribution. The character Σ (sigma) is used to indicate summation or adding the scores. N stands for the number of scores. Reading the formula then, the mean is equal to the sum of the scores in a distribution divided by the number of scores in the distribution.

If the standard deviation is an average, then we must add up something and divide by the number of somethings we have. The somethings that we will add up are not the raw scores in a distribution (represented by X in the earlier formula) but rather, deviation scores.

If we could find out how far each raw score in a distribution deviates from some reference point, then each score in the distribution could be converted into a deviation score. The logical reference point to use in calculating deviation scores is the mean. It is the measure of central tendency that is sensitive to all of the scores in a distribution, including extreme scores. We want to know how far—on average—all of the scores deviate from the central reference point. We use the mean as our reference point.

Figure 14–5 includes ten raw scores in a distribution. By calculating the mean of the distribution, we can determine how far each of the ten scores deviates from the mean by subtracting, from the mean, each score. The column in Figure 14–5 headed $(X - \overline{X})$ represents the deviation score for each student in the distribution.

Lecture Note: As a check on comprehension, ask students to define the term *deviation score.*

Journal Entry: Have students reflect on why the mean is the best index to use as a reference point.

X (Raw Scores)	$(X - \overline{X})$ (Deviation Scores)	$(X - \overline{X})^2$ (Squared Deviations)
38	−2	4
32	−8	64
43	+3	9
44	+4	16
42	+2	4
37	−3	9
44	+4	16
39	−1	1
41	+1	1
40	0	0
$\Sigma\Xi = 400$	$\Sigma(X - \overline{X}) = 0$	$\Sigma(X - \overline{X})^2 = 124$

$$\overline{X} = \frac{\Sigma x}{N}$$

$$\overline{X} = \frac{400}{10}$$

$$\overline{X} = 40$$

standard deviation =

$$\text{s.d.} = \sqrt{\frac{\Sigma(x - \overline{x})^2}{N}}$$

$$\text{s.d.} = \sqrt{\frac{124}{10}} = \sqrt{12.4}$$

$$\text{s.d.} = 3.52$$

■ **Figure 14–5** *Finding the Standard Deviation of a Distribution of Scores*

Remember the conceptual definition of the standard deviation: the average deviation. This definition suggests that we could find the standard deviation by adding up the deviation scores and dividing by the number of deviation scores we have. There is a problem, however. If you were to sum the deviation scores in this or any distribution, the sum would be zero $[\Sigma(X - \overline{X}) = 0]$. The reason is that the mean in any distribution is that point in the distribution that balances the scores above it with the scores below it. Indeed, the mean of a distribution can be defined as that point in a distribution from which all deviations sum to zero.

If all deviations sum to zero, we would be unable to differentiate between the dispersion in one distribution from the dispersion in any other distribution. Let's call this problem the "zero problem." What we want to know is how far from the mean the scores are, not whether scores are above or below the mean. Scores that are above the mean are higher than the mean. Subtracting scores from the mean in these cases yields a negative number. The total of the negative numbers (the scores above the mean) balance the scores below the mean, yielding the sum of zero. One way to get rid of the zero problem would be to simply identify the distance between each score and the mean of the distribution. The distance could be given by a number, without regard for whether that number is positive or negative, that is, above or below the mean.

Lecture Note: Check students' comprehension of standard deviation by asking them to paraphrase the "zero problem."

To get rid of negative numbers, we could also square the difference between each score and the mean. This yields the third column $(X - \overline{X})^2$ in Figure 14–5. The third column is the distribution of squared deviation scores. Although squaring the deviation scores eliminates our zero problem, it introduces another problem.

The squared deviations are, in some cases, very much larger than the actual distance of a given score from the mean. For example, a raw score that is five points above the mean yields a deviation score of five. The squared deviation is equal to 25. Even though the distances from each score to the mean are inflated, we at least have an index of distance by summing the squared deviations. We provide an index of the distances between each score in the distribution and our reference point, the mean.

If we divide the sum of squared deviations by the number of scores in the distribution, we have the following:

Lecture Note: Draw a line on the floor of your classroom or use tiles on the floor to indicate scores in a distribution. Have one student stand at a point on the distribution that represents it's mean. Have a second student stand five points below the mean, a third student five points above. By squaring the distances students are away from the mean, the estimate of deviation is much higher than the actual distance. To get a more realistic estimate of the distance, take the square root of squared deviations.

$$\frac{\Sigma(X - \overline{X})^2}{N}$$

In order to eliminate the inflated distances, we can take the square root of the mean of squared deviations. This operation yields the following formula:

$$\sqrt{\frac{\Sigma(X - \overline{X})^2}{N}}$$

This is the formula for standard deviation.

Squaring deviations and then taking the square root of the quantity are merely mathematical operations that allow us to eliminate the zero problem. At the heart of the formula is a mean. For our purposes, the essential element of the standard deviation formula is that it is an average.

Lecture Note: Remind students that standard deviation is an index of the dispersion property of distributions. Because each distribution has a degree of dispersion, we can compare distributions based on the similarity or dissimilarity of scores.

Connection: Understanding the standard deviation is the basis for explaining standardized test scores to parents (see the memo in Figure 14–2).

Chapter 15 Casebook Preview: See Please Sign This Contract.

Transparency: This figure is duplicated in the acetate transparency package. See T-25 Standardized Test Scores in Relation to the Normal Curve.

If we know how far, on average, scores in a distribution deviate from the mean, we can then compare distributions and identify those distributions in which scores are quite similar. Similar scores in a distribution yield a small standard deviation. A distribution in which scores are highly dissimilar yields a large standard deviation.

In summary, we have discussed five statistics. Three statistics serve as indices of central tendency: mean, median, and mode. Two statistics serve as indices of dispersion in a distribution: range and standard deviation. The question that remains is, How do these indices serve as the basis for standardized test scores?

The Normal Distribution

The standard deviation is a ruler applied to the normal distribution. (The normal distribution discussed earlier is given in Figure 14–6.)

Looking at Figure 14–6, we see that the normal distribution is symmetrical and that most of the scores in a normal distribution are located near the center. Because the highest point in the distribution is in the exact center of the symmetrical curve, the mean, median, and mode coincide.

The normal distribution is a theoretical distribution. It is derived from mathematical formulas. Even though the normal distribution is theoretical, it describes many naturally occurring distributions. Consider the height of human beings. If we were to measure the height of all human beings over eighteen years of age and construct a frequency polygon of that distribution, the distribution would be normal in shape. Most people would be of average

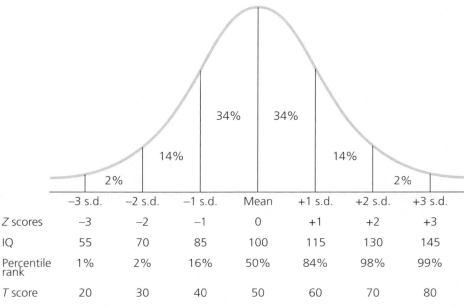

	−3 s.d.	−2 s.d.	−1 s.d.	Mean	+1 s.d.	+2 s.d.	+3 s.d.
Z scores	−3	−2	−1	0	+1	+2	+3
IQ	55	70	85	100	115	130	145
Percentile rank	1%	2%	16%	50%	84%	98%	99%
T score	20	30	40	50	60	70	80

* s.d. = standard deviation.

■ **Figure 14–6** *Standardized Test Scores in Relation to the Normal Curve*
SOURCE: From *Essentials of Educational Measurement* (5th ed., p. 69) by R. L. Ebel and D. A. Frisbie, 1991, Englewood Cliffs, NJ: Prentice Hall. Copyright 1991 by Prentice Hall. Adapted by permission.

height. As we move to the extremes of the distribution—people who are very tall or people who are very short—we should find fewer and fewer people. The mathematical theory, called the normal distribution, matches many actual distributions of psychological characteristics as well.

Measures of anxiety yield normal distributions as do measures of achievement, intelligence, and any number of personality characteristics. Because the normal curve matches many of the characteristics we measure in education, we can use the properties of the normal curve to help us understand differences among people.

As mentioned earlier, the mean of a normal distribution resides at the center of the distribution along with the median and the mode. Properties of the normal distribution include the relations of various points on the curve to the standard deviation. Suppose, for example, characteristic X is normally distributed. By adding all of the X scores in the distribution and dividing by the number of X scores in that distribution, we can calculate the average score of the X distribution.

Having calculated the mean of that distribution, we can then determine how far each score in the distribution deviates from the mean by calculating the statistic called standard deviation. The properties of the normal distribution are such that one standard deviation (the average distance of all scores from the mean of the distribution) accounts for certain percentages of the area defined by the normal distribution.

Standard Deviation and the Normal Distribution

Looking at Figure 14–6, we can see that the normal distribution has been divided into areas defined by standard deviation units. If we move in either direction from the mean of the distribution to a distance that is equal to one standard deviation unit, we find that each unit above and below the mean accounts for roughly 34 percent of the entire distribution. Taken together, the two standard deviation units on either side of the mean account for a total of 68 percent of all of the scores in the X distribution. The area of the normal curve defined by the area between one and two standard deviation units above or below the mean accounts for approximately 14 percent of all of the scores in the distribution. Figure 14–6 also includes the percentages accounted for between two and three standard deviation units. Once we are beyond three standard deviation units above or below the mean, we have accounted for approximately 99 percent of all of the scores in a distribution.

It is by using the standard deviation of a distribution to identify points on a normal curve, that we can assign standardized scores. Standardized scores tell educators how one person's performance on a test compares with other people in the same norm group.

Z Scores

One form of standardized score is called a Z score (shown in Figure 14–6). A **Z score** is a score given in standard deviation units. The mean of any normal distribution is assigned a Z score of zero. Standard deviation units define Z scores above and below the mean. A score on the normal distribution that is one standard deviation unit above the mean is assigned a Z score of +1. A score which resides two standard deviation units above the mean is assigned a Z score of +2. Scores which reside below the mean are given minus or negative Z scores. Note that we can assign Z scores to any normal distribution regardless of the mean and the standard deviation of that distribution.

Z score A score given in standard deviation units. The mean of any normal distribution is assigned a Z score of 0. Scores above the mean are plus scores; scores below the mean are minus scores.

Lecture Note: As an additional example: Ask students to imagine a perfectly symmetrical tree that is losing it's leaves in autumn. As the leaves flutter down to the ground, they form a pile. Ask students to imagine the shape of that pile and how it is related to the normal distribution.

Lecture Note: Emphasize that standard deviation units serve as the ruler or the units of measurement for interpreting the normal distribution.

Lecture Note: As an aid to students, tell them that the normal distribution of standardized test scores represents the norm group.

Lecture Note: Give students some
practice in interpreting the normal distribution by asking them to locate the
Z score, given percentages above or
below the mean or percentages between two points on the distribution.

Take a look at Figure 14–7 (A and B). Depicted in that figure are two normal distributions (A, B). The amount of dispersion in the top distribution (A) is considerably smaller than the amount of dispersion in the bottom distribution (B). The standard deviation in the top distribution is smaller than the standard deviation in the bottom distribution. In both cases, however, assigning the standard deviation units to the curve yields the same percentage areas under the curves. By noticing the Z scores assigned to the standard deviation units in both of the distributions, we can see that Z scores are based entirely on the standard deviation ruler that is used to measure the distance above or below the mean in a normal distribution.

IQ Scores

A more familiar standardized score is provided by the intelligence quotient (IQ). IQ is based on standard deviation units as well. Once we have assigned

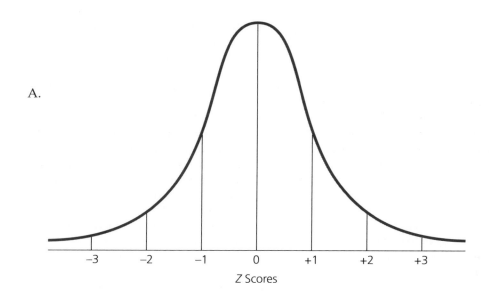

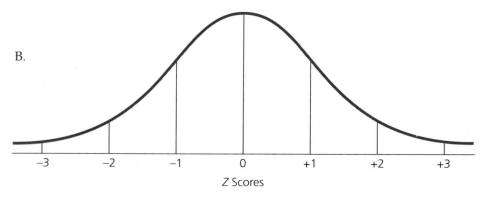

■ **Figure 14–7** *Two Normal Distributions Differing in Their Dispersion*

the standard deviation ruler to a normal curve, it is possible to compute any of the standardized scores such as Z scores, IQ scores, percentile ranks, or T scores.

Before describing some of the other standardized scores, let's look at an example of where IQ scores come from and how they are interpreted in relation to the normal curve. (IQ scores are given in Figure 14–6.) Typically, intelligence tests have a mean of 100 and a standard deviation of 15. Interpreted in terms of these standardized scores, if you had an IQ of 115, you would have an IQ that is higher than 84 percent of the general population. We can calculate that percentage by examining the areas under the normal curve defined by standard deviation units. Note also that an IQ score of 115 is equivalent to a Z score of +1.

Percentile Rank

Percentile rank, another standardized score, defines the percentage of people in the norm group above whom an individual scores. In the previous example, 84 percent is the percentile rank of the individual with an IQ of 115 and, equivalently, a Z score of +1.

Deriving Standardized Scores

Another standardized score that has been developed is called the T score. The distribution of a **T score** has a mean of 50 and a standard deviation of 10. An IQ score of 115 converts to a T score of 60. Any number of standardized scores could be derived in this way.

IQ scores, which we use most often and tend to think of as having certain numeric properties, are defined scores. Suppose you invented an IQ test. Your IQ test has sixty-three items on it. You can assign a score to any one person's performance, ranging from 0 to 63. Let's assume that you administer your IQ test to a large number of people, perhaps 5,000. After collecting 5,000 scores on your IQ test, you could then calculate the mean score. Let's assume that the mean score on your IQ test is thirty-eight items correct. With the distribution of your IQ scores in hand, you can then calculate the standard deviation of the distribution. Let's assume that the average deviation from the mean of all the 5,000 scores is 4. This is another way of saying that the standard deviation is 4.

A mean equal to 38 and a standard deviation equal to 4 are based on the obtained scores on your IQ test. Obtained scores are often called raw scores. Because of the size of your sample and the nature of the characteristic being measured, we can assume that the distribution of scores is normal around a mean of 38, with a standard deviation of 4. When the time comes for you to report the results of your IQ test, you could report the raw scores.

For example, a person who scored one standard deviation above the mean would have a raw IQ score of 42. Instead of reporting the raw score, you could also report derived scores. One such score would be the Z score. Instead of reporting the raw score of 42, you could inform the person who received the raw score of 42 that their score is a +1 in Z-score terms. Alteratively, you could report a T score of 60, or a percentile rank of 84.

You could, however, follow the more common pattern of reporting IQ scores by converting the raw score mean into a defined IQ score of 100. You could also define the standard deviation of your IQ distribution to be equal to fifteen IQ-point units. Thus, instead of the person receiving an IQ score of 42 in raw score terms, you could report that person's defined IQ score as 115.

Journal Entry: Have students reflect on why it is possible to convert from IQ scores to percentile ranks.

Lecture Note: Have your students create their own standardized score by supplying a definition of a derived score.

Chapter 15 Casebook Preview: See Bringing the Real World into the Classroom.

Teacher Interview: Have each student interview a teacher regarding the advantages of reporting standardized test scores as bands or ranges or scores during parent–teacher conferences.

Teaching Anecdote: Tell your students about the junior high social studies curriculum committee charged with revising the district's social studies program. When several members of the committee complained that elementary students coming to the junior high were poorly prepared, it was brought to their attention that the district's sixth graders performed two years above grade level on their most recent standardized tests. The committee members scoffed and replied, "But they don't know what we want them to know before coming to seventh grade."

Ask your students where the problem might lie: in the test, in the elementary social studies curriculum, or in a mismatch between the elementary and the junior high curricula.

Stanine Scores

Another fairly common standardized score is a stanine. **Stanine** scores are standardized scores that range from one to nine, each of which represents a range or band of percentages under the normal distribution. The stanine bands are depicted in Figure 14–8. A stanine score of 5 represents the middle 20 percent of the distribution and includes those students who scored at the mean of the distribution. Stanine scores greater than 5 indicate performances that are above average. Stanine scores below 5 indicate performances below the average.

One advantage of reporting stanine scores is that small differences between scores are less likely to be interpreted as real differences. It is important that we keep in mind that all standardized tests, as indeed all educational measurement, contain error.

In some instances, standardized scores will be reported with estimates of confidence limits. For example, a child's IQ may be reported as 116, plus or minus 4. Reporting standardized scores in this way is an acknowledgment of a statistical phenomenon known as standard error of measurement. Because tests are not perfectly reliable, it is important to interpret individual scores as a range of possible scores within which the true score is most likely to fall. Confidence limits are estimates of the consistency of an individual's score. Reporting scores with their confidence limits also helps in interpreting the difference between two scores within a test battery, or to interpret differences between the scores of two individual students.

Equivalent Scores

Along with stanines and percentile ranks, perhaps the most popular form of reporting standardized test results is the use of grade equivalents and age equivalents. Of the two equivalents scores, grade equivalents are used considerably more often (Carey, 1988; Kubiszyn & Borich, 1987).

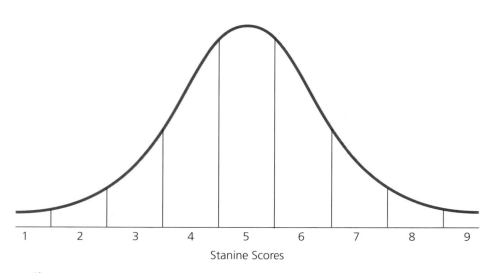

Stanine Scores

■ **Figure 14–8** *Stanine Scores in Relation to the Normal Curve*

Recall the imaginary situation early in this chapter: You learned of parent–teacher conferences and your responsibility to report and interpret the standardized scores of your students. Your senior colleague in the lounge seemed somewhat at a loss to offer an accurate interpretation of the second grader's reading score being equivalent to that of a fourth grader. On a superficial level, it seems obvious that a student in the second grade who scores at a fourth-grade reading level is capable of reading as well as the average fourth grader. As obvious as that may seem, it is not the case, and is the reason why grade equivalents are so often misinterpreted.

Connection: See the memo in Figure 14–2.

Typically, grade equivalent scores are generated by using a test to measure the performance of the target grade, and grades one level below and one level above the target grade. Thus, the norm group and the tables of scores used for that second-grader's norm group come from the performances of first, second, and third graders. Fourth graders, with whom the second grader is being compared, are not part of the group who took the second grader's test. In this example, second graders and fourth graders are not members of the same norm group. Remembering the caveat about norm groups, that only members of the norm group are eligible for comparison, we can see the mistake that is made by a parent or teacher who assumes that the second grader is performing at the same level as the average fourth grader.

Lecture Note: Remind students that standardized test scores are a form of norm-referenced measurement and that is why the norm group is so important to the interpretation of these scores.

The reason our second grader earned a grade equivalent score of fourth grade is that scores beyond one grade level above and below the target are extrapolated, or estimated, from the obtained scores of the three grades. Grade equivalent scores that are much higher or much lower than the student's actual grade level merely indicate that the student differs considerably from the average performance of his or her own norm group. Extreme grade equivalent scores say nothing about the specific skills that a student may possess.

In addition to this common problem of misinterpretation, there are additional problems related to the use of grade equivalent scores. Kubiszyn and Borich (1987) list four problems.

Teacher Interview: Have students interview teachers concerning the interpretation of grade equivalent scores, asking them to share their experiences with these scores.

1. Equal differences among grade equivalent scores do not necessarily reflect equal differences in achievement. For example, the difference between Student A who performs at a grade equivalent of 2.6 (sixth month of the second grade) and Student B who scores at a grade equivalent level of 3.6 is not the same as the difference between Student C who scores a grade equivalent of 5.6 and Student D who scores at a grade equivalent of 6.6.

2. Grade equivalents are not useful unless a subject is taught across all of the grades that are represented in the grade equivalent scores. For example, to report that a student's achievement in geometry is at the grade equivalent level of 5.4 is meaningless, since fifth graders do not generally take geometry. If this is the case, what does it mean to achieve in geometry at the level of the average fifth grader in the fourth month of that grade?

3. Grade equivalents are often interpreted as standards rather than norms. Grade equivalents are averages; a grade equivalent of 9.3 for example represents the median point in a distribution of scores obtained by students in the third month of the ninth grade. Grade

equivalents then, are based on a comparison with other students, that is, these equivalents are norm-referenced, not criterion-referenced, evaluations.

4. It is difficult to compare grade equivalents across various school subjects. A student who is a full grade level behind in math may be further behind in math than the same student who is one full grade level behind in reading. Students progress at different rates in different subjects; therefore, the norms for reading and for math are not comparable.

Despite all of these problems, it is very likely that you will receive grade equivalent scores for your students. It is also very likely that at some point you will have to interpret those scores in order to make instructional or placement decisions about your students. You will also be asked to explain the results of standardized tests to curious parents. It is important to always keep in mind the use to which the tests will be put.

The use of standardized achievement, aptitude, and diagnostic tests provide norm-referenced information. Norm-referenced evaluation provides a basis for comparing students with each other. In Chapter 13, we looked at classroom data yielded generally by criterion-referenced measures of various sorts. In recent years, there has been a greater emphasis on criterion-referenced tests in schools in order to more carefully track the progress of students across objectives. This recent trend—to track carefully on an objective-by-objective basis the instructional progress of students—has led to another trend: providing criterion-referenced information on norm-referenced tests. The information comes in the form of scores on content or skill clusters. Such information can take the form of an individual profile, the profile of a school, or the profile of an entire district.

Field Observation: Have students contact the central office of a school district and arrange to interview administrators concerning the use of individual, school, and district-wide profiles based on standardized test results.

Principles in Practice 14.2

Principles . . .
1. Every distribution of scores has a central tendency and dispersion.
2. Standardized test scores are norm referenced.
3. Standardized test scores must be interpreted with reference to appropriate norm groups.

. . . in Practice
The teacher in Teacher Chronicle 14.2 did not have a clear idea of standardized test scores in general, and of stanines in particular. As a result, the teacher spent the conference "fending off" questions requiring technical knowledge of standardized scores. He had little useful information to share, and neither the teacher nor the parent learned much that would help the student, Dan. The most obvious outcome of the conference was that the teacher lost credibility.

1. How should the teacher have used norm group information in the conference with Mr. Longley?
2. How do stanines differ from grade equivalent scores?
3. How will you communicate standardized test results without giving statistics lessons to parents?

SETTLING THE SCORE

There was a note in my mailbox from Mrs. Geiger, the principal. "Could I see you at your break to discuss the math placements for next year?"

I jotted a quick response, left it in her mailbox, and went to get my math record book. I would review it during my study hall assignment in the sixth period. But I already knew that Mrs. Geiger had decided to make next year's placements based primarily on the most recent achievement test scores. Anyone with a 7 stanine or above would be slotted for fast-track math next year.

One student I had some reservations about was Heidi. She was a good average student who worked really hard in math, which did not come easy to her. I had been surprised to see that her stanine had been 7 on the test because I had expected it to be 5, maybe 6. At the time, I felt really pleased for her.

Yet, because Mrs. Geiger was asking us to base the following year's placement on one test score for the first time, I was having second thoughts.

The announcement for this new policy was still clear in my head. It was short and direct. "Math placements for the next school year will be based upon student achievement tests. Any student scoring 7th stanine or above will be placed in the fast-track math classes."

The note left little room for discussion, but I knew I had to convince her that Heidi would be better off in a general math class next year. Taking a firm grip on my grade book, I headed for the showdown.

"Let's sit at the table while we look at the test scores."

"Fine," I said, pulling out a chair next to hers and opening my grade book.

"Are there any students you have concerns about?" she asked, catching me off guard.

"Yes, there is one in particular, Heidi Rogers. I realize that she did in fact score in the 7th stanine on the test, but I feel that it would be a disservice to her to place her in the fast track next year."

"Why?" Mrs. Geiger asked, scanning my grade book for her name.

"For two major reasons," I answered, pointing to Heidi's name. "Look at the test results. She was in the 7th stanine for computation, but only in the 5th in math reasoning. Her daily work reflects this split, too, but to a greater degree. Heidi is an extremely hard worker in class. She is attentive in every lesson, but she has to work her fingers to the bone to grasp new concepts. For example, her mother told me at the last conference that she spends at least an hour every night working on math problems. When we begin a new unit she sometimes spends two or three hours trying to understand the new material. It appears to me that her computation score is on the high side because of her sheer determination to work computations."

Mrs. Geiger nodded her head. "What's the second reason?"

"The 5 stanine reflects the difficulty she has in math reasoning. I see it in class and on her homework. She has a hard time figuring out word problems in particular. She often guesses which operation to use. When she does the computation, she is usually correct. However, more often than not she uses the wrong operation to answer the word problem."

"So she's high at one end and average on the other," Mrs. Geiger said, summing it up.

"Right," I agreed. "I would hate to have her swallowed up in the fast track based on this one test. She'd work her heart out, but the results would not be worth the effort."

"I think we should keep her in general math next year then. Is there anyone else you have concerns about?"

"No, not really. But I appreciate the opportunity to discuss Heidi with you. It is a good decision for her."

■ ■

ISSUES IN STANDARDIZED TESTING

Chap. Obj. 4–5
Test Ques. 14.71–14.104

Focus Questions: How should legitimate concerns over standardized tests govern their use? What form will standardized testing take in the near future?

Chapter 15 Casebook Preview: See Writers' Tea.

Haney and Madaus (1989) classified the complaints most commonly expressed against tests. Among those complaints are that tests are biased against some kinds of students, they reduce teaching to preparing students for the tests themselves, and they focus time on lower-order thinking skills. We will examine these criticisms in the sections that follow.

Test Bias

A major and long-standing criticism of tests is that they are biased toward certain types of students. Flaugher (1978) identified the several definitions of test bias that have been used in discussing the appropriate use of tests. For example, a test can be thought to be biased if the scores of one group of students are lower, on average, than those of other groups. Such results may indicate differences that can be attributed to test bias, but this is not necessarily the case. Differences on the test may be due to unequal educational opportunity of the groups being tested.

Some have argued that a test is biased if the following faulty assumption is made: Tests measure the same characteristics for all examinees. If we assume, for example, that all examinees taking the math achievement test can read the instructions equally well, then we would attribute differences in their scores to math ability. However, two students of equal math ability may be unequal in their ability to read and follow instructions on the test. In that case, reading ability and not math ability would account for differences on the test.

Other critics have argued that the sexist or racist content of a test is a form of bias. When the language and pictures used on a test do not represent the gender and racial balance of the examinees, or when undesirable role stereotypes are perpetuated, the test is thought to be culturally or subculturally biased. A test can also be biased if it predicts performance more accurately for one group than for another group. If, for example, the SAT did a better job of predicting success in higher education for students from urban high schools than for students from rural high schools, the test would be thought to be biased.

Teacher Interview: Have students interview teachers concerning their experiences with test bias.

For tests used to make selections, such as the Graduate Record Examination (GRE) or other tests of aptitude or achievement used to include or exclude students from instructional opportunity, bias can exist if the criteria for selection is unfair to students scoring lower on the test.

A test can be biased if it is used in the wrong way. Suppose a company tested its prospective employees using an examination that measured skills and aptitudes that were irrelevant for the job, but that systematically excluded one group or another. If the test results did not accurately predict success on the job, the use of that test would result in bias.

Tests can be biased if they are administered under conditions that unfairly affect certain groups. For example, a test might be administered that prevented someone with a physical disability from demonstrating the appropriate knowledge or skills needed to answer a question or questions.

Popham (1981) provides a general definition of test bias. **Test bias** occurs whenever aspects of tests, the way the test is administered, or the way the results are interpreted unfairly penalize or give an advantage to individuals as a result of their membership in some subgroup. Most instances of test bias are brought to light because a group has been penalized, but test bias can operate in both directions.

Bias and Anxiety

Bias can occur because of the anxiety that tests foster. Students come to learn very quickly how much importance is placed on standardized achievement tests. Standardized aptitude tests, especially those given later in a child's academic career, are even more critical to their futures. For example, tests such as the SAT are used to make decisions about college admission. Hill (1984) suggests that test anxiety affects as many as ten million elementary school students in the United States, the most serious cases occurring in formal testing situations. Students who are extremely anxious perform significantly better when testing conditions are less intimidating. They know material but cannot demonstrate their knowledge in a formal testing situation. For such students, the tests provide low and invalid estimates of their abilities.

Hill's review of the research indicates that there are three characteristics of standardized testing that contribute most heavily to test anxiety. The first is the time limits and pressures of a standardized test. The second is test difficulty. Standardized tests are norm referenced; the goal of the test is to discriminate between students. Such tests are bound to contain difficult items. The final characteristic that contributes to test anxiety is the mechanics of the test, such as the instructions and the question formats. Hill recommends that teachers can help alleviate test anxiety by teaching test-taking skills to students who suffer from this anxiety in standardized test situations.

Test-taking skills can be enhanced by familiarizing students with various item types, having them read test instructions carefully and giving them feedback on their interpretations of those instructions prior to taking the tests. Such feedback can alleviate some of the student's anxiety, and help the learner gain confidence in his or her ability to take such tests. Another recommendation is simply to provide more time for taking tests in order to alleviate that pressure.

Finally, Hill recommends that we attempt to simplify test instructions and mechanics. Practically speaking, teachers have little control over the form of standardized achievement, aptitude, and diagnostic tests. The instructions are prescribed and must be followed closely in order to maintain the validity of the test. It seems reasonable, given what we know about the human memory and information-processing techniques (see Chapter 6), to

Journal Entry: Have students reflect on their experiences of anxiety in relation to standardized tests, considering how these experiences will help them counsel future students who experience test anxiety.

Teaching Anecdote: Tell your students about the teacher who had had two poor evaluations and was scheduled for a third evaluation. In each previous evaluation, the principal had cited the poor performance of the teacher's class on standardized tests as a major problem that had to be corrected. The teacher, determined to keep his job, decided to "teach to the test" the entire year. He geared his instruction to the material he thought would most likely be on the test.

Ask your students how professional this action was and if such test-driven instruction might actually improve student performance on tests or their ability to learn.

PATRICIA WOODWARD

LINCOLN JUNIOR HIGH SCHOOL

FORT COLLINS, COLORADO

Being asked to articulate my philosophy of education brings to mind the response my mother used to make when a well-meaning friend or acquaintance would comment on one of her children's accomplishments; "I take no credit, and I take no blame." On the surface, her reply might have seemed detached or uncaring. Yet, with further thought, we realized that her attitude was truly a compliment to her son or daughter. She knew that responsibility for achievement or failure rested ultimately with the child. This is not to say that she had nothing to do with what her children were taught (or *not* taught), but that whatever resulted from that teaching was our own. We could take ownership of our achievements and/or failures. However, my mother, like any good teacher, worked long and hard to make sure that we were equipped to take on this responsibility. She challenged, she motivated, she encouraged, she corrected, she shared information, she guided. In short, she taught. In the end, she applauded, "You did it!" Teachers should give credit where credit is due, as my mother did. But we cannot be absolved of the necessity of giving our students all they need to be able to assume responsibility for their own education. We will be held accountable for developing skills, for motivating desire, for guiding inquiry.

Ours is a profession that is in the spotlight of public scrutiny. The results of our efforts do not go unnoticed. Every year, we graduate living testimonials to our teaching who go on to either higher education or employment. The skills they have acquired—or have failed to acquire—will be obvious. Whether we teach English, math, science, woodworking, or power mechanics, our students will be using the information they have stored and the talents they have developed in endeavors to which they are best suited.

Not every student will develop the same level of skills, but teachers of conscience must be able to say that every student was shown the way. We must give our students whatever guideposts they will need, whether they be punctuation rules, algebraic equations, or proper sanding techniques. Without the necessary information, critical thinking skills and decision-making abilities, all students, not only the dyslexic or the inept, but the "average learner" and even the gifted as well, will be handicapped—and who is to blame? The teacher.

Regardless of how well the information is presented, if the student does not possess the desire to learn, the teaching will be incomplete. Motivation is undoubtedly the crux of the learning process; instilling a love of learning where little or none exists and encouraging that which is

try to adapt the test-taking environment to the student. More importantly, the teacher can try to shape behaviors that are adaptive in test-taking situations.

Minimum Competency Testing

An important trend in standardized testing is the use of so-called minimum competency tests. Minimum competency testing came about as a response to the public's perception that our educational system was not teaching our students basic skills. Most states created laws requiring minimum competency testing. The most common type of minimum competency testing required that students pass comprehensive exams before being awarded high school diplomas. Minimum competency tests have also been used as a basis for promotion at various grade levels.

The purpose of minimum competency testing, as first designed, was twofold. First, these tests were to ensure that students graduating with a

Field Observation: Have students check with the local school district concerning the policy on minimum competency tests.

already there, remains our challenge. If we look to our own motivation for teaching, perhaps we will be more successful in inspiring a love of learning in our students. Do we love both our subject and our students? Are we interested and excited by words, ideas, and concepts? Do we have faith in our students' innate yearning for knowledge and ability to recognize what is important? Are we willing to look for the particular key that will unlock this unique personality, that individual mind? Not every teacher will succeed every day with every student because we are limited in our understanding of all that goes on in each of their lives. Nevertheless, we are given the charge to not only show the way, but to encourage the journey. Kahlil Gibran said it well, "The teacher . . . leads you to the threshold of your mind."

Once our protégés have embarked upon the journey—shown an interest in the subject (however small or great the journey might be)—it is the teacher's responsibility to act as a guide. We must become their mentors, encouraging them to continue their quest. Whether the student's interest is long lived or limited, the teacher must attempt to keep that interest alive. We must have a thorough knowledge of our content area and inquiring minds of our own so that we can point our students in the direction of excellence. Because our students leave our classrooms does not mean they leave our lives—or that we have left theirs. Our influence continues. When students write to say, "I remember when you told me . . .," or "My interest in social ethics began in the ninth grade when you gave me *Brave New World* to read," or "Thank you for showing me that . . .," we are reassured that, yes, we do have impact and we do have a responsibility for encouragement.

That encouragement may be just the support a student needs to achieve his or her full potential. Whether it is of a technical, intellectual, or personal nature, the teacher's support can help students achieve. In the end, we are in the race together: teachers are the coaches, the cheerleaders, and fans; the students are the track stars. Whether they win the race or not, the glory (or the chagrin) belongs to them, but without us there would be no race.

Do teachers take the credit? Do we take the blame? No. That belongs to the students, but we have our own "promises to keep." In becoming teachers, we promise, albeit tacitly, to share our knowledge, to inspire a love of learning, and to encourage excellence. To do less would be an abdication of a sacred responsibility.

high school diploma had achieved minimum skills. Second, they were to provide schools with an incentive to better educate students in basic skills. As minimum competency testing became more common, legal issues were raised, including the fairness of such tests when administered to special education students and minorities. Again, this is the issue of test bias. A major related problem that remains unsolved is that of defining precisely what competency is. An answer to the question is critical for those who must establish the cut-off scores that will be used to make judgments about graduation or promotion (Cunningham, 1986).

Measurement-driven Instruction

One result of minimum competency testing has been identified by Popham (1987) as **measurement-driven instruction,** which "occurs when a high-stakes test of educational achievement, because of the important contingencies associated with a student's performance, influences the instructional program

measurement-driven instruction An instructional program that is designed to prepare students for a test.

Minimum competency testing was designed to ensure that students who graduated from high school had mastered a prescribed set of basic skills, and by doing so, such testing provided schools with an incentive to teach these skills.

Teaching Anecdote: Tell your students about the first-grade student who had just begun to read. However, when she took a standardized reading test, she scored at a level that indicated that she needed remedial instruction. Her teacher, realizing the difference between her classroom performance and the test results, had her retested two months later. The results showed a dramatic gain in reading skill.

Ask your students what this story might reveal about testing young children. Ask them how a teacher's classroom evaluations might be taken into account when interpreting test results.

Lecture Note: Take the presentation of these criteria as an opportunity to argue that if tests are constructed to evaluate outcomes considered important or even critical, then measurement-driven instruction is desirable.

that prepares students for the test" (Popham, 1987, p. 680). A high-stakes test is one that qualifies students for promotion or graduation or one that is used to evaluate instructional quality. A high-stakes test serves as a "curricular magnet" (p. 680).

Popham argues that measurement-driven instruction can improve the quality of education if five criteria are met.

- Clearly described criterion-referenced tests must be used so that teachers can target their instruction.
- Tests must measure worthwhile content and skills.
- Tests should each be limited to a reasonable number of essential skills. Popham suggests five to ten.
- Tests should be constructed so that they lead to effective instructional sequences.
- Instructional support must be provided.

The general idea is that in those cases where measurement drives instruction, the instruments used to measure must be constructed with that effect in mind.

Tests by their very nature have the capability of driving instruction. Take, for example, a large urban school district whose students were given a state-mandated test, as were students in all of that city's schools. The test was originally designed to measure basic skills. It was administered to determine which schools within the districts had an unacceptably high percentage of students who had not achieved basic skills. The results of the tests were to be used by the state's Department of Education as the basis for its allocation of monies for remedial instruction. Thus, the purpose of the test was to formulate a plan for the allocation of instructional monies.

After the first administration of this test, a local newspaper printed the results of the test by rank, ordering the performance of the schools within the district. The publicity led some schools in the district to encourage their teachers to focus their instructional efforts on the skills represented on the test. The point is that the test became a matter of very high stakes for a number of schools. The purpose of the test changed from being the basis for allocating monies to judging which schools in the city were the best and worst. The measurement began to drive instructional programs. Again, a caveat comes into play. When using tests, we must be aware of the purpose for which they are designed. Bracey (1987) argues that measurement-driven instruction leads to a fragmented and narrow curriculum, to trivialism, and to stagnation of the curriculum and instruction.

There is movement within the educational community to address the problems associated with the tendency of standardized tests to drive instruction. One way to address the problem is to define minimum competency as consisting of a higher level of skills than have been required in the past (see Koffler, 1987). Another attempt to solve the problem of measurement-driven instruction is an approach to measurement called curriculum-based assessment (Tucker, 1985).

Although curriculum-based assessment is not a new practice, there is a renewed interest in this approach. **Curriculum-based assessment** involves testing students with materials taken directly from their school curriculum. Such testing provides on-going information that is more useful for instructional planning than standardized achievement tests because it aligns assessment with instruction. As applied to students with learning disabilities, curriculum-based assessment provides teachers with information for matching student ability with instruction, rather than simply diagnosing the disability.

Computerized Adaptive Testing

A final trend in standardized testing is computerized adaptive testing (Eller, Kaufman, & McLean, 1986–1987). **Computerized adaptive testing** uses computer programs that gather information about a student's ability and then provide test questions based on that information. The most sophisticated software systems evaluate ability after each question. Eller et al. suggest that computerized adaptive testing is one way in which technology may contribute to alternatives in testing, expanding the range of information obtained from testing. Although the widespread use of computerized adaptive testing has not yet occurred, clearly we will continue to see growth of this technique for obtaining evaluative information.

Some problems with this technology as a measurement instrument have become evident as the use of computer-based testing continues to grow (Sarvela & Noonan, 1988). Some of the computer-based testing issues being researched include the problems of human factors or how humans interact with computers. Such questions include the degree of feedback provided by computer programs and the timing of that feedback. The ability to change a previous answer raises questions about the reliability and validity of computer-based tests. Problems of item type are being addressed as well. The technology, especially the software, is not yet developed enough to handle constructed response items, even though such items seem to be the most appropriate.

curriculum-based assessment Evaluation based on materials taken directly from the school curriculum.
computerized adaptive testing Testing that uses computer programs that present items tailored to the abilities and skills of the student.

Teacher Interview: Have each student interview a teacher regarding political pressure and test performance, asking the teacher to contrast these concerns with Popham's criteria.

Lecture Note: Again, the reminder: Tests aren't bad but sometimes the uses to which tests are put are bad.

Connection: See the discussion of formative evaluation in Chapter 13.

Journal Entry: Have students reflect on computerized adaptive testing and the kinds of information it might supply them in the future, considering how they will use computerized adaptive testing for instructional planning and for evaluation.

Lecture Note: Have students form small groups. Have them imagine that they have been placed on a task force by a school district and charged with generating a plan for implementing computer-based testing. Ask each group to generate a list of five recommendations.

Teacher Interview: Have each student discuss with a practicing teacher how one balances the need for norm-referenced evaluation with the need to understand students as individuals.

Questions of motivation are also attracting the attention of researchers. The effect of negative consequences is being studied in particular. There are also questions about differential motivation effects for high and low achievers.

Using computer-based tests requires the use of many different items that address similar skill areas. This is a problem of nonequivalence of groups. Very often, students will see different numbers of items and items that are different. The order that the items are presented in will change and items will be administered at different times in a course. All of these problems result in nonequivalent comparison groups. As we have learned, in order to make norm-referenced comparisons, the norm groups must consist of people who have been tested under identical conditions.

Principles in Practice 14.3

Principles . . .

1. The use of standardized tests to make decisions requires an understanding of the possible sources of bias.
2. The use of standardized tests as a measure of competency can influence instructional programs.
3. Adaptive testing techniques take into account the student's ability level.

. . . in Practice

In Teacher Chronicle 14.3, the teacher was concerned about using the results from one standardized achievement test as the basis for placing a particular student. By analyzing the components of the overall score and corroborating the test results with classroom data, the teacher was able to convince the principal that Heidi should not be placed in the fast-track math group. Without the careful analysis of the standardized test results and a comparison with classroom work, Heidi would have "automatically" gone into that group. The analysis lead to a decision that reversed the principal's intention, but which satisfied both the teacher and the principal.

1. In what sense did the principal's "stanine score" criterion disadvantage Heidi?
2. How did the achievement test help in making the placement decision concerning Heidi?
3. How might computerized adaptive testing aid placement decisions such as the one made in Teacher Chronicle 14.3?

Assign Chapter 14 of the Study Guide.

CONCLUSION

The issues of measurement and evaluation raised in this chapter and in Chapter 13 help us as teachers to understand some important principles. First among these is the principle that as teachers we should be aware of the evaluative purposes to which measurements will be put. As consumers of standardized test information, we must be aware of the purpose for which a test is designed. We must also be aware of how standardized scores are generated. We must always be aware of the norm group from which a particular student comes, so that we avoid the tendency to read into numerical data meanings that may not be there.

Standardized tests are a means to an end, they are not the end in themselves. Such tests require adherence to a set of statistical principles from which standardized scores, in their myriad forms, are reported. Statistics are the tools we use to communicate information. And as is the case with all tools, they can be mishandled by those without the proper training to use them. Whenever teachers interpret the results of statistically generated scores, they would do well to keep in mind that statistics, as a set of procedures, are "stupid."

Statistics are stupid in the same way that computers are stupid. In order for a computer to do the job that we require of it, we must tell the computer, through a program, every single step to take. If we misinform the computer, it will misinform us.

The same is true of statistics. Statistics are a set of numerical operations waiting to be turned on. It matters not to the statistical procedures what the numbers are, where the numbers came from, or what the numbers mean. Making those determinations is the job of those of us who must consume and interpret statistically generated scores.

It would be possible, for example, to calculate the average telephone number of the students in your class. The statistical procedures would be happy to accommodate your request. But what would you do with the statistical results? If you determined that the average telephone number of your class was 563–4776.3738264, how would you use that information? We must take care in using the results of standardized tests. Not only because it is tempting to read additional information into those results, but because testing has a way of providing too easily used labels.

Many years ago, the terms *imbecile, idiot,* and *moron* were clinical diagnostic labels. Clinical psychologists would use the results of tests to categorize subjects as belonging to one of these clinical groups. We all know what happened to those clinical labels. Today we have new labels; tomorrow we will have still others. Educational labels come from measurements and from evaluative judgments based on the use of standardized tests. We are quick to convert standardized scores into labels. We are quick to say that a person with an IQ of 150 is gifted. Perhaps more importantly, our students understand labels as well as we do as adults. Students are very good at taking diagnostic labels and incorporating them into their self-evaluations.

Chapter Summary

Introduction: Professional Judgments
Teachers are required to make professional judgments. Some of the information on which judgments that are critical to students' futures are made comes from standardized tests.

Norm-referenced and Criterion-referenced Measurement
Tests are forms of measurement. All measurement is based on comparison. Norm-referenced tests compare students with other students who took the

same test (fellow members of the norm group). Criterion-referenced tests compare students' performances to a set of external criteria.

Types of Standardized Tests
Standardized tests are tests that are administered to and norm-referenced on a large number of people. The scores from standardized tests are based on the performances of the people who took the test. The results of standardized tests can be used for several different purposes.

Achievement Tests
Achievement tests are standardized tests designed to measure what students have learned.

Aptitude Tests
Aptitude tests are standardized tests designed to measure students' potential or aptitude. An aptitude test may measure potential narrowly—as in the case of a specific job, or broadly—as in the case of general academic potential.

Diagnostic Tests
Tests designed to measure specific strengths and weaknesses for the purpose of making decisions about a student's learning program are called diagnostic tests.

Comparing People and Numbers
Standardized test results are numerical descriptions of a student's performance. It is important to keep in mind that the measurement of a student's performance is not the student—tests indicate, but do not define, what a student might accomplish.

Standardized Test Scores
Standardized test scores are numerical comparisons of students' performances on a standardized test. The scores are based on statistics that describe the distribution of test scores.

Properties of Distributions
All distribution of test scores have two basic properties. *Central tendency* indicates where the middle of a distribution of score is. A distribution's *dispersion* refers to how similar or different the scores are from one another.

The Normal Distribution
The normal distribution is a theoretical distribution that accurately describes many of the characteristics important to educators. It is the basis for many standardized test scores.

Issues in Standardized Testing
Test Bias
Test bias occurs when a group of students is placed at a disadvantage when a test is administered, scored, or interpreted. Possible test bias must be considered when using the results of standardized tests to make decisions about students.

Minimum Competency Testing
Minimum competency tests are used to certify students in some way. A test that must be taken and passed in order to graduate from high school is one example of a minimum competency test. A danger to guard against with minimum competency tests is the possibility that these "high-stakes" tests may drive instruction.

Computerized Adaptive Testing
Computerized adaptive testing requires the use of sophisticated computer programs that present test items based on the abilities and skills of the test-taker. By tailoring test questions to the ability of a student, new and perhaps more useful evaluative information can be gained.

Reflections: Building Your Theory of Teaching

14.1 One of your students scores very well on a standardized test. How will you explain to her that, although she did do well on the test, you have decided she will remain in the low group/track?

14.2 Suppose you decided that one of your students—who has not demonstrated a sufficiently high IQ or produced outstanding standardized test scores—should be transferred from your school and to a gifted and talented "magnet" class in another building. How would you convince your principal that your decision is correct?

14.3 Draft a letter to parents and/or students that will accompany the report of the yearly standardized achievement scores. Include some helpful hints in interpreting the scores themselves and some caveats about the "meaning" of these scores that you would like them to keep in mind.

Key Terms

Suggested Readings

Archibald, D., & Newman, F. (1988). *Beyond standardized testing: Authentic academic achievement in the secondary school.* Reston, VA: NASSP.

Cole, N. S. (1981). Bias in testing. *American Psychologist, 36,* 1067–1077.

Ebel, R. L., & Frisbie, D. A. (1991). *Essentials of educational measurement.* Needham Heights, MA: Allyn & Bacon.

Green, B. F. (1981). A primer of testing. *American Psychologist, 36,* 1001–1011.

Gronlund, N. E., & Linn, R. L. (1990). *Measurement and evaluation in teaching* (6th ed.). New York: Macmillan.

References

Bracey, G. W. (1987). Measurement-driven instruction: Catchy phrase, dangerous practice. *Phi Delta Kappan, 68,* 683–686.

Carey, L. M. (1988). *Measuring and evaluating school learning.* Newton, MA: Allyn & Bacon.

Cunningham, G. K. (1986). *Educational and psychological measurement.* New York: Macmillan.

Eller, B. F., Kaufman, A. S., & McLean, J. E. (1986–1987). Computer-based assessment of cognitive abilities: Current status/future directions. *Journal of Educational Technology Systems, 15,* 137–147.

Flaugher, R. L. (1978). The many definitions of test bias. *American Psychologist, 33,* 671–679.

Glaser, R. (1963). Instructional technology and the measurement of learning outcomes: Some questions. *American Psychologist, 18,* 519–521.

Gronlund, N. E. (1985). *Measurement and evaluation in teaching* (5th ed.). New York: Macmillan.

Haney, W., & Madaus, G. (1989). Searching for alternatives to standardized tests: Why, whats, and whithers. *Phi Delta Kappan, 70,* 683–687.

Hill, K. T. (1984). Debilitating motivation and testing: A major educational problem—Possible solutions and policy applications. In R. E. Ames & C. Ames (Eds.), *Research on motivation in education: Vol. 1, Student motivation.* New York: Academic Press.

Koffler, S. L. (1987). Assessing the impact of a state's decision to move from minimum competency testing toward higher level testing for graduation. *Educational Evaluation and Policy Analysis, 9,* 325–336.

Kubiszyn, T., & Borich, G. D. (1987). *Educational testing and measurement.* Glenview, IL: Scott, Foresman.

Popham, W. J. (1981). *Modern educational measurement.* Englewood Cliffs, NJ: Prentice-Hall.

Popham, W. J. (1987, May). The merits of measurement-driven instruction. *Phi Delta Kappan, 68,* 679–682.

Sarvela, P. D., & Noonan, J. V. (1988). Testing and computer-based instruction: Psychometric considerations. *Educational Technology, 28*(5), 17–20.

Tucker, J. A. (1985). Curriculum-based assessment: An introduction. *Exceptional Children, 52,* 199–204.

15
Casebook of Successful Teaching

ELEMENTARY SCHOOL
  Student of the Week
  Beginning Each Day as a Learning Experience
  I Am Leo
  Responsibility Education
  Taking Control

JUNIOR HIGH/MIDDLE SCHOOL
  Around the World
  Coup D'Etat in the Classroom
  Science Is Only Real When You Do It
  Bringing the Real World into the Classroom

HIGH SCHOOL
  Gifted Achievers and Underachievers
  Improvisation and Aesthetic Appreciation
  Book Writing
  Writers' Tea
  Please Sign This Contract
  Writing Success in Science

Chapter Overview

Someday you will be standing in front of a classroom of students; it will be your responsibility to teach them. What problems will you face? What solutions will you try?

This casebook contains accounts of real problems and their successful solutions written by expert teachers. These teachers observed their students, identified problems, formulated solutions, and tested those solutions.

These cases are organized by elementary school, junior high/middle school, and high school levels. The experiences the teachers discuss range from working with individuals or small groups to entire classes of students. Each of these cases is presented by a different teacher. As a result, they differ in style and length.

As you read the cases, ask yourself how the teacher identified the problem and then went about solving it. Most importantly, ask why the solution worked. Using your knowledge of educational psychology, reflect on why the teacher in each of these cases was successful. ■

ELEMENTARY SCHOOL

Student of the Week

Connections: Chapter 4, Cultures and Values; Chapter 5, Changing Behaviors

In the following account, Nanci Maes's goal is "to promote a positive attitude and a good self-image in each of my students." To this end she created the "Student of the Week" program. In addition to working in the affective domain, Nanci's approach also demonstrates the way in which an excellent teacher brings a number of separate cognitive curricular activities together under one thematic umbrella. Through the "Student of the Week" program, Nanci gives students the opportunity to practice speaking, organizing, and demonstration skills; she links social studies to families and friends; and she provides opportunities for oral reading, all the while building each individual child's self-esteem.

In 1985, Nanci Maes was recognized as "Wisconsin Teacher of the Year."

One goal of elementary school teaching is to promote a positive attitude and a good self-image in each student. Building self-esteem, I feel, is of utmost importance. To promote this I began to implement a "Student of the Week" program. I have done this in my classroom for the past nine years with very favorable results.

At the beginning of the year, each child is assigned his or her special week. A letter goes home to the family explaining what this special week means. Children look forward to their week with great anticipation. Meanwhile, the child and his or her family can be making plans for each day of that week.

The "Student of the Week," leads the class each morning in the Pledge of Allegiance. He or she is in charge of putting up the calendar date and of conducting "Show and Tell" and "Daily News." The Student of the Week is the "Line Leader" for the week, and also the "Messenger," taking notes to the office, passing out all papers, and so on. During milk break the student is our "Milkman."

The Student of the Week has a special bulletin board to decorate with photographs of himself from babyhood on. The student is encouraged to include photos of her family, home, pets, vacations, and so on. The student is given the opportunity to tell the class all about the photos.

We set aside a table in class for the Student of the Week to set up displays. He can display any collection of favorite toys, souvenirs, and so on and is encouraged to tell about them. If the child has a hobby, she can explain it to the class and demonstrate it, or set up a display of things she has made.

During the week, the child is encouraged to read one of his favorite books to the class each day, tell his favorite jokes or riddles, and have record-books for the group to see and listen too.

The Student of the Week can make arrangements to bring pets to school to show the class and tell all about them.

The special student can also invite visitors to the classroom—Mom, Dad, grandparents and other relatives, friends, or neighbors—to tell the class about their jobs and careers or to demonstrate a craft or hobby for the group, or even show slides of special travels. This practice brings a wide range of occupational speakers and craftspeople into the classroom (and, not incidentally, correlates very well with our second-grade social studies curriculum).

The Student of the Week can bring a treat to pass out to the class. He is encouraged to bring a treat that he and his family have made together.

I have found that these "Student of the Week" activities have done a lot to increase each child's self-esteem, not only during the actual week, but in the anticipation and planning stages. The involvement of the family with the child adds to positive attitude development. I received much positive feedback from family members who enjoyed being involved in these activities with their children.

Beginning Each Day as a Learning Experience

How can a teacher present everything he or she is supposed to teach and still remain sane at the end of the day? There never seems to be enough time to teach all the required materials. When and how does one teach all the subjects and skills essential to a rich, functional curriculum?

Connections: Chapter 6, Memory Structures; Chapter 9, Level 1: Receiving or Attending; Chapter 10, Inductive Models; Chapter 12, Maintaining Attention

In the following case, Betsy F. Young of the Liholiho Elementary School in Honolulu discusses a way to integrate content and communication skills through the curriculum. Betsy F. Young, 1986 "Hawaii Teacher of the Year," has taught for fifteen years.

I begin the day by taking the daily tasks of morning business and having them serve multiple needs by integrating them with and applying to them listening, reading, writing, and thinking skills as well as the concepts and skills previously taught in content areas of science, social studies, and literature.

As one example, I will relate social studies to a foreign language. The class is currently studying about Japan so I provide for the students' exposure to the Japanese language and have them conduct morning business in Japanese. A meaningful and practical application of Japanese occurs as they learn, practice, and review their new language words of greeting, songs, days of the week, months of the year, simple requests, simple replies, counting, and weather.

Another important aspect of morning business periods is our daily sharing. A particular kind of sharing is designated for each day of the week. Mondays are teacher's sharing days. This practice gives me an excellent opportunity to model and set standards indirectly. I share poems, books, current events, and teach songs.

The students share from Tuesday to Friday. Each student is scheduled so that he or she knows what and when to share during the month and can plan accordingly. The class is divided into five groups. Each group is scheduled to present in one of three categories—current events, poetry, or books—during the week.

When sharing current events, the students search for articles related to the science, social studies, or literature units of study. For example, last month the students had to apply their newspaper reading skills in selecting articles related to our science units on plants, animals, and ecology. The following articles were shared: "Be Wary of Breakfast Foods," "How to Keep Costs Down, Nutrition Up," "Spoilage Signs in Cans," and "Guilty Dog Still Sought on Big Isle." The students prepare for the sharing by locating an appropriate article, reading it, and then writing a short summary. During their oral presentations, they point out the location of the incident discussed in the article on a map. These sharings bring additional real-life dimensions to our units.

When sharing poetry, the students choose poems related to the social studies and science topics and literature themes. They also attempt to identify specific literary elements previously taught within the poem of their choice. For example, Malie chose a poem by X. J. Kennedy, "The Whale Off Wales," and demonstrated her recognition of personification and simile in this poem. In addition, the students' own understanding of personification and simile enhanced their appreciation and comprehension of her piece. The students enjoy and appreciate the range of poems shared; these poems also serve as models for their own writing. Through exposures to poems on subjects about which they have done reading, they realize there are many ways to express ideas about a topic.

When sharing books, the students select books related to our study of literature and/or social studies topics for the month. They read, prepare, and creatively present their books. For example, upon selecting and reading a myth or tall tale, each student pretended to be a director or a member of a cast of characters for a play based on the story. In the context of enjoyable book-sharing activities, the students analyzed the qualities of the characters and identified similar qualities among their classmates.

I have found that students extend their range of reading, expand the ways they "sell" books to others beyond the traditional book report, and stimulate their own perceptions when interpreting stories through these book-sharing activities.

These morning activities directly address the students' needs for effective communication skills. The *daily* integration and application of content and communication areas has far reaching benefits for my students by providing the necessary involvement and practice to help them internalize content and refine their communication abilities. By using integration, all of this is accomplished within the limited amount of time given to the morning business periods.

Students who are assigned special topics to research and share become more involved in lessons and develop their research skills.

I Am Leo

Every school has a number of specialist teachers who serve unique student needs. Remedial teachers in elementary schools provide students with individual help outside the regular classroom environment, most commonly in math and language arts. These educators develop effective teaching techniques while working one-on-one with students. As the following case, "I Am Leo," illustrates, realizing individual student's needs and learning abilities, discovering the key to student motivation, and seeking the critical moment for making an academic connection is vital for any teacher.

Sue Misheff, now a college professor, was a K–6 reading specialist.

David could not read or write. He could recognize only the letters in his first name; he could not say the alphabet. He could not concentrate on one thing long enough to count a number of items past ten. He often confused his left hand and his right hand. He could not retell a story told to him in the proper sequence. For all appearances, David had a potentially serious learning problem as a six-year-old kindergartner.

In addition to his apparent lack of ability to achieve in school, David's home life had been unhappy until his recent adoption into a loving family. And, as if to ensure that David would be noticed somehow, nature had not endowed David with tear ducts, so that a continual tear always lingered in his eye.

When he was first referred to my remedial reading program, I learned that David could make up a wonderful story and that he enjoyed listening to books while I read to him. David exuded curiosity and a willingness to interact with the printed word that belied his underlying problems; and so I began our sessions together with a great deal of hope and a belief that one among all of the techniques that I planned to use would help him to grow.

By Christmas, however, David had made little progress and I was starting to feel as if I'd failed. None of the language experience activities that I'd used had seemed to enlighten him at all about the various forms and functions of print. The kinesthetic tactics that were supposed to increase David's awareness of individual letter patterns had obviously failed to do their job, for he still could only recognize and write the letters of his first name. Although we had read and enjoyed a number of books together, I could see no evidence that David connected what we were doing when we looked at pictures and listened to stories with the words on the page. I did not feel that I'd given David a gift of literacy for the holidays.

In late January, however, something happened that confirmed every belief in the power of stories to change the lives of people that I'd ever held. David had decided to take home a book/cassette kit of *Leo the Late Bloomer* by Robert Kraus. He chose the book himself because, as he said, he liked the cover; and I planned to have him tell me the story by using the pictures and what he remembered from listening to the tape at our next session.

When David returned the following week, he sat down, opened his book, pointed to the little lion and said, "That's me. I'm Leo." I had not seen David react so positively to a story, and I marveled as he continued pointing to the characters in the pictures.

"My dad is like Leo's dad."

"And is your mom like Leo's mom?"

"Yeah, she is."

Connections: Chapter 2, Egocentrism; Chapter 3, Stage 4: Identify versus Inferiority; Chapter 7, Self-reflective Capability; Chapter 8, Self-efficacy, Attribution Training; Chapter 14, Diagnostic Tests

So we spent that session talking about what it's like to be a late bloomer. David decided that Leo had bloomed because he *wanted* to; I said that I thought that sounded very sensible. We made word cards for three sentences—"Leo is like me," "Leo's dad is like my dad," and "Leo's mom is like my mom"—and deposited them into David's word bank. When David left to go back to his class, I knew that he'd received his overdue Christmas present. David had connected with a book.

I wondered, however, if David would remember his word-bank sentences the next week. He did, and was obviously proud of this new trick of being able to look at a sentence and tell me what it said. For the first time, he could point to the words in these three sentences and *read* them.

Since that time, David has continued to make progress. He has built his bank of words and has gained increasing control over his negotiation processes with print. David can recognize all of the letters in the alphabet now, and he is able to write letters other than the ones in his first name. His invented spelling indicates a new awareness of graphophonemic relationships; he takes delight in showing me how to spell. While David still lags behind his classmates, he's made a beginning, founded on the joy of discovering himself in a book.

Responsibility Education

Connections: Chapter 2, Organization; Chapter 3, Grade Level Characteristics/Intermediate Grades; Chapter 6, Automaticity; Chapter 7, Self-efficacy; Chapter 10, The Transfer Stages; Chapter 12, Rules-Reward-Punishment (RRP); Chapter 13, Alternatives to Grading; Chapter 14, Measures of Dispersion

How do we make students more responsible for their own learning? A major goal for many teachers is to have their students become more self-motivated and involved in taking responsibility for their own learning. We often ask students to be "more responsible," but rarely help them develop the attitudes or teach them the techniques needed for achieving more responsibility.

To overcome this difficulty, Chuck Bowen of Jefferson School in Morton, Illinois, developed a framework for responsibility education for his students. As an offshoot of his plan, Chuck had students participate in evaluating themselves, thus taking even more direct responsibility for their own learning.

Soon after I began teaching, I became frustrated with students' lack of responsibility, so I developed a responsibility education program to solve the problem. The program's goal is to have children become responsible, independent learners. They learn to set goals, evaluate their progress, and use organizational skills to succeed.

To help students become independent learners, I designed a child-centered grading system. I feel that grades should make sense to children. How else can students evaluate progress toward their own goals? Unfortunately, we often use grading systems that were designed for adults' convenience instead of children's understanding. For example, to a child limited to Piaget's "concrete operational thought," abstractions such as weighted grades seem more like magic than useful, relevant information. Furthermore, issuing report cards weeks after the work is done compounds students' confusion. I solved the problem with a weekly grading system based on concrete operations that students can understand and use as independent learners.

The skills students learn in the responsibility education program allow them to grow beyond being merely responsible. They learn to be independent and to strive for excellence. The "pay off" comes when the students take over the class.

For example, last year my fifth-grade class designed, organized, and carried out a very successful read-a-thon for world hunger. The students used their skills to set goals and organize committees. They gathered information, arranged publicity, designed ways and means to implement the project, and handled the money they raised. Along the way they taught themselves lessons in geography, earth science, political science, nutrition, and English. To further educate themselves and others they obtained a speaker and arranged a school assembly. The students examined charitable agencies to compare how well each would use their contributions to help the hungry. And of course, each student read five-hundred pages. In five weeks, the "500 For Food" read-a-thon raised about eight hundred dollars for world hunger.

As is demonstrated by the "500 For Food" read-a-thon, students can learn to be responsible, self-directed learners. It was designed, organized, and carried out by fifth graders who had learned not only to feel responsible for themselves and for others, but who had also learned how to be responsible.

Taking Control

Sometimes we are forced to ask ourselves, "Who really is in charge here?" As teachers we like to think of ourselves as being in control of the classroom, both in terms of learning and management. Our job is to instruct while smoothly coordinating a classroom filled with individuals. Sometimes, however, one student seems to have more influence on the class than we do. This student can be a disruptive child, a child with intense curiosities that override other children's interest, a child undergoing emotional problems or a student with exceptional needs.

How does one deal with a child who seems to be determined to run your room? In this case, Barbara Vinson realizes that one child in her class of moderately disabled students is controlling her room. She analyzes the problem and puts into place strategies that work toward solving the difficulties and allow her to regain control of the class.

Barbara Vinson is currently working on a doctorate in school psychology.

Connections: Chapter 5, Consequences of Behavior, Shaping; Chapter 11, Individualized Education Program

I was hired to teach a public school class for intermediate moderately mentally handicapped (MoMH) students that had a reputation for defiance of its teachers and of the school's rules. There were ten students in the classroom—nine boys and one girl. One student in particular, who had been referred by at least two teachers for emotional problems, and who had entered the primary MoMH class from a class for the seriously emotionally handicapped, was often in control of the classroom. His behaviors included making threats on the life of the teacher by imaginary uncles, kicking the wall, saying that absent students had been misbehaving, attributing behaviors to students who were incapable of performing those behaviors, and chanting.

I decided to use a form of response cost that emphasized good behavior. In other words, I wanted to catch them being good and then reward that behavior. The system was color coded, using green, yellow, and red tokens. At the beginning of the day, everyone started out in the "green." This meant that everyone had two smiley faces in the green, two in the yellow, and two frowning faces in the red. When a child exhibited a negative behavior, he was given a warning. If the behavior occurred again, the child lost a smiley face from the green and was sent to time-out for three minutes. At the end of the three minutes, if the child was calm, he or she was allowed to rejoin the class. If the child was not yet calm, the timer was reset for another three minutes. If, at the end of that time, the child was still not calm, he or she was given a choice of being calm or losing another smiley face. I explained to the child that although he or she had lost one smiley face, he or she was still in the green, but if he or she chose to continue the negative behavior, he or she would then be out of the green. Once out of the green, the child was reminded that he or she was still in the yellow.

At the end of the day, if a child was still in the green, the child was allowed to have popcorn while watching a movie. If the child was in the yellow, the child was allowed to watch the movie and still had tomorrow's recesses. If a child lost all of the smiley faces, then the child was in the "red," which meant no movie and no popcorn, but he or she could have recesses the following day. A child who had lost all of his or her frowning faces was no longer in the red and would lose recesses for the following day.

The color coding and rewards were combined with the verbal feedback that the child received from the teacher. For me, this feedback was the most important part. For example, if a child had an extremely bad day and was in the red at the end of the day, I would say to that child as he or she was leaving, "Tomorrow, you *will* have a good day." I emphasized the "will" instead of saying, "I *hope* you have a good day."

This technique resulted in a transference of external control to internal control. For example, eventually, as the students were leaving for the day, they would say to the teacher, "Mrs. V., tomorrow I *will* have a good day!" I would then praise them for being so "grown-up and mature."

A problem with this technique occurred between the time the movie and popcorn were given and the time the school bus arrived. The disruptive student would act out or display other disruptive behaviors, knowing that he had received his reward for the day. When this occurred, I began passing out candy to those who were exhibiting desired behaviors. Those who acted out were ignored. This technique was successful in reducing the negative behaviors prior to bus arrival.

The technique I used has proven to be successful in reducing negative behavior. It does need to be used with other strategies to maintain or increase positive behaviors. It, also, has not been found to be effective in increasing production or quality of work. However, it was successful in reducing the amount of time the child spent out of the classroom (e.g., in the principal's office). The best part of this approach is that I regained control of my class in a positive way.

Test Ques. 15.16–15.27

JUNIOR HIGH/MIDDLE SCHOOL

Around the World

Connections: Chapter 5, Primary Reinforcers and Conditioned Reinforcers; Chapter 6, Understanding—from a Cognitive Perspective; Chapter 8, Attention; Chapter 11, Questioning; Chapter 13, Matching Items

Teachers must continually tackle the problem of enlivening factual material. Repetitious drills, reviews before tests, and rote memorization do not necessarily ensure that students will retain the information they have learned. Every teacher faces the difficulty of directly involving students in remembering specific information.

In an effort to overcome this difficulty, William Smyth developed an instructional game called "Around the World" in which the teacher asks questions and students answer. Smyth's game, however, excites and involves students as they increase their store of factual information.

By actively involving students with their subject matter, teachers can increase attention, motivation, and understanding.

William Smyth currently teaches in a school for academically and artistically gifted students.

Every teacher encounters the problem of students not being able to remember what they learned last week, last month, last quarter, or last semester. It is a typical problem. Students remember what they need to recall for the next test and then promptly forget the material. Then when cumulative tests come, students fall apart. They do not seem to remember material they should readily have at their fingertips. Whether the test is a teacher-made exam or a national standard of measurement, students and teachers look bad.

There is a solution, however. It is a game called "Around the World" that teachers and students can enjoy. Played daily or whenever time permits, the game can be adapted to all subjects and age levels. There are virtually no limits to how the game can be employed.

Simply stated, the teacher calls out questions and students answer. Two randomly selected students seated next to each other begin. They stand and the teacher asks a question such as "What is the continent on which we live called?" The first of the two students to say "North America" wins and advances to the next student. That student stands to face the challenger. The teacher asks another question. If the student who previously won wins again, he or she advances to the third student. If not, that student sits down in the seat of the second student, and the second student advances. The game continues for several rounds or as long as time permits. Each student tries to go "Around the World" or around the classroom by defeating all the other students. A prize may be offered for doing so.

Competition requiring calculations takes students to the chalkboard. With chalk in hand, the two competitors listen to the problem and work it as quickly as possible. When they are finished, they step back and point to the correct answer. If neither is correct, the teacher might allow students to work the problem again. Normally, whoever finishes first with the correct answer challenges the next student. Variations could include letting one half of the room challenge the other half. Points for right answers are tallied. Sometimes, points are awarded to both teams if students come up with correct answers within a certain time limit.

"Around the World" works beautifully with English grammar questions. A teacher might ask students to find the verb in the sentence, "John walked to school" or the proper noun in the sentence, "I asked Mary to come to the game." In science, questions could focus on scientific terms, body systems, parts of the universe, or animals and their habitats. Social studies is perhaps the easiest subject in which to formulate questions because there is seemingly no end to the number of geography questions a teacher can generate.

The game can be lots of fun and very effective even on a field trip. While on the bus, teachers and students can review material applicable to that particular extended classroom experience. The teacher asks questions as usual but calls on one student from each side of the bus beginning with the first student. Two new students may be called each time or the winner may continue and face a new challenger each time. Regardless, students do not stand up. They keep their seats, and everyone must be very quiet in order to hear the questions and answers.

There really are no limits to this game. Teachers and students will see its advantages immediately and think up a number of variations. If played regularly, students will remember material from earlier classes and surprise themselves and test administrators with the knowledge they have accumulated.

Coup D'Etat in the Classroom

Connections: Chapter 2, Adaptation; Chapter 6, Metaphors and Analogies; Chapter 7, Learning and Performance; Chapter 9, The Psychomotor Domain

All too often we as teachers feel that the classroom "show" must revolve around us. However, we often forget that learning is central to the classroom and the teacher doesn't have to be the main focus. By capturing students' imaginations through simulations, we put our classes on center stage, creating situations that students will "buy into" and learn from. Such simulations also allow students to explore the affective realm as they experience personal empathy/understanding.

Sandy Wiley captured such a moment when she responded to a current events situation by having her students simulate a coup d'etat in Panama. Not only did her students gain an appreciation for the Panamanian situation, but they were able to empathize with the Panamanians and better understand the events unfolding at the time.

The country of Panama was in turmoil. A military leader had just replaced the former president as head of the country in a coup d'etat.

Batesville is a town of 5,000 residents located in southeastern Indiana about an hour from both Cincinnati and Indianapolis. It is home for a *Fortune* 500 corporation and has an above-average per capita income.

My eighth-grade history class at Batesville Middle School had twenty-seven students. These students were grouped by past academic performance and fell into the upper half of the eight-grade class. We had a rotating news team that reported the major news events of the past day. The news was dominated by the Panamanian coup and the United States's response to it.

During the days that followed the coup, we studied Panama's geographic location; form of government; economic condition; relationship to the United States; and, of course, the strategic importance of the Panama Canal. We asked questions such as, "How could this happen?" "What events are likely to follow?" "Could this have a serious effect on the United States?"

I decided that a kinesthetic and visual approach to investigating those questions was appropriate. We would stage a surprise classroom coup d'etat. What follows is a list of the steps I took to organize the coup.

1. Outline the main concepts to which I want the students exposed and for which I want understanding to develop.
   - vulnerability of citizens
   - educational level of citizens
   - past dependence of citizens
   - the need to know what is happening around you
   - the fight for freedom
2. Identify the leaders of the various groups within the class: athletes, higher and lower achievers, lower-income boys and girls (I already knew who they were).
3. Notify the principal of my intentions.
4. Meet in secret with the selected leaders. Emphasize and define each role. (This meeting took place only hours before the class period.)

The coup was executed without too many hitches. The lights were turned out a few minutes after class started and the overthrow team emerged from the ranks. I was taken to the rear of the room under guard before the lights were turned on again. The dictatorship was established at once, new class rules were set up in the classroom, and a few students were mistreated (but not physically). I tried to mount a counteroffensive from my position by passing notes to encourage my followers to rebel but could not get enough support. After about thirty minutes, I called a halt to the demonstration as the situation was beginning to deteriorate. The classroom was a bit disarranged; files and desks had been moved and a sliding wall had been knocked from its track when a file was moved to block my view.

We talked and mostly just settled down for the remainder of the class period. Each student was asked to write about the experience for the next class period, considering such issues as the factors that contributed to the coup, how the dictatorship could have been avoided, how it could have been overthrown, and how far it could have progressed.

The following class period was spent studying the Panamanian situation and defining criteria to use as a guide for understanding and predicting the outcome in Panama over the next few weeks. Students were encouraged to watch the news for details and student predictions of the day the new government would topple were recorded and posted.

Science Is Only Real When You Do It

Finding the right match between the content of the curriculum and the social needs of adolescents presents unique problems for the junior high/middle school teacher. The difficulty becomes even more acute when teaching ab-

Connections: Chapter 2, Abstract Reasoning, Zone of Proximal Development; Chapter 3, Building Self-esteem and Social Community; Chapter 4, Learning Styles; Chapter 5, Contingencies; Chapter 7, Peer Models; Chapter 8, Fear of Success; Chapter 10, The QAIT Model, The General Inquiry Model; Chapter 11, Cooperative Learning in Teams; Chapter 12, The Ripple Effect

In science, the use of rotating labs promotes hands-on experience, group interaction, and enthusiasm.

stract concepts of science and math. As Faye McCollum found out, involving students with hands-on activities and allowing for much-needed social interaction, engages them while they learn.

Faye was one of thirty teachers selected in 1989 to fly into the crater of Mt. St. Helens. As her case study demonstrates, she is obviously a believer in hands-on education for her students as well as herself.

A dedicated teacher must deal with the learning styles of students. Usually classroom education is sedentary, with instruction that involves lectures, demonstrations, and writing. These strategies leave most students passive and uninvolved in the learning process. Studies have shown that student learning abilities fall into three categories: Kinesthetic/tactual, auditory, and visual. If students are to succeed at learning, some method of instruction must address these needs. The first priority of any teacher should be to reach an understanding of how each student will best process the knowledge presented to him or her. Only then is it possible to develop a plan to involve and instruct these students.

In an attempt to appeal to the various learning styles of my students, I developed the concept of rotating labs. Because I am dedicated to the idea that science is only real when you actually do it, I seek to promote group interaction, enthusiasm, and learning through channels that engage the students. I worked with the hypothesis that when given the opportunity to interact with peers in a social and academic environment, students would instinctively acquire the necessary task-related scientific information, whether it be auditory, visual, or kinesthetic.

Rotating labs allow students to work in small groups of three, four, or five at different tasks in the classroom. Students are involved in five different activities on a rotational basis; they are busy experimenting, reasoning, and problem solving rather than passively listening. Students compare and discuss lab results and are encouraged to spend extra time assisting each other. I am free to roam from station to station assisting, monitoring, and evaluating their performances.

To facilitate learning each lab is designed to simulate one of the three major processing methods. This method of instruction focuses on a set of well-defined, interrelated tasks in one subject area. During a study of weather, for instance, the lab setup may include the measurement of relative humidity, plotting hurricane activity, a filmstrip or video on weather fronts and forecasting, a computer tutorial program, reading a weather map, a weather crossword, and experiments with chemicals to develop land and sea breezes. All of these labs require intense use of learning skills. Students within the group are able to assist each other with difficulties or seek assistance from the teacher when necessary. The success of this method of classroom instruction is continually evident. Frequently students ask to go to lunch in lab groups, attend pep rallies together, or stay in the same lab groups for other assignments. As a vivid example, five students came to class with the number "2" on their sweatshirts. When asked what it stood for their response was "Oh, Ms. Mac, we're lab group 2."

During the past five years laboratory stations have become an integral part of our life and earth science curricula. Other teachers in our junior high have also adopted this teaching and learning method in a variety of disciplines. English students work in lab stations to practice vocabulary words, design scenes for stories, illustrate their own manuscripts, view filmstrips of short subjects, and present plays of their own creation. Social studies teachers, too, have successfully used this method of instruction.

The results of this attempt to discover a superior method of instruction has been very successful. Improvement has been verified by a significant increase in both the level of interest and in test scores. Students are so stimulated by the laboratory involvement that they frequently ask to come back after school to complete the labs offered for extra credit. Enthusiasm, interaction, involvement, and a change in attitude toward science have clearly been noticeable. The teacher's job of motivating students is easily accomplished and students are free to assimilate knowledge in ways that assure consistent success.

Bringing the Real World into the Classroom

All too many times teachers hear the complaint, "But this doesn't have anything to with the real world." This is a recurring complaint, particularly as students get older and wish to be more "adult." Although teachers often say, "You'll need this when you graduate," many students are eager to make the connection to the real world sooner than we expect.

Patricia Woodward, an English teacher at Lincoln Junior High in Fort Collins, Colorado, heard this complaint from many of her students and realized that she had to do something to address the problem. To bring the real world into her room, she devised a classroom management plan emulating the philosophy and management style of successful businesses.

Ms. Woodward was the 1986 "Colorado Teacher of the Year."

Ten years ago, in response to an apathetic student's complaint, "English doesn't have anything to do with the real world," I devised a classroom

Connections: Chapter 4, Achievement-related Value Conflicts; Chapter 5, Token Economies; Chapter 12, Giving Clear Instructions; Chapter 13, Table of Specifications; Chapter 14, Stanine Scores

management approach that does, in fact, emulate the philosophy and management style of successful businesses. I set up my classes to be run the way a large corporation is, complete with a board of directors (parents and school board members), personnel policy, salary schedule, job descriptions, incentives, and bonus trips for top producers.

In an effort to encourage adult, responsible behavior in a typical junior high, every academic grade was translated into economic terms. Instead of giving 25 points for a vocabulary quiz, I paid up to "$25." Rather than getting 100 points for an essay or test, a student could earn as much as "$100." Outstanding class participation, asking a good question, or exhibiting exemplary behavior could earn additional income. On the other hand, tardiness, disruptive behavior, sloppy work, or general "goldbricking" would result in a dock in pay.

Students were grouped into heterogenous "departments" of five or six "employees" and a supervisor, who had qualified, applied, and interviewed for the position. These students would work both individually and as a group to turn out high-quality work which would result in high "pay," bonus trips to a local country dinner playhouse, the respect and recognition of their peers, and the approval of their boss. Of course, students were not paid in real money, but with all the other "pay-offs," students enthusiastically accepted their nonnegotiable paychecks, which were then translated into traditional grades for the official records.

This system can be adapted quite easily to any content area with as little as or as much detail as the teacher wants to incorporate. The beauty of this approach is that it not only captures the imagination of the students, but it teaches responsibility, encourages creativity and initiative, and establishes a work climate that allows students to behave like adults.

HIGH SCHOOL

Gifted Achievers and Underachievers

Test Ques. 15.28–15.45

Connections: Chapter 3, Identity: A Closer Look; Chapter 4, Physical Disabilities; Chapter 5, Punishment; Chapter 8, Attribution Theory; Chapter 10, The Conflict Resolution Model; Chapter 11, Discussion Groups

The pressures on gifted students are many: their intellects often separate them from their peers; their interests involve them in activities outside the mainstream; and their perceptions of self, added to the expectations of others, increase their difficulties. Some gifted students respond to these pressures by becoming superachievers, trying to continually outdo themselves and others. Some gifted students will take the opposite tack and become underachievers, purposely accomplishing much less than they are capable of. Finding the right balance between the affective needs and the academic needs of gifted students is an ongoing challenge.

Jean Sunde Peterson, coordinator of the gifted program at Lincoln High School in Sioux Falls, South Dakota, realizes the difficulties faced by both highly motivated as well as underachieving gifted students. Through out-of-the-classroom, noon-hour discussion groups, she is helping these students better understand themselves and others, enabling them to come closer to successfully achieving their potential.

When I was first hired five years ago to direct and teach the gifted program at Lincoln High School, I carefully examined my experiences with highly capable students in the eighteen years I had taught English and German in the classroom. I particularly remembered several very bright, sensi-

Teachers can use discussion groups as a way to discover and to balance the affective and academic needs of gifted students.

tive, talented students who had seemed to struggle academically, socially, and/or emotionally, and for whom school often was not an enjoyable place to be. I remembered some who had even dropped out. I knew that some had tried, or at least had seriously considered, suicide. Some were anorexic; several had had ulcers. Some had even felt they were not "intelligent," letting their poor grades "define" them.

I wanted to create a program that might motivate underachieving gifted students and, at the same time, help achievers deal with the stress that often is the result of their own and others' high expectations. When students of high capability are not "productive," we lose a valuable natural national resource. And the prognosis is not good for achievers who are miserable.

Fortunately, my administrators gave me a great deal of autonomy. As one of twenty options in the program, I set up noon-hour discussion groups, which would bring together students who were achievers or underachievers, affluent or poverty stricken, "all-Americans" or those who struggle socially. They would meet in groups of ten to discuss the "burdens of capability." I felt that if they could come together and discover their commonalities, could peel off their adolescent facades, could break down the stereotypes and become merely human beings with much to share, and could honestly discuss personal and school issues, the achievers might relieve some stress and the underachievers might affirm their capability and become more motivated. They could learn from each other.

Since then, participation has grown annually from 30 to 60 to 90 to 110 this year, and I can quickly name 30 to 40 underachievers who have made significant academic and/or personal progress over two or three years of participation. I am convinced that the groups have contributed to these results. These students and all the others have gained skills in articulating personal concerns, have learned to support each other, have achieved a greater self-awareness, and have learned to affirm their intellects. They seem to have borne out my assumption that when affective needs are met, academic achievement often improves, and there can be joy in this achievement.

In the discussion groups students learn to articulate strengths and weaknesses; conflicts with parents and siblings; anxieties; relationship problems; mood swings; and problems associated with perfectionism, compulsivity, hypersensitivity, procrastination, and lack of motivation. They hear presentations by adults who survived adolescence intact, in spite of sharing similar problems. They learn to assess their own needs and to separate their needs from others' needs, and they learn to be careful about who and what they allow to "define" them—including tests and grades.

I quickly learned that I needed to "unlearn" many of my classroom teaching methods, opting for a "guide-on-the-side," rather than a "sage-on-the-stage" approach. Some students need to accomplish something each time, while others are content simply with good conversation.

I believe these groups are the most important element in our complex program. Apparently the students do, too. One wrote on an evaluation, "I, for one, need help in dealing with stress that comes from being capable. Our group is the only place I receive this help." Another said, "Counselors have to devote so much time to problem kids. I was really worried about college, but I felt I had no adult that I had a right to seek advice from. Discussion group seemed almost like therapy for me. The divorce discussion was especially helpful. Knowing what people my age worry about has made me feel more normal. Sometimes kids just need to talk." Yet another remarked, "I think I discovered some reasons why I haven't been doing well in school."

There is mutuality in this kind of learning for teacher as well as students. I believe we all leave each meeting a bit more motivated—and more at peace with ourselves.

Improvisation and Aesthetic Appreciation

Connections: Chapter 3, Moral Reflection; Chapter 6, The Model of Human Information Processing: Processes; Chapter 7, Self-reflective Capability; Chapter 9, The Psychomotor Domain; Chapter 10, The Synectics Model

While concentrating on academic content at the high school level, we often do not exploit the affective domain as an instructional tool. Appreciation for literature or art—an affective outcome—is hard to measure. Many times students can get a good "content" grade in these areas, without really gaining a lifelong, personal aesthetic appreciation for a literary or artistic masterpiece.

Recognizing this problem in her students, Nancy Gorrell of Morristown High School in Morristown, New Jersey, used improvisation to encourage aesthetic appreciation of Arthur Miller's *Death of a Salesman*. By creating a situation in which they acted out a particular scenario, Nancy helped her students gain experience that could be used with advantage when reading, discussing, and viewing the play.

Several years ago, I decided to experiment with the technique of improvisation as a method of "getting into" drama. I wanted my students to identify and empathize with the character, to "get into" the character's shoes, so that they might imagine the complexity of emotions, choices, and conflicts at the heart of the work. I developed a hypothetical office scene for my students to improvise that would parallel the critical office scene in the play, *Death of a Salesman.* My goal was to improve motivation (curiosity/enthusiasm), aesthetic appreciation, dramatic sensibility, and critical thinking.

I paired the students and gave them ten minutes to plan their improvisations. I told them to decide what office they were in, what characters they would be, and their respective roles. The results were highly successful. For students with no acting experience or ability, I was surprised and delighted with the ease and execution of this scenario. Students were immediately engaged in the conflict and fell naturally into the roles of the characters. They had no difficulty imagining an appropriate office setting. Ironically, several students created scenes similar to the parallel scene in *Death of a Salesman* during which the boss fires Willy. In their corporate office scenes, the boss either fires an incompetent employee or fires a woman employee who refuses sexual favors. Another improvisation scene that was successful involved a principal and student in a discipline office and the student being expelled.

Our improvisations provided a powerful anticipatory mood. My students were highly curious and eager to read the play. They were wondering how our improvisations related to *Death of a Salesman.* I told the class we had improvised a parallel scene and to look for that scene as we read the play. I told them Character A was Willy Loman, and they could think of this while they read. Our oral reading was no longer monotonous. Students intuitively felt the character and read with expression and emotion. When we arrived at the office scene, we acted it out in front of the class. Then we compared the scene with our improvisations. Students were amazed at the similarities. Next I showed Dustin Hoffman's interpretation of the same scene. Students were struck by the heightened emotions. They were expecting anger, frustration, and desperation, but they did not anticipate the explosions they saw on screen. Here was true appreciation—the kind that comes from experience. They too had imagined or played the role and they could anticipate Hoffman's actions and reactions.

I knew our experiment had succeeded by the sustained interest and motivation of my students, their eagerness to read the play, their attention to detail, and their insightful comments when analyzing and comparing the scenes. They had gained a dramatic sensibility. I saw this when they performed their improvisations, and when they acted as an appreciative audience for each other and Dustin Hoffman.

Several students pointed out that the improvisation improved their understanding of the office scene but not the entire play. Their point is well taken. The office scene sets the emotional context for the play and begins the plot, but it does not incorporate the complex emotional relationships of the family members that eventually becomes the center of the action. I asked my students if another improvisation based on the conflict exposed in the confrontational restaurant scene might be beneficial for future class instruction. Many agreed two improvisations might be helpful.

In conclusion, all students felt the improvisations were fun. One student wrote, "Acting out the play in front of the class really caused both interest and understanding to peak." Clearly, improvisation remains a useful envoy to aesthetic appreciation and understanding.

Book Writing

Connections: Chapter 9, Using Objectives, Alternative Views; Chapter 13, Nontest Evaluation Techniques

Getting students to extend themselves academically as well as creatively is a recurring challenge. We may encourage students to put forth their best efforts, but how do we get them to commit to personally achieve what we know they are capable of accomplishing?

Terri Fields of Sunnyslope High School in Phoenix, Arizona, identified this problem in her sophomore English classes. Wishing to have her students go beyond themselves creatively while applying the English skills they had been studying, she created a "Booked for Success" project that not only accomplished her goals, but enabled her students to become models for younger pupils. This project was awarded the Golden Bell by the Arizona School Boards Association as a most innovative curriculum idea, one that motivates students toward academic achievement.

How could I make students care enough about writing to submit their very best efforts? How could I give them the opportunity to apply their knowledge of the fiction elements that had been covered earlier in the semester? These were the two questions to which I sought answers when I designed the "Booked for Success" project. It succeeded far beyond my most fervent hopes.

In its simplest concept, the project entailed having each of my sophomore English students write a personalized book for an elementary school student. "Booked for Success" was set in motion when the principal at Mountain View Elementary School agreed to let my sophomore English students interview first graders. On an assigned date, my students arrived at Mountain View. Each had a number in hand, and as he or she got off the bus, the student was instructed to find the first grader who had the matching number. The students were then given an hour to get to know each other.

After they had returned to Sunnyslope, my students were instructed to write stories using the children's names and as many personalized characteristics as possible. They didn't have to write using a first-grade reading vocabulary because I believed that would be too limiting. Instead, I asked them only to make certain that the first grader could understand the vocabulary and style if the book were read to him or her. All books were to be illustrated, bound, and at least thirty-five pages in length.

I asked each student to go back and review several books that had been read to him or her as a young child and decide what elements made those books special. We made a list that included the need for effective and interesting dialogue, rising action, climax, theme, and resolution. We discussed the need for an attention-getting opening, and students gave examples of how that might be accomplished.

Though they would have a full month to complete this project, I asked for and critiqued two drafts of their manuscripts before they turned in the completed book. Even reluctant writers seemed to want to do a good job on this book.

I emphasized the importance of good grammar, punctuation, and spelling. "After all," I told my students, "these little children admire you, and whatever way you spell or write is going to be the right way as far as they are concerned."

The books were turned in on the due date and graded based on the creativity and excellence of the story; correctness of the grammar, sentence structure, and spelling; overall appearance and neatness. The stories showed sensitivity. Creativity was abundant. There were "pop-up" books, shape books, and books with handmade puppets in them.

After the books had been graded, they were returned to the students who were asked to correct any noted spelling or grammatical errors. Students made the corrections, wrapped their books, and brought them back to class to take to the first graders.

On an appointed date, we traveled back to Mountain View for an authors' autograph party. The elementary school children had arranged for special refreshments and a short program. At its conclusion, each high school student presented his or her "little friend" with a book. The big–little pairs could be seen in every corner of the room as the sophomores autographed the books and read them to the first graders.

"I'll never ever forget you" and "This was the best present I ever got," were just a couple of the enthusiastic and tearful parting words of the first graders. Sophomores said this had been the hardest high school assignment they'd ever had, but that the final results were worth the effort.

"Booked for Success" not only met my stated objectives of having my sophomore students motivated enough to create a writing project of excellence and of having them put the elements of fiction into practical use, but it achieved several goals for the elementary school children as well. According to their teachers, it provided the first graders with a role model who liked to read and write, it made the children feel special, and it encouraged even reluctant readers to try to read the words around their names.

Writers' Tea

Engaging students' enthusiasm after they have completed an extensive project or exam is difficult. They have expended so much effort and energy in achieving the goal that there isn't much left for a dynamic wrap-up. Yet such culminating activities are vital because they help students—individually and as a group—see and understand the project's diverse connections.

Dorothy Sawyer addressed this problem by instituting the Writers' Tea as the final activity in a lengthy unit of study. Because she was frustrated by the lack of response to her final lecture following the completion of a research paper of her class, she created the Writers' Tea as a way to motivate her students to reflect on what they had done and to improve in the future.

Mrs. Sawyer was the 1986 "Oregon Teacher of the Year."

My lecture following the completion of the research paper in junior language arts class never motivated much active listening or response or change, so I instituted the Writers' Tea to celebrate the completion of the project or the return of the papers.

When students enter the room, they draw a question, pick up a sheet with all the questions that will be discussed, and serve themselves from the tea table. They arrange themselves in a circle and are asked to choose a portion of the paper from which they learned something new. They prepare that section for reading aloud and also write a response to the question they drew. Responses are to be personal, based on how the authors experienced the research process.

When the preparation time has elapsed, students read from their papers, identify their question by number, and then read their responses. Time for questions and comments is allowed after each reading.

Connections: Chapter 2, Memory and Metacognition; Chapter 4, Guilford's Multifactor View; Chapter 5, Fading; Chapter 6, Reconstructive Retrieval, Conditional Prior Knowledge; Prior Knowledge, and Don't You Forget It; Chapter 11, Individualized Instruction; Chapter 12, Providing Useful Feedback and Evaluation; Chapter 13, Techniques of Evaluation; Chapter 14, Test Bias

I love to hear, "That's good!" or "Where did you find that out?" or "I had that problem too." or "Next time. . . ."

I would never go back to the old post-research-paper lecture. We all suffered through the research and writing process, and we can catch a moment of joy and relief and celebration at the tea. Sometimes we invite the head of the department and the principal or a counselor to add a little prestige to our event.

We go over the entire research process without my saying much more than students' names, making connections, and thanking them for their contributions. If the tea is on the day papers are returned, I give students a sheet with problems I found in their papers in one column and ask them to write solutions to about half of them in the other column. I think asking for completion of half—or a specified number—of the items on any activity always gets better response than saying, "Complete this."

When we've finished, students have thought about their thinking (metacognitive skills), they have discussed time management and problem solving, and they have participated in some self and peer evaluation. The tea makes a fine ending to the research paper unit.

Research Paper Tea Questions

1. In working on the research paper, what was your worst problem?
2. In working on the research paper, what went most smoothly for you?
3. Why and how did you choose your topic?
4. What research skill or library technique have you learned that you didn't know before?
5. What is a point of interest about your topic that you didn't know when you started your research?
6. Since there was no other homework for the two weeks before the final draft of the research paper was due, how did you arrange and budget your time to get the revising, typing, and final proofing done?
7. How many times did you change your thesis statement? Why?
8. What time management skills will be strengthened for you as a result of doing the research paper?
9. What were the best and worst experiences of your work time in the library?
10. Write the requirements and deadlines of the research paper assignment in Captain Vere's (*Billy Budd*) style.
11. Write the requirements and deadlines of the research paper assignment in Thoreau's style.
12. What is your topic? If you were required to use color and music in your presentation, what music and color would you use?
13. Please list everything you can think of about the research paper that is different from any other unit we have done.
14. What process did you use to create a wham-bang-razzle-dazzle title for your paper?
15. What tool for writing the research paper did you find most useful? Why?

16. If you had had unlimited energy, motivation, and time, how would your experience with the research paper have been different?

17. Go back to Atticus in *To Kill a Mockingbird*. Write a rough draft of the advice he would give you when you are discouraged about the research paper.

18. List what you feel are the five major obstacles a person must overcome to complete a successful research paper.

19. There are two strategies to use in viewing the slide-tape set, "Writing the Research Paper." One is to view a segment (on working bibliography, for example) and then to do that portion of the work. The other is to use the entire set as an overview as we did. Which method would be best for you? Why?

20. Describe your feelings when your completed paper was handed in.

21. Describe Huck Finn doing the research paper.

22. Ask the person next to you to list the advantages and disadvantages of the research paper as an assignment. Add one advantage and disadvantage of your own.

23. Most people seem to have great difficulty getting started on the research paper. What suggestions do you have to help people get over that obstacle?

24. The research paper assignment seems to cause an extra amount of stress and frustration. What suggestion do you have to reduce that stress?

Please Sign This Contract

How can I better motivate my students? is a perennial question teachers ask themselves. Motivation difficulties are faced at all levels. The ways in which students respond to their teacher's efforts vary according to student age and content material. Shaping student commitment and attitudes and creating interests all play a role in motivating students to learn new material and to do their best in school.

Gerald Walker, a chemistry teacher at Livingston High School in Livingston, New Jersey, decided to use a contract grading system to heighten student motivation in his Advanced Placement Chemistry classes. By contracting with his students—getting them to make a deeper commitment to what they were learning—Walker involved them more in their own learning and raised their motivation.

Mr. Walker was the 1986 New Jersey "Teacher of the Year."

Teachers must be particularly concerned with the critical problem of student motivation. Embodied in motivation are factors such as commitment, attitude, and interest. A device or strategy that I recently instituted to encourage commitment, elevate level of interest, and enhance positive attitude among Advanced Placement Chemistry students is the use of a contract grading system.

Students actively participate in setting standards for grading. They do this in an informal setting through discussions of standards and expectations, as one of several preliminaries to beginning the formal course work. In addition to standards, specific course requirements are focused on in these

Connections: Chapter 7, Self-efficacy; Chapter 8, Intrinsic versus Extrinsic Goals; Chapter 9, Instructional Objectives; Chapter 12, Classroom Goal Structures; Chapter 14, Standard Deviation

discussions. The students begin to lobby with each other and with me for certain stipulations that will eventually become a formalized, written grading agreement. The one requirement in this process and its outcome(s) is that the agreement, or any portion thereof, can not violate district or school policies, mandates, or guidelines for student evaluation.

Following the development of the written agreement, each student commits himself or herself to a set of goals while working within the framework of the established standards for each of four grading periods. Once a contract has been finalized, it usually contains such things as alternatives to certain kinds of work as well as opportunities for make-up work, extra credit, and the like. The contract might stipulate that different kinds of written work be graded in different manners . . . some of these being assigned point values, letter grades, and "satisfactory" versus "unsatisfactory."

The concept of a grading agreement or contract lends itself to the achievement of higher levels of competency with an emphasis on quality rather than quantity; it aids students in realizing the importance of long-range planning and establishing priorities; it encourages student participation in setting standards. It also may be constructed in such a way that it makes provisions for the student to work at a pace more suited to his or her needs.

Each student signs the agreement with the understanding that the class and I can mutually renegotiate the agreement, or portions of it, at the beginning of each new grading period if undesirable consequences, impractical items, or unrealistic stipulations surface along the way. Using this system with very bright, conscientious students (most of whom are seniors) in small classes has helped to make it an effective technique. The use of the contract has not only helped maintain an already high level of performance, it has elevated it. The report of the A.P. chemistry students' test scores for May 1987 reflects this; the summary of scores shows 2–5s, 13–4s, 5–3s, 0–2s and 0–1s. In conjunction with this high degree of success in testing, there has been a noticeable increase in commitment and enthusiasm for the program.

Writing Success in Science

Breaking a complicated learning activity into manageable steps is one way effective teachers expand their students' learning. Writing, often viewed as torture by students, is one instructional activity that lends itself to being broken into component parts before being synthesized into a whole.

Taking writing out of the English classroom and into the science class helps students see the interconnectness of the diverse elements of their education. As the following case demonstrates, clear writing teaches a variety of skills beyond the acquisition of content material.

Linda Wygoda now teaches chemistry and environmental science in Louisiana.

As a science teacher, I always have realized how important writing and critical thinking skills are to the understanding and learning of science. I have tried several times in the past to encourage students to write about science content in an essay format. However, after years of hearing, "I don't know what to write!" and "How long does this have to be?" I finally found a formula for writing success that has been very useful in teaching writing skills to my science students.

Test Questions 15.46–15.100 apply theoretical principles presented in Chapters 2 through 14.

Connections: Chapter 6, Using Prior Knowledge to Learn; Chapter 10, Models for Teaching Thinking Skills, Transfer of Learning; Chapter 13, Grading